1995–96
BASKETBALL ALMANAC

Contributing Writers

Marty Strasen

Mike Sheridan

Nick Rousso

Michael Bradley

Pete Palmer

David Korus

Bruce Herman

Murray Rubenfeld

Marty Strasen is a sports writer for the *Waterloo Courier* in Iowa and has also written for several major newspapers, including the *Detroit Free Press.* He is a former assistant editor of *Basketball Weekly.*

Mike Sheridan is managing editor of *Basketball Times* and *Eastern Basketball.*

Nick Rousso is editor of *Ultimate Sports Basketball.* He is the former editor of *Dick Vitale's Basketball* and *Don Heinrich's College Football* and was an associate editor for *Bill Mazeroski's Baseball, The Show,* and *Don Heinrich's Pro Preview.*

Michael Bradley is a freelance writer whose work has appeared in *The Sporting News, The Philadelphia Inquirer,* and a variety of national sports publications.

Pete Palmer edited both *Total Baseball* and *The Hidden Game of Baseball* with John Thorn. He was the statistician for *1995 Baseball Almanac* and *1992*

Fantasy League Baseball. Palmer is a member of the Society for American Baseball Research (SABR).

David Korus is a freelance sports statistician who lives in Massachusetts.

Bruce Herman is a sports writer and consultant who's contributed to The Topps Company, ESPN, Tribune Media Services, Dunfey Publishing, several major-league baseball teams, *Sports Illustrated, USA Today Baseball Weekly,* and *Inside Sports.*

Murray Rubenfeld is executive producer of "The Sports Card Report Radio Show" and has written extensively on basketball for several hobby publications. He is a basketball card price-guide analyst for *The Sports Card News* and *The Confident Collectors Basketball Card Price Guide.*

Statistics in the College Basketball Review section were provided by the National Collegiate Athletic Association.

Cover Photo Credit: Ben Van Hook/Duomo

CONTENTS

4 CONTENTS

CONTENTS

NBA Veterans and Rookies

In this section, you'll find scouting reports on 300 NBA veterans and 60 NBA rookies (plus a recap of the 1994 college draft on page 308). The NBA will tip off the 1995-96 season with 348 players, so this section is sure to include most every player on each NBA roster.

Each player's scouting report begins with his vital stats: team, position, height, weight, etc. Next comes a four-part evaluation of the player. "Background" reviews the player's career, starting with college and continuing up through the 1994-95 season. "Strengths" examines his best assets, including such traits as character and leadership. "Weaknesses" assesses the player's significant flaws, including things like attitude and off-court behavior. And "analysis" tries to put the player's game into perspective.

For a quick run-down on each player, you'll find a "player summary" box. The box also includes a "fantasy value" figure, which suggests a draft price for any of the fantasy basketball games that have mushroomed throughout the country. The price range is a guide based on $260 for a 15-player roster. Some players are valued at $0, meaning they are not worth drafting. Finally, the box contains a "card value" figure, which is a suggested buying price for a mint

1995-96 basketball card of that player. The values do not reflect cards from premium sets.

The scouting reports of the NBA veterans include their college and NBA statistics. The college stats include games (G), field goal percentage (FGP), free throw percentage (FTP), rebounds per game (RPG) or assists per game (APG), and points per game (PPG). The veterans' NBA stats include the following:

- games (G)
- minutes (MIN)
- field goals made (FGs/FG)
- field goal percentage (FGs/PCT)
- 3-point field goals made (3-PT FGs/FG)
- 3-point field goal percentage (3-PT FGs/PCT)
- free throws made (FTs/FT)
- free throw percentage (FTs/PCT)
- offensive rebounds (Rebounds/OFF)
- total rebounds (Rebounds/TOT)
- assists (AST)
- steals (STL)
- blocked shots (BLK)
- points (PTS)
- points per game (PPG)

The 60 NBA rookies receive half-page write-ups with abbreviated statistics.

MAHMOUD ABDUL-RAUF

Team: Denver Nuggets
Position: Guard
Height: 6'1" **Weight:** 162
Birthdate: March 9, 1969

NBA Experience: 5 years
College: Louisiana St.
Acquired: 1st-round pick in 1990 draft
(3rd overall)

Background: In two seasons at LSU, the former Chris Jackson accomplished things most four-year players will never approach. He broke NCAA freshman records for points in a game against a Division I opponent (55), points in a season (965), and scoring average (30.2 PPG). After two lackluster NBA seasons, he won the 1992-93 Most Improved Player Award. He converted to Muslim before an impressive 1993-94 campaign, then spent much of 1994-95 as a reserve.

Strengths: Abdul-Rauf is one of the sweetest shooters in the game. Only Calvin Murphy had a better free throw shooting season than his 219-of-229 in 1993-94, and he sticks the 3-pointer with ease. Also extremely quick, Abdul-Rauf can get to the hoop. He does not use strings, but the ball is attached to his hand. A crossover dribble and quick release make him tough to defend.

Weaknesses: Abdul-Rauf should be a better defender and assist man than he is. He has the quickness to penetrate and dish, but he looks to score himself first. He's been called a shooting guard trapped in a point guard's body. He plays defense like many great shooters.

Analysis: A neurological disorder called Tourette's Syndrome and a great deal of scrutiny since his college days have not prevented Abdul-Rauf from becoming a fine NBA guard. He provides instant offense with his quick jumper and phenomenal ball-handling. However, he is not a true point guard and thus was used as a sixth man for much of last season. His 16.0 PPG was his lowest average in three years.

PLAYER SUMMARY

Will .... make his free throws
Can't .... set assist records
Expect .... instant offense
Don't Expect .... a shy shooter
Fantasy Value $8-10
Card Value .... 8-15¢

COLLEGE STATISTICS

		G	FGP	FTP	APG	PPG
88-89	LSU	32	.486	.815	4.1	30.2
89-90	LSU	32	.461	.910	3.2	27.8
Totals		64	.474	.863	3.6	29.0

NBA REGULAR-SEASON STATISTICS

		G	MIN	FGs FG	FGs PCT	3-PT FGs FG	3-PT FGs PCT	FTs FT	FTs PCT	Rebounds OFF	Rebounds TOT	AST	STL	BLK	PTS	PPG
90-91	DEN	67	1505	417	.413	24	.240	84	.857	34	121	206	55	4	942	14.1
91-92	DEN	81	1538	356	.421	31	.330	94	.870	22	114	192	44	4	837	10.3
92-93	DEN	81	2710	633	.450	70	.355	217	.935	51	225	344	84	8	1553	19.2
93-94	DEN	80	2617	588	.460	42	.316	219	.956	27	168	362	82	10	1437	18.0
94-95	DEN	73	2082	472	.470	83	.386	138	.885	32	137	263	77	9	1165	16.0
Totals		382	10452	2466	.445	250	.338	752	.914	166	765	1367	342	35	5934	15.5

MICHAEL ADAMS

Team: Charlotte Hornets
Position: Guard
Height: 5'10" **Weight:** 162
Birthdate: January 19, 1963

NBA Experience: 10 years
College: Boston College
Acquired: Traded from Bullets for
1996 and 1997 2nd-round picks, 8/94

Background: Adams was named second-team All-Big East three straight years at Boston College. The former CBA Rookie of the Year (1986) once held numerous NBA 3-point records and was an All-Star in 1992. He spent most of his career in Denver and Washington before an injury-plagued 1994-95 season with Charlotte.

Strengths: Adams thrives at a fast pace. His quickness can be matched by very few players in the league, and when they foul him he will make his free throws. His career has been dominated by 3-point bombs, which he can hit from well beyond the shortened arc. He handles the ball expertly and thrives in the open court.

Weaknesses: While Adams shoots 3-pointers like there is no tomorrow, he does not convert them at an especially good rate. The shorter 3-point arc has put a lot of other players in a class ahead of him. Adams has not used his quickness to its best advantage on defense. He does not play "bigger than his size."

Analysis: Adams will soon make his 1,000th career 3-pointer, but he will probably do so in a reserve role. He could have enjoyed a nice season backing up Muggsy Bogues in Charlotte's up-tempo offense, but he was limited to 29 regular-season games because of hamstring and calf injuries.

PLAYER SUMMARY	
Will	launch from anywhere
Can't	shoot for percentage
Expect	speed off the bench
Don't Expect	disruptive defense
Fantasy Value	$0
Card Value	5-8¢

COLLEGE STATISTICS

		G	FGP	FTP	APG	PPG
81-82	BC	26	.495	.590	1.5	5.3
82-83	BC	32	.481	.809	5.3	16.2
83-84	BC	30	.455	.756	3.5	17.3
84-85	BC	31	.467	.748	3.2	15.3
Totals		119	.470	.750	3.5	13.9

NBA REGULAR-SEASON STATISTICS

		G	MIN	FGs		3-PT FGs		FTs		Rebounds		AST	STL	BLK	PTS	PPG
				FG	PCT	FG	PCT	FT	PCT	OFF	TOT					
85-86	SAC	18	139	16	.364	0	.000	8	.667	2	6	22	9	1	40	2.2
86-87	WAS	63	1303	160	.407	28	.275	105	.847	38	123	244	85	6	453	7.2
87-88	DEN	82	2778	416	.449	139	.367	166	.834	40	223	503	168	16	1137	13.9
88-89	DEN	77	2787	468	.433	166	.356	322	.819	71	283	490	166	11	1424	18.5
89-90	DEN	79	2690	398	.402	158	.366	267	.850	49	225	495	121	3	1221	15.5
90-91	DEN	66	2346	560	.394	167	.296	465	.879	58	256	693	147	6	1752	26.5
91-92	WAS	78	2795	485	.393	125	.324	313	.869	58	310	594	145	9	1408	18.1
92-93	WAS	70	2499	365	.439	68	.321	237	.856	52	240	526	100	4	1035	14.8
93-94	WAS	70	2337	285	.408	55	.288	224	.830	37	183	480	96	6	849	12.1
94-95	CHA	29	443	67	.453	29	.358	25	.833	6	29	95	23	1	188	6.5
Totals		632	20117	3220	.415	935	.332	2132	.850	411	1878	4142	1060	63	9507	15.0

RAFAEL ADDISON

Unsigned Free Agent
Last Team: Detroit Pistons
Position: Forward/Guard
Height: 6'7" **Weight:** 245
Birthdate: July 22, 1964

NBA Experience: 4 years
College: Syracuse
Acquired: Signed as a free agent, 7/94

Background: Addison was first-team All-Big East as a junior at Syracuse, where his career scoring average was nearly 15 PPG. After a mediocre senior year, he was drafted in the second round by Phoenix in 1986 and averaged 5.8 PPG as a rookie. He then played four years in Italy, had a two-year stay with the Nets, and returned to Italy for another season. Addison averaged a career-high 8.3 PPG for the Pistons in 1994-95 but was released in April.

Strengths: Defense and attitude are Addison's selling points. He is more than willing to come off the bench and blanket his man, whether it's a guard or forward, and rebound. He has a knack for getting his hands on the ball and possesses above-average spring. He's an athlete who runs the floor, and he has a decent jump shot with range when spotting up.

Weaknesses: Addison is not your prototypical shooting guard who will torch the nets nightly. He does not do much off the dribble and gets most of his offense on open jumpers and in transition. He is not in the league for his offense. Addison has never been a very dangerous passer. On defense, quick guards and big forwards can pose matchup problems.

Analysis: Addison's third stretch as an NBA player was his best. He averaged career highs in most categories, provided his usual strong defense, and showed more offense than many knew he had. He did some spot starting for Detroit and led the Pistons in games played. A forward in his first three years of college, he is still considered a 'tweener by some. His attitude is exemplary.

PLAYER SUMMARY	
Will	play defense
Can't	create off dribble
Expect	a team player
Don't Expect	distribution
Fantasy Value	$0
Card Value	5-8¢

COLLEGE STATISTICS

		G	FGP	FTP	RPG	PPG
82-83	SYR	31	.521	.651	3.2	8.4
83-84	SYR	32	.559	.836	6.0	17.7
84-85	SYR	31	.520	.727	5.8	18.4
85-86	SYR	32	.532	.793	5.6	15.0
Totals		126	.534	.763	5.2	14.9

NBA REGULAR-SEASON STATISTICS

				FGs		3-PT FGs		FTs		Rebounds						
		G	MIN	FG	PCT	FG	PCT	FT	PCT	OFF	TOT	AST	STL	BLK	PTS	PPG
86-87	PHO	62	711	146	.441	16	.320	51	.797	41	106	45	27	7	359	5.8
91-92	NJ	76	1175	187	.433	14	.286	56	.737	65	165	68	28	28	444	5.8
92-93	NJ	68	1164	182	.443	7	.206	57	.814	45	132	53	23	11	428	6.3
94-95	DET	79	1776	279	.476	24	.289	74	.747	67	242	109	53	25	656	8.3
Totals		285	4826	794	.451	61	.282	238	.770	218	645	275	131	71	1887	6.6

DANNY AINGE

Unrestricted Free Agent
Last Team: Phoenix Suns
Position: Guard
Height: 6'5" **Weight:** 195
Birthdate: March 17, 1959

NBA Experience: 14 years
College: Brigham Young
Acquired: Signed as a free agent, 7/92

Background: Ainge was a multi-sport star at Brigham Young and played two years of professional baseball with the Toronto Blue Jays, primarily as an infielder. He batted .220. He has enjoyed much greater success in the NBA, where he was an All-Star in 1988 and won two championships with Boston. He has spent his last three years coming off the Phoenix bench.

Strengths: Ainge is a fierce competitor with championship experience and tremendous leadership skills. His single best skill remains his jump shot, which he can drill with 3-point range. He's also a reliable free throw shooter.

Weaknesses: Put kindly, Ainge is a below-average defensive player and he's not getting any quicker—though he is feisty. He does not create at the offensive end as much as he feeds off teammates. He can't light it up like he used to.

Analysis: Once a superbrat, Ainge has become a steadying influence with 14 years of experience. He has had much to do with Phoenix's rise to annual title contender. Last season, he became the third player in NBA history to make 1,000 career 3-pointers.

PLAYER SUMMARY	
Will	hit 3-pointers
Can't	score like he used to
Expect	veteran leadership
Don't Expect	two more years
Fantasy Value	$1-3
Card Value	8-15¢

COLLEGE STATISTICS

		G	FGP	FTP	RPG	PPG
77-78	BYU	30	.514	.864	5.8	21.1
78-79	BYU	27	.548	.768	3.8	18.4
79-80	BYU	29	.533	.782	3.9	19.1
80-81	BYU	32	.518	.824	4.8	24.4
Totals		118	.526	.816	4.6	20.9

NBA REGULAR-SEASON STATISTICS

		G	MIN	FGs FG	FGs PCT	3-PT FGs FG	3-PT FGs PCT	FTs FT	FTs PCT	Rebounds OFF	Rebounds TOT	AST	STL	BLK	PTS	PPG
81-82	BOS	53	564	79	.357	5	.294	56	.862	25	56	87	37	3	219	4.1
82-83	BOS	80	2048	357	.496	5	.172	72	.742	83	214	251	109	6	791	9.9
83-84	BOS	71	1154	166	.460	6	.273	46	.821	29	116	162	41	4	384	5.4
84-85	BOS	75	2564	419	.529	15	.268	118	.868	76	268	399	122	6	971	12.9
85-86	BOS	80	2407	353	.504	26	.356	123	.904	47	235	405	94	7	855	10.7
86-87	BOS	71	2499	410	.486	85	.443	148	.897	49	242	400	101	14	1053	14.8
87-88	BOS	81	3018	482	.491	148	.415	158	.878	59	249	503	115	17	1270	15.7
88-89	BOS/SAC	73	2377	480	.457	116	.380	205	.854	71	255	402	93	8	1281	17.5
89-90	SAC	75	2727	506	.438	108	.374	222	.831	69	326	453	113	18	1342	17.9
90-91	POR	80	1710	337	.472	102	.406	114	.826	45	205	285	63	13	890	11.1
91-92	POR	81	1595	299	.442	78	.339	108	.824	40	148	202	73	13	784	9.7
92-93	PHO	80	2163	337	.462	150	.403	123	.848	49	214	260	69	8	947	11.8
93-94	PHO	68	1555	224	.417	80	.328	78	.830	28	131	180	57	8	606	8.9
94-95	PHO	74	1374	194	.460	78	.364	105	.808	25	109	210	46	7	571	7.7
Totals		1042	27755	4643	.469	1002	.378	1676	.846	695	2768	4199	1133	132	11964	11.5

VICTOR ALEXANDER

Team: Golden State Warriors
Position: Center/Forward
Height: 6'10" **Weight:** 265
Birthdate: August 31, 1969

NBA Experience: 4 years
College: Iowa St.
Acquired: 1st-round pick in 1991 draft
(17th overall)

Background: Alexander weighed nearly 300 pounds as an Iowa State freshman but excelled as a sophomore, finishing third in the Big Eight in scoring and rebounding. He had an outstanding senior season, was drafted in the first round, and has had four up-and-down seasons with Golden State. Alexander has been a part-time starter in each of the last three years, but he has yet to match his 11.2-PPG scoring average of 1992-93.

Strengths: Alexander is a highly skilled offensive player. He has good post-up skills, a soft shooting touch, and tremendous hands. He knows what to do with the ball near the basket and can amaze people with some of the shots he'll pull off in traffic. He has never shot less than 50 percent from the field in his four pro seasons.

Weaknesses: Defense and rebounding have never been high priorities with Alexander, who still struggles with conditioning. Questionable commitment comes into play. He'll impress everyone in the house one game, then disappear the next. Passing is one of the weaker aspects of his game and he too often relies on offensive finesse rather than power. He's a poor free throw shooter.

Analysis: Alexander will not emerge as one of the better big men in the game unless he does a better job of keeping in shape and shows a greater desire to pound the boards and (perhaps more importantly) pound his man. Alexander is a very polished offensive player who, with more assertiveness, could give his team a man-sized boost in the paint. Thus far, he's done it only in spurts.

PLAYER SUMMARY

Will	score inside
Can't	dominate boards
Expect	peaks and valleys
Don't Expect	interior defense
Fantasy Value	$1
Card Value	8-12¢

COLLEGE STATISTICS

		G	FGP	FTP	RPG	PPG
87-88	ISU	23	.600	.500	1.4	1.7
88-89	ISU	29	.583	.651	8.8	19.9
89-90	ISU	28	.585	.578	8.7	19.7
90-91	ISU	31	.659	.677	9.0	23.4
Totals		111	.538	.635	7.3	17.0

NBA REGULAR-SEASON STATISTICS

			FGs		3-PT FGs		FTs		Rebounds						
	G	MIN	FG	PCT	FG	PCT	FT	PCT	OFF	TOT	AST	STL	BLK	PTS	PPG
91-92 GS	80	1350	243	.529	0	.000	103	.691	106	336	32	45	62	589	7.4
92-93 GS	72	1753	344	.516	10	.455	111	.685	132	420	93	34	53	809	11.2
93-94 GS	69	1318	266	.530	2	.154	68	.527	114	308	66	28	32	602	8.7
94-95 GS	50	1237	230	.515	6	.240	36	.600	87	291	60	28	29	502	10.0
Totals	271	5658	1083	.522	18	.295	318	.636	439	1355	251	135	176	2502	9.2

DERRICK ALSTON

Team: Philadelphia 76ers
Position: Forward
Height: 6'11" **Weight:** 225
Birthdate: August 20, 1972

NBA Experience: 1 year
College: Duquesne
Acquired: 2nd-round pick in 1994
draft (33rd overall)

Background: As a senior in college, Alston quietly became the first player to lead the Atlantic 10 in scoring and field goal accuracy in the same season. He scored in double figures in 97 of 114 games at Duquesne and reached No. 2 on the school's career scoring list. After strong camp showings, Alston was selected 33rd by Philadelphia in the 1994 draft and saw action in 64 games as a 76er rookie. He averaged 4.7 PPG.

Strengths: Alston has long arms, good instincts for the game, and good athletic ability. Add it up and you have the makings of a productive shot-blocker. He swatted 35 last season in very limited playing time. Alston also shot a nice jumper in college, though it failed him last season while he struggled to adjust to big-league defenders. He can be impressive on the offensive boards.

Weaknesses: Most aspects of Alston's game need a tune-up, but none more than his thin frame. Put him in a weight room and lock the door. He is not physical enough to match up with most of the forwards he runs into, and it affects everything he does. He didn't do much with his limited minutes. He did not hit many shots, he picked up a lot of fouls, and he was brutal from the free throw stripe.

Analysis: Alston has never been a sure thing. He worked hard to make a 76er team that was not exactly loaded with talent, and when the time came to play, Alston was largely ineffective. Even when he's aggressive, this former college center does not have the muscle to make a big impact on an NBA front line. Gaining some should be his next order of business.

PLAYER SUMMARY	
Will	challenge shots
Can't	dominate inside
Expect	off-season work
Don't Expect	physical play
Fantasy Value	$0
Card Value	8-15¢

COLLEGE STATS

		G	FGP	FTP	RPG	PPG
90-91	DUQ	28	.536	.598	6.3	11.3
91-92	DUQ	28	.556	.526	8.0	13.9
92-93	DUQ	28	.563	.574	9.3	19.9
93-94	DUQ	30	.578	.601	7.3	21.3
Totals		114	.561	.576	7.7	16.7

NBA REGULAR-SEASON STATISTICS

			FGs		3-PT FGs		FTs		Rebounds						
	G	MIN	FG	PCT	FG	PCT	FT	PCT	OFF	TOT	AST	STL	BLK	PTS	PPG
94-95 PHI	64	1032	120	.465	0	.000	59	.492	98	219	33	39	35	299	4.7
Totals	64	1032	120	.465	0	.000	59	.492	98	219	33	39	35	299	4.7

KENNY ANDERSON

Team: New Jersey Nets
Position: Guard
Height: 6'1" **Weight:** 170
Birthdate: October 9, 1970

NBA Experience: 4 years
College: Georgia Tech
Acquired: 1st-round pick in 1991 draft
(2nd overall)

Background: A legend at New York City's Archbishop Malloy High, Anderson was an instant hit at Georgia Tech. He led the ACC in assists as a freshman. When Dennis Scott and Brian Oliver left for the NBA, Anderson tried to carry the team as a sophomore and then turned pro. After a contract holdout and disappointing rookie season, Anderson has thrived as the Nets' point guard. He has finished among the NBA assist leaders each of the last three years and played in the 1994 All-Star Game.

Strengths: Anderson is a classic point guard with a scorer's mentality. He is a terrific ball-handler, passer, and penetrator with a special ability to see the floor that few have ever had. He can create plays and finish them and has 3-point range with his awkward-looking jumper. Defensively, he relies on quick hands and superior anticipation. He has become respected for his leadership.

Weaknesses: Size remains the biggest drawback with Anderson. His slight build makes him a tempting post-up target and he struggles to fight through screens. His shooting is inconsistent, his best year from the field being a .435 campaign in 1992-93. Defenders are best advised to keep him away from the hoop.

Analysis: This former prep and college All-American has become one of the best in the pro game as well. Few guards in the game have the ability to see their options and execute them like Anderson. His ball-handling and passing are almost unmatched and he can also flat-out score. He has averaged at least 16.9 PPG in each of the past three seasons.

PLAYER SUMMARY	
Will	hit open men
Can't	live on jump shots
Expect	offensive wizardry
Don't Expect	less than 15 PPG
Fantasy Value	$25-30
Card Value	10-25¢

COLLEGE STATISTICS

		G	FGP	FTP	APG	PPG
89-90	GT	35	.515	.733	5.3	20.6
90-91	GT	30	.437	.829	5.6	25.9
Totals		65	.473	.787	5.4	23.0

NBA REGULAR-SEASON STATISTICS

		G	MIN	FGs FG	FGs PCT	3-PT FGs FG	3-PT FGs PCT	FTs FT	FTs PCT	Rebounds OFF	Rebounds TOT	AST	STL	BLK	PTS	PPG
91-92	NJ	64	1086	187	.390	3	.231	73	.745	38	127	203	67	9	450	7.0
92-93	NJ	55	2010	370	.435	7	.280	180	.776	51	226	449	96	11	927	16.9
93-94	NJ	82	3135	576	.417	40	.303	346	.818	89	322	784	158	15	1538	18.8
94-95	NJ	72	2689	411	.399	97	.330	348	.841	73	250	680	103	14	1267	17.6
Totals		273	8920	1544	.413	147	.317	947	.811	251	925	2116	424	49	4182	15.3

NICK ANDERSON

Team: Orlando Magic
Position: Forward/Guard
Height: 6'6" **Weight:** 220
Birthdate: January 20, 1968

NBA Experience: 6 years
College: Illinois
Acquired: 1st-round pick in 1989 draft
(11th overall)

Background: Anderson was a unanimous All-Big Ten selection on the "Flying Illini" Final Four team of 1988-89 and was an instant starter and double-figure scorer in the NBA with Orlando, where he's played all six years. He led the Magic in scoring in 1991-92, the year before Shaquille O'Neal joined the team. He has averaged about 16 PPG in each of the last two years.

Strengths: Anderson can put the ball in the basket. He is one of the better 3-point shooters in the NBA and is able to get to the hoop with his tremendous quickness and leaping ability. He can play both big guard and small forward and is a fine backcourt rebounder. He has settled into a role and is willing to play hard on defense.

Weaknesses: Anderson is not the most gifted ball-handler and passer. He played small forward in college and is not the man you want beating pressure. He struggled to find his niche for the first year after the arrival of Penny Hardaway, although that seems to have been settled. He has not always been game to play second fiddle.

Analysis: Once on the verge of NBA stardom, Anderson has had to give way to young megastars O'Neal and Hardaway. Though he continues to be capable of taking over games, he has also learned to be a team player for one of the top squads in the league. Anderson has become a more complete player than he was during his highest scoring days.

PLAYER SUMMARY	
Will	...hit the trey
Can't	...overshadow Shaq
Expect	...16-plus PPG
Don't Expect	...stardom
Fantasy Value	...$30-35
Card Value	...8-15¢

COLLEGE STATISTICS

		G	FGP	FTP	RPG	PPG
87-88	ILL	33	.572	.642	6.6	15.9
88-89	ILL	36	.538	.669	7.9	18.0
Totals		69	.553	.657	7.3	17.0

NBA REGULAR-SEASON STATISTICS

		G	MIN	FGs FG	FGs PCT	3-PT FGs FG	3-PT FGs PCT	FTs FT	FTs PCT	Rebounds OFF	Rebounds TOT	AST	STL	BLK	PTS	PPG
89-90	ORL	81	1785	372	.494	1	.059	186	.705	107	316	124	69	34	931	11.5
90-91	ORL	70	1971	400	.467	17	.293	173	.668	92	386	106	74	44	990	14.1
91-92	ORL	60	2203	482	.463	30	.353	202	.667	98	384	163	97	33	1196	19.9
92-93	ORL	79	2920	594	.449	88	.353	298	.741	122	477	265	128	56	1574	19.9
93-94	ORL	81	2811	504	.478	101	.322	168	.672	113	476	294	134	33	1277	15.8
94-95	ORL	76	2588	439	.476	179	.415	143	.708	85	335	314	125	22	1200	15.8
Totals		447	14278	2791	.469	416	.360	1170	.696	617	2374	1266	627	222	7168	16.0

WILLIE ANDERSON

Team: Toronto Raptors
Position: Guard/Forward
Height: 6'8" **Weight:** 205
Birthdate: January 8, 1967

NBA Experience: 7 years
College: Georgia
Acquired: Selected from Spurs in 1995 expansion draft

Background: Anderson finished eighth on Georgia's all-time scoring list and competed on the United States Olympic team in 1988. After he averaged 18.6 PPG as a rookie with San Antonio, his scoring average declined for four straight years while leg injuries limited his playing time. The 1993-94 campaign was a comeback year, but injuries again slowed Anderson last season. Toronto grabbed him in the expansion draft.

Strengths: Anderson, who in his early years drew comparisons to former Spurs scoring great George Gervin, is known for his versatility. He plays both the two and three spots with equal success. He has been a master of the drive-and-dish and also has a soft touch from the outside. He provides unselfish leadership.

Weaknesses: Anderson is not nearly the player he used to be. The injuries and his declining scoring average have seemingly taken their toll on his confidence, and he will probably never return to the high-scoring days he enjoyed as a rookie. He does not possess the explosiveness to the bucket that became a trademark before he had rods inserted in both legs. His numbers show it.

Analysis: If Anderson's comeback two years ago was encouraging, his 1994-95 season was just the opposite. He played sparingly, spent virtually all of December on the injured list (elbow), and was not a big contributor to San Antonio's success. He will at least see floor time with the Raptors.

PLAYER SUMMARY

Will ....play two positions
Can't ....regain explosiveness
Expect ....leadership
Don't Expect ....young legs
Fantasy Value $1-3
Card Value ....5-8¢

COLLEGE STATISTICS

		G	FGP	FTP	RPG	PPG
84-85	GEOR	13	.487	.625	1.5	3.3
85-86	GEOR	29	.503	.787	3.4	8.5
86-87	GEOR	30	.500	.794	4.1	15.9
87-88	GEOR	35	.500	.784	5.1	16.7
Totals		107	.500	.784	3.9	12.6

NBA REGULAR-SEASON STATISTICS

			FGs		3-PT FGs		FTs		Rebounds						
		G	MIN	FG	PCT	FG	PCT	FT	PCT	OFF	TOT	AST	STL	BLK	PTS	PPG
88-89	SA	81	2738	640	.498	4	.190	224	.775	152	417	372	150	62	1508	18.6
89-90	SA	82	2788	532	.492	7	.269	217	.748	115	372	364	111	58	1288	15.7
90-91	SA	75	2592	453	.457	7	.200	170	.798	68	351	358	79	46	1083	14.4
91-92	SA	57	1889	312	.455	13	.232	107	.775	62	300	302	54	51	744	13.1
92-93	SA	38	560	80	.430	1	.125	22	.786	7	57	79	14	6	183	4.8
93-94	SA	80	2488	394	.471	22	.324	145	.848	68	242	347	71	46	955	11.9
94-95	SA	38	556	76	.469	3	.158	30	.732	15	55	52	26	10	185	4.9
Totals		451	13611	2487	.476	57	.245	915	.782	487	1794	1874	505	279	5946	13.2

GREG ANTHONY

Team: Vancouver Grizzlies
Position: Guard
Height: 6'2" **Weight:** 185
Birthdate: November 15, 1967

NBA Experience: 4 years
College: Portland; Nevada-Las Vegas
Acquired: Selected from Knicks in
1995 expansion draft

Background: Anthony spent his first college season at Portland, where he played shooting guard. Jerry Tarkanian moved him to point guard at UNLV, where Anthony directed the Rebels to the national title in 1990 and to the Final Four in 1991. Anthony has demonstrated only fading glimpses of promise in his four NBA seasons. The 1994-95 season was his least productive yet, and the Knicks let Vancouver take him in the expansion draft.

Strengths: Anthony is a take-charge type, although some would use less flattering words to describe his demeanor. He loves to compete and can talk a big game. He is adept at the running game and can thread the needle with his passing. He expends a lot of energy at both ends and now, with the newer arc, has 3-point range.

Weaknesses: Unless he learns to hit jumpers, Anthony will never live up to expectations. It's a safe bet he'll be left wide-open in favor of double-teams elsewhere, and his miserable field goal percentage shows why. He is not the defensive presence he was made out to be in college. He takes too many chances and is an easy post-up victim for bigger guards. He has been erratic since day one.

Analysis: Anthony underwent his share of scrutiny in New York and was not likely to ever thrive with the Knicks, whose deliberate approach did not suit his style. He will struggle to find success with the Grizzlies without a competent jump shot or the ability to run an offense in a sound manner. Considering he was chosen 12th overall in the 1991 draft, you have to call him a bust.

PLAYER SUMMARY	
Will	compete
Can't	sink jumpers
Expect	erratic play
Don't Expect	composure
Fantasy Value	$6-8
Card Value	7-12¢

COLLEGE STATISTICS

		G	FGP	FTP	APG	PPG
86-87	PORT	28	.398	.694	4.0	15.3
88-89	UNLV	36	.443	.699	6.6	12.9
89-90	UNLV	39	.457	.682	7.4	11.2
90-91	UNLV	35	.456	.775	8.9	11.6
Totals		138	.437	.707	6.9	12.6

NBA REGULAR-SEASON STATISTICS

		G	MIN	FGs FG	FGs PCT	3-PT FGs FG	3-PT FGs PCT	FTs FT	FTs PCT	Rebounds OFF	Rebounds TOT	AST	STL	BLK	PTS	PPG
91-92	NY	82	1510	161	.370	8	.145	117	.741	33	136	314	59	9	447	5.5
92-93	NY	70	1699	174	.415	4	.133	107	.673	42	170	398	113	12	459	6.6
93-94	NY	80	1994	225	.394	48	.300	130	.774	43	189	365	114	13	628	7.8
94-95	NY	61	943	128	.437	56	.361	60	.789	7	64	160	50	7	372	6.1
Totals		293	6146	688	.400	116	.290	414	.738	125	559	1237	336	41	1906	6.5

B.J. ARMSTRONG

Team: Toronto Raptors
Position: Guard
Height: 6'2" **Weight:** 185
Birthdate: September 9, 1967

NBA Experience: 6 years
College: Iowa
Acquired: Selected from Bulls in 1995 expansion draft

Background: After becoming Iowa's all-time leader in assists, Armstrong was plucked by the Bulls in the 1989 draft. He saw early action and was Chicago's top bench player during the team's 1991 and 1992 NBA championship seasons. The baby-faced guard led the league in 3-point accuracy in 1992-93 (another title year) and started in the 1994 All-Star Game. Largely because of his high salary, he was exposed in the expansion draft and snatched up by Toronto.

Strengths: Armstrong has made himself one of the most dangerous jump-shooters in the game. Leave him open and he'll kill you from behind the 3-point arc. He has converted better than 40 percent from long distance every season and ranks third on the all-time 3-point accuracy list. He rarely misses a free throw, either. Armstrong thrives in an open-court game and plays quick, solid defense.

Weaknesses: Armstrong does not possess the natural playmaking ability of other point guards in the NBA. He led the Bulls in neither steals nor assists, although having talented teammates had a lot to do with that. He's better at spotting up than creating his shots in traffic. He's not much help on the boards.

Analysis: Armstrong didn't make Chicagoans forget what John Paxson contributed to their championship triplicate, but he made sure there was no dropoff when he took over as the team's top shooter. Few in the league are more reliable from long range. Though drafted by Toronto, Armstrong was rumored to go to Golden State once the league's labor dispute was settled.

PLAYER SUMMARY	
Will	hit from deep
Can't	muscle his man
Expect	40 percent from 3
Don't Expect	rebounding
Fantasy Value	$9-11
Card Value	10-20¢

COLLEGE STATISTICS

		G	FGP	FTP	APG	PPG
85-86	IOWA	29	.485	.905	1.4	2.9
86-87	IOWA	35	.519	.794	4.2	12.4
87-88	IOWA	34	.482	.849	4.6	17.4
88-89	IOWA	32	.484	.833	5.4	18.6
Totals		130	.492	.831	4.0	13.1

NBA REGULAR-SEASON STATISTICS

		G	MIN	FGs FG	FGs PCT	3-PT FGs FG	3-PT FGs PCT	FTs FT	FTs PCT	Rebounds OFF	Rebounds TOT	AST	STL	BLK	PTS	PPG
89-90	CHI	81	1291	190	.485	3	.500	69	.885	19	102	199	46	6	452	5.6
90-91	CHI	82	1731	304	.481	15	.500	97	.874	25	149	301	70	4	720	8.8
91-92	CHI	82	1875	335	.481	35	.402	104	.806	19	145	266	46	5	809	9.9
92-93	CHI	82	2492	408	.499	63	.453	130	.861	27	149	330	66	6	1009	12.3
93-94	CHI	82	2770	479	.476	60	.444	194	.855	28	170	323	80	9	1212	14.8
94-95	CHI	82	2577	418	.468	108	.427	206	.884	25	186	244	84	8	1150	14.0
Totals		491	12736	2134	.481	284	.437	800	.861	143	901	1663	392	38	5352	10.9

VINCENT ASKEW

Team: Seattle SuperSonics
Position: Guard/Forward
Height: 6'6" **Weight:** 235
Birthdate: February 28, 1966

NBA Experience: 6 years
College: Memphis St.
Acquired: Traded from Kings for a 1993 2nd-round pick, 11/92

Background: After a three-year career at Memphis State, Askew entered the NBA draft early, was selected 39th overall by Philadelphia in 1987, and was waived after 14 games. He played in Italy and in the World Basketball League and was twice MVP of the Continental Basketball Association. He has since played for Golden State, Sacramento, and Seattle. He has posted career-high averages in several categories, including scoring, each of the last two years.

Strengths: Askew is one of the better defensive players around and continues to expand his contributions. He has greatly improved his jump shot over the past two years, can make the 3-pointer, and will find the open man. His best assets, however, are his defense and versatility. He matches up with players at three positions and hustles on both ends.

Weaknesses: Askew is best used as a complementary player rather than a featured part of a team's offense. His journeys through four pro leagues indicate that his game is not suited for every team. While he offers versatility, it can also be said he has not achieved greatness at any one position.

Analysis: Askew will not be returning to the CBA anytime soon. He once set a single-season scoring record in that league, and over the past two years he has shown he can score in the NBA as well. The defensive stalwart has been one of Seattle's key performers off the bench and can never be accused of not coming to play on game nights.

PLAYER SUMMARY

Will......................play three positions
Can't..................crack starting lineup
Expect ....valuable minutes
Don't Expect ....return to CBA
Fantasy Value $2-4
Card Value ....5-8¢

COLLEGE STATISTICS

		G	FGP	FTP	RPG	PPG
84-85	MSU	35	.511	.634	3.3	8.3
85-86	MSU	34	.490	.814	6.7	10.9
86-87	MSU	34	.483	.787	5.0	15.1
Totals		103	.492	.751	5.0	11.4

NBA REGULAR-SEASON STATISTICS

				FGs		3-PT FGs		FTs		Rebounds						
		G	MIN	FG	PCT	FG	PCT	FT	PCT	OFF	TOT	AST	STL	BLK	PTS	PPG
87-88	PHI	14	234	22	.297	0	.000	8	.727	6	22	33	10	6	52	3.7
90-91	GS	7	85	12	.480	0	.000	9	.818	7	11	13	2	0	33	4.7
91-92	GS	80	1496	193	.509	1	.100	111	.694	89	233	188	47	23	498	6.2
92-93	SAC/SEA	73	1129	152	.492	2	.333	105	.705	62	161	122	40	19	411	5.6
93-94	SEA	80	1690	273	.481	6	.194	175	.829	60	184	194	73	19	727	9.1
94-95	SEA	71	1721	248	.492	31	.330	176	.739	65	181	176	49	13	703	9.9
Totals		325	6355	900	.484	40	.284	584	.749	289	792	726	221	80	2424	7.5

STACEY AUGMON

Team: Atlanta Hawks
Position: Guard/Forward
Height: 6'8" **Weight:** 205
Birthdate: August 1, 1968

NBA Experience: 4 years
College: Nevada-Las Vegas
Acquired: 1st-round pick in 1991 draft
(9th overall)

Background: Augmon, who played four positions for UNLV, established a reputation as the nation's finest college defensive player. He played on the 1988 U.S. Olympic team and was a key player in UNLV's run to the national title in 1990. He was drafted No. 9 by Atlanta and made the NBA All-Rookie first team. He has scored about 14 PPG in the last three of his four pro seasons.

Strengths: Surprisingly, Augmon has turned as many heads with his offensive ability as he has with his gritty defense. He gets to the basket, runs the floor, and is considered one of the best finishers in the league. His post-up game is very strong. His great instincts for the ball, long wingspan, and ability to get to the boards help him live up to his defensive reputation.

Weaknesses: Augmon is a much better slasher than shooter. He has enjoyed two seasons over the 50-percent mark from the field, but his accuracy dipped to .453 last season and he does not hit the 3-pointer with regularity. He needs to develop a jump shot. He's not an especially gifted passer or dribbler and his build remains slight for his height.

Analysis: Augmon has turned out to be much more than a stopper. Yes, he remains a steady, hard-working defensive player, but he also scores his share of points and his leadership has been a bonus for the Hawks. He continues to improve in most aspects of the game, and it has earned him not only the respect that comes with being a more complete player, but also some rewarding endorsements.

PLAYER SUMMARY

Will ....post you up
Can't........stick jumpers consistently
Expect ....defense, dunks
Don't Expect ....flashy dribbling
Fantasy Value $15-18
Card Value ....8-15¢

COLLEGE STATISTICS

		G	FGP	FTP	RPG	PPG
87-88	UNLV	34	.574	.647	6.1	9.2
88-89	UNLV	37	.519	.663	7.4	15.3
89-90	UNLV	39	.553	.671	6.9	14.2
90-91	UNLV	35	.587	.727	7.3	16.5
Totals		145	.555	.677	6.9	13.7

NBA REGULAR-SEASON STATISTICS

				FGs		3-PT FGs		FTs		Rebounds						
		G	MIN	FG	PCT	FG	PCT	FT	PCT	OFF	TOT	AST	STL	BLK	PTS	PPG
91-92	ATL	82	2505	440	.489	1	.167	213	.666	191	420	201	124	27	1094	13.3
92-93	ATL	73	2112	397	.501	0	.000	227	.739	141	287	170	91	18	1021	14.0
93-94	ATL	82	2605	439	.510	1	.143	333	.764	178	394	187	149	45	1212	14.8
94-95	ATL	76	2362	397	.453	7	.269	252	.728	157	368	197	100	47	1053	13.9
Totals		313	9584	1673	.488	9	.209	1025	.727	667	1469	755	464	137	4380	14.0

ANTHONY AVENT

Team: Orlando Magic
Position: Forward
Height: 6'9" **Weight:** 235
Birthdate: October 18, 1969
NBA Experience: 3 years

College: Seton Hall
Acquired: Traded from Bucks for Anthony Cook and a 1994 1st-round pick, 1/94

Background: Avent was considered one of the best prep centers in the country while at Shabazz High School in Newark, New Jersey. He averaged 17.8 points and 9.9 rebounds per game during his senior year at Seton Hall and was drafted 15th overall by Atlanta in 1991. He spent his first pro season in Italy, joined Milwaukee in 1992-93, and was traded to Orlando in January 1994. He averaged a career-low 3.6 PPG last season.

Strengths: The strong-bodied Avent is on the floor for two reasons—defense and rebounding. He is a good athlete and hustles to stay with his man. He's blessed with a great work ethic and a team-first attitude. Avent is one of the better offensive rebounders in the league, and he uses his quickness on the glass to get many of his points.

Weaknesses: Avent is not a productive offensive player at the NBA level. He never has been. Low-post moves do not come naturally to him and his average has declined from each season to the next. He was once demoted to a lesser league in Italy, where defense often goes unappreciated. His shooting is nightmarish and it's reflected in his percentages from both the field and the free throw line.

Analysis: Avent was Milwaukee's best rebounder before his trade to Orlando for Anthony Cook and a first-round pick in 1994. However, he was not the player Orlando was looking for and has been relegated to a role of providing rest for the regulars. His defense and effort are steady, but he remains an offensive liability. He could also stand to develop a mean streak.

PLAYER SUMMARY	
Will	play defense
Can't	shoot straight
Expect	reserve minutes
Don't Expect	10 PPG
Fantasy Value	$0
Card Value	7-12¢

COLLEGE STATISTICS

		G	FGP	FTP	RPG	PPG
88-89	SH	38	.456	.653	3.0	4.4
89-90	SH	28	.488	.618	9.4	10.5
90-91	SH	34	.577	.750	9.9	17.8
Totals		100	.531	.701	7.1	10.7

NBA REGULAR-SEASON STATISTICS

				FGs		3-PT FGs		FTs		Rebounds						
		G	MIN	FG	PCT	FG	PCT	FT	PCT	OFF	TOT	AST	STL	BLK	PTS	PPG
92-93	MIL	82	2285	347	.433	0	.000	112	.651	180	512	91	57	73	806	9.8
93-94	MIL/ORL	74	1371	150	.377	0	.000	89	.724	144	338	65	33	31	389	5.3
94-95	ORL	71	1066	105	.430	0	.000	48	.640	97	293	41	28	50	258	3.6
Totals		227	4722	602	.417	0	.000	249	.673	421	1143	197	118	154	1453	6.4

VIN BAKER

Team: Milwaukee Bucks
Position: Forward/Center
Height: 6'11" **Weight:** 250
Birthdate: November 23, 1971

NBA Experience: 2 years
College: Hartford
Acquired: 1st-round pick in 1993 draft
(8th overall)

Background: Baker caught the eye of NBA scouts when he finished second in scoring in Division I as a junior. He ranked fourth in the nation in scoring and 17th in rebounding as a senior and set school records in career scoring, field goals, free throws, and blocked shots. Drafted eighth overall by Milwaukee, he made the 1994 All-Rookie Team and was named an All-Star in 1994-95, when he averaged 17.7 PPG and 10.3 RPG.

Strengths: Baker has all the tools to remain an impact player. Likened by some to Danny Manning upon entering the draft, he combines power and finesse and has a vast array of moves around the basket. Perhaps more important, he has the quickness to pull them off. He is one of the best rebounding forwards in the NBA and handles the ball very well for his size. He can fill in at center when needed.

Weaknesses: Baker does not have a strong perimeter game, clearly his most glaring weakness. He is a below-average outside shooter and puts up pitiful numbers from the free throw line (.593 last season). He is not a great passer, although he is learning to recognize double-teams, and his defense is also still in the learning phase.

Analysis: Baker is a great story. Most expected him to struggle during his early career in the NBA. After all, it was a hefty jump in competition from the lowly North Atlantic Conference. But in two years, he has raised his play to the All-Star level. His added muscle has helped him be more effective when asked to play center, and his abilities as a natural power forward are scary. What's scarier is that Baker is still developing.

PLAYER SUMMARY

Will.............................get to the hoop
Can't ....make free throws
Expect ....scoring, rebounding
Don't Expect........perimeter prowess
Fantasy Value $30-35
Card Value ....20-40¢

COLLEGE STATISTICS

		G	FGP	FTP	RPG	PPG
89-90	HART	28	.617	.390	2.9	4.7
90-91	HART	29	.491	.678	10.4	19.6
91-92	HART	27	.440	.657	9.9	27.6
92-93	HART	28	.477	.625	10.7	28.3
Totals		112	.475	.637	8.5	20.0

NBA REGULAR-SEASON STATISTICS

		G	MIN	FGs FG	FGs PCT	3-PT FGs FG	3-PT FGs PCT	FTs FT	FTs PCT	Rebounds OFF	Rebounds TOT	AST	STL	BLK	PTS	PPG
93-94	MIL	82	2560	435	.501	1	.200	234	.569	277	621	163	60	114	1105	13.5
94-95	MIL	82	3361	594	.483	7	.292	256	.593	289	846	296	86	116	1451	17.7
Totals		164	5921	1029	.490	8	.276	490	.581	566	1467	459	146	230	2556	15.6

CHARLES BARKLEY

Team: Phoenix Suns
Position: Forward
Height: 6'6" **Weight:** 252
Birthdate: February 20, 1963
NBA Experience: 11 years

College: Auburn
Acquired: Traded from 76ers for Jeff Hornacek, Tim Perry, and Andrew Lang, 6/92

Background: Barkley was known as the "Round Mound of Rebound" at Auburn, where he was named SEC Player of the Year as a junior. Since becoming a 20-PPG, 12-RPG player in his second NBA season, he has reached a level few can match. He won Olympic gold in 1992 and was named MVP in 1992-93, his first year with Phoenix. He's a perennial All-Star.

Strengths: Barkley's game features the complete package. He is among the top rebounders and scorers in the league. He shoots with range, muscles inside against seven-footers, and gets to the line. His strength and demeanor make him intimidating. He's capable of dominating, yet he has also shown great leadership on a strong team.

Weaknesses: Barkley's controversial past includes late-night bar fights, courtside spitting, and countless controversial quotes. Leg and back injuries have been nagging and he got off to a late start last year due to an abdominal strain.

Analysis: Barkley has threatened to retire soon. When he does, the NBA will lose a true superstar and one of its most colorful players over the last decade. Barkley is the kind of talent that comes along once in a great while. He still craves a championship ring.

PLAYER SUMMARY	
Will	dominate
Can't	avoid controversy
Expect	20-plus PPG
Don't Expect	off-court silence
Fantasy Value	$55-60
Card Value	35-75¢

COLLEGE STATISTICS

		G	FGP	FTP	RPG	PPG
81-82	AUB	28	.595	.636	9.8	12.7
82-83	AUB	28	.644	.631	9.5	14.4
83-84	AUB	28	.638	.683	9.5	15.1
Totals		84	.626	.652	9.6	14.1

NBA REGULAR-SEASON STATISTICS

				FGs		3-PT FGs		FTs		Rebounds						
	G	MIN	FG	PCT	FG	PCT	FT	PCT	OFF	TOT	AST	STL	BLK	PTS	PPG
84-85 PHI	82	2347	427	.545	1	.167	293	.733	266	703	155	95	80	1148	14.0
85-86 PHI	80	2952	595	.572	17	.227	396	.685	354	1026	312	173	125	1603	20.0
86-87 PHI	68	2740	557	.594	21	.202	429	.761	390	994	331	119	104	1564	23.0
87-88 PHI	80	3170	753	.587	44	.280	714	.751	385	951	254	100	103	2264	28.3
88-89 PHI	79	3088	700	.579	35	.216	602	.753	403	986	325	126	67	2037	25.8
89-90 PHI	70	3085	706	.600	20	.217	557	.749	361	909	307	148	50	1989	28.4
90-91 PHI	67	2498	665	.570	44	.284	475	.722	258	680	284	110	33	1849	27.6
91-92 PHI	75	2881	622	.552	32	.234	454	.695	271	830	308	136	44	1730	23.1
92-93 PHO	76	2859	716	.520	67	.305	445	.765	237	928	385	119	74	1944	25.6
93-94 PHO	65	2298	518	.495	48	.270	318	.704	198	727	296	101	37	1402	21.6
94-95 PHO	68	2382	554	.486	74	.338	379	.748	203	756	276	110	45	1561	23.0
Totals	810	30300	6813	.555	403	.268	5062	.735	3326	9490	3233	1337	762	19091	23.6

DANA BARROS

Unrestricted Free Agent
Last Team: Philadelphia 76ers
Position: Guard
Height: 5'11" **Weight:** 165
Birthdate: April 13, 1967
NBA Experience: 6 years

College: Boston College
Acquired: Traded from Hornets with Sidney Green, draft rights to Greg Graham, and a 1994 1st-round pick for Hersey Hawkins, 9/93

Background: Barros, who finished his career as the all-time scoring leader at Boston College, became the first player in Big East history to lead the conference in scoring in back-to-back years. He served mostly as a reserve in his four years in Seattle, and his .446 3-point average in 1991-92 was tops in the NBA. A trade to Philadelphia made him a starter in 1993-94, and he made his first All-Star Game appearance in 1994-95. He was also named the NBA's Most Improved Player.

Strengths: Barros is blessed with a beautiful stroke. He was third in the league in 3-point accuracy last season and is not shy about putting them up. Few do it better when the game is on the line. Small and extremely quick, he is adept at getting to the hole. Barros possesses loads of confidence.

Weaknesses: Barros is not as polished a playmaker as most point guards, possessing the mentality of a two guard. His assist-to-turnover ratio will not lead the league and he is sometimes too content to settle for the long-range jumper. He is suspect on defense because of his size.

Analysis: Although Philadelphia and Seattle are on opposite ends of the NBA standings, coming to the 76ers has been the best thing that could have happened to Barros. He always said he just needed the minutes to show what he could do, and he was right. He exploded for 20.6 PPG in 1994-95. His long-range shooting and dangerous quickness make him a potential All-Star regular.

PLAYER SUMMARY	
Will	score from downtown
Can't	avoid post-ups
Expect	clutch jumpers
Don't Expect	assist records
Fantasy Value	$25-30
Card Value	10-15¢

COLLEGE STATISTICS

		G	FGP	FTP	APG	PPG
85-86	BC	28	.479	.791	3.5	13.7
86-87	BC	29	.458	.850	3.8	18.7
87-88	BC	33	.480	.851	4.1	21.9
88-89	BC	29	.475	.857	3.3	23.9
Totals		119	.473	.841	3.7	19.7

NBA REGULAR-SEASON STATISTICS

			FGs		3-PT FGs		FTs		Rebounds						
	G	MIN	FG	PCT	FG	PCT	FT	PCT	OFF	TOT	AST	STL	BLK	PTS	PPG
89-90 SEA	81	1630	299	.405	95	.399	89	.809	35	132	205	53	1	782	9.7
90-91 SEA	66	750	154	.495	32	.395	78	.918	17	71	111	23	1	418	6.3
91-92 SEA	75	1331	238	.483	83	.446	60	.759	17	81	125	51	4	619	8.3
92-93 SEA	69	1243	214	.451	64	.379	49	.831	18	107	151	63	3	541	7.8
93-94 PHI	81	2519	412	.469	135	.381	116	.800	28	196	424	107	5	1075	13.3
94-95 PHI	82	3318	571	.490	197	.464	347	.899	27	274	619	149	4	1686	20.6
Totals	454	10791	1888	.465	606	.417	739	.855	142	861	1635	446	18	5121	11.3

JON BARRY

Team: Milwaukee Bucks
Position: Guard
Height: 6'5" **Weight:** 204
Birthdate: July 25, 1969

NBA Experience: 3 years
College: Pacific; Paris; Georgia Tech
Acquired: Draft rights traded from
Celtics for Alaa Abdelnaby, 12/92

Background: One of four sons of Hall of Famer Rick Barry to play Division I
basketball, Barry played at Pacific and Paris (Texas) Junior College before
leading Georgia Tech in 3-point field goals as a senior. He was drafted by Boston
in 1992 and, after not being able to agree on a contract, was traded to
Milwaukee. The best of his three years with the Bucks was his second, when he
averaged 6.2 PPG.

Strengths: Barry brings good size to the backcourt. He knows the game,
hustles, and displays above-average court sense. He is a splendid passer,
perhaps from having to give up the ball while teamed with his father during
pickup games, and he handles it very well. He owns 3-point range with his
jumper and works relentlessly at both ends of the floor, tallying over 100 steals in
his second season.

Weaknesses: Barry was known as a good shooter in college, but he has yet to
make shots in the NBA with any kind of consistency. His field goal percentage
since entering the league has been awful and is the biggest reason for his time
on the bench. He does not offer much help on the boards and lacks the
quickness to be a stopper.

Analysis: Barry has some of his dad's intangibles. He is willing to do whatever it
takes to make it, and he tries to make those around him better. However, there
are several other parts of the game he needs to hone to become a productive
player at this level. Shooting the ball is the main one. Without a reliable outside
shot, he is bound to struggle for minutes.

PLAYER SUMMARY	
Will	spot open men
Can't	find his jumper
Expect	a team player
Don't Expect	his dad's numbers
Fantasy Value	$0
Card Value	7-10¢

COLLEGE STATISTICS

		G	FGP	FTP	RPG	PPG
87-88	PAC	29	.372	.746	2.6	9.5
90-91	GT	30	.444	.732	3.7	15.9
91-92	GT	35	.429	.697	4.3	17.2
Totals		94	.421	.717	3.6	14.4

NBA REGULAR-SEASON STATISTICS

			FGs		3-PT FGs		FTs		Rebounds						
	G	MIN	FG	PCT	FG	PCT	FT	PCT	OFF	TOT	AST	STL	BLK	PTS	PPG
92-93 MIL	47	552	76	.369	21	.333	33	.673	10	43	68	35	3	206	4.4
93-94 MIL	72	1242	158	.414	32	.278	97	.795	36	146	168	102	17	445	6.2
94-95 MIL	52	602	57	.425	16	.333	61	.762	15	49	85	30	4	191	3.7
Totals	171	2396	291	.403	69	.305	191	.761	61	238	321	167	24	842	4.9

BENOIT BENJAMIN

Team: Vancouver Grizzlies
Position: Center
Height: 7'0" **Weight:** 265
Birthdate: November 22, 1964

NBA Experience: 10 years
College: Creighton
Acquired: Selected from Nets in 1995 expansion draft

Background: Benjamin played for Creighton and led the nation in blocked shots (5.1 BPG) as a junior. He gave up his final year of college eligibility to enter the NBA draft and played five-plus years with the Clippers. Benjamin has played with four different teams during the last five years, most recently starting for the Nets over the past two seasons. He'll suit up in Vancouver in 1995-96.

Strengths: Benjamin has a soft touch for a big man. He is still capable of having nights that make you wonder why he has not been a standout during his pro career. He's good for at least one blocked shot per game and has enjoyed some fine seasons on the defensive glass.

Weaknesses: The word "enigma" should be stitched on the back of Benjamin's extra-large jersey. For reasons mostly unknown, he has never displayed the desire or consistency to raise his game to the next level. He is a regular in any coach's doghouse for his tendency to disappear on the court.

Analysis: Benjamin, when he retires, will be remembered as someone who never reached his potential. He returned to 50-percent shooting last season for the first time in five years and scored in double figures for the first time in three. However, his efforts remain inconsistent and his critics ever-present.

PLAYER SUMMARY

Will ....grab defensive boards
Can't ....reach his potential
Expect...............................soft hands
Don't Expect.............consistent play
Fantasy Value $6-8
Card Value ....5-8¢

COLLEGE STATISTICS

		G	FGP	FTP	RPG	PPG
82-83	CRE	27	.555	.655	9.6	14.8
83-84	CRE	30	.543	.743	9.8	16.2
84-85	CRE	32	.582	.738	14.1	21.5
Totals		89	.562	.720	11.3	17.7

NBA REGULAR-SEASON STATISTICS

				FGs		3-PT FGs		FTs		Rebounds						
		G	MIN	FG	PCT	FG	PCT	FT	PCT	OFF	TOT	AST	STL	BLK	PTS	PPG
85-86	LAC	79	2088	324	.490	1	.333	229	.746	161	600	79	64	206	878	11.1
86-87	LAC	72	2230	320	.449	0	.000	188	.715	134	586	135	60	187	828	11.5
87-88	LAC	66	2171	340	.491	0	.000	180	.706	112	530	172	50	225	860	13.0
88-89	LAC	79	2585	491	.541	0	.000	317	.744	164	696	157	57	221	1299	16.4
89-90	LAC	71	2313	362	.526	0	.000	235	.732	156	657	159	59	187	959	13.5
90-91	LAC/SEA	70	2236	386	.496	0	.000	210	.712	157	723	119	54	145	982	14.0
91-92	SEA	63	1941	354	.478	0	.000	171	.687	130	513	76	39	118	879	14.0
92-93	SEA/LAL	59	754	133	.491	0	.000	69	.663	51	209	22	31	48	335	5.7
93-94	NJ	77	1817	283	.480	0	.000	152	.710	135	499	44	35	90	718	9.3
94-95	NJ	61	1598	271	.510	0	.000	133	.760	94	440	38	23	64	675	11.1
Totals		697	19733	3264	.497	1	.056	1884	.722	1294	5453	1001	472	1491	8413	12.1

DAVID BENOIT

Team: Utah Jazz
Position: Forward
Height: 6'8" **Weight:** 220
Birthdate: May 9, 1968

NBA Experience: 4 years
College: Tyler; Alabama
Acquired: Signed as a free agent, 8/91

Background: Benoit started playing basketball in high school and began his college career at Tyler Junior College before transferring to Alabama. He averaged ten-plus PPG in both of his years there. Benoit was the Rookie of the Year in the Spanish League in 1990-91. His first three years with Utah were spent mostly as a reserve, but he broke into the starting lineup last season and averaged career highs in most categories.

Strengths: Benoit is a relentless worker who runs the floor and ignites his team with fantastic finishes. He is at his best when blocking shots and crashing the boards. He can jump out of the gym and has long arms that help him play above his man. His defense is solid. Benoit gets much of his offense in transition, but he has also developed his jumper. He shot a career best from the field last year.

Weaknesses: Inconsistency has been the most common knock on Benoit. Sometimes he's the team sparkplug; others he's hardly noticeable. He is not as good a ball-handler as other small forwards in the NBA, but he is not asked to handle it much. He turns the ball over more often than he gets credit for an assist. Sometimes he goes too hard for his own good.

Analysis: After two down years, Benoit checked into an alcohol treatment program before last season and seems to have found some answers. "I was not the person I wanted to be," he said. "Now it's time for me to step up every aspect of my basketball game." Benoit has clearly done that, shooting .486 from the field during the 1994-95 season.

PLAYER SUMMARY	
Will	run the floor
Can't	distribute
Expect	crowd-pleasing jams
Don't Expect	a dazzling dribble
Fantasy Value	$3-5
Card Value	5-8¢

COLLEGE STATISTICS

		G	FGP	FTP	RPG	PPG
88-89	ALAB	31	.507	.738	8.0	10.8
89-90	ALAB	35	.515	.767	6.1	10.5
Totals		66	.511	.752	7.0	10.6

NBA REGULAR-SEASON STATISTICS

		G	MIN	FGs FG	FGs PCT	3-PT FGs FG	3-PT FGs PCT	FTs FT	FTs PCT	Rebounds OFF	Rebounds TOT	AST	STL	BLK	PTS	PPG
91-92	UTA	77	1161	175	.467	3	.214	81	.810	105	296	34	19	44	434	5.6
92-93	UTA	82	1712	258	.436	34	.347	114	.750	116	392	43	45	43	664	8.1
93-94	UTA	55	1070	139	.385	12	.203	68	.773	89	260	23	23	37	358	6.5
94-95	UTA	71	1841	285	.486	38	.330	132	.841	96	368	58	45	47	740	10.4
Totals		285	5784	857	.448	87	.304	395	.795	406	1316	158	132	171	2196	7.7

MOOKIE BLAYLOCK

Team: Atlanta Hawks
Position: Guard
Height: 6′1″ **Weight:** 185
Birthdate: March 20, 1967

NBA Experience: 6 years
College: Midland; Oklahoma
Acquired: Traded from Nets with Roy Hinson for Rumeal Robinson, 11/92

Background: Born Daron Oshay Blaylock, Mookie earned All-America recognition at Oklahoma and was the first NCAA player to collect 200 assists and 100 steals in back-to-back seasons. He was taken 12th by New Jersey in 1989, was acquired by Atlanta in a 1992 trade, and has enjoyed his three best seasons with the Hawks. He made his All-Star debut in 1994 and averaged a career-high 17.2 PPG during the 1994-95 season.

Strengths: Blaylock is the complete package at the point. His quickness and instincts help him rank among the league leaders in steals annually. A true hustler and great rebounder, he is an NBA All-Defensive Team player. fensively, he's a prototypical point guard with sharp passing skills who can score on drives through the lane and with his jumper. He has 3-point range, a great dribble, and leadership skills.

Weaknesses: Blaylock does not shoot for a high percentage and is still prone to ice-cold nights. There are times he should stick to driving and dishing instead of firing 3-point bombs. He could use some reps at the free throw line as well.

Analysis: Blaylock has fulfilled Lenny Wilkens's prediction that he would become one of the premier point guards in the game. There are only a handful in the same class as Mookie, who gets the Hawks going with his play on both the offensive and defensive ends of the floor. He is a consistent jump shot away from becoming a regular in the All-Star Game.

PLAYER SUMMARY	
Will	pick your pocket
Can't	shoot 45 percent
Expect	clamp-down defense
Don't Expect	free throw accuracy
Fantasy Value	$25-30
Card Value	8-15¢

COLLEGE STATISTICS

		G	FGP	FTP	APG	PPG
85-86	MIDL	34	.566	.738	—	16.8
86-87	MIDL	33	.516	.723	—	19.6
87-88	OKLA	39	.460	.684	5.9	16.4
88-89	OKLA	35	.455	.650	6.7	20.0
Totals		141	.495	.696	6.3	18.1

NBA REGULAR-SEASON STATISTICS

			FGs		3-PT FGs		FTs		Rebounds						
	G	MIN	FG	PCT	FG	PCT	FT	PCT	OFF	TOT	AST	STL	BLK	PTS	PPG
89-90 NJ	50	1267	212	.371	18	.225	63	.778	42	140	210	82	14	505	10.1
90-91 NJ	72	2585	432	.416	14	.154	139	.790	67	249	441	169	40	1017	14.1
91-92 NJ	72	2548	429	.432	12	.222	126	.712	101	269	492	170	40	996	13.8
92-93 ATL	80	2820	414	.429	118	.375	123	.728	89	280	671	203	23	1069	13.4
93-94 ATL	81	2915	444	.411	114	.334	116	.730	117	424	789	212	44	1118	13.8
94-95 ATL	80	3069	509	.425	199	.359	156	.729	117	393	616	200	26	1373	17.2
Totals	435	15204	2440	.418	475	.331	723	.741	533	1755	3219	1036	187	6078	14.0

CORIE BLOUNT

Team: Los Angeles Lakers
Position: Forward
Height: 6'10" **Weight:** 242
Birthdate: January 4, 1969

NBA Experience: 2 years
College: Rancho Santiago; Cincinnati
Acquired: Traded from Bulls for future considerations, 7/95

Background: Standing only 6'5" when he finished high school, Blount enrolled at Rancho Santiago C.C. in California and was selected Junior College Player of the Year by *Basketball Times* before transferring to Cincinnati. He averaged 9.4 PPG and blocked 85 shots in two years with the Bearcats. Chicago drafted him 25th overall in 1993 and he has averaged less than four PPG in limited playing time during his first two seasons. He was traded to the Lakers over the summer.

Strengths: Blount possesses great athletic ability and uses it best on the defensive end. He's wiry-strong, gets up and down the court, and swats shots instinctively. Blount has also demonstrated the potential to be a productive rebounder at the NBA level, although he never dominated the boards in college. He does not put up many bad shots and improved his field goal percentage considerably after his rookie year.

Weaknesses: For offense, don't dial Blount. He has no perimeter game to speak of and opponents will give him open jumpers all night. Blount never made a 3-pointer in four years of college and is no threat at all from 18 feet and beyond. His offensive skills in the paint are substandard as well, and he is an embarrassing free throw shooter. He'd be in foul trouble if he played more.

Analysis: Blount was expected to help the Bulls as a defensive presence and lend a hand on the boards, and he might well be capable of doing those things with the Lakers. Problem is, he is an offensive liability and it has caused him to labor on the bench for most of his first two years. If he could develop even one or two consistent moves and make a jumper from time to time, his minutes would increase greatly.

PLAYER SUMMARY

Will....................................block shots
Can't ....make free throws
Expect ....a defensive sub
Don't Expect.............sweet shooting
Fantasy Value.................................$0
Card Value ....8-15¢

COLLEGE STATISTICS

		G	FGP	FTP	RPG	PPG
91-92	CINC	34	.479	.556	6.3	8.2
92-93	CINC	21	.550	.566	8.1	11.3
Totals		55	.511	.559	7.0	9.4

NBA REGULAR-SEASON STATISTICS

			FGs		3-PT FGs		FTs		Rebounds						
	G	MIN	FG	PCT	FG	PCT	FT	PCT	OFF	TOT	AST	STL	BLK	PTS	PPG
93-94 CHI	67	690	76	.437	0	.000	46	.613	76	194	56	19	33	198	3.0
94-95 CHI	68	889	100	.476	0	.000	38	.567	107	240	60	26	33	238	3.5
Totals	135	1579	176	.458	0	.000	84	.592	183	434	116	45	66	436	3.2

MUGGSY BOGUES

Team: Charlotte Hornets
Position: Guard
Height: 5'3" **Weight:** 136
Birthdate: January 9, 1965

NBA Experience: 8 years
College: Wake Forest
Acquired: Selected from Bullets in 1988 expansion draft

Background: Bogues learned the game at famed Dunbar High School in Baltimore, where he teamed with Reggie Williams and the late Reggie Lewis. At Wake Forest, he set ACC career records for assists and steals. His pro career took off after Charlotte plucked him from the Bullets in the 1988 expansion draft. He has ranked among the league leaders in assists each of the last four seasons.

Strengths: Bogues makes the league's so-called quick playmakers look as though they're standing still. Always moving, he's a pest on both ends. Few can stop him from driving past his man and dishing off, and he is always a threat to swipe your dribble. He has led the league in assist-to-turnover ratio six of the last seven seasons and is one of the game's best free throw shooters.

Weaknesses: His most obvious drawback is his size. He can't shoot over anyone and Spud Webb can post him up. His shooting has improved but he is not a huge scorer and is no threat to beat you from 3-point range.

Analysis: Charlotte has given up its quest to find a point guard to replace Bogues because its mighty mite continues to get better. He has improved his scoring average in each of the last four years and he continues to burn opponents with his quickness and playmaking. No one protects the ball better and very few make things happen like he does.

PLAYER SUMMARY	
Will	create
Can't	be pressured
Expect	pinpoint passes
Don't Expect	turnovers
Fantasy Value	$5-7
Card Value	5-10¢

COLLEGE STATISTICS

		G	FGP	FTP	APG	PPG
83-84	WF	32	.304	.692	1.7	1.2
84-85	WF	29	.500	.682	7.1	6.6
85-86	WF	29	.455	.730	8.4	11.3
86-87	WF	29	.500	.806	9.5	14.8
Totals		119	.473	.749	6.6	8.3

NBA REGULAR-SEASON STATISTICS

		G	MIN	FGs FG	FGs PCT	3-PT FGs FG	3-PT FGs PCT	FTs FT	FTs PCT	Rebounds OFF	Rebounds TOT	AST	STL	BLK	PTS	PPG
87-88	WAS	79	1628	166	.390	3	.188	58	.784	35	136	404	127	3	393	5.0
88-89	CHA	79	1755	178	.426	1	.077	66	.750	53	165	620	111	7	423	5.4
89-90	CHA	81	2743	326	.491	5	.192	106	.791	48	207	867	166	3	763	9.4
90-91	CHA	81	2299	241	.460	0	.000	86	.796	58	216	669	137	3	568	7.0
91-92	CHA	82	2790	317	.472	2	.074	94	.783	58	235	743	170	6	730	8.9
92-93	CHA	81	2833	331	.453	6	.231	140	.833	51	298	711	161	5	808	10.0
93-94	CHA	77	2746	354	.471	2	.167	125	.806	78	313	780	133	2	835	10.8
94-95	CHA	78	2629	348	.477	6	.200	160	.889	51	257	675	103	0	862	11.1
Totals		638	19423	2261	.460	25	.154	835	.813	432	1827	5469	1108	29	5382	8.4

ANTHONY BONNER

Unrestricted Free Agent
Last Team: New York Knicks
Position: Forward
Height: 6'8" **Weight:** 225
Birthdate: June 8, 1968

NBA Experience: 5 years
College: St. Louis
Acquired: Signed as a free agent, 10/93

Background: Bonner led all Division I players in rebounding as a senior at St. Louis University. He finished his career as the school's all-time leader in points, rebounds, steals, and games played. After three years as a reserve and part-time starter for the Kings, Bonner signed with the Knicks before the 1993-94 season and has started 61 games over the past two years.

Strengths: Bonner is a bruising rebounder who is willing to sacrifice his body. He shows a great work ethic and mixes it up at both ends of the floor. He's strong on defense, where he lacks power-forward size but can match up with them. He's tough and downright fearless.

Weaknesses: Offense is not on Bonner's resume. His free throw percentage tells you all you need to know about his shooting touch. He has little right taking 15-footers and is at his best within about five feet from the bucket. Bonner does nothing off the dribble and is prone to turnovers when he tries to do too much. His accuracy from the field dropped 100 points last season. His scoring average has dropped each of the last four years.

Analysis: Bonner was not expected to play as much as he has with the Knicks, but his defense and rebounding earned him a shot under Pat Riley. His offense is another story. While Bonner was used as a part-time starter again last season, by the playoffs he was deep on the bench. In the event he stays in New York, he will continue to battle a numbers game.

PLAYER SUMMARY

Will ....rebound
Can't ....shoot free throws
Expect ....a bruiser
Don't Expect ....offensive touch
Fantasy Value $0
Card Value ....7-12¢

COLLEGE STATISTICS

		G	FGP	FTP	RPG	PPG
86-87	STL	35	.592	.661	9.6	10.3
87-88	STL	28	.537	.597	8.8	13.8
88-89	STL	37	.560	.582	10.4	15.5
89-90	STL	33	.500	.693	13.8	19.8
Totals		133	.539	.634	10.7	14.8

NBA REGULAR-SEASON STATISTICS

		G	MIN	FGs FG	FGs PCT	3-PT FGs FG	3-PT FGs PCT	FTs FT	FTs PCT	Rebounds OFF	Rebounds TOT	AST	STL	BLK	PTS	PPG
90-91	SAC	34	750	103	.448	0	.000	44	.579	59	161	49	39	5	250	7.4
91-92	SAC	79	2287	294	.447	1	.250	151	.627	192	485	125	94	26	740	9.4
92-93	SAC	70	1764	229	.461	0	.000	143	.593	188	455	96	86	17	601	8.6
93-94	NY	73	1402	162	.563	0	.000	50	.476	150	344	88	76	13	374	5.1
94-95	NY	58	1126	88	.456	1	.200	44	.657	113	262	80	48	23	221	3.8
Totals		314	7329	876	.469	2	.125	432	.592	702	1707	438	343	84	2186	7.0

ANTHONY BOWIE

Unrestricted Free Agent
Last Team: Orlando Magic
Position: Guard
Height: 6'6" **Weight:** 200
Birthdate: November 9, 1963

NBA Experience: 6 years
College: Oklahoma
Acquired: Signed as a free agent, 12/91

Background: Bowie played college ball at Oklahoma and was drafted by Houston in 1986, but he played his first NBA ball with San Antonio in 1988-89. He was picked up by the Rockets in '89 but was let go the following year. Bowie has played some of his best ball since being picked up by Orlando from the CBA during the 1991-92 campaign. He averaged 5.5 points in about 16 minutes per game last season.

Strengths: Bowie is a versatile player who can be used at three positions, though he is mainly a backup shooting guard. He glides up and down the court and can shoot the lights out in streaks. He has converted at a 48-percent pace from the field each of the last two years and is a good free throw shooter. He averaged 14.6 PPG in 1991-92.

Weaknesses: Bowie is not as good with the ball as most NBA guards. His handling and passing skills are suspect. He is better at finishing than starting plays. Bowie is at his best in transition and coming off screens rather than creating offense on his own. Though considered a shooter, he has not enjoyed 3-point success.

Analysis: Bowie has brought attitude, effort, and ability to fill in where needed to Orlando, one of the best teams in the league. He will never be a big scorer, but the versatile Bowie accepts his job as a role-player and fills it quite well. He works hard on defense and plays within his limits.

PLAYER SUMMARY	
Will	make free throws
Can't	thrive at the point
Expect	streak shooting
Don't Expect	loads of treys
Fantasy Value	$0
Card Value	5-10¢

COLLEGE STATISTICS

		G	FGP	FTP	RPG	PPG
84-85	OKLA	37	.515	.773	5.8	13.4
85-86	OKLA	35	.502	.808	4.6	13.3
Totals		72	.509	.787	5.2	13.4

NBA REGULAR-SEASON STATISTICS

		G	MIN	FGs FG	FGs PCT	3-PT FGs FG	3-PT FGs PCT	FTs FT	FTs PCT	Rebounds OFF	Rebounds TOT	AST	STL	BLK	PTS	PPG
88-89	SA	18	438	72	.500	1	.200	10	.667	25	56	29	18	4	155	8.6
89-90	HOU	66	918	119	.406	6	.286	40	.741	36	118	96	42	5	284	4.3
91-92	ORL	52	1721	312	.493	17	.386	117	.860	70	245	163	55	38	758	14.6
92-93	ORL	77	1761	268	.471	15	.313	67	.798	36	194	175	54	14	618	8.0
93-94	ORL	70	948	139	.481	1	.056	41	.837	29	120	102	32	12	320	4.6
94-95	ORL	77	1261	177	.480	12	.300	61	.824	54	139	159	47	21	427	5.5
Totals		360	7047	1087	.473	52	.295	336	.816	250	872	724	248	94	2562	7.1

SAM BOWIE

Unrestricted Free Agent
Last Team: Los Angeles Lakers
Position: Center
Height: 7'1" **Weight:** 263
Birthdate: March 17, 1961

NBA Experience: 10 years
College: Kentucky
Acquired: Traded from Nets for Benoit Benjamin, 6/93

Background: Bowie and Ralph Sampson came out of high school in the same year as perhaps the most heralded tandem of big men ever. Bowie was on his way to stardom at Kentucky when leg injuries forced him to miss two seasons. Portland drafted him ahead of Michael Jordan. His ten-year pro career with the Trail Blazers, Nets, and Lakers has also been plagued by injuries.

Strengths: Bowie has a soft shooting touch and is a fine passer for a big man. He hits the 18-footer, sticks free throws, finds open men, and does a decent job on the glass. He has always been able to block shots despite his chronic leg injuries.

Weaknesses: The biggest weakness with Bowie is his health, as he's lost more than six seasons to injury. The word "soft" has been used to describe his overall game. He has never been adept at attacking the basket with power. His field goal percentage is low for a center and his scoring has tailed off.

Analysis: Bowie is a finesse player all the way. He has never demonstrated much power in his game, even in those rare seasons when he's been healthy. He spent only two weeks on the injured list last season but was not one of the main reasons for the Lakers' success.

PLAYER SUMMARY	
Will	block shots
Can't	trade in his legs
Expect	crafty passing
Don't Expect	power
Fantasy Value	$0
Card Value	5-10¢

COLLEGE STATISTICS

		G	FGP	FTP	RPG	PPG
79-80	KENT	34	.531	.764	8.1	12.9
80-81	KENT	28	.520	.720	9.1	17.4
83-84	KENT	34	.516	.722	9.2	10.5
Totals		96	.522	.735	8.8	13.4

NBA REGULAR-SEASON STATISTICS

			FGs		3-PT FGs		FTs		Rebounds						
	G	MIN	FG	PCT	FG	PCT	FT	PCT	OFF	TOT	AST	STL	BLK	PTS	PPG
84-85 POR	76	2216	299	.537	0	.000	160	.711	207	656	215	55	203	758	10.0
85-86 POR	38	1132	167	.484	0	.000	114	.708	93	327	99	21	96	448	11.8
86-87 POR	5	163	30	.455	0	.000	20	.667	14	33	9	1	10	80	16.0
88-89 POR	20	412	69	.451	5	.714	28	.571	36	106	36	7	33	171	8.6
89-90 NJ	68	2207	347	.416	10	.323	294	.776	206	690	91	38	121	998	14.7
90-91 NJ	62	1916	314	.434	4	.182	169	.732	176	480	147	43	90	801	12.9
91-92 NJ	71	2179	421	.445	8	.320	212	.757	203	578	186	41	120	1062	15.0
92-93 NJ	79	2092	287	.450	2	.333	141	.779	158	556	127	32	128	717	9.1
93-94 LAL	25	556	75	.436	1	.250	72	.867	27	131	47	4	28	223	8.9
94-95 LAL	67	1225	118	.442	2	.182	68	.764	72	288	118	21	80	306	4.6
Totals	511	14098	2127	.452	32	.302	1278	.748	1192	3845	1075	263	909	5564	10.9

SHAWN BRADLEY

Team: Philadelphia 76ers
Position: Center
Height: 7'6" **Weight:** 248
Birthdate: March 22, 1972

NBA Experience: 2 years
College: Brigham Young
Acquired: 1st-round pick in 1993 draft
(2nd overall)

Background: From tiny Castle Dale, Utah, Bradley played just one season at Brigham Young (as a freshman in 1990-91) and blocked 177 shots that year. He once swatted 14 in a game. He spent two years in Australia on a Mormon mission, then entered the draft and was taken second overall by Philadelphia. A knee injury cut short his first year, and he returned last season to average 9.5 points and better than three blocks per game.

Strengths: Bradley is at his best when the other team has the ball. He rates among the leading shot-swatters in the league and has a wide wingspan to cover a lot of ground in the lane. He has plenty of potential as a rebounder and is especially effective on the offensive glass. Bradley, a star baseball player in high school, is considered a decent athlete for his size. He wants to make an impression worthy of his draft status.

Weaknesses: Bradley needs to continue hitting the weights, not to mention the refrigerator. His body is still too thin to hold its ground against physical competition. His field goal percentage is horrible for a big man, he gets in foul trouble at a startling rate, and he has shown very little feel for putting the ball in the basket. His moves are mechanical.

Analysis: The 76ers are paying Bradley a lot of money (some $5 million-plus per year) for what has amounted to a defensive specialist and an offensive liability. Every now and then, Bradley puts it all together and makes you think he can become a fine NBA pivot. So far, however, those nights are in the vast minority. He is on the verge of "bust" status unless he makes big strides.

PLAYER SUMMARY	
Will	block shots
Can't	dominate offensively
Expect	a defensive presence
Don't Expect	good shooting
Fantasy Value	$12-15
Card Value	12-20¢

COLLEGE STATISTICS

		G	FGP	FTP	RPG	PPG
90-91	BYU	34	.518	.692	7.7	14.8
Totals		34	.518	.692	7.7	14.8

NBA REGULAR-SEASON STATISTICS

			FGs		3-PT FGs		FTs		Rebounds						
		G	MIN	FG	PCT	FG	PCT	FT	PCT	OFF	TOT	AST	STL	BLK	PTS	PPG
93-94	PHI	49	1385	201	.409	0	.000	102	.607	98	306	98	45	147	504	10.3
94-95	PHI	82	2365	315	.455	0	.000	148	.638	243	659	53	54	274	778	9.5
Totals		131	3750	516	.436	0	.000	250	.625	341	965	151	99	421	1282	9.8

TERRELL BRANDON

Team: Cleveland Cavaliers
Position: Guard
Height: 5'11" **Weight:** 180
Birthdate: May 20, 1970

NBA Experience: 4 years
College: Oregon
Acquired: 1st-round pick in 1991 draft
(11th overall)

Background: After sitting out his freshman year at Oregon under Prop 40, Brandon had two terrific seasons at point guard, leading the Pac-10 in scoring and steals as a junior. He entered the NBA draft early and was selected 11th overall by Cleveland. He had been a critical performer in four years with the Cavaliers before falling victim to a broken tibia in April. He averaged a career-high 13.3 PPG in 1994-95.

Strengths: Brandon is an offensive-minded point guard with explosive speed with the basketball. He has good vision and court sense and is an excellent leaper. He was a terrific offensive player in college who finishes his drives to the hoop against top NBA guards as well. He has a quick release and 3-point range. He has been invaluable for his contributions both off the bench and as a spot starter.

Weaknesses: Brandon did not play much defense in college and it is not his strength at the NBA level. He has lots of quickness and gets back in transition but is too small to muscle up against his man in halfcourt play. His shooting percentage has been up and down, but suffice it to say he is not automatic when left open.

Analysis: Brandon has fared well in Cleveland despite having to back up Mark Price, one of the best point guards in the game. While Brandon does not have Price's shooting skills or savvy, he does offer an explosive dimension and has helped his team survive a rash of injuries over the last few years. He has earned much respect from coaches.

PLAYER SUMMARY

Will......................explode to the hoop
Can't ....beat out Price
Expect ....point-guard offense
Don't Expect ....great playmaking
Fantasy Value $9-11
Card Value ....8-12¢

COLLEGE STATISTICS

		G	FGP	FTP	APG	PPG
89-90	OREG	29	.474	.752	6.0	17.9
90-91	OREG	28	.491	.850	5.0	26.6
Totals		57	.484	.810	5.5	22.2

NBA REGULAR-SEASON STATISTICS

		G	MIN	FGs FG	FGs PCT	3-PT FGs FG	3-PT FGs PCT	FTs FT	FTs PCT	Rebounds OFF	Rebounds TOT	AST	STL	BLK	PTS	PPG
91-92	CLE	82	1605	252	.419	1	.043	100	.806	49	162	316	81	22	605	7.4
92-93	CLE	82	1622	297	.478	13	.310	118	.825	37	179	302	79	27	725	8.8
93-94	CLE	73	1548	230	.420	7	.219	139	.858	38	159	277	84	16	606	8.3
94-95	CLE	67	1961	341	.448	48	.397	159	.855	35	186	363	107	14	889	13.3
Totals		304	6736	1120	.442	69	.317	516	.839	159	686	1258	351	79	2825	9.3

FRANK BRICKOWSKI

Team: Sacramento Kings
Position: Forward/Center
Height: 6'9" **Weight:** 248
Birthdate: August 14, 1959

NBA Experience: 10 years
College: Penn St.
Acquired: Signed as a free agent, 8/94

Background: Brickowski led Penn State in scoring his junior and senior years. After being drafted in the third round by the Knicks, he played overseas for three years in Italy, France, and Israel. Brickowski has played for the Sonics, Lakers, Spurs, Bucks, and Hornets in ten pro seasons. His 11th, with Sacramento last year, was spent entirely on the injured list.

Strengths: Brickowski possesses good size and quickness around the basket and is effective as a low-post scorer. He is a reliable shooter when open and can also muscle inside. He has averaged double figures in the scoring column six of his last seven years and plays tough on the defensive end.

Weaknesses: Brickowski is not the athletic power forward who thrives in an open-court game. Injuries have slowed him, including a shoulder ailment last season. His knees are also in decline. He is not a good ball-handler or passer. His rough style results in a lot of fouls.

Analysis: Brickowski works hard and is surprisingly adept in several aspects of the game. Unfortunately, he has not stayed healthy enough to make much of an impact at any of his recent stops. He spent all last season in street clothes. One has to wonder whether Brickowski will ever again be a contributor.

PLAYER SUMMARY	
Will	mix it up
Can't	stay healthy
Expect	toughness
Don't Expect	82 games
Fantasy Value	$3-5
Card Value	5-7¢

COLLEGE STATISTICS

		G	FGP	FTP	RPG	PPG
77-78	PSU	25	.457	.840	2.6	3.8
78-79	PSU	24	.495	.792	4.5	5.7
79-80	PSU	27	.521	.781	7.5	11.3
80-81	PSU	24	.601	.778	6.3	13.0
Totals		100	.537	.788	5.3	8.5

NBA REGULAR-SEASON STATISTICS

			FGs		3-PT FGs		FTs		Rebounds						
	G	MIN	FG	PCT	FG	PCT	FT	PCT	OFF	TOT	AST	STL	BLK	PTS	PPG
84-85 SEA	78	1115	150	.492	0	.000	85	.669	76	260	100	34	15	385	4.9
85-86 SEA	40	311	30	.517	0	.000	18	.667	16	54	21	11	7	78	2.0
86-87 LAL/SA	44	487	63	.508	0	.000	50	.714	48	116	17	20	6	176	4.0
87-88 SA	70	2227	425	.528	1	.200	268	.768	167	483	266	74	36	1119	16.0
88-89 SA	64	1822	337	.515	0	.000	201	.715	148	406	131	102	35	875	13.7
89-90 SA	78	1438	211	.545	0	.000	95	.674	89	327	105	66	37	517	6.6
90-91 MIL	75	1912	372	.527	0	.000	198	.798	129	406	131	86	43	942	12.6
91-92 MIL	65	1556	306	.524	3	.500	125	.767	97	344	122	60	23	740	11.4
92-93 MIL	66	2075	456	.545	8	.308	195	.728	120	405	196	80	44	1115	16.9
93-94 MIL/CHA	71	2094	368	.488	4	.000	195	.768	85	404	222	80	27	935	13.2
Totals	651	15037	2718	.521	16	.225	1430	.742	975	3225	1311	613	273	6882	10.6

SCOTT BROOKS

Team: Dallas Mavericks
Position: Guard
Height: 5'11" **Weight:** 165
Birthdate: July 31, 1965
NBA Experience: 7 years

College: Texas Christian; San Joaquin Delta; Cal.-Irvine
Acquired: Traded from Rockets for Morlon Wiley and a 1995 2nd-round pick, 2/95

Background: Brooks divided his college career among Texas Christian, San Joaquin Delta Junior College, and finally Cal.-Irvine, where he led the Pacific Coast Athletic Association in scoring, steals, and free throw percentage. Despite being passed up in the NBA draft, he emerged from the CBA to play for Philadelphia, Minnesota, Houston, and Dallas over the last seven seasons.

Strengths: Brooks is a tireless worker who loves to pressure the ball from one end of the court to the other. His quickness, great hands, and ability to handle the ball make him a nice sparkplug off the bench. He's pesky on defense, is a good penetrator, hits the 3, and rarely misses a free throw.

Weaknesses: Most of his offense comes when nothing else is available for Brooks, who is a passer first and scorer second. His size works against him on the defensive end, where he has trouble matching up against the bigger guards in the league. He almost never gets a rebound and does not have the skills to earn a starting job with many teams.

Analysis: Brooks, a California surfer type, is a consummate point guard. He shows the floor leadership and team-first attitude that coaches love. He was playing some of his best basketball before getting caught behind Sam Cassell and Kenny Smith in Houston. Last February's trade to Dallas was a good career move for this solid reserve.

PLAYER SUMMARY

Will ....pressure the ball
Can't ....win a starting spot
Expect ....a playmaker
Don't Expect ....many shots
Fantasy Value $0
Card Value ....5-8¢

COLLEGE STATISTICS

		G	FGP	FTP	APG	PPG
83-84	TCU	27	.529	.714	1.4	3.8
84-85	SJD	31	.525	.882	—	13.1
85-86	C-I	30	.448	.886	3.2	10.3
86-87	C-I	28	.478	.845	3.8	23.8
Totals		116	.489	.860	2.8	12.8

NBA REGULAR-SEASON STATISTICS

		G	MIN	FGs FG	FGs PCT	3-PT FGs FG	3-PT FGs PCT	FTs FT	FTs PCT	Rebounds OFF	Rebounds TOT	AST	STL	BLK	PTS	PPG
88-89	PHI	82	1372	156	.420	55	.359	61	.884	19	94	306	69	3	428	5.2
89-90	PHI	72	975	119	.431	31	.392	50	.877	15	64	207	47	0	319	4.4
90-91	MIN	80	980	159	.430	45	.333	61	.847	28	72	204	53	5	424	5.3
91-92	MIN	82	1082	167	.447	32	.356	51	.810	27	99	205	66	7	417	5.1
92-93	HOU	82	1516	183	.475	41	.414	112	.830	22	99	243	79	3	519	6.3
93-94	HOU	73	1225	142	.491	23	.377	74	.871	10	102	149	51	2	381	5.2
94-95	HOU/DAL	59	808	126	.458	25	.362	64	.810	14	66	116	34	4	341	5.8
Totals		530	7958	1052	.450	252	.367	473	.845	135	596	1430	399	24	2829	5.3

CHUCKY BROWN

Unrestricted Free Agent
Last Team: Houston Rockets
Position: Forward
Height: 6'8" **Weight:** 214
Birthdate: February 29, 1968

NBA Experience: 6 years
College: North Carolina St.
Acquired: Signed as a free agent, 2/95

Background: Brown was an All-ACC first-team selection after his senior year at N.C. State, and he finished his career second on the school's career field goal percentage list. Drafted 43rd overall in 1989, he has played for all or part of six seasons with the Cavaliers, Lakers, Nets, Mavericks, and Rockets. He was signed by Houston from the CBA last February and made 14 starts in 41 games.

Strengths: Brown has a fairly impressive variety of offensive skills. He can shoot a jump hook with either hand and is a dangerous pull-up jump-shooter. He loves to run and fares well in an up-tempo style. He shot a blistering 60 percent from the field in his half-season with Houston. He hustles and loves the game.

Weaknesses: The consensus is that Brown could be a much better rebounder and defender. Whether or not it's a lack of interest is up for debate, but he is nothing close to a stopper. Brown will not create much off the dribble, nor will he spot open teammates. He has been a complementary player as opposed to a main attraction.

Analysis: Brown has struggled at times during his career, but he can hardly be called an underachiever. The fact that a late second-rounder has played six years says much about his work ethic and determination. He started last season by averaging 21.3 PPG in 31 games for the Yakima Sun Kings before Houston gave him a call. Brown averaged 6.1 PPG for the Rockets.

PLAYER SUMMARY	
Will	run the floor
Can't	find open men
Expect	enthusiasm
Don't Expect	long-term deals
Fantasy Value	$0
Card Value	5-8¢

COLLEGE STATISTICS

		G	FGP	FTP	RPG	PPG
85-86	NCST	31	.475	.618	2.2	3.1
86-87	NCST	34	.587	.762	4.3	6.6
87-88	NCST	32	.572	.636	6.0	16.6
88-89	NCST	31	.548	.648	8.8	16.4
Totals		128	.557	.667	5.3	10.6

NBA REGULAR-SEASON STATISTICS

			FGs		3-PT FGs		FTs		Rebounds						
	G	MIN	FG	PCT	FG	PCT	FT	PCT	OFF	TOT	AST	STL	BLK	PTS	PPG
89-90 CLE	75	1339	210	.470	0	.000	125	.762	83	231	50	33	26	545	7.3
90-91 CLE	74	1485	263	.524	0	.000	101	.701	78	213	80	26	24	627	8.5
91-92 CLE/LAL	42	431	60	.469	0	.000	30	.612	31	82	26	12	7	150	3.6
92-93 NJ	77	1186	160	.483	0	.000	71	.724	88	232	51	20	24	391	5.1
93-94 DAL	1	10	1	1.000	0	.000	1	1.000	0	1	0	0	0	3	3.0
94-95 HOU	41	814	105	.603	1	.333	38	.613	64	189	30	11	14	249	6.1
Totals	310	5265	799	.505	1	.045	366	.707	344	948	237	102	95	1965	6.3

DEE BROWN

Team: Boston Celtics
Position: Guard
Height: 6'1" **Weight:** 161
Birthdate: November 29, 1968

NBA Experience: 5 years
College: Jacksonville
Acquired: 1st-round pick in 1990 draft
(19th overall)

Background: Brown was Jacksonville's main man as a junior, leading the Dolphins in scoring, rebounding, and steals while splitting time between big guard and small forward. He helped solidify the Celtics' backcourt as a first-team All-Rookie performer, then missed more than half of the 1991-92 season after knee surgery. He has started for most of the last three years and has averaged over 15 PPG each of the last two.

Strengths: Brown plays both guard positions well. He has a tremendous vertical leap that helped him win the NBA's 1991 Slam Dunk Contest. Brown has lightning-quick speed and is especially dangerous on the break, where he can dish off or finish the play. He sinks his free throws, can shoot the modified 3-pointer, and is a defensive nuisance.

Weaknesses: Since he's slight in build, there is not much Brown can do defensively when his man posts him up or runs him off a solid screen. Defending off guards is a chore for him. On offense, however, he is better suited to the two than the point. He is not a ball-handling wizard like some of the other NBA players on the small and quick side.

Analysis: Brown's versatility and athletic ability have helped him become a fine pro player, and he has added to his game the ability to cause problems from the outside. The shorter 3-pointer has played to his advantage. Brown serves as co-captain of the Celtics and has become a "veteran" leader in just five seasons.

PLAYER SUMMARY

Will	play two spots
Can't	muscle his man
Expect	15 PPG
Don't Expect	slow feet
Fantasy Value	$16-19
Card Value	10-15¢

COLLEGE STATISTICS

		G	FGP	FTP	APG	PPG
86-87	JACK	21	.431	.591	0.8	3.4
87-88	JACK	28	.452	.818	2.0	10.1
88-89	JACK	30	.490	.824	3.7	19.6
89-90	JACK	29	.496	.683	5.2	19.3
Totals		108	.482	.762	3.1	13.9

NBA REGULAR-SEASON STATISTICS

				FGs		3-PT FGs		FTs		Rebounds						
		G	MIN	FG	PCT	FG	PCT	FT	PCT	OFF	TOT	AST	STL	BLK	PTS	PPG
90-91	BOS	82	1945	284	.464	7	.206	137	.873	41	182	344	83	14	712	8.7
91-92	BOS	31	883	149	.426	5	.227	60	.769	15	79	164	33	7	363	11.7
92-93	BOS	80	2254	328	.468	26	.317	192	.793	45	246	461	138	32	874	10.9
93-94	BOS	77	2867	490	.480	30	.313	182	.831	63	300	347	156	47	1192	15.5
94-95	BOS	79	2792	437	.447	126	.385	236	.852	63	249	301	110	49	1236	15.6
Totals		349	10741	1688	.461	194	.346	807	.829	227	1056	1617	520	149	4377	12.5

P.J. BROWN

Team: New Jersey Nets
Position: Forward/Center
Height: 6'11" **Weight:** 240
Birthdate: October 14, 1968

NBA Experience: 2 years
College: Louisiana Tech
Acquired: 2nd-round pick in 1992 draft (29th overall)

Background: Brown, drafted 29th overall by New Jersey in 1992, spent his first professional season in Greece after making contract demands the Nets were not prepared to meet. He averaged 17.0 PPG and 13.7 RPG overseas. New Jersey signed the former Louisiana Tech shot-blocking standout and first-team All-Sun Belt player before the 1993-94 season. He has started more than half of his pro games for the Nets and averaged a sturdy 1.7 blocks per game during the 1994-95 season.

Strengths: Brown is a relentless rebounder and defensive specialist who can play both forward spots and center. He has long arms and good timing to block shots and gets his hands on his share of steals. Opposing big men hate to see Brown as their matchup because they know it means a night of wear and tear. He is a physical presence who makes himself known inside against bigger players.

Weaknesses: Putting the ball in the basket is not Brown's specialty, and it likely never will be. He does not have much to offer on the perimeter and his shooting percentage is awful for an inside player. Ditto from the free throw line. You don't want him handling the ball outside of the paint area. Brown's physical style of play also leads to frequent foul trouble.

Analysis: Brown, who finished among rookie leaders in several categories two years ago, proved last year that he is no fluke. For a second-round pick, the Nets certainly got their money's worth when it comes to shot-blocking, defense, and rebounding. Brown has his share of work to do on the offensive end, but he's done enough good to have become a surprising regular in the starting lineup.

PLAYER SUMMARY	
Will	bang inside
Can't	stick his jumper
Expect	1.5-plus BPG
Don't Expect	10 PPG
Fantasy Value	$3-5
Card Value	5-10¢

COLLEGE STATISTICS

		G	FGP	FTP	RPG	PPG
88-89	LT	32	.415	.568	5.6	4.7
89-90	LT	27	.461	.593	8.5	8.9
90-91	LT	31	.540	.653	9.7	14.4
91-92	LT	31	.489	.730	9.9	12.7
Totals		121	.488	.654	8.4	10.1

NBA REGULAR-SEASON STATISTICS

				FGs		3-PT FGs		FTs		Rebounds						
		G	MIN	FG	PCT	FG	PCT	FT	PCT	OFF	TOT	AST	STL	BLK	PTS	PPG
93-94	NJ	79	1950	167	.415	1	.167	115	.757	188	493	93	71	450	5.7
94-95	NJ	80	2466	254	.446	4	.167	139	.671	178	487	135	69	135	651	8.1
Totals		159	4416	421	.433	5	.167	254	.708	366	980	228	140	228	1101	6.9

RANDY BROWN

Team: Sacramento Kings
Position: Guard
Height: 6'3" **Weight:** 190
Birthdate: May 22, 1968

NBA Experience: 4 years
College: Houston; New Mexico St.
Acquired: 2nd-round pick in 1991 draft (31st overall)

Background: Brown played at Collins High School in Chicago before starting his college career at Houston. He transferred to New Mexico State after his sophomore year and set school records for assists and steals while twice earning first-team All-Big West honors. A second-round choice by Sacramento, Brown has played mostly in a reserve role for four years. He has averaged four-plus PPG in each of the last two seasons.

Strengths: Brown has backed up his reputation for defense. He's quick, is tough, has good hands, and is not afraid to challenge opponents. He also rebounds from the backcourt and can defend at both guard positions. He showed during his second year that he is capable of filling in as a starter (a career-high 7.6 PPG), though he has not earned much chance since.

Weaknesses: Brown is not a good enough ball-handler or passer to thrive as a point guard, yet his jump shot will not earn him a living as a starting two. He shoots a very low percentage from the field, he struggles from the free throw line, and the 3-pointer is not his shot, either. Brown's assist-to-turnover ratio is less than 2-to-1. He has not been the same since an injury-plagued 1993-94 campaign.

Analysis: Brown has potential as a disruptive defensive player who won't back down. However, his offensive game is nothing to write home about and he does not seem to have regained his second-year form on either end of the floor. Groin and knee injuries wore him down in his third season, and he has not played himself back into a comfort zone.

PLAYER SUMMARY	
Will	hustle on defense
Can't	shoot consistently
Expect	toughness
Don't Expect	10 PPG
Fantasy Value	$1
Card Value	7-12¢

COLLEGE STATISTICS

		G	FGP	FTP	APG	PPG
86-87	HOUS	28	.506	.583	2.9	3.8
87-88	HOUS	29	.451	.750	5.6	7.0
89-90	NMST	31	.446	.712	3.5	13.2
90-91	NMST	29	.399	.691	6.4	12.1
Totals		117	.436	.703	4.6	9.1

NBA REGULAR-SEASON STATISTICS

		G	MIN	FGs FG	FGs PCT	3-PT FGs FG	3-PT FGs PCT	FTs FT	FTs PCT	Rebounds OFF	Rebounds TOT	AST	STL	BLK	PTS	PPG
91-92	SAC	56	535	77	.456	0	.000	38	.655	26	69	59	35	12	192	3.4
92-93	SAC	75	1726	225	.463	2	.333	115	.732	75	212	196	108	34	567	7.6
93-94	SAC	61	1041	110	.438	0	.000	53	.609	40	112	133	63	14	273	4.5
94-95	SAC	67	1086	124	.432	14	.298	55	.671	24	108	133	99	19	317	4.7
Totals		259	4388	536	.449	16	.254	261	.680	165	501	521	305	79	1349	5.2

MARK BRYANT

Unrestricted Free Agent
Last Team: Portland Trail Blazers
Position: Forward
Height: 6'9" **Weight:** 245
Birthdate: April 25, 1965

NBA Experience: 7 years
College: Seton Hall
Acquired: 1st-round pick in 1988 draft (21st overall)

Background: As a senior, Bryant helped take Seton Hall to its first NCAA Tournament and was an All-Big East selection. He started 32 of his first 34 games as a pro but then encountered injury problems over his first few years, including two broken bones. The 1994-95 season was one of the worst of his seven in the pros, all with the Trail Blazers.

Strengths: Bryant is physically impressive and plays tough defense. He's willing to throw his weight around and battle the league's big men. He rebounds, runs the floor, and owns a decent short-range jump shot. He shoots for a high percentage because he does not take many bad shots. He is a consistent performer.

Weaknesses: Bryant will never score a lot of points. His offensive repertoire is limited and he is not a good ball-handler or passer. He is easy to overlook in a boxscore. His range is limited and his free throw shooting is subpar. While he won't hurt his team, he does little to spark it, either.

Analysis: Bryant, never spectacular, has been a valuable banger and role-player in seven years with Portland. However, the Blazers made a statement last season when they swapped star Clyde Drexler for Otis Thorpe, a power forward with solid scoring and rebounding skills. Bryant has not panned out to be that kind of player.

PLAYER SUMMARY	
Will	bang inside
Can't	dazzle a crowd
Expect	consistency
Don't Expect	the spectacular
Fantasy Value	$0
Card Value	5-8¢

COLLEGE STATISTICS

		G	FGP	FTP	RPG	PPG
84-85	SH	26	.475	.649	6.8	12.2
85-86	SH	30	.523	.678	7.5	14.0
86-87	SH	28	.496	.706	7.1	16.8
87-88	SH	34	.564	.748	9.1	20.5
Totals		118	.521	.705	7.7	16.2

NBA REGULAR-SEASON STATISTICS

		G	MIN	FGs FG	FGs PCT	3-PT FGs FG	3-PT FGs PCT	FTs FT	FTs PCT	Rebounds OFF	Rebounds TOT	AST	STL	BLK	PTS	PPG
88-89	POR	56	803	120	.486	0	.000	40	.580	65	179	33	20	7	280	5.0
89-90	POR	58	562	70	.458	0	.000	28	.560	54	146	13	18	9	168	2.9
90-91	POR	53	781	99	.488	0	.000	74	.733	65	190	27	15	12	272	5.1
91-92	POR	56	800	95	.480	0	.000	40	.667	87	201	41	26	8	230	4.1
92-93	POR	80	1396	186	.503	0	.000	104	.703	132	324	41	37	23	476	5.9
93-94	POR	79	1441	185	.482	0	.000	72	.692	117	315	37	32	29	442	5.6
94-95	POR	49	658	101	.526	1	.500	41	.651	55	161	28	19	16	244	5.0
Totals		431	6441	856	.490	1	.125	399	.671	575	1516	22	167	104	2112	4.9

SCOTT BURRELL

Team: Charlotte Hornets
Position: Forward
Height: 6'7" **Weight:** 226
Birthdate: January 12, 1971

NBA Experience: 2 years
College: Connecticut
Acquired: 1st-round pick in 1993 draft (20th overall)

Background: A defensive star at Connecticut, Burrell became the only player in NCAA Division I history to amass 1,500 points, 750 rebounds, 300 steals, and 275 assists. He doubled as a baseball pitcher in the Toronto Blue Jays' farm system for three seasons, but he gave up baseball to play in the NBA. He was drafted 20th overall by Charlotte and became a full-time starter in his second season, averaging 11.5 PPG in 1994-95. A ruptured Achilles tendon kept him out of the playoffs.

Strengths: Burrell is known as an accomplished defender, but last year he shocked many with the addition of a first-rate perimeter game. After making only two 3-pointers as a rookie, he hit 96 of 235 last season to finish among league leaders. And yes, he plays defense. He uses his wingspan and quick hands to anticipate passes and get steals. He also gets to the boards. A great athlete who runs the floor, Burrell is built for the transition game.

Weaknesses: Now that outside shooting no longer falls under this category, Burrell needs to avoid the temptation to become strictly a gunner. With his athletic ability, there should be many more drives to the hoop for buckets of his own or easy dishes to teammates. Burrell is not the greatest ball-handler among the small-forward class. And why is he not a better free throw shooter?

Analysis: Rarely does a player improve in one aspect of the game as much as Burrell did as an outside shooter. He went from taking only six 3-point shots during his rookie year to participating in the Long Distance Shootout during the 1995 All-Star Weekend. Combined with his hustling defense, the added dimension makes Burrell a player to watch in the coming years.

PLAYER SUMMARY	
Will	sink the trey
Can't	be left open
Expect	hustling defense
Don't Expect	a baseball career
Fantasy Value	$10-13
Card Value	12-20¢

COLLEGE STATISTICS

		G	FGP	FTP	RPG	PPG
89-90	CONN	32	.386	.623	5.5	8.2
90-91	CONN	31	.440	.592	7.5	12.7
91-92	CONN	30	.453	.611	6.1	16.3
92-93	CONN	26	.411	.760	6.0	16.1
Totals		119	.426	.640	6.3	13.1

NBA REGULAR-SEASON STATISTICS

		G	MIN	FGs		3-PT FGs		FTs		Rebounds		AST	STL	BLK	PTS	PPG
				FG	PCT	FG	PCT	FT	PCT	OFF	TOT					
93-94	CHA	51	767	98	.419	2	.333	46	.657	46	132	62	37	16	244	4.8
94-95	CHA	65	2014	277	.467	96	.409	100	.694	96	368	161	75	40	750	11.5
Totals		116	2781	375	.453	98	.407	146	.682	142	500	223	112	56	994	8.6

WILLIE BURTON

Team: Philadelphia 76ers
Position: Guard/Forward
Height: 6'8" **Weight:** 217
Birthdate: May 26, 1968

NBA Experience: 5 years
College: Minnesota
Acquired: Signed as a free agent, 11/94

Background: Burton became the University of Minnesota's No. 2 career scorer (behind Mychal Thompson) and led the Gophers into the Southeast Regional finals as a senior. Miami chose him ninth in the 1990 draft, but knee injuries, a bout with depression, and a foot injury plagued him over his first four seasons. Burton signed with Philadelphia before the 1994-95 season and averaged a career-high 15.3 PPG.

Strengths: The versatile Burton can score points in heaps. He can fill in at big guard in addition to his small-forward duties and is tough to stop once he gets started. Slashing to the hoop is the bread and butter of this fine athlete, although the shorter 3-point line has made him a double threat. He also hits his free throws and plays above-average defense.

Weaknesses: Burton has never been a good or willing passer, dating back to his college days. Another reason you want to limit his ball-handling time is that he commits a lot of turnovers. He also shoots a dismal percentage. The bottom line: better decision-making is needed. Inconsistency remains the most obvious of Burton's drawbacks.

Analysis: Burton made a nice comeback under John Lucas with the Sixers. He lit up his old team, Miami, for a Spectrum-record 53 points when the Heat visited Philadelphia last December. Lucas knew he could count on Burton for some big scoring nights. You have to take the bad with the good when it comes to Burton, although the good seems to be on the rise.

PLAYER SUMMARY	
Will	score in spurts
Can't	maintain level of play
Expect	good quickness
Don't Expect	high field goal pct.
Fantasy Value	$2-4
Card Value	8-12¢

COLLEGE STATISTICS

		G	FGP	FTP	RPG	PPG
86-87	MINN	28	.455	.649	4.2	8.7
87-88	MINN	28	.516	.713	5.6	13.7
88-89	MINN	30	.529	.797	7.5	18.6
89-90	MINN	32	.519	.770	6.4	19.3
Totals		118	.511	.749	6.0	15.3

NBA REGULAR-SEASON STATISTICS

		G	MIN	FGs FG	FGs PCT	3-PT FGs FG	3-PT FGs PCT	FTs FT	FTs PCT	Rebounds OFF	Rebounds TOT	AST	STL	BLK	PTS	PPG
90-91	MIA	76	1928	341	.441	4	.133	229	.782	111	262	107	72	24	915	12.0
91-92	MIA	68	1585	280	.450	6	.400	196	.800	76	244	123	46	37	762	11.2
92-93	MIA	26	451	54	.383	5	.333	91	.717	22	70	16	13	16	204	7.8
93-94	MIA	53	697	124	.438	3	.200	120	.759	50	136	39	18	20	371	7.0
94-95	PHI	53	1564	243	.401	106	.385	220	.824	49	164	96	32	19	812	15.3
Totals		276	6225	1042	.430	124	.354	856	.785	308	876	381	181	116	3064	11.1

MITCHELL BUTLER

Team: Washington Bullets
Position: Guard
Height: 6'5" **Weight:** 210
Birthdate: December 15, 1970

NBA Experience: 2 years
College: UCLA
Acquired: Signed as a free agent, 10/93

Background: Butler was a standout on a UCLA team that also included current NBA players Don MacLean and Tracy Murray. Though he helped the Bruins back to national prominence while playing as many as four different positions in college, Butler was bypassed in the 1993 NBA draft. He made Washington's roster as a free agent and was one of the NBA's biggest rookie surprises. He averaged 7.9 PPG in his second season.

Strengths: Butler is blessed with both athletic ability and versatility. He can play both guard and forward. He can also score with his back to the basket against smaller defenders and on drives to the hoop. Butler is at his best in an up-tempo game, where he can pull up for jumpers, finish with jams, or find the open man. He has shown a great work ethic, plays tough defense, and has 3-point range.

Weaknesses: Butler is not nearly as effective in the halfcourt game as he is in transition. His shooting still has a ways to go, as his poor percentages from both the field and free throw line indicate. Butler never averaged more than 9.5 PPG in his four years of college ball. He also commits more turnovers than he dishes out assists and his rebounding numbers were down last season compared to 1993-94.

Analysis: One of Washington's more pleasant surprises two years ago, Butler maintained his level of play last season and increased his scoring output. In short, he proved he is here to stay despite being considered a marginal talent coming out of college. Butler overcomes his offensive deficiencies with tireless work and a go-get-'em attitude. He has developed into a nice player off the bench.

PLAYER SUMMARY	
Will	post up
Can't	rely on jumpers
Expect	all-out hustle
Don't Expect	10 PPG
Fantasy Value	$0
Card Value	5-8¢

COLLEGE STATISTICS

		G	FGP	FTP	RPG	PPG
89-90	UCLA	33	.538	.625	2.8	6.2
90-91	UCLA	32	.548	.513	4.2	7.9
91-92	UCLA	33	.489	.451	4.2	8.0
92-93	UCLA	32	.512	.526	5.3	9.5
Totals		130	.519	.528	4.1	7.9

NBA REGULAR-SEASON STATISTICS

		G	MIN	FGs FG	FGs PCT	3-PT FGs FG	3-PT FGs PCT	FTs FT	FTs PCT	Rebounds OFF	Rebounds TOT	AST	STL	BLK	PTS	PPG
93-94	WAS	75	1321	207	.495	0	.000	104	.578	106	225	77	54	20	518	6.9
94-95	WAS	76	1554	214	.421	46	.326	123	.665	43	170	91	61	10	597	7.9
Totals		151	2875	421	.455	46	.315	227	.622	149	395	168	115	30	1115	7.4

MICHAEL CAGE

Team: Cleveland Cavaliers
Position: Forward/Center
Height: 6'9" **Weight:** 248
Birthdate: January 28, 1962

NBA Experience: 11 years
College: San Diego St.
Acquired: Signed as a free agent, 8/94

Background: Cage was voted Western Athletic Conference Player of the Year as a senior at San Diego State. He finished as the school's career leader in scoring, rebounding, and games played. He won the NBA rebounding title in 1987-88 and has played every game over the last six seasons. The 1994-95 campaign was his first with Cleveland.

Strengths: The tough, muscular Cage has made his living off the backboard. While no longer dominant, he still contributes on the glass and with tough interior defense. He can fill in at center and he shoots a high percentage. A consummate pro, he comes to play.

Weaknesses: Cage has never been known for his offense. His low-post moves are predictable, yet he has spent a large portion of his career out of position at center. He's not a reliable ball-handler or passer and is a lousy free throw shooter.

Analysis: Cage is the kind of guy you want on your side. He comes to work ready to mix it up and keep his man off the boards. He is no longer the interior presence he once was after 11 years in the league, but he will contribute. His streak of 493 consecutive games played is second to A.C. Green's 731.

PLAYER SUMMARY	
Will	defend, rebound
Can't	shoot free throws
Expect	good work habits
Don't Expect	10 PPG
Fantasy Value	$0
Card Value	5-8¢

COLLEGE STATISTICS

		G	FGP	FTP	RPG	PPG
80-81	SDS	27	.558	.756	13.1	10.9
81-82	SDS	29	.488	.661	8.8	11.0
82-83	SDS	28	.570	.747	12.6	19.5
83-84	SDS	28	.562	.741	12.6	24.5
Totals		**112**	**.548**	**.732**	**11.8**	**16.5**

NBA REGULAR-SEASON STATISTICS

				FGs		3-PT FGs		FTs		Rebounds						
		G	MIN	FG	PCT	FG	PCT	FT	PCT	OFF	TOT	AST	STL	BLK	PTS	PPG
84-85	LAC	75	1610	216	.543	0	.000	101	.737	126	392	51	41	32	533	7.1
85-86	LAC	78	1566	204	.479	0	.000	113	.649	168	417	81	62	34	521	6.7
86-87	LAC	80	2922	457	.521	0	.000	341	.730	354	922	131	99	67	1046	15.7
87-88	LAC	72	2660	360	.470	0	.000	326	.688	371	938	110	91	58	1046	14.5
88-89	SEA	80	2536	314	.498	0	.000	197	.743	276	765	126	92	52	825	10.3
89-90	SEA	82	2595	325	.504	0	.000	148	.698	306	821	70	79	45	798	9.7
90-91	SEA	82	2141	226	.508	0	.000	70	.625	177	558	89	85	58	522	6.4
91-92	SEA	82	2461	307	.566	0	.000	106	.620	266	728	92	99	55	720	8.8
92-93	SEA	82	2156	219	.526	0	.000	61	.469	268	659	69	76	46	499	6.1
93-94	SEA	82	1708	171	.545	0	.000	36	.486	164	444	45	77	38	378	4.6
94-95	CLE	82	2040	177	.521	0	.000	53	.602	203	564	56	61	67	407	5.0
Totals		**877**	**24395**	**2976**	**.513**	**0**	**.000**	**1552**	**.674**	**2679**	**7208**	**920**	**862**	**552**	**7504**	**8.6**

ELDEN CAMPBELL

Team: Los Angeles Lakers
Position: Forward/Center
Height: 6'11" **Weight:** 250
Birthdate: July 23, 1968

NBA Experience: 5 years
College: Clemson
Acquired: 1st-round pick in 1990 draft
(27th overall)

Background: Campbell led the Atlantic Coast Conference in blocked shots three straight years and became Clemson's career scoring leader. He scored 21 points in an NBA Finals game as a Laker rookie and has rated among the league's top 15 shot-blockers three times since. He became the Lakers' starting power forward during the 1993-94 campaign and has averaged better than 12 PPG each of the last two seasons.

Strengths: Best known for his shot-blocking and defensive intimidation, Campbell displays great instincts for the ball, has a huge wingspan, and is a superb athlete and leaper. He blocks almost two shots per game. He gets up and down the floor and finishes with flair. He's an adequate rebounder and has worked on his mid-range jumper.

Weaknesses: Campbell is inconsistent and has yet to become a solid halfcourt offensive player. His field goal percentage has hovered around the .460 mark since he cracked the starting lineup because he does not own a vast repertoire of low-post moves. He's a poor free throw shooter. Campbell is a below-average passer who, overall, is better off in a transition game.

Analysis: Campbell will have some dazzling nights, but there are also many games in which he fails to make an impact. When the game slows down, his deficiencies in a halfcourt offense become apparent. He has a hook shot and he can make the jumper when he's hot. Campbell has been streaky, but he appears to have the potential to raise his game to another level.

PLAYER SUMMARY	
Will	score in transition
Can't	hit free throws
Expect	high-scoring nights
Don't Expect	great consistency
Fantasy Value	$8-10
Card Value	8-12¢

COLLEGE STATISTICS

		G	FGP	FTP	RPG	PPG
86-87	CLEM	31	.554	.702	4.1	8.8
87-88	CLEM	28	.629	.619	7.4	18.8
88-89	CLEM	29	.550	.688	7.7	17.5
89-90	CLEM	35	.522	.599	8.0	16.4
Totals		123	.562	.641	6.8	15.3

NBA REGULAR-SEASON STATISTICS

				FGs		3-PT FGs		FTs		Rebounds						
		G	MIN	FG	PCT	FG	PCT	FT	PCT	OFF	TOT	AST	STL	BLK	PTS	PPG
90-91	LAL	52	380	56	.455	0	.000	32	.653	40	96	10	11	38	144	2.8
91-92	LAL	81	1876	220	.448	0	.000	138	.619	155	423	59	53	159	578	7.1
92-93	LAL	79	1551	238	.458	0	.000	130	.637	127	332	48	59	100	606	7.7
93-94	LAL	76	2253	373	.462	0	.000	188	.689	167	519	86	64	146	934	12.3
94-95	LAL	73	2076	360	.459	0	.000	193	.666	168	445	92	69	132	913	12.5
Totals		361	8136	1247	.457	0	.000	681	.655	657	1815	295	256	575	3175	8.8

TONY CAMPBELL

Team: Cleveland Cavaliers
Position: Guard/Forward
Height: 6'7" **Weight:** 215
Birthdate: May 7, 1962

NBA Experience: 11 years
College: Ohio St.
Acquired: Signed as a free agent, 10/94

Background: Campbell was the Big Ten Player of the Year as a senior at Ohio State. His pro career started on the Detroit bench and in the CBA, but he exploded onto the scene with the Lakers in the 1989 playoffs. He was Minnesota's leading scorer in its first three years of existence and has since played reserve roles with New York, Dallas, and Cleveland.

Strengths: Putting the ball in the basket is Campbell's specialty. He can get to the hoop, draws fouls, and is not afraid to take clutch shots. He is able to play both small forward and big guard. He is always capable of torching the nets when he gets loose.

Weaknesses: Campbell is not the kind of player who makes those around him better. He looks to shoot first, so his points are not accompanied by many assists. Campbell is a below-average rebounder, and he has never been considered a standout defensive player.

Analysis: Scoring is Campbell's game. His stop with the Knicks improved his passing and defense, but he was traded to Dallas and then signed by the Cavaliers as a free agent before last season. He played about 15 minutes a game for Cleveland and shot a dismal .411 from the field.

PLAYER SUMMARY	
Will	look to score
Can't	regain major role
Expect	bench offense
Don't Expect	assists
Fantasy Value	$0
Card Value	5-8¢

COLLEGE STATISTICS

		G	FGP	FTP	RPG	PPG
80-81	OSU	14	.417	.500	0.6	1.6
81-82	OSU	31	.424	.798	5.0	12.8
82-83	OSU	30	.503	.799	8.3	19.0
83-84	OSU	29	.513	.807	7.4	18.6
Totals		104	.482	.798	6.0	14.7

NBA REGULAR-SEASON STATISTICS

		G	MIN	FGs FG	FGs PCT	3-PT FGs FG	3-PT FGs PCT	FTs FT	FTs PCT	Rebounds OFF	Rebounds TOT	AST	STL	BLK	PTS	PPG
84-85	DET	56	625	130	.496	0	.000	56	.800	41	89	24	28	3	316	5.6
85-86	DET	82	1292	294	.484	2	.222	58	.795	83	236	45	62	7	648	7.9
86-87	DET	40	332	57	.393	0	.000	24	.615	21	58	19	12	1	138	3.5
87-88	LAL	13	242	57	.564	1	.333	28	.718	8	27	15	11	2	143	11.0
88-89	LAL	63	787	158	.458	2	.095	70	.843	53	130	47	37	6	388	6.2
89-90	MIN	82	3164	723	.457	9	.167	448	.787	209	451	213	111	31	1903	23.2
90-91	MIN	77	2893	652	.434	16	.262	358	.803	161	346	214	121	48	1678	21.8
91-92	MIN	78	2441	527	.464	13	.351	240	.803	141	286	229	84	31	1307	16.8
92-93	NY	58	1062	194	.490	2	.400	59	.678	59	155	62	34	5	449	7.7
93-94	NY/DAL	63	1214	227	.443	7	.250	94	.783	76	186	82	50	15	555	8.8
94-95	CLE	78	1128	161	.411	15	.357	132	.830	60	153	69	32	8	469	6.0
Totals		690	15180	3180	.456	67	.254	1567	.790	912	2117	1019	582	157	7994	11.6

ANTOINE CARR

Team: Utah Jazz
Position: Forward
Height: 6'9" **Weight:** 255
Birthdate: July 23, 1961

NBA Experience: 11 years
College: Wichita St.
Acquired: Signed as a free agent, 10/94

Background: Carr played with Cliff Levingston and Xavier McDaniel at Wichita State, where his No. 35 was retired after an All-America career. He played five-plus years in Atlanta before becoming a big scorer in Sacramento. He spent three years in San Antonio before being signed as a free agent by Utah prior to last season.

Strengths: Carr can play both power forward and center because of his strong low-post game at both ends of the floor. He holds his position in the lane, loves to put his body on opposing players, and can put the ball in the hole. He's a fierce finisher, once shattering a backboard in warmups.

Weaknesses: When pushed away from the paint, Carr becomes largely ineffective. He has limited range and is not a great rebounder for his size. This notorious bruiser has always picked up a lot of fouls. His conditioning should be monitored.

Analysis: Carr is no longer the player he once was, but he is hardly washed up yet. He helped the Jazz to a strong season with his play off the bench. His low-post offense still causes problems for opponents and he knows what to do on defense. He's a valuable reserve.

PLAYER SUMMARY

Will ....score inside
Can't ....dominate boards
Expect ....reliable defense
Don't Expect ....starts
Fantasy Value $1
Card Value ....5-10¢

COLLEGE STATISTICS

		G	FGP	FTP	RPG	PPG
79-80	WSU	29	.501	.667	5.9	15.2
80-81	WSU	33	.586	.765	7.3	15.8
81-82	WSU	28	.566	.791	7.0	16.0
82-83	WSU	22	.575	.765	7.6	22.6
Totals		112	.557	.746	6.9	17.1

NBA REGULAR-SEASON STATISTICS

		G	MIN	FGs FG	FGs PCT	3-PT FGs FG	3-PT FGs PCT	FTs FT	FTs PCT	Rebounds OFF	Rebounds TOT	AST	STL	BLK	PTS	PPG
84-85	ATL	62	1195	198	.520	2	.333	101	.789	79	232	80	29	78	499	8.0
85-86	ATL	17	258	49	.527	0	.000	18	.667	16	52	14	7	15	116	6.8
86-87	ATL	65	695	134	.506	1	.333	73	.709	60	156	34	14	48	342	5.3
87-88	ATL	80	1483	281	.544	1	.250	142	.780	94	289	103	38	83	705	8.8
88-89	ATL	78	1488	226	.480	0	.000	130	.855	106	274	91	31	62	582	7.5
89-90	ATL/SAC	77	1727	356	.494	0	.000	237	.795	115	322	119	30	68	949	12.3
90-91	SAC	77	2527	628	.511	0	.000	295	.758	163	420	191	45	101	1551	20.1
91-92	SA	81	1867	359	.490	1	.200	162	.764	128	346	63	32	96	881	10.9
92-93	SA	71	1947	379	.538	0	.000	174	.777	107	388	97	35	87	932	13.1
93-94	SA	34	465	78	.488	0	.000	42	.724	12	51	15	9	22	198	5.8
94-95	UTA	78	1677	290	.531	1	.250	165	.821	81	265	67	24	68	746	9.6
Totals		720	15329	2978	.512	6	.154	1539	.780	961	2795	874	294	728	7501	10.4

SAM CASSELL

Team: Houston Rockets
Position: Guard
Height: 6'3" **Weight:** 195
Birthdate: November 18, 1969

NBA Experience: 2 years
College: Florida St.
Acquired: 1st-round pick in 1993 draft
(24th overall)

Background: From legendary Dunbar High School in Baltimore, Cassell had two sensational seasons at San Jacinto J.C. in Texas before transferring to Florida State. He prospered on a talented Seminole unit, leading the Atlantic Coast Conference in steals. Drafted 24th overall by Houston in 1993, he was a clutch reserve during Houston's 1994 NBA championship run and improved virtually every category in 1994-95.

Strengths: Cassell has great quickness, agility, and hands and has shown an aptitude for taking the ball to the basket. He has developed into one of the better backup point guards in the game for both his scoring and playmaking skills. Cassell is a very good free throw shooter and he also has 3-point range. He has lived up to his billing as a tough defender. He seems to be at his best when he's under big-game pressure.

Weaknesses: Cassell will turn the ball over while trying to make the spectacular play, and his field goal percentage needs a boost. Better decision-making is a must. While his defensive skills are above average for a young player, he also takes a lot of chances. Veteran guards take advantage. He commits too many turnovers, many a result of ill-advised passes.

Analysis: Cassell emerged during the 1994 playoffs with a game-winning shot in the Finals and consistently strong play. He has turned out to be a steal as a No. 24 draft pick and will likely become a starting point guard before too long. He needs only to show a little better decision-making ability on a nightly basis. "He's got all the skills to be an impact player at his position," Houston coach Rudy Tomjanovich has said. He's right.

PLAYER SUMMARY	
Will	take big shots
Can't	shoot 50 percent
Expect	quick defense
Don't Expect	a timid style
Fantasy Value	$9-11
Card Value	10-20¢

COLLEGE STATISTICS

		G	FGP	FTP	APG	PPG
91-92	FSU	31	.454	.704	3.8	18.4
92-93	FSU	35	.502	.759	4.9	18.3
Totals		66	.478	.733	4.4	18.3

NBA REGULAR-SEASON STATISTICS

		G	MIN	FGs FG	FGs PCT	3-PT FGs FG	3-PT FGs PCT	FTs FT	FTs PCT	Rebounds OFF	Rebounds TOT	AST	STL	BLK	PTS	PPG
93-94	HOU	66	1122	162	.418	26	.295	90	.841	25	134	192	59	7	440	6.7
94-95	HOU	82	1882	253	.427	63	.330	214	.843	38	211	405	94	14	783	9.5
Totals		148	3004	415	.423	89	.319	304	.842	63	345	597	153	21	1223	8.3

DUANE CAUSWELL

Team: Sacramento Kings
Position: Center
Height: 7'0" **Weight:** 240
Birthdate: May 31, 1968

NBA Experience: 5 years
College: Temple
Acquired: 1st-round pick in 1990 draft
(18th overall)

Background: Causwell's college career at Temple was cut a semester short because of academic ineligibility, but he finished second in the nation in blocked shots as a junior (4.1 BPG). He started 55 games as a rookie and finished 15th in the league in blocked shots. He improved his total during his second season but has been limited by two stress fractures since then. He averaged a career-low 3.6 PPG in 1994-95.

Strengths: With his wide wingspan and good height, Causwell is regarded mainly as a shot-blocker and defensive presence. He gets up and down the floor better than a lot of the league's centers, will hit the boards, and is a fine overall athlete. He does not force many shots.

Weaknesses: Causwell offers next to nothing at the offensive end of the floor. He is a poor outside shooter, rarely makes two free throws in a row, and has not been effective in the paint. He is not a good passer, nor does he play a very physical game on either end.

Analysis: Causwell was a pleasant surprise in his first two years, but he has not regained his second-year form since struggling with injuries. He was traded to Detroit in 1993-94, but the deal was then voided because he failed a physical. Causwell is not an adequate offensive player, and his defense is not strong enough to make up for it. If he maintains his health, he will likely settle into the role of defensive specialist off the bench.

PLAYER SUMMARY	
Will	block shots
Can't	shoot straight
Expect	limited minutes
Don't Expect	5 PPG
Fantasy Value	$0
Card Value	7-10¢

COLLEGE STATISTICS

		G	FGP	FTP	RPG	PPG
87-88	TEMP	33	.491	.433	2.6	2.0
88-89	TEMP	30	.514	.683	8.9	11.3
89-90	TEMP	12	.486	.596	8.3	11.3
Totals		75	.504	.624	6.0	7.2

NBA REGULAR-SEASON STATISTICS

		G	MIN	FGs FG	FGs PCT	3-PT FGs FG	3-PT FGs PCT	FTs FT	FTs PCT	Rebounds OFF	Rebounds TOT	AST	STL	BLK	PTS	PPG
90-91	SAC	76	1719	210	.508	0	.000	105	.636	141	391	69	49	148	525	6.9
91-92	SAC	80	2291	250	.549	0	.000	136	.613	196	580	59	47	215	636	7.9
92-93	SAC	55	1211	175	.545	0	.000	103	.624	112	303	35	32	87	453	8.2
93-94	SAC	41	674	71	.518	0	.000	40	.588	68	186	11	19	49	182	4.4
94-95	SAC	58	820	76	.517	0	.000	57	.582	57	174	15	14	80	209	3.6
Totals		310	6715	782	.531	0	.000	441	.614	574	1634	189	161	579	2005	6.5

CEDRIC CEBALLOS

Team: Los Angeles Lakers
Position: Forward
Height: 6'7" **Weight:** 225
Birthdate: August 2, 1969

NBA Experience: 5 years
College: Cal. St. Fullerton
Acquired: Traded from Suns for a
future 1st-round pick, 9/94

Background: Ceballos, a Hawaii native, played just one year of varsity basketball in high school before going on to lead the Big West in scoring as a junior and senior at Cal. State Fullerton. A No. 48 pick, he surprised many by becoming a starter in Phoenix and led the NBA in field goal percentage in 1992-93. A Laker in 1994-95 after a trade, he was selected to play in the All-Star Game and led the team in scoring at 21.7 PPG.

Strengths: Ceballos is an energetic, athletic player who can flat-out score. He plays above the rim, gets to the basket, and shoots a high percentage. He runs the floor and has great hands. Ceballos is a flashy, spirited performer who won the NBA's Slam Dunk Contest in 1992 with a blindfolded jam. He also rebounds well and has become a leader.

Weaknesses: His biggest flaw remains his lack of defensive intensity. Ceballos often perceives stopping his man as a chore. His leaping ability gives him tremendous potential as a shot-blocker, yet he has not put up big numbers in that category. He is not a great free throw shooter.

Analysis: Ceballos had a fantastic first year with the Lakers. He scored 50 points in a December game against the Timberwolves, helping him earn NBA Player of the Month honors. He can put the team on his shoulders and carry it offensively. The Suns were disenchanted with his defense and ability to move the ball around, but he has been a near-perfect fit in L.A.

PLAYER SUMMARY	
Will	get to the hoop
Can't	star on defense
Expect	20-plus PPG
Don't Expect	bad shots
Fantasy Value	$35-40
Card Value	10-20¢

COLLEGE STATISTICS

		G	FGP	FTP	RPG	PPG
88-89	CSF	29	.442	.672	8.8	21.2
89-90	CSF	29	.485	.670	12.5	23.1
Totals		58	.463	.671	10.7	22.1

NBA REGULAR-SEASON STATISTICS

				FGs		3-PT FGs		FTs		Rebounds						
		G	MIN	FG	PCT	FG	PCT	FT	PCT	OFF	TOT	AST	STL	BLK	PTS	PPG
90-91	PHO	63	730	204	.487	1	.167	110	.663	77	150	35	22	5	519	8.2
91-92	PHO	64	725	176	.482	1	.167	109	.736	60	152	50	16	11	462	7.2
92-93	PHO	74	1607	381	.576	0	.000	187	.725	172	408	77	54	28	949	12.8
93-94	PHO	53	1602	425	.535	0	.000	160	.724	153	344	91	59	23	1010	19.1
94-95	LAL	58	2029	497	.509	58	.397	209	.716	169	464	105	60	19	1261	21.7
Totals		312	6693	1683	.523	60	.355	775	.714	631	1518	358	211	86	4201	13.5

TOM CHAMBERS

Unrestricted Free Agent
Last Team: Utah Jazz
Position: Forward
Height: 6'10" **Weight:** 230
Birthdate: June 21, 1959

NBA Experience: 14 years
College: Utah
Acquired: Signed as a free agent, 8/93

Background: Chambers earned All-America recognition at the University of Utah before moving on to become one of the NBA's most productive scorers. He has played in four All-Star Games in 14 years. The first unrestricted free agent in NBA history (with Phoenix in 1988), he has spent the last two years with Utah.

Strengths: A double-figure scorer in his first 13 seasons, Chambers has always been comfortable driving to the hoop with either hand. He uses the dribble well and hits his free throws. He also provides stable leadership and plays an intelligent brand of basketball.

Weaknesses: Chambers has lost a step and is therefore not the matchup problem he once was. He was never a top-notch defender and still isn't. His field goal percentage has been subpar for five straight seasons and he struggles from 3-point range.

Analysis: Chambers is winding down his high-scoring career as a veteran reserve. No longer a primary threat to score, he has altered his game to become a complementary player. He reached the 20,000 career-point plateau last year.

PLAYER SUMMARY	
Will	use the dribble
Can't	score like he used to
Expect	reserve minutes
Don't Expect	a long-term deal
Fantasy Value	$0
Card Value	7-10¢

COLLEGE STATISTICS

		G	FGP	FTP	RPG	PPG
77-78	UTAH	28	.496	.625	3.7	6.4
78-79	UTAH	30	.544	.543	8.9	16.0
79-80	UTAH	28	.543	.713	8.7	17.2
80-81	UTAH	30	.594	.742	8.7	18.6
Totals		116	.553	.665	7.6	14.6

NBA REGULAR-SEASON STATISTICS

		G	MIN	FGs FG	FGs PCT	3-PT FGs FG	3-PT FGs PCT	FTs FT	FTs PCT	Rebounds OFF	Rebounds TOT	AST	STL	BLK	PTS	PPG
81-82	SD	81	2682	554	.525	0	.000	284	.620	211	561	146	58	46	1392	17.2
82-83	SD	79	2665	519	.472	0	.000	353	.723	218	519	192	79	57	1391	17.6
83-84	SEA	82	2570	554	.499	0	.000	375	.800	219	532	133	47	51	1483	18.1
84-85	SEA	81	2923	629	.483	6	.273	475	.832	164	579	209	70	57	1739	21.5
85-86	SEA	66	2019	432	.466	13	.271	346	.836	126	431	132	55	37	1223	18.5
86-87	SEA	82	3018	660	.456	54	.372	535	.849	163	545	245	81	50	1909	23.3
87-88	SEA	82	2680	611	.448	33	.303	419	.807	135	490	212	87	53	1674	20.4
88-89	PHO	81	3002	774	.471	28	.326	509	.851	143	684	231	87	55	2085	25.7
89-90	PHO	81	3046	810	.501	24	.279	557	.861	121	571	190	88	47	2201	27.2
90-91	PHO	76	2475	556	.437	20	.274	379	.826	104	490	194	65	52	1511	19.9
91-92	PHO	69	1948	426	.431	18	.367	258	.830	86	401	142	57	37	1128	16.3
92-93	PHO	73	1723	320	.447	11	.393	241	.837	96	345	101	43	23	892	12.2
93-94	UTA	80	1838	329	.440	14	.311	221	.786	87	326	79	40	32	893	11.2
94-95	UTA	81	1240	195	.457	4	.167	109	.807	66	213	73	25	30	503	6.2
Totals		1094	33829	7369	.469	225	.305	5061	.807	1939	6687	2279	882	627	20024	18.3

REX CHAPMAN

Team: Miami Heat
Position: Guard
Height: 6'4" **Weight:** 195
Birthdate: October 5, 1967
NBA Experience: 7 years

College: Kentucky
Acquired: Traded from Bullets with rights to Terrence Rencher for Jeff Webster and Ed Stokes, 6/95

Background: At Kentucky, Chapman became the first freshman to lead the Wildcats in scoring. He left after his sophomore season and was a 15-plus PPG scorer for Charlotte in his first three pro years. Chapman was acquired by Washington in 1991-92. He's been slowed by injuries but has averaged 18.2 and 16.2 PPG his last two years, respectively. The Heat acquired him in June.

Strengths: Chapman has always been regarded as a fine athlete with springs in his legs. Offensively, he provides a good combination of drives and shooting ability. His shooting reached a career-high level two years ago, and he is very reliable from the free throw line. He has the ability to play both guard positions.

Weaknesses: Poor shot selection has been the knock on Chapman throughout his career, and he returned to earth last season after a great shooting year in 1993-94. He has a tendency to try to do it all himself rather than get his teammates involved. He remains suspect on defense and his history of injuries is a concern.

Analysis: Chapman, who has slimmed down the last two years, opened the 1994-95 season by making eight 3-pointers in a game during the first week. His shooting tapered off, however, causing one to wonder whether the previous season was a fluke. He'll score his share of points, but the consistency is just not there on either end of the court.

PLAYER SUMMARY

Will ....get his points
Can't ....shut down his man
Expect ....free throw accuracy
Don't Expect ....consistency
Fantasy Value $6-8
Card Value ....5-10¢

COLLEGE STATISTICS

		G	FGP	FTP	RPG	PPG
86-87	KENT	29	.444	.735	2.3	16.0
87-88	KENT	32	.501	.794	2.9	19.0
Totals		61	.475	.771	2.6	17.6

NBA REGULAR-SEASON STATISTICS

			FGs		3-PT FGs		FTs		Rebounds						
		G	MIN	FG	PCT	FG	PCT	FT	PCT	OFF	TOT	AST	STL	BLK	PTS	PPG
88-89	CHA	75	2219	526	.414	60	.314	155	.795	74	187	176	70	25	1267	16.9
89-90	CHA	54	1762	377	.408	47	.331	144	.750	52	179	132	46	6	945	17.5
90-91	CHA	70	2100	410	.445	48	.324	234	.830	45	191	250	73	16	1102	15.7
91-92	CHA/WAS	22	567	113	.448	8	.276	36	.679	10	58	89	15	8	270	12.3
92-93	WAS	60	1300	287	.477	43	.371	132	.810	19	88	116	38	10	749	12.5
93-94	WAS	60	2025	431	.498	64	.388	168	.816	57	146	185	59	8	1094	18.2
94-95	WAS	45	1468	254	.397	86	.314	137	.862	23	113	128	67	15	731	16.2
Totals		386	11441	2398	.438	356	.334	1006	.805	280	962	1076	368	88	6158	16.0

CALBERT CHEANEY

Team: Washington Bullets
Position: Forward/Guard
Height: 6'7" **Weight:** 215
Birthdate: July 17, 1971

NBA Experience: 2 years
College: Indiana
Acquired: 1st-round pick in 1993 draft
(6th overall)

Background: Though not highly recruited out of high school, Cheaney received a scholarship from Indiana and developed into one of the best players in Hoosier history. He set a Big Ten record for total points and won the John Wooden and James Naismith Player of the Year awards. Drafted sixth overall by Washington in 1993, he scored in double figures as a rookie and became a fixture in the starting lineup last season.

Strengths: Cheaney is a silky-smooth player with a variety of skills. He slithers to the basket, can get his own shot, and is an accurate jump-shooter. Some called him the best pure shooter in the 1993 draft. Cheaney is quick, agile, and effective in transition. He also passes, plays tough defense, and is a gritty competitor. He makes his free throws, loves pressure, and can play the two and three spots.

Weaknesses: Cheaney could not hit the long NBA 3-pointer, although he's a little better off now that the arc has been moved in. His comfort zone, however, remains about a foot inside the arc. Cheaney is not a first-rate handler of the ball, which is his biggest weakness when asked to play the two spot. He is prone to following up a great outing with a quiet one.

Analysis: Cheaney has enjoyed a successful first two years in the NBA. He has established himself as a sweet shooter whose range has improved, and he also offers hustle and know-how on the defensive end. The Bullets used him as a starter for virtually all of the 1994-95 season and he responded by boosting his scoring average to 16.6 PPG. He has the look of a future cornerstone for the Bullets.

PLAYER SUMMARY	
Will	hit jumpers
Can't	play the point
Expect	further strides
Don't Expect	flimsy defense
Fantasy Value	$15-18
Card Value	15-30¢

COLLEGE STATISTICS

		G	FGP	FTP	RPG	PPG
89-90	IND	29	.572	.750	4.6	17.1
90-91	IND	34	.596	.801	5.5	21.6
91-92	IND	34	.522	.800	4.9	17.6
92-93	IND	35	.549	.795	6.4	22.4
Totals		132	.559	.790	5.4	19.8

NBA REGULAR-SEASON STATISTICS

		G	MIN	FGs FG	FGs PCT	3-PT FGs FG	3-PT FGs PCT	FTs FT	FTs PCT	Rebounds OFF	Rebounds TOT	AST	STL	BLK	PTS	PPG
93-94	WAS	65	1604	327	.470	1	.043	124	.770	88	190	126	63	10	779	12.0
94-95	WAS	78	2651	512	.453	96	.339	173	.812	105	321	177	80	21	1293	16.6
Totals		143	4255	839	.460	97	.317	297	.794	193	511	303	143	31	2072	14.5

PETE CHILCUTT

Unrestricted Free Agent
Last Team: Houston Rockets
Position: Forward/Center
Height: 6'11" **Weight:** 235
Birthdate: September 14, 1968

NBA Experience: 4 years
College: North Carolina
Acquired: Signed as a free agent, 11/94

Background: A solid complementary player for coach Dean Smith at North Carolina, Chilcutt was never named first- or second-team All-ACC, but he played every game during his four years with the Tar Heels. He was drafted 27th overall by Sacramento in 1991 and has played for the Kings, Pistons, and Rockets in his four seasons. He made 17 starts for Houston in 1994-95.

Strengths: Chilcutt has a soft shooting touch with good range for a big man. He poses matchup problems for power forwards and centers who like to stay near the bucket because he can hit the 3-pointer (35 of 86 last season). Chilcutt also shows a decent feel for the game. He works hard, gets some rebounds, and swats a few shots.

Weaknesses: Chilcutt doesn't possess exceptional speed, quickness, jumping ability, or any other athletic skill. In fact, nothing about his game is awe-inspiring. He does not create off the dribble and is below average with his low-post scoring. He has been called soft at both ends. He rarely gets to the line and his accuracy there is nothing to boast about. Chilcutt will not be a big scorer or a defensive stopper at this level.

Analysis: Chilcutt turned out to be a wise if unspectacular addition to the Houston roster after the Pistons opted not to renew his contract after the 1993-94 season. He averaged just short of 20 minutes per game and even did some spot starting for the Rockets. The shorter 3-point line played right to his strength of shooting from the perimeter. He can provide some points off the bench.

PLAYER SUMMARY

Will	...............pull defenders outside
Can't	..........................dominate inside
Expect	.....................3-point shooting
Don't Expect	....................many starts
Fantasy Value	...................................$0
Card Value	....................................5-7¢

COLLEGE STATISTICS

		G	FGP	FTP	RPG	PPG
87-88	NC	34	.564	.706	3.2	4.9
88-89	NC	37	.537	.623	5.4	6.9
89-90	NC	34	.514	.714	6.6	9.0
90-91	NC	35	.538	.765	6.6	12.0
Totals		140	.536	.710	5.5	8.2

NBA REGULAR-SEASON STATISTICS

				FGs		3-PT FGs		FTs		Rebounds						
		G	MIN	FG	PCT	FG	PCT	FT	PCT	OFF	TOT	AST	STL	BLK	PTS	PPG
91-92	SAC	69	817	113	.452	2	1.000	23	.821	78	187	38	32	17	251	3.6
92-93	SAC	59	834	165	.485	0	.000	32	.696	80	194	64	22	21	362	6.1
93-94	SAC/DET	76	1365	203	.453	3	.200	41	.631	129	371	86	53	39	450	5.9
94-95	HOU	68	1347	146	.445	35	.407	31	.738	106	317	66	25	43	358	5.3
Totals		272	4363	627	.459	40	.388	127	.702	393	1069	254	132	120	1421	5.2

CHRIS CHILDS

Team: New Jersey Nets
Position: Guard
Height: 6'3" **Weight:** 195
Birthdate: November 20, 1967

NBA Experience: 1 year
College: Boise St.
Acquired: Signed as a free agent, 7/94

Background: Childs was an unheralded college player at Boise State who went undrafted. He spent his first five professional seasons playing with six different teams in the CBA. A recovering alcoholic, he spent time in the Lucas Center in Houston and, after a relapse, checked into another center in Miami in the summer of 1993. After leading Quad City to the CBA title in 1994, Childs finally broke into the NBA with the Nets in 1994-95.

Strengths: Childs has demonstrated a nice shooting stroke. He hit about a third of his NBA 3-point attempts and made almost 85 percent of his free throws in five CBA seasons, though that percentage dipped in the big leagues. A journeyman since coming out of college, he is experienced in running several different styles of offense and has shown the ability to adapt. He is an unselfish player who works hard.

Weaknesses: There is a reason Childs labored for five years in the CBA without so much as a cup of coffee in the NBA. He is not the quickest or most creative point guard in the league and he has trouble finishing plays on his own. He shot a paltry .380 from the field last season, one of the worst marks in the league. He is not a great help on the boards, his assist total is nothing to boast about, and he commits a lot of fouls.

Analysis: Childs was the MVP of the 1994 CBA Finals. His play obviously impressed the Nets enough to sign him as a backup to Kenny Anderson, a role which Childs filled admirably at times. New Jersey was not the same team with Childs in the lineup, but how many Kenny Andersons are there? Childs knows he has not reached that level.

PLAYER SUMMARY	
Will	run the offense
Can't	take job for granted
Expect	reserve minutes
Don't Expect	great playmaking
Fantasy Value	$0
Card Value	7-10¢

COLLEGE STATISTICS

		G	FGP	FTP	APG	PPG
85-86	BSU	28	.413	.791	3.0	10.7
86-87	BSU	30	.448	.826	2.9	15.4
87-88	BSU	30	.476	.853	3.3	14.3
88-89	BSU	30	.444	.801	4.2	13.7
Totals		118	.443	.818	3.3	13.6

NBA REGULAR-SEASON STATISTICS

			FGs		3-PT FGs		FTs		Rebounds						
	G	MIN	FG	PCT	FG	PCT	FT	PCT	OFF	TOT	AST	STL	BLK	PTS	PPG
94-95 NJ	53	1021	106	.380	41	.328	55	.753	14	69	219	42	3	308	5.8
Totals	53	1021	106	.380	41	.328	55	.753	14	69	219	42	3	308	5.8

DERRICK COLEMAN

Team: New Jersey Nets
Position: Forward
Height: 6'10" **Weight:** 258
Birthdate: June 21, 1967

NBA Experience: 5 years
College: Syracuse
Acquired: 1st-round pick in 1990 draft (1st overall)

Background: Teamed with Billy Owens and Sherman Douglas, Coleman played on one of Syracuse's most talented squads ever. He earned several college Player of the Year awards as a senior. New Jersey selected him as the No. 1 pick in the 1990 draft and he won the Rookie of the Year Award. He has played in the All-Star Game and for Dream Team II and annually scores 20-plus points per game.

Strengths: Coleman can kill you with his jump shot, his moves to the bucket, his post-up repertoire, or his transition slams. He's supremely confident, having learned the game on the Detroit playgrounds. He blocks shots and is one of the better rebounding forwards in the league. He is virtually impossible to stop one-on-one when he's on his game.

Weaknesses: Coleman is known as a player who does not work hard enough night after night to reach his limitless potential. Several players have said as much. His shooting percentage is poor and he is not as good a 3-point shooter as he thinks he is. His attitude has rubbed people the wrong way.

Analysis: Some have called Coleman the best overall power forward in the game, but his attitude both on and off the court have drawn even more attention than his skills. Last year, he made a *Sports Illustrated* cover along with the headline, "Waaaaaaaaa." Some feel his complaining both on and off the court has kept the Nets from becoming winners. It's tough to knock his skills.

PLAYER SUMMARY	
Will	beat his man
Can't	avoid bad press
Expect	20-plus PPG
Don't Expect	congeniality awards
Fantasy Value	$30-35
Card Value	12-25¢

COLLEGE STATISTICS

		G	FGP	FTP	RPG	PPG
86-87	SYR	38	.560	.686	8.8	11.9
87-88	SYR	35	.587	.630	11.0	13.5
88-89	SYR	37	.575	.692	11.4	16.9
89-90	SYR	33	.551	.715	12.1	17.9
Totals		143	.568	.684	10.7	15.0

NBA REGULAR-SEASON STATISTICS

		G	MIN	FGs FG	FGs PCT	3-PT FGs FG	3-PT FGs PCT	FTs FT	FTs PCT	Rebounds OFF	Rebounds TOT	AST	STL	BLK	PTS	PPG
90-91	NJ	74	2602	514	.467	13	.342	323	.731	269	759	163	71	99	1364	18.4
91-92	NJ	65	2207	483	.504	23	.303	300	.763	203	618	205	54	98	1289	19.8
92-93	NJ	76	2759	564	.460	23	.232	421	.808	247	852	276	92	126	1572	20.7
93-94	NJ	77	2778	541	.447	38	.314	439	.774	262	870	262	68	142	1559	20.2
94-95	NJ	56	2103	371	.425	28	.233	376	.767	167	591	187	35	94	1146	20.5
Totals		348	12449	2473	.461	125	.275	1859	.770	1148	3690	1093	320	559	6930	19.9

BIMBO COLES

Team: Miami Heat
Position: Guard
Height: 6'2" **Weight:** 185
Birthdate: April 22, 1968

NBA Experience: 5 years
College: Virginia Tech
Acquired: Draft rights traded from Kings for Rory Sparrow, 6/90

Background: Coles left Virginia Tech as the first player to lead the Metro Conference in scoring three straight years. He also set a school record for assists and was a member of the 1988 United States Olympic team. Drafted by Miami, he has missed few games in his five seasons despite surgery to repair a torn shoulder muscle in the summer of 1994. He became the Heat's starting point guard in 1994-95.

Strengths: Coles is extremely quick and can get to the hoop against virtually anyone. He has been a productive distributor off the bench and averaged a career-high 6.1 APG as a starter last season. He is a fine transition player and is dangerous with pull-up jumpers. Defense has never been a problem for Coles. He loves to play the game.

Weaknesses: His perimeter shooting remains inconsistent, and Coles has never been comfortable shooting NBA 3-pointers. He makes well under 30 percent of them, prompting defenders to back off and let him fire. Coles will rush plays at times. His assist-to-turnover ratio is less than 3-to-1 and he is not a huge scorer.

Analysis: Coles has been called a shooting guard in the body of a point guard during his career, but he was one of the better reserve point men in the league until the departure of Brian Shaw put him into the starting lineup. He has some work to do before he will be considered a top-notch starter. He lacks consistency and his shooting percentage needs a boost.

PLAYER SUMMARY	
Will	play tough defense
Can't	thrive from long range
Expect	quickness, penetration
Don't Expect	50-percent shooting
Fantasy Value	$2-4
Card Value	5-10¢

COLLEGE STATISTICS

		G	FGP	FTP	APG	PPG
86-87	VT	28	.412	.716	4.0	10.0
87-88	VT	29	.443	.741	5.9	24.2
88-89	VT	27	.455	.785	5.2	26.6
89-90	VT	31	.404	.738	3.9	25.3
Totals		115	.429	.748	4.8	21.6

NBA REGULAR-SEASON STATISTICS

				FGs		3-PT FGs		FTs		Rebounds						
		G	MIN	FG	PCT	FG	PCT	FT	PCT	OFF	TOT	AST	STL	BLK	PTS	PPG
90-91	MIA	82	1355	162	.412	6	.176	71	.747	56	153	232	65	12	401	4.9
91-92	MIA	81	1976	295	.455	10	.192	216	.824	69	189	366	73	13	816	10.1
92-93	MIA	81	2232	318	.464	42	.307	177	.805	58	166	373	80	11	855	10.6
93-94	MIA	76	1726	233	.449	20	.202	102	.779	50	159	263	75	12	588	7.7
94-95	MIA	68	2207	261	.430	16	.211	141	.810	46	191	416	99	13	679	10.0
Totals		388	9496	1269	.445	94	.236	707	.802	279	858	1650	392	61	3339	8.6

MARTY CONLON

Unrestricted Free Agent
Last Team: Milwaukee Bucks
Position: Forward
Height: 6'11" **Weight:** 245
Birthdate: January 19, 1968

NBA Experience: 4 years
College: Providence
Acquired: Signed as a free agent, 8/94

Background: After a steady career at Providence College, Conlon went undrafted and embarked on a five-year tour of pro basketball that covered the land. He played with Seattle, Sacramento, Charlotte, and Washington of the NBA and spent much time in the CBA before landing with Milwaukee in 1994-95. He finally seems to have found a home, playing in every game for the Bucks last season and averaging 9.9 PPG.

Strengths: Conlon's biggest strength may be his ability to fool people into thinking he's not very good. Actually, he has a nice face-up shot with decent range and shoots a very high percentage from the floor. He also knows how to score with crafty moves in the lane. Conlon is an above-average passer for a big man and there are not too many players who put forth a better effort.

Weaknesses: There are reasons Conlon has bounced around for five years (four in the NBA). He does not excel in any one aspect of the game. He is not a physical specimen, he does not own any speed or quickness to speak of, and he is overmatched when trying to defend opponents on the perimeter. He would probably not get off the bench for a lot of teams.

Analysis: Conlon is a trooper. He seems to have survived the harsh world of being a marginal talent. His previous best stint had been a 16-game stretch for Charlotte late in the 1993-94 season in which he averaged 10.2 PPG. He is a hard-working reserve who won't make a lot of mistakes.

PLAYER SUMMARY	
Will	work hard
Can't	defend quickness
Expect	a role-player
Don't Expect	athletic ability
Fantasy Value	$1
Card Value	8-15¢

COLLEGE STATISTICS

		G	FGP	FTP	RPG	PPG
86-87	PROV	34	.448	.831	2.9	4.4
87-88	PROV	11	.511	.833	5.6	13.2
88-89	PROV	29	.524	.728	7.0	14.3
89-90	PROV	29	.502	.738	7.6	14.7
Totals		103	.505	.765	5.7	11.0

NBA REGULAR-SEASON STATISTICS

				FGs		3-PT FGs		FTs		Rebounds						
		G	MIN	FG	PCT	FG	PCT	FT	PCT	OFF	TOT	AST	STL	BLK	PTS	PPG
91-92	SEA	45	381	48	.475	0	.000	24	.750	33	69	12	9	7	120	2.7
92-93	SAC	46	467	81	.474	0	.000	57	.704	48	123	37	13	5	219	4.8
93-94	CHA/WAS	30	579	95	.576	0	.000	43	.811	53	139	34	9	8	233	7.8
94-95	MIL	82	2064	344	.532	8	.276	119	.613	160	426	110	42	18	815	9.9
Totals		203	3491	568	.524	8	.229	243	.675	294	757	193	73	38	1387	6.8

TYRONE CORBIN

Team: Sacramento Kings
Position: Forward
Height: 6'6" **Weight:** 222
Birthdate: December 31, 1962

NBA Experience: 10 years
College: DePaul
Acquired: Traded from Hawks for
Spud Webb, 6/95

Background: After leading DePaul in both scoring and rebounding as a junior and senior, Corbin made his NBA debut with San Antonio. He played for Cleveland, Phoenix, Minnesota, and Utah before the Jazz traded him to Atlanta before the 1994-95 season. He was traded again this past summer, this time to Sacramento. Corbin has spent most of his ten-year NBA career as a reserve.

Strengths: Corbin has rightfully earned his reputation as a hard worker and physical player. He fights for rebounds, gets good inside position, comes up with steals and loose balls, and plays strong defense on men his size or bigger. Corbin can stick the medium-range jumper and is known as a workaholic and a class act.

Weaknesses: The bumping and grinding inside are necessary because Corbin does not own the silky-smooth game that many of the league's premier small forwards possess. He does not create much off the dribble for either himself or his teammates. His shooting percentage and scoring average have dropped.

Analysis: Coaches love a player like Corbin, although last season was one of his worst as a pro. His scoring average of 6.2 PPG was his worst since his rookie year and he found quality minutes hard to come by. A new team, along with his poor shooting from the field and free throw line, were largely to blame.

PLAYER SUMMARY

Will ....dive for loose balls
Can't ....lead team in scoring
Expect ....a good example
Don't Expect ....10 PPG
Fantasy Value $0
Card Value ....5-10¢

COLLEGE STATISTICS

		G	FGP	FTP	RPG	PPG
81-82	DeP	28	.417	.718	6.1	5.1
82-83	DeP	33	.471	.773	7.9	10.6
83-84	DeP	30	.525	.744	7.4	14.2
84-85	DeP	29	.534	.814	8.1	15.9
Totals		120	.504	.764	7.4	11.5

NBA REGULAR-SEASON STATISTICS

		G	MIN	FGs FG	FGs PCT	3-PT FGs FG	3-PT FGs PCT	FTs FT	FTs PCT	Rebounds OFF	Rebounds TOT	AST	STL	BLK	PTS	PPG
85-86	SA	16	174	27	.422	0	.000	10	.714	11	25	11	11	2	64	4.0
86-87	SA/CLE	63	1170	156	.409	1	.250	91	.734	88	215	97	55	5	404	6.4
87-88	CLE/PHO	84	1739	257	.490	1	.167	110	.797	127	350	115	72	18	625	7.4
88-89	PHO	77	1655	245	.540	0	.000	141	.788	176	398	118	82	13	631	8.2
89-90	MIN	82	3011	521	.481	0	.000	161	.770	219	604	216	175	41	1203	14.7
90-91	MIN	82	3196	587	.448	2	.200	296	.798	185	589	347	162	53	1472	18.0
91-92	MIN/UTA	80	2207	303	.481	0	.000	174	.866	163	472	140	82	20	780	9.8
92-93	UTA	82	2555	385	.503	0	.000	180	.826	194	519	173	108	32	950	11.6
93-94	UTA	82	2149	268	.456	6	.207	117	.813	150	389	122	99	24	659	8.0
94-95	ATL	81	1389	205	.442	14	.250	78	.684	98	262	67	55	16	502	6.2
Totals		729	19245	2954	.471	24	.188	1358	.793	1411	3823	1406	901	224	7290	10.0

JOHN CROTTY

Unrestricted Free Agent
Last Team: Utah Jazz
Position: Guard
Height: 6'1" **Weight:** 185
Birthdate: July 15, 1969

NBA Experience: 3 years
College: Virginia
Acquired: Signed as a free agent, 9/92

Background: Crotty set career records at Virginia for assists and 3-pointers and finished his career as one of only three players in ACC history to record more than 1,500 points and 600 assists. He started the last 104 games of his college career. Undrafted, Crotty played in the Global Basketball League in 1991-92 before making Utah's roster. His 3.7 PPG during the 1994-95 season was tops for his three-year NBA career.

Strengths: Crotty treats basketball like a profession. He comes to work every day ready to play, even though he knows he'll spend most of the game on the bench. The lefty can handle the ball, shoot with range, and spot open men. He has had the luxury of learning from John Stockton, so he knows his job description. Crotty hits his free throws.

Weaknesses: One of the reasons Crotty works so hard is because he has to. He does not have the skills to get away with giving less than his all. He does not create off the dribble like the better point guards and he has not been a reliable scorer, either. He struggles to keep up with quicker players on defense. Crotty shot a career-low .403 from the field last season.

Analysis: Crotty is a class act who has paid his dues and will likely continue to pay them. He has been caught in a numbers game with the Jazz, although the pointers he's gotten from Stockton are bound to help him. He'll stick it out and continue to improve. He was part of the NBA South Africa Tour in 1994 along with Dikembe Mutombo, Alonzo Mourning, and Patrick Ewing.

PLAYER SUMMARY	
Will	be prepared
Can't	create like Stockton
Expect	first-rate effort
Don't Expect	a stopper
Fantasy Value	$0
Card Value	5-8¢

COLLEGE STATISTICS

		G	FGP	FTP	RPG	PPG
87-88	VIRG	31	.362	.586	2.3	6.3
88-89	VIRG	33	.440	.669	2.6	12.9
89-90	VIRG	32	.389	.702	2.9	16.0
90-91	VIRG	33	.443	.777	2.4	15.5
Totals		129	.415	.694	2.5	12.8

NBA REGULAR-SEASON STATISTICS

				FGs		3-PT FGs		FTs		Rebounds						
		G	MIN	FG	PCT	FG	PCT	FT	PCT	OFF	TOT	AST	STL	BLK	PTS	PPG
92-93	UTA	40	243	37	.514	2	.143	26	.684	4	17	55	11	0	102	2.6
93-94	UTA	45	313	45	.455	11	.458	41	.861	11	31	77	15	1	132	2.9
94-95	UTA	80	1019	93	.403	11	.306	98	.810	27	97	205	39	6	295	3.7
Totals		165	1575	175	.435	24	.324	155	.795	42	145	337	65	7	529	3.2

TERRY CUMMINGS

Unrestricted Free Agent
Last Team: San Antonio Spurs
Position: Forward
Height: 6'9" **Weight:** 250
Birthdate: March 15, 1961

NBA Experience: 13 years
College: DePaul
Acquired: Traded from Bucks for Alvin Robertson and Greg Anderson, 5/89

Background: Cummings led DePaul in rebounding in each of his three seasons. He was drafted second overall by San Diego in 1982 and became the first rookie since Kareem Abdul-Jabbar to rank in the top ten in scoring and rebounding. Cummings played in two All-Star Games with Milwaukee and excelled with San Antonio before undergoing reconstructive knee surgery in 1992.

Strengths: Cummings was once one of the top scoring and rebounding forwards in basketball. He has a large array of post-up moves and can still get his shot off. Few can match his smarts. He has committed himself to playing aggressive defense.

Weaknesses: Cummings is not the offensive player he was before knee surgery robbed him of a step. He is no longer a primary option in the offense and he cannot take over games like he once could. He struggles from the free throw line.

Analysis: Cummings has always played the game like he's been called to war. That much has not changed. One of the premier power forwards of his time, Cummings probably has a couple more years to build on his 17,000-plus points.

PLAYER SUMMARY	
Will	get his shot
Can't	take over games
Expect	quality defense
Don't Expect	young legs
Fantasy Value	$0
Card Value	5-12¢

COLLEGE STATISTICS

		G	FGP	FTP	RPG	PPG
79-80	DeP	28	.508	.832	9.4	14.2
80-81	DeP	29	.498	.750	9.0	13.0
81-82	DeP	28	.567	.756	11.9	22.3
Totals		85	.530	.775	10.1	16.4

NBA REGULAR-SEASON STATISTICS

		G	MIN	FGs FG	FGs PCT	3-PT FGs FG	3-PT FGs PCT	FTs FT	FTs PCT	Rebounds OFF	Rebounds TOT	AST	STL	BLK	PTS	PPG
82-83	SD	70	2531	684	.523	0	.000	292	.709	303	744	177	129	62	1660	23.7
83-84	SD	81	2907	737	.494	0	.000	380	.720	323	777	139	92	57	1854	22.9
84-85	MIL	79	2722	759	.495	0	.000	343	.741	244	716	228	117	67	1861	23.6
85-86	MIL	82	2669	681	.474	0	.000	265	.656	222	694	193	121	51	1627	19.8
86-87	MIL	82	2770	729	.511	0	.000	249	.662	214	700	229	129	81	1707	20.8
87-88	MIL	76	2629	675	.485	1	.333	270	.665	184	553	181	78	46	1621	21.3
88-89	MIL	80	2824	730	.467	7	.467	362	.787	281	650	198	106	72	1829	22.9
89-90	SA	81	2821	728	.475	19	.322	343	.780	226	677	219	110	52	1818	22.4
90-91	SA	67	2195	503	.484	7	.212	164	.683	194	521	157	61	30	1177	17.6
91-92	SA	70	2149	514	.488	5	.385	177	.711	247	631	102	58	34	1210	17.3
92-93	SA	8	76	11	.379	0	.000	5	.500	6	19	4	1	1	27	3.4
93-94	SA	59	1133	183	.428	0	.000	63	.589	132	297	50	31	13	429	7.3
94-95	SA	76	1273	224	.483	0	.000	72	.585	138	378	59	36	19	520	6.8
Totals		911	28699	7158	.487	39	.289	2985	.708	2714	7357	1936	1069	585	17340	19.0

BILL CURLEY

Team: Detroit Pistons
Position: Forward/Center
Height: 6'9" **Weight:** 245
Birthdate: May 29, 1972
NBA Experience: 1 year

College: Boston College
Acquired: Draft rights traded from Spurs with a 1997 2nd-round pick for Sean Elliott, 7/94

Background: Curley, a two-time All-Big East selection at Boston College, finished his career second on the all-time school list for scoring and rebounding. He impressed NBA scouts by leading the Golden Eagles to the 1994 NCAA regional-final round. He was drafted in the first round by San Antonio and traded to Detroit in a deal that sent Sean Elliott to the Spurs. Curley played in 53 games as a rookie with the Pistons in 1994-95.

Strengths: A blue-collar player, Curley brings his lunch pail and works overtime. He shoots a face-up jumper with a soft touch for a big man and owns a lefty hook. He passes well, is one of the more unselfish players you'll come across, and will be a good free throw shooter. He hustles to overcome his athletic deficiencies.

Weaknesses: As mentioned, Curley has some things to overcome. He is not light on his feet, is not strong enough to dominate inside, and does not jump too high off the deck. He loses some battles to better athletes. Curley does not possess dangerous post skills, nor is he consistent enough to make a living with the jumper. Like many rookies, he was called for a lot of fouls.

Analysis: Curley was a surprising first-round choice to many, but it may be too early to say the Pistons made a mistake. New Pistons coach Doug Collins likes players who bust their tails, and that is the biggest thing this big man has going for him. He is still relatively untested, having spent a month and a half on the injured list with a sprained ankle and seeing less than a quarter of action per contest.

PLAYER SUMMARY

Will ....put in the work
Can't.........................sky for rebounds
Expect ....further improvement
Don't Expect............athletic prowess
Fantasy Value $0
Card Value ....15-25¢

COLLEGE STATISTICS

		G	FGP	FTP	RPG	PPG
90-91	BC	30	.542	.691	6.9	12.6
91-92	BC	31	.577	.774	8.1	17.8
92-93	BC	31	.580	.849	7.6	15.8
93-94	BC	34	.557	.793	9.0	20.0
Totals		126	.565	.780	7.9	16.7

NBA REGULAR-SEASON STATISTICS

			FGs		3-PT FGs		FTs		Rebounds						
		G	MIN	FG	PCT	FG	PCT	FT	PCT	OFF	TOT	AST	STL	BLK	PTS	PPG
94-95	DET	53	595	58	.433	0	.000	27	.750	54	124	25	21	21	143	2.7
Totals		53	595	58	.433	0	.000	27	.750	54	124	25	21	21	143	2.7

DELL CURRY

Team: Charlotte Hornets
Position: Guard
Height: 6'5" **Weight:** 208
Birthdate: June 25, 1964

NBA Experience: 9 years
College: Virginia Tech
Acquired: Selected from Cavaliers in 1988 expansion draft

Background: Curry, the Metro Conference Player of the Year as a Virginia Tech senior, was drafted by the Baltimore Orioles as a pitcher and the Utah Jazz for basketball. He was traded to Cleveland and picked up by Charlotte in the expansion draft. He has averaged double figures in each of the last eight years and won the NBA's Sixth Man Award in 1993-94. He finished second for the award last season.

Strengths: Curry has the ability to light up the scoreboard in a hurry with a dangerous outside shot, particularly from 3-point land. He ranks among the most accurate 3-point and free throw shooters in the game. He has been described as one of the five best pure shooters in the NBA.

Weaknesses: Perhaps too congenial in his approach, Curry is neither a willing nor able defender. He's not physical with players his size or larger and lacks the quickness and desire to keep up with smaller ones. Curry is not a gifted passer and would rather shoot anyway.

Analysis: Curry's stroke is a thing of beauty. When he is hot, you want the ball to touch his hands every time down the floor. Few can match his perimeter prowess and range. Curry also offers a willingness to do his job in a reserve role. He has ignited the Hornets with his shooting off the bench.

PLAYER SUMMARY	
Will	drill the trey
Can't	shine on defense
Expect	instant offense
Don't Expect	rebounds
Fantasy Value	$5-7
Card Value	5-10¢

COLLEGE STATISTICS

		G	FGP	FTP	RPG	PPG
82-83	VT	32	.475	.850	3.0	14.5
83-84	VT	35	.522	.759	4.1	19.3
84-85	VT	29	.482	.758	5.8	18.2
85-86	VT	30	.529	.789	6.8	24.1
Totals		126	.505	.785	4.8	19.0

NBA REGULAR-SEASON STATISTICS

		G	MIN	FGs FG	FGs PCT	3-PT FGs FG	3-PT FGs PCT	FTs FT	FTs PCT	Rebounds OFF	Rebounds TOT	AST	STL	BLK	PTS	PPG
86-87	UTA	67	636	139	.426	17	.283	30	.789	30	78	58	27	4	325	4.9
87-88	CLE	79	1499	340	.458	28	.346	79	.782	43	166	149	94	22	787	10.0
88-89	CHA	48	813	256	.491	19	.345	40	.870	26	104	50	42	4	571	11.9
89-90	CHA	67	1860	461	.466	52	.354	96	.923	31	168	159	98	26	1070	16.0
90-91	CHA	76	1515	337	.471	32	.372	96	.842	47	199	166	75	25	802	10.6
91-92	CHA	77	2020	504	.486	74	.404	127	.836	57	259	177	93	20	1209	15.7
92-93	CHA	80	2094	498	.452	95	.401	136	.866	51	286	180	87	23	1227	15.3
93-94	CHA	82	2173	533	.455	152	.402	117	.873	71	262	221	98	27	1335	16.3
94-95	CHA	69	1718	343	.441	154	.427	95	.856	41	168	113	55	18	935	13.6
Totals		645	14328	3411	.462	623	.392	816	.853	397	1690	1273	669	169	8261	12.8

YINKA DARE

Team: New Jersey Nets
Position: Center
Height: 7'0" **Weight:** 265
Birthdate: October 10, 1972

NBA Experience: 1 year
College: George Washington
Acquired: 1st-round pick in 1994 draft
(14th overall)

Background: The Nigerian-born Dare did not begin playing organized basketball until 1991-92 at Milford Academy in Connecticut, and he spent only two seasons at George Washington. He led the Colonials to two NCAA Tournament bids (including a spot in the Sweet 16) and led the Atlantic 10 in rebounds and blocked shots as a freshman. After opting to skip his final two college seasons, Dare was drafted 14th by New Jersey but spent all but one game of his rookie season on the injured list.

Strengths: Dare has all the physical tools: size, agility, speed, quickness, and strength. He did not display all those qualities in college, but he tested well with NBA teams before the draft. He shows a good feel for the game considering he has not been at it for very long. Dare has a soft righty hook shot and is a potential rebounding and shot-blocking force.

Weaknesses: You don't become a well-rounded player in the time Dare has spent learning the game. He is not a good passer or ball-handler, his post moves and footwork need some refining, and he does not display a good touch on his jumper. He's horrible from the free throw line. His work ethic has been questioned, as was his decision to leave school two years early. Tendinitis in his right knee could be the biggest issue.

Analysis: Dare played three minutes as a rookie, missing the only shot he took and pulling down one rebound. He did manage to commit two fouls. There will be an NBA career for Dare, but whether or not he will become a productive NBA player is up for debate. The Nets knew they were getting a project. Time will tell whether their gamble pays off.

PLAYER SUMMARY	
Will	block shots
Can't	shoot free throws
Expect	lots of coaching
Don't Expect	refined skills
Fantasy Value	$0
Card Value	10-20¢

COLLEGE STATISTICS

		G	FGP	FTP	RPG	PPG
92-93	GW	30	.551	.473	10.3	12.2
93-94	GW	30	.538	.585	10.3	15.4
Totals		60	.544	.529	10.3	13.8

NBA REGULAR-SEASON STATISTICS

			FGs		3-PT FGs		FTs		Rebounds						
	G	MIN	FG	PCT	FG	PCT	FT	PCT	OFF	TOT	AST	STL	BLK	PTS	PPG
94-95 NJ	1	3	0	.000	0	.000	0	.000	0	1	0	0	0	0	0.0
Totals	1	3	0	.000	0	.000	0	.000	0	1	0	0	0	0	0.0

BRAD DAUGHERTY

Team: Cleveland Cavaliers
Position: Center
Height: 7'0" **Weight:** 269
Birthdate: October 19, 1965

NBA Experience: 8 years
College: North Carolina
Acquired: 1st-round pick in 1986 draft
(1st overall)

Background: Daugherty performed in the McDonald's All-America Game as a 16-year-old prep senior. At North Carolina, he led the Atlantic Coast Conference in rebounding as a junior and led the country in field goal percentage as a senior. He has appeared in the NBA All-Star Game five times in his eight seasons and surpassed 20 PPG three straight years. He was sidelined in 1994-95 following back surgery.

Strengths: Daugherty can hurt you inside or out. He has the power to muscle underneath for baskets and also has the touch to make precision passes from the high post. Rivals have called him the best passing center in the league. He also provides double-figure rebounds and solid leadership.

Weaknesses: Daugherty is not as physical as some of the other centers in the league and he won't block as many shots as you'd like—less than one per game. His defense is soft at times. He has not been as steady the last couple of years, largely because of injuries.

Analysis: Daugherty opted for surgery to repair a herniated disk, sacrificing last season for the good of his next few. When healthy, he is a complete player with one of the best attitudes you'll find among pro athletes. He has never drawn the acclaim of some of the marquee big men in the league, but the Cavs are not the same team without him.

PLAYER SUMMARY	
Will	spot open men
Can't	intimidate defensively
Expect	double-doubles
Don't Expect	Shaq-like brawn
Fantasy Value	$13-16
Card Value	10-20¢

COLLEGE STATISTICS

		G	FGP	FTP	RPG	PPG
82-83	NC	35	.558	.663	5.2	8.2
83-84	NC	30	.610	.678	5.6	10.5
84-85	NC	36	.625	.742	9.7	17.3
85-86	NC	34	.648	.684	9.0	20.2
Totals		135	.620	.700	7.4	14.2

NBA REGULAR-SEASON STATISTICS

			FGs		3-PT FGs		FTs		Rebounds					
	G	MIN	FG	PCT	FG	PCT	FT	PCT	OFF	TOT	AST	STL	BLK	PTS	PPG
86-87	CLE	80	2695	487	.538	0	.000	279	.696	152	647	304	49	63	1253	15.7
87-88	CLE	79	2957	551	.510	0	.000	378	.716	151	665	333	48	56	1480	18.7
88-89	CLE	78	2821	544	.538	1	.333	386	.737	167	718	285	63	40	1475	18.9
89-90	CLE	41	1438	244	.479	0	.000	202	.704	77	373	130	29	22	690	16.8
90-91	CLE	76	2946	605	.524	0	.000	435	.751	177	830	253	74	46	1645	21.6
91-92	CLE	73	2643	576	.570	0	.000	414	.777	191	760	262	65	78	1566	21.5
92-93	CLE	71	2691	520	.571	1	.500	391	.795	164	726	312	53	56	1432	20.2
93-94	CLE	50	1838	296	.488	0	.000	256	.785	128	508	149	41	36	848	17.0
Totals		548	20029	3823	.532	2	.143	2741	.747	1207	5227	2028	422	397	10389	19.0

ANTONIO DAVIS

Team: Indiana Pacers
Position: Forward/Center
Height: 6'9" **Weight:** 230
Birthdate: October 31, 1968

NBA Experience: 2 years
College: Texas-El Paso
Acquired: 2nd-round pick in 1990 draft (45th overall)

Background: Davis finished his career at Texas-El Paso No. 5 on the all-time rebounding chart and was named to the WAC All-Defensive Team as a senior. A second-round draft pick of Indiana in 1990, he spent his first two pro seasons in Greece and then averaged 11.1 PPG and 9.9 RPG in the Italian League in 1992-93. Davis averaged 7.7 PPG and 6.2 RPG as a Pacer rookie but was slowed last season by a back injury.

Strengths: Davis is an exceptional leaper who is capable of controlling both the offensive and defensive glass. He also plays solid defense and will block his share of shots. He works tirelessly on the boards and the defensive end. Davis has improved his offensive game by leaps and bounds since his college career. He can be a good face-up shooter within 15 feet of the bucket.

Weaknesses: Davis does not own a vast offensive repertoire despite scoring more than expected since joining the league. His range is limited and his low-post moves are nothing special. Many of his points result from his effort on the offensive glass. He is a poor free throw shooter and passer, and his effectiveness in virtually every phase of the game was diminished last season. His shooting percentage tumbled.

Analysis: The 1995-96 season will be an important one for Davis, who made great strides overseas and as an NBA rookie before his back injury kept him on the injured list for more than two months last year. He wasn't the same player when he returned. A fine rebounder and defender who never stops hustling, Davis wants to reestablish himself as a coach's dream and an opponent's nightmare. If 100 percent, he can.

PLAYER SUMMARY	
Will	go all out
Can't	hit his free throws
Expect	offensive boards
Don't Expect	great range
Fantasy Value	$1
Card Value	7-10¢

COLLEGE STATISTICS

		G	FGP	FTP	RPG	PPG
86-87	UTEP	28	.344	.433	1.8	1.3
87-88	UTEP	30	.590	.548	6.5	9.3
88-89	UTEP	32	.544	.619	8.0	14.3
89-90	UTEP	32	.522	.642	7.6	10.8
Totals		122	.540	.600	6.1	9.2

NBA REGULAR-SEASON STATISTICS

				FGs		3-PT FGs		FTs		Rebounds						
		G	MIN	FG	PCT	FG	PCT	FT	PCT	OFF	TOT	AST	STL	BLK	PTS	PPG
93-94	IND	81	1732	216	.508	0	.000	194	.642	190	505	55	45	84	626	7.7
94-95	IND	44	1030	109	.445	0	.000	117	.672	105	280	25	19	29	335	7.6
Totals		125	2762	325	.485	0	.000	311	.653	295	785	80	64	113	961	7.7

DALE DAVIS

Team: Indiana Pacers
Position: Forward
Height: 6'11" **Weight:** 230
Birthdate: March 25, 1969

NBA Experience: 4 years
College: Clemson
Acquired: 1st-round pick in 1991 draft
(13th overall)

Background: At Clemson, Davis teamed with Elden Campbell for three seasons to form the "Duo of Doom." As a senior, Davis led the ACC in rebounding for a third consecutive year. The 13th pick in the 1991 draft, he has started at power forward for the Pacers in the last three of his four campaigns and has averaged about 11 PPG in each of the last two years.

Strengths: Davis has a great body and solid instincts. He is the aggressive, hard-working type who loves a challenge. His long arms and fine athletic ability make him a force as a rebounder and shot-blocker. A fan favorite in Indianapolis, he runs the floor and shoots a high percentage from the field. Davis has made himself a better offensive player with a lot of practice.

Weaknesses: Davis's range is limited and his low-post moves are too often predictable. However, he knows his limitations on the offensive end and plays within them. Many of his nontransition points follow offensive rebounds. When it comes to passing prowess, Davis is not your man. And when he gets the ball inside, it never hurts to foul this dismal free throw shooter.

Analysis: Davis continues to emerge as one of the top power forwards in the NBA. A self-proclaimed rebounding and defensive force, he has also grown offensively into a competent performer. No, he will never threaten to lead the league in scoring. However, he was fifth in the league in field goal accuracy last season and remains among the top 20 in the league in rebounding and shot-blocking.

PLAYER SUMMARY	
Will	crash the boards
Can't	make free throws
Expect	defensive intimidation
Don't Expect	assists
Fantasy Value	$11-14
Card Value	7-12¢

COLLEGE STATISTICS

		G	FGP	FTP	RPG	PPG
87-88	CLEM	29	.532	.506	7.7	7.8
88-89	CLEM	29	.670	.646	8.9	13.3
89-90	CLEM	35	.625	.596	11.3	15.3
90-91	CLEM	28	.532	.580	12.1	17.9
Totals		121	.588	.589	10.0	13.6

NBA REGULAR-SEASON STATISTICS

				FGs		3-PT FGs		FTs		Rebounds						
		G	MIN	FG	PCT	FG	PCT	FT	PCT	OFF	TOT	AST	STL	BLK	PTS	PPG
91-92	IND	64	1301	154	.552	0	.000	87	.572	158	410	30	27	74	395	6.2
92-93	IND	82	2264	304	.568	0	.000	119	.529	291	723	69	63	148	727	8.9
93-94	IND	66	2292	308	.529	0	.000	155	.527	280	700	100	48	106	771	11.7
94-95	IND	74	2346	324	.563	0	.000	138	.533	259	696	58	72	116	786	10.6
Totals		286	8203	1090	.553	0	.000	499	.537	988	2547	257	210	444	2679	9.4

HUBERT DAVIS

Team: New York Knicks
Position: Guard
Height: 6'5" **Weight:** 183
Birthdate: May 17, 1970

NBA Experience: 3 years
College: North Carolina
Acquired: 1st-round pick in 1992 draft
(20th overall)

Background: A nephew of former North Carolina and NBA great Walter Davis, Hubert Davis gradually developed into a star at North Carolina, leading the Atlantic Coast Conference in 3-point field goal percentage as a junior and his team in scoring as a senior. He was drafted by the Knicks with the 20th pick in 1992. He has done some spot starting over the last two years and averaged 10.0 PPG in 1994-95.

Strengths: Walter Davis was one of the greatest shooters in NBA history, and his nephew has a sweet stroke as well. Hubert has range beyond the 3-point line, boasts an accurate pull-up jumper, and can be deadly when he squares up to the basket. He moves well without the ball and uses screens. He runs the floor and is a better passer than most notice.

Weaknesses: Make him put it on the floor, and Davis is more likely to miss. Creating his shot has been a problem. He is slight in build and can be shoved around by bigger guards. His lack of muscle hurts him on the defensive end, where he also does not have the raw quickness to keep his man from getting past him. He does not rebound much.

Analysis: Davis is earning more and more respect as one of the better pure shooters in the game. He made about 45 percent of his 3-pointers last year and is also capable of driving to the hoop for finishes or passes to teammates. With the added respect, however, have come tighter defenses. That had much to do with his slight dip in numbers last year. Still, Davis has the look of a double-digit scorer for years to come.

PLAYER SUMMARY

Will ....hit open jumpers
Can't ....create his own shot
Expect ....great range
Don't Expect.......................rebounds
Fantasy Value $3-5
Card Value ....7-12¢

COLLEGE STATISTICS

		G	FGP	FTP	RPG	PPG
88-89	NC	35	.512	.774	0.8	3.3
89-90	NC	34	.446	.797	1.8	9.6
90-91	NC	35	.521	.835	2.4	13.3
91-92	NC	33	.508	.828	2.3	21.4
Totals		137	.498	.819	1.8	11.8

NBA REGULAR-SEASON STATISTICS

		FGs		3-PT FGs		FTs		Rebounds							
	G	MIN	FG	PCT	FG	PCT	FT	PCT	OFF	TOT	AST	STL	BLK	PTS	PPG
92-93 NY	50	815	110	.438	6	.316	43	.796	13	56	83	22	4	269	5.4
93-94 NY	56	1333	238	.471	53	.402	85	.825	23	67	165	40	4	614	11.0
94-95 NY	82	1697	296	.480	131	.455	97	.808	30	110	150	35	11	820	10.0
Totals	188	3845	644	.469	190	.433	225	.812	66	233	398	97	19	1703	9.1

TERRY DAVIS

Team: Dallas Mavericks
Position: Forward/Center
Height: 6'10" **Weight:** 250
Birthdate: June 17, 1967

NBA Experience: 6 years
College: Virginia Union
Acquired: Signed as a free agent, 8/91

Background: From tiny Virginia Union, Davis made headlines as a two-time Central Intercollegiate Athletic Association Player of the Year. Though he wasn't drafted, he signed with Miami in 1989 and spent two years there. He enjoyed his two most productive years in Dallas before shattering his left elbow in a gruesome car accident in the spring of 1993. He has not been the same player since.

Strengths: Davis emerged as a full-time starter, big-time board man, and tough defender during his first two years in Dallas. He plays with fire in his eyes and has provided a good combination of strength and agility. He is capable of playing both forward and center and has an attitude that coaches love. He hates losing.

Weaknesses: Davis has a modest offensive game that has been further hampered by his elbow injury and the ensuing layoff. He does not possess good ball-handling skills, has never been much of a passer, and does not make consistently wise decisions with the ball. He's a terrible free throw shooter. He seems to have lost his confidence since the accident.

Analysis: Davis has a great attitude, but his future is not so certain. His 15-game comeback in 1993-94 after the injury was a little premature, but last season was a telling one. He averaged just 3.0 PPG, saw very limited action, and was no longer the rebounding and defensive presence he once was. His 1995-96 season will be pivotal in determining what worth he has to a team.

PLAYER SUMMARY

Will	play defense
Can't	regain top form
Expect	hard work
Don't Expect	10 PPG
Fantasy Value	$0
Card Value	5-8¢

COLLEGE STATISTICS

		G	FGP	FTP	RPG	PPG
85-86	VU	27	.462	.605	4.3	4.1
86-87	VU	32	.521	.690	11.3	11.5
87-88	VU	31	.566	.715	10.9	22.7
88-89	VU	31	.615	.682	11.9	22.3
Totals		121	.567	.692	9.8	15.5

NBA REGULAR-SEASON STATISTICS

				FGs		3-PT FGs		FTs		Rebounds						
		G	MIN	FG	PCT	FG	PCT	FT	PCT	OFF	TOT	AST	STL	BLK	PTS	PPG
89-90	MIA	63	884	122	.466	0	.000	54	.621	93	229	25	25	28	298	4.7
90-91	MIA	55	996	115	.487	1	.500	69	.556	107	266	39	18	28	300	5.5
91-92	DAL	68	2149	256	.482	0	.000	181	.635	228	672	57	26	29	693	10.2
92-93	DAL	75	2462	393	.455	2	.250	167	.594	259	701	68	36	28	955	12.7
93-94	DAL	15	286	24	.407	0	.000	8	.667	30	74	6	9	1	56	3.7
94-95	DAL	46	580	49	.434	0	.000	42	.636	63	156	10	6	3	140	3.0
Totals		322	7357	959	.465	3	.167	521	.609	780	2098	205	120	117	2442	7.6

JOHNNY DAWKINS

Unsigned Free Agent
Last Team: Detroit Pistons
Position: Guard
Height: 6'2" **Weight:** 170
Birthdate: September 28, 1963

NBA Experience: 9 years
College: Duke
Acquired: Signed as a free agent, 10/94

Background: Dawkins finished his college career No. 1 on Duke's all-time scoring list. He was the first ACC player to collect 2,000 points, 500 assists, and 500 rebounds. San Antonio drafted him in 1986 but he missed most of 1988-89 with a leg injury and nearly all of 1990-91 with a torn anterior cruciate ligament. He played five years in Philadelphia and was released last March after one season with the Pistons.

Strengths: Dawkins is a natural point guard who generally makes wise choices with the ball and handles it well against pressure. He is a reliable free throw shooter, has 3-point range, and has displayed fine leadership ability and court sense during his career.

Weaknesses: Dawkins has been more tentative and inconsistent since his knee injury. He has lost some of his quickness, which limits his ability to make things happen on offense and to stay in front of his man on defense. His numbers and his effectiveness have declined in each of the last four seasons.

Analysis: Dawkins, once pegged as a future star, has settled for a reserve role over the last three years because he has not been effective as a starter. He has not only lost some of his lateral quickness, but much of his confidence as well. He's a capable backup point man with a good attitude who will find work somewhere.

PLAYER SUMMARY	
Will	run the offense
Can't	regain his step
Expect	backup duty
Don't Expect	10 PPG
Fantasy Value	$0
Card Value	5-8¢

COLLEGE STATISTICS

		G	FGP	FTP	APG	PPG
82-83	DUKE	28	.500	.682	4.8	18.1
83-84	DUKE	34	.481	.831	4.1	19.4
84-85	DUKE	31	.495	.795	5.0	18.8
85-86	DUKE	40	.549	.812	3.2	20.2
Totals		133	.508	.790	4.2	19.2

NBA REGULAR-SEASON STATISTICS

		G	MIN	FGs FG	FGs PCT	3-PT FGs FG	3-PT FGs PCT	FTs FT	FTs PCT	Rebounds OFF	Rebounds TOT	AST	STL	BLK	PTS	PPG
86-87	SA	81	1682	334	.437	14	.298	153	.801	56	169	290	67	3	835	10.3
87-88	SA	65	2179	405	.485	19	.311	198	.896	66	204	480	88	2	1027	15.8
88-89	SA	32	1083	177	.443	0	.000	100	.893	32	101	224	55	0	454	14.2
89-90	PHI	81	2865	465	.489	22	.333	210	.861	48	247	601	121	9	1162	14.3
90-91	PHI	4	124	26	.634	1	.250	10	.909	0	16	28	3	0	63	15.8
91-92	PHI	82	2815	394	.437	36	.356	164	.882	42	227	567	89	5	988	12.0
92-93	PHI	74	1598	258	.437	26	.310	113	.796	33	136	339	80	4	655	8.9
93-94	PHI	72	1343	177	.418	37	.352	84	.840	28	123	263	63	5	475	6.6
94-95	DET	50	1170	125	.463	25	.342	49	.891	28	113	205	52	1	325	6.5
Totals		541	14859	2361	.456	180	.330	1081	.857	333	1336	2997	618	29	5984	11.1

TODD DAY

Team: Milwaukee Bucks
Position: Guard/Forward
Height: 6'6" **Weight:** 188
Birthdate: January 7, 1970

NBA Experience: 3 years
College: Arkansas
Acquired: 1st-round pick in 1992 draft
(8th overall)

Background: The 1988 prep Player of the Year in Memphis, Day signed with Arkansas and teamed in the backcourt with Lee Mayberry. Day led Arkansas to a 115-24 record in four seasons and earned several All-America honors as a junior and senior. He was drafted eighth overall by Milwaukee in 1992 and, after two decent seasons, he raised his average to 16.0 PPG during the 1994-95 campaign.

Strengths: Day has the look of a well-rounded player. He shoots with 3-point range, handles the ball, gets up and down the court quickly, and is a fine finisher. His quick feet, long arms, and ability to leap out of the gym make him a potentially dominant defensive player. He also rebounds well and will not back down from a challenge. He can play both the big-guard and small-forward positions.

Weaknesses: Day is a streaky player. That goes for his shooting, his control of the basketball, and his defense. His shooting percentage must improve, though he did raise it last year and made 39 percent from 3-point range. Defensively, he takes a lot of chances and picks up a multitude of fouls with his feisty style. He has a history of off-court trouble but has kept clean recently.

Analysis: Day is a splendid athlete and one of the central figures in Milwaukee's future. Last year was his first as a starter from beginning to end, and he responded with career-high numbers in most categories. He made strides toward better shooting consistency, which had been his main weakness. He may be on the verge of something big.

PLAYER SUMMARY

Will ....mix it up
Can't ....shoot 50 percent
Expect ....athletic plays
Don't Expect ....defensive slack
Fantasy Value $13-16
Card Value ....10-15¢

COLLEGE STATISTICS

		G	FGP	FTP	RPG	PPG
88-89	ARK	32	.451	.715	4.0	13.3
89-90	ARK	35	.491	.760	5.4	19.5
90-91	ARK	38	.473	.747	5.3	20.7
91-92	ARK	22	.499	.764	7.0	22.7
Totals		127	.479	.747	5.3	18.9

NBA REGULAR-SEASON STATISTICS

				FGs		3-PT FGs		FTs		Rebounds						
		G	MIN	FG	PCT	FG	PCT	FT	PCT	OFF	TOT	AST	STL	BLK	PTS	PPG
92-93	MIL	71	1931	358	.432	54	.293	213	.717	144	291	117	75	48	983	13.8
93-94	MIL	76	2127	351	.415	33	.223	231	.698	115	310	138	103	52	966	12.7
94-95	MIL	82	2717	445	.424	163	.390	257	.754	95	322	134	104	63	1310	16.0
Totals		229	6775	1154	.424	250	.333	701	.723	354	923	389	282	163	3259	14.2

TERRY DEHERE

Team: Los Angeles Clippers
Position: Guard
Height: 6'4" **Weight:** 190
Birthdate: September 12, 1971

NBA Experience: 2 years
College: Seton Hall
Acquired: 1st-round pick in 1993 draft
(13th overall)

Background: A prep teammate of Bobby Hurley, Dehere was slow to develop in high school but became a star at Seton Hall. He was the Pirates' main offensive weapon for four years, during which he surpassed Chris Mullin to become the Big East's all-time leading scorer. He was named league Player of the Year as a senior. Drafted 13th by the Clippers in 1993, he followed a slow rookie year by averaging 10.4 PPG in 1994-95.

Strengths: Dehere has quick feet and is a dangerous transition player. He came into the league with a reputation for offense and has shown signs of being a scorer. He has a very quick release and has been just about as accurate from 3-point range as from inside the arc. He's smart, he wants to succeed, and he will not back down from a challenge.

Weaknesses: Dehere has struggled to find his stroke over his first two seasons. His shooting percentage hovered around the .400 mark last season after a rookie year of .377. Even free throws trouble him despite hitting at an 82-percent clip in college. He is a bit small for shooting guard, does not possess great ball-handling skills, and has been as inconsistent on defense as he has with his jump shot. He could also stand to bulk up a little.

Analysis: Expected to be a fine scorer after a little seasoning, Dehere is a little behind schedule. His shooting has been horribly inconsistent and the rest of his game is not far behind. He played the first half of the 1994-95 season primarily as a starter before reassuming his role off the bench. Dehere does have the look of a potentially dangerous scorer and should continue to develop.

PLAYER SUMMARY

Will..............................run the court
Can't..........................find his stroke
Expect ....further development
Don't Expect ....consistency
Fantasy Value $1-3
Card Value ....8-12¢

COLLEGE STATISTICS

		G	FGP	FTP	RPG	PPG
89-90	SH	28	.402	.797	3.4	16.1
90-91	SH	34	.463	.839	3.0	19.8
91-92	SH	31	.427	.830	3.7	19.4
92-93	SH	35	.461	.818	3.0	22.0
Totals		128	.442	.822	3.2	19.5

NBA REGULAR-SEASON STATISTICS

			FGs		3-PT FGs		FTs		Rebounds						
		G	MIN	FG	PCT	FG	PCT	FT	PCT	OFF	TOT	AST	STL	BLK	PTS	PPG
93-94	LAC	64	759	129	.377	23	.404	61	.753	25	68	78	28	3	342	5.3
94-95	LAC	80	1774	279	.407	48	.294	229	.784	35	152	225	45	7	835	10.4
Totals		144	2533	408	.397	71	.323	290	.777	60	220	303	73	10	1177	8.2

VINNY DEL NEGRO

Team: San Antonio Spurs
Position: Guard
Height: 6'4" **Weight:** 200
Birthdate: August 9, 1966

NBA Experience: 5 years
College: North Carolina St.
Acquired: Signed as a free agent, 7/92

Background: Sinking nearly 45 percent of his 3-point shots as a collegian at North Carolina State, Del Negro was an All-ACC pick as a senior. He played two pro seasons with Sacramento before putting in a two-year stint in Italy. He was voted Italian A League MVP after averaging 26.0 PPG in 1992. Del Negro returned to the NBA with San Antonio three years ago, started in 1994-95, and averaged a career-high 12.5 PPG.

Strengths: Del Negro can play both guard positions and has been solid at each. He is a very accurate jump-shooter with 3-point range, can get his own shots, handles the ball, and makes the right passes. He rarely makes a mistake with the ball in his hands and is an 84-percent career free throw shooter. He's a fine defensive rebounder who boxes out.

Weaknesses: What Del Negro offers in fundamentals he lacks in sheer explosiveness. He is not quick enough to create havoc off the dribble or to enjoy much success defensively against speedy guards, although he is a better athlete than his body indicates. He is not capable of carrying a team on his back.

Analysis: Del Negro is neither one of the best point guards in the league nor one of the premier shooting guards. However, he has been invaluable to the Spurs as a starter at each position over the last two seasons. He shoots well from the perimeter, helps the offense go, and makes few mistakes. He also scores in double figures.

PLAYER SUMMARY

Will	hit open jumpers
Can't	produce highlight reels
Expect	versatility
Don't Expect	explosiveness
Fantasy Value	$3-5
Card Value	5-8¢

COLLEGE STATISTICS

		G	FGP	FTP	RPG	PPG
84-85	NCST	19	.571	.652	0.7	2.1
85-86	NCST	17	.367	.636	0.8	1.7
86-87	NCST	35	.494	.887	3.3	10.4
87-88	NCST	32	.515	.839	4.9	15.9
Totals		103	.502	.825	2.9	9.1

NBA REGULAR-SEASON STATISTICS

				FGs		3-PT FGs		FTs		Rebounds						
		G	MIN	FG	PCT	FG	PCT	FT	PCT	OFF	TOT	AST	STL	BLK	PTS	PPG
88-89	SAC	80	1556	239	.475	6	.300	85	.850	48	123	206	65	14	569	7.1
89-90	SAC	76	1858	643	.462	10	.313	135	.871	39	198	250	64	10	739	9.7
92-93	SA	73	1526	218	.507	6	.250	101	.863	19	163	291	44	1	543	7.4
93-94	SA	77	1949	309	.487	15	.349	140	.824	27	161	320	64	1	773	10.0
94-95	SA	75	2360	372	.486	66	.407	128	.790	28	192	226	61	14	938	12.5
Totals		381	9249	1435	.482	103	.367	589	.837	161	885	1293	298	40	3562	9.3

VLADE DIVAC

Team: Los Angeles Lakers
Position: Center
Height: 7'1" **Weight:** 260
Birthdate: February 3, 1968

NBA Experience: 6 years
College: None
Acquired: 1st-round pick in 1989 draft
(26th overall)

Background: Divac was a national sports hero in the former Yugoslavia before being drafted by the Lakers in 1989. His wedding was televised nationally. He led Partizan to the European club championship in 1988 and averaged 20 PPG and 11 RPG in his three years there. He was named to the 1990 NBA All-Rookie Team and has increased his scoring average every year since, including 16.0 PPG in 1994-95.

Strengths: Divac is a very skilled center in most respects. He is a gifted passer and ball-handler for a big man and his improved low-post offense has taken his low-post game to a higher level. He has always been a deft shooter with range. Divac provides good shot-blocking and rebounding and runs the floor well for a big man.

Weaknesses: Inconsistency has plagued Divac throughout his NBA career, although the reality is he has been pretty steady over the last two years. He still has his nights when he is not as intense as he needs to be. He picks up a lot of fouls despite not being the most physical center.

Analysis: The strides Divac has made since crossing the ocean have been progressive. His current play is far beyond where he stood six seasons ago. He has made himself a dangerous scorer, and last season Divac ranked among the league's top 15 in both rebounding and shot-blocking. He's not in the superstar class, but most teams would gladly take him as their starting center.

```
PLAYER SUMMARY
Will ..................rebound, block shots
Can't .........................overpower Shaq
Expect ......................double-doubles
Don't Expect......physical dominance
Fantasy Value ..........................$50-55
Card Value ..................................8-12¢
```

COLLEGE STATISTICS

—DID NOT PLAY—

NBA REGULAR-SEASON STATISTICS

			FGs		3-PT FGs		FTs		Rebounds						
		G	MIN	FG	PCT	FG	PCT	FT	PCT	OFF	TOT	AST	STL	BLK	PTS	PPG
89-90	LAL	82	1611	274	.499	0	.000	153	.708	167	512	75	79	114	701	8.5
90-91	LAL	82	2310	360	.565	5	.357	196	.703	205	666	92	106	127	921	11.2
91-92	LAL	36	979	157	.495	5	.263	86	.768	87	247	60	55	35	405	11.3
92-93	LAL	82	2525	397	.485	21	.280	235	.689	220	729	232	128	140	1050	12.8
93-94	LAL	79	2685	453	.506	9	.191	208	.686	282	851	307	92	112	1123	14.2
94-95	LAL	80	2807	485	.507	10	.189	297	.777	261	829	329	109	174	1277	16.0
Totals		441	12917	2126	.509	50	.235	1175	.720	1222	3834	1095	569	702	5477	12.4

SHERMAN DOUGLAS

Team: Boston Celtics
Position: Guard
Height: 6'1" **Weight:** 180
Birthdate: September 15, 1966

NBA Experience: 6 years
College: Syracuse
Acquired: Traded from Heat for Brian Shaw, 1/92

Background: Douglas was the catalyst on a Syracuse team that included Billy Owens and Derrick Coleman. As a senior, he became the NCAA career assists leader and a first-team All-American. Despite being drafted in the second round, he made the NBA All-Rookie Team with Miami in 1989-90. He was traded to Boston during the 1991-92 season and has served primarily as the team's starting point guard.

Strengths: A nifty ball-handler with deceptive moves to the hoop, Douglas is a tremendous penetrator who is at his best in transition. He takes care of the ball and knows where to dish it. He is an above-average scorer from the point-guard slot. He once led the Heat in scoring and has topped 13 PPG each of the last two years.

Weaknesses: Douglas is not a pure shooter from the perimeter and has big trouble from the foul line and 3-point arc. He also does not rate among the best defenders in the NBA. He does not have great quickness and comes up with few steals. He is not as effective in the halfcourt game as he is on the move.

Analysis: Douglas spent the first month of last season on the injured list with a strained knee ligament and did not regain his starting point-guard spot until the end of January. He improved his scoring by more than four points a game over the final three months of the regular season. Without a jump shot, however, his game remains incomplete.

PLAYER SUMMARY

Will ....drive and dish
Can't ....hit jumper regularly
Expect ....13 PPG
Don't Expect........3-point proficiency
Fantasy Value $13-16
Card Value ....7-12¢

COLLEGE STATISTICS

		G	FGP	FTP	APG	PPG
85-86	SYR	27	.613	.727	2.1	5.4
86-87	SYR	38	.531	.744	7.6	17.3
87-88	SYR	35	.519	.693	8.2	16.1
88-89	SYR	38	.546	.632	8.6	18.2
Totals		138	.538	.695	7.0	14.9

NBA REGULAR-SEASON STATISTICS

		G	MIN	FGs		3-PT FGs		FTs		Rebounds					
				FG	PCT	FG	PCT	FT	PCT	OFF	TOT	AST	STL	BLK	PTS	PPG
89-90	MIA	81	2470	463	.494	5	.161	224	.687	70	206	619	145	10	1155	14.3
90-91	MIA	73	2562	532	.504	4	.129	284	.686	78	209	624	121	5	1352	18.5
91-92	MIA/BOS	42	752	117	.462	1	.100	73	.682	13	63	172	25	9	308	7.3
92-93	BOS	79	1932	264	.498	6	.207	84	.560	65	162	508	49	10	618	7.8
93-94	BOS	78	2789	425	.462	13	.232	177	.641	70	193	683	89	11	1040	13.3
94-95	BOS	65	2048	365	.475	20	.244	204	.689	48	170	446	80	2	954	14.7
Totals		418	12553	2166	.485	49	.205	1046	.667	344	1003	3052	509	47	5427	13.0

CLYDE DREXLER

Team: Houston Rockets
Position: Guard
Height: 6'7" **Weight:** 222
Birthdate: June 22, 1962
NBA Experience: 12 years

College: Houston
Acquired: Traded from Trail Blazers with Tracy Murray for Otis Thorpe, draft rights to Marcelo Nicola, and a conditional 1st-round pick, 2/95

Background: Drexler gained notoriety at the University of Houston, where he played in two Final Fours, for his breathtaking dunks. He has maintained that reputation as a pro, playing his first 11-plus years in Portland and taking the Blazers' all-time lead in several categories. Drexler, a veteran of eight All-Star Games, was traded to Houston in February of 1995.

Strengths: "Clyde the Glide" established himself as a superstar with great leaping and scoring ability. He makes things happen and has produced reels of fabulous finishes. Drexler owns 3-point range and hits his free throws, and his post-up moves give small guards fits. He rebounds well and is a nifty passer.

Weaknesses: Drexler has lost some of the quickness that has helped him burn defenders for more than 18,000 career points. Injuries and a declining shooting percentage have hampered him in recent seasons.

Analysis: A rejuvenated Drexler played very well after being traded to Houston. He did not score as much with the Rockets, but his shooting accuracy was better and it looked like a great burden had been lifted from his shoulders. He averaged 20.5 PPG in the playoffs and helped lift the Rockets to another NBA title.

PLAYER SUMMARY	
Will	provide excitement
Can't	regain first step
Expect	veteran leadership
Don't Expect	less than 15 PPG
Fantasy Value	$20-25
Card Value	10-25¢

COLLEGE STATISTICS

		G	FGP	FTP	RPG	PPG
80-81	HOU	30	.505	.588	10.5	11.9
81-82	HOU	32	.569	.608	10.5	15.2
82-83	HOU	34	.536	.737	8.8	15.9
Totals		96	.538	.643	9.9	14.4

NBA REGULAR-SEASON STATISTICS

				FGs		3-PT FGs		FTs		Rebounds						
		G	MIN	FG	PCT	FG	PCT	FT	PCT	OFF	TOT	AST	STL	BLK	PTS	PPG
83-84	POR	82	1408	252	.451	1	.250	123	.728	112	235	153	107	29	628	7.7
84-85	POR	80	2555	573	.494	8	.216	223	.759	217	476	441	177	68	1377	17.2
85-86	POR	75	2576	542	.475	12	.200	293	.769	171	421	600	197	46	1389	18.5
86-87	POR	82	3114	707	.502	11	.234	357	.760	227	518	566	204	71	1782	21.7
87-88	POR	81	3060	849	.506	11	.212	476	.811	261	533	467	203	52	2185	27.0
88-89	POR	78	3064	829	.496	27	.260	438	.799	289	615	450	213	54	2123	27.2
89-90	POR	73	2683	670	.494	30	.283	333	.774	208	507	432	145	51	1703	23.3
90-91	POR	82	2852	645	.482	61	.319	416	.794	212	546	493	144	60	1767	21.5
91-92	POR	76	2751	694	.470	114	.337	401	.794	166	500	512	138	70	1903	25.0
92-93	POR	49	1671	350	.429	31	.233	245	.839	126	309	278	95	37	976	19.9
93-94	POR	68	2334	473	.428	71	.324	286	.777	154	445	333	98	34	1303	19.2
94-95	POR/HOU	76	2728	571	.461	147	.360	364	.824	152	480	362	136	45	1653	21.8
Totals		902	30796	7155	.479	524	.308	3955	.789	2295	5585	5087	1857	617	18789	20.8

KEVIN DUCKWORTH

Team: Washington Bullets
Position: Center
Height: 7'0" **Weight:** 285
Birthdate: April 1, 1964

NBA Experience: 9 years
College: Eastern Illinois
Acquired: Traded from Trail Blazers
for Harvey Grant, 6/93

Background: Duckworth established a career rebounding record at Eastern Illinois, where he posted a .631 field goal percentage as a senior. His pro career started slowly in San Antonio, but he was voted the NBA's Most Improved Player for 1987-88 with Portland and played in the 1989 All-Star Game. He was traded to Washington and has not fared well in two seasons there.

Strengths: Duckworth possesses a soft touch for a man of his size. His low-post game can be potent and polished, featuring hooks and turnaround jumpers. His range is pretty good and he is capable of big scoring nights.

Weaknesses: Weight and foul problems have always followed Duckworth, but his troubles have stretched to all aspects of his game in recent seasons. He's never been a great rebounder, shot-blocker, or defender, and offense also has become a struggle. His shooting percentages from the field and the line are embarrassing, and his big-scoring days are gone.

Analysis: Duckworth has gone from All-Star to liability in just a few years. He did some starting for the Bullets last season but had another dismal year offensively, and he does not do anything to make up for what seems like a permanent shooting slump. His weight and attitude problems have cost him. He was suspended for two weeks last February.

PLAYER SUMMARY	
Will	make hook shots
Can't	keep weight down
Expect	poor shooting
Don't Expect	an All-Star return
Fantasy Value	$0
Card Value	5-8¢

COLLEGE STATISTICS

		G	FGP	FTP	RPG	PPG
82-83	EILL	30	.528	.674	6.0	9.6
83-84	EILL	28	.597	.685	6.8	11.6
84-85	EILL	28	.516	.657	7.5	19.0
85-86	EILL	32	.631	.762	9.1	19.5
Totals		118	.577	.705	7.4	15.0

NBA REGULAR-SEASON STATISTICS

		G	MIN	FGs FG	FGs PCT	3-PT FGs FG	3-PT FGs PCT	FTs FT	FTs PCT	Rebounds OFF	Rebounds TOT	AST	STL	BLK	PTS	PPG
86-87	SA/POR	65	875	130	.476	0	.000	92	.687	76	223	29	21	21	352	5.4
87-88	POR	78	2223	450	.496	0	.000	331	.770	224	576	66	31	32	1231	15.8
88-89	POR	79	2662	554	.477	0	.000	324	.757	246	635	60	56	49	1432	18.1
89-90	POR	82	2462	548	.478	0	.000	231	.740	184	509	91	36	34	1327	16.2
90-91	POR	81	2511	521	.481	0	.000	240	.772	177	531	89	33	34	1282	15.8
91-92	POR	82	2222	362	.461	0	.000	156	.690	151	497	99	38	37	880	10.7
92-93	POR	74	1762	301	.438	0	.000	127	.730	118	387	70	45	39	729	9.9
93-94	WAS	69	1485	184	.417	0	.000	88	.667	103	325	56	37	35	456	6.6
94-95	WAS	40	818	118	.442	2	.200	45	.643	65	195	20	21	24	283	7.1
Totals		650	17020	3168	.469	2	.100	1634	.737	1344	3878	580	318	305	7972	12.3

CHRIS DUDLEY

Team: Portland Trail Blazers
Position: Center
Height: 6'11" **Weight:** 240
Birthdate: February 22, 1965

NBA Experience: 8 years
College: Yale
Acquired: Signed as a free agent, 8/93

Background: A Yale graduate, Dudley was second in the nation in rebounding as a senior. Cleveland drafted him in 1987 but sent him to New Jersey in 1989-90. He turned down a $21 million, seven-year offer from the Nets for an $11 million, seven-year deal in Portland before the 1993-94 season. He played only six games that year after breaking his ankle but returned in 1994-95.

Strengths: Dudley attacks the glass and opposing players with equal abandon. He knows how to use his large frame inside to wall off opponents from the backboards. He has an aggressive, forceful approach to just about everything he does. Dudley is a smart, tough defender who blocks shots and makes his presence felt.

Weaknesses: Dudley has proven that brains have nothing to do with shooting. He is one of the most pathetic free throw shooters in the league. In fact, his offensive game in general, including his field goal shooting and passing, is very weak. He commits a lot of fouls. His best scoring season was a 7.1-PPG effort in 1990-91.

Analysis: Not many pro players are content to pound the daylights out of people and chase every rebound without scoring, but that's how Dudley makes his living. He passed up New Jersey's big offer thinking he could do better after the 1993-94 season, but the broken ankle cost him some money. His defense and rebounding have been valuable to Portland.

PLAYER SUMMARY	
Will	pound the boards
Can't	hit two free throws
Expect	defense, rebounds
Don't Expect	much else
Fantasy Value	$1
Card Value	5-8¢

COLLEGE STATISTICS

		G	FGP	FTP	RPG	PPG
83-84	YALE	26	.464	.467	5.1	4.5
84-85	YALE	26	.446	.533	10.2	12.6
85-86	YALE	26	.539	.482	9.8	16.2
86-87	YALE	24	.569	.542	13.3	17.8
Totals		102	.513	.512	9.5	12.7

NBA REGULAR-SEASON STATISTICS

		G	MIN	FGs FG	FGs PCT	3-PT FGs FG	3-PT FGs PCT	FTs FT	FTs PCT	Rebounds OFF	Rebounds TOT	AST	STL	BLK	PTS	PPG
87-88	CLE	55	513	65	.474	0	.000	40	.563	74	144	23	13	19	170	3.1
88-89	CLE	61	544	73	.435	0	.000	39	.364	72	157	21	9	23	185	3.0
89-90	CLE/hu	64	1356	146	.411	0	.000	58	.319	174	423	39	41	72	350	5.5
90-91	NJ	61	1560	170	.408	0	.000	94	.534	229	511	37	39	153	434	7.1
91-92	NJ	82	1902	190	.403	0	.000	80	.468	343	739	58	38	179	460	5.6
92-93	NJ	71	1398	94	.353	0	.000	57	.518	215	513	16	17	103	245	3.5
93-94	POR	6	86	6	.240	0	.000	2	.500	16	24	5	4	3	14	2.3
94-95	POR	82	2245	181	.406	0	.000	85	.464	325	764	34	43	126	447	5.5
Totals		482	9604	925	.405	0	.000	455	.453	1448	3275	233	204	678	2305	4.8

JOE DUMARS

Team: Detroit Pistons
Position: Guard
Height: 6'3" **Weight:** 195
Birthdate: May 23, 1963

NBA Experience: 10 years
College: McNeese St.
Acquired: 1st-round pick in 1985 draft
(18th overall)

Background: Dumars led the Southland Conference in scoring three times at McNeese State. He got pegged early as a defensive specialist in the NBA but has surpassed 13,000 career points over ten years in Detroit. He was named MVP of the 1989 Finals and has played in five All-Star Games. He also played on Dream Team II.

Strengths: Michael Jordan will vouch for the one-on-one defensive prowess of Joe D. He is a modest, unassuming leader who is also a deadly shooter with great range. Moreover, he can penetrate and pass like a point guard when asked to fill that role. He's one of the premier clutch shooters and class players in the league.

Weaknesses: Dumars has never been a strong rebounder at all, and his field goal percentage has taken a plunge over the last couple of seasons. He has played through nagging injuries in recent years and has lost a step in the quickness department. He relies more on smarts.

Analysis: There are still very few big guards in the league you'd take over Dumars, who last year played in his fifth All-Star Game and opened a youth sports center in Shelby Township, Michigan. He remains a tough defender and big scorer, but his biggest contribution may be his classy leadership on a young Piston team.

PLAYER SUMMARY	
Will	hound his man
Can't	save the Pistons
Expect	leadership, class
Don't Expect	defensive lapses
Fantasy Value	$8-10
Card Value	10-20¢

COLLEGE STATISTICS

		G	FGP	FTP	RPG	PPG
81-82	MSU	29	.444	.719	2.2	18.2
82-83	MSU	29	.435	.711	4.4	19.6
83-84	MSU	31	.471	.824	5.3	26.4
84-85	MSU	27	.495	.852	4.9	25.8
Totals		116	.462	.788	4.2	22.5

NBA REGULAR-SEASON STATISTICS

				FGs		3-PT FGs		FTs		Rebounds						
		G	MIN	FG	PCT	FG	PCT	FT	PCT	OFF	TOT	AST	STL	BLK	PTS	PPG
85-86	DET	82	1957	287	.481	5	.313	190	.798	60	119	390	66	11	769	9.4
86-87	DET	79	2439	369	.493	9	.409	184	.748	50	167	352	83	5	931	11.8
87-88	DET	82	2732	453	.472	4	.211	251	.815	63	200	387	87	15	1161	14.2
88-89	DET	69	2408	456	.505	14	.483	260	.850	57	172	390	63	5	1186	17.2
89-90	DET	75	2578	508	.480	22	.400	297	.900	60	212	368	63	2	1335	17.8
90-91	DET	80	3046	622	.481	14	.311	371	.890	62	187	443	89	7	1629	20.4
91-92	DET	82	3192	587	.448	49	.408	412	.867	82	188	375	71	12	1635	19.9
92-93	DET	77	3094	677	.466	112	.375	343	.864	63	148	308	78	7	1809	23.5
93-94	DET	69	2591	505	.452	124	.387	276	.836	35	151	261	63	4	1410	20.4
94-95	DET	67	2544	417	.430	103	.305	277	.805	47	158	368	72	7	1214	18.1
Totals		762	26581	4881	.469	456	.361	2861	.844	579	1702	3642	735	75	13079	17.2

TONY DUMAS

Team: Dallas Mavericks
Position: Guard
Height: 6'5" **Weight:** 190
Birthdate: August 25, 1972

NBA Experience: 1 year
College: Missouri-Kansas City
Acquired: 1st-round pick in 1994 draft
(19th overall)

Background: Dumas put up huge college numbers at Missouri-Kansas City, leading the Kangaroos in scoring in each of his last three years and setting career records for points and rebounds. As a senior, he was ranked eighth nationally in scoring with 26.0 PPG and he once tallied 44 and 43 on back-to-back nights. Despite poor showings at the postseason camps, he was taken 19th by Dallas in 1994 and averaged 4.6 PPG as a rookie.

Strengths: Dumas is an athlete and a scorer. His leaping ability and quickness are the two attributes that earned him status as an NBA first-rounder. He is adept at getting to the hole and can finish his own plays. He led the nation in free throw attempts as a college senior. Dumas can keep up with anyone on the break. His athletic skills give him defensive potential.

Weaknesses: There is one overwhelming and obvious problem with Dumas—his shooting from the perimeter. His accuracy bottomed out during his senior year and he has not regained his stroke as a pro. He converted at a .384 clip last season and it was the biggest reason for his limited playing time. He struggles from the charity stripe as well. He needs to raise his level of play in virtually all aspects of the game.

Analysis: Dumas was a surprise draftee of the Mavericks, who already have Jim Jackson and Lucious Harris at shooting guard. Dumas earned many of his minutes late in the season after a March injury to Jackson, and he showed some flashes of promise. Overall, however, his struggles as a rookie have some speculating that the jump from the small-school ranks was too big. He has a lot to prove.

PLAYER SUMMARY

Will ....run, jump
Can't ....find his stroke
Expect ....athletic skills
Don't expect ....starts
Fantasy Value $0
Card Value ....10-20¢

COLLEGE STATISTICS

		G	FGP	FTP	RPG	PPG
90-91	MKC	29	.499	.754	4.6	15.9
91-92	MKC	28	.521	.775	4.6	21.5
92-93	MKC	27	.489	.718	5.5	23.8
93-94	MKC	29	.421	.757	5.7	26.0
Totals		113	.477	.753	5.1	21.8

NBA REGULAR-SEASON STATISTICS

			FGs		3-PT FGs		FTs		Rebounds						
	G	MIN	FG	PCT	FG	PCT	FT	PCT	OFF	TOT	AST	STL	BLK	PTS	PPG
94-95 DAL	58	613	96	.384	22	.301	50	.649	32	62	57	13	4	264	4.6
Totals	58	613	96	.384	22	.301	50	.649	32	62	57	13	4	264	4.6

LEDELL EACKLES

Unrestricted Free Agent
Last Team: Miami Heat
Position: Guard
Height: 6'5" **Weight:** 231
Birthdate: November 24, 1966

NBA Experience: 5 years
College: San Jacinto; New Orleans
Acquired: Signed as a free agent, 10/94

Background: Eackles led the American South Conference in scoring with 23.4 PPG as a senior at New Orleans and was named Player of the Year in the league. He was drafted in the second round by Washington and played his first four pro seasons with the Bullets. After a stint on Indiana's suspended list and a brief stay in the CBA, Eackles returned to the NBA with Miami in 1994-95 and averaged 7.3 PPG over 54 games.

Strengths: Eackles is a scorer. He can hit jumpers with 3-point range or bull his way through the lane to score or draw fouls. He has been compared to a fullback for his head-down style of attack. Eackles is underrated for his passing ability. He's averaged double figures in scoring in four of five years.

Weaknesses: Inconsistency has always been a problem for Eackles, even in his best years. His weight has ballooned at times and can be considered partly responsible for his up-and-down play. Eackles is not a strong defensive player, giving away quickness to most of his matchups. He is not much help on the boards and is not at his scoring best these days.

Analysis: Eackles has been an enigmatic player to say the least. He got off to a great start last season, torching Washington with 8-of-9 shooting for 22 points in just 26 minutes last November. However, he missed 12 games due to "coach's decision" and several others with a shoulder injury. He has the makings of a high-scoring reserve.

PLAYER SUMMARY	
Will	drive the lane
Can't	star on defense
Expect	bench scoring
Don't Expect	consistency
Fantasy Value	$0
Card Value	8-12¢

COLLEGE STATISTICS

		G	FGP	FTP	RPG	PPG
84-85	SJ	29	.550	.730	5.4	19.0
85-86	SJ	37	.583	.755	6.4	27.2
86-87	NO	28	.456	.724	4.1	22.6
87-88	NO	31	.508	.802	4.9	23.4
Totals		125	.523	.768	5.3	23.3

NBA REGULAR-SEASON STATISTICS

		G	MIN	FGs FG	FGs PCT	3-PT FGs FG	3-PT FGs PCT	FTs FT	FTs PCT	Rebounds OFF	Rebounds TOT	AST	STL	BLK	PTS	PPG
88-89	WAS	80	1459	318	.434	9	.225	272	.786	100	180	123	41	5	917	11.5
89-90	WAS	78	1696	413	.439	19	.322	210	.750	74	175	182	50	4	1055	13.5
90-91	WAS	67	1616	345	.453	14	.237	164	.739	47	128	136	47	10	868	13.0
91-92	WAS	65	1463	355	.468	7	.200	139	.743	39	178	125	47	7	856	13.2
94-95	MIA	54	898	143	.439	18	.439	91	.722	33	95	72	19	2	395	7.3
Totals		344	7132	1574	.447	67	.286	876	.755	293	756	638	204	28	4091	11.9

BLUE EDWARDS

Team: Vancouver Grizzlies
Position: Forward/Guard
Height: 6'4" **Weight:** 228
Birthdate: October 31, 1965

NBA Experience: 6 years
College: Louisburg; East Carolina
Acquired: Selected from Jazz in 1995 expansion draft

Background: Edwards was a junior college All-American before his two-year career at East Carolina. As a senior, he led the Pirates in seven statistical categories. He spent his first three years with Utah before trades brought him to Milwaukee and then Boston. He was traded back to the Jazz during the 1994-95 season in a deal that sent Jay Humphries to the Celtics.

Strengths: Edwards is a first-rate athlete who presents a rare combination of speed and strength. He's a tremendous leaper, can post up, and is blessed with a nice jumper with 3-point range. He also makes his free throws. Edwards has been a good scorer off the bench for most of his career. He can play big guard and small forward.

Weaknesses: Though he plays mostly in the backcourt, he turns the ball over almost as often as he gets credit for an assist and is not a great ball-handler. Edwards gets beaten off the dribble by guards yet lacks the size to defend forwards well. Both his shooting and scoring declined in each of his stops outside Utah.

Analysis: The Bucks and Celtics wanted Edwards for his athletic ability, but he never had a well-defined role with either team and his output suffered for it. Though he fit in nicely with the Jazz, Edwards will again face uncertainty this season with the expansion Grizzlies. A talented player, Edwards deserves to be treated better.

PLAYER SUMMARY	
Will	post up
Can't	play point guard
Expect	athletic ability
Don't Expect	assists
Fantasy Value	$5-7
Card Value	8-12¢

COLLEGE STATISTICS

		G	FGP	FTP	RPG	PPG
84-85	LOU	29	.636	.645	6.1	17.8
85-86	LOU	31	.700	.658	6.0	22.3
86-87	ECAR	28	.561	.739	5.6	14.4
88-89	ECAR	29	.551	.755	6.9	26.7
Totals		117	.612	.701	6.2	20.4

NBA REGULAR-SEASON STATISTICS

		G	MIN	FGs FG	FGs PCT	3-PT FGs FG	3-PT FGs PCT	FTs FT	FTs PCT	Rebounds OFF	Rebounds TOT	AST	STL	BLK	PTS	PPG
89-90	UTA	82	1889	286	.507	9	.300	146	.719	69	251	145	76	36	727	8.9
90-91	UTA	62	1611	244	.526	6	.250	82	.701	51	201	108	57	29	576	9.3
91-92	UTA	81	2283	433	.522	39	.379	113	.774	86	298	137	81	46	1018	12.6
92-93	MIL	82	2729	554	.512	37	.349	237	.790	123	382	214	129	45	1382	16.9
93-94	MIL	82	2322	382	.477	38	.358	151	.799	104	329	171	83	27	953	11.6
94-95	BOS/UTA	67	1112	181	.461	22	.293	75	.833	50	130	77	43	16	459	6.9
Totals		456	11946	2080	.503	151	.340	804	.769	483	1591	852	469	199	5115	11.2

KEVIN EDWARDS

Team: New Jersey Nets
Position: Guard
Height: 6'3" **Weight:** 210
Birthdate: October 30, 1965

NBA Experience: 7 years
College: Lakewood; DePaul
Acquired: Signed as a free agent, 7/93

Background: Edwards finished his college career with the best shooting percentage (.534) ever by a DePaul guard and became known as a high-flying dunker. He played in nearly every game in his first four years with the Heat, but he rarely saw action after the 1993 All-Star break and New Jersey picked him up. A torn Achilles tendon limited Edwards to 14 games in 1994-95.

Strengths: Edwards has a quick first step to the basket and isn't bashful about putting it up on his drives. He is capable of posting big-time scoring numbers and has 3-point range with his jumper, especially from the shorter arc. He averages double figures in scoring every year. He puts out a good defensive effort and comes up with a lot of steals.

Weaknesses: Inconsistency has been the trademark of Edwards throughout his career. His jump shot is streaky, especially off the dribble, and he has never converted a high percentage as a pro. He's not a reliable playmaker and he's had a history of being turnover-prone.

Analysis: Edwards had one of the better years of his career after the death of Drazen Petrovic made him a starter in 1993-94, but his torn Achilles after just 14 games last season put his emergence on hold for the rest of the season. He works hard at his game, can put the ball in the hole, and is a tough defender. When he's hot, give him the ball.

PLAYER SUMMARY

Will	score in spurts
Can't	avoid cold spells
Expect	10-plus PPG
Don't Expect	high field goal pct.
Fantasy Value	$7-9
Card Value	5-8¢

COLLEGE STATISTICS

		G	FGP	FTP	RPG	PPG
84-85	LAKE	33	.589	.715	5.4	18.6
85-86	LAKE	32	.626	.761	7.5	24.1
86-87	DeP	31	.536	.808	5.0	14.4
87-88	DeP	30	.533	.783	5.3	18.3
Totals		126	.576	.760	5.8	18.9

NBA REGULAR-SEASON STATISTICS

		G	MIN	FGs FG	FGs PCT	3-PT FGs FG	3-PT FGs PCT	FTs FT	FTs PCT	Rebounds OFF	Rebounds TOT	AST	STL	BLK	PTS	PPG
88-89	MIA	79	2349	470	.425	10	.270	144	.746	85	262	349	139	27	1094	13.8
89-90	MIA	78	2211	395	.412	9	.300	139	.760	77	282	252	125	33	938	12.0
90-91	MIA	79	2000	380	.410	24	.286	171	.803	80	205	240	130	46	955	12.1
91-92	MIA	81	1840	325	.454	7	.219	162	.848	56	211	170	99	20	819	10.1
92-93	MIA	40	1134	216	.468	5	.294	119	.844	48	121	120	68	12	556	13.9
93-94	NJ	82	2727	471	.458	35	.354	167	.770	94	281	232	120	34	1144	14.0
94-95	NJ	14	466	69	.448	18	.400	40	.952	10	37	27	19	5	196	14.0
Totals		453	12727	2326	.435	108	.314	942	.798	450	1399	1390	700	177	5702	12.6

CRAIG EHLO

Team: Atlanta Hawks
Position: Guard
Height: 6'7" **Weight:** 205
Birthdate: August 11, 1961

NBA Experience: 12 years
College: Odessa; Washington St.
Acquired: Signed as a free agent, 7/93

Background: As a senior, Ehlo set a Pac-10 record for assists at Washington State. He was a reserve for Houston before a CBA stint. He spent seven years in Cleveland as both a starter and reserve before signing as a free agent with Atlanta before 1993-94. He has given the Hawks leadership off the bench in his two seasons there.

Strengths: Ehlo can do a little of everything. He is a tough defender who throws his body around for the team. He is an underrated scorer and shooter with great range. He has averaged at least nine PPG in each of the last six seasons. He's a first-class leader to boot.

Weaknesses: "A step slow" is the knock on Ehlo. He does not possess the quickness or athletic ability to stick with faster players one-on-one. He does not create much on offense, but rather feeds off teammates. He has been bothered by his back.

Analysis: Ehlo is a fine complementary player on a good team, and he has played with two of those. He'll beat you if you leave him open and he rarely does anything to hurt his own team. He has used a hard-working style to carve out a long and successful career in the NBA.

PLAYER SUMMARY

Will ....shoot with range
Can't...........................race by his man
Expect ....veteran leadership
Don't Expect ....three more years
Fantasy Value $1
Card Value ....5-8¢

COLLEGE STATISTICS

		G	FGP	FTP	RPG	PPG
79-80	ODES	28	.487	.714	5.1	12.6
80-81	ODES	30	.500	.772	6.8	20.7
81-82	WSU	30	.479	.600	2.2	5.1
82-83	WSU	30	.547	.633	3.2	12.0
Totals		118	.505	.701	4.3	12.6

NBA REGULAR-SEASON STATISTICS

		G	MIN	FGs FG	FGs PCT	3-PT FGs FG	3-PT FGs PCT	FTs FT	FTs PCT	Rebounds OFF	Rebounds TOT	AST	STL	BLK	PTS	PPG
83-84	HOU	7	63	11	.407	0	.000	1	1.000	4	9	6	3	0	23	3.3
84-85	HOU	45	189	34	.493	0	.000	19	.633	8	25	26	11	3	87	1.9
85-86	HOU	36	199	36	.429	3	.333	23	.793	17	46	29	11	4	98	2.7
86-87	CLE	44	890	99	.414	5	.172	70	.707	55	161	92	40	30	273	6.2
87-88	CLE	79	1709	226	.466	22	.344	89	.674	86	274	206	82	30	563	7.1
88-89	CLE	82	1867	249	.475	39	.390	71	.607	100	295	266	110	19	608	7.4
89-90	CLE	81	2894	436	.464	104	.419	126	.681	147	439	371	126	23	1102	13.6
90-91	CLE	82	2766	344	.445	49	.329	95	.679	142	388	376	121	34	832	10.1
91-92	CLE	63	2016	310	.453	69	.413	87	.707	94	307	238	78	22	776	12.3
92-93	CLE	82	2559	385	.490	93	.381	86	.717	113	403	254	104	22	949	11.6
93-94	ATL	82	2147	316	.446	77	.348	112	.727	71	279	273	136	26	821	10.0
94-95	ATL	49	1166	191	.453	51	.381	44	.620	55	147	113	46	6	477	9.7
Totals		732	18465	2637	.459	512	.374	823	.685	892	2773	2250	868	219	6609	9.0

MARIO ELIE

Team: Houston Rockets
Position: Guard/Forward
Height: 6'5" **Weight:** 210
Birthdate: November 26, 1963

NBA Experience: 5 years
College: American International
Acquired: Traded from Trail Blazers
for a 1995 2nd-round pick, 8/93

Background: A world traveler, Elie played in Portugal, Argentina, Ireland, and Miami (of the USBL) after his college career at American International. He speaks four languages. He was drafted by Milwaukee in 1985 but released before the season. Elie played in the CBA during 1989-90 and saw his first NBA action in 1990-91 with Philadelphia (three games). He has since played key roles with Golden State, Portland, and Houston.

Strengths: Elie is one of the top defensive stalwarts in the league. He holds his own against big scorers on a nightly basis. He can play just about any position except center. Offensively, Elie shoots his unorthodox jump shot with 3-point range and finishes the break. He can get to the hole off the dribble, is a good passer, and is rock-solid from the free throw line.

Weaknesses: Elie is not a dominant athlete, nor is he overpowering on the offensive end. He launches an unorthodox jumper that, until last season, produced inconsistent results. He lacks quickness and does nothing that would be noticed by a casual fan. Speedy assignments cause him the most trouble on defense.

Analysis: The well-travelled Elie is a rare player who works tirelessly to keep playing in the NBA, and he has been rewarded with two championship rings with the Rockets. He does enough offensively to keep defenses honest and is one of the team's premier defenders. Elie, a former seventh-rounder, is no longer underappreciated.

PLAYER SUMMARY

Will ....hound his man
Can't ....get used to one town
Expect ....a reserve sparkplug
Don't Expect ....10 PPG
Fantasy Value $1-3
Card Value ....5-8¢

COLLEGE STATISTICS

		G	FGP	FTP	RPG	PPG
81-82	AI	25	.586	.742	8.3	15.4
82-83	AI	31	.527	.739	7.7	15.9
83-84	AI	31	.565	.794	8.6	18.9
84-85	AI	33	.549	.777	9.0	20.1
Totals		120	.555	.767	8.4	17.7

NBA REGULAR-SEASON STATISTICS

		G	MIN	FGs		3-PT FGs		FTs		Rebounds		AST	STL	BLK	PTS	PPG
				FG	PCT	FG	PCT	FT	PCT	OFF	TOT					
90-91	PHI/GS	33	644	79	.497	4	.400	75	.843	46	110	45	19	10	237	7.2
91-92	GS	79	1677	221	.521	23	.329	155	.852	69	227	174	68	15	620	7.8
92-93	POR	82	1757	240	.458	45	.349	183	.855	59	216	177	74	20	708	8.6
93-94	HOU	67	1606	208	.446	56	.335	154	.860	28	181	208	50	8	626	9.3
94-95	HOU	81	1896	243	.499	80	.398	144	.842	50	196	189	65	12	710	8.8
Totals		342	7580	991	.481	208	.360	711	.851	252	930	793	276	65	2901	8.5

SEAN ELLIOTT

Team: San Antonio Spurs
Position: Forward
Height: 6'8" **Weight:** 220
Birthdate: February 2, 1968
NBA Experience: 6 years

College: Arizona
Acquired: Traded from Pistons for draft rights to Bill Curley and a 1997 2nd-round pick, 7/94

Background: Elliott was college basketball's 1989 Player of the Year at Arizona, where he broke Lew Alcindor's Pac-10 record with 2,555 career points. He enjoyed four fine years in San Antonio before a trade (involving Dennis Rodman) sent him to Detroit and a substandard 1993-94 season. He was traded back to the Spurs in July 1994 and was second on the team in scoring last season at 18.1 PPG.

Strengths: Elliott has a diverse offensive arsenal. He can shoot from the perimeter, drive to the hoop, handle the ball, and make crisp passes. Despite his lack of bulk, he has quick hands and feet to stay in front of his man on defense. His versatility allows him to play big guard in addition to small forward. He drills both 3-pointers and free throws.

Weaknesses: Elliott does not thrive in the halfcourt game like he does in the open court, which accounts in part for his poor showing with Detroit. Also, stronger players can wear him down on defense. He is not a great rebounding forward. A 1993-94 trade from Detroit to Houston was nixed because of a kidney condition. It is not thought to be serious.

Analysis: A return to San Antonio was just what the doctor ordered. Elliott enjoyed the best scoring year of his career in 1994-95, hitting well over 40 percent from the shorter 3-point arc. This versatile swingman loves to run and has regained the look of a potential All-Star.

PLAYER SUMMARY	
Will	thrive in transition
Can't	outrebound Rodman
Expect	great versatility
Don't Expect	less than 15 PPG
Fantasy Value	$17-20
Card Value	12-20¢

COLLEGE STATISTICS

		G	FGP	FTP	RPG	PPG
85-86	ARIZ	32	.486	.749	5.3	15.6
86-87	ARIZ	30	.510	.770	6.0	19.3
87-88	ARIZ	38	.570	.793	5.8	19.6
88-89	ARIZ	33	.480	.841	7.2	22.3
Totals		133	.512	.793	6.1	19.2

NBA REGULAR-SEASON STATISTICS

				FGs		3-PT FGs		FTs		Rebounds						
		G	MIN	FG	PCT	FG	PCT	FT	PCT	OFF	TOT	AST	STL	BLK	PTS	PPG
89-90	SA	81	2032	311	.481	1	.111	187	.866	127	297	154	45	14	810	10.0
90-91	SA	82	3044	478	.490	20	.313	325	.808	142	456	238	69	33	1301	15.9
91-92	SA	82	3120	514	.494	25	.305	285	.861	143	439	214	84	29	1338	16.3
92-93	SA	70	2604	451	.491	37	.356	268	.795	85	322	265	68	28	1207	17.2
93-94	DET	73	2409	360	.455	26	.299	139	.803	68	263	197	54	27	885	12.1
94-95	SA	81	2858	502	.468	136	.408	326	.807	63	287	206	78	38	1466	18.1
Totals		469	16067	2616	.481	245	.361	1530	.821	628	2064	1274	398	169	7007	14.9

DALE ELLIS

Team: Denver Nuggets
Position: Guard/Forward
Height: 6'7" **Weight:** 215
Birthdate: August 6, 1960

NBA Experience: 12 years
College: Tennessee
Acquired: Signed as a free agent, 10/94

Background: Ellis was an All-American at Tennessee, where he averaged 22.6 PPG his senior year. He was a faceless reserve with Dallas for three years, but an infamous trade for Al Wood brought him to Seattle and stardom. Ellis signed with Denver for his 12th NBA season and scored in double figures for the ninth straight time.

Strengths: Ellis still has a picture-book jumper, and over the years it has been one of the deadliest in the league. He is particularly effective coming off screens, and he made 100-plus 3-pointers last year for the sixth time in his career. Once one of the game's greatest offensive weapons, he can still fill it up.

Weaknesses: Ellis is not a great defensive player, rebounder, or ball-handler. He creates virtually none of his offense himself, instead working off screens or spotting up for open looks. He has not been a vocal leader.

Analysis: Ellis will someday be remembered as one of the best long-range shooters in history. He holds the NBA career record for 3-pointers with 1,119, and he figures to add a few more to his total before he hangs up his holster. He doesn't consider the new 3-point arc a long-range shot.

PLAYER SUMMARY

Will ....hit from deep
Can't.........................create his shots
Expect ....instant offense
Don't Expect ....defense
Fantasy Value $1
Card Value ....7-10¢

COLLEGE STATISTICS

		G	FGP	FTP	RPG	PPG
79-80	TENN	27	.445	.775	3.6	7.1
80-81	TENN	29	.597	.748	6.4	17.7
81-82	TENN	30	.654	.796	6.3	21.2
82-83	TENN	21	.601	.751	10.0	22.6
Totals		107	.595	.765	6.3	19.3

NBA REGULAR-SEASON STATISTICS

				FGs		3-PT FGs		FTs		Rebounds						
		G	MIN	FG	PCT	FG	PCT	FT	PCT	OFF	TOT	AST	STL	BLK	PTS	PPG
83-84	DAL	67	1059	225	.456	12	.414	87	.719	106	250	56	41	9	549	8.2
84-85	DAL	72	1314	274	.454	42	.385	77	.740	100	238	56	46	7	667	9.3
85-86	DAL	72	1086	193	.411	63	.364	59	.720	86	168	37	40	9	508	7.1
86-87	SEA	82	3073	785	.516	86	.358	385	.787	187	447	238	104	32	2041	24.9
87-88	SEA	75	2790	764	.503	107	.413	303	.767	167	340	197	74	11	1938	25.8
88-89	SEA	82	3190	857	.501	162	.478	377	.816	156	342	164	108	22	2253	27.5
89-90	SEA	55	2033	502	.497	96	.375	193	.818	90	238	110	59	7	1293	23.5
90-91	SEA/MIL	51	1424	340	.474	57	.363	120	.723	66	173	95	49	8	857	16.8
91-92	MIL	81	2191	485	.469	138	.419	164	.774	92	253	104	57	18	1272	15.7
92-93	SA	82	2731	545	.499	119	.401	157	.797	81	312	107	78	18	1366	16.7
93-94	SA	77	2590	478	.494	131	.395	83	.776	70	255	80	66	11	1170	15.2
94-95	DEN	81	1996	351	.453	106	.403	110	.866	56	222	57	37	9	918	11.3
Totals		877	25477	5799	.487	1119	.402	2115	.784	1257	3238	1301	759	161	14832	16.9

HAROLD ELLIS

Team: Los Angeles Clippers   **NBA Experience:** 2 years
Position: Guard   **College:** Morehouse
Height: 6'5" **Weight:** 200   **Acquired:** Signed as a free agent,
Birthdate: October 7, 1970   1/94

Background: Ellis was named conference Player of the Year during his last three seasons at Morehouse College in Atlanta, and he was the Division II Player of the Year as a senior. He was a big scorer in the CBA before landing with the Clippers during the 1993-94 season. They signed him to another contract last season and Ellis saw action in 69 games, making seven starts. His offensive numbers, however, took a nosedive.

Strengths: There was never a doubt about the athletic ability of Ellis, who at 6'5" can play above the bucket. He is a scorer who runs the floor like the wind and finishes with high-flying jams. Moreover, he has earned his reputation as a scrappy defensive player. He has a wide wingspan and is capable of disrupting big guards and small forwards. He excels in transition.

Weaknesses: Ellis is still considered a 'tweener. He is not a good enough perimeter shooter and ball-handler to thrive at guard yet is too small to be a productive forward at the NBA level. The biggest chunk of his points comes in transition and on putbacks. He is a poor free throw shooter, has limited range, and commits turnovers more frequently than he gets assists. He's ineffective in a halfcourt game.

Analysis: Ellis surprised Clipper fans and followers of the NBA two years ago with his loud debut, scoring 20-plus points in two of his first three games and picking up a $3,500 fine for throwing an elbow. He brings tons of energy to the floor and uses it best on defense. Most of his games, however, are now spent more quietly on the bench because opponents have learned that Ellis struggles at a slower pace.

PLAYER SUMMARY	
Will	run the floor
Can't	thrive at a slow pace
Expect	high-energy defense
Don't Expect	sweet shooting
Fantasy Value	$0
Card Value	5-8¢

COLLEGE STATISTICS

		G	FGP	FTP	RPG	PPG
88-89	MORE	29	.630	.607	8.5	23.0
89-90	MORE	33	.543	.696	7.9	23.6
90-91	MORE	32	.531	.610	7.2	24.0
91-92	MORE	26	.560	.581	8.7	25.6
Totals		120	.562	.627	8.0	24.0

NBA REGULAR-SEASON STATISTICS

		G	MIN	FGs FG	FGs PCT	3-PT FGs FG	3-PT FGs PCT	FTs FT	FTs PCT	Rebounds OFF	Rebounds TOT	AST	STL	BLK	PTS	PPG
93-94	LAC	49	923	159	.545	0	.000	106	.711	94	153	31	73	2	424	8.7
94-95	LAC	69	656	91	.481	1	.077	69	.590	56	88	40	67	12	252	3.7
Totals		118	1579	250	.520	1	.059	175	.658	150	241	71	140	14	676	5.7

LaPHONSO ELLIS

Team: Denver Nuggets
Position: Forward
Height: 6'8" **Weight:** 240
Birthdate: May 5, 1970

NBA Experience: 3 years
College: Notre Dame
Acquired: 1st-round pick in 1992 draft (5th overall)

Background: Ellis finished his college career as one of only four Notre Dame players to score 1,000 points and grab 1,000 rebounds. He became the all-time Irish leader in blocked shots despite missing parts of two seasons due to academics. He was drafted fifth overall by Denver in 1992 and was a first-team All-Rookie selection. He sat out nearly all of last season because of a knee injury.

Strengths: Ellis and center Dikembe Mutombo form one of the best shot-blocking tandems in the league, combining for 398 blocks in 1992-93. Ellis has great natural instincts and is an outstanding athlete who plays above the rim. He also gives the Nuggets another big-time rebounder and produces on the offensive end. He possesses a nice shooting touch both facing the basket and in the post.

Weaknesses: Ellis is not a good free throw shooter, dating back to his college days. It's hard to understand, considering his touch. On defense, he tends to rely too much on the blocked shot as a weapon instead of muscling his man away from the hoop. He is not really a power player. He is expected to bounce back from the injury, though a bad knee is always of concern.

Analysis: Ellis was a solid performer for the Nuggets at both ends of the floor during his first two years in the league. His shot-blocking, rebounding, and scoring looked to have him on the path to stardom before he injured his knee in the 1994 preseason. This will be a telling season for Ellis, who has all the tools to be a future fixture at power forward.

PLAYER SUMMARY	
Will	rebound, block shots
Can't	shoot free throws
Expect	15 PPG
Don't Expect	physical style
Fantasy Value	$9-11
Card Value	10-20¢

COLLEGE STATISTICS

		G	FGP	FTP	RPG	PPG
88-89	ND	27	.563	.684	9.4	13.5
89-90	ND	22	.511	.675	12.6	14.0
90-91	ND	15	.573	.716	10.5	16.4
91-92	ND	33	.631	.655	11.7	17.7
Totals		97	.577	.675	11.1	15.5

NBA REGULAR-SEASON STATISTICS

				FGs		3-PT FGs		FTs		Rebounds						
		G	MIN	FG	PCT	FG	PCT	FT	PCT	OFF	TOT	AST	STL	BLK	PTS	PPG
92-93	DEN	82	2749	483	.504	2	.154	237	.748	274	744	151	72	111	1205	14.7
93-94	DEN	79	2699	483	.502	7	.304	242	.674	220	682	167	63	80	1215	15.4
94-95	DEN	6	58	9	.360	0	.000	6	1.000	7	17	4	1	5	24	4.0
Totals		167	5506	975	.501	9	.250	485	.711	501	1443	322	136	196	2444	14.6

PERVIS ELLISON

Team: Boston Celtics
Position: Forward/Center
Height: 6'10" **Weight:** 225
Birthdate: April 3, 1967

NBA Experience: 6 years
College: Louisville
Acquired: Signed as a free agent, 7/94

Background: As a freshman, Ellison was the MVP of the 1986 NCAA Tournament after lifting Louisville to the title. He recorded 2,000 points and 1,000 rebounds in college and closed his career among the Division I all-time leaders in blocked shots. The top pick in the 1989 draft, he spent four of his first five years in Washington and won the Most Improved Player Award in 1991-92. He signed with Boston before the 1994-95 season.

Strengths: Ellison has long arms and decent defensive skills. He can be an effective shot-blocker and rebounder. He possesses some nifty moves around the basket and is good with both hands. He has been a productive scorer in past years in addition to his efforts on the other end of the court.

Weaknesses: Injuries played a key role in Ellison's slow NBA start and continue to hinder him. His knees have been especially troublesome, and he spent the first part of last season in street clothes. Ellison has lost some quickness, and he has never been much of a power player. The results are evident in almost every aspect of his game, from scoring to rebounding to defense.

Analysis: Ellison has made a living on the injured list during his career, and it has clearly hampered his progress. It is not likely that his knees will allow him to have another year like he did in 1991-92, although the Celtics would even settle for some productive play off the bench. Judging from last season, they may be disappointed.

PLAYER SUMMARY

Will	use both hands
Can't	trade in his knees
Expect	reserve minutes
Don't Expect	82 games
Fantasy Value	$3-5
Card Value	8-12¢

COLLEGE STATISTICS

		G	FGP	FTP	RPG	PPG
85-86	LOU	39	.554	.682	8.2	13.1
86-87	LOU	31	.533	.719	8.7	15.2
87-88	LOU	35	.601	.692	8.3	17.6
88-89	LOU	31	.615	.652	8.7	17.6
Totals		136	.577	.687	8.4	15.8

NBA REGULAR-SEASON STATISTICS

			FGs		3-PT FGs		FTs		Rebounds						
		G	MIN	FG	PCT	FG	PCT	FT	PCT	OFF	TOT	AST	STL	BLK	PTS	PPG
89-90	SAC	34	866	111	.442	0	.000	49	.628	64	196	65	16	57	271	8.0
90-91	WAS	76	1942	326	.513	0	.000	139	.650	224	585	102	49	157	791	10.4
91-92	WAS	66	2511	547	.539	1	.333	227	.728	217	740	190	62	177	1322	20.0
92-93	WAS	49	1701	341	.521	0	.000	170	.702	138	433	117	45	108	852	17.4
93-94	WAS	47	1178	137	.469	0	.000	70	.722	77	242	70	25	50	344	7.3
94-95	BOS	55	1083	152	.507	0	.000	71	.717	124	309	34	22	54	375	6.8
Totals		327	9281	1614	.513	1	.050	726	.697	844	2505	578	219	603	3955	12.1

PATRICK EWING

Team: New York Knicks
Position: Center
Height: 7'0" **Weight:** 240
Birthdate: August 5, 1962

NBA Experience: 10 years
College: Georgetown
Acquired: 1st-round pick in 1985 draft
(1st overall)

Background: Ewing led Georgetown to three NCAA finals, including the championship in 1984, and was the consensus Player of the Year as a senior while setting records across the board. He won Olympic gold in 1984 and 1992. Ewing earned NBA Rookie of the Year honors in 1986 with the Knicks and has been a perennial All-Star. He has been at the top of his game in recent years.

Strengths: A franchise player, Ewing is the complete package in the pivot. He intimidates on defense, swats shots, hoards boards, and is virtually unstoppable one-on-one when he gets the ball in the post. He has a dangerous jump shot that no one can challenge, and he gets his points despite double- and triple-teams.

Weaknesses: There is very little Ewing can't do outside of shooting a lot of 3-pointers or trying his hand at guard. He commits a lot of turnovers, but that goes with the territory. He has played in the Finals but has yet to win a championship ring.

Analysis: Ewing has been considered one of the premier centers in the league for several years and has earned serious MVP consideration along the way. He is New York's all-time scoring leader, ahead of the great Walt Frazier, and is annually among NBA leaders in scoring, rebounding, and shot-blocking.

PLAYER SUMMARY

Will ....dominate games
Can't ....be stopped by one
Expect........points, rebounds, blocks
Don't Expect ....single-digit nights
Fantasy Value $55-60
Card Value ....25-50¢

COLLEGE STATISTICS

		G	FGP	FTP	RPG	PPG
81-82	GEOR	37	.631	.617	7.5	12.7
82-83	GEOR	32	.570	.629	10.2	17.7
83-84	GEOR	37	.658	.656	10.0	16.4
84-85	GEOR	37	.625	.637	9.2	14.6
Totals		143	.620	.635	9.2	15.3

NBA REGULAR-SEASON STATISTICS

				FGs		3-PT FGs		FTs		Rebounds						
		G	MIN	FG	PCT	FG	PCT	FT	PCT	OFF	TOT	AST	STL	BLK	PTS	PPG
85-86	NY	50	1771	386	.474	0	.000	226	.739	124	451	102	54	103	998	20.0
86-87	NY	63	2206	530	.503	0	.000	296	.713	157	555	104	89	147	1356	21.5
87-88	NY	82	2546	656	.555	0	.000	341	.716	245	676	125	104	245	1653	20.2
88-89	NY	80	2896	727	.567	0	.000	361	.746	213	740	188	117	281	1815	22.7
89-90	NY	82	3165	922	.551	1	.250	502	.775	235	893	182	78	327	2347	28.6
90-91	NY	81	3104	845	.514	0	.000	464	.745	194	905	244	80	258	2154	26.6
91-92	NY	82	3150	796	.522	1	.167	377	.738	228	921	156	88	245	1970	24.0
92-93	NY	81	3003	779	.503	1	.143	400	.719	191	980	151	74	161	1959	24.2
93-94	NY	79	2972	745	.496	4	.286	445	.765	219	885	179	90	217	1939	24.5
94-95	NY	79	2920	730	.503	6	.286	420	.750	157	867	212	68	159	1886	23.9
Totals		759	27733	7116	.520	13	.165	3832	.742	1963	7873	1643	842	2143	18077	23.8

DUANE FERRELL

Team: Indiana Pacers
Position: Forward
Height: 6'7" **Weight:** 215
Birthdate: February 28, 1965

NBA Experience: 7 years
College: Georgia Tech
Acquired: Signed as a free agent, 9/94

Background: Ferrell pumped in more than 1,800 points in his four years at Georgia Tech but was not drafted by an NBA team. He signed with Atlanta as a free agent, was cut after one season, and then re-signed with the Hawks four months later. He averaged double figures in scoring in his fourth and fifth years. Indiana signed him before the 1994-95 season and he played about 11 minutes per game.

Strengths: Ferrell appreciates his job and shows it with all-out effort. He accepts his role. He shoots the jumper well enough from 20 feet and in that defenders have to respect it. His defense is solid if unspectacular. He will not take many ill-advised shots and he runs the floor well.

Weaknesses: Ferrell was pegged as an inconsistent player in his final year with the Hawks, and he wore much the same label in Indiana. He does not create much off the dribble, either for himself or teammates, and he's prone to cold spells. He's not a good ball-handler or passer, he's not much help on the boards, and his athletic skills are marginal at best.

Analysis: It looks as though Ferrell has played his best seasons already. His minutes have shrunk over the last two years because his effectiveness has continued to slip. He does not do enough on either end of the floor to warrant 20-plus minutes, although he works hard enough to stick around.

PLAYER SUMMARY	
Will	bust his tail
Can't	create offense
Expect	reserve minutes
Don't Expect	great quickness
Fantasy Value	$0
Card Value	5-8¢

COLLEGE STATISTICS

		G	FGP	FTP	RPG	PPG
84-85	GT	32	.504	.571	4.1	9.1
85-86	GT	34	.595	.758	4.9	12.1
86-87	GT	29	.519	.812	5.9	17.9
87-88	GT	32	.532	.749	6.6	18.6
Totals		127	.537	.733	5.4	14.3

NBA REGULAR-SEASON STATISTICS

		G	MIN	FGs FG	FGs PCT	3-PT FGs FG	3-PT FGs PCT	FTs FT	FTs PCT	Rebounds OFF	Rebounds TOT	AST	STL	BLK	PTS	PPG
88-89	ATL	41	231	35	.422	0	.000	30	.682	19	41	10	7	6	100	2.4
89-90	ATL	14	29	5	.357	0	.000	2	.333	3	7	2	1	0	12	0.9
90-91	ATL	78	1165	174	.489	2	.667	125	.801	97	179	55	33	27	475	6.1
91-92	ATL	66	1598	331	.524	11	.333	166	.761	105	210	92	49	17	839	12.7
92-93	ATL	82	1736	327	.470	9	.250	176	.779	97	191	132	59	17	839	10.2
93-94	ATL	72	1155	184	.485	1	.111	144	.783	62	129	65	44	16	513	7.1
94-95	IND	56	607	83	.480	1	.167	64	.753	50	88	31	26	6	231	4.1
Totals		409	6521	1139	.488	24	.273	707	.769	433	845	387	219	89	3009	7.4

DANNY FERRY

Team: Cleveland Cavaliers
Position: Forward
Height: 6'10" **Weight:** 235
Birthdate: October 17, 1966
NBA Experience: 5 years

College: Duke
Acquired: Draft rights traded from Clippers with Reggie Williams for Ron Harper, 1990 and 1992 1st-round picks, and a 1991 2nd-round pick, 11/89

Background: After an illustrious career at Duke, in which he was named the nation's Player of the Year as a senior, Ferry snubbed the NBA and spent a year in Italy to avoid playing with the Clippers. When his rights were traded to Cleveland for Ron Harper, he came home and was a big disappointment. He has come off the bench for five years with the Cavaliers and his best scoring output has been 8.6 PPG.

Strengths: Ferry is at his best on the perimeter despite his 6'10" size. He knows where to spot up and will hit from 3-point land when given an open look. The son of former NBA player Bob Ferry has shown decent court sense. He is a precise passer and you won't find many who shoot free throws more accurately.

Weaknesses: Ferry is slow and can't work for his own shot. He feeds off others instead of making things happen himself. His biggest problem is that he is not much help on defense, where almost everyone he tries to guard can blow by him. He does not rebound well and is not capable of blocking a lot of shots.

Analysis: Ferry is a 3-point threat off the bench and a guy you want in to preserve a fourth-quarter lead because of his touch from the free throw line. However, the former college Player of the Year is far from being the kind of multi-talented player he was expected to be. He's a defensive liability with limited offensive skills.

PLAYER SUMMARY

Will	hit free throws
Can't	play defense
Expect	limited minutes
Don't Expect	10 PPG
Fantasy Value	$0
Card Value	5-8¢

COLLEGE STATISTICS

		G	FGP	FTP	RPG	PPG
85-86	DUKE	40	.460	.628	5.5	5.9
86-87	DUKE	33	.449	.844	7.8	14.0
87-88	DUKE	35	.476	.828	7.6	19.1
88-89	DUKE	35	.522	.756	7.4	22.6
Totals		143	.484	.775	7.0	15.1

NBA REGULAR-SEASON STATISTICS

		G	MIN	FGs FG	FGs PCT	3-PT FGs FG	3-PT FGs PCT	FTs FT	FTs PCT	Rebounds OFF	Rebounds TOT	AST	STL	BLK	PTS	PPG
90-91	CLE	81	1661	275	.428	23	.299	124	.816	99	286	142	43	25	697	8.6
91-92	CLE	68	937	134	.409	17	.354	61	.836	53	213	75	22	15	346	5.1
92-93	CLE	76	1461	220	.479	34	.415	99	.876	81	279	137	29	49	573	7.5
93-94	CLE	70	965	149	.446	14	.275	38	.884	47	141	74	28	22	350	5.0
94-95	CLE	82	1290	223	.446	94	.403	74	.881	30	143	96	27	22	614	7.5
Totals		377	6314	1001	.442	182	.371	396	.852	310	1062	524	149	133	2580	6.8

VERN FLEMING

Unrestricted Free Agent
Last Team: Indiana Pacers
Position: Guard
Height: 6'5" **Weight:** 185
Birthdate: February 4, 1962

NBA Experience: 11 years
College: Georgia
Acquired: 1st-round pick in 1984 draft
(18th overall)

Background: Fleming teamed with Dominique Wilkins at Georgia and, as a senior, led the SEC in scoring. He played on the 1984 Olympic team and was credited by Michael Jordan as providing his toughest defense in practices. He has played all 11 of his NBA years with the Pacers, scoring in double figures in each of the first seven.

Strengths: Fleming is a savvy player who can play either shooting or point guard. He has a height advantage over most playmakers. Fleming is the Pacers' all-time assists leader. He plays defense, rebounds, and makes few mistakes.

Weaknesses: Fleming has never had the great creativity of many point guards, possessing more of a scoring mentality. The last couple of years have seen age and nagging injuries begin to catch up with him. He is no longer an explosive scorer with drives to the hoop and he has never been a great outside shooter.

Analysis: Fleming's value is now his leadership and work ethic. He can still provide quality minutes off the bench without making many mistakes. His most productive days, however, are behind him. His last two years have been his worst statistically, and the numbers are not going to get much better.

PLAYER SUMMARY	
Will	play defense
Can't	shoot the 3
Expect	veteran leadership
Don't Expect	starts
Fantasy Value	$0
Card Value	5-8¢

COLLEGE STATISTICS

		G	FGP	FTP	RPG	PPG
80-81	GEOR	30	.480	.697	2.7	10.0
81-82	GEOR	31	.496	.640	3.9	9.9
82-83	GEOR	34	.535	.716	4.6	16.9
83-84	GEOR	30	.503	.754	4.0	19.8
Totals		125	.508	.705	3.8	14.2

NBA REGULAR-SEASON STATISTICS

		G	MIN	FGs FG	FGs PCT	3-PT FGs FG	3-PT FGs PCT	FTs FT	FTs PCT	Rebounds OFF	Rebounds TOT	AST	STL	BLK	PTS	PPG
84-85	IND	80	2486	433	.470	0	.000	260	.767	148	323	247	99	8	1126	14.1
85-86	IND	80	2870	436	.506	1	.167	263	.745	102	386	505	131	5	1136	14.2
86-87	IND	82	2549	370	.509	2	.200	238	.788	109	334	473	109	18	980	12.0
87-88	IND	80	2733	442	.523	0	.000	227	.802	106	364	568	115	11	1111	13.9
88-89	IND	76	2552	419	.515	3	.130	243	.799	85	310	494	77	12	1084	14.3
89-90	IND	82	2876	467	.508	12	.353	230	.782	118	322	610	92	10	1176	14.3
90-91	IND	69	1929	356	.531	4	.222	161	.729	83	214	369	76	13	877	12.7
91-92	IND	82	1737	294	.482	6	.222	132	.737	69	209	266	56	7	726	8.9
92-93	IND	75	1503	280	.505	7	.194	143	.726	63	169	224	63	9	710	9.5
93-94	IND	55	1053	147	.462	0	.000	64	.736	27	123	173	40	6	358	6.5
94-95	IND	55	686	93	.495	0	.000	65	.722	20	88	109	27	1	251	4.6
Totals		816	22974	3737	.503	35	.192	2026	.765	930	2842	4038	885	100	9535	11.7

GREG FOSTER

Unrestricted Free Agent
Last Team: Minnesota Timberwolves
Position: Forward/Center
Height: 6'11" **Weight:** 240
Birthdate: October 3, 1968

NBA Experience: 5 years
College: UCLA; Texas-El Paso
Acquired: Signed as a free agent, 12/94

Background: Foster led the University of Texas-El Paso to two consecutive NCAA Tournament appearances and was named MVP of the Western Athletic Conference Tournament as a senior. A 1990 second-rounder, he won a job with the Bullets and has since played with Atlanta, Milwaukee, Chicago, and Minnesota over five seasons. He was signed by the Timberwolves in December 1994 and averaged 4.9 PPG last season.

Strengths: Foster stands 6'11" and 240 pounds, and that might be his biggest plus. He has a soft touch and good range for a big man, which helps him pull opposing frontcourt players away from the basket. He canned seven 3-pointers last season. Foster is capable of being a contributor on the boards.

Weaknesses: The hope was that Foster, who was drafted as a project, would develop into a banger at the NBA level. No one is holding his breath. Foster is soft—plain and simple. He's slow, he does not have low-post scoring moves, and he is not a force on the boards or on defense. Foster seems content to shoot jumpers instead of asserting himself in the middle. He's inconsistent.

Analysis: Foster has simply not panned out. The Bulls gave him a shot last season, but they released him after 17 games and Foster wound up laboring for about 14 minutes per game on a dismal Minnesota team. He risks being pushed out of the league unless he decides to apply himself more physically in the paint. His size remains his most attractive feature.

PLAYER SUMMARY	
Will	shoot jumpers
Can't	patrol the paint
Expect	reserve minutes
Don't Expect	assertiveness
Fantasy Value	$0
Card Value	5-8¢

COLLEGE STATISTICS

		G	FGP	FTP	RPG	PPG
86-87	UCLA	31	.500	.500	2.5	3.3
87-88	UCLA	11	.527	.432	5.5	8.5
88-89	UTEP	26	.483	.651	7.3	11.1
89-90	UTEP	32	.465	.811	6.2	10.6
Totals		100	.483	.661	5.2	8.2

NBA REGULAR-SEASON STATISTICS

				FGs		3-PT FGs		FTs		Rebounds						
		G	MIN	FG	PCT	FG	PCT	FT	PCT	OFF	TOT	AST	STL	BLK	PTS	PPG
90-91	WAS	54	606	97	.460	0	.000	42	.689	52	151	37	12	22	236	4.4
91-92	WAS	49	548	89	.461	0	.000	35	.714	43	145	35	6	12	213	4.3
92-93	WAS/ATL	43	298	55	.458	0	.000	15	.714	32	83	21	3	14	125	2.9
93-94	MIL	3	19	4	.571	0	.000	2	1.000	0	3	0	0	1	10	3.3
94-95	CHI/MIN	78	1144	150	.472	7	.304	78	.703	85	259	39	15	28	385	4.9
Totals		227	2615	395	.465	7	.212	172	.705	212	641	132	36	77	969	4.3

RICK FOX

Team: Boston Celtics
Position: Guard/Forward
Height: 6'7" **Weight:** 231
Birthdate: July 24, 1969

NBA Experience: 4 years
College: North Carolina
Acquired: 1st-round pick in 1991 draft
(24th overall)

Background: Born in Canada, Fox moved to the Bahamas when he was two years old. He had a very limited basketball background before playing high school ball in Warsaw, Indiana. Though he was never a marquee player at North Carolina, he was drafted late in the first round by the Celtics in 1991. He has spent most of his four pro seasons as a reserve. He averaged 8.8 PPG in 1994-95 after a career-high 10.8 the year before.

Strengths: Fox is a hard-working player who owns a strong body and is not afraid to challenge. He's a solid defender who is not afraid to mix it up with larger men. He can play both small forward and big guard. He has 3-point range and has improved his perimeter game in general. He also drives to the hoop in transition and from the wing.

Weaknesses: Fox has been an inconsistent shooter during his career. Opponents are best advised to cut off his drive to the bucket and force him to shoot. Fox does not have great ball-handling skills and is thus better suited to forward than guard. He should be a better rebounder than he is, considering his size and athletic ability.

Analysis: Many expected Fox to have a breakthrough season in 1994-95 after posting career highs in most categories and cracking the starting lineup in his third season. Instead, he lost his starting job and saw his scoring average drop by a couple of points. Fox is a hard worker, a good defender, and a versatile athlete. With a little better decision-making and consistency, he'd earn more minutes.

PLAYER SUMMARY

Will ....play defense
Can't ....live on perimeter
Expect ....drives from the wing
Don't Expect.................pure shooting
Fantasy Value $5-7
Card Value ....8-12¢

COLLEGE STATISTICS

		G	FGP	FTP	RPG	PPG
87-88	NC	34	.628	.500	1.9	4.0
88-89	NC	37	.583	.790	3.8	11.5
89-90	NC	34	.522	.735	4.6	16.2
90-91	NC	35	.453	.804	6.6	16.9
Totals		140	.518	.757	4.2	12.2

NBA REGULAR-SEASON STATISTICS

				FGs		3-PT FGs		FTs		Rebounds						
		G	MIN	FG	PCT	FG	PCT	FT	PCT	OFF	TOT	AST	STL	BLK	PTS	PPG
91-92	BOS	81	1535	241	.459	23	.329	139	.755	73	220	126	78	30	644	8.0
92-93	BOS	71	1082	184	.484	4	.174	81	.802	55	159	113	61	21	453	6.4
93-94	BOS	82	2096	340	.467	33	.330	174	.757	105	355	217	81	52	887	10.8
94-95	BOS	53	1039	169	.481	31	.413	95	.772	61	155	139	52	19	464	8.8
Totals		287	5752	934	.471	91	.340	489	.766	294	889	595	272	122	2448	8.5

KEVIN GAMBLE

Team: Miami Heat
Position: Guard/Forward
Height: 6'5" **Weight:** 225
Birthdate: November 13, 1965

NBA Experience: 8 years
College: Lincoln; Iowa
Acquired: Signed as a free agent, 10/94

Background: After an unspectacular college career at Lincoln College and Iowa, Gamble was drafted by Portland in the third round. He wound up playing in the CBA and the Philippines. He was given one last NBA chance in 1988-89 with a rebuilding Celtics team and made the most of it over six years. He signed with Miami before the 1994-95 season and spent the year in a reserve role.

Strengths: Gamble is a reliable outside shooter who connected at better than 50 percent from the field in four of his six Celtic years. He is a 3-point threat and solid free throw shooter who also gets out on the break and finishes with either hand. He is a scrappy, hungry ballplayer who can play small forward or shooting guard.

Weaknesses: Gamble has never been a strong defender or rebounder. He has spent most of his career at small forward, where quicker players get past him and bigger ones post him up. Gamble does not possess the great lateral quickness needed to thwart the slashers. He has struggled offensively over the last two seasons.

Analysis: Gamble was once Boston's best offensive player, but the trade to Miami thrust him into a backup role behind players like Billy Owens and Glen Rice. Actually, he could become a super sixth man if he could find the stroke that helped him shoot .587 and average 15.6 PPG in 1990-91.

PLAYER SUMMARY

Will ....shoot with range
Can't ....star on defense
Expect ....instant offense
Don't Expect.......................rebounds
Fantasy Value $1
Card Value ....5-8¢

COLLEGE STATISTICS

		G	FGP	FTP	RPG	PPG
83-84	LINC	30	.559	.777	9.2	21.3
84-85	LINC	31	.579	.817	9.7	20.5
85-86	IOWA	30	.474	.700	1.7	2.6
86-87	IOWA	35	.544	.697	4.5	11.9
Totals		126	.558	.768	6.2	14.1

NBA REGULAR-SEASON STATISTICS

				FGs		3-PT FGs		FTs		Rebounds						
		G	MIN	FG	PCT	FG	PCT	FT	PCT	OFF	TOT	AST	STL	BLK	PTS	PPG
87-88	POR	9	19	0	.000	0	.000	0	.000	2	3	1	2	0	0	0.0
88-89	BOS	44	375	75	.551	2	.182	35	.636	11	42	34	14	3	187	4.3
89-90	BOS	71	990	137	.455	3	.167	85	.794	42	112	119	28	8	362	5.1
90-91	BOS	82	2706	548	.587	0	.000	185	.815	85	267	256	100	34	1281	15.6
91-92	BOS	82	2496	480	.529	9	.290	139	.885	80	286	219	75	37	1108	13.5
92-93	BOS	82	2541	459	.507	52	.374	123	.826	46	246	226	86	37	1093	13.3
93-94	BOS	75	1880	368	.458	25	.243	103	.817	41	159	149	57	22	864	11.5
94-95	MIA	77	1223	220	.489	39	.398	87	.784	29	122	119	52	10	566	7.4
Totals		522	12230	2287	.515	130	.319	757	.812	336	1237	1123	414	151	5461	10.5

WINSTON GARLAND

Unrestricted Free Agent
Last Team: Minnesota Timberwolves
Position: Guard
Height: 6'2" **Weight:** 180
Birthdate: December 19, 1964

NBA Experience: 7 years
College: Southeastern;
S.W. Missouri St.
Acquired: Signed as a free agent,
11/94

Background: Garland guided Southwest Missouri State to its first NCAA Tournament as a senior in 1987 and was named Player of the Year in the Association of Mid-Continent Universities. He led Golden State in assists and steals in his first two NBA seasons. He also played with the Clippers, Nuggets, and Rockets before spending the 1993-94 season in Italy. He signed with Minnesota in 1994-95 and started most of the season.

Strengths: Garland has earned a reputation as a good passer and tough defender. He is nearing 2,500 assists for his career and has shown the ability to run almost any offense. He hustles at both ends of the court and always seems to be in the right spot on defense. He works hard for his playing time.

Weaknesses: There is a reason Garland has been on the move during his career. He possesses neither the blinding speed nor the great creative ability the league's top starting point guards have. His jump shot is far from reliable, thus he has never converted a high percentage. His back has given him trouble.

Analysis: Garland went to training camp with Phoenix last season and was cut. The Timberwolves signed him ten days later, when Micheal Williams went on the injured list because of a bum heel. Little did Minnesota know it was hiring its starting point guard for most of the season. Garland filled in admirably, but he is by no means a fixture.

PLAYER SUMMARY	
Will	hustle on defense
Can't	find permanent home
Expect	ball-handling, passing
Don't Expect	a playmaking whiz
Fantasy Value	$0
Card Value	7-10¢

COLLEGE STATISTICS

		G	FGP	FTP	RPG	PPG
83-84	SOUT	34	.518	.836	4.4	17.0
84-85	SOUT	30	.516	.853	3.6	18.2
85-86	SMS	32	.461	.771	3.6	16.5
86-87	SMS	34	.503	.752	2.5	21.2
Totals		130	.499	.802	3.5	18.3

NBA REGULAR-SEASON STATISTICS

		G	MIN	FGs FG	FGs PCT	3-PT FGs FG	3-PT FGs PCT	FTs FT	FTs PCT	Rebounds OFF	Rebounds TOT	AST	STL	BLK	PTS	PPG
87-88	GS	67	2122	340	.439	13	.333	138	.879	68	227	429	116	7	831	12.4
88-89	GS	79	2661	466	.434	10	.233	203	.809	101	328	505	175	14	1145	14.5
89-90	GS/LAC	79	1762	230	.401	12	.333	102	.836	51	214	303	78	10	574	7.3
90-91	LAC	69	1702	221	.426	4	.154	118	.752	46	198	317	97	10	564	8.2
91-92	DEN	78	2209	333	.444	9	.321	171	.859	67	190	411	98	22	846	10.8
92-93	HOU	66	1004	152	.443	6	.462	81	.910	32	108	138	39	4	391	5.9
94-95	MIN	73	1931	170	.415	19	.253	89	.795	48	168	318	71	13	448	6.1
Totals		511	13391	1912	.430	73	.281	902	.830	413	1433	2421	674	80	4799	9.4

CHRIS GATLING

Team: Golden State Warriors
Position: Forward/Center
Height: 6'10" **Weight:** 230
Birthdate: September 3, 1967

NBA Experience: 4 years
College: Old Dominion
Acquired: 1st-round pick in 1991 draft (16th overall)

Background: Gatling did not play during his first two years in college, once under Prop 48 restrictions and once because of a transfer from Pittsburgh to Old Dominion. He was a two-time Sun Belt Conference Player of the Year, however, scoring over 20 PPG all three seasons. He has been a key reserve and spot starter in four years with Golden State, and he led the NBA in field goal percentage (.633) in 1994-95.

Strengths: Gatling is an athletic, emotional player. He's an explosive leaper who blocks shots and gets to the offensive and defensive glass. He possesses very good agility and runs the floor like a guard. He is quick to the basket with a soft touch, a nice jump hook, and good hands. Gatling shoots a phenomenal percentage from the field and averaged a career-high 13.7 PPG last season.

Weaknesses: Gatling, a post player in college, is not at his best while facing the basket. He does not dominate physically but rather with his leaping ability and long arms. Despite a lofty percentage from the floor, Gatling is no shooter. His range is limited and he is not the man you want at the free throw line. He's a poor passer and ball-handler.

Analysis: Nicknamed "The Energizer" by broadcaster Steve Albert for the spark he gives the Warriors off the bench, Gatling is an exciting player. Most of his shots are dunks, short hooks, and putbacks. He will not try to play above his head. He also likes to rebound and block shots and considers those his primary duties. The coaching of Bob Lanier helped Gatling immensely.

PLAYER SUMMARY

Will	play with emotion
Can't	make free throws
Expect	high shooting pct.
Don't Expect	3-point range
Fantasy Value	$9-11
Card Value	5-8¢

COLLEGE STATISTICS

		G	FGP	FTP	RPG	PPG
88-89	OD	27	.616	.704	9.0	22.4
89-90	OD	26	.580	.670	10.0	20.5
90-91	OD	32	.620	.692	11.1	21.0
Totals		85	.606	.689	10.1	21.3

NBA REGULAR-SEASON STATISTICS

		G	MIN	FGs FG	FGs PCT	3-PT FGs FG	3-PT FGs PCT	FTs FT	FTs PCT	Rebounds OFF	Rebounds TOT	AST	STL	BLK	PTS	PPG
91-92	GS	54	612	117	.568	0	.000	72	.661	75	182	16	31	36	306	5.7
92-93	GS	70	1248	249	.539	0	.000	150	.725	129	320	40	44	53	648	9.3
93-94	GS	82	1296	271	.588	0	.000	129	.620	143	397	41	40	63	671	8.2
94-95	GS	58	1470	324	.633	0	.000	148	.592	144	443	51	39	52	796	13.7
Totals		264	4626	961	.586	0	.000	499	.645	491	1342	148	154	204	2421	9.2

KENNY GATTISON

Team: Vancouver Grizzlies
Position: Forward/Center
Height: 6'8" **Weight:** 256
Birthdate: May 23, 1964

NBA Experience: 8 years
College: Old Dominion
Acquired: Selected from Hornets in 1995 expansion draft

Background: The Sun Belt Player of the Year in 1986, Gattison finished his career as the league's all-time leading rebounder. He ranked third nationally in field goal percentage as a senior at Old Dominion. He played with Phoenix for a year before tearing the anterior cruciate ligament in his left knee. He then played in Italy and toiled with Charlotte for six seasons. A back injury hobbled him in 1994-95, and he was selected by Vancouver in the expansion draft.

Strengths: Gattison is super-intense, the kind of player who will do whatever is asked, no matter the consequences. He sets screens, blocks out, and bangs the boards. He is versatile, having played both center and power forward, and hardly ever takes a bad shot. He goes hard on defense.

Weaknesses: Gattison has virtually no touch from beyond 12 feet, as his poor free throw shooting indicates. His reckless, physical style of play often puts him in foul trouble. He is just too small to guard centers effectively despite all the time he has spent trying to do so. Dribbling is not his forte.

Analysis: Gattison, who consistently shoots over 50 percent from the field, fits in well as a reserve role-player. You can count on him for rebounding, scoring in the paint, and physical play off the bench. His 1994-95 season was expected to be over because of a spinal injury after six games, but he battled his way back by March.

PLAYER SUMMARY	
Will	play two positions
Can't	handle the ball
Expect	inside scoring, defense
Don't Expect	bad shots
Fantasy Value	$0
Card Value	5-8¢

COLLEGE STATISTICS

		G	FGP	FTP	RPG	PPG
82-83	OD	29	.503	.705	7.5	8.4
83-84	OD	31	.494	.650	7.1	11.1
84-85	OD	31	.538	.610	9.2	16.1
85-86	OD	31	.637	.673	7.8	17.4
Totals		122	.552	.650	7.9	13.3

NBA REGULAR-SEASON STATISTICS

				FGs		3-PT FGs		FTs		Rebounds						
		G	MIN	FG	PCT	FG	PCT	FT	PCT	OFF	TOT	AST	STL	BLK	PTS	PPG
86-87	PHO	77	1104	148	.476	0	.000	108	.632	87	270	36	24	33	404	5.2
88-89	PHO	2	9	0	.000	0	.000	1	.500	0	1	0	0	0	1	0.5
89-90	CHA	63	941	148	.550	1	1.000	75	.682	75	197	39	35	31	372	5.9
90-91	CHA	72	1552	243	.532	0	.000	164	.661	136	379	44	48	67	650	9.0
91-92	CHA	82	2223	423	.529	0	.000	196	.688	177	580	131	59	69	1042	12.7
92-93	CHA	75	1475	203	.529	0	.000	102	.604	108	353	68	48	55	508	6.8
93-94	CHA	77	1644	233	.524	0	.000	126	.646	105	358	95	59	46	592	7.7
94-95	CHA	21	409	47	.470	0	.000	31	.608	21	75	17	7	15	125	6.0
Totals		469	9357	1445	.522	1	.083	803	.652	709	2213	430	280	316	3694	7.9

MATT GEIGER

Team: Miami Heat
Position: Center
Height: 7'0" **Weight:** 245
Birthdate: September 10, 1969

NBA Experience: 3 years
College: Auburn; Georgia Tech
Acquired: 2nd-round pick in 1992 draft (42nd overall)

Background: Geiger made the SEC All-Freshman team and started all 28 games as a sophomore at Auburn. He transferred to Georgia Tech, where his 65 blocked shots as a senior ranked second in school history. Once considered a lottery-type talent, Geiger slipped to 42nd in the 1992 draft. He broke into the starting lineup in his third year with the Miami Heat, posting career highs in virtually every category in 1994-95.

Strengths: Geiger is one of the quicker and more mobile seven-footers in the league. He gets up and down the court like a smaller man and can defend on the perimeter. He gets out on the break and has the ability to put it on the floor when called to do so. Geiger is willing to bang at both ends and he has become a much better low-post scorer and rebounder.

Weaknesses: Geiger has the size and ability to be a much better shot-blocker than he is, but he winds up earning a lot of reaching fouls instead. Truth is, he is still more effective in a length-of-the-floor game than in a slower affair. Geiger's face-up jumper needs work. He also shoots a poor percentage from the charity stripe.

Analysis: Geiger, considered a project coming into the league, spent a lot of time in the weight room before the 1994-95 season and it paid off. His aggressive play, along with a few Miami injuries, helped him pick up a spot in the starting lineup and he contributed with hard defense and rebounding. His high field goal percentage is a bonus.

PLAYER SUMMARY

Will	............................finish the break
Can't	......................shoot with range
Expect	........................aggressive play
Don't Expect	...........................stardom
Fantasy Value	...............................$2-4
Card Value	.....................................5-8¢

COLLEGE STATISTICS

		G	FGP	FTP	RPG	PPG
87-88	AUB	30	.513	.660	4.1	6.4
88-89	AUB	28	.504	.688	6.6	15.9
90-91	GT	27	.549	.671	6.4	11.4
91-92	GT	35	.611	.706	7.3	11.8
Totals		120	.545	.687	6.1	11.4

NBA REGULAR-SEASON STATISTICS

		G	MIN	FGs FG	FGs PCT	3-PT FGs FG	3-PT FGs PCT	FTs FT	FTs PCT	Rebounds OFF	Rebounds TOT	AST	STL	BLK	PTS	PPG
92-93	MIA	48	554	76	.524	0	.000	62	.674	46	120	14	15	18	214	4.5
93-94	MIA	72	1199	202	.574	1	.200	116	.779	119	303	32	36	29	521	7.2
94-95	MIA	74	1712	260	.536	4	.400	93	.650	146	413	55	41	51	617	8.3
Totals		194	3465	538	.548	5	.263	271	.706	311	836	101	92	98	1352	7.0

KENDALL GILL

Team: Charlotte Hornets
Position: Guard
Height: 6'5" **Weight:** 200
Birthdate: May 25, 1968
NBA Experience: 5 years

College: Illinois
Acquired: Traded from SuperSonics for Hersey Hawkins and David Wingate, 6/95

Background: Gill helped Illinois to the Final Four as a junior and the following year was named a first-team All-Big Ten selection and a UPI first-team All-American. Gill played his first three years in Charlotte and led the Hornets in scoring at 20.5 PPG during his second season. He averaged about 14 PPG in two years with Seattle, then was traded back to Charlotte this past summer.

Strengths: Gill is a great leaper who plays bigger than his 6'5" height. He is a fine open-court player who finishes with slams and can play the point when needed there. Gill is not afraid to take clutch jumpers and he can shoot them with 3-point range. He hits the boards and his quick hands help him come up with steals.

Weaknesses: Gill complains about his playing time, a problem that reached the boiling point late last season when he took a leave to deal with depression. He has never acted truly happy in either Charlotte or Seattle. Gill does play better when he sees a lot of minutes; otherwise, his game has lacked consistency. Gill has placed a premium on his individual performance.

Analysis: Gill improved his streaky shooting last season and, at times, seemed to be on the verge of big things. However, the man who griped his way out of Charlotte was not pleased with his playing time with the Sonics, either. The Hornets are taking a gamble, hoping Gill is a changed man. He has the skills to be a standout.

PLAYER SUMMARY	
Will	score in transition
Can't	accept bench time
Expect	steals, rebounds
Don't Expect	a team captain
Fantasy Value	$12-15
Card Value	8-15¢

COLLEGE STATISTICS

		G	FGP	FTP	RPG	PPG
86-87	ILL	31	.482	.642	1.4	3.7
87-88	ILL	33	.471	.753	2.2	10.4
88-89	ILL	24	.542	.793	2.9	15.4
89-90	ILL	29	.500	.777	4.9	20.0
Totals		117	.501	.755	2.8	12.0

NBA REGULAR-SEASON STATISTICS

		G	MIN	FGs FG	FGs PCT	3-PT FGs FG	3-PT FGs PCT	FTs FT	FTs PCT	Rebounds OFF	Rebounds TOT	AST	STL	BLK	PTS	PPG
90-91	CHA	82	1944	376	.450	2	.143	152	.835	105	263	303	104	39	906	11.0
91-92	CHA	79	2906	666	.467	6	.240	284	.745	165	402	329	154	46	1622	20.5
92-93	CHA	69	2430	463	.449	17	.274	224	.772	120	340	268	98	36	1167	16.9
93-94	SEA	79	2435	429	.443	38	.317	215	.782	91	268	275	151	32	1111	14.1
94-95	SEA	73	2125	392	.457	63	.368	155	.742	99	290	192	117	28	1002	13.7
Totals		382	11840	2326	.454	126	.321	1030	.770	580	1563	1367	624	181	5808	15.2

ARMON GILLIAM

Team: New Jersey Nets
Position: Forward/Center
Height: 6'9" **Weight:** 250
Birthdate: May 28, 1964

NBA Experience: 8 years
College: Independence; UNLV
Acquired: Signed as a free agent, 8/93

Background: As a college senior, Gilliam was a consensus second-team All-American while leading UNLV to the Final Four and averaging 23.2 points and 9.3 rebounds per game. Phoenix took him second in the 1987 draft and he was an All-Rookie choice. The eight-year veteran has since played in Charlotte, Philadelphia, and New Jersey. Gilliam averaged 14.8 PPG for the Nets last season.

Strengths: A versatile player, Gilliam can play both center and power forward. Nicknamed "The Hammer" for his physical style, he can be unstoppable when he gets the ball in the low post, where he beats opponents with accurate hook shots and turnaround jumpers. He uses both hands well.

Weaknesses: Gilliam is a scorer first and everything else second. Despite his size and strength, he is not a good defender. The knock has always been lack of interest in that phase of the game. He's a poor ball-handler and no better as a passer. He has never made a 3-pointer in his NBA career.

Analysis: Gilliam has been a valuable reserve for the Nets over the past two years, perhaps one of the better sixth men around. He gets his points without taking many bad shots and has done a nice job on the boards as well. He comes to play, provides leadership, and is respected league-wide for his ability to score against the big fellas.

PLAYER SUMMARY

Will ....score inside
Can't.................................dish the ball
Expect...............punch off the bench
Don't Expect......................a 3-pointer
Fantasy Value $8-10
Card Value ....7-10¢

COLLEGE STATISTICS

		G	FGP	FTP	RPG	PPG
82-83	IND	38	.621	.632	8.3	16.9
84-85	UNLV	31	.621	.653	6.8	11.9
85-86	UNLV	37	.529	.737	8.5	15.7
86-87	UNLV	39	.600	.728	9.3	23.2
Totals		145	.590	.693	8.3	17.2

NBA REGULAR-SEASON STATISTICS

				FGs		3-PT FGs		FTs		Rebounds						
		G	MIN	FG	PCT	FG	PCT	FT	PCT	OFF	TOT	AST	STL	BLK	PTS	PPG
87-88	PHO	55	1807	342	.475	0	.000	131	.679	134	434	72	58	29	815	14.8
88-89	PHO	74	2120	468	.503	0	.000	240	.743	165	541	52	54	27	1176	15.9
89-90	PHO/CHA	76	2426	484	.515	0	.000	303	.723	211	599	99	69	51	1271	16.7
90-91	CHA/PHI	75	2644	487	.487	0	.000	268	.815	220	598	105	69	53	1242	16.6
91-92	PHI	81	2771	512	.511	0	.000	343	.807	234	660	118	51	85	1367	16.9
92-93	PHI	80	1742	359	.464	0	.000	274	.843	136	472	116	37	54	992	12.4
93-94	NJ	82	1969	348	.510	0	.000	274	.759	197	500	69	38	61	970	11.8
94-95	NJ	82	2472	455	.502	0	.000	302	.770	192	613	99	67	89	1212	14.8
Totals		605	17951	3455	.497	0	.000	2135	.772	1489	4417	730	443	449	9045	15.0

GREG GRAHAM

Team: Philadelphia 76ers
Position: Guard
Height: 6'4" **Weight:** 174
Birthdate: November 26, 1970
NBA Experience: 2 years

College: Indiana
Acquired: Draft rights traded from Hornets with Dana Barros and Sidney Green for Hersey Hawkins, 9/93

Background: A high-profile recruit for Bob Knight, Graham took a couple years to become a dependable player. He helped Indiana to the Final Four as a junior and hit an amazing 51 percent from 3-point land (57 of 111) as a senior. He was drafted 17th by Charlotte, then dealt to Philadelphia before his rookie season. He averaged 4.8 PPG as a rookie and 5.0 PPG in just 50 outings last season.

Strengths: Graham, a former Big Ten Defensive Player of the Year, is tough to shake as a one-on-one defensive player. He has very good quickness. Graham also has a good stroke, though he has not converted a high percentage of his shots as a pro. He can get his own shot off the dribble, is effective in transition, and owns a quick first step to the hoop.

Weaknesses: Graham is undersized for the NBA and it hurts him in several areas. He gets out-muscled defensively and must work twice as hard at the offensive end to overcome tougher opponents. He's especially small for the off-guard post, yet he lacks the distributing, ball-handling, and leadership skills to play the point. As mentioned, Graham has not brought his accurate perimeter shot to the pro ranks. He's not a scorer.

Analysis: The 76ers obtained Graham in the deal that sent Hersey Hawkins to Charlotte before the 1993-94 season. Graham has not worked out as they had hoped. While he has demonstrated some defensive skills and there is still hope for his jump shot, he has done nothing consistently enough to emerge as a productive part of an NBA rotation. Some extra reps in the weight room might help him keep from being pushed around.

PLAYER SUMMARY

Will ....run the floor
Can't ....out-muscle his man
Expect ....defensive quickness
Don't Expect ....consistency
Fantasy Value $0
Card Value ....8-12¢

COLLEGE STATISTICS

		G	FGP	FTP	RPG	PPG
89-90	IND	29	.471	.778	2.6	9.7
90-91	IND	34	.510	.694	2.6	8.7
91-92	IND	34	.502	.741	4.0	12.8
92-93	IND	35	.551	.825	3.2	16.5
Totals		132	.514	.766	3.1	12.0

NBA REGULAR-SEASON STATISTICS

				FGs		3-PT FGs		FTs		Rebounds					
		G	MIN	FG	PCT	FG	PCT	FT	PCT	OFF	TOT	AST	STL	BLK	PTS	PPG
93-94	PHI	70	889	122	.400	2	.080	92	.836	21	86	66	61	4	338	4.8
94-95	PHI	50	775	95	.426	6	.214	55	.753	19	62	66	29	6	251	5.0
Totals		120	1664	217	.411	8	.151	147	.803	40	148	132	90	10	589	4.9

BRIAN GRANT

Team: Sacramento Kings
Position: Forward
Height: 6'9" **Weight:** 254
Birthdate: March 5, 1972

NBA Experience: 1 year
College: Xavier (Ohio)
Acquired: 1st-round pick in 1994 draft (8th overall)

Background: Despite coming out of high school with little fanfare, Grant made an early impact at Xavier. He finished second in the nation in field goal accuracy as a junior (.654), led the Musketeers in rebounding all four years, and was a two-time Midwestern Collegiate Conference Player of the Year. Drafted eighth overall by Sacramento, Grant finished the 1994-95 season ranked among rookie leaders in several categories.

Strengths: Grant was drafted for his tenacious defense and rebounding, and he did not disappoint. He led the Kings in blocked shots and was second to Olden Polynice in rebounding during his first season. He jumps well, has good hands, and is relentless in his approach. Grant proved to be a much better scorer than most expected. He runs the floor, finishes the break, and does not launch many shots out of his range.

Weaknesses: Grant does not thrive on the perimeter. His jumper is not as consistent as it will probably be after a few years of NBA seasoning, and he shoots a low percentage from the foul line. He becomes a lot less effective from beyond 16 feet. Grant will also need to expand his low-post repertoire in the coming years. He does not offer much in the passing and ball-handling departments, but that's not his job.

Analysis: One of the top all-around rookie performers in the league, Grant has a bright future. He wound up starting for most of the season in the Kings' frontcourt and was a highly productive player on several counts. Most impressive were his .511 shooting percentage and 1.5 blocks per game, and he also provided points and rebounds. His coaches love the effort he brings to work every day.

PLAYER SUMMARY	
Will	swat shots
Can't	live on perimeter
Expect	tenacious effort
Don't Expect	much bench time
Fantasy Value	$18-21
Card Value	20-40¢

COLLEGE STATISTICS

		G	FGP	FTP	RPG	PPG
90-91	XAV	32	.572	.694	8.5	11.6
91-92	XAV	26	.576	.583	9.1	11.8
92-93	XAV	30	.654	.692	9.4	18.5
93-94	XAV	29	.559	.713	9.9	16.7
Totals		117	.594	.676	9.2	14.7

NBA REGULAR-SEASON STATISTICS

		G	MIN	FGs		3-PT FGs		FTs		Rebounds		AST	STL	BLK	PTS	PPG
				FG	PCT	FG	PCT	FT	PCT	OFF	TOT					
94-95	SAC	80	2289	413	.511	1	.250	231	.636	207	598	99	49	116	1058	13.2
Totals		80	2289	413	.511	1	.250	231	.636	207	598	99	49	116	1058	13.2

GARY GRANT

Unrestricted Free Agent
Last Team: Los Angeles Clippers
Position: Guard
Height: 6'3" **Weight:** 185
Birthdate: April 21, 1965

NBA Experience: 7 years
College: Michigan
Acquired: Draft rights traded from SuperSonics with a 1989 1st-round pick for Michael Cage, 6/88

Background: A consensus All-American at Michigan, Grant concluded his career as the school's all-time leader in assists and earned Big Ten Defensive Player of the Year honors as a junior. He led all NBA rookies in steals and assists but has had an up-and-down seven-year career with the Clippers. Injuries limited Grant to 33 games during the 1994-95 season.

Strengths: Grant is known as a solid on-the-ball defender with good quickness and instincts. He has been a stopper for most of his career despite ankle surgery in 1990 and knee surgery in 1991. He has good size, handles the ball well, works hard, and has been an especially effective player in transition.

Weaknesses: Grant's decision-making on the offensive end has long been questioned. He does not penetrate consistently, he rarely gets to the line, and he is not a good enough shooter to justify staying on the perimeter. His field goal accuracy has been substandard. Injuries have become a primary concern.

Analysis: Grant has never achieved what many people thought he would as a pro. He has not enjoyed a double-figure scoring season since his second year and his shooting has been sporadic. A strained back kept him out of the lineup for more than a month late last season, adding to an already frustrating list of injuries. Grant has some work to do in 1995-96.

PLAYER SUMMARY	
Will	play defense
Can't	shake injuries
Expect	reserve playmaking
Don't Expect	10 PPG
Fantasy Value	$0
Card Value	8-12¢

COLLEGE STATISTICS

		G	FGP	FTP	APG	PPG
84-85	MICH	30	.550	.817	4.7	12.9
85-86	MICH	33	.494	.744	5.6	12.2
86-87	MICH	32	.537	.782	5.4	22.4
87-88	MICH	34	.530	.808	6.9	21.1
Totals		129	.528	.790	5.7	17.2

NBA REGULAR-SEASON STATISTICS

		G	MIN	FGs FG	FGs PCT	3-PT FGs FG	3-PT FGs PCT	FTs FT	FTs PCT	Rebounds OFF	Rebounds TOT	AST	STL	BLK	PTS	PPG
88-89	LAC	71	1924	361	.435	5	.227	119	.735	80	238	506	144	9	846	11.9
89-90	LAC	44	1529	241	.466	5	.238	88	.779	59	195	442	108	5	575	13.1
90-91	LAC	68	2105	265	.451	9	.231	51	.689	69	209	587	103	12	590	8.7
91-92	LAC	78	2049	275	.462	15	.294	44	.815	34	184	538	138	14	609	7.8
92-93	LAC	74	1624	210	.441	11	.262	55	.743	27	139	353	106	9	486	6.6
93-94	LAC	78	1533	253	.449	17	.274	65	.855	42	142	291	119	12	588	7.5
94-95	LAC	33	470	78	.470	4	.250	45	.818	8	35	93	29	3	205	6.2
Totals		446	11234	1683	.451	66	.261	467	.768	319	1142	2810	747	64	3899	8.7

HARVEY GRANT

Team: Portland Trail Blazers
Position: Forward
Height: 6'9" **Weight:** 235
Birthdate: July 4, 1965
NBA Experience: 7 years

College: Clemson; Independence; Oklahoma
Acquired: Traded from Bullets for Kevin Duckworth, 6/93

Background: Harvey is the identical twin brother of the Magic's Horace Grant. The two enrolled together at Clemson, but they were competing for the same spot and Harvey transferred to Oklahoma. He led O.U. to the NCAA title game in 1988. Grant averaged 18-plus PPG in his final three years in Washington. Since a trade to Portland two years ago, his numbers and playing time have slipped.

Strengths: Grant is known as a good face-up shooter from 18 feet and in. He possesses good athletic ability, runs the floor, and is very unselfish. He uses his lean, wiry body to the best of his ability on defense. Grant has good lateral quickness and a nice set of hands. He takes to coaching.

Weaknesses: Harvey is not as muscular as Horace and not as effective in the paint. His jump shot has been inconsistent since he joined the Blazers. He has been accused of playing soft and staying away from the boards. He is not as aggressive as he needs to be on offense and his skills with the ball are below average.

Analysis: Grant was a standout with the Bullets, but on a more talented Portland team he has found himself limited to a reserve role. He has not displayed the offensive punch the Blazers expected when they traded Kevin Duckworth for him, although they surely got the better end of that deal. Grant needs to get more assertive.

PLAYER SUMMARY	
Will	run the floor
Can't	handle the ball
Expect	16-foot jumpers
Don't Expect	Horace's muscle
Fantasy Value	$2-4
Card Value	7-10¢

COLLEGE STATISTICS

		G	FGP	FTP	RPG	PPG
84-85	CLEM	28	.496	.585	4.5	5.1
85-86	IND	33	.586	.707	11.8	22.4
86-87	OKLA	34	.534	.730	9.9	16.9
87-88	OKLA	39	.547	.729	9.4	20.9
Totals		134	.553	.712	9.1	17.0

NBA REGULAR-SEASON STATISTICS

				FGs		3-PT FGs		FTs		Rebounds						
		G	MIN	FG	PCT	FG	PCT	FT	PCT	OFF	TOT	AST	STL	BLK	PTS	PPG
88-89	WAS	71	1193	181	.464	0	.000	34	.596	75	163	79	35	29	396	5.6
89-90	WAS	81	1846	284	.473	0	.000	96	.701	138	342	131	52	43	664	8.2
90-91	WAS	77	2842	609	.498	2	.133	185	.743	179	557	204	91	61	1405	18.2
91-92	WAS	64	2388	489	.478	1	.125	176	.800	157	432	170	74	27	1155	18.0
92-93	WAS	72	2667	560	.487	1	.100	218	.727	133	412	205	72	44	1339	18.6
93-94	POR	77	2112	356	.460	2	.286	84	.641	109	351	107	70	49	798	10.4
94-95	POR	75	1771	286	.461	8	.308	103	.705	103	284	82	56	53	683	9.1
Totals		517	14819	2765	.478	14	.187	896	.723	894	2541	978	450	306	6440	12.5

HORACE GRANT

Team: Orlando Magic
Position: Forward
Height: 6'10" **Weight:** 235
Birthdate: July 4, 1965

NBA Experience: 8 years
College: Clemson
Acquired: Signed as a free agent, 7/94

Background: In his senior season at Clemson, Grant was the ACC Player of the Year after averaging 21.0 PPG. Grant, drafted tenth overall in 1987, played a key role on Chicago's three straight NBA championship teams, annually ranking among the league leaders in field goal percentage. He was an All-Star in his seventh and final year with the Bulls, then joined Orlando before 1994-95 and gave the Magic more solid play.

Strengths: Grant stands among the most talented and athletic power forwards in the game. He's a quick leaper who can outrun most power forwards while still holding his own in the strength department. He's in his element in the open court, yet he also scores in the post. He's an All-Defensive performer who will block shots and rebound.

Weaknesses: Grant has limited range and has been a poor free throw shooter. He is not a reliable ball-handler and, though he has put up some numbers, cannot be considered a great scorer. Nagging injuries the last two seasons have kept him from playing a full slate.

Analysis: Grant is considered one of the hardest-working players in basketball, and his talents have been well rewarded by Orlando. Grant made no secret of his desire to leave the Chicago management, and his free-agent deal with the Magic was big news. He gave an already talented team another strong inside presence and helped it take the next step.

PLAYER SUMMARY

Will.....................................bust his tail
Can't.............................handle the ball
Expect ....strong interior play
Don't Expect...........low field goal pct.
Fantasy Value $16-19
Card Value ....8-12¢

COLLEGE STATISTICS

		G	FGP	FTP	RPG	PPG
83-84	CLEM	28	.533	.744	4.6	5.7
84-85	CLEM	29	.555	.637	6.8	11.3
85-86	CLEM	34	.584	.725	10.5	16.4
86-87	CLEM	31	.656	.708	9.6	21.0
Totals		122	.598	.704	8.0	13.9

NBA REGULAR-SEASON STATISTICS

		G	MIN	FGs FG	FGs PCT	3-PT FGs FG	3-PT FGs PCT	FTs FT	FTs PCT	Rebounds OFF	Rebounds TOT	AST	STL	BLK	PTS	PPG
87-88	CHI	81	1827	254	.501	0	.000	114	.626	155	447	89	51	53	622	7.7
88-89	CHI	79	2809	405	.519	0	.000	140	.704	240	681	168	86	62	950	12.0
89-90	CHI	80	2753	446	.523	0	.000	179	.699	236	629	227	92	84	1071	13.4
90-91	CHI	78	2641	401	.547	1	.167	197	.711	266	659	178	95	69	1000	12.8
91-92	CHI	81	2859	457	.578	0	.000	235	.741	344	807	217	100	131	1149	14.2
92-93	CHI	77	2745	421	.508	1	.200	174	.619	341	729	201	89	96	1017	13.2
93-94	CHI	70	2570	460	.524	0	.000	137	.596	306	769	236	74	84	1057	15.1
94-95	ORL	74	2693	401	.567	0	.000	146	.692	223	715	173	76	88	948	12.8
Totals		620	20897	3245	.534	2	.059	1322	.677	2111	5436	1489	663	667	7814	12.6

JEFF GRAYER

Unrestricted Free Agent
Last Team: Philadelphia 76ers
Position: Guard/Forward
Height: 6'5" **Weight:** 215
Birthdate: December 17, 1965

NBA Experience: 7 years
College: Iowa St.
Acquired: Signed as a free agent, 1/95

Background: This second-team All-American became Iowa State's all-time leading scorer and played on the 1988 U.S. Olympic team. Though drafted in the first round by Milwaukee, Grayer has never averaged double figures in scoring in seven seasons with the Bucks, Warriors, and 76ers. He averaged 8.3 PPG in 47 games after signing with Philadelphia last season.

Strengths: Grayer brings good strength and solid defensive ability to the floor. He can match up with small forwards and big guards and helps out on the boards. Offensively, Grayer is at his best in the low post, where he knows how to maneuver for his points. He also knows that he has to work hard to earn his playing time.

Weaknesses: Grayer's outside jumper is awkward-looking and inconsistent. His free throw shooting has never been reliable, either. Grayer is a below-average ball-handler and passer who does not show a great feel for what to do with the ball. He is not a great athlete, and some have questioned his desire.

Analysis: Grayer is a role-player who is best used off the bench and who will provide a good defensive effort. He can defend at multiple positions and will get some points, but not enough to be considered an offensive threat. He was out of the league until January of last year, when the 76ers gave him a call.

PLAYER SUMMARY	
Will	post up
Can't	swish his jumper
Expect	defensive versatility
Don't Expect	10 PPG
Fantasy Value	$0
Card Value	5-8¢

COLLEGE STATISTICS

		G	FGP	FTP	RPG	PPG
84-85	ISU	33	.529	.653	6.5	12.2
85-86	ISU	33	.547	.629	6.3	20.7
86-87	ISU	27	.504	.740	7.0	22.4
87-88	ISU	32	.523	.711	9.4	25.3
Totals		125	.526	.686	7.3	20.0

NBA REGULAR-SEASON STATISTICS

		G	MIN	FGs FG	FGs PCT	3-PT FGs FG	3-PT FGs PCT	FTs FT	FTs PCT	Rebounds OFF	Rebounds TOT	AST	STL	BLK	PTS	PPG
88-89	MIL	11	200	32	.438	0	.000	17	.850	14	35	22	10	1	81	7.4
89-90	MIL	71	1427	224	.460	1	.125	99	.651	94	217	107	48	10	548	7.7
90-91	MIL	82	1422	210	.433	0	.000	101	.687	111	246	123	48	9	521	6.4
91-92	MIL	82	1659	309	.448	19	.288	102	.667	129	257	150	64	13	739	9.0
92-93	GS	48	1025	165	.467	2	.143	91	.669	71	157	70	31	8	423	8.8
93-94	GS	67	1096	191	.526	2	.167	71	.602	76	191	62	33	13	455	6.8
94-95	PHI	47	1098	163	.428	5	.333	58	.699	58	149	74	27	4	389	8.3
Totals		408	7927	1294	.457	29	.242	539	.666	553	1252	608	261	58	3156	7.7

A.C. GREEN

Team: Phoenix Suns
Position: Forward
Height: 6'9" **Weight:** 225
Birthdate: October 4, 1963

NBA Experience: 10 years
College: Oregon St.
Acquired: Signed as a free agent, 9/93

Background: Green was named Pac-10 Player of the Year as a junior at Oregon State and wound up his career as the school's second-leading rebounder and third-leading scorer. He led the Lakers in rebounding for four straight years and started in the 1990 All-Star Game. He signed with Phoenix before the 1993-94 season and has enjoyed two strong years with the Suns.

Strengths: A hard-working player, Green rebounds, scores, and gets to the line. He is a fine outside shooter and is capable of hitting from 3-point range. He's an aggressive defender, runs the floor, and provides great durability. Remarkably, he has played all 82 games in nine of his ten seasons. His skills have stood the test of time.

Weaknesses: Green is not a dominant low-post player. He gets a lot of his points on putbacks and "garbage" buckets in addition to his face-up jumpers. He won't block many shots.

Analysis: Green is pro basketball's iron man. He moved into third place on the consecutive-games-played list last season and the streak now stands at 731. He probably will never play in another All-Star Game, but his all-out hustle has been extremely valuable to the Lakers and Suns. He's a class act.

PLAYER SUMMARY	
Will	get to the glass
Can't	outscore Barkley
Expect	great leadership
Don't Expect	days off
Fantasy Value	$7-9
Card Value	7-10¢

COLLEGE STATISTICS

		G	FGP	FTP	RPG	PPG
81-82	OSU	30	.615	.610	5.3	8.6
82-83	OSU	31	.559	.689	7.6	14.0
83-84	OSU	23	.657	.770	8.7	17.8
84-85	OSU	31	.599	.680	9.2	19.1
Totals		115	.602	.696	7.7	14.7

NBA REGULAR-SEASON STATISTICS

		G	MIN	FGs FG	FGs PCT	3-PT FGs FG	3-PT FGs PCT	FTs FT	FTs PCT	Rebounds OFF	Rebounds TOT	AST	STL	BLK	PTS	PPG
85-86	LAL	82	1542	209	.539	1	.167	102	.611	160	381	54	49	49	521	6.4
86-87	LAL	79	2240	316	.538	0	.000	220	.780	210	615	84	70	80	852	10.8
87-88	LAL	82	2636	322	.503	0	.000	293	.773	245	710	93	87	45	937	11.4
88-89	LAL	82	2510	401	.529	4	.235	282	.786	258	739	103	94	55	1088	13.3
89-90	LAL	82	2709	385	.478	13	.283	278	.751	262	712	90	66	50	1061	12.9
90-91	LAL	82	2164	258	.476	11	.200	223	.738	201	516	71	59	23	750	9.1
91-92	LAL	82	2902	382	.476	12	.214	340	.744	306	762	117	91	36	1116	13.6
92-93	LAL	82	2819	379	.537	16	.348	277	.739	287	711	116	88	39	1051	12.8
93-94	PHO	82	2825	465	.502	8	.229	266	.735	275	753	137	70	38	1204	14.7
94-95	PHO	82	2687	311	.504	43	.339	251	.732	194	669	127	55	31	916	11.2
Totals		817	25034	3428	.506	108	.273	2532	.746	2398	6568	992	729	446	9496	11.6

TOM GUGLIOTTA

Team: Minnesota Timberwolves   **NBA Experience:** 3 years
Position: Forward   **College:** North Carolina St.
Height: 6'10" **Weight:** 240   **Acquired:** Traded from Warriors for
Birthdate: December 19, 1969   Donyell Marshall, 2/95

Background: "Googs" became the third North Carolina State player to record 1,500 points and 800 rebounds in a career. He led the ACC in rebounding and 3-pointers per game as a senior. His father was a high school coach and two of his brothers played professionally in Europe. After two productive years with the Bullets, the No. 6 draft choice was traded twice in three months last season, first to Golden State and then to Minnesota.

Strengths: Gugliotta has been compared to Larry Bird by none other than Michael Jordan and Pat Riley. That's because he does a little bit of everything. He shoots with range, finds open men, rebounds, handles the ball, and runs the floor. He has started at guard, forward, and center during his short career. The shorter 3-pointer is perfect for him.

Weaknesses: Gugliotta does not have a great arsenal of inside moves. He needs to develop a power game to be a more effective inside player. He is a horrible free throw shooter, which is surprising considering his outside shot. He is not one of the better young defensive players in basketball.

Analysis: Gugliotta was involved in two high-profile deals last season. He went to the Warriors with three No. 1 picks for Chris Webber early in the year, then joined the Timberwolves in a move that sent Donyell Marshall to Golden State. Gugliotta did not fare as well with Golden State as expected, but with Minnesota he has the makings of a team leader. His wife, Nikki, recently won the women's national duathlon championship (running and cycling).

PLAYER SUMMARY	
Will	hit 3-pointers
Can't	make his free throws
Expect	great versatility
Don't Expect	a stopper
Fantasy Value	$20-25
Card Value	10-20¢

COLLEGE STATISTICS

		G	FGP	FTP	RPG	PPG
88-89	NCST	21	.429	.655	1.7	2.7
89-90	NCST	30	.504	.672	7.0	11.1
90-91	NCST	31	.500	.644	9.1	15.2
91-92	NCST	30	.449	.685	9.8	22.5
Totals		112	.476	.668	7.3	13.7

NBA REGULAR-SEASON STATISTICS

		G	MIN	FGs FG	FGs PCT	3-PT FGs FG	3-PT FGs PCT	FTs FT	FTs PCT	Rebounds OFF	Rebounds TOT	AST	STL	BLK	PTS	PPG
92-93	WAS	81	2795	484	.426	38	.281	181	.644	219	781	306	134	35	1187	14.7
93-94	WAS	78	2795	540	.466	40	.270	213	.685	189	728	276	172	51	1333	17.1
94-95	WAS/GS/MIN															
		77	2568	371	.443	60	.323	174	.690	165	572	279	132	62	976	12.7
Totals		236	8158	1395	.446	138	.294	568	.673	573	2081	861	438	148	3496	14.8

TOM HAMMONDS

Unrestricted Free Agent
Last Team: Denver Nuggets
Position: Forward
Height: 6'9" **Weight:** 225
Birthdate: March 27, 1967

NBA Experience: 6 years
College: Georgia Tech
Acquired: Signed as a free agent, 2/93

Background: Hammonds was a third-team All-American as a senior at Georgia Tech. Though drafted ninth overall by Washington in 1989, Hammonds has played sparingly in his six NBA years. His best season was with the Bullets and Hornets in 1991-92, when he averaged 11.9 PPG. He has spent the last two-plus seasons coming off the Denver bench.

Strengths: Hammonds has a weight room-sculpted, NBA body. He uses it best on defense, where he can cause problems at both the three and four spots. Hammonds can play transition basketball and is comfortable as a finisher on the break. He can post up and will not launch many bad shots. He shot a career-best .535 from the field last season.

Weaknesses: Hammonds is a classic 'tweener. He is not wide or strong enough to thrive at power forward, yet his skills facing the basket are not where they need to be for the three spot. He has not shown an ability to put the ball on the floor, nor does he pass the ball well. Most of the big power forwards give him problems on defense. He has not been consistent.

Analysis: Once considered one of the best talents to come out of the Atlantic Coast Conference, Hammonds has been a major disappointment as a lottery pick. Injuries early in his career helped slow his progress, but the biggest culprit has been his inability to get comfortable facing the basket.

PLAYER SUMMARY

Will......................................play defense
Can't ....spot open men
Expect ....a fine physique
Don't Expect...........................a starter
Fantasy Value $0
Card Value ....5-7¢

COLLEGE STATISTICS

		G	FGP	FTP	RPG	PPG
85-86	GT	34	.609	.816	6.4	12.2
86-87	GT	29	.569	.722	7.2	16.2
87-88	GT	30	.568	.826	7.2	18.9
88-89	GT	30	.538	.773	8.1	20.9
Totals		123	.566	.801	7.2	16.9

NBA REGULAR-SEASON STATISTICS

				FGs		3-PT FGs		FTs		Rebounds						
		G	MIN	FG	PCT	FG	PCT	FT	PCT	OFF	TOT	AST	STL	BLK	PTS	PPG
89-90	WAS	61	805	129	.437	0	.000	63	.643	61	168	51	11	14	321	5.3
90-91	WAS	70	1023	155	.461	0	.000	57	.722	58	206	43	15	7	367	5.2
91-92	WAS/CHA	37	984	195	.488	0	.000	50	.610	49	185	36	22	13	440	11.9
92-93	CHA/DEN	54	713	105	.475	0	.000	38	.613	38	127	24	18	12	248	4.6
93-94	DEN	74	877	115	.500	0	.000	71	.683	62	199	34	20	12	301	4.1
94-95	DEN	70	956	139	.535	0	.000	132	.746	55	222	36	11	14	410	5.9
Totals		366	5358	838	.481	0	.000	411	.683	323	1107	224	97	72	2087	5.7

ANFERNEE HARDAWAY

Team: Orlando Magic
Position: Guard
Height: 6'7" **Weight:** 207
Birthdate: July 18, 1972
NBA Experience: 2 years

College: Memphis St.
Acquired: Draft rights traded from Warriors with 1996, 1998, and 2000 1st-round picks for draft rights to Chris Webber, 6/93

Background: Hardaway was *Parade's* 1989-90 national High School Player of the Year. However, he sat out his freshman year at Memphis State under Prop 48, then suffered a gunshot wound in his right foot in 1991. He recovered and became his conference's two-time Player of the Year. He was drafted No. 3 by Golden State but was immediately dealt to Orlando. It has taken him just two years to become an All-Star starter.

Strengths: "Penny" has been compared to Magic Johnson, and not without reason. He has great size for a point guard, which allows him to see the floor and spot open men. He directs the fastbreak with authority, handles the ball deftly, and knows how to get off his shot in traffic. Hardaway is a 20-plus PPG scorer and also provides quick, aggressive defense. "Pennies for Penny's Pals" raises money for charity, and Hardaway is beginning to realize his endorsement potential as well.

Weaknesses: Hardaway is a better scorer than shooter, though he raised his field goal percentage considerably last season and had a much easier time with the shorter 3-point arc. Still, defenders are advised to keep him on the outside. He commits a lot of turnovers, but he also handles the ball a lot.

Analysis: Hardaway sells tickets, especially when paired with fellow All-Star youngster Shaquille O'Neal. If there's a better inside-outside combination in basketball, let us know. Penny scored 12 points and dished out 11 assists in his first of what will probably be many All-Star starts. His rookie season was fabulous and his sophomore campaign even better in almost every aspect. It's hard to imagine, but he will probably get better.

PLAYER SUMMARY

Will ....run the show
Can't ....be kept from bucket
Expect ....superstardom
Don't Expect ....conservative passes
Fantasy Value $70-75
Card Value ....50¢-$1.25

COLLEGE STATISTICS

		G	FGP	FTP	APG	PPG
91-92	MSU	34	.433	.652	5.5	17.4
92-93	MSU	32	.477	.767	6.4	22.8
Totals		66	.456	.717	5.9	20.0

NBA REGULAR-SEASON STATISTICS

				FGs		3-PT FGs		FTs		Rebounds						
		G	MIN	FG	PCT	FG	PCT	FT	PCT	OFF	TOT	AST	STL	BLK	PTS	PPG
93-94	ORL	82	3015	509	.466	50	.267	245	.742	192	439	544	190	51	1313	16.0
94-95	ORL	77	2901	585	.512	87	.349	356	.769	139	336	551	130	26	1613	20.9
Totals		159	5916	1094	.490	137	.314	601	.758	331	775	1095	320	77	2926	18.4

TIM HARDAWAY

Team: Golden State Warriors
Position: Guard
Height: 6'0" **Weight:** 195
Birthdate: September 12, 1966

NBA Experience: 5 years
College: Texas-El Paso
Acquired: 1st-round pick in 1989 draft
(14th overall)

Background: Hardaway surpassed Nate Archibald as the all-time scoring leader at the University of Texas-El Paso. In 1989-90, he led all rookies in assists and steals while directing the high-powered Golden State offense. Hardaway has since appeared in three All-Star Games. A Dream Team II choice, he sat out the entire 1993-94 campaign after surgery to his left knee. Wrist surgery cut short his comeback season in 1994-95.

Strengths: Few can handle the ball like Hardaway. His between-the-legs crossover dribble, dubbed the "UTEP two-step," mesmerizes even the best of defenders and usually opens a clear lane to the basket. His long-range shot is unorthodox but he shoots it with 3-point range. Hardaway is a quick, effective floor leader who gets the ball into the right hands, which are often his own. He is a hardnosed defender.

Weaknesses: Injuries have stalled (temporarily, at least) Hardaway's heroics over the last couple of seasons. Also, his small frame makes him vulnerable against bigger guards, especially on defense. His shooting percentage is substandard and he takes a few too many chances defensively.

Analysis: Hardaway made a splendid comeback from the famed anterior cruciate tear before breaking his wrist during one of his high-scoring games. The king of the crossover is a bona fide superstar and one tough cookie. Without him, the Warriors are nowhere near the team they are when he's healthy. He is one of the most explosive and competitive point guards in the game.

PLAYER SUMMARY	
Will	get past his man
Can't	be left open
Expect	20-plus points
Don't Expect	slack defense
Fantasy Value	$19-22
Card Value	10-20¢

COLLEGE STATISTICS

		G	FGP	FTP	APG	PPG
85-86	UTEP	28	.521	.651	1.9	4.1
86-87	UTEP	31	.490	.663	4.8	10.0
87-88	UTEP	32	.449	.754	5.7	13.6
88-89	UTEP	33	.501	.741	5.4	22.0
Totals		124	.484	.718	4.5	12.8

NBA REGULAR-SEASON STATISTICS

		G	MIN	FGs		3-PT FGs		FTs		Rebounds		AST	STL	BLK	PTS	PPG
				FG	PCT	FG	PCT	FT	PCT	OFF	TOT					
89-90	GS	79	2663	464	.471	23	.274	211	.764	57	310	689	165	12	1162	14.7
90-91	GS	82	3215	739	.476	97	.385	306	.803	87	332	793	214	12	1881	22.9
91-92	GS	81	3332	734	.461	127	.338	298	.766	81	310	807	164	13	1893	23.4
92-93	GS	66	2609	522	.447	102	.330	273	.744	60	263	699	116	12	1419	21.5
94-95	GS	62	2321	430	.427	168	.378	219	.760	46	190	578	88	12	1247	20.1
Totals		370	14140	2889	.458	517	.353	1307	.768	331	1405	3566	747	61	7602	20.5

DEREK HARPER

Team: New York Knicks
Position: Guard
Height: 6'4" **Weight:** 206
Birthdate: October 13, 1961
NBA Experience: 12 years

College: Illinois
Acquired: Traded from Mavericks for Tony Campbell and a 1997 1st-round pick, 1/94

Background: Harper led the Big Ten in steals for two years, then declared for the NBA draft after his junior season. He was the first player in league history to improve his scoring average in each of his first eight years. After ten-plus years in Dallas, he was traded to New York and, in his first full season with the Knicks, started nearly every game in 1994-95.

Strengths: A respected all-around talent who plays both guard spots, Harper is respected league-wide for his willingness to play belly-up defense. He is also a solid 3-point shooter, a reliable ball-handler and passer, and a veteran leader who gives all he's got. He is not afraid to take clutch shots.

Weaknesses: Harper is not the scoring machine he was for several years in Dallas, and he is also not the most creative playmaker. He has lost a little of the quickness that helped him become one of the league's top thieves.

Analysis: It took Harper a while to adjust to the Knicks, but he enjoyed a fine 1994-95 season. He returned to double-figure scoring, racked up a nice assist total, and fashioned a 3-to-1 assist-to-turnover ratio. His leadership skills should keep him around awhile.

PLAYER SUMMARY

Will ....score, pass, defend
Can't ....shoot 50 percent
Expect ....veteran leadership
Don't Expect................late-game fear
Fantasy Value $1-3
Card Value ....7-12¢

COLLEGE STATISTICS

		G	FGP	FTP	APG	PPG
80-81	ILL	29	.413	.717	5.4	8.3
81-82	ILL	29	.457	.756	5.0	8.4
82-83	ILL	32	.537	.675	3.7	15.4
Totals		90	.478	.701	4.7	10.9

NBA REGULAR-SEASON STATISTICS

				FGs		3-PT FGs		FTs		Rebounds						
		G	MIN	FG	PCT	FG	PCT	FT	PCT	OFF	TOT	AST	STL	BLK	PTS	PPG
83-84	DAL	82	1712	200	.443	3	.115	66	.673	53	172	239	95	21	469	5.7
84-85	DAL	82	2218	329	.520	21	.344	111	.721	47	199	360	144	37	790	9.6
85-86	DAL	79	2150	390	.534	12	.235	171	.747	75	226	416	153	23	963	12.2
86-87	DAL	77	2556	497	.501	76	.358	160	.684	51	199	609	167	25	1230	16.0
87-88	DAL	82	3032	536	.459	60	.313	261	.759	71	246	634	168	35	1393	17.0
88-89	DAL	81	2968	538	.477	99	.356	229	.806	46	228	570	172	41	1404	17.3
89-90	DAL	82	3007	567	.488	89	.371	250	.794	54	244	609	187	26	1473	18.0
90-91	DAL	77	2879	572	.467	89	.362	286	.731	59	233	548	147	14	1519	19.7
91-92	DAL	65	2252	448	.443	58	.312	198	.759	49	170	373	101	17	1152	17.7
92-93	DAL	62	2108	393	.419	101	.393	239	.756	42	123	334	80	16	1126	18.2
93-94	DAL/NY	82	2204	303	.407	73	.360	112	.687	20	141	334	125	8	791	9.6
94-95	NY	80	2716	337	.446	106	.363	139	.724	31	194	458	79	10	919	11.5
Totals		931	29802	5110	.467	787	.351	2222	.745	598	2375	5484	1618	273	13229	14.2

RON HARPER

Team: Chicago Bulls
Position: Guard
Height: 6'6" **Weight:** 198
Birthdate: January 20, 1964

NBA Experience: 9 years
College: Miami (OH)
Acquired: Signed as a free agent, 9/94

Background: Harper left Miami of Ohio with the all-time Mid-American Conference scoring record and finished second in Rookie of the Year voting with Cleveland. He was traded to the Clippers in November 1989, but his first year there was cut short when he tore the anterior cruciate ligament in his right knee. He made a nice comeback, but he struggled last season with the Bulls after signing a rich free-agent contract.

Strengths: Harper has been a dominant open-court player with slashing moves to the hoop and tremendous finishing ability. More a scorer than a shooter, he has put up some big numbers during his career. He is an accomplished rebounding guard and also finds open men.

Weaknesses: Poor shot selection has been a career-long knock on Harper, who never managed to find a comfort zone last season in Chicago's triangle offense. He has never been a steady shooter, and his field goal percentage reflects that. Harper does not play great defense, and his overall game seems out of sorts.

Analysis: Harper has been a borderline marquee player during his career. Before coming to Chicago, he had averaged at least 18 PPG in seven of his eight seasons. Much was expected of Harper when he joined the Bulls, but he wound up taking a back seat to the team's premier attractions.

PLAYER SUMMARY	
Will	finish with both hands
Can't	rely on jumpers
Expect	open-court moves
Don't Expect	a leader
Fantasy Value	$4-6
Card Value	7-10¢

COLLEGE STATISTICS

		G	FGP	FTP	RPG	PPG
82-83	MIA	28	.497	.674	7.0	12.9
83-84	MIA	30	.537	.570	7.6	14.9
84-85	MIA	31	.541	.661	10.7	24.9
85-86	MIA	31	.545	.665	11.7	24.4
Totals		120	.534	.642	9.3	19.5

NBA REGULAR-SEASON STATISTICS

			FGs		3-PT FGs		FTs		Rebounds						
	G	MIN	FG	PCT	FG	PCT	FT	PCT	OFF	TOT	AST	STL	BLK	PTS	PPG
86-87 CLE	82	3064	734	.455	20	.213	386	.684	169	392	394	209	84	1874	22.9
87-88 CLE	57	1830	340	.464	3	.150	196	.705	64	223	281	122	52	879	15.4
88-89 CLE	82	2851	587	.511	29	.250	323	.751	122	409	434	185	74	1526	18.6
89-90 CLE/LAC	35	1367	301	.473	14	.275	182	.788	74	206	182	81	41	798	22.8
90-91 LAC	39	1383	285	.391	48	.324	145	.668	58	188	209	66	35	763	19.6
91-92 LAC	82	3144	569	.440	64	.303	293	.736	120	447	417	152	72	1495	18.2
92-93 LAC	80	2970	542	.451	52	.280	307	.769	117	425	360	177	73	1443	18.0
93-94 LAC	75	2856	569	.426	71	.301	299	.715	129	460	344	144	54	1508	20.1
94-95 CHI	77	1536	209	.426	31	.282	81	.618	51	180	157	97	27	530	6.9
Totals	609	21001	4136	.450	332	.283	2212	.721	904	2930	2778	1233	512	10816	17.8

LUCIOUS HARRIS

Team: Dallas Mavericks
Position: Guard
Height: 6'5" **Weight:** 190
Birthdate: December 18, 1970

NBA Experience: 2 years
College: Long Beach St.
Acquired: 2nd-round pick in 1993 draft (28th overall)

Background: Harris completed his four years at Long Beach State as the leading scorer in Big West history. He averaged 23.1 PPG as a senior and earned all-conference first-team honors in each of his last two years. He was the first pick in the second round of the 1993 draft, ahead of college teammate Bryon Russell (Utah). Harris has missed only eight games in his first two seasons and averaged 9.5 PPG in 1994-95.

Strengths: Harris is known for his long-range shooting skills. He made 39 percent of his 3-point tries last season. He is especially dangerous in transition, where he can pull up for jumpers or take it all the way to the hole. Harris has good size for a guard and is not afraid to help out on the boards. He's a willing passer, a promising defender, and a reliable free throw shooter.

Weaknesses: Harris has played both guard positions in his two pro seasons, but it is clear he does not have the playmaking instincts of a point guard. He is not an expert ball-handler, either. Harris is not as comfortable in a halfcourt game as he is when the pace is fast and furious. He could stand to add some muscle for the defensive requirements of the NBA. He's not going to dominate with speed or strength.

Analysis: Harris did an admirable job filling in as a starter at big guard last season while Jim Jackson was out for 31 games. The second-year pro dumped in 31 points one night and came closer than many believed he could to averaging double figures for the season. Harris figures to come off the bench most of the time, providing instant offense with his dangerous stroke.

PLAYER SUMMARY	
Will	shoot the trey
Can't	beat out J.J.
Expect	instant offense
Don't Expect	muscle
Fantasy Value	$2-4
Card Value	8-12¢

COLLEGE STATISTICS

		G	FGP	FTP	RPG	PPG
89-90	LBS	32	.430	.694	4.8	14.3
90-91	LBS	28	.396	.700	4.7	19.7
91-92	LBS	30	.471	.734	4.3	18.8
92-93	LBS	32	.525	.774	5.3	23.1
Totals		122	.458	.727	4.8	19.0

NBA REGULAR-SEASON STATISTICS

		G	MIN	FGs FG	FGs PCT	3-PT FGs FG	3-PT FGs PCT	FTs FT	FTs PCT	Rebounds OFF	Rebounds TOT	AST	STL	BLK	PTS	PPG
93-94	DAL	77	1165	162	.421	7	.212	87	.731	45	157	106	49	10	418	5.4
94-95	DAL	79	1695	280	.459	55	.387	136	.800	85	220	132	58	14	751	9.5
Totals		156	2860	442	.444	62	.354	223	.772	130	377	238	107	24	1169	7.5

ANTONIO HARVEY

Team: Vancouver Grizzlies
Position: Forward/Center
Height: 6'11" **Weight:** 225
Birthdate: July 9, 1970
NBA Experience: 2 years

College: Southern Illinois; Georgia; Pfeiffer
Acquired: Selected from Lakers in 1995 expansion draft

Background: Harvey played in obscurity at Pfeiffer College in Misenheimer, North Carolina, and was not selected in the 1993 draft. He impressed the Lakers with his strong play in the Southern California Summer League and was signed for the 1993-94 season. He played in 27 games as a rookie. The Lakers re-signed him as a free agent before the 1994-95 season and Harvey improved slightly to 3.0 PPG in 59 contests. The Grizzlies grabbed him in the expansion draft.

Strengths: Harvey's best attribute at this point in his career is his shot-blocking. He swatted 41 last season despite limited playing time and would be a 100-plus guy if he managed to play even 20 minutes a contest. He has good size, has nice timing, and can really get off the floor. Harvey also has the potential to be a productive rebounder with his energy and athletic ability.

Weaknesses: To call Harvey's skills raw would be an understatement. Recall, he has had only two years of experience against top-flight competition since finishing his small-college career. He needs some serious work on his low-post footwork, and his face-up game is not going to have defenders quivering anytime soon. He is shaky with the dribble, is not a good passer, and shoots an embarrassing percentage from the free throw line.

Analysis: Did anyone really expect Harvey to make an impact? He has learned a great deal in two years, but unfortunately some of his deficiencies might not be curable. He made eight starts for the Lakers last season, a break from his more frequent role of mop-up man. He does have the size and athletic potential to stick around, especially with an expansion team like Vancouver.

PLAYER SUMMARY	
Will	block shots
Can't	score points
Expect	a project
Don't Expect	slick moves
Fantasy Value	$0
Card Value	8-12¢

COLLEGE STATISTICS

		G	FGP	FTP	RPG	PPG
88-89	SILL	34	.464	.484	5.2	6.9
90-91	GEOR	29	.455	.507	4.3	7.2
91-92	PFEI	29	.533	.693	8.1	13.7
92-93	PFEI	29	.525	.574	10.1	18.3
Totals		121	.504	.578	6.9	11.3

NBA REGULAR-SEASON STATISTICS

		G	MIN	FG	PCT	FG	PCT	FT	PCT	OFF	TOT	AST	STL	BLK	PTS	PPG
93-94	LAL	27	247	29	.367	0	.000	12	.462	26	59	5	8	19	70	2.6
94-95	LAL	59	572	77	.438	1	1.000	24	.533	39	102	23	16	41	179	3.0
Totals		86	819	106	.416	1	1.000	36	.507	65	161	28	24	60	249	2.9

HERSEY HAWKINS

Team: Seattle SuperSonics
Position: Guard
Height: 6'3" **Weight:** 204
Birthdate: September 29, 1966

NBA Experience: 7 years
College: Bradley
Acquired: Traded from Hornets with David Wingate for Kendall Gill, 6/95

Background: Hawkins went from being a 6'3", all-city center at Westinghouse High School in Chicago to an outside gunner at Bradley. As a senior, he led the nation in scoring and was named the nation's Player of the Year. He left college as the fourth-leading scorer in NCAA history. He was one of the NBA's top 25 scorers with Philadelphia before a trade two years ago boosted Charlotte's backcourt. Seattle acquired him over the summer.

Strengths: Hawkins is one of the most dangerous 3-point shooters in the league. The decision to shorten the arc last season made treys like layups for him. He also knows how to get to the hoop off the bounce. He is close to automatic from the free throw line. Hawkins has surprised some people with his defense.

Weaknesses: Hawkins is not an All-Star player on a good team. He is at his best when his team runs plays for him rather than creating things himself. Hawkins is not among the better passing and ball-handling guards in the league. His coaches would like to see more of a mean streak at times.

Analysis: Hawkins was a bit of a disappointment during his first year in Charlotte, but he came back with a productive 1994-95 season as more than just a long-range shooting specialist. His rebounding, defense, and durability have turned out to be nice bonuses. And his stroke is as good as ever. Sonics fans won't miss Kendall Gill.

PLAYER SUMMARY

Will	drain 3-pointers
Can't	run the point
Expect	about 14 PPG
Don't Expect	missed free throws
Fantasy Value	$20-25
Card Value	7-10¢

COLLEGE STATISTICS

		G	FGP	FTP	RPG	PPG
84-85	BRAD	30	.581	.771	6.1	14.6
85-86	BRAD	35	.542	.768	5.7	18.7
86-87	BRAD	29	.533	.793	6.7	27.2
87-88	BRAD	31	.524	.848	7.8	36.3
Totals		125	.539	.806	6.5	24.1

NBA REGULAR-SEASON STATISTICS

		G	MIN	FGs FG	FGs PCT	3-PT FGs FG	3-PT FGs PCT	FTs FT	FTs PCT	Rebounds OFF	Rebounds TOT	AST	STL	BLK	PTS	PPG
88-89	PHI	79	2577	442	.455	71	.428	241	.831	51	225	239	120	37	1196	15.1
89-90	PHI	82	2856	522	.460	84	.420	387	.888	85	304	261	130	28	1515	18.5
90-91	PHI	80	3110	590	.472	108	.400	479	.871	48	310	299	178	39	1767	22.1
91-92	PHI	81	3013	521	.462	91	.397	403	.874	53	271	248	157	43	1536	19.0
92-93	PHI	81	2977	551	.470	122	.397	419	.860	91	346	317	137	30	1643	20.3
93-94	CHA	82	2648	395	.460	78	.332	312	.862	89	377	216	135	22	1180	14.4
94-95	CHA	82	2731	390	.482	131	.440	261	.867	60	314	262	122	18	1172	14.3
Totals		567	19912	3411	.466	685	.402	2502	.867	477	2147	1842	979	217	10009	17.7

CARL HERRERA

Team: Houston Rockets
Position: Forward
Height: 6'9" **Weight:** 225
Birthdate: December 14, 1966
NBA Experience: 4 years

College: Jacksonville; Houston
Acquired: Draft rights traded from Heat with draft rights to Dave Jamerson for draft rights to Alec Kessler, 6/90

Background: Born in Trinidad and raised in Venezuela, Herrera did not play basketball until the age of 13. He was noticed by colleges for his play as a 16-year-old point guard on the Venezuelan national team in the Pan-Am Games. He spent two years at Jacksonville (Texas) Junior College and one at the University of Houston. After starting his pro career in Spain, Herrera has spent four years with the Rockets, mostly as a reserve.

Strengths: Herrera is a magnificent athlete who was a volleyball star as a teenager. It's not difficult to see what made him a standout in that sport— tremendous leaping ability. He also possesses a great pair of hands. He can play both forward spots and gets up and down the floor like a guard. He has provided a forceful defensive presence and has a decent hook and mid-range jumper.

Weaknesses: Herrera is by no means a skilled offensive player. Though his face-up jumper works well at times, he is far from consistent on the perimeter or the blocks. He is also a weak free throw shooter. Herrera does not make anything happen via the pass and lacks court sense. He does not have a real good understanding of the game.

Analysis: Herrera has been a valuable player at times, including Houston's championship run in 1994. He plays inspired defense and leaves most of the scoring to his teammates. He seems better suited to a reserve role than that of a starter. Hamstring injuries sent him to the injured list near the end of the 1994-95 season and limited his contributions somewhat.

PLAYER SUMMARY

Will	get off his feet
Can't	hit his free throws
Expect	reliable defense
Don't Expect	10 PPG
Fantasy Value	$0
Card Value	7-10¢

COLLEGE STATISTICS

		G	FGP	FTP	RPG	PPG
89-90	HOUS	33	.565	.804	9.2	16.7
Totals		33	.565	.804	9.2	16.7

NBA REGULAR-SEASON STATISTICS

				FGs		3-PT FGs		FTs		Rebounds						
		G	MIN	FG	PCT	FG	PCT	FT	PCT	OFF	TOT	AST	STL	BLK	PTS	PPG
91-92	HOU	43	566	83	.516	0	.000	25	.568	33	99	27	16	25	191	4.4
92-93	HOU	81	1800	240	.541	0	.000	125	.710	148	454	61	47	35	605	7.5
93-94	HOU	75	1292	142	.458	0	.000	69	.711	101	285	37	32	26	353	4.7
94-95	HOU	61	1331	171	.523	0	.000	73	.624	98	278	44	40	38	415	6.8
Totals		260	4989	636	.512	0	.000	292	.673	380	1116	169	135	124	1564	6.0

GRANT HILL

Team: Detroit Pistons
Position: Forward
Height: 6'8" **Weight:** 225
Birthdate: October 5, 1972

NBA Experience: 1 year
College: Duke
Acquired: 1st-round pick in 1994 draft
(3rd overall)

Background: Hill, along with Bobby Hurley and Christian Laettner, formed the core of back-to-back national championship teams at Duke in 1991 and 1992. Hill was a consensus All-American in 1993-94 and became the first ACC player with 1,900 points, 700 rebounds, 400 assists, 200 steals, and 100 blocks. The third pick in the 1994 draft, he was second among all rookies in scoring and assists and was the top vote-getter in the All-Star balloting.

Strengths: Hill quite literally does it all. He led the Pistons in scoring and steals in his rookie season, a testament to his play at both ends of the floor. He is a tremendous slasher with the ability to get to the bucket from almost anywhere on the court. He possesses a great crossover dribble and can finish his own plays or find open teammates. He was considered one of the best defensive prospects to come along the pike in a while and has not disappointed. He sets a great example.

Weaknesses: Shooting range is about the only significant flaw in Hill's game. He made only four 3-pointers during his rookie season, but his percentage from the field was admirable for a first-year player. He is not the best free throw shooter in the game.

Analysis: The son of former NFL star Calvin Hill is a coach's dream both on and off the court. He had 25 points, ten boards, five assists, and three blocks in his pro debut. He became the first rookie ever to lead the All-Star fan balloting when he edged Shaquille O'Neal. The versatile Hill is capable of playing three positions and burning the opposition from any one of them. Expect him to be a franchise player for years to come.

PLAYER SUMMARY	
Will	score, pass, rebound
Can't	pour in 3-pointers
Expect	an All-Star regular
Don't Expect	many mistakes
Fantasy Value	$65-70
Card Value	$3.00-8.00

COLLEGE STATISTICS

		G	FGP	FTP	RPG	PPG
90-91	DUKE	36	.516	.609	5.1	11.2
91-92	DUKE	33	.611	.733	5.7	14.0
92-93	DUKE	26	.578	.746	6.4	18.0
93-94	DUKE	34	.462	.703	6.9	17.4
Totals		129	.532	.698	6.0	14.9

NBA REGULAR-SEASON STATISTICS

			FGs		3-PT FGs		FTs		Rebounds						
	G	MIN	FG	PCT	FG	PCT	FT	PCT	OFF	TOT	AST	STL	BLK	PTS	PPG
94-95 DET	70	2678	508	.477	4	.148	374	.732	125	445	353	124	62	1394	19.9
Totals	70	2678	508	.477	4	.148	374	.732	125	445	353	124	62	1394	19.9

TYRONE HILL

Team: Cleveland Cavaliers
Position: Forward
Height: 6'9" **Weight:** 243
Birthdate: March 17, 1968

NBA Experience: 5 years
College: Xavier (OH)
Acquired: Signed as a free agent, 7/93

Background: Hill joined an exclusive group of college players to score 2,000 points and grab 1,000 rebounds in a career. He was among the top three nationally in rebounding as a junior and senior at Xavier. He spent his first three NBA years banging the boards for Golden State before landing in Cleveland as a free agent. In 1994-95, his second season with the Cavaliers, Hill was selected to play in the All-Star Game.

Strengths: Hill is one of the best rebounding forwards in the NBA. He has a muscular body and uses it to get inside position. He snares boards with great instincts, leaping ability, and quickness. Hill is also a top-notch, hard-working defensive player and has made himself a reliable low-post scorer. He runs the floor and is rewarded with transition slams.

Weaknesses: Though his low-post offense is much improved, Hill remains a below-average outside shooter and is ineffective from the free throw line. He has no feel for getting the ball to teammates at the right time and his assist total is embarrassing. He picks up a lot of fouls.

Analysis: Hill spent the last off-season working on his inside game with Pete Newell and Danny Manning. The work paid dividends, as he averaged a career-high 13.8 PPG and earned a spot in the All-Star Game. His scoring has improved in each of his years in the league and he remains a force on the boards. With even a decent outside jumper, he'd be scary.

PLAYER SUMMARY

Will ....control the boards
Can't ....shoot with range
Expect ....emerging offense
Don't Expect ......free throw accuracy
Fantasy Value $12-15
Card Value ....8-12¢

COLLEGE STATISTICS

		G	FGP	FTP	RPG	PPG
86-87	XAV	31	.552	.672	8.4	8.8
87-88	XAV	30	.557	.745	10.5	15.3
88-89	XAV	33	.606	.701	12.2	18.9
89-90	XAV	32	.581	.658	12.6	20.2
Totals		126	.579	.692	11.0	15.9

NBA REGULAR-SEASON STATISTICS

				FGs		3-PT FGs		FTs		Rebounds						
		G	MIN	FG	PCT	FG	PCT	FT	PCT	OFF	TOT	AST	STL	BLK	PTS	PPG
90-91	GS	74	1192	147	.492	0	.000	96	.632	157	383	19	33	30	390	5.3
91-92	GS	82	1886	254	.522	0	.000	163	.694	182	593	47	73	43	671	8.2
92-93	GS	74	2070	251	.508	0	.000	138	.624	255	754	68	41	40	640	8.6
93-94	CLE	57	1447	216	.543	0	.000	171	.668	184	499	46	53	35	603	10.6
94-95	CLE	70	2397	350	.504	0	.000	263	.662	269	765	55	55	41	963	13.8
Totals		357	8992	1218	.513	0	.000	831	.659	1047	2994	235	255	189	3267	9.2

JEFF HORNACEK

Team: Utah Jazz
Position: Guard
Height: 6'4" **Weight:** 190
Birthdate: May 3, 1963
NBA Experience: 9 years

College: Iowa St.
Acquired: Traded from 76ers with Sean Green and a conditional 2nd-round pick for Jeff Malone and a conditional 1st-round pick, 2/94

Background: Hornacek walked on at Iowa State, earned a scholarship, and wound up setting a Big Eight career assist record with 665. His nine-year pro career has evolved in a similar pattern—from unheralded to highly respected. He led the Suns in 1991-92 with 20.1 PPG and earned a spot in the 1992 All-Star Game. Hornacek was Utah's second-leading scorer in 1994-95 with 16.5 PPG.

Strengths: A dead-eye gunner, Hornacek can kill you from anywhere on the court—inside or outside the 3-point line. He rates among NBA leaders in free throw and 3-point accuracy. He makes few mistakes, is good with both hands, and approaches the game with a great work ethic. He can handle both guard positions.

Weaknesses: The fact that Hornacek is not a great athlete has not stopped him from achieving at every level. His size (or lack of it) works against him on defense, but he makes up for it with savvy play.

Analysis: A coach's son, Hornacek has a thorough understanding of the game and plays it at a high level. He started alongside John Stockton during 1994-95 in what proved to be one of the league's premier backcourts. Hornacek set an NBA record early last season by going 8-of-8 from 3-point range against Seattle. He also eclipsed the 10,000 career point plateau.

PLAYER SUMMARY

Will ....hit open jumpers
Can't ....jump out of gyms
Expect ....skills, smarts, savvy
Don't Expect ....poor decisions
Fantasy Value $25-30
Card Value ....8-12¢

COLLEGE STATISTICS

		G	FGP	FTP	RPG	PPG
82-83	ISU	27	.422	.711	2.3	5.4
83-84	ISU	29	.500	.790	3.5	10.0
84-85	ISU	34	.521	.844	3.6	12.5
85-86	ISU	33	.478	.776	3.8	13.7
Totals		123	.489	.790	3.3	10.7

NBA REGULAR-SEASON STATISTICS

				FGs		3-PT FGs		FTs		Rebounds						
		G	MIN	FG	PCT	FG	PCT	FT	PCT	OFF	TOT	AST	STL	BLK	PTS	PPG
86-87	PHO	80	1561	159	.454	12	.279	94	.777	41	184	361	70	5	424	5.3
87-88	PHO	82	2243	306	.506	17	.293	152	.822	71	262	540	107	10	781	9.5
88-89	PHO	78	2487	440	.495	27	.333	147	.826	75	266	465	129	8	1054	13.5
89-90	PHO	67	2278	483	.536	40	.408	173	.856	86	313	337	117	14	1179	17.6
90-91	PHO	80	2733	544	.518	61	.418	201	.897	74	321	409	111	16	1350	16.9
91-92	PHO	81	3078	635	.512	83	.439	279	.886	106	407	411	158	31	1632	20.1
92-93	PHI	79	2860	582	.470	97	.390	250	.865	84	342	548	131	21	1511	19.1
93-94	PHI/UTA	80	2820	472	.470	70	.337	260	.878	60	279	419	127	13	1274	15.9
94-95	UTA	81	2696	482	.514	89	.406	284	.882	53	210	347	129	17	1337	16.5
Totals		708	22756	4103	.499	496	.384	1840	.863	650	2584	3837	1079	135	10542	14.9

ROBERT HORRY

Team: Houston Rockets
Position: Forward
Height: 6'10" **Weight:** 220
Birthdate: August 25, 1970

NBA Experience: 3 years
College: Alabama
Acquired: 1st-round pick in 1992 draft
(11th overall)

Background: Named Alabama prep Player of the Year at Andalusia High, Horry stayed at home and helped the Tide to the final 16 of the NCAA Tournament twice. He finished his career as the all-time school leader in blocked shots. The 11th pick in the 1992 draft, Horry has been a three-year Houston starter at small forward. He has averaged right around ten points per game in each of his pro seasons.

Strengths: Horry is a splendid athlete who loves to challenge shots. The former SEC All-Defensive player has a nose for the ball and rejects a high number of shots for a small forward. He's also a capable scorer with a quick first step, a dangerous jumper, and good range. He moves well without the ball and finds open men. Horry is a talented transition player.

Weaknesses: Horry is not the scoring machine many starting small forwards are, nor is he a great ball-handler. He has not yet developed the night-to-night offensive consistency his coaches would like to see from him. He tends to disappear in too many games, passing up open scoring chances. His back has bothered him.

Analysis: Horry had a large hand in Houston's run to the 1994 NBA championship and also stepped it up in the 1995 playoffs. He had actually been traded to Detroit in 1993-94, but the deal was called off when Sean Elliott failed a Rockets physical. Horry is rare in that he has started on a quality team since day one of his NBA career. Houston fans would like to see more offensive assertiveness.

PLAYER SUMMARY

Will ....swat shots
Can't ....dribble like a guard
Expect.......................................10 PPG
Don't Expect ....timid defense
Fantasy Value $14-17
Card Value ....10-20¢

COLLEGE STATISTICS

		G	FGP	FTP	RPG	PPG
88-89	ALAB	31	.427	.644	5.0	6.5
89-90	ALAB	35	.467	.760	6.2	13.1
90-91	ALAB	32	.449	.804	8.1	11.9
91-92	ALAB	35	.470	.727	8.5	15.8
Totals		133	.458	.742	7.0	12.0

NBA REGULAR-SEASON STATISTICS

		G	MIN	FGs FG	FGs PCT	3-PT FGs FG	3-PT FGs PCT	FTs FT	FTs PCT	Rebounds OFF	Rebounds TOT	AST	STL	BLK	PTS	PPG
92-93	HOU	79	2330	323	.474	12	.255	143	.715	113	392	191	80	83	801	10.1
93-94	HOU	81	2370	322	.459	44	.324	115	.732	128	440	231	119	75	803	9.9
94-95	HOU	64	2074	240	.447	86	.379	86	.761	81	324	216	94	76	652	10.2
Totals		224	6774	885	.461	142	.346	344	.732	322	1156	638	293	234	2256	10.1

ALLAN HOUSTON

Team: Detroit Pistons
Position: Guard
Height: 6'6" **Weight:** 200
Birthdate: April 4, 1971

NBA Experience: 2 years
College: Tennessee
Acquired: 1st-round pick in 1993 draft
(11th overall)

Background: Kentucky's Mr. Basketball as a prep, Houston was headed to the University of Louisville, where his father Wade was an assistant. Plans changed when the elder Houston was offered the head-coaching job at Tennessee. Allan enjoyed a bang-up career with the Vols, finishing second in SEC history to Pete Maravich in career points. Houston was drafted 11th by the Pistons and, in his second year, he led the team in 3-pointers while scoring 14.5 PPG. He averaged 22 PPG over his last 36 games.

Strengths: Houston is a pure shooter with excellent mechanics. He can score on pull-up jumpers or after spotting up behind a screen. He has range beyond the NBA 3-point line and also possesses the ability to get to the hoop off the dribble. He is a very good free throw shooter. The son of a coach, he knows the game inside and out, spots open men, and handles the ball well.

Weaknesses: Houston was not expected to be a first-rate NBA defensive player, and he is not. His slight build works against him and he has not shown the ability to belly up to his man for long stretches. He does not contribute much on the boards, either. Houston tends to rely too much on his great range rather than attacking the basket and cashing in at the line.

Analysis: Houston had a nice sophomore season, raising hopes that he will one day take over for Joe Dumars as a scoring machine at the two slot. He has the jump shot, the quickness, and the know-how. He put a great deal of off-season effort into his game and it resulted in a much better field goal rate and scoring average in 1994-95. He should only get better.

PLAYER SUMMARY

Will ....hit from deep
Can't ....muscle up
Expect ....good court sense
Don't Expect ....tough defense
Fantasy Value $12-15
Card Value ....8-12¢

COLLEGE STATISTICS

		G	FGP	FTP	RPG	PPG
89-90	TENN	30	.437	.805	2.9	20.3
90-91	TENN	34	.482	.863	3.1	23.7
91-92	TENN	34	.453	.840	5.3	21.1
92-93	TENN	30	.465	.878	4.8	22.3
Totals		128	.460	.849	4.0	21.9

NBA REGULAR-SEASON STATISTICS

			FGs		3-PT FGs		FTs		Rebounds						
		G	MIN	FG	PCT	FG	PCT	FT	PCT	OFF	TOT	AST	STL	BLK	PTS	PPG
93-94	DET	79	1519	272	.405	35	.299	89	.824	19	120	100	34	13	668	8.5
94-95	DET	76	1996	398	.463	158	.424	147	.860	29	167	164	61	14	1101	14.5
Totals		155	3515	670	.438	193	.394	236	.846	48	287	264	95	27	1769	11.4

BYRON HOUSTON

Team: Seattle SuperSonics
Position: Forward
Height: 6'5" **Weight:** 250
Birthdate: November 22, 1969
NBA Experience: 3 years

College: Oklahoma St.
Acquired: Traded from Warriors with Sarunas Marciulionis for Ricky Pierce, draft rights to Carlos Rogers, and two 1995 2nd-round picks, 7/94

Background: Houston was an All-American at Oklahoma State, finishing his career as the school's all-time leader in nine statistical categories, including scoring, rebounding, and blocks. He joined Danny Manning and Wayman Tisdale as the only Big Eight players with 2,000 points, 1,000 rebounds, and 200 blocks. Houston, the last pick of the 1992 first round, has played two seasons with Golden State and one with Seattle.

Strengths: Owner of a body that's been sculpted in the weight room, Houston is extremely strong. He is not afraid to bump and bruise, and he can play physical defense against opponents with seven or eight inches on him. Houston has improved his jump shot.

Weaknesses: When playing significant minutes, the physical Houston was always a high risk to foul out. He tends to use his frame rather than his feet on defense. A bigger problem with Houston, however, has been his inability to score inside. Though his frame resembles that of Charles Barkley, there has been no similarity between their scoring and rebounding prowess. Houston has a long way to go in most areas.

Analysis: Houston was pretty much an extra in a deal that involved Sarunas Marciulionis, Ricky Pierce, and Carlos Rogers before the 1994-95 season. He was a nonfactor for most of the year as Seattle ran off another fine regular season before collapsing in the first round of the playoffs. Houston does not do enough to crack the regular rotation of a team like the Sonics, and he's not improving his skills on the bench.

PLAYER SUMMARY	
Will	hit the weights
Can't	score inside
Expect	physical defense
Don't Expect	another Barkley
Fantasy Value	$0
Card Value	10-15¢

COLLEGE STATISTICS

		G	FGP	FTP	RPG	PPG
88-89	OSU	30	.583	.745	8.4	13.0
89-90	OSU	31	.528	.731	10.0	18.5
90-91	OSU	32	.573	.743	10.5	22.7
91-92	OSU	34	.533	.700	8.6	20.2
Totals		127	.552	.729	9.4	18.7

NBA REGULAR-SEASON STATISTICS

		G	MIN	FGs		3-PT FGs		FTs		Rebounds		AST	STL	BLK	PTS	PPG
				FG	PCT	FG	PCT	FT	PCT	OFF	TOT					
92-93	GS	79	1274	145	.446	2	.286	129	.665	119	315	69	44	43	421	5.3
93-94	GS	71	866	81	.458	1	.143	33	.611	67	194	32	33	31	196	2.8
94-95	SEA	39	258	49	.458	6	.273	28	.737	20	55	6	13	5	132	3.4
Totals		189	2398	275	.452	9	.250	190	.664	206	564	107	90	79	749	4.0

JUWAN HOWARD

Team: Washington Bullets
Position: Forward
Height: 6'9" **Weight:** 250
Birthdate: February 7, 1973

NBA Experience: 1 year
College: Michigan
Acquired: 1st-round pick in 1994 draft
(5th overall)

Background: Howard was the first of Michigan's heralded Fab Five recruiting class to sign with the Wolverines; the others followed. Together, they played in two national championship games before the early exit of Chris Webber allowed Howard to grab more of the spotlight. He went pro after his junior year and was drafted fifth by Washington. Howard led all rookies in rebounding at 8.4 per game and was among the top first-year scorers as well.

Strengths: Howard is a schooled low-post player with the makings of a big-time scorer. He has a nice array of moves in the post and can also step out and knock down 16-foot jumpers. He has a great set of hands and is a good high-post passer. Howard hustles up and down the court and gives a workmanlike effort on the glass. His defense was better than that of most rookies. He is a proven winner who plays with intensity.

Weaknesses: Howard does not have the best springs in his legs and, though he plays solid position defense, is not a threat to block many shots. His shooting range is limited to 16-17 feet and he sinks a poor percentage from the free throw line. He is not much of a ball-handler, and his handling of double-teams in the low post could stand some work.

Analysis: All in all, the Bullets have very few complaints about Howard. He displayed surprising poise and consistency for a first-year player, especially one who signed late with his club. But those players who have watched him play since high school were not as surprised as some of his teammates. "Juwan's more mature than most rookies," said point guard Scott Skiles. "He's got an inner confidence about him."

PLAYER SUMMARY

Will	score inside
Can't	block many shots
Expect	tough rebounding
Don't Expect	passive defense
Fantasy Value	$19-22
Card Value	75¢-$2.00

COLLEGE STATISTICS

		G	FGP	FTP	RPG	PPG
91-92	MICH	34	.450	.688	6.2	11.1
92-93	MICH	36	.506	.700	7.4	14.6
93-94	MICH	30	.557	.675	8.9	20.8
Totals		100	.510	.688	7.5	15.3

NBA REGULAR-SEASON STATISTICS

		G	MIN	FGs FG	FGs PCT	3-PT FGs FG	3-PT FGs PCT	FTs FT	FTs PCT	Rebounds OFF	Rebounds TOT	AST	STL	BLK	PTS	PPG
94-95	WAS	65	2348	455	.489	0	.000	194	.664	184	545	165	52	15	1104	17.0
Totals		65	2348	455	.489	0	.000	194	.664	184	545	165	52	15	1104	17.0

JAY HUMPHRIES

Unrestricted Free Agent
Last Team: Boston Celtics
Position: Guard
Height: 6'3" **Weight:** 185
Birthdate: October 17, 1962

NBA Experience: 11 years
College: Colorado
Acquired: Traded from Jazz with a 1995 2nd-round pick for Blue Edwards, 2/95

Background: An All-Big Eight selection as a senior at Colorado, Humphries set 16 school records, including career assists, steals, and games played. He was drafted by Phoenix in 1984 and has since seen action with Milwaukee, Utah, and Boston over 11 seasons, primarily as a reserve. Knee injuries limited Humphries to 18 games in 1994-95.

Strengths: Humphries is a versatile veteran who can play both guard positions. His all-around abilities include scoring, handling the ball, solid passing, and tough defense. He's good with both hands. He was once Milwaukee's captain and is respected for his leadership.

Weaknesses: Humphries lacks the creativity of the league's more spectacular playmakers and does not shoot consistently enough to be a top-tier off guard. He plays conservatively on offense and does not hit a high percentage of his shots. Bad knees are a big concern at this late stage of his career.

Analysis: Humphries is a steadying hand who plays tough defense and leads by example. He underwent knee surgery before the 1994-95 season, but he was never 100 percent and spent three terms on the injured list. Ironically, he was traded for Blue Edwards for the second time in his career last February.

PLAYER SUMMARY	
Will	play two positions
Can't	overcome knee injuries
Expect	leadership
Don't Expect	peak performance
Fantasy Value	$0
Card Value	5-8¢

COLLEGE STATISTICS

		G	FGP	FTP	APG	PPG
80-81	COLO	28	.517	.660	3.5	6.4
81-82	COLO	27	.467	.639	4.3	10.3
82-83	COLO	28	.501	.632	6.2	14.3
83-84	COLO	29	.509	.788	6.0	15.4
Totals		112	.498	.696	5.0	11.7

NBA REGULAR-SEASON STATISTICS

		G	MIN	FGs FG	FGs PCT	3-PT FGs FG	3-PT FGs PCT	FTs FT	FTs PCT	Rebounds OFF	Rebounds TOT	AST	STL	BLK	PTS	PPG
84-85	PHO	80	2062	279	.446	4	.200	141	.829	32	164	350	107	8	703	8.8
85-86	PHO	82	2733	352	.479	4	.138	197	.767	56	260	526	132	9	905	11.0
86-87	PHO	82	2579	359	.477	5	.185	200	.769	62	260	632	112	9	923	11.3
87-88	PHO/MIL	68	1809	284	.528	3	.167	112	.732	49	174	395	81	5	683	10.0
88-89	MIL	73	2220	345	.483	25	.266	129	.816	70	189	405	142	5	844	11.6
89-90	MIL	81	2818	496	.494	21	.300	224	.786	80	269	472	156	11	1237	15.3
90-91	MIL	80	2726	482	.502	60	.373	191	.799	57	220	538	129	7	1215	15.2
91-92	MIL	71	2261	377	.469	42	.292	195	.783	44	184	466	119	13	991	14.0
92-93	UTA	78	2034	287	.436	15	.200	101	.777	40	143	317	101	11	690	8.8
93-94	UTA	75	1619	233	.436	38	.396	57	.750	35	127	219	65	11	561	7.5
94-95	UTA/BOS	18	201	8	.235	2	.500	2	.500	4	13	19	9	0	20	1.1
Totals		788	23062	3502	.476	219	.297	1549	.782	529	2003	4339	1153	89	8772	11.1

LINDSEY HUNTER

Team: Detroit Pistons
Position: Guard
Height: 6'2" **Weight:** 195
Birthdate: December 3, 1970

NBA Experience: 2 years
College: Alcorn St.; Jackson St.
Acquired: 1st-round pick in 1993 draft
(10th overall)

Background: After playing high school ball in Jackson, Mississippi, Hunter played a year at Alcorn State but transferred to Jackson State for the 1990-91 season. He was an immediate success there and averaged 26.7 PPG as a senior, fifth highest in the nation. The tenth draft choice in 1993, Hunter was a second-team All-Rookie selection who averaged 10.3 PPG for Detroit. However, a broken foot cost him about half of his second season.

Strengths: Hunter is a lightning-quick point guard who can get his shot off against virtually anybody one-on-one. He also has a quick release and outstanding range. A great athlete, Hunter is lethal in the open court and explosive taking the ball to the rim. He knows how to find open men. He has the makings of a fine defensive player, with quick hands and a knack for steals.

Weaknesses: Hunter is a respectable 3-point shooter but has been dismal from closer to the basket. He found it much more difficult to finish his drives to the hoop against bigger NBA defenders. He has yet to shoot even 40 percent from the floor. Hunter does not always play under great control and is still learning the point-guard position. He was strictly a shooting guard in college.

Analysis: Expectations are high in Detroit for Hunter, who has a long way to go before he will be compared to former Piston great Isiah Thomas. Last season could have been a big one in his development, but he broke a foot in December and failed to improve on his rookie performance. Better decision-making, better finishing, and better mid-range shooting are musts for this exciting bundle of Piston potential.

PLAYER SUMMARY	
Will	get past his man
Can't	finish his drives
Expect	quick hands
Don't Expect	conservative play
Fantasy Value	$4-6
Card Value	10-20¢

COLLEGE STATISTICS

		G	FGP	FTP	APG	PPG
88-89	ASU	28	.393	.719	3.5	6.0
90-91	JSU	30	.409	.695	3.5	20.9
91-92	JSU	28	.412	.637	4.3	24.8
92-93	JSU	34	.412	.771	3.4	26.7
Totals		120	.409	.709	3.7	19.9

NBA REGULAR-SEASON STATISTICS

		G	MIN	FGs FG	FGs PCT	3-PT FGs FG	3-PT FGs PCT	FTs FT	FTs PCT	Rebounds OFF	Rebounds TOT	AST	STL	BLK	PTS	PPG
93-94	DET	82	2172	335	.375	69	.333	104	.732	47	189	390	121	10	843	10.3
94-95	DET	42	944	119	.374	36	.333	40	.727	24	75	159	51	7	314	7.5
Totals		124	3116	454	.375	105	.333	144	.731	71	264	549	172	17	1157	9.3

BOBBY HURLEY

Team: Sacramento Kings
Position: Guard
Height: 6'0" **Weight:** 165
Birthdate: June 28, 1971

NBA Experience: 2 years
College: Duke
Acquired: 1st-round pick in 1993 draft
(7th overall)

Background: One of many quality players from St. Anthony's, a prep powerhouse in New Jersey, Hurley went to Duke and did nothing but win. The Blue Devils went to three Final Fours and won two national crowns (1991 and 1992) with Hurley, who set the NCAA career assists record (1,076). A decent rookie year ended in December 1993 when he suffered life-threatening injuries in an auto accident. However, he came back in 1994-95 to play a reserve role with Sacramento.

Strengths: Hurley is a prototypical point guard. He's quick, anticipates well in transition, and can break down a defense with his dribble. He runs a precise offense and delivers the ball. He has good range and craves the ball when the game is on the line. That he came back at all shows how tough this lifelong gym rat truly is. No challenge, it seems, is too steep.

Weaknesses: Hurley's injuries have provided a huge hurdle for him to clear, though he appears to have lost less than most would have guessed. Now he must prove he can shoot the ball at the NBA level. He has yet to break the 40-percent barrier from the field. Finishing his drives has been a problem, as has making his jump shots and keeping pace on defense. He expressed unhappiness about his playing time last year.

Analysis: Hurley, who has been compared to the likes of Bob Cousy and John Stockton, might never approach the level of those greats. But in 1994-95, he was without a doubt the comeback story of the year. His injuries (lung, ribs, shoulder, back, knee) would have discouraged a lot of people. That Hurley is playing basketball at all is a wonderful accomplishment.

PLAYER SUMMARY	
Will	work at his game
Can't	hit a high percentage
Expect	masterful ball-handling
Don't Expect	a quitter
Fantasy Value	$1-3
Card Value	15-30¢

COLLEGE STATISTICS

		G	FGP	FTP	APG	PPG
89-90	DUKE	38	.351	.769	7.6	8.8
90-91	DUKE	39	.423	.728	7.4	11.3
91-92	DUKE	31	.433	.789	7.6	13.2
92-93	DUKE	32	.421	.803	8.2	17.0
Totals		140	.410	.776	7.7	12.4

NBA REGULAR-SEASON STATISTICS

				FGs		3-PT FGs		FTs		Rebounds						
		G	MIN	FG	PCT	FG	PCT	FT	PCT	OFF	TOT	AST	STL	BLK	PTS	PPG
93-94	SAC	19	499	54	.370	2	.125	24	.800	6	34	115	13	1	134	7.1
94-95	SAC	68	1105	103	.363	21	.276	58	.763	14	70	226	29	0	285	4.2
Totals		87	1604	157	.365	23	.250	82	.774	20	104	341	42	1	419	4.8

JIM JACKSON

Team: Dallas Mavericks
Position: Guard
Height: 6'6" **Weight:** 220
Birthdate: October 14, 1970

NBA Experience: 3 years
College: Ohio St.
Acquired: 1st-round pick in 1992 draft
(4th overall)

Background: A rare two-time Mr. Basketball in Ohio, Jackson led Toledo Macomber to a state championship as a senior. He started all 93 games in his three years at Ohio State. Jackson was named Big Ten Freshman of the Year and was a consensus All-American as a junior. After a bitter rookie contract holdout with Dallas, the fourth player taken in the 1992 draft has emerged as one of the NBA's leading scorers.

Strengths: Jackson is a tremendous talent and a big-time scorer. He is blessed with the ability to post up, drive to the hoop, or hit from the perimeter (although he's shaky from 3-point land). He's also the kind of player who can make those around him look better, which is quite a feat with the Mavericks. His passing skills are highly advanced, he gets to the boards, and he has made himself an 80-percent free throw shooter.

Weaknesses: Jackson does not rate as one of the better ball-handling guards in the league. While his shooting has improved, he is still not as consistent from long range as most of the good shooting guards are. He has made a habit of trying to do too much at times.

Analysis: Jackson, who did not play a full 1994-95 season because of an ankle injury, is the kind of player who can help a team like Dallas reach the playoff level and perhaps better. He scored 50 points at Denver last season and averaged 25.7 per game, a number only a few players in the league can match. If he keeps improving at the rate he has been, Jackson will be an All-Star.

PLAYER SUMMARY	
Will	get his points
Can't	save Mavs himself
Expect	an All-Star future
Don't Expect	dribbling wizardry
Fantasy Value	$45-50
Card Value	25-75¢

COLLEGE STATISTICS

		G	FGP	FTP	RPG	PPG
89-90	OSU	30	.499	.785	5.5	16.1
90-91	OSU	31	.517	.752	5.5	18.9
91-92	OSU	32	.493	.811	6.8	22.4
Totals		93	.503	.784	5.9	19.2

NBA REGULAR-SEASON STATISTICS

				FGs		3-PT FGs		FTs		Rebounds						
		G	MIN	FG	PCT	FG	PCT	FT	PCT	OFF	TOT	AST	STL	BLK	PTS	PPG
92-93	DAL	28	938	184	.395	21	.288	68	.739	42	122	131	40	11	457	16.3
93-94	DAL	82	3066	637	.445	17	.283	285	.821	169	388	374	87	25	1576	19.2
94-95	DAL	51	1982	484	.472	35	.318	306	.805	120	260	191	28	12	1309	25.7
Totals		161	5986	1305	.446	73	.300	659	.805	331	770	696	155	48	3342	20.8

MARK JACKSON

Team: Indiana Pacers
Position: Guard
Height: 6'1" **Weight:** 180
Birthdate: April 1, 1965
NBA Experience: 8 years

College: St. John's
Acquired: Traded from Clippers with draft rights to Greg Minor for Pooh Richardson, Malik Sealy, and draft rights to Eric Piatkowski, 6/94

Background: Jackson was a second-team All-American as a senior at St. John's and finished his career with the school's all-time assist record. With the Knicks, he earned the unanimous vote for NBA Rookie of the Year in 1988 and won a trip to the 1989 All-Star Game. He spent two years with the Clippers before a trade took him to Indiana for the 1994-95 season. He averaged a career-low 7.6 PPG.

Strengths: When Jackson drives toward the bucket, he has the ability to either find the open man or make acrobatic shots. His court vision is superb and he remains one of the best passers in the league. He has been a good scorer and has a surprising post-up game. He is also one of the better rebounding point guards.

Weaknesses: Jackson is not regarded as a great outside shooter, and his percentage has fallen rapidly in recent years. Opponents are best off keeping him on the perimeter. Jackson is not among the quicker guards around and defense is not his forte. Inconsistency has crept into his game.

Analysis: Indiana, not pleased with the job Jackson was doing as a starter, sent him to the bench at one point last year in favor of Haywoode Workman. Jackson won the job back, however, and played very well down the stretch as the Pacers won their division. He still has some fire left in him.

PLAYER SUMMARY

Will	make off-balance shots
Can't	rely on his jumper
Expect	pinpoint passing
Don't Expect	a stopper
Fantasy Value	$5-7
Card Value	7-10¢

COLLEGE STATISTICS

		G	FGP	FTP	APG	PPG
83-84	STJ	30	.575	.688	3.6	5.8
84-85	STJ	35	.564	.725	3.1	5.1
85-86	STJ	36	.478	.739	9.1	11.3
86-87	STJ	30	.504	.806	6.4	18.9
Totals		131	.510	.751	5.6	10.1

NBA REGULAR-SEASON STATISTICS

				FGs		3-PT FGs		FTs		Rebounds						
		G	MIN	FG	PCT	FG	PCT	FT	PCT	OFF	TOT	AST	STL	BLK	PTS	PPG
87-88	NY	82	3249	438	.432	32	.254	206	.774	120	396	868	205	6	1114	13.6
88-89	NY	72	2477	479	.467	81	.338	180	.698	106	341	619	139	7	1219	16.9
89-90	NY	82	2428	327	.437	35	.267	120	.727	106	318	604	109	4	809	9.9
90-91	NY	72	1595	250	.492	13	.255	117	.731	62	197	452	60	9	630	8.8
91-92	NY	81	2461	367	.491	11	.256	171	.770	95	305	694	112	13	916	11.3
92-93	LAC	82	3117	459	.486	22	.268	241	.803	129	388	724	136	12	1181	14.4
93-94	LAC	79	2711	331	.452	36	.283	167	.791	107	348	678	120	6	865	10.9
94-95	IND	82	2402	239	.422	27	.310	119	.778	73	306	616	105	16	624	7.6
Totals		632	20440	2890	.460	257	.290	1321	.761	798	2599	5255	986	73	7358	11.6

KEITH JENNINGS

Team: Toronto Raptors
Position: Guard
Height: 5'7" **Weight:** 160
Birthdate: November 2, 1968

NBA Experience: 3 years
College: East Tennessee St.
Acquired: Selected from Warriors in 1995 expansion draft

Background: Nicknamed "Mister," the 5'7" Jennings was named Southern Conference MVP as a junior and senior at East Tennessee State and finished his career as the all-time NCAA leader in 3-point accuracy (.493). Undrafted, he spent the 1991-92 season in Germany. Golden State then signed him but major knee surgery limited his rookie year to eight games. He primarily played backup point guard the last two years. Toronto selected him in the expansion draft.

Strengths: Jennings is as quick as lightning and the ball is attached to his hand. He gets past his man and is a creative playmaker. He relies on the 3-pointer for most of his scoring and almost never misses a free throw. Jennings is a promising NBA defender because of his quickness, and he is tougher than his frame might indicate.

Weaknesses: Size is the obvious drawback, and it's the main reason Jennings was bypassed by everyone in the 1991 draft. Opponents can post him up or shoot over him at will. He's not much help on the boards for obvious reasons. Jennings sports a poor field goal percentage for two reasons. One, about a third of his shots are 3-pointers. Two, he can't score in traffic.

Analysis: Jennings zips around the floor like Muggsy Bogues and has his nights where he plays close to that level. However, his best offensive weapons are the 3-pointer and the free throw, and it's too easy to defend a 3-pointer when you know it's coming. Jennings came into the NBA with a scorer's mind-set, but he has not demonstrated the ability or confidence to get it done. As a reserve playmaker, he'll do.

PLAYER SUMMARY

Will .... spot open men
Can't .... score among giants
Expect .... 3-pointers, playmaking
Don't Expect .... 10 PPG
Fantasy Value $3-5
Card Value ....5-8¢

COLLEGE STATISTICS

		G	FGP	FTP	APG	PPG
87-88	ETST	29	.489	.826	6.3	12.9
88-89	ETST	31	.510	.847	6.5	14.5
89-90	ETST	34	.575	.877	8.7	14.8
90-91	ETST	33	.596	.895	9.1	20.1
Totals		127	.549	.861	7.7	15.7

NBA REGULAR-SEASON STATISTICS

				FGs		3-PT FGs		FTs		Rebounds						
		G	MIN	FG	PCT	FG	PCT	FT	PCT	OFF	TOT	AST	STL	BLK	PTS	PPG
92-93	GS	8	136	25	.595	5	.556	14	.778	2	11	23	4	0	69	8.6
93-94	GS	76	1097	138	.404	56	.371	100	.833	16	89	218	65	0	432	5.7
94-95	GS	80	1722	190	.447	75	.368	134	.876	26	148	373	95	2	589	7.4
Totals		164	2955	353	.436	136	.374	248	.852	44	248	614	164	2	1090	6.6

AVERY JOHNSON

Team: San Antonio Spurs
Position: Guard
Height: 5'11" **Weight:** 180
Birthdate: March 25, 1965

NBA Experience: 7 years
College: Cameron; Southern
Acquired: Signed as a free agent, 7/94

Background: Johnson led the nation in assists as a junior and senior at Southern University, where he was a two-time Southwestern Athletic Conference Player of the Year. He was not drafted but he latched on in Seattle as a free agent and played two years there. He has since seen action for Denver, San Antonio, Houston, and Golden State. The 1994-95 season marked his third stint with the Spurs and was his best yet.

Strengths: A pure point guard, Johnson covers the court like a pinball. His quickness allows him to penetrate and show off his crafty passing skills. He sees the court better than most. His 8.2 APG ranked among the best in the league last season. Johnson is a tough customer who gives it all he's got and has become a significant force.

Weaknesses: The younger brother of former NBA guard Vinnie Johnson is not the shooting machine his brother once was for the Pistons. Avery prefers creating to finishing, although he has made himself a scoring threat. His range does not extend to the 3-point line and he is a poor free throw shooter.

Analysis: Johnson appears to have found his home. He was happy to have played under Don Nelson for a year with Golden State, but he was happier to be back with San Antonio via free agency. Johnson has improved his overall game tremendously in the last few years, becoming a leader on a talented team.

PLAYER SUMMARY

Will ....drive and dish
Can't ....shoot 3-pointers
Expect ....playmaking, leadership
Don't Expect ......free throw accuracy
Fantasy Value $10-13
Card Value ....5-8¢

COLLEGE STATISTICS

		G	FGP	FTP	APG	PPG
84-85	CAM	33	.509	.618	3.2	4.3
86-87	SOUT	31	.439	.615	10.7	7.1
87-88	SOUT	30	.537	.688	13.3	11.4
Totals		94	.497	.641	8.9	7.5

NBA REGULAR-SEASON STATISTICS

				FGs		3-PT FGs		FTs		Rebounds						
		G	MIN	FG	PCT	FG	PCT	FT	PCT	OFF	TOT	AST	STL	BLK	PTS	PPG
88-89	SEA	43	291	29	.349	1	.111	9	.563	11	24	73	21	3	68	1.6
89-90	SEA	53	575	55	.387	1	.250	29	.725	21	43	162	26	1	140	2.6
90-91	DEN/SA	68	959	130	.469	1	.111	59	.678	22	77	230	47	4	320	4.7
91-92	SA/HOU	69	1235	158	.479	4	.267	66	.653	13	80	266	61	9	386	5.6
92-93	SA	75	2030	256	.502	0	.000	144	.791	20	146	561	85	16	656	8.7
93-94	GS	82	2332	356	.492	0	.000	178	.704	41	176	433	113	8	890	10.9
94-95	SA	82	3011	448	.519	3	.136	202	.685	49	208	670	114	13	1101	13.4
Totals		472	10433	1432	.489	10	.127	687	.705	177	754	2395	467	54	3561	7.5

ERVIN JOHNSON

Team: Seattle SuperSonics
Position: Center
Height: 6'11" **Weight:** 245
Birthdate: December 21, 1967

NBA Experience: 2 years
College: New Orleans
Acquired: 1st-round pick in 1993 draft (23rd overall)

Background: Johnson didn't play high school basketball and nearly passed on college too. He bagged groceries in a Baton Rouge, Louisiana, store for nearly three years before soliciting a scholarship from New Orleans, where he set several school records. He was drafted 23rd by Seattle and played sparingly as a rookie. Johnson made 30 starts in 1994-95 and finished second on the Sonics in blocked shots.

Strengths: Johnson is from Block High School, and blocks are what he does best. He averaged more than one per game last season despite playing limited minutes. E.J. was a defensive specialist in college who has done a decent job in the pros as well. He has shown signs of being a solid rebounder at both ends. Johnson gives maximum effort, makes his fouls count, and gets up and down the floor.

Weaknesses: For offense, Johnson is not your man. He is very limited with the ball in his hands, capable of scoring only on tips and simple plays. One problem is his hands; they're small and stiff and they prevent him from catching the ball surely. He does not show good touch from the field or the free throw line. He is not a good passer. In fact, he had 54 turnovers and just 16 assists last season.

Analysis: Johnson will not become a first-rate offensive player at this level. However, he needs to become at least reliable enough to justify an increase in minutes. If he does, Johnson has the potential to really emerge as a defensive specialist, shot-blocker, and rebounder. If he continues to struggle offensively, Johnson will continue to spend most of his time on the bench. His contract expires after 1995-96.

PLAYER SUMMARY	
Will	swat shots
Can't	shoot, score
Expect	low-post coaching
Don't Expect	10 PPG
Fantasy Value	$0
Card Value	7-12¢

COLLEGE STATISTICS

		G	FGP	FTP	RPG	PPG
89-90	NO	32	.579	.561	6.8	6.3
90-91	NO	30	.572	.537	12.2	12.7
91-92	NO	32	.584	.714	11.1	15.4
92-93	NO	29	.619	.674	11.9	18.4
Totals		123	.591	.646	10.5	13.1

NBA REGULAR-SEASON STATISTICS

		G	MIN	FGs FG	FGs PCT	3-PT FGs FG	3-PT FGs PCT	FTs FT	FTs PCT	Rebounds OFF	Rebounds TOT	AST	STL	BLK	PTS	PPG
93-94	SEA	45	280	44	.415	0	.000	29	.630	48	118	7	10	22	117	2.6
94-95	SEA	64	907	85	.443	0	.000	29	.630	101	289	16	17	67	199	3.1
Totals		109	1187	129	.433	0	.000	58	.630	149	407	23	27	89	316	2.9

KEVIN JOHNSON

Team: Phoenix Suns
Position: Guard
Height: 6'1" **Weight:** 190
Birthdate: March 4, 1966
NBA Experience: 8 years
College: California

Acquired: Traded from Cavaliers with Mark West, Tyrone Corbin, 1988 1st- and 2nd-round picks, and a 1989 2nd-round pick for Larry Nance, Mike Sanders, and a 1988 1st-round pick, 2/88

Background: Johnson concluded his college career as California's all-time leader in scoring, assists, and steals. He averaged more than 21 points and 11 assists per game in his first four full seasons with Phoenix. Johnson won the Most Improved Player Award in 1988-89. The three-time All-Star and Dream Team II member has been held back by groin, hamstring, and knee injuries.

Strengths: When Johnson is at full speed, there is virtually no one capable of stopping his one-on-one penetration. Leave him open from outside and he will bury jumpers up to 20 feet. His passing skills are made more devastating because he draws multiple defenders when he goes to the hoop. He is an accomplished defensive thief. Johnson was one of five pro athletes to receive the 1995 Most Caring Athlete Award.

Weaknesses: Injuries are the primary concern. Without him in the lineup, Phoenix is simply not the same team. Johnson is not a good 3-point shooter and he is not much help on the boards.

Analysis: When playing at 100 percent, Johnson is clearly one of the dominant lead guards in the NBA. However, he has spent a considerable amount of time on the injured list recently and his knees have become an issue. His quickness is essential, because a healthy Johnson can take the Suns to great heights.

PLAYER SUMMARY	
Will	penetrate
Can't	stay healthy
Expect	veteran playmaking
Don't Expect	rebounds
Fantasy Value	$35-40
Card Value	10-20¢

COLLEGE STATISTICS

		G	FGP	FTP	APG	PPG
83-84	CAL	28	.510	.721	2.3	9.7
84-85	CAL	27	.450	.662	4.1	12.9
85-86	CAL	29	.490	.815	6.0	15.6
86-87	CAL	34	.471	.819	5.0	17.2
Totals		118	.477	.757	4.4	14.0

NBA REGULAR-SEASON STATISTICS

		G	MIN	FGs FG	FGs PCT	3-PT FGs FG	3-PT FGs PCT	FTs FT	FTs PCT	Rebounds OFF	Rebounds TOT	AST	STL	BLK	PTS	PPG
87-88	CLE/PHO	80	1917	275	.461	5	.208	177	.839	36	191	437	103	24	732	9.1
88-89	PHO	81	3179	570	.505	2	.091	508	.882	46	340	991	135	24	1650	20.4
89-90	PHO	74	2782	578	.499	8	.195	501	.838	42	270	846	95	14	1665	22.5
90-91	PHO	77	2772	591	.516	9	.205	519	.843	54	271	781	163	11	1710	22.2
91-92	PHO	78	2899	539	.479	10	.217	448	.807	61	292	836	116	23	1536	19.7
92-93	PHO	49	1643	282	.499	1	.125	226	.819	30	104	384	85	20	791	16.1
93-94	PHO	67	2449	477	.487	6	.222	380	.819	55	167	637	125	10	1340	20.0
94-95	PHO	47	1352	246	.470	4	.154	234	.810	32	115	360	47	18	730	15.5
Totals		553	18993	3558	.493	45	.189	2993	.835	356	1750	5272	869	144	10154	18.4

LARRY JOHNSON

Team: Charlotte Hornets
Position: Forward
Height: 6'7" **Weight:** 263
Birthdate: March 14, 1969

NBA Experience: 4 years
College: Odessa; Nevada-Las Vegas
Acquired: 1st-round pick in 1991 draft
(1st overall)

Background: L.J. originally signed with Southern Methodist, but he ended up at Odessa (Texas) Junior College after SMU officials questioned his retake of the SAT. UNLV won the national title in his first season and he was the nation's consensus Player of the Year in 1990-91. He was drafted No. 1 overall by Charlotte in 1991 and won Rookie of the Year honors. He has since played in two All-Star Games and for Dream Team II.

Strengths: Johnson possesses incredible strength that carries over into virtually every aspect of the game. He can't be moved once he gets position on the low blocks. He scores in the post and can shoot jumpers with 3-point range. He's a superb passer, rebounds with a vengeance, and is a capable defensive player. L.J. is one of the game's most popular personalities.

Weaknesses: A bad back kept Johnson on the injured list for much of the 1993-94 season and out of the 1994 All-Star Game. He has bounced back nicely from surgery but was not as dominant on the boards last season as he is capable of being. Johnson is a physical player, but defense would not be considered his strength. He is not a productive shot-blocker.

Analysis: Johnson fought through a rigorous off-season regimen to strengthen his back and surprised some people with a strong return in 1994-95. Many wondered whether he could regain his form. His numbers are down from those of his second season, but keep in mind that his teammates are a lot better. He has even added the 3-point shot to his arsenal.

PLAYER SUMMARY

Will ....score inside and out
Can't ....sky for blocks
Expect ....an All-Star regular
Don't Expect..................shy shooting
Fantasy Value $40-45
Card Value ....25-50¢

COLLEGE STATISTICS

		G	FGP	FTP	RPG	PPG
87-88	ODE	35	.649	.794	12.3	22.3
88-89	ODE	35	.653	.760	10.9	29.8
89-90	UNLV	40	.624	.767	11.4	20.6
90-91	UNLV	35	.662	.818	10.9	22.7
Totals		145	.648	.780	11.4	23.7

NBA REGULAR-SEASON STATISTICS

		G	MIN	FGs FG	FGs PCT	3-PT FGs FG	3-PT FGs PCT	FTs FT	FTs PCT	Rebounds OFF	Rebounds TOT	AST	STL	BLK	PTS	PPG
91-92	CHA	82	3047	616	.490	5	.227	339	.829	323	899	292	81	51	1576	19.2
92-93	CHA	82	3323	728	.526	18	.254	336	.767	281	864	353	53	27	1810	22.1
93-94	CHA	51	1757	346	.515	5	.238	137	.695	143	448	184	29	14	834	16.4
94-95	CHA	81	3234	585	.480	81	.386	274	.774	190	585	369	78	28	1525	18.8
Totals		296	11361	2275	.502	109	.336	1086	.777	937	2796	1198	241	120	5745	19.4

EDDIE JONES

Team: Los Angeles Lakers
Position: Guard/Forward
Height: 6'6" **Weight:** 190
Birthdate: October 20, 1971

NBA Experience: 1 year
College: Temple
Acquired: 1st-round pick in 1994 draft
(10th overall)

Background: Jones sat out his freshman year at Temple for academic reasons before easing into his college career. A two-year starter, he became the Atlantic 10 Conference's best player and finished his career as the first player in Temple history with 100 assists and 100 blocked shots. Jones, drafted tenth overall in 1994, won a starting job in the Lakers' training camp and was one of the top rookie scorers and assist men despite missing more than a month with a shoulder injury.

Strengths: Jones is extraordinarily quick and loves to run. He flies up-court and is often rewarded with crowd-pleasing slams. He is a splendid leaper. Jones also uses his quickness and wide wingspan to block shots and come up with steals. He has the ability to create his own shot and is comfortable from 3-point range. He can be productive at big guard or small forward. Jones is fearless.

Weaknesses: Jones is a streaky player in most regards. He is capable of hitting for 30 points one night and dropping off to single digits the next. His jump shot has plenty of potential but is not yet as reliable as it could be. Slight in build, Jones can be worn down physically by the more bruising forwards. He is not a great ball-handler.

Analysis: A starter in his first NBA game, Jones enjoyed a highly successful rookie year and was a big reason for the Lakers' revival. Said team V.P. Jerry West: "We're impressed with not just his basketball ability. It's his character too. He's a great kid." Jones sprained his right shoulder in February and was out until late March, but that was one of the only things that could slow down this exciting young athlete.

PLAYER SUMMARY	
Will	play above the rim
Can't	dribble through pressure
Expect	transition highlights
Don't Expect	less than 10 PPG
Fantasy Value	$17-20
Card Value	75¢-$2.00

COLLEGE STATISTICS

		G	FGP	FTP	RPG	PPG
91-92	TEMP	29	.437	.547	4.2	11.4
92-93	TEMP	32	.458	.604	7.0	17.0
93-94	TEMP	31	.470	.662	6.8	19.2
Totals		92	.458	.614	6.1	16.0

NBA REGULAR-SEASON STATISTICS

			FGs		3-PT FGs		FTs		Rebounds						
	G	MIN	FG	PCT	FG	PCT	FT	PCT	OFF	TOT	AST	STL	BLK	PTS	PPG
94-95 LAL	64	1981	342	.460	91	.370	122	.722	79	249	128	131	41	897	14.0
Totals	64	1981	342	.460	91	.370	122	.722	79	249	128	131	41	897	14.0

POPEYE JONES

Team: Dallas Mavericks
Position: Forward
Height: 6'8" **Weight:** 250
Birthdate: June 17, 1970
NBA Experience: 2 years

College: Murray St.
Acquired: Draft rights traded from Rockets for draft rights to Eric Riley, 6/93

Background: A two-time Ohio Valley Conference Player of the Year and an NCAA Tournament regular at Murray State, Jones was drafted by Houston in the second round in 1992. He spent his first professional season in the Italian A2 League, averaging 21.1 points and 13.3 rebounds a game. His rights were traded to Dallas and he set a Mavs rookie record for rebounding. He was the league's 12th-best rebounder in 1994-95.

Strengths: He's Popeye the rebounding man. Jones has a massive frame and knows how to get to the boards on both ends of the floor. He really works at it and is quick off his feet for a big man. Jones has a great set of hands and there's a pretty good hook shot in his bag of tricks. He is also an outstanding passer. He has improved his defense and is a team player.

Weaknesses: Although he scored a ton of points in college and in Italy, Jones is not an offensive force. His outside shot is unreliable and his range very limited. He does not display power moves inside. His field goal percentage is atrocious for an inside player. Jones does not block many shots and he picks up a lot of fouls. His weight problem appears to be behind him.

Analysis: Jones became a double-figure rebounder and scorer during his second season, but he is much better at the former than the latter. He craves rebounds more than points. "He is our Dennis Rodman," Dallas teammate Jamal Mashburn has said. Jones has not reached that level quite yet, but he has shed 60 pounds since his freshman year of college and seems determined to make an impact.

PLAYER SUMMARY	
Will	crash the boards
Can't	shoot straight
Expect	10 RPG
Don't Expect	fluid moves
Fantasy Value	$1
Card Value	7-12¢

COLLEGE STATISTICS

		G	FGP	FTP	RPG	PPG
88-89	MSU	30	.489	.754	4.6	5.8
89-90	MSU	30	.500	.757	11.2	19.5
90-91	MSU	33	.493	.711	14.2	20.2
91-92	MSU	30	.488	.778	14.4	21.1
Totals		123	.493	.751	11.2	16.7

NBA REGULAR-SEASON STATISTICS

				FGs		3-PT FGs		FTs		Rebounds						
		G	MIN	FG	PCT	FG	PCT	FT	PCT	OFF	TOT	AST	STL	BLK	PTS	PPG
93-94	DAL	81	1773	195	.479	0	.000	78	.729	299	605	99	61	31	468	5.8
94-95	DAL	80	2385	372	.443	1	.083	80	.645	329	844	163	35	27	825	10.3
Totals		161	4158	567	.455	1	.077	158	.684	628	1449	262	96	58	1293	8.0

MICHAEL JORDAN

Team: Chicago Bulls
Position: Guard
Height: 6'6" **Weight:** 198
Birthdate: February 17, 1963

NBA Experience: 10 years
College: North Carolina
Acquired: 1st-round pick in 1984 draft (3rd overall)

Background: Jordan hit the winning basket in the 1982 NCAA championship game and went on to earn consensus All-America recognition. He earned NBA Rookie of the Year honors, was an All-Star in his first nine seasons, and has won three NBA championships, three league MVP Awards, three Finals MVP honors, and two Olympic golds. He retired before the 1993-94 season but returned in March of 1995.

Strengths: Jordan is one of the most intense competitors in the history of the sport. He plays virtually every aspect of the game at its highest level. Sometimes his outstanding defensive ability, uncanny playmaking, and aggressive rebounding are overshadowed by his unparalleled drives and shot-making.

Weaknesses: Hitting the curveball, hitting for power, and hitting the cutoff man are some of the rare things Jordan cannot do. His attempt at professional baseball stalled in Double-A after the outfielder barely hoisted his average above the .200 mark.

Analysis: Jordan is considered by his peers to be the greatest basketball player in history. His career scoring average is the highest in NBA/ABA annals, and he led the Bulls to three consecutive crowns before he retired for more than a year and a half. In his fifth game back, Jordan lit up the Knicks for a staggering 55 points. His return has rejuvenated the league.

PLAYER SUMMARY	
Will	dominate games
Can't	stand losing
Expect	Hall of Fame honors
Don't Expect	more baseball
Fantasy Value	$75-80
Card Value	$1.50-5.00

COLLEGE STATISTICS

		G	FGP	FTP	RPG	PPG
81-82	NC	34	.534	.722	4.4	13.5
82-83	NC	36	.535	.737	5.5	20.0
83-84	NC	31	.551	.779	5.3	19.6
Totals		101	.465	.748	5.0	17.7

NBA REGULAR-SEASON STATISTICS

		G	MIN	FGs FG	FGs PCT	3-PT FGs FG	3-PT FGs PCT	FTs FT	FTs PCT	Rebounds OFF	Rebounds TOT	AST	STL	BLK	PTS	PPG
84-85	CHI	82	3144	837	.515	9	.173	630	.845	167	534	481	196	69	2313	28.2
85-86	CHI	18	451	150	.457	3	.167	105	.840	23	64	53	37	21	408	22.7
86-87	CHI	82	3281	1098	.482	12	.182	833	.857	166	430	377	236	125	3041	37.1
87-88	CHI	82	3311	1069	.535	7	.132	723	.841	139	449	485	259	131	2868	35.0
88-89	CHI	81	3255	966	.538	27	.276	674	.850	149	652	650	234	65	2633	32.5
89-90	CHI	82	3197	1034	.526	92	.376	593	.848	143	565	519	227	54	2753	33.6
90-91	CHI	82	3034	990	.539	29	.312	571	.851	118	492	453	223	83	2580	31.5
91-92	CHI	80	3102	943	.519	27	.270	491	.832	91	511	489	182	75	2404	30.0
92-93	CHI	78	3067	992	.495	81	.352	476	.837	135	522	428	221	61	2541	32.6
94-95	CHI	17	668	166	.411	16	.500	109	.801	25	117	90	30	13	457	26.9
Totals		684	26510	8245	.514	303	.307	5205	.845	1156	4336	4025	1845	697	21998	32.2

ADAM KEEFE

Team: Utah Jazz
Position: Forward
Height: 6'9" **Weight:** 240
Birthdate: February 22, 1970
NBA Experience: 3 years

College: Stanford
Acquired: Traded from Hawks for Tyrone Corbin and a 1995 2nd-round pick, 9/94

Background: Keefe was Stanford's rock in the middle, a three-time Pac-10 rebounding champion. The MVP of the NIT as a junior, Keefe was also a world-class volleyball player. The tenth choice in the 1992 draft, Keefe played in 82 games as an Atlanta rookie before struggling for time the next season. He was traded to Utah before the 1994-95 campaign and finished second on the Jazz in field goal percentage (.577).

Strengths: Keefe is big, strong, and smart. He plays within himself and thus has raised his field goal percentage to new heights. He bangs the boards aggressively and is especially adept on the offensive glass. He is not afraid of contact and he gets to the free throw line. He is also a pretty good face-up shooter within his limited range. Keefe is a team player.

Weaknesses: Keefe is very limited in his back-to-the-basket moves and is a step slow when he goes to the hoop. He often struggles to convert in traffic and gets his share of shots blocked. He gets most of his points by hitting the boards and running the floor. Keefe does not intimidate defensively.

Analysis: The big redhead is clearly not one of the ten best players in his draft class. However, he enjoyed something of a revival after being traded to the Jazz for Tyrone Corbin. He averaged 4.4 rebounds in just 16.9 minutes per game and pulled down 15 boards in a game against Indiana. He has developed a better feel for the game and is becoming an intelligent role-player off the bench. His high field goal percentage is impressive.

PLAYER SUMMARY

Will ....hit the boards
Can't.........................dominate inside
Expect ....a role-playing reserve
Don't Expect.....................many starts
Fantasy Value $1
Card Value ....5-10¢

COLLEGE STATISTICS

		G	FGP	FTP	RPG	PPG
88-89	STAN	33	.633	.689	5.4	8.4
89-90	STAN	30	.627	.725	9.1	20.0
90-91	STAN	33	.609	.760	9.5	21.5
91-92	STAN	29	.564	.746	12.2	25.3
Totals		125	.600	.736	9.0	18.6

NBA REGULAR-SEASON STATISTICS

				FGs		3-PT FGs		FTs		Rebounds						
		G	MIN	FG	PCT	FG	PCT	FT	PCT	OFF	TOT	AST	STL	BLK	PTS	PPG
92-93	ATL	82	1549	188	.500	0	.000	166	.700	171	432	80	57	16	542	6.6
93-94	ATL	63	763	96	.451	0	.000	81	.730	77	201	34	20	9	273	4.3
94-95	UTA	75	1270	172	.577	0	.000	117	.676	135	327	30	36	25	461	6.1
Totals		220	3582	456	.514	0	.000	364	.699	383	960	144	113	50	1276	5.8

SHAWN KEMP

Team: Seattle SuperSonics
Position: Forward
Height: 6'10" **Weight:** 245
Birthdate: November 26, 1969

NBA Experience: 6 years
College: None
Acquired: 1st-round pick in 1989 draft
(17th overall)

Background: Kemp never played a minute of college basketball. He was a Prop 48 casualty at Kentucky, transferred to Trinity Junior College amid scrutiny, then opted for the draft. He became a starter for the Sonics in his second season and has played in the last three All-Star Games. A Dream Team II veteran, Kemp rates among the league leaders in rebounding, field goal percentage, shot-blocking, and dunks.

Strengths: Kemp's dunks are almost a nightly feature on the TV sports highlights. He is blessed with great quickness to the hoop and dominating physical ability. He is strong and has a great vertical leap. Kemp is one of the best rebounding forwards in basketball and he also plays physical defense and blocks shots. He scores, shoots a great percentage, and gets to the line.

Weaknesses: Kemp's biggest weakness is in the area of fouling. He has been averaging about ten disqualifications per season because of his relentless and physical play. He needs to learn how to turn it down a notch when his man's not a threat to score. Kemp also commits an inordinate number of turnovers.

Analysis: Kemp, a crowd-pleaser from the moment he stepped onto the NBA hardwood, has been an integral part in Seattle's rise to prominence. He is a franchise player who started in the All-Star Game last year and will make several return appearances. He is capable of dominating the opposition on any given night. He energizes crowds and throws down dunks like few others can.

PLAYER SUMMARY	
Will	electrify crowds
Can't	avoid fouling
Expect	10 RPG, 18 PPG
Don't Expect	3-pointers
Fantasy Value	$50-55
Card Value	30-75¢

COLLEGE STATISTICS

—DID NOT PLAY—

NBA REGULAR-SEASON STATISTICS

		G	MIN	FGs FG	FGs PCT	3-PT FGs FG	3-PT FGs PCT	FTs FT	FTs PCT	Rebounds OFF	Rebounds TOT	AST	STL	BLK	PTS	PPG
89-90	SEA	81	1120	203	.479	2	.167	117	.736	146	346	26	47	70	525	6.5
90-91	SEA	81	2442	462	.508	2	.167	288	.661	267	679	144	77	123	1214	15.0
91-92	SEA	64	1808	362	.504	0	.000	270	.748	264	665	86	70	124	994	15.5
92-93	SEA	78	2582	515	.492	0	.000	358	.712	287	833	155	119	146	1388	17.8
93-94	SEA	79	2597	533	.538	1	.250	364	.741	312	851	207	142	166	1431	18.1
94-95	SEA	82	2679	545	.547	2	.286	438	.749	318	893	149	102	122	1530	18.7
Totals		465	13228	2620	.515	7	.167	1835	.724	1594	4267	767	557	751	7082	15.2

STEVE KERR

Team: Chicago Bulls
Position: Guard
Height: 6'3" **Weight:** 180
Birthdate: September 27, 1965

NBA Experience: 7 years
College: Arizona
Acquired: Signed as a free agent, 9/93

Background: Kerr was a second-team All-American as a senior at Arizona, where he set a Pac-10 record in 1987-88 by shooting an incredible .573 from 3-point range. He is the NBA's all-time leader in 3-point field goal percentage, although he has served mostly in a reserve role with Phoenix, Cleveland, Orlando, and Chicago. Kerr set an NBA season record in 3-point percentage in 1994-95 (.524).

Strengths: Kerr can flat-out shoot the ball from virtually anywhere. He hit better than 50 percent of his 3-point shots when the arc was deeper in 1989-90. The shorter distance adopted last year is a layup for him. Kerr is also a good free throw shooter. He handles the ball, finds open men, and works his tail off.

Weaknesses: Kerr is not the most creative player around, largely because he is a step slower than the average NBA guard. Take away his open looks at the basket and he has a hard time. He hustles defensively but again is limited by his lack of speed. He has never been quite good enough to start.

Analysis: No one has hit long-range jumpers at a better rate than Kerr during his career. He has come off the bench in his two years with Chicago. Thanks to Kerr and B.J. Armstrong, few teams could boast a better long-range tandem over the last two years. Kerr is a coach's dream, the kind of player who leads by example and never complains.

PLAYER SUMMARY

Will ....hit half his treys
Can't............................create his shot
Expect ....a steady hand
Don't Expect ....starts
Fantasy Value $1-3
Card Value ....5-8¢

COLLEGE STATISTICS

		G	FGP	FTP	RPG	PPG
83-84	ARIZ	28	.516	.692	1.2	7.1
84-85	ARIZ	31	.568	.803	2.4	10.0
85-86	ARIZ	32	.540	.899	3.2	14.4
87-88	ARIZ	38	.559	.824	2.0	12.6
Totals		129	.548	.815	2.2	11.2

NBA REGULAR-SEASON STATISTICS

		G	MIN	FGs FG	FGs PCT	3-PT FGs FG	3-PT FGs PCT	FTs FT	FTs PCT	Rebounds OFF	Rebounds TOT	AST	STL	BLK	PTS	PPG
88-89	PHO	26	157	20	.435	8	.471	6	.667	3	17	24	7	0	54	2.1
89-90	CLE	78	1664	192	.444	73	.507	63	.863	12	98	248	45	7	520	6.7
90-91	CLE	57	905	99	.444	28	.452	45	.849	5	37	131	29	4	271	4.8
91-92	CLE	48	847	121	.511	32	.432	45	.833	14	78	110	27	10	319	6.6
92-93	CLE/ORL	52	481	53	.434	6	.231	22	.917	5	45	70	10	1	134	2.6
93-94	CHI	82	2036	287	.497	52	.419	83	.856	26	131	210	75	3	709	8.6
94-95	CHI	82	1839	261	.527	89	.524	63	.778	20	119	151	44	3	674	8.2
Totals		425	7929	1033	.485	288	.467	327	.836	85	525	944	237	28	2681	6.3

JEROME KERSEY

Team: Toronto Raptors
Position: Forward
Height: 6'7" **Weight:** 225
Birthdate: June 26, 1962

NBA Experience: 11 years
College: Longwood College
Acquired: Selected from Trail Blazers in 1995 expansion draft

Background: Kersey rewrote the record books at NAIA Longwood College, where he became the all-time leader in points, rebounds, steals, and blocked shots. Kersey started his pro career modestly before receiving consideration for the Most Improved Player Award in 1987-88, when he tallied 19.2 PPG. His scoring then dipped for six straight years before he averaged 8.1 PPG last season. Toronto grabbed him in the '95 expansion draft.

Strengths: Kersey remains an exciting player in the open court. He punctuates the fastbreak for many of his points and chases down opponents to block their layup attempts. He has been an above-average rebounder for a small forward. Kersey hustles and knows how to score.

Weaknesses: Kersey has always struggled with shot selection, and his field goal percentage reflects it. His conversion rate continues to decline (.415 last season). He is horribly inconsistent and does not know when to give up the ball. He has lost some of his explosiveness and is now used in a reserve role.

Analysis: Kersey finally reversed the slide of his scoring average, but he cannot do the same for his career. Since losing his starting job to Cliff Robinson three years ago, Kersey has struggled. He no longer possesses the great quickness and scoring ability to cause much trouble for opponents.

PLAYER SUMMARY	
Will	run the floor
Can't	pass up shots
Expect	reserve minutes
Don't Expect	high percentages
Fantasy Value	$1
Card Value	5-8¢

COLLEGE STATISTICS

		G	FGP	FTP	RPG	PPG
80-81	LONG	28	.629	.586	8.9	16.9
81-82	LONG	23	.585	.633	11.3	17.0
82-83	LONG	25	.560	.608	10.8	14.6
83-84	LONG	27	.521	.606	14.2	19.6
Totals		103	.570	.607	11.3	17.0

NBA REGULAR-SEASON STATISTICS

				FGs		3-PT FGs		FTs		Rebounds						
		G	MIN	FG	PCT	FG	PCT	FT	PCT	OFF	TOT	AST	STL	BLK	PTS	PPG
84-85	POR	77	958	178	.478	0	.000	117	.646	95	206	63	49	29	473	6.1
85-86	POR	79	1217	258	.549	0	.000	156	.681	137	293	83	85	32	672	8.5
86-87	POR	82	2088	373	.509	1	.043	262	.720	201	496	194	122	77	1009	12.3
87-88	POR	79	2888	611	.499	3	.200	291	.735	211	657	243	127	65	1516	19.2
88-89	POR	76	2716	533	.469	6	.286	258	.694	246	629	243	137	84	1330	17.5
89-90	POR	82	2843	519	.478	3	.150	269	.690	251	690	188	121	63	1310	16.0
90-91	POR	73	2359	424	.478	4	.308	232	.709	169	481	227	101	76	1084	14.8
91-92	POR	77	2553	398	.467	1	.125	174	.664	241	633	243	114	71	971	12.6
92-93	POR	65	1719	281	.438	8	.286	116	.634	126	406	121	80	41	686	10.6
93-94	POR	78	1276	203	.433	1	.125	101	.748	130	331	75	71	49	508	6.5
94-95	POR	63	1143	203	.415	7	.259	95	.766	93	256	82	52	35	508	8.1
Totals		831	21760	3981	.476	34	.198	2071	.699	1900	5078	1762	1059	622	10067	12.1

JASON KIDD

Team: Dallas Mavericks
Position: Guard
Height: 6'4" **Weight:** 205
Birthdate: March 23, 1973

NBA Experience: 1 year
College: California
Acquired: 1st-round pick in 1994 draft
(2nd overall)

Background: A hotly recruited prep star in Oakland, California, Kidd stayed close to home with the Cal Bears and led the nation in steals per game as a freshman. He was the country's top assist man as a sophomore, earning All-America and Pac-10 Player of the Year honors. He skipped his final two college seasons to join Dallas as the second overall draft pick. An impact player, Kidd led all NBA rookies in assists and steals.

Strengths: Kidd was considered the NBA's best pure point-guard prospect in several years and he has not disappointed. He has good quickness and strength, uncanny playmaking skills, and a knack for delivering the ball to the right place at the right time. He has been compared quite favorably to the likes of Magic Johnson and John Stockton. Kidd brings good size and rebounding ability to the backcourt and plays tough defense.

Weaknesses: The most glaring deficiency in this rising star's game is his perimeter shooting. He is not reliable from the outside, which begs defenders to sag. Though he has 3-point range, Kidd connected on less than 30 percent of his attempts from the NBA arc. He has also been involved in some off-the-court troubles during his young career.

Analysis: Kidd could wage an assault on Stockton's growing career assist record before he is through. He already rates as one of the most creative playmakers and precise passers in the game after just one year. He nearly had a triple-double in his first NBA game with ten points, 11 assists, and nine steals. He did not let up after that. If Kidd can develop a consistent jump shot, he will leave defenders absolutely helpless.

PLAYER SUMMARY	
Will	make things happen
Can't	rely on his jumper
Expect	first-rate playmaking
Don't Expect	soft defense
Fantasy Value	$20-25
Card Value	$2.50-5.00

COLLEGE STATISTICS

		G	FGP	FTP	APG	PPG
92-93	CAL	29	.463	.657	7.7	13.0
93-94	CAL	30	.472	.692	9.1	16.7
Totals		59	.468	.677	8.4	14.9

NBA REGULAR-SEASON STATISTICS

				FGs		3-PT FGs		FTs		Rebounds						
		G	MIN	FG	PCT	FG	PCT	FT	PCT	OFF	TOT	AST	STL	BLK	PTS	PPG
94-95	DAL	79	2668	330	.385	70	.272	192	.698	152	430	607	151	24	922	11.7
Totals		79	2668	330	.385	70	.272	192	.698	152	430	607	151	24	922	11.7

STACEY KING

Unrestricted Free Agent
Last Team: Minnesota Timberwolves
Position: Forward/Center
Height: 6'11" **Weight:** 250
Birthdate: January 29, 1967

NBA Experience: 6 years
College: Oklahoma
Acquired: Traded from Bulls for Luc Longley, 2/94

Background: King earned All-America and Big Eight Player of the Year honors as a senior at Oklahoma, where he led the conference in scoring and rebounding as a senior. He was named second-team All-Rookie with Chicago in 1989-90. He was inconsistent with the Bulls but was a member of three straight NBA title teams. He spent the last year and a half with Minnesota, playing mainly as a reserve last season. The Wolves did not offer him a contract after last season.

Strengths: King runs the floor well for a big man and has shown some promise offensively. He looks to score whenever he touches the ball. He possesses a decent hook shot and a turnaround jumper in the post. While not a banger on defense, King does a decent job of pressuring the ball.

Weaknesses: King's biggest problem has been his inability to control the boards. He is not physical in the post on either end of the court and gets murdered on the glass by opposing centers. Inconsistency in all aspects of the game has dragged him down. He takes bad shots, almost never looks for open teammates, and shoots a poor percentage from the field and line.

Analysis: King was Minnesota's starting center to close the 1993-94 season, but last year he resumed his familiar post on the bench. The acquisition of Sean Rooks gave the Timberwolves a better all-around player in the pivot. King has simply never panned out as a productive NBA center. Ankle and knee injuries have also slowed his progress.

PLAYER SUMMARY	
Will	run the floor
Can't	dominate the glass
Expect	reserve minutes
Don't Expect	good shooting
Fantasy Value	$0
Card Value	5-8¢

COLLEGE STATISTICS

		G	FGP	FTP	RPG	PPG
85-86	OKLA	14	.388	.744	3.8	6.0
86-87	OKLA	28	.438	.621	3.9	7.0
87-88	OKLA	39	.543	.675	8.5	22.3
88-89	OKLA	33	.524	.718	10.1	26.0
Totals		114	.516	.690	7.2	17.6

NBA REGULAR-SEASON STATISTICS

		G	MIN	FGs FG	FGs PCT	3-PT FGs FG	3-PT FGs PCT	FTs FT	FTs PCT	Rebounds OFF	Rebounds TOT	AST	STL	BLK	PTS	PPG
89-90	CHI	82	1777	267	.504	0	.000	194	.727	169	384	87	38	58	728	8.9
90-91	CHI	76	1198	156	.467	0	.000	107	.704	72	208	65	24	42	419	5.5
91-92	CHI	79	1268	215	.506	2	.400	119	.753	87	205	77	21	25	551	7.0
92-93	CHI	76	1059	160	.471	2	.333	86	.705	105	207	71	26	20	408	5.4
93-94	CHI/MIN	49	1053	146	.428	0	.000	93	.684	90	241	58	31	42	385	7.9
94-95	MIN	50	792	99	.467	0	.000	68	.667	54	165	26	24	20	266	5.3
Totals		412	7147	1043	.478	4	.235	667	.712	577	1410	384	164	207	2757	6.7

JOE KLEINE

Team: Phoenix Suns
Position: Center
Height: 7'0" **Weight:** 271
Birthdate: January 4, 1962

NBA Experience: 10 years
College: Notre Dame; Arkansas
Acquired: Signed as a free agent, 8/93

Background: Kleine, who transferred to Arkansas after a year at Notre Dame, led the Razorbacks in scoring as a junior and senior and was a member of the gold medal-winning 1984 U.S. Olympic team. He averaged 9.8 PPG with Sacramento in 1987-88, his best statistical year. He has mainly been a reserve in four-plus years with Boston and two with Phoenix.

Strengths: Opponents cringe when Kleine checks into the game. He uses his huge body to put the hurt on people. He rebounds, sets hard picks, and plays a style of defense that results in bruises. He shoots with decent range and hits his free throws. His work ethic and attitude are exemplary.

Weaknesses: Finesse has no place in Kleine's game. He possesses poor hands, should be forbidden to dribble the ball, and is a below-average passer. His main role in the offense is as a screen-setter. Foul trouble would be a problem if he saw more than about 12 minutes per game.

Analysis: Kleine is a favorite of teammates, fans, and coaches because he does whatever is asked of him. He rebounds, plays defense, throws his weight around, and gets the most out of his six fouls. Kleine is better suited to coming off the bench than starting, although he played with the Suns' first team much of last season.

PLAYER SUMMARY	
Will	do the dirty work
Can't	handle the ball
Expect	bumps and bruises
Don't Expect	even 5 PPG
Fantasy Value	$0
Card Value	5-7¢

COLLEGE STATISTICS

		G	FGP	FTP	RPG	PPG
80-81	ND	29	.640	.750	2.4	2.6
81-82	ARK	30	.537	.633	7.3	13.3
83-84	ARK	32	.595	.773	9.2	18.2
84-85	ARK	35	.607	.720	8.4	22.1
Totals		126	.587	.723	7.0	14.5

NBA REGULAR-SEASON STATISTICS

		G	MIN	FGs FG	FGs PCT	3-PT FGs FG	3-PT FGs PCT	FTs FT	FTs PCT	Rebounds OFF	Rebounds TOT	AST	STL	BLK	PTS	PPG
85-86	SAC	80	1180	160	.465	0	.000	94	.723	113	373	46	24	34	414	5.2
86-87	SAC	79	1658	256	.471	0	.000	110	.786	173	483	71	35	30	622	7.9
87-88	SAC	82	1999	324	.472	0	.000	153	.814	179	579	93	28	59	801	9.8
88-89	SAC/BOS	75	1411	175	.405	0	.000	134	.882	124	378	67	33	23	484	6.5
89-90	BOS	81	1365	176	.480	0	.000	83	.830	117	355	46	15	27	435	5.4
90-91	BOS	72	850	102	.468	0	.000	54	.783	71	244	21	15	14	258	3.6
91-92	BOS	70	991	144	.491	4	.500	34	.708	94	296	32	23	14	326	4.7
92-93	BOS	78	1129	108	.404	0	.000	41	.707	113	346	39	17	17	257	3.3
93-94	PHO	74	848	125	.488	5	.455	30	.769	50	193	45	14	19	285	3.9
94-95	PHO	75	968	119	.449	0	.000	42	.857	82	259	39	14	18	280	3.7
Totals		766	12399	1689	.460	9	.250	775	.797	1116	3506	499	218	255	4162	5.4

NEGELE KNIGHT

Unrestricted Free Agent
Last Team: Detroit Pistons
Position: Guard
Height: 6'1" **Weight:** 182
Birthdate: March 6, 1967

NBA Experience: 5 years
College: Dayton
Acquired: Signed as a free agent,
12/94

Background: Knight left Dayton as the school's all-time assists leader. He enjoyed some success backing up Kevin Johnson in three-plus seasons in Phoenix before a 1993-94 trade took him to San Antonio. He played three games with Portland last season before being released and picked up by Detroit. Knight made 17 starts but averaged a career-low 4.2 PPG.

Strengths: Knight is very quick and has shown the ability to get to the hoop. He fares well in an open-court game. He is capable of hitting jumpers with good range or scoring on drives through the lane. He is a tough defender who stands his ground. He plays bigger than his size and can be a spark off the bench.

Weaknesses: Knight's inconsistency has made him expendable at each of his previous stops. He is capable of putting up some numbers, but more often than not he struggles. He has not displayed the playmaking that made him highly sought-after during his first two seasons. Knight is prone to horrible shooting slumps and does not come up with many steals on defense.

Analysis: Knight's career seems to be going in the wrong direction. Once considered a second-round steal, he was traded to San Antonio for a second-round pick and has since been let go by the Spurs and Blazers. A look at his field goal percentage tells all you need to know about his troubles. Knight looks good in stretches but has not gotten the job done on a steady basis.

PLAYER SUMMARY

Will	handle the ball
Can't	unpack his bags
Expect	impressive stretches
Don't Expect	consistency
Fantasy Value	$0
Card Value	5-10¢

COLLEGE STATISTICS

		G	FGP	FTP	APG	PPG
85-86	DAY	30	.379	.670	4.3	7.1
87-88	DAY	31	.472	.713	4.9	14.8
88-89	DAY	29	.366	.735	5.8	13.9
89-90	DAY	32	.503	.800	6.8	22.8
Totals		122	.440	.746	5.4	14.8

NBA REGULAR-SEASON STATISTICS

		G	MIN	FGs FG	FGs PCT	3-PT FGs FG	3-PT FGs PCT	FTs FT	FTs PCT	Rebounds OFF	Rebounds TOT	AST	STL	BLK	PTS	PPG
90-91	PHO	64	792	131	.425	6	.240	71	.602	20	71	191	20	7	339	5.3
91-92	PHO	42	631	103	.475	4	.308	33	.688	16	46	112	24	3	243	5.8
92-93	PHO	52	888	124	.391	0	.000	67	.779	28	64	145	23	4	315	6.1
93-94	PHO/SA	65	1438	225	.474	4	.190	141	.810	28	103	197	34	11	595	9.2
94-95	POR/DET	47	708	85	.397	11	.393	18	.720	21	61	127	21	5	199	4.2
Totals		270	4457	668	.436	25	.266	330	.732	113	345	772	122	30	1691	6.3

JON KONCAK

Unrestricted Free Agent
Last Team: Atlanta Hawks
Position: Center
Height: 7'0" **Weight:** 250
Birthdate: May 17, 1963

NBA Experience: 10 years
College: Southern Methodist
Acquired: 1st-round pick in 1985 draft
(5th overall)

Background: Koncak concluded his career at Southern Methodist as the school's all-time leader in rebounds, blocked shots, and field goal percentage. He played for the gold medal-winning U.S. Olympic team in 1984. He has spent each of his ten NBA seasons with Atlanta, primarily as a backup center.

Strengths: Koncak is a solid defensive player. He understands the concept of position defense and is willing to fight for his spot. He brings good size to the middle and is unselfish on offense, perhaps too much so. He almost never turns the ball over. He knows his role and accepts it.

Weaknesses: Koncak offers next to nothing offensively, which is why Atlanta fans have viewed him as a bust. He hasn't averaged more than six PPG since his rookie year and he shoots a poor percentage from the field and the line. His low-post offense is virtually nonexistent. You don't want him handling the ball.

Analysis: Koncak sounds like contract, and he first became famous for signing a six-year, $13.2 million deal in 1989 that had fans in Atlanta scratching their heads. As the years have passed and other deals have dwarfed that one, Koncak has been known in Atlanta more for the role he's played. It has not been a glamorous one.

PLAYER SUMMARY

Will ....bang on defense
Can't ....score inside
Expect.........................limited minutes
Don't Expect ....much offense
Fantasy Value $0
Card Value ....5-7¢

COLLEGE STATISTICS

		G	FGP	FTP	RPG	PPG
81-82	SMU	27	.461	.620	5.7	10.0
82-83	SMU	30	.527	.691	9.4	14.6
83-84	SMU	33	.621	.607	11.5	15.5
84-85	SMU	33	.592	.667	10.7	17.2
Totals		123	.559	.649	9.5	14.5

NBA REGULAR-SEASON STATISTICS

				FGs		3-PT FGs		FTs		Rebounds						
		G	MIN	FG	PCT	FG	PCT	FT	PCT	OFF	TOT	AST	STL	BLK	PTS	PPG
85-86	ATL	82	1695	263	.507	0	.000	156	.607	171	467	55	37	69	682	8.3
86-87	ATL	82	1684	169	.480	0	.000	125	.654	153	493	31	52	76	463	5.6
87-88	ATL	49	1073	98	.483	0	.000	83	.610	103	333	19	36	56	279	5.7
88-89	ATL	74	1531	141	.524	0	.000	63	.553	147	453	56	54	98	345	4.7
89-90	ATL	54	977	78	.614	0	.000	42	.532	58	226	23	38	34	198	3.7
90-91	ATL	77	1931	140	.436	1	.125	32	.593	101	375	124	74	76	313	4.1
91-92	ATL	77	1489	111	.391	0	.000	19	.655	62	261	132	50	67	241	3.1
92-93	ATL	78	1975	124	.464	3	.375	24	.480	100	427	140	75	100	275	3.5
93-94	ATL	82	1823	159	.431	0	.000	24	.667	83	365	102	63	125	342	4.2
94-95	ATL	62	943	77	.412	12	.333	13	.542	23	184	52	36	45	179	2.9
Totals		717	15121	1360	.469	16	.213	581	.599	1001	3584	734	515	746	3317	4.6

TONI KUKOC

Team: Chicago Bulls
Position: Forward/Guard
Height: 6'10" **Weight:** 230
Birthdate: September 18, 1968

NBA Experience: 2 years
College: None
Acquired: 2nd-round pick in 1990 draft (29th overall)

Background: Kukoc was considered one of the greatest players ever in Europe, starring for Benetton Treviso of the Italian 1A League and earning several Player of the Year honors. He averaged 19 points, six rebounds, and five assists a game in his final year overseas. The Bulls took him in the second round in 1990 and finally lured him in 1993-94. Kukoc made great strides from his first year to his second in almost every phase.

Strengths: Kukoc is a tremendous all-around talent whose best assets are his court vision and unselfishness. He does a little bit of everything, including shooting with 3-point range, handling the ball, and finding the open man. He had more assists than point guard B.J. Armstrong last season. Kukoc also hits the boards and is a veteran of top-notch competition. He uses both hands well and is not afraid to take game-deciding shots.

Weaknesses: Kukoc is not a physically strong player, and he could use some added muscle for the grinding style of defense required in the NBA. He was accustomed to playing zone in Europe and is still learning man-to-man. He has struggled to decipher his role at times, including late last year when Michael Jordan returned.

Analysis: Kukoc was first seen by many American basketball fans on Croatia's silver medal-winning Olympic team in 1992. Some dubbed him a disappointment as an NBA rookie, but he came into last season more fit than ever and enjoyed a fine all-around year as both a starter and a sixth man. He took a backseat to M.J. down the stretch, but who didn't? Kukoc remains an extraordinary talent who is capable of great things.

PLAYER SUMMARY	
Will	drive with either hand
Can't	overshadow Jordan
Expect	great versatility
Don't Expect	physical dominance
Fantasy Value	$20-25
Card Value	20-50¢

COLLEGE STATISTICS

—DID NOT PLAY—

NBA REGULAR-SEASON STATISTICS

			FGs		3-PT FGs		FTs		Rebounds						
	G	MIN	FG	PCT	FG	PCT	FT	PCT	OFF	TOT	AST	STL	BLK	PTS	PPG
93-94 CHI	75	1808	313	.431	32	.271	156	.743	98	297	252	81	33	814	10.9
94-95 CHI	81	2584	487	.504	62	.313	235	.748	155	440	372	102	16	1271	15.7
Totals	156	4392	800	.473	94	.297	391	.746	253	737	624	183	49	2085	13.4

CHRISTIAN LAETTNER

Team: Minnesota Timberwolves
Position: Forward
Height: 6'11" **Weight:** 245
Birthdate: August 17, 1969

NBA Experience: 3 years
College: Duke
Acquired: 1st-round pick in 1992 draft
(3rd overall)

Background: The only college player on the 1992 Olympic Dream Team, Laettner was named national Player of the Year as a senior and was the catalyst behind Duke's back-to-back national championships in 1991 and 1992. He became the only player in history to start in four Final Fours. The third selection in the 1992 draft, he has led the Timberwolves in rebounds and blocked shots in each of his three seasons.

Strengths: Laettner can score from inside and out. He has good range with his jumper, yet is strong enough to muscle inside for short bank shots and dunks. He is solid fundamentally. Mentally tough, Laettner has never been afraid to take clutch shots and likes to have the ball in his hands. He gets to the boards and blocks a little more than a shot per game.

Weaknesses: Abrasive. Annoying. Cocky. All have been used to describe Laettner, a difficult personality to size up. Teammates have called him selfish, although he racks up the assists. He turns the ball over too often, draws a lot of whistles, and does not shoot for a high percentage. His scoring average has declined since his rookie year.

Analysis: Laettner is an interesting case study. For a player so supremely confident in his abilities, he has not progressed at nearly the rate he was expected to. Chalk part of that up to his great rookie season. However, his scoring has decreased in each of his years since and he has not made strides in other areas. Some contend that Laettner has already reached his peak. His role has not been well defined.

PLAYER SUMMARY	
Will	take big shots
Can't	avoid turnovers
Expect	a little of everything
Don't Expect	congeniality awards
Fantasy Value	$35-40
Card Value	12-20¢

COLLEGE STATISTICS

		G	FGP	FTP	RPG	PPG
88-89	DUKE	36	.723	.717	4.7	8.9
89-90	DUKE	38	.511	.836	9.6	16.3
90-91	DUKE	39	.575	.802	8.7	19.8
91-92	DUKE	35	.575	.815	7.9	21.5
Totals		148	.574	.806	7.8	16.6

NBA REGULAR-SEASON STATISTICS

				FGs		3-PT FGs		FTs		Rebounds						
		G	MIN	FG	PCT	FG	PCT	FT	PCT	OFF	TOT	AST	STL	BLK	PTS	PPG
92-93	MIN	81	2823	503	.474	4	.100	462	.835	171	708	223	105	83	1472	18.2
93-94	MIN	70	2428	396	.448	6	.240	375	.783	160	602	307	87	86	1173	16.8
94-95	MIN	81	2770	450	.489	13	.325	409	.818	164	613	234	101	87	1322	16.3
Totals		232	8021	1349	.471	23	.219	1246	.813	495	1923	764	293	256	3967	17.1

ANDREW LANG

Team: Atlanta Hawks
Position: Center
Height: 6'11" **Weight:** 250
Birthdate: June 28, 1966

NBA Experience: 7 years
College: Arkansas
Acquired: Signed as a free agent, 9/93

Background: Lang completed his collegiate career at Arkansas as the school's all-time leader in blocked shots. His playing time increased in each of his four years with Phoenix and he blocked 201 shots in 1991-92. He went to Philadelphia in the 1992 trade that sent Charles Barkley to Phoenix and has spent the last two years with Atlanta. He started at center for most of the 1994-95 season.

Strengths: When it comes to defensive middle men, Lang is a good one. He has blocked close to 900 shots in his seven seasons and ranked among the league's top 15 last year. He is blessed with lateral quickness and good instincts. Lang has some inside moves and has dramatically improved his free throw shooting.

Weaknesses: Lang has never been a big scorer. Most of his points come from within a few feet of the hoop. After four years of shooting better than 50 percent with the Suns, he has dropped off the last three years. He does not handle the ball well, even in the pivot, and he commits a lot of fouls. He's not a great rebounder.

Analysis: Considered an offensive liability for most of his career, Lang hit for a career-high 9.7 PPG last season and started for most of the year. He also maintained his stature as a fine shot-blocker, regaining some of the confidence he lost in Philadelphia. Want improvement? Lang was a .575 free throw shooter in college but hit .809 in 1994-95.

PLAYER SUMMARY

Will ....swat shots
Can't.............................handle the ball
Expect ....inside quickness
Don't Expect ....a scoring leader
Fantasy Value $1-3
Card Value ....7-10¢

COLLEGE STATISTICS

		G	FGP	FTP	RPG	PPG
84-85	ARK	33	.405	.563	2.0	2.6
85-86	ARK	26	.466	.607	6.5	8.2
86-87	ARK	32	.500	.644	7.5	8.1
87-88	ARK	30	.527	.450	7.3	9.3
Totals		121	.489	.575	5.7	6.9

NBA REGULAR-SEASON STATISTICS

				FGs		3-PT FGs		FTs		Rebounds						
		G	MIN	FG	PCT	FG	PCT	FT	PCT	OFF	TOT	AST	STL	BLK	PTS	PPG
88-89	PHO	62	526	60	.513	0	.000	39	.650	54	147	9	17	48	159	2.6
89-90	PHO	74	1011	97	.557	0	.000	64	.653	83	271	21	22	133	258	3.5
90-91	PHO	63	1152	109	.577	0	.000	93	.715	113	303	27	17	127	311	4.9
91-92	PHO	81	1965	248	.522	0	.000	126	.768	170	546	43	48	201	622	7.7
92-93	PHI	73	1861	149	.425	1	.200	87	.763	136	436	79	46	141	386	5.3
93-94	ATL	82	1608	215	.469	1	.250	73	.689	126	313	51	38	87	504	6.1
94-95	ATL	82	2340	320	.473	2	.667	152	.809	154	456	72	45	144	794	9.7
Totals		517	10463	1198	.491	4	.286	634	.737	836	2472	302	233	881	3034	5.9

ERIC LECKNER

Unrestricted Free Agent
Last Team: Detroit Pistons
Position: Center
Height: 6'11" **Weight:** 265
Birthdate: May 27, 1966

NBA Experience: 6 years
College: Wyoming
Acquired: Traded from 76ers for a future 2nd-round pick, 7/94

Background: Leckner was named Most Valuable Player of the Western Athletic Conference Tournament for three straight years at Wyoming, where he ranked among NCAA leaders in field goal percentage as a senior. He has played for five different teams in his six NBA seasons and spent the 1992-93 campaign in the Italian League. He made 11 starts in 57 games with Detroit last season.

Strengths: Leckner sets hard picks, works hard on defense, rebounds, and does not try to play above and beyond his capabilities. Leckner is well liked for his personality and his willingness to play the game with all he's got. He has a decent catch-and-shoot jumper within 15 feet.

Weaknesses: Leckner is a marginal talent at best. He's been a backup center for most of his career because he possesses neither the game skills nor the athletic ability to score a lot of points. He is not an impact player in any phase of the game. He's a step slow, has "hard hands," and can be outrebounded by smaller, quicker opponents.

Analysis: Leckner's name will not pop up in conversations about athletic ability among big men. He is a third-teamer for a lot of clubs, although he started for the 76ers two years ago and saw some significant action with the Pistons as well. Not altogether coincidentally, neither team made the playoffs. Most of Leckner's limited contributions don't show up in a boxscore. He's a role-player.

PLAYER SUMMARY	
Will	give his all
Can't	outscore his man
Expect	hard picks, fouls
Don't Expect	athletic ability
Fantasy Value	$0
Card Value	5-8¢

COLLEGE STATISTICS

		G	FGP	FTP	RPG	PPG
84-85	WYO	29	.583	.615	3.9	8.4
85-86	WYO	36	.582	.612	5.8	15.8
86-87	WYO	34	.631	.706	7.2	18.6
87-88	WYO	32	.644	.756	6.6	15.4
Totals		131	.612	.681	5.9	14.8

NBA REGULAR-SEASON STATISTICS

			FGs		3-PT FGs		FTs		Rebounds						
	G	MIN	FG	PCT	FG	PCT	FT	PCT	OFF	TOT	AST	STL	BLK	PTS	PPG
88-89 UTA	75	779	120	.545	0	.000	79	.699	48	199	16	8	22	319	4.3
89-90 UTA	77	764	125	.563	0	.000	81	.743	48	192	19	15	23	331	4.3
90-91 SAC/CHA	72	1122	131	.446	0	.000	62	.559	82	295	39	14	22	324	4.5
91-92 CHA	59	716	79	.513	0	.000	38	.745	49	206	31	9	18	196	3.3
93-94 PHI	71	1163	139	.486	0	.000	84	.646	75	282	86	18	34	362	5.1
94-95 DET	57	623	87	.527	0	.000	51	.708	47	174	14	15	15	225	3.9
Totals	411	5167	681	.508	0	.000	395	.674	349	1348	205	79	134	1757	4.3

BRAD LOHAUS

Unrestricted Free Agent
Last Team: Miami Heat
Position: Forward/Center
Height: 6′11″ **Weight:** 235
Birthdate: September 29, 1964

NBA Experience: 8 years
College: Iowa
Acquired: Signed as a free agent, 10/94

Background: In his senior year at Iowa, Lohaus increased his scoring average by nearly eight points per game and shot 54 percent from the field. He has played with five NBA teams in eight years, his best numbers coming with expansion Minnesota in 1989. Lohaus saw action in a career-low 61 games with Miami during 1994-95 after signing with the Heat before the season.

Strengths: Lohaus is loaded with perimeter punch. He shoots with unlimited range and has a quick release. He's hit more than 300 treys in his career and converted them at a .406 clip last season. Lohaus will also block some shots and he gets up and down the court quickly for a seven-footer.

Weaknesses: If ever there was a guard in a center's body, Lohaus is the man. Despite his height, he possesses virtually no inside game. His back-to-the-basket skills are forgettable. He does not create his own shots with the dribble like he catches and fires. Lohaus plays soft, especially on the boards.

Analysis: At his best, Lohaus is the definition of a matchup problem. What seven-footer wants to defend beyond the 3-point line? On the flip side, he does not stack up with opposing big men in the paint on either end of the court. He has found minutes harder and harder to come by, missing 21 games due to "coach's decision" in Miami last season.

PLAYER SUMMARY

Will	hit 3-pointers
Can't	score inside
Expect	matchup problems
Don't Expect	physical play
Fantasy Value	$0
Card Value	5-8¢

COLLEGE STATISTICS

		G	FGP	FTP	RPG	PPG
82-83	IOWA	20	.310	.538	0.6	1.3
83-84	IOWA	28	.404	.673	5.2	6.8
85-86	IOWA	32	.431	.794	3.2	3.6
86-87	IOWA	35	.540	.692	7.7	11.3
Totals		115	.467	.695	4.6	6.3

NBA REGULAR-SEASON STATISTICS

		G	MIN	FGs FG	FGs PCT	3-PT FGs FG	3-PT FGs PCT	FTs FT	FTs PCT	Rebounds OFF	Rebounds TOT	AST	STL	BLK	PTS	PPG
87-88	BOS	70	718	122	.496	3	.231	50	.806	46	138	49	20	41	297	4.2
88-89	BOS/SAC	77	1214	210	.432	1	.091	81	.786	84	256	66	30	56	502	6.5
89-90	MIN/MIL	80	1943	305	.460	47	.343	75	.728	98	398	168	58	88	732	9.1
90-91	MIL	81	1219	179	.431	33	.277	37	.685	59	217	75	50	74	428	5.3
91-92	MIL	70	1081	162	.450	57	.396	27	.659	65	249	74	40	71	408	5.8
92-93	MIL	80	1766	283	.461	85	.370	73	.723	59	276	127	47	74	724	9.1
93-94	MIL	67	962	102	.363	46	.343	20	.690	33	150	62	30	55	270	4.0
94-95	MIA	61	730	97	.420	63	.406	10	.667	28	102	43	20	25	267	4.4
Totals		586	9633	1460	.443	335	.355	373	.734	472	1786	664	295	484	3628	6.2

GRANT LONG

Team: Atlanta Hawks
Position: Forward
Height: 6'8" **Weight:** 248
Birthdate: March 12, 1966
NBA Experience: 7 years

College: Eastern Michigan
Acquired: Traded from Heat with
Steve Smith and a future 2nd-round
pick for Kevin Willis and a future
1st-round pick, 11/94

Background: As a senior at Eastern Michigan, Long was named Mid-American Conference Player of the Year and MVP of the MAC Tournament. He was one of the league's most improved players with Miami during the 1991-92 campaign and became a double-figure scorer. Long was traded to Atlanta two games into the 1994-95 season and averaged 11.6 PPG.

Strengths: Long is a hard-working player who attacks the boards, runs the floor, plays go-get-'em defense, and can also score. Coaches love his attitude and his willingness to give 100 percent every night. He is a fine medium-range jump-shooter who excels in transition. He anticipates well and gets his hands on a lot of steals.

Weaknesses: Long is not a finesse player. He's not a smooth driver and his skills with the ball are nothing to boast about. He was among the league leaders in fouls early in his career and still commits his share. He has trouble against some of the bigger power forwards and won't alter many shots.

Analysis: Coaches love players like Long—guys who work their tails off whether they're scoring 20 points or two. Atlanta got an energetic, enthusiastic forward when they traded Kevin Willis and a No. 1 draft pick for Long and Steve Smith. Long is not the most gifted player you'll find, but there are few who work harder. You know what you're going to get from him.

PLAYER SUMMARY

Will	energize his team
Can't	keep his fouls down
Expect	110 percent
Don't Expect	All-Star recognition
Fantasy Value	$8-10
Card Value	5-8¢

COLLEGE STATISTICS

		G	FGP	FTP	RPG	PPG
84-85	EMU	28	.564	.609	4.0	4.1
85-86	EMU	27	.526	.644	6.6	8.6
86-87	EMU	29	.549	.725	9.0	14.9
87-88	EMU	30	.555	.765	10.4	23.0
Totals		114	.549	.725	7.6	12.9

NBA REGULAR-SEASON STATISTICS

		G	MIN	FGs FG	FGs PCT	3-PT FGs FG	3-PT FGs PCT	FTs FT	FTs PCT	Rebounds OFF	Rebounds TOT	AST	STL	BLK	PTS	PPG
88-89	MIA	82	2435	336	.486	0	.000	304	.749	240	546	149	122	48	976	11.9
89-90	MIA	81	1856	257	.483	0	.000	172	.714	156	402	96	91	38	686	8.5
90-91	MIA	80	2514	276	.492	1	.167	181	.787	225	568	176	119	43	734	9.2
91-92	MIA	82	3063	440	.494	6	.273	326	.807	259	691	225	139	40	1212	14.8
92-93	MIA	76	2728	397	.469	6	.231	261	.765	197	568	182	104	31	1061	14.0
93-94	MIA	69	2201	300	.446	1	.167	187	.786	190	495	170	89	26	788	11.4
94-95	MIA/ATL	81	2641	342	.478	11	.355	244	.751	191	606	131	109	34	939	11.6
Totals		551	17438	2348	.478	25	.253	1675	.767	1458	3876	1129	773	260	6396	11.6

LUC LONGLEY

Team: Chicago Bulls
Position: Center
Height: 7'2" **Weight:** 265
Birthdate: January 19, 1969

NBA Experience: 4 years
College: New Mexico
Acquired: Traded from Timberwolves
for Stacey King, 2/94

Background: Originally from Perth, Australia, Longley was coveted by pro scouts from the day he set foot on the New Mexico campus. He never emerged as a consistent force in college despite becoming the school's all-time leading scorer and rebounder. Longley was drafted seventh by Minnesota in 1991, struggled, and was traded to Chicago in February 1994 for Stacey King. He missed much of 1994-95 with a stress fracture.

Strengths: Longley has refined skills for a big man. He is a very good passer, moves pretty well, and can score in the post or with the jumper to about 16 feet. His primary weapon, of course, is his size. But along with it, Longley owns a nice touch. He is a pretty steady free throw shooter and he also rebounds and blocks shots.

Weaknesses: The big Aussie has been inconsistent for as long as anyone can recall. His intensity, desire, and ability to take the game seriously have been questioned. Longley has never applied himself physically to reach his potential. His low-post offense needs to become much stronger. On defense, he gets whistled for a lot of reaching fouls.

Analysis: Longley, once considered a natural and still blessed with nice skills, has been a big-time disappointment for a No. 7 pick. He is not the high-scoring center people thought he would be and has yet to shoot better than 48 percent from the field. His defense is just as sporadic. He does contribute some with the Bulls, but mostly as a result of his teammates.

PLAYER SUMMARY

Will........................make crisp passes
Can't.........................gain consistency
Expect ....soft hands
Don't Expect ....fulfilled potential
Fantasy Value $1
Card Value ....5-8¢

COLLEGE STATISTICS

		G	FGP	FTP	RPG	PPG
87-88	NM	35	.500	.392	2.7	4.0
88-89	NM	33	.578	.769	6.8	13.0
89-90	NM	34	.559	.821	9.7	18.4
90-91	NM	30	.656	.716	9.2	19.1
Totals		132	.586	.735	7.0	13.4

NBA REGULAR-SEASON STATISTICS

				FGs		3-PT FGs		FTs		Rebounds						
		G	MIN	FG	PCT	FG	PCT	FT	PCT	OFF	TOT	AST	STL	BLK	PTS	PPG
91-92	MIN	66	991	114	.458	0	.000	53	.663	67	257	53	35	64	281	4.3
92-93	MIN	55	1045	133	.455	0	.000	53	.716	71	240	51	47	77	319	5.8
93-94	MIN/CHI	76	1502	219	.471	0	.000	90	.720	129	433	109	45	79	528	6.9
94-95	CHI	55	1001	135	.447	0	.000	88	.822	82	263	73	24	45	358	6.5
Totals		252	4539	601	.459	0	.000	284	.736	349	1193	286	151	265	1486	5.9

RYAN LORTHRIDGE

Team: Golden State Warriors
Position: Guard
Height: 6'4" **Weight:** 190
Birthdate: July 27, 1972

NBA Experience: 1 year
College: Jackson St.
Acquired: Signed as a free agent, 1/95

Background: Lorthridge stayed home to play college ball at Jackson State. As a senior, he led the team in steals, 3-point shooting, and scoring (19.4 PPG) and was named to the All-SWAC first team. Bypassed in the 1994 NBA draft, he was cut from the Nets before the season and started his pro career in the CBA. He was signed by Golden State last January and wound up averaging 7.4 PPG in 37 contests.

Strengths: Lorthridge knows how to score. He can get his shot off with a man in his face and is a dangerous pull-up shooter, especially when the game is moving at a fast pace. He hit his field goals at a .475 clip last season, a remarkable number for a rookie guard. Lorthridge has 3-point range, is a pretty good passer, and has the quickness to become a disruptive defensive player.

Weaknesses: Slow the pace and Lorthridge is not nearly as effective. He played at a breakneck pace (by design) during college, so he does not have much experience creating offense in a halfcourt set. He is more a rhythm shooter than a pure long-range marksman, and he struggled from the free throw and 3-point lines last season. He has a lot to learn about defense at the NBA level, and he could stand to add some muscle.

Analysis: Lorthridge was one pleasant surprise in a down year for Golden State. After turning some heads in the CBA, he was signed to a ten-day contract and eventually inked for the rest of the season. He wound up with better numbers than a lot of the drafted rookies. Lorthridge averaged more than 18 minutes a game, giving him a chance to make some progress.

PLAYER SUMMARY	
Will	pick up the pace
Can't	muscle his man
Expect	improved shooting
Don't Expect	stardom
Fantasy Value	$0
Card Value	7-10¢

COLLEGE STATISTICS

		G	FGP	FTP	RPG	PPG
91-92	JSU	24	.472	.583	1.4	5.5
92-93	JSU	34	.536	.697	2.4	8.8
93-94	JSU	29	.442	.761	4.1	19.4
Totals		87	.473	.713	2.7	11.4

NBA REGULAR-SEASON STATISTICS

			FGs		3-PT FGs		FTs		Rebounds						
	G	MIN	FG	PCT	FG	PCT	FT	PCT	OFF	TOT	AST	STL	BLK	PTS	PPG
94-95 GS	37	672	106	.475	3	.214	57	.648	24	71	101	28	1	272	7.4
Totals	37	672	106	.475	3	.214	57	.648	24	71	101	28	1	272	7.4

GEORGE LYNCH

Team: Los Angeles Lakers
Position: Forward
Height: 6'8" **Weight:** 223
Birthdate: September 3, 1970

NBA Experience: 2 years
College: North Carolina
Acquired: 1st-round pick in 1993 draft
(12th overall)

Background: Lynch never became the college superstar some thought he would be, but he found a niche and flourished in Dean Smith's North Carolina system. He set a school record with 241 career steals and became the second-leading rebounder in Tar Heels history. After winning a national title as a senior, he was drafted 12th by the Lakers. He came on in the second half of his rookie year, then averaged 6.1 PPG last season.

Strengths: Lynch goes after every loose ball, plays aggressive defense, and is not afraid to throw his body around. He can play both forward positions because he makes up in heart what he lacks in size. Lynch is a fine rebounder who is especially effective on the offensive glass, getting a lot of putbacks. He hustles for steals and has demonstrated some potential as a scorer.

Weaknesses: Poor ball-handling and perimeter-shooting skills could keep Lynch from making a big impact. His jumper is inconsistent, and he plays the perimeter like a power forward. Problem is, his body has small forward written all over it. He has limited range on his jump shot and does not own a great variety of post-up moves. Many of his points come after steals or offensive rebounds.

Analysis: The verdict is still out on Lynch, who was drafted much sooner than expected but has had some moments when he's looked legitimate. The decline in his minutes and scoring average last season had more to do with the Lakers' addition of more young talent than anything Lynch did or did not do. He could make a great pitch for more time with the addition of a consistent jump shot and more confidence with the ball.

PLAYER SUMMARY	
Will	hustle on defense
Can't	set up the offense
Expect	offensive boards
Don't Expect	3-point accuracy
Fantasy Value	$2-4
Card Value	10-15¢

COLLEGE STATISTICS

		G	FGP	FTP	RPG	PPG
89-90	NC	34	.521	.663	5.4	8.6
90-91	NC	35	.523	.630	7.4	12.5
91-92	NC	33	.539	.649	8.8	13.9
92-93	NC	38	.501	.667	9.6	14.7
Totals		140	.519	.651	7.8	12.5

NBA REGULAR-SEASON STATISTICS

		G	MIN	FGs FG	FGs PCT	3-PT FGs FG	3-PT FGs PCT	FTs FT	FTs PCT	Rebounds OFF	Rebounds TOT	AST	STL	BLK	PTS	PPG
93-94	LAL	71	1762	291	.508	0	.000	99	.596	220	410	96	102	27	681	9.6
94-95	LAL	56	953	138	.468	3	.143	62	.721	75	184	62	51	10	341	6.1
Totals		127	2715	429	.494	3	.115	161	.639	295	594	158	153	37	1022	8.0

DON MacLEAN

Team: Washington Bullets
Position: Forward
Height: 6'10" **Weight:** 235
Birthdate: January 16, 1970
NBA Experience: 3 years

College: UCLA
Acquired: Draft rights traded from Clippers with William Bedford for John Williams, 10/92

Background: MacLean finished his UCLA career as the leading scorer in school and Pac-10 history. He led all Division I players in free throw percentage as a senior and was a first-team all-conference selection three years in a row. Detroit drafted MacLean and traded him to the Clippers, but he wound up in Washington via another deal. He won the 1994 Most Improved Player Award before an injury-plagued 1994-95 season.

Strengths: MacLean has a scorer's mind-set and a game to match. He knows how to put the ball in the hole. He is a deadly perimeter marksman with a quick release and is a reliable free throw shooter. He knows how to get open. MacLean also helps out on the boards. He possesses leadership qualities, boundless confidence, and a great work ethic.

Weaknesses: MacLean is not yet a great 3-point shooter, although he can hit from the shorter arc. In general, his accuracy tapers off beyond about 18-20 feet. MacLean has never been much for giving up the ball, thus he turns it over about as frequently as he gets an assist. He has worked at it, but defense is still one of the weaker aspects of his game.

Analysis: MacLean's incredible progress was slowed last year by tendinitis in his knees, which kept him on the injured list from mid-December until late February. It's too bad, because his hours of off-season work the previous year helped him earn league-wide respect as a player. Never one to quit, the ever-confident MacLean can be expected to bounce back after another hard-working summer.

PLAYER SUMMARY

Will	hit the jumper
Can't	star on defense
Expect	supreme confidence
Don't Expect	2 APG
Fantasy Value	$8-10
Card Value	8-12¢

COLLEGE STATISTICS

		G	FGP	FTP	RPG	PPG
88-89	UCLA	31	.555	.816	7.5	18.6
89-90	UCLA	33	.516	.848	8.7	19.9
90-91	UCLA	31	.551	.846	7.3	23.0
91-92	UCLA	32	.504	.921	7.8	20.7
Totals		127	.531	.860	7.8	20.5

NBA REGULAR-SEASON STATISTICS

				FGs		3-PT FGs		FTs		Rebounds						
		G	MIN	FG	PCT	FG	PCT	FT	PCT	OFF	TOT	AST	STL	BLK	PTS	PPG
92-93	WAS	62	674	157	.435	3	.500	90	.811	33	122	39	11	4	407	6.6
93-94	WAS	75	2487	517	.502	3	.143	328	.824	140	467	160	47	22	1365	18.2
94-95	WAS	39	1052	158	.438	10	.250	104	.765	46	165	51	15	3	430	11.0
Totals		176	4213	832	.475	16	.239	522	.809	219	754	250	73	29	2202	12.5

MARK MACON

Team: Detroit Pistons
Position: Guard
Height: 6'5" **Weight:** 200
Birthdate: April 14, 1969
NBA Experience: 4 years

College: Temple
Acquired: Traded from Nuggets with Marcus Liberty for Alvin Robertson and a 1995 2nd-round pick, 11/93

Background: Macon was a superstar from day one at Temple. He was the nation's leading freshman scorer and led the Owls to a 32-2 mark. He struggled after that but still finished as the school's career scoring leader. As a rookie with Denver, his field goal percentage of 37.5 was the lowest of any starter in the league. He has yet to shoot much better, even after a 1993-94 trade to the Pistons.

Strengths: Macon is known for his intense combativeness at the defensive end of the court. He can flat-out cover just about any guy in the league. He has excellent lateral quickness and is a good leaper. He has good size to go along with his quick hands and feet, and he comes up with his share of steals. He hits his free throws.

Weaknesses: "Embarrassing" is the best way to describe Macon's offense. He simply cannot shoot the ball with any consistency. He has converted less than 40 percent from the field in three of his four years. It's hard to figure when you look at his progress at the free throw line. His poor assist-to-turnover ratio keeps him from playing the point.

Analysis: For defense, there are few better. For offense, there are few worse. Such has been the plight of Macon, who started out last season in Detroit like a reborn player but slipped back into his career-long slump as the season progressed. His contract expires after the 1995-96 season, so it could be a make-or-break year.

PLAYER SUMMARY

Will ....hound his man
Can't ....shoot 40 percent
Expect...........................superb defense
Don't Expect ....offensive output
Fantasy Value $0
Card Value ....8-12¢

COLLEGE STATISTICS

		G	FGP	FTP	RPG	PPG
87-88	TEMP	34	.454	.771	5.6	20.6
88-89	TEMP	30	.407	.776	5.6	18.3
89-90	TEMP	31	.389	.798	6.0	21.9
90-91	TEMP	31	.440	.766	4.9	22.0
Totals		126	.423	.780	5.6	20.7

NBA REGULAR-SEASON STATISTICS

				FGs		3-PT FGs		FTs		Rebounds						
		G	MIN	FG	PCT	FG	PCT	FT	PCT	OFF	TOT	AST	STL	BLK	PTS	PPG
91-92	DEN	76	2304	333	.375	4	.133	135	.730	80	220	168	154	14	805	10.6
92-93	DEN	48	1141	158	.415	0	.000	42	.700	33	103	126	69	3	358	7.5
93-94	DEN/DET	42	496	69	.375	2	.200	23	.676	18	41	51	39	1	163	3.9
94-95	DET	55	721	101	.381	20	.323	55	.809	29	76	63	67	1	276	5.0
Totals		221	4662	661	.385	26	.241	255	.735	160	440	408	329	19	1602	7.2

DAN MAJERLE

Team: Phoenix Suns
Position: Guard/Forward
Height: 6'6" **Weight:** 220
Birthdate: September 9, 1965

NBA Experience: 7 years
College: Central Michigan
Acquired: 1st-round pick in 1988 draft
(14th overall)

Background: Majerle was a three-time All-Mid-American Conference selection at Central Michigan, where he ranked second on the all-time scoring, steals, and field goal percentage lists. In seven years, he has emerged as one of the NBA's premier all-around players. A Dream Team II member, he has played in three All-Star Games and has twice led the league in 3-pointers made and attempted.

Strengths: Majerle is one of the most versatile stars in the game. He handles the ball, rebounds, plays tough defense, and scores from inside and outside. "Thunder Dan" possesses great leaping ability and gets to the bucket, yet he is also one of the top long-range marksmen in the league. His work ethic and hustle are contagious.

Weaknesses: Majerle's role has changed, and some contend it has not been for the better. He does not burn the opposition with nearly as many drives and dunks now that he has become a designated long-range shooter. He is not as talented a big guard as he is a small forward.

Analysis: Majerle, whose Phoenix restaurant is booming, was voted an All-Star starter in 1995 and remains one of the most popular people in Arizona. There are not many things on a basketball floor he is unable to do. He came off the bench for much of the 1994-95 season, however, and he might be better off mixing some "Thunder Dan" moves with his bombs.

PLAYER SUMMARY

Will ....shoot 3-pointers
Can't ....forget what got him here
Expect..........................great versatility
Don't Expect......50-percent shooting
Fantasy Value $14-17
Card Value ....8-20¢

COLLEGE STATISTICS

		G	FGP	FTP	RPG	PPG
84-85	CMU	12	.568	.582	6.7	18.6
85-86	CMU	27	.527	.718	7.9	21.4
86-87	CMU	23	.555	.552	8.5	21.1
87-88	CMU	32	.521	.645	10.8	23.7
Totals		94	.536	.631	8.9	21.8

NBA REGULAR-SEASON STATISTICS

		G	MIN	FGs FG	FGs PCT	3-PT FGs FG	3-PT FGs PCT	FTs FT	FTs PCT	Rebounds OFF	Rebounds TOT	AST	STL	BLK	PTS	PPG
88-89	PHO	54	1354	181	.419	27	.329	78	.614	62	209	130	63	14	467	8.6
89-90	PHO	73	2244	296	.424	19	.237	198	.762	144	430	188	100	32	809	11.1
90-91	PHO	77	2281	397	.484	30	.349	227	.762	168	418	216	106	40	1051	13.6
91-92	PHO	82	2853	551	.478	87	.382	229	.756	148	483	274	131	43	1418	17.3
92-93	PHO	82	3199	509	.464	167	.381	203	.778	120	383	311	138	33	1388	16.9
93-94	PHO	80	3207	476	.418	192	.382	176	.739	120	349	275	129	43	1320	16.5
94-95	PHO	82	3091	438	.425	199	.363	206	.730	104	375	340	96	38	1281	15.6
Totals		530	18229	2848	.447	721	.367	1317	.744	866	2647	1734	763	243	7734	14.6

JEFF MALONE

Team: Philadelphia 76ers
Position: Guard
Height: 6'4" **Weight:** 205
Birthdate: June 28, 1961
NBA Experience: 12 years

College: Mississippi St.
Acquired: Traded from Jazz with a conditional 1st-round pick for Jeff Hornacek, Sean Green, and a conditional 2nd-round pick, 2/94

Background: Malone broke Bailey Howell's career scoring record as a four-year starter at Mississippi State. He spent his first seven pro seasons with Washington and played in two All-Star Games. He has continued as one of the league's best shooters with Utah and Philadelphia. Injuries limited him to 19 games in 1994-95.

Strengths: You'll have to search to find a better pure shooter than Malone, who annually hovers around 50 percent from the perimeter and rarely misses from the free throw line. Malone fills the basket from anywhere, including the shorter 3-point arc. The longer distance was a little out of his range.

Weaknesses: Malone does not run the floor well for a guard, nor does he create. He will not provide assists, steals, rebounds, or blocked shots. Defense has never been his forte, and injuries have become a concern for the first time in his career.

Analysis: After 12 NBA seasons, Malone can still put the ball in the bucket against just about anyone. He has more than 17,000 career points and is good for 16-18 a night. His right heel dragged him down late last season, and he is not getting any younger. He's in the proverbial twilight, but he's still shooting well.

PLAYER SUMMARY	
Will	fill the net
Can't	shine on defense
Expect	16-18 PPG
Don't Expect	three more years
Fantasy Value	$1-3
Card Value	5-8¢

COLLEGE STATISTICS

		G	FGP	FTP	RPG	PPG
79-80	MSU	27	.459	.824	3.3	11.9
80-81	MSU	27	.490	.820	4.2	20.1
81-82	MSU	27	.549	.743	4.1	18.6
82-83	MSU	29	.531	.824	3.7	26.8
Totals		110	.512	.809	3.8	19.5

NBA REGULAR-SEASON STATISTICS

		G	MIN	FGs FG	FGs PCT	3-PT FGs FG	3-PT FGs PCT	FTs FT	FTs PCT	Rebounds OFF	Rebounds TOT	AST	STL	BLK	PTS	PPG
83-84	WAS	81	1976	408	.444	24	.324	142	.826	57	155	151	23	13	982	12.1
84-85	WAS	76	2613	605	.499	15	.208	211	.844	60	206	184	52	9	1436	18.9
85-86	WAS	80	2992	735	.483	3	.176	322	.868	66	288	191	70	12	1795	22.4
86-87	WAS	80	2763	689	.457	4	.154	376	.885	50	218	298	75	13	1758	22.0
87-88	WAS	80	2655	648	.476	10	.417	335	.882	44	206	237	51	13	1641	20.5
88-89	WAS	76	2418	677	.480	1	.053	296	.871	55	179	219	39	14	1651	21.7
89-90	WAS	75	2567	781	.491	1	.167	257	.877	54	206	243	48	6	1820	24.3
90-91	UTA	69	2466	525	.508	1	.167	231	.917	36	206	143	50	6	1282	18.6
91-92	UTA	81	2922	691	.511	1	.083	256	.898	49	233	180	56	5	1639	20.2
92-93	UTA	79	2558	595	.494	3	.333	236	.852	31	173	128	42	4	1429	18.1
93-94	UTA/PHI	77	2560	525	.486	7	.583	205	.830	51	199	125	40	5	1262	16.4
94-95	PHI	19	660	144	.507	11	.393	51	.864	11	55	29	15	0	350	18.4
Totals		873	29150	7023	.485	81	.266	2918	.871	564	2324	2128	561	100	17045	19.5

KARL MALONE

Team: Utah Jazz
Position: Forward
Height: 6'9" **Weight:** 256
Birthdate: July 24, 1963

NBA Experience: 10 years
College: Louisiana Tech
Acquired: 1st-round pick in 1985 draft (13th overall)

Background: Malone finished third on the all-time scoring list at Louisiana Tech despite playing just three years. In ten years with Utah, he has missed only four games. He has played in eight All-Star Games, winning MVP honors in 1989 and 1993, and won gold in the 1992 Olympics. Malone has finished second to Michael Jordan in scoring four times and is annually in the top five.

Strengths: Nicknamed "The Mailman" because he delivers, Malone is virtually impossible for one man to stop. He is big, quick, and incredibly strong. If he fails to score, he almost always draws a foul. He has gone to the line more than anyone in the NBA in five of the last seven years. He plays defense and is one of the top rebounding forwards in basketball.

Weaknesses: Malone commits a lot of turnovers, largely because defenders swarm him almost every time he touches the ball. He has to work on his free throw shooting, as it does not come naturally.

Analysis: The Mailman deserved serious MVP consideration for another outstanding year in 1994-95. He has established himself as one of the premier forwards basketball has seen in recent years. No one can stop him from scoring or getting to the line when he gets the ball down low. Malone topped the 21,000 career-point mark last season.

PLAYER SUMMARY

Will ....get to the line
Can't ....be stopped in post
Expect ....10,000 career boards
Don't Expect ....less than 20 PPG
Fantasy Value $75-80
Card Value ....25-40¢

COLLEGE STATISTICS

		G	FGP	FTP	RPG	PPG
82-83	LT	28	.582	.623	10.3	20.9
83-84	LT	32	.576	.682	8.8	18.8
84-85	LT	32	.541	.571	9.0	16.5
Totals		92	.566	.631	9.3	18.7

NBA REGULAR-SEASON STATISTICS

		G	MIN	FGs FG	PCT	3-PT FGs FG	PCT	FTs FT	PCT	Rebounds OFF	TOT	AST	STL	BLK	PTS	PPG
85-86	UTA	81	2475	504	.496	0	.000	195	.481	174	718	236	105	44	1203	14.9
86-87	UTA	82	2857	728	.512	0	.000	323	.598	278	855	158	104	60	1779	21.7
87-88	UTA	82	3198	858	.520	0	.000	552	.700	277	986	199	117	50	2268	27.7
88-89	UTA	80	3126	809	.519	5	.313	703	.766	259	853	219	144	70	2326	29.1
89-90	UTA	82	3122	914	.562	16	.372	696	.762	232	911	226	121	50	2540	31.0
90-91	UTA	82	3302	847	.527	4	.286	684	.770	236	967	270	89	79	2382	29.0
91-92	UTA	81	3054	798	.526	3	.176	673	.778	225	909	241	108	51	2272	28.0
92-93	UTA	82	3099	797	.552	4	.200	619	.740	227	919	308	124	85	2217	27.0
93-94	UTA	82	3329	772	.497	8	.250	511	.694	235	940	328	125	126	2063	25.2
94-95	UTA	82	3126	830	.536	11	.268	516	.742	156	871	285	129	85	2187	26.7
Totals		816	30688	7857	.526	51	.259	5472	.721	2299	8929	2470	1166	700	21237	26.0

DANNY MANNING

Unrestricted Free Agent
Last Team: Phoenix Suns
Position: Forward
Height: 6'10" **Weight:** 235
Birthdate: May 17, 1966

NBA Experience: 7 years
College: Kansas
Acquired: Signed as a free agent, 8/94

Background: Manning was voted college Player of the Year in 1988, when he led Kansas to the national title. He ended his college career with more than three dozen school, conference, and NCAA records. His early NBA years were slowed by a tear of the anterior cruciate (knee) ligament, and a similar injury in February ended Manning's 1994-95 season early. He has played in two All-Star Games in seven years.

Strengths: Manning is a big-time scorer who drills his quick-release jumper and owns a deadly half-hook that he throws in from all angles. He moves well without the ball and has been called a point guard in the body of a forward—a tribute to his passing skills. His career average is nearly 19 PPG. He also has shot-blocking ability.

Weaknesses: Manning is known as a subpar defensive player and he is not a much better rebounder. He commits a truckload of fouls. He has struggled from the free throw line and is not a 3-point specialist. The biggest question mark, of course, is his knee. Will he be able to stage another comeback?

Analysis: Phoenix coach Paul Westphal called Manning the Suns' MVP before another knee injury threatened to change his career. That's high praise on a team loaded with stars. Manning is the kind of player who makes those around him better. He's overcome one knee injury; perhaps he can do it again.

PLAYER SUMMARY	
Will	spot open men
Can't	trade in his knee
Expect	more rehab
Don't Expect	great defense
Fantasy Value	$9-11
Card Value	15-25¢

COLLEGE STATISTICS

		G	FGP	FTP	RPG	PPG
84-85	KANS	34	.566	.765	7.6	14.6
85-86	KANS	39	.600	.748	6.3	16.7
86-87	KANS	36	.617	.730	9.5	23.9
87-88	KANS	38	.583	.734	9.0	24.8
Totals		147	.593	.740	8.1	20.1

NBA REGULAR-SEASON STATISTICS

		G	MIN	FGs		3-PT FGs		FTs		Rebounds		AST	STL	BLK	PTS	PPG
				FG	PCT	FG	PCT	FT	PCT	OFF	TOT					
88-89	LAC	26	950	177	.494	1	.200	79	.767	70	171	81	44	25	434	16.7
89-90	LAC	71	2269	440	.533	0	.000	274	.741	142	422	187	91	39	1154	16.3
90-91	LAC	73	2197	470	.519	0	.000	219	.716	169	426	196	117	62	1159	15.9
91-92	LAC	82	2904	650	.542	0	.000	279	.725	229	564	285	135	122	1579	19.3
92-93	LAC	79	2761	702	.509	8	.267	388	.802	198	520	207	108	101	1800	22.8
93-94	LAC/ATL	68	2520	586	.488	3	.176	228	.669	131	465	261	99	82	1403	20.6
94-95	PHO	46	1510	340	.547	6	.286	136	.673	97	276	154	41	57	822	17.9
Totals		445	15111	3365	.518	18	.209	1603	.732	1036	2844	1371	635	488	8351	18.8

SARUNAS MARCIULIONIS

Team: Seattle SuperSonics
Position: Guard
Height: 6'5" **Weight:** 215
Birthdate: June 13, 1964
NBA Experience: 5 years

College: Vilnius St.
Acquired: Traded from Warriors with Byron Houston for Ricky Pierce, draft rights to Carlos Rogers, and two 1995 2nd-round picks, 7/94

Background: The Lithuanian Marciulionis was the leading scorer on the Soviet Union's 1988 Olympic gold medal-winning team in Seoul, South Korea, and played for Lithuania in the 1992 Games. The first Soviet player in the NBA, he led all nonstarters in scoring (18.9 PPG) and all guards in field goal percentage (.538) in 1991-92. He was dealt to Seattle before 1994-95 after knee surgery wiped out his entire 1993-94 slate.

Strengths: Although he plays left-handed, Marciulionis is ambidextrous. Anyone unconvinced should watch him handle the ball. He has a nice jumper with 3-point range and also uses his strength to drive inside. He is capable of scoring in traffic, racking up the assists, and going to the free throw line. His work habits are exceptional.

Weaknesses: Marciulionis is not a good rebounder or defensive player. He never has been. Injuries remain a concern. He spent much of last year fighting to regain his confidence after missing a year because of a torn anterior cruciate ligament in his right knee. The year before, he fractured a fibula, dislocated an ankle, and suffered from Achilles tendinitis.

Analysis: Marciulionis is known for his uncanny ability to drive to the hole, and after such drives he can finish or distribute. If he can regain his offensive form, he could become one of the top sixth men in the game. His injuries appear to have robbed him of some confidence, but Marciulionis is a fighter who will continue to battle his way back into form.

PLAYER SUMMARY

Will ....drive with either hand
Can't ....dominate defensively
Expect ....productive offense
Don't Expect........................rebounds
Fantasy Value $4-6
Card Value ....7-10¢

COLLEGE STATISTICS

—DID NOT PLAY—

NBA REGULAR-SEASON STATISTICS

		MIN	FGs		3-PT FGs		FTs		Rebounds						
	G	MIN	FG	PCT	FG	PCT	FT	PCT	OFF	TOT	AST	STL	BLK	PTS	PPG
89-90 GS	75	1695	289	.519	10	.256	317	.787	84	221	121	94	7	905	12.1
90-91 GS	50	987	183	.501	1	.167	178	.724	51	118	85	62	4	545	10.9
91-92 GS	72	2117	491	.538	3	.300	376	.788	68	208	243	116	10	1361	18.9
92-93 GS	30	836	178	.543	3	.200	162	.761	40	97	105	51	2	521	17.4
94-95 SEA	66	1194	216	.473	35	.402	145	.732	17	68	110	72	3	612	9.3
Totals	293	6829	1357	.518	52	.331	1178	.766	260	712	664	395	26	3944	13.5

DONYELL MARSHALL

Team: Golden State Warriors
Position: Forward
Height: 6'9" **Weight:** 218
Birthdate: May 18, 1973

NBA Experience: 1 year
College: Connecticut
Acquired: Traded from Timberwolves for Tom Gugliotta, 2/95

Background: Out of Reading, Pennsylvania, Marshall was the most heralded recruit in UConn history. He did not disappoint, leading the Huskies to two NCAA Tournament bids and the 1994 Big East title. He set a school record for career blocked shots and a league scoring mark as a senior. The fourth pick in the 1994 draft, he was traded from Minnesota to Golden State midway through his rookie year. He finished among rookie leaders in blocked shots with 1.2 per game.

Strengths: Marshall is a quick leaper with a penchant for scoring. He runs the floor like a guard, is a splendid finisher, and simply knows how to put the ball in the basket. He is an accomplished dunk artist. His quickness off the floor, wide wingspan, and great timing make him a potential force as a shot-blocker and rebounder. Marshall overcomes his slight build with his speed.

Weaknesses: Shooting is the biggest downfall in Marshall's game right now. He hit less than 40 percent of his field goals with Minnesota before being traded for Tom Gugliotta last season, though he was a little better with Golden State. He also struggled from the free throw line and should not be launching as many treys. NBA defense requires more than challenging shots. His work ethic has been questioned.

Analysis: Marshall got off to a great start, coming off the bench in his first NBA game to score 26 points, including five 3-pointers, and grab four rebounds. But he never fit in with the Timberwolves. He spent most of his first season as a reserve and struggled to find consistency. He started coming around after the trade, contributing 15 PPG in a Warrior uniform. He remains a bundle of potential.

PLAYER SUMMARY

Will....................................block shots
Can't.....................overpower his man
Expect ....transition buckets
Don't Expect ....physical defense
Fantasy Value $5-7
Card Value ....60¢-$1.25

COLLEGE STATISTICS

		G	FGP	FTP	RPG	PPG
91-92	CONN	30	.424	.742	6.1	11.1
92-93	CONN	27	.500	.829	7.8	17.0
93-94	CONN	34	.511	.752	8.9	25.1
Totals		91	.487	.770	7.6	18.1

NBA REGULAR-SEASON STATISTICS

		G	MIN	FGs FG	FGs PCT	3-PT FGs FG	3-PT FGs PCT	FTs FT	FTs PCT	Rebounds OFF	Rebounds TOT	AST	STL	BLK	PTS	PPG
94-95	MIN/GS	72	2086	345	.394	69	.284	147	.662	137	405	105	45	88	906	12.6
Totals		72	2086	345	.394	69	.284	147	.662	137	405	105	45	88	906	12.6

JAMAL MASHBURN

Team: Dallas Mavericks
Position: Forward
Height: 6'8" **Weight:** 240
Birthdate: November 29, 1972

NBA Experience: 2 years
College: Kentucky
Acquired: 1st-round pick in 1993 draft
(4th overall)

Background: Dan Issel, Kenny Walker, and Jack Givens are the only Kentucky players to score more points than Mashburn, who started every game in his three years in Lexington. As a senior, he was runnerup for the Wooden Award as the national Player of the Year. Mashburn, who bypassed his senior year, was taken fourth by Dallas in 1993 and led all rookies in scoring. He improved to 24.1 PPG last season, sixth in the league.

Strengths: Mashburn is a big-time scorer who can muscle in the paint, drive from the wing, or stretch a defense with his 3-point shooting. His athletic, "Monster Mash" dunks and fluid style make him a favorite with fans. He runs the floor, finds open men, handles the ball, and is tough for one man to defend because of his inside-outside combination. He has the versatility to play both forward spots.

Weaknesses: Mashburn cannot be called an accomplished defender. He hardly ever blocks a shot and gets lit up on occasion. A symptom of his scoring mentality, he is much better on the offensive boards than he is on the defensive glass. His field goal percentage reflects his poor shot selection. He does not need to take 300-plus 3-pointers. He's also been turnover-prone.

Analysis: Mashburn is the kind of player you'd pay money to watch, and he's the kind of player expected to join fellow youngsters Jim Jackson and Jason Kidd in leading the Mavericks back into contention. Mashburn scored 50 points against Chicago in last season's opening week and has already become one of the league's best scorers. He's got the look of a future All-Star, and he probably won't be waiting long.

PLAYER SUMMARY

Will	score inside and out
Can't	avoid turnovers
Expect	20-plus PPG
Don't Expect	shot-blocking
Fantasy Value	$20-25
Card Value	50¢-$1.00

COLLEGE STATISTICS

		G	FGP	FTP	RPG	PPG
90-91	KENT	28	.474	.727	7.0	12.9
91-92	KENT	36	.567	.709	7.8	21.3
92-93	KENT	34	.492	.670	8.4	21.0
Totals		98	.516	.697	7.8	18.8

NBA REGULAR-SEASON STATISTICS

				FGs		3-PT FGs		FTs		Rebounds						
		G	MIN	FG	PCT	FG	PCT	FT	PCT	OFF	TOT	AST	STL	BLK	PTS	PPG
93-94	DAL	79	2896	561	.406	85	.284	306	.699	107	353	266	89	14	1513	19.2
94-95	DAL	80	2980	683	.436	113	.328	447	.739	116	331	298	82	8	1926	24.1
Totals		159	5876	1244	.422	198	.308	753	.722	223	684	564	171	22	3439	21.6

ANTHONY MASON

Unrestricted Free Agent
Last Team: New York Knicks
Position: Forward
Height: 6'7" **Weight:** 250
Birthdate: December 14, 1966

NBA Experience: 6 years
College: Tennessee St.
Acquired: Signed as a free agent, 7/91

Background: Mason finished his career at Tennessee State with more than 2,000 career points. He was drafted by Portland in the third round in 1988 but spent his first pro season in Turkey. He played 21 games for the Nets in 1989-90, spent the 1990-91 campaign in the CBA (save for three games with Denver), and was a top reserve for the Knicks over the last four seasons.

Strengths: Mason is a menace to opponents who have the misfortune of running into him. He owns a bruising body and uses it to establish a physical presence. He bangs, plays ferocious defense, is a dominant rebounder, and runs the court. He handles the ball well enough to beat pressure. Mason shoots a high percentage from the field and has upped his scoring.

Weaknesses: The downside with Mason is his brash attitude. He was suspended for ten days by the Knicks last season for actions detrimental to the team. He's been a near-constant complainer. Mason is not known for his shooting and is dismal from the foul line. He has never made a 3-pointer in his career. His defensive skills don't include shot-blocking.

Analysis: Mason won the NBA's Sixth Man Award last year. He lives up to his name in that he's built like a brick wall, and he gave the Knicks a physical presence, rebounding, and scoring off the bench. However, he also gives coaches fits because, while he plays exceptionally hard, he also thinks very highly of himself.

PLAYER SUMMARY

Will ....handle the ball
Can't ....shoot 3-pointers
Expect ....bruising defense
Don't Expect ....off-court silence
Fantasy Value $6-8
Card Value ....7-12¢

COLLEGE STATISTICS

		G	FGP	FTP	RPG	PPG
84-85	TSU	28	.469	.648	5.3	10.0
85-86	TSU	28	.482	.715	6.9	18.0
86-87	TSU	27	.448	.659	9.7	18.8
87-88	TSU	28	.454	.773	10.4	28.0
Totals		111	.461	.713	8.1	18.7

NBA REGULAR-SEASON STATISTICS

				FGs		3-PT FGs		FTs		Rebounds						
		G	MIN	FG	PCT	FG	PCT	FT	PCT	OFF	TOT	AST	STL	BLK	PTS	PPG
89-90	NJ	21	108	14	.350	0	.000	9	.600	11	34	7	2	2	37	1.8
90-91	DEN	3	21	2	.500	0	.000	6	.750	3	5	0	1	0	10	3.3
91-92	NY	82	2198	203	.509	0	.000	167	.642	216	573	106	46	20	573	7.0
92-93	NY	81	2482	316	.502	0	.000	199	.682	231	640	170	43	19	831	10.3
93-94	NY	73	1903	206	.476	0	.000	116	.720	158	427	151	31	9	528	7.2
94-95	NY	77	2496	287	.566	0	.000	191	.641	182	650	240	69	21	765	9.9
Totals		337	9208	1028	.511	0	.000	688	.665	801	2329	674	192	71	2744	8.1

TONY MASSENBURG

Team: Toronto Raptors
Position: Forward
Height: 6'9" **Weight:** 245
Birthdate: July 31, 1967

NBA Experience: 3 years
College: Maryland
Acquired: Selected from Clippers in 1995 expansion draft

Background: Massenburg played on a Maryland team that featured Walt Williams and Jerrod Mustaf and was a two-time All-Atlantic Coast Conference performer. He averaged 18.0 PPG and 10.1 RPG as a senior in 1989-90. A second-round choice of the Spurs, he played with four NBA teams in his first two seasons before spending two years in Spain. He signed with the Clippers and started for most of the 1994-95 season, then was nabbed by Toronto in the expansion draft.

Strengths: Massenburg is a fine athlete who hustles up and down the floor and fares well in a transition game. He loves to bang the boards and is quite proficient at it, having averaged 5.7 RPG during his return to the NBA in 1994-95. He gets a lot of his points on the offensive glass. Massenburg is an unselfish player who works at his game and goes all-out on defense.

Weaknesses: Facing the basket, Massenburg is not nearly the player he is on the blocks. He has never found a comfort zone on the perimeter, either with his jump shot or his dribble. His range is limited, he is not a great passer of the ball, and he picks up a lot of reaching and over-the-back fouls. He'll put up big numbers one night and disappear the next.

Analysis: The 1994-95 season was an encouraging one for Massenburg, who obviously benefitted from two years in the Spanish League. He averaged 15.5 points and 7.9 rebounds per game in Barcelona and made an impact on the Clippers' summer-league team, playing his way into a prominent role on a bad team. He'll fight for a starting spot with the expansion Raptors.

PLAYER SUMMARY

Will ....run the floor
Can't ....shoot 3-pointers
Expect......................................rebounds
Don't Expect..............perimeter skills
Fantasy Value $4-6
Card Value..................................7-10¢

COLLEGE STATISTICS

		G	FGP	FTP	RPG	PPG
85-86	MARY	29	.500	.563	2.1	2.9
87-88	MARY	23	.520	.573	5.3	10.1
88-89	MARY	29	.550	.600	7.8	16.6
89-90	MARY	31	.505	.721	10.1	18.0
Totals		112	.523	.643	6.4	12.1

NBA REGULAR-SEASON STATISTICS

				FGs		3-PT FGs		FTs		Rebounds						
		G	MIN	FG	PCT	FG	PCT	FT	PCT	OFF	TOT	AST	STL	BLK	PTS	PPG
90-91	SA	35	161	27	.450	0	.000	28	.622	23	58	4	4	9	82	2.3
91-92	SA/CHA/BOS/GS	18	90	10	.400	0	.000	9	.600	7	25	0	1	1	29	1.6
94-95	LAC	80	2127	282	.469	0	.000	177	.753	160	455	67	48	58	741	9.3
Totals		133	2378	319	.465	0	.000	214	.725	190	538	71	53	68	852	6.4

VERNON MAXWELL

Unsigned Free Agent
Last Team: Houston Rockets
Position: Guard
Height: 6'4" **Weight:** 190
Birthdate: September 12, 1965

NBA Experience: 7 years
College: Florida
Acquired: Acquired from Spurs for cash, 2/90

Background: Maxwell broke Florida's all-time scoring record but later admitted to using cocaine and accepting cash payments. He has been in and out of trouble as a pro in both San Antonio and Houston. He helped the Rockets to the 1994 NBA title but was suspended for ten games last season after a physical altercation with a foul-mouthed fan. He was released after the season.

Strengths: Maxwell throws his weight around on defense and he backs down from no one. He can match up effectively with big guards and smaller point men. He is fifth on the all-time Rockets steals list. Maxwell is one of the most prolific 3-point shooters in the league but can also use his quickness to get to the hoop. He plays the game with exuberance and hits some clutch shots.

Weaknesses: Though "Mad Max" is annually among the most frequent 3-point shooters in the league, he has never been among the most accurate. He also misfires frequently from the foul line. He's something of a loose cannon. He was arrested on a weapons charge two years ago.

Analysis: With Maxwell, you take the bad with the good. Without his clutch shooting in the playoffs, the Rockets would not have won their championship two years ago. His ten-game suspension by the league last year, however, is typical of the way his career has progressed. He certainly keeps things interesting.

PLAYER SUMMARY	
Will	slow down his man
Can't	control his temper
Expect	a long-range barrage
Don't Expect	high percentages
Fantasy Value	$4-6
Card Value	8-12¢

COLLEGE STATISTICS

		G	FGP	FTP	RPG	PPG
84-85	FLOR	30	.445	.686	2.4	13.3
85-86	FLOR	33	.463	.701	4.5	19.6
86-87	FLOR	34	.485	.742	3.7	21.7
87-88	FLOR	33	.447	.715	4.2	20.2
Totals		130	.462	.715	3.7	18.8

NBA REGULAR-SEASON STATISTICS

		G	MIN	FGs FG	FGs PCT	3-PT FGs FG	3-PT FGs PCT	FTs FT	FTs PCT	Rebounds OFF	Rebounds TOT	AST	STL	BLK	PTS	PPG
88-89	SA	79	2065	357	.432	32	.248	181	.745	49	202	301	86	8	927	11.7
89-90	SA/HOU	79	1987	275	.439	28	.267	136	.645	50	228	296	84	10	714	9.0
90-91	HOU	82	2870	504	.404	172	.337	217	.733	41	238	303	127	15	1397	17.0
91-92	HOU	80	2700	502	.413	162	.342	206	.772	37	243	326	104	28	1372	17.1
92-93	HOU	71	2251	349	.407	120	.332	164	.719	29	221	297	86	8	982	13.8
93-94	HOU	75	2571	380	.389	120	.298	143	.749	42	229	380	125	20	1023	13.6
94-95	HOU	64	2038	306	.394	143	.324	99	.688	18	164	274	75	13	854	13.3
Totals		530	16482	2673	.409	777	.321	1146	.725	266	1525	2177	687	102	7269	13.7

LEE MAYBERRY

Team: Milwaukee Bucks
Position: Guard
Height: 6'1" **Weight:** 175
Birthdate: June 12, 1970

NBA Experience: 3 years
College: Arkansas
Acquired: 1st-round pick in 1992 draft
(23rd overall)

Background: Mayberry, a prep star in Tulsa, Oklahoma, led Arkansas to nine NCAA Tournament wins in four years and finished as the school's career leader in assists, steals, and 3-point field goal percentage. A first-round draft choice of the Bucks, he has not missed a game in his three years and played his way into Milwaukee's starting lineup for most of the 1994-95 campaign. He led his team in 3-point percentage.

Strengths: Mayberry is a solid defensive point guard. Though he does not come up with a lot of steals, his on-the-ball defense has been very reliable. He is a good 3-point shooter and can get his shot off in spite of his size. He has leadership qualities, is durable, takes care of the ball, and runs the offense. He loves the transition game and does not commit a lot of turnovers.

Weaknesses: Mayberry has not been as aggressive as he needs to be at the offensive end. He runs a steady ship, but his coaches would like to see him look for his shot more often and make more things happen as a playmaker. He does not contribute much on the backboards. Mayberry has struggled from the free throw line.

Analysis: Mayberry started the first 27 games of the 1994-95 season, came off the bench for the next 32, and regained his starting job from Eric Murdock with better play late in the year. Mayberry takes care of the ball, gives the Bucks a 3-point threat, and plays tough defense. What he does not yet offer is a great sense of offensive urgency, preferring to play a background role in the scoring column.

PLAYER SUMMARY

Will..............................run the offense
Can't ....own the boards
Expect ....a 3-point threat
Don't Expect ....10 PPG
Fantasy Value..................................$0
Card Value ....8-15¢

COLLEGE STATISTICS

		G	FGP	FTP	APG	PPG
88-89	ARK	32	.500	.736	4.2	12.9
89-90	ARK	35	.507	.792	5.2	14.5
90-91	ARK	38	.484	.634	5.5	13.2
91-92	ARK	34	.492	.744	5.9	15.2
Totals		139	.495	.724	5.2	14.0

NBA REGULAR-SEASON STATISTICS

		G	MIN	FGs		3-PT FGs		FTs		Rebounds		AST	STL	BLK	PTS	PPG
				FG	PCT	FG	PCT	FT	PCT	OFF	TOT					
92-93	MIL	82	1503	171	.456	43	.391	39	.574	26	118	273	59	7	424	5.2
93-94	MIL	82	1472	167	.415	41	.345	58	.690	26	101	215	46	4	433	5.3
94-95	MIL	82	1744	172	.422	72	.407	58	.699	21	82	276	51	4	474	5.8
Totals		246	4719	510	.430	156	.384	155	.660	73	301	764	156	15	1331	5.4

GEORGE McCLOUD

Unrestricted Free Agent
Last Team: Dallas Mavericks
Position: Forward/Guard
Height: 6'8" **Weight:** 215
Birthdate: May 27, 1967

NBA Experience: 5 years
College: Florida St.
Acquired: Signed as a free agent, 1/95

Background: McCloud was named Metro Conference Player of the Year as a senior at Florida State, where he finished his career ranked third on the career scoring list. Drafted seventh overall by Indiana, he started his pro career slowly before averaging 7.2 PPG in his fourth season. The Pacers let McCloud go, however, and he served time in the CBA before making his NBA return with Dallas in the latter half of 1994-95.

Strengths: McCloud can shoot the basketball. He was drafted seventh in 1989 because of his perimeter shooting and 3-point range, and he hit at a 38-percent clip from behind the arc with the Mavericks last season. He hits his free throws and has improved his ability to get shots off the dribble. McCloud is capable of playing tough defense.

Weaknesses: The main reason McCloud has not lived up to his draft status has been his inconsistency. He is prone to ugly cold spells. McCloud, who had three different surgeries in his first three pro seasons, is not a great ball-handler and has trouble defending his quicker assignments.

Analysis: After a disappointing career with the Pacers and some humbling games in the CBA, McCloud signed two ten-day pacts with Dallas last winter and snapped out of his doldrums. He was a sparkplug off the bench in 42 games with the Mavericks, averaging a career-high 9.6 PPG. He's still not a No. 7 pick, but at least he's back.

PLAYER SUMMARY	
Will	shoot with range
Can't	live up to draft status
Expect	instant offense
Don't Expect	a dazzling dribble
Fantasy Value	$0
Card Value	5-8¢

COLLEGE STATISTICS

		G	FGP	FTP	RPG	PPG
85-86	FSU	27	.483	.633	1.8	4.3
86-87	FSU	30	.442	.618	4.2	7.7
87-88	FSU	30	.479	.786	3.7	18.2
88-89	FSU	30	.448	.875	3.6	22.8
Totals		117	.460	.778	3.4	13.5

NBA REGULAR-SEASON STATISTICS

			FGs		3-PT FGs		FTs		Rebounds						
	G	MIN	FG	PCT	FG	PCT	FT	PCT	OFF	TOT	AST	STL	BLK	PTS	PPG
89-90 IND	44	413	45	.313	13	.325	15	.789	12	42	45	19	3	118	2.7
90-91 IND	74	1070	131	.373	43	.347	38	.776	35	118	150	40	11	343	4.6
91-92 IND	51	892	128	.409	32	.340	50	.781	45	132	116	26	11	338	6.6
92-93 IND	78	1500	216	.411	58	.320	75	.735	60	205	192	53	11	565	7.2
94-95 DAL	42	802	144	.439	34	.382	80	.833	82	147	53	23	9	402	9.6
Totals	289	4677	664	.400	180	.341	258	.782	234	644	55	161	45	1766	6.1

XAVIER McDANIEL

Team: Boston Celtics
Position: Forward
Height: 6'7" **Weight:** 205
Birthdate: June 4, 1963

NBA Experience: 10 years
College: Wichita St.
Acquired: Signed as a free agent, 9/92

Background: McDaniel led Wichita State in scoring, rebounding, and field goal percentage as a junior and senior and was an All-American in 1985. He earned All-Rookie honors with Seattle and scored more than 20 PPG in each of his next four years, making the All-Star Game in 1988. He has since played with Phoenix, New York, and Boston.

Strengths: At his best, McDaniel has what you look for in a small forward. He puts points on the board with a turnaround jump shot and is a fine finisher. He also rebounds and provides a physical presence. McDaniel backs down from no one. He's been known as a big-game player.

Weaknesses: McDaniel has seen his better days. He seems to go through frequent lapses and his numbers reflect it. His last two seasons have been his worst. He is not a pure shooter, nor is he a polished or willing passer. He has lost a step on his drives and has been resigned to reserve duty.

Analysis: The "X-Man" has been one of the more explosive forwards in the league during his ten-year career. His play over the last two seasons, however, has been largely uninspired. His streak of 350 consecutive games played ended last November, and he played in a career-low 68 contests.

PLAYER SUMMARY	
Will	show flashes
Can't	regain top form
Expect	a physical reserve
Don't Expect	20 PPG
Fantasy Value	$1-3
Card Value	7-10¢

COLLEGE STATISTICS

		G	FGP	FTP	RPG	PPG
81-82	WSU	28	.504	.628	3.7	5.8
82-83	WSU	28	.593	.541	14.4	18.8
83-84	WSU	30	.564	.680	13.1	20.6
84-85	WSU	31	.559	.634	14.8	27.2
Totals		117	.564	.624	11.6	18.4

NBA REGULAR-SEASON STATISTICS

		G	MIN	FGs FG	FGs PCT	3-PT FGs FG	3-PT FGs PCT	FTs FT	FTs PCT	Rebounds OFF	Rebounds TOT	AST	STL	BLK	PTS	PPG
85-86	SEA	82	2706	576	.490	2	.200	250	.687	307	655	193	101	37	1404	17.1
86-87	SEA	82	3031	806	.509	3	.214	275	.696	338	705	207	115	52	1890	23.0
87-88	SEA	78	2803	687	.488	14	.280	281	.715	206	518	263	96	52	1669	21.4
88-89	SEA	82	2385	677	.489	11	.306	312	.732	177	433	134	84	40	1677	20.5
89-90	SEA	69	2432	611	.496	5	.294	244	.733	165	447	171	73	36	1471	21.3
90-91	SEA/PHO	81	2634	590	.497	0	.000	193	.723	173	557	187	76	46	1373	17.0
91-92	NY	82	2344	488	.478	12	.308	137	.714	176	460	149	57	24	1125	13.7
92-93	BOS	82	2215	457	.495	6	.273	191	.793	168	489	163	72	51	1111	13.5
93-94	BOS	82	1971	387	.461	10	.244	144	.676	142	400	126	48	39	928	11.3
94-95	BOS	68	1430	246	.451	6	.286	89	.712	94	300	108	30	20	587	8.6
Totals		788	23951	5525	.489	69	.267	2116	.718	1946	4964	1701	752	397	13235	16.8

JIM McILVAINE

Team: Washington Bullets
Position: Center
Height: 7'1" **Weight:** 240
Birthdate: July 30, 1972

NBA Experience: 1 year
College: Marquette
Acquired: 2nd-round pick in 1994
draft (32nd overall)

Background: McIlvaine led the nation as a senior by blocking 4.3 shots per game at Marquette. He finished his career with nearly as many blocks (399) as field goals (467). His draft stock dipped when he chose to miss the NBA's postseason camps, and Washington selected him 32nd overall in 1994. McIlvaine blocked 60 shots but scored only 96 points in 55 contests as a rookie. He played less than ten minutes per game.

Strengths: Great extension and timing make McIlvaine a threat to block just about any shot his man puts up. He swatted one shot every 8.9 minutes last season, one of the most efficient ratios in the NBA. He's not a top-flight athlete but he moves pretty well for a seven-footer. McIlvaine has good hands. He will hit the glass and pass the basketball. He won't try to exceed his limited offensive skills.

Weaknesses: McIlvaine is a raw offensive player. He does have a jump hook, but this is a guy who averaged less than 11 points per game during his college career despite towering over most of his defenders. He has to develop a few moves in the post and/or improve his face-up jumper. He also needs to add some upper-body strength for the rigors of rebounding and defense. There's more to it than blocking shots.

Analysis: Height can keep you in the NBA for several years, and McIlvaine has at least one skill to go along with his size. No matter how slowly the rest of his game develops, you know this guy is going to alter his share of shots in the paint. The emergence of Gheorghe Muresan last season limited McIlvaine's opportunities as a rookie. He needs more coaching anyway.

PLAYER SUMMARY	
Will	.....swat shots
Can't	do much else
Expect	a defensive presence
Don't Expect	offense
Fantasy Value	$0
Card Value	8-15¢

COLLEGE STATISTICS

		G	FGP	FTP	RPG	PPG
90-91	MARQ	28	.579	.598	4.7	8.0
91-92	MARQ	29	.545	.754	4.6	10.3
92-93	MARQ	28	.578	.714	4.8	11.0
93-94	MARQ	33	.528	.665	8.3	13.6
Totals		118	.552	.687	5.7	10.8

NBA REGULAR-SEASON STATISTICS

		G	MIN	FGs FG	FGs PCT	3-PT FGs FG	3-PT FGs PCT	FTs FT	FTs PCT	Rebounds OFF	Rebounds TOT	AST	STL	BLK	PTS	PPG
94-95	WAS	55	534	34	.479	0	.000	28	.683	40	105	10	10	60	96	1.7
Totals		55	534	34	.479	0	.000	28	.683	40	105	10	10	60	96	1.7

DERRICK McKEY

Team: Indiana Pacers
Position: Forward
Height: 6'10" **Weight:** 225
Birthdate: October 10, 1966
NBA Experience: 8 years

College: Alabama
Acquired: Traded from SuperSonics
with Gerald Paddio for Detlef
Schrempf, 11/93

Background: McKey earned Southeastern Conference Player of the Year accolades after leading Alabama to a conference title as a junior. He entered the draft a year early and was named to the 1988 All-Rookie Team in his first of six seasons with Seattle. McKey has spent the last two years with Indiana and he halted a five-year decline in his scoring average in 1994-95.

Strengths: All the athletic skills are at McKey's disposal. He has great leaping ability and handles the ball like a big guard. He has quick moves to the hoop, is a solid passer, and uses both hands effectively. He's a pure scorer who shoots well, has 3-point range, and plays rock-solid defense against some of the league's best.

Weaknesses: The knock on McKey has been his inability to play with intensity on a nightly basis, although he was "there" most nights last season. The feeling is he could be a more dominant offensive player if he ever put his mind to it, rather than being content with a supporting role. He picks up a lot of fouls.

Analysis: McKey never met his expectations with Seattle, and his trade for Detlef Schrempf before the 1993-94 season drew criticism from the Indianapolis media. His second season with the Pacers was much better than his first. In fact, were Schrempf not doing so well, people in the Hoosier state might change their opinions.

PLAYER SUMMARY	
Will	stick jumpers
Can't	shake low-key rep
Expect	team play, defense
Don't Expect	tons of shots
Fantasy Value	$19-22
Card Value	8-12¢

COLLEGE STATISTICS

		G	FGP	FTP	RPG	PPG
84-85	ALAB	33	.477	.606	4.1	5.1
85-86	ALAB	33	.636	.786	7.9	13.6
86-87	ALAB	33	.581	.862	7.5	18.6
Totals		99	.580	.797	6.5	12.4

NBA REGULAR-SEASON STATISTICS

		G	MIN	FGs FG	FGs PCT	3-PT FGs FG	3-PT FGs PCT	FTs FT	FTs PCT	Rebounds OFF	Rebounds TOT	AST	STL	BLK	PTS	PPG
87-88	SEA	82	1706	255	.491	11	.367	173	.772	115	328	107	70	63	694	8.5
88-89	SEA	82	2804	487	.502	30	.337	301	.803	167	464	219	105	70	1305	15.9
89-90	SEA	80	2748	468	.493	3	.130	315	.782	170	489	187	87	81	1254	15.7
90-91	SEA	73	2503	438	.517	4	.211	235	.845	172	423	169	91	56	1115	15.3
91-92	SEA	52	1757	285	.472	19	.380	188	.847	95	268	120	61	47	777	14.9
92-93	SEA	77	2439	387	.496	40	.357	220	.741	121	327	197	105	58	1034	13.4
93-94	IND	76	2613	355	.500	9	.290	192	.756	129	402	327	111	49	911	12.0
94-95	IND	81	2805	411	.493	32	.360	221	.744	125	394	276	125	49	1075	13.3
Totals		603	19375	3086	.497	148	.334	1845	.785	1094	3095	1602	755	473	8165	13.5

AARON McKIE

Team: Portland Trail Blazers
Position: Guard
Height: 6'5" **Weight:** 209
Birthdate: October 2, 1972

NBA Experience: 1 year
College: Temple
Acquired: 1st-round pick in 1994 draft (17th overall)

Background: McKie, a product of Philadelphia's Simon Gratz High, stayed home to attend Temple and enjoyed a fine career after sitting out his freshman year because of academics. He started all 92 of his college games and became the Owls' No. 6 career scorer. He and Temple teammate Eddie Jones were both drafted in the first round in 1994. With Portland, McKie saw most of his minutes in the latter half of the 1994-95 season.

Strengths: McKie is a workhorse who plays hard at both ends of the court. He presents the right combination of size, aggressiveness, and quickness to be a solid defensive player at the NBA level. He's not afraid to get physical. On offense, McKie is capable of knocking down 3-pointers but is considered a scorer more than a shooter. He handles the ball well and runs the floor. He'll drive if you give him room.

Weaknesses: As indicated, McKie is not a pure shooter. While he'll make some 3-pointers and pull up for jumpers from time to time, he will also launch his share of bad shots and is not likely to sink a high percentage from the field. He does not have a great feel for where and when to distribute the ball. His defense was not quite as steady as advertised, although McKie has all the tools.

Analysis: McKie spent much of 1994-95 on the injured list, including a month with a sprained right shoulder. After Portland traded Clyde Drexler and Tracy Murray, however, the energetic rookie got his chance and made the most of it. He wound up raising his scoring average to 6.5 PPG and making 20 starts in his 45 contests. He has the look of a regular rotation player who will improve with more seasoning.

PLAYER SUMMARY

Will ....play defense
Can't..............................play the point
Expect............................improvement
Don't Expect..............sweet shooting
Fantasy Value $4-6
Card Value ....20-40¢

COLLEGE STATISTICS

		G	FGP	FTP	RPG	PPG
91-92	TEMP	28	.433	.754	6.0	13.9
92-93	TEMP	33	.432	.789	5.9	20.6
93-94	TEMP	31	.401	.815	7.2	18.8
Totals		92	.421	.790	6.4	17.9

NBA REGULAR-SEASON STATISTICS

				FGs		3-PT FGs		FTs		Rebounds						
		G	MIN	FG	PCT	FG	PCT	FT	PCT	OFF	TOT	AST	STL	BLK	PTS	PPG
94-95	POR	45	827	116	.444	11	.393	50	.685	35	129	89	36	16	293	6.5
Totals		45	827	116	.444	11	.393	50	.685	35	129	89	36	16	293	6.5

NATE McMILLAN

Team: Seattle SuperSonics
Position: Guard/Forward
Height: 6'5" **Weight:** 200
Birthdate: August 3, 1964

NBA Experience: 9 years
College: Chowan; North Carolina St.
Acquired: 2nd-round pick in 1986 draft (30th overall)

Background: McMillan was a junior college All-American before transferring to North Carolina State and averaging nearly seven assists per game as a senior. As a pro, he finished among the NBA's top ten in assists in each of his first three years and is annually among the best in steals. He is Seattle's career assists leader.

Strengths: McMillan is known for his defense, rebounding, and passing. His good size, deceiving quickness, and relentless effort help him shut down opponents at three different positions. Few are better pickpockets. McMillan is a steady ball-handler and an unselfish leader who comes off the bench. He can also shoot the 3-pointer.

Weaknesses: McMillan has never been much of a scorer. The last time he averaged double figures in scoring was his second year of junior college. McMillan is brutal from the free throw line, an oddity considering his long-range stroke.

Analysis: McMillan is one of the top sixth men in the league because of his leadership and defensive ability. "This team has a lot of talent on it," Seattle head coach George Karl said last season, "but I consider Nate to be our most valuable player." McMillan, a team player who led the league in steals in 1993-94, is still sharp after nine NBA seasons.

PLAYER SUMMARY	
Will	pick your pocket
Can't	leave him open
Expect	unselfish leadership
Don't Expect	double-figure scoring
Fantasy Value	$4-6
Card Value	5-8¢

COLLEGE STATISTICS

		G	FGP	FTP	RPG	PPG
82-83	CHOW	27	.580	.696	5.0	9.9
83-84	CHOW	35	.544	.769	9.8	13.1
84-85	NCST	33	.454	.674	5.7	7.6
85-86	NCST	34	.485	.733	4.6	9.4
Totals		129	.515	.722	6.4	10.1

NBA REGULAR-SEASON STATISTICS

				FGs		3-PT FGs		FTs		Rebounds						
		G	MIN	FG	PCT	FG	PCT	FT	PCT	OFF	TOT	AST	STL	BLK	PTS	PPG
86-87	SEA	71	1972	143	.475	0	.000	87	.617	101	331	583	125	45	373	5.3
87-88	SEA	82	2453	235	.474	9	.375	145	.707	117	338	702	169	47	624	7.6
88-89	SEA	75	2341	199	.410	15	.214	119	.630	143	388	696	156	42	532	7.1
89-90	SEA	82	2338	207	.473	11	.355	98	.641	127	403	598	140	37	523	6.4
90-91	SEA	78	1434	132	.433	17	.354	57	.613	71	251	371	104	20	338	4.3
91-92	SEA	72	1652	177	.437	27	.276	54	.643	92	252	359	129	29	435	6.0
92-93	SEA	73	1977	213	.464	25	.385	95	.709	84	306	384	173	33	546	7.5
93-94	SEA	73	1887	177	.447	52	.391	31	.564	50	283	387	216	22	437	6.0
94-95	SEA	80	2070	166	.418	53	.342	34	.586	65	302	421	165	53	419	5.2
Totals		686	18124	1649	.448	209	.331	720	.647	850	2854	4501	1377	328	4227	6.2

OLIVER MILLER

Team: Toronto Raptors
Position: Center
Height: 6'9" **Weight:** 280
Birthdate: April 6, 1970

NBA Experience: 3 years
College: Arkansas
Acquired: Selected from Pistons in
1995 expansion draft

Background: Miller never gained as much attention as Arkansas teammates Todd Day and Lee Mayberry, yet he finished as the school's career leader in blocked shots (345) and field goal percentage (.636) and was second in rebounds (886). A late first-round choice by Phoenix in 1992, Miller spent two years with the Suns before Detroit signed him last season. The Raptors then grabbed him in the expansion draft.

Strengths: Miller is a tremendous all-around talent when in the 280-pound range. He is a phenomenal outlet passer, owns a great pair of hands, and is very agile for his size. His touch with the basketball is extraordinary. Miller is a good mid-range shooter who blocks a lot of shots and seals his man off the boards. He shoots for a great percentage.

Weaknesses: Miller's weight has ballooned over the 300-pound mark in the past, and it has caused him problems with his back, legs, and feet. It will always have to be monitored. Miller's game-night dedication has also been questioned, as he will disappear in certain stretches. He is a dismal free throw shooter and he is still working on his post moves.

Analysis: The verdict is not yet in on Miller, who still has not become a double-figure scorer or even a regular starter despite above-average skills. Miller rates among the top shot-blockers in the league at about two per game and his passing is superb for a big man. A hearty helping of commitment is needed to reach the next level.

PLAYER SUMMARY	
Will	block shots
Can't	make free throws
Expect	superb touch
Don't Expect	muscle definition
Fantasy Value	$7-9
Card Value	8-12¢

COLLEGE STATISTICS

		G	FGP	FTP	RPG	PPG
88-89	ARK	30	.547	.641	3.7	7.7
89-90	ARK	35	.639	.652	6.3	11.1
90-91	ARK	38	.704	.644	7.7	15.7
91-92	ARK	34	.602	.647	7.7	13.5
Totals		137	.636	.646	6.5	12.2

NBA REGULAR-SEASON STATISTICS

			FGs		3-PT FGs		FTs		Rebounds						
		G	MIN	FG	PCT	FG	PCT	FT	PCT	OFF	TOT	AST	STL	BLK	PTS	PPG
92-93	PHO	56	1069	121	.475	0	.000	71	.710	70	275	118	38	100	313	5.6
93-94	PHO	69	1786	277	.609	2	.222	80	.584	140	476	244	83	156	636	9.2
94-95	DET	64	1558	232	.555	3	.231	78	.629	162	475	93	60	116	545	8.5
Totals		189	4413	630	.559	5	.200	229	.634	372	1226	455	181	372	1494	7.9

REGGIE MILLER

Team: Indiana Pacers
Position: Guard
Height: 6'7" **Weight:** 185
Birthdate: August 24, 1965

NBA Experience: 8 years
College: UCLA
Acquired: 1st-round pick in 1987 draft
(11th overall)

Background: Miller was an All-Pac-10 selection as a senior and left UCLA ranked second to Lew Alcindor on the school's career scoring list. He has spent all eight NBA seasons with Indiana, first establishing himself as a 3-point shooter before becoming an All-Star and Dream Team II member. His 91.8-percent free throw accuracy led the league in 1990-91. He has more than 1,000 career 3-pointers and 12,000 points.

Strengths: Miller is not only one of the league's premier shooters, but also one of its best offensive players. He's virtually automatic from the line and deadly from long range. The shorter 3-point arc is a layup for Miller. He creates his own shots and gets to the basket. He is also one of the best in the league at freeing himself behind screens.

Weaknesses: Miller is rail thin and has been knocked for his defensive commitment. He has made great strides on that end, but defense is clearly not the best part of his game. He rarely blocks a shot and is not a great rebounder or ball-handler.

Analysis: Miller, the Pacers' career scoring leader, is a hard-working, durable player who was voted a starter for the 1995 All-Star Game. He is a franchise player who led the once-laughable Pacers to the Central Division championship last season. Miller is a fierce competitor who raises the level of play of those around him.

PLAYER SUMMARY	
Will	shoot the lights out
Can't	give him an opening
Expect	more All-Star showings
Don't Expect	blocked shots
Fantasy Value	$30-35
Card Value	15-35¢

COLLEGE STATISTICS

		G	FGP	FTP	RPG	PPG
83-84	UCLA	28	.509	.643	1.5	4.6
84-85	UCLA	33	.553	.804	4.3	15.2
85-86	UCLA	29	.556	.882	5.3	25.9
86-87	UCLA	32	.543	.832	5.4	22.3
Totals		122	.547	.836	4.2	17.2

NBA REGULAR-SEASON STATISTICS

				FGs		3-PT FGs		FTs		Rebounds						
		G	MIN	FG	PCT	FG	PCT	FT	PCT	OFF	TOT	AST	STL	BLK	PTS	PPG
87-88	IND	82	1840	306	.488	61	.355	149	.801	95	190	132	53	19	822	10.0
88-89	IND	74	2536	398	.479	98	.402	287	.844	73	292	227	93	29	1181	16.0
89-90	IND	82	3192	661	.514	150	.414	544	.868	95	295	311	110	18	2016	24.6
90-91	IND	82	2972	596	.512	112	.348	551	.918	81	281	331	109	13	1855	22.6
91-92	IND	82	3120	562	.501	129	.378	442	.858	82	318	314	105	26	1695	20.7
92-93	IND	82	2954	571	.479	167	.399	427	.880	67	258	262	120	26	1736	21.2
93-94	IND	79	2638	524	.503	123	.421	403	.908	30	212	248	119	24	1574	19.9
94-95	IND	81	2665	505	.462	195	.415	383	.897	30	210	242	98	16	1588	19.6
Totals		644	21917	4123	.493	1035	.395	3186	.879	553	2056	2067	807	171	12467	19.4

CHRIS MILLS

Team: Cleveland Cavaliers
Position: Forward
Height: 6'6" **Weight:** 216
Birthdate: January 25, 1970

NBA Experience: 2 years
College: Kentucky; Arizona
Acquired: 1st-round pick in 1993 draft
(22nd overall)

Background: Though he started every college game he played and won Pac-10 Player of the Year honors, Mills had a star-crossed college career. He spent one year at Kentucky but was forced to leave because of an illegal-payments scandal. Mills transferred to Arizona, where he fought an underachiever label. Drafted 22nd in 1993, he has become Cleveland's starting small forward and averaged 12.3 PPG in 1994-95.

Strengths: Mills is a fine athlete and an accomplished perimeter shooter. He can score on 3-pointers and drives to the hoop, and he can fill it up in a hurry if you leave him open. He runs the floor and finishes on the break. Mills has been a surprisingly effective defensive player who rebounds well at both ends. He has a winning attitude and shoots better than 80 percent from the line.

Weaknesses: Mills has been a little too content to take the outside shot during his first two years. He would hoist his field goal percentage and do more damage at the line if he mixed in more drives from the wing. Mills's aggressive play on defense draws its share of whistles. He needs to make better decisions with the ball if the Cavaliers want to use him a little in the backcourt.

Analysis: The Cavaliers saw something in Mills that a lot of other teams missed. He is every bit the shooter and potential scoring machine the draftniks made him out to be, and his defense and attitude have been much better than advertised. After a promising rookie campaign, he grabbed a full-time starting role and is not likely to give it up in the near future. He led the Cavaliers in minutes played last season.

PLAYER SUMMARY

Will ....shoot with range
Can't ....avoid fouling
Expect ....aggressive defense
Don't Expect......50-percent shooting
Fantasy Value $5-7
Card Value ....10-20¢

COLLEGE STATISTICS

		G	FGP	FTP	RPG	PPG
88-89	KENT	32	.484	.713	8.7	14.3
90-91	ARIZ	35	.519	.746	6.2	15.6
91-92	ARIZ	31	.506	.777	7.9	16.3
92-93	ARIZ	28	.520	.836	7.9	20.4
Totals		126	.508	.767	7.6	16.5

NBA REGULAR-SEASON STATISTICS

			FGs		3-PT FGs		FTs		Rebounds						
		G	MIN	FG	PCT	FG	PCT	FT	PCT	OFF	TOT	AST	STL	BLK	PTS	PPG
93-94	CLE	79	2022	284	.419	38	.311	137	.778	134	401	128	54	50	743	9.4
94-95	CLE	80	2814	359	.420	94	.392	174	.817	99	366	154	59	35	986	12.3
Totals		159	4836	643	.420	132	.365	311	.799	233	767	282	113	85	1729	10.9

TERRY MILLS

Team: Detroit Pistons
Position: Forward
Height: 6'10" **Weight:** 250
Birthdate: December 21, 1967

NBA Experience: 5 years
College: Michigan
Acquired: Signed as a free agent, 10/92

Background: Mills helped lead Michigan to the 1989 NCAA championship as a junior, then earned honorable-mention All-America status as a senior. He was drafted by Milwaukee, traded, and spent his rookie year with Denver and New Jersey. Detroit signed him before the 1992-93 campaign and Mills has enjoyed his three most productive years. He's led the team in rebounds the last two seasons.

Strengths: Mills is that rare power forward who can shoot with great range. The shortened 3-point arc fit him to a tee, as he converted more than 100 treys last season. He also uses his backside effectively to score in the post and can get to the hoop with the dribble. Mills is a good rebounder, has a nice feel for the game, and hits his free throws.

Weaknesses: Mills was second in the league in fouls two years ago even though he is neither a physical nor overly interested defender. He puts a lot more stock in offense. He did not block as many shots last season. He does more damage from the perimeter these days than he does on the inside. Mills has to watch his weight.

Analysis: Mills, considered by some to be an underachiever after becoming a big-name high school player, has found his hometown team to his liking. He poses all kinds of matchup problems, mainly because of his deft 3-point touch. The bombs hurt his shooting percentage, but he takes them within the flow of the game and it's tough to argue with the results.

PLAYER SUMMARY	
Will	score inside and out
Can't	be left open
Expect	matchup problems
Don't Expect	tough defense
Fantasy Value	$9-11
Card Value	5-8¢

COLLEGE STATISTICS

		G	FGP	FTP	RPG	PPG
87-88	MICH	34	.531	.729	6.4	12.1
88-89	MICH	37	.564	.769	5.9	11.6
89-90	MICH	31	.585	.759	8.0	18.1
Totals		102	.562	.755	6.7	13.8

NBA REGULAR-SEASON STATISTICS

		G	MIN	FGs FG	FGs PCT	3-PT FGs FG	3-PT FGs PCT	FTs FT	FTs PCT	Rebounds OFF	Rebounds TOT	AST	STL	BLK	PTS	PPG
90-91	DEN/NJ	55	819	134	.465	0	.000	47	.712	82	229	33	35	29	315	5.7
91-92	NJ	82	1714	310	.463	8	.348	114	.750	187	453	84	48	41	742	9.0
92-93	DET	81	2183	494	.461	10	.278	201	.791	176	472	111	44	50	1199	14.8
93-94	DET	80	2773	588	.511	24	.329	181	.797	193	672	177	64	62	1381	17.3
94-95	DET	72	2514	417	.447	109	.382	175	.799	124	558	160	68	33	1118	15.5
Totals		370	10003	1943	.472	151	.359	718	.782	762	2384	565	259	215	4755	12.9

HAROLD MINER

Team: Cleveland Cavaliers
Position: Guard
Height: 6'4" **Weight:** 214
Birthdate: May 5, 1971
NBA Experience: 3 years

College: Southern California
Acquired: Traded from Heat with a 1995 2nd-round pick for a 1995 2nd-round pick and future considerations, 6/95

Background: A prized recruit of George Raveling at Southern Cal, Miner led the previously woeful Trojans to the NCAA Tournament in 1991 and 1992. He joined Lew Alcindor as the only players in Pac-10 lore to score more than 2,000 points in three seasons. Miner was nicknamed "Baby Jordan" for his similarities to Michael in appearance and style. Miami drafted him 12th overall but his playing time in three years has been limited. Cleveland acquired him in June.

Strengths: Miner gets off his feet better than most players on the planet. His great hang time and explosive dunks often send crowds into a frenzy and helped him win the NBA's Slam Dunk Contest for the second time in 1995. The left-handed Miner is capable of going either around people or over them as he attacks the basket. He will seldom lose a game of one-on-one.

Weaknesses: Miner studies basketball and its history. But does he understand the game? There's a big difference. He does not show a great feel for team basketball. His jump shot is flat and inconsistent and he is not a proficient drive-and-dish guy. In addition, Miner does not qualify for comparisons to Jordan when it comes to defense, although he has improved.

Analysis: Miner was caught in a numbers game in the Miami backcourt. His trade to Cleveland, however, has opened the door for him to make his mark at the shooting-guard position. The 1995-96 season will be an important one for him. Miner is advised to bring an improved jump shot along with better court awareness and defense. He has the rest.

PLAYER SUMMARY	
Will	dazzle with dunks
Can't	rely on jumper
Expect	one-on-one scoring
Don't Expect	another Jordan
Fantasy Value	$1
Card Value	10-20¢

COLLEGE STATISTICS

		G	FGP	FTP	RPG	PPG
89-90	USC	28	.473	.841	3.6	20.8
90-91	USC	29	.453	.800	5.5	23.5
91-92	USC	30	.438	.811	7.0	26.3
Totals		87	.453	.814	5.4	23.6

NBA REGULAR-SEASON STATISTICS

		G	MIN	FGs FG	FGs PCT	3-PT FGs FG	3-PT FGs PCT	FTs FT	FTs PCT	Rebounds OFF	Rebounds TOT	AST	STL	BLK	PTS	PPG
92-93	MIA	73	1383	292	.475	3	.333	163	.762	74	147	73	34	8	750	10.3
93-94	MIA	63	1358	254	.477	4	.667	149	.828	75	156	95	31	13	661	10.5
94-95	MIA	45	871	123	.403	14	.286	69	.726	38	117	69	15	6	329	7.3
Totals		181	3612	669	.461	21	.328	381	.779	187	420	237	80	27	1740	9.6

GREG MINOR

Team: Boston Celtics
Position: Forward/Guard
Height: 6'6" **Weight:** 210
Birthdate: September 18, 1971

NBA Experience: 1 year
College: Louisville
Acquired: Signed as a free agent, 10/94

Background: Minor was an All-Metro Conference performer at Louisville despite playing in the shadow of Dwayne Morton and Clifford Rozier. He led the Cards in rebounding as a sophomore, in minutes as a junior, and in steals as a senior. He vaulted to the first round after his camp showings. Minor was traded from the Clippers to Indiana, then signed as a free agent with Boston before the season and averaged 6.0 PPG.

Strengths: Since he's a splendid athlete, many feel Minor has the ability to become a stopper. He can cover guards and forwards and puts out maximum effort at that end of the floor. His frame can handle the wear and tear. Minor has also demonstrated some scoring ability, including a 31-point game last season. He converts a high percentage from the field and the free throw line, runs the floor, and finishes.

Weaknesses: Minor is capable of doing a lot of things on the basketball court. It remains to be seen how well he does them on a night-to-night basis. He was not a consistent performer in college, but even the best of players struggle to gain consistency as rookies. He has the potential to do better in the rebounding department, and his shooting range is limited.

Analysis: Minor's career got off to a strange start. After the Pacers traded for his draft rights, they made him a qualifying offer that was $50,000 below the minimum required for first-round picks. The NBA took the case and ruled in favor of Minor, making him a free agent. Boston was happy to sign him, and Minor treated the Celtics to a pretty encouraging season for the most part. He seems to have a strong upside.

PLAYER SUMMARY	
Will	play two positions
Can't	launch 3-pointers
Expect	defensive potential
Don't Expect	stardom
Fantasy Value	$1
Card Value	8-12¢

COLLEGE STATISTICS

		G	FGP	FTP	RPG	PPG
91-92	LOU	30	.473	.733	5.1	9.7
92-93	LOU	31	.527	.750	5.5	14.1
93-94	LOU	34	.513	.729	6.1	13.8
Totals		95	.507	.739	5.6	12.6

NBA REGULAR-SEASON STATISTICS

	G	MIN	FGs FG	FGs PCT	3-PT FGs FG	3-PT FGs PCT	FTs FT	FTs PCT	Rebounds OFF	Rebounds TOT	AST	STL	BLK	PTS	PPG
94-95 BOS	63	945	155	.515	2	.167	65	.833	49	137	66	32	16	377	6.0
Totals	63	945	155	.515	2	.167	65	.833	49	137	66	32	16	377	6.0

SAM MITCHELL

Unrestricted Free Agent
Last Team: Indiana Pacers
Position: Forward
Height: 6'7" **Weight:** 210
Birthdate: September 2, 1963

NBA Experience: 6 years
College: Mercer
Acquired: Traded from Timberwolves with Pooh Richardson for Chuck Person and Micheal Williams, 9/92

Background: Mitchell finished his career as the all-time leading scorer at Mercer, but he got a late start as a pro. After being drafted and cut by Houston in 1985, he began a teaching career. His comeback carried him to the USBL, the CBA, and France before he became the NBA's oldest rookie (26) in 1989-90. Mitchell was a double-figure scorer for three years in Minnesota before a 1992 trade to Indiana.

Strengths: Mitchell is a versatile forward who plays with intensity and smarts. He is tough, both mentally and physically, and has a great work ethic. Mitchell runs the floor, drives, and gets to the line. He plays hard on defense and is a team player all the way. You can't knock his effort.

Weaknesses: Mitchell does nothing spectacular. His shooting range is limited and he is not much of a scorer. He got his points in Minnesota because no one else could. You'd worry about foul trouble if he logged starter's minutes, as he led the league with 338 fouls during his second season. Mitchell is a below-average ball-handler and passer and is not the biggest or quickest player around.

Analysis: Mitchell bounced back from his worst season (1993-94) with a nice 1994-95 campaign. While he did not score a ton of points and probably never will again, he converted about half of his shots from the field and showed better decision-making on an emerging team. Coaches love his work ethic, his hustle, and his unselfish approach to the game.

PLAYER SUMMARY	
Will	run the floor
Can't	shoot with range
Expect	hard work
Don't Expect	10 PPG
Fantasy Value	$0
Card Value	7-10¢

COLLEGE STATISTICS

		G	FGP	FTP	RPG	PPG
81-82	MERC	27	.497	.717	3.7	7.1
82-83	MERC	28	.519	.784	5.9	16.5
83-84	MERC	26	.507	.781	7.1	21.5
84-85	MERC	31	.516	.750	8.2	25.0
Totals		112	.512	.763	6.3	17.7

NBA REGULAR-SEASON STATISTICS

			FGs		3-PT FGs		FTs		Rebounds						
		G	MIN	FG	PCT	FG	PCT	FT	PCT	OFF	TOT	AST	STL	BLK	PTS	PPG
89-90	MIN	80	2414	372	.446	0	.000	268	.768	180	462	89	66	54	1012	12.6
90-91	MIN	82	3121	445	.441	0	.000	307	.775	188	520	133	66	57	1197	14.6
91-92	MIN	82	2151	307	.423	2	.182	209	.786	158	473	94	53	39	825	10.1
92-93	IND	81	1402	215	.445	4	.174	150	.811	93	248	76	23	10	584	7.2
93-94	IND	75	1084	140	.458	0	.000	82	.745	71	190	65	33	9	362	4.8
94-95	IND	81	1377	201	.487	1	.100	126	.724	95	243	61	43	20	529	6.5
Totals		481	11549	1680	.446	7	.104	1142	.772	785	2136	518	284	189	4509	9.4

ERIC MOBLEY

Team: Milwaukee Bucks
Position: Center
Height: 6'11" **Weight:** 250
Birthdate: February 1, 1970

NBA Experience: 1 year
College: Allegany; Pittsburgh
Acquired: 1st-round pick in 1994 draft
(18th overall)

Background: Mobley, a top recruit out of New Rochelle, New York, was diverted to a community college in Maryland before transferring to Pittsburgh. He developed slowly with the Panthers but averaged almost three blocked shots per game as a senior. He improved his stock at the Phoenix Desert Classic and went 18th in the 1994 draft. He wound up starting 26 games for Milwaukee and shot .591 from the field.

Strengths: A true center, Mobley has good athletic skills. He's strong and agile and runs well for a big man. He is a defensive intimidator with the ability to block shots, and he also makes his presence felt on the boards. Mobley gets his points in the paint and will not take many bad shots. He takes well to coaching and wants to become a force in the middle.

Weaknesses: Mobley is raw. He does not have a good feel for the game, especially at the offensive end. He gets his points on putbacks and garbage buckets. His low-post moves will not scare many defenders and his touch from the perimeter is poor. He continued an embarrassing college trend in the pros by hitting a higher percentage of his field goals than his free throws. He's one of the worst in the league from the stripe.

Analysis: Mobley started his first NBA game before the aging Alton Lister took over last season. Mobley made an extended appearance as the starter late in the season and enjoyed some success, including his 12-point, 12-rebound, four-block night against Washington. He borders on being a project, but his size, athletic ability, and defensive potential make him a likely bet to continue earning quality minutes.

PLAYER SUMMARY	
Will	block shots
Can't	shoot free throws
Expect	athletic skills
Don't Expect	much offense
Fantasy Value	$0
Card Value	12-20¢

COLLEGE STATISTICS

		G	FGP	FTP	RPG	PPG
91-92	PITT	33	.559	.410	4.6	7.2
92-93	PITT	28	.542	.553	7.5	10.4
93-94	PITT	27	.568	.492	8.8	13.7
Totals		88	.557	.486	6.8	10.2

NBA REGULAR-SEASON STATISTICS

		G	MIN	FGs FG	FGs PCT	3-PT FGs FG	3-PT FGs PCT	FTs FT	FTs PCT	Rebounds OFF	Rebounds TOT	AST	STL	BLK	PTS	PPG
94-95	MIL	46	587	78	.591	2	1.000	22	.489	55	153	21	8	27	180	3.9
Totals		46	587	78	.591	2	1.000	22	.489	55	153	21	8	27	180	3.9

ERIC MONTROSS

Team: Boston Celtics
Position: Center
Height: 7'0" **Weight:** 275
Birthdate: September 23, 1971

NBA Experience: 1 year
College: North Carolina
Acquired: 1st-round pick in 1994 draft
(9th overall)

Background: Montross, an Indianapolis prep star, disappointed Hoosier fans by choosing to play his college ball at North Carolina. He helped the Tar Heels to a national championship as a junior and shot .585 from the field as a collegian. Montross finished his career fourth on the school's all-time blocked-shots list and sixth in rebounding. Drafted ninth by Boston, he was among rookie leaders in rebounding and field goal percentage.

Strengths: Montross uses his big frame to do the kinds of things centers are supposed to do. He rebounds, takes up space in the middle, provides a physical presence, and scores on the interior. He has always shot a high percentage from the field and he displays nice touch on his jumper to about 14 feet. He brings a great attitude and work ethic to the floor, and he will not back down from a challenge.

Weaknesses: If you're looking for a great athlete, Montross is not your man. He does not have the potential to dominate games like a Patrick Ewing or a David Robinson. Montross does not own a wide variety of post moves, relying instead on power. He is not a great NBA shot-blocking threat and he is overmatched by the game's premier centers. He must cut down on his fouling and learn how to pass the basketball.

Analysis: Montross was something of a pleasant surprise in his first year. He led the Celtics in field goal percentage, finished second on the team in rebounding, and surprised a lot of people by scoring in double figures. He wants to raise his game a level or two higher and said, "It's going to be a busy (1995) summer." Expect an even better Montross in the coming years.

PLAYER SUMMARY	
Will	.....................rebound
Can't	...............avoid whistles
Expect	...........further strides
Don't Expect	....................assists
Fantasy Value	......................$6-8
Card Value	.............50¢-$1.00

COLLEGE STATISTICS

		G	FGP	FTP	RPG	PPG
90-91	NC	35	.587	.612	4.2	5.8
91-92	NC	31	.574	.624	7.0	11.2
92-93	NC	38	.615	.684	7.6	15.8
93-94	NC	35	.560	.558	8.1	13.6
Totals		139	.585	.624	6.8	11.7

NBA REGULAR-SEASON STATISTICS

			FGs		3-PT FGs		FTs		Rebounds						
	G	MIN	FG	PCT	FG	PCT	FT	PCT	OFF	TOT	AST	STL	BLK	PTS	PPG
94-95 BOS	78	2315	307	.534	0	.000	167	.635	196	566	36	29	61	781	10.0
Totals	78	2315	307	.534	0	.000	167	.635	196	566	36	29	61	781	10.0

CHRIS MORRIS

Unrestricted Free Agent
Last Team: New Jersey Nets
Position: Forward
Height: 6'8" **Weight:** 220
Birthdate: January 20, 1966

NBA Experience: 7 years
College: Auburn
Acquired: 1st-round pick in 1988 draft (4th overall)

Background: Following in the footsteps of past Auburn greats Charles Barkley and Chuck Person, Morris was the fourth player selected in the 1988 NBA draft. The Nets looked like geniuses for taking him when they did after his first two years. He leveled off after that, however, and has averaged 10-15 PPG in each of his seven NBA seasons.

Strengths: Morris matches up athletically with just about any small forward in the NBA. He runs the floor, drives to the hoop, and has become a productive 3-point shooter. He will have his share of big-scoring nights. He is an exciting finisher who gets his share of slams off the offensive glass. He also plays some defense.

Weaknesses: Morris has been plagued by inconsistency, poor shot selection, and an attitude that has gotten him in trouble with some of his coaches. The focus is not always there, although he handles himself better than he used to. He has never developed a go-to move on offense and struggles in a halfcourt game.

Analysis: Great athlete, yes. Great basketball player, not really. Morris gets his 10-15 points—sometimes a lot more or a lot less—because he runs the floor, rebounds, and has added the 3-pointer to his arsenal. He'll guard his man too. Consider, however, that Dan Majerle was selected ten spots below him in the 1988 draft. For a No. 4 pick, Morris has not lived up to his billing.

PLAYER SUMMARY	
Will	hit the 3-pointer
Can't	thrive at a slow pace
Expect	fabulous finishes
Don't Expect	an All-Star
Fantasy Value	$5-7
Card Value	5-8¢

COLLEGE STATISTICS

		G	FGP	FTP	RPG	PPG
84-85	AUB	34	.477	.620	5.0	10.4
85-86	AUB	33	.500	.670	5.2	9.8
86-87	AUB	31	.559	.711	7.3	13.5
87-88	AUB	30	.481	.795	9.8	20.7
Totals		128	.501	.712	6.7	13.4

NBA REGULAR-SEASON STATISTICS

				FGs		3-PT FGs		FTs		Rebounds						
		G	MIN	FG	PCT	FG	PCT	FT	PCT	OFF	TOT	AST	STL	BLK	PTS	PPG
88-89	NJ	76	2096	414	.457	64	.366	182	.717	188	397	119	102	60	1074	14.1
89-90	NJ	80	2449	449	.422	61	.316	228	.722	194	422	143	130	79	1187	14.8
90-91	NJ	79	2553	409	.425	45	.251	179	.734	210	521	220	138	96	1042	13.2
91-92	NJ	77	2394	346	.477	22	.200	165	.714	199	494	197	129	81	879	11.4
92-93	NJ	77	2302	436	.481	17	.224	197	.794	227	454	106	144	52	1086	14.1
93-94	NJ	50	1349	203	.447	53	.361	85	.720	91	228	83	55	49	544	10.9
94-95	NJ	71	2131	351	.410	106	.334	142	.728	181	402	147	86	51	950	13.4
Totals		510	15274	2608	.444	368	.307	1178	.733	1290	2918	1015	784	468	6762	13.3

ALONZO MOURNING

Team: Charlotte Hornets
Position: Center
Height: 6'10" **Weight:** 260
Birthdate: February 8, 1970

NBA Experience: 3 years
College: Georgetown
Acquired: 1st-round pick in 1992 draft (2nd overall)

Background: From Chesapeake, Virginia, Mourning was a coveted high school star, rating ahead of Shawn Kemp, Chris Jackson, and Billy Owens in the class of 1988. He set the NCAA record for career blocks (453) at Georgetown and became the first player named Big East Player of the Year and Defensive Player of the Year in the same season. A No. 2 overall draft pick, he played with Dream Team II and in the 1995 All-Star Game.

Strengths: Mourning can be dominant in almost every phase of the game. He scores, rebounds, blocks three shots a night, and is a ferocious competitor who loves contact and hates to lose. Mourning is a polished and productive offensive player, with a vast array of low-post moves (including a hook) and the ability to score from the perimeter. He gets to the line several times a night and plays hardnosed defense.

Weaknesses: Mourning often seems to go it alone. He turns the ball over too frequently—more than twice as often as he gets an assist. He much prefers shooting to passing, even when it means fighting a double-team. Mourning plays with a combative style that leads to a lot of personal fouls.

Analysis: Mourning has been remarkably consistent over his first three years. You know he's going to give you about 21 points, ten rebounds, and three blocked shots per night. He'll make more than half of his shots and will fight his man on the defensive end. It's a package for which all but about four coaches in the league would trade their starting center. Passing the basketball is his only glaring weakness.

PLAYER SUMMARY	
Will	score, rebound, defend
Can't	find open men
Expect	more All-Star trips
Don't Expect	soft defense
Fantasy Value	$60-65
Card Value	30-75¢

COLLEGE STATISTICS

		G	FGP	FTP	RPG	PPG
88-89	GEOR	34	.603	.667	7.3	13.1
89-90	GEOR	31	.525	.783	8.5	16.5
90-91	GEOR	23	.522	.793	7.7	15.8
91-92	GEOR	32	.595	.758	10.7	21.3
Totals		120	.566	.754	8.6	16.7

NBA REGULAR-SEASON STATISTICS

				FGs		3-PT FGs		FTs		Rebounds						
		G	MIN	FG	PCT	FG	PCT	FT	PCT	OFF	TOT	AST	STL	BLK	PTS	PPG
92-93	CHA	78	2644	572	.511	0	.000	495	.781	263	805	76	27	271	1639	21.0
93-94	CHA	60	2018	427	.505	0	.000	433	.762	177	610	86	27	188	1287	21.5
94-95	CHA	77	2941	571	.519	11	.324	490	.761	200	761	111	49	225	1643	21.3
Totals		215	7603	1570	.512	11	.282	1418	.768	640	2176	273	103	684	4569	21.3

CHRIS MULLIN

Team: Golden State Warriors
Position: Forward
Height: 6'7" **Weight:** 215
Birthdate: July 30, 1963

NBA Experience: 10 years
College: St. John's
Acquired: 1st-round pick in 1985 draft (7th overall)

Background: Mullin made every All-America team as a senior and virtually every one as a junior at St. John's. He graduated as the Big East's all-time scoring leader. His professional career began with two good years, but after voluntarily entering alcohol rehab in 1987-88, he hit his peak. He's a four-time All-Star selection and was a 1992 U.S. Olympian. He spent all but 25 games last season on the injured list.

Strengths: Mullin shoots with great touch and 3-point range, and he can kill you even with a hand in his face. He is a superb passer and plays heady defense. He's among the best free throw shooters in the NBA. Mullin is a leader with a great feel for the game.

Weaknesses: Mullin will never win any awards for his athletic ability, and injuries are starting to take their toll. Finger and thumb injuries began three years ago, then last season it was knee and ankle problems that hampered him.

Analysis: Mullin has been likened to Larry Bird in terms of his shooting, his scoring, his craftiness, and his nonstop effort. When healthy, he's dynamite. A chip fracture and sprained left knee kept him out of the lineup until January last year, and an ankle injury one week later sidelined him for another two months. The Warriors need him back.

PLAYER SUMMARY

Will ....swish his shots
Can't ....stay healthy
Expect ....crafty moves
Don't Expect...................lots of dunks
Fantasy Value $20-25
Card Value ....15-25¢

COLLEGE STATISTICS

		G	FGP	FTP	RPG	PPG
81-82	STJ	30	.534	.791	3.2	16.6
82-83	STJ	33	.577	.878	3.7	19.1
83-84	STJ	27	.571	.904	4.4	22.9
84-85	STJ	35	.521	.824	4.8	19.8
Totals		125	.550	.848	4.1	19.5

NBA REGULAR-SEASON STATISTICS

				FGs		3-PT FGs		FTs		Rebounds						
		G	MIN	FG	PCT	FG	PCT	FT	PCT	OFF	TOT	AST	STL	BLK	PTS	PPG
85-86	GS	55	1391	287	.463	5	.185	189	.896	42	115	105	70	23	768	14.0
86-87	GS	82	2377	477	.514	19	.302	269	.825	39	181	261	98	36	1242	15.1
87-88	GS	60	2033	470	.508	34	.351	239	.885	58	205	290	113	32	1213	20.2
88-89	GS	82	3093	830	.509	23	.230	493	.892	152	483	415	176	39	2176	26.5
89-90	GS	78	2830	682	.536	87	.372	505	.889	130	463	319	123	45	1956	25.1
90-91	GS	82	3315	777	.536	40	.301	513	.884	141	443	329	173	63	2107	25.7
91-92	GS	81	3346	830	.524	64	.366	350	.833	127	450	286	173	62	2074	25.6
92-93	GS	46	1902	474	.510	60	.451	183	.810	42	232	166	68	41	1191	25.9
93-94	GS	62	2324	410	.472	55	.364	165	.753	64	345	315	107	53	1040	16.8
94-95	GS	25	890	170	.489	42	.452	94	.879	25	115	125	38	19	476	19.0
Totals		653	23501	5407	.512	429	.356	3000	.862	820	3032	2611	1139	413	14243	21.8

ERIC MURDOCK

Team: Milwaukee Bucks
Position: Guard
Height: 6'1" **Weight:** 200
Birthdate: June 14, 1968
NBA Experience: 4 years

College: Providence
Acquired: Traded from Jazz with Blue Edwards and a 1992 1st-round pick for Jay Humphries and Larry Krystkowiak, 6/92

Background: As a junior at Providence, Murdock suffered a stress fracture in his leg and was hospitalized with an irregular heartbeat. He followed it up with a terrific senior year, however, and set an NCAA record with 376 career steals. Drafted by Utah, he was traded to Milwaukee after one season and was one of the league's most improved players in 1992-93. He led the Bucks in assists last season.

Strengths: Murdock brings good scoring ability to the point-guard spot. He is quick to the hoop and is a reliable 3-point shooter. Once thought to be most interested in scoring, he has improved his playmaking and is among the league's top 20 in assists. His quick hands make him an expert thief and he brings a lot of energy to both ends of the floor.

Weaknesses: Murdock does not shoot a high percentage from the field. Some of it has to do with his 3-point attempts, but another factor is his decision-making. He still tends to shoot at times when he should dump it off, and vice versa. While he gets his share of steals, he is not the kind of defender who will shut down the top lead guards.

Analysis: Murdock started last season on the injured list, eventually stole the starting point-guard duties from Lee Mayberry for 32 straight games, and then finished the season primarily as a reserve. He posts impressive numbers in several areas (six treys against the Blazers, 14 assists against the Rockets, six steals against the Heat). Steadier decision-making will make him a starter somewhere.

PLAYER SUMMARY

Will ....look to score
Can't ....shoot 50 percent
Expect ....quick hands
Don't Expect ....a shy shooter
Fantasy Value $13-16
Card Value ....7-10¢

COLLEGE STATISTICS

		G	FGP	FTP	APG	PPG
87-88	PROV	28	.413	.738	3.8	10.7
88-89	PROV	29	.457	.762	4.9	16.2
89-90	PROV	28	.419	.762	3.3	15.4
90-91	PROV	32	.445	.812	4.6	25.6
Totals		117	.436	.783	4.2	17.3

NBA REGULAR-SEASON STATISTICS

				FGs		3-PT FGs		FTs		Rebounds						
		G	MIN	FG	PCT	FG	PCT	FT	PCT	OFF	TOT	AST	STL	BLK	PTS	PPG
91-92	UTA	50	478	76	.415	5	.192	46	.754	21	54	92	30	7	203	4.1
92-93	MIL	79	2437	438	.468	31	.261	231	.780	95	284	603	174	7	1138	14.4
93-94	MIL	82	2533	477	.468	69	.411	234	.813	91	261	546	197	12	1257	15.3
94-95	MIL	75	2158	338	.415	90	.375	211	.790	48	214	482	113	12	977	13.0
Totals		286	7606	1329	.450	195	.353	722	.792	255	813	1723	514	38	3575	12.5

GHEORGHE MURESAN

Team: Washington Bullets
Position: Center
Height: 7'7" **Weight:** 303
Birthdate: February 14, 1971

NBA Experience: 2 years
College: Cluj
Acquired: 2nd-round pick in 1993 draft (30th overall)

Background: Muresan is a 24-year-old giant who is taller than even Shawn Bradley and weighs more by a lot. He is, in fact, the largest player in the history of the NBA. He played well for a professional team in France, averaging 18.7 points and 10.3 rebounds per game, before being drafted in the second round by Washington in 1993. He started for most of his second season and nearly doubled his rookie averages.

Strengths: Muresan is a mountain of a man. His massive bulk is his most obvious and clearly his greatest attribute. He takes up space on defense, rates among the top 20 in blocks, and can score when he gets the ball on the blocks. He has an accurate hook and a decent turnaround. Muresan has soft hands and can rebound without leaving the floor. He has improved steadily since coming to America.

Weaknesses: Athletic ability does not show up on Muresan's resume. He is slow on his feet and cannot get off the floor at all. He has a history of ankle and knee injuries that have caused him to fail several physical exams. He's not a good passer and you don't want him dribbling the ball. His range is limited, as is his stamina. He's not a good free throw shooter and he commits a ton of fouls.

Analysis: Muresan is a gamble that's paying off. The Bullets never envisioned him as a starting center, but injuries have forced their hand, which in turn has forced big Gheorghe to improve rapidly. Said Knicks center Patrick Ewing: "He's big and slow, but he affects your shots." Muresan is no athlete, but his size alone can cause a change in an opponent's game plan.

PLAYER SUMMARY	
Will	eat up space
Can't	get off his feet
Expect	defensive intimidation
Don't Expect	quickness
Fantasy Value	$7-9
Card Value	8-20¢

COLLEGE STATISTICS

—DID NOT PLAY—

NBA REGULAR-SEASON STATISTICS

			FGs		3-PT FGs		FTs		Rebounds						
		G	MIN	FG	PCT	FG	PCT	FT	PCT	OFF	TOT	AST	STL	BLK	PTS	PPG
93-94	WAS	54	650	128	.545	0	.000	48	.676	66	192	18	28	48	304	5.6
94-95	WAS	73	1720	303	.560	0	.000	124	.709	179	488	38	48	127	730	10.0
Totals		127	2370	431	.555	0	.000	172	.699	245	680	56	76	175	1034	8.1

LAMOND MURRAY

Team: Los Angeles Clippers
Position: Forward
Height: 6'7" **Weight:** 236
Birthdate: April 20, 1973

NBA Experience: 1 year
College: California
Acquired: 1st-round pick in 1994 draft
(7th overall)

Background: Murray and fellow 1994 lottery pick Jason Kidd played together at California. Murray led the Pac-10 in scoring as a senior and broke Kevin Johnson's all-time school scoring record in just three seasons with the Bears. The cousin of NBA forward Tracy Murray, Lamond was drafted seventh overall by the Clippers and finished the 1994-95 season among the league's top five rookie scorers at 14.1 PPG.

Strengths: Murray qualifies as both shooter and scorer. He was considered by many the best pure shooter in the 1994 draft class, possessing 3-point range and the ability to get his shot off the dribble. He also gets to the hoop, scores in transition, and has a nice post-up game. In short, he knows his way around the offensive end. Murray is also a savvy passer with a great feel for the game. He's a high riser.

Weaknesses: Most of the questions about Murray surround his commitment. His intensity and willingness to play hard on a consistent basis have been questioned, although the Clippers seem pleased with the one-year return on their investment. Murray is not as promising a defensive player as he is on offense. He played a lot of zone in college and will have to learn what pro-style defense is all about.

Analysis: The Clippers appear to have plucked a future scoring leader in Murray, who finished second on the team to Loy Vaught last season. His field goal and 3-point percentages will improve as he gets accustomed to the NBA's grind, and his first-year consistency was better than some expected. If he continues to focus on the task at hand, Murray will become a marquee-type player.

PLAYER SUMMARY

Will	get his shots
Can't	dominate physically
Expect	smooth offense
Don't Expect	a stopper
Fantasy Value	$7-9
Card Value	25-60¢

COLLEGE STATISTICS

		G	FGP	FTP	RPG	PPG
91-92	CAL	28	.474	.710	6.1	13.8
92-93	CAL	30	.517	.628	6.3	19.1
93-94	CAL	30	.476	.764	7.9	24.3
Totals		88	.489	.713	6.8	19.2

NBA REGULAR-SEASON STATISTICS

			FGs		3-PT FGs		FTs		Rebounds						
	G	MIN	FG	PCT	FG	PCT	FT	PCT	OFF	TOT	AST	STL	BLK	PTS	PPG
94-95 LAC	81	2556	439	.402	65	.298	199	.754	132	354	133	72	55	1142	14.1
Totals	81	2556	439	.402	65	.298	199	.754	132	354	133	72	55	1142	14.1

TRACY MURRAY

Team: Houston Rockets
Position: Forward
Height: 6'7" **Weight:** 228
Birthdate: July 25, 1971
NBA Experience: 3 years

College: UCLA
Acquired: Traded from Trail Blazers with Clyde Drexler for Otis Thorpe, draft rights to Marcelo Nicola, and a conditional 1st-round pick, 2/95

Background: Murray was the highest-scoring player in California prep history when he signed to play at UCLA. While sharing the ball with Don MacLean, Murray finished his college career second in Pac-10 history in 3-point field goals (197) and hit them at a 50-percent clip as a junior. He led the NBA in 3-point percentage (.459) in 1993-94 but was traded from Portland to Houston and saw limited action last season.

Strengths: Murray can flat-out shoot the ball from deep. There was no better 3-point shooter in the NBA in its final season with the long arc, and last year he made 40-plus percent from the shorter distance. He creates matchup problems because big men are forced to play him outside the arc. Murray is also a good passer.

Weaknesses: Murray lacks the quickness and strength to be a solid NBA defensive player. He does not have a body made for physical play. While he can shoot the lights out when open, he does virtually nothing off the dribble and struggles in the paint. He's a very poor rebounder for his size. Murray's work ethic has been questioned. He does little well other than shoot.

Analysis: Being the league leader in 3-point shooting does not make one a premier player, as Murray discovered last season. He does nothing else well enough to justify a starting job or even a steady supply of quality minutes. He averaged less than ten minutes per game last year and was little more than a throw-in for the Rockets in the Clyde Drexler-Otis Thorpe deal. His stroke will keep him around.

PLAYER SUMMARY

Will ....drill 3-pointers
Can't ....play tough defense
Expect ....matchup problems
Don't Expect ....all-around ability
Fantasy Value.................................$0
Card Value ....8-12¢

COLLEGE STATISTICS

		G	FGP	FTP	RPG	PPG
89-90	UCLA	33	.442	.767	5.5	12.3
90-91	UCLA	32	.503	.794	6.7	21.2
91-92	UCLA	33	.538	.800	7.0	21.4
Totals		98	.500	.791	6.4	18.3

NBA REGULAR-SEASON STATISTICS

				FGs		3-PT FGs		FTs		Rebounds						
		G	MIN	FG	PCT	FG	PCT	FT	PCT	OFF	TOT	AST	STL	BLK	PTS	PPG
92-93	POR	48	495	108	.415	21	.300	35	.875	40	83	11	8	5	272	5.7
93-94	POR	66	820	167	.470	50	.459	50	.694	43	111	31	21	20	434	6.6
94-95	POR/HOU	54	516	95	.408	35	.407	33	.786	20	59	19	14	4	258	4.8
Totals		168	1831	370	.436	106	.400	118	.766	103	253	61	43	29	964	5.7

DIKEMBE MUTOMBO

Team: Denver Nuggets   **NBA Experience:** 4 years
Position: Center   **College:** Georgetown
Height: 7'2" **Weight:** 250   **Acquired:** 1st-round pick in 1991 draft
Birthdate: June 25, 1966   (4th overall)

Background: Mutombo was raised in Zaire, a French-speaking African nation, and was forced to sit out his freshman season at Georgetown because the SAT was not offered in French. His college scoring was modest, but he won Big East Defensive Player of the Year honors in 1990 and 1991. He was the only rookie to play in the 1992 All-Star Game and has led the league in blocked shots each of the last two years.

Strengths: Great size, a giant wingspan, and underrated quickness make Mutombo a force to be reckoned with. He has blocked about four shots per game over the last two years and is also one of the top rebounders in the league (second to Dennis Rodman last season). Considered a below-average offensive player out of college, Mutombo has developed an accurate hook and can score on the inside.

Weaknesses: Mutombo does not have the shooting touch of a Patrick Ewing, David Robinson, or Hakeem Olajuwon. He also lags well behind those post men in terms of knowledge of the game, especially where and when to deliver his passes. He is an awful free throw shooter and his scoring average has decreased every year since his rookie season.

Analysis: Mutombo, an international spokesman for CARE, made a commitment to becoming the best defensive player in the league. Mutombo's scoring average has suffered for it, but he was never the most schooled offensive force anyway. He is quite simply the best combination rebounder/shot-blocker in basketball today. He's also a caring man and a class act.

PLAYER SUMMARY	
Will	intimidate
Can't	make free throws
Expect	12 RPG, 4 BPG
Don't Expect	passing, dribbling
Fantasy Value	$25-30
Card Value	15-25¢

COLLEGE STATISTICS

		G	FGP	FTP	RPG	PPG
88-89	GEOR	33	.707	.479	3.3	3.9
89-90	GEOR	31	.709	.598	10.5	10.7
90-91	GEOR	32	.586	.703	12.2	15.2
Totals		96	.644	.641	8.6	9.9

NBA REGULAR-SEASON STATISTICS

		G	MIN	FGs FG	FGs PCT	3-PT FGs FG	3-PT FGs PCT	FTs FT	FTs PCT	Rebounds OFF	Rebounds TOT	AST	STL	BLK	PTS	PPG
91-92	DEN	71	2716	428	.493	0	.000	321	.642	316	870	156	43	210	1177	16.6
92-93	DEN	82	3029	398	.510	0	.000	335	.681	344	1070	147	43	287	1131	13.8
93-94	DEN	82	2853	365	.569	0	.000	256	.583	286	971	127	59	336	986	12.0
94-95	DEN	82	3100	349	.556	0	.000	248	.654	319	1029	113	40	321	946	11.5
Totals		317	11698	1540	.527	0	.000	1160	.641	1265	3940	543	185	1154	4240	13.4

PETE MYERS

Unrestricted Free Agent
Last Team: Chicago Bulls
Position: Guard
Height: 6'6" **Weight:** 180
Birthdate: September 15, 1963

NBA Experience: 7 years
College: Faulkner St.; Arkansas-Little Rock
Acquired: Signed as a free agent, 11/94

Background: Myers, who played in relative obscurity at Arkansas-Little Rock, has been the definition of a journeyman. He saw action with five different teams in his first five years, including two stints with the Spurs, and also played in the CBA and Europe. Myers signed with Chicago in 1993-94 and started 81 games. He was used as a reserve last season.

Strengths: Myers is a valuable defensive player. He brings good size to the backcourt and will not back down from anyone. He also has pretty good quickness and gets out on the break. On offense, he keeps the ball moving and does not need to score a lot of points. He'll hit an occasional 3-pointer. Myers plays hard.

Weaknesses: The reason Myers bounced around for so long was his lack of a consistent offensive strength. He is not a great pure shooter or a dominant attack-the-basket type. He needs a go-to move. His accuracy from the field and the line is subpar. Myers has trouble matching up with with the quicker guards in the league.

Analysis: Myers had the unenviable task two years ago of taking over Michael Jordan's starting spot. He played a much less significant role last season, and now that Jordan is back in basketball, the future of this journeyman is again cloudy. He provides defense and hard work, but his offensive skills are marginal.

PLAYER SUMMARY	
Will	guard his man
Can't	displace Jordan
Expect	defensive smarts
Don't Expect	10 PPG
Fantasy Value	$0
Card Value	5-8¢

COLLEGE STATISTICS

		G	FGP	FTP	RPG	PPG
81-82	FAUL	26	.548	.743	5.1	12.4
82-83	FAUL	26	.578	.627	7.5	15.2
84-85	ALR	30	.451	.719	7.1	14.8
85-86	ALR	34	.534	.747	7.9	19.2
Totals		116	.521	.712	7.0	15.6

NBA REGULAR-SEASON STATISTICS

				FGs		3-PT FGs		FTs		Rebounds						
		G	MIN	FG	PCT	FG	PCT	FT	PCT	OFF	TOT	AST	STL	BLK	PTS	PPG
86-87	CHI	29	155	19	.365	0	.000	28	.651	8	17	21	14	2	66	2.3
87-88	SA	22	328	43	.453	0	.000	26	.667	11	37	48	17	6	112	5.1
88-89	PHI/NY	33	270	31	.425	0	.000	33	.688	15	33	48	20	2	95	2.9
89-90	NY/NJ	52	751	89	.396	0	.000	66	.660	33	96	135	35	11	244	4.7
90-91	SA	8	103	10	.435	0	.000	9	.818	2	18	14	3	3	29	3.6
93-94	CHI	82	2030	253	.455	8	.276	136	.701	54	181	245	78	20	650	7.9
94-95	CHI	71	1270	119	.415	10	.256	70	.614	57	139	148	58	15	318	4.5
Totals		297	4907	564	.430	18	.205	368	.670	180	521	659	225	59	1514	5.1

JOHNNY NEWMAN

Unrestricted Free Agent
Last Team: Milwaukee Bucks
Position: Forward
Height: 6'7" **Weight:** 205
Birthdate: November 28, 1963

NBA Experience: 9 years
College: Richmond
Acquired: Signed as a free agent, 10/94

Background: Newman, who set a career scoring record at Richmond, spent one year with Cleveland before being waived. He has since played for New York, Charlotte, New Jersey, and Milwaukee in his nine-year NBA career. Signed by the Bucks as a free agent before the 1994-95 season, he averaged 7.7 PPG.

Strengths: Newman is the definition of a slasher. He loves to attack the basket in the open court and will challenge in a halfcourt set as well. He is an impressive athlete who has always had a scoring bent. He gets his points in bunches. Newman is able to play either the small-forward or big-guard spot.

Weaknesses: Newman cares more about getting his own shots than making his teammates look better. His career average is well under two assists per game despite playing a lot of guard. He picks up a lot of reaching fouls and is not a great rebounder. His outside shooting is streaky and he has complained about playing time.

Analysis: Four different teams have allowed Newman to sign elsewhere, which says something about his outlook on the game. Scoring points has always been important to him, and last season he failed to reach ten PPG for the first time since his rookie season. He will still light it up on occasion.

PLAYER SUMMARY

Will .... slash to the hoop
Can't .... involve his teammates
Expect .... a scoring bent
Don't Expect .... 2 APG
Fantasy Value $0
Card Value .... 5-8¢

COLLEGE STATISTICS

		G	FGP	FTP	RPG	PPG
82-83	RICH	28	.529	.719	3.1	12.3
83-84	RICH	32	.528	.787	6.1	21.9
84-85	RICH	32	.551	.773	5.2	21.3
85-86	RICH	30	.517	.890	7.3	22.0
Totals		122	.532	.800	5.5	19.5

NBA REGULAR-SEASON STATISTICS

			FGs		3-PT FGs		FTs		Rebounds						
		G	MIN	FG	PCT	FG	PCT	FT	PCT	OFF	TOT	AST	STL	BLK	PTS	PPG
86-87	CLE	59	630	113	.411	1	.045	66	.868	36	70	27	20	7	293	5.0
87-88	NY	77	1589	270	.435	26	.280	207	.841	87	159	62	72	11	773	10.0
88-89	NY	81	2336	455	.475	97	.338	286	.815	93	206	162	111	23	1293	16.0
89-90	NY	80	2277	374	.476	45	.317	239	.709	60	191	180	95	22	1032	12.9
90-91	CHA	81	2477	478	.470	30	.357	385	.809	94	254	188	100	17	1371	16.9
91-92	CHA	55	1651	295	.477	13	.283	236	.766	71	179	146	70	14	839	15.3
92-93	CHA	64	1471	279	.522	12	.267	194	.808	72	143	117	45	19	764	11.9
93-94	CHA/NJ	81	1697	313	.471	24	.267	182	.809	86	180	72	69	27	832	10.3
94-95	MIL	82	1896	226	.463	45	.352	137	.801	72	173	91	69	13	634	7.7
Totals		660	16024	2803	.470	293	.313	1932	.808	671	1555	1045	651	153	7831	11.9

KEN NORMAN

Team: Atlanta Hawks
Position: Forward
Height: 6'8" **Weight:** 228
Birthdate: September 5, 1964

NBA Experience: 8 years
College: Wabash Valley; Illinois
Acquired: Traded from Bucks for Roy Hinson, 6/94

Background: Norman was a two-time All-Big Ten selection at Illinois, where he set a school record for field goal percentage. He became a starter for the Clippers late in his rookie year and increased his scoring output by nearly ten points in 1988-89. After six years in L.A., he has spent one season apiece in Milwaukee and Atlanta.

Strengths: Norman considers himself a banger and loves to rebound and play defense. Nicknamed "Snake" for his slithering moves around the basket, he can score points in bunches and thrives in an open-court game. Big for a small forward, Norman also puts up a reliable mid-range jumper and has hit the 3-pointer in his last two seasons.

Weaknesses: The glaring weakness in Norman's game is his horrendous free throw shooting, which stands at less than 60 percent for his career and was under 50 last season. It's perplexing because he almost hits an equal percentage from 3-point range. He is not a good ball-handler. Norman has yet to match his second-year numbers.

Analysis: Norman has earned a reputation for toughness. Now he must avoid the temptation to abandon his inside game because he can make 3-pointers. Though one of the league's worst free throw shooters, when he is on his game Norman commands respect—both on and off the court. He owns several dogs, attack rottweilers among them.

PLAYER SUMMARY	
Will	score inside and out
Can't	make free throws
Expect	transition buckets
Don't Expect	a nifty dribble
Fantasy Value	$2-4
Card Value	7-10¢

COLLEGE STATISTICS

		G	FGP	FTP	RPG	PPG
82-83	WAB	35	.605	.673	10.3	20.4
84-85	ILL	29	.632	.663	3.7	7.8
85-86	ILL	32	.641	.802	7.1	16.4
86-87	ILL	31	.578	.727	9.8	20.7
Totals		127	.608	.717	7.9	16.6

NBA REGULAR-SEASON STATISTICS

		G	MIN	FGs FG	FGs PCT	3-PT FGs FG	3-PT FGs PCT	FTs FT	FTs PCT	Rebounds OFF	Rebounds TOT	AST	STL	BLK	PTS	PPG
87-88	LAC	66	1435	241	.482	0	.000	87	.512	100	263	78	44	34	569	8.6
88-89	LAC	80	3020	638	.502	4	.190	170	.630	245	667	277	106	66	1450	18.1
89-90	LAC	70	2334	484	.510	7	.438	153	.632	143	470	160	78	59	1128	16.1
90-91	LAC	70	2309	520	.501	6	.188	173	.629	177	497	159	63	63	1219	17.4
91-92	LAC	77	2009	402	.490	4	.143	121	.535	158	448	125	53	66	929	12.1
92-93	LAC	76	2477	498	.511	10	.263	131	.595	209	571	165	59	58	1137	15.0
93-94	MIL	82	2539	412	.448	63	.333	92	.503	169	500	222	58	46	979	11.9
94-95	ATL	74	1879	388	.453	98	.344	64	.457	103	362	94	34	20	938	12.7
Totals		595	18002	3583	.489	192	.310	991	.574	1304	3778	1280	495	412	8349	14.0

CHARLES OAKLEY

Team: New York Knicks
Position: Forward
Height: 6'9" **Weight:** 245
Birthdate: December 18, 1963
NBA Experience: 10 years

College: Virginia Union
Acquired: Traded from Bulls with 1988 first- and third-round picks for Bill Cartwright and 1988 first- and third-round picks, 6/88

Background: The top Division II rebounder in the country in 1984-85, Oakley grabbed more than 17 per game at Virginia Union. He made the NBA All-Rookie Team and became one of the league's best rebounders with Chicago, but he was traded to New York for Bill Cartwright in 1988. Oakley was a 1994 All-Star and All-Defensive player.

Strengths: Oakley rebounds and plays punishing defense. Once the NBA's "Chairman of the Boards," Oakley still uses his wide body around the glass. It requires great courage to drive toward him. He has been a key for the Knicks in setting a physical tone, and he also buries his open jumpers.

Weaknesses: Oakley does not jump well, relying more on brute strength and positioning to get his boards. He commits a lot of fouls and is not the most popular guy in the league among opponents. His defense does not include blocked shots.

Analysis: An enforcer in every sense of the word, Oakley sat out two months last season following toe surgery. The Knicks sorely missed him. He enjoyed one of the best all-around seasons of his ten-year career in 1993-94 and will look to duplicate those numbers in 1995-96. He is a huge reason the Knicks are considered title contenders.

PLAYER SUMMARY	
Will	battle on defense
Can't	jump out of the gym
Expect	double-doubles
Don't Expect	blocked shots
Fantasy Value	$8-10
Card Value	7-12¢

COLLEGE STATISTICS

		G	FGP	FTP	RPG	PPG
81-82	VU	28	.620	.610	12.5	15.9
82-83	VU	28	.582	.588	13.0	19.3
83-84	VU	30	.612	.621	13.1	21.7
84-85	VU	31	.625	.669	17.3	24.0
Totals		117	.611	.626	14.0	20.3

NBA REGULAR-SEASON STATISTICS

				FGs		3-PT FGs		FTs		Rebounds						
		G	MIN	FG	PCT	FG	PCT	FT	PCT	OFF	TOT	AST	STL	BLK	PTS	PPG
85-86	CHI	77	1772	281	.519	0	.000	178	.662	255	664	133	68	30	740	9.6
86-87	CHI	82	2980	468	.445	11	.367	245	.686	299	1074	296	85	36	1192	14.5
87-88	CHI	82	2816	375	.483	3	.250	261	.727	326	1066	248	68	28	1014	12.4
88-89	NY	82	2604	426	.510	12	.250	197	.773	343	861	187	104	14	1061	12.9
89-90	NY	61	2196	336	.524	0	.000	217	.761	258	727	146	64	16	889	14.6
90-91	NY	76	2739	307	.516	0	.000	239	.784	305	920	204	62	17	853	11.2
91-92	NY	82	2309	210	.522	0	.000	86	.735	256	700	133	67	15	506	6.2
92-93	NY	82	2230	219	.508	0	.000	127	.722	288	708	126	85	15	565	6.9
93-94	NY	82	2932	363	.478	0	.000	243	.776	349	965	218	110	18	969	11.8
94-95	NY	50	1567	192	.489	3	.250	119	.793	155	445	126	60	7	506	10.1
Totals		756	24145	3177	.494	29	.248	1912	.739	2834	8130	1817	773	196	8295	11.0

HAKEEM OLAJUWON

Team: Houston Rockets
Position: Center
Height: 7'0" **Weight:** 255
Birthdate: January 21, 1963

NBA Experience: 11 years
College: Houston
Acquired: 1st-round pick in 1984 draft
(1st overall)

Background: Olajuwon led Houston to the Final Four three consecutive years, and he led the nation in rebounding and field goal accuracy as a senior. He was selected Southwest Conference Player of the 1980s. The former soccer goalie in Nigeria has made ten All-Star trips in 11 seasons. He was the NBA's MVP and Defensive Player of the Year while leading the Rockets to the 1994 NBA championship. He was the MVP of the last two NBA Finals.

Strengths: Olajuwon is one of the most talented and versatile centers ever. He is one of the best scorers, rebounders, and shot-blockers in the game. He has an amazing touch for a center, is an excellent passer, and is the leader of a talented team. Few play with his intensity and effectiveness on a nightly basis.

Weaknesses: Olajuwon piles up fouls and turnovers, but that's because he's always in the middle of everything. His career free throw shooting is just over 70 percent.

Analysis: A year after winning the MVP Award and a championship ring, Olajuwon carried the Rockets to the promised land again. He outdueled league MVP David Robinson in the Western Conference finals and then humbled Shaquille O'Neal in the championship round. He has already secured his spot as one of the all-time greats.

PLAYER SUMMARY	
Will	dominate nightly
Can't	be shut down
Expect	great leadership
Don't Expect	single-digit nights
Fantasy Value	$85-90
Card Value	40-75¢

COLLEGE STATISTICS

		G	FGP	FTP	RPG	PPG
81-82	HOUS	29	.607	.563	6.2	8.3
82-83	HOUS	34	.611	.595	11.4	13.9
83-84	HOUS	37	.675	.526	13.5	16.8
Totals		100	.639	.555	10.7	13.3

NBA REGULAR-SEASON STATISTICS

				FGs		3-PT FGs		FTs		Rebounds						
		G	MIN	FG	PCT	FG	PCT	FT	PCT	OFF	TOT	AST	STL	BLK	PTS	PPG
84-85	HOU	82	2914	677	.538	0	.000	338	.613	440	974	111	99	220	1692	20.6
85-86	HOU	68	2467	625	.526	0	.000	347	.645	333	781	137	134	231	1597	23.5
86-87	HOU	75	2760	677	.508	1	.200	400	.702	315	858	220	140	254	1755	23.4
87-88	HOU	79	2825	712	.514	0	.000	381	.695	302	959	163	162	214	1805	22.8
88-89	HOU	82	3024	790	.508	0	.000	454	.696	338	1105	149	213	282	2034	24.8
89-90	HOU	82	3124	806	.501	1	.167	382	.713	299	1149	234	174	376	1995	24.3
90-91	HOU	56	2062	487	.508	0	.000	213	.769	219	770	131	121	221	1187	21.2
91-92	HOU	70	2636	591	.502	0	.000	328	.766	246	845	157	127	304	1510	21.6
92-93	HOU	82	3242	848	.529	0	.000	444	.779	283	1068	291	150	342	2140	26.1
93-94	HOU	80	3277	894	.528	8	.421	388	.716	229	955	287	128	297	2184	27.3
94-95	HOU	72	2853	798	.517	3	.188	406	.756	172	775	255	133	242	2005	27.8
Totals		828	31184	7905	.516	13	.178	4081	.710	3176	10239	2135	1581	2983	19904	24.0

SHAQUILLE O'NEAL

Team: Orlando Magic
Position: Center
Height: 7'1" **Weight:** 303
Birthdate: March 6, 1972

NBA Experience: 3 years
College: Louisiana St.
Acquired: 1st-round pick in 1992 draft
(1st overall)

Background: Shaq was a two-time All-American in his three years at Louisiana State and earned a handful of Player of the Year honors after his sophomore campaign. Few Rookie of the Year winners have ever made as big an impact as Shaq did. He was the first rookie since Michael Jordan to start in the All-Star Game and has started each year since. He also played on Dream Team II and won last year's NBA scoring title.

Strengths: O'Neal is as powerful as any player in the game. He has torn down two backboards on slam dunks and is virtually unstoppable when he gets the ball in the paint. He scores, rebounds, and swats shots with the best of them. His field goal percentage is also among the best in the league and his offensive arsenal continues to grow. He's a fan favorite who has made the Magic a title contender.

Weaknesses: The biggest struggles for this mega-star come from the free throw line, and he gets there more than any player. He has yet to make more than 60 percent and seems to get worse instead of better. Foul trouble is often an issue with O'Neal.

Analysis: O'Neal has earned the right to be called the NBA's superstar of the present and future. He is the most physically dominant player in the league. What's scarier, he has added a turnaround jumper and a nifty set of post moves to complement his raw power. He has also cut a successful rap album, has starred in a movie (*Blue Chips*), and is one of the biggest names in the entire entertainment industry.

PLAYER SUMMARY	
Will	overpower opponents
Can't	be stopped inside
Expect	multiple MVP Awards
Don't Expect	free throw titles
Fantasy Value	$70-75
Card Value	$1.25-4.00

COLLEGE STATISTICS

		G	FGP	FTP	RPG	PPG
89-90	LSU	32	.573	.556	12.0	13.9
90-91	LSU	28	.628	.638	14.7	27.6
91-92	LSU	30	.615	.528	14.0	24.1
Totals		90	.610	.575	13.5	21.6

NBA REGULAR-SEASON STATISTICS

				FGs		3-PT FGs		FTs		Rebounds						
		G	MIN	FG	PCT	FG	PCT	FT	PCT	OFF	TOT	AST	STL	BLK	PTS	PPG
92-93	ORL	81	3071	733	.562	0	.000	427	.592	342	1122	152	60	286	1893	23.4
93-94	ORL	81	3224	953	.599	0	.000	471	.554	384	1072	195	76	231	2377	29.3
94-95	ORL	79	2923	930	.583	0	.000	455	.533	328	901	214	73	192	2315	29.3
Totals		241	9218	2616	.583	0	.000	1353	.558	1054	3095	561	209	709	6585	27.3

BO OUTLAW

Team: Los Angeles Clippers
Position: Forward
Height: 6′8″ **Weight:** 210
Birthdate: April 13, 1971

NBA Experience: 2 years
College: South Plains; Houston
Acquired: Signed as a free agent, 2/94

Background: Charles "Bo" Outlaw led the nation in field goal percentage in 1992 and 1993 at the University of Houston, but he was bypassed in the 1993 NBA draft. He was tearing up the CBA in Grand Rapids before the Clippers signed him in February 1994. Outlaw stuck with the Clippers and has been a part-time starter in his season and a half of NBA experience. He finished ninth in the league at 1.86 BPG last season.

Strengths: Outlaw gives the Clippers something they have sorely needed— defense. Everyone above him on the list of NBA shot-blocking leaders is considerably taller than this 6′8″ power forward. What he gives up in size he makes up for in leaping ability, hustle, and heart. He even guards centers. Outlaw is a dangerous offensive rebounder who also bangs the defensive boards. He does not play over his head.

Weaknesses: Outlaw is small for a post player and has no perimeter game to bail him out. He has horrible mechanics and poor touch on his outside shot, and he is one of the worst free throw shooters you'll find. He gets most of his points on the offensive glass, as his low-post arsenal is nothing spectacular. Outlaw won't make a living with his ball-handling or passing, either.

Analysis: Outlaw has a good chance of sticking around because of his splendid defense. He makes it a challenge to stay in his man's jersey, and he blocks shots better than anyone in the NBA his size. Outlaw knows he has to work to keep his job and he does just that. He is also a class act off the court. He played Santa Claus for 5,000 underprivileged children in Los Angeles last Christmas.

PLAYER SUMMARY

Will.............................block shots
Can't ....shoot straight
Expect ....hardnosed defense
Don't Expect ....10 PPG
Fantasy Value...............................$1
Card Value ....7-10¢

COLLEGE STATISTICS

		G	FGP	FTP	RPG	PPG
89-90	SP	30	.563	.507	9.6	12.1
90-91	SP	30	.661	.574	10.9	13.2
91-92	HOUS	31	.684	.442	8.2	11.9
92-93	HOUS	30	.658	.495	10.0	16.2
Totals		121	.640	.503	9.7	13.3

NBA REGULAR-SEASON STATISTICS

			FGs		3-PT FGs		FTs		Rebounds						
	G	MIN	FG	PCT	FG	PCT	FT	PCT	OFF	TOT	AST	STL	BLK	PTS	PPG
93-94 LAC	37	871	98	.587	0	.000	61	.592	81	212	36	36	37	257	6.9
94-95 LAC	81	1655	170	.523	0	.000	82	.441	121	313	84	90	151	422	5.2
Totals	118	2526	268	.545	0	.000	143	.495	202	525	120	126	188	679	5.8

DOUG OVERTON

Team: Washington Bullets
Position: Guard
Height: 6'3" **Weight:** 190
Birthdate: August 3, 1969

NBA Experience: 3 years
College: LaSalle
Acquired: Signed as a free agent, 10/92

Background: Overton, a high school teammate of Bo Kimble and the late Hank Gathers at Philadelphia's Dobbins Tech, was a solid complementary player to Lionel Simmons at LaSalle but struggled after Simmons graduated. Overton was drafted in the second round by Detroit in 1991 but was released without playing a game. He's played his three pro seasons with Washington and appeared in all 82 games last season.

Strengths: Overton's greatest asset is his defense. His Philadelphia years taught him about toughness and he will not back down from anyone. He can defend at both backcourt spots. Overton is an excellent free throw shooter and can hit the 3-pointer as well. He made 42 percent from behind the arc last season. Overton also finished with a career-high assist total and scored 30 points in a game.

Weaknesses: Overton possesses only average quickness and does not penetrate as easily or as often as coaches would like. He is not a prototypical point guard, as he looks for his own shot more often than he sets up a teammate. He's not a great finisher in traffic. In fact, he shot better from outside the arc last season than he did from 2-point range. He won't come up with a lot of steals.

Analysis: Overton is a streetwise player who plays defense, can ignite his team with 3-pointers, and will handle the offense well enough to give your starter a rest. Whether he can develop as a starting point guard at the NBA level remains to be seen. After a disappointing sophomore campaign, he was the only Bullet to play a full 82 games last season.

PLAYER SUMMARY	
Will	hit from deep
Can't	set assist records
Expect	toughness
Don't Expect	finishes in traffic
Fantasy Value	$0
Card Value	5-8¢

COLLEGE STATISTICS

		G	FGP	FTP	APG	PPG
87-88	LaS	34	.498	.841	2.7	7.8
88-89	LaS	32	.494	.787	7.6	13.2
89-90	LaS	32	.519	.798	6.6	17.2
90-91	LaS	25	.445	.818	5.0	22.3
Totals		123	.486	.814	5.5	14.6

NBA REGULAR-SEASON STATISTICS

		G	MIN	FGs FG	FGs PCT	3-PT FGs FG	3-PT FGs PCT	FTs FT	FTs PCT	Rebounds OFF	Rebounds TOT	AST	STL	BLK	PTS	PPG
92-93	WAS	45	990	152	.471	3	.231	59	.728	25	106	157	31	6	366	8.1
93-94	WAS	61	749	87	.403	1	.091	43	.827	19	69	92	21	1	218	3.6
94-95	WAS	82	1704	207	.416	53	.424	109	.872	26	143	246	53	2	576	7.0
Totals		188	3443	446	.430	57	.383	211	.818	70	318	495	105	9	1160	6.2

BILLY OWENS

Team: Miami Heat
Position: Forward/Guard
Height: 6'9" **Weight:** 225
Birthdate: May 1, 1969
NBA Experience: 4 years

College: Syracuse
Acquired: Traded from Warriors with draft rights to Predrag Danilovic for Rony Seikaly, 11/94

Background: Owens, the 1988 A.P. High School Player of the Year at Carlisle (Pennsylvania) High, finished his three-year career at Syracuse ranked among the school's top seven in scoring, rebounds, blocked shots, steals, and assists. Owens was one of the top NBA rookies with Golden State but has since had surgery on both knees. He was traded to Miami before the 1994-95 season and was third on the Heat in scoring.

Strengths: Owens brings tremendous versatility to the court. He plays small forward, but he is capable of filling in at either big forward or small guard and he triggers the break like a point guard. He's a strong finisher, can break his man down off the dribble, and can also score with wing jumpers. He is an exceptional offensive rebounder and has a keen passing eye.

Weaknesses: Owens has limited range and has never been a good free throw shooter. In fact, shooting jumpers is not the best part of his offensive game. His decision-making still needs some work, as indicated by his 2-of-22 3-point shooting last season. Owens too often tries to do the spectacular instead of the logical. He draws a lot of whistles and is not a star defender.

Analysis: Owens, fully recovered from the knee problems that slowed his second season, was traded to the Heat in a deal that sent former Syracuse teammate Rony Seikaly to Golden State. Owens is capable of triple-doubles with his scoring, passing, and rebounding abilities. He wants to be an All-Star but has not attained that level of consistency yet.

PLAYER SUMMARY

Will	shine in transition
Can't	pump in treys
Expect	great versatility
Don't Expect	pure shooting
Fantasy Value	$25-30
Card Value	10-15¢

COLLEGE STATISTICS

		G	FGP	FTP	RPG	PPG
88-89	SYR	38	.521	.648	6.9	13.0
89-90	SYR	33	.486	.722	8.4	18.2
90-91	SYR	32	.509	.674	11.6	23.3
Totals		103	.505	.682	8.8	17.7

NBA REGULAR-SEASON STATISTICS

				FGs		3-PT FGs		FTs		Rebounds						
		G	MIN	FG	PCT	FG	PCT	FT	PCT	OFF	TOT	AST	STL	BLK	PTS	PPG
91-92	GS	80	2510	468	.525	1	.111	204	.654	243	639	188	90	65	1141	14.3
92-93	GS	37	1201	247	.501	1	.091	117	.639	108	264	144	35	28	612	16.5
93-94	GS	79	2738	492	.507	3	.200	199	.610	230	640	326	83	60	1186	15.0
94-95	MIA	70	2296	403	.491	2	.091	194	.620	203	502	246	80	30	1002	14.3
Totals		266	8745	1610	.507	7	.123	714	.630	784	2045	904	288	183	3941	14.8

ROBERT PACK

Team: Denver Nuggets
Position: Guard
Height: 6'2" **Weight:** 190
Birthdate: February 3, 1969

NBA Experience: 4 years
College: Tyler; Southern California
Acquired: Traded from Trail Blazers for a 1993 2nd-round pick, 10/92

Background: Pack totaled 319 assists in just two years at Southern Cal. He joined former USC stars Gus Williams, Jacque Hill, and Larry Friend when he recorded back-to-back years of 100 or more assists. He was not drafted but spent a year with Portland and has been with the Nuggets the past three years. Pack had won a starting job last season before knee surgery in early March sidelined him.

Strengths: Pack has lightning quickness and good strength, and he uses them to drive past just about anyone. He distributes, has 3-point range, and upped his scoring to a career-high 12.1 PPG after injuring his left knee last season. Pack is as tough as nails on defense. The feisty sort, he comes up with steals and plays a very intense brand of basketball. He recorded his first triple-double last season.

Weaknesses: Pack is not a pure shooter, although he has worked very hard on that aspect of his game. His offensive play in general is hot-and-cold and he is not great fundamentally. He takes a few too many chances on both ends of the floor and commits a lot of turnovers. Keep an eye on the knee, because quickness is his calling card.

Analysis: One of the fastest emerging players in basketball saw his momentum come to a halt because of the famed anterior cruciate tear. His March 1 surgery was said to be successful, and Pack undoubtedly spent many off-season hours strengthening it in preparation for the 1995-96 season. Such an off-season work ethic has helped him become a reliable all-around player.

PLAYER SUMMARY	
Will	get past his man
Can't	eliminate turnovers
Expect	off-season work
Don't Expect	pure shooting
Fantasy Value	$1-3
Card Value	5-8¢

COLLEGE STATISTICS

		G	FGP	FTP	APG	PPG
89-90	USC	28	.472	.677	5.9	12.1
90-91	USC	29	.480	.794	5.3	14.7
Totals		57	.476	.742	5.6	13.4

NBA REGULAR-SEASON STATISTICS

				FGs		3-PT FGs		FTs		Rebounds						
		G	MIN	FG	PCT	FG	PCT	FT	PCT	OFF	TOT	AST	STL	BLK	PTS	PPG
91-92	POR	72	894	115	.423	0	.000	102	.803	32	97	140	40	4	332	4.6
92-93	DEN	77	1579	285	.470	1	.125	239	.768	52	160	335	81	10	810	10.5
93-94	DEN	66	1382	223	.443	6	.207	179	.758	25	123	356	81	9	631	9.6
94-95	DEN	42	1144	170	.430	30	.417	137	.783	19	113	290	61	6	507	12.1
Totals		257	4999	793	.447	37	.311	657	.774	128	493	1121	263	29	2280	8.9

ROBERT PARISH

Team: Charlotte Hornets
Position: Center
Height: 7'0" **Weight:** 244
Birthdate: August 30, 1953

NBA Experience: 19 years
College: Centenary
Acquired: Signed as a free agent, 7/94

Background: The best player in Centenary history, "Chief" enjoyed four solid seasons with Golden State before his career blossomed in Boston. Parish helped the Celtics to championships in 1981, '84, and '86. The oldest player in the league at 41 last season, he played in 81 games with Charlotte.

Strengths: Parish remains a productive rebounder, though his high-arching jumpers are less frequent. He will finish his career among the all-time leaders in scoring, rebounding, and blocked shots. Parish needs to play 66 more games to catch Kareem Abdul-Jabbar (1,560) for the all-time lead.

Weaknesses: Parish is no longer effective for long chunks of minutes. He is but a shadow of his former self in all phases of the game.

Analysis: Parish is headed for the Hall of Fame the first year he's eligible. However, one of the most productive and durable big men in history is also headed for retirement.

PLAYER SUMMARY	
Will	be remembered
Can't	do what he used to
Expect	the Hall to call
Don't Expect	two more years
Fantasy Value	$0
Card Value	8-15¢

COLLEGE STATISTICS

		G	FGP	FTP	RPG	PPG
72-73	CENT	27	.579	.610	18.7	23.0
73-74	CENT	25	.523	.628	15.3	19.9
74-75	CENT	29	.560	.661	15.4	18.9
75-76	CENT	27	.589	.694	18.0	24.8
Totals		108	.564	.655	16.9	21.6

NBA REGULAR-SEASON STATISTICS

				FGs		3-PT FGs		FTs		Rebounds						
		G	MIN	FG	PCT	FG	PCT	FT	PCT	OFF	TOT	AST	STL	BLK	PTS	PPG
76-77	GS	77	1384	288	.503	0	.000	121	.708	201	543	74	55	94	697	9.1
77-78	GS	82	1969	430	.472	0	.000	165	.625	211	679	95	79	123	1025	12.5
78-79	GS	76	2411	554	.499	0	.000	196	.698	265	916	115	100	217	1304	17.2
79-80	GS	72	2119	510	.507	0	.000	203	.715	257	793	122	58	115	1223	17.0
80-81	BOS	82	2298	635	.545	0	.000	282	.710	245	777	144	81	214	1552	18.9
81-82	BOS	80	2534	669	.542	0	.000	252	.710	288	866	140	68	192	1590	19.9
82-83	BOS	78	2459	619	.550	0	.000	271	.698	260	827	141	79	148	1509	19.3
83-84	BOS	80	2867	623	.542	0	.000	274	.745	243	857	139	55	116	1520	19.0
84-85	BOS	79	2850	551	.542	0	.000	292	.743	263	840	125	56	101	1394	17.6
85-86	BOS	81	2567	530	.549	0	.000	245	.731	246	770	145	65	116	1305	16.1
86-87	BOS	80	2995	588	.556	0	.000	227	.735	254	851	173	64	144	1403	17.5
87-88	BOS	74	2312	442	.589	0	.000	177	.734	173	628	115	55	84	1061	14.3
88-89	BOS	80	2840	596	.570	0	.000	294	.719	342	996	175	79	116	1486	18.6
89-90	BOS	79	2396	505	.580	0	.000	233	.747	259	796	103	38	69	1243	15.7
90-91	BOS	81	2441	485	.598	0	.000	237	.767	271	856	66	66	103	1207	14.9
91-92	BOS	79	2285	468	.535	0	.000	179	.772	219	705	70	68	97	1115	14.1
92-93	BOS	79	2146	416	.535	0	.000	162	.689	246	740	61	57	107	994	12.6
93-94	BOS	74	1987	356	.491	0	.000	154	.740	141	542	82	42	96	866	11.7
94-95	CHA	81	1352	159	.427	0	.000	71	.703	93	350	44	27	36	389	4.8
Totals		1494	44212	9424	.537	0	.000	4035	.722	4477	14332	2129	1192	2288	22883	15.3

GARY PAYTON

Team: Seattle SuperSonics
Position: Guard
Height: 6'4" **Weight:** 190
Birthdate: July 23, 1968

NBA Experience: 5 years
College: Oregon St.
Acquired: 1st-round pick in 1990 draft (2nd overall)

Background: Payton was an All-American as a senior at Oregon State, where he set a school scoring record, ended his career second on the NCAA assists list, and set a Pac-10 record with 100 steals in his final season. He has started all but seven games of his first five NBA seasons, has played in the last two All-Star Games, and annually ranks among league leaders in steals.

Strengths: Payton lives up to his defensive reputation and can now be considered one of the premier all-around point guards in the game. He hounds the ball, makes his opponent work for everything he gets, and is among the top thieves in basketball. He finishes his drives and has also improved his playmaking. He has improved his scoring average each season to its current 20.6 PPG.

Weaknesses: A noted trash talker, Payton tends to make opponents want to cram the ball down his throat. Sometimes his teammates feel the same way. Shooting has never been Payton's forte, although he has improved a great deal. He's not one of the better 3-point or free throw shooters.

Analysis: Payton has gone from a reckless defensive whiz to someone who deserves MVP consideration on an annual basis. Even though he had a tremendous 1993-94 season (sixth in the MVP vote), one could safely call him one of the most improved players in the league in 1994-95. He upped his scoring and assist output while retaining his stopper status. Payton is still the best defensive point guard in basketball.

PLAYER SUMMARY	
Will	shut down his man
Can't	shut his mouth
Expect	more All-Star nods
Don't Expect	missed starts
Fantasy Value	$45-50
Card Value	10-20¢

COLLEGE STATISTICS

		G	FGP	FTP	APG	PPG
86-87	OSU	30	.459	.671	7.6	12.5
87-88	OSU	31	.489	.699	7.4	14.5
88-89	OSU	30	.475	.677	8.1	20.1
89-90	OSU	29	.504	.690	8.1	25.7
Totals		120	.485	.684	7.8	18.1

NBA REGULAR-SEASON STATISTICS

				FGs		3-PT FGs		FTs		Rebounds						
		G	MIN	FG	PCT	FG	PCT	FT	PCT	OFF	TOT	AST	STL	BLK	PTS	PPG
90-91	SEA	82	2244	259	.450	1	.077	69	.711	108	243	528	165	15	588	7.2
91-92	SEA	81	2549	331	.451	3	.130	99	.669	123	295	506	147	21	764	9.4
92-93	SEA	82	2548	476	.494	7	.206	151	.770	95	281	399	177	21	1110	13.5
93-94	SEA	82	2881	584	.504	15	.278	166	.595	105	269	494	188	19	1349	16.5
94-95	SEA	82	3015	685	.509	70	.302	249	.716	108	281	583	204	13	1689	20.6
Totals		409	13237	2335	.489	96	.270	734	.687	539	1369	2510	881	89	5500	13.4

ANTHONY PEELER

Team: Los Angeles Lakers
Position: Guard
Height: 6'4" **Weight:** 212
Birthdate: November 25, 1969

NBA Experience: 3 years
College: Missouri
Acquired: 1st-round pick in 1992 draft
(15th overall)

Background: Perhaps the most heralded recruit in Missouri history, Peeler lived up to expectations despite an inability to stay out of trouble. He was named Big Eight Player of the Year after averaging 23.4 PPG, 5.5 RPG, and 3.9 APG as a senior. Peeler slipped to 15th in the 1992 draft but enjoyed a fine rookie year. He came back from second-year leg injuries last season but his scoring dipped to 10.4 PPG.

Strengths: A tremendous athlete, Peeler was drafted by the Texas Rangers in 1988 as a left-handed pitcher/outfielder. He has a sweet stroke from the perimeter with 3-point range and is also capable of beating his man off the dribble. Peeler is an accomplished passer who has even been tried by the Lakers as a point guard. He has some defensive potential.

Weaknesses: Peeler could stand to apply himself more on defense and on the backboards, because all the tools are at his disposal. His commitment has been questioned by some and he has not always reported to work in the best of shape. He needs to improve his consistency and make better decisions with the basketball. His checkered off-court record includes a conviction on a felony weapons charge.

Analysis: Peeler has loads of natural ability and the potential to become a star. His first step should be coming to camp in great shape and solidifying a starting spot in a Laker lineup loaded with young talent. If he can do that, stay out of trouble, and keep his health, there is no reason to think Peeler can't become a 15-PPG scorer and a key ingredient on a winning team.

PLAYER SUMMARY	
Will	shoot with range
Can't	defend consistently
Expect	scoring ability
Don't Expect	a team captain
Fantasy Value	$2-4
Card Value	15-25¢

COLLEGE STATISTICS

		G	FGP	FTP	RPG	PPG
88-89	MISS	36	.504	.754	3.7	10.1
89-90	MISS	31	.446	.769	5.4	16.8
90-91	MISS	21	.475	.768	6.2	19.4
91-92	MISS	29	.459	.806	5.5	23.4
Totals		117	.466	.779	5.1	16.8

NBA REGULAR-SEASON STATISTICS

			FGs		3-PT FGs		FTs		Rebounds						
		G	MIN	FG	PCT	FG	PCT	FT	PCT	OFF	TOT	AST	STL	BLK	PTS	PPG
92-93	LAL	77	1656	297	.468	46	.390	162	.786	64	179	166	60	14	802	10.4
93-94	LAL	30	923	176	.430	14	.222	57	.803	48	109	94	43	8	423	14.1
94-95	LAL	73	1559	285	.432	84	.389	102	.797	62	168	122	52	13	756	10.4
Totals		180	4138	758	.445	144	.363	321	.793	174	456	382	155	35	1981	11.0

WILL PERDUE

Team: Chicago Bulls
Position: Center
Height: 7'0" **Weight:** 240
Birthdate: August 29, 1965

NBA Experience: 7 years
College: Vanderbilt
Acquired: 1st-round pick in 1988 draft
(11th overall)

Background: As a senior at Vanderbilt, Perdue led the league in rebounding and was named Southeastern Conference Player of the Year. Drafted by the Bulls in 1988, he played less than any other first-round pick as a rookie. He failed to score even five PPG in any of his first six seasons before starting at center in 1994-95 and averaging 8.0 PPG.

Strengths: Perdue knows his limitations and plays within them. He gives some of the league's better centers a strong effort on the defensive end and goes after rebounds. Perdue has a decent face-up jumper and made about 55 percent of his shots in 1994-95.

Weaknesses: A gifted athlete Perdue is not. He doesn't jump well at all and he's even worse at anticipating the ball. His high-scoring days ended in college, as he does not have a reliable low-post game. His best shot remains the "Per-dunk," and he is also a poor passer and free throw shooter. He does not have the skills to be a legitimate starter in the NBA.

Analysis: Perdue has three NBA championship rings but did not play a huge role on those teams. In fact, he is coming off the only season in which he has played a significant part, although his numbers are far below those of most starting centers. On a team stocked with scorers, Perdue's biggest asset might be that he doesn't need to get a lot of points.

PLAYER SUMMARY	
Will	grab offensive boards
Can't	dominate inside
Expect	a role-player
Don't Expect	10 PPG
Fantasy Value	$2-4
Card Value	5-7¢

COLLEGE STATISTICS

		G	FGP	FTP	RPG	PPG
83-84	VAND	17	.467	.444	2.2	2.7
85-86	VAND	22	.585	.438	2.8	3.5
86-87	VAND	34	.599	.618	8.7	17.4
87-88	VAND	31	.634	.673	10.1	18.3
Totals		104	.606	.620	6.8	12.3

NBA REGULAR-SEASON STATISTICS

		G	MIN	FGs FG	FGs PCT	3-PT FGs FG	3-PT FGs PCT	FTs FT	FTs PCT	Rebounds OFF	Rebounds TOT	AST	STL	BLK	PTS	PPG
88-89	CHI	30	190	29	.403	0	.000	8	.571	18	45	11	4	6	66	2.2
89-90	CHI	77	884	111	.414	0	.000	72	.692	88	214	46	19	26	294	3.8
90-91	CHI	74	972	116	.494	0	.000	75	.670	122	336	47	23	57	307	4.1
91-92	CHI	77	1007	152	.547	1	.500	45	.495	108	312	80	16	43	350	4.5
92-93	CHI	72	998	137	.557	0	.000	67	.604	103	287	74	22	47	341	4.7
93-94	CHI	43	397	47	.420	0	.000	23	.719	40	126	34	8	11	117	2.7
94-95	CHI	78	1592	254	.553	0	.000	113	.582	211	522	90	26	56	621	8.0
Totals		451	6040	846	.507	1	.077	403	.612	690	1842	382	118	246	2096	4.6

SAM PERKINS

Team: Seattle SuperSonics
Position: Forward/Center
Height: 6'9" **Weight:** 255
Birthdate: June 14, 1961
NBA Experience: 11 years

College: North Carolina
Acquired: Traded from Lakers for Benoit Benjamin and draft rights to Doug Christie, 2/93

Background: Perkins was a three-time All-American at North Carolina, where he earned an NCAA title in 1982 and won the Lapchick Award as the nation's outstanding senior in 1984. In six seasons with Dallas, he became the club's all-time leader in rebounds. He has spent his last five years with the Lakers and Sonics.

Strengths: Perkins scores from both the post and the perimeter. He hits 3-pointers like few players his size and is also a good free throw shooter. Perkins plays heady defense, is an accomplished rebounder, and leads by example with an intelligent brand of ball. He has never averaged less than 11.0 PPG.

Weaknesses: Perkins is not the defensive player and rebounder he used to be. Eleven years in the league can do that to you. He no longer alters many shots in the paint, nor does he dominate the boards with his quickness.

Analysis: Perkins has given the talented Sonics veteran leadership and steady scoring from both inside and long range. He provides matchup problems, whether in a reserve role or as a starter. Perkins has scored nearly 12,000 career points and has 6,000-plus career rebounds. He still averages 12-plus PPG for a contending team.

PLAYER SUMMARY	
Will	score inside and out
Can't	dominate on defense
Expect	matchup problems
Don't Expect	young legs
Fantasy Value	$6-8
Card Value	7-10¢

COLLEGE STATISTICS

		G	FGP	FTP	RPG	PPG
80-81	NC	37	.626	.741	7.8	14.9
81-82	NC	32	.578	.768	7.8	14.3
82-83	NC	35	.527	.819	9.4	16.9
83-84	NC	31	.589	.856	9.6	17.6
Totals		135	.576	.796	8.6	15.9

NBA REGULAR-SEASON STATISTICS

				FGs		3-PT FGs		FTs		Rebounds						
		G	MIN	FG	PCT	FG	PCT	FT	PCT	OFF	TOT	AST	STL	BLK	PTS	PPG
84-85	DAL	82	2317	347	.471	9	.250	200	.820	189	605	135	63	63	903	11.0
85-86	DAL	80	2626	458	.503	11	.333	307	.814	195	685	153	75	94	1234	15.4
86-87	DAL	80	2687	461	.482	19	.352	245	.828	197	616	146	109	77	1186	14.8
87-88	DAL	75	2499	394	.450	5	.167	273	.822	201	601	118	74	54	1066	14.2
88-89	DAL	78	2860	445	.464	7	.184	274	.833	235	688	127	76	92	1171	15.0
89-90	DAL	76	2668	435	.493	6	.214	330	.778	209	572	175	88	64	1206	15.9
90-91	LAL	73	2504	368	.495	18	.281	229	.821	167	538	108	64	78	983	13.5
91-92	LAL	63	2332	361	.450	15	.217	304	.817	192	556	141	64	62	1041	16.5
92-93	LAL/SEA	79	2351	381	.477	24	.338	250	.820	163	524	156	60	82	1036	13.1
93-94	SEA	81	2170	341	.438	99	.367	218	.801	120	366	111	67	31	999	12.3
94-95	SEA	82	2356	346	.466	136	.397	215	.799	96	398	135	72	45	1043	12.7
Totals		849	27370	4337	.472	349	.337	2845	.813	1964	6149	1505	812	742	11868	14.0

ELLIOT PERRY

Unrestricted Free Agent
Last Team: Phoenix Suns
Position: Guard
Height: 6'0" **Weight:** 160
Birthdate: March 28, 1969

NBA Experience: 3 years
College: Memphis St.
Acquired: Signed as a free agent, 1/94

Background: A product of the fertile Memphis prep ranks, Perry was a four-year standout at Memphis State who finished his college career with more than 2,200 points and 500 assists. He was a second-round draftee of the Clippers in 1991 but saw more action with Charlotte as a rookie. He became a CBA standout before the Suns signed him during the latter half of 1993-94. He then led Phoenix with 394 assists last season.

Strengths: Perry has all the intangibles coaches love. He works his knee-high socks off in practice and in games and is ready when called upon, whether as a starter or a reserve. He is a pain in the rear for opposing ball-handlers, as he ranked eighth in the league in steals last season with 1.9 per game. He makes his free throws, sticks an occasional 3-pointer, and distributes.

Weaknesses: While Perry has made a name for himself, his extra minutes also helped him lead the Suns in turnovers. He is not as creative a playmaker as some of the top point guards in the league and he will not shoot the lights out on a consistent basis, despite his surprising .520 field goal percentage last season. There's not much to knock anymore.

Analysis: The Suns needed a replacement for K.J. last season and Perry was in the right place at the right time. Given the chance to start, he raised his game to a new level. Perry's aggressive style is contagious and he has impressed everyone with his leadership. "He's established himself as a fine NBA point guard," says Suns coach Paul Westphal.

PLAYER SUMMARY

Will ....pick your pocket
Can't..................eliminate turnovers
Expect ....an aggressive approach
Don't Expect..................a CBA return
Fantasy Value $2-4
Card Value ....10-20¢

COLLEGE STATISTICS

		G	FGP	FTP	RPG	PPG
87-88	MSU	32	.417	.806	3.5	13.1
88-89	MSU	32	.462	.821	3.4	19.4
89-90	MSU	30	.418	.753	3.7	16.8
90-91	MSU	32	.464	.793	3.5	20.8
Totals		126	.443	.794	3.5	17.5

NBA REGULAR-SEASON STATISTICS

		G	MIN	FGs FG	FGs PCT	3-PT FGs FG	3-PT FGs PCT	FTs FT	FTs PCT	Rebounds OFF	Rebounds TOT	AST	STL	BLK	PTS	PPG
91-92	LAC/CHA	50	437	49	.380	1	.143	27	.659	14	39	78	34	3	126	2.5
93-94	PHO	27	432	42	.372	0	.000	21	.750	12	39	125	25	1	105	3.9
94-95	PHO	82	1977	306	.520	25	.417	158	.810	51	151	394	156	4	795	9.7
Totals		159	2846	397	.478	26	.371	206	.780	77	229	597	215	8	1026	6.5

TIM PERRY

Team: Philadelphia 76ers
Position: Forward
Height: 6'9" **Weight:** 220
Birthdate: June 4, 1965
NBA Experience: 7 years

College: Temple
Acquired: Traded from Suns with Jeff Hornacek and Andrew Lang for Charles Barkley, 6/92

Background: Perry was named Atlantic 10 Player of the Year as a senior at Temple, where he finished as the school's career leader in blocked shots. Although he was taken seventh in the 1988 draft, he spent most of his four years in Phoenix as a reserve before being traded to Philadelphia in the Charles Barkley deal. The 1994-95 season was by far his worst.

Strengths: Defense and rebounding are the best aspects of Perry's game. He has the athletic ability to stick with his man, crash the boards, and block some shots. He gets up and down the floor quickly and was a threat from beyond the 3-point arc before last season.

Weaknesses: Perry has been inconsistent, and last season his play and his playing time deteriorated. His offensive game is very weak. Perry is not a good shooter (he can't buy a free throw) and he does not make up for it with a low-post game. He is a subpar passer and ball-handler. Even Perry's defense is not what it once was.

Analysis: Inconsistency has haunted Perry throughout his career, but last season that changed when he was consistently unable to produce. He averaged only about 11 minutes per game and was a mere shadow of the defensive presence he used to be. He is not likely to crack anyone's starting lineup, thanks to an offensive game that seems to have shut down.

PLAYER SUMMARY	
Will	run the floor
Can't	make free throws
Expect	limited minutes
Don't Expect	big numbers
Fantasy Value	$0
Card Value	5-8¢

COLLEGE STATISTICS

		G	FGP	FTP	RPG	PPG
84-85	TEMP	30	.414	.500	3.9	2.3
85-86	TEMP	31	.566	.575	9.5	11.6
86-87	TEMP	36	.514	.620	8.6	12.9
87-88	TEMP	33	.585	.637	8.0	14.5
Totals		130	.544	.605	7.6	10.5

NBA REGULAR-SEASON STATISTICS

				FGs		3-PT FGs		FTs		Rebounds						
		G	MIN	FG	PCT	FG	PCT	FT	PCT	OFF	TOT	AST	STL	BLK	PTS	PPG
88-89	PHO	62	614	108	.537	1	.250	40	.615	61	132	18	19	32	257	4.1
89-90	PHO	60	612	100	.513	1	1.000	53	.589	79	152	17	21	22	254	4.2
90-91	PHO	46	587	75	.521	0	.000	43	.614	53	126	27	23	43	193	4.2
91-92	PHO	80	2483	413	.523	3	.375	153	.712	204	551	134	44	116	982	12.3
92-93	PHI	81	2104	287	.468	10	.204	147	.710	154	409	126	40	91	731	9.0
93-94	PHI	80	2336	272	.435	73	.365	102	.580	117	404	94	60	82	719	9.0
94-95	PHI	42	446	27	.346	0	.000	22	.550	38	89	12	10	15	76	1.8
Totals		451	9182	1282	.485	88	.313	560	.649	706	1863	428	217	401	3212	7.1

CHUCK PERSON

Team: San Antonio Spurs
Position: Forward
Height: 6'8" **Weight:** 230
Birthdate: June 27, 1964

NBA Experience: 9 years
College: Auburn
Acquired: Signed as a free agent, 8/94

Background: The all-time leading scorer in Auburn history when he graduated from college, Person won NBA Rookie of the Year honors in 1986-87. In six seasons, he became Indiana's all-time leading NBA scorer before spending two years with Minnesota. He was signed by San Antonio before 1994-95 as a top reserve.

Strengths: Person has been one of those rare players who can take over games by himself. Blessed with great range, he has hit countless clutch shots from both the 3-point line and the post. He also handles the ball and distributes. Person has great confidence, works hard, rebounds, and is a student of the game.

Weaknesses: The main knock on Person throughout his career has not been his play, but rather his mouth. He is known for jawing at opponents, officials, and teammates alike, though he has toned down his act. He is not the league's best defender or free throw shooter, and he has seen better scoring days.

Analysis: San Antonio made a good move in signing "The Rifleman," who has never averaged below double figures in scoring during his nine-year career. One of the more valuable sixth men in the league last year, he helped the Spurs to the best record in basketball with his adept 3-point shooting. His confidence is contagious.

PLAYER SUMMARY	
Will	hit 3-pointers
Can't	keep quiet
Expect	supreme confidence
Don't Expect	20 PPG
Fantasy Value	$1-3
Card Value	8-12¢

COLLEGE STATISTICS

		G	FGP	FTP	RPG	PPG
82-83	AUB	28	.541	.758	4.6	9.3
83-84	AUB	31	.543	.728	8.0	19.1
84-85	AUB	34	.544	.738	8.9	22.0
85-86	AUB	33	.519	.804	7.9	21.5
Totals		126	.536	.757	7.5	18.3

NBA REGULAR-SEASON STATISTICS

			FGs		3-PT FGs		FTs		Rebounds						
	G	MIN	FG	PCT	FG	PCT	FT	PCT	OFF	TOT	AST	STL	BLK	PTS	PPG
86-87 IND	82	2956	635	.468	49	.355	222	.747	168	677	295	90	16	1541	18.8
87-88 IND	79	2807	575	.459	59	.333	132	.670	171	536	309	73	8	1341	17.0
88-89 IND	80	3012	711	.489	63	.307	243	.792	144	516	289	83	18	1728	21.6
89-90 IND	77	2714	605	.407	94	.372	211	.781	126	445	230	53	20	1515	19.7
90-91 IND	80	2566	620	.504	69	.340	165	.721	121	417	238	56	17	1474	18.4
91-92 IND	81	2923	616	.480	132	.373	133	.675	114	426	382	68	18	1497	18.5
92-93 MIN	78	2985	541	.433	118	.355	109	.649	98	433	343	67	30	1309	16.8
93-94 MIN	77	2029	356	.422	100	.368	82	.759	55	253	185	45	12	894	11.6
94-95 SA	81	2033	317	.423	172	.387	66	.647	49	258	106	45	12	872	10.8
Totals	715	24025	4976	.467	856	.360	1363	.727	1046	3961	2377	580	151	12171	17.0

WESLEY PERSON

Team: Phoenix Suns
Position: Guard
Height: 6'6" **Weight:** 195
Birthdate: March 28, 1971

NBA Experience: 1 year
College: Auburn
Acquired: 1st-round pick in 1994 draft
(23rd overall)

Background: The younger brother of San Antonio's Chuck Person, Wesley kept up the family tradition by attending Auburn but wound up playing on some bad teams. He finished third on the school's career scoring list behind his brother and former NBA player Mike Mitchell, and he was its all-time leader in 3-point percentage and 3-pointers made and attempted. Person fell to 23rd in the draft but led all rookies in 3-point accuracy.

Strengths: Those who tabbed Person the best 3-point shooter in the 1994 draft class were on the mark. He is about as good as they come when he gets the ball in rhythm, and he is also capable of creating his own shots off the dribble. Person can also score from inside the arc, as his overall field goal percentage (.484) reflects. He makes his free throws and helps on the boards.

Weaknesses: Person is not the precise passer his big brother has been. He turned the ball over three times for every four assists. He's not one of the better ball-handlers in the game. He is also rail thin and needs to spend some hours in the weight room to improve his defense. Person does not possess blinding speed and quickness.

Analysis: Person was a steal for the Suns at No. 23 in the draft. His stock apparently dropped when he chose not to attend some of the pre-draft camps, but he wound up starting for a Phoenix team that featured six All-Stars or former All-Stars. His 3-point and overall field goal percentages were remarkable for a rookie, and he even beat his big brother in a 3-point shooting contest during the All-Star break.

PLAYER SUMMARY

Will ....hit from deep
Can't ....push his brother around
Expect ....a sweet stroke
Don't Expect ....Chuck's mouth
Fantasy Value $2-4
Card Value ....20-50¢

COLLEGE STATISTICS

		G	FGP	FTP	RPG	PPG
90-91	AUB	26	.471	.765	5.7	15.4
91-92	AUB	27	.506	.726	6.8	19.9
92-93	AUB	27	.556	.772	7.1	18.8
93-94	AUB	28	.484	.734	6.4	22.2
Totals		108	.504	.747	6.5	19.1

NBA REGULAR-SEASON STATISTICS

		G	MIN	FGs FG	PCT	3-PT FGs FG	PCT	FTs FT	PCT	Rebounds OFF	TOT	AST	STL	BLK	PTS	PPG
94-95	PHO	78	1800	309	.484	116	.436	80	.792	67	201	105	48	24	814	10.4
Totals		78	1800	309	.484	116	.436	80	.792	67	201	105	48	24	814	10.4

BOBBY PHILLS

Team: Cleveland Cavaliers
Position: Guard
Height: 6'5" **Weight:** 217
Birthdate: December 20, 1969

NBA Experience: 4 years
College: Southern
Acquired: Signed as a free agent, 3/92

Background: Phills, the son of a college dean, stayed home in Baton Rouge, Louisiana, to play at Southern U. He wound up launching 788 3-point attempts in his career, making 4.4 a game as a senior. Milwaukee took him in the 1991 draft, but Phills was released and the Cavaliers signed him after a CBA stint. He became a starter in the third of his four years with Cleveland and averaged 11.0 PPG last season.

Strengths: A gunner in college, Phills is now gaining recognition for his defensive play. He brings a nice combination of strength and quickness to the floor and can check either forwards or guards. He's a fine athlete who runs like the wind and throws down his share of dunks. He also has a quick first step to the hoop and has become a double-figure scoring threat.

Weaknesses: Phills has been a little inconsistent in his four-year career, mostly with his streaky jump shot. He does not convert readily enough from the outside to dissuade defenders from backing off a step or two. He is not nearly as proficient from long range as he was in college. He is not a great ball-handler, and he has the ability to do better on the boards.

Analysis: Phills no longer has to worry about sticking around in the league. His versatility, defense, athletic skills, and work ethic have ensured that. He starts on a perennial playoff team and last year scored in double figures for the first time. If he could consistently knock down his jumper, the athletic Phills would really be an offensive force.

PLAYER SUMMARY	
Will ....dunk in transition	
Can't ....rely on his jumper	
Expect ....defensive versatility	
Don't Expect......50-percent shooting	
Fantasy Value.................................$1	
Card Value ....5-8¢	

COLLEGE STATISTICS

		G	FGP	FTP	RPG	PPG
87-88	SOUT	23	.491	.714	1.8	3.7
88-89	SOUT	31	.431	.733	4.6	13.5
89-90	SOUT	31	.451	.657	4.3	20.1
90-91	SOUT	28	.407	.720	4.7	28.4
Totals		113	.413	.710	4.0	17.0

NBA REGULAR-SEASON STATISTICS

		G	MIN	FGs FG	FGs PCT	3-PT FGs FG	3-PT FGs PCT	FTs FT	FTs PCT	Rebounds OFF	Rebounds TOT	AST	STL	BLK	PTS	PPG
91-92	CLE	10	65	12	.429	0	.000	7	.636	4	8	4	3	1	31	3.1
92-93	CLE	31	139	38	.463	2	.400	15	.600	6	17	10	10	2	93	3.0
93-94	CLE	72	1531	242	.471	1	.083	113	.720	71	212	133	67	12	598	8.3
94-95	CLE	80	2500	338	.414	19	.345	183	.779	90	265	180	115	25	878	11.0
Totals		193	4235	630	.438	22	.297	318	.743	171	502	327	195	40	1600	8.3

ERIC PIATKOWSKI

Team: Los Angeles Clippers
Position: Guard/Forward
Height: 6'7" **Weight:** 215
Birthdate: September 30, 1970
NBA Experience: 1 year

College: Nebraska
Acquired: Draft rights traded from Pacers with Pooh Richardson and Malik Sealy for Mark Jackson and draft rights to Greg Minor, 6/94

Background: Nicknamed "The Polish Rifle," Piatkowski made a Nebraska-record 202 3-pointers in his college career and scored 1,934 points, second most in school history. He scored 21.5 PPG in his senior year and then improved his draft stock by winning MVP honors at the Desert Classic pre-draft camp. He was drafted 15th by Indiana and had his rights traded to the Clippers, for whom he averaged 7.0 PPG.

Strengths: Piatkowski was one of the better pure shooters among last year's rookie class. He has a picture-perfect release and range beyond the shortened NBA 3-point arc. He made better than 37 percent of his long ones last year and can be expected to improve on that. The son of a former ABA player (Walt), he has a nice feel for the game. He's a nifty passer and capable ball-handler who can play forward or guard.

Weaknesses: Piatkowski needs some work on his defense. He has trouble stopping the big-scoring small forwards of the league, and most of the shooting guards he's assigned to have a step on him. He is a below-average defensive rebounder despite doing a nice job on the offensive boards. His shot is not as dangerous when he takes it off the dribble as it is when he catches and fires.

Analysis: Shooting percentage can be deceiving, and such is the case with Piatkowski. More than 40 percent of his buckets were 3-pointers, so his overall accuracy was a little better than the numbers indicate. His stroke is a thing of beauty. A tough, tireless worker, Piatkowski took some first-year lumps on defense while showing signs of becoming a decent NBA scorer. The Clippers expect good things in 1995-96.

PLAYER SUMMARY	
Will	work for his shot
Can't	stop quick guards
Expect	perfect rotation
Don't Expect	tons of boards
Fantasy Value	$1
Card Value	12-25¢

COLLEGE STATISTICS

		G	FGP	FTP	RPG	PPG
90-91	NEBR	34	.465	.837	3.7	10.9
91-92	NEBR	29	.426	.725	6.3	14.3
92-93	NEBR	30	.485	.760	5.7	16.7
93-94	NEBR	30	.496	.794	6.3	21.5
Totals		123	.471	.777	5.4	15.7

NBA REGULAR-SEASON STATISTICS

			FGs		3-PT FGs		FTs		Rebounds						
	G	MIN	FG	PCT	FG	PCT	FT	PCT	OFF	TOT	AST	STL	BLK	PTS	PPG
94-95 LAC	81	1208	201	.441	74	.374	90	.783	63	133	77	37	15	566	7.0
Totals	81	1208	201	.441	74	.374	90	.783	63	133	77	37	15	566	7.0

RICKY PIERCE

Unrestricted Free Agent
Last Team: Golden State Warriors
Position: Guard
Height: 6'4" **Weight:** 215
Birthdate: August 19, 1959
NBA Experience: 13 years

College: Rice
Acquired: Traded from SuperSonics with draft rights to Carlos Rogers and two 1995 2nd-round picks for Sarunas Marciulionis and Byron Houston, 7/94

Background: Pierce led Rice in scoring and rebounding for three straight years. The 13-year veteran played single seasons in Detroit and San Diego, then became a celebrated reserve in Milwaukee, winning two Sixth Man Awards. A 1991 All-Star with Seattle, Pierce played for Golden State in 1994-95.

Strengths: Pierce has been one of the league's best pure shooters during his career. He hits 3-pointers and his strong upper body also helps him get to the hoop. He has been a great clutch player who almost never misses a free throw.

Weaknesses: Ball-handling, passing, and defense have never been strengths of Pierce, who is not among the quicker guards in the game. Bone spurs and a bulged disc have dragged him down over the past two seasons.

Analysis: Pierce, one of the top free throw shooters in league history, is now most valuable for the level of professionalism he gives to a team after 13 seasons. He can still score when healthy and will build on his total of almost 13,000 career points. Few players have provided more offense off the bench.

PLAYER SUMMARY	
Will	score off the bench
Can't	stay off injured list
Expect	automatic free throws
Don't Expect	three more years
Fantasy Value	$0
Card Value	5-10¢

COLLEGE STATISTICS

		G	FGP	FTP	RPG	PPG
79-80	RICE	26	.480	.718	8.2	19.2
80-81	RICE	26	.518	.706	7.0	20.9
81-82	RICE	30	.511	.794	7.5	26.8
Totals		82	.504	.751	7.6	22.5

NBA REGULAR-SEASON STATISTICS

			FGs		3-PT FGs		FTs		Rebounds						
		G	MIN	FG	PCT	FG	PCT	FT	PCT	OFF	TOT	AST	STL	BLK	PTS	PPG
82-83	DET	39	265	33	.375	1	.143	18	.563	15	35	14	8	4	85	2.2
83-84	SD	69	1280	268	.470	0	.000	149	.861	59	135	60	27	13	685	9.9
84-85	MIL	44	882	165	.537	1	.250	102	.823	49	117	94	34	5	433	9.8
85-86	MIL	81	2147	429	.538	3	.130	266	.858	94	231	177	83	6	1127	13.9
86-87	MIL	79	2505	575	.534	3	.107	387	.880	117	266	144	64	24	1540	19.5
87-88	MIL	37	965	248	.510	3	.214	107	.877	30	83	73	21	7	606	16.4
88-89	MIL	75	2078	527	.518	8	.222	255	.859	82	197	156	77	19	1317	17.6
89-90	MIL	59	1709	503	.510	46	.346	307	.839	64	167	133	50	7	1359	23.0
90-91	MIL/SEA	78	2167	561	.485	46	.397	430	.913	67	191	168	60	13	1598	20.5
91-92	SEA	78	2658	620	.475	33	.268	417	.916	93	233	241	86	20	1690	21.7
92-93	SEA	77	2218	524	.489	42	.372	313	.889	58	192	220	100	7	1403	18.2
93-94	SEA	51	1022	272	.471	6	.188	189	.896	29	83	91	42	5	739	14.5
94-95	GS	27	673	111	.437	23	.329	93	.877	12	64	40	22	2	338	12.5
Totals		794	20569	4836	.499	215	.304	3033	.877	769	1994	1611	674	132	12920	16.3

ED PINCKNEY

Team: Toronto Raptors
Position: Forward
Height: 6'9" **Weight:** 215
Birthdate: March 27, 1963

NBA Experience: 10 years
College: Villanova
Acquired: Selected from Bucks in 1995 expansion draft.

Background: The highlight of Pinckney's career was leading Villanova to a national title in 1985 and being named tournament MVP. His ten-year NBA career started in Phoenix and has since included stops in Sacramento, Boston, and Milwaukee. He has averaged double figures in scoring twice in his career. Toronto picked Pinckney in the expansion draft.

Strengths: Pinckney provides rebounding on both ends and plays solid defense. In fact, he collected more rebounds last year than points. He is capable of providing a shot-blocking presence. Pinckney always hits for a high percentage from the field because he does not take bad shots.

Weaknesses: "Easy Ed" has never mastered the kind of low-post moves that would help him become a decent scorer. He relies on offensive boards for many of his points, as his offensive range is very limited. He's not much of a passer or ball-handler, either. Pinckney has not been as productive on either end of the floor since undergoing arthroscopic knee surgery in 1992.

Analysis: Overall, Pinckney has been a disappointment. He has never become the rebounding force some expected him to be and offers very little in the way of offensive ability. His trade from Boston to Milwaukee before last year gave the Bucks little more than a bench-warmer and fill-in player. He averaged 2.3 PPG.

PLAYER SUMMARY	
Will	snare rebounds
Can't	light up scoreboard
Expect	reserve minutes
Don't Expect	much offense
Fantasy Value	$0
Card Value	5-8¢

COLLEGE STATISTICS

		G	FGP	FTP	RPG	PPG
81-82	VILL	32	.640	.714	7.8	14.2
82-83	VILL	31	.568	.760	9.7	12.5
83-84	VILL	31	.604	.694	7.9	15.4
84-85	VILL	35	.600	.730	8.9	15.6
Totals		129	.604	.723	8.6	14.5

NBA REGULAR-SEASON STATISTICS

			FGs		3-PT FGs		FTs		Rebounds						
	G	MIN	FG	PCT	FG	PCT	FT	PCT	OFF	TOT	AST	STL	BLK	PTS	PPG
85-86 PHO	80	1602	255	.558	0	.000	171	.673	95	308	90	71	37	681	8.5
86-87 PHO	80	2250	290	.584	0	.000	257	.739	179	580	116	86	54	837	10.5
87-88 SAC	79	1177	179	.522	0	.000	133	.747	94	230	66	39	32	491	6.2
88-89 SAC/BOS	80	2012	319	.513	0	.000	280	.800	166	449	118	83	66	918	11.5
89-90 BOS	77	1082	135	.542	0	.000	92	.773	93	225	68	34	42	362	4.7
90-91 BOS	70	1165	131	.539	0	.000	104	.897	155	341	45	61	43	366	5.2
91-92 BOS	81	1917	203	.537	0	.000	207	.812	252	564	62	70	56	613	7.6
92-93 BOS	7	151	10	.417	0	.000	12	.923	14	43	1	4	7	32	4.6
93-94 BOS	76	1524	151	.522	0	.000	92	.736	160	478	62	58	44	394	5.2
94-95 MIL	62	835	48	.495	0	.000	44	.710	65	211	21	34	17	140	2.3
Totals	692	13715	1721	.538	0	.000	1392	.765	1273	3429	649	540	398	4834	7.0

SCOTTIE PIPPEN

Team: Chicago Bulls
Position: Forward
Height: 6'7" **Weight:** 225
Birthdate: September 25, 1965
NBA Experience: 8 years
College: Central Arkansas

Acquired: Draft rights traded from SuperSonics for draft rights to Olden Polynice, a 1989 2nd-round pick, and the option to exchange 1989 1st-round picks, 6/87

Background: An NAIA All-American as a senior at Central Arkansas, Pippen arrived in Chicago in the 1987 draft. He improved rapidly and helped the Bulls to three straight NBA championships. No forward in the NBA has as many assists over the last four seasons. Pippen has played in five All-Star Games and won Olympic gold with Dream Team I. He led the league in steals in 1994-95.

Strengths: The acrobatic Pippen does things few forwards in the league can do. His long arms and quick hands help him swipe the ball better than anyone in basketball, and no forward passes the ball better. He has countless moves to the basket, is an electrifying transition player, and shoots with 3-point range. He led the Bulls in points, rebounds, assists, and steals last season.

Weaknesses: Pippen has received attention for some less-than-professional playoff episodes like refusing to re-enter a game and his infamous migraine headache. Last year, he was suspended for throwing a chair. He has been outspoken in his contempt for Chicago management.

Analysis: Pippen is one of the premier players in the league, with or without Michael Jordan by his side. Not many men have led their team in four major categories in the same season as Pippen did last year. The MVP of the 1994 All-Star Game, Pippen is one of the most explosive players in the league.

PLAYER SUMMARY	
Will	pick your pocket
Can't	overshadow Jordan
Expect	all-around dominance
Don't Expect	off-court silence
Fantasy Value	$70-75
Card Value	20-50¢

COLLEGE STATISTICS

		G	FGP	FTP	RPG	PPG
83-84	CA	20	.456	.684	3.0	4.3
84-85	CA	19	.564	.676	9.2	18.5
85-86	CA	29	.556	.686	9.2	19.8
86-87	CA	25	.592	.719	10.0	23.6
Totals		93	.563	.695	8.1	17.2

NBA REGULAR-SEASON STATISTICS

		G	MIN	FGs FG	FGs PCT	3-PT FGs FG	3-PT FGs PCT	FTs FT	FTs PCT	Rebounds OFF	Rebounds TOT	AST	STL	BLK	PTS	PPG
87-88	CHI	79	1650	261	.463	4	.174	99	.576	115	298	169	91	52	625	7.9
88-89	CHI	73	2413	413	.476	21	.273	201	.668	138	445	256	139	61	1048	14.4
89-90	CHI	82	3148	562	.489	28	.250	199	.675	150	547	444	211	101	1351	16.5
90-91	CHI	82	3014	600	.520	21	.309	240	.706	163	595	511	193	93	1461	17.8
91-92	CHI	82	3164	687	.506	16	.200	330	.760	185	630	572	155	93	1720	21.0
92-93	CHI	81	3123	628	.473	22	.237	232	.663	203	621	507	173	73	1510	18.6
93-94	CHI	72	2759	627	.491	63	.320	270	.660	173	629	403	211	58	1587	22.0
94-95	CHI	79	3014	634	.480	109	.345	315	.716	175	639	409	232	89	1692	21.4
Totals		630	22285	4412	.489	284	.294	1886	.688	1302	4404	3271	1405	620	10994	17.5

OLDEN POLYNICE

Team: Sacramento Kings
Position: Center
Height: 7'0" **Weight:** 250
Birthdate: November 21, 1964
NBA Experience: 8 years

College: Virginia
Acquired: Traded from Pistons for Pete Chilcutt, a 1994 2nd-round pick, and a conditional 1st-round pick, 2/94

Background: Polynice led Virginia in scoring and rebounding for two seasons and was a three-year leader in field goal accuracy. He began his NBA career as a backup center with Seattle and has started for the L.A. Clippers, Detroit, and Sacramento. He averaged a double-double two years ago and was the Kings' rebounding leader again last season.

Strengths: Polynice is respected for his rebounding and he also provides tough defense. He can bang with big men yet is quick enough to get out and harass smaller players on the perimeter. He loves crashing the boards. He shoots for a high percentage and has a reliable low-post hook shot.

Weaknesses: Polynice has a limited offensive arsenal. He is a poor ball-handler and perimeter shooter and his free throw shooting is atrocious. He is one of the worst passing centers in the league. Polynice has made a habit of rubbing coaches and teammates the wrong way. He tends to do his own thing.

Analysis: Polynice, who once went on a brief hunger strike for starving people in his native Haiti, has become a double-figure scorer over the last two seasons while maintaining a solid effort on the boards. He does not take too many shots he can't make. On a contending team, however, Polynice would be no better than a second-teamer.

PLAYER SUMMARY	
Will	toss in hooks
Can't	shoot free throws
Expect	rebounds, 10 PPG
Don't Expect	All-Star trips
Fantasy Value	$5-7
Card Value	5-8¢

COLLEGE STATISTICS

		G	FGP	FTP	RPG	PPG
83-84	VIRG	33	.551	.588	5.6	7.7
84-85	VIRG	32	.603	.599	7.6	13.0
85-86	VIRG	30	.572	.637	8.0	16.1
Totals		95	.578	.612	7.0	12.1

NBA REGULAR-SEASON STATISTICS

				FGs		3-PT FGs		FTs		Rebounds						
		G	MIN	FG	PCT	FG	PCT	FT	PCT	OFF	TOT	AST	STL	BLK	PTS	PPG
87-88	SEA	82	1080	118	.465	0	.000	101	.639	122	330	33	32	26	337	4.1
88-89	SEA	80	835	91	.506	0	.000	51	.593	98	206	21	37	30	233	2.9
89-90	SEA	79	1085	156	.540	1	.500	47	.475	128	300	15	25	21	360	4.6
90-91	SEA/LAC	79	2092	316	.560	0	.000	146	.579	220	553	42	43	32	778	9.8
91-92	LAC	76	1834	244	.519	0	.000	125	.622	195	536	46	45	20	613	8.1
92-93	DET	67	1299	210	.490	0	.000	66	.465	181	418	29	31	21	486	7.3
93-94	DET/SAC	68	2402	346	.523	0	.000	97	.508	299	809	41	42	67	789	11.6
94-95	SAC	81	2534	376	.544	1	1.000	124	.639	277	725	62	48	52	877	10.8
Totals		612	13161	1857	.525	2	.167	757	.572	1520	3877	289	303	269	4473	7.3

TERRY PORTER

Unrestricted Free Agent
Last Team: Portland Trail Blazers
Position: Guard
Height: 6'3" **Weight:** 195
Birthdate: April 8, 1963

NBA Experience: 10 years
College: Wisconsin-Stevens Point
Acquired: 1st-round pick in 1985 draft (24th overall)

Background: Porter was an NAIA All-American as a junior and senior at Wisconsin-Stevens Point, where his shooting accuracy was remarkable for a guard. He has spent all ten pro seasons in Portland, where he has played in the NBA Finals and been a two-time All-Star. Ankle surgery sidelined him for the first half of the 1994-95 season.

Strengths: Porter still boasts deadly long-range shooting skills. He can get his shots off the dribble and has made 773 from behind the arc during his career. He is good with both hands and uses his strength well on defense. Porter has earned respect for his clutch performances and his leadership.

Weaknesses: Age and injuries have slowed Porter, who did not possess blinding speed in the first place. He was never among the most creative guards in the league and has been reduced to a reserve role over the last couple of years. His shooting percentage and overall effectiveness are in decline.

Analysis: Perhaps Porter could use a change of scenery. He failed to score in double figures last season for the first time since his rookie year. His best days are certainly behind him and he is slowing physically, but Porter could still help a team (a contender, perhaps?) with his shooting and leadership off the bench.

PLAYER SUMMARY

Will ....knock down treys
Can't...........................regain his step
Expect ....veteran leadership
Don't Expect ....more All-Star trips
Fantasy Value....................................$1
Card Value....................................7-12¢

COLLEGE STATISTICS

		G	FGP	FTP	APG	PPG
81-82	WSP	25	.368	.692	0.8	2.0
82-83	WSP	30	.611	.697	5.2	11.4
83-84	WSP	32	.622	.830	4.2	18.8
84-85	WSP	30	.575	.834	4.3	19.7
Totals		117	.589	.796	3.8	13.5

NBA REGULAR-SEASON STATISTICS

		G	MIN	FGs FG	FGs PCT	3-PT FGs FG	3-PT FGs PCT	FTs FT	FTs PCT	Rebounds OFF	Rebounds TOT	AST	STL	BLK	PTS	PPG
85-86	POR	79	1214	212	.474	13	.310	125	.806	35	117	198	81	1	562	7.1
86-87	POR	80	2714	376	.488	13	.217	280	.838	70	337	715	159	9	1045	13.1
87-88	POR	82	2991	462	.519	24	.348	274	.846	65	378	831	150	16	1222	14.9
88-89	POR	81	3102	540	.471	79	.361	272	.840	85	367	770	146	8	1431	17.7
89-90	POR	80	2781	448	.462	89	.374	421	.892	59	272	726	151	4	1406	17.6
90-91	POR	81	2665	486	.515	130	.415	279	.823	52	282	649	158	12	1381	17.0
91-92	POR	82	2784	521	.461	128	.395	315	.856	51	255	477	127	12	1485	18.1
92-93	POR	81	2883	503	.454	143	.414	327	.843	58	316	419	101	10	1476	18.2
93-94	POR	77	2074	348	.416	110	.390	204	.872	45	215	401	79	18	1010	13.1
94-95	POR	35	770	105	.393	44	.386	58	.707	18	81	133	30	2	312	8.9
Totals		758	23978	4001	.470	773	.385	2555	.846	538	2620	5319	1182	92	11330	14.9

MARK PRICE

Team: Cleveland Cavaliers
Position: Guard
Height: 6'0" **Weight:** 178
Birthdate: February 16, 1964
NBA Experience: 9 years

College: Georgia Tech
Acquired: Draft rights traded from Mavericks for a 1989 2nd-round pick and cash, 6/86

Background: Price, Georgia Tech's second all-time leading scorer when he graduated in 1986, was drafted by Dallas and immediately traded to the Cavs. Despite an emergency appendectomy as a rookie, a tear of the anterior cruciate ligament in 1990, and wrist surgery last season, he has played in four All-Star Games and was a Dream Team II member.

Strengths: Price is one of the most dangerous shooters in the game, ranking among the all-time leaders from 3-point range and having won two Long Distance Shootout titles on All-Star Weekend. He also owns the highest career free throw average of all time. He is deceivingly quick, a splendid passer, and an underrated defender.

Weaknesses: Price does not have good size, allowing bigger guards to shoot and rebound over him. He has suffered his share of injuries in nine seasons. Right wrist surgery kept him from trying for a third straight Shootout title in 1995.

Analysis: Price is one of the premier point guards in the NBA. He owns an All-Star Game record of six 3-pointers and could finish his career as the best free throw shooter in history. Although he is not the flamboyant type, his leadership and overall play qualify him as a superstar. He is an avid church singer and charity supporter.

PLAYER SUMMARY

Will	make his shots
Can't	avoid the injury bug
Expect	All-Star leadership
Don't Expect	missed free throws
Fantasy Value	$17-20
Card Value	15-25¢

COLLEGE STATISTICS

		G	FGP	FTP	APG	PPG
82-83	GT	28	.435	.877	3.3	20.3
83-84	GT	29	.509	.824	4.2	15.6
84-85	GT	35	.483	.840	4.3	16.7
85-86	GT	34	.528	.855	4.4	17.4
Totals		126	.487	.850	4.0	17.4

NBA REGULAR-SEASON STATISTICS

		G	MIN	FGs FG	FGs PCT	3-PT FGs FG	3-PT FGs PCT	FTs FT	FTs PCT	Rebounds OFF	Rebounds TOT	AST	STL	BLK	PTS	PPG
86-87	CLE	67	1217	173	.408	23	.329	95	.833	33	117	202	43	4	464	6.9
87-88	CLE	80	2626	493	.506	72	.486	221	.877	54	180	480	99	12	1279	16.0
88-89	CLE	75	2728	529	.526	93	.441	263	.901	48	226	631	115	7	1414	18.9
89-90	CLE	73	2706	489	.459	152	.406	300	.888	66	251	666	114	5	1430	19.6
90-91	CLE	16	571	97	.497	18	.340	59	.952	8	45	166	42	2	271	16.9
91-92	CLE	72	2138	438	.488	101	.387	270	.947	38	173	535	94	12	1247	17.3
92-93	CLE	75	2380	477	.484	122	.416	289	.948	37	201	602	89	11	1365	18.2
93-94	CLE	76	2386	480	.478	118	.397	238	.888	39	228	589	103	11	1316	17.3
94-95	CLE	48	1375	253	.413	103	.407	148	.914	25	112	335	35	4	757	15.8
Totals		582	18127	3429	.479	802	.409	1883	.906	348	1533	4206	734	68	9543	16.4

DINO RADJA

Team: Boston Celtics
Position: Forward
Height: 6'11" **Weight:** 225
Birthdate: April 24, 1967

NBA Experience: 2 years
College: None
Acquired: 2nd-round pick in 1989 draft (40th overall)

Background: The Celtics had to wait four years for Radja, who continued playing in Europe despite being taken in the second round of the 1989 draft. He won a silver medal with Croatia in the 1992 Olympics before averaging 21.5 points and 10.2 rebounds per game in the Italian 1A League. He was a second-team All-Rookie performer and upped his average to 17.2 PPG, second on the team, during the 1994-95 season.

Strengths: Radja brings a fine set of offensive skills to the power-forward position. He owns a good touch from the perimeter and has some aggressive moves with his back to the basket. Some guys simply know how to score, and he's one of them. The big guy can get out in transition. Radja is a solid rebounder on both ends of the court and he also blocks shots. He displays a nice feel for the game.

Weaknesses: The one flaw that stands out is common to many European imports—defense. Radja is willing to work on that end of the court and will alter some shots, but he also commits a lot of fouls and does not have great footwork. To his credit, he wants to get better. Radja is no Toni Kukoc when it comes to handling and passing the ball. He gets credit for more turnovers than assists.

Analysis: Once considered the second-best player in Europe (behind Kukoc), Radja continues to progress as an NBA player as well. He was the Celtics' second-leading scorer last season, behind Dominique Wilkins, despite the fact that defenders were taking his game a little more seriously. Radja offers a nice blend of clever moves and aggressive play in the post and has a proven knack for scoring.

PLAYER SUMMARY

Will ....score inside
Can't ....avoid fouls
Expect ....soft touch
Don't Expect ....physical defense
Fantasy Value $17-20
Card Value ....20-40¢

COLLEGE STATISTICS

—DID NOT PLAY—

NBA REGULAR-SEASON STATISTICS

			FGs		3-PT FGs		FTs		Rebounds						
		G	MIN	FG	PCT	FG	PCT	FT	PCT	OFF	TOT	AST	STL	BLK	PTS	PPG
93-94	BOS	80	2303	491	.521	0	.000	226	.751	191	577	114	70	67	1208	15.1
94-95	BOS	66	2147	450	.490	0	.000	233	.759	149	573	111	60	86	1133	17.2
Totals		146	4450	941	.506	0	.000	459	.755	340	1150	225	130	153	2341	16.0

KHALID REEVES

Team: Miami Heat
Position: Guard
Height: 6'3" **Weight:** 200
Birthdate: July 15, 1972

NBA Experience: 1 year
College: Arizona
Acquired: 1st-round pick in 1994 draft (12th overall)

Background: A high-profile recruit from New York City, Reeves was considered a disappointment during his first three years at Arizona. As a senior, however, he nearly doubled his scoring average to 24.2 PPG and was third on the all-time school scoring list when he finished his career at the Final Four. Drafted 12th overall by Miami in 1994, Reeves ranked second on the Heat and fourth among rookies with 4.3 APG last season.

Strengths: Reeves provides versatility in that he can play both guard positions, making him an ideal player to bring off the bench. He looks to score and can do so in a variety of ways. He scores in transition, shoots with 3-point range, and can create his own opportunities off the dribble. He is a solid defensive player who can help on the boards.

Weaknesses: While Reeves's versatility is a strength, the fact that he seems to be stuck between backcourt positions can be seen as a weakness. As a shooting guard, he does not possess great size and is susceptible on defense. He struggles more at the point. He does not have blinding speed and his assist-to-turnover ratio is not much better than 2-to-1. He should improve his free throw shooting.

Analysis: All in all, Reeves enjoyed a quietly productive rookie season. The NBA 3-pointer is well within his range, and thus his future appears to be as a shooting guard. On the other hand, it's nice to know you have a guy who handles the ball well enough to fill in at the point when you need him. Reeves must continue to improve his defense and learn to involve his teammates more often. He's got a future.

PLAYER SUMMARY	
Will	play two positions
Can't	burn point guards
Expect	3-point shooting
Don't Expect	blinding speed
Fantasy Value	$9-11
Card Value	30-60¢

COLLEGE STATISTICS

		G	FGP	FTP	APG	PPG
90-91	ARIZ	35	.454	.690	2.9	9.1
91-92	ARIZ	30	.476	.788	3.7	13.9
92-93	ARIZ	28	.498	.727	2.9	12.2
93-94	ARIZ	35	.483	.799	2.9	24.2
Totals		128	.479	.763	3.1	15.0

NBA REGULAR-SEASON STATISTICS

			FGs		3-PT FGs		FTs		Rebounds						
		G	MIN	FG	PCT	FG	PCT	FT	PCT	OFF	TOT	AST	STL	BLK	PTS	PPG
94-95	MIA	67	1462	206	.443	67	.392	140	.714	52	186	288	77	10	619	9.2
Totals		67	1462	206	.443	67	.392	140	.714	52	186	288	77	10	619	9.2

J.R. REID

Team: San Antonio Spurs
Position: Forward
Height: 6'9" **Weight:** 255
Birthdate: March 31, 1968
NBA Experience: 6 years

College: North Carolina
Acquired: Traded from Hornets for Sidney Green, a 1993 1st-round pick, and a 1996 2nd-round pick, 12/92

Background: Coming out of high school in 1986, Reid was the No. 1-ranked player in America. A 1988 U.S. Olympian, he was a consensus All-American as a North Carolina sophomore. A second-team All-Rookie pick with Charlotte, he averaged 11-plus PPG over his first three years before a trade to San Antonio. Reid averaged a career-low 7.0 PPG last season.

Strengths: Reid possesses a soft shooting touch from up to 15 feet and a nice all-around offensive game, both facing the bucket and in the post. He can use his size, strength, and speed to beat opposing forwards off the dribble and get to the hoop. He shoots for a high percentage. Reid is also a decent low-post defender. He has kept himself in better shape over the last two years.

Weaknesses: Reid's biggest problems have to do with his inconsistency. He'll score 20 points one night and three the next. His intensity has been questioned, although he has shown better commitment in recent years. Reid rarely passes once he gets the ball. He is not a great ball-handler and could be a better rebounder.

Analysis: There will be no All-Star showings for this one-time can't-miss superstar. After becoming something of an enigma early in his career, he has played well in his role off the bench. And although his scoring average has dipped into single digits, his commitment to the game has improved and he seems to be having more fun.

PLAYER SUMMARY	
Will	hit 15-footers
Can't	pass the ball
Expect	bench scoring
Don't Expect	stardom
Fantasy Value	$1
Card Value	5-8¢

COLLEGE STATISTICS

		G	FGP	FTP	RPG	PPG
86-87	NC	36	.584	.653	7.4	14.7
87-88	NC	33	.607	.680	8.9	18.0
88-89	NC	27	.614	.669	6.3	15.9
Totals		96	.601	.668	7.6	16.2

NBA REGULAR-SEASON STATISTICS

			FGs		3-PT FGs		FTs		Rebounds						
	G	MIN	FG	PCT	FG	PCT	FT	PCT	OFF	TOT	AST	STL	BLK	PTS	PPG
89-90 CHA	82	2757	358	.440	0	.000	192	.664	199	691	101	92	54	908	11.1
90-91 CHA	80	2467	360	.466	0	.000	182	.703	154	502	89	87	47	902	11.3
91-92 CHA	51	1257	213	.490	0	.000	134	.705	96	317	81	49	23	560	11.0
92-93 CHA/SA	83	1887	283	.476	0	.000	214	.764	120	456	80	47	31	780	9.4
93-94 SA	70	1344	260	.491	0	.000	107	.699	91	220	73	43	25	627	9.0
94-95 SA	81	1566	201	.508	1	.500	160	.687	120	393	55	60	32	563	7.0
Totals	447	11278	1675	.473	1	.050	989	.704	780	2579	479	378	212	4340	9.7

GLEN RICE

Team: Miami Heat
Position: Forward/Guard
Height: 6'7" **Weight:** 220
Birthdate: May 28, 1967

NBA Experience: 6 years
College: Michigan
Acquired: 1st-round pick in 1989 draft (4th overall)

Background: Rice led Michigan to a national title in 1989 while averaging nearly 31 PPG in NCAA Tournament play. He finished his college career as the leading scorer in Big Ten history. After being selected second-team All-Rookie in 1989-90, Rice has become one of the league's top scorers and 3-point shooters. He finished among the league's ten leading scorers (ninth) for the third time last season.

Strengths: Rice makes his living filling the nets. He rarely misses a free throw and has his nights when he rarely misses anything. He netted 56 points against Orlando last April, the top single-game effort in the league last year. He complements his perimeter prowess with effective drives to the bucket. Rice also plays good defense.

Weaknesses: Rice is not a great ball-handler or passer. In fact, he does not rack up many more assists than he does turnovers, making his overall floor game the weakest aspect of his play. Quicker players cause him problems on defense. He is invisible on the offensive glass, though he does get to the boards on D.

Analysis: After a disappointing rookie season in which he was out of shape and overweight, Rice has become one of the best pure shooters and scorers in basketball. He captured the Long Distance Shootout on All-Star Weekend last season and is capable of burning the nets from anywhere on the court. He has yet to fulfill his dream of playing in an All-Star Game.

PLAYER SUMMARY

Will ....hit from deep
Can't.................clear offensive glass
Expect.........................40-point games
Don't Expect ....fancy moves
Fantasy Value $40-45
Card Value....................................7-12¢

COLLEGE STATISTICS

		G	FGP	FTP	RPG	PPG
85-86	MICH	32	.550	.600	3.0	7.0
86-87	MICH	32	.562	.787	9.2	16.9
87-88	MICH	33	.571	.806	7.2	22.1
88-89	MICH	37	.577	.832	6.3	25.6
Totals		134	.569	.797	6.4	18.2

NBA REGULAR-SEASON STATISTICS

				FGs		3-PT FGs		FTs		Rebounds							
		G	MIN	FG	PCT	FG	PCT	FT	PCT	OFF	TOT	AST	STL	BLK	PTS	PPG
89-90	MIA	77	2311	470	.439	17	.246	91	.734	100	352	138	67	27	1048	13.6
90-91	MIA	77	2646	550	.461	71	.386	171	.818	85	381	189	101	26	1342	17.4
91-92	MIA	79	3007	672	.469	155	.391	266	.836	84	394	184	90	35	1765	22.3
92-93	MIA	82	3082	582	.440	148	.383	242	.820	92	424	180	92	25	1554	19.0
93-94	MIA	81	2999	663	.467	132	.382	250	.880	76	434	184	110	32	1708	21.1
94-95	MIA	82	3014	667	.475	185	.410	312	.855	99	378	192	112	14	1831	22.3
Totals		478	17059	3604	.459	708	.386	1332	.835	536	2363	1067	572	159	9248	19.3

POOH RICHARDSON

Team: Los Angeles Clippers
Position: Guard
Height: 6'1" **Weight:** 180
Birthdate: May 14, 1966
NBA Experience: 6 years

College: UCLA
Acquired: Traded from Pacers with Malik Sealy and draft rights to Eric Piatkowski for Mark Jackson and draft rights to Greg Minor, 6/94

Background: Richardson was a four-year starter and three-time All-Pac-10 star at UCLA, where he set a conference record for assists. He spent his first three pro seasons in Minnesota, but after asking to be traded he finally was. He spent two frustrating seasons with Indiana before another trade made him the Clippers' starting point guard during the 1994-95 campaign.

Strengths: Richardson brings both scoring and playmaking ability to the point-guard position. He shoots with 3-point range, drives to the basket, and finished eighth in the league with 7.9 APG last season. He loves to run and makes crisp passes at high speed. Richardson is also a solid defensive player and defensive rebounder.

Weaknesses: Richardson earned a reputation as a chronic complainer in Minnesota, and he failed to gain the respect of teammates and coaches in Indiana too. His decision-making and ability to steer a steady ship have been questioned. Richardson shot less than 40 percent from the field last season and he has not been an accurate free throw shooter.

Analysis: Inconsistency and injuries have kept Richardson from living up to his potential through six NBA seasons. He has most of the tools of a quality point guard. He is a fine passer, a capable shooter and scorer, and a good defender when he sets his mind to it. For a number of reasons, however, he has yet to put it all together. He hopes his second year in L.A. will be much better than the first.

PLAYER SUMMARY

Will ....find open men
Can't ....put it together
Expect ....bright moments
Don't Expect..........steady leadership
Fantasy Value $5-7
Card Value ....5-8¢

COLLEGE STATISTICS

		G	FGP	FTP	APG	PPG
85-86	UCLA	29	.492	.689	6.2	10.6
86-87	UCLA	32	.527	.582	6.5	10.5
87-88	UCLA	30	.470	.667	7.0	11.6
88-89	UCLA	31	.555	.562	7.6	15.2
Totals		122	.513	.624	6.8	12.0

NBA REGULAR-SEASON STATISTICS

				FGs		3-PT FGs		FTs		Rebounds						
		G	MIN	FG	PCT	FG	PCT	FT	PCT	OFF	TOT	AST	STL	BLK	PTS	PPG
89-90	MIN	82	2581	426	.461	23	.277	63	.589	55	217	554	133	25	938	11.4
90-91	MIN	82	3154	635	.470	42	.328	89	.539	82	286	734	131	13	1401	17.1
91-92	MIN	82	2922	587	.466	53	.342	123	.691	91	301	685	119	25	1350	16.5
92-93	IND	74	2396	337	.479	3	.103	92	.742	63	267	573	94	12	769	10.4
93-94	IND	37	1022	160	.452	3	.250	47	.610	28	110	237	32	3	370	10.0
94-95	LAC	80	2864	353	.394	87	.357	81	.648	38	261	632	129	12	874	10.9
Totals		437	14939	2498	.455	211	.324	495	.638	357	1442	3415	638	90	5702	13.0

MITCH RICHMOND

Team: Sacramento Kings
Position: Guard
Height: 6'5" **Weight:** 215
Birthdate: June 30, 1965
NBA Experience: 7 years

College: Moberly Area; Kansas St.
Acquired: Traded from Warriors with Les Jepsen and a 1995 2nd-round pick for draft rights to Billy Owens, 11/91

Background: Richmond was a junior college All-American before he spent two years at Kansas State, where he set a single-season record for points. He was a near-unanimous choice for Rookie of the Year with Golden State in 1989 and has never averaged less than 21.9 PPG in seven seasons. He was traded to Sacramento on the eve of the 1991-92 opener and has played in the last two All-Star Games.

Strengths: Look up "pure scorer" in the dictionary and it should mention Richmond. He nails jumpers with men all over him, hits 3-pointers, and drives through traffic without fear. When he sets his muscular frame in the post, he is almost impossible for smaller defenders to stop. He runs the floor, rebounds, and gets his teammates involved. Richmond also decided to make a defensive statement last season.

Weaknesses: Richmond is not one of the better ball-handling guards in the game. He does not possess blinding speed and commits a fair number of turnovers. The knocks on his defense may have become a thing of the past.

Analysis: Richmond has been one of the league's best offensive players for several years, but his efforts have gone largely unnoticed on lottery teams. His performance in the 1995 All-Star Game, which included 23 points in 22 minutes on 10-of-13 field goal shooting, earned him game MVP honors. It's about time some recognition came his way.

PLAYER SUMMARY	
Will	torch the nets
Can't	dribble against pressure
Expect	at least 22 PPG
Don't Expect	blazing speed
Fantasy Value	$30-35
Card Value	10-20¢

COLLEGE STATISTICS

		G	FGP	FTP	RPG	PPG
84-85	MA	40	.480	.647	4.6	10.4
85-86	MA	38	.478	.689	6.6	16.0
86-87	KSU	30	.447	.761	5.7	18.6
87-88	KSU	34	.514	.775	6.3	22.6
Totals		142	.481	.732	5.8	16.5

NBA REGULAR-SEASON STATISTICS

		G	MIN	FGs FG	FGs PCT	3-PT FGs FG	3-PT FGs PCT	FTs FT	FTs PCT	Rebounds OFF	Rebounds TOT	AST	STL	BLK	PTS	PPG
88-89	GS	79	2717	649	.468	33	.367	410	.810	158	468	334	82	13	1741	22.0
89-90	GS	78	2799	640	.497	34	.358	406	.866	98	360	223	98	24	1720	22.1
90-91	GS	77	3027	703	.494	40	.348	394	.847	147	452	238	126	34	1840	23.9
91-92	SAC	80	3095	685	.468	103	.384	330	.813	62	319	411	92	34	1803	22.5
92-93	SAC	45	1728	371	.474	48	.369	197	.845	18	154	221	53	9	987	21.9
93-94	SAC	78	2897	635	.445	127	.407	426	.834	70	286	313	103	17	1823	23.4
94-95	SAC	82	3172	668	.446	156	.368	375	.843	69	357	311	91	29	1867	22.8
Totals		519	19435	4351	.469	541	.377	2538	.836	622	2396	2051	645	160	11781	22.7

ISAIAH RIDER

Team: Minnesota Timberwolves
Position: Guard/Forward
Height: 6'5" **Weight:** 215
Birthdate: March 12, 1971

NBA Experience: 2 years
College: Nevada-Las Vegas
Acquired: 1st-round pick in 1993 draft (5th overall)

Background: Upon graduating from an Alameda high school in California, Rider committed to Kansas State but failed to qualify academically. He transferred to a junior college in Kansas, then to another in California, and finally to UNLV. He was second nationally in scoring in 1992-93 with 29.1 PPG. Called J.R. in college, he announced his preference for Isaiah before his All-Rookie 1993-94 season. Rider led Minnesota with 20.4 PPG last season.

Strengths: Rider is a highly skilled offensive player and an explosive athlete who plays with great intensity and confidence. He shoots with 3-point range, posts up, and finishes his drives with crowd-pleasing jams. He guaranteed a victory in the 1994 Slam Dunk Contest and won with his "East Bay Funk" dunk. The energetic Rider is also a reliable free throw shooter and an underrated passer and rebounder.

Weaknesses: Rider is not among the better ball-handling guards in basketball and he needs to continue to fine-tune his decision-making. He commits a lot of turnovers. While he hustles on both ends, he still needs to learn the ins and outs of NBA defense. Rider has been a controversial off-court celebrity at times. His resume includes habitual tardiness to practice.

Analysis: Rider is one who talks the talk and walks the walk. He is a tremendous talent with a boundless confidence to go along with it. He gets the idea no one can stop him when he gets the ball in his hands, and much of the time he is correct. Certainly few can stop him when he's hovering above the rim. With his scoring skills, he has potential as a franchise player for years to come.

PLAYER SUMMARY

Will ....get his points
Can't ....run the point
Expect ....20-plus PPG
Don't Expect ....poor confidence
Fantasy Value $17-20
Card Value ....20-40¢

COLLEGE STATISTICS

		G	FGP	FTP	RPG	PPG
91-92	UNLV	27	.490	.747	5.2	20.7
92-93	UNLV	28	.515	.826	8.9	29.1
Totals		55	.505	.805	7.1	24.9

NBA REGULAR-SEASON STATISTICS

			FGs		3-PT FGs		FTs		Rebounds						
		G	MIN	FG	PCT	FG	PCT	FT	PCT	OFF	TOT	AST	STL	BLK	PTS	PPG
93-94	MIN	79	2415	522	.468	54	.360	215	.811	118	315	202	54	28	1313	16.6
94-95	MIN	75	2645	558	.447	139	.351	277	.817	90	249	245	69	23	1532	20.4
Totals		154	5060	1080	.457	193	.353	492	.815	208	564	447	123	51	2845	18.5

DOC RIVERS

Unrestricted Free Agent
Last Team: San Antonio Spurs
Position: Guard
Height: 6'4" **Weight:** 185
Birthdate: October 13, 1961

NBA Experience: 12 years
College: Marquette
Acquired: Signed as a free agent, 12/94

Background: A Marquette product, Rivers spent his first eight seasons with Atlanta and was an All-Star in 1989. He spent a year with the Clippers and was dealt to the Knicks before the 1992-93 season. Rivers suffered a season-ending knee injury in December 1993 and, after surgery, was released by New York three games into 1994-95. He signed with the Spurs and played in 60 games.

Strengths: Rivers does nothing flashy; he just gets the job done. He's a world-class citizen who plays defense, delivers the ball, can score with drives and jumpers, and provides great leadership. Rivers can play both guard positions.

Weaknesses: Knee surgery has robbed Rivers of much of his effectiveness at both ends. He was slipping a notch before the injury and his days as a major offensive force are over. Rivers has seen a decline in his shooting, scoring, and defensive abilities in recent years.

Analysis: Rivers has probably seen the last of his days as a starter, thanks to the wear and tear of 12 seasons. He is now most valuable for the lessons young players will learn from watching his approach to the game. Having Rivers in your locker room is like hiring an extra coach.

PLAYER SUMMARY

Will..............................lead by example
Can't ....turn back the clock
Expect ....a coach on the floor
Don't Expect ....10 PPG
Fantasy Value.................................$0
Card Value ....5-8¢

COLLEGE STATISTICS

		G	FGP	FTP	APG	PPG
80-81	MARQ	31	.553	.588	3.6	14.0
81-82	MARQ	29	.453	.648	5.9	14.3
82-83	MARQ	29	.437	.611	4.3	13.2
Totals		89	.478	.615	4.6	13.9

NBA REGULAR-SEASON STATISTICS

				FGs		3-PT FGs		FTs		Rebounds							
		G	MIN	FG	PCT	FG	PCT	FT	PCT	OFF	TOT	AST	STL	BLK	PTS	PPG
83-84	ATL	81	1938	250	.462	2	.167	255	.785	72	220	314	127	30	757	9.3
84-85	ATL	69	2126	334	.476	15	.417	291	.770	66	214	410	163	53	974	14.1
85-86	ATL	53	1571	220	.474	0	.000	172	.608	49	162	443	120	13	612	11.5
86-87	ATL	82	2590	342	.451	4	.190	365	.828	83	299	823	171	30	1053	12.8
87-88	ATL	80	2502	403	.453	9	.273	319	.758	83	366	747	140	41	1134	14.2
88-89	ATL	76	2462	371	.455	43	.347	247	.861	89	286	525	181	40	1032	13.6
89-90	ATL	48	1526	218	.454	24	.364	138	.812	47	200	264	116	22	598	12.5
90-91	ATL	79	2586	444	.435	88	.336	221	.844	47	253	340	148	47	1197	15.2
91-92	LAC	59	1657	226	.424	26	.283	163	.832	23	147	233	111	19	641	10.9
92-93	NY	77	1886	216	.437	39	.317	133	.821	26	192	405	123	9	604	7.8
93-94	NY	19	499	55	.433	19	.365	14	.636	4	39	100	25	5	143	7.5
94-95	NY/SA	63	989	108	.358	45	.354	60	.732	15	109	162	65	21	321	5.1
Totals		786	22332	3187	.447	314	.326	2378	.785	604	2487	4766	1490	330	9066	11.5

STANLEY ROBERTS

Team: Los Angeles Clippers
Position: Center
Height: 7'0" **Weight:** 295
Birthdate: February 7, 1970

NBA Experience: 3 years
College: Louisiana St.
Acquired: Traded from Magic in three-team, multi-player deal, 9/92

Background: Roberts teamed with Shaquille O'Neal at LSU, but academic problems plagued Roberts and he signed with a pro team in Spain. Though his rookie year with Orlando began with jokes about his weight, he ended up averaging 10.4 PPG. He was traded to the Clippers before the 1992-93 campaign and averaged 11.3 PPG and 6.2 RPG. An Achilles injury has limited him to 14 games over the last two years.

Strengths: Roberts can be an offensive force around the basket. He has a killer spin move, is virtually impossible to budge once he gets position on the interior, and has good hands and footwork despite his bulk. Roberts has blocked 1.7 shots per game during his career. He can also be effective on the boards when he sets his mind to it.

Weaknesses: Weight and foul trouble have long been the biggest problems for Roberts, who has reported as large as 320 pounds and ballooned close to 340 while on the injured list. Fat jokes have followed him. Roberts led the league in personal fouls (332) and disqualifications (15) in his last full season. He does not run the floor well and his passing and free throw shooting are substandard.

Analysis: Roberts is a huge (pun intended) question mark after playing just 14 games in 1993-94 and sitting out all last year after left Achilles tendon surgery. At his best, he can be dominant offensively. Working against him, however, are his weight, his inconsistency, and his time spent on the bench while hurt or in foul trouble. Injuries will probably continue to plague Roberts unless he makes a commitment to stay in shape.

PLAYER SUMMARY	
Will	spin to the hole
Can't	pass up a meal
Expect	blocked shots
Don't Expect	conditioning
Fantasy Value	$1-3
Card Value	5-8¢

COLLEGE STATISTICS

		G	FGP	FTP	RPG	PPG
89-90	LSU	32	.576	.460	9.8	14.1
Totals		32	.576	.460	9.8	14.1

NBA REGULAR-SEASON STATISTICS

		G	MIN	FGs FG	FGs PCT	3-PT FGs FG	3-PT FGs PCT	FTs FT	FTs PCT	Rebounds OFF	Rebounds TOT	AST	STL	BLK	PTS	PPG
91-92	ORL	55	1118	236	.529	0	.000	101	.515	113	336	39	22	83	573	10.4
92-93	LAC	77	1816	375	.527	0	.000	120	.488	181	478	59	34	141	870	11.3
93-94	LAC	14	350	43	.430	0	.000	18	.409	27	93	11	6	25	104	7.4
Totals		146	3284	654	.520	0	.000	239	.492	321	907	109	62	249	1547	10.6

CLIFFORD ROBINSON

Team: Portland Trail Blazers
Position: Forward
Height: 6'10" **Weight:** 225
Birthdate: December 16, 1966

NBA Experience: 6 years
College: Connecticut
Acquired: 2nd-round pick in 1989 draft (36th overall)

Background: Robinson led Connecticut in scoring for three consecutive years. Bypassed until the second round of the 1989 draft, the six-year Portland pro did not miss a game in his first five years and has improved his scoring every season. He won the league's Sixth Man Award for 1992-93. A starter the past two years, Robinson played in the 1994 All-Star Game and averaged 21.3 PPG last season.

Strengths: Explosive athletic ability, versatility, and the ability to light up the scoreboard make Robinson an invaluable player. He is an elusive driver and tremendous open-court player who gets to the hoop for dazzling finishes. Robinson also became a prolific 3-point shooter last season while maintaining his contributions as a decent shot-blocker and rebounder.

Weaknesses: Robinson has had some off-court incidents, including speeding tickets for driving 110 and 89 mph. He has also had some personality conflicts with teammates and former teammates, and he's developed a history of coming up short in big games. His name doesn't come to mind when talking about team players. He's a below-average free throw shooter.

Analysis: Robinson's string of consecutive games ended after five-plus seasons, but his remarkable ability to increase his scoring average every year continues. The shorter 3-point arc last season helped him as much as anyone else in the league. Now that he has established himself as a 20-point man, Robinson's next trick should be looking to involve his teammates more often.

PLAYER SUMMARY	
Will	finish with slams
Can't	be left open
Expect	athletic drives
Don't Expect	tons of assists
Fantasy Value	$30-35
Card Value	7-12¢

COLLEGE STATISTICS

		G	FGP	FTP	RPG	PPG
85-86	CONN	28	.366	.610	3.1	5.6
86-87	CONN	16	.420	.570	7.4	18.1
87-88	CONN	34	.479	.655	6.9	17.6
88-89	CONN	31	.470	.684	7.4	20.0
Totals		109	.452	.644	6.1	15.3

NBA REGULAR-SEASON STATISTICS

		G	MIN	FGs FG	FGs PCT	3-PT FGs FG	3-PT FGs PCT	FTs FT	FTs PCT	Rebounds OFF	Rebounds TOT	AST	STL	BLK	PTS	PPG
89-90	POR	82	1565	298	.397	12	.273	138	.550	110	308	72	53	53	746	9.1
90-91	POR	82	1940	373	.463	6	.316	205	.653	123	349	151	78	76	957	11.7
91-92	POR	82	2124	398	.466	1	.091	219	.664	140	416	137	85	107	1016	12.4
92-93	POR	82	2575	632	.473	19	.247	287	.690	165	542	182	98	163	1570	19.1
93-94	POR	82	2853	641	.457	13	.245	352	.765	164	550	159	118	111	1647	20.1
94-95	POR	75	2725	597	.452	142	.371	265	.694	152	423	198	79	82	1601	21.3
Totals		485	13782	2939	.454	193	.329	1466	.681	854	2588	899	511	592	7537	15.5

DAVID ROBINSON

Team: San Antonio Spurs
Position: Center
Height: 7'1" **Weight:** 235
Birthdate: August 6, 1965

NBA Experience: 6 years
College: Navy
Acquired: 1st-round pick in 1987 draft
(1st overall)

Background: As a senior at Navy, Robinson led the nation in blocked shots and was college basketball's consensus Player of the Year. He set NCAA records for blocks in a game and a season. After a two-year stint in the Navy, he exploded onto the pro scene in 1989-90, winning unanimous Rookie of the Year honors. He won gold in the 1992 Olympics and has played in the last five All-Star Games. Robinson was the league MVP in 1994-95.

Strengths: Robinson is dominant in most aspects of the game. His quickness allows him to explode to the hoop with unstoppable low-post spin moves. He can stick jumpers or swing the ball back outside for assists. He clears the boards, runs the floor, blocks shots, and comes up with steals. Robinson was named Defensive Player of the Year in 1992 and won the league scoring title in 1993-94. He's also a class act off the court.

Weaknesses: For lack of anything else in this category, Robinson led the Spurs in turnovers last year. What do you expect from a player who's constantly double-teamed?

Analysis: Mr. Robinson, who clinched the 1993-94 scoring title with a 71-point game on the last day of the season, enjoyed an even better overall year in 1994-95. He led San Antonio to the best record in the NBA and beat out Hakeem Olajuwon for league MVP honors. Robinson has never averaged below 23.2 PPG while making his teammates look better as well. He is a Hall of Fame shoo-in at his current pace.

PLAYER SUMMARY	
Will	dominate nightly
Can't	be single-teamed
Expect	the total package
Don't Expect	a weakness
Fantasy Value	$85-90
Card Value	40-80¢

COLLEGE STATISTICS

		G	FGP	FTP	RPG	PPG
83-84	NAVY	28	.623	.575	4.0	7.6
84-85	NAVY	32	.644	.626	11.6	23.6
85-86	NAVY	35	.607	.628	13.0	22.7
86-87	NAVY	32	.591	.637	11.8	28.2
Totals		127	.613	.627	10.3	21.0

NBA REGULAR-SEASON STATISTICS

			FGs		3-PT FGs		FTs		Rebounds						
	G	MIN	FG	PCT	FG	PCT	FT	PCT	OFF	TOT	AST	STL	BLK	PTS	PPG
89-90 SA	82	3002	690	.531	0	.000	613	.732	303	983	164	138	319	1993	24.3
90-91 SA	82	3095	754	.552	1	.143	592	.762	335	1063	208	127	320	2101	25.6
91-92 SA	68	2564	592	.551	1	.125	393	.701	261	829	181	158	305	1578	23.2
92-93 SA	82	3211	676	.501	3	.176	561	.732	229	956	301	127	264	1916	23.4
93-94 SA	80	3241	840	.507	10	.345	693	.749	241	855	381	139	265	2383	29.8
94-95 SA	81	3074	788	.530	6	.300	656	.774	234	877	236	134	262	2238	27.6
Totals	475	18187	4340	.527	21	.253	3508	.744	1603	5563	1471	823	1735	12209	25.7

GLENN ROBINSON

Team: Milwaukee Bucks
Position: Forward
Height: 6'7" **Weight:** 240
Birthdate: January 10, 1973

NBA Experience: 1 year
College: Purdue
Acquired: 1st-round pick in 1994 draft
(1st overall)

Background: A former prep phenom from Gary, Indiana, Robinson sat out his freshman year at Purdue because of academics before becoming the best college player in the country. He led the nation in 1993-94 with 30.3 PPG and became the first player to lead the Big Ten in both scoring and rebounding since Mychal Thompson turned the trick in 1978. Milwaukee made the consensus Player of the Year the top overall draft choice, and Robinson led all rookies with 21.9 PPG.

Strengths: "Big Dog" is a dominant player in most aspects of the game. He will probably average 20-plus PPG for the rest of his NBA life thanks to an offensive game that features a soft jumper with 3-point range, a strong post-up game, and the ability to get his shot whenever he wants it. Few players his size can do the things he does with the ball. He's a clutch performer who also rebounds, runs the floor, and finds open men.

Weaknesses: There is very little Robinson is unable to do on the basketball court. He does not block a lot of shots and his defense, while solid at times, needs to get better. He did not sink a high percentage from the field or the 3-point line last season, but that's true of virtually all rookies. He ranked as the NBA leader in turnovers.

Analysis: Robinson will be a franchise player for years to come. After a lengthy contract holdout (he was asking for a deal worth $100 million before settling for a mere eight-figure pact), he adjusted quickly to life in the NBA and established himself as a force. He learned to make teams pay for double-teaming him, and few in the league stand a chance against him one-on-one.

PLAYER SUMMARY

Will ....get his shot
Can't ....be left alone
Expect ....an All-Star future
Don't Expect ....slack defense
Fantasy Value $30-35
Card Value $1.50-5.00

COLLEGE STATISTICS

		G	FGP	FTP	RPG	PPG
92-93	PURD	28	.474	.741	9.2	24.1
93-94	PURD	34	.483	.796	10.1	30.3
Totals		62	.479	.773	9.7	27.5

NBA REGULAR-SEASON STATISTICS

			FGs		3-PT FGs		FTs		Rebounds						
	G	MIN	FG	PCT	FG	PCT	FT	PCT	OFF	TOT	AST	STL	BLK	PTS	PPG
94-95 MIL	80	2958	636	.451	86	.321	397	.796	169	513	197	115	22	1755	21.9
Totals	80	2958	636	.451	86	.321	397	.796	169	513	197	115	22	1755	21.9

JAMES ROBINSON

Team: Portland Trail Blazers
Position: Guard
Height: 6'2" **Weight:** 180
Birthdate: August 31, 1970

NBA Experience: 2 years
College: Alabama
Acquired: 1st-round pick in 1993 draft
(21st overall)

Background: Robinson scored 40 PPG as a senior at Murrah High School in Mississippi. He was a marquee recruit for Alabama but sat out his first year because of a questionable ACT score. He eventually was given four full years of eligibility. He became the first freshman to lead the Tide in scoring since 1953 and, after three years, was drafted by Portland. He improved his scoring from 4.8 PPG as a rookie to 9.2 PPG last season.

Strengths: A top-flight athlete, Robinson explodes to the basket and can be a fine one-on-one player. He once set a Mississippi high school record in the 300-meter hurdles and won the slam-dunk competition at the McDonald's All-America Game. Robinson has great quickness, shoots with 3-point range, and has loads of confidence. He plays enthusiastic defense and can give his man length-of-the-floor fits.

Weaknesses: Robinson is a classic 'tweener. His questionable decision-making keeps him from being a pure point guard, yet he is too small to be a standout at the two spot. He plays out of control at times and some would say his substantial ego obscures the team concept. He does not convert a high percentage from the field and is a terrible free throw shooter.

Analysis: Robinson has demonstrated a knack for scoring. He uses his quickness to get to the hoop and can bury the jumper in streaks when his man gives him a step. He scored 30 points in a game last year and was a 25-game starter for the Blazers. He does not yet show enough consistency to be used with the No. 1 unit on a regular basis, but you can't coach quickness.

PLAYER SUMMARY

Will ....hustle on defense
Can't ....shoot free throws
Expect.....................superb quickness
Don't Expect ....great consistency
Fantasy Value $1-3
Card Value ....7-10¢

COLLEGE STATISTICS

		G	FGP	FTP	APG	PPG
90-91	ALAB	33	.470	.699	1.2	16.8
91-92	ALAB	34	.445	.712	2.2	19.4
92-93	ALAB	29	.420	.682	2.3	20.6
Totals		96	.444	.695	1.9	18.9

NBA REGULAR-SEASON STATISTICS

			MIN	FGs		3-PT FGs		FTs		Rebounds						
		G	MIN	FG	PCT	FG	PCT	FT	PCT	OFF	TOT	AST	STL	BLK	PTS	PPG
93-94	POR	58	673	104	.365	23	.315	45	.672	34	78	68	30	15	276	4.8
94-95	POR	71	1539	255	.409	76	.341	65	.591	42	132	180	48	13	651	9.2
Totals		129	2212	359	.395	99	.334	110	.621	76	210	248	78	28	927	7.2

DENNIS RODMAN

Team: San Antonio Spurs
Position: Forward
Height: 6'8" **Weight:** 210
Birthdate: May 13, 1961
NBA Experience: 9 years

College: Cooke County;
S.E. Oklahoma St.
Acquired: Traded from Pistons with
Isaiah Morris for Sean Elliott and David
Wood, 10/93

Background: Only 5'11" as a high school senior, Rodman went to work as an airport laborer. An incredible nine-inch growth spurt convinced him to give basketball a try. He was a three-time NAIA All-American at S.E. Oklahoma State. He played in two All-Star Games with Detroit, was twice named Defensive Player of the Year, and has led the league in rebounding four years in a row.

Strengths: No forward in recent history has been as dominant defensively and on the glass as Rodman. His 18.7 RPG in 1991-92 was the highest average since Wilt Chamberlain had 19.2 in 1971-72. "Worm" can cover players at all five positions and smothers them with quickness, speed, and strength. He's always moving and can even trigger the break.

Weaknesses: Rodman is not in the NBA for his scoring or his shooting touch. He has been a public-relations nightmare, including a bizarre weapons incident three years ago and countless instances of absence or tardiness. He draws a lot of technical fouls.

Analysis: Rodman might be the most intriguing player in the game today. He is one of the hardest working and most productive rebounders ever to play the game, yet he gains more notoriety for his constantly changing hair color, tattoos, and general rebel image. He has made big contributions to winning teams.

PLAYER SUMMARY	
Will	rebound, defend
Can't	avoid controversy
Expect	15-plus RPG
Don't Expect	predictability
Fantasy Value	$7-9
Card Value	8-15¢

COLLEGE STATISTICS

		G	FGP	FTP	RPG	PPG
82-83	CC	16	.616	.582	13.3	17.6
83-84	SOS	30	.618	.655	13.1	26.0
84-85	SOS	32	.648	.566	15.9	26.8
85-86	SOS	34	.645	.655	17.8	24.4
Totals		112	.635	.620	15.3	24.5

NBA REGULAR-SEASON STATISTICS

		G	MIN	FGs FG	FGs PCT	3-PT FGs FG	3-PT FGs PCT	FTs FT	FTs PCT	Rebounds OFF	Rebounds TOT	AST	STL	BLK	PTS	PPG
86-87	DET	77	1155	213	.545	0	.000	74	.587	163	332	56	38	48	500	6.5
87-88	DET	82	2147	398	.561	5	.294	152	.535	318	715	110	75	45	953	11.6
88-89	DET	82	2208	316	.595	6	.231	97	.626	327	772	99	55	76	735	9.0
89-90	DET	82	2377	288	.581	1	.111	142	.654	336	792	72	52	60	719	8.8
90-91	DET	82	2747	276	.493	6	.200	111	.631	361	1026	85	65	55	669	8.2
91-92	DET	82	3301	342	.539	32	.317	84	.600	523	1530	191	68	70	800	9.8
92-93	DET	62	2410	183	.427	15	.205	87	.534	367	1132	102	48	45	468	7.5
93-94	SA	79	2989	156	.534	5	.208	53	.520	453	1367	184	52	32	370	4.7
94-95	SA	49	1568	137	.571	0	.000	75	.676	274	823	97	31	23	349	7.1
Totals		677	20902	2309	.539	70	.247	875	.594	3122	8489	996	484	454	5563	8.2

CARLOS ROGERS

Team: Golden State Warriors
Position: Forward/Center
Height: 6'11" **Weight:** 220
Birthdate: February 6, 1971
NBA Experience: 1 year
College: Arkansas-Little Rock;

Tennessee St.
Acquired: Draft rights traded from
SuperSonics with Ricky Pierce and a
1995 2nd-round pick for Sarunas
Marciulionis and Byron Houston, 7/94

Background: Rogers sat out two of his first three years in college, once because of academics and again because he transferred from Arkansas-Little Rock to Tennessee State. He was a two-time Ohio Valley Player of the Year and the only collegian in 1993-94 to finish in the top 15 nationally in scoring, rebounding, field goal accuracy, and blocked shots. Drafted 11th by Seattle and traded to Golden State, he averaged 8.9 PPG.

Strengths: Rogers is blessed with great quickness and athletic ability for his size. He gets off the floor in a heartbeat, makes an impact on the boards, and blocks better than a shot per game. He has the potential to be a very good defensive player in the NBA. He runs the floor and plays within his limitations on offense. He shoots for a high percentage.

Weaknesses: Some contend Rogers is more athlete than basketball player. He certainly has a lot of work to do on the offensive end. He does not shoot the ball well at all, has no touch from the free throw line, and needs to develop a couple of reliable moves in the post to be considered a great threat. He is not a steady ball-handler or passer and he picks up a lot of fouls.

Analysis: Rogers is a power forward with the build of a small forward. However, he does not have anything resembling a small forward's offensive game. He gets the job done on the glass and holds his own on defense because of his superior quickness and athletic skills. His best scoring move at this stage, however, is the putback. Rogers has the skills to develop quickly, but his offensive game is raw.

PLAYER SUMMARY	
Will	block shots
Can't	shoot free throws
Expect	athletic ability
Don't Expect	offensive touch
Fantasy Value	$3-5
Card Value	20-40¢

COLLEGE STATISTICS

		G	FGP	FTP	RPG	PPG
90-91	ALR	19	.508	.554	6.9	8.4
92-93	TSU	29	.621	.624	11.7	20.3
93-94	TSU	31	.614	.649	11.5	24.5
Totals		79	.603	.629	10.5	19.1

NBA REGULAR-SEASON STATISTICS

			FGs		3-PT FGs		FTs		Rebounds						
	G	MIN	FG	PCT	FG	PCT	FT	PCT	OFF	TOT	AST	STL	BLK	PTS	PPG
94-95 GS	49	1017	180	.529	2	.143	76	.521	108	278	37	22	52	438	8.9
Totals	49	1017	180	.529	2	.143	76	.521	108	278	37	22	52	438	8.9

RODNEY ROGERS

Team: Los Angeles Clippers
Position: Forward
Height: 6'7" **Weight:** 255
Birthdate: June 20, 1971
NBA Experience: 2 years

College: Wake Forest
Acquired: Traded from Nuggets with draft rights to Brent Barry for Randy Woods and draft rights to Antonio McDyess, 6/95

Background: Rogers earned second-team all-league honors as a freshman at Wake Forest and went on to become 1992-93 Player of the Year in the ACC, averaging 21.2 points and 7.4 rebounds per game. An early entrant into the NBA draft, Rogers slipped to the ninth pick in 1993 and did not make the All-Rookie first or second team. He became a Denver starter in his second season, however, and averaged 12.2 PPG. He was dealt to the Clippers in June.

Strengths: The muscular Rogers has called himself a cross between Charles Barkley and Karl Malone. He has the build. Rogers does not back down from contact and can score from inside or the perimeter. He owns a surprisingly accurate 3-point stroke and cannot be left open from that range. He also has some strong post moves. Rogers has played both forward positions. He has the makings of a tough defensive player.

Weaknesses: Rogers tends to go too hard for his own good at times. He commits an extraordinary number of fouls, ranking among the league leaders in that category last season. For someone with a nice long-range touch, Rogers should be a much better free throw shooter. He also has the potential to do a more consistent job on the boards at both ends. He gets frustrated too easily.

Analysis: Rogers, who was used as a reserve small forward for most of his rookie year, wound up starting 77 games last season at power forward because of an injury to LaPhonso Ellis. This created a matchup problem for just about every opponent, whose big men did not want to chase Rogers beyond the 3-point arc. After a mildly disappointing rookie year, Rogers is beginning to emerge.

PLAYER SUMMARY	
Will	shoot the 3-pointer
Can't	keep from fouling
Expect	matchup problems
Don't Expect	soft defense
Fantasy Value	$10-13
Card Value	15-30¢

COLLEGE STATISTICS

		G	FGP	FTP	RPG	PPG
90-91	WF	30	.570	.669	7.9	16.3
91-92	WF	29	.614	.683	8.5	20.5
92-93	WF	30	.555	.717	7.4	21.2
Totals		89	.579	.694	7.9	19.3

NBA REGULAR-SEASON STATISTICS

				FGs		3-PT FGs		FTs		Rebounds						
		G	MIN	FG	PCT	FG	PCT	FT	PCT	OFF	TOT	AST	STL	BLK	PTS	PPG
93-94	DEN	79	1406	239	.439	35	.380	127	.672	90	226	101	63	48	640	8.1
94-95	DEN	80	2142	375	.488	50	.338	179	.651	132	385	161	95	46	979	12.2
Totals		159	3548	614	.467	85	.354	306	.659	222	611	262	158	94	1619	10.2

SEAN ROOKS

Team: Minnesota Timberwolves
Position: Center/Forward
Height: 6'10" **Weight:** 250
Birthdate: September 9, 1969

NBA Experience: 3 years
College: Arizona
Acquired: Traded from Mavericks for a future 1st-round pick, 11/94

Background: After joining Brian Williams and Ed Stokes on the "Tucson Skyline," Rooks led Arizona in scoring and was second in rebounding as a senior. He was a first-team All-Pac-10 selection. A second-round choice of Dallas in 1992, Rooks played well as a rookie and had his second year cut short by injuries. He returned healthy with Minnesota in 1994-95 and started 70 games at center.

Strengths: Rooks has a wide body and knows what to do with the ball in the low post. He works his way around opposing centers and has a soft touch on the blocks. He can also hit face-up jumpers within his range of about 15 feet. Rooks owns good hands and a nice feel for the game. He'll block a few shots. His work ethic is commendable.

Weaknesses: Rooks remains an inconsistent player in most areas. He seems lost at times against the better centers in the league and goes into a shell. His rebounding and defense have not been selling points. The Timberwolves' starting forwards both grabbed more boards than Rooks last season—a bad sign. He is not much of a passer or ball-handler and his field goal accuracy could use a boost.

Analysis: "Wookie," nicknamed after the *Star Wars* character, shows flashes of top-notch scoring ability but has been unable to sustain them. He has his best success against the game's second-tier big men, which will ultimately put him in a reserve role unless he develops some consistency and confidence. He needs to get hungry on defense and the boards.

PLAYER SUMMARY

Will ....post up
Can't.....................dominate boards
Expect........................streaky scoring
Don't Expect ....an enforcer
Fantasy Value $5-7
Card Value ....7-12¢

COLLEGE STATISTICS

		G	FGP	FTP	RPG	PPG
88-89	ARIZ	32	.598	.615	2.8	5.6
89-90	ARIZ	31	.532	.708	4.9	12.7
90-91	ARIZ	35	.562	.658	5.7	11.9
91-92	ARIZ	31	.560	.651	6.9	16.3
Totals		129	.558	.664	5.0	11.6

NBA REGULAR-SEASON STATISTICS

				FGs	3-PT FGs		FTs		Rebounds						
		G	MIN	FG	PCT	FG	PCT	FT	PCT	OFF	TOT	AST	STL	BLK	PTS	PPG
92-93	DAL	72	2087	368	.493	0	.000	234	.602	196	536	95	38	81	970	13.5
93-94	DAL	47	1255	193	.491	0	.000	150	.714	84	259	49	21	44	536	11.4
94-95	MIN	80	2405	289	.470	0	.000	290	.761	165	486	97	29	71	868	10.9
Totals		199	5747	850	.484	0	.000	674	.688	445	1281	241	88	196	2374	11.9

JALEN ROSE

Team: Denver Nuggets
Position: Guard
Height: 6'8" **Weight:** 210
Birthdate: January 20, 1973

NBA Experience: 1 year
College: Michigan
Acquired: 1st-round pick in 1994 draft
(13th overall)

Background: Rose became the second player in Michigan history to amass 1,500 points, 400 rebounds, 300 assists, and 100 steals. He played in two NCAA championship games during his three years and helped Michigan to a 13-3 record in tourney play. He was the third member of the Fab Five to be selected in the first round of the NBA draft. He was a 37-game starter as a rookie with the Nuggets and he led the team in assists.

Strengths: Rose is an extremely versatile and street-wise player. He can play both backcourt positions and even some small forward, although he has been used most effectively as a point guard. He is an experienced runner of offenses who sees the floor well and knows where and when to deliver the ball. He penetrates, can finish with either hand, and is a good off-balance shooter with range. Rose exudes confidence.

Weaknesses: While his versatility on offense provides problems for the opposition, it also makes him a hard-to-define player. Quicker point guards give him trouble on defense, yet he does not shoot consistently enough to become an All-Star shooting guard. His thin frame does not lend itself to banging with forwards. Rose will play a little out of control at times, a habit that was tolerated at Michigan but not as much in the NBA.

Analysis: The Nuggets got a good one in Rose, a brash competitor who will not back down from a challenge. He is not afraid to take big shots or make something happen off the dribble when his team needs a bucket. He set a Denver rookie record for assists despite coming off the bench for most of the season. He is capable of starting the offense from any of three positions.

PLAYER SUMMARY	
Will	use both hands
Can't	be easily defined
Expect	great versatility
Don't Expect	selfish play
Fantasy Value	$8-10
Card Value	25-60¢

COLLEGE STATISTICS

		G	FGP	FTP	APG	PPG
91-92	MICH	34	.486	.756	4.0	17.6
92-93	MICH	36	.446	.720	3.9	15.4
93-94	MICH	32	.461	.734	3.9	19.9
Totals		102	.464	.738	3.9	17.5

NBA REGULAR-SEASON STATISTICS

			FGs		3-PT FGs		FTs		Rebounds						
	G	MIN	FG	PCT	FG	PCT	FT	PCT	OFF	TOT	AST	STL	BLK	PTS	PPG
94-95 DEN	81	1798	227	.454	36	.316	173	.739	57	217	389	65	22	663	8.2
Totals	81	1798	227	.454	36	.316	173	.739	57	217	389	65	22	663	8.2

DONALD ROYAL

Team: Orlando Magic
Position: Forward
Height: 6'8" **Weight:** 210
Birthdate: May 2, 1966

NBA Experience: 5 years
College: Notre Dame
Acquired: Signed as a free agent, 8/92

Background: Royal averaged 15.8 PPG and 7.0 RPG during his senior year at Notre Dame, after which he was a third-round draft choice of Cleveland in 1987. He spent his first two pro seasons in the CBA and played his first NBA ball with Minnesota in 1989-90. He has since played in Israel, San Antonio, and Orlando. He's been a key role-player for the Magic over the last three seasons. He made 68 starts last year.

Strengths: The owner of a great first step, Royal makes a living with the drive. He is a slashing penetrator who knows no fear when taking the ball to the hole. He gets a dunk or usually gets fouled trying. Royal runs the floor, works hard, and plays with enthusiasm. He is also a tough defender who can match up with twos, threes, and fours.

Weaknesses: Royal's biggest problem is his lack of a reliable jump shot. Defenders can afford to back off, knowing to expect a drive. The 3-point shot is out of his range. Royal has gotten better at spotting and dishing off to open teammates but still tends to force the issue himself.

Analysis: Royal makes defenders work. Even though they know a drive is coming, his first step is so quick that there's often nothing to do but look for help or foul him. If Royal could add a steady jumper with range, he could become a primary scoring threat. As it is, he plays a major role with his hustle on both ends of the court.

PLAYER SUMMARY	
Will	get to the line
Can't	shoot 3-pointers
Expect	quick drives
Don't Expect	pull-up jumpers
Fantasy Value	$1-3
Card Value	5-8¢

COLLEGE STATISTICS

		G	FGP	FTP	RPG	PPG
83-84	ND	31	.594	.622	2.3	3.4
84-85	ND	30	.497	.782	5.5	9.1
85-86	ND	28	.583	.766	4.9	10.6
86-87	ND	28	.576	.820	7.0	15.8
Totals		117	.560	.780	4.9	9.5

NBA REGULAR-SEASON STATISTICS

				FGs		3-PT FGs		FTs		Rebounds						
		G	MIN	FG	PCT	FG	PCT	FT	PCT	OFF	TOT	AST	STL	BLK	PTS	PPG
89-90	MIN	66	746	117	.459	0	.000	153	.777	69	137	43	32	8	387	5.9
91-92	SA	60	718	80	.449	0	.000	92	.692	65	124	34	25	7	252	4.2
92-93	ORL	77	1636	194	.496	0	.000	318	.815	116	295	80	36	25	706	9.2
93-94	ORL	74	1357	174	.501	0	.000	199	.740	94	248	61	50	16	547	7.4
94-95	ORL	70	1841	206	.475	0	.000	223	.746	83	279	198	45	16	635	9.1
Totals		347	6298	771	.480	0	.000	985	.765	427	1083	416	188	72	2527	7.3

CLIFFORD ROZIER

Team: Golden State Warriors
Position: Center/Forward
Height: 6'10" **Weight:** 245
Birthdate: October 31, 1972

NBA Experience: 1 year
College: North Carolina; Louisville
Acquired: 1st-round pick in 1994 draft
(16th overall)

Background: One of the top high school talents in the nation out of Bradenton, Florida, Rozier played a nondescript freshman year at North Carolina before transferring to Louisville. He was voted Metro Conference Player of the Year in each of his two seasons with the Cardinals and set an NCAA record by going 15-for-15 against Eastern Kentucky as a junior. A first-round choice of Golden State, he led the team in total rebounds as a rookie.

Strengths: Rozier is a physically strong inside player. He has an NBA body, as scouts like to say, and he uses it to seal his man off the boards. He finished third among rookie rebounders during the 1994-95 season with 7.4 per game. Rozier has a nice set of hands, which combined with his strength gives him inside scoring potential. He's willing to throw his weight around.

Weaknesses: A center in college, Rozier does not have much of a face-up game. He'll take some off-balance shots and is not a good shooter even when his feet are set. His disgraceful free throw percentage says a lot about his touch. Rozier does not own a great set of post moves, either. Passing and ball-handling are not recommended. He needs to get serious in the off-season.

Analysis: Rozier played well at times last season, but he was not the answer the Warriors were looking for in the middle. Yes, he rebounds. He uses his strength to get position and has a nose for the ball. The rest of Rozier's game, however, lags behind his board work. He's a little too small to compete at the center position, and without a decent jumper, his contributions in the scoring column will likely be limited.

PLAYER SUMMARY

Will ....get to the boards
Can't ....hit two free throws
Expect ....good strength
Don't Expect..............perimeter skills
Fantasy Value....................................$1
Card Value ....12-30¢

COLLEGE STATISTICS

		G	FGP	FTP	RPG	PPG
90-91	NC	34	.471	.565	3.0	4.9
92-93	LOU	31	.561	.568	10.9	15.7
93-94	LOU	34	.618	.545	11.1	18.1
Totals		99	.573	.557	8.2	12.8

NBA REGULAR-SEASON STATISTICS

		G	MIN	FGs		3-PT FGs		FTs		Rebounds		AST	STL	BLK	PTS	PPG
				FG	PCT	FG	PCT	FT	PCT	OFF	TOT					
94-95	GS	66	1494	189	.485	2	.286	68	.447	200	486	45	35	39	448	6.8
Totals		66	1494	189	.485	2	.286	68	.447	200	486	45	35	39	448	6.8

BRYON RUSSELL

Team: Utah Jazz
Position: Forward
Height: 6'7" **Weight:** 225
Birthdate: December 31, 1970

NBA Experience: 2 years
College: Long Beach St.
Acquired: 2nd-round pick in 1993 draft (45th overall)

Background: Russell sat out a year of basketball at Long Beach State to become academically eligible, then steadily progressed the next three seasons while teaming with fellow 1993 second-round pick Lucious Harris. Russell led the 49ers in rebounding and blocked shots as a senior. Considered a surprise draft choice by the Jazz, he wound up starting 48 games as a rookie but was used mostly off the bench in 1994-95.

Strengths: Russell does not take his job in the NBA for granted and is willing to do the dirty work to earn his minutes. He's tough and physical and isn't afraid to wrestle with bigger players on defense. Russell has good instincts for the ball and will come up with his share of steals. He brings a lot of energy to the floor and makes things happen in transition.

Weaknesses: Russell is not a talented offensive player. He does not put the ball on the floor with great confidence, will not rack up the assists, and is prone to poor offensive decision-making. Much of this could be overlooked if he made jumpers at a decent rate, but he does not have a stroke you'd want to bank on. He is also a poor free throw shooter and a below-average rebounder for a forward.

Analysis: For someone who easily could have started his career in the CBA, Russell has been somewhat of a surprise. His defensive energy and work habits have served him well. Last season, however, Russell saw his playing time limited to less than 14 minutes per game and was rarely a factor on offense. He'll have to keep up his off-season regimen to improve his stock.

PLAYER SUMMARY

Will ....hustle on defense
Can't ....rely on jumper
Expect ....boundless energy
Don't Expect ....10 PPG
Fantasy Value..................................$0
Card Value ....7-10¢

COLLEGE STATISTICS

		G	FGP	FTP	RPG	PPG
90-91	LBS	28	.430	.652	5.8	7.9
91-92	LBS	26	.555	.656	7.4	13.9
92-93	LBS	32	.537	.727	6.7	13.2
Totals		86	.513	.683	6.6	11.7

NBA REGULAR-SEASON STATISTICS

				FGs		3-PT FGs		FTs		Rebounds						
		G	MIN	FG	PCT	FG	PCT	FT	PCT	OFF	TOT	AST	STL	BLK	PTS	PPG
93-94	UTA	67	1121	135	.484	2	.091	62	.614	61	181	54	68	19	334	5.0
94-95	UTA	63	860	104	.437	13	.295	62	.667	44	141	34	48	11	283	4.5
Totals		130	1981	239	.462	15	.227	124	.639	105	322	88	116	30	617	4.7

JOHN SALLEY

Team: Toronto Raptors
Position: Forward/Center
Height: 6'11" **Weight:** 250
Birthdate: May 16, 1964

NBA Experience: 9 years
College: Georgia Tech
Acquired: Selected from Heat in 1995 expansion draft

Background: "Spider" was Georgia Tech's all-time leader in blocked shots before being selected by the Pistons (along with Dennis Rodman) in the 1986 draft. He won two NBA championship rings with Detroit while earning a talented-but-inconsistent tag. Salley was in and out of the starting lineup with Miami. He was selected by Toronto in the expansion draft.

Strengths: Salley is at his best on defense. He has good quickness to go along with his size, can match up with centers and forwards, and will soon block the 1,000th shot of his career. He runs the floor and has shown some inside scoring ability. He has a spin move, a hook shot, and a jumper with 15-foot range.

Weaknesses: Salley has been famous for thinking more about his contract than his game. He has never been very consistent, even in his best seasons. He does not own a powerful low-post game and he has never averaged double figures in the scoring column. He picks up a lot of fouls.

Analysis: Salley is an aspiring comedian who has worked night-club gigs. Some would argue that he should spend more time working on his game. Miami expected leadership and defense when it signed him, and he does provide some of the latter. As for leadership, he has never been a great example of consistency.

PLAYER SUMMARY

Will ....crack jokes
Can't ....crack double figures
Expect ....blocked shots
Don't expect.....................consistency
Fantasy Value $1-3
Card Value ....5-8¢

COLLEGE STATISTICS

		G	FGP	FTP	RPG	PPG
82-83	GT	27	.502	.637	5.7	11.5
83-84	GT	29	.589	.674	5.8	11.8
84-85	GT	35	.627	.636	7.1	14.0
85-86	GT	34	.606	.594	6.7	13.1
Totals		125	.587	.633	6.4	12.7

NBA REGULAR-SEASON STATISTICS

				FGs		3-PT FGs		FTs		Rebounds						
		G	MIN	FG	PCT	FG	PCT	FT	PCT	OFF	TOT	AST	STL	BLK	PTS	PPG
86-87	DET	82	1463	163	.562	0	.000	105	.614	108	296	54	44	125	431	5.3
87-88	DET	82	2003	258	.566	0	.000	185	.709	166	402	113	53	137	701	8.5
88-89	DET	67	1458	166	.498	0	.000	135	.692	134	335	75	40	72	467	7.0
89-90	DET	82	1914	209	.512	1	.250	174	.713	154	439	67	51	153	593	7.2
90-91	DET	74	1649	179	.475	0	.000	186	.727	137	327	70	52	112	544	7.4
91-92	DET	72	1774	249	.512	0	.000	186	.715	106	296	116	49	110	684	9.5
92-93	MIA	51	1422	154	.502	0	.000	115	.799	113	313	83	32	70	423	8.3
93-94	MIA	76	1910	208	.477	2	.667	164	.729	132	407	135	56	78	582	7.7
94-95	MIA	76	1955	197	.499	0	.000	153	.739	110	336	123	47	85	547	7.2
Totals		662	15548	1783	.511	3	.214	1403	.715	1160	3151	836	424	942	4972	7.5

DANNY SCHAYES

Unrestricted Free Agent
Last Team: Phoenix Suns
Position: Center
Height: 6'11" **Weight:** 276
Birthdate: May 10, 1959

NBA Experience: 14 years
College: Syracuse
Acquired: Signed as a free agent, 9/94

Background: The son of Hall of Famer Dolph Schayes, Danny was a late bloomer who did not start at Syracuse until his senior year. Drafted by Utah in 1981, he spent the largest portion of his 14 NBA years with Denver. He was signed as a free agent by Phoenix last season and wound up starting 27 games.

Strengths: Schayes provides good size and toughness in the middle. He's a banger who is rarely caught out of position. He's learned some tricks over 14 seasons. He shot .508 from the field last season.

Weaknesses: Schayes, who has undergone major knee surgery in his career, is not among the athletic centers in the game. He is slow on his feet. Schayes no longer makes much happen offensively or dominates the boards.

Analysis: The Suns were looking for a big body who did not need to score, and they found one in Schayes. However, they also discovered that the 14-year veteran is not the guy you want in your starting lineup. He will not join his father in the Hall of Fame, but he's made a nice living.

PLAYER SUMMARY	
Will	bang on defense
Can't	play above the rim
Expect	backup minutes
Don't Expect	two more years
Fantasy Value	$0
Card Value	5-7¢

COLLEGE STATISTICS

		G	FGP	FTP	RPG	PPG
77-78	SYR	24	.565	.756	4.0	4.7
78-79	SYR	29	.530	.833	4.2	6.2
79-80	SYR	30	.509	.769	4.5	5.9
80-81	SYR	34	.579	.822	8.4	14.6
Totals		117	.554	.806	5.4	8.2

NBA REGULAR-SEASON STATISTICS

				FGs		3-PT FGs		FTs		Rebounds						
		G	MIN	FG	PCT	FG	PCT	FT	PCT	OFF	TOT	AST	STL	BLK	PTS	PPG
81-82	UTA	82	1623	252	.481	0	.000	140	.757	131	427	146	46	72	644	7.9
82-83	UTA/DEN	82	2284	342	.457	0	.000	228	.773	200	635	205	54	98	912	11.1
83-84	DEN	82	1420	183	.493	0	.000	215	.790	145	433	91	32	60	581	7.1
84-85	DEN	56	542	60	.465	0	.000	79	.814	48	144	38	20	25	199	3.6
85-86	DEN	80	1654	221	.502	0	.000	216	.777	154	439	79	42	63	658	8.2
86-87	DEN	76	1556	210	.519	0	.000	229	.779	120	380	85	20	74	649	8.5
87-88	DEN	81	2166	361	.540	0	.000	407	.836	200	662	106	62	92	1129	13.9
88-89	DEN	76	1918	317	.522	3	.333	332	.826	142	500	105	42	81	969	12.8
89-90	DEN	53	1194	163	.494	0	.000	225	.852	117	342	61	41	45	551	10.4
90-91	MIL	82	2228	298	.499	0	.000	274	.835	174	535	98	55	61	870	10.6
91-92	MIL	43	726	83	.417	0	.000	74	.771	58	168	34	19	19	240	5.6
92-93	MIL	70	1124	105	.399	0	.000	112	.818	72	249	78	36	36	322	4.6
93-94	MIL/LAL	36	363	28	.333	0	.000	29	.906	31	79	13	10	10	85	2.4
94-95	PHO	69	823	126	.508	1	1.000	50	.725	57	208	89	20	37	303	4.4
Totals		968	19621	2749	.490	4	.138	2610	.807	1649	5201	1228	499	773	8112	8.4

DETLEF SCHREMPF

Team: Seattle SuperSonics
Position: Forward
Height: 6'10" **Weight:** 235
Birthdate: January 21, 1963
NBA Experience: 10 years

College: Washington
Acquired: Traded from Pacers for Derrick McKey and Gerald Paddio, 11/93

Background: A graduate of the University of Washington, Schrempf spent the first three-plus years of his NBA career in Dallas. He was traded to Indiana in 1989 and won the NBA Sixth Man Award in 1991 and 1992. He began starting and was traded before the 1993-94 season to Seattle. Schrempf made a remarkable 51.4 percent of his 3-point attempts in 1994-95.

Strengths: Schrempf is one of the league's most complete, versatile, and consistent players. He's a superb ball-handler, shooter, and passer. He can drive for dunks, but if you give him a few feet he'll bury 3-pointers all night. He also runs, rebounds, and plays relentless defense. Schrempf is that rare player who never gives less than 100 percent in a game or practice.

Weaknesses: One of the few weaknesses in Schrempf's game has been his tendency to spend too much time pleading his case to the refs. He does not reject many shots and is not the quickest player in the league.

Analysis: This one-time reserve never ceases to amaze. As if he didn't give opponents enough trouble, he made a joke of the shorter 3-point arc last season by finishing second in the league for accuracy. Schrempf was very deserving of his 1993 and 1995 All-Star invitations and is likely to see more before he is through.

PLAYER SUMMARY	
Will	give you his all
Can't	be left open
Expect	scoring, defense
Don't Expect	missed treys
Fantasy Value	$35-40
Card Value	10-20¢

COLLEGE STATISTICS

		G	FGP	FTP	RPG	PPG
81-82	WASH	28	.452	.553	2.0	3.3
82-83	WASH	31	.466	.717	6.8	10.6
83-84	WASH	31	.539	.736	7.4	16.8
84-85	WASH	32	.558	.714	8.0	15.8
Totals		**122**	**.521**	**.708**	**6.2**	**11.9**

NBA REGULAR-SEASON STATISTICS

		G	MIN	FGs FG	FGs PCT	3-PT FGs FG	3-PT FGs PCT	FTs FT	FTs PCT	Rebounds OFF	Rebounds TOT	AST	STL	BLK	PTS	PPG
85-86	DAL	64	969	142	.451	3	.429	110	.724	70	198	88	23	10	397	6.2
86-87	DAL	81	1711	265	.472	33	.478	193	.742	87	303	161	50	16	756	9.3
87-88	DAL	82	1587	246	.456	5	.156	201	.756	102	279	159	42	32	698	8.5
88-89	DAL/IND	69	1850	274	.474	7	.200	273	.780	126	395	179	53	19	828	12.0
89-90	IND	78	2573	424	.516	17	.354	402	.820	149	620	247	59	16	1267	16.2
90-91	IND	82	2632	432	.520	15	.375	441	.818	178	660	301	58	22	1320	16.1
91-92	IND	80	2605	496	.536	23	.324	365	.828	202	770	312	62	37	1380	17.3
92-93	IND	82	3098	517	.476	8	.154	525	.804	210	780	493	79	27	1567	19.1
93-94	SEA	81	2728	445	.493	22	.324	300	.769	144	454	275	73	9	1212	15.0
94-95	SEA	82	2886	521	.523	93	.514	437	.839	135	508	310	93	35	1572	19.2
Totals		**781**	**22639**	**3762**	**.498**	**226**	**.375**	**3247**	**.799**	**1403**	**4967**	**2525**	**592**	**223**	**10997**	**14.1**

BYRON SCOTT

Team: Vancouver Grizzlies
Position: Guard
Height: 6'4" **Weight:** 200
Birthdate: March 28, 1961

NBA Experience: 12 years
College: Arizona St.
Acquired: Selected from Pacers in 1995 expansion draft

Background: In three years, Scott became Arizona State's career scoring leader. He worked his way into the Lakers' starting lineup as a rookie and broke Michael Cooper's team record for career 3-pointers. Scott helped the Lakers to three NBA championships in the 1980s. He spent the last two years as an Indiana reserve and was selected by Vancouver in the 1995 expansion draft.

Strengths: Scott is a classic spot-up shooter who is deadly when he gets his feet together. He has great range and does not mind taking the pressure shot. He has made plenty of them. He can also get to the hoop, drill free throws, and provide veteran leadership. In short, Scott is a winner.

Weaknesses: Scott is no longer a primary scoring threat despite his almost 14,000 career points. He is average, at best, with the dribble and is not a playmaker. He is nothing close to a force on defense or on the boards.

Analysis: Indiana filled a leadership void when it signed Scott as a free agent two years ago. The Grizzlies will be impressed with Scott's veteran savvy, as well as his ability to put the ball in the hole. To score in double figures for 12 straight seasons says something about one's abilities.

PLAYER SUMMARY

Will	spot up for jumpers
Can't	shut down his man
Expect	professionalism
Don't Expect	15 PPG
Fantasy Value	$1
Card Value	5-10¢

COLLEGE STATISTICS

		G	FGP	FTP	RPG	PPG
79-80	ASU	29	.500	.733	2.7	13.6
80-81	ASU	28	.505	.693	3.8	16.6
82-83	ASU	33	.513	.782	5.4	21.6
Totals		90	.507	.747	4.0	17.5

NBA REGULAR-SEASON STATISTICS

			FGs		3-PT FGs		FTs		Rebounds						
	G	MIN	FG	PCT	FG	PCT	FT	PCT	OFF	TOT	AST	STL	BLK	PTS	PPG
83-84 LAL	74	1637	334	.484	8	.235	112	.806	50	164	177	81	19	788	10.6
84-85 LAL	81	2305	541	.539	26	.433	187	.820	57	210	244	100	17	1295	16.0
85-86 LAL	76	2190	507	.513	22	.361	138	.784	55	189	164	85	15	1174	15.4
86-87 LAL	82	2729	554	.489	65	.436	224	.892	63	286	281	125	18	1397	17.0
87-88 LAL	81	3048	710	.527	62	.346	272	.858	76	333	335	155	27	1754	21.7
88-89 LAL	74	2605	588	.491	77	.399	195	.863	72	302	231	114	27	1448	19.6
89-90 LAL	77	2593	472	.470	93	.423	160	.766	51	242	274	77	31	1197	15.5
90-91 LAL	82	2630	501	.477	71	.324	118	.797	54	246	177	95	21	1191	14.5
91-92 LAL	82	2679	460	.458	54	.344	244	.838	74	310	226	105	28	1218	14.9
92-93 LAL	58	1677	296	.449	44	.326	156	.848	27	134	157	55	13	792	13.7
93-94 IND	67	1197	256	.467	27	.365	157	.805	19	110	133	62	9	696	10.4
94-95 IND	80	1528	265	.455	79	.389	193	.850	18	151	108	61	13	802	10.0
Totals	914	26818	5484	.489	628	.373	2156	.832	616	2677	2507	1115	238	13752	15.0

DENNIS SCOTT

Team: Orlando Magic
Position: Forward/Guard
Height: 6'8" **Weight:** 230
Birthdate: September 5, 1968

NBA Experience: 5 years
College: Georgia Tech
Acquired: 1st-round pick in 1990 draft (4th overall)

Background: Scott led Georgia Tech to the NCAA Final Four as a senior. That year, he recorded the highest single-season point total in Atlantic Coast Conference history and was named ACC Player of the Year. He earned All-Rookie honors in 1990-91, setting a rookie record for 3-pointers, but right knee surgery and other injuries cut short his next two seasons. Scott was one of the top sixth men in the league last season.

Strengths: The sweet-shooting Scott has range well beyond the 3-point line. He once made nine 3-pointers in a game and annually ranks among the NBA's most accurate trey shooters. He is tall enough to shoot over defenders and heats up in a hurry. Scott handles the ball well, makes crisp passes, and has good court awareness.

Weaknesses: Scott does not possess great quickness, which hurts him most on defense. He also has a history of leg injuries and of playing with a few extra pounds, with each problem contributing to the other. He does not get to the line much and does not convert a good percentage from inside the arc. He's not much help on the boards.

Analysis: When first moved into a reserve role two years ago, Scott was not a happy camper. He seemed to accept it much better a year ago, when his play off the bench helped spark Orlando to a divisional title and the best record in the Eastern Conference. His long-range shooting is capable of stretching defenses, even with Shaq roaming inside.

PLAYER SUMMARY	
Will	stretch a defense
Can't	control the boards
Expect	instant offense
Don't Expect	a stopper
Fantasy Value	$5-7
Card Value	7-10¢

COLLEGE STATISTICS

		G	FGP	FTP	RPG	PPG
87-88	GT	32	.440	.655	5.0	15.5
88-89	GT	32	.443	.814	4.1	20.3
89-90	GT	35	.465	.793	6.6	27.7
Totals		99	.452	.777	5.3	21.4

NBA REGULAR-SEASON STATISTICS

				FGs		3-PT FGs		FTs		Rebounds						
		G	MIN	FG	PCT	FG	PCT	FT	PCT	OFF	TOT	AST	STL	BLK	PTS	PPG
90-91	ORL	82	2336	503	.425	125	.374	153	.750	62	235	134	62	25	1284	15.7
91-92	ORL	18	608	133	.402	29	.326	64	.901	14	66	35	20	9	359	19.9
92-93	ORL	54	1759	329	.431	108	.403	92	.786	38	186	136	57	18	858	15.9
93-94	ORL	82	2283	384	.405	155	.399	123	.774	54	218	216	81	32	1046	12.8
94-95	ORL	62	1499	283	.439	150	.426	86	.754	25	146	131	45	14	802	12.9
Totals		298	8485	1632	.422	567	.396	518	.779	193	851	652	265	98	4349	14.6

MALIK SEALY

Team: Los Angeles Clippers
Position: Forward
Height: 6'8" **Weight:** 190
Birthdate: February 1, 1970
NBA Experience: 3 years

College: St. John's
Acquired: Traded from Pacers with Pooh Richardson and draft rights to Eric Piatkowski for Mark Jackson and draft rights to Greg Minor, 6/94

Background: Sealy starred at Tolentine High in the Bronx. He led all Big East players in scoring as a senior (22.6 PPG) at hometown St. John's while earning his second straight spot on the all-conference first team. He finished his career as St. John's' all-time steals leader and was second to Chris Mullin in scoring. He played minimally with the Pacers for two years before averaging 13.0 PPG last year after a trade to the Clippers.

Strengths: Sealy is an energetic, versatile player. He plays both big guard and small forward, has great quickness, and is tougher than he appears. He thrives in a transition game and has the tools to play disruptive on-the-ball defense. More scorer than shooter, Sealy can finish his drives to the hoop with either hand. He gets his own shot and has 3-point range.

Weaknesses: Sealy needs more work on his jump shot. He can hit from long range but has not found much consistency in his three pro seasons. His free throw shooting has improved. Sealy is not adept at handling the ball against pressure, nor is he an accomplished playmaker. Injuries (a hip last season) have kept him from playing more than 60 games in a year.

Analysis: Sealy, who once lost his playbook on a 1993 playoff trip to New York and heard the scouting reports read over the radio, was happy to be traded from Indiana. With the Clippers, he earned the chance to start for 41 of his 60 games and posted career highs in most categories. Staying healthy and becoming more consistent would take his career a step further.

PLAYER SUMMARY

Will...................................play defense
Can't ....shoot consistently
Expect ....further improvement
Don't Expect ....playmaking
Fantasy Value $5-7
Card Value ....8-15¢

COLLEGE STATISTICS

		G	FGP	FTP	RPG	PPG
88-89	STJ	31	.489	.558	6.4	12.9
89-90	STJ	34	.525	.746	6.9	18.1
90-91	STJ	32	.492	.743	7.7	22.1
91-92	STJ	30	.472	.793	6.8	22.6
Totals		127	.494	.729	6.9	18.9

NBA REGULAR-SEASON STATISTICS

			FGs		3-PT FGs		FTs		Rebounds						
		G	MIN	FG	PCT	FG	PCT	FT	PCT	OFF	TOT	AST	STL	BLK	PTS	PPG
92-93	IND	58	672	136	.426	7	.226	51	.689	60	112	47	36	7	330	5.7
93-94	IND	43	623	111	.405	4	.250	59	.678	43	118	48	31	8	285	6.6
94-95	LAC	60	1604	291	.435	22	.301	174	.780	77	214	107	72	25	778	13.0
Totals		161	2899	538	.426	33	.275	284	.740	180	444	202	139	40	1393	8.7

RONY SEIKALY

Team: Golden State Warriors
Position: Center
Height: 6'11" **Weight:** 252
Birthdate: May 10, 1965
NBA Experience: 7 years

College: Syracuse
Acquired: Traded from Heat for Billy Owens and draft rights to Predrag Danilovic, 11/94

Background: A native of Greece, Seikaly was one of Syracuse's all-time great big men. He was inconsistent as a rookie in 1988-89 but won the NBA's Most Improved Player Award in 1989-90. In six years with Miami, he averaged 15.4 PPG and 10.4 RPG, but tendinitis in his right ankle limited his 1994-95 season with Golden State to 36 games.

Strengths: Seikaly has been dominant on the boards at times. He once grabbed 34 rebounds in a game against Washington, more than the Bullets nabbed as a team. He has good quickness, speed, jumping ability, and confidence. He owns a polished low-post offensive game and can also be a defensive presence who alters shots.

Weaknesses: Seikaly is not one of the league's better-passing big men and he commits a large number of turnovers. He draws a lot of fouls and has not been a consistent force at the defensive end. The ankle injury kept his contributions down last season. He is not a good face-up or free throw shooter.

Analysis: Long in need of a productive center, Golden State traded Billy Owens for fellow Syracuse product Seikaly before the 1994-95 season. The Warriors figured on getting a steady 15 points and ten rebounds per game from the big guy. Instead, they got less than half a season of a much less effective Seikaly before his ankle got the best of him.

PLAYER SUMMARY	
Will	hit the boards
Can't	shoot with range
Expect	low-post offense
Don't Expect	All-Star play
Fantasy Value	$16-19
Card Value	7-12¢

COLLEGE STATISTICS

		G	FGP	FTP	RPG	PPG
84-85	SYR	31	.542	.558	6.4	8.1
85-86	SYR	32	.547	.563	7.8	10.1
86-87	SYR	38	.568	.600	8.2	15.1
87-88	SYR	35	.566	.568	9.6	16.3
Totals		136	.560	.576	8.0	12.6

NBA REGULAR-SEASON STATISTICS

				FGs		3-PT FGs		FTs		Rebounds						
		G	MIN	FG	PCT	FG	PCT	FT	PCT	OFF	TOT	AST	STL	BLK	PTS	PPG
88-89	MIA	78	1962	333	.448	1	.250	181	.511	204	549	55	46	96	848	10.9
89-90	MIA	74	2409	486	.502	0	.000	256	.594	253	766	78	78	124	1228	16.6
90-91	MIA	64	2171	395	.481	2	.333	258	.619	207	709	95	51	86	1050	16.4
91-92	MIA	79	2800	463	.489	0	.000	370	.733	307	934	109	40	121	1296	16.4
92-93	MIA	72	2456	417	.480	1	.125	397	.735	259	846	100	38	83	1232	17.1
93-94	MIA	72	2410	392	.488	0	.000	244	.720	244	740	136	59	100	1088	15.1
94-95	GS	36	1035	162	.516	0	.000	111	.694	77	266	45	20	37	435	12.1
Totals		475	15243	2648	.484	4	.167	1877	.663	1551	4810	618	332	647	7177	15.1

BRIAN SHAW

Unrestricted Free Agent
Last Team: Orlando Magic
Position: Guard
Height: 6'6" **Weight:** 194
Birthdate: March 22, 1966

NBA Experience: 6 years
College: St. Mary's (CA);
Cal.-Santa Barbara
Acquired: Signed as a free agent,
9/94

Background: Shaw, the Pacific Coast Athletic Association Player of the Year as a senior at Cal.-Santa Barbara, was a second-team All-Rookie performer with the Celtics in 1988-89. He spent 1989-90 in Italy before returning to Boston and later playing two-plus years in Miami. He signed as a free agent with Orlando before the 1994-95 season and was second on the team in assists.

Strengths: Shaw brings good size and a wide array of skills to the backcourt. He is an above-average rebounding guard, can play two positions, delivers the ball to the right people, and plays defense. This former college forward can shoot 3's, handles the ball well, and makes accurate passes, even at high speed.

Weaknesses: Though he has made himself a 3-point threat, Shaw has never been a pure shooter and his percentages reflect it. He hit less than 39 percent from the field last season and his free throw shooting was not great, either. He struggles to convert on his drives into traffic and is better off giving it up to a teammate. He has not been very consistent.

Analysis: Shaw is a versatile guard who helped the Magic by providing quality minutes when Anfernee Hardaway needed a breather. At better than five per contest, Shaw was one of the leading reserve assist men in the league. He works hard, has good leadership skills, and can help an offense with his ball-handling and passing skills.

PLAYER SUMMARY	
Will	handle the ball
Can't	beat out Penny
Expect	crisp passes
Don't Expect	Magic starts
Fantasy Value	$1
Card Value	8-15¢

COLLEGE STATISTICS

		G	FGP	FTP	RPG	PPG
83-84	SM	14	.361	.737	0.9	2.9
84-85	SM	27	.402	.724	5.3	9.4
86-87	CSB	29	.434	.712	7.7	10.9
87-88	CSB	30	.466	.740	8.7	13.3
Totals		100	.434	.728	6.4	10.1

NBA REGULAR-SEASON STATISTICS

		G	MIN	FGs FG	FGs PCT	3-PT FGs FG	3-PT FGs PCT	FTs FT	FTs PCT	Rebounds OFF	Rebounds TOT	AST	STL	BLK	PTS	PPG
88-89	BOS	82	2301	297	.433	0	.000	109	.826	119	376	472	78	27	703	8.6
90-91	BOS	79	2772	442	.469	3	.111	204	.819	104	370	602	105	34	1091	13.8
91-92	BOS/MIA	63	1423	209	.407	5	.217	72	.791	50	204	250	57	22	495	7.9
92-93	MIA	68	1603	197	.393	43	.331	61	.782	70	257	235	48	19	498	7.3
93-94	MIA	77	2037	278	.417	73	.338	64	.719	104	350	385	71	21	693	9.0
94-95	ORL	78	1836	192	.389	48	.261	70	.737	52	241	406	73	18	502	6.4
Totals		447	11972	1615	.425	172	.290	580	.790	499	1798	2350	432	141	3982	8.9

LIONEL SIMMONS

Team: Sacramento Kings
Position: Forward
Height: 6'7" **Weight:** 210
Birthdate: November 14, 1968

NBA Experience: 5 years
College: La Salle
Acquired: 1st-round pick in 1990 draft (7th overall)

Background: Simmons, who won the Wooden Award in 1990 as college basketball's Player of the Year, finished his career at La Salle third on the all-time NCAA scoring list. He was the first player in college history to amass more than 3,000 points and 1,100 rebounds. Simmons was second in the 1990-91 Rookie of the Year balloting with the Kings, but after three strong seasons he was reduced to a reserve role in 1994-95.

Strengths: Simmons brings a variety of skills to the wing. He can score, rebound, pass, and play defense. He understands the game and makes those around him better with his good recognition. Despite being blessed with above-average athletic ability, Simmons also works hard. He blocked 132 shots in his second season.

Weaknesses: If you're looking for a shooter, look elsewhere. The gaping flaw with Simmons is his inability to hit the jump shot on a regular basis. He does not possess a great deal of confidence in his jumper, and with reason. He does not convert even 45 percent from the field. He has not been a take-charge type, and his knee has given him trouble.

Analysis: Simmons averaged at least 15 points and seven rebounds per game before last season, when right knee surgery cost him the first 19 games of the year and he never played well enough to regain his starting job. He does a lot of things, but Simmons has not been the high-profile leader the Kings thought they were getting with the seventh overall pick in the 1990 draft.

PLAYER SUMMARY	
Will	score, rebound
Can't	shoot straight
Expect	unselfish play
Don't Expect	a franchise player
Fantasy Value	$4-6
Card Value	10-20¢

COLLEGE STATISTICS

		G	FGP	FTP	RPG	PPG
86-87	LaS	33	.526	.763	9.8	20.3
87-88	LaS	34	.485	.757	11.4	23.3
88-89	LaS	32	.487	.711	11.4	28.4
89-90	LaS	32	.513	.661	11.1	26.5
Totals		131	.501	.722	10.9	24.6

NBA REGULAR-SEASON STATISTICS

				FGs		3-PT FGs		FTs		Rebounds						
		G	MIN	FG	PCT	FG	PCT	FT	PCT	OFF	TOT	AST	STL	BLK	PTS	PPG
90-91	SAC	79	2978	549	.422	3	.273	320	.736	193	697	315	113	85	1421	18.0
91-92	SAC	78	2895	527	.454	1	.200	281	.770	149	634	337	135	132	1336	17.1
92-93	SAC	69	2502	468	.444	1	.091	298	.819	156	495	312	95	38	1235	17.9
93-94	SAC	75	2702	436	.438	6	.353	251	.777	168	562	305	104	50	1129	15.1
94-95	SAC	58	1064	131	.420	6	.375	59	.702	61	196	89	28	23	327	5.6
Totals		359	12141	2111	.437	17	.283	1209	.770	727	2584	1358	475	328	5448	15.2

DICKEY SIMPKINS

Team: Chicago Bulls
Position: Forward
Height: 6'10" **Weight:** 250
Birthdate: April 6, 1972

NBA Experience: 1 year
College: Providence
Acquired: 1st-round pick in 1994 draft
(21st overall)

Background: A largely anonymous player at Providence, Simpkins vaulted himself into the first round of the 1994 draft with his showings at the Portsmouth Invitational and Phoenix Desert Classic. He fared much better in those camps than he did in college, where he averaged 9.8 points and 6.3 rebounds per game. Chicago drafted him 21st overall but left Simpkins off its 1995 playoff roster after he averaged less than ten minutes per game.

Strengths: Simpkins was drafted for his defensive potential. He has good size, strength, and quickness to get after NBA forwards. He plays the passing angles, is willing to bang with bigger players in the post, and goes after offensive and defensive rebounds. He runs the floor very well for a big man. His work ethic has been commended, and he is anything but selfish.

Weaknesses: Simpkins is a very limited offensive player. He does not possess a great variety of moves in the post and his jump shot is not a weapon. He does not have good range and is a poor free throw shooter. He simply does not look comfortable with the ball. Simpkins is also not a passing or ball-handling threat, and Chicago expected more of a shot-blocker than they wound up with. He has a long way to go.

Analysis: Simpkins did not have a distinguished rookie season, with one exception. He was the player who went on the injured list March 18 when Michael Jordan came out of retirement. The official listing was Achilles tendinitis. What was really ailing Simpkins, however, was his inability to contribute on the offensive end of the floor. He has a lot of work to do before he begins to earn more than garbage minutes.

PLAYER SUMMARY	
Will	work on defense
Can't	knock down jumpers
Expect	reserve minutes
Don't Expect	10 PPG
Fantasy Value	$0
Card Value	8-15¢

COLLEGE STATISTICS

		G	FGP	FTP	RPG	PPG
90-91	PROV	32	.492	.609	6.6	7.8
91-92	PROV	30	.492	.703	5.8	9.0
92-93	PROV	33	.450	.596	6.5	10.6
93-94	PROV	30	.516	.686	6.3	11.8
Totals		125	.486	.646	6.3	9.8

NBA REGULAR-SEASON STATISTICS

			FGs		3-PT FGs		FTs		Rebounds						
		G	MIN	FG	PCT	FG	PCT	FT	PCT	OFF	TOT	AST	STL	BLK	PTS	PPG
94-95	CHI	59	586	78	.424	0	.000	50	.694	60	151	37	10	7	206	3.5
Totals		59	586	78	.424	0	.000	50	.694	60	151	37	10	7	206	3.5

SCOTT SKILES

Unrestricted Free Agent
Last Team: Washington Bullets
Position: Guard
Height: 6'1" **Weight:** 180
Birthdate: March 5, 1964

NBA Experience: 9 years
College: Michigan St.
Acquired: Traded from Magic with a 1996 1st-round pick for a 1996 2nd-round pick, 7/94

Background: Skiles was an All-American as a senior at Michigan State, finishing second in the nation in scoring and setting school records for points, assists, steals, and free throw accuracy. However, he also spent time in jail. The nine-year veteran came into his own as a starter with Orlando in 1990-91. He averaged 7.3 APG last season after a trade to Washington.

Strengths: They do not come any more competitive than Skiles, who despises losing. He knows how to run an offense and find open men. He set a league record in 1990-91 by dishing out 30 assists in a single game. He penetrates and passes with precision, hits the 3-pointer, and is almost automatic from the free throw line.

Weaknesses: Skiles is not quick enough to keep opposing point guards from driving and is not big enough to keep from being posted up. He's not able to pressure the ball fullcourt and does not rank with the ball-handling wizards.

Analysis: Skiles is the consummate playmaker. He's tough as nails, and you know his wrist and knee injuries had to be painful to limit him to 62 games last season. He had played in at least 70 contests each of the previous six years. If everyone on the Bullets had his drive to win, the team would not be a perennial lottery club.

PLAYER SUMMARY	
Will	distribute
Can't	stop quick guards
Expect	3-point accuracy
Don't Expect	world-class speed
Fantasy Value	$7-9
Card Value	5-10¢

COLLEGE STATISTICS

		G	FGP	FTP	APG	PPG
82-83	MSU	30	.493	.831	4.9	12.5
83-84	MSU	28	.480	.832	4.6	14.5
84-85	MSU	29	.505	.789	5.8	17.7
85-86	MSU	31	.554	.900	6.3	27.4
Totals		118	.516	.850	5.4	18.2

NBA REGULAR-SEASON STATISTICS

		G	MIN	FGs FG	FGs PCT	3-PT FGs FG	3-PT FGs PCT	FTs FT	FTs PCT	Rebounds OFF	Rebounds TOT	AST	STL	BLK	PTS	PPG
86-87	MIL	13	205	18	.290	3	.214	10	.833	6	26	45	5	1	49	3.8
87-88	IND	51	760	86	.411	6	.300	45	.833	11	66	180	22	3	223	4.4
88-89	IND	80	1571	198	.448	20	.267	130	.903	21	149	390	64	2	546	6.8
89-90	ORL	70	1460	190	.409	52	.394	104	.874	23	159	334	36	4	536	7.7
90-91	ORL	79	2714	462	.445	93	.408	340	.902	57	270	660	89	4	1357	17.2
91-92	ORL	75	2377	359	.414	91	.364	248	.895	36	202	544	74	5	1057	14.1
92-93	ORL	78	3086	416	.467	80	.340	289	.892	52	290	735	86	2	1201	15.4
93-94	ORL	82	2303	276	.429	68	.412	195	.878	42	189	503	47	2	815	9.9
94-95	WAS	62	2077	265	.455	96	.421	179	.886	26	159	452	70	6	805	13.0
Totals		590	16553	2270	.436	509	.378	1540	.890	274	1510	3843	493	29	6589	11.2

CHARLES SMITH

Team: New York Knicks
Position: Forward
Height: 6'10" **Weight:** 244
Birthdate: July 16, 1965

NBA Experience: 7 years
College: Pittsburgh
Acquired: Traded from Clippers in three-team, multi-player deal, 9/92

Background: Smith, the Big East Player of the Year as a senior, left Pitt with the school's career records for points and blocked shots. He earned All-Rookie honors in 1988-89 with the Clippers, for whom he became a 20-point scorer and leading rebounder and shot-blocker. Knee injuries and a trade to the Knicks before the 1992-93 season have caused his numbers to decline.

Strengths: Smith is a versatile athlete who can play both forward positions. He is a very good ball-handler for his size and uses the dribble to get to the hoop. Smith owns some fluid moves in the post and also has good range on his jumper. His timing and wide wingspan help him block more than a shot per game.

Weaknesses: Inconsistent play, partly due to the poor condition of his knees, has caused Smith to be booed by New York fans. He's there one night, gone the next. He does not pass the ball well and too often settles for outside shots, including 3-pointers. He has been a below-average rebounder since leaving Los Angeles.

Analysis: Smith made greater contributions to the Knicks last season than he did in his two previous years, largely due to better health. He seemed to regain some of the confidence he lost after arthroscopic surgery on his right knee in December 1993. However, Smith will probably never regain the magic of his first few years.

PLAYER SUMMARY	
Will	block shots
Can't	trade in his knees
Expect	low-post offense
Don't Expect	20 PPG
Fantasy Value	$9-11
Card Value	7-12¢

COLLEGE STATISTICS

		G	FGP	FTP	RPG	PPG
84-85	PITT	29	.502	.706	8.0	15.0
85-86	PITT	29	.404	.762	8.1	15.9
86-87	PITT	33	.550	.735	8.5	17.0
87-88	PITT	31	.558	.764	7.7	18.9
Totals		122	.500	.753	8.1	16.8

NBA REGULAR-SEASON STATISTICS

		G	MIN	FGs FG	FGs PCT	3-PT FGs FG	3-PT FGs PCT	FTs FT	FTs PCT	Rebounds OFF	Rebounds TOT	AST	STL	BLK	PTS	PPG
88-89	LAC	71	2161	435	.495	0	.000	285	.725	173	465	103	68	89	1155	16.3
89-90	LAC	78	2732	595	.520	1	.083	454	.794	177	524	114	86	119	1645	21.1
90-91	LAC	74	2703	548	.469	0	.000	384	.793	216	608	134	81	145	1480	20.0
91-92	LAC	49	1310	251	.466	0	.000	212	.785	95	301	56	41	98	714	14.6
92-93	NY	81	2172	358	.469	0	.000	285	.782	170	432	142	48	96	1003	12.4
93-94	NY	43	1105	176	.443	8	.500	87	.719	66	165	50	26	45	447	10.4
94-95	NY	76	2150	352	.471	7	.226	255	.792	144	324	120	49	95	966	12.7
Totals		472	14333	2715	.482	16	.208	1964	.777	1041	2819	719	399	687	7410	15.7

CHRIS SMITH

Team: Minnesota Timberwolves
Position: Guard
Height: 6'3" **Weight:** 191
Birthdate: May 17, 1970

NBA Experience: 3 years
College: Connecticut
Acquired: 2nd-round pick in 1992 draft (34th overall)

Background: Smith became the first player in University of Connecticut history to surpass the 2,000-point barrier. He finished his career as the Huskies' all-time leader in 3-pointers made and attempted and he led the Big East with 21.2 PPG as a senior. A second-round pick of the Timberwolves, he has averaged between four and six points a game in each of his three NBA seasons. He made 17 starts last year.

Strengths: Smith brings a scorer's mentality and the ability to hit 3-pointers to the point-guard position. He shot .435 from 3-point range last season. Smith has a nifty crossover dribble that he uses to get his shots. He handles the ball adequately and makes solid passes. His best defensive attributes are his toughness and his willingness to work.

Weaknesses: Smith has been called a shooting guard in a point guard's body, and not without reason. He does not make his teammates look better like the good lead guards do, nor does he shoot the ball with much consistency. He has hit between 43 and 44 percent of his field goals each year. Smith is not a standout defensive player, he's no help on the boards, and he's a poor free throw shooter.

Analysis: After three years, Smith has shown far less progress than the Timberwolves had hoped. He has not improved in much other than 3-point shooting, and that has as much to do with the shorter arc adopted by the league. His numbers were much better in his 17 starts last season (.467 from the field, 7.9 PPG), but this former college shooting guard is not a first-rate point.

PLAYER SUMMARY

Will ....hit some 3's
Can't ....make others look better
Expect ....about 5 PPG
Don't Expect ....5 APG
Fantasy Value $0
Card Value ....7-10¢

COLLEGE STATISTICS

		G	FGP	FTP	RPG	PPG
88-89	CONN	29	.405	.565	2.8	9.9
89-90	CONN	37	.417	.811	2.5	17.2
90-91	CONN	31	.439	.719	2.9	18.9
91-92	CONN	30	.415	.800	3.3	21.2
Totals		127	.421	.761	2.9	16.9

NBA REGULAR-SEASON STATISTICS

				FGs		3-PT FGs		FTs		Rebounds						
		G	MIN	FG	PCT	FG	PCT	FT	PCT	OFF	TOT	AST	STL	BLK	PTS	PPG
92-93	MIN	80	1266	125	.433	2	.143	95	.792	32	96	196	48	16	347	4.3
93-94	MIN	80	1617	184	.435	10	.256	95	.674	15	122	285	38	18	473	5.9
94-95	MIN	64	1073	116	.439	47	.435	41	.651	14	73	146	32	22	320	5.0
Totals		224	3956	425	.435	59	.366	231	.713	61	291	627	118	56	1140	5.1

DOUG SMITH

Team: Toronto Raptors
Position: Forward
Height: 6'10" **Weight:** 240
Birthdate: September 17, 1969

NBA Experience: 4 years
College: Missouri
Acquired: Selected from Mavericks in 1995 expansion draft

Background: Smith went from Detroit's MacKenzie High to immediate stardom at Missouri. He starred as the Tigers went 94-35 in his four seasons. He was drafted sixth overall by Dallas in 1991 and was among rookie leaders with 5.1 RPG. He raised his scoring average to 10.4 PPG in his second season but it has fallen in each of the two years since, to a career-low 5.1 PPG last season. Toronto selected Smith in the expansion draft.

Strengths: Smith handles the ball, delivers passes, and runs the floor well for a player his size. He is considered to have above-average awareness and instincts. Smith has the ability to go coast-to-coast after he grabs a rebound. He has come off the bench at both forward positions. He seems to be at his best in an up-tempo game.

Weaknesses: Smith does not have the low-post game nor the shooting touch to be a big-time player in the league. His around-the-basket moves are limited and predictable and his shooting percentage is frighteningly low for a big man. Smith is not the hardest-working player on his team. He does not control the boards like many expected him to.

Analysis: Smith will probably never live up to his status as a No. 6 overall draft choice. He can be an exciting player in the open court and has some athletic ability, but his inability to make shots, rebound, or play defense has reduced him to a reserve role, and a limited one at that. Smith caught a break when he was drafted by the Grizzlies. It gives him one more chance to emerge as a legitimate NBA forward.

PLAYER SUMMARY	
Will	handle the ball
Can't	live up to draft status
Expect	transition points
Don't Expect	good shooting
Fantasy Value	$0
Card Value	5-10¢

COLLEGE STATISTICS

		G	FGP	FTP	RPG	PPG
87-88	MISS	30	.504	.640	6.6	11.3
88-89	MISS	36	.477	.736	6.9	13.9
89-90	MISS	32	.563	.714	9.2	19.8
90-91	MISS	30	.497	.821	10.4	23.6
Totals		128	.510	.747	8.2	17.1

NBA REGULAR-SEASON STATISTICS

				FGs		3-PT FGs		FTs		Rebounds						
		G	MIN	FG	PCT	FG	PCT	FT	PCT	OFF	TOT	AST	STL	BLK	PTS	PPG
91-92	DAL	76	1707	291	.415	0	.000	89	.736	129	391	129	62	34	671	8.8
92-93	DAL	61	1524	289	.434	0	.000	56	.757	96	328	104	48	52	634	10.4
93-94	DAL	79	1684	295	.435	2	.222	106	.835	114	349	119	82	38	698	8.8
94-95	DAL	63	826	131	.417	1	.083	57	.760	43	144	44	29	26	320	5.1
Totals		279	5741	1006	.426	3	.083	308	.776	382	1212	396	221	150	2323	8.3

KENNY SMITH

Team: Houston Rockets
Position: Guard
Height: 6'3" **Weight:** 170
Birthdate: March 8, 1965
NBA Experience: 8 years

College: North Carolina
Acquired: Traded from Hawks with Roy Marble for Tim McCormick and John Lucas, 9/90

Background: Smith established all-time school records for assists and steals at North Carolina, where he was named All-Atlantic Coast Conference as a senior. He averaged double figures in scoring in his first three NBA seasons with Sacramento and Atlanta, but he did not truly shine until a 1990 trade brought him to Houston, where he won championship rings in 1994 and 1995.

Strengths: Smith is capable of filling both guard positions and is one of the better shooters around. He led all guards in field goal percentage three years ago, he makes almost every free throw, and he finished eighth in the league in 3-point accuracy last season (.429). He's a class act who provides double-figure scoring.

Weaknesses: Smith's scoring average has declined in each of the past four seasons, and Sam Cassell appears to be the heir to his starting point-guard spot. Smith is not a great defensive player and he's not been as aggressive at either end of the floor. His drives to the hole and trips to the line have become infrequent.

Analysis: Smith has provided a steady hand over the past few years, feeding his teammates, knocking down long jumpers, and scoring when the Rockets have needed him to. He makes wise decisions and keeps the ball in the hands of the right people. He is not a spectacular or creative point man, but he does his job.

PLAYER SUMMARY

Will ....knock down treys
Can't ....shut down his man
Expect ....a steady hand
Don't Expect..........aggressive drives
Fantasy Value $4-6
Card Value ....5-10¢

COLLEGE STATISTICS

		G	FGP	FTP	APG	PPG
83-84	NC	23	.519	.800	5.0	9.1
84-85	NC	36	.518	.860	6.5	12.3
85-86	NC	34	.516	.808	6.2	12.0
86-87	NC	34	.502	.807	6.1	16.9
Totals		127	.512	.823	6.0	12.9

NBA REGULAR-SEASON STATISTICS

		G	MIN	FGs		3-PT FGs		FTs		Rebounds		AST	STL	BLK	PTS	PPG
				FG	PCT	FG	PCT	FT	PCT	OFF	TOT					
87-88	SAC	61	2170	331	.477	12	.308	167	.819	40	138	434	92	8	841	13.8
88-89	SAC	81	3145	547	.462	46	.359	263	.737	49	226	621	102	7	1403	17.3
89-90	SAC/ATL	79	2421	378	.466	26	.313	161	.821	18	157	445	79	8	943	11.9
90-91	HOU	78	2699	522	.520	49	.363	287	.844	36	163	554	106	11	1380	17.7
91-92	HOU	81	2735	432	.475	54	.394	219	.866	34	177	562	104	7	1137	14.0
92-93	HOU	82	2422	387	.520	96	.438	195	.878	28	160	446	80	7	1065	13.0
93-94	HOU	78	2209	341	.480	89	.405	135	.871	24	138	327	59	4	906	11.6
94-95	HOU	81	2030	287	.484	142	.429	126	.851	27	155	323	71	10	842	10.4
Totals		621	19831	3225	.485	514	.398	1553	.828	256	1314	3712	693	62	8517	13.7

MICHAEL SMITH

Team: Sacramento Kings
Position: Forward
Height: 6'8" **Weight:** 233
Birthdate: March 28, 1972

NBA Experience: 1 year
College: Providence
Acquired: 2nd-round pick in 1994 draft (35th overall)

Background: Smith attended the same Dunbar High in Baltimore that produced Reggie Lewis, David Wingate, and Muggsy Bogues. After sitting out his freshman year for academic reasons, he led the Big East in rebounding for three straight years at Providence. He was the first player ever to do so. The MVP of the 1994 conference tournament, Smith was a second-round choice of Sacramento who played in all 82 games as a rookie.

Strengths: Rebounding, rebounding, and rebounding. Smith was third on the Kings in that category last season despite not starting a game. He comes off the bench and pounds the boards relentlessly. He also runs the floor like a guard and plays physical defense. He can defend both small forwards and power forwards. Smith will not shy away from contact and does not try to play above his head offensively.

Weaknesses: Smith is no scorer. He does not own great moves in the post, and his perimeter game is nonexistent. He converted less than 50 percent of his free throws last season and is not much better from ten or 12 feet away. Passing and dribbling also fall into this category. Smith is undersized for the big-forward spot but is not equipped with the skills of a three. His offensive skills in general are subpar.

Analysis: All in all, Smith was one of the more surprising rookies last season. He proved to be an important player off the Kings' bench because of his contagious energy, his rebounding, and his defensive efforts. Says Sacramento coach Garry St. Jean: "He thinks every rebound is his." The Kings have needed someone like that for the last several years. Now if they could just teach Smith how to shoot the ball....

PLAYER SUMMARY	
Will	rebound
Can't	shoot free throws
Expect	defensive energy
Don't Expect	much offense
Fantasy Value	$1-3
Card Value	20-40¢

COLLEGE STATISTICS

		G	FGP	FTP	RPG	PPG
91-92	PROV	31	.495	.579	10.3	10.7
92-93	PROV	33	.514	.546	11.4	11.8
93-94	PROV	30	.605	.714	11.5	12.9
Totals		94	.539	.600	11.0	11.8

NBA REGULAR-SEASON STATISTICS

			FGs		3-PT FGs		FTs		Rebounds						
	G	MIN	FG	PCT	FG	PCT	FT	PCT	OFF	TOT	AST	STL	BLK	PTS	PPG
94-95 SAC	82	1736	220	.542	0	.000	127	.485	174	486	67	61	49	567	6.9
Totals	82	1736	220	.542	0	.000	127	.485	174	486	67	61	49	567	6.9

STEVE SMITH

Team: Atlanta Hawks
Position: Guard
Height: 6'7" **Weight:** 215
Birthdate: March 31, 1969
NBA Experience: 4 years

College: Michigan St.
Acquired: Traded from Heat with Grant Long and a future 2nd-round pick for Kevin Willis and a future 1st-round pick, 11/94

Background: A Detroit product, Smith surpassed Scott Skiles as Michigan State's all-time leading scorer. He led the Big Ten in scoring as a junior and senior and set a conference record by hitting 45 consecutive free throws. Despite two knee surgeries while with Miami, Smith emerged as a 1994 Olympic Dream Team II member. He was traded to Atlanta early in the 1994-95 season and averaged 16.3 PPG.

Strengths: Smith is a versatile athlete who plays both backcourt positions. Not unlike another Spartan product named Magic Johnson, he brings great size and court sense to the point-guard spot—and a long-range stroke to the two spot. He is an outstanding post-up guard who also handles the ball and makes crisp passes. Smith rates among the game's better free throw shooters.

Weaknesses: Smith is a below-average defensive player, just as he was in college. He's slight in build and does not have great lateral quickness. Point guards give him fits. He commits a very high number of fouls for a guard. Smith is a notorious trash talker. He made less than a third of his 3-pointers (.329) last season—an unexpected drop.

Analysis: Smith does most everything with an air of confidence, and it serves him well on the offensive end. The 1994-95 season was one of adjustment for him after being traded with Grant Long to the Hawks for Kevin Willis and a first-round draft choice. He played mostly big guard for Atlanta, and he will be expected to hoist his shooting percentage in the years to come. With his stroke, it shouldn't be a problem.

PLAYER SUMMARY
Will......................dribble, shoot, pass
Can't ....defend quickness
Expect ....versatile leadership
Don't Expect ....lack of confidence
Fantasy Value $15-18
Card Value ....10-20¢

COLLEGE STATISTICS

		G	FGP	FTP	APG	PPG
87-88	MSU	28	.466	.758	4.0	10.7
88-89	MSU	33	.478	.763	6.9	17.7
89-90	MSU	31	.526	.695	7.0	20.2
90-91	MSU	30	.474	.802	6.1	25.1
Totals		122	.487	.756	6.1	18.5

NBA REGULAR-SEASON STATISTICS

				FGs		3-PT FGs		FTs		Rebounds						
		G	MIN	FG	PCT	FG	PCT	FT	PCT	OFF	TOT	AST	STL	BLK	PTS	PPG
91-92	MIA	61	1806	297	.454	40	.320	95	.748	81	188	278	59	19	729	12.0
92-93	MIA	48	1610	279	.451	53	.402	155	.787	56	197	267	50	16	766	16.0
93-94	MIA	78	2776	491	.456	91	.347	273	.835	156	352	394	84	35	1346	17.3
94-95	MIA/ATL	80	2665	428	.426	137	.329	312	.841	104	276	274	62	33	1305	16.3
Totals		267	8857	1495	.446	321	.343	835	.817	397	1013	1213	255	103	4146	15.5

TONY SMITH

Unrestricted Free Agent
Last Team: Los Angeles Lakers
Position: Guard
Height: 6'4" **Weight:** 205
Birthdate: June 14, 1968

NBA Experience: 5 years
College: Marquette
Acquired: 2nd-round pick in 1990 draft (51st overall)

Background: As a senior, Smith set Marquette single-season records for points and scoring average, earning All-Midwestern Collegiate Conference honors. He climbed to second on the all-time school assists list. Smith has spent his first five pro seasons primarily as a Laker reserve. His playing time was shaved to about 17 minutes per game last season.

Strengths: A big scorer in college, Smith has been somewhat of a defensive specialist as a pro. He first proved himself as such against Michael Jordan in the 1991 NBA Finals. Smith has good strength, speed, and quickness to stick with his man, whether it's a one or a two. Smith can also play both guard spots on offense.

Weaknesses: Smith has not brought his prolific college scoring ability to the NBA. He is not a great outside shooter and has not fared well from beyond the 3-point arc or the free throw line. And Smith has never been a natural point guard. He does not handle or pass the ball particularly well and is not a creative sort. He is not a threat to score in double figures.

Analysis: Smith found himself caught in a numbers game last season as the Lakers added several young players to their rotation. He was used in a limited role for most of the year. He is a better defender than most expected when he came into the league, but his offensive contributions have been minimal. His contract expired after the season and he could find success elsewhere.

PLAYER SUMMARY	
Will	play defense
Can't	score like in college
Expect	versatility
Don't Expect	starts
Fantasy Value	$0
Card Value	7-10¢

COLLEGE STATISTICS

		G	FGP	FTP	APG	PPG
86-87	MARQ	29	.534	.753	2.1	8.1
87-88	MARQ	28	.523	.739	2.9	13.1
88-89	MARQ	28	.556	.730	5.6	14.2
89-90	MARQ	29	.495	.856	5.8	23.8
Totals		114	.521	.785	4.1	14.8

NBA REGULAR-SEASON STATISTICS

			FGs		3-PT FGs		FTs		Rebounds						
	G	MIN	FG	PCT	FG	PCT	FT	PCT	OFF	TOT	AST	STL	BLK	PTS	PPG
90-91 LAL	64	695	97	.441	0	.000	40	.702	24	71	135	28	12	234	3.7
91-92 LAL	63	820	113	.399	0	.000	49	.653	31	76	109	39	8	275	4.4
92-93 LAL	55	752	133	.484	2	.182	62	.756	46	87	63	50	7	330	6.0
93-94 LAL	73	1617	272	.441	16	.320	85	.714	106	195	148	59	14	645	8.8
94-95 LAL	61	1024	132	.427	32	.352	44	.698	43	107	102	46	7	340	5.6
Totals	316	4908	747	.438	50	.294	280	.707	250	536	557	222	48	1824	5.8

RIK SMITS

Team: Indiana Pacers
Position: Center
Height: 7'4" **Weight:** 265
Birthdate: August 23, 1966

NBA Experience: 7 years
College: Marist
Acquired: 1st-round pick in 1988 draft (2nd overall)

Background: Smits, a two-time East Coast Athletic Conference Player of the Year at Marist, was the second overall pick in the 1988 draft. He was named to the NBA All-Rookie Team but led the league in disqualifications his first two years. He has also been among its more accurate field goal shooters. Smits enjoyed his best year in 1994-95, averaging 17.9 PPG during the regular season and 20.1 PPG in the playoffs.

Strengths: Smits is one of the most dangerous offensive centers in basketball. He has great touch on his low-post hook shots and can also drill face-up jumpers with range up to 18 feet. His above-average mobility and coordination help him create space to shoot. Smits has blocked more than 700 shots during his seven seasons.

Weaknesses: Though he has improved in this area, Smits is still below the norm on the boards. With his size, he should be pulling down nine or ten boards a night. He has been slowed by tendinitis in both knees. Smits has been one of the most prolific foulers in basketball. His shot-swatting has declined.

Analysis: Smits seems to be enjoying the game more over the last few years, and it is reflected in his play. On the offensive end, few centers in the league stack up. He can fill the net facing the basket or with his back to it. However, he has not been one of the better centers in the league when it comes to rebounding and defense.

PLAYER SUMMARY	
Will	score inside
Can't	avoid whistles
Expect	soft touch
Don't Expect	9 RPG
Fantasy Value	$16-19
Card Value	5-8¢

COLLEGE STATISTICS

		G	FGP	FTP	RPG	PPG
84-85	MAR	29	.567	.577	5.6	11.2
85-86	MAR	30	.622	.681	8.1	17.7
86-87	MAR	21	.609	.722	8.1	20.1
87-88	MAR	27	.623	.735	8.7	24.7
Totals		107	.609	.693	7.6	18.2

NBA REGULAR-SEASON STATISTICS

				FGs		3-PT FGs		FTs		Rebounds						
		G	MIN	FG	PCT	FG	PCT	FT	PCT	OFF	TOT	AST	STL	BLK	PTS	PPG
88-89	IND	82	2041	386	.517	0	.000	184	.722	185	500	70	37	151	956	11.7
89-90	IND	82	2404	515	.533	0	.000	241	.811	135	512	142	45	169	1271	15.5
90-91	IND	76	1690	342	.485	0	.000	144	.762	116	357	84	24	111	828	10.9
91-92	IND	74	1772	436	.510	0	.000	152	.788	124	417	116	29	100	1024	13.8
92-93	IND	81	2072	494	.486	0	.000	167	.732	126	432	121	27	75	1155	14.3
93-94	IND	78	2113	493	.534	0	.000	238	.793	135	483	156	49	82	1224	15.7
94-95	IND	78	2381	558	.526	0	.000	284	.753	192	601	111	40	79	1400	17.9
Totals		551	14473	3224	.514	0	.000	1410	.767	1013	3302	800	251	767	7858	14.3

ELMORE SPENCER

Team: Los Angeles Clippers
Position: Center
Height: 7'0" **Weight:** 270
Birthdate: December 6, 1969
NBA Experience: 3 years

College: Georgia; Connors St.;
Nevada-Las Vegas
Acquired: 1st-round pick in 1992 draft
(25th overall)

Background: Spencer started his college career at Georgia before becoming the nation's hottest junior college prospect while leading Connors State (Oklahoma) to the national title. In two years at Nevada-Las Vegas, he set a school record for career blocked shots. Drafted 25th by the Clippers, he spent his rookie year on the bench, his second year in the starting lineup, and much of his third season on the injured list.

Strengths: Spencer is a fine shot-blocker, finishing among the league's top 15 two years ago and swatting 23 in 19 games last season. He offers good size and a decent feel for the game. He has a soft touch inside with his left hand and moves well for a big man. He plays tough defense and has potential as a rebounder.

Weaknesses: Get Spencer away from the basket a little bit and his game takes a nosedive. He does not shoot with respectable range and his free throw touch is embarrassing. He commits a lot of fouls and turns the ball over about twice as often as he gets credit for an assist. He has had problems with his weight and his overall consistency.

Analysis: An injury to the Clippers' Stanley Roberts two years ago thrust Spencer into a starting role for which he was not ready. He rarely played as a rookie, and he saw another year all but wasted in 1994-95 when two stints on the injured list limited him to 19 games. He missed the last two months after going out with a sprained ankle. So far, the only thing Spencer has been able to do consistently is block shots.

PLAYER SUMMARY

Will ....challenge shots
Can't ....make his free throws
Expect............................growing pains
Don't Expect..................ball-handling
Fantasy Value $1
Card Value ....7-10¢

COLLEGE STATISTICS

		G	FGP	FTP	RPG	PPG
88-89	GEOR	11	.641	.500	5.3	12.0
90-91	UNLV	31	.522	.471	4.0	6.4
91-92	UNLV	28	.637	.546	8.1	14.8
Totals		70	.603	.516	5.9	10.6

NBA REGULAR-SEASON STATISTICS

				FGs		3-PT FGs		FTs		Rebounds						
		G	MIN	FG	PCT	FG	PCT	FT	PCT	OFF	TOT	AST	STL	BLK	PTS	PPG
92-93	LAC	44	280	44	.537	0	.000	16	.500	17	62	8	8	18	104	2.4
93-94	LAC	76	1930	288	.533	0	.000	97	.599	96	415	75	30	127	673	8.9
94-95	LAC	19	368	52	.441	0	.000	28	.560	11	65	25	14	23	132	6.9
Totals		139	2578	384	.519	0	.000	141	.578	124	542	108	52	168	909	6.5

FELTON SPENCER

Team: Utah Jazz
Position: Center
Height: 7'0" **Weight:** 265
Birthdate: January 5, 1968

NBA Experience: 5 years
College: Louisville
Acquired: Traded from Timberwolves for Mike Brown, 6/93

Background: Spencer ended his college career as Louisville's all-time leader in field goal percentage and was third in the nation in that category in 1989-90. He was one of college basketball's most improved players as a senior. He earned second-team NBA All-Rookie honors with Minnesota but has played his best ball since a trade to Utah two years ago. Achilles tendon surgery ended his 1994-95 season after 34 games.

Strengths: Spencer takes up a lot of space and does not back away from contact. He hits the boards, blocks shots, and holds his defensive ground. He has also become a more confident and productive offensive player. He gets points off the offensive glass but also has a decent variety of post moves. He uses the pump-fake well.

Weaknesses: Spencer is a below-average offensive center, especially when facing the basket. His jumper is simply not reliable, even from short to mid-range. He remains one of the worst passing big men in basketball, averaging about one assist every two games. He's slow on his feet, picks up a lot of fouls, and is prone to injuries.

Analysis: Just as Spencer was enjoying some success, his surgery last January derailed him. Before the injury, he seemed like a new man in his season and a half with Utah. He was more confident on offense and provided solid rebounding and defense to complement the play of Karl Malone inside. He'll put in the hours and be back in the lineup for 1995-96.

PLAYER SUMMARY	
Will	block shots
Can't	pass
Expect	8 RPG
Don't Expect	quickness
Fantasy Value	$3-5
Card Value	8-12¢

COLLEGE STATISTICS

		G	FGP	FTP	RPG	PPG
86-87	LOU	31	.551	.492	2.7	3.8
87-88	LOU	35	.592	.640	4.2	7.4
88-89	LOU	33	.607	.733	5.1	8.2
89-90	LOU	35	.681	.716	8.5	14.9
Totals		134	.628	.676	5.2	8.7

NBA REGULAR-SEASON STATISTICS

		G	MIN	FGs		3-PT FGs		FTs		Rebounds		AST	STL	BLK	PTS	PPG
				FG	PCT	FG	PCT	FT	PCT	OFF	TOT					
90-91	MIN	81	2099	195	.512	0	.000	182	.722	272	641	25	48	121	572	7.1
91-92	MIN	61	1481	141	.426	0	.000	123	.691	167	435	53	27	79	405	6.6
92-93	MIN	71	1296	105	.465	0	.000	83	.654	134	324	17	23	66	293	4.1
93-94	UTA	79	2210	256	.505	0	.000	165	.607	235	658	43	41	67	677	8.6
94-95	UTA	34	905	105	.488	0	.000	107	.793	90	260	17	12	32	317	9.3
Totals		326	7991	802	.483	0	.000	660	.685	898	2318	155	151	365	2264	6.9

LATRELL SPREWELL

Team: Golden State Warriors
Position: Guard
Height: 6'5" **Weight:** 190
Birthdate: September 8, 1970

NBA Experience: 3 years
College: Three Rivers; Alabama
Acquired: 1st-round pick in 1992 draft
(24th overall)

Background: Though not recruited by a Division I school, Sprewell was a first-team All-SEC choice at Alabama and also made the All-Defensive team as a senior, when he averaged 17.8 points, 5.2 rebounds, and 1.8 steals per contest. Drafted 24th by Golden State, he made the All-Rookie second team and has been an All-Star in his two years since. Sprewell started in the All-Star Game last season.

Strengths: Sprewell is a high-energy player who excels on both ends of the court. He has a devastating first step to the bucket, and once he gets started he can finish with a dunk or pull up for a jumper. He also has 3-point range. On defense, Sprewell has been a legitimate stopper who has long arms and great instincts. He can run and jump with virtually anyone in the league and matches up at three different positions.

Weaknesses: Sound decisions are not always made when Sprewell has the ball. He has turned it over more than 200 times each year and he chucks up far too many 3-pointers than his accuracy says he should. His shooting percentage suffers for it. He has been in the doghouse for tardiness and unexcused absences.

Analysis: Sprewell, who did not play organized basketball until his senior year of high school, has all the tools to remain a star. He made the All-NBA first team in his second season, a rare feat for a late first-rounder, and is already an All-Star regular. There are some negatives, however, that could hold him back if he lets them. Sprewell needs to add more control.

PLAYER SUMMARY	
Will	hound his man
Can't	pass up treys
Expect	20 PPG
Don't Expect	a slow pace
Fantasy Value	$30-35
Card Value	30-60¢

COLLEGE STATISTICS

		G	FGP	FTP	RPG	PPG
90-91	ALAB	33	.511	.690	5.0	8.9
91-92	ALAB	35	.493	.771	5.2	17.8
Totals		68	.499	.740	5.1	13.5

NBA REGULAR-SEASON STATISTICS

		G	MIN	FGs FG	FGs PCT	3-PT FGs FG	3-PT FGs PCT	FTs FT	FTs PCT	Rebounds OFF	Rebounds TOT	AST	STL	BLK	PTS	PPG
92-93	GS	77	2741	449	.464	73	.369	211	.746	79	271	295	126	52	1182	15.4
93-94	GS	82	3533	613	.433	141	.361	353	.774	80	401	385	180	76	1720	21.0
94-95	GS	69	2771	490	.418	90	.276	350	.781	58	256	279	112	46	1420	20.6
Totals		228	9045	1552	.436	304	.332	914	.770	217	928	959	418	174	4322	19.0

JOHN STARKS

Team: New York Knicks
Position: Guard
Height: 6'5" **Weight:** 185
Birthdate: August 10, 1965
NBA Experience: 6 years

College: Northern Oklahoma;
Oklahoma St.
Acquired: Signed as a free agent,
10/90

Background: Starks is a product of four colleges in four years, including Oklahoma State as a senior (1987-88). He signed on with Golden State as a free agent but a back injury ended his rookie season prematurely. He became a CBA All-Star with Cedar Rapids and also played for Memphis in the WBL before making the Knicks' roster in 1990. Starks has finished second on the team in scoring three years in a row.

Strengths: Starks jump-starts the Knicks with his competitive fire, long-range shooting, and outstanding defense. He set NBA records last season for 3-pointers made (217) and attempted (611). He penetrates and finds open men. Starks wreaks havoc defensively with his supreme quickness and get-out-of-my-face attitude.

Weaknesses: Starks has become known for his flagrant fouls. He commits nearly as many personal fouls as his team's bruising big men and has earned a reputation as a hothead. He is prone to woeful cold spells, which do not dissuade him from shooting. At his success rate, 611 trey attempts is a mite too many.

Analysis: Starks, who worked at a grocery store before gaining success in pro basketball, has been a sparkplug for the Knicks. He's the kind of player a coach loves taking to a battle. Despite the 3-point records, the 1994-95 season was not one of Starks's best. He spent much of the year trying to find his stroke and converted less than 40 percent from the field. His scoring dropped to 15.3 PPG.

PLAYER SUMMARY	
Will	launch from anywhere
Can't	avoid confrontations
Expect	combative defense
Don't Expect	shy shooting
Fantasy Value	$10-13
Card Value	8-15¢

COLLEGE STATISTICS

		G	FGP	FTP	RPG	PPG
84-85	NOK	14	.463	.774	2.4	11.1
87-88	OSU	30	.497	.838	4.7	15.4
Totals		44	.487	.820	4.0	14.0

NBA REGULAR-SEASON STATISTICS

				FGs		3-PT FGs		FTs		Rebounds						
		G	MIN	FG	PCT	FG	PCT	FT	PCT	OFF	TOT	AST	STL	BLK	PTS	PPG
88-89	GS	36	316	51	.408	10	.385	34	.654	15	41	27	23	3	146	4.1
90-91	NY	61	1173	180	.439	27	.290	79	.752	30	131	204	59	17	466	7.6
91-92	NY	82	2118	405	.449	94	.348	235	.778	45	191	276	103	18	1139	13.9
92-93	NY	80	2477	513	.428	108	.321	263	.795	54	204	404	91	12	1397	17.5
93-94	NY	59	2057	410	.420	113	.335	187	.754	37	185	348	95	6	1120	19.0
94-95	NY	80	2725	419	.395	217	.355	168	.737	34	219	411	92	4	1223	15.3
Totals		398	10866	1978	.423	569	.340	966	.763	215	971	1670	463	60	5491	13.8

LARRY STEWART

Team: Vancouver Grizzlies
Position: Forward
Height: 6'8" **Weight:** 230
Birthdate: September 21, 1968

NBA Experience: 4 years
College: Coppin St.
Acquired: Selected from Bullets in 1995 expansion draft

Background: Stewart played high school ball at the famed Dobbins Tech in Philadelphia, then was a two-time Mid-Eastern Athletic Conference Player of the Year at Coppin State. He finished his career as the school's all-time rebounding king. Though not drafted in 1991, he won second-team All-Rookie honors with the Bullets and played in 81 games the next year. He has played in just 43 games over the last two years. Vancouver selected him in the 1995 expansion draft.

Strengths: Stewart is a fine athlete who supplements his ability with desire. He's not afraid to battle in the paint against much bigger players. He can be productive on the offensive glass and in an up-tempo style. He handles the ball and passes pretty well for a power forward, and he does not take many bad shots. He'll work on defense too.

Weaknesses: The undersized Stewart gives away a couple of inches to most of his matchups. It hurts him on both ends of the floor. There's no way he can pull his game outside with any success, yet he does not have the ability to score in the post on a consistent basis. In general, Stewart offers very little offensively.

Analysis: After missing all but three games of the 1993-94 season because of a broken foot as well as injuries suffered when he was shot and stabbed in a robbery attempt, Stewart has not been the same. It does not appear to be any physical problem holding him back, but rather an inability to regain the confidence level he showed over his first two seasons.

PLAYER SUMMARY	
Will	battle bigger men
Can't	regain early form
Expect	reserve minutes
Don't Expect	much offense
Fantasy Value	$0
Card Value	5-8¢

COLLEGE STATISTICS

		G	FGP	FTP	RPG	PPG
88-89	CSC	28	.659	.691	10.0	17.6
89-90	CSC	33	.645	.701	11.2	18.7
90-91	CSC	30	.635	.785	13.4	23.9
Totals		91	.646	.737	11.6	20.0

NBA REGULAR-SEASON STATISTICS

				FGs		3-PT FGs		FTs		Rebounds						
		G	MIN	FG	PCT	FG	PCT	FT	PCT	OFF	TOT	AST	STL	BLK	PTS	PPG
91-92	WAS	76	2229	303	.514	0	.000	188	.807	186	449	120	51	44	794	10.4
92-93	WAS	81	1823	306	.543	0	.000	184	.727	154	383	146	47	29	796	9.8
93-94	WAS	3	35	3	.375	0	.000	7	.700	1	7	2	2	1	13	4.3
94-95	WAS	40	346	41	.461	0	.000	20	.667	28	67	18	16	9	102	2.6
Totals		200	4433	653	.522	0	.000	399	.759	369	906	286	116	83	1705	8.5

BRYANT STITH

Team: Denver Nuggets
Position: Guard
Height: 6'5" **Weight:** 210
Birthdate: December 10, 1970

NBA Experience: 3 years
College: Virginia
Acquired: 1st-round pick in 1992 draft
(13th overall)

Background: Without much national fanfare, Stith was named All-ACC three consecutive seasons and led Virginia to the 1992 NIT championship as tournament MVP. He finished his career as the Cavaliers' all-time leader in scoring, minutes, and free throws made. The MVP of the 1992 pre-draft Orlando Classic, he was taken 13th overall by Denver. He has averaged double figures in scoring in his last two seasons.

Strengths: Stith brings great intangibles to the floor. He's a natural leader who comes up big under pressure and, in just his third year, was named team captain. He is the Nuggets' best backcourt defender. He has great anticipation and toughness. Stith moves well without the ball, draws fouls on his drives, and hits his free throws. He is a good outside shooter who can get on deadly streaks.

Weaknesses: Nothing about Stith's game is flashy. He does not possess great quickness or athletic ability, although he makes up for it with his hustle, savvy, and court sense. He will not startle anyone with his ball-handling or passing, and his jumper has been streaky. Stith has not found much success outside the 3-point stripe, though he does have the range.

Analysis: Stith is the heart and soul of the Nuggets. His teammates look to him for leadership and he provides it, seemingly raising his game a level during crunch time. He does not bring explosive scoring ability to the floor, but you have to admire his defense, his unselfishness, and his knack for making the right play. Stith shared time as a starter with Mahmoud Abdul-Rauf last season.

PLAYER SUMMARY	
Will	make wise decisions
Can't	pump in treys
Expect	savvy leadership
Don't Expect	explosiveness
Fantasy Value	$8-10
Card Value	8-15¢

COLLEGE STATISTICS

		G	FGP	FTP	RPG	PPG
88-89	VIRG	33	.548	.769	6.5	15.5
89-90	VIRG	32	.481	.777	6.9	20.8
90-91	VIRG	33	.471	.791	6.2	19.8
91-92	VIRG	33	.452	.815	6.6	20.7
Totals		131	.483	.789	6.6	19.2

NBA REGULAR-SEASON STATISTICS

				FGs		3-PT FGs		FTs		Rebounds						
		G	MIN	FG	PCT	FG	PCT	FT	PCT	OFF	TOT	AST	STL	BLK	PTS	PPG
92-93	DEN	39	865	124	.446	0	.000	99	.832	39	124	49	24	5	347	8.9
93-94	DEN	82	2853	365	.450	2	.222	291	.829	119	349	199	116	16	1023	12.5
94-95	DEN	81	2329	312	.472	20	.294	267	.824	95	268	153	91	18	911	11.2
Totals		202	6047	801	.458	22	.272	657	.827	253	741	401	231	39	2281	11.3

JOHN STOCKTON

Team: Utah Jazz
Position: Guard
Height: 6'1" **Weight:** 175
Birthdate: March 26, 1962

NBA Experience: 11 years
College: Gonzaga
Acquired: 1st-round pick in 1984 draft
(16th overall)

Background: Stockton led the West Coast Athletic Conference in points as a senior at Gonzaga, and in assists and steals for three years. He has shattered NBA assists records in 11 years with Utah. He is the only player in league history with more than 10,000 career assists and he has led the league for eight consecutive seasons. He has played in seven straight All-Star Games and was a 1992 Olympic gold-medalist.

Strengths: Stockton remains the best playmaker in basketball, and he's perhaps the best ever. He is quick and masterful with the ball, with an uncanny ability to take it to the hole and create easy shots for teammates. He is a great 3-point and free throw shooter. Stockton is also an accomplished defensive player with more than 2,200 career steals.

Weaknesses: Stockton does not have great size, but it has not held him back. He's not asked to rebound.

Analysis: Is John Stockton the best playmaker in history? Says Magic Johnson, whose career assist record fell last season: "There's nobody who could distribute the ball and lead his team like John Stockton." Stockton tied Bob Cousy's record by winning an eighth straight league assist crown. He also leads the league with his 445 consecutive starts.

PLAYER SUMMARY	
Will	distribute
Can't	be left open
Expect	12-plus APG
Don't Expect	days off
Fantasy Value	$40-45
Card Value	20-40¢

COLLEGE STATISTICS

		G	FGP	FTP	APG	PPG
80-81	GONZ	25	.578	.743	1.4	3.1
81-82	GONZ	27	.576	.676	5.0	11.2
82-83	GONZ	27	.518	.791	6.8	13.9
83-84	GONZ	28	.577	.692	7.2	20.9
Totals		107	.559	.719	5.2	12.5

NBA REGULAR-SEASON STATISTICS

		G	MIN	FGs FG	FGs PCT	3-PT FGs FG	3-PT FGs PCT	FTs FT	FTs PCT	Rebounds OFF	Rebounds TOT	AST	STL	BLK	PTS	PPG
84-85	UTA	82	1490	157	.471	2	.182	142	.736	26	105	415	109	11	458	5.6
85-86	UTA	82	1935	228	.489	2	.133	172	.839	33	179	610	157	10	630	7.7
86-87	UTA	82	1858	231	.499	7	.184	179	.782	32	151	670	177	14	648	7.9
87-88	UTA	82	2842	454	.574	24	.358	272	.840	54	237	1128	242	16	1204	14.7
88-89	UTA	82	3171	497	.538	16	.242	390	.863	83	248	1118	263	14	1400	17.1
89-90	UTA	78	2915	472	.514	47	.416	354	.819	57	206	1134	207	18	1345	17.2
90-91	UTA	82	3103	496	.507	58	.345	363	.836	46	237	1164	234	16	1413	17.2
91-92	UTA	82	3002	453	.482	83	.407	308	.842	68	270	1126	244	22	1297	15.8
92-93	UTA	82	2863	437	.486	72	.385	293	.798	64	237	987	199	21	1239	15.1
93-94	UTA	82	2969	458	.528	48	.492	272	.805	72	258	1031	199	22	1236	15.1
94-95	UTA	82	2867	429	.542	102	.449	246	.804	57	251	1011	194	22	1206	14.7
Totals		898	29015	4312	.515	461	.370	2991	.820	592	2379	10394	2225	186	12076	13.4

ROD STRICKLAND

Team: Portland Trail Blazers
Position: Guard
Height: 6'3" **Weight:** 185
Birthdate: July 11, 1966

NBA Experience: 7 years
College: DePaul
Acquired: Signed as a free agent, 7/92

Background: Strickland left DePaul for the pros a year early, but not before he led the Blue Demons in scoring, assists, and steals as a junior and climbed among the school's career leaders in each category. He was a backup point guard with New York as a rookie before becoming a starter in San Antonio. He signed as a free agent with Portland in 1992. Strickland averaged a career-high 18.9 PPG last season.

Strengths: Few penetrate as easily and frequently as Strickland, whose nifty ball-handling and great quickness allow him to get past even the best defenders. He was fourth in the league with 8.8 APG last season. He hits acrobatic shots off his drives and is a potent scorer. Strickland excels in transition and plays solid defense.

Weaknesses: Strickland has had some off-court slip-ups and earned a reputation as a troublemaker in New York and San Antonio. He has become a better citizen. He has not enjoyed great success from behind the 3-point arc.

Analysis: With his lethal combination of scoring and playmaking ability, Strickland is capable of giving any defender fits. Few guards in the league possess his range of offensive skills. He has taken his play to another level since arriving in Portland, becoming more of a leader. It is probably a matter of time before he earns an All-Star invitation in a conference loaded with star guards.

PLAYER SUMMARY	
Will	drive and dish
Can't	rely on 3-point shot
Expect	18 PPG, 9 APG
Don't Expect	passive play
Fantasy Value	$45-50
Card Value	5-8¢

COLLEGE STATISTICS

		G	FGP	FTP	APG	PPG
85-86	DeP	31	.497	.675	5.1	14.1
86-87	DeP	30	.582	.606	6.5	16.3
87-88	DeP	26	.528	.606	7.8	20.0
Totals		87	.534	.626	6.4	16.6

NBA REGULAR-SEASON STATISTICS

				FGs		3-PT FGs		FTs		Rebounds						
		G	MIN	FG	PCT	FG	PCT	FT	PCT	OFF	TOT	AST	STL	BLK	PTS	PPG
88-89	NY	81	1358	265	.467	19	.322	172	.745	51	160	319	98	3	721	8.9
89-90	NY/SA	82	2140	343	.454	8	.267	174	.626	90	259	468	127	14	868	10.6
90-91	SA	58	2076	314	.482	11	.333	161	.763	57	219	463	117	11	800	13.8
91-92	SA	57	2053	300	.455	5	.333	182	.687	92	265	491	118	17	787	13.8
92-93	POR	78	2474	396	.485	4	.133	273	.717	120	337	559	131	24	1069	13.7
93-94	POR	82	2889	528	.483	2	.200	353	.749	122	370	740	147	24	1411	17.2
94-95	POR	64	2267	441	.466	46	.374	283	.745	73	317	562	123	9	1211	18.9
Totals		502	15257	2587	.471	95	.317	1598	.721	605	1927	3602	861	102	6867	13.7

DEREK STRONG

Unrestricted Free Agent
Last Team: Boston Celtics
Position: Forward
Height: 6'8" **Weight:** 220
Birthdate: February 9, 1968

NBA Experience: 4 years
College: Xavier
Acquired: Traded from Bucks with Blue Edwards for Ed Pinckney and draft rights to Andrei Fetisov, 6/94

Background: Strong played with Tyrone Hill as a collegian at Xavier (Ohio), where he averaged 9.9 RPG as a senior. He was drafted late in the second round by Philadelphia but was cut. He played one game while on a ten-day contract with Washington in 1991-92 and was the CBA MVP in 1992-93. After one full season with Milwaukee, Strong was traded to Boston before the 1994-95 season and made 24 starts for the Celtics.

Strengths: Strong lives up to his name on the boards. No matter what position you line him up in, he will rebound. Though undersized for a power forward, he challenges his opponents on defense. He does not shy away from contact and has good athletic skills. Strong runs the floor, gets to the line, and is a good free throw shooter.

Weaknesses: Strong is caught between the two forward positions. He is not quick enough to do a good defensive job against small forwards, yet his size puts him at a disadvantage against the power forwards. His post-up game is nothing extraordinary and he makes his jumper only in streaks. He is not a confident ball-handler or an aware passer. His game is rough around the edges.

Analysis: For starters, Strong does not have the ability to become a big-time NBA player. That said, he has loads of potential as a rebounding specialist off the bench. He averaged more than five boards per game last season despite playing just 19 minutes per contest. If the rest of his game develops to the point where he earns more time, he could be a double-figure board man.

PLAYER SUMMARY	
Will	hit the boards
Can't	shoot 50 percent
Expect	further improvement
Don't Expect	10 PPG
Fantasy Value	$1
Card Value	10-20¢

COLLEGE STATISTICS

		G	FGP	FTP	RPG	PPG
87-88	XAV	30	.569	.718	7.1	10.6
88-89	XAV	33	.617	.817	8.0	15.3
89-90	XAV	33	.533	.839	9.9	14.2
Totals		96	.573	.802	8.4	13.4

NBA REGULAR-SEASON STATISTICS

			FGs		3-PT FGs		FTs		Rebounds						
	G	MIN	FG	PCT	FG	PCT	FT	PCT	OFF	TOT	AST	STL	BLK	PTS	PPG
91-92 WAS	1	12	0	.000	0	.000	3	.750	1	5	1	0	0	3	3.0
92-93 MIL	23	339	42	.457	4	.500	68	.800	40	115	14	11	1	156	6.8
93-94 MIL	67	1131	141	.413	3	.231	159	.772	109	281	48	38	14	444	6.6
94-95 BOS	70	1344	149	.453	2	.286	141	.820	136	375	44	24	13	441	6.3
Totals	161	2826	332	.433	9	.321	371	.794	286	776	107	73	28	1044	6.5

ROY TARPLEY

Team: Dallas Mavericks
Position: Forward
Height: 6'11" **Weight:** 250
Birthdate: November 28, 1964

NBA Experience: 6 years
College: Michigan
Acquired: Signed as a free agent,
10/94

Background: Tarpley powered Michigan to back-to-back Big Ten titles, winning league Player of the Year honors as a junior and All-America recognition in his final two seasons. He won the 1987-88 Sixth Man Award and emerged as a dominant player before being suspended from the NBA in 1990-91 for his third violation of the anti-drug policy. After stints in the CBA, the USBL, and Greece, he returned as a Dallas reserve in 1994-95.

Strengths: There is no denying Tarpley's ability to be a force on the boards. He has averaged more than ten rebounds per game in four of his six seasons and contributed better than eight per game last year despite his sixth-man role. Tarpley is also a fine shooter with good range for a big man. He makes his free throws.

Weaknesses: Tarpley is a head case. Dallas has taken a big chance with him, knowing that the possibility of a relapse always exists. Tarpley has shown a disdain for team and league rules in his career. He'll show up late for practices and team functions. On the court, he is not the defensive force he could be.

Analysis: Tarpley has returned to a role that served him well early in his career—that of a sixth man. He was not nearly as dominant last year as he had been before his dismissal from the NBA, but three years of inferior competition can do that. The proverbial bad apple, Tarpley will always be one slip-up away from disaster.

PLAYER SUMMARY	
Will	rebound
Can't	afford to slip
Expect	double-doubles
Don't Expect	a good example
Fantasy Value	$7-9
Card Value	5-8¢

COLLEGE STATISTICS

		G	FGP	FTP	RPG	PPG
82-83	MICH	26	.407	.579	3.2	3.5
83-84	MICH	33	.527	.794	8.1	12.5
84-85	MICH	30	.525	.775	10.4	19.0
85-86	MICH	33	.541	.811	8.8	15.9
Totals		122	.522	.774	7.8	13.1

NBA REGULAR-SEASON STATISTICS

				FGs		3-PT FGs		FTs		Rebounds						
		G	MIN	FG	PCT	FG	PCT	FT	PCT	OFF	TOT	AST	STL	BLK	PTS	PPG
86-87	DAL	75	1405	233	.467	1	.333	94	.676	180	533	52	56	79	561	7.5
87-88	DAL	81	2307	444	.500	0	.000	205	.740	360	959	86	103	86	1093	13.5
88-89	DAL	19	591	131	.541	0	.000	66	.688	77	218	17	28	30	328	17.3
89-90	DAL	45	1648	314	.451	0	.000	130	.756	189	589	67	79	70	758	16.8
90-91	DAL	5	171	43	.544	0	.000	16	.889	16	55	12	6	9	102	20.4
94-95	DAL	55	1354	292	.479	5	.278	102	.836	142	449	58	45	55	691	12.6
Totals		280	7476	1457	.483	6	.176	613	.744	964	2803	292	317	329	3533	12.6

OTIS THORPE

Team: Portland Trail Blazers
Position: Forward
Height: 6'10" **Weight:** 245
Birthdate: August 5, 1962
NBA Experience: 11 years

College: Providence
Acquired: Traded from Rockets with draft rights to Marcelo Nicola and a conditional 1st-round pick for Clyde Drexler and Tracy Murray, 2/95

Background: Thorpe left Providence with the all-time Big East record for rebounds and was a consensus all-conference selection as a senior. He started his pro career with the Kings, played six-plus years in Houston, and was traded to Portland in February 1995. Thorpe was a 1992 All-Star and has played all 82 games in eight of his 11 seasons.

Strengths: Thorpe is annually one of the most accurate field goal shooters in the league. He gets a lot of points on putbacks and does not take unwise shots. He uses his muscular frame to bang in the post and has amassed nearly 8,000 rebounds in his career. He handles the ball and never lets up.

Weaknesses: Thorpe does not shoot well and is not a threat to take over games offensively. He is a poor free throw shooter and gets his points because of hustle rather than great skills. He picks up a lot of fouls.

Analysis: You know what you'll get from Thorpe on a nightly basis. He'll score in double figures, ignite the break, chase rebounds, and provide aggressive defense. Houston missed his rebounding after trading him in the Clyde Drexler deal last season. Thorpe is the ultimate team player.

PLAYER SUMMARY	
Will	rebound, defend
Can't	make his free throws
Expect	high field goal pct.
Don't Expect	selfish play
Fantasy Value	$9-11
Card Value	7-12¢

COLLEGE STATISTICS

		G	FGP	FTP	RPG	PPG
80-81	PROV	26	.515	.658	5.3	9.6
81-82	PROV	27	.541	.643	8.0	14.1
82-83	PROV	31	.636	.659	8.0	16.1
83-84	PROV	29	.580	.653	10.3	17.1
Totals		113	.575	.653	8.0	14.4

NBA REGULAR-SEASON STATISTICS

		G	MIN	FGs FG	FGs PCT	3-PT FGs FG	3-PT FGs PCT	FTs FT	FTs PCT	Rebounds OFF	Rebounds TOT	AST	STL	BLK	PTS	PPG
84-85	KC	82	1918	411	.600	0	.000	230	.620	187	556	111	34	37	1052	12.8
85-86	SAC	75	1675	289	.587	0	.000	164	.661	137	420	84	35	34	742	9.9
86-87	SAC	82	2956	567	.540	0	.000	413	.761	259	819	201	46	60	1547	18.9
87-88	SAC	82	3072	622	.507	0	.000	460	.755	279	837	266	62	56	1704	20.8
88-89	HOU	82	3135	521	.542	0	.000	328	.729	272	787	202	82	37	1370	16.7
89-90	HOU	82	2947	547	.548	0	.000	307	.688	258	734	261	66	24	1401	17.1
90-91	HOU	82	3039	549	.556	3	.429	334	.696	287	846	197	73	20	1435	17.5
91-92	HOU	82	3056	558	.592	0	.000	304	.657	285	862	250	52	37	1420	17.3
92-93	HOU	72	2357	385	.558	0	.000	153	.598	219	589	181	43	19	923	12.8
93-94	HOU	82	2909	449	.561	0	.000	251	.657	271	870	189	66	28	1149	14.0
94-95	HOU/POR	70	2096	385	.565	0	.000	167	.594	202	558	112	41	28	937	13.4
Totals		873	29160	5283	.555	3	.063	3111	.687	2656	7878	2054	600	380	13680	15.7

SEDALE THREATT

Team: Los Angeles Lakers
Position: Guard
Height: 6'2" **Weight:** 185
Birthdate: September 10, 1961
NBA Experience: 12 years

College: West Virginia Tech
Acquired: Traded from SuperSonics for 1994, 1995, and 1996 2nd-round picks, 10/91

Background: Threatt was an NAIA All-American at West Virginia Tech, where he finished his career as the school's all-time scoring leader. Originally a sixth-round draft pick by Philadelphia, he has played 12 seasons with the 76ers, Bulls, SuperSonics, and Lakers. His scoring dropped to 9.5 PPG for the Lakers last season.

Strengths: Threatt is a pure shooter. He can create his own shot off the dribble and is an 80-percent career free throw shooter. He is a heady transition player, can run the offense, and is an accomplished thief. Threatt is capable of playing both guard positions.

Weaknesses: The knock on Threatt has been his lack of leadership skills. He is more of a gunner than the kind of guard who makes those around him look better. An abdominal injury kept him out of the playoffs last season.

Analysis: The Lakers used Threatt wisely as a third guard last season, giving the starting point-guard job to the emerging Nick Van Exel. Threatt did an admirable if unspectacular job as the starter after Magic Johnson's retirement, but he is better suited for a role in which the offense is not dependent on him.

PLAYER SUMMARY

Will ....play two positions
Can't ....create like Magic
Expect..............................a steal a game
Don't Expect....................Laker starts
Fantasy Value $2-4
Card Value ....5-8¢

COLLEGE STATISTICS

		G	FGP	FTP	APG	PPG
79-80	WVT	28	.481	.714	3.9	17.8
80-81	WVT	31	.452	.712	5.7	17.7
81-82	WVT	34	.500	.729	5.9	22.2
82-83	WVT	27	.557	.732	6.7	25.5
Totals		120	.498	.724	5.5	20.7

NBA REGULAR-SEASON STATISTICS

				FGs		3-PT FGs		FTs		Rebounds							
		G	MIN	FG	PCT	FG	PCT	FT	PCT	OFF	TOT	AST	STL	BLK	PTS	PPG
83-84	PHI	45	464	62	.419	1	.125	23	.821	17	40	41	13	2	148	3.3
84-85	PHI	82	1304	188	.452	4	.182	66	.733	21	99	175	80	16	446	5.4
85-86	PHI	70	1754	310	.453	1	.042	75	.833	21	121	193	93	5	696	9.9
86-87	PHI/CHI	68	1446	239	.448	7	.219	95	.798	26	108	259	74	13	580	8.5
87-88	CHI/SEA	71	1055	216	.508	3	.111	57	.803	23	88	160	60	8	492	6.9
88-89	SEA	63	1220	235	.494	11	.367	63	.818	31	117	238	83	4	544	8.6
89-90	SEA	65	1481	303	.506	8	.250	130	.828	43	115	216	65	8	744	11.4
90-91	SEA	80	2066	433	.519	10	.286	137	.792	25	99	273	113	8	1013	12.7
91-92	LAL	82	3070	509	.489	20	.323	202	.831	43	253	593	168	16	1240	15.1
92-93	LAL	82	2893	522	.508	14	.264	177	.823	47	273	564	142	11	1235	15.1
93-94	LAL	81	2278	411	.482	5	.152	138	.890	28	153	344	110	19	965	11.9
94-95	LAL	59	1384	217	.497	36	.379	88	.793	21	124	248	54	12	558	9.5
Totals		848	20415	3645	.488	120	.265	1251	.818	346	1590	3304	1055	122	8661	10.2

WAYMAN TISDALE

Unrestricted Free Agent
Last Team: Phoenix Suns
Position: Forward/Center
Height: 6'9" **Weight:** 260
Birthdate: June 9, 1964

NBA Experience: 10 years
College: Oklahoma
Acquired: Signed as a free agent, 9/94

Background: Tisdale became the first player in college basketball history to be named first-team All-America in his first three seasons. He starred on the 1984 gold medal-winning U.S. Olympic team and finished college with 17 Oklahoma records. He averaged 17.0 PPG over his first nine years with Indiana and Sacramento before dropping to 10.0 PPG with Phoenix last season.

Strengths: Tisdale is an accomplished low-post scorer who gets his shots off despite his relatively small size. His offensive arsenal includes a variety of twisting moves in the lane and a consistent short-range jumper. He once averaged 22.3 PPG. He also hits the boards.

Weaknesses: Defense has never been Tisdale's forte. His size does not serve him well and he expends a lot of energy on offense. He does not pass well out of double-teams and does not have great range.

Analysis: The Suns signed Tisdale to a free-agent contract before last season, giving a ten-year veteran his first chance to play for a contender. His numbers and minutes were bound to drop, but he did give the team a reliable scorer off the bench. Tisdale is also an accomplished bass player whose band, Fifth Quarter, cut an album in the summer of 1994.

PLAYER SUMMARY

Will ....score inside
Can't ....shut down his man
Expect ....instant offense
Don't Expect ....nifty passes
Fantasy Value $2-4
Card Value ....7-12¢

COLLEGE STATISTICS

		G	FGP	FTP	RPG	PPG
82-83	OKLA	33	.580	.635	10.3	24.5
83-84	OKLA	34	.577	.640	9.7	27.0
84-85	OKLA	37	.578	.703	10.2	25.2
Totals		104	.578	.661	10.1	25.6

NBA REGULAR-SEASON STATISTICS

			FGs		3-PT FGs		FTs		Rebounds						
	G	MIN	FG	PCT	FG	PCT	FT	PCT	OFF	TOT	AST	STL	BLK	PTS	PPG
85-86 IND	81	2277	516	.515	0	.000	160	.684	191	584	79	32	44	1192	14.7
86-87 IND	81	2159	458	.513	0	.000	258	.709	217	475	117	50	26	1174	14.5
87-88 IND	79	2378	511	.512	0	.000	246	.783	168	491	103	54	34	1268	16.1
88-89 IND/SAC	79	2434	532	.514	0	.000	317	.773	187	609	128	55	52	1381	17.5
89-90 SAC	79	2937	726	.525	0	.000	306	.783	185	595	108	54	54	1758	22.3
90-91 SAC	33	1116	262	.483	0	.000	136	.800	75	253	66	23	28	660	20.0
91-92 SAC	72	2521	522	.500	0	.000	151	.763	135	469	106	55	79	1195	16.6
92-93 SAC	76	2283	544	.509	0	.000	175	.758	127	500	108	52	47	1263	16.6
93-94 SAC	79	2557	552	.501	0	.000	215	.808	159	560	139	37	52	1319	16.7
94-95 PHO	65	1276	278	.484	0	.000	94	.770	83	247	45	29	27	650	10.0
Totals	724	21938	4901	.508	0	.000	2058	.762	1527	4783	999	441	443	11860	16.4

JEFF TURNER

Team: Orlando Magic
Position: Forward
Height: 6'9" **Weight:** 240
Birthdate: April 9, 1962

NBA Experience: 9 years
College: Vanderbilt
Acquired: Signed as a free agent, 7/89

Background: Turner was a two-time SEC All-Academic selection at Vanderbilt and played for the 1984 gold medal-winning U.S. Olympic team. He struggled with New Jersey for three pro seasons before playing in Italy for two years. Turner returned to the NBA with Orlando, where he has spent the past six years primarily as a reserve. He averaged 11.8 minutes and 4.1 points in 49 games last season.

Strengths: A perimeter-oriented forward, Turner has a soft touch with his lefty jump shot and can stroke it with 3-point range. He uses his head, boxes out, and does not try to do more than he is capable of offensively. He made 26 of 29 free throws last season.

Weaknesses: Turner does little offensively other than shoot. He cannot put the ball on the floor and does not possess an inside game to bail him out. He lacks quickness for the perimeter and muscle for the paint. The same dilemma haunts him on defense.

Analysis: Turner made a comeback last season from a torn anterior cruciate he suffered in April 1994. No one can question his work ethic and his team-first approach to the game. However, he failed to be called from the bench in 33 outings last season and shot a career-low 41 percent from the floor. Those aren't good signs.

PLAYER SUMMARY

Will	make free throws
Can't	shove people around
Expect	a shooting specialist
Don't Expect	headlines
Fantasy Value	$0
Card Value	5-8¢

COLLEGE STATISTICS

		G	FGP	FTP	RPG	PPG
80-81	VAND	28	.417	.645	3.0	3.6
81-82	VAND	27	.524	.732	5.4	9.3
82-83	VAND	33	.492	.765	5.5	13.2
83-84	VAND	29	.533	.843	7.3	16.8
Totals		117	.506	.772	5.3	10.9

NBA REGULAR-SEASON STATISTICS

				FGs		3-PT FGs		FTs		Rebounds						
		G	MIN	FG	PCT	FG	PCT	FT	PCT	OFF	TOT	AST	STL	BLK	PTS	PPG
84-85	NJ	72	1429	171	.454	0	.000	79	.859	88	218	108	29	7	421	5.8
85-86	NJ	53	650	84	.491	0	.000	58	.744	45	137	14	21	3	226	4.3
86-87	NJ	76	1003	151	.465	0	.000	76	.731	80	197	60	33	13	378	5.0
89-90	ORL	60	1105	132	.429	2	.200	42	.778	52	227	53	23	12	308	5.1
90-91	ORL	71	1683	259	.487	6	.400	85	.759	108	363	97	29	10	609	8.6
91-92	ORL	75	1591	225	.451	1	.125	79	.693	62	246	92	24	16	530	7.1
92-93	ORL	75	1479	231	.529	10	.588	56	.800	74	252	107	19	9	528	7.0
93-94	ORL	68	1536	199	.467	18	.327	35	.778	79	271	60	23	11	451	6.6
94-95	ORL	49	576	73	.410	27	.360	26	.897	23	97	38	12	3	199	4.1
Totals		599	11052	1525	.469	64	.346	536	.768	611	2008	629	213	84	3650	6.1

B.J. TYLER

Team: Toronto Raptors
Position: Guard
Height: 6'1" **Weight:** 185
Birthdate: April 30, 1971

NBA Experience: 1 year
College: DePaul; Texas
Acquired: Selected from 76ers in
1995 expansion draft

Background: Though he played high school ball in Port Arthur, Texas, Tyler chose to attend DePaul. After a dismal freshman year, however, he returned home to play for the Longhorns. After allegedly failing a drug test and spending time in John Lucas's clinic, Tyler became a big scorer at Texas and finished his career second on the school's all-time assists list. He played for Lucas as a Philadelphia rookie but averaged just 3.5 PPG. The 76ers exposed Tyler in the expansion draft and the Raptors snatched him up.

Strengths: Tyler has big-league quickness in everything he does. He can beat his man off the dribble and fly down the court on the break. Known as a scorer, he can get to the hoop or pull up for jumpers from the 3-point arc. He also creates opportunities for his teammates. Tyler is a potential defensive whiz because of his quick hands and feet. He makes things happen.

Weaknesses: Not all the things Tyler makes happen are good. He commits a high number of turnovers because he tries to do too much with the ball. His shot selection is also questionable at times, as his shooting percentage indicates. You have to wonder whether he might be going too fast for his own good. Largely due to his sporadic minutes, Tyler has yet to show any consistency.

Analysis: Tyler is a speedy bundle of potential who is prone to erratic stretches. He spent two stints on the injured list last season with abdominal and shoulder injuries, and the greatly improved play of Dana Barros at the point served to keep him on the bench for all but about 15 minutes a game. Tyler will likely be a backup for the expansion Raptors, caddying for star rookie Damon Stoudamire.

PLAYER SUMMARY	
Will	run, run, run
Can't	slow down
Expect	quickness, 3-pointers
Don't Expect	consistency
Fantasy Value	$0
Card Value	10-30¢

COLLEGE STATISTICS

		G	FGP	FTP	APG	PPG
89-90	DeP	17	.333	.786	2.1	2.9
91-92	TEX	35	.435	.792	6.5	18.3
92-93	TEX	13	.446	.632	6.1	17.3
93-94	TEX	28	.443	.727	6.3	22.8
Totals		93	.435	.741	2.8	16.7

NBA REGULAR-SEASON STATISTICS

			FGs		3-PT FGs		FTs		Rebounds						
	G	MIN	FG	PCT	FG	PCT	FT	PCT	OFF	TOT	AST	STL	BLK	PTS	PPG
94-95 PHI	55	809	72	.381	16	.314	35	.700	13	62	174	36	2	195	3.5
Totals	55	809	72	.381	16	.314	35	.700	13	62	174	36	2	195	3.5

NICK VAN EXEL

Team: Los Angeles Lakers
Position: Guard
Height: 6'1" **Weight:** 171
Birthdate: November 27, 1971

NBA Experience: 2 years
College: Cincinnati
Acquired: 2nd-round pick in 1993 draft (37th overall)

Background: After spending his first two years at a junior college, Van Exel was the ringleader of a Cincinnati team that advanced to the Final Four in 1992 and the regional finals in 1993. He slipped to the second round of the 1993 draft but was second among all rookies in assists during the 1993-94 season with 5.8 per game with the Lakers. Van Exel upped his contributions to 16.9 PPG and 8.3 APG in 1994-95.

Strengths: Van Exel brings great quickness, confidence, and ability to the point-guard position. He handles the ball, gets past his man, and finds open teammates. He also shoots with great range and was among NBA leaders with 183 3-pointers made last season. He can light up the scoreboard in a hurry. Van Exel uses his quickness to his advantage on the defensive end. He wants to be a star and plays with determination.

Weaknesses: About the only legitimate knock on Van Exel after two years is his night-to-night consistency. He will continue to hoist treys despite some harsh cold spells, and he is also susceptible to lapses on defense. Van Exel has alienated some (ex-Laker coach Randy Pfund among them), but by no means has he been a problem off the court. His field goal percentage reflects his large number of 3-point tries.

Analysis: Van Exel has been a surprise to some. Others, like Cincinnati coach Bob Huggins, predicted stardom for the player overlooked 36 times in the 1993 draft. Van Exel is the trigger man of a rejuvenated L.A. Laker team, leading the attack with drives, dishes, and long-range fireworks. He is a high-energy player who is tough to slow down when he gets on a roll.

PLAYER SUMMARY

Will.............................score, distribute
Can't...............................pass up treys
Expect.......................competitive fire
Don't Expect.....................a slow pace
Fantasy Value $15-18
Card Value ....40-75¢

COLLEGE STATISTICS

		G	FGP	FTP	APG	PPG
91-92	CINC	34	.446	.673	2.9	12.3
92-93	CINC	31	.386	.725	4.5	18.3
Totals		65	.409	.701	3.6	15.2

NBA REGULAR-SEASON STATISTICS

				FGs		3-PT FGs		FTs		Rebounds						
		G	MIN	FG	PCT	FG	PCT	FT	PCT	OFF	TOT	AST	STL	BLK	PTS	PPG
93-94	LAL	81	2700	413	.394	123	.338	150	.781	47	238	466	85	8	1099	13.6
94-95	LAL	80	2944	465	.420	183	.358	235	.783	27	223	660	97	6	1348	16.9
Totals		161	5644	878	.407	306	.350	385	.783	74	461	1126	182	14	2447	15.2

LOY VAUGHT

Team: Los Angeles Clippers
Position: Forward
Height: 6'9" **Weight:** 240
Birthdate: February 27, 1967

NBA Experience: 5 years
College: Michigan
Acquired: 1st-round pick in 1990 draft
(13th overall)

Background: Vaught led the Big Ten in field goal percentage as a junior and senior and was the first Michigan player since Roy Tarpley to average double-figure points and rebounds. He also led the conference in rebounding as a senior. The five-year pro has improved his numbers every season and enjoyed by far his best year in 1994-95, leading the Clippers in both scoring and rebounding.

Strengths: Vaught is known for his shooting touch and his work on the boards. He approaches basketball in workmanlike fashion. He's deadly when coming around a pick and refuses to take a bad shot. He always hits for a high percentage. Vaught has a muscular frame and uses it to seal his man off the boards. His 9.7 RPG last season ranked 15th in the NBA.

Weaknesses: Vaught does very little off the dribble. He could be a devastating offensive player if he mastered a driving move to the hoop. His defense has always been a weak aspect of his game. He should block a lot more shots and he too often resorts to fouling instead of staying in front of his man. His turnovers still outnumber his assists.

Analysis: Not expected to be much of an offensive force five years ago, all Vaught did last season was raise his scoring average by almost six points to 17.5 per game. He very nearly averaged a double-double while becoming the leader of an inexperienced club. A talented artist, Vaught has drawings on display in an art gallery.

PLAYER SUMMARY	
Will	catch and shoot
Can't	master the dribble
Expect	double-doubles
Don't Expect	great passing
Fantasy Value	$16-19
Card Value	5-10¢

COLLEGE STATISTICS

		G	FGP	FTP	RPG	PPG
86-87	MICH	32	.557	.500	3.9	4.6
87-88	MICH	34	.621	.724	4.4	10.5
88-89	MICH	37	.661	.778	8.0	12.6
89-90	MICH	31	.595	.804	11.2	15.5
Totals		134	.617	.752	6.8	10.8

NBA REGULAR-SEASON STATISTICS

				FGs		3-PT FGs		FTs		Rebounds						
		G	MIN	FG	PCT	FG	PCT	FT	PCT	OFF	TOT	AST	STL	BLK	PTS	PPG
90-91	LAC	73	1178	175	.487	0	.000	49	.662	124	349	40	20	23	399	5.5
91-92	LAC	79	1687	271	.492	4	.800	55	.797	160	512	71	37	31	601	7.6
92-93	LAC	79	1653	313	.508	1	.250	116	.748	164	492	54	55	39	743	9.4
93-94	LAC	75	2118	373	.537	0	.000	131	.720	218	656	74	76	22	877	11.7
94-95	LAC	80	2966	609	.514	7	.212	176	.710	261	772	139	104	29	1401	17.5
Totals		386	9602	1741	.511	12	.245	527	.724	927	2781	378	292	144	4021	10.4

REX WALTERS

Team: New Jersey Nets
Position: Guard
Height: 6'4" **Weight:** 190
Birthdate: March 12, 1970

NBA Experience: 2 years
College: Northwestern; Kansas
Acquired: 1st-round pick in 1993 draft
(16th overall)

Background: Walters was ignored by Kansas University as a high school senior, but he transferred there after a strong sophomore campaign at Northwestern. He was a two-time All-Big Eight choice and played in the Final Four as a senior. He hit 43 percent of his college 3-point tries. Drafted 16th by New Jersey in 1993, Walters played sparingly as a rookie but made 30 starts during the 1994-95 campaign.

Strengths: Walters is a fine outside shooter with a quick release and fantastic range. He converted half of his 28 3-point attempts as a rookie and hit better than 36 percent last season. He is also a top-notch free throw shooter. He's left-handed, which makes him tricky to guard, and he plays the game with fire. Few players practice and play as hard as Walters, who can play either guard position.

Weaknesses: Walters is not the biggest or quickest or strongest guy who plays in an NBA backcourt. He does not do enough off the dribble to be a big-scoring two guard and he lacks the quickness and playmaking prowess to thrive at the point. He does not get to the line much. Walters is highly combative, but he has a long way to go with his defensive game. Quick players give him fits.

Analysis: Walters has something to contribute. He brings a tough, aggressive attitude and a great work ethic to the floor. He's relentless, a coach's player. He can also flat-out shoot the basketball. However, there are some physical limitations that probably will prevent him from becoming a featured player. Moreover, his defense needs to improve and he needs to get more comfortable creating chances off the dribble.

PLAYER SUMMARY

Will ....shoot with range
Can't.......................stop quick guards
Expect ....relentlessness
Don't Expect ....lethal drives
Fantasy Value...................................$0
Card Value ....10-20¢

COLLEGE STATISTICS

		G	FGP	FTP	APG	PPG
88-89	NORT	24	.378	.917	1.4	2.1
89-90	NORT	28	.503	.794	4.5	17.6
91-92	KANS	32	.525	.827	3.9	16.0
92-93	KANS	36	.490	.873	4.3	15.3
Totals		120	.500	.837	3.6	13.4

NBA REGULAR-SEASON STATISTICS

				FGs		3-PT FGs		FTs		Rebounds						
		G	MIN	FG	PCT	FG	PCT	FT	PCT	OFF	TOT	AST	STL	BLK	PTS	PPG
93-94	NJ	48	386	60	.522	14	.500	28	.824	6	38	71	15	3	162	3.4
94-95	NJ	80	1435	206	.439	71	.362	40	.769	18	93	121	37	16	523	6.5
Totals		128	1821	266	.455	85	.379	68	.791	24	131	192	52	19	685	5.4

CHARLIE WARD

Team: New York Knicks
Position: Guard
Height: 6'2" **Weight:** 190
Birthdate: October 12, 1970

NBA Experience: 1 year
College: Florida St.
Acquired: 1st-round pick in 1994 draft
(26th overall)

Background: One of the most exciting college football players in recent years, Ward won the Heisman Trophy in 1993 after quarterbacking Florida State to a national championship. He also played basketball and became the Seminoles' all-time steals leader despite playing just one full season. He was bypassed in the NFL draft but was selected by the Knicks late in the first round. As a rookie, Ward played in only ten games.

Strengths: Ward is an accomplished athlete. Only a handful of people have played two college sports at such a high level. He has good speed and quickness, and his leadership ability may be the biggest asset going for him. He is a take-charge type with a lot of heart and character. Ward is a natural point guard who will get the basketball where it needs to be. He's also got defensive potential.

Weaknesses: There are many who questioned the Knicks' decision to draft Ward. He is not a good shooter, and he may also lack the playmaking ability to become an NBA regular. He did not even convert college shots at a respectable rate and will have trouble finishing against the giants of the pro game. He did not play enough college basketball to become sharp. He has had to fight through some injuries.

Analysis: Ward has a well-deserved reputation as a winner. As an NBA prospect, however, a conclusive assessment is impossible at this point. He was slowed by wrist and shoulder injuries last season, but mostly he was made to wait while New York handed the ball to its backcourt veterans. The hope is that Ward has used his first basketball-only year to prepare for his opportunity to play.

PLAYER SUMMARY

Will ....wait for his chance
Can't ....throw more spirals
Expect ....leadership skills
Don't Expect ....an accurate shot
Fantasy Value $0
Card Value ....15-35¢

COLLEGE STATISTICS

		G	FGP	FTP	APG	PPG
90-91	FSU	30	.455	.713	3.4	8.0
91-92	FSU	28	.497	.530	4.4	7.2
92-93	FSU	17	.462	.667	5.5	7.8
93-94	FSU	16	.365	.625	4.9	10.5
Totals		91	.441	.636	4.4	8.1

NBA REGULAR-SEASON STATISTICS

			FGs		3-PT FGs		FTs		Rebounds						
	G	MIN	FG	PCT	FG	PCT	FT	PCT	OFF	TOT	AST	STL	BLK	PTS	PPG
94-95 NY	10	44	4	.211	1	.100	7	.700	1	6	4	2	0	16	1.6
Totals	10	44	4	.211	1	.100	7	.700	1	6	4	2	0	16	1.6

JAMIE WATSON

Team: Utah Jazz
Position: Forward
Height: 6'7" **Weight:** 190
Birthdate: February 23, 1972

NBA Experience: 1 year
College: South Carolina
Acquired: 2nd-round pick in 1994 draft (47th overall)

Background: Watson averaged 18.1 PPG as a senior at South Carolina but was a fairly obscure player by SEC standards. He led the team in scoring as a junior and senior and was a second-team all-conference pick. Watson impressed scouts at the pre-draft all-star camps and was selected by Utah 47th overall in the 1994 draft. He saw action in 60 games as a rookie and he scored in double figures seven times.

Strengths: Watson was one of the top athletes in his draft class. He runs like the wind and can get off his feet. Watson is capable of playing the two and three spots and brings good size to the backcourt. He has the potential to produce on the boards and on defense, though he's a little raw at this stage. He made half of his shots as a rookie, which came as a pleasant surprise.

Weaknesses: While he can play two positions, small and power forward, there are some who feel Watson will not stand out at either spot. He will struggle against the more physical forwards, yet he is not the reliable shooter and ball-handler a team wants in the backcourt. He is not a good free throw shooter and was somewhat turnover-prone in his initial NBA season. He has some things to learn about pro defense.

Analysis: Watson was not expected to contribute much as a rookie on a 60-game winner, and he did not. He averaged only about 11 minutes and 3.3 points per contest last year. The biggest surprise was his field goal percentage, because Watson averaged less than 45 percent as a collegian. All in all, Utah has to be pleased with the progress of a player who did not attract much interest elsewhere.

PLAYER SUMMARY	
Will	run the floor
Can't	rely on jumpers
Expect	athletic ability
Don't Expect	early minutes
Fantasy Value	$0
Card Value	8-15¢

COLLEGE STATISTICS

		G	FGP	FTP	RPG	PPG
90-91	SC	33	.420	.568	2.5	6.0
91-92	SC	28	.440	.524	4.5	7.5
92-93	SC	27	.461	.642	5.0	14.7
93-94	SC	27	.459	.674	7.0	18.1
Totals		115	.450	.630	4.7	11.3

NBA REGULAR-SEASON STATISTICS

| | | G | MIN | FGs | | 3-PT FGs | | FTs | | Rebounds | | AST | STL | BLK | PTS | PPG |
				FG	PCT	FG	PCT	FT	PCT	OFF	TOT					
94-95	UTA	60	673	76	.500	5	.263	38	.679	16	74	59	35	11	195	3.3
Totals		60	673	76	.500	5	.263	38	.679	16	74	59	35	11	195	3.3

CLARENCE WEATHERSPOON

Team: Philadelphia 76ers
Position: Forward
Height: 6'7" **Weight:** 240
Birthdate: September 8, 1970

NBA Experience: 3 years
College: Southern Mississippi
Acquired: 1st-round pick in 1992 draft
(9th overall)

Background: Weatherspoon attended Motley High in Crawford, Mississippi, the same school that produced NFL star Jerry Rice. "Spoon" finished his college career as the all-time Southern Mississippi leader in scoring, rebounding, and blocked shots. Weatherspoon, drafted ninth in 1992, was a second-team All-Rookie choice before averaging a double-double in 1993-94. He has averaged 18-plus PPG in each of the last two seasons.

Strengths: Weatherspoon has been compared to Charles Barkley, and not without foundation. He has the same powerful build and leaping ability, plays hard at both ends, and can dominate the boards. Weatherspoon can face the basket and shoot or post up his man. He is agile, runs well, and finishes with a flourish. He also blocks shots and was second on the team in assists last season.

Weaknesses: Spoon is no Sir Charles just yet. He does not handle the ball like Barkley and he has not displayed the kind of consistency it takes to be an All-Star. Weatherspoon has not been a steady shooter from the outside and his field goal percentage is subpar. Moreover, he did not rebound nearly as well last year as he did the year before. He has expressed some discontent in Philly.

Analysis: Weatherspoon is a tremendous talent. He can score, rebound, and defend at a very high level. However, he is not the kind of talent who can get away with going at half speed. Some of his statistical decline can be attributed to the overdue improvement of center Shawn Bradley, but Weatherspoon also needs to maintain his mean streak. He's capable of dominating.

PLAYER SUMMARY	
Will	score, rebound
Can't	shoot 50 percent
Expect	explosiveness
Don't Expect	another Barkley
Fantasy Value	$30-35
Card Value	12-20¢

COLLEGE STATISTICS

		G	FGP	FTP	RPG	PPG
88-89	SMU	27	.545	.590	10.7	14.7
89-90	SMU	32	.605	.691	11.6	17.8
90-91	SMU	29	.589	.745	12.2	17.8
91-92	SMU	29	.563	.675	10.5	22.3
Totals		117	.576	.677	11.3	18.7

NBA REGULAR-SEASON STATISTICS

		G	MIN	FGs		3-PT FGs		FTs		Rebounds		AST	STL	BLK	PTS	PPG
				FG	PCT	FG	PCT	FT	PCT	OFF	TOT					
92-93	PHI	82	2654	494	.469	1	.250	291	.713	179	589	147	85	67	1280	15.6
93-94	PHI	82	3147	602	.483	4	.235	298	.693	254	832	192	100	116	1506	18.4
94-95	PHI	76	2991	543	.439	4	.190	283	.751	144	526	215	115	67	1373	18.1
Totals		240	8792	1639	.463	9	.214	872	.718	577	1947	554	300	250	4159	17.3

SPUD WEBB

Team: Atlanta Hawks
Position: Guard
Height: 5'7" **Weight:** 135
Birthdate: July 13, 1963

NBA Experience: 10 years
College: Midland; North Carolina St.
Acquired: Traded from Kings for
Tyrone Corbin, 6/95

Background: After pacing North Carolina State in assists for two straight seasons, Webb was drafted by Detroit in 1985 but signed as a free agent with Atlanta before his rookie season, when he won the NBA's Slam Dunk Contest. He spent his first six years with the Hawks and his last four in Sacramento. Webb was the league's top free throw shooter (.934) in 1994-95 before being reacquired by the Hawks in June.

Strengths: Webb overcomes his small stature by playing big. Almost everything he does starts with his quickness. He hits jumpers with 3-point range, sinks his free throws, and has scored in double figures the last five years. He's a great leaper who finishes breaks with slams. Webb has improved his playmaking.

Weaknesses: For obvious reasons, Webb is always going to be susceptible to being posted up and shot over by bigger players. He has never been a great defensive player or prolific pickpocket, nor has he ranked among the league's first-rate distributors. He'll take his share of bad shots.

Analysis: Webb played very well at times for the Kings, but the fact remains that he is not a point guard who raises his teammates' level of play to new heights. Webb will no longer be asked to log starter's minutes. Mookie Blaylock is the premier point guard in Atlanta and Webb will serve as his backup.

PLAYER SUMMARY	
Will	overcome his size
Can't	defend like Muggsy
Expect	10-plus PPG
Don't Expect	10 APG
Fantasy Value	$1-3
Card Value	7-12¢

COLLEGE STATISTICS

		G	FGP	FTP	APG	PPG
81-82	MID	38	.515	.781	—	20.8
82-83	MID	35	.445	.774	—	14.6
83-84	NCST	33	.459	.761	6.0	9.8
84-85	NCST	33	.481	.761	5.3	11.1
Totals		139	.479	.773	5.7	14.3

NBA REGULAR-SEASON STATISTICS

				FGs		3-PT FGs		FTs		Rebounds						
		G	MIN	FG	PCT	FG	PCT	FT	PCT	OFF	TOT	AST	STL	BLK	PTS	PPG
85-86	ATL	79	1229	199	.483	2	.182	216	.785	27	123	337	82	5	616	7.8
86-87	ATL	33	532	71	.438	1	.167	80	.762	6	60	167	34	2	223	6.8
87-88	ATL	82	1347	191	.475	1	.053	107	.817	16	146	337	63	11	490	6.0
88-89	ATL	81	1219	133	.459	1	.045	52	.867	21	123	284	70	6	319	3.9
89-90	ATL	82	2184	294	.477	1	.053	162	.871	38	201	477	105	12	751	9.2
90-91	ATL	75	2197	359	.447	54	.321	231	.868	41	174	417	118	6	1003	13.4
91-92	SAC	77	2724	448	.445	73	.367	262	.859	30	223	547	125	24	1231	16.0
92-93	SAC	69	2335	342	.433	37	.274	279	.851	44	193	481	104	6	1000	14.5
93-94	SAC	79	2567	373	.460	55	.335	204	.813	44	222	528	93	23	1005	12.7
94-95	SAC	76	2458	302	.438	48	.331	226	.934	29	174	468	75	8	878	11.6
Totals		733	18792	2712	.454	273	.307	1819	.846	296	1639	4043	869	103	7516	10.3

CHRIS WEBBER

Team: Washington Bullets
Position: Forward/Center
Height: 6'10" **Weight:** 250
Birthdate: March 1, 1973
NBA Experience: 2 years

College: Michigan
Acquired: Traded from Warriors for Tom Gugliotta and three future 1st-round picks, 11/94

Background: The cornerstone of Michigan's Fab Five class, Webber led the Wolverines to back-to-back appearances in the NCAA championship game. He was the first player to make the All-Final Four team as a freshman and sophomore. The top pick in the 1993 draft, he was traded from Orlando to Golden State on draft day and won Rookie of the Year honors. He was traded again last season to Washington, where he averaged 20.1 PPG.

Strengths: Webber has been a dominant inside player at every level. His strength and quickness give him a great edge around the basket, and he runs the floor like a guard. Webber has soft but strong hands and uses them to dominate the offensive boards. His dunks make the highlight packages. Webber also blocks a lot of shots, finds open men, leads the break, and plays the game with abandon.

Weaknesses: There are scorers and there are shooters. Webber is 100 percent the former. He is one of the worst free throw shooters in basketball despite getting to the line almost five times a game. He is not a reliable 3-point shooter (.276 last season), but that didn't stop him from launching 145 long ones. He's been cast as a bad apple for his run-ins with former coach Don Nelson.

Analysis: Webber was destined to be an NBA star from the time he was a Detroit Country Day prep All-American. He is blessed with skills that most others can only wish for. In the near future, he is likely to emerge as an All-Star regular. He dislocated his left shoulder last season (ironically, in his first game back in Oakland) and missed more than a month of action.

PLAYER SUMMARY	
Will	be an All-Star
Can't	shoot free throws
Expect	triple-doubles
Don't Expect	less than 20 PPG
Fantasy Value	$65-70
Card Value	30-60¢

COLLEGE STATISTICS

		G	FGP	FTP	RPG	PPG
91-92	MICH	34	.556	.496	10.0	15.5
92-93	MICH	36	.619	.552	10.1	19.2
Totals		70	.589	.530	10.0	17.4

NBA REGULAR-SEASON STATISTICS

		G	MIN	FGs FG	FGs PCT	3-PT FGs FG	3-PT FGs PCT	FTs FT	FTs PCT	Rebounds OFF	Rebounds TOT	AST	STL	BLK	PTS	PPG
93-94	GS	76	2438	572	.552	0	.000	189	.532	305	694	272	93	164	1333	17.5
94-95	WAS	54	2067	464	.495	40	.276	117	.502	200	518	256	83	85	1085	20.1
Totals		130	4505	1036	.525	40	.252	306	.520	505	1212	528	176	249	2418	18.6

BILL WENNINGTON

Team: Chicago Bulls
Position: Center
Height: 7'0" **Weight:** 260
Birthdate: April 26, 1963

NBA Experience: 8 years
College: St. John's
Acquired: Signed as a free agent, 9/93

Background: Wennington improved his scoring and rebounding numbers in each of his four years at St. John's, where he teamed with Walter Berry and Chris Mullin. The Montreal native spent his first five pro years in a reserve role in Dallas before stints with Sacramento and in the Italian League. He's rejoined the reserve ranks for two years with Chicago.

Strengths: Wennington has good size but has always had the ability to pull his offensive game away from the basket. He is an accurate jump-shooter from medium range. He also hits his free throws, runs the floor well for a center, and is willing to fill whatever role he is given. He's a team player all the way.

Weaknesses: For low-post play, Wennington is not your man on either end of the court. He is more comfortable facing the bucket on offense and he possesses neither the size nor the know-how to wear down his man with strong defense. He's below average in many respects for a seven-footer, including rebounding and shot-blocking.

Analysis: Wennington has given the Bulls some solid play off the bench at times over the last two years. However, his time is usually very limited. He was the team's No. 3 center for most of the 1994-95 season and saw only about 13 minutes per outing. His best attributes are his work ethic and his unselfishness.

PLAYER SUMMARY	
Will	play hard
Can't	defend star centers
Expect	a role-player
Don't Expect	starts
Fantasy Value	$0
Card Value	5-7¢

COLLEGE STATISTICS

		G	FGP	FTP	RPG	PPG
81-82	STJ	30	.435	.676	4.2	3.2
82-83	STJ	33	.605	.698	4.4	5.5
83-84	STJ	26	.593	.675	5.7	11.7
84-85	STJ	35	.602	.816	6.4	12.5
Totals		124	.579	.738	5.2	8.2

NBA REGULAR-SEASON STATISTICS

		G	MIN	FGs FG	FGs PCT	3-PT FGs FG	3-PT FGs PCT	FTs FT	FTs PCT	Rebounds OFF	Rebounds TOT	AST	STL	BLK	PTS	PPG
85-86	DAL	56	562	72	.471	0	.000	45	.726	32	132	21	11	22	189	3.4
86-87	DAL	58	560	56	.424	0	.000	45	.750	53	129	24	13	10	157	2.7
87-88	DAL	30	125	25	.510	1	.500	12	.632	14	39	4	5	9	63	2.1
88-89	DAL	65	1074	119	.433	1	.111	61	.744	82	286	46	16	35	300	4.6
89-90	DAL	60	814	105	.449	0	.000	60	.800	64	198	41	20	21	270	4.5
90-91	SAC	77	1455	181	.436	1	.200	74	.787	101	340	69	46	59	437	5.7
93-94	CHI	76	1371	235	.488	0	.000	72	.818	117	353	70	43	29	542	7.1
94-95	CHI	73	956	156	.492	0	.000	51	.810	64	190	40	22	17	363	5.0
Totals		495	6917	949	.461	3	.094	420	.773	527	1667	315	176	202	2321	4.7

DAVID WESLEY

Team: Boston Celtics
Position: Guard
Height: 6'0" **Weight:** 190
Birthdate: November 14, 1970

NBA Experience: 2 years
College: Temple J.C.; Baylor
Acquired: Signed as a free agent, 7/94

Background: Wesley was named the Southwest Conference's Player of the Year as a senior at Baylor after averaging 20.9 points, 4.7 assists, and 4.9 rebounds a game. Undrafted in 1992, he was cut by the Rockets and made the CBA All-Rookie Team. He spent his first NBA season as a backup to Kenny Anderson with New Jersey in 1993-94, and he made 36 starts for Boston before knee surgery ended his 1994-95 season.

Strengths: Wesley is a versatile guard who brings a nice mix of shooting and defense to the floor. He was impressive in New Jersey mostly for his hustling brand of defense, but he lit up the nets at about a 43-percent rate from 3-point range with the Celtics last season. He also came up with more than a steal and a half per game in Boston before his February knee surgery. His enthusiasm is contagious.

Weaknesses: Wesley can play both guard positions, but there are drawbacks in both cases. A shooting guard in college and the CBA, he does not have the drive-and-dish mentality of the better point men in the league. As a two guard, however, he is undersized and does not do enough offensively. Wesley does not create much off the dribble and has not shown a consistent ability to score inside the 3-point arc.

Analysis: Boston did not expect Wesley to emerge as a starter when they signed him during the summer of 1994, but stranger things have happened. His hard-working defense and long-range shooting made him a fine addition to the Celtics until he injured his knee. With his ability to play both guard spots, Wesley would seem to make a decent third guard who could spark a team off the bench.

PLAYER SUMMARY	
Will	defend aggressively
Can't	drive and dish
Expect	3-point shooting
Don't Expect	stardom
Fantasy Value	$0
Card Value	8-12¢

COLLEGE STATISTICS

		G	FGP	FTP	RPG	PPG
89-90	BAYL	18	.455	.836	2.2	11.6
90-91	BAYL	26	.424	.839	2.9	16.5
91-92	BAYL	28	.450	.817	4.9	20.9
Totals		72	.441	.828	3.5	17.0

NBA REGULAR-SEASON STATISTICS

				FGs		3-PT FGs		FTs		Rebounds						
		G	MIN	FG	PCT	FG	PCT	FT	PCT	OFF	TOT	AST	STL	BLK	PTS	PPG
93-94	NJ	60	542	64	.368	11	.234	44	.830	10	44	123	38	4	183	3.1
94-95	BOS	51	1380	128	.409	51	.429	71	.755	31	117	266	82	9	378	7.4
Totals		111	1922	192	.394	62	.373	115	.782	41	161	389	120	13	561	5.1

DOUG WEST

Team: Minnesota Timberwolves
Position: Guard
Height: 6'6" **Weight:** 200
Birthdate: May 27, 1967

NBA Experience: 6 years
College: Villanova
Acquired: 2nd-round pick in 1989 draft (38th overall)

Background: West was a four-year starter at Villanova, finishing his career third on the school's all-time scoring list. He served as a reserve for Minnesota in each of his first two NBA seasons before being promoted to the starting lineup in 1991-92. He led the Timberwolves in scoring with a career-high 19.3 PPG in 1992-93, but his scoring average has declined in the two seasons since.

Strengths: West is an explosive player with a sweet jumper and fabulous finishing ability. His athletic dunks are some of the best in the league. He can be lethal from 18 feet and in. He is also a solid free throw shooter. West is a dedicated, hard-working player who goes after his man on defense. He can play small forward or big guard.

Weaknesses: One of the main knocks on West has been his reluctance to take the ball aggressively to the basket in the halfcourt game. He has the quickness and athletic ability to get through traffic for jams and more trips to the line. He's not as potent off the dribble as he is catching and shooting. He fouls frequently and he's not a gifted passer.

Analysis: West has the distinction of being the lone holdover from the original Timberwolves team. Thus, he has plied his trade in a quiet, humble, and relatively obscure fashion despite putting up some decent numbers. Many figured Donyell Marshall would take his starting small-forward spot last season, but it never happened and Marshall was traded.

PLAYER SUMMARY	
Will	dunk in transition
Can't	save the Wolves
Expect	spot-up shooting
Don't Expect	national recognition
Fantasy Value	$6-8
Card Value	5-8¢

COLLEGE STATISTICS

		G	FGP	FTP	RPG	PPG
85-86	VILL	37	.515	.682	3.7	10.2
86-87	VILL	31	.479	.729	4.9	15.2
87-88	VILL	37	.497	.724	4.9	15.8
88-89	VILL	33	.463	.720	4.9	18.4
Totals		138	.486	.716	4.6	14.8

NBA REGULAR-SEASON STATISTICS

		G	MIN	FGs FG	FGs PCT	3-PT FGs FG	3-PT FGs PCT	FTs FT	FTs PCT	Rebounds OFF	Rebounds TOT	AST	STL	BLK	PTS	PPG
89-90	MIN	52	378	53	.393	3	.273	26	.813	24	70	18	10	6	135	2.6
90-91	MIN	75	824	118	.480	0	.000	58	.690	56	136	48	35	23	294	3.9
91-92	MIN	80	2540	463	.518	4	.174	186	.805	107	257	281	66	26	1116	13.9
92-93	MIN	80	3104	646	.517	2	.087	249	.841	89	247	235	85	21	1543	19.3
93-94	MIN	72	2182	434	.487	1	.125	187	.810	61	231	172	65	24	1056	14.7
94-95	MIN	71	2328	351	.461	11	.180	206	.837	60	227	185	65	24	919	12.9
Totals		430	11356	2065	.494	21	.165	912	.814	397	1168	939	326	124	5063	11.8

MARK WEST

Team: Detroit Pistons
Position: Center
Height: 6'10" **Weight:** 246
Birthdate: November 5, 1960

NBA Experience: 12 years
College: Old Dominion
Acquired: Traded from Suns for 1996 and 1999 2nd-round picks, 8/94

Background: West ended his college career at Old Dominion as the third-leading shot-blocker in NCAA history. He played with Dallas, Milwaukee, and Cleveland in his first five years before landing with Phoenix for six-plus seasons. West led the league in field goal accuracy in 1989-90. He spent the 1994-95 season in Detroit after a trade.

Strengths: West is a workhorse who blocks shots, rebounds, and plays tough interior defense. He rarely takes a bad shot. He hasn't shot below 54 percent since his rookie year. An iron man, West saw his streak of 521 consecutive games played snapped last year because of an injured knee.

Weaknesses: Foul trouble follows West. He was disqualified from eight of his 67 games last season. A very limited offensive player, he has averaged double figures in scoring only once in his 12-year career. West can't dribble or pass and he's a dismal free throw shooter.

Analysis: West is an old pro who helps his team with defense and hard work. His amazing health record was finally spotted last year when he required surgery on his left knee. Offensively, his game has always been ailing. Still a valuable role-player, he started all but nine of his games last season.

PLAYER SUMMARY	
Will	block shots
Can't	hit free throws
Expect	rebounds, defense
Don't Expect	10 PPG
Fantasy Value	$0
Card Value	5-8¢

COLLEGE STATISTICS

		G	FGP	FTP	RPG	PPG
79-80	OD	30	.475	.370	7.1	4.8
80-81	OD	28	.527	.578	10.3	10.9
81-82	OD	30	.610	.531	10.0	15.7
82-83	OD	29	.569	.491	10.8	14.4
Totals		117	.559	.514	9.5	11.4

NBA REGULAR-SEASON STATISTICS

		G	MIN	FGs FG	FGs PCT	3-PT FGs FG	3-PT FGs PCT	FTs FT	FTs PCT	Rebounds OFF	Rebounds TOT	AST	STL	BLK	PTS	PPG
83-84	DAL	34	202	15	.357	0	.000	7	.318	19	46	13	1	15	37	1.1
84-85	MIL/CLE	66	888	106	.546	0	.000	43	.494	90	251	15	13	49	255	3.9
85-86	CLE	67	1172	113	.541	0	.000	54	.524	97	322	20	27	62	280	4.2
86-87	CLE	78	1333	209	.543	0	.000	89	.514	126	339	41	22	81	507	6.5
87-88	CLE/PHO	83	2098	316	.551	0	.000	170	.596	165	523	74	47	147	802	9.7
88-89	PHO	82	2019	243	.653	0	.000	108	.535	167	551	39	35	187	594	7.2
89-90	PHO	82	2399	331	.625	0	.000	199	.691	212	728	45	36	184	861	10.5
90-91	PHO	82	1957	247	.647	0	.000	135	.655	171	564	37	32	161	629	7.7
91-92	PHO	82	1436	196	.632	0	.000	109	.637	134	372	22	14	81	501	6.1
92-93	PHO	82	1558	175	.614	0	.000	86	.518	153	458	29	16	103	436	5.3
93-94	PHO	82	1236	162	.566	0	.000	58	.500	112	295	33	31	109	382	4.7
94-95	DET	67	1543	217	.556	0	.000	66	.478	160	408	18	27	102	500	7.5
Totals		887	17841	2330	.589	0	.000	1124	.574	1606	4857	386	301	1281	5784	6.5

GERALD WILKINS

Team: Vancouver Grizzlies
Position: Guard
Height: 6'6" **Weight:** 218
Birthdate: September 11, 1963
NBA Experience: 9 years

College: Moberly Area; Tennessee-Chattanooga
Acquired: Selected from Cavaliers in 1995 expansion draft

Background: Dominique's little brother, Gerald slam-dunked his way to three outstanding collegiate seasons at Tennessee-Chattanooga. He spent his first seven seasons with the Knicks before Cleveland picked him up in 1992-93. He logged 80 or more games in eight of his first nine pro campaigns before a ruptured Achilles tendon cost him the entire 1994-95 season. Vancouver selected him in the expansion draft.

Strengths: Wilkins is a fine defensive player because of his quickness, strength, leaping ability, and long arms. He also has some of his big brother's offensive explosiveness, although Gerald has not been nearly as consistent as Dominique. He drives the entire lane with a single stride and is a dangerous 3-point shooter.

Weaknesses: Wilkins is a streaky shooter. He's capable of shooting the lights out one night and going 1-for-12 the next. He has tended to try the dramatic during his career instead of making sound decisions with the ball.

Analysis: Wilkins had come a long way before his injury in the 1994 preseason forced him to sit out a year. He is respected league-wide for his defense and he takes great pride in it. Wilkins has also worked to improve his jump shot. Dominique suffered the same injury in 1992 and made an impressive return. Little brother may do likewise.

PLAYER SUMMARY

Will	get in your face
Can't	outscore his brother
Expect	scoring binges
Don't Expect	.500 shooting
Fantasy Value	$5-7
Card Value	7-10¢

COLLEGE STATISTICS

		G	FGP	FTP	RPG	PPG
81-82	MA	39	.551	.770	5.9	18.5
82-83	T-C	30	.483	.661	3.8	12.6
83-84	T-C	23	.542	.695	4.0	17.3
84-85	T-C	32	.519	.632	4.6	21.0
Totals		124	.526	.685	4.7	17.5

NBA REGULAR-SEASON STATISTICS

		G	MIN	FGs FG	FGs PCT	3-PT FGs FG	3-PT FGs PCT	FTs FT	FTs PCT	Rebounds OFF	Rebounds TOT	AST	STL	BLK	PTS	PPG
85-86	NY	81	2025	437	.468	7	.280	132	.557	92	208	161	68	9	1013	12.5
86-87	NY	80	2758	633	.486	26	.351	235	.701	120	294	354	88	18	1527	19.1
87-88	NY	81	2703	591	.446	39	.302	191	.786	106	270	326	90	22	1412	17.4
88-89	NY	81	2414	462	.451	51	.297	186	.756	95	244	274	115	22	1161	14.3
89-90	NY	82	2609	472	.457	39	.312	208	.803	133	371	330	95	21	1191	14.5
90-91	NY	68	2164	380	.473	9	.209	169	.820	78	207	275	82	23	938	13.8
91-92	NY	82	2344	431	.447	38	.352	116	.730	74	206	219	76	17	1016	12.4
92-93	CLE	80	2079	361	.453	16	.276	152	.840	74	214	183	78	18	890	11.1
93-94	CLE	82	2768	446	.457	84	.396	194	.776	106	303	255	105	38	1170	14.3
Totals		717	21864	4213	.460	309	.327	1583	.748	878	2317	2377	797	188	10318	14.4

BRIAN WILLIAMS

Team: Denver Nuggets
Position: Forward/Center
Height: 6'11" **Weight:** 260
Birthdate: April 6, 1969
NBA Experience: 4 years

College: Maryland; Arizona
Acquired: Traded from Magic for Todd Lichti, Anthony Cook, and a 1994 2nd-round pick, 8/93

Background: Williams, who played at three different high schools, had a terrific freshman season at Maryland but then transferred to Arizona. The Wildcats went 53-14 in his two seasons there. Drafted tenth by Orlando, Williams missed most of his second season because of a bout with clinical depression and a broken hand. He has fared much better in two seasons since a trade to Denver in August 1993.

Strengths: Williams has an abundance of physical gifts. He is quick, jumps well, and runs the floor like a small forward. He rebounds and plays tough defense both in the post and on the perimeter. Williams owns a soft touch in the paint and is solid with either hand. He has a nice little hook shot that's tough to stop. He shoots for a high percentage.

Weaknesses: Williams is tough to figure. He's been pretty successful since his second-year emotional troubles, but he still has not gained great consistency. He has missed many games due to injury already in his career, including 19 last season. He's not a good free throw shooter, he picks up a lot of fouls (he fouled out seven times last season), and he does not do much passing.

Analysis: The Nuggets have been very pleased with the play of Williams, who was acquired two years ago for two players they deemed expendable and a second-round draft choice. He has been fully capable of giving solid minutes off the bench with his defense, inside scoring, and hustle. Further improvement, more consistency, and better health could make Williams a starter before long.

PLAYER SUMMARY	
Will	toss in hooks
Can't	stay healthy
Expect	tough defense
Don't Expect	shooting range
Fantasy Value	$2-4
Card Value	8-12¢

COLLEGE STATISTICS

		G	FGP	FTP	RPG	PPG
87-88	MARY	29	.600	.671	6.1	12.5
89-90	ARIZ	32	.553	.727	5.7	10.6
90-91	ARIZ	35	.619	.673	7.8	14.0
Totals		96	.594	.691	6.6	12.4

NBA REGULAR-SEASON STATISTICS

		G	MIN	FGs FG	FGs PCT	3-PT FGs FG	3-PT FGs PCT	FTs FT	FTs PCT	Rebounds OFF	Rebounds TOT	AST	STL	BLK	PTS	PPG
91-92	ORL	48	905	171	.528	0	.000	95	.669	115	272	33	41	53	437	9.1
92-93	ORL	21	240	40	.513	0	.000	16	.800	24	56	5	14	17	96	4.6
93-94	DEN	80	1507	251	.541	0	.000	137	.649	138	446	50	49	87	639	8.0
94-95	DEN	63	1261	196	.589	0	.000	106	.654	98	298	53	38	43	498	7.9
Totals		212	3913	658	.549	0	.000	354	.662	375	1072	141	142	200	1670	7.9

BUCK WILLIAMS

Team: Portland Trail Blazers
Position: Forward
Height: 6'8" **Weight:** 225
Birthdate: March 8, 1960

NBA Experience: 14 years
College: Maryland
Acquired: Traded from Nets for Sam Bowie and a 1989 1st-round pick, 6/89

Background: Williams turned pro after his junior season at Maryland, was named 1982 NBA Rookie of the Year, and played in three All-Star Games as a Net. He won the NBA's field goal-percentage crown in 1990-91 and 1991-92 with Portland. Williams has played in 80-plus games in 12 of his 14 seasons.

Strengths: For rebounds and low-post defense, few players of his time have been as steady as Williams. Offensively, he converts short jumpers and hooks and never takes a bad shot. He has never shot less than 51 percent from the field. He brings a great attitude to work.

Weaknesses: Williams is a below-average passer and ball-handler and a poor free throw shooter. He does not score or dominate the boards like he used to, though he can still get it done.

Analysis: Williams, one of the hardest-working men the game has known, continues to lead by example. His businesslike approach is contagious. He started all 82 games again last season and became the eighth player in NBA history to record 15,000 points and 12,000 rebounds. He's got Hall of Fame-type credentials.

PLAYER SUMMARY	
Will	rebound, defend
Can't	score like he used to
Expect	a consummate pro
Don't Expect	missed games
Fantasy Value	$2-4
Card Value	5-8¢

COLLEGE STATISTICS

		G	FGP	FTP	RPG	PPG
78-79	MARY	30	.583	.550	10.8	10.0
79-80	MARY	24	.606	.664	10.1	15.5
80-81	MARY	31	.647	.637	11.7	15.5
Totals		85	.615	.623	10.9	13.6

NBA REGULAR-SEASON STATISTICS

		G	MIN	FGs FG	FGs PCT	3-PT FGs FG	3-PT FGs PCT	FTs FT	FTs PCT	Rebounds OFF	Rebounds TOT	AST	STL	BLK	PTS	PPG
81-82	NJ	82	2825	513	.582	0	.000	242	.624	347	1005	107	84	84	1268	15.5
82-83	NJ	82	2961	536	.588	0	.000	324	.620	365	1027	125	91	110	1396	17.0
83-84	NJ	81	3003	495	.535	0	.000	284	.570	355	1000	130	81	125	1274	15.7
84-85	NJ	82	3182	577	.530	1	.250	336	.625	323	1005	167	63	110	1491	18.2
85-86	NJ	82	3070	500	.523	0	.000	301	.676	329	986	131	73	96	1301	15.9
86-87	NJ	82	2976	521	.557	0	.000	430	.731	322	1023	129	78	91	1472	18.0
87-88	NJ	70	2637	466	.560	1	1.000	346	.668	298	834	109	68	44	1279	18.3
88-89	NJ	74	2446	373	.531	0	.000	213	.666	249	696	78	61	36	959	13.0
89-90	POR	82	2801	413	.548	0	.000	250	.706	250	800	116	69	39	1114	13.6
90-91	POR	80	2582	358	.602	0	.000	217	.705	227	751	97	47	47	933	11.7
91-92	POR	80	2519	340	.604	0	.000	221	.754	260	704	108	62	41	901	11.3
92-93	POR	82	2498	270	.511	0	.000	138	.645	232	690	75	81	61	678	8.3
93-94	POR	81	2636	291	.555	0	.000	201	.679	315	843	80	58	47	783	9.7
94-95	POR	82	2422	309	.512	1	.500	138	.673	251	669	78	67	69	757	9.2
Totals		1122	38558	5962	.552	3	.115	3679	.664	4123	12033	1530	983	1000	15606	13.9

JAYSON WILLIAMS

Unrestricted Free Agent
Last Team: New Jersey Nets
Position: Forward
Height: 6'10" **Weight:** 245
Birthdate: February 22, 1968

NBA Experience: 5 years
College: St. John's
Acquired: Traded from 76ers for conditional draft picks, 10/92

Background: After guiding St. John's to an NIT title in 1989 as a junior (he was tourney MVP), Williams broke his foot halfway through his senior season. He was drafted by Phoenix in 1990 but spent his five seasons with Philadelphia and New Jersey because of trades. His career has been highlighted mainly by time on the injured list, on the bench, and in the doghouse.

Strengths: Williams is blessed with good athletic skills for a player his size, and he also sculpts his body in the weight room. He is a very good offensive rebounder who gets a lot of his points on putbacks. He can also be a factor on the defensive glass, and he has improved his low-post moves. He can play center in a pinch.

Weaknesses: If his maturity and work ethic have been questioned, it is with reason. The fun-loving Williams has been arrested for allegedly firing a gun in a parking lot after a game and is known for his carousing. He takes bad shots, his range is limited, he's dismal from the free throw line, and he's not a consistent defender.

Analysis: After five years in the league, it is safe to call Williams a classic underachiever. He has yet to average even five points per game in a season in spite of his physical ability. Williams has spent most of his career on the bench because he's a liability in several areas. The Nets have tried to trade him, but what could they get?

PLAYER SUMMARY	
Will	hit offensive boards
Can't	avoid controversy
Expect	reserve minutes
Don't Expect	commitment
Fantasy Value	$1
Card Value	7-10¢

COLLEGE STATISTICS

		G	FGP	FTP	RPG	PPG
87-88	STJ	28	.513	.600	5.1	9.9
88-89	STJ	31	.573	.702	7.9	19.5
89-90	STJ	13	.534	.613	7.8	14.6
Totals		72	.550	.652	6.8	14.9

NBA REGULAR-SEASON STATISTICS

				FGs		3-PT FGs		FTs		Rebounds						
		G	MIN	FG	PCT	FG	PCT	FT	PCT	OFF	TOT	AST	STL	BLK	PTS	PPG
90-91	PHI	52	508	72	.447	1	.500	37	.661	41	111	16	9	6	182	3.5
91-92	PHI	50	646	75	.364	0	.000	56	.636	62	145	12	20	20	206	4.1
92-93	NJ	12	139	21	.457	0	.000	7	.389	22	41	0	4	4	49	4.1
93-94	NJ	70	877	125	.427	0	.000	72	.605	109	263	26	17	36	322	4.6
94-95	NJ	75	982	149	.461	0	.000	65	.533	179	425	35	26	33	363	4.8
Totals		259	3152	442	.430	1	.143	237	.588	413	985	89	76	99	1122	4.3

JOHN WILLIAMS

Team: Cleveland Cavaliers
Position: Forward/Center
Height: 6'11" **Weight:** 250
Birthdate: August 9, 1962

NBA Experience: 9 years
College: Tulane
Acquired: 2nd-round pick in 1985 draft (45th overall)

Background: Williams's involvement in an alleged point-fixing scandal at Tulane rocked the college basketball world in the mid-1980s. He paced the Green Wave in scoring three of his four years. Williams has played all nine pro seasons with Cleveland, going from All-Rookie performer to top reserve to starter. He averaged 12.6 PPG last season.

Strengths: Williams can shoot, go hard to the basket, draw fouls, block shots, crash the boards, and muscle people off the ball. His ability to play shut-down defense at multiple positions may be his greatest asset. Williams gives his team a lift with his aggressive, unselfish play.

Weaknesses: Williams almost never goes to his left because that hand is shaky. This fact is not lost on defenders. "Hot Rod" is not a steady free throw shooter and his field goal accuracy also took a dive last year. At times, he is too unselfish. He charges about $4 million a season.

Analysis: A lot of coaches would love to have a Williams—someone who works hard on both ends of the floor, even when he's having an "off" night. He tries to earn his paycheck. He can defend just about any forward and has blocked more than 100 shots in eight of his nine pro seasons. Williams consistently gives you between 11 and 14 PPG.

PLAYER SUMMARY

Will ....play defense
Can't ....use his left
Expect ....11-14 PPG
Don't Expect ....selfishness
Fantasy Value $10-13
Card Value ....8-12¢

COLLEGE STATISTICS

		G	FGP	FTP	RPG	PPG
81-82	TUL	28	.584	.662	7.2	14.8
82-83	TUL	31	.476	.703	5.4	12.4
83-84	TUL	28	.569	.761	7.9	19.4
84-85	TUL	28	.566	.774	7.8	17.8
Totals		115	.549	.731	7.0	16.0

NBA REGULAR-SEASON STATISTICS

		G	MIN	FGs FG	FGs PCT	3-PT FGs FG	3-PT FGs PCT	FTs FT	FTs PCT	Rebounds OFF	Rebounds TOT	AST	STL	BLK	PTS	PPG
86-87	CLE	80	2714	435	.485	0	.000	298	.745	222	629	154	58	167	1168	14.6
87-88	CLE	77	2106	316	.477	0	.000	211	.756	159	506	103	61	145	843	10.9
88-89	CLE	82	2125	356	.509	1	.250	235	.748	173	477	108	77	134	948	11.6
89-90	CLE	82	2776	528	.493	0	.000	325	.739	220	663	168	86	167	1381	16.8
90-91	CLE	43	1293	199	.463	0	.000	107	.652	111	290	100	36	69	505	11.7
91-92	CLE	80	2432	341	.503	0	.000	270	.752	228	607	196	60	182	952	11.9
92-93	CLE	67	2055	263	.470	0	.000	212	.716	127	415	152	48	105	738	11.0
93-94	CLE	76	2660	394	.478	0	.000	252	.728	207	575	193	78	130	1040	13.7
94-95	CLE	74	2641	366	.452	1	.200	196	.685	173	507	192	83	101	929	12.6
Totals		661	20802	3198	.482	2	.125	2106	.730	1620	4669	1366	587	1200	8504	12.9

LORENZO WILLIAMS

Team: Dallas Mavericks
Position: Forward/Center
Height: 6'9" **Weight:** 218
Birthdate: July 15, 1969

NBA Experience: 3 years
College: Stetson
Acquired: Signed as a free agent, 2/94

Background: Williams played two seasons at Polk Community College in Florida before becoming the all-time Trans America Athletic Conference leader in blocked shots at Stetson. He was not drafted in 1991, so he played in the USBL, CBA, and Global Basketball Association before reaching the NBA. Williams played with three teams in each of his first two NBA seasons before starting at center for Dallas in 1994-95.

Strengths: Shot-blocking and rebounding have helped Williams arrive in the NBA. He was 12th in the league in swats last season with 1.8 per game and 20th in rebounding at 8.4 per contest. Not bad for a guy who was in the "minors" not long ago. He has good athletic ability and timing. He works hard on defense and can live with a limited role. He's happy to be in the NBA.

Weaknesses: Everything having to do with offense falls into this category. No one in the league is a worse free throw shooter (.376) and no starting center does less in the scoring column. Williams knows his shooting range is limited to putbacks, so that's about all he does. He's undersized for a center and he commits too many fouls trying to make up for it.

Analysis: Williams reminds you of a smaller Charles Jones. His offense is nowhere near NBA-caliber, but he has made an impression with shot-blocking and rebounding. It says a great deal about his character and work ethic that Williams started 81 games last season, just one year removed from his travels. It also says that the Mavericks have enough scorers already.

PLAYER SUMMARY	
Will	block shots
Can't	hit a free throw
Expect	defensive hustle
Don't Expect	scoring
Fantasy Value	$1
Card Value	5-8¢

COLLEGE STATISTICS

		G	FGP	FTP	RPG	PPG
89-90	STET	32	.520	.295	8.4	7.8
90-91	STET	31	.540	.667	10.1	9.2
Totals		63	.530	.484	9.2	8.5

NBA REGULAR-SEASON STATISTICS

		G	MIN	FGs FG	FGs PCT	3-PT FGs FG	3-PT FGs PCT	FTs FT	FTs PCT	Rebounds OFF	Rebounds TOT	AST	STL	BLK	PTS	PPG
92-93	CHA/ORL/BOS	27	179	17	.472	0	.000	2	.286	17	55	5	5	17	36	1.3
93-94	ORL/CHA/DAL	38	716	49	.445	0	.000	12	.429	95	217	25	18	46	110	2.9
94-95	DAL	82	2383	145	.477	0	.000	38	.376	291	690	124	52	148	328	4.0
Totals		147	3278	211	.469	0	.000	52	.382	403	962	154	75	211	474	3.2

MICHEAL WILLIAMS

Team: Minnesota Timberwolves
Position: Guard
Height: 6'2" **Weight:** 175
Birthdate: July 23, 1966
NBA Experience: 7 years

College: Baylor
Acquired: Traded from Pacers with
Chuck Person for Pooh Richardson
and Sam Mitchell, 9/92

Background: Williams, a two-time all-league selection at Baylor, has played for a slew of pro teams. A member of Detroit's championship team in 1988-89, he spent the next season with Phoenix, Dallas, Charlotte, and the CBA's Rapid City Thrillers. He became one of the NBA's top thieves in Indiana. He was Minnesota's leader in steals and assists for two years before missing all but one game last season with a heel injury.

Strengths: Williams has blistering speed, quick hands, and improved playmaking. He possesses a lightning-quick first step and an above-average pull-up jumper. He has been a hustling defender who comes up with a lot of steals. He set a league record by making 97 consecutive free throws.

Weaknesses: Williams is not the defensive player his numbers say he is. He gets beaten routinely by his man and comes up with steals because he gambles for them. He is not a consistent outside shooter and there are a lot more effective set-up men in the game. Some call him selfish.

Analysis: Williams has been a statistical success for much of his NBA career, but the fact remains he has yet to lead a team to any degree of success in the win column. With the Timberwolves, he is not the only one to blame. Williams required surgery for a torn tendon in his left heel after just one game last season. He'll be back.

PLAYER SUMMARY	
Will	swipe the ball
Can't	rescue the T'Wolves
Expect	great quickness
Don't Expect	missed free throws
Fantasy Value	$12-15
Card Value	5-8¢

COLLEGE STATISTICS

		G	FGP	FTP	APG	PPG
84-85	BAYL	28	.487	.793	2.4	14.6
85-86	BAYL	22	.462	.806	2.7	13.0
86-87	BAYL	31	.475	.714	5.1	17.2
87-88	BAYL	34	.505	.697	5.4	18.4
Totals		115	.485	.738	4.0	16.1

NBA REGULAR-SEASON STATISTICS

		G	MIN	FGs		3-PT FGs		FTs		Rebounds						
				FG	PCT	FG	PCT	FT	PCT	OFF	TOT	AST	STL	BLK	PTS	PPG
88-89	DET	49	358	47	.364	2	.222	31	.660	9	27	70	13	3	127	2.6
89-90	PHO/CHA	28	329	60	.504	0	.000	36	.783	12	32	81	22	1	156	5.6
90-91	IND	73	1706	261	.499	1	.143	290	.879	49	176	348	150	17	813	11.1
91-92	IND	79	2750	404	.490	8	.242	372	.871	73	282	647	233	22	1188	15.0
92-93	MIN	76	2661	353	.446	26	.243	419	.907	84	273	661	165	23	1151	15.1
93-94	MIN	71	2206	314	.457	10	.222	333	.839	67	221	512	118	24	971	13.7
94-95	MIN	1	28	1	.250	0	.000	4	.800	0	1	3	2	0	6	6.0
Totals		377	10038	1440	.468	47	.230	1485	.866	294	1012	2322	703	90	4412	11.7

MONTY WILLIAMS

Team: New York Knicks
Position: Forward
Height: 6'8" **Weight:** 225
Birthdate: October 8, 1971

NBA Experience: 1 year
College: Notre Dame
Acquired: 1st-round pick in 1994 draft
(24th overall)

Background: A heralded recruit at Notre Dame, Williams was forced to miss two seasons after being diagnosed with a heart condition that involves thickening of the muscle. Cleared to play in 1992, he returned to lead the Irish in scoring as a junior and upped his average to 22.4 PPG as a senior. He was drafted 24th by the Knicks and made 23 starts early in his rookie season. He wound up averaging 3.3 PPG in 41 contests.

Strengths: Williams follows the mold of a typical high-scoring small forward. He can shoot from 18-20 feet and is adept at getting to the basket off the dribble. However, he did not do either with much success in his one pro season. Williams is a workaholic who keeps himself in peak condition, can run the floor all night, and is expected to help out with passes and rebounds as well.

Weaknesses: While Williams is a good athlete, he does not possess lightning speed. He will have to have some success shooting the ball before defenders give him a chance to drive. He has had some troubles from the free throw line and he is not a 3-point threat. Like a lot of rookies, he has also struggled on the defensive end. He won't block many shots, but he needs to maintain better position.

Analysis: The heart does not appear to be a major concern with Williams, though it will be monitored closely. He was thought to be a lottery-type talent otherwise. Williams got his starts early in the season when Charles Oakley was out of the lineup with an injury, but even in the games he started Williams averaged only about 15 minutes a game. The goal, for now, should be gaining respect as a backup.

PLAYER SUMMARY

Will..improve
Can't..intimidate
Expect.........................a scoring bent
Don't Expect ....early stardom
Fantasy Value $0
Card Value ....10-20¢

COLLEGE STATISTICS

		G	FGP	FTP	RPG	PPG
89-90	ND	29	.483	.740	3.7	7.7
92-93	ND	27	.461	.791	9.3	18.5
93-94	ND	29	.511	.698	8.2	22.4
Totals		85	.487	.738	7.0	16.1

NBA REGULAR-SEASON STATISTICS

			FGs		3-PT FGs		FTs		Rebounds						
	G	MIN	FG	PCT	FG	PCT	FT	PCT	OFF	TOT	AST	STL	BLK	PTS	PPG
94-95 NY	41	503	60	.451	0	.000	17	.447	42	98	49	20	4	137	3.3
Totals	41	503	60	.451	0	.000	17	.447	42	98	49	20	4	137	3.3

REGGIE WILLIAMS

Team: Denver Nuggets
Position: Forward/Guard
Height: 6'7" **Weight:** 195
Birthdate: March 5, 1964

NBA Experience: 8 years
College: Georgetown
Acquired: Signed as a free agent, 1/91

Background: As a senior at Georgetown, Williams was an All-American and Big East Player of the Year. He was named NCAA Tournament MVP when the Hoyas won the title in 1984. Drafted fourth, he was a letdown with the Clippers, Cleveland, and San Antonio before signing with Denver in 1991. Williams has since averaged at least 13 PPG in four-plus years with the Nuggets.

Strengths: Williams is a slasher who thrives in transition and brings a scorer's mentality to the court. He shoots with 3-point range. He also rebounds, blocks shots, comes up with steals, finds open men, and has a quick first step to the hoop. He'll take the clutch shots and has converted his share.

Weaknesses: Williams is not at his best in a halfcourt attack. He tends to force shots and has not hit a high percentage of his 3-point tries (32 percent last year). Williams picks up a lot of fouls. He's also a below-average ball-handler. His overall play has been streaky.

Analysis: Projected as a star coming out of college, Williams was a first-rate flop for three-plus years before finding new life in the Rockies. He has overcome a lot in his career to become a productive starter who shines at times. Williams recorded his first career triple-double last season but resigned his co-captainship of the Nuggets in January.

PLAYER SUMMARY	
Will	finish the break
Can't	thrive at slow pace
Expect	about 13 PPG
Don't Expect	All-Star status
Fantasy Value	$9-11
Card Value	7-10¢

COLLEGE STATISTICS

		G	FGP	FTP	RPG	PPG
83-84	GEOR	37	.433	.768	3.5	9.1
84-85	GEOR	35	.506	.755	5.7	11.9
85-86	GEOR	32	.528	.732	8.2	17.6
86-87	GEOR	34	.482	.804	8.6	23.6
Totals		138	.490	.768	6.4	15.3

NBA REGULAR-SEASON STATISTICS

			FGs		3-PT FGs		FTs		Rebounds						
	G	MIN	FG	PCT	FG	PCT	FT	PCT	OFF	TOT	AST	STL	BLK	PTS	PPG
87-88 LAC	35	857	152	.356	13	.224	48	.727	55	118	58	29	21	365	10.4
88-89 LAC	63	1303	260	.438	30	.288	92	.754	70	179	103	81	29	642	10.2
89-90 LAC/CLE/SA	47	743	131	.388	6	.162	52	.765	28	83	53	32	14	320	6.8
90-91 SA/DEN	73	1896	384	.449	57	.363	166	.843	133	306	133	113	41	991	13.6
91-92 DEN	81	2623	601	.471	56	.359	216	.803	145	405	235	148	68	1474	18.2
92-93 DEN	79	2722	535	.458	33	.270	238	.804	132	428	295	126	76	1341	17.0
93-94 DEN	82	2654	418	.412	64	.278	165	.733	98	392	300	117	66	1065	13.0
94-95 DEN	74	2198	388	.459	85	.320	132	.759	94	329	231	114	67	993	13.4
Totals	534	14996	2869	.440	344	.304	1109	.783	755	2240	1408	760	382	7191	13.5

SCOTT WILLIAMS

Team: Philadelphia 76ers   **NBA Experience:** 5 years
Position: Forward/Center   **College:** North Carolina
Height: 6'10" **Weight:** 230   **Acquired:** Signed as a free agent,
Birthdate: March 21, 1968   7/94

Background: Williams was Dean Smith's first West Coast recruit. He led
Carolina in rebounding and blocked shots as a senior but was bypassed in the
1990 NBA draft. Williams made the Bulls as a free agent and won three
championship rings. A knee injury shortened his final year in Chicago. He signed
a long-term deal with Philadelphia in 1994 and averaged 6.4 PPG for the 76ers
last season.

Strengths: Williams can play forward or center and his best attributes are his
defense and energy. He has good quickness and agility for his size and is not
afraid to put his body on the big guys. He rebounds and blocks shots. He gets his
points on short jumpers and putbacks. Williams has big, strong hands and an
above-average feel for the game.

Weaknesses: Williams has yet to develop a wide range of effective post moves
or the confidence to attack the hoop against the league's more talented big men.
His shooting stroke is far from reliable, as a check of his free throw percentage
will confirm. He has been plagued by shoulder and knee injuries through most of
his five years.

Analysis: Williams, who spent most of his career as part of a four-headed center
situation in Chicago, got the chance to start 43 games for the 76ers after signing
a lucrative seven-year deal with the team. His ability to play the four and five
spots seems to make him suited for sixth man, especially considering his
unreliable offensive game.

PLAYER SUMMARY

Will ....play two positions
Can't.........................create his shots
Expect.........................tough defense
Don't Expect ....10 PPG
Fantasy Value $1
Card Value ....5-8¢

COLLEGE STATISTICS

		G	FGP	FTP	RPG	PPG
86-87	NC	36	.497	.558	4.2	5.5
87-88	NC	34	.572	.673	6.4	12.8
88-89	NC	35	.556	.654	7.3	11.4
89-90	NC	33	.554	.615	7.3	14.5
Totals		138	.551	.636	6.2	10.9

NBA REGULAR-SEASON STATISTICS

				FGs		3-PT FGs		FTs		Rebounds						
		G	MIN	FG	PCT	FG	PCT	FT	PCT	OFF	TOT	AST	STL	BLK	PTS	PPG
90-91	CHI	51	337	53	.510	1	.500	20	.714	42	98	16	12	13	127	2.5
91-92	CHI	63	690	83	.483	0	.000	48	.649	90	247	50	13	36	214	3.4
92-93	CHI	71	1369	166	.466	0	.000	90	.714	168	451	68	55	66	422	5.9
93-94	CHI	38	638	114	.483	1	.200	60	.612	69	181	39	16	21	289	7.6
94-95	PHI	77	1781	206	.475	0	.000	79	.738	173	485	59	71	40	491	6.4
Totals		300	4815	622	.478	2	.083	297	.686	542	1462	232	167	176	1543	5.1

WALT WILLIAMS

Team: Sacramento Kings
Position: Guard/Forward
Height: 6'8" **Weight:** 230
Birthdate: April 16, 1970

NBA Experience: 3 years
College: Maryland
Acquired: 1st-round pick in 1992 draft
(7th overall)

Background: Williams, the Washington, D.C.-area prep Player of the Year in 1988, broke Len Bias's Maryland record for points in a season as a senior. He averaged 26.8 points, 5.6 rebounds, 3.6 assists, and 2.1 steals per outing in his final season. Drafted seventh in 1992 by Sacramento, Williams has not matched his rookie-year scoring average of 17.0 PPG in two subsequent seasons. He started 77 games last year.

Strengths: By two months into his rookie season, Williams had seen action at all five positions. He can play three positions fairly comfortably. Williams is a fine offensive talent with the ability to hit 3-pointers, drive to the hoop, or post up. He has a lot of weapons at his disposal and the ability to create. He's a good passer, he comes up with steals, and he'll block some shots.

Weaknesses: Williams plays defense like a lot of scorers, which is to say his interests are elsewhere a lot of the time. He picks up a lot of reaching fouls and does not always fight to hold his position. Williams is not a great pure athlete and has had some trouble with his weight and conditioning in the past. He is not a steady free throw shooter.

Analysis: While he did not equal his rookie scoring average, the 1994-95 season was a decent all-around campaign for Williams. It would have been a great year for a lot of other players, but much is expected of this versatile talent who needs to become more consistent in most phases of the game. Williams seems to be settling in as a small forward and the Kings are expecting better days ahead.

PLAYER SUMMARY

Will ....create his shot
Can't ....avoid fouls
Expect ....steals, blocks
Don't Expect........................a stopper
Fantasy Value $20-25
Card Value ....12-25¢

COLLEGE STATISTICS

		G	FGP	FTP	RPG	PPG
88-89	MARY	26	.441	.623	3.5	7.3
89-90	MARY	33	.483	.776	4.2	12.7
90-91	MARY	17	.449	.837	5.1	18.7
91-92	MARY	29	.472	.758	5.6	26.8
Totals		105	.466	.762	4.6	16.2

NBA REGULAR-SEASON STATISTICS

			FGs		3-PT FGs		FTs		Rebounds						
		G	MIN	FG	PCT	FG	PCT	FT	PCT	OFF	TOT	AST	STL	BLK	PTS	PPG
92-93	SAC	59	1673	358	.435	61	.319	224	.742	115	265	178	66	29	1001	17.0
93-94	SAC	57	1356	226	.390	38	.288	148	.635	71	235	132	52	23	638	11.2
94-95	SAC	77	2739	445	.446	103	.348	266	.731	100	345	316	123	63	1259	16.4
Totals		193	5768	1029	.429	202	.326	638	.710	286	845	626	241	115	2898	15.0

KEVIN WILLIS

Team: Miami Heat
Position: Forward/Center
Height: 7'0" **Weight:** 240
Birthdate: September 6, 1962
NBA Experience: 10 years

College: Michigan St.
Acquired: Traded from Hawks with a future 1st-round pick for Steve Smith, Grant Long, and a future 2nd-round pick, 11/94

Background: Willis led the Big Ten in rebounding and field goal percentage as a junior at Michigan State, where he received all-conference mention as a senior. He played nine-plus seasons with Atlanta (he missed 1988-89 with a broken foot) and was a 1992 All-Star. He was traded to Miami two games into the 1994-95 season.

Strengths: Willis is a strong rebounder and a productive low-post scorer. He has been one of the better rebounding forwards in the league over the last four years. His jump hook is almost unstoppable and he also hits mid-range jumpers. He runs the floor well for a seven-footer and has shed his inconsistent label.

Weaknesses: Willis is not an accomplished passer, ball-handler, or free throw shooter. He does not make opponents pay for double-teaming him, as he dished out only 86 assists all last season. Some feel he thinks more about himself than his team. He should be a much better shot-blocker than he is.

Analysis: Once seen as a hot-and-cold performer, Willis now has to be considered one of the top power forwards in basketball. He has averaged a double-double in each of his last three seasons, putting him in elite company. His coaches would like to see his assist total rise.

PLAYER SUMMARY	
Will	score, rebound
Can't	find open men
Expect	lethal jump hooks
Don't Expect	dribbling
Fantasy Value	$25-30
Card Value	5-10¢

COLLEGE STATISTICS

		G	FGP	FTP	RPG	PPG
81-82	MSU	27	.474	.567	4.2	6.0
82-83	MSU	27	.596	.514	9.6	13.3
83-84	MSU	25	.492	.661	7.7	11.0
Totals		79	.530	.579	7.1	10.1

NBA REGULAR-SEASON STATISTICS

				FGs		3-PT FGs		FTs		Rebounds						
		G	MIN	FG	PCT	FG	PCT	FT	PCT	OFF	TOT	AST	STL	BLK	PTS	PPG
84-85	ATL	82	1785	322	.467	2	.222	119	.657	177	522	36	31	49	765	9.3
85-86	ATL	82	2300	419	.517	0	.000	172	.654	243	704	45	66	44	1010	12.3
86-87	ATL	81	2626	538	.536	1	.250	227	.709	321	849	62	65	61	1304	16.1
87-88	ATL	75	2091	356	.518	0	.000	159	.649	235	547	28	68	42	871	11.6
89-90	ATL	81	2273	418	.519	2	.286	168	.683	253	645	57	63	47	1006	12.4
90-91	ATL	80	2373	444	.504	4	.400	159	.668	259	704	99	60	40	1051	13.1
91-92	ATL	81	2962	591	.483	6	.162	292	.804	418	1258	173	72	54	1480	18.3
92-93	ATL	80	2878	616	.506	7	.241	196	.653	335	1028	165	68	41	1435	17.9
93-94	ATL	80	2867	627	.499	9	.375	268	.713	335	963	150	79	38	1531	19.1
94-95	ATL/MIA	67	2390	473	.466	3	.200	205	.690	227	732	86	60	36	1154	17.2
Totals		789	24545	4804	.501	34	.238	1965	.695	2803	7952	901	632	452	11607	14.7

DAVID WINGATE

Team: Seattle SuperSonics
Position: Guard
Height: 6'5" **Weight:** 195
Birthdate: December 15, 1963

NBA Experience: 9 years
College: Georgetown
Acquired: Traded from Hornets with Hersey Hawkins for Kendall Gill, 6/95

Background: Wingate was a member of the great Georgetown teams of the mid-1980s. He was drafted by Philadelphia and played three years with the 76ers. He spent two years with the Spurs, who once placed him on the suspended list following two off-court legal incidents. Charges were dropped. Wingate started with Washington in 1991-92 and spent the last three years in Charlotte primarily as a reserve. Seattle acquired him this past summer.

Strengths: Wingate has been a certified stopper for much of his career. He stays in front of his man and goes after the ball. He can defend players at three positions. Wingate is a pretty reliable ball-handler and passer who will also hit the boards and get out on the break.

Weaknesses: Wingate is not a confident shooter or scorer. Many of his points come in transition and very few of them come from 3-point range (13 treys over the last seven years). As mentioned, Wingate has had some problems off the court. He also had knee surgery two years ago.

Analysis: Wingate provided the Hornets with tough defense off the bench, but his minutes were limited last season largely due to the emergence of Scott Burrell at the small-forward spot. Wingate was on the court for an average of ten minutes per night, and that allotment probably won't increase with Seattle.

PLAYER SUMMARY	
Will	hound his man
Can't	be a scorer
Expect	a versatile defender
Don't Expect	10 PPG
Fantasy Value	$0
Card Value	5-8¢

COLLEGE STATISTICS

		G	FGP	FTP	RPG	PPG
82-83	GEOR	32	.445	.702	3.0	12.0
83-84	GEOR	37	.435	.721	3.6	11.2
84-85	GEOR	38	.484	.689	3.6	12.4
85-86	GEOR	32	.497	.755	4.0	15.9
Totals		139	.467	.719	3.6	12.8

NBA REGULAR-SEASON STATISTICS

				FGs		3-PT FGs		FTs		Rebounds						
		G	MIN	FG	PCT	FG	PCT	FT	PCT	OFF	TOT	AST	STL	BLK	PTS	PPG
86-87	PHI	77	1612	259	.430	13	.250	149	.741	70	156	155	93	19	680	8.8
87-88	PHI	61	1419	218	.400	10	.250	99	.750	44	101	119	47	22	545	8.9
88-89	PHI	33	372	54	.470	2	.333	27	.794	12	37	73	9	2	137	4.2
89-90	SA	78	1856	220	.448	0	.000	87	.777	62	195	208	89	18	527	6.8
90-91	SA	25	563	53	.384	1	.111	29	.707	24	75	46	19	5	136	5.4
91-92	WAS	81	2127	266	.465	1	.056	105	.719	80	269	247	123	21	638	7.9
92-93	CHA	72	1471	180	.536	1	.167	79	.738	49	174	183	66	9	440	6.1
93-94	CHA	50	1005	136	.481	4	.333	34	.667	30	134	104	42	6	310	6.2
94-95	CHA	52	515	50	.410	4	.182	18	.750	11	60	56	19	6	122	2.3
Totals		529	10940	1436	.448	36	.202	627	.739	382	1201	1191	507	108	3535	6.7

DONTONIO WINGFIELD

Team: Toronto Raptors
Position: Forward
Height: 6'8" **Weight:** 256
Birthdate: June 23, 1974

NBA Experience: 1 year
College: Cincinnati
Acquired: Selected from SuperSonics in 1995 expansion draft

Background: Wingfield was a prep sensation in Albany, Georgia, and was one of Bob Huggins's marquee recruits at Cincinnati. He was the top freshman scorer and rebounder in the Great Midwest Conference before bypassing his final three seasons to enter the NBA draft. He slipped into the second round, primarily because some questioned his off-the-court behavior. He played in only 20 games for Seattle as a rookie and was selected by Toronto in the 1995 expansion draft.

Strengths: Wingfield is a tremendously versatile talent. Not only can he play both guard and forward, but he brings a wide variety of skills to the floor. He was a 40-percent 3-point shooter in college and he also made an impact on the glass with 9.0 RPG. He has the strength, speed, and leaping ability to compete at the NBA level, and he knows how to put the ball in the hole.

Weaknesses: Several incidents, including paternity suits and a domestic dispute with his mother, spotted Wingfield's record before he came into the NBA. His character remains in question. Wingfield is just two years removed from high school basketball and has not had to show consistency over a long season. There are questions about his ability to play defense and get his points at this level of competition.

Analysis: At 20, Wingfield was the youngest player in the NBA last season. He played only 81 total minutes, spent plenty of time watching games in street clothes, and scored no more than six points in any one game. A dazzling rookie year it was not. If anyone needs time to get adjusted to life in the big leagues, it's Wingfield. He has the ability. Now he needs to show the dedication, the mettle, and the character to make it.

PLAYER SUMMARY	
Will	bide his time
Can't	crack the rotation
Expect	growing pains
Don't Expect	a team captain
Fantasy Value	$0
Card Value	10-20¢

COLLEGE STATISTICS

		G	FGP	FTP	RPG	PPG
93-94	CINC	29	.422	.669	9.0	16.0
Totals		29	.422	.669	9.0	16.0

NBA REGULAR-SEASON STATISTICS

		G	MIN	FGs FG	FGs PCT	3-PT FGs FG	3-PT FGs PCT	FTs FT	FTs PCT	Rebounds OFF	Rebounds TOT	AST	STL	BLK	PTS	PPG
94-95	SEA	20	81	18	.353	2	.167	8	.800	11	30	3	5	3	46	2.3
Totals		20	81	18	.353	2	.167	8	.800	11	30	3	5	3	46	2.3

DAVID WOOD

Unrestricted Free Agent
Last Team: Golden State Warriors
Position: Forward
Height: 6'9" **Weight:** 230
Birthdate: November 30, 1964

NBA Experience: 5 years
College: Skagit Valley; Nevada-Reno
Acquired: Signed as a free agent, 10/94

Background: Wood was a center at Nevada-Reno, where he transferred after beginning his career at Skagit Valley Junior College. He played two games for Chicago in 1988-89 but served most of his first three years in the CBA and Europe. Wood has never played two straight years with the same NBA team. He was with the Warriors last season after one year each in Houston, Spain, San Antonio, and Detroit.

Strengths: Wood plays the game with a lot of heart and helps his teammates look better. He hustles, takes charges, makes sound decisions, plays defense, rebounds, and is not afraid to mix it up. He is a good 3-point marksman when he's able to get a good look at the basket. He wears his hard hat to work.

Weaknesses: Offense has not been Wood's ticket back to the NBA. He does not create his own shot or shoot well on the move, he has a slow release, and he does not use his dribble effectively. His defense comes from the heart, not the feet. Wood lacks the physical gifts like quickness, speed, and leaping ability.

Analysis: Wood is sorely lacking in natural talent. He will never score 15 PPG as he did in Spain, although he will come to work every night, play defense, and sink some 3-pointers. With a good team, this yeoman forward would spend most of his time on the bench. With Golden State last year, he started 13 of his 78 games. His 5.5 PPG was a career high.

PLAYER SUMMARY	
Will	set hard picks
Can't	buy a house
Expect	an honest day's work
Don't Expect	athletic skills
Fantasy Value	$0
Card Value	5-8¢

COLLEGE STATISTICS

		G	FGP	FTP	RPG	PPG
83-84	SV	29	.546	.704	7.3	9.7
84-85	SV	26	.609	.719	11.6	18.2
86-87	N-R	28	.511	.662	6.0	9.0
87-88	N-R	30	.472	.726	9.4	12.1
Totals		113	.538	.709	8.5	12.1

NBA REGULAR-SEASON STATISTICS

		G	MIN	FGs FG	FGs PCT	3-PT FGs FG	3-PT FGs PCT	FTs FT	FTs PCT	Rebounds OFF	Rebounds TOT	AST	STL	BLK	PTS	PPG
88-89	CHI	2	2	0	.000	0	.000	0	.000	0	0	0	0	0	0	0.0
90-91	HOU	82	1421	148	.424	28	.311	108	.812	107	246	94	58	16	432	5.3
92-93	SA	64	598	52	.444	5	.238	46	.836	38	97	34	13	12	155	2.4
93-94	DET	78	1182	119	.459	22	.449	62	.756	104	239	51	39	19	322	4.1
94-95	GS	78	1336	153	.469	31	.341	91	.778	83	241	65	28	13	428	5.5
Totals		304	4539	472	.449	86	.343	307	.793	332	823	244	138	60	1337	4.4

HAYWOODE WORKMAN

Unrestricted Free Agent
Last Team: Indiana Pacers
Position: Guard
Height: 6'3" **Weight:** 180
Birthdate: January 23, 1966

NBA Experience: 4 years
College: Winston-Salem St.;
Oral Roberts
Acquired: Signed as a free agent,
8/93

Background: A three-year starter at Oral Roberts after starting his college career at Winston-Salem State, Workman posted averages of 17.9 points and 5.2 rebounds per game for the Monarchs. He was drafted in the second round by Atlanta in 1989 but played just six games with the Hawks before making the CBA All-Rookie Team. After a year in Washington, he's played two seasons apiece in the Italian League and with Indiana.

Strengths: Workman is aptly named. He knows his role involves playing tough defense, so that's what he does. He can guard point guards or shooting guards and he limits their options. He also comes up with steals. Workman is an unselfish player who keeps the ball moving. He runs the offense with a steady hand and shoots with 3-point range.

Weaknesses: Workman is not the type of point guard who will keep the opposition on its toes with his scoring ability. He looks more to pass and for good reason. He has never been a consistent shooter and he dipped to .375 from the field last season. He does not attack the basket enough to spend much time at the line. Workman is not the most creative guard in basketball.

Analysis: Workman was a vital cog in Indiana's fine playoff run two years ago, but the addition of Mark Jackson last season gave the Pacers better playmaking and ultimately put Workman in a more limited role. It was difficult for Workman to develop any consistency with his up-and-down playing time, but a coach can count on him to play solid defense.

PLAYER SUMMARY	
Will	play defense
Can't	shoot the lights out
Expect	a feisty reserve
Don't Expect	10 PPG
Fantasy Value	$0
Card Value	5-10¢

COLLEGE STATISTICS

		G	FGP	FTP	RPG	PPG
84-85	WSS	25	.457	.589	3.0	10.3
86-87	OR	28	.365	.796	3.3	13.8
87-88	OR	29	.415	.755	6.0	19.4
88-89	OR	28	.483	.815	6.1	19.9
Totals		110	.430	.754	4.7	16.0

NBA REGULAR-SEASON STATISTICS

		G	MIN	FGs FG	FGs PCT	3-PT FGs FG	3-PT FGs PCT	FTs FT	FTs PCT	Rebounds OFF	Rebounds TOT	AST	STL	BLK	PTS	PPG
89-90	ATL	6	16	2	.667	0	.000	2	1.000	0	3	2	3	0	6	1.0
90-91	WAS	73	2034	234	.454	12	.240	101	.759	51	242	353	87	7	581	8.0
93-94	IND	65	1714	195	.424	18	.321	93	.802	32	204	404	85	4	501	7.7
94-95	IND	69	1028	101	.375	35	.357	55	.743	21	111	194	59	5	292	4.2
Totals		213	4792	532	.427	65	.319	251	.772	104	560	953	234	16	1380	6.5

SHARONE WRIGHT

Team: Philadelphia 76ers
Position: Forward/Center
Height: 6'11" **Weight:** 260
Birthdate: January 30, 1973

NBA Experience: 1 year
College: Clemson
Acquired: 1st-round pick in 1994 draft
(6th overall)

Background: Wright attended the same Southwest High School in Macon, Georgia, that produced Norm Nixon and Jeff Malone. He averaged a double-double in his last two seasons at Clemson and was among the nation's top shot-blockers as a sophomore. He was drafted sixth overall by Philadelphia, started his first NBA game, and wound up averaging 11.4 PPG and 6.0 RPG for the 76ers in his rookie season.

Strengths: Wright provides a physical presence in the paint. He has a strong body and uses it to get to the boards and play defense. He finished seventh among rookies in rebounding last year and was also one of the top first-year shot-blockers with 104 on the season. Wright works for his points in the paint and is able to play some center (in addition to his power-forward position) when the need arises.

Weaknesses: Not one of the more polished low-post scorers in the league, Wright will need to develop his array of offensive moves. He relies basically on sheer strength and his ability on the offensive glass for points. He's not a shooter and he hits a low percentage of his free throws. Wright amasses too many turnovers and personal fouls and not enough assists. He's just learning to look for open teammates.

Analysis: Wright scored 23 points and grabbed 15 rebounds in his second NBA game. He leveled off after that, of course, but Philadelphia was encouraged by his rookie season. He made 49 starts and will be the team's top power forward coming into the 1995-96 campaign. Offers Wright: "I'd like to lead the league in rebounding in a couple of years and be an All-Star." That's the spirit.

PLAYER SUMMARY

Will.....................................block shots
Can't ....shoot free throws
Expect ....aggressive rebounding
Don't Expect ....smooth offense
Fantasy Value $8-10
Card Value ....25-50¢

COLLEGE STATISTICS

		G	FGP	FTP	RPG	PPG
91-92	CLEM	28	.498	.563	8.1	12.0
92-93	CLEM	30	.567	.669	10.5	15.0
93-94	CLEM	34	.525	.644	10.6	15.4
Totals		92	.531	.632	9.8	14.2

NBA REGULAR-SEASON STATISTICS

				FGs		3-PT FGs		FTs		Rebounds						
		G	MIN	FG	PCT	FG	PCT	FT	PCT	OFF	TOT	AST	STL	BLK	PTS	PPG
94-95	PHI	79	2044	361	.465	0	.000	182	.645	191	472	48	37	104	904	11.4
Totals		79	2044	361	.465	0	.000	182	.645	191	472	48	37	104	904	11.4

1995 NBA Draft

	Player	College	Team
1)	Joe Smith	Maryland	Golden State
2)	Antonio McDyess	Alabama	L.A. Clippers
3)	Jerry Stackhouse	North Carolina	Philadelphia
4)	Rasheed Wallace	North Carolina	Washington
5)	Kevin Garnett	(Farragut Academy)	Minnesota
6)	Bryant Reeves	Oklahoma State	Vancouver
7)	Damon Stoudamire	Arizona	Toronto
8)	Shawn Respert	Michigan State	Portland
9)	Ed O'Bannon	UCLA	New Jersey
10)	Kurt Thomas	Texas Christian	Miami
11)	Gary Trent	Ohio	Milwaukee
12)	Cherokee Parks	Duke	Dallas
13)	Corliss Williamson	Arkansas	Sacramento
14)	Eric Williams	Providence	Boston
15)	Brent Barry	Oregon State	Denver
16)	Alan Henderson	Indiana	Atlanta
17)	Bob Sura	Florida State	Cleveland
18)	Theo Ratliff	Wyoming	Detroit
19)	Randolph Childress	Wake Forest	Detroit
20)	Jason Caffey	Alabama	Chicago
21)	Michael Finley	Wisconsin	Phoenix
22)	George Zidek	UCLA	Charlotte
23)	Travis Best	Georgia Tech	Indiana
24)	Loren Meyer	Iowa State	Dallas
25)	David Vaughn	Memphis	Orlando
26)	Sherell Ford	Illinois-Chicago	Seattle
27)	Mario Bennett	Arizona State	Phoenix
28)	Greg Ostertag	Kansas	Utah
29)	Cory Alexander	Virginia	San Antonio

	Player	College	Team
30)	Lou Roe	Massachusetts	Detroit
31)	Dragan Tarlac	(Greece)	Chicago
32)	Terrence Rencher	Texas	Washington
33)	Junior Burrough	Virginia	Boston
34)	Andrew DeClercq	Florida	Golden State
35)	Jimmy King	Michigan	Toronto
36)	Lawrence Moten	Syracuse	Vancouver
37)	Frankie King	Western Carolina	L.A. Lakers
38)	Rashard Griffith	Wisconsin	Milwaukee
39)	Donny Marshall	Connecticut	Cleveland
40)	Dwayne Whitfield	Jackson State	Golden State
41)	Erik Meek	Duke	Houston
42)	Donnie Boyce	Colorado	Atlanta
43)	Eric Snow	Michigan State	Milwaukee
44)	Anthony Pelle	Fresno State	Denver
45)	Troy Brown	Providence	Atlanta
46)	George Banks	Texas-El Paso	Miami
47)	Tyus Edney	UCLA	Sacramento
48)	Mark Davis	Texas Tech	Minnesota
49)	Jerome Allen	Pennsylvania	Minnesota
50)	Martin Lewis	Seward County C.C.	Golden State
51)	Dejan Bodiroga	(Italy)	Sacramento
52)	Fred Hoiberg	Iowa State	Indiana
53)	Constantin Popa	Miami (FL)	L.A. Clippers
54)	Eurelejus Zukauskas	(Lithuania)	Seattle
55)	Michael McDonald	New Orleans	Golden State
56)	Chris Carr	Southern Illinois	Phoenix
57)	Cuonzo Martin	Purdue	Atlanta
58)	Don Reid	Georgetown	Detroit

CORY ALEXANDER

Team: San Antonio Spurs
Position: Guard
Height: 6'1" **Weight:** 183
Birthdate: June 22, 1973
College: Virginia
Acquired: 1st-round pick in 1995 draft (29th overall)

PLAYER SUMMARY	
Will	drive, draw, and dish
Can't	stay healthy
Expect	spark off the bench
Don't Expect	lack of effort
Fantasy	$0 Card......12-20¢

Background: Alexander began his career at Virginia with much promise, but he suffered ankle injuries that derailed him for the 1993-94 season and six weeks of the 1994-95 campaign. He averaged 4.7 assists for his career, second in school history. He left school with a year's eligibility remaining.

Strengths: Alexander is a true point guard, capable of running a team and setting up the designated scorers. He has exceptional quickness. He can score either with jump shots or penetration.

Weaknesses: Considering his scoring proficiency, he should make more than 69.8 percent of his free throw attempts. Most of the questions about Alexander concern his right ankle, which he's broken twice and still contains surgical pins.

Analysis: Alexander slipped to the last player selected in the first round because of fears that he's too brittle. He was an excellent pick for San Antonio, which had a glaring need for a backup point guard.

COLLEGE STATISTICS

		G	FGP	FTP	RPG	APG	PPG
91-92	VIRG	33	.376	.686	3.2	4.4	11.2
92-93	VIRG	31	.453	.705	3.5	4.6	18.8
93-94	VIRG	1	—	—	1.0	2.0	—
94-95	VIRG	20	.452	.701	4.2	5.5	16.7
Totals		85	.427	.698	3.5	4.7	15.1

JEROME ALLEN

Team: Minnesota Timberwolves
Position: Guard
Height: 6'3" **Weight:** 184
Birthdate: January 28, 1973
College: Pennsylvania
Acquired: 2nd-round pick in 1995 draft (49th overall)

PLAYER SUMMARY	
Will	guard his man
Can't	shake the rafters
Expect	a legit player
Don't Expect	a head case
Fantasy	$0 Card......20-35¢

Background: A two-time Ivy League Player of the Year, Allen is Penn's all-time leader in assists and steals. He played for the U.S. team at the Goodwill Games. In his final college game, he had 30 points against Alabama in the 1995 NCAA Tournament.

Strengths: Allen is a much better athlete than most players from the Ivy League. He's quick enough to play the point and smart enough to run a team. He's a positive factor on the fastbreak. He digs in defensively.

Weaknesses: Allen's outside shot isn't as consistent as it will need to be in the NBA. Likewise, he'll need to upgrade his ball-handling. Some people count his Ivy background as a strike against him.

Analysis: While he played only sporadic minutes at point guard in college, Allen has a chance to develop into a good backup point man in the NBA. He was drafted by a Minnesota team that needs a transfusion of new blood. He has the athleticism to survive training camp.

COLLEGE STATISTICS

		G	FGP	FTP	RPG	APG	PPG
91-92	PENN	26	.411	.684	3.6	3.2	12.2
92-93	PENN	27	.423	.667	4.7	4.9	13.1
93-94	PENN	28	.401	.787	4.5	4.6	14.5
94-95	PENN	28	.429	.712	4.8	5.7	14.7
Totals		109	.417	.722	4.4	4.6	13.7

GEORGE BANKS

Team: Miami Heat
Position: Forward
Height: 6'7" **Weight:** 210
Birthdate: October 9, 1972
College: Central Arizona; Texas-El Paso
Acquired: 2nd-round pick in 1995 draft (46th overall)

PLAYER SUMMARY	
Will	play hard
Can't	convert from outside
Expect	a CBA detour
Don't Expect	a banger
Fantasy	$0 Card ...... 10-15¢

Background: Banks played two seasons at Central Arizona J.C. before transferring to Texas-El Paso, where he twice led the Miners in rebounding and earned All-WAC honors as a senior. He had 122 blocked shots and 91 steals in 59 college games. He came on like gangbusters in the second half of the 1994-95 season, regularly outplaying his more heralded teammate, Antoine Gillespie, who wasn't drafted.

Strengths: Banks is extremely quick, which enables him to beat bigger players to rebounds and loose balls. A fluid runner, he makes things happen on the fastbreak. He became an outstanding defensive player during his senior season.

Weaknesses: He lacks a consistent stroke from the perimeter. Very thin, he's liable to get pounded in training camp.

Analysis: Banks got a lot of his minutes in college at center, but he's really an undersized power forward. He'll need a lot of work on his floor game and outside shot to have a chance to make it in the NBA. Miami needs depth in its frontcourt, but it's doubtful Banks will be good enough to stick.

COLLEGE STATISTICS

	G	FGP	FTP	RPG	APG	PPG
93-94 UTEP	30	.494	.588	8.3	0.7	8.3
94-95 UTEP	29	.566	.740	8.6	0.7	15.2
Totals	59	.536	.686	8.4	0.7	11.7

BRENT BARRY

Team: Los Angeles Clippers
Position: Guard
Height: 6'6" **Weight:** 185
Birthdate: December 31, 1971
College: Oregon St.
Acquired: Draft rights traded from Nuggets with Rodney Rogers for Randy Woods and draft rights to Antonio McDyess, 6/95

PLAYER SUMMARY	
Will	flourish on the break
Can't	bang the boards
Expect	an exciting talent
Don't Expect	a prima donna
Fantasy	$3-5 Card ...... 20-35¢

Background: Brent is the son of Rick and brother of Scooter, Jon, and Drew. Barry progressed slowly at Oregon State and didn't move into first-round draft consideration until his senior season, when he ranked second in the Pac-10 in scoring and steals.

Strengths: Like his father, Barry has great feel for the game. He displays terrific court vision and passing skills, and he's as quick as many point guards. He's not strong, but he has ideal size for a shooting guard.

Weaknesses: There's little not to like. He'll have to add some muscle to his body to survive the NBA grind, and he must smooth out the mechanics on his jump shot.

Analysis: Barry has the potential to develop into a starting shooting guard, even on a good team, though the Clippers' summer roster was loaded with similar players. Minutes might be scarce his rookie season. In the long run, he could be one of the steals of the draft.

COLLEGE STATISTICS

	G	FGP	FTP	RPG	APG	PPG
91-92 OSU	31	.419	.667	1.5	2.3	5.2
92-93 OSU	23	.411	.851	2.1	3.6	7.2
93-94 OSU	27	.498	.759	5.2	3.5	15.2
94-95 OSU	27	.514	.823	5.9	3.9	21.0
Totals	108	.480	.794	3.7	3.3	12.1

MARIO BENNETT

Team: Phoenix Suns
Position: Forward
Height: 6'9" **Weight:** 235
Birthdate: August 1, 1973
College: Arizona St.
Acquired: 1st-round pick in 1995 draft (27th overall)

PLAYER SUMMARY	
Will	throw it down
Can't	dodge medical concerns
Expect	a Shaq at the line
Don't Expect	much P.T.
Fantasy	$0 Card......20-35¢

Background: Though he played just three seasons at Arizona State, Bennett is the school's all-time leading shot-blocker. He also holds the school record for career field goal accuracy. He missed the 1992-93 season because of a knee injury. In 1994-95, he averaged 19 points and 9.1 rebounds in 12 games against ranked opponents.

Strengths: A sensational talent, Bennett probably would have been a lottery pick if not for his history of injuries. He has ideal size for a power forward, runs the court well, finishes plays on the break, and poses problems for defenders in the halfcourt. He's a quick, instinctive shot-blocker.

Weaknesses: Bennett has had two anterior cruciate tears in his left knee and tested poorly in medical exams before the draft. He's an awful free throw shooter.

Analysis: Taking Bennett was a calculated gamble for the Suns, who watched him play in their own backyard for three years. If he stays healthy, he could work his way into a starting role in a couple of years. He's a boom-or-bust draft pick.

COLLEGE STATISTICS

		G	FGP	FTP	RPG	APG	PPG
91-92	ASU	33	.574	.614	6.8	0.8	12.5
93-94	ASU	21	.593	.508	8.6	1.5	16.2
94-95	ASU	33	.592	.491	8.2	2.4	18.7
Totals		87	.587	.530	7.8	1.6	15.7

TRAVIS BEST

Team: Indiana Pacers
Position: Guard
Height: 5'11" **Weight:** 182
Birthdate: July 12, 1972
College: Georgia Tech
Acquired: 1st-round pick in 1995 draft (23rd overall)

PLAYER SUMMARY	
Will	fill it up
Can't	dish it up
Expect	a quiet leader
Don't Expect	a big splash
Fantasy	$0 Card......12-20¢

Background: A three-time All-ACC choice, Best ranks among Georgia Tech's top five in points, assists, 3-pointers, and steals. He and Phil Ford are the only players in ACC history with 2,000 points and 600 assists.

Strengths: Scoring. Few little guards do it better than Best, who can beat opponents with jump shots or darting moves to the basket. He was one of the best free throw shooters in the nation the past two seasons. Durable, he can play a lot of minutes and hold up physically.

Weaknesses: He's not a pure point guard and will need to work to get his teammates involved at the next level. Otherwise, he's solid as a rock.

Analysis: Best fits the new profile of the scoring point guard. His ability to stick the jump shot could earn him a lot of money in the NBA. Indiana needed help in its backcourt because it lost Byron Scott to expansion and feared losing two other guards to free agency. Best could work his way into the rotation as the season wears on.

COLLEGE STATISTICS

		G	FGP	FTP	RPG	APG	PPG
91-92	GT	35	.449	.735	2.5	5.7	12.3
92-93	GT	30	.472	.752	3.1	5.9	16.3
93-94	GT	29	.462	.866	3.6	5.8	18.3
94-95	GT	30	.446	.847	3.2	5.0	20.2
Totals		124	.456	.809	3.1	5.6	16.6

DONNIE BOYCE

Team: Atlanta Hawks
Position: Guard
Height: 6'5" **Weight:** 195
Birthdate: September 2, 1973
College: Colorado
Acquired: 2nd-round pick in 1995 draft (42nd overall)

```
PLAYER SUMMARY
Will.......................score in bunches
Can't...................keep an even keel
Expect.....................hits and misses
Don't Expect........a rookie phenom
Fantasy............$0   Card......12-20¢
```

Background: Boyce and Proviso East High School teammates Michael Finley and Sherell Ford were all taken in the 1995 draft. A two-time All-Big Eight choice, Boyce left Colorado as the school's all-time leading scorer. His career ended when he suffered a broken leg in the 1995 Big Eight Tournament.

Strengths: Though he looks like all skin and bones, Boyce is a great athlete who reminds scouts of Gerald Wilkins. He runs the floor quickly and dunks with authority. He rebounds well for a guard.

Weaknesses: Boyce has a scorer's mentality, which is both good and bad. He needs better shot selection and consistency with his jump shot. He plays out of control at times. His character has been questioned.

Analysis: The leg injury Boyce suffered in March may sideline him for the entire 1995-96 season. It's doubtful Atlanta will pay him if he can't play, so he'll probably get cut. He has a good chance to make it in the NBA down the road.

COLLEGE STATISTICS

	G	FGP	FTP	RPG	APG	PPG
91-92 COLO	28	.419	.564	4.8	3.1	14.9
92-93 COLO	27	.455	.639	6.2	3.6	19.1
93-94 COLO	26	.401	.708	6.7	4.5	22.4
94-95 COLO	26	.409	.706	6.5	4.1	18.5
Totals	107	.421	.666	6.0	3.8	18.6

TROY BROWN

Team: Atlanta Hawks
Position: Forward
Height: 6'8" **Weight:** 238
Birthdate: April 3, 1971
College: Providence
Acquired: 2nd-round pick in 1995 draft (45th overall)

```
PLAYER SUMMARY
Will.........................fight for caroms
Can't .........................create offense
Expect ...............a struggle to stick
Don't Expect ..........any guarantees
Fantasy ............$0   Card ......10-15¢
```

Background: A late-bloomer, Brown sat out 1993-94 as a redshirt because Providence was overstocked with good forwards (Dickey Simpkins, Michael Smith, Eric Williams). Brown started 29 games as a senior, grabbing ten or more rebounds eight times.

Strengths: Similar to Smith, Brown is a rebounder deluxe who's willing to do the dirty work. He's strong and physical and wants the ball. A top-flight athlete, he runs the floor well. He displays a steadily improving post game on offense.

Weaknesses: Brown's skills will dictate that he play power forward at the next level; he's not skilled enough for the three spot. He lacks any semblance of a game facing the basket. He had just 36 assists in college.

Analysis: The ability to rebound gives Brown a chance to play in the NBA, but it probably won't be in 1995-96. Atlanta drafted another power forward, Alan Henderson, in the first round. Brown may have to be content with the CBA for a year or two, though scouts like his potential.

COLLEGE STATISTICS

	G	FGP	FTP	RPG	APG	PPG
90-91 PROV	26	.459	.435	2.7	0.4	3.0
91-92 PROV	29	.475	.625	2.3	0.1	3.9
92-93 PROV	33	.397	.703	3.8	0.3	4.5
94-95 PROV	30	.529	.758	7.9	0.4	12.0
Totals	118	.480	.688	4.2	0.3	5.9

JUNIOR BURROUGH
Team: Boston Celtics
Position: Forward
Height: 6'7" **Weight:** 242
Birthdate: January 18, 1973
College: Virginia
Acquired: 2nd-round pick in 1995 draft (33rd overall)

PLAYER SUMMARY	
Will	hit the 12-footer
Can't	hit the 22-footer
Expect	a struggle to stick
Don't Expect	a rim-rattler
Fantasy	$0 Card	15-25¢

Background: Burrough ranks among Virginia's all-time top five in scoring, rebounding, and blocked shots. He scored 20 or more points 13 times as a senior, picking up the slack after Cory Alexander was lost because of an injury.

Strengths: A wide-body, Burrough gets his share of rebounds, but offense is the best part of his game. He can hit the foul-line and corner jump shots, and he steps up in big games.

Weaknesses: While he plays a power forward's game, Burrough lacks ideal size for the position. He's not good enough to rebound consistently against NBA players, nor does he do a good job driving to the basket. He needs to add versatility to his game.

Analysis: Each year, only a handful of second-round picks begin the season on NBA rosters. The others go to the CBA or overseas to work on their game. The latter figures to apply to Burrough, a good all-around player but perhaps not quite good enough yet for the big leagues.

COLLEGE STATISTICS

	G	FGP	FTP	RPG	APG	PPG
91-92 VIRG	33	.446	.695	5.8	0.2	13.2
92-93 VIRG	31	.438	.638	7.2	0.6	14.6
93-94 VIRG	31	.405	.638	7.0	0.9	15.0
94-95 VIRG	34	.501	.710	8.7	1.6	18.1
Totals	129	.449	.673	7.2	0.9	15.3

JASON CAFFEY
Team: Chicago Bulls
Position: Forward
Height: 6'8" **Weight:** 255
Birthdate: June 12, 1973
College: Alabama
Acquired: 1st-round pick in 1995 draft (20th overall)

PLAYER SUMMARY	
Will	bang the boards
Can't	scrape the rafters
Expect	a two-year project
Don't Expect	Robert Horry
Fantasy	$0 Card	15-30¢

Background: Though he averaged just 10.4 points at Alabama, Caffey attracted the interest of NBA scouts and earned an invitation to the pre-draft Desert Classic. He was named second-team All-SEC as a senior.

Strengths: Caffey has good size and strength as well as long arms. He's a beast on the boards. Unlike some big players, he can get to the basket with his dribble. If he expands his shooting range, he could find some minutes at small forward.

Weaknesses: He made only four 3-pointers in college, so he needs to hone his stroke from beyond 12 feet. Caffey's a bad free throw shooter. Injuries have been a concern.

Analysis: Caffey was the first major surprise of the draft. Many scouts projected him as a mid-second-round pick. He comes from a program that has produced several quality NBA players, which could bode well for his future. He probably won't be a starter anytime soon and could be hard-pressed to earn more than spot minutes in 1995-96.

COLLEGE STATISTICS

	G	FGP	FTP	RPG	APG	PPG
91-92 ALAB	30	.425	.333	2.2	0.3	2.4
92-93 ALAB	29	.518	.615	8.7	1.3	14.5
93-94 ALAB	29	.520	.629	6.3	0.7	12.8
94-95 ALAB	31	.509	.545	8.0	1.6	12.1
Totals	119	.509	.578	6.3	1.0	10.4

CHRIS CARR

Team: Phoenix Suns
Position: Forward/Guard
Height: 6'5" **Weight:** 200
Birthdate: March 12, 1974
College: Southern Illinois
Acquired: 2nd-round pick in 1995 draft (56th overall)

PLAYER SUMMARY	
Will	run and jump
Can't	stop his man
Expect	a used Carr
Don't Expect	a Cadillac
Fantasy	$0 Card	10-15¢

Background: Carr improved his scoring average strongly each year at Southern Illinois before leaving school after his junior season. He was the Player of the Year in the Missouri Valley Conference in 1994-95 and scored 26 points against Syracuse in the NCAA Tournament.

Strengths: Carr runs the floor easily and handles the ball well on the fastbreak, though he tends to make poor decisions as a passer. He scores in bunches.

Weaknesses: Scouts aren't sure why Carr came out early, because there's nothing impressive about his game. His jump shot comes and goes and he doesn't accomplish much defensively. He's supposed to be a great athlete but didn't test well in the pre-draft camps. He's too thin.

Analysis: Carr made two mistakes: leaving school early and hiring an agent, which prevents him from returning to college. His dismal showing at the Chicago camp indicates that he has no chance to make an NBA team, especially one as good as Phoenix. He looks like CBA material.

COLLEGE STATISTICS

		G	FGP	FTP	RPG	APG	PPG
92-93	SILL	31	.591	.545	3.5	0.4	3.9
93-94	SILL	30	.518	.807	6.6	1.8	14.1
94-95	SILL	32	.480	.771	7.3	2.1	22.0
Totals		93	.503	.757	5.8	1.5	13.5

RANDOLPH CHILDRESS

Team: Detroit Pistons
Position: Guard
Height: 6'1" **Weight:** 188
Birthdate: September 21, 1972
College: Wake Forest
Acquired: 1st-round pick in 1995 draft (19th overall)

PLAYER SUMMARY	
Will	stop and pop
Can't	shadow the jets
Expect	a big-game presence
Don't Expect	a big rookie splash
Fantasy	$1 Card	25-40¢

Background: Childress is No. 2 on Wake Forest's all-time scoring list and is the second-most prolific 3-point shooter in ACC history. He made 329 treys in 120 games and finished his career with 40, 30, and 37 points in consecutive games in the 1995 ACC Tournament. He missed the 1991-92 season because of a knee injury.

Strengths: Childress has a smooth shooting stroke and deep range. He's capable of taking over a game. He forces contact, gets to the line, and makes 80 percent of his foul shots. He has adequate playmaking skills.

Weaknesses: He's too small to play shooting guard, and he's not as quick as you'd like at the point. He could be vulnerable defensively against the waterbug types.

Analysis: Childress was drafted by Detroit amid rumors that he would be traded to Portland as soon as the NBA reached labor peace with its players. He's a long shot to earn a starting position in the next few years, but his shooting ability suggests he should have a solid career.

COLLEGE STATISTICS

		G	FGP	FTP	RPG	APG	PPG
90-91	WF	29	.449	.772	2.1	2.2	14.0
92-93	WF	30	.484	.810	2.8	4.2	19.7
93-94	WF	29	.415	.789	3.4	3.9	19.6
94-95	WF	32	.438	.833	3.6	5.2	20.1
Totals		120	.446	.804	3.0	3.9	18.4

PREDRAG DANILOVIC

Team: Miami Heat
Position: Guard
Height: 6'6" **Weight:** 200
Birthdate: February 26, 1970
College: None
Acquired: Traded from Golden State with Billy Owens for Rony Seikaly, 11/94

PLAYER SUMMARY	
Will	stop and pop
Can't	shake the rafters
Expect	a sixth man
Don't Expect	a bust
Fantasy	$1-3 Card ....N/A

Background: A native of Yugoslavia, Danilovic has played professionally in Belgrade and in Bologna, Italy, the past several seasons. He led the Yugoslavian national team to a berth in the 1996 Olympics. He was selected by Golden State in the second round (43rd overall) of the 1992 draft. His rights were acquired by Miami before the 1994-95 season.

Strengths: Danilovic was the best player in Europe last season. He's exceptionally strong for his size, which enables him to get his shot when he wants it, and he hits the 3-pointer consistently. He reminds some scouts of Jeff Hornacek. He has a lot of experience in big games.

Weaknesses: While Danilovic needs to upgrade his ball-handling and defense to flourish in the NBA, he has no glaring weaknesses.

Analysis: In the long run, Danilovic could be better than Billy Owens, the principal player in the Rony Seikaly trade. For now, he'll probably come off the bench at both shooting guard and small forward. Don't be surprised if he contends for a spot on the NBA All-Rookie Team.

COLLEGE STATISTICS

—DID NOT PLAY—

MARK DAVIS

Team: Minnesota Timberwolves
Position: Guard/Forward
Height: 6'6" **Weight:** 210
Birthdate: April 26, 1973
College: Howard; Texas Tech
Acquired: 2nd-round pick in 1995 draft (48th overall)

PLAYER SUMMARY	
Will	stick and stay
Can't	stand charity
Expect	a sleeper
Don't Expect	a slacker
Fantasy	$0 Card ......10-15¢

Background: Davis played two seasons at Howard College in Texas before surfacing at Texas Tech, where he played every position as a junior and became the first player in school history with 200 rebounds and 100 assists in the same season. He ranked in the top ten in the Southwest Conference in six statistical categories as a senior.

Strengths: A quality athlete, Davis has the quickness and feel for the game to be an outstanding defensive player in the NBA. He's fundamentally sound on offense and finishes plays well on the break. A team player, he passes the ball selflessly. He's versatile enough to play small forward or shooting guard.

Weaknesses: Davis needs to work on his jump shot. He has awkward mechanics and a habit of letting his elbow fly out. He commits a lot of turnovers.

Analysis: Minnesota is starting anew with Kevin McHale calling the personnel shots, and that could mean a thorough housecleaning, giving Davis an excellent chance to make the team. Davis could develop into a deluxe backup swingman.

COLLEGE STATISTICS

		G	FGP	FTP	RPG	APG	PPG
93-94	TT	28	.496	.660	8.1	3.9	18.5
94-95	TT	30	.499	.614	8.5	4.7	17.3
Totals		58	.497	.639	8.3	4.3	17.9

ANDREW DeCLERCQ

Team: Golden State
Position: Forward/Center
Height: 6'9" **Weight:** 230
Birthdate: February 1, 1973
College: Florida
Acquired: 2nd-round pick in 1995 draft (34th overall)

PLAYER SUMMARY	
Will	bust his tail
Can't	contribute offensively
Expect	a garbage man
Don't Expect	anything soon
Fantasy	$0 Card ...... 12-20¢

Background: While he never averaged more than 13.2 points in a season, DeClercq earned a spot on the 1994 Goodwill Games team and garnered first-team All-SEC honors in 1994-95. He's the second-leading shot-blocker and third-leading rebounder in Florida history. He started all 128 games during his career.

Strengths: DeClercq makes effort plays (deflections, loose balls, taking a charge) that don't show up in the boxscore. He has good lateral movement and footwork on defense. He pushes himself to run the floor.

Weaknesses: He's a woeful offensive player and didn't improve much at Florida. He's neither big enough nor strong enough to play center in the NBA, and he lacks the skills to play on the perimeter.

Analysis: If DeClercq can be compared to a current NBA player, it would be Jack Haley, the towel-waver at the end of San Antonio's bench in 1994-95. Like Haley, DeClercq will be a fringe player at best. He is a long shot to make the Warriors.

COLLEGE STATISTICS

	G	FGP	FTP	RPG	APG	PPG
91-92 FLOR	33	.507	.655	6.2	0.8	8.8
92-93 FLOR	28	.567	.584	7.1	0.5	10.5
93-94 FLOR	37	.544	.654	7.9	1.5	8.8
94-95 FLOR	30	.511	.723	8.8	1.4	13.2
Totals	128	.531	.663	7.5	1.1	10.2

TYUS EDNEY

Team: Sacramento Kings
Position: Guard
Height: 5'10" **Weight:** 152
Birthdate: February 14, 1973
College: UCLA
Acquired: 2nd-round pick in 1995 draft (47th overall)

PLAYER SUMMARY	
Will	push it hard
Can't	avoid injuries
Expect	a slow start
Don't Expect	lack of heart
Fantasy	$1 Card ...... 20-35¢

Background: A hero of the 1995 NCAA Tournament, Edney lifted UCLA past Missouri with a last-second basket in the second round. Edney had 38 assists and only ten turnovers in the tournament. He won the 1995 Frances Pomeroy Naismith Award as the top college senior under six feet.

Strengths: A gamer, Edney brings all the intangibles to the table. He has superb quickness. He's adept at knifing into the lane for a pass or a running lob shot. His fast hands serve him well defensively.

Weaknesses: Edney needs to become a better outside shooter or else opposing defenders will back off and take away his penetration. His lack of size poses problems, and he's been injury-prone.

Analysis: Edney outplayed Damon Stoudamire both times they met in 1994-95, but Stoudamire is a better NBA prospect because of his shooting ability. Edney would be a lock to make Sacramento's roster, but there are concerns about his wrist injury. He could be a dandy backup point guard.

COLLEGE STATISTICS

	G	FGP	FTP	RPG	APG	PPG
91-92 UCLA	32	.472	.797	2.1	2.8	5.6
92-93 UCLA	33	.483	.841	3.5	5.6	13.6
93-94 UCLA	28	.466	.820	3.4	5.8	15.4
94-95 UCLA	32	.497	.764	3.1	6.8	14.3
Totals	125	.481	.805	3.0	5.2	12.1

MICHAEL FINLEY

Team: Phoenix Suns
Position: Guard/Forward
Height: 6'7" **Weight:** 215
Birthdate: March 6, 1973
College: Wisconsin
Acquired: 1st-round pick in 1995 draft
(21st overall)

PLAYER SUMMARY	
Will	look to score
Can't	get in a groove
Expect	a competent pro
Don't Expect	a sudden impact
Fantasy	$1 Card ......30-60¢

Background: Wisconsin's all-time leading scorer, Finley earned honorable-mention All-America honors from the Associated Press each of the past three seasons. In 1994-95, he led the Badgers in points, assists, and steals while scoring in double figures in 26 of 27 games.

Strengths: One of the best athletes in the draft, Finley has the quickness and ball-handling skills to beat foes with his dribble, and he's a good rebounder for his size. He's experienced in international competition.

Weaknesses: While he's an accomplished scorer, Finley needs a lot of shots to get his points. He averaged 17.4 attempts as a senior while shooting just 37.9 percent from the field and 28.4 from 3-point range. He plays out of control at times.

Analysis: Finley could be a good NBA player or just another guy. He isn't a pure shooter, and he was drafted by a team that's chock-full of talent. He should make the roster but probably will have to be content to sit and watch for a year or more.

COLLEGE STATISTICS

		G	FGP	FTP	RPG	APG	PPG
91-92	WISC	31	.453	.742	4.9	2.7	12.3
92-93	WISC	28	.467	.771	5.8	3.1	22.1
93-94	WISC	29	.466	.786	6.7	3.2	20.4
94-95	WISC	27	.379	.773	5.2	4.0	20.5
Totals		115	.440	.768	5.6	3.2	18.7

SHERELL FORD

Team: Seattle SuperSonics
Position: Forward/Guard
Height: 6'7" **Weight:** 210
Birthdate: August 26, 1972
College: Illinois-Chicago
Acquired: 1st-round pick in 1995 draft
(26th overall)

PLAYER SUMMARY	
Will	stroke it good
Can't	guard anybody
Expect	a designated shooter
Don't Expect	a lemon
Fantasy	$1 Card ......35-75¢

Background: Ford played at Proviso East High School in Illinois with Donnie Boyce and Michael Finley. Ford sat out 1991-92 at Illinois-Chicago to become academically eligible. He ranked fourth nationally in scoring as a senior and earned MVP kudos at the pre-draft Desert Classic.

Strengths: Shooting is Ford's greatest attribute. He has smooth actions and 3-point range. He can put the ball on the floor and get to the basket. He has a strong body and good leaping ability, which serves him well as a rebounder.

Weaknesses: A poor defensive player, Ford lacks the intensity and desire to stop his man consistently. He played in a run-and-gun system in college that didn't emphasize defense.

Analysis: Ford looks like a good fit for Seattle, which lacked punch on the perimeter in 1994-95. He might be limited to spot minutes as a rookie because of his defensive deficiencies. After playing at a low-level Division I school, he'll need time to adjust to the quality of NBA play.

COLLEGE STATISTICS

		G	FGP	FTP	RPG	APG	PPG
92-93	I-C	32	.477	.630	8.4	1.3	18.8
93-94	I-C	29	.498	.698	8.8	1.1	24.3
94-95	I-C	27	.472	.765	10.5	1.4	26.2
Totals		88	.482	.704	9.2	1.3	22.9

JAMES FORREST

Team: Unsigned
Position: Forward
Height: 6'8" **Weight:** 243
Birthdate: August 13, 1972
College: Georgia Tech

PLAYER SUMMARY	
Will	shoot with touch
Can't	stay in shape
Expect	a quick exit
Don't Expect	any guarantees
Fantasy	$0 Card	N/A

Background: One of the best high school players in the nation in 1991, Forrest adapted easily at Georgia Tech, finishing as the runnerup to Bob Sura for the ACC Rookie of the Year award. Forrest plateaued after that, however, ranking fourth in the conference in scoring each of the next three years and slipping to third-team All-ACC as a senior.

Strengths: A good athlete, Forrest has the strength to play power forward and the agility to work at the three spot. He makes the 15-foot jumper consistently.

Weaknesses: Forrest tends to gain weight; he was 260 pounds two weeks before the draft. He has a questionable work ethic. His ball-handling and one-on-one moves need refinement for him to play small forward.

Analysis: Once considered a lock for the first round, Forrest played poorly before the draft and fell off the face of the Earth. To make it in the NBA, he'll have to get in shape and dedicate himself to becoming a better player. He has a chance, but he'll probably have to come up through the bush leagues.

COLLEGE STATISTICS

		G	FGP	FTP	RPG	APG	PPG
91-92	GT	35	.509	.708	6.4	1.8	13.3
92-93	GT	30	.542	.687	7.5	1.4	19.5
93-94	GT	25	.468	.716	7.9	1.4	19.0
94-95	GT	24	.488	.664	8.3	1.6	18.8
Totals		114	.503	.694	7.4	1.6	17.4

KEVIN GARNETT

Team: Minnesota Timberwolves
Position: Forward
Height: 6'11" **Weight:** 220
Birthdate: May 19, 1976
College: None
Acquired: 1st-round pick in 1995 draft (5th overall)

PLAYER SUMMARY	
Will	get a chance early
Can't	body-up against giants
Expect	a fluid runner
Don't Expect	immediate returns
Fantasy	$1-3 Card	$2.00-4.00

Background: Rumors about Garnett going directly from Chicago's Farragut Academy to the NBA began percolating months before the draft. He wowed scouts with an MVP performance at the McDonald's All-America Game, and he was sensational in workouts leading up to the draft. He played three seasons at Mauldin (South Carolina) High School before transferring to Farragut.

Strengths: You name it, Garnett's got it. He's a greyhound in transition, sticks the 3-pointer, passes with grace and precision, and explodes to the basket with his dribble. He's been called a cross between Danny Manning and Ralph Sampson.

Weaknesses: Garnett had just turned 19 when he was drafted, which speaks volumes about his readiness for the NBA. His body, and his whole game in general, has room for continued growth. He needs to build stamina.

Analysis: It's going to take time, and the lowly Timberwolves have plenty of that. Shawn Kemp, the last player to bypass college for the NBA, averaged just 13 minutes his rookie season. Garnett will get more minutes than that because he's on a worse team. Eventually, he should be an All-Star.

COLLEGE STATISTICS

—DID NOT PLAY—

RASHARD GRIFFITH

Team: Milwaukee Bucks
Position: Center
Height: 6'10" **Weight:** 270
Birthdate: October 8, 1974
College: Wisconsin
Acquired: 2nd-round pick in 1995 draft (38th overall)

PLAYER SUMMARY	
Will	knock down jumpers
Can't	rely on press clippings
Expect	a lot of beef
Don't Expect	a lot of sizzle
Fantasy	$0 Card .....15-25¢

Background: The Illinois Player of the Year in 1993, Griffith was considered a recruiting coup for former Wisconsin coach Stu Jackson. The Badgers struggled during Griffith's tenure, but he led the Big Ten in rebounding and blocks in 1994-95 and was named team MVP ahead of Michael Finley. Griffith left school after his sophomore season.

Strengths: A space-eater defensively, Griffith has a pro body. He's a good shooter, capable of making the 12-footer or wheeling into the lane for the jump hook. He runs the court well.

Weaknesses: There are questions about Griffith's work ethic. Scouts didn't see much improvement from him in two years at Wisconsin. He has stiff, robotic movements and often seems to be a step behind the action.

Analysis: Considering the hype surrounding Griffith in high school, he had to be considered a disappointment in college, and he probably isn't ready for the NBA. Nonetheless, he figures to make Milwaukee's roster because the Bucks are woefully thin at center. Griffith looks like a three- or four-year project.

COLLEGE STATISTICS

	G	FGP	FTP	RPG	APG	PPG
93-94 WISC	25	.538	.580	8.5	1.0	13.9
94-95 WISC	26	.566	.579	10.8	0.8	17.2
Totals	51	.554	.580	9.7	0.9	15.6

ALAN HENDERSON

Team: Atlanta Hawks
Position: Forward
Height: 6'9" **Weight:** 225
Birthdate: December 12, 1972
College: Indiana
Acquired: 1st-round pick in 1995 draft (16th overall)

PLAYER SUMMARY	
Will	find a way to win
Can't	stick the 3-pointer
Expect	a well-rounded player
Don't Expect	a go-to guy
Fantasy	$1 Card .....25-40¢

Background: A four-year starter at Indiana, Henderson finished his career as the Hoosiers' all-time leading rebounder and shot-blocker and ranks fifth all-time in scoring. He was the leading rebounder for the U.S. Goodwill Games team in 1994.

Strengths: A smooth operator with good court sense, Henderson put up big numbers against good competition in college. He can operate with his back to the basket or hit the jumper from the perimeter. He rebounds aggressively and responds to coaching.

Weaknesses: Though he blocks shots, Henderson lacks the explosiveness of the top power forwards. He's strong but a tad undersized for the position. He misses too many free throws.

Analysis: While scouts remain unconvinced that Henderson can be a front-line player in the NBA, it's hard to argue with his productivity. His ability to play either forward spot enhances his chances. He'll be a backup in 1995-96, perhaps working his way into the rotation by the end of the season.

COLLEGE STATISTICS

		G	FGP	FTP	RPG	APG	PPG
91-92	IND	33	.508	.661	7.2	0.5	11.6
92-93	IND	30	.487	.637	8.1	0.9	11.1
93-94	IND	30	.531	.657	10.3	1.2	17.8
94-95	IND	31	.597	.634	9.7	1.7	23.5
Totals		124	.540	.646	8.8	1.1	16.0

FRED HOIBERG

Team: Indiana Pacers
Position: Guard
Height: 6'3" **Weight:** 203
Birthdate: October 15, 1972
College: Iowa St.
Acquired: 2nd-round pick in 1995 draft (52nd overall)

PLAYER SUMMARY	
Will	let it fly
Can't	distribute the orb
Expect	deep range
Don't Expect	a roster spot now
Fantasy	$0 Card ......12-20¢

Background: In high school, Hoiberg was nicknamed "The Mayor" because he was the most popular guy in town. He finished his career ranked third in Iowa State history in scoring, first in 3-point field goals, third in steals, fifth in assists, and sixth in rebounding. He was an academic All-American.

Strengths: Long-range shooting is Hoiberg's claim to fame. He was 40-percent accurate on college 3-pointers and showed a willingness to take the big shot. He's a better driver than generally given credit for. He's smart and has a solid work ethic.

Weaknesses: His ball-handling and overall floor game need to get better. His athletic abilities are nothing to get excited about. Though a competent defender, he's vulnerable against quickness.

Analysis: Indiana is expected to have some openings in its backcourt, but it's doubtful Hoiberg will make the team in 1995-96. Eventually, after some seasoning in the CBA or overseas, he could play in the NBA as a backup shooting guard.

COLLEGE STATISTICS

		G	FGP	FTP	RPG	APG	PPG
91-92	ISU	34	.573	.806	5.3	2.5	12.1
92-93	ISU	31	.550	.816	6.3	3.0	11.6
93-94	ISU	27	.535	.864	6.7	3.6	20.2
94-95	ISU	34	.438	.861	5.6	2.2	19.9
Totals		126	.511	.844	5.9	2.8	15.8

FRANKIE KING

Team: Los Angeles Lakers
Position: Guard
Height: 6'1" **Weight:** 185
Birthdate: June 6, 1972
College: Brunswick; Western Carolina
Acquired: 2nd-round pick in 1995 draft (37th overall)

PLAYER SUMMARY	
Will	attack the middle
Can't	be a starter
Expect	a roster spot
Don't Expect	a pass master
Fantasy	$0 Card ......20-35¢

Background: A two-time Southern Conference Player of the Year, King ranked second nationally in scoring in 1994-95. He played two seasons at a junior college in Georgia before going to Western Carolina in 1993. He scored 30 or more points 22 times for the Catamounts, including outbursts of 30 against Duke, 35 against Tennessee, and 41 against Louisville.

Strengths: Though short, King is built like a tank. He competes hard, is tough, and can penetrate with the ball. He's an excellent free throw shooter and a willing passer.

Weaknesses: A shooting guard in a point guard's body, King will have to be something special to make it in the NBA. He'll need to make big adjustments defensively.

Analysis: Without a pick in the 1995 draft, Lakers G.M. Jerry West made a deal with Detroit to acquire the 37th selection and take King. The Lakers are hoping for as much success with King as they've had with Nick Van Exel, the 37th pick in the 1993 draft. King has a strong upside and, as L.A.'s only pick, probably will make the team.

COLLEGE STATISTICS

		G	FGP	FTP	RPG	APG	PPG
93-94	WC	28	.490	.737	7.5	2.1	26.9
94-95	WC	28	.479	.832	7.3	3.4	26.5
Totals		56	.484	.780	7.4	2.7	26.7

JIMMY KING

Team: Toronto Raptors
Position: Guard
Height: 6'5" **Weight:** 210
Birthdate: August 9, 1973
College: Michigan
Acquired: 2nd-round pick in 1995 draft (35th overall)

PLAYER SUMMARY	
Will	run and dunk
Can't	make his free throws
Expect	growing pains
Don't Expect	sleight of hand
Fantasy	$1 Card 20-35¢

Background: One of Michigan's Fab Five recruits in 1991, King was the fourth to be drafted. He had a mediocre senior season, shooting 25.7 percent from 3-point range, but made the all-tournament team at the Portsmouth Invitational. He played in a school-record 17 NCAA Tournament games.

Strengths: King is an exceptional athlete with cat-like quickness and explosive jumping ability. He can be a defensive stopper when he wants to be. He passes willingly.

Weaknesses: After relying on his athleticism to this point, King needs to refine his skills. His shooting stroke in particular needs a lot of work, as do his ball-handling and passing. He's too small and too weak to play small forward in the NBA.

Analysis: King is a class guy who may be a consistent jump shot away from making it in the NBA. He could help himself by adding a little more aggressiveness to his game. He has a chance to make Toronto's roster in 1995-96 because the Raptors are expected to emphasize youth.

COLLEGE STATISTICS

		G	FGP	FTP	RPG	APG	PPG
91-92	MICH	34	.496	.736	3.3	2.3	9.9
92-93	MICH	36	.509	.648	4.4	3.1	10.8
93-94	MICH	29	.489	.646	3.8	2.6	12.3
94-95	MICH	31	.433	.679	5.0	2.9	14.7
Totals		130	.477	.676	4.1	2.7	11.9

MARTIN LEWIS

Team: Golden State Warriors
Position: Forward
Height: 6'5" **Weight:** 210
Birthdate: April 28, 1975
College: Butler County; Seward County
Acquired: 2nd-round pick in 1995 draft (50th overall)

PLAYER SUMMARY	
Will	finish on the break
Can't	nail foul shots
Expect	a skywalker
Don't Expect	anything now
Fantasy	$0 Card 10-15¢

Background: Lewis played one season at Butler County C.C. before transferring to Seward County in his hometown of Liberal, Kansas. Seward, with Lewis as its leading scorer, was the nation's top-ranked team for much of the 1994-95 season. He signed with Oklahoma State before declaring himself eligible for the draft.

Strengths: One of the best athletes in the '95 draft, Lewis runs the court swiftly and jumps out of the gym. He's a great dunker and shows good range on his jump shot.

Weaknesses: Other than free throw shooting, Lewis has no glaring weaknesses. He'll have to make the switch from inside player to outside player and prove that he can handle the leap from J.C. ball to the NBA.

Analysis: Golden State drafted Lewis intending to trade him to Toronto as part of a deal involving B.J. Armstrong. Because they're starting from scratch, the Raptors may have room for a rough gem such as Lewis, who was a complete unknown to NBA scouts before the draft. More likely, he will have to develop his game in the basketball bush leagues.

COLLEGE STATISTICS

		G	FGP	FTP	RPG	APG	PPG
93-94	BUTL	33	.552	.651	6.3	1.6	17.4
94-95	SEW	37	.650	.658	8.2	1.7	22.6
Totals		70	.639	.655	7.3	1.7	20.2

DONNY MARSHALL

Team: Cleveland Cavaliers
Position: Forward
Height: 6'7" **Weight:** 230
Birthdate: July 17, 1972
College: Connecticut
Acquired: 2nd-round pick in 1995 draft
(39th overall)

PLAYER SUMMARY	
Will	run and press
Can't	draw and dish
Expect	a roster spot
Don't Expect	lack of effort
Fantasy	$1 Card ......12-20¢

Background: Marshall increased his scoring and rebounding averages each season at Connecticut and saved his best for last, averaging 22.3 points in four games in the 1995 NCAA Tournament. He was the leading scorer at the pre-draft Desert Classic.

Strengths: Marshall has a strong upside. A superb athlete, he runs the floor easily and gets in his man's face defensively. His jump shot improved dramatically over the course of four college seasons, to the point where he can stick the 18-footer routinely. He plays with a lot of enthusiasm.

Weaknesses: While he's a competent ball-handler, Marshall must work on his overall floor game. His passing is substandard and he lacks creativity with the ball. He's a bit undersized for an NBA small forward.

Analysis: Marshall made waves at the Desert Classic and probably would have been a first-round pick had he not skipped the Chicago camp. He's good enough to play in the NBA and is the kind of hardnosed player Cleveland coach Mike Fratello likes.

COLLEGE STATISTICS

	G	FGP	FTP	RPG	APG	PPG
91-92 CONN	27	.370	.708	1.6	0.4	1.9
92-93 CONN	28	.466	.761	4.2	1.1	7.8
93-94 CONN	34	.517	.774	5.5	1.3	12.4
94-95 CONN	32	.456	.829	5.8	1.4	15.8
Totals	121	.474	.791	4.4	1.1	9.9

CUONZO MARTIN

Team: Atlanta Hawks
Position: Guard
Height: 6'4" **Weight:** 215
Birthdate: September 23, 1971
College: Purdue
Acquired: 2nd-round pick in 1995 draft
(57th overall)

PLAYER SUMMARY	
Will	jack it up
Can't	be a forward
Expect	a solid technician
Don't Expect	pyrotechnics
Fantasy	$0 Card ......10-15¢

Background: Martin had a good run at Purdue, first as a complement to Glenn Robinson, then as the main man after Robinson left for the NBA in 1994. Martin played a school-record 127 games. He made 91 3-pointers his senior season while earning first-team All-Big Ten recognition.

Strengths: Martin is an outstanding stand-still jump-shooter and a tenacious, hard-nosed defensive player. He shot 45.1 percent from 3-point range as a collegian. He's well coached in basketball fundamentals.

Weaknesses: A small forward in college, Martin will have to move to shooting guard after measuring just 6'4" before the draft. Consequently, he needs to expand his game on the perimeter and learn to create scoring opportunities with his dribble.

Analysis: Seldom does the 57th pick in the draft make an NBA roster, but Martin has a fighting chance. Atlanta needs his aggressiveness. He would have gone earlier in the draft had he not skipped the Chicago camp because of illness.

COLLEGE STATISTICS

	G	FGP	FTP	RPG	APG	PPG
91-92 PURD	33	.521	.759	3.3	1.5	5.8
92-93 PURD	28	.522	.807	3.7	2.4	11.9
93-94 PURD	34	.463	.735	4.3	1.9	16.3
94-95 PURD	32	.439	.799	3.9	2.2	18.4
Totals	127	.472	.777	3.8	2.0	13.1

MICHAEL McDONALD

Team: Golden State Warriors
Position: Center
Height: 6'10" **Weight:** 232
Birthdate: February 13, 1969
College: Utah Valley; New Orleans
Acquired: 2nd-round pick in 1995 draft
(55th overall)

PLAYER SUMMARY	
Will	send it back
Can't	face and score
Expect	a fringe guy
Don't Expect	nifty assists
Fantasy	$0 Card ..... 10-15¢

Background: The oldest player selected in the 1995 draft, McDonald never played high school basketball and didn't begin college until he was 21. He spent one year at Utah Valley C.C. before going to New Orleans, where as a senior he led the Privateers in rebounding, blocked shots, and field goal accuracy. He averaged a school-record 2.5 blocks for his career.

Strengths: A fine athlete, McDonald runs the floor smoothly and has good quickness. His 7'4" wingspan enables him to block shots, and he works hard for rebounds. He's still growing as a basketball player.

Weaknesses: McDonald's offensive game is raw. His moves are rudimentary and he's a poor free throw shooter. He showed no above-average skills at the pre-draft Portsmouth and Chicago camps.

Analysis: McDonald isn't ready for the NBA, and he's not nearly as good as former New Orleans center Ervin Johnson. McDonald could play in the CBA or overseas for a couple of years, then perhaps have a shot at making it. He's 26, so time is of the essence.

COLLEGE STATISTICS

		G	FGP	FTP	RPG	APG	PPG
92-93	NO	29	.657	.648	2.5	0.1	4.2
93-94	NO	30	.597	.509	6.9	0.5	5.7
94-95	NO	29	.573	.585	9.7	0.8	11.1
Totals		88	.593	.581	6.3	0.5	7.0

ANTONIO McDYESS

Team: Denver Nuggets
Position: Forward
Height: 6'9" **Weight:** 220
Birthdate: September 7, 1974
College: Alabama
Acquired: Draft rights traded from Clippers with Randy Woods for Rodney Rogers and draft rights to Brent Barry, 6/95

PLAYER SUMMARY	
Will	snare offensive rebounds
Can't	stick the 3-pointer
Expect	a good team player
Don't Expect	a finished product
Fantasy ..$10-13 Card ..$1.75-3.50	

Background: Before leaving school after his sophomore season, McDyess had a 39-point, 19-rebound breakout against Penn in the NCAA Tournament. At Alabama, he played alongside Jason Caffey, a forward selected in the first round by Chicago.

Strengths: McDyess has an enormous upside. He has prototypical size for a power forward, and he moves easily for his size. He grades above average in strength, wingspan, vertical leap, and end-to-end speed. He has no trouble beating defenders one-on-one with quickness in the post.

Weaknesses: McDyess is still learning how to play. He lacks any semblance of a perimeter game (he never made a college 3-pointer), and he's a below-average passer. His free throw shooting needs work.

Analysis: Even some NBA scouts had no idea who McDyess was a year ago. Now they agree that McDyess can become an All-Star a few years down the road. For now, he gives the Nuggets insurance against the health of LaPhonso Ellis.

COLLEGE STATISTICS

		G	FGP	FTP	RPG	APG	PPG
93-94	ALAB	26	.564	.533	8.1	0.4	11.4
94-95	ALAB	33	.512	.667	10.2	0.6	13.9
Totals		59	.533	.625	9.3	0.5	12.8

ERIK MEEK

Team: Houston Rockets
Position: Forward/Center
Height: 6'10" **Weight:** 245
Birthdate: January 17, 1973
College: Duke
Acquired: 2nd-round pick in 1995 draft
(41st overall)

PLAYER SUMMARY	
Will	shoot a high pct.
Can't	inherit the Earth
Expect	an honest effort
Don't Expect	instant impact
Fantasy	$0 Card ......12-20¢

Background: Meek was never more than a role-player at Duke, averaging five points and 15 minutes for his career, but he wowed NBA scouts at the Portsmouth Invitational with averages of 14.7 points and 14.3 rebounds. He had eight double-doubles in 31 games his senior season.

Strengths: A hustler, Meek plays hard and pushes himself to run the floor. He can make the 12- to 15-footer consistently. He's a good position rebounder.

Weaknesses: Meek lacks the athletic ability of many of the NBA's players. He was inconsistent from game to game in college and in the postseason camps. He's a bad free throw shooter.

Analysis: A five-star high school player, Meek was slowed at Duke because of injuries suffered when he was hit by a car. Consequently, some NBA scouts think he's just gaining his best form and has a chance to stick. He's helped by the fact that Houston didn't have a first-round pick and is weak at backup center.

COLLEGE STATISTICS

	G	FGP	FTP	RPG	APG	PPG
91-92 DUKE	25	.579	.500	1.2	0.2	2.5
92-93 DUKE	32	.594	.571	2.9	0.2	3.5
93-94 DUKE	34	.545	.600	4.2	0.4	3.5
94-95 DUKE	31	.621	.580	8.3	0.8	10.3
Totals	**122**	**.598**	**.575**	**4.3**	**0.4**	**5.0**

LOREN MEYER

Team: Dallas Mavericks
Position: Center
Height: 6'10" **Weight:** 257
Birthdate: December 30, 1972
College: Iowa St.
Acquired: 1st-round pick in 1995 draft
(24th overall)

PLAYER SUMMARY	
Will	fill on the break
Can't	rattle the rafters
Expect	a pure stroke
Don't Expect	pure power
Fantasy	$0 Card ......10-15¢

Background: Meyer missed 15 games in 1993-94 because of injuries sustained in a truck/train collision. His scoring average dipped by 6.6 points per game, but he averaged 12 rebounds over the final seven games of the season.

Strengths: Meyer runs the floor easily, knocks down his jump shot consistently, and has range to near the 3-point line. He's a decent foul shooter and he gets to the line often. He plays sound position defense and, while not a fearsome shot-blocker, does a good job clogging the middle.

Weaknesses: Consistency has eluded Meyer. He's just discovering how good he can be. He lacks an offensive repertoire with his back to the basket.

Analysis: A happy-go-lucky guy from a small town in Iowa, Meyer can have as good a career in the NBA as he wants to have. If he turns up the intensity, he can be a legitimate starter on a good team. His athletic ability gives him a big edge over most power players. This is a solid pick for Dallas.

COLLEGE STATISTICS

	G	FGP	FTP	RPG	APG	PPG
91-92 ISU	34	.514	.596	3.1	0.4	5.1
92-93 ISU	31	.542	.710	4.9	1.3	9.8
93-94 ISU	12	.610	.737	9.5	1.7	22.2
94-95 ISU	34	.556	.732	8.9	1.5	15.7
Totals	**111**	**.556**	**.713**	**6.1**	**1.1**	**11.5**

LAWRENCE MOTEN

Team: Vancouver Grizzlies
Position: Guard
Height: 6'5" **Weight:** 185
Birthdate: March 25, 1972
College: Syracuse
Acquired: 2nd-round pick in 1995 draft (36th overall)

PLAYER SUMMARY	
Will	score early and often
Can't	do anything else
Expect	a slacker
Don't Expect	a sudden impact
Fantasy	$0 Card .....15-25¢

Background: Moten began his career as the national Freshman of the Year and ended it as the leading scorer in Syracuse and Big East history. Remarkably consistent, he scored in double figures in 118 of 121 college games.

Strengths: A stone scorer, Moten knows how to get off his shot in nearly any situation. He has good touch on his jumper and deceptive moves off the dribble. He's adept at finishing plays on the break. He has ideal size for a shooting guard.

Weaknesses: Moten's a terrible defensive player who displays little desire to get better. He moves in slow motion and apparently has a false sense of his abilities. His rebounding average got progressively smaller each season at Syracuse.

Analysis: Moten was lucky to get drafted by an expansion team, because he lacks the overall game to stick with an established club. The Grizzlies, though, are stocked with shooting guards, the position Moten will have to play in the NBA.

COLLEGE STATISTICS

		G	FGP	FTP	RPG	APG	PPG
91-92	SYR	32	.497	.752	6.0	2.0	18.2
92-93	SYR	29	.473	.652	4.8	2.7	17.9
93-94	SYR	30	.501	.698	4.5	2.2	21.5
94-95	SYR	30	.459	.743	4.2	3.3	19.6
Totals		121	.483	.716	4.9	2.5	19.3

ED O'BANNON

Team: New Jersey Nets
Position: Forward
Height: 6'8" **Weight:** 217
Birthdate: August 14, 1972
College: UCLA
Acquired: 1st-round pick in 1995 draft (9th overall)

PLAYER SUMMARY	
Will	lead by example
Can't	miss as a pro
Expect	class
Don't Expect	durability
Fantasy	...$5-7 Card $1.00-2.50

Background: Several media outlets named O'Bannon national Player of the Year in 1994-95, when he led UCLA to the national championship. He suffered an injury to his left knee in 1990 that sidelined him for more than a year. He is the fourth-leading scorer in UCLA history.

Strengths: Intelligence, leadership, moxie—and those are just the intangibles. O'Bannon displays a rock-solid all-around game, runs the court easily, finishes plays at the rim, and rebounds aggressively. An unorthodox left-hander, he's difficult to defend.

Weaknesses: His perimeter stroke and perimeter defense need refinement. The only other concern is his bum knee.

Analysis: Concerns about O'Bannon's damaged knee caused him to slip in the draft. He may not have a long career because of the injury, but he should be an impact player for as long as he stays healthy. Look for him to work his way into the starting lineup by the middle of his rookie season.

COLLEGE STATISTICS

		G	FGP	FTP	RPG	APG	PPG
91-92	UCLA	23	.416	.630	3.0	0.5	3.6
92-93	UCLA	33	.539	.707	7.0	1.7	16.7
93-94	UCLA	28	.484	.745	8.8	2.1	18.2
94-95	UCLA	33	.533	.785	8.3	2.5	20.4
Totals		117	.513	.739	7.0	1.8	15.5

GREG OSTERTAG

Team: Utah Jazz
Position: Center
Height: 7'2" **Weight:** 279
Birthdate: March 6, 1973
College: Kansas
Acquired: 1st-round pick in 1995 draft (28th overall)

PLAYER SUMMARY	
Will	make the team
Can't	score facing up
Expect	a big body
Don't Expect	a big somebody
Fantasy	$0 Card ...... 10-15¢

Background: Ostertag never averaged more than 10.3 points in any season at Kansas, but he became the leading shot-blocker in Big Eight Conference history with 258 rejections. He didn't become a regular starter until his junior season. He led the Jayhawks in field goal accuracy as a senior.

Strengths: You can't teach seven feet, and you can't teach 7'2", either. Ostertag bangs around in the post, rebounds, defends, and blocks shots—all the things a backup center is supposed to do.

Weaknesses: A poor offensive player, Ostertag lacks a move he can rely on. He has minimal shooting range, doesn't run well, and rarely passes. He tends to gain weight and has a questionable work ethic. He'll commit a lot of fouls as a rookie.

Analysis: Utah suffered in the 1995 playoffs without an injured Felton Spencer, so drafting a backup center was a priority. Ostertag is another in the long line of Utah mountain men. He can help in spot minutes as a rookie. He figures to stick.

COLLEGE STATISTICS

	G	FGP	FTP	RPG	APG	PPG
91-92 KANS	32	.545	.653	3.5	0.2	4.8
92-93 KANS	29	.517	.600	4.1	0.4	5.3
93-94 KANS	35	.533	.631	8.8	0.3	10.3
94-95 KANS	31	.596	.553	7.5	0.4	9.6
Totals	127	.550	.604	6.1	0.3	7.6

CHEROKEE PARKS

Team: Dallas Mavericks
Position: Forward/Center
Height: 6'10" **Weight:** 235
Birthdate: October 11, 1972
College: Duke
Acquired: 1st-round pick in 1995 draft (12th overall)

PLAYER SUMMARY	
Will	mix it up inside
Can't	jump out of the gym
Expect	a serviceable backup
Don't Expect	a scoring machine
Fantasy	$3-5 Card ...... 20-35¢

Background: Parks was a reserve on Duke's 1992 national championship team before moving into the starting lineup as a sophomore. He improved his production in points, rebounds, and assists in each of his four seasons. He ranks second in school history in blocked shots.

Strengths: Parks plays with emotion and knows how to win. He expanded his shooting range as a senior. He's a willing defender and rebounder as well as a good free throw shooter. He handles the ball well.

Weaknesses: Parks has a slow trigger on his shot and doesn't run very well. He needs to add some muscle to his body and expand his low-post game. Rumors of an apparent heart condition surfaced before the draft, sending up red flags around the NBA.

Analysis: Dallas drafted two big men—Parks and Loren Meyer—to complement its perimeter players. Parks has the skills to play spot minutes in the middle or slide to power forward. Most likely, he will be a reserve for the first few years of his career.

COLLEGE STATISTICS

	G	FGP	FTP	RPG	APG	PPG
91-92 DUKE	34	.571	.725	2.4	0.4	5.0
92-93 DUKE	32	.652	.720	6.9	0.4	12.3
93-94 DUKE	34	.536	.772	8.4	0.9	14.4
94-95 DUKE	31	.501	.776	9.3	1.5	19.0
Totals	131	.551	.755	6.7	0.8	12.5

ANTHONY PELLE

Team: Denver Nuggets
Position: Center
Height: 7'0" **Weight:** 260
Birthdate: December 1, 1972
College: Villanova; Fresno St.
Acquired: 2nd-round pick in 1995 draft (44th overall)

PLAYER SUMMARY	
Will	reject shots
Can't	do much else
Expect	a project
Don't Expect	Dikembe
Fantasy	$0 Card .....10-15¢

Background: A scrub at Villanova for three seasons, Pelle transferred to Fresno State for the 1994-95 season and emerged as the Bulldogs' starting center. He blocked 53 shots in 26 games. A strong showing at the Portsmouth Invitational convinced scouts that he could play in the NBA.

Strengths: Pelle has all the physical tools: size, strength, speed, quickness. An excellent shot-blocker, he anticipates well and re-acts instantaneously. He shows good touch from ten feet and has a nice jump hook from closer. He runs the court easily.

Weaknesses: Despite his many strengths, Pelle doesn't get much done on the court. His stats in college were nothing to get excited about. He doesn't get the clutch rebounds.

Analysis: Pelle's a good shot-blocker and Denver needs a backup center, so he has a chance to make the team. His value is enhanced because he can swing to power forward. It's doubtful he'll ever be more than a backup, and he may just be a tease.

COLLEGE STATISTICS

		G	FGP	FTP	RPG	APG	PPG
90-91	VILL	30	.500	.629	1.7	0.1	2.0
91-92	VILL	27	.367	.750	2.5	0.1	2.3
92-93	VILL	24	.480	.569	3.3	0.5	5.4
94-95	FSU	26	.510	.650	8.0	1.1	10.8
Totals		107	.483	.642	3.8	0.4	5.0

CONSTANTIN POPA

Team: Los Angeles Clippers
Position: Center
Height: 7'2" **Weight:** 235
Birthdate: February 18, 1971
College: Miami (FL)
Acquired: 2nd-round pick in 1995 draft (53rd overall)

PLAYER SUMMARY	
Will	hook with either hand
Can't	muscle underneath
Expect	growing pains
Don't Expect	anything pretty
Fantasy	$0 Card .....10-15¢

Background: Born in Bucharest, Popa played for the Romanian junior and senior national teams before attending Fork Union Academy in Virginia. He is Miami's all-time leader in blocked shots with 263 and ranks in the top ten in steals and rebounding.

Strengths: Popa has the best hook shot of any player in the 1995 draft (George Zidek is next). That is his main offensive weapon. He progressed steadily each season in college. He gets up and down the floor fairly well and blocks a few shots.

Weaknesses: Thin and gangly, Popa has a bad body for NBA purposes. He's foul-prone and a below-average rebounder. Lack of strength is his greatest shortcoming.

Analysis: Popa has a lot of room for growth as a player, and he may get the chance with the Clippers, who are weak at center and uncertain about the health of starter Stanley Roberts. Even if Popa makes the team, he won't play much as a rookie. More likely, he'll end up overseas, perhaps in Greece, for a couple of years.

COLLEGE STATISTICS

		G	FGP	FTP	RPG	APG	PPG
91-92	MIAM	32	.433	.540	4.8	0.6	6.8
92-93	MIAM	27	.527	.595	7.3	0.7	13.2
93-94	MIAM	27	.463	.701	6.0	1.1	9.1
94-95	MIAM	27	.527	.726	7.0	0.7	11.6
Totals		113	.493	.630	6.2	0.8	10.0

THEO RATLIFF

Team: Detroit Pistons
Position: Forward/Center
Height: 6'10" **Weight:** 215
Birthdate: April 17, 1973
College: Wyoming
Acquired: 1st-round pick in 1995 draft (18th overall)

PLAYER SUMMARY	
Will	run and jump
Can't	stick the jumper
Expect	a swatmeister
Don't Expect	a finished product
Fantasy	$1 Card	20-35¢

Background: Ratliff contributed almost nothing as a freshman at Wyoming. A year later, he led the nation in blocked shots, averaging 4.4 per game. He finished his career as the second-leading shot-blocker in NCAA history with 425 swats.

Strengths: An extraordinary shot-blocker, Ratliff has good size, long arms, and explosive leaping ability—plus terrific instincts for the task. He runs the floor well and is a high-percentage shooter.

Weaknesses: Thinly built at 215 pounds, Ratliff will suffer regular beatings against NBA power forwards. Chances are, he will struggle to rebound. Offensively, he lacks range on his shot and proficiency at the foul line. He had just 74 assists in college.

Analysis: Detroit traded the eighth pick in the draft for two later picks, one of which it used to draft Ratliff. The Pistons needed a rejector after losing their best shot-blocker, Oliver Miller, in the expansion draft. On most teams, Ratliff would be too raw to start, but Doug Collins might put him in the lineup.

COLLEGE STATISTICS

	G	FGP	FTP	RPG	APG	PPG
91-92 WYOM	27	.438	.583	2.0	0.3	1.8
92-93 WYOM	28	.538	.517	6.2	0.3	9.2
93-94 WYOM	28	.569	.649	7.8	1.0	15.4
94-95 WYOM	28	.544	.633	7.5	1.1	14.4
Totals	111	.547	.608	5.9	0.7	10.3

BRYANT REEVES

Team: Vancouver Grizzlies
Position: Center
Height: 7'0" **Weight:** 292
Birthdate: June 8, 1973
College: Oklahoma St.
Acquired: 1st-round pick in 1995 draft (6th overall)

PLAYER SUMMARY	
Will	establish position
Can't	shoot with range
Expect	steady improvement
Don't Expect	a skywalker
Fantasy	$6-8 Card	50¢-$1.00

Background: Reeves was a big nobody when he arrived on campus from tiny Gans, Oklahoma, in 1991, but he quickly became a dominating player, winning Big Eight Player of the Year honors in 1993 and 1995, and led Oklahoma State to the 1995 Final Four. He exceeded 2,000 points and 1,000 rebounds.

Strengths: His massive body gives Reeves an edge in most one-on-one matchups near the basket. He has a knack for getting his opponent into foul trouble. He seals off well on the defensive glass and he blocks shots.

Weaknesses: Reeves lacks the explosive athletic ability of many NBA players, and he'll be vulnerable against quickness in the post and in transition. He doesn't jump well and he's a mediocre passer.

Analysis: The best pure center in the 1995 draft, Reeves should have a long, prosperous career, though some scouts aren't convinced that he can be a front-line player. He could be a force if surrounded by good perimeter players.

COLLEGE STATISTICS

	G	FGP	FTP	RPG	APG	PPG
91-92 OSU	36	.521	.633	5.1	0.7	8.1
92-93 OSU	29	.621	.650	10.0	1.2	19.5
93-94 OSU	34	.585	.595	9.7	1.5	21.0
94-95 OSU	37	.586	.706	9.5	0.8	21.5
Totals	136	.585	.648	8.5	1.0	17.4

DON REID

Team: Detroit Pistons
Position: Forward
Height: 6'8" **Weight:** 250
Birthdate: December 30, 1973
College: Georgetown
Acquired: 2nd-round pick in 1995 draft (58th overall)

PLAYER SUMMARY	
Will	dunk in your face
Can't	operate outside
Expect	a hasty exit
Don't Expect	a Don Reid video
Fantasy	$0 Card	10-15¢

Background: A role-playing defender and rebounder, Reid averaged just 15.9 minutes per game during his career at Georgetown. The Hoyas' captain as a senior, he blocked 60 shots in 31 games and had four double-doubles.

Strengths: Reid got lost in the shuffle at Georgetown but showed NBA scouts a lot of talent in workouts before the draft. He's agile, runs the court smoothly, and fills on the break. He finishes plays inside and will accept contact. He blocks shots.

Weaknesses: Reid needs a consistent jumper to have a chance in the pros. He needs to generate some offense after averaging 4.5 points in college. He's well-built but perhaps an inch short for an NBA power forward. He's a bad free throw shooter.

Analysis: The last player selected in the 1995 draft, Reid is an intriguing prospect who nonetheless figures to lose a numbers game the first time around. With further development, perhaps overseas, he'll have a chance to play in the NBA someday.

COLLEGE STATISTICS

	G	FGP	FTP	RPG	APG	PPG
91-92 GEOR	28	.433	.600	2.1	0.3	1.6
92-93 GEOR	32	.419	.452	2.1	0.1	1.6
93-94 GEOR	31	.643	.630	5.9	0.9	7.7
94-95 GEOR	31	.595	.516	5.7	0.8	7.2
Totals	122	.579	.561	4.0	0.5	4.5

TERRENCE RENCHER

Team: Miami Heat
Position: Guard
Height: 6'3" **Weight:** 185
Birthdate: February 19, 1973
College: Texas
Acquired: Draft rights traded by Bullets with Rex Chapman for Jeff Webster and Ed Stokes, 6/95

PLAYER SUMMARY	
Will	push the pace
Can't	stoke the trifecta
Expect	a lefty sparkplug
Don't Expect	Nate Archibald
Fantasy	$0 Card	12-20¢

Background: Rencher surpassed former Texas player Travis Mays as the leading scorer in Southwest Conference history. Rencher scored in double figures in 111 of 124 games. His draft status improved with strong showings at the pre-draft camps.

Strengths: Rencher is exceptionally quick with the ball. He can stick the pull-up jumper or drive and finish plays in close. He's a good ball-handler against pressure and knows how to get a team into its offense. He's quick-handed defensively.

Weaknesses: Rencher never played point guard for the Longhorns, so he needs to learn the position. He was a gunner in college, making less than 30 percent of his 3-point attempts. He needs to add strength.

Analysis: Selected by Washington with the 32nd pick in the draft, Rencher was sent to Miami. The Heat have a lot of guards on their roster, but Rencher is good enough to stick. A late-bloomer, he could be one of the best sleeper picks of the 1995 draft.

COLLEGE STATISTICS

	G	FGP	FTP	RPG	APG	PPG
91-92 TEX	34	.463	.706	4.3	3.6	19.1
92-93 TEX	26	.377	.697	5.0	3.5	19.1
93-94 TEX	34	.413	.706	5.4	3.1	15.9
93-95 TEX	30	.475	.676	5.3	4.0	20.8
Totals	124	.434	.696	5.0	3.5	18.6

SHAWN RESPERT

Team: Milwaukee Bucks
Position: Guard
Height: 6'3" **Weight:** 195
Birthdate: February 6, 1972
College: Michigan St.
Acquired: Draft rights traded from Trail Blazers for draft rights to Gary Trent and a 1996 1st-round pick, 6/95

PLAYER SUMMARY	
Will	light it up
Can't	apply the clamps
Expect	a role as a rookie
Don't Expect	a dominator
Fantasy	$6-8 Card......$1.50-3.00

Background: Respert, picked eighth in the first round, missed the 1990-91 season because of a knee injury. He ranked eighth nationally in scoring as a senior and ranks No. 2 in scoring in Big Ten history.

Strengths: Respert's a stone scorer, capable of getting on a roll with his jump shot and putting up 30 points in a hurry. He was a 46-percent shooter from college 3-point range. He converts at the free throw line.

Weaknesses: Just 6'3", Respert will have to learn how to play the point. Consequently, his ball-handling and passing need to be upgraded. He's not especially quick and he's below average defensively.

Analysis: Every good team has a third guard capable of coming off the bench to spark a rally. Preferably, that player can swing between the point and shooting guard. Respert fits the prototype, though he'll need to grow as a playmaker. A productive career awaits.

COLLEGE STATISTICS

	G	FGP	FTP	RPG	APG	PPG
90-91 MSU	1	—	—	—	—	—
91-92 MSU	30	.503	.872	2.1	2.1	15.8
92-93 MSU	28	.481	.856	4.0	2.6	20.1
93-94 MSU	32	.484	.840	4.0	2.5	24.3
94-95 MSU	28	.473	.869	4.0	3.0	25.6
Totals	119	.483	.857	3.5	2.5	21.3

LOU ROE

Team: Detroit Pistons
Position: Forward
Height: 6'6" **Weight:** 220
Birthdate: July 14, 1972
College: Massachusetts
Acquired: 2nd-round pick in 1995 draft (30th overall)

PLAYER SUMMARY	
Will	get down and dirty
Can't	fill it up
Expect	a blue-collar worker
Don't Expect	Curtis Rowe
Fantasy	$0 Card......20-35¢

Background: The 1994-95 Atlantic 10 Player of the Year, Roe was the key ingredient in Massachusetts' rise as a national power. He's the leading rebounder in school history and ranks second to Jim McCoy in scoring.

Strengths: Roe competes fiercely and has a solid all-around game. He displays above-average athletic tools. He rebounds as well as any other player his size, and he's a top-flight defender.

Weaknesses: Until he improves his ball-handling and perimeter shooting, Roe will be a man without a position in the NBA. He's too small to survive at power forward. He scores on effort plays inside but lacks a refined post game.

Analysis: Undersized power players can make it in the NBA, particularly if they're drafted by the right team. Detroit is starting over with Doug Collins as coach, and the Pistons need some toughness in their frontcourt. Roe figures to stick, though playing time could be scarce.

COLLEGE STATISTICS

	G	FGP	FTP	RPG	APG	PPG
91-92 MASS	34	.529	.672	6.4	0.9	7.8
92-93 MASS	31	.564	.725	9.2	1.3	13.8
93-94 MASS	35	.505	.667	8.3	1.7	18.6
94-95 MASS	34	.532	.706	8.1	1.7	16.5
Totals	134	.529	.690	8.0	1.4	14.2

STEFANO RUSCONI

Team: Phoenix Suns
Position: Forward/Center
Height: 6'10" **Weight:** 240
Birthdate: February 10, 1968
College: None
Acquired: Draft rights traded from Cavaliers for draft rights to Milos Babic and other considerations, 6/90

PLAYER SUMMARY	
Will	push and shove
Can't	run and gun
Expect	a backup
Don't Expect	a go-to guy
Fantasy	$0 Card N/A

Background: Rusconi goes from Italy to the NBA after signing a three-year, $3.2 million contract with Phoenix, which acquired him in a draft-day deal in 1990. Rusconi played the past four seasons for Benetton Treviso, one of the best teams in Europe. He also played for the Italian national team.

Strengths: Rusconi has good size for a power forward and will throw his weight around under the boards. He plays hard and blocks shots. He shows good touch on the short-range jump shot. He can play some spot minutes at center.

Weaknesses: A lumbering athlete, he doesn't run the floor particularly well. His low-post game on offense needs to be upgraded.

Analysis: Phoenix signed Rusconi as an insurance policy against the health and possible retirement of Charles Barkley. If Barkley retires, Rusconi could get substantial minutes. If not, he'll see most of the action from a seat at the end of bench. He may need a year or more to adapt to the higher quality of play in the NBA.

COLLEGE STATISTICS

—DID NOT PLAY—

ARVYDAS SABONIS

Team: Portland Trail Blazers
Position: Center
Height: 7'3" **Weight:** 290
College: None
Acquired: 1st-round pick in 1986 draft (24th overall)

PLAYER SUMMARY	
Will	post and score
Can't	elevate
Expect	a big body
Don't Expect	a savior
Fantasy	$1 Card N/A

Background: Nine years after being drafted by Portland, Sabonis finally agreed to play in the NBA, though no contract had been signed before the NBA player lockout kicked in. A Lithuanian, Sabonis led the Soviet team to a gold medal at the 1988 Olympics. He led Real Madrid of Spain to the European club championship in 1995. He's widely regarded as the best player in Europe over the last decade.

Strengths: Sabonis could have been one of the best NBA centers ever. A big man who can score, Sabonis shows nice touch around the basket. He's strong and he moves easily. He's an exceptional passer and he dribbles the ball well for his size.

Weaknesses: At age 30, after a couple of Achilles tendon injuries, it remains to be seen how much Sabonis has left physically. He's never had a good work ethic, and his character has been questioned many times. Can he hold up to an 82-game schedule?

Analysis: Sabonis gives the Blazers an immediate offensive upgrade in the middle. Chances are, he'll split time with Chris Dudley in 1995-96. He won't be the monster he once was, but he'll be a better-than-average NBA center.

COLLEGE STATISTICS

—DID NOT PLAY—

JOE SMITH

Team: Golden State Warriors
Position: Forward
Height: 6'10" **Weight:** 225
Birthdate: July 26, 1975
College: Maryland
Acquired: 1st-round pick in 1995 draft (1st overall)

```
PLAYER SUMMARY
Will ...............................block shots
Can't .....................survive at center
Expect ......continued improvement
Don't Expect...........a selfish player
Fantasy ..$13-16  Card ...$3.50-6.00
```

Background: It took just two years for Smith to advance from an obscure high school player to the top pick in the NBA draft. During his brief tenure at Maryland, he garnered consensus national Freshman of the Year honors in 1993-94 and won the Naismith Award as the best player in the nation in 1994-95.

Strengths: Smith has the versatility that NBA teams covet in a big man. A quick jumper, he snatches rebounds from opponents, blocks shots, and has an assortment of scoring moves in the post. He runs the court easily and is an above-average ballhandler. He plays with great enthusiasm.

Weaknesses: Smith didn't turn 20 until July. He needs to add bulk to his lanky body and make the adjustment from college center to pro power forward.

Analysis: If history repeats itself, Smith will be an elite player. Thirteen of the past 16 top picks have made the All-Star team at least once, and Glenn Robinson and Chris Webber will make it soon. Smith eventually should produce 20 points and ten rebounds a night.

COLLEGE STATISTICS

	G	FGP	FTP	RPG	APG	PPG
93-94 MARY	30	.522	.734	10.7	0.8	19.4
94-95 MARY	34	.578	.741	10.6	1.2	20.8
Totals	64	.550	.737	10.7	1.0	20.1

ERIC SNOW

Team: Seattle SuperSonics
Position: Guard
Height: 6'3" **Weight:** 190
Birthdate: April 24, 1973
College: Michigan St.
Acquired: Draft rights traded from Bucks for draft rights to Eurelejus Zukaukas, 6/95

```
PLAYER SUMMARY
Will .......................distribute the pill
Can't .........................stroke the "J"
Expect ..............................machismo
Don't Expect..............anything now
Fantasy .............$0   Card ......20-35¢
```

Background: Snow moved into Michigan State's lineup as a sophomore and quickly established himself as the best assist man in the Big Ten. He ranked fourth nationally in assists in 1994-95. Snow's brother Percy is a former All-America linebacker at MSU.

Strengths: Snow may have been the best pure point guard in the 1995 draft. He knows how to control the game's tempo, penetrate the cracks, and distribute the ball to the shooters. He's strong physically and has superb leadership qualities. He defends aggressively.

Weaknesses: His future would be bright if he could make a jump shot, but Snow's a terrible shooter from the field and from the free throw line. Most of his baskets are layups.

Analysis: Selected by Milwaukee with the 43rd pick in the draft, Snow was shipped to Seattle, a team without a classic point guard. However, the Sonics have a lot of talent. If Snow makes it, it will be as the 12th man.

COLLEGE STATISTICS

		G	FGP	FTP	RPG	APG	PPG
91-92	MSU	25	.480	.200	0.6	1.0	1.1
92-93	MSU	28	.546	.268	2.6	5.2	4.3
93-94	MSU	32	.514	.449	3.5	6.7	6.8
94-95	MSU	28	.520	.608	3.3	7.8	10.8
Totals		113	.521	.459	2.6	5.3	5.9

JERRY STACKHOUSE

Team: Philadelphia 76ers
Position: Guard/Forward
Height: 6'6" **Weight:** 218
Birthdate: November 5, 1974
College: North Carolina
Acquired: 1st-round pick in 1995 draft (3rd overall)

PLAYER SUMMARY	
Will	start immediately
Can't	miss as a pro
Expect	the Rookie of the Year
Don't Expect	a head case
Fantasy ..$15-18	Card ...$4.00-8.00

Background: Out of powerful Oak Hill Academy in Virginia, Stackhouse adapted quickly at North Carolina, earning MVP honors at the ACC Tournament as a freshman and accolades from *Sports Illustrated* as the best player in the nation in 1994-95. The Tar Heels were 56-13 in his two seasons.

Strengths: Strength, speed, tenacity, character—Stackhouse has it all. He's a sensational rebounder for his size, and a willing passer. He's capable of shutting out opponents defensively. Offensively, he excels at beating defenders to the basket. He's been well schooled in basketball fundamentals.

Weaknesses: Stackhouse lacks a pure stroke from the perimeter. An average ballhandler, he's apt to commit a lot of turnovers as a rookie.

Analysis: Stackhouse is the rookie most likely to make a sudden impact in 1995-96. The 76ers need someone to take charge offensively, and Stackhouse can do that. While he averaged less than 16 points as a collegian, he attempted just ten shots a game. Expect both numbers to increase immediately.

COLLEGE STATISTICS

	G	FGP	FTP	RPG	APG	PPG
93-94	NC	35	.466	.732	5.0	2.0	12.2
94-95	NC	34	.517	.712	8.2	2.7	19.2
Totals		69	.496	.720	6.6	2.3	15.7

DAMON STOUDAMIRE

Team: Toronto Raptors
Position: Guard
Height: 5'10" **Weight:** 171
Birthdate: September 3, 1973
College: Arizona
Acquired: 1st-round pick in 1995 draft (7th overall)

PLAYER SUMMARY	
Will	dominate the rock
Can't	pass up an open look
Expect	plenty of opportunity
Don't Expect	a defensive stopper
Fantasy $4-6	Card ....60¢-$1.25

Background: A three-time All-Pac-10 selection, Stoudamire shared 1995 conference Player of the Year honors with UCLA's Ed O'Bannon. Stoudamire and Gary Payton are the only players in Pac-10 history with 1,800 points, 600 assists, and 400 rebounds.

Strengths: A left-handed waterbug, Stoudamire pushes a furious pace with the basketball, has shooting range to 25 feet, and can get to the basket with his dribble. He sets up his jump shot with a devilish crossover move. His quick hands serve him well defensively.

Weaknesses: While he's a productive player, Stoudamire isn't a true point guard. He looks for his own offense too often, and his shot selection ranges from good to awful. Can he lead an NBA team? The jury is out.

Analysis: The trend toward scoring point guards bodes well for Stoudamire. So does the endorsement of Isiah Thomas, one of the all-time great point men and now G.M. of the Raptors. Stoudamire could average 14 points and five assists his rookie season.

COLLEGE STATISTICS

		G	FGP	FTP	RPG	APG	PPG
91-92	ARIZ	30	.455	.771	2.2	2.5	7.2
92-93	ARIZ	28	.438	.791	4.1	5.7	11.0
93-94	ARIZ	35	.448	.800	4.5	5.9	18.3
94-95	ARIZ	30	.476	.826	4.3	7.3	22.8
Totals		123	.457	.804	3.8	5.4	15.0

BOB SURA

Team: Cleveland Cavaliers
Position: Guard
Height: 6'4" **Weight:** 200
Birthdate: March 25, 1973
College: Florida St.
Acquired: 1st-round pick in 1995 draft
(17th overall)

PLAYER SUMMARY	
Will	shoot the rock
Can't	resist temptation
Expect	some hits and misses
Don't Expect	a wallflower
Fantasy	$1 Card ...... 20-35¢

Background: Sura became the only player in ACC history with 2,000 points, 700 rebounds, 400 assists, and 200 steals. As a freshman, he was the third wheel in a backcourt that included Sam Cassell and Charlie Ward. Sura is FSU's all-time leading scorer.

Strengths: Sura's a top-notch scorer and a superb athlete with speed and leaping ability. A streaky shooter, he can get white-hot with his jumper. He rebounds better than most guards.

Weaknesses: While he's a good passer, he's turnover-prone, tending to play out of control at times. Sura needs to develop more consistency from 3-point range. He's a surprisingly poor free throw shooter.

Analysis: Many scouts rated Sura the best shooting guard in the 1995 draft, but he slipped to the 17th slot overall, behind Shawn Respert (eighth) and Brent Barry (15th). Sura has NBA-level offensive skills and landed with a team that finished last in the league in scoring in 1994-95. He couldn't ask for a better opportunity.

COLLEGE STATISTICS

	G	FGP	FTP	RPG	APG	PPG
91-92 FSU	31	.461	.627	3.5	2.5	12.3
92-93 FSU	34	.452	.638	6.1	2.7	19.9
93-94 FSU	27	.469	.654	7.9	4.5	21.2
94-95 FSU	27	.417	.687	6.9	5.4	18.6
Totals	119	.450	.652	6.0	3.7	17.9

KURT THOMAS

Team: Miami Heat
Position: Forward
Height: 6'9" **Weight:** 230
Birthdate: October 4, 1972
College: Texas Christian
Acquired: 1st-round pick in 1995 draft
(10th overall)

PLAYER SUMMARY	
Will	attack the rack
Can't	bury the bomb
Expect	1,000 minutes in 1995-96
Don't Expect	a difference-maker
Fantasy	$1 Card ...... 30-75¢

Background: In 1994-95, Thomas joined Hank Gathers and Xavier McDaniel as the only players to lead the NCAA Division I in scoring and rebounding in the same season. Thomas finished his career with a school-record 166 blocks. He sat out the 1992-93 season because of a broken leg.

Strengths: Thomas is a good all-around player. He has sticky hands, a soft shooting touch in close, and several go-to moves. He jumps well and has good instincts for rebounding and shot-blocking.

Weaknesses: While he improved his shooting percentage each season at TCU, Thomas lacks range. He made just 24 percent of his 3-point attempts. Injuries have been a concern, and his attitude has been questioned on occasion.

Analysis: Anticipating the imminent decline of veteran Kevin Willis, Miami drafted a potential replacement in Thomas, who might need a couple of years to get the hang of the NBA. He could be a good player down the road, but he's no sure thing.

COLLEGE STATISTICS

	G	FGP	FTP	RPG	APG	PPG
90-91 TC	28	.444	.500	0.5	0.1	1.9
91-92 TC	21	.487	.667	5.4	1.1	7.1
93-94 TC	27	.509	.645	9.7	1.9	20.7
94-95 TC	27	.548	.714	14.6	1.2	28.9
Totals	103	.524	.682	7.6	1.0	14.7

SCOTTY THURMAN

Team: Unsigned
Position: Forward/Guard
Height: 6'6" **Weight:** 210
Birthdate: November 10, 1974
College: Arkansas

PLAYER SUMMARY	
Will	apply deep heat
Can't	apply the clamps
Expect	a CBA detour
Don't Expect	Hog Heaven
Fantasy	$0 Card .... N/A

Background: Thurman was the hero of the 1994 NCAA Tournament; his 3-pointer in the final seconds gave Arkansas a victory against Duke in the championship game. He ranks first in Razorbacks history in 3-pointers, ninth in scoring, ninth in assists, and 11th in steals. Arkansas was 83-19 in games he played. He left school after his junior season.

Strengths: Thurman is a long-range jump-shooting specialist. He has beautiful form on his shot. He's a good athlete. He converts a high percentage from the field and from the free throw line.

Weaknesses: Thurman needs to develop some versatility to have a chance in the pros. He's a weak passer and ball-handler and struggles to create offense with his dribble. His defense leaves a lot to be desired. He might not be quick enough to survive at guard in the NBA.

Analysis: Thurman thought he was a top-20 talent, but scouts disagreed and he went undrafted. Someone will invite him to training camp, but he has no chance to play in the NBA right now. He's looking at the CBA, assuming he rules out a return to school.

COLLEGE STATISTICS

	G	FGP	FTP	RPG	APG	PPG
92-93 ARK	31	.465	.800	4.4	2.2	17.4
93-94 ARK	34	.469	.732	4.5	3.0	15.9
94-95 ARK	37	.458	.781	3.9	2.3	15.4
Totals	102	.464	.770	4.3	2.5	16.2

GARY TRENT

Team: Portland Trail Blazers
Position: Forward
Height: 6'7" **Weight:** 240
Birthdate: September 22, 1974
College: Ohio
Acquired: Draft rights traded from Bucks with a 1996 1st-round pick for draft rights to Shawn Respert, 6/95

PLAYER SUMMARY	
Will	maul in the middle
Can't	play the facing game
Expect	growing pains
Don't Expect	lack of effort
Fantasy	$1 Card ...... 25-50¢

Background: Dubbed "The Shaq of the MAC," Trent led the Mid-American Conference in scoring three straight seasons and in rebounding twice. He and Ron Harper are the only MAC players with 2,000 points and 1,000 rebounds. Trent left school after his junior season and was drafted 11th overall.

Strengths: Trent overpowers players his size in the post. He runs and jumps well and has some explosiveness. He rebounds relentlessly and makes a high percentage of his field goal attempts.

Weaknesses: Trent lacks the size to play power forward in the NBA and isn't quick enough to guard the better "three" men. He can't hit the outside jump shot consistently. His ball-handling needs work.

Analysis: Portland swung a deal to acquire Trent and landed a 1996 first-round pick to boot. The Trail Blazers are dismantling their aging team and probably will give Trent a long look as a rookie. He needs to expand his skills, especially on the perimeter, to make it into the playing rotation.

COLLEGE STATISTICS

	G	FGP	FTP	RPG	APG	PPG
92-93 OHIO	27	.651	.696	9.3	1.6	19.0
93-94 OHIO	33	.576	.722	11.4	2.0	25.4
94-95 OHIO	33	.527	.642	12.8	2.4	22.9
Totals	93	.573	.687	11.3	2.0	22.7

DAVID VAUGHN

Team: Orlando Magic
Position: Forward/Center
Height: 6'10" **Weight:** 240
Birthdate: March 23, 1973
College: Memphis
Acquired: 1st-round pick in 1995 draft
(25th overall)

PLAYER SUMMARY	
Will ....look like an NBA player	
Can't ....make it at center	
Expect...............a low-key approach	
Don't Expect....much P.T. this year	
Fantasy ....$0 Card ......20-40¢	

Background: Son of former ABA player David Vaughn and nephew of Memphis coach Larry Finch, Vaughn missed his sophomore season because of a knee injury. Returning in 1993-94, he ranked fourth nationally in blocked shots and sixth in rebounding. He forfeited a year of eligibility to enter the NBA draft.

Strengths: While he lacks any above-average skills by NBA standards, Vaughn has a solid all-around power game. He has good shooting touch inside. He blocks shots and gets his share of rebounds.

Weaknesses: Vaughn has neither the strength nor the intensity to play center in the NBA. He's never been a take-charge type of player. Scouts have concerns about his injuries and propensity for turnovers.

Analysis: Vaughn was reunited with former Memphis teammate Anfernee Hardaway when Orlando selected him with the 25th pick in the draft. He should make the Magic roster as a backup power forward. Minutes could be scarce.

COLLEGE STATISTICS

	G	FGP	FTP	RPG	APG	PPG
91-92 MEMP	34	.513	.761	8.3	0.7	13.4
92-93 MEMP	1	.364	—	8.0	2.0	10.0
93-94 MEMP	28	.496	.757	12.0	1.1	16.6
94-95 MEMP	29	.450	.729	9.6	1.0	12.9
Totals	92	.486	.749	9.8	0.9	14.2

RASHEED WALLACE

Team: Washington Bullets
Position: Forward/Center
Height: 6'10" **Weight:** 225
Birthdate: September 17, 1974
College: North Carolina
Acquired: 1st-round pick in 1995 draft
(4th overall)

PLAYER SUMMARY	
Will................................run and jump	
Can't................defend consistently	
Expect ....film at 11:00	
Don't Expect ......a good playmaker	
Fantasy ...$5-7 Card $1.75-3.50	

Background: Wallace was heralded as the best prep big man to come out of Philadelphia since Wilt Chamberlain. Wallace had a good run at North Carolina, finishing his two-year career as the leading field goal marksman in ACC history and setting a Tar Heels record with 93 blocks in 1994-95.

Strengths: Wallace runs the floor exceptionally well for a man his size, and he finishes plays around the basket with authority. He has good instincts and springs for blocking shots and rebounding, and he can hit the 15-foot jumper. He has a strong upside because he's still maturing physically.

Weaknesses: Most of the questions about Wallace before the draft centered on his apparent immaturity and lack of toughness. Basketball-wise, he needs to add muscle to his body and hone his stroke from the free throw line.

Analysis: Wallace won't be a center in the NBA, as he's too slight for the position. However, he's perfectly suited for power forward, where he'll have an edge in quickness and speed over most of his opponents. He should be a ten-year starter.

COLLEGE STATISTICS

	G	FGP	FTP	RPG	APG	PPG
93-94 NC	35	.604	.604	6.6	0.5	9.5
94-95 NC	34	.654	.631	8.2	1.0	16.6
Totals	69	.635	.621	7.4	0.8	13.0

DWAYNE WHITFIELD

Team: Golden State
Position: Forward
Height: 6'6" **Weight:** 240
Birthdate: August 21, 1972
College: Jackson St.
Acquired: 2nd-round pick in 1995 draft (40th overall)

PLAYER SUMMARY	
Will	fight for the rock
Can't	face and shoot
Expect	a work in progress
Don't Expect	anything now
Fantasy	$0 Card ...... 10-15¢

Background: Whitfield sat out his freshman season to become academically eligible and missed most of his sophomore season because of a broken foot. As a senior, he led Jackson State in scoring, rebounding, field goal accuracy, and blocks and had 21 rebounds in a game against Louisville.

Strengths: Whitfield runs the court easily and rebounds aggressively. He's built to withstand the rigors of playing small forward in the NBA. He comes from a program that has produced several pro players in recent seasons, including Lindsey Hunter and Ryan Lorthridge.

Weaknesses: A center and power forward throughout his career, Whitfield will have to improve his game facing the basket to play the three spot in the pros. He never made a 3-pointer and had only 34 assists in 67 games. Listed at 6'9" in college, he measured 6'6" before the draft.

Analysis: A late-bloomer with a solid work ethic, Whitfield has a chance to play in the NBA some day. Before that happens, he'll probably have to pay his dues in the CBA.

COLLEGE STATISTICS

	G	FGP	FTP	RPG	APG	PPG
92-93 JSU	12	.483	.577	3.8	0.2	6.1
93-94 JSU	29	.574	.715	6.7	0.6	12.4
94-95 JSU	26	.610	.621	10.5	0.6	19.6
Totals	67	.584	.651	7.7	0.5	14.1

ERIC WILLIAMS

Team: Boston Celtics
Position: Forward
Height: 6'7" **Weight:** 220
Birthdate: July 17, 1972
College: Vincennes; Providence
Acquired: 1st-round pick in 1995 draft (14th overall)

PLAYER SUMMARY	
Will	get a big shot early
Can't	be a power forward
Expect	points in transition
Don't Expect	a franchise-maker
Fantasy	$0 Card ...... 20-35¢

Background: Williams seemingly came out of nowhere to be recognized as a top-15 draft pick. He played two seasons at Vincennes (Indiana) Junior College before going to Providence in 1993. In a game against St. John's during his senior season, Williams scored 19 consecutive points. He cemented his draft status with stellar work at the pre-draft Desert Classic.

Strengths: A fluid runner, Williams does some damage on the fastbreak. He jumps quickly and has good scoring sense around the basket. He passes selflessly and he works hard on defense. He was well coached at Providence.

Weaknesses: While he shot 37.2 percent from 3-point range as a senior, Williams needs more work on his shot. At 220 pounds, he needs to add some meat to his bones.

Analysis: This is the top sleeper pick of the draft. Scouting guru Marty Blake said Williams could start for Boston, especially now that Dominique Wilkins is gone. Williams is still growing as a player and should have a fruitful career.

COLLEGE STATISTICS

	G	FGP	FTP	RPG	APG	PPG
93-94 PROV	30	.508	.660	5.0	1.2	15.7
94-95 PROV	30	.410	.687	6.7	2.5	17.7
Totals	60	.453	.673	5.9	1.9	16.7

CORLISS WILLIAMSON

Team: Sacramento Kings
Position: Forward
Height: 6'7" **Weight:** 245
Birthdate: December 4, 1973
College: Arkansas
Acquired: 1st-round pick in 1995 draft (13th overall)

```
         PLAYER SUMMARY
Will .........................bump and grind
Can't .......................post the giants
Expect ................a low-post scorer
Don't Expect ................Sir Charles
Fantasy ...$1-3  Card......$1.50-3.00
```

Background: "Big Nasty" overpowered most of his opponents during his three seasons at Arkansas. He led the Razorbacks to the 1994 national championship and averaged 20.2 points and 7.5 rebounds in 15 career NCAA Tournament games. Arkansas was 74-17 in games he played.

Strengths: A determined inside force, Williamson scatters opponents like bowling pins. He has good scoring sense and a nice touch around the basket. He seldom takes a bad shot and he gets the big rebounds. He has great hands.

Weaknesses: Williamson lacks scoring punch from the perimeter and struggles to finish against bigger players inside. He commits a lot of fouls. He needs to improve his ball-handling and free throw shooting. He tends to gain weight.

Analysis: Sacramento, already loaded at power forward, surprised some people when it selected Williamson. Williamson slipped badly in 1994-95 in the eyes of some scouts, who doubt he can make an impact at power forward at his size. The jury is out.

COLLEGE STATISTICS

		G	FGP	FTP	RPG	APG	PPG
92-93	ARK	18	.574	.622	5.1	1.7	14.6
93-94	ARK	34	.626	.700	7.7	2.2	20.4
94-95	ARK	39	.550	.668	7.5	2.3	19.7
Totals		91	.583	.672	7.1	2.1	19.0

GEORGE ZIDEK

Team: Charlotte Hornets
Position: Center
Height: 7'0" **Weight:** 250
Birthdate: August 2, 1973
College: UCLA
Acquired: 1st-round pick in 1995 draft (22nd overall)

```
         PLAYER SUMMARY
Will ...............eat space defensively
Can't .......................outrun anybody
Expect ........hooks with either hand
Don't Expect .......................a rejector
Fantasy ............$0  Card ......10-15¢
```

Background: Zidek played with the Czech junior national team for three years, averaging 20 points and ten rebounds, before coming to UCLA, where he averaged just 1.1 points as a freshman. He took a quantum leap his junior season when he moved into the starting lineup. He moved into first-round draft consideration with strong play in the 1995 NCAA Tournament.

Strengths: As he showed against Arkansas in the NCAA championship game, Zidek can close down the middle defensively. On offense, he displays a soft touch on his trusty hook shot.

Weaknesses: A lumbering athlete, Zidek struggles to keep pace in an up-tempo game. Despite his large frame, he's not a good shot-blocker. He had only 15 assists in 33 games as a senior.

Analysis: Zidek made himself a lot of money in the NCAA Tournament, as most experts had him penciled into the second round. Even if Zidek continues to improve, he'll probably be a career backup.

COLLEGE STATISTICS

		G	FGP	FTP	RPG	APG	PPG
91-92	UCLA	17	.381	.500	1.1	0.1	1.1
92-93	UCLA	26	.423	.760	1.7	0.3	2.4
93-94	UCLA	28	.517	.763	7.0	0.5	11.1
94-95	UCLA	33	.553	.731	5.4	0.5	10.6
Totals		104	.520	.744	4.2	0.4	7.1

NBA Team Overviews

This section evaluates all 29 NBA teams, sectioning them off by their divisions. For each team, you'll find:

- the club's address
- arena information
- a listing of the team's owner, general manager (or equivalent thereof), and head coach
- the head coach's record (lifetime and with team)
- a review of the team's history
- team finishes over the last five years
- a review of the team's 1994-95 season
- the club's 1995-96 roster
- a preview of the 1995-96 season

The team rosters include players who were drafted in June. The rosters list each player's 1994-95 statistics. Stats include games (G), points per game (PPG), rebounds per game (RPG), and assists per game (APG). The category "Exp." (experience) indicates the number of years the player has played in the NBA. An (∗) indicates the player was an unrestricted free agent as of late August.

Each 1995-96 season preview tips off with an "opening line," which looks at the players the team lost and those that are coming in. The preview then examines the team at each position, including guard, forward, center, and coaching. "Analysis" evaluates the team's strengths and weaknesses and puts it all into perspective.

BOSTON CELTICS

Home: FleetCenter
Capacity: 19,600
Year Built: 1995

Chairman of the Board: Paul E.Gaston
Director of Basketball Operations: M.L. Carr

Address:
FleetCenter
Boston, MA 02114

Head Coach: M.L. Carr
NBA: 0-0   Celtics: 0-0

Celtics History

The Celtics, winners of 16 world championships, began as a member of the old BAA in 1946-47 and joined the NBA at its inception. Red Auerbach took over as coach of the team in 1950-51 and began assembling the pieces of the Celtic machine. He started with guard Bob Cousy (perhaps the best ever on the fastbreak), added Bill Sharman, and in 1956 bagged the big one—Bill Russell.

Boston won its first championship in 1956-57, then won every title from 1958-59 through 1965-66, thoroughly dominating pro basketball. Russell, famous for his battles with Wilt Chamberlain, redefined post defense. His supporting cast included Sam and K.C. Jones, Tom Heinsohn, Frank Ramsey, and John Havlicek.

Auerbach moved to the front office in 1966 and Russell took over as player/coach, but the Celtics didn't falter, winning championships in 1968 and '69. Heinsohn assumed control of the bench in 1969 and won titles in 1974 and '76 with stars like Havlicek, center Dave Cowens, and guard Jo Jo White.

The Celtics' modern era dawned in 1979, when the team drafted forward Larry Bird. Behind Bird and frontcourt partners Robert Parish and Kevin McHale, Boston shared the 1980s spotlight with the Los Angeles Lakers, taking world championships in 1981, '84, and '86.

Last Five Years

Season	W	L	Playoffs
1990-91	56	26	L-East Semis
1991-92	51	31	L-East Semis
1992-93	48	34	L-Round 1
1993-94	32	50	DNQ
1994-95	35	47	L-Round 1

1994-95 Review

When Celtic fans think back to the great basketball seen during the history of the venerable Boston Garden, they won't spend too much time lingering over the 1994-95 season. The Celts took advantage of the devalued Eastern Conference to skulk into the playoffs with a 35-47 record, but even the excitement of a first-round near-miss against Orlando couldn't provide a proper send-off for one of sports' most historic gymnasiums.

None of the current Boston players will ever see his number raised to the rafters with the greats of yore, and the chance of any championship banners heading skyward in the near future is equally as slim. And if the play on the court wasn't bad enough, the reports about alleged drug use by former Celt Reggie Lewis made a sour season even less palatable.

The Celtics lacked scoring punch in 1994-95, played poor defense, and even had a losing record (20-21) at home. Among the few highlights was the play of power forward Dino Radja (17.2 PPG, 8.7 RPG) and the encouraging first year of rookie pivotman Eric Montross (10.0 PPG, 7.3 RPG). The backcourt tandem of Sherman Douglas (14.7 PPG, 6.9 APG) and Dee Brown (15.6 PPG) was its usual inconsistent self.

The arrival of forward Dominique Wilkins (17.8 PPG) didn't provide the significant scoring boost the team needed, and Pervis Ellison's cranky knees prohibited him from approaching his former performances. Frontcourt role-players like Rick Fox, Xavier McDaniel, and Derek Strong inspired fear in no one, and backcourt reserves Greg Minor and David Wesley were inadequate.

Boston Celtics
1995-96 Season Preview

Opening Line: At least M.L. Carr knew what he was getting when he took over as coach of the Celtics. As director of basketball operations, he helped create the team's current struggling incarnation and now must try to coach it back into contention—no mean feat. Let's hope Carr the executive has patience with Carr the coach and vice versa, since the Celtic draft was of questionable quality.

Guard: Dee Brown and Sherman Douglas are a veteran, but severely flawed, backcourt tandem. Brown is a notch below most off guards from the perimeter, something his excellent quickness and leaping ability can't overcome. Douglas isn't the greatest shooter, either, and though he can penetrate well, his lack of quickness hurts him on defense. David Wesley is an adequate backup point man with solid 3-point skills.

Forward: After signing selfish free agent Dominique Wilkins last year, Carr looks to fill the former All-Star's shoes now that 'Nique went to Greece in the off-season. Power forward Dino Radja, a reliable inside scorer and an above-average rebounder, is one of the few Celtics who wouldn't have been out of place on the title teams of yore. Soft Rick Fox and Xavier McDaniel, no longer the imposing force he once was, fill the small-forward slot, with rookies Eric Williams of Providence and Junior Burrough of Virginia bringing incomplete offensive games to the Celts.

Center: Give Eric Montross a truth-in-advertising award for his rookie season. Montross is not that fast or very athletic, but he has the basic skills, a good attitude, and a sound work ethic to make him a capable NBA center for many years. Backup pivot Pervis Ellison may flash his old game every now and then, but his cranky knees have limited him substantially.

Analysis: If Carr thinks the Celtics are anywhere close to serious contention, he is deluding himself. Boston needs a new backcourt and some frontcourt scoring pop before it will again be a serious threat. It will be a while before the Celtics' performance looks as sharp as its new FleetCenter home.

1995-96 Roster

No.	Player	Pos.	Ht.	Wt.	Exp.	College	G	RPG	APG	PPG
							\multicolumn{4}{c}{—1994-95—}			
7	Dee Brown	G	6'1"	161	5	Jacksonville	79	3.1	3.8	15.6
—	Junior Burrough	F	6'7"	242	R	Virginia	—	—	—	—
20	Sherman Douglas	G	6'1"	180	6	Syracuse	65	2.6	6.9	14.7
29	Pervis Ellison	F/C	6'10"	225	6	Louisville	55	5.6	0.6	6.8
44	Rick Fox	F/G	6'7"	231	4	North Carolina	53	2.9	2.6	8.8
*5	Jay Humphries	G	6'3"	185	11	Colorado	18	0.7	1.1	1.1
34	Xavier McDaniel	F	6'7"	205	10	Wichita St.	68	4.4	1.6	8.6
9	Greg Minor	F/G	6'6"	210	1	Louisville	63	2.1	1.0	6.0
0	Eric Montross	C	7'0"	275	1	North Carolina	78	7.3	0.5	10.0
40	Dino Radja	F	6'11"	225	2	(Croatia)	66	8.7	1.7	17.2
*31	Derek Strong	F	6'8"	220	4	Xavier	70	5.3	0.6	6.3
4	David Wesley	G	6'0"	190	2	Baylor	51	2.3	5.2	7.4
55	Eric Williams	F	6'7"	220	R	Providence	—	—	—	—

MIAMI HEAT

Home: Miami Arena
Capacity: 15,200
Year Built: 1988

Owner: Ted Arison
V.P./Operations: Dave Wohl

Address:
Miami Arena
Miami, FL 33136

Head Coach: TBA

Heat History

In its first three years of existence, Miami won 57 games—combined. But the Heat finally rose in 1991-92, becoming the first of the league's recent expansion teams to make the playoffs.

The city was awarded a franchise in April 1987 and entered the league in 1988-89 under the direction of coach Ron Rothstein. The Heat stumbled to a 15-67 record in its inaugural campaign, relying on rookies Rony Seikaly and Kevin Edwards. The following year brought rookies Glen Rice and Sherman Douglas to the Heat, but only three more wins.

Miami fans got to vent their frustrations on a new rival—the expansion Orlando Magic; and the arrival of the 1990 All-Star Game in Miami helped perk up the season. However, the team struggled through another bad campaign in 1990-91, going 24-58. In May 1991, Rothstein resigned.

New coach Kevin Loughery arrived in 1991-92 and all of a sudden the Heat came alive. With the help of rookie guard Steve Smith, Seikaly in the middle, and an improved Rice, Miami snuck into the playoffs. Once there, however, they were quickly swept by the world-champion Bulls.

Despite its young nucleus, the team has not improved much because of injuries and a lack of a physical presence. Miami broke the .500 mark in 1993-94 but lost a nail-biting series to Atlanta in the first round.

Last Five Years

Season	W	L	Playoffs
1990-91	24	58	DNQ
1991-92	38	44	L-Round 1
1992-93	36	46	DNQ
1993-94	42	40	L-Round 1
1994-95	32	50	DNQ

1994-95 Review

It would have been interesting to see how the Heat would have fared last season if it hadn't made a pair of trades that robbed the team of the bulk of its leadership. Miami started the season by dishing center Rony Seikaly to Golden State for Billy Owens, and then pulled the trigger on an ill-advised deal that brought power forward Kevin Willis from Atlanta for guard Steve Smith and forward Grant Long.

The resulting aggregation lacked defensive resolve and consistent performance and slumped home at 32-50, its worst record since 1990-91. The Heat's slow start cost Kevin Loughery his job, and its poor finish didn't exactly do much for the job prospects of interim boss Alvin Gentry.

Small forward Glen Rice (22.3 PPG) had his best season, sustaining his scoring ability all year and registering 56 points against Orlando in mid-April. Rookie guard Khalid Reeves (9.2 PPG, 4.3 APG) made a slow but sure adjustment to the point and had a strong second half, demonstrating more potential than starting point Bimbo Coles. Owens (14.3 PPG, 7.2 RPG) again struggled with finding a true position, and off guard Harold Miner continued to disappoint after such a promising college career.

Willis (17.2 PPG, 10.9 RPG) and John Salley (7.3 PPG, 4.5 RPG) continued to be among the league's more overrated seven-footers. Though Willis grabbed his share of rebounds, he shot too often and was rarely a defensive force. Salley continued his cavalier approach to the game and rarely was a force for an entire game. Reserve centers Matt Geiger and Brad Lohaus made steady contributions, but neither could be considered the long-term solution to Miami's pivot problems.

Miami Heat
1995-96 Season Preview

Opening Line: Last year's nasty 32-50 season did more than just place the Heat squarely in second place among Florida teams; it demonstrated the franchise's considerable need for a massive redirection. Although there is some talent on the roster, most notably Billy Owens and Glen Rice, the Heat lacks the intensity needed to win in the league.

Guard: When Rice is on, there are few shooters in the NBA who can match him. He torched Orlando for 56 last year and had perhaps his most consistent season as a pro. Khalid Reeves looked like an exciting creator by the end of last season and appears to be the point guard of the future. Bimbo Coles is a solid reserve and a good distributor, while ex-Bullet Rex Chapman can score when healthy and Texas rookie Terrence Rencher can get his shot off in just about any situation. Keep an eye on import Predrag Danilovic.

Forward: If Texas Christian rookie Kurt Thomas can replicate his collegiate ability to score and rebound at high levels, he could combine with Owens in an athletic, versatile tandem. The 6'9" Thomas led the nation in scoring and rebounding last year and is a polished offensive player near the basket who can also block some shots. Owens does a little bit of everything but needs a better perimeter game. Kevin Gamble is a scoring threat off the bench, and Keith Askins can get on the backboards a little.

Center: There is no doubt Kevin Willis is one of the game's biggest rebound accumulators, but his offensive game is limited, he doesn't get to the free throw line too often, and he blocks far too few shots for an athletic seven-footer. Matt Geiger hustles, rebounds, and doesn't try to do too much offensively, while Brad Lohaus is a seven-foot jump-shooter.

Analysis: Figure the Heat for somewhere between 35-40 wins this year and a shot at a playoff berth in the devalued Eastern Conference. That isn't much, considering Miami was the first of the expansion teams to reach the postseason and has slid slowly backward since then. A heart transplant would be a good step back toward respectability.

1995-96 Roster

No.	Player	Pos.	Ht.	Wt.	Exp.	College	G	RPG	APG	PPG
									—1994-95—	
*2	Keith Askins	G/F	6'8"	223	5	Alabama	50	4.0	0.8	4.6
34	George Banks	F	6'7"	210	R	UTEP	—	—	—	—
7	Rex Chapman	G	6'4"	195	7	Kentucky	45	2.5	2.8	16.2
12	Bimbo Coles	G	6'2"	185	5	Virginia Tech	68	2.8	6.1	10.0
—	Predrag Danilovic	G	6'6"	200	R	(Serbia)	—	—	—	—
*21	Ledell Eackles	G	6'5"	231	5	New Orleans	54	1.8	1.3	7.3
35	Kevin Gamble	G/F	6'5"	210	8	Iowa	77	1.5	1.5	7.4
52	Matt Geiger	C	7'0"	245	3	Georgia Tech	74	5.6	0.7	8.3
*54	Brad Lohaus	F/C	6'11"	238	8	Iowa	61	1.6	0.7	4.4
32	Billy Owens	F/G	6'9"	220	4	Syracuse	70	7.2	3.5	14.3
3	Khalid Reeves	G	6'3"	207	1	Arizona	67	2.8	4.3	9.2
15	Terrence Rencher	G	6'3"	185	R	Texas	—	—	—	—
41	Glen Rice	G/F	6'7"	220	6	Michigan	82	4.6	2.3	22.3
40	Kurt Thomas	F	6'9"	230	R	Texas Christ.	—	—	—	—
42	Kevin Willis	F/C	7'0"	240	10	Michigan St.	67	10.9	1.3	17.2

NEW JERSEY NETS

Home: Meadowlands Arena
Capacity: 20,039
Year Built: 1981

Address:
405 Murray Hill Pkwy.
East Rutherford, NJ 07073

Chairman of the Board: Alan L. Aufzien
Executive V.P./General Manager: Willis Reed

Head Coach: Butch Beard
NBA: 30-52　　Nets: 30-52

Nets History

Fans can choose from two images of the Nets. The first is from the mid-1970s, back in the days of the ABA. Back then, the team featured Julius Erving, the man who carried the Nets to the 1976 league title. The second image is that of the late '80s/early '90s club, one that posted six straight awful seasons in New Jersey.

The franchise was born in 1967 as the New Jersey Americans, a charter member of the ABA. The team moved to Long Island the next year, became the New York Nets, and acquired high-scoring Rick Barry for the 1970-71 season. The Nets made it to the ABA Finals the next year, but they lost Barry to the NBA. Erving came aboard in 1973-74 and led the team to the league title in 1975-76. When the Nets became one of four teams to merge with the NBA, they appeared to be in great shape.

Then the problems started. Erving had a contract dispute with owner Roy Boe, who sold him to Philadelphia. The Nets made the playoffs six of the next ten years but won only one series. That team featured an impressive frontcourt of Buck Williams, Albert King, and Darryl Dawkins.

The years 1986-91 were dismal, as management made poor draft decisions. The Nets improved over the next three years, thanks to forward Derrick Coleman and guard Kenny Anderson, but couldn't do much better than .500.

Last Five Years

Season	W	L	Playoffs
1990-91	26	56	DNQ
1991-92	40	42	L-Round 1
1992-93	43	39	L-Round 1
1993-94	45	37	L-Round 1
1994-95	30	52	DNQ

1994-95 Review

After watching the Nets slog through an injury-plagued and controversy-filled season, one had to wonder just how a team that had so much promise just two seasons ago had deteriorated into the NBA's version of a day-care center.

The tone was set early on, when power forward Derrick Coleman handed new coach Butch Beard a blank check to handle the fines he planned to incur by not adhering to Beard's new dress code. Forward Chris Morris joined the fun by refusing to tie his shoes during a practice session, and the rest of the Nets contributed to Beard's nightmare rookie season by playing selfish and uninspired basketball.

The Nets' 30-52 record included a 4-15 finish. It also prevented them from making the playoffs after a three-year run. What made the slide most maddening was that New Jersey still had two of the best players at their positions in the league—Coleman and point guard Kenny Anderson—when they wanted to be. Coleman (20.5 PPG, 10.6 RPG) also missed 26 games because of injuries, while Anderson (17.6 PPG, 9.4 APG) mixed inconsistent play with his usual bursts of magic.

The rest of the roster was generally overmatched. Forwards Armon Gilliam (14.8 PPG 7.5 RPG), Rick Mahorn, and P.J. Brown were capable backups, although they were pressed into starting service at times. Morris (13.4 PPG) shot just 41 percent from the field, and center was a nightmare spot, with Benoit Benjamin and Dwayne Schintzius providing little consistency. First-round draft pick Yinka Dare missed all but a few minutes of the season with a bad knee.

New Jersey Nets
1995-96 Season Preview

Opening Line: There is little hope that the free-falling Nets will bounce back into contention anytime soon. Despite a roster with some All-Star talent on it, New Jersey has been mismanaged and victimized by some of the league's most selfish players. Adding forward Ed O'Bannon through the draft should help, but the Nets remain one of the league's prime rudderless teams.

Guard: Nobody can deny the magic Kenny Anderson is capable of creating, when he's healthy and happy—two things that are no guarantee. The wispy point man has All-Star talent but isn't very consistent and remains an awful shooter. New Jersey doesn't have much to pair him with, since neither Rex Walters nor Kevin Edwards can be considered a front-line NBA backcourt gunner.

Forward: On paper, the Nets seem to be set here, but paper often lies. Power forward Derrick Coleman is one of the few NBA players capable of dominating a game from the four spot. He has countless abilities and numerous personality problems. On some nights, he and the multitalented O'Bannon could be a top forward tandem. But if Coleman's attitude is bad and O'Bannon's knee doesn't hold up, New Jersey will have plenty of trouble. The backup crew isn't exactly stellar. Three man Chris Morris can be crankier than Coleman, and Armon Gilliam is just a stat machine.

Center: With Benoit Benjamin gone to Vancouver via the expansion draft, the Nets are hoping raw second-year man Yinka Dare can develop in the pivot. Dare played three minutes last year before being shelved by knee troubles. P.J. Brown is a respected interior performer, but he's better off as a backup four and five man.

Analysis: If the Nets could somehow get Anderson and Coleman to play a whole, happy season, they might just have something. But that isn't going to happen, so the franchise will continue to underachieve. Grabbing O'Bannon was a good move, but New Jersey still needs a reliable shooting guard and a center. G.M. Willis Reed has held onto his job for a long time, but he had better have his resume updated. He built this team, and he deserves the blame for it.

1995-96 Roster

No.	Player	Pos.	Ht.	Wt.	Exp.	College	1994-95			
							G	RPG	APG	PPG
7	Kenny Anderson	G	6'1"	168	4	Georgia Tech	72	3.5	9.4	17.6
42	P.J. Brown	F/C	6'11"	240	2	Louisiana Tech	80	6.1	1.7	8.1
1	Chris Childs	G	6'3"	195	1	Boise St.	53	1.3	4.1	5.8
44	Derrick Coleman	F	6'10"	258	5	Syracuse	56	10.6	3.3	20.5
11	Yinka Dare	C	7'0"	265	1	G. Washington	1	1.0	0.0	0.0
21	Kevin Edwards	G	6'3"	210	7	DePaul	14	2.6	1.9	14.0
*12	Eric Floyd	G	6'3"	185	13	Georgetown	48	1.1	2.6	4.1
43	Armon Gilliam	F	6'9"	250	8	UNLV	82	7.5	1.2	14.8
9	Sean Higgins	G/F	6'9"	215	4	Michigan	57	1.4	0.5	4.7
*4	Rick Mahorn	F	6'10"	260	14	Hampton Inst.	58	2.8	0.4	3.4
*34	Chris Morris	F	6'8"	220	7	Auburn	71	5.7	2.1	13.4
31	Ed O'Bannon	F	6'8"	222	R	UCLA	—	—	—	—
*33	Dwayne Schintzius	C	7'2"	285	5	Florida	43	1.9	0.3	2.0
2	Rex Walters	G	6'4"	190	2	Kansas	80	1.2	1.5	6.5
*55	Jayson Williams	F	6'10"	245	5	St. John's	75	5.7	0.5	4.8

NEW YORK KNICKS

Home: Madison Square Garden
Capacity: 19,763
Year Built: 1968

Governor: Robert M. Gutkowski
V.P./General Manager: Ernie Grunfeld

Address:
Two Pennsylvania Plaza
New York, NY 10121

Head Coach: Don Nelson
NBA: 817-604　　Knicks: 0-0

Knicks History

The Knicks have spent much of their existence in the shadow of their rival to the north—Boston. Soon after the franchise's inception as a BAA member, the Knicks made trips to the NBA Finals—in 1951, '52, and '53. Hall of Fame coach Joe Lapchick melded forward Carl Braun with Harry Gallatin, Dick McGuire, and Nat "Sweetwater" Clifton and reached the playoffs nine consecutive years (1947-55).

The following ten years were not so kind, as the Knicks made the playoffs only once, in 1959. But fortunes changed quickly when Red Holzman took over in 1967-68. The Knicks built a powerhouse on the backs of center Willis Reed, forwards Bill Bradley and Dave DeBusschere, and guards Walt "Clyde" Frazier and Dick Barnett. In 1969-70, they defeated the Lakers in seven games for the title.

Jerry Lucas replaced Reed in the middle, and flashy Earl Monroe joined Frazier to form an outstanding backcourt. Together, they won the NBA title in 1973.

The subsequent 22 seasons have featured only modest success. High-scoring Bernard King provided some thrills in the mid-1980s, and star center Patrick Ewing sparked the team to the Atlantic Division title in 1988-89. New coach Pat Riley won three straight division titles but has fallen short in his quest for an NBA title, losing in the 1994 Finals to Houston.

1994-95 Review

Patrick Ewing's unsuccessful layup in the waning seconds of the Knicks' seventh-game playoff loss to Indiana had been out of the basket for just a few seconds when the questions started about whether New York's window for winning an NBA title had just slammed shut. The team was left with great uncertainty in the wake of its Eastern Conference semifinal loss to the Pacers.

Everybody wanted to know whether demanding coach Pat Riley would re-enlist for another draining tour of duty, if Ewing's troubled knees could sustain another high-caliber season, and how quickly disgruntled forward Anthony Mason would take his act elsewhere when free-agent time came around. New York lost its Atlantic Division title to Orlando but still finished with 55 wins and was considered a title threat, despite some highly publicized incidents throughout the season—including Mason's suspension and Riley's public criticism of the team's unprofessional attitude.

Ewing (23.9 PPG, 11.0 RPG) continued to prove himself as one of the league's premier players and did so with his customary class. He and power forward Charles Oakley (10.1 PPG, 8.9 RPG) provided the Knicks with an excellent inside presence. Mason (9.9 PPG, 8.4 RPG) provided fire and muscle off the bench but trouble off the court, and Charles Smith (12.7 PPG) was one of the league's softer 6'10" players.

The backcourt of Derek Harper (11.5 PPG, 5.7 APG) and John Starks (15.3 PPG, NBA-record 217 3's) was top-shelf, although Starks had some prolonged shooting slumps, and backup Hubert Davis (10.0 PPG) continued to be a solid outside weapon.

Last Five Years

Season	W	L	Playoffs
1990-91	39	43	L-Round 1
1991-92	51	31	L-East Semis
1992-93	60	22	L-East Finals
1993-94	57	25	L-NBA Finals
1994-95	55	27	L-East Semis

New York Knicks
1995-96 Season Preview

Opening Line: Now that Pat Riley has fled Manhattan over a dispute about control, Don Nelson moves into one of the NBA's most pressure-packed jobs less than a year after leaving Golden State when the circus-like atmosphere there deteriorated his health. New York has plenty of talent, but if Riley couldn't will the Knicks to the NBA title, it's debatable whether Nelson can cajole them to the top.

Guard: Derek Harper and John Starks may not be the prettiest backcourt tandem in the league, but each has considerable talent. Harper is a tenacious defender, excellent leader, and capable scorer, while Starks is an emotional scorer whose production can swing as dramatically as his moods. He does, however, play excellent defense and can carry a team for significant stretches if hot. Hubert Davis appears ready to emerge as a top-flight scorer, and Greg Anthony's departure via the expansion draft creates room for Charlie Ward at point guard.

Forward: Charles Oakley and Charles Smith are veteran producers with disparate talents. Oakley lives underneath, grabbing rebounds, bouncing bodies, and scoring effectively from close range. Smith is a softer forward, better in the open court, and not willing to mix it up so much. The loss of enforcer Anthony Mason to free agency means Anthony Bonner and Monty Williams will have to emerge as the Knicks' primary bench performers here. Williams might become a capable scorer if Nelson opens things up, but Bonner is too one-dimensional to be a reliable third forward.

Center: Patrick Ewing may be getting a little old, but there isn't a better outside-shooting center in the league. Ewing can still be counted on for almost 25 a game, but he needs Oakley in the lineup to help with the heavy lifting inside. Veteran Herb Williams keeps the pivot warm when Ewing sits down.

Analysis: Maybe a change in personality will make a difference for the Knicks, but Nelson alone won't bring New York to the top. The Knicks are an aging team with only a year or two left before a complete overhaul is needed. For now, New York needs bench support in the frontcourt and someone to back up Harper.

1995-96 Roster

No.	Player	Pos.	Ht.	Wt.	Exp.	College	G	RPG	APG	PPG
*4	Anthony Bonner	F	6'8"	225	5	St. Louis	58	4.5	1.4	3.8
7	Doug Christie	G/F	6'6"	205	3	Pepperdine	12	1.1	0.7	1.3
44	Hubert Davis	G	6'5"	183	3	North Carolina	82	1.3	1.8	10.0
33	Patrick Ewing	C	7'0"	240	10	Georgetown	79	11.0	2.7	23.9
11	Derek Harper	G	6'4"	206	12	Illinois	80	2.4	5.7	11.5
*14	Anthony Mason	F	6'7"	250	6	Tennessee St.	77	8.4	3.1	9.9
34	Charles Oakley	F	6'9"	245	10	Virginia Union	50	8.9	2.5	10.1
54	Charles Smith	F	6'10"	244	7	Pittsburgh	76	4.2	1.6	12.7
3	John Starks	G	6'5"	185	6	Oklahoma St.	80	2.7	5.1	15.3
21	Charlie Ward	G	6'2"	190	1	Florida St.	10	0.6	0.4	1.6
32	Herb Williams	C/F	6'11"	260	14	Ohio St.	56	2.4	0.5	3.3
2	Monty Williams	F	6'8"	225	1	Notre Dame	41	2.4	1.2	3.3

ORLANDO MAGIC

Home: Orlando Arena
Capacity: 15,998
Year Built: 1989

Chairman: Rich DeVos
General Manager: Pat Williams

Address:
One Magic Place
Orlando, FL 32801

Head Coach: Brian Hill
NBA: 107-57   Magic: 107-57

Magic History

Magic fans have ridden a roller-coaster over the last six years. After an 18-64 debut in 1989-90, Orlando improved to 31-51 in 1990-91. Injuries ruined the next season, but Shaquille O'Neal brought glittering new magic to Orlando in 1992-93.

In Orlando's inaugural season, coach Matt Guokas blended expansion-draft acquisitions Reggie Theus, Sam Vincent, Otis Smith, and Scott Skiles with rookie Nick Anderson into a team that was exciting, though not very successful.

Things perked up in 1990-91. Orlando drafted sharp-shooter Dennis Scott, and Skiles developed into one of the league's top point guards. However, Skiles fizzled out in 1991-92 and Scott missed most of the year with an injury. Orlando finished the year as the East's worst team.

With the No. 1 pick in the 1992 draft, the Magic grabbed O'Neal, a mega-star who improved the club by 20 games in 1992-93. Orlando barely missed the 1993 playoff but amazingly won the pre-draft lottery again. The team drafted Chris Webber, traded him for rookie Anfernee Hardaway, and dreamed of bright days ahead.

Orlando won 50 games in 1993-94 but was swept in the opening playoff round by Indiana. The club added the final piece of the puzzle in 1994-95, free-agent power forward Horace Grant, and finished with the best record in the conference.

1994-95 Review

If the 1994-95 season was about any one thing for the young Magic, it was about paying dues. The old, proven adage in the NBA is that no one ever wins the title without enduring a few years of lumps along the way. In 1993-94, that meant Orlando had to suffer the humiliation of a first-round playoff sweep. Last season, it meant another sweep, although this one came in the NBA Finals after the Magic had proven itself worthy of wearing the Atlantic Division crown.

Although no one knows for sure what lies ahead for Orlando, it can certainly mark its NBA-dues voucher "paid in full." By whipping Chicago and Indiana in its run to the Finals, the Magic displayed a maturity few thought it had and proved that it wasn't just a team comprised of precocious, young stars with no heart or drive. These guys could play and win—big.

Center Shaquille O'Neal (29.3 PPG, 11.4 RPG, 2.4 BPG) endured criticism about his Chamberlain-esque foul shooting, his rap records, and his youth to continue his rise into the current pantheon of NBA pivotmen. In 1994-95, he actually received some help inside from free-agent acquisition Horace Grant (12.8 PPG, 9.7 RPG), whose leadership and rebounding at the power-forward position meant plenty to the young Magic.

Point guard Penny Hardaway (20.9 PPG, 7.2 APG) continued his development into one of the game's brightest young stars, while the perimeter tandem of Nick Anderson (15.8 PPG) and Dennis Scott (12.9 PPG) were excellent complementary components. Brian Shaw was a solid backup point man, and Donald Royal and Anthony Bowie filled in admirably.

Last Five Years

Season	W	L	Playoffs
1990-91	31	51	DNQ
1991-92	21	61	DNQ
1992-93	41	41	DNQ
1993-94	50	32	L-Round 1
1994-95	57	25	L-NBA Finals

Orlando Magic
1995-96 Season Preview

Opening Line: Their four-game loss to Houston in the '95 NBA Finals notwithstanding, the Magic remains the league title favorite. They enter this year hardened by the reality of last year's championship-series sweep and vowing that their dues have been paid in full. Management didn't do too much to upgrade its team during the off-season and didn't really have to, since it is solid just about everywhere.

Guard: Anfernee Hardaway may not have as many endorsement deals as Shaquille O'Neal, but he is certainly among the best at his position. Although Hardaway is not a classic distributor, he has excellent penetration skills and is lethal in post-up situations. Backcourt mate Dennis Scott is one of the league's top gunners and can go on unconscious 3-point binges at any time. Brian Shaw is an athletic backup who can play either guard spot, and Donald Royal is a solid defender.

Forward: The Nick Anderson-Horace Grant team is one of the more consistent and talented in the league. Even though Anderson struggled mightily in the Finals, he is an excellent inside-outside scorer, while Grant provides rebounding help inside and some limited point production close to the basket. Reserve Jeff Turner is a 6'9" jump-shooter, but rookie David Vaughn is an intriguing addition with excellent rebounding and shot-blocking skills.

Center: A lot of people may not like it, but O'Neal has developed into one of the game's elite players and is still improving. He may still shoot fouls like Wilt Chamberlain, but he does a lot of other things like Wilt too. He is immovable down low, has tremendous power moves, has an emerging jump hook, and can run the floor like few other pivots. Like him or not, this is Shaq's time.

Analysis: There doesn't seem to be a team in the Eastern Conference with enough to stop the Magic, provided O'Neal and Hardaway stay healthy. And even though the Rockets blitzed Orlando in last year's Finals, a repeat is highly unlikely. If the Magic don't win the 1995-96 title, something is wrong.

1995-96 Roster

No.	Player	Pos.	Ht.	Wt.	Exp.	College	G	RPG	APG	PPG
25	Nick Anderson	G/F	6'6"	220	6	Illinois	76	4.4	4.1	15.8
10	Darrell Armstrong	G	6'1"	180	1	Fayetteville	3	0.3	1.0	3.3
00	Anthony Avent	F	6'9"	235	3	Seton Hall	71	4.1	0.6	3.6
*14	Anthony Bowie	G	6'6"	200	6	Oklahoma	77	1.8	2.1	5.5
54	Horace Grant	F	6'10"	235	8	Clemson	74	9.7	2.3	12.8
43	Geert Hammink	F/C	7'0"	262	2	Louisiana St.	1	2.0	1.0	4.0
1	Anfernee Hardaway	G/F	6'7"	200	2	Memphis St.	77	4.4	7.2	20.9
32	Shaquille O'Neal	C	7'1"	301	3	Louisiana St.	79	11.4	2.7	29.3
*30	Tree Rollins	C	7'1"	255	18	Clemson	51	1.9	0.2	1.2
5	Donald Royal	F	6'8"	210	5	Notre Dame	70	4.0	2.8	9.1
3	Dennis Scott	G/F	6'8"	229	5	Georgia Tech	62	2.4	2.1	12.9
*20	Brian Shaw	G	6'6"	194	6	Cal.-Santa Bar.	78	3.1	5.2	6.4
22	Brooks Thompson	G	6'4"	195	1	Oklahoma St.	38	0.6	1.1	3.1
31	Jeff Turner	F	6'9"	240	9	Vanderbilt	49	2.0	0.8	4.1
—	David Vaughn	F	6'10"	240	R	Memphis	—	—	—	—

PHILADELPHIA 76ERS

Home: The Spectrum
Capacity: 18,168
Year Built: 1967

Owner: Harold Katz
General Manager: John Lucas

Address:
P.O. Box 25040
Philadelphia, PA 19147

Head Coach: John Lucas
NBA: 118-107   76ers: 24-58

Sixers History

The 76ers own the distinction of having the Alpha and Omega of NBA basketball history, going 68-13 in 1966-67 and 9-73 in 1972-73. The Sixers began in 1949-50 as the Syracuse Nationals and reached the first NBA Finals series, losing in six games to Minneapolis. Hall of Fame center Dolph Schayes was the big gun on both that team and the 1953-54 squad that fell again in the NBA Finals, this time to the Lakers.

The team moved to Philadelphia in 1963-64 and acquired Wilt Chamberlain in a trade in early 1965. They moved onto a level with the Boston Celtics and began to challenge them for league supremacy. In fact, the Nationals/Sixers have met the Celtics in 17 playoff series, winning seven. Philly beat Boston in the 1967 East finals on the way to the NBA title.

The Sixers nosedived in the early 1970s, but the arrival of coach Gene Shue and ABA imports George McGinnis and Julius Erving signaled a renaissance. Philly advanced to the NBA Finals in 1976-77 but lost to Portland. Similar excursions were made in 1979-80 and 1981-82, thanks to Erving, Bobby Jones, and Maurice Cheeks.

Moses Malone arrived for the 1982-83 season, and the Sixers won another NBA title. In 1984, Philly drafted forward Charles Barkley, who led the team to the 1989-90 Atlantic Division title. The team has struggled since trading Barkley in 1992.

Last Five Years

Season	W	L	Playoffs
1990-91	44	38	L-East Semis
1991-92	35	47	DNQ
1992-93	26	56	DNQ
1993-94	25	57	DNQ
1994-95	24	58	DNQ

1994-95 Review

By the time Year One of the John Lucas Era fizzled to a close, it was actually possible to see signs of improvement on the floundering Sixers. Although the team remained well removed from the playoff chase, Philadelphia certainly finished 1994-95 better than it began. Even though the team won 24 games—one less than the previous year—the Sixers were far more competitive after the All-Star break.

Much of the credit for the team's increased resolve went to popular Philadelphia whipping boy Shawn Bradley (9.5 PPG, 8.0 RPG, 3.3 BPG), who actually began to assert himself during the final 25 games. The spindly 7'6" center remained clearly overmatched, but he was more fluid and aggressive as the season wore on. The season-long performance of Dana Barros (20.6 PPG, 46.4 percent 3-point) gave Sixer fans most of their few reasons to cheer. The 5'11" point guard was one of the league's top 3-point shooters and won the NBA's Most Improved Player Award.

Forward Clarence Weatherspoon (18.1, 6.9 RPG), however, was uncomfortable in his small-forward role and was unable to score from the perimeter effectively. The men for whom he made room, free-agent power forward Scott Williams and rookie big man Sharone Wright (11.4 PPG, 6.0 RPG), showed moments of promise but were inconsistent.

Outside of Barros, the Sixer backcourt was a mess. Veteran shooting guard Jeff Malone was sidelined for much of the season with a heel injury, and preseason acquisition Willie Burton mixed periodic outbursts with the same problems with injury and occasional disinterest that sabotaged his early years in the league.

Philadelphia 76ers
1995-96 Season Preview

Opening Line: Year Two of the John Lucas Reclamation Project appears to have a much brighter outlook than its predecessor. The continued development of center Shawn Bradley and power forward Sharone Wright, together with the addition of lottery pick Jerry Stackhouse, should give the Sixers a solid nucleus for future success.

Guard: Though Stackhouse played forward at North Carolina, he will make the move to off guard in the NBA and has all the physical tools to handle the transition smoothly. Should his jump shot develop quickly, Stackhouse could be a superstar. He'll apprentice behind veteran Jeff Malone, provided Malone's cranky heel is healthy. Add in 3-point bombing point guard Dana Barros, and the Sixers should have a high-scoring backcourt. They won't, however, have too much in the passing department. Philadelphia was last in the NBA in that category in 1994-95.

Forward: Though Philadelphia has several options up front, two of its top players are being asked to perform out of position. Veteran Clarence Weatherspoon is a force inside, but he's only 6'6" and hasn't shown the quickness or outside shooting needed for the small-forward spot. Wright is a solid 6'11" at the four, but he played pivot in college and has little game away from the hoop. Meanwhile, Scott Williams is earning a lot of money but hasn't produced at power forward consistently enough to warrant the big outlay. Free-agent acquisition Willie Burton is a high-scoring "X factor" with a history of physical and personal problems.

Center: By the last 20 games of the 1994-95 season, Bradley had begun to evolve into a more productive center. He was scoring, rebounding, blocking shots, and cutting down on fouls. But the 7'6" flagpole has a long way to go. He must get stronger, more versatile on offense, and much nastier. Wright and Williams can both back him up.

Analysis: Philadelphia should win more than 24 games this year, but don't count on the Sixers to be fighting for a playoff spot. Bradley, Wright, and Stackhouse all still have plenty of developing left to do, and the point-guard and small-forward positions must still be addressed properly. The Sixers are making progress, but it is slow going.

1995-96 Roster

No.	Player	Pos.	Ht.	Wt.	Exp.	College	G	RPG	APG	PPG
21	Derrick Alston	F	6'11"	225	1	Duquesne	64	3.4	0.5	4.7
*3	Dana Barros	G	5'11"	163	6	Boston College	82	3.3	7.5	20.6
76	Shawn Bradley	C	7'6"	248	2	Brigham Young	82	8.0	0.6	9.5
*9	Willie Burton	G/F	6'8"	219	5	Minnesota	53	3.1	1.8	15.3
*5	Corey Gaines	G	6'4"	195	6	Loyola Mary.	11	1.6	3.0	5.0
20	Greg Graham	G	6'4"	174	2	Indiana	50	1.2	1.3	5.0
*14	Jeff Grayer	G	6'5"	215	7	Iowa St.	47	3.1	1.6	8.3
25	Jeff Malone	G	6'4"	205	12	Mississippi St.	19	2.9	1.5	18.4
23	Tim Perry	F	6'9"	220	7	Temple	42	2.1	0.3	1.8
42	Jerry Stackhouse	G/F	6'6"	218	R	North Carolina	—	—	—	—
35	C. Weatherspoon	F	6'7"	240	3	S. Mississippi	76	6.9	2.8	18.1
—	Scott Williams	F	6'10"	230	5	North Carolina	77	6.3	0.8	6.4
4	Sharone Wright	F/C	6'11"	260	1	Clemson	79	6.0	0.6	11.4

WASHINGTON BULLETS

Home: USAir Arena
Capacity: 18,756
Year Built: 1973

Chairman of the Board: Abe Pollin
V.P./General Manager: John Nash

Address:
USAir Arena
Landover, MD 20785

Head Coach: Jim Lynam
NBA: 267-325   Bullets: 21-61

Bullets History

The Bullets' greatest years came in the 1970s, but the franchise rolled off the assembly line in 1961-62 as the Chicago Packers. In 1963, it moved to Baltimore and adopted its current nickname.

In 1964-65, the Bullets advanced to the Western finals behind center Walt Bellamy and forward Bailey Howell. Prior to the 1968-69 season, Baltimore drafted huge Wes Unseld, and he went on to win the MVP Award in his first season. Unseld teamed with slick Earl "The Pearl" Monroe to help the Bullets win the Eastern Division.

The Bullets made their first trip to the NBA Finals in 1970-71, but they were dispatched in four games by Milwaukee. They made it back in 1974-75, this time as Washington, but Golden State swept them 4-0. Dick Motta took over the Bullets in 1976-77 and led them to the Finals the following year. This time, Unseld, Elvin Hayes, Bob Dandridge, and company whipped Seattle in seven games. The Sonics got revenge in the Finals the next year, closing out the Bullets' big decade.

The 1980s featured some talented players (Jeff Ruland, Rick Mahorn, Greg Ballard, Jeff Malone) but few highlights. Unseld took over as coach in 1987-88 but—outside of Bernard King and then Pervis Ellison—had little to work with. The club has been moribund throughout the 1990s.

Last Five Years

Season	W	L	Playoffs
1990-91	30	52	DNQ
1991-92	25	57	DNQ
1992-93	22	60	DNQ
1993-94	24	58	DNQ
1994-95	21	61	DNQ

1994-95 Review

Given all the changes and supposed improvements made by the Bullets before and during the 1994-95 season, it seems almost impossible that the team finished the year with only 21 wins. The Bullets had the fewest wins in franchise history since the 1966-67 Baltimore incarnation (20). Lowlights included a 13-game losing streak, eight of which came at home, and a franchise-worst 13-28 home mark.

Still, the 1994-95 Bullets actually generated considerable excitement. The early-season acquisition of power forward Chris Webber from Golden State for forward Tom Gugliotta and future draft picks gave Washington a forward tandem of Webber and former Fab Five teammate Juwan Howard that should develop into one of the league's best within the next few years. Though Webber (20.1 PPG, 9.6 RPG) missed several weeks with a shoulder injury, he sparkled when he played, and Howard (17.0 PPG, 8.4 RPG) was his usual businesslike self.

Those two weren't enough. The Bullets played poor defense, had an inadequate backcourt, and were weak in the pivot. Veteran point man Scott Skiles (13.0 PPG, 7.3 APG) hustled, but he missed the last quarter of the season with a wrist injury. Second-year shooting guard Calbert Cheaney (16.6 PPG) showed flashes of improvement, but veteran two man Rex Chapman (16.2 PPG) shot just 39.7 percent from the field.

Center Gheorghe Muresan (10.0 PPG, 6.7 RPG) played the entire season in the middle, thanks to Kevin Duckworth's continued losing battle with corpulence, but the slow 7'7" Romanian was clearly not made to be a first-line NBA pivot.

Washington Bullets
1995-96 Season Preview

Opening Line: After spending three years stockpiling young talent, it would appear the Bullets are ready to win some games. Don't count on Washington moving into the playoffs this year, but the franchise should certainly break out of its six-year funk and provide fans with something to cheer about.

Guard: The Bullets have a problem here, since the tandem of Scott Skiles and Calbert Cheaney is a notch below playoff-caliber rivals. Skiles would make a great backup man on just about any team, but he lacks the quickness to be a first-teamer. Cheaney, meanwhile, needs to refine his outside shooting and ball-handling in order to become a quality off guard. Unlike Skiles, however, he has the talent to blossom. Two man Mitchell Butler and point guard Doug Overton are mediocre reserves.

Forward: Juwan Howard and Chris Webber may both be power forwards, but they both have tremendous talent and could very well develop into a complementary tandem. Webber is slowly developing a modest perimeter game that could keep him out of Howard's way, but he still does his best work down low. Howard is an all-around rock, capable of handling the four or five spots and clearly a potential star. Don MacLean has a soft touch from the outside but little stomach for the rough stuff.

Center: Even though he may be playing out of position, North Carolina rookie Rasheed Wallace should have an impact in the middle this year. He blocks shots well, runs the floor like a stretched-out gazelle, and can finish well around the basket. He is, however, raw, young, and somewhat immature. Gheorge Muresan will be a valuable reserve because of his size and proficiency inside, and Jim McIlvaine will provide some more heft in case Wallace gets pushed around.

Analysis: The Bullets are definitely headed in the right direction, but the road ahead of them is long and crowded with other rebuilding teams. In Webber, Howard, and Wallace, they have three budding frontcourt stars, but the key is putting them together in a configuration that works. If the backcourt comes around, expect plenty of excitement in the nation's capital.

1995-96 Roster

| No. | Player | Pos. | Ht. | Wt. | Exp. | College | —1994-95— | | | |
							G	RPG	APG	PPG
32	Mitchell Butler	G	6'5"	210	2	UCLA	76	2.2	1.2	7.9
40	Calbert Cheaney	F/G	6'7"	215	2	Indiana	78	4.1	2.3	16.6
00	Kevin Duckworth	C	7'0"	275	9	E. Illinois	40	4.9	0.5	7.0
5	Juwan Howard	F/C	6'9"	250	1	Michigan	65	8.4	2.5	17.0
34	Don MacLean	F	6'10"	235	3	UCLA	39	4.2	1.3	11.0
22	Jim McIlvaine	C	7'1"	240	1	Marquette	55	1.9	0.2	1.7
77	Gheorghe Muresan	C	7'7"	315	2	(Cluj)	73	6.7	0.5	10.0
14	Doug Overton	G	6'3"	190	3	La Salle	82	1.7	3.0	7.0
*4	Scott Skiles	G	6'1"	180	9	Michigan St.	62	2.6	7.3	13.0
*15	Kenny Walker	F	6'8"	220	7	Kentucky	24	2.0	0.3	2.4
30	Rasheed Wallace	F/C	6'10"	225	R	North Carolina	—	—	—	—
4	Chris Webber	F/C	6'10"	245	2	Michigan	54	9.6	4.7	20.1

ATLANTA HAWKS

Home: The Omni
Capacity: 16,365
Year Built: 1972

Owner: Ted Turner
V.P./General Manager: Pete Babcock

Address:
One CNN Center, #405 South
Atlanta, GA 30303

Head Coach: Lenny Wilkens
NBA: 968-957　　Hawks: 99-65

Hawks History

Few teams have had as many different addresses as the Hawks. Before settling in Georgia, the franchise roamed the Midwest, calling Moline, Rock Island, Davenport, Milwaukee, and St. Louis home.

An original member of the NBA, the franchise was first known as the Tri-City Blackhawks. Two years later, it moved to Milwaukee and changed its nickname to the Hawks. Though active off the court, it wasn't until the team drafted Bob Pettit in 1954 that it started to show some life on it.

The Hawks moved to St. Louis in 1955, won consecutive Western Conference championships from 1957-61, and defeated Boston in 1958 for the franchise's lone NBA title. Pettit, Cliff Hagan, Ed Macauley, Charlie Share, and Slater Martin formed the nucleus of those teams.

The 1960s featured talented players like Lou Hudson, Joe Caldwell, and Zelmo Beatty, but the Hawks could not get back to the Finals. The team moved to Atlanta for the 1968-69 season and staggered through the next decade as a .500 team.

Things started to change in 1982, when Atlanta drafted exciting forward Dominique Wilkins. The Hawks won the NBA Central Division title in 1986-87 and recorded a franchise-record 57 wins. The team hovered around .500 in the early 1990s before a 57-win season under new coach Lenny Wilkens in 1993-94.

1994-95 Review

Although Hawks coach Lenny Wilkens passed Red Auerbach as the NBA's all-time winningest coach, it wasn't the greatest year for pro basketball in Atlanta. One year after tying a franchise record with 57 wins, the Hawks slipped to 42-40 and were bounced in the first round of the playoffs by Indiana, the same team that dispatched them the previous year.

It was a year of highs, lows, and curious moves in Atlanta, which continued to play good defense but lacked offensive firepower and came under criticism from fans and media for lacking a big-name star. While Wilkens's milestone was certainly worth celebrating, the Hawks' overall play was inconsistent and often bland. Atlanta scored the fourth-fewest points in the league (96.6).

Not even an early-season trade that sent Kevin Willis to Miami for guard Steve Smith and power forward Grant Long could shake things up. Point man Mookie Blaylock (17.2 PPG, 7.7 APG) proved again he was one of the best at his position, although his assists dropped by two a game. He and the versatile Smith (16.3 PPG) formed a sturdy backcourt, but the Hawks did miss injured gunner Craig Ehlo, who played only half the season.

Stacey Augmon (13.9 PPG, 4.8 RPG) continued to shine on defense and in the open court, but his shooting was again below the standard for his position. Long (11.6 PPG, 7.5 RPG) provided his usual steady presence up front, while veteran Ken Norman (12.7 PPG) did what he does best—score. The center tandem of Andrew Lang and Jon Koncak was again inadequate, a fact proved by the team's overall rebounding deficit.

Last Five Years

Season	W	L	Playoffs
1990-91	43	39	L-Round 1
1991-92	38	44	DNQ
1992-93	43	39	L-Round 1
1993-94	57	25	L-East Semis
1994-95	42	40	L-Round 1

Atlanta Hawks
1995-96 Season Preview

Opening Line: By the end of last season, the Omni was a mausoleum, and Hawks fans were yawning through boring basketball. Lenny Wilkens may top the all-time NBA coaching win list, but he has quite a challenge bringing Atlanta back toward the 50-win plateau. Atlanta has deficiencies up front and lacks the kind of star power that creates excitement.

Guard: This should be an undeniable strength, thanks to the returning tandem of Mookie Blaylock and Steve Smith and the off-season acquisition of veteran Spud Webb. Spud should be an excellent backup to Blaylock, one of the NBA's most underrated performers whose offensive game has matched his considerable defensive acumen. Smith does a little of everything from the two spot and has the potential to become a big-time scorer. Rookie Donnie Boyce should provide some excellent bench pop, provided his leg heals.

Forward: Stacey Augmon is a great defender and stellar open-court player with enough athletic skills to get to the basket in just about any situation, but his poor jump shot prevents him from being a big-time frontcourt scorer. Kenny Norman can score, but he does little else, and Grant Long is a tremendous rebounder and defender with limited offensive skills. Add in Indiana rookie Alan Henderson, a 6'9" player who isn't sure whether he is a small forward or a power man, and Wilkens has more questions than solutions.

Center: Speaking of trouble, how does an Andrew Lang/Jon Koncak pivot tandem sound to you? We thought so. Both are slow and unpolished offensively. Lang is game, but he can't last 35-40 minutes against the big boys, and Koncak has been a well-paid bust.

Analysis: The Hawks will sneak into the playoffs, largely because of their backcourt and Wilkens. But Atlanta fans shouldn't expect too much more than about 44 wins and a first-round exit, since the lack of a solid frontcourt will always doom the Hawks. If Atlanta doesn't act quickly, it might find itself sliding behind Milwaukee and Detroit.

1995-96 Roster

No.	Player	Pos.	Ht.	Wt.	Exp.	College	—1994-95—		
							G	RPG	APG	PPG
*22	Greg Anderson	F/C	6'10"	230	7	Houston	51	3.7	0.3	2.9
2	Stacey Augmon	G/F	6'8"	205	4	UNLV	76	4.8	2.6	13.9
10	Mookie Blaylock	G	6'1"	185	6	Oklahoma	80	4.9	7.7	17.2
—	Donnie Boyce	G	6'5"	196	R	Colorado	—	—	—	—
—	Troy Brown	F	6'8"	238	R	Providence	—	—	—	—
3	Craig Ehlo	G/F	6'7"	205	12	Washington St.	49	3.0	2.3	9.7
—	Alan Henderson	F	6'9"	235	R	Indiana	—	—	—	—
*32	Jon Koncak	C	7'0"	250	10	Southern Meth.	62	3.0	0.8	2.9
28	Andrew Lang	C	6'11"	250	7	Arkansas	82	5.5	0.8	9.7
*14	Jim Les	G	5'11"	175	7	Bradley	24	1.1	1.8	2.1
43	Grant Long	F	6'8"	248	7	E. Michigan	81	7.5	1.6	11.6
—	Cuonzo Martin	G/F	6'4"	213	R	Purdue	—	—	—	—
—	Gaylon Nickerson	G	6'3"	190	R	N.W. Okla. St.	—	—	—	—
4	Ken Norman	F	6'8"	223	8	Illinois	74	4.9	1.3	12.7
41	Blair Rasmussen	C	7'0"	250	8	Oregon	—	—	—	—
8	Steve Smith	G	6'7"	213	4	Michigan St.	80	3.5	3.4	16.3
—	Spud Webb	G	5'7"	135	10	N. Carolina St.	76	2.3	6.2	11.6
*1	Ennis Whatley	G	6'3"	180	9	Alabama	27	1.1	2.0	2.6

CHARLOTTE HORNETS

Home: Charlotte Coliseum
Capacity: 23,698
Year Built: 1988

Owner: George Shinn
V.P./Basketball Operations: Bob Bass

Address:
Hive Drive
Charlotte, NC 28217

Head Coach: Allan Bristow
NBA: 166-162   Hornets: 166-162

Hornets History

They've always loved college basketball down on Tobacco Road, so it was a natural for the NBA to try and tap into that market. In the first three years, the level of play was below the high expectations of spoiled Carolina fans. However, the club has improved greatly over the last three years.

The 1988-89 Hornets may have looked sharp in their teal-and-blue pinstriped duds, but their 20-62 record wasn't as fashionable. Among the highlights of that first season was the play of veteran Kelly Tripucka and exciting guards Muggsy Bogues and Rex Chapman.

Charlotte took a step back in 1989-90, winning only 19 games, and coach Dick Harter was replaced by Gene Littles. Littles boosted the team's production to 26 wins in 1990-91, as rookie guard Kendall Gill showed flashes of a brilliant future. In 1991-92, Allan Bristow took over as coach and the team added thunder-dunking rookie Larry Johnson, who helped improve the team by five games.

With the addition of yet another stellar rookie—tenacious center Alonzo Mourning—Charlotte took a monster step in 1992-93, knocking off Boston in the first round of the playoffs. Injuries ruined the 1993-94 season, but the nucleus of Johnson, Mourning, Bogues, and sharp-shooters Hersey Hawkins and Dell Curry helped the team win 50 games in 1994-95.

1994-95 Review

It's tough to get too angry at the Hornets for winning 50 games during the regular season, only to fall apart in the first round of the playoffs against Chicago. After all, who could have forecast that Michael Jordan would take one of the first steps in his triumphant return to basketball at the expense of Charlotte?

Though the Hornets appeared as if they could create some trouble for the Bulls early on in the series, they eventually succumbed in four games and entered the off-season an angry group in need of more depth, with a coach (Allan Bristow) under fire. The positive side to the season was the season-long inspired play of forward Larry Johnson, who appeared fully recovered from his back surgery and ready to take his place again among the top front-court players in the country.

Johnson (18.8 PPG, 7.2 RPG) played in every game but one and was once again a dangerous scorer inside and out. He and center Alonzo Mourning (21.3 PPG, 9.9 RPG, 2.9 BPG) provided a stout one-two punch up front, one that was complemented for most of the season by the inspired play of athletic forward Scott Burrell (11.5 PPG, 5.7 RPG), who was a candidate for Most Improved Player honors until he tore his Achilles tendon in April.

Kenny Gattison bravely played on after recovering from a career-threatening neck injury, while the backcourt gunning tandem of Hersey Hawkins (14.3 PPG) and Dell Curry (13.6 PPG) continued to light it up from the outside. Point guard Muggsy Bogues (11.1 PPG, 8.7 APG) was again productive throughout the year but hurt the team during the playoffs with his poor outside shooting.

| | **Last Five Years** | | |
Season	W	L	Playoffs
1990-91	26	56	DNQ
1991-92	31	51	DNQ
1992-93	44	38	L-East Semis
1993-94	41	41	DNQ
1994-95	50	32	L-Round 1

Charlotte Hornets
1995-96 Season Preview

Opening Line: In the coming season, it will be interesting to see whether the Hornets will be able to stave off the charging Chicago Bulls and take aim at the Indiana Pacers within the Central Division, or if they are still floating conspiracy theories about the league favoring Air Jordan and Co. This is certainly a big year for coach Allan Bristow, who needs to get the promising Bugs past the early rounds of the playoffs and into the Eastern Conference's upper reaches.

Guard: Hersey Hawkins may not have been the perfect off guard, but dealing him to Seattle for recalcitrant prodigal son Kendall Gill doesn't make a whole lot of sense. The Hornets get back a guy who grouched about playing time when he was with them before and really isn't more talented than Hawkins. Meanwhile, tiny point man Muggsy Bogues was again exposed as an offensive liability during the playoffs. Veteran shooter Dell Curry is about the only sure thing in the Hornet backcourt.

Forward: Larry Johnson enjoyed an excellent return from his aching back last year and should be even stronger this year—a good sign for the Hornets. But now Charlotte has to worry about whether Scott Burrell can rebound from his torn Achilles tendon. Until getting hurt, Burrell was having a great year and he has the talent to become an excellent all-around forward. Depth could be a problem, since reliable rebounder Kenny Gattison was lost to expansion.

Center: Alonzo Mourning has proven he can be counted on for about 20 points and ten boards each night, but he needs to become even more productive in each area if the Hornets are to move ahead. He has the talent but needs more consistency and maturity. Plodding UCLA rookie George Zidek will back him up.

Analysis: In Mourning and Johnson, the Hornets have an excellent start, but the big questions in Charlotte are whether Burrell will be healthy and if Gill can grow up enough to be a reliable producer at off guard. Charlotte has been a team on the come for three years now and must arrive in 1995-96 or risk an overhaul.

1995-96 Roster

No.	Player	Pos.	Ht.	Wt.	Exp.	College	G	RPG	APG	PPG
								—1994-95—		
23	Michael Adams	G	5'10"	162	10	Boston College	29	1.0	3.3	6.5
25	Tony Bennett •	G	6'0"	186	3	Wisc.-Green Bay	3	0.7	1.3	4.7
1	Muggsy Bogues	G	5'3"	140	8	Wake Forest	78	3.3	8.7	11.1
24	Scott Burrell	G/F	6'7"	218	2	Connecticut	65	5.7	2.5	11.5
30	Dell Curry	G	6'5"	200	9	Virginia Tech	69	2.4	1.6	13.6
13	Kendall Gill	G	6'5"	200	5	Illinois	73	4.0	2.6	13.7
4	Darrin Hancock	G/F	6'6"	205	1	Kansas	46	1.2	0.7	3.3
2	Larry Johnson	F	6'7"	250	4	UNLV	81	7.2	4.6	18.8
33	Alonzo Mourning	C	6'10"	260	3	Georgetown	77	9.9	1.4	21.3
00	Robert Parish	C	7'0"	244	19	Centenary	81	4.3	0.5	4.8
*12	Greg Sutton	G	6'2"	170	2	Oral Roberts	53	1.1	1.7	5.0
*43	Joe Wolf	F/C	6'11"	230	7	North Carolina	63	2.0	0.6	1.4
—	George Zidek	C	7'0"	250	R	UCLA	—	—	—	—

CHICAGO BULLS

Home: United Center
Capacity: 21,500
Year Built: 1994

Address:
1901 W. Madison
Chicago, IL 60612

Chairman: Jerry Reinsdorf
V.P./Basketball Operations: Jerry Krause

Head Coach: Phil Jackson
NBA: 342-150   Bulls: 342-150

Bulls History

The Bulls were defined in the early '90s by the atmospheric antics of Michael Jordan, but the team's 29-year history has not always been so spectacular.

Chicago joined the league in 1966. After four losing seasons, the Bulls enjoyed regular-season success during their next five. Coach Dick Motta pulled together Chet Walker, Bob Love, Jerry Sloan, and Norm Van Lier to form a quick team that advanced to the West finals in 1973-74, losing in four games to Milwaukee. The next year, the Bulls acquired Nate Thurmond from Golden State and won the Midwest Division, only to drop a 4-3 decision to the Warriors in the West finals.

Chicago managed only two winning seasons during the next 12 and won just one playoff series, but the Bulls' fortunes changed radically in 1984 when they selected Jordan with the third pick in the draft. Almost instantly, Jordan became an ambassador for basketball everywhere.

By 1987, the results matched the enthusiasm. Chicago surrounded Jordan with Scottie Pippen and Horace Grant and advanced to the Eastern finals in 1988-89 and 1989-90, losing both times to Detroit. The Bulls matured in 1990-91 and knocked off the L.A. Lakers in the NBA Finals. In 1991-92, Chicago defeated Portland for its second world crown, then, in 1992-93, three-peated with a win over Phoenix.

1994-95 Review

Lost in the maddening hoopla of Michael Jordan's return to the game was a basic tenet of basketball: One man can't do it all. Just as the early part of Jordan's career was characterized by his inability to carry a team with glaring weaknesses to the NBA summit, so too was his 1995 reappearance marked by Chicago's inadequacies.

Even Jordan was a few notches below his amazing self, mixing moments of mastery with some performances that won't find their way onto his highlight reel. In 1995, however, Jordan's rust was only part of the problem. The Bulls lacked the inside presence to battle the stronger teams in the league, and the entire unit looked out of sync as it tried to readjust to being part of Jordan's on-court entourage.

The resulting six-game playoff loss to Orlando in the Eastern semifinals magnified the team's weaknesses and gave its management a clear assignment for the off-season: Find some big people who can play. Jordan averaged 26.9 PPG in his 17-game regular-season return, but he shot only 41.1 percent from the field. His superstar partner, Scottie Pippen (21.4 PPG, 8.1 RPG, 5.2 APG), led the team in rebounds and assists but had to withstand a year of uncertainty about his future with the team.

Toni Kukoc (15.7 PPG) continued to contribute in many ways, but he was inadequate inside as a power forward once Jordan returned and seemed reluctant to assert himself when the Great One was on the floor. B.J. Armstrong (42.7 percent from 3) and Steve Kerr (league-high 52.4 percent from deep) were brilliant bombardiers, but the three-headed pivot of Will Perdue, Luc Longley, and Bill Wennington was barely equal to a half-Shaq.

Season	W	L	Playoffs
1990-91	61	21	NBA Champs
1991-92	67	15	NBA Champs
1992-93	57	25	NBA Champs
1993-94	55	27	L-East Semis
1994-95	47	35	L-East Semis

Last Five Years

Chicago Bulls
1995-96 Season Preview

Opening Line: When Michael Jordan returned to the NBA late last year, he didn't come back to finish second. He wants to win this season and will try to carry the Bulls to one more championship before he departs for good and the team is reinvented. This year Chicago will have to overcome another personnel loss in B.J. Armstrong.

Guard: Jordan was great last year, but he wasn't able to reach the ethereal heights he did before "retiring" after the 1992-93 season. Though it is never a good idea to bet against Jordan, there is certainly a little doubt about whether he'll ever be as dominant as he was before. If so, he is certainly capable of carrying Chicago to the title. There is some question about who will line up beside him, since Armstrong was selected by Toronto in the expansion draft. Toni Kukoc could handle the point role, but he's too slow to defend rival one guards. Brilliant bomber Steve Kerr is another possibility, but he's better suited for a reserve role.

Forward: Scottie Pippen thought he was leaving Chicago, but he's back and should again be a perfect complement to Jordan. Pippen has sensational skills, but he is clearly better suited for the right-hand man spot, largely because of his limited perimeter game. If Kukoc doesn't play the point, he'll fit in at power forward, which doesn't suit his finesse personality. Alabama rookie Jason Caffey has a good body but is raw.

Center: Chicago fans must really appreciate Bill Cartwright now that they've watched Will Perdue, Luc Longley, and Bill Wennington add up to a journeyman pivot. None is quick enough to play the position with the league's best, and each has some serious offensive deficiencies. Jordan can do a lot by himself, but he might not be able to make up for this ensemble.

Analysis: At his best, Jordan is Hercules, but the Bulls may be even too heavy for him to lift to the summit. There are huge questions at the point and power-forward positions, and the center situation is a mess. Chicago can't be dismissed, but it will take a near miracle for it to win everything in 1995-96.

1995-96 Roster

No.	Player	Pos.	Ht.	Wt.	Exp.	College	—1994-95—		
							G	RPG	APG	PPG
*35	Jud Buechler	F/G	6'6"	220	5	Arizona	57	1.7	0.9	3.8
—	Jason Caffey	F	6'8"	255	R	Alabama	—	—	—	—
9	Ron Harper	G	6'6"	198	9	Miami (OH)	77	2.3	2.0	6.9
23	Michael Jordan	G	6'6"	198	10	North Carolina	17	6.9	5.3	26.9
25	Steve Kerr	G	6'3"	180	7	Arizona	82	1.5	1.8	8.2
*42	Larry Krystkowiak	F	6'9"	240	8	Montana	19	3.1	1.4	4.4
7	Toni Kukoc	F/G	6'11"	230	2	(Croatia)	81	5.4	4.6	15.7
13	Luc Longley	C	7'2"	265	4	New Mexico	55	4.8	1.3	6.5
*20	Pete Myers	G/F	6'6"	180	7	Ark.-Little Rock	71	2.0	2.1	4.5
32	Will Perdue	C	7'0"	240	7	Vanderbilt	78	6.7	1.2	8.0
33	Scottie Pippen	F	6'7"	225	8	Cent. Arkansas	79	8.1	5.2	21.4
8	Dickey Simpkins	F	6'10"	250	1	Providence	59	2.6	0.6	3.5
34	Bill Wennington	C	7'0"	260	8	St. John's	73	2.6	0.5	5.0

CLEVELAND CAVALIERS

Home: Gateway Arena
Capacity: 20,562
Year Built: 1994

Chairman of the Board: Gordon Gund
President: Wayne Embry

Address:
1 Center Court
Cleveland, OH 44115

Head Coach: Mike Fratello
NBA: 414-327   Cavaliers: 90-74

Cavaliers History

After their debut in 1970, the Cavaliers won only one playoff series in their first 21 seasons. In their early years, the Cavs didn't have many marquee players—the result of some poor drafting and trades during the 1970s. Things changed in the late 1980s thanks to smarter drafting and the stewardship of coach Lenny Wilkens.

Cleveland spent its first four seasons in the Central basement. In 1975-76, coach Bill Fitch was rewarded for his patience with a division title, as well as the team's first playoff series win. They beat Washington in the Eastern Conference semis.

Center Jim Chones, forwards Campy Russell and Jim Brewer, and guard Bobby "Bingo" Smith were the main performers on that team, but the good times ended soon thereafter. Cleveland qualified for the playoffs the next two seasons but made it back only once (1984-85) in the ensuing nine years.

In 1986, the Cavs began their renaissance by drafting center Brad Daugherty. Daugherty, guards Ron Harper and Mark Price, and forward Larry Nance led the Cavs to a 42-40 record in 1987-88 and a 57-25 mark the next year. After two disappointing seasons, Cleveland put it together again in 1991-92. The Cavs went 57-25 and roared to the conference finals, where they lost to Chicago. They again lost to the Bulls in the 1993 and 1994 playoffs.

Last Five Years

Season	W	L	Playoffs
1990-91	33	49	DNQ
1991-92	57	25	L-East Finals
1992-93	54	28	L-East Semis
1993-94	47	35	L-Round 1
1994-95	43	39	L-Round 1

1994-95 Review

Faced with the prospect of not having injured center Brad Daugherty (back), injured off guard Gerald Wilkins (Achilles tendon), or retired forward Larry Nance at his disposal for the 1994-95 season, Cavs coach Mike Fratello decided the only way to make his team competitive was to employ an excruciating style of play that featured strangulating defense and patient offensive patterns.

Fratello achieved the desired results, making the Cavaliers competitive in just about every game but also consigning them to a season of ugly, boring basketball. Cleveland's new Gund Arena home and wild new uniforms may have created some excitement, but the Cavs' play was often difficult to watch. En route to a respectable 43-39 record and a first-round playoff loss to the Knicks, Cleveland held its foes to a NBA-record 89.8 points per game but scored a league-worst 90.5.

As usual, point guard Mark Price (15.8 PPG, 7.0 APG) led the Cavaliers, but he played only 48 games due to injury. His backup, Terrell Brandon (13.3 PPG), continued his development into a fine point man, while Tyrone Hill (13.8 PPG, 10.9 RPG) blossomed into a quality forward. Veteran John Williams (12.6 PPG, 6.9 RPG) was unselfish while playing out of position in the pivot, while veteran Michael Cage banged the boards.

Chris Mills (12.3 PPG) and Bobby Phills (11.0 PPG) provided adequate scoring within the framework of the slowdown system. Mills was particularly impressive, making 39.2 percent of his 3-point tries. There were even a few signs of life from Danny Ferry, who turned into a strong 3-point shooter (40.3 percent).

Cleveland Cavaliers
1995-96 Season Preview

Opening Line: Last year's brief playoff appearance was accomplished without center Brad Daugherty and guard Gerald Wilkins, whose absences forced coach Mike Fratello to house his team in a defensive cocoon. Daugherty's expected return and some new faces should help the Cav offense considerably and make Cleveland a Central threat.

Guard: Veteran Mark Price remains an excellent blend of outside shooting and creative penetration, although the identity of his partner remains a mystery. Newly acquired shooter Harold Miner hasn't lived up to his advance notices, and rookie Bob Sura from Florida State has tremendous athletic skills but a tendency toward playing out of control. Two guard Bobby Phills is a solid all-around player. Terrell Brandon has been the "point guard of the future" for four seasons now and might be close to getting the starting job.

Forward: Daugherty's return should allow John Williams to return to his customary power-forward position and join Tyrone Hill and Chris Mills in a versatile tandem. Williams may be getting old, but he is still an active inside scorer and rebounder, while Hill is an excellent banger who showed surprising scoring ability last year. Mills is an athletic three man with a good outside shot but needs to improve his defense.

Center: Daugherty had back surgery last season, and it's difficult to judge how soon he'll be back to full power. When healthy, Daugherty is an excellent finesse pivotman with good passing ability and sound rebounding fundamentals. He won't, however, intimidate too many people. Veteran Michael Cage is a rebounding machine in reserve.

Analysis: The Cavaliers are an interesting club, largely because of Fratello, an excellent coach with the ability to adapt his system to the talent he has. If Daugherty is healthy and Miner and Sura produce, don't expect a repeat of last year's boring basketball. Cleveland will still play good defense, but expect a lot more scoring, something that could make them quite dangerous by the end of the year.

1995-96 Roster

No.	Player	Pos.	Ht.	Wt.	Exp.	College	G	RPG	APG	PPG
10	John Battle	G	6'2"	190	10	Rutgers	28	0.4	1.3	4.1
1	Terrell Brandon	G	5'11"	180	4	Oregon	67	2.8	5.4	13.3
44	Michael Cage	C/F	6'9"	240	11	San Diego St.	82	6.9	0.7	5.0
*9	Tony Campbell	G/F	6'7"	215	11	Ohio St.	78	2.0	0.9	6.0
*5	Steve Colter	G	6'3"	175	8	N. Mexico St.	57	1.0	1.8	3.4
43	Brad Daugherty	C	7'0"	269	8	North Carolina	—	—	—	—
*30	Greg Dreiling	C	7'1"	250	9	Kansas	58	2.0	0.4	1.9
35	Danny Ferry	F	6'10"	245	5	Duke	82	1.7	1.2	7.5
32	Tyrone Hill	F	6'9"	245	5	Xavier (OH)	70	10.9	0.8	13.8
—	Donny Marshall	F	6'7"	230	R	Connecticut	—	—	—	—
24	Chris Mills	F	6'6"	216	2	Arizona	80	4.6	1.9	12.3
—	Harold Miner	G	6'4"	215	3	Southern Cal.	45	2.6	1.5	7.3
14	Bobby Phills	G	6'5"	217	4	Southern	80	3.3	2.3	11.0
25	Mark Price	G	6'0"	178	9	Georgia Tech	48	2.3	7.0	15.8
*31	Fred Roberts	F	6'10"	218	11	Brigham Young	21	1.6	0.4	3.8
—	Bob Sura	G	6'4"	200	R	Florida St.	—	—	—	—
18	John Williams	F/C	6'11"	245	9	Tulane	74	6.9	2.6	12.6

DETROIT PISTONS

Home: The Palace
Capacity: 21,454
Year Built: 1988

Managing Partner: William Davidson
Director of Player Personnel: Doug Collins

Address:
Two Championship Dr.
Auburn Hills, MI 48326

Head Coach: Doug Collins
NBA: 137-109   Pistons: 0-0

Pistons History

Any discussion of Pistons history is bound to be a little heavy on the "Bad Boy" years. After three fruitless decades, the Pistons won back-to-back NBA titles in 1988-89 and 1989-90.

The Fort Wayne Pistons joined the NBA in 1949. Fort Wayne, led by high-scoring George Yardley, advanced to the Finals twice during the 1950s, losing to Syracuse in 1954-55 and Philadelphia in 1955-56.

The Pistons moved to Detroit in 1957 but began to falter, finishing below .500 for the next 13 seasons. Detroit made some news during the period, naming 24-year-old Dave DeBusschere player/coach in 1964 and drafting hot-shot guard Dave Bing in 1966. Things got a little better in the mid-1970s. Detroit posted a 52-30 record in 1973-74, due largely to the play of Bing and center Bob Lanier. But the Pistons were eliminated in the Western semis and had to wait another nine seasons for a strong team.

That came in 1983-84 when Chuck Daly took over as coach. Daly, building his team around point guard Isiah Thomas, won the Central Division title in 1987-88. They advanced to the NBA Finals that season, losing to Los Angeles in seven games. Thomas, Bill Laimbeer, Dennis Rodman, and Joe Dumars were not denied the next two years, sweeping the Lakers in 1988-89 and whipping Portland in 1989-90.

Last Five Years

Season	W	L	Playoffs
1990-91	50	32	L-East Finals
1991-92	48	34	L-Round 1
1992-93	40	42	DNQ
1993-94	20	62	DNQ
1994-95	28	54	DNQ

1994-95 Review

If Grant Hill had been able to redeem all of his magazine covers, talk show appearances, and endorsement deals for Piston wins, then maybe Don Chaney would still have a head-coaching job in the NBA. As it turned out, no amount of goodwill generated by Hill could save Chaney and the Pistons from an unpleasant 1994-95 fate. Despite the remarkable season from Hill—on and off the court—Detroit stumbled home with a 28-54 record, worst in the Central Division and well removed from playoff consideration.

Even though the Pistons managed eight more wins than their 1993-94 counterpart, it's hard to imagine this team was a two-time NBA champion just five seasons ago. No one could fault Hill (19.9 PPG), who was one of the league's most exciting players, capable of scoring in a variety of ways and one of the more flashy finishers around the basket. But Hill alone wasn't enough to save Chaney's neck, although much of the coach's trouble was self-inflicted.

It took Chaney more than half the season to insert Allan Houston (14.5 PPG) into the starting lineup at two guard. Houston closed the year on fire, draining 3-pointers from the deep recesses of the Palace and scoring like a veteran. To make room for Houston, Chaney slid classy star Joe Dumars (18.1 PPG) to the point ahead of second-year man Lindsey Hunter, who struggled again with the position. Up front, veteran power forward Terry Mills (15.5 PPG, 7.8 RPG) continued his steady play, but the center tandem of Mark West and Oliver Miller was inconsistent, and Chaney lost big points for not insisting that the bloated Miller stay in shape.

Detroit Pistons
1995-96 Season Preview

Opening Line: Doug Collins returns to the bench after an extended TV analyst hiatus to help the Pistons build back to contention. Although Collins has quite a weapon with which to start—second-year forward Grant Hill—Detroit's glaring weaknesses at center and point guard make the road back to contention a potentially long one.

Guard: Now that the Pistons have found that their shooting guard of the future, Allan Houston, can play in the NBA, they need to find a point guard of the present. Last year, Lindsey Hunter continued to struggle running the team, and veteran off guard Joe Dumars was forced to handle the floor-general duties when Houston blossomed—a job he performed with customary effectiveness. Collins hopes draft pick Randolph Childress from Wake Forest can make the switch from off guard to the point, but that's no guarantee. Actually, it was rumored that Childress would be traded to Portland for yeoman power forward Otis Thorpe.

Forward: Hill's future is incandescent, thanks to his multifaceted game and tremendous off-court charisma. He is clearly one of the NBA's finest young building blocks and should be an even deadlier offensive weapon this year. Fellow forward Terry Mills gets little credit for his consistent scoring, but he isn't chastised enough for his inadequate defense either. Collins drafted for depth, grabbing Wyoming rebounder and shot-blocker Theo Ratliff, hard-working but undersized Lou Roe of Massachusetts, and Georgetown enforcer Don Reid. They'll fight for minutes with Bill Curley.

Center: By letting corpulent Oliver Miller go to Toronto in the expansion draft, the Pistons were left with veterans Mark West and Eric Leckner in the middle. Each works hard but neither is a front-line NBA center. Look for Ratliff to see time here too.

Analysis: Collins brings a recharged battery to the Pistons, and he'll need it since Detroit has problems throughout the lineup and an inadequate bench. Hill is the perfect starting point, and should Houston continue his excellent play from the second half of last year, Detroit will have a good, young nucleus. But the Pistons need big help at the point and more inside pop before they can start winning consistently again.

1995-96 Roster

No.	Player	Pos.	Ht.	Wt.	Exp.	College	G	RPG	APG	PPG
17	Bill Curley	F	6'9"	245	1	Boston College	53	2.3	0.5	2.7
4	Joe Dumars	G	6'3"	195	10	McNeese St.	67	2.4	5.5	18.1
33	Grant Hill	F	6'8"	225	1	Duke	70	6.4	5.0	19.9
20	Allan Houston	G	6'6"	200	2	Tennessee	76	2.2	2.2	14.5
1	Lindsey Hunter	G	6'2"	195	2	Jackson St.	42	1.8	3.8	7.5
*32	Negele Knight	G	6'1"	182	5	Dayton	47	1.3	2.7	4.2
*45	Eric Leckner	C	6'11"	265	6	Wyoming	57	3.1	0.2	4.0
2	Mark Macon	G	6'5"	200	4	Temple	55	1.4	1.1	5.0
6	Terry Mills	F	6'10"	250	5	Michigan	72	7.8	2.2	15.5
42	Theo Ratliff	F/C	6'10"	225	R	Wyoming	—	—	—	—
52	Don Reid	F	6'8"	250	R	Georgetown	—	—	—	—
3	Lou Roe	F	6'6"	220	R	Massachusetts	—	—	—	—
41	Mark West	C	6'10"	246	12	Old Dominion	67	6.1	0.3	7.5

INDIANA PACERS

Home: Market Square Arena
Capacity: 16,530
Year Built: 1974

Owners: Melvin Simon, Herbert Simon
President/G.M.: Don Walsh

Address:
300 E. Market St.
Indianapolis, IN 46204

Head Coach: Larry Brown
NBA: 533-407   Pacers: 99-65

Pacers History

If there could be such a thing as the "Boston Celtics of the ABA," it would have been the Indiana Pacers. The Pacers won three ABA titles and finished second twice from 1968-69 through 1974-75.

The old days were something in Indianapolis. Led by Mel Daniels, a 6'9" bull of a center, the early Pacers featured a lineup that was equal to many NBA teams. Guard Freddie Lewis and forward Roger Brown were deadly scorers, and power forward Bob Netolicky was a bruiser. In 1971, Indiana signed forward George McGinnis. It later added guard Bill Keller and forward Billy Knight to a potent rotation.

Yet the same penchant for accumulating talented personnel did not carry over to Indiana's years in the NBA. The Pacers had only two winning seasons from 1976-77 through 1992-93, and in recent years they became known for their perennial mediocrity. Indiana had the offense in the early 1990s—from long-range bombers Chuck Person and Reggie Miller to do-everything forward Detlef Schrempf—but it lacked the defense, team chemistry, and mental toughness to excel in the playoffs.

New coach Larry Brown addressed all of those concerns, and the Pacers gutted out some tough wins in the 1994 and 1995 playoffs. Led by Miller and center Rik Smits, Indiana lost a seven-game war to New York in the '94 Eastern finals.

Last Five Years

Season	W	L	Playoffs
1990-91	41	41	L-Round 1
1991-92	40	42	L-Round 1
1992-93	41	41	L-Round 1
1993-94	47	35	L-East Finals
1994-95	52	30	L-East Finals

1994-95 Review

For the second straight season, the Pacers enjoyed a trip to the brink of the NBA Finals, only to fall short in yet another seventh game of the Eastern finals. Unlike 1994's near miss against the Knicks, which served as a harbinger of future success, last year's conference-finals loss to Orlando raised some significant questions about whether the Pacers had enough in their current incarnation to win it all.

Though the team did a great job to exorcise the ghosts of 1994's loss to the Knicks by eliminating New York in the conference semis, it lacked the necessary inside scoring and overall athletic ability to compete with the younger Magic.

There is no question that the team's one-two punch of guard Reggie Miller and center Rik Smits did the job. Miller (19.6 PPG) shot 41.5 percent from 3-point land and reiterated his status as one of the league's top scoring guards. Smits (17.9 PPG, 7.7 RPG), now arguably one of the league's top five or six centers, continued his strong play in the pivot and out away from the basket and hit a big shot at the buzzer to win the fourth game of the Orlando series.

After those two, however, the scoring options were limited. The forward triumvirate of Derrick McKey (13.3 PPG), Dale Davis (10.6 PPG, 9.4 RPG), and Antonio Davis (7.6 PPG) was again physical and at times imposing, but none of the three could be considered explosive. Backup point guard Byron Scott (10.0 PPG) had his moments, but he couldn't be counted on for big-time production every night. And even though Mark Jackson (7.6 PPG, 7.5 APG) was a solid floor leader, his scoring abilities were severely limited.

Indiana Pacers
1995-96 Season Preview

Opening Line: Following the 1993-94 season, the Pacers appeared close to competing for the NBA title. Now they just seem to be treading water, and cynics might be wondering when coach Larry Brown is going to bolt. If Indiana wants to reach the Finals, it must find some more scoring up front and get more pop from its backcourt reserves.

Guard: In Mark Jackson and Reggie Miller, Indiana has quite a complementary backcourt pair. Jackson runs the show, makes smart decisions, and isn't much of a scorer. Miller, on the other hand, could be the NBA's top long-range shooter and is capable of some remarkable outbursts. The Pacers grabbed backcourt help in the draft, landing lightning-quick point man Travis Best from Georgia Tech and machine-gunning two man Fred Hoiberg of Iowa State. Haywoode Workman is a tough point guard who can't score.

Forward: Few teams in the NBA can boast such a formidable trio of forwards as the Pacers can. In Derrick McKey, Dale Davis, and Antonio Davis, Indiana has considerable heft and strength. And little scoring. Only McKey can be considered an offensive threat, and he doesn't seem too interested in the role of primary offensive option. The Davises may rebound and play strong defense, but they struggle outside the paint.

Center: It seems like Rik Smits just keeps getting better every year. His scoring and rebounding averages improved during 1994-95, and he continued to develop into a valuable pivotman. Smits won't overpower too many players, and he blocks far too few shots for a big man, but he has made significant improvement from his awkward early years.

Analysis: Even though the Pacers have failed to make it to the Finals the past two seasons, they haven't yet reached a point where their star is waning. Indiana has a solid nucleus of players but needs more scoring in order to move on to the next level. Brown is an excellent coach who can motivate, but even he can't conjure up a title without all the pieces.

1995-96 Roster

								—1994-95—		
No.	Player	Pos.	Ht.	Wt.	Exp.	College	G	RPG	APG	PPG
22	Damon Bailey	G	6'3"	201	R	Indiana	—	—	—	—
—	Travis Best	G	5'11"	182	R	Georgia Tech	—	—	—	—
33	Antonio Davis	F/C	6'9"	230	2	Texas-El Paso	44	6.4	0.6	7.6
32	Dale Davis	F	6'11"	230	4	Clemson	74	9.4	0.8	10.6
27	Duane Ferrell	F	6'7"	215	7	Georgia Tech	56	1.6	0.6	4.1
*10	Vern Fleming	G	6'5"	185	11	Georgia	55	1.6	2.0	4.6
44	Scott Haskin	G	6'11"	250	1	Oregon St.	—	—	—	—
—	Fred Hoiberg	G	6'4"	203	R	Iowa St.	—	—	—	—
13	Mark Jackson	G	6'1"	180	8	St. John's	82	3.7	7.5	7.6
*54	Greg Kite	C	6'11"	263	12	Brigham Young	11	2.0	0.1	0.7
9	Derrick McKey	F	6'10"	225	8	Alabama	81	4.9	3.4	13.3
31	Reggie Miller	G	6'7"	185	8	UCLA	81	2.5	3.0	19.6
*5	Sam Mitchell	F	6'7"	210	6	Mercer	81	3.0	0.8	6.5
45	Rik Smits	C	7'4"	265	7	Marist	78	7.7	1.4	17.9
*41	LaSalle Thompson	F/C	6'10"	260	13	Texas	38	2.3	0.5	2.9
*3	Haywoode Workman	G	6'3"	180	4	Oral Roberts	69	1.6	2.8	4.2

MILWAUKEE BUCKS

Home: Bradley Center
Capacity: 18,633
Year Built: 1988

Owner: Herb Kohl
V.P./Player Personnel: Lee Rose

Address:
1001 N. Fourth St.
Milwaukee, WI 53203

Head Coach: Mike Dunleavy
NBA: 183-227   Bucks: 82-164

Bucks History

In their first 23 years of existence (through 1990-91), the Bucks missed out on postseason play only four times. But despite that gleaming record, the franchise's glory period is long past.

Milwaukee stumbled through its rookie season in 1968-69, but the Bucks signed UCLA star Lew Alcindor and embarked on a five-year run of success. In 1969-70, Milwaukee reached the Eastern finals, and the arrival of guard Oscar Robertson during the off-season was the final piece in coach Larry Costello's puzzle. In 1970-71, Alcindor, Robertson, Bob Dandridge, Greg Smith, and Jon McGlocklin led the Bucks to a 66-16 record and the NBA title.

Alcindor changed his name to Kareem Abdul-Jabbar, and in 1973-74 the Bucks made it back to the title series. However, they lost to Boston in seven games. Jabbar was dealt to Los Angeles for four players following the 1974-75 season, and the Bucks floundered for the next four years.

Don Nelson became coach in 1976-77 and directed the team back into the playoffs on a regular basis. But although the nucleus of Sidney Moncrief, Junior Bridgeman, Marques Johnson, and Terry Cummings was strong enough to win 50-plus games each year from 1980-81 to 1986-87, the Bucks couldn't get back to the Finals. The club had grown too old by the early '90s and began a rebuilding program.

Last Five Years

Season	W	L	Playoffs
1990-91	48	34	L-Round 1
1991-92	31	51	DNQ
1992-93	28	54	DNQ
1993-94	20	62	DNQ
1994-95	34	48	DNQ

1994-95 Review

After struggling for the first two years under Mike Dunleavy, the Bucks made significant strides in 1994-95, improving their won-loss record by 14 games (to 34-48) and finally showing signs that their youth movement would be paying dividends. The Bucks challenged for the final playoff spot in the East and generated some excitement with their frontcourt-oriented club.

The Bucks were considerably more competitive than their previous three clubs and appeared to have finally found a player around whom they could center their rebuilding efforts—forward Glenn Robinson. Once Robinson (21.9 PPG, 6.4 RPG), the first pick in last year's draft, abandoned his highly publicized quest to become sports' first $100 million man, Milwaukee began its methodical improvement, centering the team around Robinson's myriad skills and the inspired play of sophomore forward Vin Baker.

Baker (17.7 PPG, 10.3 PPG) did whatever the team needed, even if that meant playing out of position again in the middle. Veteran forward Johnny Newman (7.7 PPG) provided his customary wing scoring, rookie Eric Mobley proved to be a capable backup pivotman, and veteran forward Marty Conlon did a little bit of everything.

But the Bucks remained unsettled in the backcourt. The tandem of Todd Day (16.0 PPG) and Lee Mayberry showed some improvement, but neither was consistent enough to be considered among the top half of the performers at his position. Day's shooting remained suspect (42.4 percent), and Mayberry offered little offensively at the point. Third guard Eric Murdock (13.0 PPG) provided defense and quickness.

Milwaukee Bucks
1995-96 Season Preview

Opening Line: This could very well be the year Mike Dunleavy's patient rebuilding work lands the Bucks in the playoffs. Milwaukee has been accumulating young talent for the last few years, and the 1995 draft may have provided the last pieces needed for a postseason berth. Milwaukee fans shouldn't get too excited, however, since real contention is still a long way off.

Guard: By acquiring Shawn Respert from Portland on draft day, the Bucks may have finally found themselves a real shooting guard. Although he showed some life last year, Todd Day has struggled from the outside and will have to fend off the sweet-shooting Respert to keep his starting job. Eric Murdock might be ready to take over the point duties full-time, but he needs to mix a little more offense in with his good distributing and defensive skills. Lee Mayberry is an inconsistent backup at the point.

Forward: The Bucks are in great shape here with two of the league's best young frontcourt performers. Second-year man Glenn Robinson can score inside and out, is strong on the backboards, and should continue to blossom into a star. Vin Baker, meanwhile, gets more and more recognition for his complete game and is one of the league's most reliable four men. There isn't much depth, however. Marty Conlon hustles every night and Johnny Newman can shoot it, but the Bucks need an upgrade behind the starters.

Center: Adding raw, immature Wisconsin rookie Rashard Griffith to Eric Mobley and Alton Lister didn't do too much to help the Bucks' pivot picture for this season. Griffith needs a lot of time to develop, while Mobley is limited to banging close to the hoop and Lister is near the end of his career.

Analysis: Respert is another good piece in the Buck puzzle, but there are still questions at the point and in the middle. Milwaukee will threaten the .500 mark and create some excitement this season, but Dunleavy has more work to do before real contention is a possibility.

1995-96 Roster

No.	Player	Pos.	Ht.	Wt.	Exp.	College	G	RPG	APG	PPG
							\-1994-95\-			
42	Vin Baker	F	6'11"	250	2	Hartford	82	10.3	3.6	17.7
17	Jon Barry	G	6'5"	204	3	Georgia Tech	52	0.9	1.6	3.7
*30	Marty Conlon	F	6'11"	245	4	Providence	82	5.2	1.3	9.9
10	Todd Day	G/F	6'6"	200	3	Arkansas	82	3.9	1.6	16.0
—	Andrei Fetisov	F	6'10"	225	R	(Russia)	—	—	—	—
*12	Tate George	G	6'5"	208	4	Connecticut	3	0.3	0.0	1.3
—	Rashard Griffith	C	6'10"	274	R	Wisconsin	—	—	—	—
*53	Alton Lister	C	7'0"	245	13	Arizona St.	60	3.9	0.2	2.8
11	Lee Mayberry	G	6'1"	172	3	Arkansas	82	1.0	3.4	5.8
52	Eric Mobley	C	6'11"	250	1	Pittsburgh	46	3.3	0.5	3.9
5	Eric Murdock	G	6'1"	200	4	Providence	75	2.9	6.4	13.0
*22	Johnny Newman	F	6'7"	205	9	Richmond	82	2.1	1.1	7.7
—	Shawn Respert	G	6'3"	195	R	Michigan St.	—	—	—	—
13	Glenn Robinson	F	6'7"	240	1	Purdue	80	6.4	2.5	21.9

TORONTO RAPTORS

Home: SkyDome
Capacity: 23,000
Year Built: 1989

President: John Bitove
V.P./Basketball Operations: Isiah Thomas

Address:
20 Bay St. #702
Toronto, ONT M5J 2N8

Head Coach: Brendan Malone
NBA: 0-0   Raptors: 0-0

1995-96 Season Preview

Opening Line: Well, they wanted the NBA in Canada, and here it comes. It won't be pretty. Players like B.J. Armstrong and John Salley may have familiar names, but neither is good enough to carry a team.

Guard: This figures to be the strength of the Raptors, with Armstrong, San Antonio expatriate Willie Anderson, and draft pick Damon Stoudamire of Arizona providing the nucleus. If he's not traded (as rumored), expect steady Armstrong and machine-gunning Anderson to start, but look for Toronto to groom the multi-talented Stoudamire and super-quick B.J. Tyler for the future. Pesky Keith Jennings can push the tempo off the bench.

Forward: A career underachiever, Salley is hardly a quality power man. Veteran Jerome Kersey's skills have been eroding, while Ed Pinckney's game is limited to

within five feet of the basket. Second-year pro Dontonio Wingfield has potential but is terribly raw, while Dallas castaway Doug Smith has disappointed for years. Tony Massenburg will grab some boards.

Center: If he could shed 50 or 60 pounds, Oliver Miller could be an active force in the middle. That's not likely, given his track record. Boston gave up on Acie Earl pretty quickly, and with good reason. He's slow and unpolished offensively.

Analysis: It's going to be a long time before Toronto comes close to the playoffs, thanks to the collection of castoffs that has come north through the expansion draft and the NBA's decision to keep the new teams away from the top five picks in the draft for a few seasons. Such is the price for entry into the world's top sports/entertainment conglomerate.

1995-96 Roster

Player	Pos.	Ht.	Wt.	Exp.	College	G	RPG	APG	PPG
							—1994-95—		
Willie Anderson	G/F	6'8"	200	7	Georgia	38	1.4	1.4	4.9
B.J. Armstrong	G	6'2"	185	6	Iowa	82	2.3	3.0	14.0
Acie Earl	C/F	6'10"	240	2	Iowa	30	1.5	0.1	2.2
Keith Jennings	G	5'7"	160	3	E. Tenn. St.	80	1.9	4.7	7.4
Jerome Kersey	F	6'7"	225	11	Longwood	63	4.1	1.3	8.1
Jimmy King	G	6'5"	210	R	Michigan	—	—	—	—
Tony Massenburg	F	6'9"	245	3	Maryland	80	5.7	0.8	9.3
Oliver Miller	C/F	6'9"	280	3	Arkansas	64	7.4	1.5	8.5
Ed Pinckney	F	6'9"	215	10	Villanova	62	3.4	0.3	2.3
John Salley	F/C	6'11"	250	9	Georgia Tech	75	4.5	1.6	7.3
Doug Smith	F	6'10"	238	4	Missouri	63	2.3	0.7	5.1
Damon Stoudamire	G	5'10"	171	R	Arizona	—	—	—	—
Zan Tabak	C/F	7'0"	245	1	(Croatia)	37	1.5	0.1	2.0
B.J. Tyler	G	6'1"	185	1	Texas	55	1.1	3.2	3.5
Dontonio Wingfield	F	6'8"	246	1	Cincinnati	20	1.5	0.2	2.3

DALLAS MAVERICKS

Home: Reunion Arena
Capacity: 17,502
Year Built: 1980

Owner: Donald Carter
General Manager: Norm Sonju

Address:
777 Sports St.
Dallas, TX 75207

Head Coach: Dick Motta
NBA: 948-979   Mavericks: 282-353

Mavericks History

Most NBA franchises start out bad and then get better. The Mavericks started out well but then went down the tubes.

Dallas entered the league in 1980 and soon made its mark. In the 1981 draft, the Mavs selected Mark Aguirre, Rolando Blackman, and Jay Vincent. In 1983, they brought in standout guards Dale Ellis and Derek Harper. That high-scoring nucleus, coached by Dick Motta, won 43 games in 1983-84 and advanced to the West semis.

Dallas won the Midwest in 1986-87, buoyed by mammoth center James Donaldson and rookie forward Roy Tarpley, but the Mavs bowed out in the first round of the playoffs. The excitement really ran high the next year, as Dallas stretched Los Angeles to seven games in the Western finals.

Things started to sour in 1988-89. Aguirre was traded to Detroit for mercurial Adrian Dantley, and Tarpley played only 19 games due to substance abuse. The Mavericks fell to 38-44 in 1988-89, and though they rebounded to 47-35 the next season, MacLeod was fired and Dallas lost in the first round of the 1990 playoffs.

The next four seasons were disastrous. The downfall was triggered by a lifetime ban on Tarpley, but injuries, bad trades, and dissension also crippled the Mavericks. High draft picks Jimmy Jackson, Jamal Mashburn, and Jason Kidd did give the Mavs hope for the future.

Last Five Years

Season	W	L	Playoffs
1990-91	28	54	DNQ
1991-92	22	60	DNQ
1992-93	11	71	DNQ
1993-94	13	69	DNQ
1994-95	36	46	DNQ

1994-95 Review

After four years as one of the league's true laughingstocks, the Mavs road back into the NBA spotlight with a 23-win improvement and a cadre of young stars that should serve as an exciting nucleus for plenty of future success.

Under coach Dick Motta, who returned to the scene of his successes with early Maverick teams, Dallas played captivating basketball and was even in the hunt for the playoffs until the last few weeks of the season. If it hadn't been for a midseason injury to emerging shooting guard Jim Jackson, the Mavs might have finished above .500 for the first time since the 1989-90 season.

Leading the way was the perimeter triumvirate of Jackson, Jason Kidd, and Jamal Mashburn, each of whom has a chance to be among the best at his position one day. Jackson (25.7 PPG) was on his way to a great year when a grisly ankle injury put him on the shelf. Dallas continued to remain competitive, thanks to the play of Mashburn (24.1 PPG), whose myriad skills made him a threat inside or outside from the small-forward position, and Kidd (11.7 PPG, 7.7 APG), who played the point with aplomb.

Motta surrounded the trio with some fine complementary players, including hardworking rebounding machine Popeye Jones (10.3 PPG, 10.6 RPG); George McCloud (9.6 PPG), a CBA reclamation project who shined along the perimeter; and Lucious Harris, a shooter who backed up Jackson. Roy Tarpley (12.6 PPG, 8.2 RPG) made his return to the league from drug-induced exile and was alternately moody and productive. Center Lorenzo Williams offered boards and blocks.

Dallas Mavericks
1995-96 Season Preview

Opening Line: They're not exactly clearing space for championship banners in Reunion Arena, but the mood in Dallas is decidedly more upbeat than in recent seasons. By winning 36 games last year and playing some exciting basketball, the young Mavericks took a big step back toward the playoffs and now appear to have considerable hope for the future.

Guard: The tandem of Jason Kidd and Jimmy Jackson has the potential to be the best in the league in a few years. Kidd may have an awful shot, but he is a marvel in the open court, distributes it well, and plays relentless defense. Jackson needs only to expand his shooting range to become one of the league's top three or four off guards. He already has tremendous strength off the dribble. CBA reclamation project George McCloud is effective in short bursts, and Lucious Harris is a versatile reserve.

Forward: Jamal Mashburn has proven he can score. Now he must show some maturity and restraint. Only one player in the NBA—Shaquille O'Neal—launched more shots than Mashburn last year, and though plenty fell, it's time for Mashburn to become more efficient. The Mavs helped their front-line picture considerably on draft day, adding big men Cherokee Parks from Duke and Loren Meyer of Iowa State. Together with ferocious rebounder Popeye Jones, they should help upgrade the four spot. Parks has an excellent shooting touch, while Meyer's size and deceptive quickness make him tough to handle down low.

Center: It's difficult to tell whether the Mavs will be able to count on Roy Tarpley for an extended period of time. If they can, they get a solid player who shoots well inside and can clear the glass. If not, it's a mishmash of undersized Lorenzo Williams, Parks, and Meyer.

Analysis: The Mavs will definitely be a team to watch in 1995-96, if only to chart the increased productivity of their Big Three (Kidd, Jackson, and Mashburn) and watch whether the frontcourt newcomers can help them move into true playoff contention. Even if the Mavs slip into the lottery again, it should be their last visit for a long time.

1995-96 Roster

No.	Player	Pos.	Ht.	Wt.	Exp.	College	G	RPG	APG	PPG
1	Scott Brooks	G	5'11"	165	7	Cal.-Irvine	59	1.1	2.0	5.8
43	Terry Davis	F/C	6'10"	250	6	Virginia Union	46	3.4	0.2	3.0
7	Tony Dumas	G	6'6"	190	1	Missouri-K.C.	58	1.1	1.0	4.6
30	Lucious Harris	G	6'5"	190	2	Long Beach St.	79	2.8	1.7	9.5
35	Donald Hodge	C	7'0"	240	4	Temple	54	2.3	0.8	3.9
24	Jimmy Jackson	G	6'6"	220	3	Ohio St.	51	5.1	3.7	25.7
54	Popeye Jones	F	6'8"	250	2	Murray St.	80	10.6	2.0	10.3
5	Jason Kidd	G	6'4"	205	1	California	79	5.4	7.7	11.7
32	Jamal Mashburn	F	6'8"	240	2	Kentucky	80	4.1	3.7	24.1
*21	George McCloud	G/F	6'8"	215	5	Florida St.	42	3.5	1.3	9.6
40	Loren Meyer	C	6'10"	257	R	Iowa St.	—	—	—	—
4	Cherokee Parks	C	6'10"	235	R	Duke	—	—	—	—
42	Roy Tarpley	C/F	7'0"	245	6	Michigan	55	8.2	1.1	12.6
44	Lorenzo Williams	F/C	6'9"	213	3	Stetson	82	8.4	1.5	4.0

DENVER NUGGETS

Home: McNichols Sports Arena
Capacity: 17,171
Year Built: 1975

Address:
1635 Clay St.
Denver, CO 80204

Owner: COMSAT Denver, Inc.
General Manager: Bernie Bickerstaff

Head Coach: Bernie Bickerstaff
NBA: 221-215   Nuggets: 20-12

Nuggets History

The Nuggets were one of the rarities of the old ABA—a team that stayed in the same place throughout the league's tumultuous nine-year history.

Early on, Denver Rocket fans were thrilled by the high-flying exploits of forward Spencer Haywood, who led Denver to the Western Conference finals in 1969-70. But Haywood soon left and the franchise's fortunes dimmed until 1974, when G.M. Carl Scheer and coach Larry Brown came to the Rockies from the Carolina Cougars.

Scheer immediately changed the team nickname to the Nuggets. Denver won 65 games in 1974-75 but lost in the Western finals. The next season, the Nuggets acquired star guard David Thompson and made it to the league championship series.

The Nuggets were one of four ABA teams to merge with the NBA in 1976, and they won the Midwest Division in their first two seasons. Denver won Midwest titles in 1984-85 and 1987-88 under Doug Moe and made it to the Western finals in 1985.

Following the 1989-90 season, Denver fired Moe and hired Paul Westhead. Westhead's high-octane running game didn't bring too many results, as Denver registered the league's worst record in 1990-91. Young stars like Dikembe Mutombo and Mahmoud Abdul-Rauf helped the team take a healthy step forward over the next three seasons.

Last Five Years

Season	W	L	Playoffs
1990-91	20	62	DNQ
1991-92	24	58	DNQ
1992-93	36	46	DNQ
1993-94	42	40	L-West Semis
1994-95	41	41	L-Round 1

1994-95 Review

This time last year, the folks in Denver couldn't line up fast enough to heap praise on the young team that had shocked the NBA by whipping heavily favored Seattle in the playoffs. The future looked bright in the Rocky Mountains. Year One of that hereafter didn't quite develop like the Nuggets and their faithful had planned.

Instead of moving deeper into the playoffs, Denver had to scrap just to qualify. A quick, three-game dispatch at the hands of San Antonio was its reward and provided none of the drama of 1993-94's postseason journey. The Nuggets entered the playoffs without coach Dan Issel, who quit in midseason citing health concerns. G.M. Bernie Bickerstaff assumed the coaching reins and guided Denver to a solid second half, but he saw first-hand that the team still had a long way to go.

Injuries didn't help matters. Power forward LaPhonso Ellis missed all but six games with a busted knee, and point guard Robert Pack (12.1 PPG, 6.9 APG) played just a half-season due to knee problems. Center Dikembe Mutombo (11.5 PPG, 12.5 RPG, 3.9 BPG) was again a defensive force, although he complained plenty about his lack of offensive opportunities.

Veteran Reggie Williams (13.4 PPG) was adequate from the perimeter, and guard Mahmoud Abdul-Rauf (16.0 PPG) still couldn't find a set backcourt position. Bickerstaff had to be pleased with the play of second-year forward Rodney Rogers (12.2 PPG, 4.8 RPG), while rookie Jalen Rose (8.2 PPG, 4.8 APG) did a little bit of everything at guard. Veteran Dale Ellis (11.3 PPG) shot 40.3 percent from 3-point range, and off guard Bryant Stith (11.2 PPG) scored well from 15 feet and in.

Denver Nuggets
1995-96 Season Preview

Opening Line: Although injuries and reality brought the Nuggets back to Earth last season, Denver remains a young team on the rise—a good reason for interim coach, and G.M., Bernie Bickerstaff to make himself the permanent bench jockey. Denver is still a player or two away from true contention, but the addition of rookie power forward Antonio McDyess is a good start.

Guard: If Robert Pack can rebound from knee surgery, the Nuggets will be set with a blazing point man who can also score a little bit. Who lines up next to him is the big question. Mahmoud Abdul-Rauf is too small to be a full-time two guard, and neither Jalen Rose nor Bryant Stith has proven himself a strong enough shooter. Veteran Dale Ellis is an effective bomber off the bench.

Forward: McDyess has a bright future ahead of him at the four position, largely because of his strength, excellent rebounding skills, and tremendous leaping ability, but he plays the same position as LaPhonso Ellis and neither is particularly suited to move to the small-forward spot. Veteran Reggie Williams can still score enough to play the three, but it seems odd that the Nuggets would acquire McDyess on top of Ellis and Brian Williams, another solid four man.

Center: Dikembe Mutombo's offensive game may lag behind those of the league's premier pivotmen, but his defensive skills and rebounding are second to none. Mutombo is a relentless worker and one of the more imposing centers in the league. Rookie Anthony Pelle of Fresno State, who impressed during postseason workouts, will back him up. Williams can also handle the pivot in small doses.

Analysis: The Nuggets are a big-time perimeter scorer away from being one of the best in the West. And though that guy isn't around this year, Denver is still a strong bet to get back into the playoffs. Should Bickerstaff find himself a Clyde Drexler type, the Nuggets will do more than just surprise some big shots.

1995-96 Roster

No.	Player	Pos.	Ht.	Wt.	Exp.	College	G	RPG	APG	PPG
							\-1994-95\-			
1	Mahmoud Abdul-Rauf	G	6'1"	162	5	Louisiana St.	73	1.9	3.6	16.0
3	Dale Ellis	G/F	6'7"	215	12	Tennessee	81	2.7	0.7	11.3
20	LaPhonso Ellis	F	6'8"	240	3	Notre Dame	6	2.8	0.7	4.0
9	Greg Grant	G	5'7"	140	6	Trenton St.	14	0.6	3.1	2.2
*21	Tom Hammonds	F	6'9"	225	6	Georgia Tech	70	3.2	0.5	5.9
*53	Cliff Levingston	C/F	6'8"	225	11	Wichita St.	57	2.2	0.5	2.3
—	Antonio McDyess	F	6'9"	220	R	Alabama	—	—	—	—
55	Dikembe Mutombo	C	7'2"	250	4	Georgetown	82	12.5	1.4	11.5
14	Robert Pack	G	6'2"	190	4	Southern Cal.	42	2.7	6.9	12.1
—	Anthony Pelle	C	7'0"	260	R	Fresno St.	—	—	—	—
*42	Mark Randall	F	6'9"	235	4	Kansas	8	1.5	0.1	0.8
5	Jalen Rose	G	6'8"	210	1	Michigan	81	2.7	4.8	8.2
23	Bryant Stith	G	6'5"	208	3	Virginia	81	3.3	1.9	11.2
8	Brian Williams	F	6'11"	250	4	Arizona	63	4.7	0.8	8.0
34	Reggie Williams	F/G	6'7"	195	8	Georgetown	74	4.4	3.1	13.4
—	Randy Woods	G	6'0"	190	3	La Salle	62	0.7	2.2	2.0

HOUSTON ROCKETS

Home: The Summit
Capacity: 16,311
Year Built: 1975

Owner: Les Alexander
V.P./Basketball Operations: Bob Weinhauer

Address:
10 Greenway Plaza
Houston, TX 77046

Head Coach: Rudy Tomjanovich
NBA: 176-100   Rockets: 176-100

Rockets History

Throughout their 28 seasons in San Diego and Houston, the Rockets have featured some of the NBA's finest big men. The tradition began during the team's second year. Behind rookie Elvin Hayes, the league's leading scorer, San Diego advanced to the 1968-69 Western Conference semis, losing to Atlanta.

The Rockets moved to Houston in 1971, but Hayes spent only one season there before being dealt to Baltimore. Houston then built its team around considerably shorter players such as 5'11" guard Calvin Murphy and forwards Mike Newlin and Rudy Tomjanovich.

Star center No. 2 came in 1976, when Moses Malone moved over from the defunct ABA. Houston won the Central Division crown in 1976-77 and advanced to the NBA Finals in 1980-81, losing in six games to Boston. In 1983, the Rockets drafted 7'4" Ralph Sampson from Virginia; one year later, they selected the dominating Akeem Olajuwon. In 1985-86, Houston made it back to the Finals behind its "Twin Towers," only to lose to Boston in six.

The Rockets lost in the first round of playoffs from 1988-91. Houston won its division under Tomjanovich in 1992-93, but it lost in the West semis. True success didn't come until 1993-94, when Olajuwon carried Houston to its first NBA championship. They repeated the trick in 1994-95.

1994-95 Review

Nothing proves the relative meaninglessness of the NBA's regular season than Houston's run to its second straight title. In rising from sixth seed in the Western Conference to the league championship, the Rockets proved that it doesn't matter what happens during the regular season so long as everything is in place come money time. By beating Utah, Phoenix, San Antonio, and Orlando during its improbable march to repeating, Houston overcame the teams with the four best regular-season records and showed the value of team play and strict adherence to a winning system.

When the playoffs began, no one would have been blamed for dismissing Houston's chances. A midseason trade that brought Clyde Drexler from Portland for warrior power forward Otis Thorpe appeared to leave the Rockets woefully thin up front. A subsequent shoulder injury to valuable reserve forward Carl Herrera—plus the leave of absence granted troubled shooting guard Vernon Maxwell—made Houston an even less likely champion.

But coach Rudy Tomjanovich strapped his team to the back of center Hakeem Olajuwon (27.8 PPG, 10.8 RPG, 3.4 BPG), clearly the best player in the game today, and made excellent use of his personnel. Drexler (21.8 PPG) provided much needed consistency from the off-guard spot and finally got his championship ring.

Point men Kenny Smith (10.4 PPG) and Sam Cassell (9.5 PPG) took turns running the team and making big shots, while Robert Horry (10.2 PPG, 5.1 RPG) blossomed at power forward, despite playing out of position. Mario Elie entered the starting lineup in the playoffs and was quietly effective at small forward.

Last Five Years

Season	W	L	Playoffs
1990-91	52	30	L-Round 1
1991-92	42	40	DNQ
1992-93	55	27	L-West Semis
1993-94	58	24	NBA Champs
1994-95	47	35	NBA Champs

Houston Rockets
1995-96 Season Preview

Opening Line: As long as Hakeem Olajuwon is on the court, Houston cannot be counted out of the title chase. The Rockets may have a glaring weakness at the power-forward spot, but Olajuwon's magic and the team's excellent backcourt make them dangerous during a seven-game series.

Guard: Many howled when the Rockets traded Otis Thorpe for Clyde Drexler, but Drexler was invaluable during the playoffs, scoring from the perimeter and in the open court. If Sam Cassell improves his consistency, he may join Drexler in the starting backcourt. If not, steady vet Kenny Smith will hold fort, although he is better suited for long-distance bombing than creativity. The "X factor" is mercurial Vernon Maxwell, a great scorer with some big personal problems.

Forward: It's hard to believe the Rockets won an NBA title with the tandem of Mario Elie and Robert Horry, but that just proves Olajuwon's talent even more. Elie is an adequate perimeter threat and solid transition player, while Horry played out of place in the four spot last year. He has tremendous physical skills and can score from all over the court, but he doesn't rebound very well. Carl Herrera is a spirited backup who performs well close to the basket, while Pete Chilcutt and Chucky Brown are valuable role-players inside.

Center: Just when it seems Olajuwon can't get any better, he adds something else to his repertoire. In 1994-95 it was the medium-range jumper, and this year it could be the 3-pointer. Olajuwon is the complete player, capable of dominating on offense, defense, or the backboards, and he has proven himself the best in the game. Duke rookie Erik Meek, who impressed during postseason workouts, will carry Hakeem's bags.

Analysis: Imagining Houston as a three-time champion may be difficult, but just think back to last year's title run and appreciate what it accomplished. Olajuwon and Drexler are a fabulous inside-outside tandem; Horry, Cassell, Smith, and Elie are excellent complementary parts; and coach Rudy Tomjanovich gets nowhere near enough credit for his work. The only thing standing in their way this year could be a lack of hunger.

1995-96 Roster

No.	Player	Pos.	Ht.	Wt.	Exp.	College	G	RPG	APG	PPG
15	Tim Breaux	G/F	6'7"	215	1	Wyoming	42	0.8	0.4	3.0
*52	Chucky Brown	F	6'8"	215	6	N. Carolina St.	41	4.6	0.7	6.1
10	Sam Cassell	G	6'3"	195	2	Florida St.	82	2.6	4.9	9.5
*32	Pete Chilcutt	F/C	6'11"	232	4	North Carolina	68	4.7	0.9	5.3
22	Clyde Drexler	G	6'7"	222	12	Houston	76	6.3	4.8	21.8
17	Mario Elie	F/G	6'5"	210	5	American Inter.	81	2.4	2.3	8.8
7	Carl Herrera	F	6'9"	225	4	Houston	61	4.6	0.7	6.8
25	Robert Horry	F	6'10"	220	3	Alabama	64	5.1	3.4	10.2
27	Charles Jones	C	6'9"	215	11	Albany St.	3	2.3	0.0	1.0
11	Vernon Maxwell	G	6'4"	190	7	Florida	64	2.6	4.3	13.3
—	Erik Meek	C	6'10"	245	R	Duke	—	—	—	—
—	Tracy Murray	G/F	6'8"	225	3	UCLA	54	1.1	0.4	4.8
34	Hakeem Olajuwon	C	7'0"	255	11	Houston	72	10.8	3.5	27.8
30	Kenny Smith	G	6'3"	170	8	North Carolina	81	1.9	4.0	10.4

MINNESOTA TIMBERWOLVES

Home: Target Center
Capacity: 19,006
Year Built: 1990

Address:
600 First Ave. North
Minneapolis, MN 55403

Owners: Harvey Ratner, Marv Wolfenson
V.P./Basketball Operations: Kevin McHale

Head Coach: Bill Blair
NBA: 21-61   T'Wolves: 21-61

Timberwolves History

After six years in the NBA, Minnesota finds itself right where it started—at the bottom rung of the ladder.

The Timberwolves first took to the court in 1989-90, and the initial year's results were predictable—22-60. The team featured some bright spots that first year. Forward Tony Campbell emerged as a top scoring threat, and rookie guard Pooh Richardson was an adroit playmaker and scorer. Under defensive-minded coach Bill Musselman, the T'Wolves were one of the league's best at maintaining tempo and stopping opponents from scoring.

For 1990-91, Minnesota added 7'0" center Felton Spencer and forward Gerald Glass, and they moved into the brand new Target Center in downtown Minneapolis. The team improved to 29-53, good for fifth place in the Midwest Division. But despite the six-game improvement, Musselman got the axe and was replaced by Jimmy Rodgers.

The change did nothing to help the team, as the 1991-92 T'Wolves finished with the league's worst record. After the season, Minnesota drafted Christian Laettner and landed standouts Chuck Person and Micheal Williams in a trade. Nevertheless, the 1992-93 club still lacked the talent to win 20 games. High-scoring rookie Isaiah Rider couldn't improve the Wolves in 1993-94.

1994-95 Review

At least no one can accuse the T'Wolves of failing to make progress the last few years. After winning just 19 games during 1992-93, they improved to 20-62 in 1993-94. The headway continued last season with another one-game jump up to 21 victories.

Minnesota remains the only member of the recent expansion quartet never to have won 30 games, much less qualified for the playoffs, and improvement doesn't appear too imminent. Making the season even more difficult to bear was the big improvement by Dallas, which had joined the Timberwolves in the Midwest Division basement for the past few years. The Wolves' continued struggle with inadequate talent in the middle and at the point-guard position was exacerbated by another season of grousing by the club's better players, particularly off guard Isaiah Rider.

Though Rider (20.4 PPG) continued to prove himself capable of ascending to the upper echelon of NBA scorers, his poor attitude sabotaged his sustained progress. Forward Christian Laettner (16.3 PPG, 7.6 RPG) produced strong numbers consistently once again and even steered clear of controversy for much of the year, but his pairing with multi-talented Tom Gugliotta (12.7 PPG, 7.4 RPG)—acquired midyear from Golden State for 1994 first-round draft pick Donyell Marshall—didn't pay off as T'Wolves management thought it might.

Sean Rooks (10.9 PPG, 6.1 RPG) was game but overmatched in the pivot, and point guard Winston Garland was erratic at the point in relief of Micheal Williams, who missed the year with a heel injury. Aside from swingman Doug West (12.9 PPG), the rest of the Wolves were atrocious.

Last Five Years

Season	W	L	Playoffs
1990-91	29	53	DNQ
1991-92	15	67	DNQ
1992-93	19	63	DNQ
1993-94	20	62	DNQ
1994-95	21	61	DNQ

Minnesota Timberwolves
1995-96 Season Preview

Opening Line: Pity Kevin McHale. The former Celtic great has been entrusted with trying to make something out of the awful T'Wolves and must do so with many of the same players who precipitated the team's misery during the past six years. The addition of high school prodigy Kevin Garnett leaves little doubt that this will be a long, tedious reclamation project.

Guard: If Isaiah Rider would just concentrate on playing basketball and not mouthing off or getting into trouble with civilians, he might just become a great off guard. Chances are, however, he'll continue to gripe and never reach stardom. While Rider stands firm at the two spot, Micheal Williams's heel causes concern at the point. He missed all but one game last year and is needed to provide some stability on offense. Veteran Winston Garland is a serviceable backup, while Doug West is a capable scorer at the two or three spots. Rookie Jerome Allen from Penn is an intense defender with a weak shot.

Forward: The pairing of Tom Gugliotta with Christian Laettner makes little sense, since neither is particularly quick and both are better suited for the four spot. But that's Minnesota. Laettner will never be a superstar, but he is formidable inside, and Googs is a multi-talented scorer/passer/rebounder. West is featured at the three spot at times, and rookie Mark Davis of Texas Tech should bring some needed athletic ability up front.

Center: Garnett has tremendous skills for a 6'11" player but is only 19 years old. He may revolutionize the position or be so overwhelmed that his skills will become flash-frozen and he'll never grow into the player he would have if he had gone to college. He'll share the middle with Sean Rooks, a somewhat soft three-year vet.

Analysis: McHale should visit Boston's new FleetCenter every now and then, just to reassure himself that he is a winner. Looking at the Celtic championship banners would help assuage some of the frustration he'll experience while trying to steer the Wolves to respectability. Garnett could be a great first step, or he could be another T'Wolves draft-day mistake.

1995-96 Roster

No.	Player	Pos.	Ht.	Wt.	Exp.	College	G	RPG	APG	PPG
—	Jerome Allen	G	6'3"	184	R	Pennsylvania	—	—	—	—
*40	Mike Brown	F/C	6'10"	260	9	G. Washington	27	1.7	0.4	1.3
—	Mark Davis	G/F	6'6"	210	R	Texas Tech	—	—	—	—
*30	Pat Durham	G/F	6'8"	220	2	Colorado St.	59	1.6	0.9	5.1
*44	Greg Foster	F/C	6'11"	240	5	Texas-El Paso	78	3.3	0.5	4.9
*22	Winston Garland	G	6'2"	180	7	S.W. Missou. St.	73	2.3	4.4	6.1
—	Kevin Garnett	F	6'11"	220	R	None	—	—	—	—
24	Tom Gugliotta	F	6'10"	240	3	N. Carolina St.	77	7.4	3.6	12.7
32	Christian Laettner	F	6'11"	245	3	Duke	81	7.6	2.9	16.3
*15	Darrick Martin	G	5'11"	170	1	UCLA	34	1.9	3.9	7.5
34	Isaiah Rider	G/F	6'5"	215	2	UNLV	75	3.3	3.3	20.4
45	Sean Rooks	C/F	6'10"	250	3	Arizona	80	6.1	1.2	10.9
3	Chris Smith	G	6'3"	190	3	Connecticut	64	1.1	2.3	5.0
5	Doug West	G	6'6"	200	6	Villanova	71	3.2	2.6	12.9
4	Micheal Williams	G	6'2"	175	7	Baylor	1	1.0	3.0	6.0

SAN ANTONIO SPURS

Home: Alamodome
Capacity: 20,662
Year Built: 1993

Address:
100 Montana St.
San Antonio, TX 78203

Chairman of the Board: Robert McDermott
V.P./Basketball Operations: Gregg Popovich

Head Coach: Bob Hill
NBA: 195-174   Spurs: 62-20

Spurs History

This Texas franchise was born as a charter member of the ABA. Its name? The Dallas Chaparrals. The stay in Dallas was rocky, featuring six coaches in six years.

Angelo Drossos moved the club to San Antonio in 1973, and the team was renamed the Spurs. The club had 50-plus-win seasons in 1974-75 and 1975-76 and moved into the NBA at full gallop.

Led by unstoppable guard George Gervin, mammoth center Artis Gilmore, and a supporting cast of Johnny Moore, Larry Kenon, and James Silas, the Spurs won two Central and three Midwest Division titles in six years. Gervin was the NBA scoring champ four times. However, San Antonio fell in the conference finals three times.

The Spurs' nucleus began to age in the mid-1980s, and the team fell from its lofty status. In 1987, the Spurs drafted David Robinson of Navy. The team continued to sag in the next two seasons while Robinson completed his military obligation, but he joined the Spurs in 1989-90.

Robinson immediately emerged as one of the NBA's best centers. He teamed with Terry Cummings and Sean Elliott to help San Antonio win the Midwest title in both 1989-90 and 1990-91. Despite fine records throughout the 1990s, the Spurs weren't able to reach the conference finals until 1995, when they lost to Houston.

Last Five Years

Season	W	L	Playoffs
1990-91	55	27	L-Round 1
1991-92	47	35	L-Round 1
1992-93	49	33	L-West Semis
1993-94	55	27	L-Round 1
1994-95	62	20	L-West Finals

1994-95 Review

It's unfortunate that the Spurs' excellent 1994-95 season will be remembered more for Dennis Rodman's wild behavior than it will be for David Robinson's MVP performance or San Antonio's Midwest Division title. But while people may be tempted to characterize the Spurs' inability to win the NBA title as a function of Rodman's antics, they must remember that San Antonio went as far as it could with a team that had glaring deficiencies in the backcourt.

That the Spurs won the division and then made it to the Western Conference finals says a lot for a team that was adjusting to a new coach, Bob Hill. But once the season got rolling, the expectations grew, and the Spurs' playoff loss to the Rockets was indeed disappointing.

Rodman's season-long grab for attention played a role in disintegrating the team's chemistry. The guy could rebound (16.8 RPG), but he sure didn't like following rules. Robinson (27.6 PPG, 10.8 RPG, 3.2 BPG), meanwhile, was a model citizen. He scored down low and from outside. He did it in the halfcourt and on the run. He rebounded. He played defense. He certainly deserved the MVP trophy.

Forward Sean Elliott (18.1 PPG) enjoyed one of his best seasons, while point guard Avery Johnson (13.4 PPG, 8.2 APG) came out of nowhere to be quite productive, although his outside shooting was woeful. Backcourt mate Vinny Del Negro (12.5 PPG) was solid but hardly a front-line gunner. And while Chuck Person (10.8 PPG) had his moments from the outside, his outbursts weren't too consistent. Veterans J.R. Reid, Terry Cummings, and Doc Rivers joined Person in a solid bench unit.

San Antonio Spurs
1995-96 Season Preview

Opening Line: The Spurs are still stinging from last year's Western Conference finals loss to the Rockets, but they nonetheless enter the 1995-96 season as one of the league's top teams and are still considered a threat to win it all. The keys to success are whether the Spurs can control (or even choose to keep) talented but troubled power forward Dennis Rodman, and if their mediocre backcourt will be upgraded by the addition of rookie Cory Alexander.

Guard: It's still amazing that the Spurs posted the best record in basketball with a starting backcourt of Avery Johnson and Vinny Del Negro. Johnson is a quick penetrator who passes well, but he has little range on his shot and isn't the best defender, while Del Negro is somewhat slow and liable to be exposed on defense. Despite their limitations, they do get the job done. The backup tandem of point Doc Rivers and gunner Chuck Person is aging but effective, and though Alexander has marvelous skills, he is young and still recovering from a broken ankle.

Forward: Sean Elliott came back to San Antonio and flourished—offensively. There is no question Elliott can score from just about anywhere on the court, but his rebounding and defense are below par. Rodman is just the opposite—a board machine and stopper with no offensive game and the league's most volatile character. When he decides to play, the Spurs are almost impossible to beat. When he's acting up, San Antonio loses a lot. J.R. Reid has found a solid niche as a low-post backup.

Center: David Robinson certainly deserved the MVP Award last season and is certainly among the top three or four players in the league right now. He scores, rebounds, blocks shots, and runs the floor with equal ability and is a fine balance to Rodman's unpredictable behavior.

Analysis: As long as Robinson is performing at his customary high level, the Spurs are a threat to go far, but their title hopes rely on better backcourt play and solid citizenship by Rodman. Until all that comes together, the Spurs will be a great regular-season team with no championship rings.

1995-96 Roster

| No. | Player | Pos. | Ht. | Wt. | Exp. | College | —1994-95— | | |
							G	RPG	APG	PPG
1	Cory Alexander	G	6'1"	185	R	Virginia	—	—	—	—
*34	Terry Cummings	F	6'9"	245	13	DePaul	76	5.0	0.8	6.8
15	Vinny Del Negro	G	6'4"	200	5	N. Carolina St.	75	2.6	3.0	12.5
32	Sean Elliott	F	6'8"	215	6	Arizona	81	3.5	2.5	18.1
*54	Jack Haley	F/C	6'10"	250	6	UCLA	31	0.9	0.2	2.4
6	Avery Johnson	G	5'11"	175	7	Southern	82	2.5	8.2	13.4
*2	Moses Malone	C	6'10"	260	19	None	17	2.7	0.4	2.9
00	Julius Nwosu	F	6'10"	255	1	Liberty	23	1.0	0.1	1.3
45	Chuck Person	F	6'8"	225	9	Auburn	81	3.1	1.3	10.8
7	J.R. Reid	F/C	6'9"	255	6	North Carolina	81	4.9	0.7	7.0
*25	Doc Rivers	G	6'4"	185	12	Marquette	63	1.7	2.6	5.1
50	David Robinson	C	7'1"	235	6	Navy	81	10.8	2.9	27.6
10	Dennis Rodman	F	6'8"	210	9	S.E. Okla. St.	49	16.8	2.0	7.1

UTAH JAZZ

Home: Delta Center
Capacity: 19,911
Year Built: 1991

Owner: Larry H. Miller
General Manager: Tim Howells

Address:
301 W. South Temple
Salt Lake City, UT 84101

Head Coach: Jerry Sloan
NBA: 458-314   Jazz: 364-193

Jazz History

About the last city you'd expect to find a team named the Jazz would be in puritan Salt Lake City, Utah. However, the name comes with an easy explanation. When the franchise was born back in 1974, its home-town was New Orleans, a jazzy place if ever there was one. When it moved west in 1979, it decided to hold on to the name.

The early days did have their moments. In the mid-1970s, Louisiana native "Pistol" Pete Maravich lit up the Bayou, scoring baskets in bushels and once torching the Knicks for 68. Maravich's knee went out in 1977-78 and, despite the emergence of all-world rebounder Leonard "Truck" Robinson, the Jazz limped along.

Under coach Frank Layden, the Jazz captured the Midwest Division crown in 1983-84 and advanced to the conference semifinals, relying on league scoring leader Adrian Dantley, quick backcourt men Darrell Griffith and Ricky Green, and mammoth, 7'4" center Mark Eaton.

The Jazz selected power forward Karl Malone in the 1985 draft, and he was an immediate sensation, teaming with assist machine John Stockton to form a solid nucleus. Utah won the 1988-89 Midwest title under new coach Jerry Sloan before falling in the first round of the playoffs. Utah advanced to the Western finals in 1991-92 and 1993-94 but was beaten by Portland and Houston, respectively.

1994-95 Review

By falling to Houston in the first round of the playoffs, the Jazz earned the dubious distinction of becoming the second team in NBA history (last year's Sonics were the first) to win 60 games during the regular season and then exit in the conference quarterfinals.

It was ironic that the Jazz, who used a sparkling 27-14 road record to help them to their 60-22 second-place finish in the Midwest Division, was unable to subdue the Rockets at home in the decisive fifth game. The Jazz finally appeared to have enough to represent the Western Conference in the NBA Finals, but it couldn't deliver in the playoffs, a tough thing to accept for their fans, underrated coach Jerry Sloan, and the All-Star tandem of Karl Malone and John Stockton.

Once again the pair was among the best in the league at their respective positions, only to find themselves playing golf in June. Malone (26.7 PPG, 10.6 RPG) was a pillar of strength down low, but he was hurt by the team's lack of a center—a situation created by the torn Achilles tendon suffered by workmanlike pivotman Felton Spencer (9.3 PPG, 7.6 RPG) after just 34 games. Stockton (14.7 PPG, 12.3 APG) again led the league in assists and teamed with Jeff Hornacek (16.5 PPG) to give the Jazz one of the league's most productive backcourts.

Forward David Benoit (10.4 PPG) was an excellent complement up front, veteran Antoine Carr performed yeoman's work in the middle when Spencer went down, and forward Adam Keefe showed some life off the bench. But though the Jazz had a lot going for it during the regular season, it didn't have enough come playoff time.

Last Five Years

Season	W	L	Playoffs
1990-91	54	28	L-West Semis
1991-92	55	27	L-West Finals
1992-93	47	35	L-Round 1
1993-94	53	29	L-West Finals
1994-95	60	22	L-Round 1

Utah Jazz
1995-96 Season Preview

Opening Line: After another typical year in Salt Lake City—great regular season, early playoff exit—the Jazz enters 1995-96 with the sound of a ticking clock providing the soundtrack. Karl Malone and John Stockton aren't getting any younger, and the Jazz haven't done much in the past few years to revitalize their team through the draft. This year's pick, plodding Kansas rookie center Greg Ostertag, isn't exactly the best foundation for the future.

Guard: As long as they keep assist totals, Stockton will have a job in the NBA. No one can set up teammates better than Stockton, who also manages to shoot above 50 percent from the field. Backcourt mate Jeff Hornacek is a steady outside shooter, a good creator, and a smart defender, but the Utah backcourt isn't exactly the fastest around. John Crotty is an adequate playmaker in reserve.

Forward: Karl Malone may not be as brutally effective as he was in his youth, but the Mailman remains among the league's top power men and can still be counted on for about 25 points and ten boards a night. He teams with David Benoit, a solid complementary weapon on offense who could use a little better perimeter game. Adam Keefe, who began to show signs of some life last year on the interior, is the main forward off the bench. Aging Antoine Carr took on the pivot job when Felton Spencer suffered an Achilles injury, but Carr doesn't have much left.

Center: It doesn't seem possible, but Spencer's injury was a crushing blow to the Jazz. Spencer isn't going to make any top-ten lists among NBA pivotmen, but he is huge and can clear the glass. Ostertag may be even slower than Spencer, but he gives the Jazz six more fouls inside.

Analysis: It may be difficult for the rabid Utah fans to comprehend, but there is little hope of this team winning a championship without a significant injection of athletic ability on the perimeter and an upgrade in the middle. Sure, the Jazz might well win 60 games again and even advance as far as the Western Conference finals, but that's it.

1995-96 Roster

No.	Player	Pos.	Ht.	Wt.	Exp.	College	G	—1994-95— RPG	APG	PPG
21	David Benoit	F	6'8"	220	4	Alabama	71	5.2	0.8	10.4
55	Antoine Carr	F	6'9"	255	11	Wichita St.	78	3.4	0.9	9.6
*42	Tom Chambers	F	6'10"	230	14	Utah	81	2.6	0.9	6.2
*25	John Crotty	G	6'1"	185	3	Virginia	80	1.2	2.6	3.7
14	Jeff Hornacek	G	6'4"	190	9	Iowa St.	81	2.6	4.3	16.5
31	Adam Keefe	F	6'9"	241	3	Stanford	75	4.4	0.4	6.1
32	Karl Malone	F	6'9"	256	10	Louisiana Tech	82	10.6	3.5	26.7
00	Greg Ostertag	C	7'2"	280	R	Kansas	—	—	—	—
34	Bryon Russell	F	6'7"	225	2	Long Beach St.	63	2.2	0.5	4.5
50	Felton Spencer	C	7'0"	265	5	Louisville	34	7.6	0.5	9.3
12	John Stockton	G	6'1"	175	11	Gonzaga	82	3.1	12.3	14.7
5	Andy Toolson	G/F	6'6"	210	1	Brigham Young	—	—	—	—
15	Jamie Watson	F	6'7"	190	1	South Carolina	60	1.2	1.0	3.3

VANCOUVER GRIZZLIES

Home: General Motors Place
Capacity: 20,004
Year Built: 1989

Chairman: Arthur Griffiths
V.P./Basketball Operations: Stu Jackson

Address:
788 Beatty St. #201
Vancouver, BC V6B 2M1

Head Coach: Brian Winters
NBA: 0-0   Grizzlies: 0-0

1995-96 Season Preview

Opening Line: The Grizzlies will accomplish at least one thing this season: making the Clippers feel good. The Big Bears will try to build around rookie center Bryant Reeves and hope that coach Brian Winters has plenty of patience with the usual collection of rag-tag expansion fodder.

Guard: Greg Anthony finally gets a chance to run a team now that he has escaped New York. He's quick and aggressive, but his shot is weak and his play inconsistent. If veteran Gerald Wilkins's Achilles tendon is healed, he'll score plenty at the two spot, with veteran Byron Scott providing 3-point sniping from the bench. Syracuse rookie Lawrence Moten needs to improve his jump shot but has potential, and Trevor Ruffin could be a good bench gunner.

Forward: Blue Edwards is a proven slasher at the three spot, but he doesn't have very much from the outside. Pencil him in at one starting spot. Winters will choose the power man from among Kenny Gattison, who is game if his neck is healed, capable Larry Stewart, and unproven youngsters Doug Edwards, Reggie Slater, Rodney Dent, and Antonio Harvey.

Center: Reeves developed into a solid pivot at Oklahoma State and brings a big body and fairly well-developed inside game to Vancouver. Benoit Benjamin, a career dud, will form the other half of the center tandem.

Analysis: The Grizzlies roster is packed with question marks, although Gattison, Wilkins, and Scott might prove valuable for a couple seasons. Since Vancouver is in the same boat as Toronto—no draft picks in the top five until 1998—its fans should expect years of pain and bad basketball.

1995-96 Roster

Player	Pos.	Ht.	Wt.	Exp.	College	G	RPG	APG	PPG
Greg Anthony	G	6'2"	185	4	UNLV	61	1.0	2.6	6.1
Benoit Benjamin	C	7'0"	265	10	Creighton	61	7.2	0.6	11.1
Rodney Dent	F/C	6'10"	256	1	Kentucky	—	—	—	—
Blue Edwards	G/F	6'4"	228	6	East Carolina	67	1.9	1.1	6.9
Doug Edwards	F	6'7"	235	2	Florida St.	38	1.3	0.3	1.8
Kenny Gattison	F	6'8"	252	8	Old Dominion	21	3.6	0.8	6.0
Antonio Harvey	C/F	6'11"	225	2	Pfeiffer	59	1.7	0.4	3.0
Lawrence Moten	G	6'5"	185	R	Syracuse	—	—	—	—
Derrick Phelps	G	6'4"	180	1	North Carolina	3	0.0	0.3	0.0
Bryant Reeves	C	7'0"	292	R	Oklahoma St.	—	—	—	—
Trevor Ruffin	G	6'1"	185	1	Hawaii	49	0.5	1.0	4.8
Byron Scott	G	6'4"	200	12	Arizona St.	80	1.9	1.4	10.0
Reggie Slater	F	6'7"	250	1	Wyoming	25	2.3	0.5	4.8
Larry Stewart	F	6'8"	230	4	Coppin St.	40	1.7	0.5	2.6
Gerald Wilkins	G	6'6"	210	9	Tenn.-Chattan.	—	—	—	—

GOLDEN STATE WARRIORS

Home: Oakland Coliseum Arena
Capacity: 15,025
Year Built: 1966

Chairman: Chris Cohan
General Manager: Dave Twardzik

Address:
Oakland Coliseum Arena
Oakland, CA 94621

Head Coach: Rick Adelman
NBA: 291-154   Warriors: 0-0

Warriors History

Not many fans know that this club began as the Philadelphia Warriors, a team that won the first BAA title in 1946-47 behind scoring machine Joe Fulks.

The Warriors advanced to the BAA finals in 1948, losing to Baltimore. But they defeated Fort Wayne in 1956 to win the NBA title behind Paul Arizin, Neil Johnston, and Tom Gola. In 1959, Wilt Chamberlain joined the team and won the MVP Award in his rookie season. The team moved to San Francisco in 1962 and lost to Boston in the NBA Finals in 1963-64. The Warriors traded Chamberlain to the new Philadelphia 76ers in 1964-65, then lost to the Sixers in the NBA Finals two years later.

The Warriors changed their name to Golden State in 1971 and moved across the bay to Oakland, where the championship drought continued until 1974-75. That year, coach Al Attles incorporated a ten-man rotation around Rick Barry and took the Warriors to the NBA title.

The Warriors didn't rebound again until 1988, when Don Nelson took over as coach. Using a small lineup built around Chris Mullin and Mitch Richmond, the Warriors made it to the Western semis in 1988-89. Point guard Tim Hardaway was added for the 1989-90 season, and in 1990-91 Golden State again advanced to the West semis, losing to Los Angeles. Injuries have plagued the team since.

1994-95 Review

No one could have forecast the controversy and sheer confusion that conspired before and during the 1994-95 season to transform the Warriors from a rising star in the West into a franchise in considerable disarray. By the time Golden State slunk home with a 26-56 record, Don Nelson had been replaced as coach by Bob Lanier, and two players who had helped the Warriors move to the threshold of power had been dished to other teams.

The preseason was highlighted by the Warriors' trade of Billy Owens to the Miami Heat for center Rony Seikaly, as well as acrimony between Nelson and second-year forward Chris Webber. In November, Golden State traded Webber to Washington for draft picks and forward Tom Gugliotta (who was later sent to Minnesota for rookie forward Donyell Marshall).

Nelson finally resigned his post in midseason, citing health concerns. Lanier inherited a team with little cohesiveness or spirit, and plenty of anger. Third-year guard Latrell Sprewell (20.6 PPG) was particularly grouchy, and his bad attitude was evident in some selfish play. Point man Tim Hardaway (20.1 PPG, 9.3 APG) was marvelous, but a wrist injury forced him to miss the last quarter of the season.

Veteran forward Chris Mullin (19.0 PPG) played only 25 games because of lingering injuries, while Seikaly (12.1 PPG, 7.4 RPG) played only 36 games because of leg problems. Power forward Chris Gatling (13.7 PPG, 63.3 FGP) was his usual reliable self around the basket, and Marshall showed flashes of future greatness. Rookie Carlos Rogers looked promising up front, but fellow first-year man Clifford Rozier struggled in the middle.

Last Five Years

Season	W	L	Playoffs
1990-91	44	38	L-West Semis
1991-92	55	27	L-Round 1
1992-93	34	48	DNQ
1993-94	50	32	L-Round 1
1994-95	26	56	DNQ

Golden State Warriors
1995-96 Season Preview

Opening Line: If the off-again, on-again Warriors hold form, this should be a pretty good year. The additions of G.M. Dave Twardzik, coach Rick Adelman, and No. 1 pick Joe Smith will help erase the controversy that caused last season's dreadful performance.

Guard: If Tim Hardaway is healthy, and Latrell Sprewell is happy, the Warriors should have one of the league's best tandems. When 100 percent, Hardaway is a lightning-quick penetrator and reliable perimeter scorer. Off guard Sprewell sulked through most of last year but should respond well to Twardzik and Adelman, two of the league's more accommodating souls. That should mean 20-plus points a night and some spectacular play. Depth is a problem, although veteran Ricky Pierce may see more time after spending much of last year on the D.L.

Forward: The addition of Smith gives Adelman some tremendous options here. He can go with youth and athletic ability, pairing Smith and Donyell Marshall in an exciting, albeit a little thin, pairing. Or he can inject veteran sharpshooter Chris Mullin for a better halfcourt look. He could even play all three at the same time. Backup support will be supplied by near-automatic inside scorer Chris Gatling, corpulent Victor Alexander, and second-year man Carlos Rogers, who has great skills to go with his 6'11" frame.

Center: Rony Seikaly isn't going to dominate anybody, but he is a hard-working, reliable pivotman who is capable of grabbing a bunch of rebounds every night. Gatling, Alexander, and Smith should all be able to handle backup assignments.

Analysis: Expect the Warriors to make a quick transformation from the smallish teams of the Don Nelson era to a more versatile unit with more frontcourt pop. The metamorphosis isn't finished yet, but Golden State has enough raw talent to scare some people this year.

1995-96 Roster

No.	Player	Pos.	Ht.	Wt.	Exp.	College	G	RPG	APG	PPG
								—1994-95—		
52	Victor Alexander	C/F	6'9"	265	4	Iowa St.	50	5.8	1.2	10.0
—	Andrew DeClercq	F	6'9"	230	R	Florida	—	—	—	—
25	Chris Gatling	F/C	6'10"	225	4	Old Dominion	58	7.6	0.9	13.7
10	Tim Hardaway	G	6'0"	195	5	Texas-El Paso	62	3.1	9.3	20.1
*20	Tim Legler	G	6'4"	210	5	La Salle	24	1.7	1.1	7.3
—	Martin Lewis	G/F	6'5"	210	R	Seward County	—	—	—	—
9	Ryan Lorthridge	G	6'4"	190	1	Jackson St.	37	1.9	2.7	7.4
3	Donyell Marshall	F	6'9"	218	1	Connecticut	72	5.6	1.5	12.6
—	Michael McDonald	C	6'10"	232	R	New Orleans	—	—	—	—
50	Dwayne Morton	G/F	6'6"	190	1	Louisville	41	1.4	0.4	4.1
17	Chris Mullin	F	6'7"	215	10	St. John's	25	4.6	5.0	19.0
*22	Ricky Pierce	G	6'4"	215	13	Rice	27	2.4	1.5	12.5
34	Carlos Rogers	F	6'11"	220	1	Tennessee St.	49	5.7	0.8	8.9
44	Clifford Rozier	C/F	6'10"	245	1	Louisville	66	7.4	0.7	6.8
4	Rony Seikaly	C	6'11"	252	7	Syracuse	36	7.4	1.3	12.1
—	Joe Smith	F	6'10"	225	R	Maryland	—	—	—	—
15	Latrell Sprewell	G	6'5"	190	3	Alabama	69	3.7	4.0	20.6
—	Dwayne Whitfield	F	6'6"	240	R	Jackson St.	—	—	—	—
*12	David Wood	F	6'9"	230	5	Nevada-Reno	78	3.1	0.8	5.5

LOS ANGELES CLIPPERS

Home: L.A. Memorial Sports Arena
Capacity: 16,021
Year Built: 1959

Owner: Donald T. Sterling
V.P./Basketball Operations: Elgin Baylor

Address:
3939 S. Figueroa St.
Los Angeles, CA 90037

Head Coach: Bill Fitch
NBA: 862-942   Clippers: 17-65

Clippers History

Despite brief periods of success, the Clippers have been one of the league's weakest and most poorly managed teams.

Born the Buffalo Braves in 1970, the team flourished briefly under the direction of Jack Ramsay. The Braves crept above the .500 mark (42-40) in 1973-74, behind NBA scoring leader Bob McAdoo, slick playmaker Ernie DiGregorio, and sharp-shooting forward Jim McMillian. The Braves improved to 49-33 the next season with MVP McAdoo again leading the way. But the Braves lost to Washington in the Eastern semifinals that year, then lost to Boston in the semis the following season.

Thus ended the good times for Braves/Clippers fans. Prior to the 1978-79 season, Braves owner John Y. Brown traded the team to Irving Levin in return for control of the Celtics. Levin moved the club to San Diego, renamed it the Clippers, and watched it register a 17-65 record in 1981-82. The Clippers moved north to L.A. for the 1984-85 season and were an immediate poor cousin to the flourishing Lakers.

Though they won 30-plus games in 1984-85 and 1985-86, the Clippers embarked on three straight miserable seasons, with the lowlight being a 12-70 mark in 1986-87. Despite young talent such as Ron Harper and Danny Manning, the Clippers failed to rise above mediocrity in the late '80s and early '90s.

Last Five Years

Season	W	L	Playoffs
1990-91	31	51	DNQ
1991-92	45	37	L-Round 1
1992-93	41	41	L-Round 1
1993-94	27	55	DNQ
1994-95	17	65	DNQ

1994-95 Review

Give coach Bill Fitch credit. He didn't lose his sense of humor as the Clippers bumbled to their worst record, 17-65, since 1987-88. Fitch squired his young, over-matched charges through the treacherous NBA waters with humor and class.

The Clipper players didn't quit too many nights, either, despite glaring weaknesses in the middle and a dearth of talent in the backcourt. The season could have been better, had hulking center Stanley Roberts not torn his Achilles tendon during training camp. His absence forced Fitch to copy the Golden State model of the 1980s, without the talent. The Clippers shot only 44.4 percent from the field, fourth worst in the NBA, and allowed opponents to score at a 49.6-percent clip, the league's poorest field goal defense total.

Veteran power forward Loy Vaught (17.5 PPG, 9.7 RPG) enjoyed his best year as a pro but did so in near anonymity. He and rookie small forward Lamond Murray (14.1 PPG) were a solid frontcourt tandem, although Murray shot only 40.2 percent from the field and made a miserable 29.8 percent of 218 3-point attempts. The rest of the forwards had few sustained periods of effectiveness, although Malik Sealy (13.0 PPG) did have his best year as a pro.

Third-year man Tony Massenburg (9.3 PPG, 5.7 RPG) was mere fodder as a 6'9" center, while Charles Outlaw scored well near the basket and grabbed a few rebounds. The backcourt featured 39.4-percent shooting by point man Pooh Richardson (10.9 PPG, 7.9 APG) and slight improvement by off guard Terry Dehere (10.4 PPG). Rookie Eric Piatkowski shot a respectable 37.4 percent from 3-point range.

Los Angeles Clippers
1995-96 Season Preview

Opening Line: The fact that Jerry Stackhouse didn't want to have anything to do with the Clippers says it all for this sad-sack franchise. L.A. remains one of the most muddled teams in the NBA, and there is little hope that it will be climbing out of the Pacific basement any time soon.

Guard: By swinging a draft-day deal that brought Oregon State rookie Brent Barry to town, the Clippers served notice that off guards Terry Dehere and Eric Piatkowski—their first-round picks in the last two drafts—weren't getting it done. Barry has a world of skills but needs time to adapt them to the NBA game. Pooh Richardson lines up next to him at the point and is among the worst-shooting guards in the league. Malik Sealy sees some time at the two spot, but he doesn't have much of an outside game.

Forward: This isn't such a bad area, since starters Loy Vaught and Lamond Murray were the two most productive Clips last year and Rodney Rogers, acquired from the Nuggets with Barry, should provide some good depth. Vaught is an underrated power man with surprising scoring ability and a relentless attitude on the boards. Murray has plenty of flash and dash but needs to become more consistent, as does Rogers, who is largely a four man trapped in a small forward's body.

Center: Coach Bill Fitch will be thrilled if hulking center Stanley Roberts can return from Achilles-tendon surgery and clog things up in the middle. Roberts won't score too much, but he is a legitimate seven-footer who can rebound and block about two shots a game. Equally enormous Elmore Spencer is a plodding backup who should lend some of his bulk to skinny, 7'2" Miami of Florida rookie Constantin Popa.

Analysis: Pencil the Clippers in for last in the Pacific this year, next year, and maybe the year after. Fitch has maintained his sense of humor while coaching the hapless team, but he won't be laughing if L.A. can't break the 20-win plateau this year. With a little health and some development by Murray, Barry, and Rogers, the Clips might even win 25. Whoopee.

1995-96 Roster

No.	Player	Pos.	Ht.	Wt.	Exp.	College	G	—1994-95—		
								RPG	APG	PPG
31	Brent Barry	G	6'6"	185	R	Oregon St.	—	—	—	—
24	Terry Dehere	G	6'4"	190	2	Seton Hall	80	1.9	2.8	10.4
30	Harold Ellis	G	6'5"	220	2	Morehouse	69	1.3	0.6	3.7
23	Gary Grant	G	6'3"	185	7	Michigan	33	1.1	2.8	6.2
7	Lamond Murray	F	6'7"	236	1	California	81	4.4	1.6	14.1
45	Bo Outlaw	F	6'8"	210	2	Houston	81	3.9	1.0	5.2
52	Eric Piatkowski	G/F	6'7"	215	1	Nebraska	81	1.6	1.0	7.0
—	Constantin Popa	C	7'2"	235	R	Miami (FL)	—	—	—	—
2	Pooh Richardson	G	6'1"	180	6	UCLA	80	3.2	7.9	10.9
42	Eric Riley	C	7'0"	245	2	Michigan	40	2.8	0.3	4.4
53	Stanley Roberts	C	7'0"	290	3	Louisiana St.	—	—	—	—
54	Rodney Rogers	F	6'7"	250	2	Wake Forest	80	4.9	2.0	12.2
21	Malik Sealy	G/F	6'8"	192	3	St. John's	60	3.6	1.8	13.0
4	Michael Smith	F	6'10"	225	3	Brigham Young	29	1.9	0.7	5.3
27	Elmore Spencer	C	7'0"	270	3	UNLV	19	3.4	1.3	6.9
35	Loy Vaught	F	6'9"	240	5	Michigan	80	9.7	1.7	17.5

LOS ANGELES LAKERS

Home: The Great Western Forum
Capacity: 17,505
Year Built: 1967

Owner: Dr. Jerry Buss
V.P./Basketball Operations: Jerry West

Address:
3900 W. Manchester Blvd.
Inglewood, CA 90306

Head Coach: Del Harris
NBA: 380-375   Lakers: 48-34

Lakers History

In their 45 years of existence, the Lakers have put a dazzling array of talent onto NBA courts. Along the way, they have won 11 world championships.

The Laker magic began in Minneapolis and was built around 6'10" center George Mikan, clearly the premier player of his day. With Mikan, Bob Pollard, Vern Mikkelsen, and Slater Martin, the Minneapolis Lakers won five titles in six years from 1949-54.

In 1960, the team moved to L.A. But the early years there led to heartbreak, as the Lakers lost in the NBA Finals to the Celtics six times, despite the heroics of guard Jerry West and forward Elgin Baylor.

Even the arrival of Wilt Chamberlain in 1968-69 couldn't stop the string of runnerup finishes. L.A. dropped the 1968-69 series to the Celtics and the 1969-70 title series to the Knicks. The Lakers gained revenge two years later by going 69-13 (including a 33-game winning streak) and beating New York 4-1 in the Finals.

Kareem Abdul-Jabbar continued the tradition of Hall of Fame pivot men for the Lakers when he was acquired from Milwaukee in 1975. But it wasn't until Magic Johnson was drafted in 1979 that the Lakers truly began to shine. The team won five titles in the 1980s, including two over Boston, and assumed the "Showtime" image that predominated its home city.

Last Five Years

Season	W	L	Playoffs
1990-91	58	24	L-NBA Finals
1991-92	43	39	L-Round 1
1992-93	39	43	L-Round 1
1993-94	33	49	DNQ
1994-95	48	34	L-West Semis

1994-95 Review

The young Lakers scored a dramatic first-round playoff upset of Seattle, but L.A. was more than just a Cinderella team. By winning 48 games and advancing to the Western Conference semifinals, the Lakers established themselves as one of the NBA's teams on the rise, boasting a lineup packed with young talent that was just a player or two away from serious contention.

Credit G.M. Jerry West with the lightning-fast rebuilding job of a lottery team that cemented his reputation as the league's top executive. West snookered Phoenix out of forward Cedric Ceballos, continued his recent drafting success by adding guard Eddie Jones, and made the right choice by hiring Del Harris as coach for the 1994-95 season.

Though nicknamed "Dull" by scribes, Harris managed the young Lakers with a combination of patience and old-fashioned teaching. He gave the ball to sparkplug Nick Van Exel (16.9 PPG, 8.3 APG) and was rewarded with a great year.

Ceballos (21.7 PPG) was tremendous as well, despite battling injury problems, and Jones (14.0 PPG) had some spectacular moments at the two spot, despite missing time with a bad shoulder. Power forward Elden Campbell (12.5 PPG, 6.1 RPG) continued his development and showed promise of future greatness, while center Vlade Divac (16.0 PPG, 10.4 RPG) had his best year as a professional.

The Laker bench was a little weak. Veteran point guard Sedale Threatt missed much time with injuries, and two man Anthony Peeler was erratic. George Lynch was troubled by injuries, and Sam Bowie put up the worst numbers of his career.

Los Angeles Lakers
1995-96 Season Preview

Opening Line: Lakers G.M. Jerry West has done a fabulous job of building a young, exciting team out of the wreckage of Showtime's waning years, and coach Del Harris's firm hand and excellent teaching skills have been a perfect match. Last year's 48 wins and startling first-round playoff upset of Seattle were merely a precursor to future successes.

Guard: Nick Van Exel may take too many shots and make some poor decisions, but he needs only a little more self-control and some more experience to become a big-time floor leader. This fearless leader teams with second-year pro Eddie Jones, who has a reliable outside shot, has great quickness off the dribble, and plays excellent defense. Anthony Peeler and his inconsistent shooting come off the bench, and rookie Frankie King is a smallish gunner. Veteran Sedale Threatt, who was plagued by injuries last year, could be a solid backup.

Forward: That really was Elden Campbell tearing it up during the playoffs, and you can't blame the Lakers for wondering whether it was just a tease. Should he come to play every night, Campbell could be one of the NBA's best power forwards. His running mate, Cedric Ceballos, doesn't have the best outside shot and plays little defense, but he gets to the hoop for bushels of points. Third-year man George Lynch is an adequate rebounder with limited athletic ability.

Center: Vlade Divac had one of his best seasons in 1994-95 and finally seems to have adopted a more physical mindset in the post. While Divac isn't exactly David Robinson, he has strong offensive skills and can be counted upon for consistent production in the pivot. Backup Sam Bowie was particularly ineffective last year and appears too slow for the modern NBA game.

Analysis: With Seattle in flux and Phoenix getting older, it would appear the Lakers are well positioned for a return to the top of the Pacific. It won't happen this year, unless Campbell develops into the star he could be and the bench improves its production considerably, but the Lakers are looming. Expect another playoff appearance and big trouble for a couple postseason opponents.

1995-96 Roster

No.	Player	Pos.	Ht.	Wt.	Exp.	College	G	RPG	APG	PPG
00	Corie Blount	F/C	6'10"	242	2	Cincinnati	68	3.5	0.9	3.5
*31	Sam Bowie	C	7'1"	263	10	Kentucky	67	4.3	1.8	4.6
41	Elden Campbell	F/C	6'11"	250	5	Clemson	73	6.1	1.3	12.5
23	Cedric Ceballos	F	6'7"	225	5	Cal. St. Fuller.	58	8.0	1.8	21.7
12	Vlade Divac	C	7'1"	260	6	(Serbia)	80	10.4	4.1	16.0
25	Eddie Jones	G/F	6'6"	190	1	Temple	64	3.9	2.0	14.0
4	Frankie King	G	6'1"	185	R	W. Carolina	—	—	—	—
30	George Lynch	F	6'8"	220	2	North Carolina	56	3.3	1.1	6.1
2	Anthony Miller	F	6'9"	255	1	Michigan St.	46	3.3	0.8	4.1
1	Anthony Peeler	G	6'4"	212	3	Missouri	73	2.3	1.7	10.4
*34	Tony Smith	G	6'4"	205	5	Marquette	61	1.8	1.7	5.6
3	Sedale Threatt	G	6'2"	185	12	W. Virg. Tech	59	2.1	4.2	9.5
9	Nick Van Exel	G	6'1"	171	2	Cincinnati	80	2.8	8.3	16.9

PHOENIX SUNS

Home: America West Arena
Capacity: 19,023
Year Built: 1992

Chief Executive Officer: Jerry Colangelo
V.P./Player Personnel: Dick Van Arsdale

Address:
201 E. Jefferson St.
Phoenix, AZ 85004

Head Coach: Paul Westphal
NBA: 177-69   Suns: 177-69

Suns History

The Phoenix Suns are synonymous with the term "near miss." The Suns have missed out on superstars and championships by the narrowest of margins.

The team's destiny was shaped by a coin toss following the 1968-69 season, when the Suns lost the draft rights to Lew Alcindor to Milwaukee and continued a seven-year run of mediocrity. Connie Hawkins and Dick Van Arsdale made things exciting, but the Suns could only make the playoffs once during the period.

The next close call came during the 1976 playoffs, when underdog Phoenix advanced to the NBA Finals against Boston. With the series tied 2-2, the Suns lost Game 5 in triple-overtime, 128-126. In 1978-79, center Alvan Adams, forward Truck Robinson, and superb guard Paul Westphal formed a solid nucleus that again fell just short, losing to Seattle in a seven-game Western Conference finals.

The Suns enjoyed some success in the early 1980s and won the Pacific Division in 1980-81. They dropped off in the middle of the decade but picked up the slack again in the late 1980s. Tom Chambers, Kevin Johnson, and Dan Majerle led Phoenix to four straight 50-plus-win seasons. The addition of Charles Barkley pushed Phoenix past the 60-win plateau in 1992-93, and they made it all the way to the NBA Finals before losing to Chicago.

1994-95 Review

For the second year in a row, the Suns' hopes for their first NBA title were dashed by a combination of injuries, a woefully inadequate presence in the middle, and the Houston Rockets. Although Phoenix finished the regular season atop the Pacific Division, it was unable to overcome the game Rockets and fell in a dramatic seven-game Western Conference semifinal series, in which Phoenix blew a 3-1 lead.

When it was over, the Suns were left with several questions, the biggest of which surrounding forward Charles Barkley (23.0 PPG, 11.1 RPG), who was again contemplating retirement after a postseason in which his battered body broke down once more. Barkley, who was again one of the NBA's best during his 68-game regular season, fell prey to back and knee problems in the playoffs.

Suns management also had to address the pivot problem, since the combination of Joe Kleine and Danny Schayes just didn't get it done. Of course, had Danny Manning (17.9 PPG) not hurt his knee in midseason, the Suns might not have needed the pivot contributions. Phoenix's backcourt of Kevin Johnson (15.5 PPG, 7.7 APG) and Dan Majerle (15.6 PPG) looked good on paper, but Johnson again missed 30-plus games with injuries, and Majerle was ineffective against Houston.

Forward A.C. Green (11.2 PPG, 8.2 RPG) provided consistent play inside, while the reserve backcourt of rookie Wesley Person (10.4 PPG) and a resurgent Elliot Perry provided hope for the future. Danny Ainge's contribution dipped some as his career headed toward its twilight, and Wayman Tisdale (10.0 PPG) was a valuable forward reserve.

Last Five Years

Season	W	L	Playoffs
1990-91	55	27	L-Round 1
1991-92	53	29	L-West Semis
1992-93	62	20	L-NBA Finals
1993-94	56	26	L-West Semis
1994-95	59	23	L-West Semis

Phoenix Suns
1995-96 Season Preview

Opening Line: Time is clearly running out for the Suns, a veteran team that has moved further away from the NBA title each of the last two years. Phoenix has a solid, albeit aging, nucleus constructed around Charles Barkley and could be staring at its last chance at a championship in its current configuration.

Guard: Is this the year Kevin Johnson plays an entire season? Injuries have plagued the talented but unreliable point man during the past three seasons, and Phoenix officials have to be wondering if they should look elsewhere. When healthy, he teams with kamikaze bombardier Dan Majerle in a dangerous backcourt. Elliot Perry had a big year as a fill-in but lacks the size and strength to play 35 minutes every night. Second-year man Wesley Person has the potential to blossom into a fine off guard.

Forward: This should finally be Barkley's final season, and he would love to go out a winner. He remains one of the game's most dynamic forces—when his cranky knees and back comply—and can still dominate a game. If Danny Manning returns completely healthy from midseason knee surgery, the Suns may have the league's best forward lineup. Backboard warrior A.C. Green and two high-scoring rookies, Wisconsin's Michael Finley and Arizona State's Mario Bennett, give coach Paul Westphal plenty of options.

Center: Here's where the trouble starts. Joe Kleine and Danny Schayes are not the type of pivotmen championship teams feature. Neither is particularly athletic or successful on the backboards. Until Phoenix can upgrade this position, Suns fans can forget about a championship.

Analysis: Phoenix will again be one of the best teams in the Western Conference, but it needs good health and a better pivot situation if it wants to win it all. Even without a good center, however, the Suns have a lot of firepower and could win the Pacific Division. The trouble should start in the playoffs, when Houston and San Antonio come calling.

1995-96 Roster

No.	Player	Pos.	Ht.	Wt.	Exp.	College	G	RPG	APG	PPG
									—1994-95—	
*22	Danny Ainge	G	6'5"	195	14	Brigham Young	74	1.5	2.8	7.7
34	Charles Barkley	F	6'6"	250	11	Auburn	68	11.1	4.1	23.0
—	Mario Bennett	F	6'9"	235	R	Arizona St.	—	—	—	—
—	Chris Carr	G	6'5"	207	R	S. Illinois	—	—	—	—
—	Michael Finley	F	6'7"	215	R	Wisconsin	—	—	—	—
45	A.C. Green	F	6'9"	224	10	Oregon St.	82	8.2	1.5	11.2
7	Kevin Johnson	G	6'1"	190	8	California	47	2.4	7.7	15.5
35	Joe Kleine	C	7'0"	271	10	Arkansas	75	3.5	0.5	3.7
21	Antonio Lang	F/G	6'8"	201	1	Duke	12	0.3	0.1	0.9
9	Dan Majerle	G/F	6'6"	220	7	Cent. Michigan	82	4.6	4.1	15.6
*15	Danny Manning	F	6'10"	234	7	Kansas	46	6.0	3.3	17.9
*2	Elliot Perry	G	6'0"	160	3	Memphis	82	1.8	4.8	9.7
11	Wesley Person	G/F	6'6"	195	1	Auburn	78	2.6	1.3	10.4
—	Stefano Rusconi	F/C	6'10"	240	R	(Italy)	—	—	—	—
*24	Dan Schayes	C	6'11"	276	14	Syracuse	69	3.0	1.3	4.4
*23	Wayman Tisdale	C/F	6'9"	260	10	Oklahoma	65	3.8	0.7	10.0

PORTLAND TRAIL BLAZERS

Home: Rose Garden
Capacity: 20,300
Year Built: 1995

Chairman: Paul Allen
President: Bob Whitsitt

Address:
1 N. Center Ct. #200
Portland, OR 97227

Head Coach: P.J. Carlesimo
NBA: 44-38   Blazers: 44-38

Trail Blazers History

Few teams in sports can boast of fan loyalty the way Portland can. The Blazers sold out Memorial Coliseum more than 800 consecutive times, believed to be a record for any sport.

Portland was a typical expansion team in the early 1970s, shuttling players and coaches in and out. Early stars included Geoff Petrie, Sidney Wicks, and future Blazers coach Rick Adelman.

Things began to change in 1974 when the Blazers drafted UCLA center Bill Walton. Two years later, Jack Ramsay became coach and led the team to its only NBA title. With Walton serving as a do-everything high-post in Ramsay's motion offense, Portland upset Philadelphia in the 1977 Finals 4-2. Bob Gross, Maurice Lucas, Dave Twardzik, and Lionel Hollins comprised the rest of that starting unit. The Blazers appeared primed to repeat in 1977-78, but Walton injured his foot and Portland was eliminated by Seattle in the West semifinals.

In the 1980s, management drafted star guards Clyde Drexler and Terry Porter, and in 1989 Portland traded for rebounding forward Buck Williams. The Blazers had world-championship talent, but they couldn't quite win the big one. Portland fell to Detroit in the 1990 NBA Finals, lost to the Lakers in the 1991 West finals, and fell to Chicago in the 1992 NBA Finals.

Last Five Years

Season	W	L	Playoffs
1990-91	63	19	L-West Finals
1991-92	57	25	L-NBA Finals
1992-93	51	31	L-Round 1
1993-94	47	35	L-Round 1
1994-95	44	38	L-Round 1

1994-95 Review

By the time the Blazers' season fizzled to a close with a quick, three-game, first-round playoff loss to Phoenix, the team appeared no closer to solving its identity problems than it was when the year started. A new coach, a controversial trade, and some of the same old faces combined to produce a largely uninspired campaign.

First-year coach P.J. Carlesimo's NBA baptism was not without its rough moments. Besides the disappointing 44-38 record that dropped the Blazers below the surging Lakers and into fourth place in the Pacific Division, there were some grumblings from players who didn't like Carlesimo's style. The coach couldn't have been too pleased with his charges, either. Portland shot just 45.1 percent as a team. And though it outrebounded its rivals by a sizeable margin, Portland lacked perimeter scoring options in the halfcourt.

At midseason, the Blazers sent fan favorite and long-time meal ticket Clyde Drexler to Houston for power forward Otis Thorpe. Clifford Robinson (21.3 PPG, 5.6 RPG) stepped into the main scorer's role, reinventing himself as a small forward. He and underrated point guard Rod Strickland (18.9 PPG, 8.8 APG) were the Blazers' primary offensive weapons.

James Robinson (9.2 PPG) and rookie Aaron McKie (6.5 PPG) struggled somewhat to fill Drexler's shoes, but Thorpe (13.4 PPG, 8.0 RPG) and veteran Buck Williams (9.2 PPG, 8.2 RPG) were a strong inside tandem. They joined center Chris Dudley—who played his usual strong defense, rebounded well, and shot as if the ball were made of plutonium—to give Carlesimo several options down low.

Portland Trail Blazers
1995-96 Season Preview

Opening Line: The change continues in the City of Roses. Last year it was a new coach, P.J. Carlesimo, and this season the Blazers move into a spanking new arena. The shiny digs may make fans happy, but the play within isn't guaranteed to bring a smile. Portland remains in a transition period and needs help at a variety of positions before it can contend again.

Guard: Though Rod Strickland was dangled as trade bait before the draft, he's back to solidify at least a half of the backcourt and is quickly becoming one of the league's best point men. The big question for Carlesimo is if either Aaron McKie or James Robinson can emerge as a big-time off guard, now that Clyde Drexler is polishing his championship ring in Houston. Neither shot the ball particularly well last year, and McKie is particularly unsteady from 3-point range. Steady veteran Terry Porter stands in reserve at the point-guard position.

Forward: Carlesimo has all sorts of options here, but none can be guaranteed to yield great results. Clifford Robinson scores like the big-time force he claims he is, but he isn't particularly dependable in the clutch and launches a lot of shots. Power forward Buck Williams will turn 36 in March and can't be counted on for too many more rebounds. That's fine, since Otis Thorpe is an excellent inside operator. Rookie Gary Trent can bang some and has the potential to operate along the perimeter too. Harvey Grant is a stone scorer off the bench.

Center: Chris Dudley plays defense, rebounds, and can't be counted on for anything offensively. Dudley can't shoot free throws and is almost as bad from the field. Mark Bryant and Lithuanian mountain man Arvydas Sabonis will spell him.

Analysis: Portland better watch out, or it may find itself looking up at Golden State and Sacramento—as well as the Sonics, Suns, and Lakers. The Blazers lack big-time perimeter scoring and have a huge hole in the middle, no matter how many boards Dudley gets. The new Rose Garden arena will create excitement, but a couple more seasons just above .500 won't.

1995-96 Roster

No.	Player	Pos.	Ht.	Wt.	Exp.	College	G	RPG	APG	PPG
*2	Mark Bryant	F	6'9"	245	7	Seton Hall	49	3.3	0.6	5.0
24	Chris Dudley	C	6'11"	240	8	Yale	82	9.3	0.4	5.5
53	James Edwards	C	7'1"	252	18	Washington	28	1.5	0.3	2.7
44	Harvey Grant	F	6'9"	235	7	Oklahoma	75	3.8	1.1	9.1
*12	Steve Henson	G	6'1"	180	5	Kansas St.	37	0.7	2.3	3.2
23	Aaron McKie	G	6'5"	209	1	Temple	45	2.9	1.9	6.5
*30	Terry Porter	G	6'3"	195	10	Wis.-Stevens Pt.	35	2.3	3.8	8.9
3	Clifford Robinson	F	6'10"	225	6	Connecticut	75	5.6	2.6	21.3
26	James Robinson	G	6'2"	180	2	Alabama	71	1.9	2.5	9.2
1	Rod Strickland	G	6'3"	185	7	DePaul	64	5.0	8.8	18.9
33	Otis Thorpe	F	6'10"	246	11	Providence	70	8.0	1.6	13.4
—	Gary Trent	F	6'7"	250	R	Ohio	—	—	—	—
52	Buck Williams	F	6'8"	225	14	Maryland	82	8.2	1.0	9.2

Table subheader: —1994-95—

SACRAMENTO KINGS

Home: ARCO Arena
Capacity: 17,317
Year Built: 1988

Managing General Partner: Jim Thomas
V.P./Basketball Operations: Geoff Petrie

Address:
One Sports Parkway
Sacramento, CA 95834

Head Coach: Garry St. Jean
NBA: 92-154   Kings: 92-154

Kings History

Like the sun rises in the East and sets in the West, so has the Royals/Kings franchise. The Rochester (New York) Royals won the franchise's only league title in 1950-51. But cross-country moves, ending in Sacramento, have only led to futility.

That Rochester championship team featured a slick backcourt of Bob Davies, Bobby Wanzer, and Red Holzman, with Arnie Risen in the middle. The Royals made the playoffs only once from 1956-61, though they featured a potent forecourt of Maurice Stokes, Jack Twyman, and Clyde Lovellette.

The team moved to Cincinnati for 1957-58 and added rookie Oscar Robertson in 1960. The Royals advanced to the Eastern finals in 1962-63 and 1963-64, thanks to Robertson, Twyman, and Jerry Lucas, but the success was short-lived. The team didn't have a winning season from 1966-67 to 1973-74 and moved again in 1972, splitting time between Kansas City and Omaha as the Kings.

In 1974-75, the team won 44 games and featured brilliant point guard Nate "Tiny" Archibald. The 1980-81 edition lost to Houston in the conference finals. The most recent move came in 1985, when the franchise landed in Sacramento. Aside from a brief playoff appearance that season, the club has been a perennial lottery team ever since.

1994-95 Review

It may seem completely implausible, but the Kings actually were one game away from the playoffs during 1994-95. Had Sacramento defeated Denver in the regular-season finale, it would have celebrated its tenth season in Northern California with a spot in the postseason for the first time since the club arrived on the West Coast. Although the Kings stumbled in their quest to play in May, they did create substantial excitement and provided their fans with hope for the first time in years.

Sacramento coach Garry St. Jean blended the Kings' mix of veterans and youngsters into a team that played solid defense—for a change—and was one of the conference's better teams at home. Mitch Richmond (22.8 PPG) led the team in scoring and stayed healthy for the full year. He teamed with ageless watch-charm point guard Spud Webb (11.6 PPG, 6.2 APG) in a productive backcourt that suffered somewhat from a lack of depth. Fourth-year man Randy Brown and second-year man Bobby Hurley, still not completely recovered from his life-threatening 1993 auto accident, were a definite step down from the starters.

The frontcourt was a little deeper, thanks to the draft-day acquisitions of forwards Michael Smith and Brian Grant (13.2 PPG, 7.5 RPG), who was one of the league's most underrated rookies. Walt Williams (16.4 PPG) finally found a home at the three spot after two seasons of wandering throughout the lineup, although his shooting wasn't all that great. Veteran Olden Polynice (10.8 PPG, 9.0 RPG) was his usual self in the pivot, rebounding well and scoring in the low double figures.

Last Five Years

Season	W	L	Playoffs
1990-91	25	57	DNQ
1991-92	29	53	DNQ
1992-93	25	57	DNQ
1993-94	28	54	DNQ
1994-95	39	43	DNQ

Sacramento Kings
1995-96 Season Preview

Opening Line: The Kings came within one game of making the playoffs last year—quite an accomplishment for a team that was once the dregs of the Pacific Division. Sacramento should again challenge for a postseason berth, and the Kings continue to accumulate good, young talent through the draft, as evidenced by the recent arrivals of Corliss Williamson and Tyus Edney.

Guard: Selecting the ultra-quick Edney from UCLA made long-time Kings point man Spud Webb expendable, and he was dealt to Atlanta. Edney is a little taller than Webb but has many of the same attributes. His penetration will help set up two man Mitch Richmond's considerable outside game and create opportunities for Sacramento's growing stable of inside performers. If healthy again, Richmond will be one of the NBA's best at his position, although depth here is a problem. Point man Bobby Hurley is still wildly inconsistent, and Randy Brown has a limited outside game.

Forward: Brian Grant had a fabulous rookie season in just about all facets of power-forward life, and he teams with Walt Williams in a young, productive forward tandem. Now that Williams has found a home at the three spot, he can concentrate on unleashing his multiple skills every night. Second-year man Michael Smith is an excellent backup banger, but veteran Lionel Simmons is fading somewhat. That could make room for Williamson, who could be a future starter or struggle as a four man in a small forward's body.

Center: Olden Polynice is a reliable rebounder and adequate scorer, but he hardly provides the kind of intimidating presence in the middle the Kings need. Backup Duane Causwell can block shots and scare some people, but his offensive game is rudimentary.

Analysis: The Kings are on the rise, but they still have some work to do before they'll challenge for more than just the eighth playoff berth. The center position needs to be upgraded, and Edney or Hurley has to contribute right away or else the offense will stall. But Sacramento has built slowly and properly, and the effects of its work are becoming quite evident.

1995-96 Roster

No.	Player	Pos.	Ht.	Wt.	Exp.	College	G	RPG	APG	PPG
43	Frank Brickowski	F/C	6'9"	248	11	Penn St.	—	—	—	—
3	Randy Brown	G	6'3"	190	4	New Mexico St.	67	1.6	2.0	4.7
31	Duane Causwell	C	7'0"	240	5	Temple	58	3.0	0.3	3.6
—	Tyrone Corbin	F	6'6"	222	10	DePaul	81	3.2	0.8	6.2
—	Tyus Edney	G	5'10"	152	R	UCLA	—	—	—	—
33	Brian Grant	F	6'9"	254	1	Xavier	80	7.5	1.2	13.2
7	Bobby Hurley	G	6'0"	165	2	Duke	68	1.0	3.3	4.2
*20	Doug Lee	G	6'6"	210	3	Purdue	22	0.2	0.2	2.0
0	Olden Polynice	C	7'0"	250	8	Virginia	81	9.0	0.8	10.8
2	Mitch Richmond	G	6'5"	215	7	Kansas St.	82	4.4	3.8	22.8
22	Lionel Simmons	F	6'7"	210	5	La Salle	58	3.4	1.5	5.6
34	Michael Smith	F	6'8"	233	1	Providence	82	5.9	0.8	6.9
9	Henry Turner	G/F	6'7"	200	2	Cal. St.-Fuller.	30	0.9	0.2	2.3
42	Walt Williams	G/F	6'8"	230	3	Maryland	77	4.5	4.1	16.4
—	Corliss Williamson	F	6'7"	245	R	Arkansas	—	—	—	—

SEATTLE SUPERSONICS

Home: The Key Arena
Capacity: 17,100
Year Built: 1995

Owner: Barry Ackerley
President/G.M.: Wally Walker

Address:
190 Queen Anne Ave. N. #200
Seattle, WA 98109

Head Coach: George Karl
NBA: 321-262   Sonics: 202-86

SuperSonics History

Prior to Seattle's resurgence in the 1990s, there was only one Sonic boom. It came in the late 1970s.

Seattle's 1977-78 team featured rookie center Jack Sikma, rebounding machine Paul Silas, and the guard triumvirate of Gus Johnson, Dennis Johnson, and "Downtown" Fred Brown. They fell in seven games to Washington in the NBA Finals. The team was not denied the following season. The Sonics soared to the Pacific Division championship and won the title in five games over the Bullets.

That two-year period stands in stark contrast to the team's early years. Born in 1967, the team failed to qualify for the playoffs for seven seasons and boasted few stars, other than enigmatic Spencer Haywood. Seattle made it to the Western semifinals in 1974-75 and 1975-76, setting the stage for its runs to the Finals.

After a 56-26 season in 1979-80, the Sonics wallowed through a decade of mediocrity. The 1986-87 season was a stunner, however. Despite finishing with a losing record, the Sonics advanced to the Western finals, thanks to the high-scoring trio of Xavier McDaniel, Dale Ellis, and Tom Chambers. A new cast of characters emerged in the early 1990s, headed by Shawn Kemp and Gary Payton. They roared to the 1993 Western finals, where they lost to Phoenix in seven games.

Last Five Years

Season	W	L	Playoffs
1990-91	41	41	L-Round 1
1991-92	47	35	L-West Semis
1992-93	55	27	L-West Finals
1993-94	63	19	L-Round 1
1994-95	57	25	L-Round 1

1994-95 Review

If Seattle's 1994 first-round playoff swoon was a fluke, then the Sonics' collapse against the Lakers in the opening postseason series in '95 was an indictment of a selfish team that thrived during the regular season but collapsed when the pressure heightened. For the second straight year, the Sonics followed up a strong 82-game showing with a complete flop in its next five.

At least Seattle took Denver to five games in 1994's first-round loss. In 1995, the Sonics lasted only four. When it was over, the finger-pointing and excuse-making couldn't mask the message that Seattle was filled with players who functioned only as individuals, not a unit. While fans and media called for coach George Karl's scalp, they conveniently forgot that the 12 men on the roster shared responsibility too.

Once again, the Sonics had a pile of highlights in the regular season. Point guard Gary Payton (20.6 PPG, 7.1 APG) was particularly strong in the second half, while veteran forward Detlef Schrempf (19.2 PPG, 6.2 RPG, 51.4 3-point) continued to prove to be one of the game's most versatile players. Powerful Shawn Kemp (18.7 PPG, 10.9 PPG) was again a force inside.

However, off guard Kendall Gill (13.7 PPG) pouted all year and continued to be an inadequate perimeter weapon. Veteran Sam Perkins (12.7 PPG) produced again, although he spent too much time on the perimeter, and bench stalwarts Vincent Askew (9.9 PPG) and Nate McMillan were solid. It added up to another great regular season, a quick playoff exit, and more turmoil.

Seattle SuperSonics
1995-96 Season Preview

Opening Line: With two first-round playoff losses looming over their heads like an eager guillotine, the Sonics enter 1995-96 as the best team never to accomplish anything in NBA history. Much of the same interchangeable cast returns, although malcontent Kendall Gill was dispatched to Charlotte (for Hersey Hawkins), a move that should make coach George Karl's life a little easier.

Guard: The Sonics helped themselves by adding Hawkins and subtracting the cranky Gill. Hawkins is a much better outside shooter and should form a versatile duo with point man Gary Payton. Payton has blossomed into a dangerous scorer and is a shut-down defender. Nate McMillan can handle the ball, play excellent defense, and shoot it some, while Sarunas Marciulionis is a valuable all-around threat if healthy. Rookie Eric Snow is an accomplished ball-handler and thrives in the open court.

Forward: There may not be a better forward tandem in the league than Shawn Kemp and Detlef Schrempf. Kemp is one of the game's preeminent power players and nearly unstoppable underneath, while Schrempf does a little bit of everything and is becoming a better shooter as his career moves on. Vincent Askew is a slasher with a little bit of range to his shot, and rookie Sherell Ford should develop into a valuable scorer but needs to improve his defense.

Center: Sam Perkins continues to light it up from the outside, but that isn't exactly what you want a center to do. His inability to handle the heavy stuff inside is as big a reason for the Sonics' postseason troubles as anything else. Ervin Johnson is improving slowly.

Analysis: There is no question the Sonics have talent galore and the potential to challenge for the NBA title, but they had better accomplish something this year or else Karl and most of the team's main components could be putting their homes on the market. Seattle plays excellent defense and is a solid open-court team, but it needs to solidify its pivot situation and develop a less selfish team culture if it wants to succeed.

1995-96 Roster

No.	Player	Pos.	Ht.	Wt.	Exp.	College	G	RPG	APG	PPG
								|---1994-95---|		
2	Vincent Askew	G/F	6'6"	235	6	Memphis	71	2.5	2.5	9.9
24	Bill Cartwright	C	7'1"	245	15	San Francisco	29	3.0	0.3	2.4
—	Sherell Ford	F	6'7"	210	R	Ill.-Chicago	—	—	—	—
33	Hersey Hawkins	G	6'3"	190	7	Bradley	82	3.8	3.2	14.3
21	Byron Houston	F	6'5"	250	3	Oklahoma St.	39	1.4	0.2	3.4
50	Ervin Johnson	C	6'11"	242	2	New Orleans	64	4.5	0.3	3.1
40	Shawn Kemp	F	6'10"	245	6	None	82	10.9	1.8	18.7
45	Rich King	C	7'2"	265	4	Nebraska	2	0.0	0.0	0.0
30	S. Marciulionis	G	6'5"	215	5	(Lithuania)	66	1.0	1.7	9.3
10	Nate McMillan	G/F	6'5"	197	9	N. Carolina St.	80	3.8	5.3	5.2
20	Gary Payton	G	6'4"	190	5	Oregon St.	82	3.4	7.1	20.6
14	Sam Perkins	F/C	6'9"	257	11	North Carolina	82	4.9	1.6	12.7
*55	Steve Scheffler	C	6'9"	250	5	Purdue	18	1.3	0.2	2.2
11	Detlef Schrempf	F	6'10"	230	10	Washington	82	6.2	3.8	19.2
—	Eric Snow	G	6'3"	200	R	Michigan St.	—	—	—	—
—	David Wingate	G/F	6'5"	185	9	Georgetown	52	1.2	1.1	2.3

N B A Awards and Records

This section showcases the NBA's champions, award-winners, and record-setters—as well as a history of No. 1 draft picks. Here is a breakdown of what you'll find:

- World Champions
- Most Valuable Players
- Rookies of the Year
- Most Improved Players
- NBA Finals MVPs
- Defensive Players of the Year
- Sixth Man Award winners
- Coaches of the Year
- All-NBA Teams
- All-Rookie Teams
- All-Defensive Teams

- All-Star Game results
- career leaders
- active career leaders
- regular-season records
- game records
- team records—season
- team records—game
- playoff records—career
- playoff records—game
- playoff records—team
- history of No. 1 draft picks

WORLD CHAMPIONS

	CHAMPION	FINALIST	RESULT		CHAMPION	FINALIST	RESULT
1946-47	Philadelphia	Chicago	4-1	1971-72	Los Angeles	New York	4-1
1947-48	Baltimore	Philadelphia	4-2	1972-73	New York	Los Angeles	4-1
1948-49	Minneapolis	Washington	4-2	1973-74	Boston	Milwaukee	4-3
1949-50	Minneapolis	Syracuse	4-2	1974-75	Golden State	Washington	4-0
1950-51	Rochester	New York	4-3	1975-76	Boston	Phoenix	4-2
1951-52	Minneapolis	New York	4-3	1976-77	Portland	Philadelphia	4-2
1952-53	Minneapolis	New York	4-1	1977-78	Washington	Seattle	4-3
1953-54	Minneapolis	Syracuse	4-3	1978-79	Seattle	Washington	4-1
1954-55	Syracuse	Fort Wayne	4-3	1979-80	Los Angeles	Philadelphia	4-2
1955-56	Philadelphia	Fort Wayne	4-1	1980-81	Boston	Houston	4-2
1956-57	Boston	St. Louis	4-3	1981-82	Los Angeles	Philadelphia	4-2
1957-58	St. Louis	Boston	4-2	1982-83	Philadelphia	Los Angeles	4-0
1958-59	Boston	Minneapolis	4-0	1983-84	Boston	Los Angeles	4-3
1959-60	Boston	St. Louis	4-3	1984-85	L.A. Lakers	Boston	4-2
1960-61	Boston	St. Louis	4-1	1985-86	Boston	Houston	4-2
1961-62	Boston	Los Angeles	4-3	1986-87	L.A. Lakers	Boston	4-2
1962-63	Boston	Los Angeles	4-2	1987-88	L.A. Lakers	Detroit	4-3
1963-64	Boston	San Francisco	4-1	1988-89	Detroit	L.A. Lakers	4-0
1964-65	Boston	Los Angeles	4-1	1989-90	Detroit	Portland	4-1
1965-66	Boston	Los Angeles	4-3	1990-91	Chicago	L.A. Lakers	4-1
1966-67	Philadelphia	San Francisco	4-2	1991-92	Chicago	Portland	4-2
1967-68	Boston	Los Angeles	4-2	1992-93	Chicago	Phoenix	4-2
1968-69	Boston	Los Angeles	4-3	1993-94	Houston	New York	4-3
1969-70	New York	Los Angeles	4-3	1994-95	Houston	Orlando	4-0
1970-71	Milwaukee	Baltimore	4-0				

MOST VALUABLE PLAYERS

	PLAYER	PPG		PLAYER	PPG
1955-56	Bob Pettit, St. Louis	25.7	1975-76	Kareem Abdul-Jabbar, L.A.	27.7
1956-57	Bob Cousy, Boston	20.6	1976-77	Kareem Abdul-Jabbar, L.A.	26.2
1957-58	Bill Russell, Boston	16.6	1977-78	Bill Walton, Portland	18.9
1958-59	Bob Pettit, St. Louis	29.2	1978-79	Moses Malone, Houston	24.8
1959-60	Wilt Chamberlain, Phil.	37.6	1979-80	Kareem Abdul-Jabbar, L.A.	24.8
1960-61	Bill Russell, Boston	16.9	1980-81	Julius Erving, Philadelphia	24.6
1961-62	Bill Russell, Boston	18.9	1981-82	Moses Malone, Houston	31.1
1962-63	Bill Russell, Boston	16.8	1982-83	Moses Malone, Philadelphia	24.5
1963-64	Oscar Robertson, Cincinnati	31.4	1983-84	Larry Bird, Boston	24.2
1964-65	Bill Russell, Boston	14.1	1984-85	Larry Bird, Boston	28.7
1965-66	Wilt Chamberlain, Phil.	33.5	1985-86	Larry Bird, Boston	25.8
1966-67	Wilt Chamberlain, Phil.	24.1	1986-87	Magic Johnson, L.A. Lakers	23.9
1967-68	Wilt Chamberlain, Phil.	24.3	1987-88	Michael Jordan, Chicago	35.0
1968-69	Wes Unseld, Baltimore	13.8	1988-89	Magic Johnson, L.A. Lakers	22.5
1969-70	Willis Reed, New York	21.7	1989-90	Magic Johnson, L.A. Lakers	22.3
1970-71	Lew Alcindor, Milwaukee	31.7	1990-91	Michael Jordan, Chicago	31.5
1971-72	Kareem Abdul-Jabbar, Mil.	34.8	1991-92	Michael Jordan, Chicago	30.1
1972-73	Dave Cowens, Boston	20.5	1992-93	Charles Barkley, Phoenix	25.6
1973-74	Kareem Abdul-Jabbar, Mil.	27.0	1993-94	Hakeem Olajuwon, Houston	27.3
1974-75	Bob McAdoo, Buffalo	34.5	1994-95	David Robinson, San Antonio	27.6

ROOKIES OF THE YEAR

1952-53	Don Meineke, Fort Wayne	1974-75	Keith Wilkes, Golden State
1953-54	Ray Felix, Baltimore	1975-76	Alvan Adams, Phoenix
1954-55	Bob Pettit, Milwaukee	1976-77	Adrian Dantley, Buffalo
1955-56	Maurice Stokes, Rochester	1977-78	Walter Davis, Phoenix
1956-57	Tom Heinsohn, Boston	1978-79	Phil Ford, Kansas City
1957-58	Woody Sauldsberry, Philadelphia	1979-80	Larry Bird, Boston
1958-59	Elgin Baylor, Minneapolis	1980-81	Darrell Griffith, Utah
1959-60	Wilt Chamberlain, Philadelphia	1981-82	Buck Williams, New Jersey
1960-61	Oscar Robertson, Cincinnati	1982-83	Terry Cummings, San Diego
1961-62	Walt Bellamy, Chicago	1983-84	Ralph Sampson, Houston
1962-63	Terry Dischinger, Chicago	1984-85	Michael Jordan, Chicago
1963-64	Jerry Lucas, Cincinnati	1985-86	Patrick Ewing, New York
1964-65	Willis Reed, New York	1986-87	Chuck Person, Indiana
1965-66	Rick Barry, San Francisco	1987-88	Mark Jackson, New York
1966-67	Dave Bing, Detroit	1988-89	Mitch Richmond, Golden State
1967-68	Earl Monroe, Baltimore	1989-90	David Robinson, San Antonio
1968-69	Wes Unseld, Baltimore	1990-91	Derrick Coleman, New Jersey
1969-70	Lew Alcindor, Milwaukee	1991-92	Larry Johnson, Charlotte
1970-71	Dave Cowens, Boston	1992-93	Shaquille O'Neal, Orlando
	Geoff Petrie, Portland	1993-94	Chris Webber, Golden State
1971-72	Sidney Wicks, Portland	1994-95	Grant Hill, Detroit
1972-73	Bob McAdoo, Buffalo		Jason Kidd, Dallas
1973-74	Ernie DiGregorio, Buffalo		

MOST IMPROVED PLAYERS

1985-86	Alvin Robertson, San Antonio	1990-91	Scott Skiles, Orlando
1986-87	Dale Ellis, Seattle	1991-92	Pervis Ellison, Washington
1987-88	Kevin Duckworth, Portland	1992-93	Chris Jackson, Denver
1988-89	Kevin Johnson, Phoenix	1993-94	Don MacLean, Washington
1989-90	Rony Seikaly, Miami	1994-95	Dana Barros, Philadelphia

NBA FINALS MVPS

1969	Jerry West, Los Angeles	1983	Moses Malone, Philadelphia
1970	Willis Reed, New York	1984	Larry Bird, Boston
1971	Lew Alcindor, Milwaukee	1985	Kareem Abdul-Jabbar, L.A. Lakers
1972	Wilt Chamberlain, Los Angeles	1986	Larry Bird, Boston
1973	Willis Reed, New York	1987	Magic Johnson, L.A. Lakers
1974	John Havlicek, Boston	1988	James Worthy, L.A. Lakers
1975	Rick Barry, Golden State	1989	Joe Dumars, Detroit
1976	Jo Jo White, Boston	1990	Isiah Thomas, Detroit
1977	Bill Walton, Portland	1991	Michael Jordan, Chicago
1978	Wes Unseld, Washington	1992	Michael Jordan, Chicago
1979	Dennis Johnson, Seattle	1993	Michael Jordan, Chicago
1980	Magic Johnson, Los Angeles	1994	Hakeem Olajuwon, Houston
1981	Cedric Maxwell, Boston	1995	Hakeem Olajuwon, Houston
1982	Magic Johnson, Los Angeles		

DEFENSIVE PLAYERS OF THE YEAR

1982-83	Sidney Moncrief, Milwaukee	1989-90	Dennis Rodman, Detroit
1983-84	Sidney Moncrief, Milwaukee	1990-91	Dennis Rodman, Detroit
1984-85	Mark Eaton, Utah	1991-92	David Robinson, San Antonio
1985-86	Alvin Robertson, San Antonio	1992-93	Hakeem Olajuwon, Houston
1986-87	Michael Cooper, L.A. Lakers	1993-94	Hakeem Olajuwon, Houston
1987-88	Michael Jordan, Chicago	1994-95	Dikembe Mutombo, Denver
1988-89	Mark Eaton, Utah		

SIXTH MAN AWARD WINNERS

1982-83	Bobby Jones, Philadelphia	1989-90	Ricky Pierce, Milwaukee
1983-84	Kevin McHale, Boston	1990-91	Detlef Schrempf, Indiana
1984-85	Kevin McHale, Boston	1991-92	Detlef Schrempf, Indiana
1985-86	Bill Walton, Boston	1992-93	Cliff Robinson, Portland
1986-87	Ricky Pierce, Milwaukee	1993-94	Dell Curry, Charlotte
1987-88	Roy Tarpley, Dallas	1994-95	Anthony Mason, New York
1988-89	Eddie Johnson, Phoenix		

COACHES OF THE YEAR

1962-63	Harry Gallatin, St. Louis	1979-80	Bill Fitch, Boston
1963-64	Alex Hannum, San Francisco	1980-81	Jack McKinney, Indiana
1964-65	Red Auerbach, Boston	1981-82	Gene Shue, Washington
1965-66	Dolph Schayes, Philadelphia	1982-83	Don Nelson, Milwaukee
1966-67	Johnny Kerr, Chicago	1983-84	Frank Layden, Utah
1967-68	Richie Guerin, St. Louis	1984-85	Don Nelson, Milwaukee
1968-69	Gene Shue, Baltimore	1985-86	Mike Fratello, Atlanta
1969-70	Red Holzman, New York	1986-87	Mike Schuler, Portland
1970-71	Dick Motta, Chicago	1987-88	Doug Moe, Denver
1971-72	Bill Sharman, Los Angeles	1988-89	Cotton Fitzsimmons, Phoenix
1972-73	Tom Heinsohn, Boston	1989-90	Pat Riley, L.A. Lakers
1973-74	Ray Scott, Detroit	1990-91	Don Chaney, Houston
1974-75	Phil Johnson, K.C.-Omaha	1991-92	Don Nelson, Golden State
1975-76	Bill Fitch, Cleveland	1992-93	Pat Riley, New York
1976-77	Tom Nissalke, Houston	1993-94	Lenny Wilkens, Atlanta
1977-78	Hubie Brown, Atlanta	1994-95	Del Harris, L.A. Lakers
1978-79	Cotton Fitzsimmons, Kansas City		

ALL-NBA TEAMS

1946-47
Joe Fulks, PHI
Bob Feerick, WAS
Stan Miasek, DET
Bones McKinney, WAS
Max Zaslofsky, CHI

1947-48
Joe Fulks, PHI
Max Zaslofsky, CHI
Ed Sadowski, BOS
Howie Dallmar, PHI
Bob Feerick, WAS

1948-49
George Mikan, MIN
Joe Fulks, PHI
Bob Davies, ROC
Max Zaslofsky, CHI
Jim Pollard, MIN

1949-50
George Mikan, MIN
Jim Pollard, MIN
Alex Groza, IND
Bob Davies, ROC
Max Zaslofsky, CHI

1950-51
George Mikan, MIN
Alex Groza, IND
Ed Macauley, BOS
Bob Davies, ROC
Ralph Beard, IND

1951-52
George Mikan, MIN
Ed Macauley, BOS
Paul Arizin, PHI
Bob Cousy, BOS
Bob Davies, ROC
Dolph Schayes, SYR

1952-53
George Mikan, MIN
Bob Cousy, BOS
Neil Johnston, PHI
Ed Macauley, BOS
Dolph Schayes, SYR

1953-54
Bob Cousy, BOS
Neil Johnston, PHI

George Mikan, MIN
Dolph Schayes, SYR
Harry Gallatin, NY

1954-55
Neil Johnston, PHI
Bob Cousy, BOS
Dolph Schayes, SYR
Bob Pettit, MIL
Larry Foust, FTW

1955-56
Bob Pettit, STL
Paul Arizin, PHI
Neil Johnston, PHI
Bob Cousy, BOS
Bill Sharman, BOS

1956-57
Paul Arizin, PHI
Dolph Schayes, SYR
Bob Pettit, STL
Bob Cousy, BOS
Bill Sharman, BOS

1957-58
Dolph Schayes, SYR
George Yardley, DET
Bob Pettit, STL
Bob Cousy, BOS
Bill Sharman, BOS

1958-59
Bob Pettit, STL
Elgin Baylor, MIN
Bill Russell, BOS
Bob Cousy, BOS
Bill Sharman, BOS

1959-60
Bob Pettit, STL
Elgin Baylor, MIN
Wilt Chamberlain, PHI
Bob Cousy, BOS
Gene Shue, DET

1960-61
Elgin Baylor, LA
Bob Pettit, STL
Wilt Chamberlain, PHI
Bob Cousy, BOS
Oscar Robertson, CIN

1961-62
Bob Pettit, STL
Elgin Baylor, LA
Wilt Chamberlain, PHI
Jerry West, LA
Oscar Robertson, CIN

1962-63
Elgin Baylor, LA
Bob Pettit, STL
Bill Russell, BOS
Oscar Robertson, CIN
Jerry West, LA

1963-64
Bob Pettit, STL
Elgin Baylor, LA
Wilt Chamberlain, SF
Oscar Robertson, CIN
Jerry West, LA

1964-65
Elgin Baylor, LA
Jerry Lucas, CIN
Bill Russell, BOS
Oscar Robertson, CIN
Jerry West, LA

1965-66
Rick Barry, SF
Jerry Lucas, CIN
Wilt Chamberlain, PHI
Oscar Robertson, CIN
Jerry West, LA

1966-67
Rick Barry, SF
Elgin Baylor, LA
Wilt Chamberlain, PHI
Jerry West, LA
Oscar Robertson, CIN

1967-68
Elgin Baylor, LA
Jerry Lucas, CIN
Wilt Chamberlain, PHI
Dave Bing, DET
Oscar Robertson, CIN

1968-69
Billy Cunningham, PHI
Elgin Baylor, LA
Wes Unseld, BAL

Earl Monroe, BAL
Oscar Robertson, CIN

1969-70
Billy Cunningham, PHI
Connie Hawkins, PHO
Willis Reed, NY
Jerry West, LA
Walt Frazier, NY

1970-71
John Havlicek, BOS
Billy Cunningham, PHI
Lew Alcindor, MIL
Jerry West, LA
Dave Bing, DET

1971-72
John Havlicek, BOS
S. Haywood, SEA
K. Abdul-Jabbar, MIL
Jerry West, LA
Walt Frazier, NY

1972-73
John Havlicek, BOS
S. Haywood, SEA
K. Abdul-Jabbar, MIL
Nate Archibald, KCO
Jerry West, LA

1973-74
John Havlicek, BOS
Rick Barry, GS
K. Abdul-Jabbar, MIL
Walt Frazier, NY
Gail Goodrich, LA

1974-75
Rick Barry, GS
Elvin Hayes, WAS
Bob McAdoo, BUF
Nate Archibald, KCO
Walt Frazier, NY

1975-76
Rick Barry, GS
George McGinnis, PHI
K. Abdul-Jabbar, LA
Nate Archibald, KC
Pete Maravich, NO

1976-77
Elvin Hayes, WAS
D. Thompson, DEN
K. Abdul-Jabbar, LA
Pete Maravich, NO
Paul Westphal, PHO

1977-78
Truck Robinson, NO
Julius Erving, PHI
Bill Walton, POR
George Gervin, SA
D. Thompson, DEN

1978-79
M. Johnson, MIL
Elvin Hayes, WAS
Moses Malone, HOU
George Gervin, SA
Paul Westphal, PHO

1979-80
Julius Erving, PHI
Larry Bird, BOS
K. Abdul-Jabbar, LA
George Gervin, SA
Paul Westphal, PHO

1980-81
Julius Erving, PHI
Larry Bird, BOS
K. Abdul-Jabbar, LA
George Gervin, SA
Dennis Johnson, PHO

1981-82
Larry Bird, BOS
Julius Erving, PHI
Moses Malone, HOU
George Gervin, SA
Gus Williams, SEA

1982-83
Larry Bird, BOS
Julius Erving, PHI
Moses Malone, PHI
Magic Johnson, LA
Sidney Moncrief, MIL

1983-84
Larry Bird, BOS
Bernard King, NY
K. Abdul-Jabbar, LA
Magic Johnson, LA
Isiah Thomas, DET

1984-85
Larry Bird, BOS
Bernard King, NY
Moses Malone, PHI
Magic Johnson, LAL
Isiah Thomas, DET

1985-86
Larry Bird, BOS
D. Wilkins, ATL
K. Abdul-Jabbar, LAL
Magic Johnson, LAL
Isiah Thomas, DET

1986-87
Larry Bird, BOS
Kevin McHale, BOS
A. Olajuwon, HOU
Magic Johnson, LAL
Michael Jordan, CHI

1987-88
Larry Bird, BOS
Charles Barkley, PHI
A. Olajuwon, HOU
Michael Jordan, CHI
Magic Johnson, LAL

1988-89
Karl Malone, UTA
Charles Barkley, PHI
A. Olajuwon, HOU
Magic Johnson, LAL
Michael Jordan, CHI

1989-90
Karl Malone, UTA
Charles Barkley, PHI
Patrick Ewing, NY
Magic Johnson, LAL
Michael Jordan, CHI

1990-91
Karl Malone, UTA
Charles Barkley, PHI
David Robinson, SA
Michael Jordan, CHI
Magic Johnson, LAL

1991-92
Karl Malone, UTA
Chris Mullin, GS
David Robinson, SA
Michael Jordan, CHI
Clyde Drexler, POR

1992-93
Charles Barkley, PHO
Karl Malone, UTA
H. Olajuwon, HOU
Michael Jordan, CHI
Mark Price, CLE

1993-94
Scottie Pippen, CHI
Karl Malone, UTA
H. Olajuwon, HOU
John Stockton, UTA
Latrell Sprewell, GS

1994-95
FIRST
Karl Malone, UTA
Scottie Pippen, CHI
David Robinson, SA
John Stockton, UTA
A. Hardaway, ORL

SECOND
Charles Barkley, PHO
Shawn Kemp, SEA
Shaquille O'Neal, ORL
Gary Payton, SEA
Mitch Richmond, SAC

ALL-ROOKIE TEAMS

1962-63
Terry Dischinger, CHI
Chet Walker, SYR
Zelmo Beaty, STL
John Havlicek, BOS
D. DeBusschere, DET

1963-64
Jerry Lucas, CIN
Gus Johnson, BAL
Nate Thurmond, SF
Art Heyman, NY
Rod Thorn, BAL

1964-65
Willis Reed, NY
Jim Barnes, NY
Howard Komives, NY
Lucious Jackson, PHI
Wally Jones, BAL
Joe Caldwell, DET

1965-66
Rick Barry, SF
Billy Cunningham, PHI
T. Van Arsdale, DET
Dick Van Arsdale, NY
Fred Hetzel, SF

1966-67
Lou Hudson, STL
Jack Marin, BAL
Erwin Mueller, CHI
Cazzie Russell, NY
Dave Bing, DET

1967-68
Earl Monroe, BAL
Bob Rule, SEA
Walt Frazier, NY
Al Tucker, SEA
Phil Jackson, NY

1968-69
Wes Unseld, BAL
Elvin Hayes, SD
Bill Hewitt, LA
Art Harris, SEA
Gary Gregor, PHO

1969-70
Lew Alcindor, MIL
Bob Dandridge, MIL
Jo Jo White, BOS
Mike Davis, BAL
Dick Garrett, LA

1970-71
Geoff Petrie, POR
Dave Cowens, BOS
Pete Maravich, ATL
Calvin Murphy, SD
Bob Lanier, DET

1971-72
Elmore Smith, BUF
Sidney Wicks, POR
Austin Carr, CLE
Phil Chenier, BAL
Clifford Ray, CHI

1972-73
Bob McAdoo, BUF
Lloyd Neal, POR
Fred Boyd, PHI
Dwight Davis, CLE
Jim Price, LA

1973-74
Ernie DiGregorio, BUF
Ron Behagen, KCO
Mike Bantom, PHO
John Brown, ATL
N. Weatherspoon, CAP

1974-75
Keith Wilkes, GS
John Drew, ATL
Scott Wedman, KCO
Tom Burleson, SEA
Brian Winters, LA

1975-76
Alvan Adams, PHO
Gus Williams, GS
J. Meriweather, HOU
J. Shumate, PHO/BUF
Lionel Hollins, POR

1976-77
Adrian Dantley, BUF
Scott May, CHI
Mitch Kupchak, WAS
John Lucas, HOU
Ron Lee, PHO

1977-78
Walter Davis, PHO
M. Johnson, MIL
Bernard King, NJ
Jack Sikma, SEA
Norm Nixon, LA

1978-79
Phil Ford, KC
M.Thompson, POR
Ron Brewer, POR
Reggie Theus, CHI
Terry Tyler, DET

1979-80
Larry Bird, BOS
Magic Johnson, LA
Bill Cartwright, NY
Calvin Natt, POR
D. Greenwood, CHI

1980-81
Joe Barry Carroll, GS
Darrell Griffith, UTA
Larry Smith, GS
Kevin McHale, BOS
Kelvin Ransey, POR

1981-82
Kelly Tripucka, DET
Jay Vincent, DAL
Isiah Thomas, DET
Buck Williams, NJ
Jeff Ruland, WAS

1982-83
Terry Cummings, SD
Clark Kellogg, IND
D. Wilkins, ATL
James Worthy, LA
Quintin Dailey, CHI

1983-84
Ralph Sampson, HOU
S. Stipanovich, IND
Byron Scott, LA
Jeff Malone, WAS
Thurl Bailey, UTA
Darrell Walker, NY

1984-85
Michael Jordan, CHI
A. Olajuwon, HOU
Sam Bowie, POR
Charles Barkley, PHI
Sam Perkins, DAL

1985-86
Xavier McDaniel, SEA
Patrick Ewing, NY
Karl Malone, UTA
Joe Dumars, DET
Charles Oakley, CHI

1986-87
Brad Daugherty, CLE
Ron Harper, CLE
Chuck Person, IND
Roy Tarpley, DAL
John Williams, CLE

1987-88
Mark Jackson, NY
Armon Gilliam, PHO
Kenny Smith, SAC
Greg Anderson, SA
Derrick McKey, SEA

1988-89
Mitch Richmond, GS
Willie Anderson, SA
Hersey Hawkins, PHI
Rik Smits, IND
Charles Smith, LAC

1989-90
David Robinson, SA
Tim Hardaway, GS
Vlade Divac, LAL
S. Douglas, MIA
Pooh Richardson, MIN

1990-91
Derrick Coleman, NJ
Lionel Simmons, SAC
Dee Brown, BOS
Kendall Gill, CHA
Dennis Scott, ORL

1991-92
Larry Johnson, CHA
D. Mutombo, DEN
Billy Owens, GS
Steve Smith, MIA
Stacey Augmon, ATL

1992-93
Shaquille O'Neal, ORL
A. Mourning, CHA
C. Laettner, MIN
Tom Gugliotta, WAS
LaPhonso Ellis, DEN

1993-94
Chris Webber, GS
A. Hardaway, ORL
Vin Baker, MIL
Jamal Mashburn, DAL
Isaiah Rider, MIN

1994-95
FIRST
Jason Kidd, DAL
Grant Hill, DET
Glenn Robinson, MIL
Eddie Jones, LAL
Brian Grant, SAC

SECOND
Juwan Howard, WAS
Eric Montross, BOS
Wesley Person, PHO
Jalen Rose, DEN
D. Marshall, MIN/GS
Sharone Wright, PHI

ALL-DEFENSIVE TEAMS

1968-69
D. DeBusschere, NY
Nate Thurmond, SF
Bill Russell, BOS
Walt Frazier, NY
Jerry Sloan, CHI

1969-70
D. DeBusschere, NY
Gus Johnson, BAL
Willis Reed, NY
Walt Frazier, NY
Jerry West, LA

1970-71
D. DeBusschere, NY
Gus Johnson, BAL
Nate Thurmond, SF
Walt Frazier, NY
Jerry West, LA

1971-72
D. DeBusschere, NY
John Havlicek, BOS
Wilt Chamberlain, LA
Jerry West, LA
Walt Frazier, NY
Jerry Sloan, CHI

1972-73
D. DeBusschere, NY
John Havlicek, BOS
Wilt Chamberlain, LA
Jerry West, LA
Walt Frazier, NY

1973-74
D. DeBusschere, NY
John Havlicek, BOS
K. Abdul-Jabbar, MIL
Norm Van Lier, CHI
Walt Frazier, NY
Jerry Sloan, CHI

1974-75
John Havlicek, BOS
Paul Silas, BOS
K. Abdul-Jabbar, MIL
Jerry Sloan, CHI
Walt Frazier, NY

1975-76
Paul Silas, BOS
John Havlicek, BOS
Dave Cowens, BOS
Norm Van Lier, CHI
Don Watts, SEA

1976-77
Bobby Jones, DEN
E.C. Coleman, NO
Bill Walton, POR
Don Buse, IND
Norm Van Lier, CHI

1977-78
Bobby Jones, DEN
Maurice Lucas, POR
Bill Walton, POR
Lionel Hollins, POR
Don Buse, PHO

1978-79
Bobby Jones, PHI
B. Dandridge, WAS
K. Abdul-Jabbar, LA
Dennis Johnson, SEA
Don Buse, PHO

1979-80
Bobby Jones, PHI
Dan Roundfield, ATL
K. Abdul-Jabbar, LA
Dennis Johnson, SEA
Don Buse, PHO
M.R. Richardson, NY

1980-81
Bobby Jones, PHI
Caldwell Jones, PHI
K. Abdul-Jabbar, LA
Dennis Johnson, PHO
M.R. Richardson, NY

1981-82
Bobby Jones, PHI
Dan Roundfield, ATL
Caldwell Jones, PHI
Michael Cooper, LA
Dennis Johnson, PHO

1982-83
Bobby Jones, PHI
Dan Roundfield, ATL
Moses Malone, PHI
Sidney Moncrief, MIL
Dennis Johnson, PHO
Maurice Cheeks, PHI

1983-84
Bobby Jones, PHI
Michael Cooper, LA
Tree Rollins, ATL
Maurice Cheeks, PHI
Sidney Moncrief, MIL

1984-85
Sidney Moncrief, MIL
Paul Pressey, MIL
Mark Eaton, UTA
Michael Cooper, LAL
Maurice Cheeks, PHI

1985-86
Paul Pressey, MIL
Kevin McHale, BOS
Mark Eaton, UTA
Sidney Moncrief, MIL
Maurice Cheeks, PHI

1986-87
Kevin McHale, BOS
Michael Cooper, LAL
A. Olajuwon, HOU
Alvin Robertson, SA
Dennis Johnson, BOS

1987-88
Kevin McHale, BOS
Rodney McCray, HOU
A. Olajuwon, HOU
Michael Cooper, LAL
Michael Jordan, CHI

1988-89
Dennis Rodman, DET
Larry Nance, CLE
Mark Eaton, UTA
Michael Jordan, CHI
Joe Dumars, DET

1989-90
Dennis Rodman, DET
Buck Williams, POR
A. Olajuwon, HOU
Michael Jordan, CHI
Joe Dumars, DET

1990-91
Dennis Rodman, DET
Buck Williams, POR
David Robinson, SA
Michael Jordan, CHI
Alvin Robertson, MIL

1991-92
Dennis Rodman, DET
Scottie Pippen, CHI
David Robinson, SA
Michael Jordan, CHI
Joe Dumars, DET

1992-93
Dennis Rodman, DET
Scottie Pippen, CHI
H. Olajuwon, HOU
Michael Jordan, CHI
Joe Dumars, DET

1993-94
Scottie Pippen, CHI
Charles Oakley, NY
H. Olajuwon, HOU
Gary Payton, SEA
Mookie Blaylock, ATL

1994-95

FIRST
Scottie Pippen, CHI
Dennis Rodman, SA
David Robinson, SA
Gary Payton, SEA
Mookie Blaylock, ATL

SECOND
Horace Grant, ORL
Derrick McKey, IND
D. Mutombo, DEN
John Stockton, UTA
Nate McMillan, SEA

ALL-STAR GAMES

	RESULT	SITE	MVP
1950-51	East 111, West 94	Boston	Ed Macauley, Boston
1951-52	East 108, West 91	Boston	Paul Arizin, Philadelphia
1952-53	West 79, East 75	Fort Wayne	George Mikan, Minneapolis
1953-54	East 98, West 93 (OT)	New York	Bob Cousy, Boston
1954-55	East 100, West 91	New York	Bill Sharman, Boston
1955-56	West 108, East 94	Rochester	Bob Pettit, St. Louis
1956-57	East 109, West 97	Boston	Bob Cousy, Boston
1957-58	East 130, West 118	St. Louis	Bob Pettit, St. Louis
1958-59	West 124, East 108	Detroit	Elgin Baylor, Minnisota/ Bob Pettit, St. Louis
1959-60	East 125, West 115	Philadelphia	Wilt Chamberlain, Philadelphia
1960-61	West 153, East 131	Syracuse	Oscar Robertson, Cincinnati
1961-62	West 150, East 130	St. Louis	Bob Pettit, St. Louis
1962-63	East 115, West 108	Los Angeles	Bill Russell, Boston
1963-64	East 111, West 107	Boston	Oscar Robertson, Cincinnati
1964-65	East 124, West 123	St. Louis	Jerry Lucas, Cincinnati
1965-66	East 137, West 94	Cincinnati	Adrian Smith, Cincinnati
1966-67	West 135, East 120	San Francisco	Rick Barry, San Francisco
1967-68	East 144, West 124	New York	Hal Greer, Philadelphia
1968-69	East 123, West 112	Baltimore	Oscar Robertson, Cincinnati
1969-70	East 142, West 135	Philadelphia	Willis Reed, New York
1970-71	West 108, East 107	San Diego	Lenny Wilkens, Seattle
1971-72	West 112, East 110	Los Angeles	Jerry West, Los Angeles
1972-73	East 104, West 84	Chicago	Dave Cowens, Boston
1973-74	West 134, East 123	Seattle	Bob Lanier, Detroit
1974-75	East 108, West 102	Phoenix	Walt Frazier, New York
1975-76	East 123, West 109	Philadelphia	Dave Bing, Washington
1976-77	West 125, East 124	Milwaukee	Julius Erving, Philadelphia
1977-78	East 133, West 125	Atlanta	Randy Smith, Buffalo
1978-79	West 134, East 129	Detroit	David Thompson, Denver
1979-80	East 144, West 135 (OT)	Washington	George Gervin, San Antonio
1980-81	East 123, West 120	Cleveland	Nate Archibald, Boston
1981-82	East 120, West 118	E. Rutherford	Larry Bird, Boston
1982-83	East 132, West 123	Los Angeles	Julius Erving, Philadelphia
1983-84	East 154, West 145 (OT)	Denver	Isiah Thomas, Detroit
1984-85	West 140, East 129	Indianapolis	Ralph Sampson, Houston
1985-86	East 139, West 132	Dallas	Isiah Thomas, Detroit
1986-87	West 154, East 149 (OT)	Seattle	Tom Chambers, Seattle
1987-88	East 138, West 133	Chicago	Michael Jordan, Chicago
1988-89	West 143, East 134	Houston	Karl Malone, Utah
1989-90	East 130, West 113	Miami	Magic Johnson, L.A. Lakers
1990-91	East 116, West 114	Charlotte	Charles Barkley, Philadelphia
1991-92	West 153, East 113	Orlando	Magic Johnson, L.A. Lakers
1992-93	West 135, East 132 (OT)	Utah	Karl Malone, Utah/ John Stockton, Utah
1993-94	East 127, West 118	Minneapolis	Scottie Pippen, Chicago
1994-95	West 139, East 112	Phoenix	Mitch Richmond, Sacramento

CAREER LEADERS

(Players active at the close of 1994-95
are listed in bold)

POINTS

Kareem Abdul-Jabbar	38,387
Wilt Chamberlain	31,419
Moses Malone	**27,409**
Elvin Hayes	27,313
Oscar Robertson	26,710
John Havlicek	26,395
Alex English	25,613
Dominique Wilkins	**25,389**
Jerry West	25,192
Adrian Dantley	23,177
Elgin Baylor	23,149
Robert Parish	**22,883**
Michael Jordan	**21,998**
Larry Bird	21,791
Hal Greer	21,586
Karl Malone	**21,237**
Walt Bellamy	20,941
Bob Pettit	20,880
George Gervin	20,708
Tom Chambers	**20,024**

GAMES

Kareem Abdul-Jabbar	1,560
Robert Parish	**1,494**
Moses Malone	**1,329**
Elvin Hayes	1,303
John Havlicek	1,270
Paul Silas	1,254
Alex English	1,193
Tree Rollins	**1,155**
James Edwards	**1,140**
Buck Williams	**1,122**
Hal Greer	1,122

MINUTES

Kareem Abdul-Jabbar	57,446
Elvin Hayes	50,000
Wilt Chamberlain	47,859
John Havlicek	46,471
Moses Malone	**45,071**
Robert Parish	**44,212**
Oscar Robertson	43,886
Bill Russell	40,726
Hal Greer	39,788
Walt Bellamy	38,940

SCORING AVERAGE

(Minimum 400 Games or 10,000 Points)

Michael Jordan	**32.2**
Wilt Chamberlain	30.1
Elgin Baylor	27.4
Jerry West	27.0
Bob Pettit	26.4
George Gervin	26.2
Karl Malone	**26.0**
Dominique Wilkins	**25.8**
David Robinson	**25.7**
Oscar Robertson	25.7

REBOUNDS

Wilt Chamberlain	23,924
Bill Russell	21,620
Kareem Abdul-Jabbar	17,440
Elvin Hayes	16,279
Moses Malone	**16,212**
Nate Thurmond	14,464
Robert Parish	**14,323**
Walt Bellamy	14,241
Wes Unseld	13,769
Jerry Lucas	12,942

ASSISTS

John Stockton	**10,394**
Magic Johnson	9,921
Oscar Robertson	9,887
Isiah Thomas	9,061
Maurice Cheeks	7,392
Lenny Wilkens	7,211
Bob Cousy	6,955
Guy Rodgers	6,917
Nate Archibald	6,476
John Lucas	6,454

STEALS

Maurice Cheeks	2,310
John Stockton	**2,225**
Alvin Robertson	1,946
Isiah Thomas	1,861
Clyde Drexler	**1,857**
Michael Jordan	**1,845**
Magic Johnson	1,698
Lafayette Lever	1,666
Gus Williams	1,638
Derek Harper	**1,618**

BLOCKED SHOTS

Kareem Abdul-Jabbar	3,189
Mark Eaton	3,064
Hakeem Olajuwon	2,983
Tree Rollins	2,542
Robert Parish	2,288
Patrick Ewing	2,143
Manute Bol	2,086
George T. Johnson	2,082
Larry Nance	2,027
Elvin Hayes	1,771

PERSONAL FOULS

Kareem Abdul-Jabbar	4,657
Robert Parish	4,323
Elvin Hayes	4,193
James Edwards	3,981
Jack Sikma	3,879
Hal Greer	3,855
Buck Williams	3,783
Tom Chambers	3,726
Dolph Schayes	3,664
Bill Laimbeer	3,633

FIELD GOALS ATTEMPTED

Kareem Abdul-Jabbar	28,307
Elvin Hayes	24,272
John Havlicek	23,930
Wilt Chamberlain	23,497
Alex English	21,036
Dominique Wilkins	20,504
Elgin Baylor	20,171
Oscar Robertson	19,620
Moses Malone	19,225
Jerry West	19,032

FIELD GOALS MADE

Kareem Abdul-Jabbar	15,837
Wilt Chamberlain	12,681
Elvin Hayes	10,976
Alex English	10,659
John Havlicek	10,513
Dominique Wilkins	9,516
Oscar Robertson	9,508
Moses Malone	9,435
Robert Parish	9,424
Jerry West	9,016

FIELD GOAL PCT.
(Minimum 2,000 FGM)

Artis Gilmore	.599
Mark West	.589
Shaquille O'Neal	.583
Steve Johnson	.572
Darryl Dawkins	.572
James Donaldson	.571
Jeff Ruland	.564
Kareem Abdul-Jabbar	.559
Otis Thorpe	.555
Charles Barkley	.555

FREE THROWS ATTEMPTED

Wilt Chamberlain	11,862
Moses Malone	11,090
Kareem Abdul-Jabbar	9,304
Oscar Robertson	9,185
Jerry West	8,801
Adrian Dantley	8,351
Dolph Schayes	8,273
Bob Pettit	8,119
Walt Bellamy	8,088
Elvin Hayes	7,999

FREE THROWS MADE

Moses Malone	8,531
Oscar Robertson	7,694
Jerry West	7,160
Dolph Schayes	6,979
Adrian Dantley	6,832
Kareem Abdul-Jabbar	6,712
Bob Pettit	6,182
Wilt Chamberlain	6,057
Elgin Baylor	5,763
Dominique Wilkins	5,721

FREE THROW PCT.
(Minimum 1,200 FTM)

Mark Price	.906
Rick Barry	.900
Calvin Murphy	.892
Scott Skiles	.890
Larry Bird	.886
Bill Sharman	.883
Reggie Miller	.879
Ricky Pierce	.877
Kiki Vandeweghe	.872
Jeff Malone	.871

3-PT. FIELD GOALS ATTEMPTED

Michael Adams	2,816
Dale Ellis	2,783
Danny Ainge	2,651
Reggie Miller	2,622
Vernon Maxwell	2,422
Chuck Person	2,379
Derek Harper	2,244
Terry Porter	2,006
Dominique Wilkins	1,973
Dan Majerle	1,965

3-PT. FIELD GOALS MADE

Dale Ellis	1,119
Reggie Miller	1,035
Danny Ainge	1,002
Michael Adams	935
Chuck Person	856
Mark Price	802
Derek Harper	787
Vernon Maxwell	777
Terry Porter	766
Dan Majerle	721

3-PT. FIELD GOAL PCT.
(Minimum 250 Made)

Steve Kerr	.467
Drazen Petrovic	.437
B.J. Armstrong	.437
Dana Barros	.417

Mark Price	.409
Trent Tucker	.408
Dale Ellis	.402
Hersey Hawkins	.402
Craig Hodges	.400
Kenny Smith	.398

MOST VICTORIES, COACH

Lenny Wilkens	968
Red Auerbach	938
Dick Motta	892
Jack Ramsay	864
Bill Fitch	862
Don Nelson	817
Cotton Fitzsimmons	805
Gene Shue	784
Pat Riley	756
John MacLeod	707

ACTIVE CAREER LEADERS

(Includes players active at the close
of the 1994-95 season)

POINTS

Moses Malone	27,409
Dominique Wilkins	25,389
Robert Parish	22,883
Michael Jordan	21,998
Karl Malone	21,237
Tom Chambers	20,024
Hakeem Olajuwon	19,904
Charles Barkley	19,091
Clyde Drexler	18,789
Patrick Ewing	18,077

GAMES

Robert Parish	1,494
Moses Malone	1,329
Tree Rollins	1,155
James Edwards	1,140
Buck Williams	1,122
Tom Chambers	1,094
Danny Ainge	1,042
Herb Williams	1,004
Dominique Wilkins	984
Rick Mahorn	970

MINUTES

Moses Malone	45,071
Robert Parish	44,212
Buck Williams	38,558
Dominique Wilkins	35,916

Tom Chambers	33,829
Hakeem Olajuwon	31,184
Clyde Drexler	30,796
Karl Malone	30,688
Charles Barkley	30,300
Derek Harper	29,802

SCORING AVERAGE
(Minimum 400 Games or 10,000 Points)

Michael Jordan	32.2
Karl Malone	26.0
Dominique Wilkins	25.8
David Robinson	25.7
Hakeem Olajuwon	24.0
Patrick Ewing	23.8
Charles Barkley	23.3
Mitch Richmond	22.7
Chris Mullin	21.8
Clyde Drexler	20.8

REBOUNDS

Moses Malone	16,212
Robert Parish	14,323
Buck Williams	12,033
Hakeem Olajuwon	10,239
Charles Barkley	9,490
Karl Malone	8,929
Dennis Rodman	8,489
Charles Oakley	8,130
Kevin Willis	7,952
Otis Thorpe	7,878

ASSISTS

John Stockton	10,394
Derek Harper	5,484
Muggsy Bogues	5,469
Terry Porter	5,319
Kevin Johnson	5,272
Mark Jackson	5,255
Sleepy Floyd	5,175
Clyde Drexler	5,087
Doc Rivers	4,766
Nate McMillan	4,501

STEALS

John Stockton	2,225
Clyde Drexler	1,857
Michael Jordan	1,845
Derek Harper	1,618
Hakeem Olajuwon	1,581
Doc Rivers	1,490
Scottie Pippen	1,405
Nate McMillan	1,377
Charles Barkley	1,337
Dominique Wilkins	1,335

BLOCKED SHOTS

Hakeem Olajuwon	2,983
Tree Rollins	2,542
Robert Parish	2,288
Patrick Ewing	2,143
Manute Bol	2,086
David Robinson	1,735
Moses Malone	1,733
Herb Williams	1,556
Benoit Benjamin	1,491
Alton Lister	1,416

PERSONAL FOULS

Robert Parish	4,323
James Edwards	3,981
Buck Williams	3,783
Tom Chambers	3,726
Tree Rollins	3,377
Rick Mahorn	3,248
Hakeem Olajuwon	3,204
Dan Schayes	3,155
Moses Malone	3,076
Terry Cummings	3,037

FIELD GOALS ATTEMPTED

Dominique Wilkins	20,504
Moses Malone	19,225
Robert Parish	17,530
Michael Jordan	16,051
Tom Chambers	15,716
Hakeem Olajuwon	15,306
Clyde Drexler	14,951
Karl Malone	14,941
Terry Cummings	14,696
Jeff Malone	14,481

FIELD GOALS MADE

Dominique Wilkins	9,516
Moses Malone	9,435
Robert Parish	9,424
Michael Jordan	8,245
Hakeem Olajuwon	7,905
Karl Malone	7,857
Tom Chambers	7,369
Terry Cummings	7,158
Clyde Drexler	7,155
Patrick Ewing	7,116

FIELD GOAL PCT.
(Minimum 2,000 FGM)

Mark West	.589
Shaquille O'Neal	.583
James Donaldson	.571
Otis Thorpe	.555
Charles Barkley	.555
Buck Williams	.552
Dennis Rodman	.539
Robert Parish	.537
Horace Grant	.534
David Robinson	.527

FREE THROWS ATTEMPTED

Moses Malone	11,090
Karl Malone	7,585
Dominique Wilkins	7,046
Charles Barkley	6,888
Tom Chambers	6,268
Michael Jordan	6,161
Hakeem Olajuwon	5,749
Robert Parish	5,592
Buck Williams	5,542
Patrick Ewing	5,161

FREE THROWS MADE

Moses Malone	8,531
Dominique Wilkins	5,721
Karl Malone	5,472
Michael Jordan	5,205
Charles Barkley	5,062
Tom Chambers	5,061
Hakeem Olajuwon	4,081
Robert Parish	4,035
Clyde Drexler	3,955
Patrick Ewing	3,832

FREE THROW PCT.
(Minimum 1,200 FTM)

Mark Price	.906
Scott Skiles	.890
Reggie Miller	.879
Ricky Pierce	.877
Jeff Malone	.871
Hersey Hawkins	.867
Micheal Williams	.866
Jeff Hornacek	.863
Chris Mullin	.862
Michael Adams	.850

3-PT. FIELD GOALS ATTEMPTED

Michael Adams	2,816
Dale Ellis	2,783
Danny Ainge	2,651
Reggie Miller	2,622
Vernon Maxwell	2,422
Chuck Person	2,379
Derek Harper	2,244
Terry Porter	2,006
Dominique Wilkins	1,973
Dan Majerle	1,965

3-PT. FIELD GOALS MADE

Dale Ellis	1,119
Reggie Miller	1,035
Danny Ainge	1,002
Michael Adams	935
Chuck Person	856

Mark Price	.802
Derek Harper	.787
Vernon Maxwell	.777
Terry Porter	.766
Dan Majerle	.721

3-PT. FIELD GOAL PCT.
(Minimum 250 Made)

Steve Kerr	.467
B.J. Armstrong	.437
Dana Barros	.417
Mark Price	.409
Dale Ellis	.402
Hersey Hawkins	.402
Kenny Smith	.398
Dennis Scott	.396
Reggie Miller	.395
Dell Curry	.392

MOST VICTORIES, COACH

Lenny Wilkens	968
Dick Motta	892
Bill Fitch	862
Pat Riley	756
Larry Brown	533
Jerry Sloan	458
Mike Fratello	414
Del Harris	380
Phil Jackson	342
George Karl	321

REGULAR-SEASON RECORDS

MINUTES
(First Kept in 1951-52)

3,882	Wilt Chamberlain, PHI	1961-62
3,836	Wilt Chamberlain, PHI	1967-68
3,806	Wilt Chamberlain, SF	1962-63
3,773	Wilt Chamberlain, PHI	1960-61
3,737	Wilt Chamberlain, PHI	1965-66
3,698	John Havlicek, BOS	1971-72
3,689	Wilt Chamberlain, SF	1963-64
3,682	Wilt Chamberlain, PHI	1966-67
3,681	Nate Archibald, KCO	1972-73
3,678	John Havlicek, BOS	1970-71

POINTS

4,029	Wilt Chamberlain, PHI	1961-62
3,586	Wilt Chamberlain, SF	1962-63
3,041	Michael Jordan, CHI	1986-87
3,033	Wilt Chamberlain, PHI	1960-61
2,948	Wilt Chamberlain, SF	1963-64

2,868	Michael Jordan, CHI	1987-88
2,831	Bob McAdoo, BUF	1974-75
2,822	Kareem Abdul-Jabbar, MIL	1971-72
2,775	Rick Barry, SF	1966-67
2,753	Michael Jordan, CHI	1989-90

SCORING AVERAGE
(Minimum 70 Games or 1,400 Points)

50.4	Wilt Chamberlain, PHI	1961-62
44.8	Wilt Chamberlain, SF	1962-63
38.4	Wilt Chamberlain, PHI	1960-61
37.6	Wilt Chamberlain, PHI	1959-60
37.1	Michael Jordan, CHI	1986-87
36.9	Wilt Chamberlain, SF	1963-64
35.6	Rick Barry, SF	1966-67
35.0	Michael Jordan, CHI	1987-88
34.8	Kareem Abdul-Jabbar, MIL	1971-72
34.7	Wilt Chamberlain, SF/PHI	1964-65

REBOUNDS
(First Kept in 1950-51)

2,149	Wilt Chamberlain, PHI	1960-61
2,052	Wilt Chamberlain, PHI	1961-62
1,957	Wilt Chamberlain, PHI	1966-67
1,952	Wilt Chamberlain, PHI	1967-68
1,946	Wilt Chamberlain, SF	1962-63
1,943	Wilt Chamberlain, PHI	1965-66
1,941	Wilt Chamberlain, PHI	1959-60
1,930	Bill Russell, BOS	1963-64
1,878	Bill Russell, BOS	1964-65
1,868	Bill Russell, BOS	1960-61

ASSISTS

1,164	John Stockton, UTA	1990-91
1,134	John Stockton, UTA	1989-90
1,128	John Stockton, UTA	1987-88
1,126	John Stockton, UTA	1991-92
1,123	Isiah Thomas, DET	1984-85
1,118	John Stockton, UTA	1988-89
1,099	Kevin Porter, DET	1978-79
1,031	John Stockton, UTA	1993-94
1,011	John Stockton, UTA	1994-95
991	Kevin Johnson, PHO	1988-89

STEALS
(First Kept in 1973-74)

301	Alvin Robertson, SA	1985-86
281	Don Buse, IND	1976-77
265	Micheal Richardson, NY	1979-80
263	John Stockton, UTA	1988-89
261	Slick Watts, SEA	1975-76
260	Alvin Robertson, SA	1986-87
259	Michael Jordan, CHI	1987-88
246	Alvin Robertson, MIL	1990-91
244	John Stockton, UTA	1991-92
243	Micheal Richardson, NJ	1984-85
243	Alvin Robertson, SA	1987-88

BLOCKED SHOTS
(First Kept in 1973-74)

456	Mark Eaton, UTA	1984-85
397	Manute Bol, WAS	1985-86
393	Elmore Smith, LA	1973-74
376	Akeem Olajuwon, HOU	1989-90
369	Mark Eaton, UTA	1985-86
351	Mark Eaton, UTA	1982-83
345	Manute Bol, GS	1988-89
343	Tree Rollins, ATL	1982-83
342	Hakeem Olajuwon, HOU	1992-93
338	Kareem Abdul-Jabbar, LA	1975-76

PERSONAL FOULS

386	Darryl Dawkins, NJ	1983-84
382	Darryl Dawkins, NJ	1982-83
372	Steve Johnson, KC	1981-82
367	Bill Robinzine, KC	1978-79
366	Bill Bridges, STL	1967-68
363	Lonnie Shelton, NY	1976-77
363	James Edwards, IND	1978-79
361	Kevin Kunnert, HOU	1976-77
358	Dan Roundfield, ATL	1978-79
358	Rick Mahorn, WAS	1983-84

DISQUALIFICATIONS
(First Kept in 1950-51)

26	Don Meineke, FTW	1952-53
25	Steve Johnson, KC	1981-82
23	Darryl Dawkins, NJ	1982-83
22	Walter Dukes, DET	1958-59
22	Darryl Dawkins, NJ	1983-84
21	Joe Meriweather, ATL	1976-77
20	Joe Fulks, PHI	1952-53
20	Vern Mikkelsen, MIN	1957-58
20	Walter Dukes, DET	1959-60
20	Walter Dukes, DET	1961-62
20	George Johnson, NJ	1977-78

FIELD GOALS ATTEMPTED

3,159	Wilt Chamberlain, PHI	1961-62
2,770	Wilt Chamberlain, SF	1962-63
2,457	Wilt Chamberlain, PHI	1960-61
2,311	Wilt Chamberlain, PHI	1959-60
2,298	Wilt Chamberlain, SF	1963-64
2,279	Michael Jordan, CHI	1986-87
2,273	Elgin Baylor, LA	1962-63
2,217	Rick Barry, GS	1974-75
2,215	Elvin Hayes, SD	1970-71
2,166	Elgin Baylor, LA	1960-61

FIELD GOALS MADE

1,597	Wilt Chamberlain, PHI	1961-62
1,463	Wilt Chamberlain, SF	1962-63
1,251	Wilt Chamberlain, PHI	1960-61
1,204	Wilt Chamberlain, SF	1963-64
1,159	Kareem Abdul-Jabbar, MIL	1971-72
1,098	Michael Jordan, CHI	1986-87
1,095	Bob McAdoo, BUF	1974-75
1,074	Wilt Chamberlain, PHI	1965-66
1,069	Michael Jordan, CHI	1987-88
1,065	Wilt Chamberlain, PHI	1959-60

FIELD GOAL PCT.
(Minimum 300 FGM)

.727	Wilt Chamberlain, LA	1972-73
.683	Wilt Chamberlain, PHI	1966-67
.670	Artis Gilmore, CHI	1980-81
.652	Artis Gilmore, CHI	1981-82
.649	Wilt Chamberlain, LA	1971-72
.637	James Donaldson, LAC	1984-85
.633	Chris Gatling, GS	1994-95

.632 ....Steve Johnson, SA.............1985-86
.626 ....Artis Gilmore, SA................1982-83
.625 ....Mark West, PHO.................1989-90

FREE THROWS ATTEMPTED

1,363 ......Wilt Chamberlain, PHI.......1961-62
1,113 ......Wilt Chamberlain, SF..........1962-63
1,054 ......Wilt Chamberlain, PHI.......1960-61
1,016 ......Wilt Chamberlain, SF..........1963-64
991.......Wilt Chamberlain, SF..........1959-60
977.......Jerry West, LA 1965-66
976.......Wilt Chamberlain, PHI.......1965-66
972.......Michael Jordan, CHI............1986-87
951.......Charles Barkley, PHI............1987-88
946.......Adrian Dantley, UTA............1983-84

FREE THROWS MADE

840 ....Jerry West, LA 1965-66
835 ....Wilt Chamberlain, PHI.......1961-62
833 ....Michael Jordan, CHI............1986-87
813 ....Adrian Dantley, UTA............1983-84
800 ....Oscar Robertson, CIN........1963-64
753 ....Rick Barry, SF.....................1966-67
742 ....Oscar Robertson, CIN........1965-66
737 ....Moses Malone, PHI 1984-85
736 ....Oscar Robertson, CIN........1966-67
723 ....Michael Jordan, CHI............1987-88

FREE THROW PCT.
(Minimum 125 FTM)
.958 ....Calvin Murphy, HOU............1980-81
.956 ....M. Abdul-Rauf, DEN.............1993-94
.948 ....Mark Price, CLE 1992-93
.947 ....Mark Price, CLE 1991-92
.947 ....Rick Barry, HOU 1978-79
.945 ....Ernie DiGregorio, BUF.........1976-77
.935 ....Chris Jackson, DEN 1992-93
.935 ....Ricky Sobers, CHI 1980-81
.935 ....Rick Barry, HOU 1979-80
.934 ....Spud Webb, SAC 1994-95

3-PT. FIELD GOALS ATTEMPTED
(Rule went into effect in 1979-80)
611 ....John Starks, NY...................1994-95
564 ....Michael Adams, DEN 1990-91
555 ....Mookie Blaylock, ATL...........1994-95
548 ....Dan Majerle, PHO.................1994-95
511 ....Nick Van Exel, LAL...............1994-95
510 ....Vernon Maxwell, HOU...........1990-91
503 ....Dan Majerle, PHO.................1993-94
473 ....Vernon Maxwell, HOU...........1991-92
470 ....Reggie Miller, IND 1994-95
466 ....Michael Adams, DEN 1988-89

3-PT. FIELD GOALS MADE
217 ....John Starks, NY...................1994-95
199 ....Mookie Blaylock, ATL...........1994-95
199 ....Dan Majerle, PHO.................1994-95
197 ....Dana Barros, PHI..................1994-95
195 ....Reggie Miller, IND.................1994-95
192 ....Dan Majerle, PHO.................1993-94
185 ....Glen Rice, MIA......................1994-95
183 ....Nick Van Exel, LAL...............1994-95
179 ....Nick Anderson, ORL.............1994-95
172 ....Vernon Maxwell, HOU...........1990-91
172 ....Chuck Person, SA 1994-95

3-PT. FIELD GOAL PCT.
(Minimum 50 Made; 1994-95: 82 Made)
.524........Steve Kerr, CHI 1994-95
.514........Detlef Schrempf, SEA 1994-95
.507........Steve Kerr, CLE 1989-90
.491........Craig Hodges, MIL/PHO.........1987-88
.486........Mark Price, CLE 1987-88
.481........Craig Hodges, CHI 1989-90
.478........Dale Ellis, SEA 1988-89
.462........Dana Barros, PHI 1994-95
.461........Jim Les, SAC 1990-91
.459........Tracy Murray, POR 1993-94

GAME RECORDS

POINTS
100 ...Wilt Chamberlain, PHI vs. NY, March 2, 1962
78 .....Wilt Chamberlain, PHI vs. LA, Dec. 8, 1961 (3 OT)
73 .....Wilt Chamberlain, PHI vs. CHI, Jan. 13, 1962
73 .....Wilt Chamberlain, SF vs. NY, Nov. 6, 1962
73 .....David Thompson, DEN vs. DET, April 9, 1978
72 .....Wilt Chamberlain, SF vs. LA, Nov. 3, 1962
71 .....Elgin Baylor, LA vs. NY, Nov. 15, 1960

71......David Robinson, SA vs. LAC, Apr. 24, 1994
70 .....Wilt Chamberlain, SF vs. SYR, March 10, 1963
69 .....Michael Jordan, CHI vs. CLE, March 28, 1990 (OT)
68 .....Wilt Chamberlain, PHI vs. CHI, Dec. 16, 1967
68 .....Pete Maravich, NO vs. NY, Feb. 25, 1977

REBOUNDS
55 .....Wilt Chamberlain, PHI vs. BOS, Nov. 24, 1960
51 .....Bill Russell, BOS vs. SYR, Feb. 5, 1960

49 .....Bill Russell, BOS vs. PHI, Nov. 16, 1957
49 .....Bill Russell, BOS vs. DET, March 11, 1965
45 .....Wilt Chamberlain, PHI vs. SYR, Feb. 6, 1960
45 .....Wilt Chamberlain, PHI vs. LA, Jan. 21, 1961

ASSISTS
30 .....Scott Skiles, ORL vs. DEN, Dec. 30, 1990
29 .....Kevin Porter, NJ vs. HOU, Feb. 24, 1978
28 .....Bob Cousy, BOS vs. MIN, Feb. 27, 1959
28 .....Guy Rodgers, SF vs. STL, March 14, 1963
28 .....John Stockton, UTA vs. SA, Jan. 15, 1991

STEALS
11 .....Larry Kenon, SA vs. KC, Dec. 26, 1976
10 .....Jerry West, LA vs. SEA, Dec. 7, 1973
10 .....Larry Steele, POR vs. L.A., Nov. 16, 1974
10 .....Fred Brown, SEA vs. PHI, Dec. 3, 1976
10 .....Gus Williams, SEA vs. NJ, Feb. 22, 1978
10 .....Eddie Jordan, NJ vs. PHI, March 23, 1979
10 .....Johnny Moore, SA vs. IND, March 6, 1985
10 .....Fat Lever, DEN vs. IND, March 9, 1985
10 ......Clyde Drexler, POR vs. MIL, Jan. 10, 1986
10 .....Alvin Robertson, SA vs. PHO, Feb. 18, 1986
10 .....Ron Harper, CLE vs. PHI, March 10, 1987
10 .....Michael Jordan, CHI vs. NJ, Jan. 29, 1988
10 .....Alvin Robertson, SA vs. HOU, Jan. 11, 1989 (OT)
10 .....Alvin Robertson, MIL vs. UTA, Nov. 19, 1990
10 .....Kevin Johnson, PHO vs. WAS, Dec. 9, 1993

BLOCKED SHOTS
17 .....Elmore Smith, LA vs. POR, Oct. 28, 1973
15 .....Manute Bol, WAS vs. ATL, Jan. 25, 1986
15 .....Manute Bol, WAS vs. IND, Feb. 26, 1987
15 .....Shaquille O'Neal, ORL vs. NJ, Nov. 20, 1993

FIELD GOALS ATTEMPTED
63 .....Wilt Chamberlain, PHI vs. NY, March 2, 1962
62 .....Wilt Chamberlain, PHI vs. LA, Dec. 8, 1961 (3 OT)
60 .....Wilt Chamberlain, SF vs. CIN, Oct. 28, 1962 (OT)
58 .....Wilt Chamberlain, SF vs. PHI, Nov. 26, 1964

FIELD GOALS MADE
36 .....Wilt Chamberlain, PHI vs. NY, March 2, 1962

31 .....Wilt Chamberlain, PHI vs. LA, Dec. 8, 1961 (3 OT)
30 .....Wilt Chamberlain, PHI vs. CHI, Dec. 16, 1967
30 .....Rick Barry, GS vs. POR, March 26, 1974

FIELD GOAL PCT.
(Minimum 15 Attempts)
1.000.Wilt Chamberlain, PHI vs. BAL, Feb. 24, 1967 (18/18)
1.000.Wilt Chamberlain, PHI vs. BAL, March 19, 1967 (16/16)
1.000.Wilt Chamberlain, PHI vs. LA, Jan. 20, 1967 (15/15)
.947 ..Wilt Chamberlain, SF vs. NY, Nov. 27, 1963 (18/19)
.941 ..Wilt Chamberlain, PHI vs. BAL, Nov. 25, 1966 (16/17)

FREE THROWS ATTEMPTED
34 .....Wilt Chamberlain, PHI vs. STL, Feb. 22, 1962
32 .....Wilt Chamberlain, PHI vs. NY, March 2, 1962
31 .....Adrian Dantley, UTA vs. DEN, Nov. 25, 1983
29 .....Lloyd Free, SD vs. ATL, Jan. 13, 1979
29 .....Adrian Dantley, UTA vs. DAL, Oct. 31, 1980
29 .....Adrian Dantley, UTA vs. HOU, Jan. 4, 1984

FREE THROWS MADE
28 .....Wilt Chamberlain, PHI vs. NY, March 2, 1962
28 .....Adrian Dantley, UTA vs. HOU, Jan. 4, 1984
27 .....Adrian Dantley, UTA vs. DEN, Nov. 25, 1983
26 .....Adrian Dantley, UTA vs. DAL, Oct. 31, 1980
26 .....Michael Jordan, CHI vs. NJ, Feb. 26, 1987

FREE THROW PCT.
(Most with No Misses)
1.000..Dominique Wilkins, ATL vs. CHI, Dec. 8, 1992 (23/23)
1.000..Bob Pettit, STL vs. BOS, Nov. 22, 1961 (19/19)
1.000..Bill Cartwright, NY vs. KC, Nov. 17, 1981 (19/19)
1.000..Adrian Dantley, DET vs. CHI, Dec. 15, 1987 (19/19) (OT)

3-PT. FIELD GOALS ATTEMPTED
20 .....Michael Adams, DEN vs. LAC, April 12, 1991
19 .....Dennis Scott, ORL vs. MIL, April 13, 1993
18 .....Joe Dumars, DET vs. MIN, Nov. 8, 1994

3-PT. FIELD GOALS MADE
10 .....Brian Shaw, MIA vs. MIL, April 8, 1993
10 .....Joe Dumars, DET vs. MIN, Nov. 8, 1994
9 ....Dale Ellis, SEA vs. LAC, April 20, 1990
9 ....Michael Adams, DEN vs. LAC, April 12, 1991
9 ....Dennis Scott, ORL vs. MIL, April 13, 1993

TEAM RECORDS—SEASON

HIGHEST WINNING PCT.
.841 .....69-13 Los Angeles, 1971-72
.840 .....68-13 Philadelphia, 1966-67
.829 .....68-14 Boston, 1972-73

LOWEST WINNING PCT.
.110 ..... 9-73 Philadelphia, 1972-73
.125 ..... 6-42 Providence, 1947-48
.134 .....11-71 Dallas, 1992-93

HIGHEST WINNING PCT., HOME
.976 .....40-1 Boston, 1985-86
.971 .....33-1 Rochester, 1949-50
.969 .....31-1 Syracuse, 1949-50

HIGHEST WINNING PCT., ROAD
.816 .....31-7 Los Angeles, 1971-72
.800 .....32-8 Boston, 1972-73
.780 .....32-9 Boston, 1974-75

CONSECUTIVE WINS
33 ....Los Angeles, Nov. 5, 1971-Jan. 7, 1972
20 ....Milwaukee, Feb. 6-March 8, 1971
20 ....Washington, March 13-Dec. 4, 1948
          (overlapping seasons)

CONSECUTIVE WINS
(Start of Season)
15 ....Washington, Nov. 3-Dec. 4, 1948
14 ....Boston, Oct. 22-Nov. 27, 1957
12 ....Seattle, Oct. 29-Nov. 19, 1982

CONSECUTIVE LOSSES
24 ....Cleveland, March 19-Nov. 5, 1982
          (overlapping seasons)
21 ....Detroit, March 7-Oct. 22, 1980
          (overlapping seasons)
20 ....Philadelphia, Jan. 9-Feb. 11, 1973
20 ....Dallas, Nov. 13-Dec. 22, 1993

CONSECUTIVE WINS, HOME
38 ....Boston, Dec. 10, 1985-Nov. 28, 1986
          (overlapping seasons)
36 ....Philadelphia, Jan. 14, 1966-Jan. 20, 1967 (overlapping seasons)
34 ....Portland, March 5, 1977-Feb. 3, 1978 (overlapping seasons)

CONSECUTIVE WINS, ROAD
16 ....Los Angeles, Nov. 6, 1971-Jan. 7, 1972
15 ....Utah, Nov. 27, 1994-Jan. 26, 1995
13 ....Boston, Dec. 5, 1964-Jan. 20, 1965

HIGHEST SCORING AVERAGE
126.5 ...Denver, 1981-82
125.4 ...Philadelphia, 1961-62
125.2 ...Philadelphia, 1966-67

LOWEST SCORING AVERAGE
(Since 1954-55, first year of the 24-second clock)
87.4 .....Milwaukee, 1954-55
90.5 .....Cleveland, 1994-95
90.8 .....Rochester, 1954-55

FEWEST POINTS ALLOWED PER GAME
(Since 1954-55, first year of the 24-second clock)
89.8 .....Cleveland, 1994-95
89.9 .....Syracuse, 1954-55
90.0 .....Ft. Wayne, 1954-55

MOST POINTS ALLOWED PER GAME
130.8 ...Denver, 1990-91
126.0 ...Denver, 1981-82
125.1 ...Seattle, 1967-68

TEAM RECORDS—GAME

MOST POINTS
186 ......Detroit vs. Denver, Dec. 13, 1983 (3 OT)
184 ......Denver vs. Detroit, Dec. 13, 1983 (3 OT)
173 ......Boston vs. Minneapolis, Feb. 27, 1959
173 ......Phoenix vs. Denver, Nov. 10, 1990
171 ......San Antonio vs. Milwaukee, March 6, 1982 (3 OT)
169 ......Philadelphia vs. New York, March 2, 1962

FEWEST POINTS
(Since 1954-55, first year of the 24-second clock)
57 ....Milwaukee vs. Boston, Feb. 27, 1955
59 ....Sacramento vs. Charlotte, Jan. 10, 1991
61 ....New York vs. Detroit, April 12, 1992
61 ....Indiana vs. Cleveland, March 22, 1994

MOST POINTS, BOTH TEAMS
370 ...Detroit (186) vs. Denver (184), Dec. 13, 1983 (3 OT)
337 ...San Antonio (171) vs. Milwaukee (166), March 6, 1982 (3 OT)
318 ...Denver (163) vs. San Antonio (155), Jan. 11, 1984
316 ...Philadelphia (169) vs. New York (147), March 2, 1962

316 ...Cincinnati (165) vs. San Diego (151), March 12, 1970
316 ...Phoenix (173) vs. Denver (143), Nov. 10, 1990

FEWEST POINTS, BOTH TEAMS
(Since 1954-55, first year of the 24-second clock)
119 ...Milwaukee (57) vs. Boston (62), Feb. 27, 1955
133 ...New York (61) vs. Detroit (72), April 12, 1992
135 ...Syracuse (66) vs. Ft. Wayne (69), Jan. 25, 1955

LARGEST MARGIN OF VICTORY
68 .....Cleveland (148) vs. Miami (80), Dec. 17, 1991
63 .....Los Angeles (162) vs. Golden State (99), March 19, 1972
62 .....Syracuse (162) vs. New York (100), Dec. 25, 1960
59 .....Golden State (150) vs. Indiana (91), March 19, 1977
59 .....Milwaukee (143) vs. Detroit (84), Dec. 26, 1978

PLAYOFF RECORDS—CAREER

POINTS
5,762 ...Kareem Abdul-Jabbar
4,457 ...Jerry West
4,165 ...Michael Jordan
3,897 ...Larry Bird
3,776 ...John Havlicek

SCORING AVERAGE
(Minimum 25 Games)
34.4 .....Michael Jordan
29.1 .....Jerry West
28.3 .....Hakeem Olajuwon
27.5 .....Karl Malone
27.0 .....Elgin Baylor

REBOUNDS
4,104 ...Bill Russell
3,913 ...Wilt Chamberlain
2,481 ...Kareem Abdul-Jabbar
1,777 ...Wes Unseld
1,761 ...Robert Parish

ASSISTS
2,320 ...Magic Johnson
1,062 ...Larry Bird
1,006 ...Dennis Johnson
987 ...Isiah Thomas
980 ...John Stockton

STEALS
358 ...Magic Johnson
296 ...Larry Bird
295 ...Maurice Cheeks
281 ...Michael Jordan
247 ...Dennis Johnson

BLOCKED SHOTS
476 ...Kareem Adul-Jabbar
391 ...Hakeem Olajuwon
306 ...Robert Parish
281 ...Kevin McHale
239 ...Julius Erving

PLAYOFF RECORDS—GAME

POINTS
63 ..... Michael Jordan, CHI vs. BOS, April 20, 1986 (2 OT)
61 ..... Elgin Baylor, LA vs. BOS, April 14, 1962
56 ..... Wilt Chamberlain, PHI vs. SYR, March 22, 1962
56 ..... Michael Jordan, CHI vs. MIA, Apr. 29, 1992
56 ..... Charles Barkley, PHO vs. GS, May 4, 1994

REBOUNDS
41 ..... Wilt Chamberlain, PHI vs. BOS, April 5, 1967
40 ..... Bill Russell, BOS vs. PHI, March 23, 1958
40 ..... Bill Russell, BOS vs. STL, March 29, 1960
40 ..... Bill Russell, BOS vs. LA, April 18, 1962 (OT)

ASSISTS
24 ...... Magic Johnson, LA vs. PHO, May 15, 1984
24 ..... John Stockton, UTA vs. LAL, May 17, 1988
23 ..... Magic Johnson, LAL vs. POR, May 3, 1985

STEALS
8 .... Rick Barry, GS vs. SEA, April 14, 1975
8 .... Lionel Hollins, POR vs. LA, May 8, 1977
8 .... Maurice Cheeks, PHI vs. NJ, April 11, 1979
8 .... Craig Hodges, MIL vs. PHI, May 9, 1986
8 .... Tim Hardaway, GS vs. LAL, May 8, 1991

BLOCKED SHOTS
10 ..... Mark Eaton, UTA vs. HOU, April 26, 1985
10 ..... Akeem Olajuwon, HOU vs. LAL, April 29, 1990

PLAYOFF RECORDS—TEAM

CONSECUTIVE GAMES WON
13 ..... L.A. Lakers, 1988-89
12 ..... Detroit, 1989-90
9 ..... Los Angeles, 1982
9 ..... Chicago, 1992-93

CONSECUTIVE GAMES LOST
11 ..... Baltimore, 1965-66 and 1969-70
11 ..... Denver, 1988-90 and 1994
10 ..... New Jersey, 1984-86 and 1992

CONSECUTIVE SERIES WON
18 ..... Boston, 1959-1967
13 ..... Chicago, 1991-94
11 ..... L.A. Lakers, 1987-89

MOST POINTS, GAME
157 ... Boston vs. New York, April 28, 1990
156 ... Milwaukee vs. Philadelphia, March 30, 1970
153 ... L.A. Lakers vs. Denver, May 22, 1985
153 ... Portland vs. Phoenix, May 11, 1992 (2 OT)

FEWEST POINTS, GAME
(Since 1954-55, first year of the 24-second clock)
68 ..... New York vs. Indiana, May 28, 1994
69 ..... Indiana vs. Atlanta, May 12, 1994

70 ..... Golden State vs. Los Angeles, April 21, 1973
70 ..... Seattle vs. Houston, April 23, 1982

MOST POINTS, BOTH TEAMS, GAME
304 ... Portland (153) vs. Phoenix (151), May 11, 1992 (2 OT)
285 ... San Antonio (152) vs. Denver (133), April 26, 1983
285 ... Boston (157) vs. New York (128), April 28, 1990

FEWEST POINTS, BOTH TEAMS, GAME
145 ... Syracuse (71) vs. Ft. Wayne (74), March 24, 1956
156 ... New York (68) vs. Indiana (88), May 28, 1994
157 ... Kansas City (76) vs. Phoenix (81), April 17, 1981
157 ... Detroit (78) vs. Boston (79), May 30, 1988

LARGEST MARGIN OF VICTORY, GAME
58 ..... Minneapolis (133) vs. St. Louis (75), March 19, 1956
56 ..... Los Angeles (126) vs. Golden State (70), April 21, 1973
50 ..... Milwaukee (136) vs. San Francisco (86), April 4, 1971

NBA FIRST-ROUND PICKS
(Since 1972)

ATLANTA HAWKS
1995	Alan Henderson, Indiana
1994	(no 1st-round pick)
1993	Doug Edwards, Florida St.
1992	Adam Keefe, Stanford
1991	Stacey Augmon, UNLV
	Anthony Avent, Seton Hall
1990	Rumeal Robinson, Michigan
1989	Roy Marble, Iowa
1988	(no 1st-round pick)
1987	Dallas Comegys, DePaul
1986	Billy Thompson, Louisville
1985	Jon Koncak, Southern Methodist
1984	Kevin Willis, Michigan St.
1983	(no 1st-round pick)
1982	Keith Edmonson, Purdue
1981	Al Wood, N. Carolina
1980	Don Collins, Washington St.
1979	(no 1st-round pick)
1978	Butch Lee, Marquette
	Jack Givens, Kentucky
1977	Tree Rollins, Clemson
1976	Armond Hill, Princeton
1975	David Thompson, N. Carolina St.
	Marvin Webster, Morgan St.
1974	Tom Henderson, Hawaii
	Mike Sojourner, Utah
1973	Dwight Jones, Houston
	John Brown, Missouri
1972	(no 1st-round pick)

BOSTON CELTICS
1995	Eric Williams, Providence
1994	Eric Montross, N. Carolina
1993	Acie Earl, Iowa
1992	Jon Barry, Georgia Tech
1991	Rick Fox, N. Carolina
1990	Dee Brown, Jacksonville
1989	Michael Smith, Brigham Young
1988	Brian Shaw, Cal.-Santa Barbara
1987	Reggie Lewis, Northeastern
1986	Len Bias, Maryland
1985	Sam Vincent, Michigan St.
1984	Michael Young, Houston
1983	Greg Kite, Brigham Young
1982	Darren Tillis, Cleveland St.
1981	Charles Bradley, Wyoming
1980	Kevin McHale, Minnesota
1979	(no 1st-round pick)
1978	Larry Bird, Indiana St.
	Freeman Williams, Portland St.
1977	Cedric Maxwell, N.C.-Charlotte
1976	Norm Cook, Kansas
1975	Tom Boswell, S. Carolina
1974	Glenn McDonald, Long Beach St.

1973	Steve Downing, Indiana
1972	Paul Westphal, Southern Cal.

CHARLOTTE HORNETS
1995	George Zidek, UCLA
1994	(no 1st-round pick)
1993	Greg Graham, Indiana
	Scott Burrell, Connecticut
1992	Alonzo Mourning, Georgetown
1991	Larry Johnson, UNLV
1990	Kendall Gill, Illinois
1989	J.R. Reid, N. Carolina
1988	Rex Chapman, Kentucky

CHICAGO BULLS
1995	Jason Caffey, Alabama
1994	Dickey Simpkins, Providence
1993	Corie Blount, Cincinnati
1992	Byron Houston, Oklahoma St.
1991	Mark Randall, Kansas
1990	(no 1st-round pick)
1989	Stacey King, Oklahoma
	B.J. Armstrong, Iowa
	Jeff Sanders, Georgia Southern
1988	Will Perdue, Vanderbilt
1987	Olden Polynice, Virginia
	Horace Grant, Clemson
1986	Brad Sellers, Ohio St.
1985	Keith Lee, Memphis St.
1984	Michael Jordan, N. Carolina
1983	Sidney Green, UNLV
1982	Quintin Dailey, San Francisco
1981	Orlando Woolridge, Notre Dame
1980	Kelvin Ransey, Ohio St.
1979	David Greenwood, UCLA
1978	Reggie Theus, UNLV
1977	Tate Armstrong, Duke
1976	Scott May, Indiana
1975	(no 1st-round pick)
1974	Maurice Lucas, Marquette
	Cliff Pondexter, Long Beach St.
1973	Kevin Kunnert, Iowa
1972	Ralph Simpson, Michigan St.

CLEVELAND CAVALIERS
1995	Bob Sura, Florida St.
1994	(no 1st-round pick)
1993	Chris Mills, Arizona
1992	(no 1st-round pick)
1991	Terrell Brandon, Oregon
1990	(no 1st-round pick)
1989	John Morton, Seton Hall
1988	Randolph Keys, Southern Miss.
1987	Kevin Johnson, California
1986	Brad Daugherty, N. Carolina
	Ron Harper, Miami (OH)
1985	Charles Oakley, Virginia Union

1984	Tim McCormick, Michigan
1983	Roy Hinson, Rutgers
	Stewart Granger, Villanova
1982	John Bagley, Boston College
1981	(no 1st-round pick)
1980	Chad Kinch, N.C.-Charlotte
1979	(no 1st-round pick)
1978	Mike Mitchell, Auburn
1977	(no 1st-round pick)
1976	Chuckie Williams, Kansas St.
1975	John Lambert, Southern Cal.
1974	Campy Russell, Michigan
1973	Jim Brewer, Minnesota
1972	Dwight Davis, Houston

DALLAS MAVERICKS

1995	Cherokee Parks, Duke
	Loren Meyer, Iowa St.
1994	Jason Kidd, California
	Tony Dumas, Missouri-K.C.
1993	Jamal Mashburn, Kentucky
1992	Jim Jackson, Ohio St.
1991	Doug Smith, Missouri
1990	(no 1st-round pick)
1989	Randy White, Louisiana Tech
1988	(no 1st-round pick)
1987	Jim Farmer, Alabama
1986	Roy Tarpley, Michigan
1985	Detlef Schrempf, Washington
	Bill Wennington, St. John's
	Uwe Blab, Indiana
1984	Sam Perkins, N. Carolina
	Terence Stansbury, Temple
1983	Dale Ellis, Tennessee
	Derek Harper, Illinois
1982	Bill Garnett, Wyoming
1981	Mark Aguirre, DePaul
	Rolando Blackman, Kansas St.
1980	Kiki Vandeweghe, UCLA

DENVER NUGGETS

1995	Brent Barry, Oregon St.
1994	Jalen Rose, Michigan
1993	Rodney Rogers, Wake Forest
1992	LaPhonso Ellis, Notre Dame
	Bryant Stith, Virginia
1991	Dikembe Mutombo, Georgetown
	Mark Macon, Temple
1990	Chris Jackson, Louisiana St.
1989	Todd Lichti, Stanford
1988	Jerome Lane, Pittsburgh
1987	(no 1st-round pick)
1986	Maurice Martin, St. Joseph's
	Mark Alarie, Duke
1985	Blair Rasmussen, Oregon
1984	(no 1st-round pick)
1983	Howard Carter, Louisiana St.
1982	Rob Williams, Houston
1981	(no 1st-round pick)
1980	James Ray, Jacksonville

	Carl Nicks, Indiana St.
1979	(no 1st-round pick)
1978	Rod Griffin, Wake Forest
	Mike Evans, Kansas St.
1977	Tom LaGarde, N. Carolina
	Anthony Roberts, Oral Roberts
1976	(no 1st-round pick)

DETROIT PISTONS

1995	Theo Ratliff, Wyoming
	Randolph Childress, Wake Forest
1994	Grant Hill, Duke
1993	Lindsey Hunter, Jackson St.
	Allan Houston, Tennessee
1992	Don MacLean, UCLA
1991	(no 1st-round pick)
1990	Lance Blanks, Texas
1989	Kenny Battle, Illinois
1988	(no 1st-round pick)
1987	(no 1st-round pick)
1986	John Salley, Georgia Tech
1985	Joe Dumars, McNeese St.
1984	Tony Campbell, Ohio St.
1983	Antoine Carr, Wichita St.
1982	Cliff Levingston, Wichita St.
	Ricky Pierce, Rice
1981	Isiah Thomas, Indiana
	Kelly Tripucka, Notre Dame
1980	Larry Drew, Missouri
1979	Greg Kelser, Michigan St.
	Roy Hamilton, UCLA
	Phil Hubbard, Michigan
1978	(no 1st-round pick)
1977	(no 1st-round pick)
1976	Leon Douglas, Alabama
1975	(no 1st-round pick)
1974	Al Eberhard, Missouri
1973	(no 1st-round pick)
1972	Bob Nash, Hawaii

GOLDEN ST. WARRIORS

1995	Joe Smith, Maryland
1994	Clifford Rozier, Louisville
1993	Anfernee Hardaway, Memphis St.
1992	Latrell Sprewell, Alabama
1991	Chris Gatling, Old Dominion
	Victor Alexander, Iowa St.
	Shaun Vandiver, Colorado
1990	Tyrone Hill, Xavier
1989	Tim Hardaway, Texas-El Paso
1988	Mitch Richmond, Kansas St.
1987	Tellis Frank, Western Kentucky
1986	Chris Washburn, N. Carolina St.
1985	Chris Mullin, St. John's
1984	(no 1st-round pick)
1983	Russell Cross, Purdue
1982	Lester Conner, Oregon St.
1981	(no 1st-round pick)
1980	Joe Barry Carroll, Purdue
	Rickey Brown, Mississippi St.

1979	(no 1st-round pick)
1978	Purvis Short, Jackson St.
	Raymond Townsend, UCLA
1977	Rickey Green, Michigan
	Wesley Cox, Louisville
1976	Robert Parish, Centenary
	Sonny Parker, Texas A&M
1975	Joe Bryant, La Salle
1974	Jamaal Wilkes, UCLA
1973	Kevin Joyce, S. Carolina
1972	(no 1st-round pick)

HOUSTON ROCKETS

1995	(no 1st-round pick)
1994	(no 1st-round pick)
1993	Sam Cassell, Florida St.
1992	Robert Horry, Alabama
1991	John Turner, Phillips
1990	Alec Kessler, Georgia
1989	(no 1st-round pick)
1988	Derrick Chievous, Missouri
1987	(no 1st-round pick)
1986	Buck Johnson, Alabama
1985	Steve Harris, Tulsa
1984	Akeem Olajuwon, Houston
1983	Ralph Sampson, Virginia
	Rodney McCray, Louisville
1982	Terry Teagle, Baylor
1981	(no 1st-round pick)
1980	(no 1st-round pick)
1979	Lee Johnson, E. Texas St.
1978	(no 1st-round pick)
1977	(no 1st-round pick)
1976	John Lucas, Maryland
1975	Joe Meriweather, Southern Illinois
1974	Bobby Jones, N. Carolina
1973	Ed Ratleff, Long Beach St.
1972	(no 1st-round pick)

INDIANA PACERS

1995	Travis Best, Georgia Tech
1994	Eric Piatkowski, Nebraska
1993	Scott Haskin, Oregon St.
1992	Malik Sealy, St. John's
1991	Dale Davis, Clemson
1990	(no 1st-round pick)
1989	George McCloud, Florida St.
1988	Rik Smits, Marist
1987	Reggie Miller, UCLA
1986	Chuck Person, Auburn
1985	Wayman Tisdale, Oklahoma
1984	Vern Fleming, Georgia
1983	Steve Stipanovich, Missouri
	Mitchell Wiggins, Florida St.
1982	Clark Kellogg, Ohio St.
1981	Herb Williams, Ohio St.
1980	(no 1st-round pick)
1979	Dudley Bradley, N. Carolina
1978	Rick Robey, Kentucky
1977	(no 1st-round pick)
1976	

LOS ANGELES CLIPPERS

1995	Antonio McDyess, Alabama
1994	Lamond Murray, California
	Greg Minor, Louisville
1993	Terry Dehere, Seton Hall
1992	Randy Woods, La Salle
	Elmore Spencer, UNLV
1991	LeRon Ellis, Syracuse
1990	Bo Kimble, Loyola Marymount
	Loy Vaught, Michigan
1989	Danny Ferry, Duke
1988	Danny Manning, Kansas
	Hersey Hawkins, Bradley
1987	Reggie Williams, Georgetown
	Joe Wolf, N. Carolina
	Ken Norman, Illinois
1986	(no 1st-round pick)
1985	Benoit Benjamin, Creighton
1984	Lancaster Gordon, Louisville
	Michael Cage, San Diego St.
1983	Byron Scott, Arizona St.
1982	Terry Cummings, DePaul
1981	Tom Chambers, Utah
1980	Michael Brooks, La Salle
1979	(no 1st-round pick)
1978	(no 1st-round pick)
1977	(no 1st-round pick)
1976	Adrian Dantley, Notre Dame
1975	(no 1st-round pick)
1974	Tom McMillen, Maryland
1973	Ernie DiGregorio, Providence
1972	Bob McAdoo, N. Carolina

LOS ANGELES LAKERS

1995	(no 1st-round pick)
1994	Eddie Jones, Temple
1993	George Lynch, North Carolina
1992	Anthony Peeler, Missouri
1991	(no 1st-round pick)
1990	Elden Campbell, Clemson
1989	Vlade Divac, Yugoslavia
1988	David Rivers, Notre Dame
1987	(no 1st-round pick)
1986	Ken Barlow, Notre Dame
1985	A.C. Green, Oregon St.
1984	Earl Jones, District of Columbia
1983	(no 1st-round pick)
1982	James Worthy, N. Carolina
1981	Mike McGee, Michigan
1980	(no 1st-round pick)
1979	Earvin Johnson, Michigan St.
	Brad Holland, UCLA
1978	(no 1st-round pick)
1977	Ken Carr, N. Carolina St.
	Brad Davis, Maryland
	Norm Nixon, Duquesne
1976	(no 1st-round pick)
1975	David Meyers, UCLA
	Junior Bridgeman, Louisville
1974	Brian Winters, S. Carolina

1973	Kermit Washington, American
1972	Travis Grant, Kentucky St.

MIAMI HEAT

1995	Kurt Thomas, Texas Christian
1994	Khalid Reeves, Arizona
1993	(no 1st-round pick)
1992	Harold Miner, Southern Cal.
1991	Steve Smith, Michigan St.
1990	Willie Burton, Minnesota
	Dave Jamerson, Ohio
1989	Glen Rice, Michigan
1988	Rony Seikaly, Syracuse
	Kevin Edwards, DePaul

MILWAUKEE BUCKS

1995	Gary Trent, Ohio
1994	Glenn Robinson, Purdue
	Eric Mobley, Pittsburgh
1993	Vin Baker, Hartford
1992	Todd Day, Arkansas
	Lee Mayberry, Arkansas
1991	Kevin Brooks, S.W. Louisiana
1990	Terry Mills, Michigan
1989	(no 1st-round pick)
1988	Jeff Grayer, Iowa St.
1987	(no 1st-round pick)
1986	Scott Skiles, Michigan St.
1985	Jerry Reynolds, Louisiana St.
1984	Kenny Fields, UCLA
1983	Randy Breuer, Minnesota
1982	Paul Pressey, Tulsa
1981	Alton Lister, Arizona St.
1980	(no 1st-round pick)
1979	Sidney Moncrief, Arkansas
1978	George Johnson, St. John's
1977	Kent Benson, Indiana
	Marques Johnson, UCLA
	Ernie Grunfeld, Tennessee
1976	Quinn Buckner, Indiana
1975	(no 1st-round pick)
1974	Gary Brokaw, Notre Dame
1973	Swen Nater, UCLA
1972	Russell Lee, Marshall
	Julius Erving, Massachusetts

MINNESOTA TIMBERWOLVES

1995	Kevin Garnett, Farragut Academy
1994	Donyell Marshall, Connecticut
1993	Isaiah (J.R.) Rider, UNLV
1992	Christian Laettner, Duke
1991	Luc Longley, New Mexico
1990	Felton Spencer, Louisville
	Gerald Glass, Mississippi
1989	Pooh Richardson, UCLA

NEW JERSEY NETS

1995	Ed O'Bannon, UCLA
1994	Yinka Dare, G. Washington
1993	Rex Walters, Kansas
1992	(no 1st-round pick)

1991	Kenny Anderson, Georgia Tech
1990	Derrick Coleman, Syracuse
	Tate George, Connecticut
1989	Mookie Blaylock, Oklahoma
1988	Chris Morris, Auburn
1987	Dennis Hopson, Ohio St.
1986	Dwayne Washington, Syracuse
1985	(no 1st-round pick)
1984	Jeff Turner, Vanderbilt
1983	(no 1st-round pick)
1982	Sleepy Floyd, Georgetown
	Eddie Phillips, Alabama
1981	Buck Williams, Maryland
	Albert King, Maryland
	Ray Tolbert, Indiana
1980	Mike O'Koren, N. Carolina
	Mike Gminski, Duke
1979	Calvin Natt, N.E. Louisiana
	Cliff Robinson, Southern Cal.
1978	Winford Boynes, San Francisco
1977	Bernard King, Tennessee
1976	(no 1st-round pick)

NEW YORK KNICKS

1995	(no 1st-round pick)
1994	Monty Williams, Notre Dame
	Charlie Ward, Florida St.
1993	(no 1st-round pick)
1992	Hubert Davis, North Carolina
1991	Greg Anthony, UNLV
1990	Jerrod Mustaf, Maryland
1989	(no 1st-round pick)
1988	Rod Strickland, DePaul
1987	Mark Jackson, St. John's
1986	Kenny Walker, Kentucky
1985	Patrick Ewing, Georgetown
1984	(no 1st-round pick)
1983	Darrell Walker, Arkansas
1982	Trent Tucker, Minnesota
1981	(no 1st-round pick)
1980	Mike Woodson, Indiana
1979	Bill Cartwright, San Francisco
	Larry Demic, Arizona
	Sly Williams, Rhode Island
1978	Micheal Ray Richardson, Montana
1977	Ray Williams, Minnesota
1976	(no 1st-round pick)
1975	Eugene Short, Jackson St.
1974	(no 1st-round pick)
1973	Mel Davis, St. John's
1972	Tom Riker, S. Carolina

ORLANDO MAGIC

1995	David Vaughn, Memphis
1994	Brooks Thompson, Oklahoma St.
1993	Chris Webber, Michigan
	Geert Hammink, Louisiana St.
1992	Shaquille O'Neal, Louisiana St.
1991	Brian Williams, Arizona
	Stanley Roberts, Louisiana St.

| 1990 | Dennis Scott, Georgia Tech |
| 1989 | Nick Anderson, Illinois |

PHILADELPHIA 76ERS

1995	Jerry Stackhouse, North Carolina
1994	Sharone Wright, Clemson
	B.J. Tyler, Texas
1993	Shawn Bradley, Brigham Young
1992	Clarence Weatherspoon, S. Miss.
1991	(no 1st-round pick)
1990	(no 1st-round pick)
1989	Kenny Payne, Louisville
1988	Charles Smith, Pittsburgh
1987	Chris Welp, Washington
1986	(no 1st-round pick)
1985	Terry Catledge, S. Alabama
1984	Charles Barkley, Auburn
	Leon Wood, Fullerton St.
	Tom Sewell, Lamar
1983	Leo Rautins, Syracuse
1982	Mark McNamara, California
1981	Franklin Edwards, Cleveland St.
1980	Andrew Toney, S.W. Louisiana
	Monti Davis, Tennessee St.
1979	Jim Spanarkel, Duke
1978	(no 1st-round pick)
1977	Glenn Mosley, Seton Hall
1976	Terry Furlow, Michigan St.
1975	Darryl Dawkins, Evans High School
1974	Marvin Barnes, Providence
1973	Doug Collins, Illinois St.
	Raymond Lewis, Los Angeles St.
1972	Fred Boyd, Oregon St.

PHOENIX SUNS

1995	Michael Finley, Wisconsin
	Mario Bennett, Arizona St.
1994	Wesley Person, Auburn
1993	Malcolm Mackey, Georgia Tech
1992	Oliver Miller, Arkansas
1991	(no 1st-round pick)
1990	Jayson Williams, St. John's
1989	Anthony Cook, Arizona
1988	Tim Perry, Temple
	Dan Majerle, Central Michigan
1987	Armon Gilliam, UNLV
1986	William Bedford, Memphis St.
1985	Ed Pinckney, Villanova
1984	Jay Humphries, Colorado
1983	(no 1st-round pick)
1982	David Thirdkill, Bradley
1981	Larry Nance, Clemson
1980	(no 1st-round pick)
1979	Kyle Macy, Kentucky
1978	Marty Byrnes, Syracuse
1977	Walter Davis, N. Carolina
1976	Ron Lee, Oregon
1975	Alvan Adams, Oklahoma
	Ricky Sobers, UNLV
1974	John Shumate, Notre Dame

| 1973 | Mike Bantom, St. Joseph's |
| 1972 | Corky Calhoun, Pennsylvania |

PORTLAND TRAIL BLAZERS

1995	Shawn Respert, Michigan St.
1994	Aaron McKie, Temple
1993	James Robinson, Alabama
1992	Dave Johnson, Syracuse
1991	(no 1st-round pick)
1990	Alaa Abdelnaby, Duke
1989	Byron Irvin, Missouri
1988	Mark Bryant, Seton Hall
1987	Ronnie Murphy, Jacksonville
1986	Walter Berry, St. John's
	Arvidas Sabonis, Soviet Union
1985	Terry Porter, Wisc.-Stevens Point
1984	Sam Bowie, Kentucky
	Bernard Thompson, Fresno St.
1983	Clyde Drexler, Houston
1982	Lafayette Lever, Arizona St.
1981	Jeff Lamp, Virginia
	Darnell Valentine, Kansas
1980	Ronnie Lester, Iowa
1979	Jim Paxson, Dayton
1978	Mychal Thompson, Minnesota
	Ron Brewer, Arkansas
1977	Rich Laurel, Hofstra
1976	Wally Walker, Virginia
1975	Lionel Hollins, Arizona St.
1974	Bill Walton, UCLA
1973	Barry Parkhill, Virginia
1972	LaRue Martin, Loyola (IL)

SACRAMENTO KINGS

1995	Corliss Williamson, Arkansas
1994	Brian Grant, Xavier
1993	Bobby Hurley, Duke
1992	Walt Williams, Maryland
1991	Billy Owens, Syracuse
	Pete Chilcutt, N. Carolina
1990	Lionel Simmons, La Salle
	Travis Mays, Texas
	Duane Causwell, Temple
	Anthony Bonner, St. Louis
1989	Pervis Ellison, Louisville
1988	Ricky Berry, San Jose St.
1987	Kenny Smith, N. Carolina
1986	Harold Pressley, Villanova
1985	Joe Kleine, Arkansas
1984	Otis Thorpe, Providence
1983	Ennis Whatley, Alabama
1982	LaSalle Thompson, Texas
	Brook Steppe, Georgia Tech
1981	Steve Johnson, Oregon St.
	Kevin Loder, Alabama St.
1980	Hawkeye Whitney, N. Carolina St.
1979	Reggie King, Alabama
1978	Phil Ford, N. Carolina
1977	Otis Birdsong, Houston
1976	Richard Washington, UCLA

1975	Bill Robinzine, DePaul
	Bob Bigelow, Pennsylvania
1974	Scott Wedman, Colorado
1973	Ron Behagen, Minnesota
1972	(no 1st-round pick)

SAN ANTONIO SPURS

1995	Cory Alexander, Virginia
1994	Bill Curley, Boston College
1993	(no 1st-round pick)
1992	Tracy Murray, UCLA
1991	(no 1st-round pick)
1990	Dwayne Schintzius, Florida
1989	Sean Elliott, Arizona
1988	Willie Anderson, Georgia
1987	David Robinson, Navy
	Greg Anderson, Houston
1986	Johnny Dawkins, Duke
1985	Alfredrick Hughes, Loyola (IL)
1984	Alvin Robertson, Arkansas
1983	John Paxson, Notre Dame
1982	(no 1st-round pick)
1981	(no 1st-round pick)
1980	Reggie Johnson, Tennessee
1979	Wiley Peck, Mississippi St.
1978	Frankie Sanders, Southern
1977	(no 1st-round pick)
1976	(no 1st-round pick)

SEATTLE SUPERSONICS

1995	Sherell Ford, Illinois-Chicago
1994	Carlos Rogers, Tennessee St.
1993	Ervin Johnson, New Orleans
1992	Doug Christie, Pepperdine
1991	Rich King, Nebraska
1990	Gary Payton, Oregon St.
1989	Dana Barros, Boston College
	Shawn Kemp, Trinity J.C.
1988	Gary Grant, Michigan
1987	Scottie Pippen, Central Arkansas
	Derrick McKey, Alabama
1986	(no 1st-round pick)
1985	Xavier McDaniel, Wichita St.
1984	(no 1st-round pick)
1983	Jon Sundvold, Missouri
1982	(no 1st-round pick)
1981	Danny Vranes, Utah
1980	Bill Hanzlik, Notre Dame
1979	James Bailey, Rutgers
	Vinnie Johnson, Baylor
1978	(no 1st-round pick)
1977	Jack Sikma, Illinois Wesleyan
1976	Bob Wilkerson, Indiana
1975	Frank Oleynick, Seattle
1974	Tom Burleson, N. Carolina St.
1973	Mike Green, Louisiana Tech
1972	Bud Stallworth, Kansas

TORONTO RAPTORS

1995	Damon Stoudamire, Arizona

UTAH JAZZ

1995	Greg Ostertag, Kansas
1994	(no 1st-round pick)
1993	Luther Wright, Seton Hall
1992	(no 1st-round pick)
1991	Eric Murdock, Providence
1990	(no 1st-round pick)
1989	Blue Edwards, E. Carolina
1988	Eric Leckner, Wyoming
1987	Jose Ortiz, Oregon St.
1986	Dell Curry, Virginia Tech
1985	Karl Malone, Louisiana Tech
1984	John Stockton, Gonzaga
1983	Thurl Bailey, N. Carolina St.
1982	Dominique Wilkins, Georgia
1981	Danny Schayes, Syracuse
1980	Darrell Griffith, Louisville
	John Duren, Georgetown
1979	Larry Knight, Loyola (IL)
1978	James Hardy, San Francisco
1977	(no 1st-round pick)
1976	(no 1st-round pick)
1975	Rich Kelley, Stanford
1974	(no 1st-round pick)

VANCOUVER GRIZZLIES

1995	Bryant Reeves, Oklahoma St.

WASHINGTON BULLETS

1995	Rasheed Wallace, North Carolina
1994	Juwan Howard, Michigan
1993	Calbert Cheaney, Indiana
1992	Tom Gugliotta, N. Carolina St.
1991	LaBradford Smith, Louisville
1990	(no 1st-round pick)
1989	Tom Hammonds, Georgia Tech
1988	Harvey Grant, Oklahoma
1987	Muggsy Bogues, Wake Forest
1986	John Williams, Louisiana St.
	Anthony Jones, UNLV
1985	Kenny Green, Wake Forest
1984	Melvin Turpin, Kentucky
1983	Jeff Malone, Mississippi St.
	Randy Wittman, Indiana
1982	(no 1st-round pick)
1981	Frank Johnson, Wake Forest
1980	Wes Matthews, Wisconsin
1979	(no 1st-round pick)
1978	Roger Phegley, Bradley
	Dave Corzine, DePaul
1977	Greg Ballard, Oregon
	Bo Ellis, Marquette
1976	Mitch Kupchak, N. Carolina
	Larry Wright, Grambling
1975	Kevin Grevey, Kentucky
1974	Len Elmore, Maryland
1973	Nick Weatherspoon, Illinois
1972	(no 1st-round pick)

N B A Year-By-Year Results

This section lists the final standings of every NBA season since its inception in 1946-47. Actually, in its first three years of existence, the league was called the BAA (Basketball Association of America), but it is still considered part of NBA history.

This section also includes league leaders in every major category since 1946-47. In its first four years of existence, the league kept track of only four statistics—scoring, assists, field goal percentage, and free throw percentage. In 1950-51, it began keeping track of rebounds. In 1973-74, the league added blocked shots and steals to the stat sheets. In 1979-80, the 3-point shot arrived in the NBA.

Because most statistical categories are based on averages, the NBA has had to establish qualifying criteria (e.g., a player can only qualify for the scoring championship if he appears in at least 70 games). Through the years, the league has frequently changed its qualifying criteria. These are the standards that players have had to meet in order to qualify:

Scoring
• 1946-47 to 1968-69: Based on total points, not on an average.
• 1969-70 to 1973-74: Minimum 70 games.
• 1974-75 to present: Minimum 70 games or 1,400 points.

Rebounds
• 1950-51 to 1968-69: Based on total rebounds, not on an average.
• 1969-70 to 1973-74: Minimum 70 games.
• 1974-75 to present: Minimum 70 games or 800 rebounds.

Assists
• 1946-47 to 1968-69: Based on total assists, not on an average.
• 1969-70 to 1973-74: Minimum 70 games.
• 1974-75 to present: Minimum 70 games or 400 assists.

Steals
• 1973-74: Minimum 70 games.
• 1974-75 to present: Minimum 70 games or 125 steals.

Blocked Shots
• 1973-74: Minimum 70 games.
• 1974-75 to present: Minimum 70 games or 100 blocks.

Field Goal Pct.
The NBA has changed the qualifications for field goal percentage 14 times. Since 1974-75, a player has needed to make 300 field goals to qualify.

Free Throw Pct.
Since its inception, the league has changed the qualifications for free throw percentage 13 times. Since 1974-75, a player has needed to make 125 free throws in order to qualify.

3-Point Field Goal Pct.
• 1979-80 to 1989-90: Minimum 25 3-point field goals made.
• 1990-91 to 1993-94: Minimum 50 3-point field goals made.
• 1994-95: Minimum 82 3-point field goals made.

This section also contains results of every playoff series of every season. The last year of this section, 1994-95, has been expanded to include more statistical information.

1946-47 FINAL STANDINGS

Eastern Division

	W	L	PCT.	GB
Washington	49	11	.817	
Philadelphia	35	25	.583	14
New York	33	27	.550	16
Providence	28	32	.467	21
Toronto	22	38	.367	27
Boston	22	38	.367	27

Western Division

	W	L	PCT.	GB
Chicago	39	22	.639	
St. Louis	38	23	.623	1
Cleveland	30	30	.500	8.5
Detroit	20	40	.333	18.5
Pittsburgh	15	45	.250	23.5

POINTS

	AVG.	NO.
J. Fulks, PHI	23.2	1389
B. Feerick, WAS	16.3	926
S. Miasek, DET	14.9	895
E. Sadowski, TOR/CLE	16.5	877
M. Zaslofsky, CHI	14.4	877
E. Calverley, PRO	14.3	845
C. Halbert, CHI	12.7	773
J. Logan, STL	12.6	770
L. Mogus, CLE/TOR	13.0	753
C. Gunther, PIT	14.1	734

ASSISTS

	AVG.	NO.
E. Calverley, PRO	3.4	202
K. Sailors, CLE	2.3	134
O. Schectman, NY	2.0	109
H. Dallmar, PHI	1.7	104
M. Rottner, CHI	1.7	93

FIELD GOAL PCT.

Bob Feerick, WAS	.401
Ed Sadowski, TOR/CLE	.369
Earl Shannon, PRO	.339
Coulby Gunther, PIT	.336

FREE THROW PCT.

Fred Scolari, WAS	.811
Tony Kapper, PIT/BOS	.795
Stan Stutz, NY	.782
Bob Feerick, WAS	.762

QUARTERFINALS
Philadelphia 2, St. Louis 1
New York 2, Cleveland 1

SEMIFINALS
Chicago 4, Washington 2
Philadelphia 2, New York 0

BAA FINALS
Philadelphia 4, Chicago 1

1947-48 FINAL STANDINGS

Eastern Division

	W	L	PCT.	GB
Philadelphia	27	21	.563	
New York	26	22	.542	1
Boston	20	28	.417	7
Providence	6	42	.125	21

Western Division

	W	L	PCT.	GB
St. Louis	29	19	.604	
Baltimore	28	20	.583	1
Chicago	28	20	.583	1
Washington	28	20	.583	1

POINTS

	AVG.	NO.
M. Zaslofsky, CHI	21.0	1007
J. Fulks, PHI	22.1	949
E. Sadowski, BOS	19.4	910
B. Feerick, WAS	16.1	775
S. Miasek, CHI	14.9	716
C. Braun, NY	14.3	671
J. Logan, STL	13.4	644
J. Palmer, NY	13.0	622
R. Rocha, STL	12.7	611
F. Scolari, WAS	12.5	589

ASSISTS

	AVG.	NO.
H. Dallmar, PHI	2.5	120
E. Calverley, PRO	2.5	119
J. Seminoff, CHI	1.8	89
C. Gilmur, CHI	1.6	77
A. Phillip, CHI	2.3	74

FIELD GOAL PCT.

Bob Feerick, WAS	.340
Ed Sadowski, BOS	.323
Carl Braun, NY	.323
Max Zaslofsky, CHI	.323
Chick Reiser, BAL	.322

FREE THROW PCT.

Bob Feerick, WAS	.788
Max Zaslofsky, CHI	.784
Joe Fulks, PHI	.762
Buddy Jeannette, BAL	.758
Howie Dallmar, PHI	.744

QUARTERFINALS
Baltimore 2, New York 1
Chicago 2, Boston 1

SEMIFINALS
Philadelphia 4, St. Louis 3
Baltimore 2, Chicago 0

BAA FINALS
Baltimore 4, Philadelphia 2

1948-49 FINAL STANDINGS

Eastern Division

	W	L	PCT.	GB
Washington	38	22	.633	
New York	32	28	.533	6
Baltimore	29	31	.483	9
Philadelphia	28	32	.467	10
Boston	25	35	.417	13
Providence	12	48	.200	26

Western Division

	W	L	PCT.	GB
Rochester	45	15	.750	
Minneapolis	44	16	.733	1
Chicago	38	22	.633	7
St. Louis	29	31	.483	16
Fort Wayne	22	38	.367	23
Indianapolis	18	42	.300	27

POINTS	AVG.	NO.
G. Mikan, MIN	28.3	1698
J. Fulks, PHI	26.0	1560
M. Zaslofsky, CHI	20.6	1197
A. Risen, ROC	16.6	995
E. Sadowski, PHI	15.3	920
B. Smawley, STL	15.5	914
B. Davies, ROC	15.1	904
K. Sailors, PRO	15.8	899
C. Braun, NY	14.2	810
J. Logan, STL	14.1	803

ASSISTS	AVG.	NO.
B. Davies, ROC	5.4	321
A. Phillip, CHI	5.3	319

| E. Calverley, PRO | 4.3 | 251 |
| G. Senesky, PHI | 3.9 | 233 |

FIELD GOAL PCT.

Arnie Risen, ROC	.423
George Mikan, MIN	.416
Ed Sadowski, PHI	.405
Jim Pollard, MIN	.396
Red Rocha, STL	.389

FREE THROW PCT.

Bob Feerick, WAS	.859
Max Zaslofsky, CHI	.840
Bob Wanzer, ROC	.823
Herm Schaefer, MIN	.817

EAST SEMIFINALS
Washington 2, Philadelphia 0
New York 2, Baltimore 1

EAST FINALS
Washington 2, New York 1

WEST SEMIFINALS
Rochester 2, St. Louis 0
Minneapolis 2, Chicago 0

WEST FINALS
Minneapolis 2, Rochester 0

BAA FINALS
Minneapolis 4, Washington 2

1949-50 FINAL STANDINGS

Eastern Division

	W	L	GB
Syracuse	51	13	
New York	40	28	13
Washington	32	36	21
Philadelphia	26	42	27
Baltimore	25	43	28
Boston	22	46	31

Western Division

	W	L	GB
Indianapolis	39	25	
Anderson	37	27	2
Tri-Cities	29	35	10
Sheboygan	22	40	16
Waterloo	19	43	19
Denver	11	51	27

Central Division

	W	L	GB
Minneapolis	51	17	
Rochester	51	17	
Fort Wayne	40	28	11
Chicago	40	28	11
St. Louis	26	42	25

POINTS	AVG.	NO.
G. Mikan, MIN	27.4	1865
A. Groza, IND	23.4	1496
F. Brian, AND	17.8	1138
M. Zaslofsky, CHI	16.4	1115
E. Macauley, STL	16.1	1081

ASSISTS	AVG.	NO.
D. McGuire, NY	5.7	386
A. Phillip, CHI	5.8	377

FIELD GOAL PCT.

| Alex Groza, IND | .478 |
| Dick Mehen, WAT | .420 |

FREE THROW PCT.

| Max Zaslofsky, CHI | .843 |
| Chick Reiser, WAS | .835 |

EAST SEMIFINALS
Syracuse 2, Philadelphia 0
New York 2, Washington 0

EAST FINALS
Syracuse 2, New York 1

CENTRAL SEMIFINALS
Minneapolis 2, Chicago 0
Fort Wayne 2, Rochester 0

CENTRAL FINALS
Minneapolis 2, Fort Wayne 0

WEST SEMIFINALS
Indianapolis 2, Sheboygan 1
Anderson 2, Tri-Cities 1

WEST FINALS
Anderson 2, Indianapolis 1

NBA SEMIFINALS
Minneapolis 2, Anderson 0

NBA FINALS
Minneapolis 4, Syracuse 2

1950-51 FINAL STANDINGS

Eastern Division

	W	L	PCT.	GB
Philadelphia	40	26	.606	
Boston	39	30	.565	2.5
New York	36	30	.545	4
Syracuse	32	34	.485	8
Baltimore	24	42	.364	16
Washington	10	25	.286	14.5

Western Division

	W	L	PCT.	GB
Minneapolis	44	24	.647	
Rochester	41	27	.603	3
Fort Wayne	32	36	.471	12
Indianapolis	31	37	.456	13
Tri-Cities	25	43	.368	19

POINTS

	AVG.	NO.
G. Mikan, MIN	28.4	1932
A. Groza, IND	21.7	1429
E. Macauley, BOS	20.4	1384
J. Fulks, PHI	18.7	1236
F. Brian, TC	16.8	1144
P. Arizin, PHI	17.2	1121
D. Schayes, SYR	17.0	1121
B. Beard, IND	16.8	1111

REBOUNDS

	AVG.	NO.
D. Schayes, SYR	16.4	1080
G. Mikan, MIN	14.1	958
H. Gallatin, NY	12.1	800
A. Risen, ROC	12.0	795

ASSISTS

	AVG.	NO.
A. Phillip, PHI	6.3	414
D. McGuire, NY	6.3	400
G. Senesky, PHI	5.3	342
B. Cousy, BOS	4.9	341

FIELD GOAL PCT.

Alex Groza, IND	.470
Ed Macauley, BOS	.466
George Mikan, MIN	.428

FREE THROW PCT.

Joe Fulks, PHI	.855
Belus Smawley, SYR/BAL	.850
Bob Wanzer, ROC	.850

EAST SEMIFINALS
Syracuse 2, Philadelphia 0
New York 2, Boston 0

EAST FINALS
New York 3, Syracuse 2

WEST SEMIFINALS
Minneapolis 2, Indian. 1
Rochester 2, Fort Wayne 1

WEST FINALS
Rochester 3, Minneapolis 1

NBA FINALS
Rochester 4, New York 3

1951-52 FINAL STANDINGS

Eastern Division

	W	L	PCT.	GB
Syracuse	40	26	.606	
Boston	39	27	.591	1
New York	37	29	.561	3
Philadelphia	33	33	.500	7
Boston	20	46	.303	20

Western Division

	W	L	PCT.	GB
Rochester	41	25	.621	
Minneapolis	40	26	.606	1
Indianapolis	34	32	.515	7
Fort Wayne	29	37	.439	12
Milwaukee	17	49	.258	24

POINTS

	AVG.	NO.
P. Arizin, PHI	25.4	1674
G. Mikan, MIN	23.8	1523
B. Cousy, BOS	21.7	1433
E. Macauley, BOS	19.2	1264
B. Davies, ROC	16.2	1052
F. Brian, FTW	15.9	1051
L. Foust, FTW	15.9	1047
Bob Wanzer, ROC	15.7	1033

REBOUNDS

	AVG.	NO.
L. Foust, FTW	13.3	880
M. Hutchins, MIL	13.3	880
G. Mikan, MIN	13.5	866
A. Risen, ROC	12.7	841

ASSISTS

	AVG.	NO.
A. Phillip, PHI	8.2	539
B. Cousy, BOS	6.7	441
B. Davies, ROC	6.0	390
D. McGuire, NY	6.1	388

FIELD GOAL PCT.

Paul Arizin, PHI	.448
Harry Gallatin, NY	.442
Ed Macauley, BOS	.432

FREE THROW PCT.

Bob Wanzer, ROC	.904
Al Cervi, SYR	.883
Bill Sharman, BOS	.859

EAST SEMIFINALS
Syracuse 2, Phil. 1
New York 2, Boston 1

EAST FINALS
New York 3, Syracuse 1

WEST SEMIFINALS
Rochester 2, Fort Wayne 0
Minneapolis 2, Indian. 0

WEST FINALS
Minneapolis 3, Roch. 1

NBA FINALS
Minneapolis 4, New York 3

1952-53 FINAL STANDINGS

Eastern Division

	W	L	PCT.	GB
New York	47	23	.671	
Syracuse	47	24	.662	.5
Boston	46	25	.648	1.5
Baltimore	16	54	.229	31
Philadelphia	12	57	.174	34.5

Western Division

	W	L	PCT.	GB
Minneapolis	48	22	.686	
Rochester	44	26	.629	4
Fort Wayne	36	33	.522	11.5
Indianapolis	28	43	.394	20.5
Milwaukee	27	44	.380	21.5

POINTS

	AVG.	NO.
N. Johnston, PHI	22.3	1564
G. Mikan, MIN	20.6	1442
B. Cousy, BOS	19.8	1407
E. Macauley, BOS	20.3	1402
D. Schayes, SYR	17.8	1262
B. Sharman, BOS	16.2	1147
J. Nichols, MIL	15.8	1090
V. Mikkelsen, MIN	15.0	1047
B. Davies, ROC	15.6	1029

REBOUNDS

	AVG.	NO.
G. Mikan, MIN	14.4	1007
N. Johnston, PHI	13.9	979
D. Schayes, SYR	13.0	920
H. Gallatin, NY	13.1	916

ASSISTS

	AVG.	NO.
B. Cousy, BOS	7.7	547
A. Phillip, PHI/FTW	5.7	397
G. King, SYR	5.1	364
D. McGuire, NY	4.9	296

FIELD GOAL PCT.

Neil Johnston, PHI	.45242
Ed Macauley, BOS	.45236
Harry Gallatin, NY	.444

FREE THROW PCT.

Bill Sharman, BOS	.850
Fred Scolari, FTW	.844
Dolph Schayes, SYR	.827

EAST SEMIFINALS
New York 2, Baltimore 0
Boston 2, Syracuse 0

EAST FINALS
New York 3, Boston 1

WEST SEMIFINALS
Minneapolis 2, Indian. 0
Fort Wayne 2, Rochester 1

WEST FINALS
Minneapolis 3, Fort Wayne 2

NBA FINALS
Minneapolis 4, New York 1

1953-54 FINAL STANDINGS

Eastern Division

	W	L	PCT.	GB
New York	44	28	.611	
Boston	42	30	.583	2
Syracuse	42	30	.583	2
Philadelphia	29	43	.403	15
Baltimore	16	56	.222	28

Western Division

	W	L	PCT.	GB
Minneapolis	46	26	.639	
Rochester	44	28	.611	2
Fort Wayne	40	32	.556	6
Milwaukee	21	51	.292	25

POINTS

	AVG.	NO.
N. Johnston, PHI	24.4	1759
B. Cousy, BOS	19.2	1383
E. Macauley, BOS	18.9	1344
G. Mikan, MIN	18.1	1306
R. Felix, BAL	17.6	1269
D. Schayes, SYR	17.1	1228
B. Sharman, BOS	16.0	1155
L. Foust, FTW	15.1	1090
C. Braun, NY	14.8	1062

REBOUNDS

	AVG.	NO.
H. Gallatin, NY	15.3	1098
G. Mikan, MIN	14.3	1028
L. Foust, FTW	13.4	967
R. Felix, BAL	13.3	958

ASSISTS

	AVG.	NO.
B. Cousy, BOS	7.2	518
A. Phillip, FTW	6.3	449
P. Seymour, SYR	5.1	364
D. McGuire, NY	5.2	354

FIELD GOAL PCT.

Ed Macauley, BOS	.486
Bill Sharman, BOS	.450
Neil Johnston, PHI	.449

FREE THROW PCT.

Bill Sharman, BOS	.844
Dolph Schayes, SYR	.827
Carl Braun, NY	.825

EAST ROUND ROBIN
Syracuse 4, Boston 2, N.Y. 0

EAST FINALS
Syracuse 2, Boston 0

WEST ROUND ROBIN
Minneapolis 3, Rochester 2,
Fort Wayne 0

WEST FINALS
Minneapolis 2, Rochester 1

NBA FINALS
Minneapolis 4, Syracuse 3

1954-55 FINAL STANDINGS

Eastern Division

	W	L	PCT.	GB
Syracuse	43	29	.597	
New York	38	34	.528	5
Boston	36	36	.500	7
Philadelphia	33	39	.458	10

Western Division

	W	L	PCT.	GB
Fort Wayne	43	29	.597	
Minneapolis	40	32	.556	3
Rochester	29	43	.403	14
Milwaukee	26	46	.361	17

POINTS	AVG.	NO.
N. Johnston, PHI	22.7	1631
P. Arizin, PHI	21.0	1512
B. Cousy, BOS	21.2	1504
B. Pettit, MIL	20.4	1466
F. Selvy, BAL/MIL	19.0	1348
D. Schayes, SYR	18.8	1333
V. Mikkelsen, MIN	18.4	1327
C. Lovellette, MIN	18.7	1311
B. Sharman, BOS	18.4	1253
E. Macauley, BOS	17.6	1248

REBOUNDS	AVG.	NO.
N. Johnston, PHI	15.1	1085
H. Gallatin, NY	13.8	995
B. Pettit, MIL	13.8	994
D. Schayes, SYR	12.3	887

ASSISTS	AVG.	NO.
B. Cousy, BOS	7.8	557
D. McGuire, NY	7.6	542
A. Phillip, FTW	7.7	491
P. Seymour, SYR	6.7	483

FIELD GOAL PCT.	
Larry Foust, FTW	.487
Jack Coleman, ROC	.462
Neil Johnston, PHI	.440
Ray Felix, NY	.438

FREE THROW PCT.	
Bill Sharman, BOS	.897
Frank Brian, FTW	.851
Dolph Schayes, SYR	.833

EAST SEMIFINALS
Boston 2, New York 1

EAST FINALS
Syracuse 3, Boston 1

WEST SEMIFINALS
Minneapolis 2, Rochester 1

WEST FINALS
Fort Wayne 3, Minn. 1

NBA FINALS
Syracuse 4, Fort Wayne 3

1955-56 FINAL STANDINGS

Eastern Division

	W	L	PCT.	GB
Philadelphia	45	27	.625	
Boston	39	33	.542	6
Syracuse	35	37	.486	10
New York	35	37	.486	10

Western Division

	W	L	PCT.	GB
Fort Wayne	37	35	.514	
Minneapolis	33	39	.458	4
St. Louis	33	39	.458	4
Rochester	31	41	.431	6

POINTS	AVG.	NO.
B. Pettit, STL	25.7	1849
P. Arizin, PHI	24.2	1741
N. Johnston, PHI	22.1	1547
C. Lovellette, MIN	21.5	1526
D. Schayes, SYR	20.4	1472
B. Sharman, BOS	19.9	1434
B. Cousy, BOS	18.8	1356
E. Macauley, BOS	17.5	1240
G. Yardley, FTW	17.4	1233
L. Foust, FTW	16.2	1166

REBOUNDS	AVG.	NO.
B. Pettit, STL	16.2	1164
M. Stokes, ROC	16.3	1094
C. Lovellette, MIN	14.0	992
D. Schayes, SYR	12.4	891

ASSISTS	AVG.	NO.
B. Cousy, BOS	8.9	642
J. George, PHI	6.3	457
S. Martin, MIN	6.2	445
A. Phillip, FTW	5.9	410

FIELD GOAL PCT.	
Neil Johnston, PHI	.457
Paul Arizin, PHI	.448
Larry Foust, FTW	.447
Ken Sears, NY	.438

FREE THROW PCT.	
Bill Sharman, BOS	.867
Dolph Schayes, SYR	.858
Dick Schnittker, MIN	.856

EAST SEMIFINALS
Syracuse 2, Boston 1

EAST FINALS
Philadelphia 3, Syracuse 2

WEST SEMIFINALS
St. Louis 2, Minneapolis 1

WEST FINALS
Fort Wayne 3, St. Louis 2

NBA FINALS
Philadelphia 4, Fort Wayne 1

1956-57 FINAL STANDINGS

Eastern Division

	W	L	PCT.	GB
Boston	44	28	.611	
Syracuse	38	34	.528	6
Philadelphia	37	35	.514	7
New York	36	36	.500	8

Western Division

	W	L	PCT.	GB
St. Louis	34	38	.472	
Minneapolis	34	38	.472	
Fort Wayne	34	38	.472	
Rochester	31	41	.431	3

POINTS — AVG. NO.
- P. Arizin, PHI 25.6 1817
- B. Pettit, STL 24.7 1755
- D. Schayes, SYR....22.5 1617
- N. Johnston, PHI 22.8 1575
- G. Yardley, FTW......21.5 1547
- C. Lovellette, MIN ...20.8 1434
- B. Sharman, BOS....21.1 1413
- B. Cousy, BOS 20.6 1319
- E. Macauley, STL....16.5 1187
- D. Garmaker, MIN ...16.3 1177

REBOUNDS — AVG. NO.
- M. Stokes, ROC 17.4 1256
- B. Pettit, STL 14.6 1037
- D. Schayes, SYR.....14.0 1008
- B. Russell, BOS.......19.6 943

ASSISTS — AVG. NO.
- B. Cousy, BOS......... 7.5 478
- J. McMahon, STL..... 5.1 367
- M. Stokes, ROC....... 4.6 331
- J. George, PHI 4.6 307

FIELD GOAL PCT.
- Neil Johnston, PHI.............447
- Charles Share, STL...........439
- Jack Twyman, ROC 439
- Bob Houbregs, FTW..........432

FREE THROW PCT.
- Bill Sharman, BOS 905
- Dolph Schayes, SYR........904
- Dick Garmaker, MIN.........839

EAST SEMIFINALS
Syracuse 2, Philadelphia 0

EAST FINALS
Boston 3, Syracuse 0

WEST SEMIFINALS
Minneapolis 2, Fort Wayne 0

WEST FINALS
St. Louis 3, Minn. 0

NBA FINALS
Boston 4, St. Louis 3

1957-58 FINAL STANDINGS

Eastern Division

	W	L	PCT.	GB
Boston	49	23	.681	
Syracuse	41	31	.569	8
Philadelphia	37	35	.514	12
New York	35	37	.486	14

Western Division

	W	L	PCT.	GB
St. Louis	41	31	.569	
Detroit	33	39	.458	8
Cincinnati	33	39	.458	8
Minneapolis	19	53	.264	22

POINTS — AVG. NO.
- G. Yardley, DET 27.8 2001
- D. Schayes, SYR....24.9 1791
- B. Pettit, STL 24.6 1719
- C. Lovellette, CIN ...23.4 1659
- P. Arizin, PHI 20.7 1406
- B. Sharman, BOS....22.3 1402
- C. Hagan, STL..........19.9 1391
- N. Johnston, PHI 19.5 1388
- K. Sears, NY............18.6 1342
- V. Mikkelsen, MIN ...17.3 1248

REBOUNDS — AVG. NO.
- B. Russell, BOS.......22.7 1564
- B. Pettit, STL 17.4 1216
- M. Stokes, CIN 18.1 1142
- D. Schayes, SYR.....14.2 1022

ASSISTS — AVG. NO.
- B. Cousy, BOS......... 7.1 463
- D. McGuire, DET...... 6.6 454
- M. Stokes, CIN........ 6.4 403
- C. Braun, NY............ 5.5 393

FIELD GOAL PCT.
- Jack Twyman, CIN 452
- Cliff Hagan, STL...............443
- Bill Russell, BOS..............442
- Ray Felix, NY 442

FREE THROW PCT.
- Dolph Schayes, SYR........904
- Bill Sharman, BOS 893
- Bob Cousy, BOS 850

EAST SEMIFINALS
Philadelphia 2, Syracuse 1

EAST FINALS
Boston 4, Philadelphia 1

WEST SEMIFINALS
Detroit 2, Cincinnati 0

WEST FINALS
St. Louis 4, Detroit 1

NBA FINALS
St. Louis 4, Boston 2

1958-59 FINAL STANDINGS

Eastern Division

	W	L	PCT.	GB
Boston	52	20	.722	
New York	40	32	.556	12
Syracuse	35	37	.486	17
Philadelphia	32	40	.444	20

Western Division

	W	L	PCT.	GB
St. Louis	49	23	.681	
Minneapolis	33	39	.458	16
Detroit	28	44	.389	21
Cincinnati	19	53	.264	30

POINTS

	AVG.	NO.
B. Pettit, STL	29.2	2105
J. Twyman, CIN	25.8	1857
P. Arizin, PHI	26.4	1851
E. Baylor, MIN	24.9	1742
C. Hagan, STL	23.7	1707
D. Schayes, SYR	21.3	1534
K. Sears, NY	21.0	1488
B. Sharman, BOS	20.4	1466
B. Cousy, BOS	20.0	1297
R. Guerin, NY	18.2	1291

REBOUNDS

	AVG.	NO.
B. Russell, BOS	23.0	1612
B. Pettit, STL	16.4	1182
E. Baylor, MIN	15.0	1050
J. Kerr, SYR	14.0	1008

ASSISTS

	AVG.	NO.
B. Cousy, BOS	8.6	557
D. McGuire, DET	6.2	443
L. Costello, SYR	5.4	379
R. Guerin, NY	5.1	364

FIELD GOAL PCT.

Ken Sears, NY	.490
Bill Russell, BOS	.457
Cliff Hagan, STL	.456
Clyde Lovellette, STL	.454

FREE THROW PCT.

Bill Sharman, BOS	.932
Dolph Schayes, SYR	.864
Ken Sears, NY	.861
Bob Cousy, BOS	.855

EAST SEMIFINALS
Syracuse 2, New York 0

EAST FINALS
Boston 4, Syracuse 3

WEST SEMIFINALS
Minneapolis 2, Detroit 1

WEST FINALS
Minneapolis 4, St. Louis 2

NBA FINALS
Boston 4, Minneapolis 0

1959-60 FINAL STANDINGS

Eastern Division

	W	L	PCT.	GB
Boston	59	16	.787	
Philadelphia	49	26	.653	10
Syracuse	45	30	.600	14
New York	27	48	.360	32

Western Division

	W	L	PCT.	GB
St. Louis	46	29	.613	
Detroit	30	45	.400	16
Minneapolis	25	50	.333	21
Cincinnati	19	56	.253	27

POINTS

	AVG.	NO.
W. Chamberlain, PHI	37.6	2707
J. Twyman, CIN	31.2	2338
E. Baylor, MIN	29.6	2074
B. Pettit, STL	26.1	1882
C. Hagan, STL	24.8	1859
G. Shue, DET	22.8	1712
D. Schayes, SYR	22.5	1689
T. Heinsohn, BOS	21.7	1629
R. Guerin, NY	21.8	1615
P. Arizin, PHI	22.3	1606

REBOUNDS

	AVG.	NO.
W. Chamberlain, PHI	27.0	1941
B. Russell, BOS	24.0	1778
B. Pettit, STL	17.0	1221
E. Baylor, MIN	16.4	1150

ASSISTS

	AVG.	NO.
B. Cousy, BOS	9.5	715
G. Rodgers, PHI	7.1	482
R. Guerin, NY	6.3	468
L. Costello, SYR	6.3	449

FIELD GOAL PCT.

Ken Sears, NY	.477
Hal Greer, SYR	.476
Clyde Lovellette, STL	.468
Bill Russell, BOS	.467

FREE THROW PCT.

Dolph Schayes, SYR	.893
Gene Shue, DET	.872
Ken Sears, NY	.868
Bill Sharman, BOS	.866

EAST SEMIFINALS
Philadelphia 2, Syrac. 1

EAST FINALS
Boston 4, Philadelphia 2

WEST SEMIFINALS
Minneapolis 2, Detroit 0

WEST FINALS
St. Louis 4, Minneapolis 3

NBA FINALS
Boston 4, St. Louis 3

1960-61 FINAL STANDINGS

Eastern Division

	W	L	PCT.	GB
Boston	57	22	.722	
Philadelphia	46	33	.582	11
Syracuse	38	41	.481	19
New York	21	58	.266	36

Western Division

	W	L	PCT.	GB
St. Louis	51	28	.646	
Los Angeles	36	43	.456	15
Detroit	34	45	.430	17
Cincinnati	33	46	.418	18

POINTS	AVG.	NO.
W. Chamberlain, PHI..	38.4	3033
E. Baylor, LA	34.8	2538
O. Robertson, CIN	30.5	2165
B. Pettit, STL	27.9	2120
J. Twyman, CIN	25.3	1997
D. Schayes, SYR	23.6	1868
W. Naulls, NY	23.4	1846
P. Arizin, PHI	23.2	1832
B. Howell, DET	23.6	1815
G. Shue, DET	22.6	1765

REBOUNDS	AVG.	NO.
W. Chamberlain, PHI..	27.2	2149
B. Russell, BOS	23.9	1868
B. Pettit, STL	20.3	1540
E. Baylor, LA	19.8	1447

ASSISTS	AVG.	NO.
O. Robertson, CIN....	9.7	690
G. Rodgers, PHI	8.7	677
B. Cousy, BOS	7.7	587
G. Shue, DET	6.8	530

FIELD GOAL PCT.	
W. Chamberlain, PHI	.509
Jack Twyman, CIN	.488
Larry Costello, SYR	.482
Oscar Robertson, CIN	.473

FREE THROW PCT.	
Bill Sharman, BOS	.921
Dolph Schayes, SYR	.868
Gene Shue, DET	.856
Frank Ramsey, BOS	.833

EAST SEMIFINALS
Syracuse 3, Phil. 0

EAST FINALS
Boston 4, Syracuse 1

WEST SEMIFINALS
Los Angeles 3, Detroit 2

WEST FINALS
St. Louis 4, Los Angeles 3

NBA FINALS
Boston 4, St. Louis 1

1961-62 FINAL STANDINGS

Eastern Division

	W	L	PCT.	GB
Boston	60	20	.750	
Philadelphia	49	31	.613	11
Syracuse	41	39	.513	19
New York	29	51	.363	31

Western Division

	W	L	PCT.	GB
Los Angeles	54	26	.675	
Cincinnati	43	37	.538	11
Detroit	37	43	.463	17
St. Louis	29	51	.363	25
Chicago	18	62	.225	36

POINTS	AVG.	NO.
W. Chamberlain, PHI..	50.4	4029
W. Bellamy, CHI	31.6	2495
O. Robertson, CIN...	30.8	2432
B. Pettit, STL	31.1	2429
J. West, LA	30.8	2310
R. Guerin, NY	29.5	2303
W. Naulls, NY	25.0	1877
E. Baylor, LA	38.3	1836
J. Twyman, CIN	22.9	1831

REBOUNDS	AVG.	NO.
W. Chamberlain, PHI..	25.7	2052
B. Russell, BOS	23.6	1790
W. Bellamy, CHI	19.0	1500
B. Pettit, STL	18.7	1459

ASSISTS	AVG.	NO.
O. Robertson, CIN...	11.4	899
G. Rodgers, PHI	7.9	663
B. Cousy, BOS	7.8	584
R. Guerin, NY	6.9	539

FIELD GOAL PCT.	
Walt Bellamy, CHI	.519
W. Chamberlain, PHI	.506
Jack Twyman, CIN	.479
Oscar Robertson, CIN	.478

FREE THROW PCT.	
Dolph Schayes, SYR	.896
Willie Naulls, NY	.842
Larry Costello, SYR	.837

EAST SEMIFINALS
Philadelphia 3, Syrac. 2

EAST FINALS
Boston 4, Philadelphia 3

WEST SEMIFINALS
Detroit 3, Cincinnati 1

WEST FINALS
Los Angeles 4, Detroit 2

NBA FINALS
Boston 4, Los Angeles 3

1962-63 FINAL STANDINGS

Eastern Division

	W	L	PCT.	GB
Boston	58	22	.725	
Syracuse	48	32	.600	10
Cincinnati	42	38	.525	16
New York	21	59	.263	37

Western Division

	W	L	PCT.	GB
Los Angeles	53	27	.663	
St. Louis	48	32	.600	5
Detroit	34	46	.425	19
San Francisco	31	49	.388	22
Chicago	25	55	.313	28

POINTS

	AVG.	NO.
W. Chamberlain, SF	44.8	3586
E. Baylor, LA	34.0	2719
O. Robertson, CIN	28.3	2264
B. Pettit, STL	28.4	2241
W. Bellamy, CHI	27.9	2233
B. Howell, DET	22.7	1793
R. Guerin, NY	21.5	1701
J. Twyman, CIN	19.8	1586
H. Greer, SYR	19.5	1562

REBOUNDS

	AVG.	NO.
W. Chamberlain, SF	24.3	1946
B. Russell, BOS	23.0	1843
W. Bellamy, CHI	16.4	1309
B. Pettit, STL	15.1	1191

ASSISTS

	AVG.	NO.
G. Rodgers, SF	10.4	825
O. Robertson, CIN	9.5	758
B. Cousy, BOS	6.8	515
S. Green, CHI	5.8	422

FIELD GOAL PCT.

W. Chamberlain, SF	.528
Walt Bellamy, CHI	.527
Oscar Robertson, CIN	.518
Bailey Howell, DET	.516

FREE THROW PCT.

Larry Costello, SYR	.881
Richie Guerin, NY	.848
Elgin Baylor, LA	.837

EAST SEMIFINALS
Cincinnati 3, Syracuse 2

EAST FINALS
Boston 4, Cincinnati 3

WEST SEMIFINALS
St. Louis 3, Detroit 1

WEST FINALS
Los Angeles 4, St. Louis 3

NBA FINALS
Boston 4, Los Angeles 2

1963-64 FINAL STANDINGS

Eastern Division

	W	L	PCT.	GB
Boston	59	21	.738	
Cincinnati	55	25	.688	4
Philadelphia	34	46	.425	25
New York	22	58	.275	37

Western Division

	W	L	PCT.	GB
San Francisco	48	32	.600	
St. Louis	46	34	.575	2
Los Angeles	42	38	.525	6
Baltimore	31	49	.388	17
Detroit	23	57	.288	25

POINTS

	AVG.	NO.
W. Chamberlain, SF	36.9	2948
O. Robertson, CIN	31.4	2480
B. Pettit, STL	27.4	2190
W. Bellamy, BAL	27.0	2159
J. West, LA	28.7	2064
E. Baylor, LA	25.4	1983
H. Greer, PHI	23.3	1865
B. Howell, DET	21.6	1666
T. Dischinger, BAL	20.8	1662

REBOUNDS

	AVG.	NO.
B. Russell, BOS	24.7	1930
W. Chamberlain, SF	22.3	1787
J. Lucas, CIN	17.4	1375
W. Bellamy, BAL	17.0	1361

ASSISTS

	AVG.	NO.
O. Robertson, CIN	11.0	868
G. Rodgers, SF	7.0	556
K. Jones, BOS	5.1	407
J. West, LA	5.6	403

FIELD GOAL PCT.

Jerry Lucas, CIN	.527
W. Chamberlain, SF	.524
Walt Bellamy, BAL	.513
Terry Dischinger, BAL	.496

FREE THROW PCT.

Oscar Robertson, CIN	.853
Jerry West, LA	.832
Hal Greer, PHI	.829

EAST SEMIFINALS
Cincinnati 3, Philadelphia 2

EAST FINALS
Boston 4, Cincinnati 1

WEST SEMIFINALS
St. Louis 3, Los Angeles 2

WEST FINALS
San Francisco 4, St. L. 3

NBA FINALS
Boston 4, San Francisco 1

1964-65 FINAL STANDINGS

Eastern Division

	W	L	PCT.	GB
Boston	62	18	.715	
Cincinnati	48	32	.600	14
Philadelphia	40	40	.500	22
New York	31	49	.388	31

Western Division

	W	L	PCT.	GB
Los Angeles	49	31	.613	
St. Louis	45	35	.563	4
Baltimore	37	43	.463	12
Detroit	31	49	.388	18
San Francisco	17	63	.213	32

POINTS	AVG.	NO.
W. Chamber., SF/PHI	34.7	2534
J. West, LA	31.0	2292
O. Robertson, CIN	30.4	2279
S. Jones, BOS	25.9	2070
E. Baylor, LA	27.1	2009
W. Bellamy, BAL	24.8	1981
W. Reed, NY	19.5	1560
B. Howell, BAL	19.2	1534
T. Dischinger, DET	18.2	1456

REBOUNDS	AVG.	NO.
B. Russell, BOS	24.1	1878
W. Chamber., SF/PHI	22.9	1673
N. Thurmond, SF	18.1	1395
J. Lucas, CIN	20.0	1321

ASSISTS	AVG.	NO.
O. Robertson, CIN	11.5	861
G. Rodgers, SF	7.3	565
K. Jones, BOS	5.6	437
L. Wilkens, STL	5.5	431

FIELD GOAL PCT.	
W. Chamberlain, SF/PHI	.510
Walt Bellamy, BAL	.509
Jerry Lucas, CIN	.498
Jerry West, LA	.497

FREE THROW PCT.	
Larry Costello, PHI	.877
Oscar Robertson, CIN	.839
Howard Komives, NY	.835

EAST SEMIFINALS
Philadelphia 3, Cincinnati 1

EAST FINALS
Boston 4, Philadelphia 3

WEST SEMIFINALS
Baltimore 3, St. Louis 1

WEST FINALS
Los Angeles 4, Baltimore 2

NBA FINALS
Boston 4, Los Angeles 1

1965-66 FINAL STANDINGS

Eastern Division

	W	L	PCT.	GB
Philadelphia	55	25	.688	
Boston	54	26	.675	1
Cincinnati	45	35	.563	10
New York	30	50	.375	25

Western Division

	W	L	PCT.	GB
Los Angeles	45	35	.563	
Baltimore	38	42	.475	7
St. Louis	36	44	.450	9
San Francisco	35	45	.438	10
Detroit	22	58	.275	23

POINTS	AVG.	NO.
W. Chamberlain, PHI	33.5	2649
J. West, LA	31.3	2476
O. Robertson, CIN	31.3	2378
R. Barry, SF	25.7	2059
W. Bellamy, BAL/NY	22.8	1820
H. Greer, PHI	22.7	1819
D. Barnett, NY	23.1	1729
J. Lucas, CIN	21.5	1697
Z. Beaty, STL	20.7	1656

REBOUNDS	AVG.	NO.
W. Chamberlain, PHI	24.6	1943
B. Russell, BOS	22.8	1779
J. Lucas, CIN	21.1	1668
N. Thurmond, SF	18.0	1312

ASSISTS	AVG.	NO.
O. Robertson, CIN	11.1	847
G. Rodgers, SF	10.7	846
K. Jones, BOS	6.3	503
J. West, LA	6.1	480

FIELD GOAL PCT.	
W. Chamberlain, PHI	.540
John Green, NY/BAL	.536
Walt Bellamy, BAL/NY	.506
Al Attles, SF	.503

FREE THROW PCT.	
Larry Siegfried, BOS	.881
Rick Barry, SF	.862
Howard Komives, NY	.861

EAST SEMIFINALS
Boston 3, Cincinnati 2

EAST FINALS
Boston 4, Philadelphia 1

WEST SEMIFINALS
St. Louis 3, Baltimore 0

WEST FINALS
Los Angeles 4, St. Louis 3

NBA FINALS
Boston 4, Los Angeles 3

1966-67
FINAL STANDINGS

Eastern Division

	W	L	PCT.	GB
Philadelphia	68	13	.840	
Boston	60	21	.741	8
Cincinnati	39	42	.481	29
New York	36	45	.444	32
Baltimore	20	61	.247	48

Western Division

	W	L	PCT.	GB
San Francisco	44	37	.543	
St. Louis	39	42	.481	5
Los Angeles	36	45	.444	8
Chicago	33	48	.407	11
Detroit	30	51	.370	14

POINTS	AVG.	NO.
R. Barry, SF	35.6	2775
O. Robertson, CIN	30.5	2412
W. Chamberlain, PHI	24.1	1956
J. West, LA	28.7	1892
E. Baylor, LA	26.6	1862
H. Greer, PHI	22.1	1765
J. Havlicek, BOS	21.4	1733
W. Reed, NY	20.9	1628
B. Howell, BOS	20.0	1621
D. Bing, DET	20.0	1601
S. Jones, BOS	22.1	1594
C. Walker, PHI	19.3	1567
G. Johnson, BAL	20.7	1511
W. Bellamy, NY	19.0	1499
B. Cunningham, PHI	18.5	1495
L. Hudson, STL	18.4	1471
G. Rodgers, CHI	18.0	1459
J. Lucas, CIN	17.8	1438
B. Boozer, CHI	18.0	1436
E. Miles, DET	17.6	1425

REBOUNDS	AVG.	NO.
W. Chamberlain, PHI	24.2	1957
B. Russell, BOS	21.0	1700
J. Lucas, CIN	19.1	1547
N. Thurmond, SF	21.3	1382
B. Bridges, STL	15.1	1190
W. Reed, NY	14.6	1136
D. Imhoff, LA	13.3	1080
W. Bellamy, NY	13.5	1064
L. Ellis, BAL	12.0	970
D. DeBusschere, DET	11.8	924

ASSISTS	AVG.	NO.
G. Rodgers, CHI	11.2	908
O. Robertson, CIN	10.7	845
W. Chamberlain, PHI	7.8	630
B. Russell, BOS	5.8	472
J. West, LA	6.8	447
L. Wilkens, STL	5.7	442
H. Komives, NY	6.2	401
K. Jones, BOS	5.0	389
R. Guerin, STL	4.4	345
P. Neumann, SF	4.4	342

FIELD GOAL PCT.

W. Chamberlain, PHI	.683
Walt Bellamy, NY	.521
Bailey Howell, BOS	.512
Oscar Robertson, CIN	.493
Willis Reed, NY	.490
Chet Walker, PHI	.488
Bob Boozer, CHI	.487
Tom Hawkins, LA	.481
Happy Hairston, CIN	.479
Dick Barnett, NY	.478

FREE THROW PCT.

Adrian Smith, CIN	.903
Rick Barry, SF	.884
Jerry West, LA	.878
Oscar Robertson, CIN	.873
Sam Jones, BOS	.857
Larry Siegfried, BOS	.847
Wally Jones, PHI	.838
John Havlicek, BOS	.828

EAST SEMIFINALS

Philadelphia 3, Cincinnati 1
Boston 3, New York 1

EAST FINALS

Philadelphia 127, Boston 113
Philadelphia 107, Boston 102
Philadelphia 115, Boston 104
Boston 121, Philadelphia 117
Philadelphia 140, Boston 116

WEST SEMIFINALS

San Francisco 3, L.A. 0
St. Louis 3, Chicago 0

WEST FINALS

San Francisco 117, St. L. 115
San Francisco 143, St. L. 136
St. Louis 115, S.F. 109
St. Louis 109, S.F. 104
San Francisco 123, St. L. 102
San Francisco 112, St. L. 107

NBA FINALS

Phil. 141, S.F. 135 (OT)
Philadelphia 126, S.F. 95
San Francisco 130, Phil. 124
Philadelphia 122, S.F. 108
San Francisco 117, Phil. 109
Philadelphia 125, S.F. 122

1967-68
FINAL STANDINGS

Eastern Division

	W	L	PCT.	GB
Philadelphia	62	20	.756	
Boston	54	28	.659	8
New York	43	39	.524	19
Detroit	40	42	.488	22
Cincinnati	39	43	.476	23
Baltimore	36	46	.439	26

Western Division

	W	L	PCT.	GB
St. Louis	56	26	.683	
Los Angeles	52	30	.634	4
San Francisco	43	39	.524	13
Chicago	29	53	.354	27
Seattle	23	59	.280	33
San Diego	15	67	.183	41

POINTS

	AVG.	NO.
D. Bing, DET	27.1	2142
E. Baylor, LA	26.0	2002
W. Chamberlain, PHI	24.3	1992
E. Monroe, BAL	24.3	1991
H. Greer, PHI	24.1	1976
O. Robertson, CIN	29.2	1896
W. Hazzard, SEA	23.9	1894
J. Lucas, CIN	21.4	1760
Z. Beaty, STL	21.1	1733
R. LaRusso, SF	21.8	1726
J. Havlicek, BOS	20.7	1700
W. Reed, NY	20.8	1685
B. Boozer, CHI	21.5	1655
L. Wilkens, STL	20.0	1638
B. Howell, BOS	19.8	1621
A. Clark, LA	19.9	1612
S. Jones, BOS	21.3	1553
J. Mullins, SF	18.9	1493
B. Rule, SEA	18.1	1484
C. Walker, PHI	17.9	1465

REBOUNDS

	AVG.	NO.
W. Chamberlain, PHI	23.8	1952
J. Lucas, CIN	19.0	1560
B. Russell, BOS	18.6	1451
C. Lee, SF	13.9	1141
N. Thurmond, SF	22.0	1121
R. Scott, BAL	13.7	1111
B. Bridges, STL	13.4	1102
D. DeBusschere, DET	13.5	1081
W. Reed, NY	13.2	1073
W. Bellamy, NY	11.7	961

ASSISTS

	AVG.	NO.
W. Chamberlain, PHI	8.6	702
L. Wilkens, STL	8.3	679
O. Robertson, CIN	9.7	633
D. Bing, DET	6.4	509
W. Hazzard, SEA	6.2	493
A. Williams, SD	4.9	391
A. Attles, SF	5.8	390
J. Havlicek, BOS	4.7	384
G. Rodgers, CHI/CIN	4.8	380
H. Greer, PHI	4.5	372

FIELD GOAL PCT.

W. Chamberlain, PHI	.595
Walt Bellamy, NY	.541
Jerry Lucas, CIN	.519
Jerry West, LA	.514
Len Chappell, CIN/DET	.513
Oscar Robertson, CIN	.500
Tom Hawkins, LA	.499
Terry Dischinger, DET	.494
Don Nelson, BOS	.494
Henry Finkel, SD	.492

FREE THROW PCT.

Oscar Robertson, CIN	.873
Larry Siegfried, BOS	.868
Dave Gambee, SD	.847
Fred Hetzel, SF	.833
Adrian Smith, CIN	.829
Sam Jones, BOS	.827
Flynn Robinson, CIN/CHI	.821
John Havlicek, BOS	.812

EAST SEMIFINALS

Philadelphia 4, New York 2

Boston 4, Detroit 2

EAST FINALS

Boston 127, Philadelphia 118

Philadelphia 115, Boston 106

Philadelphia 122, Boston 114

Philadelphia 110, Boston 105

Boston 122, Philadelphia 104

Boston 114, Philadelphia 106

Boston 100, Philadelphia 96

WEST SEMIFINALS

San Francisco 4, St. Louis 2

Los Angeles 4, Chicago 1

WEST FINALS

Los Angeles 133, S.F. 105

Los Angeles 115, S.F. 112

Los Angeles 128, S.F. 124

Los Angeles 106, S.F. 100

NBA FINALS

Boston 107, Los Angeles 101

Los Angeles 123, Boston 113

Boston 127, Los Angeles 119

Los Angeles 119, Boston 105

Boston 120, L.A. 117 (OT)

Boston 124, Los Angeles 109

1968-69
FINAL STANDINGS

Eastern Division

	W	L	PCT.	GB
Baltimore	57	25	.695	
Philadelphia	55	27	.671	2
New York	54	28	.659	3
Boston	48	34	.585	9
Cincinnati	41	41	.500	16
Detroit	32	50	.390	25
Milwaukee	27	55	.329	30

Western Division

	W	L	PCT.	GB
Los Angeles	55	27	.671	
Atlanta	48	34	.585	7
San Francisco	41	41	.500	14
San Diego	37	45	.451	18
Chicago	33	49	.402	22
Seattle	30	52	.366	25
Phoenix	16	66	.195	39

POINTS	AVG.	NO.
E. Hayes, SD	28.4	2327
E. Monroe, BAL	25.8	2065
B. Cunningham, PHI	24.8	2034
B. Rule, SEA	24.0	1965
O. Robertson, CIN	24.7	1955
G. Goodrich, PHO	23.8	1931
H. Greer, PHI	23.1	1896
E. Baylor, LA	24.8	1881
L. Wilkens, SEA	22.4	1835
D. Kojis, SD	22.5	1820
K. Loughery, BAL	22.6	1806
D. Bing, DET	23.4	1800
J. Mullins, SF	22.8	1775
J. Havlicek, BOS	21.6	1771
L. Hudson, ATL	21.9	1770
W. Reed, NY	21.1	1733
B. Boozer, CHI	21.7	1716
D. Van Arsdale, PHO	21.0	1678
W. Chamberlain, LA	20.5	1664
F. Robinson, CHI/MIL	20.0	1662

REBOUNDS	AVG.	NO.
W. Chamberlain, LA	21.1	1712
W. Unseld, BAL	18.2	1491
B. Russell, BOS	19.3	1484
E. Hayes, SD	17.1	1406
N. Thurmond, SF	19.7	1402
J. Lucas, CIN	18.4	1360
W. Reed, NY	14.5	1191
B. Bridges, ATL	14.2	1132
W. Bellamy, NY/DET	12.5	1101
B. Cunningham, PHI	12.8	1050

ASSISTS	AVG.	NO.
O. Robertson, CIN	9.8	772
L. Wilkens, SEA	8.2	674
W. Frazier, NY	7.9	635
G. Rodgers, MIL	6.9	561
D. Bing, DET	7.1	546
A. Williams, SD	6.6	524
G. Goodrich, PHO	6.4	518
W. Hazzard, ATL	5.9	474
J. Havlicek, BOS	5.4	441
J. West, LA	6.9	423

FIELD GOAL PCT.

W. Chamberlain, LA	.583
Jerry Lucas, CIN	.551
Willis Reed, NY	.521
Terry Dischinger, DET	.515
Walt Bellamy, NY/DET	.510
Joe Caldwell, ATL	.507
Walt Frazier, NY	.505
Tom Hawkins, LA	.499
Lou Hudson, ATL	.492
Jon McGlocklin, MIL	.487

FREE THROW PCT.

Larry Siegfried, BOS	.864
Jeff Mullins, SF	.843
Jon McGlocklin, MIL	.842
Flynn Robinson, CHI/MIL	.839
Oscar Robertson, CIN	.838
Fred Hetzel, MIL/CIN	.838
Jack Marin, BAL	.830
Jerry West, LA	.821

EAST SEMIFINALS
New York 4, Baltimore 0
Boston 4, Philadelphia 1

EAST FINALS
Boston 108, New York 100
Boston 112, New York 97
New York 101, Boston 91
Boston 97, New York 96
New York 112, Boston 104
Boston 106, New York 105

WEST SEMIFINALS
Los Angeles 4, San Fran. 2
Atlanta 4, San Diego 2

WEST FINALS
Los Angeles 95, Atlanta 93
Los Angeles 104, Atlanta 102
Atlanta 99, Los Angeles 86
Los Angeles 100, Atlanta 85
Los Angeles 104, Atlanta 96

NBA FINALS
Los Angeles 120, Boston 118
Los Angeles 118, Boston 112
Boston 111, Los Angeles 105
Boston 89, Los Angeles 88
Los Angeles 117, Boston 104
Boston 99, Los Angeles 90
Boston 108, Los Angeles 106

1969-70
FINAL STANDINGS

Eastern Division

	W	L	PCT.	GB
New York	60	22	.732	
Milwaukee	56	26	.683	4
Baltimore	50	32	.610	10
Philadelphia	42	40	.512	18
Cincinnati	36	46	.439	24
Boston	34	48	.415	26
Detroit	31	51	.378	29

Western Division

	W	L	PCT.	GB
Atlanta	48	34	.585	
Los Angeles	46	36	.561	2
Chicago	39	43	.476	9
Phoenix	39	43	.476	9
Seattle	36	46	.439	12
San Francisco	30	52	.366	18
San Diego	27	55	.329	21

SCORING

Jerry West, LA	31.2
Lew Alcindor, MIL	28.8
Elvin Hayes, SD	27.5
Billy Cunningham, PHI	26.1
Lou Hudson, ATL	25.4
Connie Hawkins, PHO	24.6
Bob Rule, SEA	24.6
John Havlicek, BOS	24.2
Earl Monroe, BAL	23.4
Dave Bing, DET	22.9
Tom Van Arsdale, CIN	22.8
Jeff Mullins, SF	22.1
Hal Greer, PHI	22.0
Flynn Robinson, MIL	21.8
Willis Reed, NY	21.7
Chet Walker, CHI	21.5
Dick Van Arsdale, PHO	21.3
Joe Caldwell, ATL	21.1
Bob Love, CHI	21.0
Walt Frazier, NY	20.9

REBOUNDS

Elvin Hayes, SD	16.9
Wes Unseld, BAL	16.7
Lew Alcindor, MIL	14.5
Bill Bridges, ATL	14.4
Gus Johnson, BAL	13.9
Willis Reed, NY	13.9
Billy Cunningham, PHI	13.6
Tom Boerwinkle, CHI	12.5
Paul Silas, PHO	11.7
Clyde Lee, SF	11.3

ASSISTS

Len Wilkens, SEA	9.1
Walt Frazier, NY	8.2
Clem Haskins, CHI	7.6
Jerry West, LA	7.5
Gail Goodrich, PHO	7.5
Walt Hazzard, ATL	6.8
John Havlicek, BOS	6.8
Art Williams, SD	6.3
Norm Van Lier, CIN	6.2
Dave Bing, DET	6.0

FIELD GOAL PCT.

Johnny Green, CIN	.559
Darrall Imhoff, PHI	.540
Lou Hudson, ATL	.531
Jon McGlocklin, MIL	.530
Dick Snyder, SEA	.528
Jim Fox, PHO	.524
Lew Alcindor, MIL	.518
Wes Unseld, BAL	.518
Walt Frazier, NY	.518
Dick Van Arsdale, PHO	.508

FREE THROW PCT.

Flynn Robinson, MIL	.898
Chet Walker, CHI	.850
Jeff Mullins, SF	.847
John Havlicek, BOS	.844
Bob Love, CHI	.842
Earl Monroe, BAL	.830
Lou Hudson, ATL	.824
Jerry West, LA	.824

EAST SEMIFINALS

New York 4, Baltimore 3
Milwaukee 4, Philadelphia 1

EAST FINALS

New York 110, Milwaukee 102
New York 112, Milwaukee 111
Milwaukee 101, New York 96
New York 117, Milwaukee 105
New York 132, Milwaukee 96

WEST SEMIFINALS

Atlanta 4, Chicago 1
Los Angeles 4, Phoenix 3

WEST FINALS

Los Angeles 119, Atlanta 115
Los Angeles 105, Atlanta 94
Los Angeles 115, Atl. 114 (OT)
Los Angeles 133, Atlanta 114

NBA FINALS

New York 124, L.A. 112
Los Angeles 105, N.Y. 103
New York 111, L.A. 108 (OT)
Los Angeles 121, N.Y. 115 (OT)
New York 107, L.A. 100
Los Angeles 135, N.Y. 113
New York 113, L.A. 99

1970-71
FINAL STANDINGS

Eastern Conference
Atlantic Division

	W	L	PCT.	GB
New York	52	30	.634	
Philadelphia	47	35	.573	5
Boston	44	38	.537	8
Buffalo	22	60	.268	30

Central Division

	W	L	PCT.	GB
Baltimore	42	40	.512	
Atlanta	36	46	.439	6
Cincinnati	33	49	.402	9
Cleveland	15	67	.183	27

Western Conference
Midwest Division

	W	L	PCT.	GB
Milwaukee	66	16	.805	
Chicago	51	31	.622	15
Phoenix	48	34	.585	18
Detroit	45	37	.549	21

Pacific Division

	W	L	PCT.	GB
Los Angeles	48	34	.585	
San Francisco	41	41	.500	7
San Diego	40	42	.488	8
Seattle	38	44	.463	10
Portland	29	53	.354	19

SCORING
Lew Alcindor, MIL 31.7
John Havlicek, BOS 28.9
Elvin Hayes, SD 28.7
Dave Bing, DET 27.0
Lou Hudson, ATL 26.8
Bob Love, CHI 25.2
Geoff Petrie, POR 24.8
Pete Maravich, ATL 23.2
Billy Cunningham, PHI 23.0
Tom Van Arsdale, CIN 22.9
Chet Walker, CHI 22.0
Dick Van Arsdale, PHO.....21.9
Walt Frazier, NY................21.7
Earl Monroe, BAL..............21.4
Jo Jo White, BOS..............21.3
Archie Clark, PHI 21.3
Willis Reed, NY 20.9
Connie Hawkins, PHO 20.9
Jeff Mullins, SF 20.8

REBOUNDS
W. Chamberlain, LA..........18.2
Wes Unseld, BAL..............16.9
Elvin Hayes, SD 16.6
Lew Alcindor, MIL 16.0
Jerry Lucas, SF.................15.8
Bill Bridges, ATL 15.0
Dave Cowens, BOS..........15.0
Tom Boerwinkle, CHI 13.8
Nate Thurmond, SF 13.8
Willis Reed, NY 13.7

ASSISTS
Norm Van Lier, CIN...........10.1
Len Wilkens, SEA 9.2
Oscar Robertson, MIL 8.2
John Havlicek, BOS 7.5
Walt Frazier, NY 6.7
Walt Hazzard, ATL 6.3
Ron Williams, SF 5.9
Nate Archibald, CIN 5.5
Archie Clark, PHI 5.4
Dave Bing, DET 5.0

FIELD GOAL PCT.
Johnny Green, CIN............ .587
Lew Alcindor, MIL.............. .577
W. Chamberlain, LA .... .545
Jon McGlocklin, MIL .... .535
Dick Snyder, SEA .... .531
Greg Smith, MIL .... .512
Bob Dandridge, MIL .... .509
Wes Unseld, BAL .... .501
Jerry Lucas, SF .... .498

FREE THROW PCT.
Chet Walker, CHI .... .859
Oscar Robertson, MIL ...... .850
Ron Williams, SF............... .844
Jeff Mullins, SF................. .844
Dick Snyder, SEA.............. .837
Stan McKenzie, POR .... .836
Jerry West, LA................... .832
Jimmy Walker, DET........... .831

EAST SEMIFINALS
New York 4, Atlanta 1
Baltimore 4, Philadelphia 3

EAST FINALS
New York 112, Baltimore 111
New York 107, Baltimore 88
Baltimore 114, New York 88
Baltimore 101, New York 80
New York 89, Baltimore 84
Baltimore 113, New York 96
Baltimore 93, New York 91

WEST SEMIFINALS
Milwaukee 4, San Francisco 1
Los Angeles 4, Chicago 3

WEST FINALS
Milwaukee 106, L.A. 85
Milwaukee 91, Los Angeles 73
Los Angeles 118, Milw. 107
Milwaukee 117, L.A. 94
Milwaukee 116, L.A. 98

NBA FINALS
Milwaukee 98, Baltimore 88
Milwaukee 102, Baltimore 83
Milwaukee 107, Baltimore 99
Milwaukee 118, Baltimore 106

1971-72
FINAL STANDINGS

Eastern Conference
Atlantic Division

	W	L	PCT.	GB
Boston	56	26	.683	
New York	48	34	.585	8
Philadelphia	30	52	.366	26
Buffalo	22	60	.268	34

Central Division

	W	L	PCT.	GB
Baltimore	38	44	.463	
Atlanta	36	46	.439	2
Cincinnati	30	52	.366	8
Cleveland	23	59	.280	15

Western Conference
Midwest Division

	W	L	PCT.	GB
Milwaukee	63	19	.768	
Chicago	57	25	.695	6
Phoenix	49	33	.598	14
Detroit	26	56	.317	37

Pacific Division

	W	L	PCT.	GB
Los Angeles	69	13	.841	
Golden State	51	31	.622	18
Seattle	47	35	.573	22
Houston	34	48	.415	35
Portland	18	64	.220	51

SCORING
K. Abdul-Jabbar, MIL........34.8
Nate Archibald, CIN 28.2
John Havlicek, BOS...........27.5
Spencer Haywood, SEA ...26.2
Gail Goodrich, LA..............25.9
Bob Love, CHI....................25.8
Jerry West, LA...................25.8
Bob Lanier, DET 25.7
Archie Clark, BAL..............25.2
Elvin Hayes, HOU..............25.2
Lou Hudson, ATL................24.7
Sidney Wicks, POR...........24.5
Billy Cunningham, PHI 23.3
Walt Frazier, NY.................23.2
Jo Jo White, BOS...............23.1
Jack Marin, BAL.................22.3
Chet Walker, CHI...............22.0
Jeff Mullins, GS.................21.5
Nate Thurmond, GS..........21.4
Cazzie Russell, GS...........21.4

REBOUNDS
W. Chamberlain, LA...........19.2
Wes Unseld, BAL...............17.6
K. Abdul-Jabbar, MIL..........16.6
Nate Thurmond, GS...........16.1
Dave Cowens, BOS...........15.2
Elmore Smith, BUF.............15.2
Elvin Hayes, HOU..............14.6
Clyde Lee, GS....................14.5
Bob Lanier, DET 14.2

ASSISTS
Jerry West, LA................... 9.7
Len Wilkens, SEA.............. 9.6
Nate Archibald, CIN........... 9.2
Archie Clark, BAL.............. 8.0
John Havlicek, BOS 7.5
Norm Van Lier, CIN/CHI 6.9
Billy Cunningham, PHI 5.9
Jeff Mullins, GS 5.9
Walt Frazier, NY................ 5.8
Walt Hazzard, BUF............ 5.6

FIELD GOAL PCT.
W. Chamberlain, LA 649
K. Abdul-Jabbar, MIL.........574
Walt Bellamy, ATL.............545
Dick Snyder, SEA..............529
Jerry Lucas, NY.................512
Walt Frazier, NY................512
Jon McGlocklin, MIL...........510
Chet Walker, CHI...............505
Lucius Allen, MIL...............505

FREE THROW PCT.
Jack Marin, BAL 894
Calvin Murphy, HOU 890
Gail Goodrich, LA..............850
Chet Walker, CHI 847
Dick Van Arsdale, PHO 845
Stu Lantz, HOU..................838
John Havlicek, BOS 834
Cazzie Russell, GS 833

EAST SEMIFINALS
Boston 4, Atlanta 2
New York 4, Baltimore 2

EAST FINALS
New York 116, Boston 94
New York 106, Boston 105
Boston 115, New York 109
New York 116, Boston 98
New York 111, Boston 103

WEST SEMIFINALS
Los Angeles 4, Chicago 0
Milwaukee 4, Golden St. 1

WEST FINALS
Milwaukee 93, Los Angeles 72
Los Angeles 135, Milw. 134
Los Angeles 108, Milw. 105
Milwaukee 114, L.A. 88
Los Angeles 115, Milw. 90
Los Angeles 104, Milw. 100

NBA FINALS
New York 114, Los Angeles 92
Los Angeles 106, New York 92
Los Angeles 107, New York 96
Los Angeles 116, N.Y. 111 (OT)
Los Angeles 114, N.Y. 100

1972-73
FINAL STANDINGS

Eastern Conference
Atlantic Division

	W	L	PCT.	GB
Boston	68	14	.829	
New York	57	25	.695	11
Buffalo	21	61	.256	47
Philadelphia	9	73	.110	59

Central Division

	W	L	PCT.	GB
Baltimore	52	30	.634	
Atlanta	46	36	.561	6
Houston	33	49	.402	19
Cleveland	32	50	.390	20

Western Conference
Midwest Division

	W	L	PCT.	GB
Milwaukee	60	22	.732	
Chicago	51	31	.622	9
Detroit	40	42	.488	20
K.C.-Omaha	36	46	.439	24

Pacific Division

	W	L	PCT.	GB
Los Angeles	60	22	.732	
Golden State	47	35	.573	13
Phoenix	38	44	.463	22
Seattle	26	56	.317	34
Portland	21	61	.256	39

SCORING
Nate Archibald, KCO.........34.0
K. Abdul-Jabbar, MIL 30.2
Spencer Haywood, SEA ...29.2
Lou Hudson, ATL..............27.1
Pete Maravich, ATL 26.1
Charlie Scott, PHO............25.3
Geoff Petrie, POR.............24.9
Gail Goodrich, LA..............23.9
Sidney Wicks, POR............23.8
Bob Lanier, DET...............23.8
John Havlicek, BOS 23.8
Bob Love, CHI...................23.1
Dave Bing, DET 22.4
Rick Barry, GS 22.3
Elvin Hayes, BAL 21.2
Walt Frazier, NY................21.1
Austin Carr, CLE...............20.5
Dave Cowens, BOS..........20.5
Len Wilkens, CLE 20.5

REBOUNDS
W. Chamberlain, LA..........18.6
Nate Thurmond, GS..........17.1
Dave Cowens, BOS...........16.2
K. Abdul-Jabbar, MIL 16.1
Wes Unseld, BAL..............15.9
Bob Lanier, DET 14.9
Elvin Hayes, BAL 14.5
Walt Bellamy, ATL 13.0
Paul Silas, BOS 13.0
Spencer Haywood, SEA ...12.9

ASSISTS
Nate Archibald, KCO 11.4
Len Wilkens, CLE............. 8.4
Dave Bing, DET 7.8
Oscar Robertson, MIL........ 7.5
Norm Van Lier, CHI 7.1
Pete Maravich, ATL 6.9
John Havlicek, BOS........... 6.6
Herm Gilliam, ATL 6.3
Charlie Scott, PHO 6.1
Jo Jo White, BOS 6.1

FIELD GOAL PCT.
W. Chamberlain, LA 727
Matt Guokas, KCO 570
K. Abdul-Jabbar, MIL 554
Curtis Rowe, DET.............519
Jim Fox, SEA...................515
Jerry Lucas, NY 513
Mike Riordan, BAL 510
Archie Clark, BAL..............507
Bob Kauffman, BUF 505

FREE THROW PCT.
Rick Barry, GS..................902
Calvin Murphy, HOU 888
Mike Newlin, HOU 886
Jimmy Walker, HOU...........884
Bill Bradley, NY 871
Cazzie Russell, GS 864
Dick Snyder, SEA..............861
Dick Van Arsdale, PHO .... .859

EAST SEMIFINALS
Boston 4, Atlanta 2
New York 4, Baltimore 1

EAST FINALS
Boston 134, New York 108
New York 129, Boston 96
New York 98, Boston 91
New York 117, Bost. 110 (2OT)
Boston 98, New York 97
Boston 110, New York 100
New York 94, Boston 78

WEST SEMIFINALS
Los Angeles 4, Chicago 3
Golden St. 4, Milwaukee 2

WEST FINALS
Los Angeles 101, G.S. 99
Los Angeles 104, G.S. 93
Los Angeles 126, G.S. 70
Golden St. 117, L.A. 109
Los Angeles 128, G.S. 118

NBA FINALS
Los Angeles 115, N.Y. 112
New York 99, Los Angeles 95
New York 87, Los Angeles 83
New York 103, Los Angeles 98
New York 102, Los Angeles 93

1973-74
FINAL STANDINGS

Eastern Conference
Atlantic Division

	W	L	PCT.	GB
Boston	56	26	.683	
New York	49	33	.598	7
Buffalo	42	40	.512	14
Philadelphia	25	57	.305	31

Central Division

	W	L	PCT.	GB
Capital	47	35	.573	
Atlanta	35	47	.427	12
Houston	32	50	.390	15
Cleveland	29	53	.354	18

Western Conference
Midwest Division

	W	L	PCT.	GB
Milwaukee	59	23	.720	
Chicago	54	28	.659	5
Detroit	52	30	.634	7
K.C.-Omaha	33	49	.402	26

Pacific Division

	W	L	PCT.	GB
Los Angeles	47	35	.573	
Golden State	44	38	.537	3
Seattle	36	46	.439	11
Phoenix	30	52	.366	17
Portland	27	55	.329	20

SCORING
Bob McAdoo, BUF 30.6
Pete Maravich, ATL 27.7
K. Abdul-Jabbar, MIL 27.0
Gail Goodrich, LA..............25.3
Rick Barry, GS 25.1
Rudy Tomjanovich, HOU ..24.5
Geoff Petrie, POR 24.3
Spencer Haywood, SEA ...23.5
John Havlicek, BOS 22.6
Bob Lanier, DET 22.5

REBOUNDS
Elvin Hayes, CAP...............18.1
Dave Cowens, BOS ...15.7
Bob McAdoo, BUF 15.1
K. Abdul-Jabbar, MIL 14.5
Happy Hairston, LA 13.5
Spencer Haywood, SEA ...13.4
Sam Lacey, KCO 13.4
Bob Lanier, DET 13.3
Clifford Ray, CHI 12.2

ASSISTS
Ernie DiGregorio, BUF 8.2
Calvin Murphy, HOU 7.4
Len Wilkens, CLE.............. 7.1
Walt Frazier, NY 6.9
Dave Bing, DET 6.9
Norm Van Lier, CHI 6.9
Oscar Robertson, MIL 6.4
Rick Barry, GS................... 6.1

STEALS
Larry Steele, POR............2.68
Steve Mix, PHI 2.59
Randy Smith, BUF 2.48
Jerry Sloan, CHI...............2.38
Rick Barry, GS 2.11
Phil Chenier, CAP.............2.04

BLOCKED SHOTS
Elmore Smith, LA 4.85
K. Abdul-Jabbar, MIL 3.49
Bob McAdoo, BUF 3.32
Bob Lanier, DET 3.04
Elvin Hayes, CAP...............2.96
Garfield Heard, BUF 2.84

FIELD GOAL PCT.
Bob McAdoo, BUF............. .547
K. Abdul-Jabbar, MIL........ .539
Rudy Tomjanovich, HOU.. .536
Calvin Murphy, HOU .... .522
Butch Beard, GS .... .512
Clifford Ray, CHI .... .511

FREE THROW PCT.
Ernie DiGregorio, BUF ..... .902
Rick Barry, GS.................. .899
Jeff Mullins, GS................ .875
Chet Walker, CHI .... .875
Bill Bradley, NY .... .874
Calvin Murphy, HOU .... .868

EAST SEMIFINALS
Boston 4, Buffalo 2
New York 4, Capital 3

EAST FINALS
Boston 113, New York 88
Boston 111, New York 99
New York 103, Boston 100
Boston 98, New York 91
Boston 105, New York 94

WEST SEMIFINALS
Milwaukee 4, Los Angeles 1
Chicago 4, Detroit 3

WEST FINALS
Milwaukee 101, Chicago 85
Milwaukee 113, Chicago 111
Milwaukee 113, Chicago 90
Milwaukee 115, Chicago 99

NBA FINALS
Boston 98, Milwaukee 83
Milwaukee 105, Bos. 96 (OT)
Boston 95, Milwaukee 83
Milwaukee 97, Boston 89
Boston 96, Milwaukee 87
Milwaukee 102, Bos. 101 (2OT)
Boston 102, Milwaukee 87

1974-75
FINAL STANDINGS

Eastern Conference
Atlantic Division

	W	L	PCT.	GB
Boston	60	22	.732	
Buffalo	49	33	.598	11
New York	40	42	.488	20
Philadelphia	34	48	.415	26

Central Division

	W	L	PCT.	GB
Washington	60	22	.732	
Houston	41	41	.500	19
Cleveland	40	42	.488	20
Atlanta	31	61	.378	29
New Orleans	23	59	.280	37

Western Conference
Midwest Division

	W	L	PCT.	GB
Chicago	47	35	.573	
K.C.-Omaha	44	38	.537	3
Detroit	40	42	.488	7
Milwaukee	38	44	.463	9

Pacific Division

	W	L	PCT.	GB
Golden State	48	34	.585	
Seattle	43	39	.524	5
Portland	38	44	.463	10
Phoenix	32	50	.390	16
Los Angeles	30	52	.366	18

SCORING
Bob McAdoo, BUF 34.5
Rick Barry, GS 30.6
K. Abdul-Jabbar, MIL 30.0
Nate Archibald, KCO........26.5
Charlie Scott, PHO...........24.3
Bob Lanier, DET 24.0
Elvin Hayes, WAS.............23.0
Gail Goodrich, LA.............22.6
Spencer Haywood, SEA ...22.4
Fred Carter, PHI................21.9

REBOUNDS
Wes Unseld, WAS 14.8
Dave Cowens, BOS..........14.7
Sam Lacey, KCO 14.2
Bob McAdoo, BUF 14.1
K. Abdul-Jabbar, MIL 14.0
Happy Hairston, LA...........12.8
Paul Silas, BOS 12.5
Elvin Hayes, WAS.............12.2
Bob Lanier, DET 12.0

ASSISTS
Kevin Porter, WAS 8.0
Dave Bing, DET.................. 7.7
Nate Archibald, KCO 6.8
Randy Smith, BUF.............. 6.5
Pete Maravich, NO 6.2
Rick Barry, GS................... 6.2
Slick Watts, SEA 6.1

STEALS
Rick Barry, GS 2.85
Walt Frazier, NY................2.44
Larry Steele, POR.............2.41
Slick Watts, SEA 2.32
Fred Brown, SEA 2.31
Phil Chenier, WAS 2.29

BLOCKED SHOTS
K. Abdul-Jabbar, MIL 3.26
Elmore Smith, LA 2.92
Nate Thurmond, CHI..........2.44
Elvin Hayes, WAS..............2.28
Bob Lanier, DET 2.26
Bob McAdoo, BUF 2.12

FIELD GOAL PCT.
Don Nelson, BOS .... .539
Butch Beard, GS .... .528
Rudy Tomjanovich, HOU... .525
K. Abdul-Jabbar, MIL........ .513
Bob McAdoo, BUF............. .512
Kevin Kunnert, HOU .... .512

FREE THROW PCT.
Rick Barry, GS................... .904
Calvin Murphy, HOU .... .883
Bill Bradley, NY .... .873
Nate Archibald, KCO .... .872
Jim Price, LA/MIL .... .871
John Havlicek, BOS .... .870

EAST FIRST ROUND
Houston 2, New York 1

EAST SEMIFINALS
Washington 4, Buffalo 3
Boston 4, Houston 1

EAST FINALS
Washington 4, Boston 2

WEST FIRST ROUND
Seattle 2, Detroit 1

WEST SEMIFINALS
Golden St. 4, Seattle 2
Chicago 4, K.C.-Omaha 2

WEST FINALS
Golden St. 4, Chicago 3

NBA FINALS
Golden St. 101, Washington 95
Golden St. 92, Washington 91
Golden St. 109, Wash. 101
Golden St. 96, Washington 95

1975-76
FINAL STANDINGS

Eastern Conference
Atlantic Division

	W	L	PCT.	GB
Boston	54	28	.659	
Buffalo	46	36	.561	8
Philadelphia	46	36	.561	8
New York	38	44	.463	16

Central Division

	W	L	PCT.	GB
Cleveland	49	33	.598	
Washington	48	34	.585	1
Houston	40	42	.488	9
New Orleans	38	44	.463	11
Atlanta	29	53	.354	20

Western Conference
Midwest Division

	W	L	PCT.	GB
Milwaukee	38	44	.463	
Detroit	36	46	.439	2
Kansas City	31	51	.378	7
Chicago	24	58	.293	14

Pacific Division

	W	L	PCT.	GB
Golden State	59	23	.720	
Seattle	43	39	.524	16
Phoenix	42	40	.512	17
Los Angeles	40	42	.488	19
Portland	37	45	.451	22

SCORING
Bob McAdoo, BUF 31.1
K. Abdul-Jabbar, LA........27.7
Pete Maravich, NO...........25.9
Nate Archibald, KC 24.8
Fred Brown, SEA...............23.1
George McGinnis, PHI......23.0
Randy Smith, BUF.............21.8
John Drew, ATL................21.6
Bob Dandridge, MIL..........21.5
Rick Barry, GS 21.0

REBOUNDS
K. Abdul-Jabbar, LA........16.9
Dave Cowens, BOS..........16.0
Wes Unseld, WAS 13.3
Paul Silas, BOS 12.7
Sam Lacey, KC 12.6
George McGinnis, PHI......12.6
Bob McAdoo, BUF.............12.4
Elmore Smith, MIL 11.4
Spencer Haywood, NY......11.3

ASSISTS
Slick Watts, SEA 8.1
Nate Archibald, KC........... 7.9
Calvin Murphy, HOU 7.3
Norm Van Lier, CHI........... 6.6
Rick Barry, GS.................. 6.1
Dave Bing, WAS................ 6.0
Randy Smith, BUF............. 5.9

STEALS
Slick Watts, SEA...............3.18
George McGinnis, PHI......2.57
Paul Westphal, PHO.........2.56
Rick Barry, GS 2.49
Chris Ford, DET................2.17
Larry Steele, POR............2.10

BLOCKED SHOTS
K. Abdul-Jabbar, LA........4.12
Elmore Smith, MIL 3.05
Elvin Hayes, WAS............2.53
Harvey Catchings, PHI.....2.19
George Johnson, GS........2.12
Bob McAdoo, BUF 2.05

FIELD GOAL PCT.
Wes Unseld, WAS ..... .56085
John Shumate, BUF ..... .56081
Jim McMillian, BUF........... .536
Bob Lanier, DET............... .532
K. Abdul-Jabbar, LA .... .529
Elmore Smith, MIL............ .518

FREE THROW PCT.
Rick Barry, GS................... .923
Calvin Murphy, HOU .... .907
Cazzie Russell, LA .... .892
Bill Bradley, NY .... .878
Fred Brown, SEA.............. .869
Mike Newlin, HOU............. .865

EAST FIRST ROUND
Buffalo 2, Philadelphia 1

EAST SEMIFINALS
Boston 4, Buffalo 2
Cleveland 4, Washington 3

EAST FINALS
Boston 4, Cleveland 2

WEST FIRST ROUND
Detroit 2, Milwaukee 1

WEST SEMIFINALS
Golden St. 4, Detroit 2
Phoenix 4, Seattle 2

WEST FINALS
Phoenix 4, Golden St. 3

NBA FINALS
Boston 98, Phoenix 87
Boston 105, Phoenix 90
Phoenix 105, Boston 98
Phoenix 109, Boston 107
Boston 128, Phoe. 126 (3OT)
Boston 87, Phoenix 80

1976-77
FINAL STANDINGS

Eastern Conference
Atlantic Division

	W	L	PCT.	GB
Philadelphia	50	32	.610	
Boston	44	38	.537	6
N.Y. Knicks	40	42	.488	10
Buffalo	30	52	.366	20
N.Y. Nets	22	60	.288	28

Central Division

	W	L	PCT.	GB
Houston	49	33	.598	
Washington	48	34	.585	1
San Antonio	44	38	.537	5
Cleveland	43	39	.524	6
New Orleans	35	47	.427	14
Atlanta	31	51	.378	18

Western Conference
Midwest Division

	W	L	PCT.	GB
Denver	50	32	.610	
Detroit	44	38	.537	6
Chicago	44	38	.537	6
Kansas City	40	42	.488	10
Indiana	36	46	.439	14
Milwaukee	30	52	.366	20

Pacific Division

	W	L	PCT.	GB
Los Angeles	53	29	.646	
Portland	49	33	.598	4
Golden State	46	36	.561	7
Seattle	40	42	.488	13
Phoenix	34	48	.415	19

SCORING
Pete Maravich, NO............31.1
Billy Knight, IND..............26.6
K. Abdul-Jabbar, LA........26.2
David Thompson, DEN 25.9
Bob McAdoo, BUF/NYK.....25.8
Bob Lanier, DET 25.3
John Drew, ATL 24.2
Elvin Hayes, WAS............23.7
George Gervin, SA............23.1
Dan Issel, DEN 22.3

REBOUNDS
Bill Walton, POR 14.4
K. Abdul-Jabbar, LA..........13.3
Moses Malone, BUF/HOU 13.1
Artis Gilmore, CHI............13.0
Bob McAdoo, BUF/NYK......12.9
Elvin Hayes, WAS.............12.5
Swen Nater, MIL...............12.0
George McGinnis, PHI......11.5

ASSISTS
Don Buse, IND 8.5
Slick Watts, SEA 8.0
Norm Van Lier, CHI 7.8
Kevin Porter, DET 7.3
Tom Henderson, ATL/WAS... 6.9
Rick Barry, GS.................. 6.0
Jo Jo White, BOS 6.0

STEALS
Don Buse, IND 3.47
Brian Taylor, KC...............2.76
Slick Watts, SEA..............2.71
Quinn Buckner, MIL 2.43
Mike Gale, SA..................2.33
Bobby Jones, DEN............2.27

BLOCKED SHOTS
Bill Walton, POR 3.25
K. Abdul-Jabbar, LA..........3.18
Elvin Hayes, WAS.............2.68
Artis Gilmore, CHI............2.48
Caldwell Jones, PHI..........2.44
George Johnson, GS/BUF ...2.27

FIELD GOAL PCT.
K. Abdul-Jabbar, LA .... .579
Mitch Kupchak, WAS........ .572
Bobby Jones, DEN .... .570
George Gervin, SA........... .544
Bob Lanier, DET .... .534
Bob Gross, POR............... .529

FREE THROW PCT.
Ernie DiGregorio, BUF ..... .945
Rick Barry, GS................. .916
Calvin Murphy, HOU .... .886
Mike Newlin, HOU .... .885
Fred Brown, SEA.............. .884

EAST FIRST ROUND
Washington 2, Cleveland 1
Boston 2, San Antonio 0

EAST SEMIFINALS
Philadelphia 4, Boston 3
Houston 4, Washington 2

EAST FINALS
Philadelphia 4, Houston 2

WEST FIRST ROUND
Portland 2, Chicago 1
Golden St. 2, Detroit 1

WEST SEMIFINALS
Los Angeles 4, Golden St. 3
Portland 4, Denver 2

WEST FINALS
Portland 4, Los Angeles 0

NBA FINALS
Philadelphia 107, Portland 101
Philadelphia 107, Portland 89
Portland 129, Philadelphia 107
Portland 130, Philadelphia 98
Portland 110, Philadelphia 104
Portland 109, Philadelphia 107

1977-78
FINAL STANDINGS

Eastern Conference
Atlantic Division

	W	L	PCT.	GB
Philadelphia	55	27	.671	
New York	43	39	.524	12
Boston	32	50	.390	23
Buffalo	27	55	.329	28
New Jersey	24	58	.293	31

Central Division

	W	L	PCT.	GB
San Antonio	52	30	.634	
Washington	44	38	.537	8
Cleveland	43	39	.524	9
Atlanta	41	41	.500	11
New Orleans	39	43	.476	13
Houston	28	54	.341	24

Western Conference
Midwest Division

	W	L	PCT.	GB
Denver	48	34	.585	
Milwaukee	44	38	.537	4
Chicago	40	42	.488	8
Detroit	38	44	.463	10
Indiana	31	51	.378	17
Kansas City	31	51	.378	17

Pacific Division

	W	L	PCT.	GB
Portland	58	24	.707	
Phoenix	49	33	.598	9
Seattle	47	35	.573	11
Los Angeles	45	37	.549	13
Golden State	43	39	.524	15

SCORING
George Gervin, SA 27.22
David Thompson, DEN 27.15
Bob McAdoo, NY 26.5
K. Abdul-Jabbar, LA 25.8
Calvin Murphy, HOU 25.6
Paul Westphal, PHO 25.2
Randy Smith, BUF 24.6
Bob Lanier, DET 24.5
Walter Davis, PHO..............24.2
Bernard King, NJ 24.2

REBOUNDS
Truck Robinson, NO 15.7
Moses Malone, HOU..........15.0
Dave Cowens, BOS..........14.0
Elvin Hayes, WAS..............13.3
Swen Nater, BUF 13.2
Artis Gilmore, CHI 13.1
K. Abdul-Jabbar, LA 12.9
Bob McAdoo, NY 12.8

ASSISTS
Kevin Porter, DET/NJ..........10.2
John Lucas, HOU 9.4
Ricky Sobers, IND 7.4
Norm Nixon, LA 6.8
Norm Van Lier, CHI 6.8
Henry Bibby, PHI................5.7

STEALS
Ron Lee, PHO....................2.74
Gus Williams, SEA.............2.34
Quinn Buckner, MIL............2.29
Mike Gale, SA....................2.27
Don Buse, PHO 2.26
Foots Walker, CLE.............2.17

BLOCKED SHOTS
George Johnson, NJ 3.38
K. Abdul-Jabbar, LA...........2.98
Tree Rollins, ATL................2.73
Bill Walton, POR 2.52
Billy Paultz, SA...................2.43
Artis Gilmore, CHI 2.21

FIELD GOAL PCT.
Bobby Jones, DEN 578
Darryl Dawkins, PHI .... .575
Artis Gilmore, CHI 559
K. Abdul-Jabbar, LA .... .550
Alex English, MIL................542

FREE THROW PCT.
Rick Barry, GS...................924
Calvin Murphy, HOU 918
Fred Brown, SEA...............898
Mike Newlin, HOU .... .874
Scott Wedman, KC............870

EAST FIRST ROUND
Washington 2, Atlanta 0
New York 2, Cleveland 0

EAST SEMIFINALS
Philadelphia 4, New York 0
Washington 4, San Antonio 2

EAST FINALS
Washington 4, Philadelphia 2

WEST FIRST ROUND
Seattle 2, Los Angeles 1
Milwaukee 2, Phoenix 0

WEST SEMIFINALS
Seattle 4, Portland 2
Denver 4, Milwaukee 3

WEST FINALS
Seattle 4, Denver 2

NBA FINALS
Seattle 106, Washington 102
Washington 106, Seattle 98
Seattle 93, Washington 92
Washington 120, Seat. 116 (OT)
Seattle 98, Washington 94
Washington 117, Seattle 82
Washington 105, Seattle 99

1978-79
FINAL STANDINGS

Eastern Conference
Atlantic Division

	W	L	PCT.	GB
Washington	54	28	.659	
Philadelphia	47	35	.573	7
New Jersey	37	45	.451	17
New York	31	51	.378	23
Boston	29	53	.354	25

Central Division

	W	L	PCT.	GB
San Antonio	48	34	.585	
Houston	47	35	.573	1
Atlanta	46	36	.561	2
Cleveland	30	52	.366	18
Detroit	30	52	.366	18
New Orleans	26	56	.317	22

Western Conference
Midwest Division

	W	L	PCT.	GB
Kansas City	48	34	.585	
Denver	47	35	.573	1
Indiana	38	44	.463	10
Milwaukee	38	44	.463	10
Chicago	31	51	.378	17

Pacific Division

	W	L	PCT.	GB
Seattle	52	30	.634	
Phoenix	50	32	.610	2
Los Angeles	47	35	.573	5
Portland	45	37	.549	7
San Diego	43	39	.524	9
Golden State	38	44	.463	14

SCORING
George Gervin, SA............29.6
Lloyd Free, SD.................28.8
Marques Johnson, MIL 25.6
Bob McAdoo, NY/BOS 24.8
Moses Malone, HOU......24.8
David Thompson, DEN 24.0
Paul Westphal, PHO.........24.0
K. Abdul-Jabbar, LA 23.8
Artis Gilmore, CHI 23.7
Walter Davis, PHO............23.6

REBOUNDS
Moses Malone, HOU........17.6
Rich Kelley, NO................12.8
K. Abdul-Jabbar, LA.........12.8
Artis Gilmore, CHI 12.7
Jack Sikma, SEA 12.4
Elvin Hayes, WAS.............12.1
Robert Parish, GS.............12.1

ASSISTS
Kevin Porter, DET 13.4
John Lucas, GS 9.3
Norm Nixon, LA.................. 9.0
Phil Ford, KC...................... 8.6
Paul Westphal, PHO.......... 6.5
Rick Barry, HOU 6.3

STEALS
M.L. Carr, DET..................2.46
Ed Jordan, NJ 2.45
Norm Nixon, LA.................2.45
Foots Walker, CLE............2.36
Phil Ford, KC....................2.20
Randy Smith, SD 2.16

BLOCKED SHOTS
K. Abdul-Jabbar, LA..........3.95
George Johnson, NJ.........3.24
Tree Rollins, ATL 3.14
Robert Parish, GS.............2.86
Terry Tyler, DET 2.45

FIELD GOAL PCT.
Cedric Maxwell, BOS .... .584
K. Abdul-Jabbar, LA .... .577
Wes Unseld, WAS............. .577
Artis Gilmore, CHI .... .575
Swen Nater, SD................ .569

FREE THROW PCT.
Rick Barry, HOU............... .947
Calvin Murphy, HOU .... .928
Fred Brown, SEA.............. .888
Robert Smith, DEN........... .883
Ricky Sobers, IND .... .882

EAST FIRST ROUND
Philadelphia 2, New Jersey 0
Atlanta 2, Houston 0

EAST SEMIFINALS
Washington 4, Atlanta 3
San Antonio 4, Philadelphia 3

EAST FINALS
Washington 4, San Antonio 3

WEST FIRST ROUND
Phoenix 2, Portland 1
Los Angeles 2, Denver 1

WEST SEMIFINALS
Seattle 4, Los Angeles 1
Phoenix 4, Kansas City 1

WEST FINALS
Seattle 4, Phoenix 3

NBA FINALS
Washington 99, Seattle 97
Seattle 92, Washington 82
Seattle 105, Washington 95
Seattle 114, Wash. 112 (OT)
Seattle 97, Washington 93

1979-80
FINAL STANDINGS

Eastern Conference
Atlantic Division

	W	L	PCT.	GB
Boston	61	21	.744	
Philadelphia	59	23	.720	2
Washington	39	43	.476	22
New York	39	43	.476	22
New Jersey	34	48	.415	27

Central Division

	W	L	PCT.	GB
Atlanta	50	32	.610	
Houston	41	41	.500	9
San Antonio	41	41	.500	9
Indiana	37	45	.451	13
Cleveland	37	45	.451	13
Detroit	16	66	.195	34

Western Conference
Midwest Division

	W	L	PCT.	GB
Milwaukee	49	33	.598	
Kansas City	47	35	.573	2
Denver	30	52	.366	19
Chicago	30	52	.366	19
Utah	24	58	.293	25

Pacific Division

	W	L	PCT.	GB
Los Angeles	60	22	.732	
Seattle	56	26	.683	4
Phoenix	55	27	.671	5
Portland	38	44	.463	22
San Diego	35	47	.427	25
Golden State	24	58	.293	36

SCORING

George Gervin, SA	33.1
Lloyd Free, SD	30.2
Adrian Dantley, UTA	28.0
Julius Erving, PHI	26.9
Moses Malone, HOU	25.8
K. Abdul-Jabbar, LA	24.8
Dan Issel, DEN	23.8
Elvin Hayes, WAS	23.0
Otis Birdsong, KC	22.7
Mike Mitchell, CLE	22.2

REBOUNDS

Swen Nater, SD	15.0
Moses Malone, HOU	14.5
Wes Unseld, WAS	13.3
Caldwell Jones, PHI	11.9
Jack Sikma, SEA	11.1

ASSISTS

Micheal Richardson, NY	10.1
Nate Archibald, BOS	8.4
Foots Walker, CLE	8.0
Norm Nixon, LA	7.8
John Lucas, GS	7.5

STEALS

Micheal Richardson, NY	3.23
Ed Jordan, NJ	2.72
Dudley Bradley, IND	2.57
Gus Williams, SEA	2.44
Magic Johnson, LA	2.43

BLOCKED SHOTS

K. Abdul-Jabbar, LA	3.41
George Johnson, NJ	3.19
Tree Rollins, ATL	2.98
Terry Tyler, DET	2.68
Elvin Hayes, WAS	2.33

FIELD GOAL PCT.

Cedric Maxwell, BOS	.609
K. Abdul-Jabbar, LA	.604
Artis Gilmore, CHI	.595
Adrian Dantley, UTA	.576
Tom Boswell, DEN/UTA	.564

FREE THROW PCT.

Rick Barry, HOU	.935
Calvin Murphy, HOU	.897
Ron Boone, UTA	.893
Paul Silas, SA	.887

3-PT. FIELD GOAL PCT.

Fred Brown, SEA	.443
Chris Ford, BOS	.427
Larry Bird, BOS	.406
John Roche, DEN	.380

EAST FIRST ROUND
Philadelphia 2, Washington 0
Houston 2, San Antonio 1

EAST SEMIFINALS
Boston 4, Houston 0
Philadelphia 4, Atlanta 1

EAST FINALS
Philadelphia 4, Boston 1

WEST FIRST ROUND
Seattle 2, Portland 1
Phoenix 2, Kansas City 1

WEST SEMIFINALS
Los Angeles 4, Phoenix 1
Seattle 4, Milwaukee 3

WEST FINALS
Los Angeles 4, Seattle 1

NBA FINALS
Los Angeles 109, Phil. 102
Philadelphia 107, L.A. 104
Los Angeles 111, Phil. 101
Philadelphia 105, L.A. 102
Los Angeles 108, Phil. 103
Los Angeles 123, Phil. 107

1980-81
FINAL STANDINGS

Eastern Conference

Atlantic Division

	W	L	PCT.	GB
Boston	62	20	.756	
Philadelphia	62	20	.756	
New York	50	32	.610	12
Washington	39	43	.476	23
New Jersey	24	58	.293	38

Central Division

	W	L	PCT.	GB
Milwaukee	60	22	.732	
Chicago	45	37	.549	15
Indiana	44	38	.537	16
Atlanta	31	51	.378	29
Cleveland	28	54	.341	32
Detroit	21	61	.256	39

Western Conference

Midwest Division

	W	L	PCT.	GB
San Antonio	52	30	.634	
Kansas City	40	42	.488	12
Houston	40	42	.488	12
Denver	37	45	.451	15
Utah	28	54	.341	24
Dallas	15	67	.183	37

Pacific Division

	W	L	PCT.	GB
Phoenix	57	25	.695	
Los Angeles	54	28	.659	3
Portland	45	37	.549	12
Golden State	39	43	.476	18
San Diego	36	46	.439	21
Seattle	34	48	.415	23

SCORING
Adrian Dantley, UTA 30.7
Moses Malone, HOU.........27.8
George Gervin, SA............27.1
K. Abdul-Jabbar, LA..........26.2
David Thompson, DEN 25.5
Otis Birdsong, KC 24.6
Julius Erving, PHI..............24.6
Mike Mitchell, CLE............24.5
Lloyd Free, GS..................24.1
Alex English, DEN.............23.8

REBOUNDS
Moses Malone, HOU........14.8
Swen Nater, SD 12.4
Larry Smith, GS................12.1
Larry Bird, BOS.................10.9
Jack Sikma, SEA 10.4

ASSISTS
Kevin Porter, WAS 9.1
Norm Nixon, LA................. 8.8
Phil Ford, KC 8.8
Micheal Richardson, NY 7.9
Nate Archibald, BOS 7.7

STEALS
Magic Johnson, LA 3.43
Micheal Richardson, NY ...2.94

Quinn Buckner, MIL 2.40
Maurice Cheeks, PHI 2.38
Ray Williams, NY 2.34

BLOCKED SHOTS
George Johnson, SA........3.39
Tree Rollins, ATL 2.93
K. Abdul-Jabbar, LA..........2.85
Robert Parish, BOS 2.61
Artis Gilmore, CHI 2.41

FIELD GOAL PCT.
Artis Gilmore, CHI .... .670
Darryl Dawkins, PHI .... .607
Cedric Maxwell, BOS .... .588
Bernard King, GS .... .588
K. Abdul-Jabbar, LA .... .574

FREE THROW PCT.
Calvin Murphy, HOU .... .958
Ricky Sobers, CHI .... .935
Mike Newlin, NJ................ .888
Jim Spanarkel, DAL.......... .887

3-PT. FIELD GOAL PCT.
Brian Taylor, SD .... .383
Freeman Williams, SD...... .340
Joe Hassett, DAL/GS........... .340
Mike Bratz, CLE .... .337

EAST FIRST ROUND
Philadelphia 2, Indiana 0
Chicago 2, New York 0

EAST SEMIFINALS
Boston 4, Chicago 0
Philadelphia 4, Milwaukee 3

EAST FINALS
Boston 4, Philadelphia 3

WEST FIRST ROUND
Houston 2, Los Angeles 1
Kansas City 2, Portland 1

WEST SEMIFINALS
Kansas City 4, Phoenix 3
Houston 4, San Antonio 3

WEST FINALS
Houston 4, Kansas City 1

NBA FINALS
Boston 98, Houston 95
Houston 92, Boston 90
Boston 94, Houston 71
Houston 91, Boston 86
Boston 109, Houston 80
Boston 102, Houston 91

1981-82
FINAL STANDINGS

Eastern Conference
Atlantic Division

	W	L	PCT.	GB
Boston	63	19	.768	
Philadelphia	58	24	.707	5
New Jersey	44	38	.537	19
Washington	43	39	.524	20
New York	33	49	.402	30

Central Division

	W	L	PCT.	GB
Milwaukee	55	27	.671	
Atlanta	42	40	.512	13
Detroit	39	43	.476	16
Indiana	35	47	.427	20
Chicago	34	48	.415	21
Cleveland	15	67	.183	40

Western Conference
Midwest Division

	W	L	PCT.	GB
San Antonio	48	34	.585	
Denver	46	36	.561	2
Houston	46	36	.561	2
Kansas City	30	52	.366	18
Dallas	28	54	.341	20
Utah	25	57	.305	23

Pacific Division

	W	L	PCT.	GB
Los Angeles	57	25	.695	
Seattle	52	30	.634	5
Phoenix	46	36	.561	11
Golden State	45	37	.549	12
Portland	42	40	.512	15
San Diego	17	65	.207	40

SCORING
George Gervin, SA.............32.3
Moses Malone, HOU.........31.1
Adrian Dantley, UTA 30.3
Alex English, DEN.............25.4
Julius Erving, PHI..............24.4
K. Abdul-Jabbar, LA..........23.9
Gus Williams, SEA.............23.4
Bernard King, GS..............23.2
World B. Free, GS..............22.9
Larry Bird, BOS.................22.9

REBOUNDS
Moses Malone, HOU.........14.7
Jack Sikma, SEA................12.7
Buck Williams, NJ.............12.3
Mychal Thompson, POR....11.7
Maurice Lucas, NY............11.3

ASSISTS
Johnny Moore, SA.............. 9.6
Magic Johnson, LA.............. 9.5
Maurice Cheeks, PHI 8.4
Nate Archibald, BOS 8.0
Norm Nixon, LA................... 8.0

STEALS
Magic Johnson, LA............2.67
Maurice Cheeks, PHI 2.65

Micheal Richardson, NY ...2.60
Quinn Buckner, MIL 2.49
Ray Williams, NJ................2.43

BLOCKED SHOTS
George Johnson, SA...........3.12
Tree Rollins, ATL 2.84
K. Abdul-Jabbar, LA..........2.72
Artis Gilmore, CHI 2.70
Robert Parish, BOS 2.40

FIELD GOAL PCT.
Artis Gilmore, CHI .... .652
Steve Johnson, KC............ .613
Buck Williams, NJ............. .582
K. Abdul-Jabbar, LA .... .579
Calvin Natt, POR............... .576

FREE THROW PCT.
Kyle Macy, PHO .... .899
Charlie Criss, SD .... .887
John Long, DET .... .865
George Gervin, SA .... .864

3-PT. FIELD GOAL PCT.
Campy Russell, NY .... .439
Andrew Toney, PHI .... .424
Kyle Macy, PHO .... .390
Brian Winters, MIL............. .387

EAST FIRST ROUND
Philadelphia 2, Atlanta 0
Washington 2, New Jersey 0

EAST SEMIFINALS
Boston 4, Washington 1
Philadelphia 4, Milwaukee 2

EAST FINALS
Philadelphia 4, Boston 3

WEST FIRST ROUND
Seattle 2, Houston 1
Phoenix 2, Denver 1

WEST SEMIFINALS
Los Angeles 4, Phoenix 0
San Antonio 4, Seattle 1

WEST FINALS
Los Angeles 4, San Antonio 0

NBA FINALS
Los Angeles 124, Phil. 117
Philadelphia 110, L.A. 94
Los Angeles 129, Phil. 108
Los Angeles 111, Phil. 101
Philadelphia 135, L.A. 102
Los Angeles 114, Phil. 104

1982-83
FINAL STANDINGS

Eastern Conference
Atlantic Division

	W	L	PCT.	GB
Philadelphia	65	17	.793	
Boston	56	26	.683	9
New Jersey	49	33	.598	16
New York	44	38	.537	21
Washington	42	40	.512	23

Central Division

	W	L	PCT.	GB
Milwaukee	51	31	.622	
Atlanta	43	39	.524	8
Detroit	37	45	.451	14
Chicago	28	54	.341	23
Cleveland	23	59	.280	28
Indiana	20	62	.244	31

Western Conference
Midwest Division

	W	L	PCT.	GB
San Antonio	53	29	.646	
Denver	45	37	.549	8
Kansas City	45	37	.549	8
Dallas	38	44	.463	15
Utah	30	52	.366	23
Houston	14	68	.171	39

Pacific Division

	W	L	PCT.	GB
Los Angeles	58	24	.707	
Phoenix	53	29	.646	5
Seattle	48	34	.585	10
Portland	46	36	.561	12
Golden State	30	52	.366	28
San Diego	25	57	.305	33

SCORING
Alex English, DEN.............28.4
Kiki Vandeweghe, DEN.....26.7
Kelly Tripucka, DET 26.5
George Gervin, SA............26.2
Moses Malone, PHI...........24.5
Mark Aguirre, DAL.............24.4
Joe Barry Carroll, GS........24.1
World B. Free, GS/CLE......23.9
Reggie Theus, CHI 23.8
Terry Cummings, SD 23.7

REBOUNDS
Moses Malone, PHI...........15.3
Buck Williams, NJ 12.5
Bill Laimbeer, DET 12.1
Artis Gilmore, SA 12.0
Jack Sikma, SEA 11.4

ASSISTS
Magic Johnson, LA 10.5
Johnny Moore, SA............. 9.8
Rickey Green, UTA 8.9
Larry Drew, KC 8.1
Frank Johnson, WAS 8.1

STEALS
Micheal Richardson, GS/NJ...2.84
Rickey Green, UTA...........2.82

Johnny Moore, SA 2.52
Isiah Thomas, DET 2.46
Darwin Cook, NJ................2.37

BLOCKED SHOTS
Tree Rollins, ATL 4.29
Bill Walton, POR 3.61
Mark Eaton, UTA 3.40
Larry Nance, PHO.............2.65
Artis Gilmore, CHI 2.34

FIELD GOAL PCT.
Artis Gilmore, SA............... .626
Steve Johnson, KC............ .624
Darryl Dawkins, NJ............ .599
K. Abdul-Jabbar, LA .... .588
Buck Williams, NJ.............. .588

FREE THROW PCT.
Calvin Murphy, HOU .... .920
Kiki Vandeweghe, DEN..... .875
Kyle Macy, PHO .... .872
George Gervin, SA............ .853

3-PT. FIELD GOAL PCT.
Mike Dunleavy, SA............ .345
Isiah Thomas, DET............ .288
Darrell Griffith, UTA........... .288
Allen Leavell, HOU .... .240

EAST FIRST ROUND
Boston 2, Atlanta 1
New York 2, New Jersey 0

EAST SEMIFINALS
Philadelphia 4, New York 0
Milwaukee 4, Boston 0

EAST FINALS
Philadelphia 4, Milwaukee 1

WEST FIRST ROUND
Denver 2, Phoenix 1
Portland 2, Seattle 0

WEST SEMIFINALS
Los Angeles 4, Portland 1
San Antonio 4, Denver 1

WEST FINALS
Los Angeles 4, San Antonio 2

NBA FINALS
Philadelphia 113, L.A. 107
Philadelphia 103, L.A. 93
Philadelphia 111, L.A. 94
Philadelphia 115, L.A. 108

1983-84
FINAL STANDINGS

Eastern Conference
Atlantic Division

	W	L	PCT.	GB
Boston	62	20	.756	
Philadelphia	52	30	.634	10
New York	47	35	.573	15
New Jersey	45	37	.549	17
Washington	35	47	.427	27

Central Division

	W	L	PCT.	GB
Milwaukee	50	32	.610	
Detroit	49	33	.598	1
Atlanta	40	42	.488	10
Cleveland	28	54	.341	22
Chicago	27	55	.329	23
Indiana	26	56	.317	24

Western Conference
Midwest Division

	W	L	PCT.	GB
Utah	45	37	.549	
Dallas	43	39	.524	2
Denver	38	44	.463	7
Kansas City	38	44	.463	7
San Antonio	37	45	.451	8
Houston	29	53	.354	16

Pacific Division

	W	L	PCT.	GB
Los Angeles	54	28	.659	
Portland	48	34	.585	6
Seattle	42	40	.512	12
Phoenix	41	41	.500	13
Golden State	37	45	.451	17
San Diego	30	52	.366	24

SCORING
Adrian Dantley, UTA 30.6
Mark Aguirre, DAL 29.5
Kiki Vandeweghe, DEN....29.4
Alex English, DEN............26.4
Bernard King, NY 26.3
George Gervin, SA............25.9
Larry Bird, BOS................24.2
Mike Mitchell, SA 23.3
Terry Cummings, SD 22.9
Purvis Short, GS 22.8

REBOUNDS
Moses Malone, PHI..........13.4
Buck Williams, NJ 12.3
Jeff Ruland, WAS.............12.3
Bill Laimbeer, DET 12.2
Ralph Sampson, HOU 11.1

ASSISTS
Magic Johnson, LA 13.1
Norm Nixon, SD...............11.1
Isiah Thomas, DET 11.1
John Lucas, SA................10.7
Johnny Moore, SA............ 9.6

STEALS
Rickey Green, UTA 2.65
Isiah Thomas, DET 2.49

Gus Williams, SEA............2.36
Maurice Cheeks, PHI 2.28
Magic Johnson, LA 2.24

BLOCKED SHOTS
Mark Eaton, UTA 4.28
Tree Rollins, ATL 3.60
Ralph Sampson, HOU 2.40
Larry Nance, PHO............2.11
Artis Gilmore, SA 2.06

FIELD GOAL PCT.
Artis Gilmore, SA..............631
James Donaldson, SD.......596
Mike McGee, LA...............594
Darryl Dawkins, NJ...........593
Calvin Natt, POR 583

FREE THROW PCT.
Larry Bird, BOS 888
John Long, DET 884
Bill Laimbeer, DET 866
Walter Davis, PHO 863

3-PT. FIELD GOAL PCT.
Darrell Griffith, UTA...........361
Mike Evans, DEN..............360
Johnny Moore, SA.............322
Michael Cooper, LA...........314

EAST FIRST ROUND
Boston 3, Washington 1
Milwaukee 3, Atlanta 2
New Jersey 3 Philadelphia 2
New York 3, Detroit 2
EAST SEMIFINALS
Boston 4, New York 3
Milwaukee 4, New Jersey 2
EAST FINALS
Boston 4, Milwaukee 1
WEST FIRST ROUND
Los Angeles 3, Kansas City 0
Utah 3, Denver 2
Phoenix 3, Portland 2
Dallas 3, Seattle 2
WEST SEMIFINALS
Los Angeles 4, Dallas 1
Phoenix 4, Utah 2
WEST FINALS
Los Angeles 4, Phoenix 2
NBA FINALS
Los Angeles 115, Boston 109
Boston 124, L.A. 121 (OT)
Los Angeles 137, Boston 104
Boston 129, L.A. 125 (OT)
Boston 121, Los Angeles 103
Los Angeles 119, Boston 108
Boston 111, Los Angeles 102

1984-85
FINAL STANDINGS

Eastern Conference
Atlantic Division

	W	L	PCT.	GB
Boston	63	19	.768	
Philadelphia	58	24	.707	5
New Jersey	42	40	.512	21
Washington	40	42	.488	23
New York	24	58	.293	39

Central Division

	W	L	PCT.	GB
Milwaukee	59	23	.720	
Detroit	46	36	.561	13
Chicago	38	44	.463	21
Cleveland	36	46	.439	23
Atlanta	34	48	.415	25
Indiana	22	60	.268	37

Western Conference
Midwest Division

	W	L	PCT.	GB
Denver	52	30	.634	
Houston	48	34	.585	4
Dallas	44	38	.537	8
San Antonio	41	41	.500	11
Utah	41	41	.500	11
Kansas City	31	51	.378	21

Pacific Division

	W	L	PCT.	GB
L.A. Lakers	62	20	.756	
Portland	42	40	.512	20
Phoenix	36	46	.439	26
L.A. Clippers	31	51	.378	31
Seattle	31	51	.378	31
Golden State	22	60	.268	40

SCORING
Bernard King, NY 32.9
Larry Bird, BOS................28.7
Michael Jordan, CHI 28.2
Purvis Short, GS 28.0
Alex English, DEN.............27.9
Dominique Wilkins, ATL.....27.4
Adrian Dantley, UTA 26.6
Mark Aguirre, DAL 25.7
Moses Malone, PHI..........24.6
Terry Cummings, MIL 23.6

REBOUNDS
Moses Malone, PHI..........13.1
Bill Laimbeer, DET............12.4
Buck Williams, NJ 12.3
Akeem Olajuwon, HOU......11.9
Mark Eaton, UTA 11.3

ASSISTS
Isiah Thomas, DET............13.9
Magic Johnson, LAL..........12.6
Johnny Moore, SA.............10.0
Norm Nixon, LAC 8.8
John Bagley, CLE.............. 8.6

STEALS
Micheal Richardson, NJ....2.96
Johnny Moore, SA 2.79
Lafayette Lever, DEN........2.46
Michael Jordan, CHI 2.39
Doc Rivers, ATL.................2.36

BLOCKED SHOTS
Mark Eaton, UTA 5.56
Akeem Olajuwon, HOU.....2.68
Sam Bowie, POR...............2.67
Wayne Cooper, DEN 2.46
Tree Rollins, ATL 2.39

FIELD GOAL PCT.
James Donaldson, LAC.... .637
Artis Gilmore, SA............... .623
Otis Thorpe, KC................. .600
K. Abdul-Jabbar, LAL .... .599
Larry Nance, PHO .... .587

FREE THROW PCT.
Kyle Macy, PHO................ .907
Kiki Vandeweghe, POR...... .896
Brad Davis, DAL................. .888
Kelly Tripucka, DET.......... .885

3-PT. FIELD GOAL PCT.
Byron Scott, LAL .... .433
Larry Bird, BOS .... .427
Brad Davis, DAL................. .409
Trent Tucker, NY .... .403

EAST FIRST ROUND
Boston 3, Cleveland 1
Milwaukee 3, Chicago 1
Philadelphia 3, Washington 1
Detroit 3, New Jersey 0

EAST SEMIFINALS
Boston 4, Detroit 2
Philadelphia 4, Milwaukee 0

EAST FINALS
Boston 4, Philadelphia 1

WEST FIRST ROUND
L.A. Lakers 3, Phoenix 0
Denver 3, San Antonio 2
Utah 3, Houston 2
Portland 3, Dallas 1

WEST SEMIFINALS
L.A. Lakers 4, Portland 1
Denver 4, Utah 1

WEST FINALS
L.A. Lakers 4, Denver 1

NBA FINALS
Boston 148, L.A. Lakers 114
L.A. Lakers 109, Boston 102
L.A. Lakers 136, Boston 111
Boston 107, L.A. Lakers 105
L.A. Lakers 120, Boston 111
L.A. Lakers 111, Boston 100

1985-86
FINAL STANDINGS

Eastern Conference
Atlantic Division

	W	L	PCT.	GB
Boston	67	15	.817	
Philadelphia	54	28	.659	13
Washington	39	43	.476	28
New Jersey	39	43	.476	28
New York	23	59	.280	44

Central Division

	W	L	PCT.	GB
Milwaukee	57	25	.695	
Atlanta	50	32	.610	7
Detroit	46	36	.561	11
Chicago	30	52	.366	27
Cleveland	29	53	.354	28
Indiana	26	56	.317	31

Western Conference
Midwest Division

	W	L	PCT.	GB
Houston	51	31	.622	
Denver	47	35	.573	4
Dallas	44	38	.537	7
Utah	42	40	.512	9
Sacramento	37	45	.451	14
San Antonio	35	47	.427	16

Pacific Division

	W	L	PCT.	GB
L.A. Lakers	62	20	.756	
Portland	40	42	.488	22
L.A. Clippers	32	50	.390	30
Phoenix	32	50	.390	30
Seattle	31	51	.378	31
Golden State	30	52	.366	32

SCORING
Dominique Wilkins, ATL....30.3
Adrian Dantley, UTA 29.8
Alex English, DEN.............29.8
Larry Bird, BOS.................25.8
Purvis Short, GS 25.5
Kiki Vandeweghe, POR 24.8
Moses Malone, PHI............23.8
Akeem Olajuwon, HOU.....23.5
Mike Mitchell, SA 23.4
World B. Free, CLE............23.4

REBOUNDS
Bill Laimbeer, DET 13.1
Charles Barkley, PHI.........12.8
Buck Williams, NJ 12.0
Moses Malone, PHI...........11.8
Ralph Sampson, HOU 11.1

ASSISTS
Magic Johnson, LAL 12.6
Isiah Thomas, DET 10.8
Reggie Theus, SAC............ 9.6
John Bagley, CLE............... 9.4
Maurice Cheeks, PHI 9.2

STEALS
Alvin Robertson, SA..........3.67
Micheal Richardson, NJ....2.66

Clyde Drexler, POR 2.63
Maurice Cheeks, PHI........2.52
Lafayette Lever, DEN........2.28

BLOCKED SHOTS
Manute Bol, WAS..............4.96
Mark Eaton, UTA..............4.61
Akeem Olajuwon, HOU.....3.40
Wayne Cooper, DEN 2.91
Benoit Benjamin, LAC.......2.61

FIELD GOAL PCT.
Steve Johnson, SA .... .632
Artis Gilmore, SA .... .618
Larry Nance, PHO............ .581
James Worthy, LAL........... .579
Kevin McHale, BOS .... .574

FREE THROW PCT.
Larry Bird, BOS............... .8963
Chris Mullin, GS.............. .8957
Mike Gminski, NJ............. .893
Jim Paxson, POR............. .889

3-PT. FIELD GOAL PCT.
Craig Hodges, MIL........... .4506
Trent Tucker, NY............. .4505
Ernie Grunfeld, NY.......... .426
Larry Bird, BOS................ .423

EAST FIRST ROUND
Boston 3, Chicago 0
Milwaukee 3, New Jersey 0
Philadelphia 3, Washington 2
Atlanta 3, Detroit 1

EAST SEMIFINALS
Boston 4, Atlanta 1
Milwaukee 4, Philadelphia 3

EAST FINALS
Boston 4, Milwaukee 0

WEST FIRST ROUND
L.A. Lakers 3, San Antonio 0
Houston 3, Sacramento 0
Denver 3, Portland 1
Dallas 3, Utah 1

WEST SEMIFINALS
L.A. Lakers 4, Dallas 2
Houston 4, Denver 2

WEST FINALS
Houston 4, L.A. Lakers 1

NBA FINALS
Boston 112, Houston 100
Boston 117, Houston 95
Houston 106, Boston 104
Boston 106, Houston 103
Houston 111, Boston 96
Boston 114, Houston 97

1986-87
FINAL STANDINGS

Eastern Conference
Atlantic Division

	W	L	PCT.	GB
Boston	59	23	.720	
Philadelphia	45	37	.549	14
Washington	42	40	.512	17
New Jersey	24	58	.293	35
New York	24	58	.293	35

Central Division

	W	L	PCT.	GB
Atlanta	57	25	.695	
Detroit	52	30	.634	5
Milwaukee	50	32	.610	7
Indiana	41	41	.500	16
Chicago	40	42	.488	17
Cleveland	31	51	.378	26

Western Conference
Midwest Division

	W	L	PCT.	GB
Dallas	55	27	.671	
Utah	44	38	.537	11
Houston	42	40	.512	13
Denver	37	45	.451	18
Sacramento	29	53	.354	26
San Antonio	28	54	.341	27

Pacific Division

	W	L	PCT.	GB
L.A. Lakers	65	17	.793	
Portland	49	33	.598	16
Golden State	42	40	.512	23
Seattle	39	43	.476	26
Phoenix	36	46	.439	29
L.A. Clippers	12	70	.146	53

SCORING
Michael Jordan, CHI 37.1
Dominique Wilkins, ATL....29.0
Alex English, DEN............28.6
Larry Bird, BOS.................28.1
Kiki Vandeweghe, POR 26.9
Kevin McHale, BOS...........26.1
Mark Aguirre, DAL 25.7
Dale Ellis, SEA.................24.9
Moses Malone, WAS 24.1
Magic Johnson, LAL 23.9

REBOUNDS
Charles Barkley, PHI.......14.6
Charles Oakley, CHI 13.1
Buck Williams, NJ 12.5
James Donaldson, DAL 11.9
Bill Laimbeer, DET 11.6

ASSISTS
Magic Johnson, LAL 12.2
Sleepy Floyd, GS.............10.3
Isiah Thomas, DET 10.0
Doc Rivers, ATL................10.0
Terry Porter, POR 8.9

STEALS
Alvin Robertson, SA..........3.21
Michael Jordan, CHI 2.88

Maurice Cheeks, PHI........2.65
Ron Harper, CLE 2.55
Clyde Drexler, POR 2.49

BLOCKED SHOTS
Mark Eaton, UTA 4.06
Manute Bol, WAS..............3.68
Akeem Olajuwon, HOU.....3.39
Benoit Benjamin, LAC.......2.60
Alton Lister, SEA...............2.40

FIELD GOAL PCT.
Kevin McHale, BOS...........604
Artis Gilmore, SA..............597
Charles Barkley, PHI 594
James Donaldson, DAL....586
K. Abdul-Jabbar, LAL 564

FREE THROW PCT.
Larry Bird, BOS 910
Danny Ainge, BOS............897
Bill Laimbeer, DET 894
Byron Scott, LAL 892

3-PT. FIELD GOAL PCT.
Kiki Vandeweghe, POR.....481
Detlef Schrempf, DAL........478
Danny Ainge, BOS 443
Byron Scott, LAL 436

EAST FIRST ROUND
Boston 3, Chicago 0
Atlanta 3, Indiana 1
Detroit 3, Washington 0
Milwaukee 3, Philadelphia 2

EAST SEMIFINALS
Boston 4, Milwaukee 3
Detroit 4, Atlanta 1

EAST FINALS
Boston 4, Detroit 3

WEST FIRST ROUND
L.A. Lakers 3, Denver 0
Seattle 3, Dallas 1
Houston 3, Portland 1
Golden St. 3, Utah 2

WEST SEMIFINALS
L.A. Lakers 4, Golden St. 1
Seattle 4, Houston 2

WEST FINALS
L.A. Lakers 4, Seattle 0

NBA FINALS
L.A. Lakers 126, Boston 113
L.A. Lakers 141, Boston 122
Boston 109, L.A. Lakers 103
L.A. Lakers 107, Boston 106
Boston 123, L.A. Lakers 108
L.A. Lakers 106, Boston 93

1987-88
FINAL STANDINGS

Eastern Conference
Atlantic Division

	W	L	PCT.	GB
Boston	57	25	.695	
Washington	38	44	.463	19
New York	38	44	.463	19
Philadelphia	36	46	.439	21
New Jersey	19	63	.232	38

Central Division

	W	L	PCT.	GB
Detroit	54	28	.659	
Atlanta	50	32	.610	4
Chicago	50	32	.610	4
Cleveland	42	40	.512	12
Milwaukee	42	40	.512	12
Indiana	38	44	.463	16

Western Conference
Midwest Division

	W	L	PCT.	GB
Denver	54	28	.659	
Dallas	53	29	.646	1
Utah	47	35	.573	7
Houston	46	36	.561	8
San Antonio	31	51	.378	23
Sacramento	24	58	.293	30

Pacific Division

	W	L	PCT.	GB
L.A. Lakers	62	20	.756	
Portland	53	29	.646	9
Seattle	44	38	.537	18
Phoenix	28	54	.341	34
Golden State	20	62	.244	42
L.A. Clippers	17	65	.207	45

SCORING
Michael Jordan, CHI 35.0
Dominique Wilkins, ATL...30.7
Larry Bird, BOS................29.9
Charles Barkley, PHI.........28.3
Karl Malone, UTA..............27.7
Clyde Drexler, POR 27.0
Dale Ellis, SEA.................25.8
Mark Aguirre, DAL 25.1
Alex English, DEN............25.0
Akeem Olajuwon, HOU.....22.8

REBOUNDS
Michael Cage, LAC 13.03
Charles Oakley, CHI 13.00
Akeem Olajuwon, HOU.....12.1
Karl Malone, UTA..............12.0
Buck Williams, NJ 11.9

ASSISTS
John Stockton, UTA..........13.8
Magic Johnson, LAL 11.9
Mark Jackson, NY 10.6
Terry Porter, POR.............10.1
Doc Rivers, ATL 9.3

STEALS
Michael Jordan, CHI 3.16
Alvin Robertson, SA..........2.96

John Stockton, UTA..........2.95
Lafayette Lever, DEN.........2.72
Clyde Drexler, POR 2.51

BLOCKED SHOTS
Mark Eaton, UTA 3.71
Benoit Benjamin, LAC........3.41
Patrick Ewing, NY 2.99
Akeem Olajuwon, HOU......2.71
Manute Bol, WAS..............2.70

FIELD GOAL PCT.
Kevin McHale, BOS........... .604
Robert Parish, BOS.......... .589
Charles Barkley, PHI......... .587
John Stockton, UTA........... .574
Walter Berry, SA............... .563

FREE THROW PCT.
Jack Sikma, MIL .... .922
Larry Bird, BOS .... .916
John Long, IND .... .907
Mike Gminski, NJ/PHI .... .906

3-PT. FIELD GOAL PCT.
Craig Hodges, MIL/PHO ...... .491
Mark Price, CLE .... .486
John Long, IND .... .442
G. Henderson, NY/PHI .... .423

EAST FIRST ROUND
Boston 3, New York 1
Detroit 3, Washington 2
Atlanta 3, Milwaukee 2
Chicago 3, Cleveland 2

EAST SEMIFINALS
Boston 4, Atlanta 3
Detroit 4, Chicago 1

EAST FINALS
Detroit 4, Boston 2

WEST FIRST ROUND
L.A. Lakers 3, San Antonio 0
Denver 3, Seattle 2
Utah 3, Portland 1
Dallas 3, Houston 1

WEST SEMIFINALS
L.A. Lakers 4, Utah 3
Dallas 4, Denver 2

WEST FINALS
L.A. Lakers 4, Dallas 3

NBA FINALS
Detroit 105, L.A. Lakers 93
L.A. Lakers 108, Detroit 96
L.A. Lakers 99, Detroit 86
Detroit 111, L.A. Lakers 86
Detroit 104, L.A. Lakers 94
L.A. Lakers 103, Detroit 102
L.A. Lakers 108, Detroit 105

1988-89 FINAL STANDINGS

Eastern Conference
Atlantic Division

	W	L	PCT.	GB
New York	52	30	.634	
Philadelphia	46	36	.561	6
Boston	42	40	.512	10
Washington	40	42	.488	12
New Jersey	26	56	.317	26
Charlotte	20	62	.244	32

Central Division

	W	L	PCT.	GB
Detroit	63	19	.768	
Cleveland	57	25	.695	6
Atlanta	52	30	.634	11
Milwaukee	49	33	.598	14
Chicago	47	35	.573	16
Indiana	28	54	.341	35

Western Conference
Midwest Division

	W	L	PCT.	GB
Utah	51	31	.622	
Houston	45	37	.549	6
Denver	44	38	.537	7
Dallas	38	44	.463	13
San Antonio	21	61	.256	30
Miami	15	67	.183	36

Pacific Division

	W	L	PCT.	GB
L.A. Lakers	57	25	.695	
Phoenix	55	27	.671	2
Seattle	47	35	.573	10
Golden State	43	39	.524	14
Portland	39	43	.476	18
Sacramento	27	55	.329	30
L.A. Clippers	21	61	.256	36

SCORING
Michael Jordan, CHI 32.5
Karl Malone, UTA...............29.1
Dale Ellis, SEA...................27.5
Clyde Drexler, POR 27.2
Chris Mullin, GS...............26.5
Alex English, DEN.............26.5
Dominique Wilkins, ATL....26.2
Charles Barkley, PHI.........25.8
Tom Chambers, PHO 25.7
Akeem Olajuwon, HOU 24.8

REBOUNDS
Akeem Olajuwon, HOU....13.5
Charles Barkley, PHI........12.5
Robert Parish, BOS 12.5
Moses Malone, ATL.........11.8
Karl Malone, UTA.............10.7

ASSISTS
John Stockton, UTA..........13.6
Magic Johnson, LAL 12.8
Kevin Johnson, PHO.........12.2
Terry Porter, POR 9.5
Nate McMillan, SEA 9.3

STEALS
John Stockton, UTA..........3.21
Alvin Robertson, SA..........3.03

Michael Jordan, CHI 2.89
Lafayette Lever, DEN........2.75
Clyde Drexler, POR 2.73

BLOCKED SHOTS
Manute Bol, GS.................4.31
Mark Eaton, UTA...............3.84
Patrick Ewing, NY 3.51
Akeem Olajuwon, HOU....3.44
Larry Nance, CLE 2.82

FIELD GOAL PCT.
Dennis Rodman, DET .... .595
Charles Barkley, PHI.......... .579
Robert Parish, BOS........... .570
Patrick Ewing, BOS........... .567
James Worthy, LAL .... .548

FREE THROW PCT.
Magic Johnson, LAL .... .911
Jack Sikma, MIL................. .905
Scott Skiles, IND................ .903
Mark Price, CLE .... .901

3-PT. FIELD GOAL PCT.
Jon Sundvold, MIA .... .522
Dale Ellis, SEA .... .478
Mark Price, CLE .... .441
Hersey Hawkins, PHI .... .428

EAST FIRST ROUND
Detroit 3, Boston 0
New York 3, Philadelphia 0
Chicago 3, Cleveland 2
Milwaukee 3, Atlanta 2

EAST SEMIFINALS
Detroit 4, Milwaukee 0
Chicago 4, New York 2

EAST FINALS
Detroit 4, Chicago 2

WEST FIRST ROUND
L.A. Lakers 3, Portland 0
Golden St. 3, Utah 0
Phoenix 3, Denver 0
Seattle 3, Houston 1

WEST SEMIFINALS
L.A. Lakers 4, Seattle 0
Phoenix 4, Golden St. 1

WEST FINALS
L.A. Lakers 4, Phoenix 0

NBA FINALS
Detroit 109, L.A. Lakers 97
Detroit 108, L.A. Lakers 105
Detroit 114, L.A. Lakers 110
Detroit 105, L.A. Lakers 97

1989-90 FINAL STANDINGS

Eastern Conference

Atlantic Division

	W	L	PCT.	GB
Philadelphia	53	29	.646	
Boston	52	30	.634	1
New York	45	37	.549	8
Washington	31	51	.378	22
Miami	18	64	.220	35
New Jersey	17	65	.207	36

Central Division

	W	L	PCT.	GB
Detroit	59	23	.720	
Chicago	55	27	.671	4
Milwaukee	44	38	.537	15
Cleveland	42	40	.512	17
Indiana	42	40	.512	17
Atlanta	41	41	.500	18
Orlando	18	64	.220	41

Western Conference

Midwest Division

	W	L	PCT.	GB
San Antonio	56	26	.683	
Utah	55	27	.671	1
Dallas	47	35	.573	9
Denver	43	39	.524	13
Houston	41	41	.500	15
Minnesota	22	60	.268	34
Charlotte	19	63	.232	37

Pacific Division

	W	L	PCT.	GB
L.A. Lakers	63	19	.768	
Portland	59	23	.720	4
Phoenix	54	28	.659	9
Seattle	41	41	.500	22
Golden State	37	45	.451	26
L.A. Clippers	30	52	.366	33
Sacramento	23	59	.280	40

SCORING

Michael Jordan, CHI	33.6
Karl Malone, UTA	31.0
Patrick Ewing, NY	28.6
Tom Chambers, PHO	27.2
Dominique Wilkins, ATL	26.7
Charles Barkley, PHI	25.2
Chris Mullin, GS	25.1
Reggie Miller, IND	24.6
Akeem Olajuwon, HOU	24.3
David Robinson, SA	24.3

REBOUNDS

Akeem Olajuwon, HOU	14.0
David Robinson, SA	12.0
Charles Barkley, PHI	11.5
Karl Malone, UTA	11.1
Patrick Ewing, NY	10.9

ASSISTS

John Stockton, UTA	14.5
Magic Johnson, LAL	11.5
Kevin Johnson, PHO	11.4
Muggsy Bogues, CHA	10.7

STEALS

Michael Jordan, CHI	2.77
John Stockton, UTA	2.65
Scottie Pippen, CHI	2.57
Alvin Robertson, MIL	2.56
Derek Harper, DAL	2.28

BLOCKED SHOTS

Akeem Olajuwon, HOU	4.59
Patrick Ewing, NY	3.99
David Robinson, SA	3.89
Manute Bol, GS	3.17
Benoit Benjamin, LAC	2.63

FIELD GOAL PCT.

Mark West, PHO	.625
Charles Barkley, PHI	.600
Robert Parish, BOS	.580
Karl Malone, UTA	.562

FREE THROW PCT.

Larry Bird, BOS	.930
Eddie Johnson, PHO	.917
Walter Davis, DEN	.912
Joe Dumars, DET	.900

3-PT. FIELD GOAL PCT.

Steve Kerr, CLE	.507
Craig Hodges, CHI	.481
Drazen Petrovic, POR	.459
Jon Sundvold, MIA	.440

EAST FIRST ROUND
Detroit 3, Indiana 0
Philadelphia 3, Cleveland 2
Chicago 3, Milwaukee 1
New York 3, Boston 2

EAST SEMIFINALS
Detroit 4, New York 1
Chicago 4, Philadelphia 1

EAST FINALS
Detroit 4, Chicago 3

WEST FIRST ROUND
L.A. Lakers 3, Houston 1
San Antonio 3, Denver 0
Portland 3, Dallas 0
Phoenix 3, Utah 2

WEST SEMIFINALS
Phoenix 4, L.A. Lakers 1
Portland 4, San Antonio 3

WEST FINALS
Portland 4, Phoenix 2

NBA FINALS
Detroit 105, Portland 99
Portland 106, Detroit 105 (OT)
Detroit 121, Portland 106
Detroit 112, Portland 109
Detroit 92, Portland 90

1990-91 FINAL STANDINGS

Eastern Conference
Atlantic Division

	W	L	PCT.	GB
Boston	56	26	.683	
Philadelphia	44	38	.537	12
New York	39	43	.476	17
Washington	30	52	.366	26
New Jersey	26	56	.317	30
Miami	24	58	.293	32

Central Division

	W	L	PCT.	GB
Chicago	61	21	.744	
Detroit	50	32	.610	11
Milwaukee	48	34	.585	13
Atlanta	43	39	.524	18
Indiana	41	41	.500	20
Cleveland	33	49	.402	28
Charlotte	26	56	.317	35

Western Conference
Midwest Division

	W	L	PCT.	GB
San Antonio	55	27	.671	
Utah	54	28	.659	1
Houston	52	30	.634	3
Orlando	31	51	.378	24
Minnesota	29	53	.354	26
Dallas	28	54	.341	27
Denver	20	62	.244	35

Pacific Division

	W	L	PCT.	GB
Portland	63	19	.768	
L.A. Lakers	58	24	.707	5
Phoenix	55	27	.671	8
Golden State	44	38	.537	19
Seattle	41	41	.500	22
L.A. Clippers	31	51	.378	32
Sacramento	25	57	.305	38

SCORING
Michael Jordan, CHI	31.5
Karl Malone, UTA	29.0
Bernard King, WAS	28.4
Charles Barkley, PHI	27.6
Patrick Ewing, NY	26.6
Michael Adams, DEN	26.5
Dominique Wilkins, ATL	25.9
Chris Mullin, GS	25.7
David Robinson, SA	25.6
Mitch Richmond, GS	23.9

REBOUNDS
David Robinson, SA	13.0
Dennis Rodman, DET	12.5
Charles Oakley, NY	12.1
Karl Malone, UTA	11.8
Patrick Ewing, NY	11.2

ASSISTS
John Stockton, UTA	14.2
Magic Johnson, LAL	12.5
Michael Adams, DEN	10.5
Kevin Johnson, PHO	10.1

STEALS
Alvin Robertson, MIL	3.04
John Stockton, UTA	2.85

Michael Jordan, CHI	2.72
Tim Hardaway, GS	2.61
Scottie Pippen, CHI	2.35

BLOCKED SHOTS
Hakeem Olajuwon, HOU	3.95
David Robinson, SA	3.90
Patrick Ewing, NY	3.19
Manute Bol, PHI	3.01
Chris Dudley, NJ	2.51

FIELD GOAL PCT.
Buck Williams, POR	.602
Robert Parish, BOS	.598
Kevin Gamble, BOS	.587
Charles Barkley, PHI	.570

FREE THROW PCT.
Reggie Miller, IND	.918
Jeff Malone, UTA	.917
Ricky Pierce, MIL/SEA	.913
Kelly Tripucka, CHA	.910

3-PT. FIELD GOAL PCT.
Jim Les, SAC	.461
Trent Tucker, NY	.418
Jeff Hornacek, PHO	.418
Terry Porter, POR	.415

EAST FIRST ROUND
Chicago 3, New York 0
Boston 3, Indiana 2
Detroit 3, Atlanta 2
Philadelphia 3, Milwaukee 0

EAST SEMIFINALS
Chicago 4, Philadelphia 1
Detroit 4, Boston 2

EAST FINALS
Chicago 4, Detroit 0

WEST FIRST ROUND
Portland 3, Seattle 2
Golden St. 3, San Antonio 1
L.A. Lakers 3, Houston 0
Utah 3, Phoenix 1

WEST SEMIFINALS
Portland 4, Utah 1
L.A. Lakers 4, Golden St. 1

WEST FINALS
L.A. Lakers 4, Portland 2

NBA FINALS
L.A. Lakers 93, Chicago 91
Chicago 107, L.A. Lakers 86
Chicago 104, L.A. 96 (OT)
Chicago 97, L.A. Lakers 82
Chicago 108, L.A. Lakers 101

1991-92 FINAL STANDINGS

Eastern Conference

Atlantic Division

	W	L	PCT.	GB
Boston	51	31	.622	
New York	51	31	.622	
New Jersey	40	42	.488	11
Miami	38	44	.463	13
Philadelphia	35	47	.427	16
Washington	25	57	.305	26
Orlando	21	61	.256	30

Central Division

	W	L	PCT.	GB
Chicago	67	15	.817	
Cleveland	57	25	.695	10
Detroit	48	34	.585	19
Indiana	40	42	.488	27
Atlanta	38	44	.463	29
Charlotte	31	51	.378	36
Milwaukee	31	51	.378	36

Western Conference

Midwest Division

	W	L	PCT.	GB
Utah	55	27	.671	
San Antonio	47	35	.573	8
Houston	42	40	.512	13
Denver	24	58	.293	31
Dallas	22	60	.268	33
Minnesota	15	67	.183	40

Pacific Division

	W	L	PCT.	GB
Portland	57	25	.695	
Golden State	55	27	.671	2
Phoenix	53	29	.646	4
Seattle	47	35	.573	10
L.A. Clippers	45	37	.549	12
L.A. Lakers	43	39	.524	14
Sacramento	29	53	.347	28

SCORING
Michael Jordan, CHI 30.1
Karl Malone, UTA 28.0
Chris Mullin, GS................25.6
Clyde Drexler, POR 25.0
Patrick Ewing, NY 24.0
Tim Hardaway, GS 23.4
David Robinson, SA 23.2
Charles Barkley, PHI 23.1
Mitch Richmond, SAC.......22.5
Glen Rice, MIA 22.3

REBOUNDS
Dennis Rodman, DET.......18.7
Kevin Willis, ATL...............15.5
Dikembe Mutombo, DEN..12.3
David Robinson, SA 12.2
Hakeem Olajuwon, HOU ..12.1

ASSISTS
John Stockton, UTA 13.7
Kevin Johnson, PHO 10.7
Tim Hardaway, GS 10.0
Muggsy Bogues, CHA 9.1

STEALS
John Stockton, UTA 2.98
Micheal Williams, IND......2.95

Alvin Robertson, MIL 2.56
Mookie Blaylock, NJ 2.36
David Robinson, SA 2.32

BLOCKED SHOTS
David Robinson, SA 4.49
Hakeem Olajuwon, HOU ..4.34
Larry Nance, CLE 3.00
Patrick Ewing, NY 2.99
Dikembe Mutombo, DEN ..2.96

FIELD GOAL PCT.
Buck Williams, POR.......... .604
Otis Thorpe, HOU .... .592
Horace Grant, CHI .... .578
Brad Daugherty, CLE ...... .570

FREE THROW PCT.
Mark Price, CLE .... .947
Larry Bird, BOS................ .926
Ricky Pierce, SEA............ .916
Rolando Blackman, DAL.. .898

3-PT. FIELD GOAL PCT.
Dana Barros, SEA .... .446
Drazen Petrovic, NJ......... .444
Jeff Hornacek, PHO......... .439
Mike Iuzzolino, DAL......... .434

EAST FIRST ROUND
Chicago 3, Miami 0
Boston 3, Indiana 1
Cleveland 3, New Jersey 1
New York 3, Detroit 2

EAST SEMIFINALS
Chicago 4, New York 3
Cleveland 4, Boston 3

EAST FINALS
Chicago 4, Cleveland 2

WEST FIRST ROUND
Portland 3, L.A. Lakers 1
Utah 3, L.A. Clippers 2
Seattle 3, Golden St. 1
Phoenix 3, San Antonio 0

WEST SEMIFINALS
Portland 4, Phoenix 1
Utah 4, Seattle 1

WEST FINALS
Portland 4, Utah 2

NBA FINALS
Chicago 122, Portland 89
Portland 115, Chi. 104 (OT)
Chicago 94, Portland 84
Portland 93, Chicago 88
Chicago 119, Portland 106
Chicago 97, Portland 93

1992-93 FINAL STANDINGS

Eastern Conference

Atlantic Division

	W	L	PCT.	GB
New York	60	22	.732	
Boston	48	34	.585	12
New Jersey	43	39	.524	17
Orlando	41	41	.500	19
Miami	36	46	.439	24
Philadelphia	26	56	.317	34
Washington	22	60	.268	38

Central Division

	W	L	PCT.	GB
Chicago	57	25	.695	
Cleveland	54	28	.659	3
Charlotte	44	38	.537	13
Atlanta	43	39	.524	14
Indiana	41	41	.500	16
Detroit	40	42	.488	17
Milwaukee	28	54	.341	29

Western Conference

Midwest Division

	W	L	PCT.	GB
Houston	55	27	.671	
San Antonio	49	33	.598	6
Utah	47	35	.573	8
Denver	36	46	.439	19
Minnesota	19	63	.232	36
Dallas	11	71	.134	44

Pacific Division

	W	L	PCT.	GB
Phoenix	62	20	.756	
Seattle	55	27	.671	7
Portland	51	31	.622	11
L.A. Clippers	41	41	.500	21
L.A. Lakers	39	43	.476	23
Golden State	34	48	.415	28
Sacramento	25	57	.305	37

SCORING
Michael Jordan, CHI 32.6
Dominique Wilkins, ATL....29.9
Karl Malone, UTA 27.0
Hakeem Olajuwon, HOU ..26.1
Charles Barkley, PHO......25.6
Patrick Ewing, NY 24.2
Joe Dumars, DET 23.5
Shaquille O'Neal, ORL......23.4
David Robinson, SA..........23.4
Danny Manning, LAC........22.8

REBOUNDS
Dennis Rodman, DET.......18.3
Shaquille O'Neal, ORL.....13.9
Dikembe Mutombo, DEN...13.0
Hakeem Olajuwon, HOU ..13.0
Kevin Willis, ATL................12.9

ASSISTS
John Stockton, UTA..........12.0
Tim Hardaway, GS 10.6
Scott Skiles, ORL...............9.4
Mark Jackson, LAC 8.8

STEALS
Michael Jordan, CHI 2.83
Mookie Blaylock, ATL 2.54

John Stockton, UTA..........2.43
Nate McMillan, SEA..........2.37
Alvin Robertson, MIL/DET 2.25

BLOCKED SHOTS
Hakeem Olajuwon, HOU ..4.17
Shaquille O'Neal, ORL......3.53
Dikembe Mutombo, DEN ..3.50
Alonzo Mourning, CHA 3.47
David Robinson, SA..........3.22

FIELD GOAL PCT.
Cedric Ceballos, PHO...... .576
Brad Daugherty, CLE .... .571
Dale Davis, IND .... .568
Shaquille O'Neal, ORL .... .562

FREE THROW PCT.
Mark Price, CLE .... .948
Chris Jackson, DEN .... .935
Eddie Johnson, SEA......... .911
Micheal Williams, MIN .... .907

3-PT. FIELD GOAL PCT.
B.J. Armstrong, CHI .... .453
Chris Mullin, GS .... .451
Drazen Petrovic, NJ .... .449
Kenny Smith, HOU .... .438

EAST FIRST ROUND
New York 3, Indiana 1
Chicago 3, Atlanta 0
Cleveland 3, New Jersey 2
Charlotte 3, Boston 1

EAST SEMIFINALS
New York 4, Charlotte 1
Chicago 4, Cleveland 0

EAST FINALS
Chicago 4, New York 2

WEST FIRST ROUND
Phoenix 3, L.A. Lakers 2
Houston 3, L.A. Clippers 2
Seattle 3, Utah 2
San Antonio 3, Portland 1

WEST SEMIFINALS
Seattle 4, Houston 3
Phoenix 4, San Antonio 2

WEST FINALS
Phoenix 4, Seattle 3

NBA FINALS
Chicago 100, Phoenix 92
Chicago 111, Phoenix 108
Phoenix 129, Chic. 121 (3OT)
Chicago 111, Phoenix 105
Phoenix 108, Chicago 98
Chicago 99, Phoenix 98

1993-94 FINAL STANDINGS

Eastern Conference

Atlantic Division

	W	L	PCT.	GB
New York	57	25	.695	
Orlando	50	32	.610	7
New Jersey	45	37	.549	12
Miami	42	40	.512	15
Boston	32	50	.390	25
Philadelphia	25	57	.305	32
Washington	24	58	.234	33

Central Division

	W	L	PCT.	GB
Atlanta	57	25	.695	
Chicago	55	27	.671	2
Indiana	47	35	.573	10
Cleveland	47	35	.573	10
Charlotte	41	41	.500	16
Detroit	20	62	.244	37
Milwaukee	20	62	.244	37

Western Conference

Midwest Division

	W	L	PCT.	GB
Houston	58	24	.707	
San Antonio	55	27	.671	3
Utah	53	29	.646	5
Denver	42	40	.512	16
Minnesota	20	62	.244	38
Dallas	13	69	.159	45

Pacific Division

	W	L	PCT.	GB
Seattle	63	19	.768	
Phoenix	56	26	.683	7
Golden State	50	32	.610	13
Portland	47	35	.573	16
L.A. Lakers	33	49	.402	30
Sacramento	28	54	.341	35
L.A. Clippers	27	55	.329	36

SCORING
David Robinson, SA....29.8
Shaquille O'Neal, ORL....29.3
Hakeem Olajuwon, HOU...27.3
Dominique Wilkins, ATL/LAC 26.0
Karl Malone, UTA 25.2
Patrick Ewing, NY 24.5
Mitch Richmond, SAC 23.4
Scottie Pippen, CHI 22.0
Charles Barkley, PHO 21.6
Glen Rice, MIA................21.1

REBOUNDS
Dennis Rodman, SA 17.3
Shaquille O'Neal, ORL......13.2
Kevin Willis, ATL 12.0
Hakeem Olajuwon, HOU ..11.9
Olden Polynice, DET/SAC....11.9

ASSISTS
John Stockton, UTA..........12.6
Muggsy Bogues, CHA 10.1
Mookie Blaylock, ATL 9.7
Kenny Anderson, NJ 9.6

STEALS
Nate McMillan, SEA.........2.96
Scottie Pippen, CHI 2.93

Mookie Blaylock, ATL 2.62
John Stockton, UTA..........2.43
Eric Murdock, MIL 2.40

BLOCKED SHOTS
Hakeem Olajuwon, HOU ..3.71
David Robinson, SA...........3.31
Alonzo Mourning, CHA 3.13
Shawn Bradley, PHI..........3.00
Shaquille O'Neal, ORL......2.85

FIELD GOAL PCT.
Shaquille O'Neal, ORL .... .599
Dikembe Mutombo, DEN .569
Otis Thorpe, HOU 561
Chris Webber, GS.............552

FREE THROW PCT.
M. Abdul-Rauf, DEN .... .956
Reggie Miller, IND............. .908
Ricky Pierce, SEA............. .896
Sedale Threatt, LAL .... .890

3-PT. FIELD GOAL PCT.
Tracy Murray, POR........... .459
B.J. Armstrong, CHI .... .444
Reggie Miller, IND............. .421
Steve Kerr, CHI................. .419

EAST FIRST ROUND
Atlanta 3, Miami 2
New York 3, New Jersey 1
Chicago 3, Cleveland 0
Indiana 3, Orlando 0

EAST SEMIFINALS
New York 4, Chicago 3
Indiana 4, Atlanta 2

EAST FINALS
New York 4, Indiana 3

WEST FIRST ROUND
Denver 3, Seattle 2
Houston 3, Portland 1
Phoenix 3, Golden St. 0
Utah 3, San Antonio 1

WEST SEMIFINALS
Houston 4, Phoenix 3
Utah 4, Denver 3

WEST FINALS
Houston 4, Utah 1

NBA FINALS
Houston 85, New York 78
New York 91, Houston 83
Houston 93, New York 89
New York 91, Houston 82
New York 91, Houston 84
Houston 86, New York 84
Houston 90, New York 84

1994-95 FINAL STANDINGS

Eastern Conference
Atlantic Division

	W	L	PCT.	GB
Orlando	57	25	.695	
New York	55	27	.671	2
Boston	35	47	.427	22
Miami	32	50	.390	25
New Jersey	30	52	.366	27
Philadelphia	24	58	.293	33
Washington	21	61	.256	36

Central Division

	W	L	PCT.	GB
Indiana	52	30	.634	
Charlotte	50	32	.610	2
Chicago	47	35	.573	5
Cleveland	43	39	.524	9
Atlanta	42	40	.512	10
Milwaukee	34	48	.415	18
Detroit	28	54	.341	24

Western Conference
Midwest Division

	W	L	PCT.	GB
San Antonio	62	20	.756	
Utah	60	22	.732	2
Houston	47	35	.573	15
Denver	41	41	.500	21
Dallas	36	46	.439	26
Minnesota	21	61	.256	41

Pacific Division

	W	L	PCT.	GB
Phoenix	59	23	.720	
Seattle	57	25	.695	2
L.A. Lakers	48	34	.585	11
Portland	44	38	.537	15
Sacramento	39	43	.476	20
Golden State	26	56	.317	33
L.A. Clippers	17	65	.207	42

SCORING
Shaquille O'Neal, ORL......29.3
Hakeem Olajuwon, HOU ..27.8
David Robinson, SA........27.6
Karl Malone, UTA 26.7
Jamal Mashburn, DAL 24.1
Patrick Ewing, NY 23.9
Charles Barkley, PHO........23.0
Mitch Richmond, SAC........22.8
Glen Rice, MIA...................22.3
Glenn Robinson, MIL.........21.9
Clyde Drexler, POR/HOU 21.8
Scottie Pippen, CHI 21.4
Clifford Robinson, POR 21.3
Alonzo Mourning, CHA 21.3
A. Hardaway, ORL.............20.9
Gary Payton, SEA.............20.6
Latrell Sprewell, GS 20.6

REBOUNDS
Dennis Rodman, SA 16.8
Dikembe Mutombo, DEN...12.5
Shaquille O'Neal, ORL......11.4
Patrick Ewing, NY 11.0
Tyrone Hill, CLE................10.9
Shawn Kemp, SEA 10.9
David Robinson, SA...........10.8
Hakeem Olajuwon, HOU ..10.8

ASSISTS
John Stockton, UTA..........12.3
Kenny Anderson, NJ...........9.4
Tim Hardaway, GS 9.3
Rod Strickland, POR...........8.8
Tyrone Bogues, CHA..........8.7
Nick Van Exel, LAL.............8.3
Avery Johnson, SA.............8.2
Pooh Richardson, LAC 7.9

STEALS
Scottie Pippen, CHI 2.94
Mookie Blaylock, ATL........2.50
Gary Payton, SEA..............2.49
John Stockton, UTA...........2.37
Nate McMillan, SEA...........2.06
Eddie Jones, LAL...............2.05
Jason Kidd, DAL................1.91
Elliot Perry, PHO................1.90

BLOCKED SHOTS
Dikembe Mutombo, DEN..3.91
Hakeem Olajuwon, HOU ..3.36
Shawn Bradley, PHI...........3.34
David Robinson, SA...........3.23
Alonzo Mourning, CHA 2.92
Shaquille O'Neal, ORL.......2.43
Vlade Divac, LAL...............2.18

FIELD GOAL PCT.
Chris Gatling, GS..............633
Shaquille O'Neal, ORL......583
Horace Grant, ORL............567
Otis Thorpe, HOU/POR..........565
Dale Davis, IND 563
Gheorghe Muresan, WAS .560
Dikembe Mutombo, DEN .556

FREE THROW PCT.
Spud Webb, SAC...............934
Mark Price, CLE.................914
Dana Barros, PHI..............899
Reggie Miller, IND..............897
Muggsy Bogues, CHA 889
Scott Skiles, WAS.............886
M. Abdul-Rauf, DEN...........885
B.J. Armstrong, CHI..........884

3-POINT PCT.
Steve Kerr, CHI.................524
Detlef Schrempf, SEA........514
Dana Barros, PHI..............464
Hubert Davis, NY 455
John Stockton, UTA...........449
Hersey Hawkins, CHA 440
Wesley Person, PHO.........436
Kenny Smith, HOU 429

1994-95 HOME-AWAY RECORDS

	HOME	AWAY	TOTAL		HOME	AWAY	TOTAL
San Antonio	33-8	29-12	62-20	Denver	23-18	18-23	41-41
Utah	33-8	27-14	60-22	Sacramento	27-14	12-29	39-43
Phoenix	32-9	27-14	59-23	Dallas	19-22	17-24	36-46
Orlando	39-2	18-23	57-25	Boston	20-21	15-26	35-47
Seattle	32-9	25-16	57-25	Milwaukee	22-19	12-29	34-48
New York	29-12	26-15	55-27	Miami	22-19	10-31	32-50
Indiana	33-8	19-22	52-30	New Jersey	20-21	10-31	30-52
Charlotte	29-12	21-20	50-32	Detroit	22-19	6-35	28-54
L.A. Lakers	29-12	19-22	48-34	Golden State	15-26	11-30	26-56
Chicago	28-13	19-22	47-35	Philadelphia	14-27	10-31	24-58
Houston	25-16	22-19	47-35	Minnesota	13-28	8-33	21-61
Portland	26-15	18-23	44-38	Washington	13-28	8-33	21-61
Cleveland	26-15	17-24	43-39	L.A. Clippers	13-28	4-37	17-65
Atlanta	24-17	18-23	42-40				

1995 PLAYOFFS

EAST FIRST ROUND
Orlando 124, Boston 77
Boston 99, Orlando 92
Orlando 82, Boston 77
Orlando 95, Boston 92

Indiana 90, Atlanta 82
Indiana 105, Atlanta 97
Indiana 105, Atlanta 89

New York 103, Cleveland 79
Cleveland 90, New York 84
New York 83, Cleveland 81
New York 93, Cleveland 80

Chicago 108, Char. 100 (OT)
Charlotte 106, Chicago 89
Chicago 103, Charlotte 80
Chicago 85, Charlotte 84

EAST SEMIFINALS
Indiana 107, New York 105
New York 96, Indiana 77
Indiana 97, New York 95 (OT)
Indiana 98, New York 84
New York 96, Indiana 95
New York 92, Indiana 82
Indiana 97, New York 95

Orlando 94, Chicago 91
Chicago 104, Orlando 94
Orlando 110, Chicago 101

Chicago 106, Orlando 95
Orlando 103, Chicago 95
Orlando 108, Chicago 102

EAST FINALS
Orlando 105, Indiana 101
Orlando 119, Indiana 114
Indiana 105, Orlando 100
Indiana 94, Orlando 93
Orlando 108, Indiana 106
Indiana 123, Orlando 96
Orlando 105, Indiana 81

WEST FIRST ROUND
San Antonio 104, Denver 88
San Antonio 122, Denver 96
San Antonio 99, Denver 95

Phoenix 129, Portland 102
Phoenix 103, Portland 94
Phoenix 117, Portland 109

Utah 102, Houston 100
Houston 140, Utah 126
Utah 95, Houston 82
Houston 123, Utah 106
Houston 95, Utah 91

Seattle 96, L.A. Lakers 71
L.A. Lakers 84, Seattle 82
L.A. Lakers 105, Seattle 101
L.A. Lakers 114, Seattle 110

WEST SEMIFINALS
San Antonio 110, L.A. 94
San Antonio 97, L.A. 90 (OT)
L.A. 92, San Antonio 85
San Antonio 80, L.A. 71
L.A. 98, San Antonio 96 (OT)
San Antonio 100, L.A. 88

Phoenix 130, Houston 108
Phoenix 118, Houston 94
Houston 118, Phoenix 85
Phoenix 114, Houston 110
Houston 103, Phoenix 97 (OT)
Houston 116, Phoenix 103
Houston 115, Phoenix 114

WEST FINALS
Houston 94, San Antonio 93
Houston 106, San Antonio 96
San Antonio 107, Houston 102
San Antonio 103, Houston 81
Houston 111, San Antonio 90
Houston 100, San Antonio 95

NBA FINALS
Houston 120, Orl. 118 (OT)
Houston 117, Orlando 106
Houston 106, Orlando 103
Houston 113, Orlando 101

1994-95 OFFENSIVE TEAM STATISTICS

TEAM	FIELD GOALS			FREE THROWS			REBOUNDS			MISCELLANEOUS						SCORING	
	ATT	FGs	PCT	ATT	FTs	PCT	OFF	DEF	TOT	AST	PFs	DQ	STL	TO	BLK	PTS	AVG
Orlando	6899	3460	.502	2465	1648	.669	1149	2457	3606	2281	1726	11	672	1297	488	9091	110.9
Phoenix	6967	3356	.482	2352	1777	.756	1027	2403	3430	2198	1839	10	687	1167	312	9073	110.6
Seattle	6741	3310	.491	2564	1944	.758	1068	2337	3405	2115	2067	21	917	1295	392	9055	110.4
San Antonio	6687	3236	.484	2487	1836	.738	1029	2661	3690	1919	1871	11	656	1246	456	8742	106.6
Utah	6339	3243	.512	2483	1939	.781	874	2412	3286	2256	2045	16	758	1289	392	8726	106.4
Golden State	6873	3217	.468	2395	1687	.704	1101	2371	3472	2017	1804	20	649	1497	391	8667	105.7
L.A. Lakers	7088	3284	.463	2072	1523	.735	1126	2316	3442	2078	1933	22	750	1243	563	8616	105.1
Houston	6579	3159	.480	2039	1527	.749	880	2440	3320	2060	1714	10	721	1322	514	8491	103.5
Dallas	7342	3227	.440	2210	1622	.734	1514	2433	3947	1941	1811	17	579	1345	348	8462	103.2
Portland	7134	3217	.451	2230	1555	.697	1352	2443	3795	1846	2024	17	668	1212	467	8451	103.1
Boston	6847	3179	.464	2268	1708	.753	1156	2320	3476	1783	1975	21	612	1305	361	8428	102.8
Chicago	6710	3191	.476	2065	1500	.726	1106	2294	3400	1970	1962	20	797	1297	352	8325	101.5
Denver	6461	3098	.479	2305	1700	.738	1040	2402	3442	1836	2063	23	660	1381	585	8309	101.3
Miami	6738	3144	.467	2133	1569	.736	1092	2272	3364	1779	2000	25	662	1291	298	8293	101.1
Charlotte	6438	3051	.474	2042	1587	.777	832	2395	3227	2072	1685	11	620	1224	399	8240	100.6
Washington	6899	3176	.460	2013	1457	.724	1044	2219	3263	1749	1949	16	648	1301	404	8242	100.5
Milwaukee	6586	3022	.459	2259	1608	.712	1063	2187	3250	1737	1858	22	674	1393	359	8146	99.3
Indiana	6248	2983	.477	2390	1796	.751	1051	2290	3341	1877	1939	16	703	1340	363	8136	99.2
Sacramento	6463	3025	.468	2317	1647	.711	1073	2325	3398	1824	2040	15	650	1449	457	8056	98.2
New York	6394	2985	.467	2114	1552	.734	929	2473	3402	2055	2102	22	591	1305	387	8054	98.2
Detroit	6633	3060	.461	1941	1439	.741	958	2204	3162	1872	2151	24	705	1318	420	8053	98.2
New Jersey	6738	2939	.436	2305	1750	.759	1213	2569	3782	1884	1844	18	544	1300	548	8042	98.1
L.A. Clippers	6888	3060	.444	2079	1476	.710	1064	2076	3140	1805	2152	19	787	1334	435	7927	96.7
Atlanta	6680	2986	.447	1948	1410	.724	1104	2272	3376	1757	1804	13	738	1221	412	7921	96.6
Philadelphia	6577	2949	.448	2125	1567	.737	1105	2230	3335	1566	1835	34	643	1355	576	7820	95.4
Minnesota	6219	2792	.449	2355	1824	.775	883	2090	2973	1780	2074	14	609	1400	402	7726	94.2
Cleveland	6255	2756	.441	1982	1507	.760	1045	2237	3282	1672	1694	11	630	1176	349	7417	90.5

1994-95 DEFENSIVE TEAM STATISTICS

TEAM	FIELD GOALS			FREE THROWS			REBOUNDS			MISCELLANEOUS						SCORING		
	ATT	FGs	PCT	ATT	FTs	PCT	OFF	DEF	TOT	AST	PFs	DQ	STL	TO	BLK	PTS	AVG	DIF
Cleveland	6083	2803	.461	1801	1364	.757	851	2246	3097	1812	1770	14	556	1213	433	7366	89.8	+0.6
New York	6410	2800	.437	2449	1802	.736	1021	2317	3338	1584	1907	21	639	1264	324	7799	95.1	+3.1
Atlanta	6485	3001	.463	1919	1394	.726	1051	2391	3442	1733	1815	12	608	1359	320	7816	95.3	+1.3
Indiana	6408	2921	.456	2089	1516	.726	1048	2156	3204	1804	2058	24	691	1370	416	7833	95.5	+3.7
Chicago	6399	2923	.457	2280	1682	.738	1068	2252	3320	1713	1892	14	687	1485	369	7924	96.7	+4.8
Charlotte	6807	3088	.454	1859	1375	.740	1102	2365	3467	1898	1859	20	535	1216	368	7980	97.3	+3.3
Utah	6282	2845	.453	2477	1835	.741	917	2125	3042	1713	2053	15	648	1353	429	8071	98.4	+8.0
Sacramento	6549	2964	.453	2473	1833	.741	1145	2268	3413	1820	2033	18	756	1348	515	8138	99.2	-1.0
Portland	6465	2951	.456	2380	1794	.754	883	2295	3178	1789	1938	21	638	1302	405	8138	99.2	+3.8
Philadelphia	6663	3100	.465	2057	1569	.763	1143	2317	3460	1992	1859	22	712	1299	422	8236	100.4	-5.1
Denver	6695	3050	.456	2296	1721	.750	1021	2207	3228	1784	1956	24	640	1167	460	8240	100.5	+0.8
San Antonio	6974	3168	.454	2089	1491	.714	1017	2303	3320	1878	2063	25	633	1182	408	8253	100.6	+6.0
New Jersey	6904	3182	.461	2073	1495	.721	1056	2435	3491	1826	1911	21	733	1104	440	8299	101.2	-3.1
Houston	7061	3202	.453	1874	1407	.751	1165	2386	3551	1940	1779	12	744	1274	365	8317	101.4	+2.1
Seattle	6637	3008	.453	2514	1848	.735	1064	2207	3271	1849	2024	17	652	1485	493	8384	102.2	+8.2
Miami	6566	3092	.471	2340	1732	.740	1036	2355	3391	1860	1896	21	656	1332	385	8464	103.2	-1.6
Minnesota	6509	3088	.474	2491	1820	.731	1169	2305	3474	2069	1982	15	703	1323	512	8464	103.2	-9.0
Milwaukee	6589	3248	.493	2081	1517	.729	1014	2337	3351	2103	1973	18	770	1359	407	8504	103.7	-4.4
Orlando	7093	3242	.457	2106	1560	.741	1136	2226	3362	1986	1954	21	700	1234	367	8512	103.8	+7.1
Boston	6820	3303	.484	2225	1601	.720	1064	2335	3399	1999	1922	17	653	1232	454	8582	104.7	-1.9
L.A. Lakers	7050	3299	.468	2233	1580	.708	1283	2474	3757	2203	1807	16	644	1390	489	8634	105.3	-0.2
Detroit	6558	3120	.476	2720	1963	.722	1147	2432	3579	2013	1746	9	693	1286	439	8651	105.5	-7.3
L.A. Clippers	6470	3207	.496	2503	1876	.750	1083	2536	3619	1917	1905	9	693	1506	459	8678	105.8	-9.2
Dallas	6982	3407	.488	1981	1454	.734	1053	2379	3432	1991	1925	17	722	1250	502	8700	106.1	-2.9
Washington	6768	3246	.480	2315	1771	.765	1107	2521	3628	1959	1775	13	701	1359	446	8701	106.1	-5.6
Phoenix	6963	3320	.477	2138	1590	.744	1038	2431	3469	2149	2026	22	658	1285	391	8755	106.8	+3.9
Golden State	7233	3527	.488	2175	1565	.720	1196	2527	3723	2345	2133	21	865	1326	412	9111	111.1	-5.4

1995 NBA FINALS COMPOSITE BOX

Orlando	G	AVG MIN	FGs FG-ATT	PCT	FTs FT-ATT	PCT	REB	AST	STL	BLK	TOT PTS	AVG PTS
Shaquille O'Neal	4	45.0	44-74	.595	24-42	.571	50	25	1	10	112	28.0
Anfernee Hardaway	4	43.0	35-70	.500	21-23	.913	19	32	4	3	102	25.5
Horace Grant	4	42.0	25-47	.532	4-5	.800	48	6	2	2	54	13.5
Brian Shaw	4	21.0	20-47	.426	0-0	.000	13	13	2	1	50	12.5
Nick Anderson	4	40.3	18-50	.360	3-10	.300	34	17	8	2	49	12.3
Dennis Scott	4	37.5	13-42	.310	9-9	1.00	14	9	4	1	42	10.5
Anthony Bowie	4	6.5	6-10	.600	0-0	.000	2	6	0	1	13	3.3
Jeff Turner	4	10.8	2-10	.200	0-0	.000	4	2	0	0	6	1.5
Donald Royal	1	1.0	0-0	.000	0-0	.000	0	0	0	0	0	0.0
Totals	**4**	**49.3**	**163-350**	**.466**	**61-89**	**.685**	**184**	**110**	**21**	**20**	**428**	**107.0**

3-PT. FGP—41-118, .347 (Hardaway 11-24, Shaw 10-26, Anderson 10-31, Scott 7-29, Turner 2-6, Bowie 1-2)

Houston	G	AVG MIN	FGs FG-ATT	PCT	FTs FT-ATT	PCT	REB	AST	STL	BLK	TOT PTS	AVG PTS
Hakeem Olajuwon	4	44.8	56-116	.483	18-26	.692	46	22	8	8	131	32.8
Clyde Drexler	4	40.5	27-60	.450	30-38	.789	38	27	4	1	86	21.5
Robert Horry	4	46.8	23-53	.434	14-21	.667	40	15	12	9	71	17.8
Mario Elie	4	40.3	24-37	.649	9-10	.900	17	13	8	0	65	16.3
Sam Cassell	4	23.3	15-35	.429	20-24	.833	7	12	7	0	57	14.3
Kenny Smith	4	26.3	11-29	.379	0-0	.000	7	16	1	0	30	7.5
Chucky Brown	4	9.5	5-11	.455	2-2	1.00	11	0	0	2	12	3.0
Charles Jones	4	14.3	1-2	.500	2-2	1.00	7	0	0	0	4	1.0
Pete Chilcutt	3	1.0	0-0	.000	0-0	.000	0	0	0	0	0	0.0
Totals	**4**	**49.3**	**162-343**	**.472**	**95-123**	**.772**	**173**	**105**	**40**	**20**	**456**	**114.0**

3-PT. FGP—37-92, .402 (Horry 11-29, Elie 8-14, Smith 8-19, Cassell 7-15, Drexler 2-13, Olajuwon 1-1, Brown 0-1)

1994-95 MOST VALUABLE PLAYER VOTING

D. Robinson, SA (73)	901	C. Barkley, PHO (1)	96	Michael Jordan, CHI	12
S. O'Neal, ORL (12)	605	S. Pippen, CHI (1)	83	Dennis Rodman, SA	9
K. Malone, UTA (14)	532	J. Stockton, UTA (1)	47	Jason Kidd, DAL	7
P. Ewing, NY (2)	230	Gary Payton, SEA	34	Clyde Drexler, POR/HOU	3
H. Olajuwon, HOU (1)	147	Anfernee Hardaway, ORL	23	Cedric Ceballos, LAL	1

* 1st-place votes in parentheses.

DEFENSIVE PLAYER OF THE YEAR

D. Mutombo, DEN	45
Scottie Pippen, CHI	16
H. Olajuwon, HOU	13
David Robinson, SA	12
Dennis Rodman, SA	11
Derrick McKey, IND	2
Nate McMillan, SEA	2
Alonzo Mourning, CHA	2
Gary Payton, SEA	2

SIXTH MAN AWARD

Anthony Mason, NY	47
Dell Curry, CHA	18
Chuck Person, SA	12
Nate McMillan, SEA	9
Dennis Scott, ORL	7
Byron Scott, IND	6
Antoine Carr, UTA	3
Chris Gatling, GS	2
Armon Gilliam, NJ	1

ROOKIE OF THE YEAR

Grant Hill, DET	43
Jason Kidd, DAL	43
Glenn Robinson, MIL	15
Eddie Jones, LAL	2
Brian Grant, SAC	1
Juwan Howard, WAS	1

COACH OF THE YEAR

Del Harris, LAL	62
Mike Fratello, CLE	15
Bob Hill, SA	12
Jerry Sloan, UTA	11
Dick Motta, DAL	5

1995-96 NBA Schedule

Below is the NBA schedule for the 1995-96 season. All game times listed are local. TNT telecasts are denoted by a "•", TBS games by a "+", and NBC games by a "#". The symbol "@" indicates more games that NBC may telecast; the network will make its decision at a later date.

Fri Nov 3
Mil at Bos, 7:30
Was at Phi, 7:30
Cle at Orl, 7:30
Ind at Atl, 7:30
NJ at Tor, 9:00
NY at Det, 7:30
•Cha at Chi, 7:00
GS at Hou, 7:30
Dal at SA, 7:30
Sea at Uta, 7:00
Pho at LAC, 7:30
Den at LAL, 7:30
Min at Sac, 7:30
Van at Por, 7:00

Sat Nov 4
Det at Was, 7:30
Cle at Mia, 7:30
Phi at Cha, 7:30
Orl at Atl, 7:30
Tor at Ind, 7:30
Bos at Chi, 7:30
NY at Mil, 7:30
GS at Dal, 7:30
SA at Den, 7:00
LAL at Sea, 7:00

Sun Nov 5
Hou at Pho, 7:00
LAC at Sac, 6:00
Uta at Por, 5:00
Min at Van, 6:00

Mon Nov 6
Was at Orl, 7:30
Atl at Uta, 7:00

Tue Nov 7
•Pho at NY, 8:00
Por at NJ, 7:30
Sac at Phi, 7:30
Det at Cha, 7:30
Ind at Cle, 7:30
Tor at Chi, 7:30
LAL at Min, 7:00
Van at Dal, 7:30
Mil at Hou, 7:30
Den at GS, 7:30
LAC at Sea, 7:00

Wed Nov 8
Pho at Bos, 7:30
Cha at Was, 7:30
NJ at Orl, 7:30

Hou at Mia, 7:30
Sac at Tor, 7:00
Por at Det, 7:30
Van at SA, 7:30
Sea at Den, 7:00
LAL at Uta, 7:00
Atl at LAC, 7:30

Thu Nov 9
Ind at NY, 7:30
Chi at Cle, 7:30
Mil at Dal, 7:30
Atl at GS, 7:30

Fri Nov 10
•Orl at Bos, 8:00
Cha at Phi, 7:30
NY at Was, 7:30
NJ at Mia, 7:30
Pho at Tor, 7:00
Cle at Det, 7:30
Sac at Ind, 7:30
Por at Min, 7:00
Mil at SA, 7:30
Den at Uta, 7:00
Sea at LAL, 7:30
•LAC at Van, 7:30

Sat Nov 11
Sac at NJ, 8:00
Mia at Orl, 7:30
Tor at Cha, 7:30
Por at Chi, 7:30
Atl at Dal, 7:30
Min at Hou, 7:30
LAL at GS, 7:30
Van at Sea, 7:00

Sun Nov 12
Uta at NY, 6:00
SA at Cle, 7:30
GS at Pho, 7:00
Den at LAC, 6:00

Mon Nov 13
Uta at Tor, 7:00
Dal at Van, 7:00

Tue Nov 14
Sea at Phi, 7:30

Wed Nov 15
Uta at Bos, 7:30
Cha at NJ, 7:30
Phi at Was, 7:30
Ind at Mia, 7:30
Hou at Tor, 7:00

Sea at Det, 7:30
Cle at Chi, 7:30
SA at Min, 7:00
+Den at Pho, 6:00
+Dal at LAL, 7:30

Thu Nov 16
Ind at Orl, 7:30
Hou at Mil, 7:30
Van at LAC (Ana), 7:30
NY at GS, 7:30
Sac at Por, 7:00

Fri Nov 17
Was at Bos, 7:30
Cle at Phi, 7:30
Sea at Cha, 7:30
Mia at Atl, 7:30
Min at Tor, 7:00
•Uta at Det, 8:00
NJ at Chi, 7:30
NY at Den, 7:00
Dal at LAC, 7:30
Pho at Sac, 7:30
LAL at Van, 7:00

Sat Nov 18
Phi at NJ, 8:00
Tor at Was, 7:30
Orl at Mia, 7:30
Det at Cle, 7:30
Sea at Ind, 7:30
Bos at Mil, 7:30
Uta at Min, 7:00
Den at Hou, 7:30
Cha at SA, 7:30
Por at Pho, 7:00
Dal at GS, 7:30

Sun Nov 19
Van at NY, 8:00
LAC at LAL, 6:30
Atl at Sac, 6:00

Mon Nov 20
Hou at Bos, 7:30
GS at Orl, 7:30
NJ at Uta, 7:00
LAC at Por, 7:00

Tue Nov 21
•Sea at Tor, 8:00
Chi at Dal, 7:30
Atl at Den, 7:00
Por at LAL, 7:30

Wed Nov 22
Hou at Phi, 7:30
Van at Orl, 7:30
GS at Mia, 7:30
Bos at Cha, 7:30
NY at Cle, 7:30
Was at Det, 7:30
Tor at Mil, 7:30
Sea at Min, 7:00
+Chi at SA, 7:00
Sac at Uta, 7:00
Atl at Pho, 7:00
NJ at LAC, 7:30

Thu Nov 23
Hou at Ind, 7:30

Fri Nov 24
GS at Bos, 7:30
Mia at Was (Bal), 7:30
Van at Cha, 7:30
Phi at Det, 7:30
Cle at Ind, 7:30
Orl at Min, 7:00
Den at Dal, 7:30
•Chi at Uta, 6:00
Sac at LAL, 7:30
NJ at Por, 7:00
SA at Sea, 7:00

Sat Nov 25
Hou at NY, 1:00
GS at Phi, 7:30
Orl at Was, 7:30
Van at Mia, 7:30
Tor at Atl, 7:30
Mil at Cle, 7:30
Uta at Den, 7:00
LAL at Pho, 7:00
SA at LAC, 7:30

Sun Nov 26
Cha at Bos, 7:00
Hou at Det, 7:00
Min at Mil, 6:00
NJ at Sac, 6:00
Chi at Sea, 5:00

Mon Nov 27
Det at Orl, 7:30
GS at Tor, 7:00
Uta at Pho, 7:00
Chi at Por, 7:00

Tue Nov 28
Atl at NY, 7:30

Was at NJ, 7:30
Dal at Mia, 7:30
Tor at Cle, 7:30
•Cha at Mil, 7:00
Van at Min, 7:00
LAC at Hou, 7:30
Den at Sac, 7:30
Ind at Sea, 7:00

Wed Nov 29
Det at Bos, 7:30
+NY at Cha, 8:00
Phi at Atl, 7:30
LAC at SA, 7:30
Pho at LAL, 7:30
Por at GS, 7:30

Thu Nov 30
Cle at Was, 7:30
Dal at Orl, 7:30
Mia at Det, 7:30
Uta at Hou, 7:30
Ind at Sac, 7:30
Mil at Por, 7:00
Chi at Van, 7:00

Fri Dec 1
NJ at Bos, 7:30
Cha at Mia, 7:30
•Dal at Atl, 8:00
Phi at Tor, 7:00
Min at Pho, 7:00
Van at LAL, 7:30
Mil at Sea, 7:00

Sat Dec 2
Cle at NJ, 7:30
NY at Phi, 7:30
Bos at Was (Bal), 7:30
Atl at Det, 7:30
Cha at Hou, 7:30
Pho at SA, 7:30
Min at Den, 7:00
Chi at LAC (Ana), 7:30
Ind at GS, 7:30
Orl at Sac, 7:30

Sun Dec 3
Was at NY, 6:00
Mia at Tor, 5:30
Dal at Cle, 7:30
Ind at LAL, 6:30
Orl at Por, 6:00
Mil at Van, 2:00

Mon Dec 4
Mia at Bos, 7:30
Det at Den, 7:00

Tue Dec 5
Dal at NY, 7:30
Phi at Ind, 7:30
LAL at SA, 7:30
•Hou at Uta, 6:00

Van at Pho, 7:00
Orl at LAC, 7:30
Tor at Sea, 7:00

Wed Dec 6
Dal at Phi, 7:30
Atl at Was, 7:30
Bos at Mia, 7:30
Cle at Cha, 7:30
+NY at Chi, 7:30
NJ at Min, 7:00
LAL at Hou, 7:30
Orl at GS, 7:30

Thu Dec 7
SA at Atl, 7:30
LAC at Mil, 7:30
Den at Uta, 7:00
Tor at Por, 7:00
Det at Van, 7:00

Fri Dec 8
Ind at NJ, 7:30
•Cha at Orl, 8:00
Phi at Cle, 7:30
SA at Chi, 7:30
LAC at Min, 7:00
Was at Hou, 7:30
Pho at Den, 7:00
Tor at LAL, 7:30
Det at GS, 7:30
Sea at Sac, 7:30

Sat Dec 9
Bos at Phi, 7:30
Min at Cha, 7:30
NY at Atl, 7:30
NJ at Cle, 7:30
Chi at Mil, 7:30
Was at Dal, 7:30
GS at Uta, 7:00
Mia at Pho, 7:00
Por at Sea, 7:30

Sun Dec 10
SA at NY, 6:00
LAC at Ind, 2:30
Det at LAL, 6:30
Mia at Sac, 6:00
Hou at Por, 7:00
Tor at Van, 5:30

Mon Dec 11
Den at Phi, 7:30
Cha at Uta, 7:00

Tue Dec 12
•LAL at NY, 8:00
Orl at NJ, 7:30
Mil at Was, 7:30
Min at Atl, 7:30
Bos at Tor, 7:00
LAC at Cle, 7:30
Den at Ind, 7:30
Sea at Dal, 7:30

Cha at Pho, 7:00
Mia at GS, 7:30
Hou at Sac, 7:30

Wed Dec 13
Phi at Bos, 7:30
LAL at Det, 7:30
+Orl at Chi, 7:00
Sea at SA, 7:30
Hou at Van, 7:00

Thu Dec 14
Den at NY, 7:30
Chi at Atl, 7:30
Ind at Tor, 7:00
SA at Dal, 7:30
Mia at LAC, 7:30
Cha at Por, 7:00

Fri Dec 15
Tor at Bos, 7:30
LAL at Was, 7:30
•Uta at Orl, 8:00
NJ at Det, 7:30
Mil at Ind, 7:30
Cle at Min, 7:00
Sac at Hou, 7:30
GS at Sea, 7:00
Por at Van, 7:00

Sat Dec 16
Det at NY, 7:30
Uta at Mia, 7:30
Den at Atl, 7:30
LAL at Chi, 7:30
Pho at Dal, 7:30
Sac at SA, 7:30
Cha at LAC, 7:30
GS at Van, 7:00

Sun Dec 17
Orl at Tor, 5:30
Den at Cle, 7:30
Ind at Mil, 6:00
Phi at Min, 5:00
Was at Por, 1:00

Mon Dec 18
Chi at Bos, 7:30
Uta at NJ, 7:30
Van at Sac, 7:30

Tue Dec 19
Mia at NY, 7:30
Det at Tor, 7:30
Min at Cle, 7:30
Dal at Chi, 7:30
LAL at Mil, 7:30
•Pho at Hou, 7:00
Por at SA, 7:30
Was at LAC, 7:30
Cha at GS, 7:30
Sea at Van, 7:00

Wed Dec 20
Mia at NJ, 7:30

Uta at Phi, 7:30
Min at Orl, 7:30
+Mil at Det, 8:00
LAL at Ind, 7:30
GS at Den, 7:00
Was at Pho, 7:00

Thu Dec 21
Bos at Cha, 7:30
Uta at Cle, 7:30
Por at Hou, 7:30
Den at SA, 7:30
Sac at LAC, 7:30
Van at Sea, 7:00

Fri Dec 22
Min at Bos, 7:30
Mil at Phi, 7:30
•NY at Orl, 8:00
Det at Mia, 7:30
NJ at Atl, 7:30
Dal at Ind, 6:00
Tor at Chi, 7:30
•Sac at LAL, 7:30
Was at GS, 7:30
Pho at Van, 7:00

Sat Dec 23
Tor at NY, 7:30
NJ at Phi, 7:30
Mia at Cha, 7:30
Ind at Cle, 7:30
Orl at Det, 7:30
Uta at Mil, 7:30
Atl at Mil, 7:30
Dal at Min, 7:00
Hou at SA, 7:30
LAC at Den, 7:00
LAL at Por, 7:30
Was at Sea, 7:00

Mon Dec 25
#Hou at Orl, 6:00
#SA at Pho, 1:30

Tue Dec 26
NJ at Mia, 7:30
LAC at Atl, 7:30
Mil at Tor (Ham), 1:30
GS at Det, 7:30
•Chi at Ind, 8:00
Van at Hou, 7:30
Dal at Den, 7:00
Por at Uta, 7:00
Bos at LAL, 7:30
SA at Sac, 7:30

Wed Dec 27
+GS at Was, 8:00
LAC at Cha, 7:30
Mil at Min, 7:30
Phi at Pho, 7:00
Bos at Por, 7:00
Den at Sea, 7:00

Thu Dec 28
Cle at NY, 7:30
Tor at Det, 7:30
Mia at Ind, 6:00
Van at Dal, 7:30
NJ at Hou, 7:30
Min at Uta, 7:00
SA at LAL, 7:30
Fri Dec 29
NY at Was, 7:30
LAC at Orl, 7:30
Por at Cha, 7:30
GS at Atl, 7:30
Ind at Chi, 7:30
Den at Pho, 7:00
Phi at Sac, 7:00
Bos at Sea, 7:00
Sat Dec 30
GS at NJ, 7:30
LAC at Mia, 7:30
Por at Cle, 7:30
Cha at Det, 7:30
Atl at Chi, 7:30
Was at Mil, 7:30
Hou at Dal, 7:30
Min at SA, 7:30
Phi at Den, 7:00
LAL at Uta, 1:00
Sea at Pho, 7:00
Bos at Van, 7:00
Tue Jan 2
Por at NY, 7:30
Mil at NJ, 7:30
Cle at Was, 7:30
Sea at Atl, 7:30
Hou at Min, 7:00
Uta at Dal, 7:30
Ind at Den, 7:00
Phi at LAL, 7:30
Wed Jan 3
Por at Bos, 7:30
Tor at Orl, 7:30
+Hou at Chi, 7:00
Det at Mil, 7:30
Uta at SA, 7:30
Ind at LAC, 7:30
Phi at GS, 7:30
Thu Jan 4
NJ at NY, 7:30
Dal at Was, 7:30
Sea at Mia, 7:30
Chi at Cha, 7:30
Tor at Atl, 7:30
Min at Pho, 7:00
Den at Sac, 7:30
Fri Jan 5
Cle at Bos, 7:30
Dal at NJ, 7:30

Sea at Orl, 7:30
Por at Mil, 7:30
•Ind at SA, 7:00
Pho at LAC, 7:30
Uta at LAL, 7:30
Min at GS, 7:30
Phi at Van, 7:00
Sat Jan 6
Atl at Cha, 7:30
Orl at Cle, 7:30
Was at Det, 7:30
Mil at Chi, 7:30
Ind at Hou, 7:30
Mia at Den, 7:00
GS at Sac, 7:30
Sun Jan 7
Dal at Bos, 7:00
Sea at NY, 8:00
Atl at NJ, 7:30
Den at LAL, 6:30
Min at Por, 7:00
LAC at Van, 2:00
Mon Jan 8
Orl at Phi, 7:30
Was at Cle, 7:30
Mia at Uta, 7:00
Tue Jan 9
Bos at NY, 7:30
NJ at Orl, 7:30
Sac at Atl, 7:30
Cha at Tor, 7:00
Sea at Mil, 7:30
Ind at Dal, 7:30
•SA at Hou, 7:00
LAC at Pho, 7:30
Min at LAL, 7:30
Van at GS, 7:30
Wed Jan 10
Sac at Bos, 7:30
NY at NJ, 7:30
Was at Phi, 7:30
+Sea at Chi, 7:00
Cle at SA, 7:30
Mia at Por, 7:00
Den at Van, 7:00
Thu Jan 11
Det at Cha, 7:30
Atl at Tor, 7:00
Mil at Ind, 7:30
Min at LAC, 7:30
Pho at GS, 7:30
Fri Jan 12
NY at Bos, 7:30
Phi at NJ, 7:30
Sac at Was, 7:30
Mil at Orl, 7:30
Cle at Den, 7:00
SA at Uta, 7:00

•Dal at Pho, 6:00
Hou at LAL, 7:30
Mia at Sea, 7:00
GS at Van, 7:00
Sat Jan 13
Sac at NY, 7:30
Det at NJ, 7:30
Chi at Phi, 7:30
Bos at Atl, 7:30
Was at Tor, 6:00
Min at Ind, 2:30
Cha at Dal, 7:30
Orl at SA, 7:30
Por at Den, 7:00
Hou at LAC, 7:30
Mia at Van, 7:00
Sun Jan 14
Cle at Pho, 7:00
Mon Jan 15
Mil at NY, 1:00
Tor at NJ, 7:30
Chi at Was, 1:00
Det at Atl, 1:00
Sac at Min, 2:30
Orl at Dal, 7:30
Uta at Hou, 7:30
Mia at LAL, 1:30
Sea at GS, 2:00
Tue Jan 16
Ind at Tor, 7:00
Phi at Chi, 7:30
Bos at SA, 7:30
Den at Por, 7:30
•Cle at Sea, 5:00
Wed Jan 17
Mil at Phi, 7:30
Was at Mia, 7:30
NJ at Cha, 7:30
Ind at Atl, 7:30
GS at Min, 7:00
Hou at Den, 7:00
+Orl at Pho, 6:00
NY at LAC, 7:30
Thu Jan 18
Chi at Tor, 7:00
SA at Det, 7:30
GS at Mil, 7:30
Bos at Hou, 7:30
Por at Sac, 7:30
Cle at Van, 7:00
Fri Jan 19
Atl at Phi, 7:30
NJ at Was (Bal), 7:30
•Cha at Mia, 8:00
Det at Ind, 7:30
SA at Min, 7:00
Bos at Dal, 7:30
Orl at Uta, 7:00

LAL at LAC, 7:30
Pho at Por, 7:00
NY at Sea, 7:00
Sat Jan 20
Min at NJ, 7:30
GS at Cha, 7:30
Mia at Atl, 7:30
Sac at Den, 7:00
Uta at LAC (Ana), 7:30
Cle at LAL, 7:30
NY at Van, 7:00
Sun Jan 21
SA at Phi, 7:00
Bos at Tor, 12:00
#Chi at Det, 12:00
Was at Ind, 2:30
#Orl at Hou, 1:30
Sac at Pho, 7:00
Cle at Por, 6:00
Dal at Sea, 5:00
Mon Jan 22
SA at Mia, 7:30
Hou at Atl, 7:30
Van at Mil, 7:30
Tue Jan 23
•Chi at NY, 8:00
Phi at Orl, 7:30
NJ at Tor, 7:00
Atl at Cle, 7:30
Pho at Ind, 7:30
Por at Uta, 7:00
Dal at Sac, 7:30
Wed Jan 24
LAL at Bos, 7:30
Hou at NJ, 7:30
Cle at Phi, 7:30
NY at Mia, 7:30
Was at Cha, 7:30
Van at Chi, 7:30
Ind at Mil, 7:30
+Pho at Min, 7:00
Det at SA, 7:30
Uta at GS, 7:30
Den at Sea, 7:00
Thu Jan 25
Hou at Was, 7:30
Van at Tor, 8:30
Det at Dal, 7:30
Den at LAC, 7:30
Fri Jan 26
Ind at Bos, 7:30
Cha at NJ, 7:30
•LAL at Phi, 8:00
Orl at Atl, 7:30
Mia at Chi, 7:30
Pho at Mil, 7:30
Por at SA, 7:30

Sac at GS, 7:30
Uta at Sea, 7:00

Sat Jan 27
Atl at Bos, 7:30
Min at NY, 7:30
LAL at NJ, 7:30
Van at Was, 7:30
Phi at Cha, 7:30
Mia at Cle, 7:30
Orl at Ind, 7:30
Por at Dal, 7:30
Det at Hou, 7:30
Tor at Den, 7:00
GS at Uta, 7:00
Sea at LAC (Ana), 7:30

Sun Jan 28
#Pho at Chi, 12:00

Mon Jan 29
Mia at NY, 7:30
Van at Phi, 7:30
Cle at Cha, 7:30
Det at Uta, 7:00
Sea at Por, 7:00

Tue Jan 30
Bos at Orl, 7:30
Pho at Mia, 7:30
Atl at Ind, 7:30
Den at Min, 7:00
LAC at Dal, 7:30
•Chi at Hou, 7:00
GS at LAL, 7:30
Tor at Sac, 7:30
NJ at Sea, 7:00

Wed Jan 31
Van at Bos, 7:30
Pho at Atl, 7:30
Mil at Cle, 7:30
LAC at SA, 7:30
+Uta at Por, 5:00

Thu Feb 1
Orl at NY, 7:30
Phi at Mia, 7:30
Hou at Cha, 7:30
Ind at Det, 7:30
Den at Mil, 7:30
Sea at Dal, 7:30
Chi at Sac, 7:30

Fri Feb 2
Por at Was, 7:30
Atl at Orl, 7:30
•Pho at Cle, 8:00
Bos at Ind, 7:30
Min at SA, 7:30
LAC at Uta, 7:00
Chi at LAL, 7:30
Tor at GS, 7:30
NJ at Van, 7:00

Sat Feb 3
Por at Phi, 7:30
Bos at Mia, 7:30
Sac at Det, 7:30
Cle at Mil, 7:30
Min at Dal, 7:30
Sea at Hou, 7:30
Tor at LAC, 7:30

Sun Feb 4
Pho at Was, 1:00
#SA at Orl, 3:30
Cha at Atl, 7:00
#NY at Ind, 1:00
Chi at Den, 7:00
Uta at LAL, 6:30
NJ at GS, 7:30

Mon Feb 5
Det at NY, 7:30
Sac at Mia, 7:30
Por at Tor, 7:00
Dal at Min, 7:00
GS at LAC, 7:30
Uta at Van, 7:00

Tue Feb 6
Sac at Orl, 7:30
SA at Cha, 7:30
Bos at Cle, 7:30
Dal at Mil, 7:30
LAL at Den, 7:00
•Chi at Pho, 6:00
Hou at Sea, 7:00

Wed Feb 7
SA at Bos, 7:30
Was at NY, 7:30
Ind at Phi, 7:30
Atl at Mia, 7:30
Mil at Tor, 7:00
+Orl at Det, 8:00
Por at Min, 7:00
Van at Den, 7:30
Hou at LAC, 7:30
+NJ at LAL, 7:30
Chi at GS, 7:30

Thu Feb 8
Sac at Cha, 7:30
Was at Atl, 7:30
Utah at Dal, 7:30
LAC at Den, 7:00
NJ at Pho, 7:00

Sun Feb 11
#All-Star Game (SA), 5:00

Tue Feb 13
Den at Orl, 7:30
Tor at Mia, 7:30
Cha at Cle, 7:30
NJ at Ind, 7:30
Was at Chi, 7:30

Phi at Mil, 7:30
•Dal at Hou, 7:00
Uta at SA, 7:30
Sea at Pho, 7:00
Bos at LAC, 7:30
Min at Sac, 7:30
GS at Por, 7:00

Wed Feb 14
Ind at NJ, 7:30
Det at Phi, 7:30
+NY at Cha, 8:00
Atl at LAL, 7:30
Bos at GS, 7:30
Min at Sea, 7:00
Sac at Van, 7:00

Thu Feb 15
Den at Mia, 7:30
Cle at Tor (Ham), 7:00
Chi at Det, 7:30
Was at Mil, 7:30
SA at Hou, 7:30
Dal at Uta, 7:00
Pho at Por, 7:00

Fri Feb 16
Phi at NY, 7:30
Ind at Was (Bal), 7:30
Mil at Orl, 7:30
•Den at Cha, 8:00
Chi at Min, 7:00
GS at SA, 7:30
Dal at LAL, 7:30
Bos at Sac, 7:30
Pho at Sea, 7:00
Atl at Van, 7:00

Sat Feb 17
NY at NJ, 7:30
Orl at Mia, 7:30
Phi at Cle, 7:30
Tor at Det, 7:30
Por at LAC (Ana), 7:30

Sun Feb 18
#Mil at Cha, 3:30
#Chi at Ind, 1:00
Was at Min, 2:30
#Hou at SA, 2:30
Bos at Den, 7:00
Atl at Por, 7:00
Sea at Van, 12:30

Mon Feb 19
NJ at Was, 7:00
Mia at Cle, 3:30
Min at Det, 7:30
GS at Dal, 7:30
Sac at Hou, 7:30
Van at Pho, 7:00
Atl at Sea, 7:00

Tue Feb 20
Mil at NY, 7:30

Phi at Orl, 7:30
•Cle at Chi, 7:00
Bos at Uta, 7:00
LAC at LAL, 7:30
SA at Por, 7:00

Wed Feb 21
Mia at Phi, 7:30
Was at Cha, 7:30
NY at Det, 7:30
+Orl at Ind, 8:00
NJ at Mil, 7:30
Hou at Min, 7:00
Sac at Dal, 7:30
Bos at Pho, 7:00
LAL at LAC, 7:30
SA at GS, 7:30

Thu Feb 22
Chi at Atl, 7:30
Hou at Cle, 7:30
Tor at Uta, 7:00
Den at Por, 7:00
GS at Sea, 7:00

Fri Feb 23
Atl at NY, 7:30
Cha at Was, 7:30
Chi at Mia, 7:30
Phi at Ind, 7:30
Orl at Mil, 7:30
Det at Min, 7:30
•LAL at Dal, 7:00
Tor at Pho, 7:00
SA at Sac, 7:30

Sat Feb 24
Ind at Cha, 7:30
NJ at Cle, 7:30
LAL at Hou, 7:30
Uta at Den, 7:00
LAC at GS, 7:30
Sac at Sea, 7:00

Sun Feb 25
Bos at NJ, 7:00
Mil at Was, 1:00
Phi at Mia, 6:00
#Orl at Chi, 12:00
Atl at Min, 2:30
Tor at Dal, 7:00
#NY at Pho, 1:30
Sea at LAC, 6:00
Det at Por, 3:00
SA at Van, 12:30

Mon Feb 26
Ind at Bos, 7:30
Pho at Uta, 7:00
NY at LAL, 7:30
Det at Sac, 7:30

Tue Feb 27
Mia at NJ, 7:30
GS at Cle, 7:30

Por at Ind, 7:30
Min at Chi, 7:30
•Cha at Mil, 7:00
Phi at Dal, 7:30
Tor at Hou, 7:30
Was at Den, 7:00
SA at LAC (Ana), 7:30

Wed Feb 28
Cha at Bos, 7:30
Mia at Orl, 7:30
Por at Atl, 7:30
Pho at Min, 7:00
Was at Uta, 7:00
NY at Sac, 7:30
+Det at Sea, 5:00
LAL at Van, 7:00

Thu Feb 29
Orl at NJ, 7:30
GS at Ind, 7:30
Cle at Mil, 7:30
Phi at Hou, 7:30
Tor at SA, 7:30
Dal at Den, 7:00
Sac at LAC, 7:30

Fri Mar 1
Sea at Bos, 7:30
Por at Mia, 7:30
Cle at Atl, 7:30
GS at Chi, 7:30
Cha at Min, 7:00
•NY at Uta, 6:00
Det at Pho, 7:00
Was at LAL, 7:30
Dal at Van, 7:00

Sat Mar 2
Sea at NJ, 7:30
Por at Orl, 7:30
Bos at Chi, 7:30
Atl at Mil, 7:30
Phi at SA, 7:30
Van at Den, 7:00
Det at LAC, 7:30

Sun Mar 3
GS at NY, 6:00
Tor at Cle, 3:00
#Cha at Ind, 3:30
Mia at Min, 2:30
#Pho at Dal, 12:00
#Hou at LAL, 12:30
Was at Sac, 6:00

Mon Mar 4
Mil at Bos, 7:30
Atl at Det, 7:30
SA at Den, 7:00
Was at Van, 7:00

Tue Mar 5
LAC at NY, 7:30
Min at Mia, 7:30

•Orl at Cha, 8:00
Det at Tor, 7:00
Sea at Cle, 7:30
Mil at Chi, 7:30
NJ at Dal, 7:30
Ind at Pho, 7:00
Van at GS, 7:30
Uta at Sac, 7:30
Hou at Por, 7:00

Wed Mar 6
LAC at Bos, 7:30
Min at Phi, 7:30
Sea at Was, 7:30
NY at Tor, 7:30
+Den at SA, 7:00
Ind at Uta, 7:00

Thu Mar 7
Dal at Cha, 7:30
Atl at Cle, 7:30
Det at Chi, 7:30
Pho at Den, 7:00
Hou at GS, 7:30
LAL at Sac, 7:30

Fri Mar 8
Cle at Bos, 7:30
NY at Phi, 7:30
LAC at Was, 7:30
Cha at Orl, 7:30
Tor at Mia, 7:30
Mil at Atl, 7:30
Sea at Min, 7:00
NJ at SA, 7:30
Hou at Uta, 7:00
LAL at Pho, 7:00
Sac at Por, 7:00
Ind at Van, 7:00

Sat Mar 9
Dal at Det, 7:30
GS at Den, 7:00

Sun Mar 10
#Chi at NY, 5:30
LAC at Phi, 1:00
Atl at Was, 3:00
#Pho at Orl, 12:30
Cle at Mia, 1:00
Dal at Tor, 8:00
Bos at Min, 2:30
Uta at Min, 2:30
NJ at Den, 7:00
Sac at GS, 7:30
Ind at Por, 12:00
SA at Sea, 5:00
Hou at Van, 12:00

Mon Mar 11
LAC at Det, 7:30
Van at Sac, 7:30

Tue Mar 12
Pho at NJ, 7:30

Tor at Phi, 7:30
Uta at Atl, 7:30
Mia at Dal, 7:30
•Orl at Den, 6:00
Por at LAL, 7:30
SA at GS, 7:30

Wed Mar 13
Phi at Bos, 7:30
Uta at Cha, 7:30
+Pho at Det, 8:00
Was at Chi, 7:30
NY at Min, 7:00
Mil at Sac, 7:30
Orl at Sea, 7:00

Thu Mar 14
Was at NJ, 7:30
Bos at Cle, 7:30
Atl at Hou, 7:30
Mia at SA, 7:30
Dal at LAC (Ana), 7:30
LAL at GS, 7:30

Fri Mar 15
Pho at Phi, 7:30
Tor at Cha, 7:30
Cle at Det, 7:30
Uta at Ind, 7:30
Den at Chi, 7:30
Sac at Min, 7:00
Mil at LAL, 7:30
LAC at Por, 7:00
Dal at Sea, 7:00
Orl at Van, 7:00

Sat Mar 16
Phi at NY, 7:30
Chi at NJ, 7:30
Uta at Was, 7:30
Mia at Hou, 7:30
Atl at SA, 7:30
Mil at GS, 7:30

Sun Mar 17
NJ at Bos, 7:30
#Pho at Cha, 12:00
Sac at Cle, 1:00
#Den at Det, 12:00
Tor at Ind, 3:00
Van at Min, 2:30
Orl at LAL, 6:30
Dal at Por, 1:00

Mon Mar 18
Chi at Phi, 7:30
Den at Tor, 7:00
Uta at Mil, 7:30
GS at SA, 7:30
LAC at Sea, 7:00

Tue Mar 19
Van at NJ, 7:30
Det at Orl, 7:30

Ind at Cha, 7:30
Sac at Chi, 7:30
Cle at Dal, 7:30
•GS at Hou, 7:00
Sea at LAL, 7:30
Min at Por, 7:00

Wed Mar 20
Orl at Bos, 7:30
+Ind at NY, 8:00
SA at Was, 7:30
Det at Mia, 7:30
Van at Atl, 7:30
Cha at Tor, 7:00
Sac at Mil, 7:30
Phi at Uta, 7:00
Min at LAC, 7:30

Thu Mar 21
Den at NJ, 7:30
NY at Chi, 7:30
Cle at Hou, 7:30
GS at Pho, 7:00
LAL at Sea, 7:00

Fri Mar 22
Den at Bos, 7:30
Orl at Was, 7:30
Atl at Cha, 7:30
SA at Tor, 7:00
NJ at Det, 7:30
Van at Ind, 7:30
Mia at Mil, 7:30
Min at Dal, 7:30
Cle at Uta, 7:00
Phi at LAC, 7:30
Por at Sac, 7:30

Sat Mar 23
Det at Atl, 7:30
Min at Hou, 7:30
Pho at GS, 7:30
Phi at Sea, 7:00

Sun Mar 24
Mia at Bos, 7:00
Den at Was, 3:30
Chi at Tor, 3:30
Van at Cle, 1:00
#SA at Ind, 1:00
NJ at Mil, 2:30
#NY at Dal, 12:00
LAC at Pho, 7:00
Cha at LAL, 6:30
Sea at Sac, 6:00

Mon Mar 25
SA at NJ, 7:30
Dal at Uta, 7:00
Phi at Por, 7:00

Tue Mar 26
•LAL at Orl, 8:00
Atl at Tor, 7:00
Was at Cle, 7:30

Van at Det, 7:30
Bos at Ind, 7:30
NY at Hou, 7:30
Cha at Den, 7:00
Sac at Pho, 7:00
Mil at LAC, 7:30
Sea at GS, 7:30

Wed Mar 27
Tor at Phi, 7:30
Ind at Was, 7:30
LAL at Mia, 7:30
Bos at Min, 7:00
Hou at Dal, 7:30
+NY at SA, 7:00
Mil at Uta, 7:00
Cha at Sea, 7:00

Thu Mar 28
Atl at Chi, 7:30
Cle at LAC, 7:30
GS at Por, 7:00
Den at Van, 7:00

Fri Mar 29
NJ at NY, 7:30
Bos at Phi, 7:30
Was at Mia, 7:30
LAL at Atl, 7:30
Orl at Tor, 7:00
Ind at Min, 7:00
•SA at Dal, 7:00
Van at Uta, 7:00
Mil at Pho, 7:00
Cha at Sac, 7:30

Sat Mar 30
Phi at Was, 7:30
Mia at Det, 7:30
LAC at Chi, 12:00
Por at Hou, 7:30
Mil at Den, 7:00
Cle at GS, 7:30
Uta at Sea, 7:00

Sun Mar 31
Atl at Bos, 2:30
#NY at Orl, 12:00
LAL at Tor, 3:00
NJ at Ind, 2:30
LAC at Min, 2:30
Por at Dal, 7:00
Pho at SA, 2:30
Cle at Sac, 6:00
Cha at Van, 2:00

Tue Apr 2
Chi at Mia, 7:30
•LAL at Cha, 8:00
Bos at Atl, 7:30
LAC at Tor, 7:00
NY at Ind, 7:30
Det at Mil, 7:30
Sac at Dal, 7:30

Min at Den, 7:00
Sea at Uta, 7:00
SA at Pho, 7:00
Hou at GS, 7:30
Van at Por, 7:00

Wed Apr 3
+Orl at NY, 8:00
LAC at NJ, 7:30
Ind at Phi, 7:30
LAL at Cle, 7:30
Cha at Det, 7:30
Sac at SA, 7:30
Hou at Sea, 7:00
Min at Van, 7:00

Thu Apr 4
Bos at Orl, 7:30
Was at Atl, 7:30
Cle at Tor, 7:00
Mia at Chi, 7:30
Uta at Pho, 7:00
Den at GS, 7:30

Fri Apr 5
Det at Phi, 7:30
•Chi at Cha, 8:00
NY at Mil, 7:30
Was at SA, 7:30
Por at Den, 7:00
Min at Uta, 7:00
Van at LAL, 7:30
Hou at Sac, 7:30
Pho at Sea, 7:00

Sat Apr 6
Mil at NJ, 7:30
Phi at Atl, 7:30
NY at Tor, 6:00
Cha at Cle, 7:30
Mia at Ind, 6:00
LAC at Dal, 7:30
Min at GS, 7:30
Sea at Por, 7:00

Sun Apr 7
Det at Bos, 12:30
#Chi at Orl, 5:30
#Hou at Den, 1:00
#SA at LAL, 12:00
Uta at Sac, 6:00
Pho at Van, 12:00

Mon Apr 8
NJ at Phi, 7:30
Mia at Was, 7:30
Atl at Ind, 7:30
Cha at Chi, 7:30
Tor at Min, 7:00
SA at Uta, 7:00
Por at LAC, 7:30
Dal at GS, 7:30

Tue Apr 9
Bos at NY, 7:30

Det at NJ, 7:30
Tor at Mil, 7:30
Van at Hou, 7:30
•LAL at Den, 6:00
Por at Pho, 7:00
Dal at Sac, 7:30

Wed Apr 10
Was at Bos, 7:30
Cle at Orl, 7:30
Mia at Cha, 7:30
Phi at Det, 7:30
LAL at Min, 7:00
Van at SA, 7:30
+Pho at Uta, 6:00
Sac at Sea, 7:00

Thu Apr 11
Cle at NY, 7:30
Chi at NJ, 7:30
Mil at Mia, 7:30
Den at Hou, 7:30
GS at LAC (Ana), 7:30

Fri Apr 12
Tor at Bos, 7:30
Min at Was, 7:30
•Ind at Orl, 8:00
Mil at Atl, 7:30
Phi at Chi, 7:30
GS at LAL, 7:30
Sac at Van, 7:00

Sat Apr 13
@NY at Mia, 3:30
Det at Ind, 6:00
@Dal at Hou, 2:30
@Sea at SA, 2:30
Uta at LAC, 7:30

Sun Apr 14
Atl at NJ, 1:00
Cha at Phi, 1:00
Tor at Was, 1:00
#Chi at Cle, 1:00
Bos at Det, 7:00
Orl at Mil, 5:00
Den at Min, 2:30
#Pho at LAL, 12:30
Uta at GS, 7:30
LAC at Sac, 6:00
Por at Van, 12:00

Mon Apr 15
Tor at NY, 7:30
NJ at Mia, 7:30
Cha at Ind, 7:30
Sea at Hou, 7:30
Sac at Den, 7:00
SA at Por, 7:00

Tue Apr 16
Was at Orl, 7:30

Cle at Atl, 7:30
Chi at Mil, 7:30
LAL at Dal, 7:30
LAC at Uta, 7:00
•Hou at Pho, 6:00
SA at Van, 7:00

Wed Apr 17
Tor at NJ, 7:30
Mia at Phi, 7:30
Bos at Was, 7:30
+Ind at Det, 8:00
GS at Min, 7:00
Pho at Sac, 7:30
Por at Sea, 7:00

Thu Apr 18
Atl at Orl, 7:30
Mil at Cha, 7:30
NY at Cle, 7:30
Det at Chi, 7:30
Den at Dal, 7:30
LAC at Hou, 7:30
LAL at SA, 7:30
Uta at Van, 7:00

Fri Apr 19
•Cha at NY, 8:00
Bos at NJ, 7:30
Orl at Phi, 7:30
Was at Tor, 7:00
Mia at Mil, 7:30
Den at Hou, 7:00
Dal at Pho, 7:00
Por at GS, 7:30
Min at Sea, 7:00

Sat Apr 20
NJ at Atl, 7:30
Det at Cle, 1:00
#Ind at Chi, 2:30
Sac at Uta, 7:00
Min at LAL, 7:30

Sun Apr 21
NY at Bos, 1:00
Chi at Was, 1:00
Atl at Mia, 6:00
@Orl at Cha, 3:30
Phi at Tor, 1:00
@Mil at Det, 3:30
Cle at Ind, 2:30
@Pho at Hou, 2:30
@Dal at SA, 2:30
@Sea at Den, 1:30
Van at LAC, 3:00
GS at Sac, 6:00
LAL at Por, 6:00

BASKETBALL HALL OF FAME

This section honors the 103 players that are enshrined in the Naismith Memorial Basketball Hall of Fame in Springfield, Massachusetts. The section includes bios on each player in the Hall. At the end of each bio is a date in parentheses; this is the year the member was enshrined. A list of the coaches, contributors, referees, and teams enshrined in the Hall of Fame is on page 479.

Abbreviations include BAA (Basketball Association of America), NBL (National Basketball League), ABA (American Basketball Association), AAU (American Athletic Union), and NIT (National Invitational Tournament).

PLAYERS

KAREEM ABDUL-JABBAR
Center: The former Lew Alcindor led UCLA to an 88-2 record and three NCAA titles (1967-69). With his patented "sky hook," the 7'2" Jabbar won six NBA MVP Awards, was named to 19 All-Star Games, and won six NBA titles with Milwaukee and the L.A. Lakers. He holds NBA career records for scoring (38,387), seasons (20), games (1,560), minutes (57,446), blocked shots (3,189), and playoff scoring (5,762). (1995)

NATE ARCHIBALD
Guard: Small in stature at 6'1", "Tiny" Archibald was a giant on the court. After starring at Texas-El Paso, he began his pro career in Cincinnati in 1970-71. In 1972-73, he led the NBA in assists (11.4) and scoring (34.0). In 1980-81, he helped Boston win the NBA title. Archibald was league MVP in 1981. (1991)

PAUL ARIZIN
Forward: A star at Villanova, where he was college Player of the Year in 1950, the sharp-shooting Arizin averaged better than 22 PPG over his ten-year NBA career in Philadelphia. Known for his deadly jump shot, Arizin led the league in scoring in 1952 and '57 and led the Warriors to the NBA title in 1956. He made ten All-Star Game appearances. (1977)

TOM BARLOW
Forward: When the Eastern League was popular, "Babe" Barlow was among the game's most exciting players. A pro at age 16, Babe enjoyed 20 seasons of roundball (from 1912-32). Barlow was known as much for his defensive skills as for his scoring. (1980)

RICK BARRY
Forward: One of the game's most accurate shooters, Barry starred at Miami of Florida. In 1965, Rick led the NCAA with 37.4 PPG. As a pro, he played in both the ABA and NBA and is the only player to lead both leagues in scoring. His career NBA free throw pct. was .900, a record that held until 1992-93. In 1975, he led Golden State to the NBA title. (1986)

ELGIN BAYLOR
Forward: Baylor was considered the most devastating, artistic forward of his era. After a spectacular college career in which he led Seattle to the NCAA finals in 1958, Baylor debuted in the NBA in 1958-59. He averaged 24.9 PPG as a rookie with Minneapolis and won Rookie of the Year honors. Over his 14-year career, he averaged 27.4 PPG. (1976)

JOHNNY BECKMAN
Forward: From 1910 until the 1940s, Beckman was often called the Babe Ruth of basketball. A star in the Interstate, New York State, and Eastern Leagues, Beckman eventually joined the Original Celtics. As their captain, he led them to some of their greatest years. (1972)

WALT BELLAMY
Center: After playing for Indiana University, Bellamy became NBA Rookie of the Year with the 1962 Chicago Packers, averaging 31.6 PPG and 19.0 RPG. He played 14 NBA seasons with six different teams, averaging 20.1 PPG and 13.7 RPG. (1993)

SERGEI BELOV

Guard: Belov was considered a basketball magician who could score at will. The 6'3" guard led the Russian national team to four European and two world championships. In the Olympics, he helped the Soviet national team to one gold medal (1972) and three bronze medals. (1992)

DAVE BING

Guard: Born to score, Bing averaged 24.8 PPG in four years at Syracuse. The off guard was named NBA Rookie of the Year with Detroit in 1966-67 and won the scoring title the next year (27.1 PPG). Bing played in seven All-Star Games in his 12 NBA seasons. (1989)

CAROL BLAZEJOWSKI

Guard: Only Pete Maravich scored more points in college than Blazejowski. At 5'10", the "Blaze" totaled 3,199 points during her career (31.7 PPG) at New Jersey's Montclair State College. She was a three-time All-American. (1994)

BENNIE BORGMANN

Guard: Though only 5'8", Borgmann was one of the most popular touring pros on the East Coast in the early years. It wasn't unusual for Borgmann to score half of his team's points during any given game. He later coached both at the college and professional level. (1961)

BILL BRADLEY

Forward: "Dollar Bill" Bradley was an intelligent player with a graceful, deadly shooting touch. A three-time All-American at Princeton, he averaged 30 PPG and was the 1965 college Player of the Year. A Rhodes Scholar, Bradley played ten seasons with the New York Knicks, amassing 9,217 points, 2,533 assists, and two NBA championship rings. He is currently a U.S. senator in New Jersey. (1982)

JOE BRENNAN

Forward: "Poison Joe" Brennan enjoyed a 17-year pro career, starting at age 19 when he joined the Brooklyn Visitation and led them to their greatest years. In 1950, the New York Basketball Old-Timers voted Brennan the second-greatest player of his era. (1974)

AL CERVI

Guard: An outstanding clutch performer, Cervi was an immediate star with the NBL's Buffalo Bisons. His pro career was interrupted by a five-year stint in World War II, but he resumed his career in 1945, playing for the Rochester Royals. In 1948, he became a player/coach for the Syracuse Nats. He was named Coach of the Year five times in the next eight seasons. (1984)

WILT CHAMBERLAIN

Center: At 7'1", Wilt "The Stilt" Chamberlain was an awesome, dominant figure on the court. After two All-America years at Kansas, Wilt spent a year with the Harlem Globetrotters before entering the NBA in 1959. In just his first year, he was named the NBA's MVP. During 14 years, he was the league MVP four times (1960, 1966-68). He still holds NBA records for career rebounds (23,924), season scoring average (50.4 in 1961-62), and most points in a game (100). He won world titles with Philadelphia (1967) and Los Angeles ('72). (1978)

CHARLES COOPER

Center: In his day, "Tarzan" Cooper was a giant among men. The 6'4", 214-pound Cooper was a consistent winner for 20 years of pro basketball. In 11 years with the New York Renaissance, his teams compiled a record of 1,303-203. He has been called the greatest center of his day. (1976)

BOB COUSY

Guard: At 6'1", Cousy made his name as the most sensational passer the game had ever known. After three All-America years at Holy Cross, "Mr. Basketball" joined the Boston Celtics in 1950. Eventually, he led them to six NBA titles, including five in a row (1959-63). He led the league in assists for eight straight years and played in 13 All-Star Games. (1970)

DAVE COWENS

Center: Cowens was a tough, physical player. "The Redhead" starred at Florida State, where he averaged 19 points and 17 rebounds per game. In ten seasons with the Celtics, he won two championships (1974 and '76) and was player/coach for a year. In his career, Cowens averaged 17.6 PPG and collected 10,444 rebounds. (1991)

BILLY CUNNINGHAM

Guard: A scrappy playmaker at North Carolina, Cunningham debuted with the 76ers in 1965. In 11 pro seasons, Cunningham made the All-NBA first team three times and was named ABA MVP in 1973. In 770 pro games, he averaged 21.8 PPG. He became the 76ers' coach in 1978, bringing them a 454-196 record over eight seasons, including a league title in 1983. (1985)

BOB DAVIES

Guard: Davies has been called the "first superstar of modern pro basketball." A two-time All-American at Seton Hall, Davies turned pro in 1945 with Rochester. In ten BAA and NBA seasons, he was all-league seven times. He led the Royals to league titles in 1946, '47, and '51. (1969)

FORREST DeBERNARDI

Forward/Guard/Center: DeBernardi's career revolved around AAU tournaments. He was an AAU All-American in 1921, '22, and '23 and won four AAU titles. In 11 AAU tournaments, "De" was all-tournament seven times. (1961)

DAVE DeBUSSCHERE

Forward: DeBusschere was one of the game's great defensive forwards. After three All-America years at the University of Detroit, DeBusschere debuted with the Pistons in 1962. At age 24, he became the Pistons' player/coach. He was traded to the Knicks in 1969 and helped them to two championships (1970 and '73). He amassed 14,053 points and 9,618 rebounds. (1982)

DUTCH DEHNERT

Guard: Back in the 1920s, playing for the powerful Celtics, Dehnert inadvertently invented pivot play when he routinely stationed himself at the foul line to relay passes back and forth to weaving teammates. Though he didn't play either high school or college ball, Dehnert honed his skills in Eastern pro leagues. (1968)

ANNE DONOVAN

Center: The 6'8" Donovan led Old Dominion to the 1980 AIAW title as a freshman. She was a three-time All-American, averaging 20.0 PPG and 14.5 RPG. Donovan helped the U.S. to the 1984 and 1988 Olympic gold medals. (1995)

PAUL ENDACOTT

Guard: Endacott achieved status as "the greatest player ever coached" by Kansas' Phog Allen. Endacott was Player of the Year in 1923. In 1969, he received the Sportsmen's World Award in basketball, because his "exemplary personal conduct has made him an outstanding inspiration for youth to emulate." (1971)

JULIUS ERVING

Forward: An extraordinary leaper, the spectacular Dr. J. had the ability to change directions in mid-air. The Massachusetts alum brought attention to the ABA, where he averaged 28.7 PPG and 12.1 RPG in five seasons. With the NBA's 76ers, he was named to 11 All-Star Games, averaged 22.0 PPG, and led his 1983 team to the world title. (1993)

BUD FOSTER

Guard: Harold "Bud" Foster, a star player in college, also excelled as a coach. As a senior at Wisconsin in 1930, he earned All-America honors. Foster played briefly as a pro before embarking on a glorious 25-year career as a coach. He guided Wisconsin to three Big Ten titles and the NCAA title (1941). (1964)

WALT FRAZIER

Guard: A smooth guard known for sleek passing and laser-accurate shooting, "Clyde" Frazier played 13 seasons in the NBA. Frazier helped the Knicks to league titles in 1970 and 1973, played in seven All-Star Games, was a celebrated defensive wizard, and finished his career with an average of 18.9 PPG. (1986)

MARTY FRIEDMAN

Guard: Max "Marty" Friedman was one of a pair of hoops stars known as the "Heavenly Twins" (his counterpart was Barney Sedran). Friedman was one of the great defensive players of his era. He played in six Eastern leagues and, in 1915, helped Carbondale win 35 straight games. He later won accolades as well as championships as a coach. (1971)

JOE FULKS

Forward: "Jumping Joe" Fulks was one of the first scoring superstars of the BAA and NBA. An ambidextrous jump-shot artist, Fulks shocked the BAA in 1946-47 by scoring 23.2 PPG for Philadelphia. Two years later, he averaged 26.0 PPG and was named *The Sporting News* Athlete of the Year for 1949. (1977)

LADDIE GALE

Forward: Lauren "Laddie" Gale's excellence on the court helped bring recognition to the basketball programs in the Pacific Northwest. Gale was an All-American at Oregon, and in 1939 he led his school to the NCAA title. Gale played professionally and was also a successful coach. (1976)

HARRY GALLATIN

Center: A large center for his time (6'6"), Harry "The Horse" Gallatin was the centerpiece of the New York Knicks for nine years. In 1953-54, he led the NBA in rebounds (1,098). He later went on to a successful coaching career at the pro and college levels. (1991)

WILLIAM GATES

Guard: "Pop" Gates helped the New York Renaissance to 68 straight victories and a World Professional Championship. In his 12-year career, he played for many outstanding teams, including the Harlem Globetrotters, where he was a player/coach from 1950-55. (1988)

TOM GOLA

Forward: Gola combined outstanding scoring prowess with defensive wizardry. At La Salle in the mid-1950s, Gola was a four-year All-American, averaging 21 points and 20 rebounds per game. He played ten years professionally with Philadelphia, San Francisco, and New York, scoring 7,871 points. He was often high in assists and rebounds. (1975)

HAL GREER

Guard: Greer was the first black scholarship athlete to attend Marshall (1955-59). He played five years with the Syracuse Nationals before joining the powerful Philadelphia 76ers for another ten seasons. He recorded 21,586 career points, was named to ten All-Star Games, and won a world title in 1967. (1981)

ROBERT GRUENIG

Center: A 6'8" center with a shooter's touch, "Ace" Gruenig was a brilliant AAU performer. From 1937-48, he was the annual choice as first-team all-tournament center. In 1943, he received the Los Angeles Sports Award Medallion as the nation's greatest player. (1963)

CLIFF HAGAN

Forward: Hagan was a two-time All-American (1952 and '54) who led Kentucky to an NCAA title in 1951 and a perfect 25-0 record in 1954. During ten years in the NBA with the St. Louis Hawks, he scored 13,447 points, relying heavily on his amazingly accurate hook shot. He appeared in four All-Star Games and helped the Hawks win the league title in 1958. He also played three years in the ABA, serving as player/coach for the Dallas Chaparrals. (1977)

VICTOR HANSON

Guard: Hanson starred at Syracuse in basketball, football, and baseball. He was a three-time All-American in hoops (1925-27), winning a national championship in 1926. In his senior campaign, Hanson was the college Player of the Year. He later played pro ball with the Cleveland Rosenblums, and he also played minor-league baseball. (1960)

LUSIA HARRIS

Center: The 6'3" Harris became one of women's basketball's early superstars. She finished her career at Delta State with 2,981 points (25.9 PPG) and 1,662 rebounds (14.4 RPG). Harris was a three-time All-American and won three national titles (1975-77). She also played on the 1976 Olympic team. (1992)

JOHN HAVLICEK

Forward: After leading Ohio State to three NCAA finals and one championship, "Hondo" Havlicek embarked on a 16-year NBA career with Boston. Havlicek began as the Celts' sixth man and was later named team captain. In his career, he scored 26,395 points, appeared in 13 All-Star Games, and was an eight-time member of the NBA All-Defensive Team. (1983)

CONNIE HAWKINS

Forward: Hawkins, similar in style to Julius Erving, left Iowa during his freshman year and played two years with the Harlem Globetrotters (1964-66). In the ABA's inaugural season, he was named league MVP after leading Pittsburgh to the title. Hawkins played seven NBA seasons with Phoenix, Los Angeles, and Atlanta, averaging 16.5 PPG and 7.9 RPG. (1992)

ELVIN HAYES

Forward: The 6'9" Hayes used strength, speed, and grace to achieve amazing results. At Houston, "The Big E." was the 1968 college Player of the Year. Hayes led the NBA in scoring as a rookie and went on to play 16 years with San Diego, the Bullets, and Houston. In 1977-78, he led the Bullets to the NBA title. He played exactly 50,000 NBA minutes—second most in league history. He scored 27,313 points. (1989)

TOMMY HEINSOHN

Forward: A two-time All-American at Holy Cross, Heinsohn became the NBA Rookie of the Year for Boston in 1957 and started for the champion Celtics for the next eight seasons. Heinsohn, who was named to six All-Star Games, averaged 18.6 PPG over his career. In 1970, he took over as coach. He guided Boston to two NBA titles. (1985)

NAT HOLMAN

Guard: Holman, who gained fame as coach of the City College of New York Beavers, was also a player of note from 1916-33. Holman joined the Original Celtics in 1920, stayed nine seasons, and was one of their greatest players, exploiting his skills as a passer, shooter, and strategist. In 1950, his Beavers won both the NIT and NCAA titles, which no team had ever done before. (1964)

BOB HOUBREGS

Center: Houbregs was an All-American with Washington in 1953. He held the second-highest scoring average in NCAA Tournament history (34.8 PPG) before being drafted by Milwaukee. He played five years in the NBA and later served as G.M. of the Seattle SuperSonics from 1970-73. (1986)

CHUCK HYATT

Forward: A great amateur player, Hyatt starred at the University of Pittsburgh from 1927-30 and was a three-time All-American. He was the top scorer in the nation in 1930. The Panthers won national titles in 1928 and '30. He later joined the Phillips 66 Oilers and became a legend of the AAU circuit. (1959)

DAN ISSEL

Forward: After averaging 25.8 PPG in college at Kentucky, Issel continued to smoke the nets in the ABA (six years, 25.6 PPG) and the NBA (nine years, all with Denver, 20.4 PPG). Though a solid rebounder, Issel will forever be known for his scoring, as he tallied 27,482 points in his pro career. He became coach of the Nuggets in 1992-93. (1993)

HARRY JEANNETTE

Guard: From 1938-48, "Buddy" Jeannette was regarded as basketball's top backcourt player. He was adept at passing, clutch shooting, and defense. Jeannette garnered four MVP Awards in the NBL and ABL and played on five championship teams. He also coached for Georgetown and in the NBA (Baltimore). (1994)

WILLIAM JOHNSON

Center: Tall and lanky, "Skinny" Johnson was a dominant center for Kansas from 1930-33. He guided his squad to a record of 42-11 and three Big Six championships. In 1975, he was named an All-Time Great in Oklahoma, his home state. (1976)

NEIL JOHNSTON

Center: After two years at Ohio State, the 6'8" Johnston tried his luck as a pitcher, signing a pro baseball contract. A sore arm turned him back to basketball, where he joined the Philadelphia Warriors in 1951. In eight seasons, he led the NBA in scoring and field goal percentage three times, led in rebounding once, and helped the Warriors win the title in 1956. (1989)

K.C. JONES

Guard: After starring in college at San Francisco, Jones joined the Boston Celtics in 1958 and was a dependable guard on their great teams. As a coach, Jones won more than 500 NBA games, including 308 with the Celts. He was involved in 11 titles in Boston—eight as a player, one as an assistant coach, and two as head coach (1984 and '86). (1988)

SAM JONES

Guard: After playing brilliantly at tiny North Carolina College, Jones cracked the Celtics lineup in 1958 and became part of ten championship teams. He led the club in scoring three times and averaged 25.9 PPG in 1964-65. His patented jump shot off the glass was feared around the NBA. (1983)

EDWARD KRAUSE

Center: A star at Notre Dame in the early 1930s, Krause was a three-time All-American in two sports—basketball and football. At 6'3", 215 pounds, he was considered the first "agile" center. "Moose" later played professionally before returning to the college scene as a coach and athletic director. (1975)

BOB KURLAND

Center: The first of the truly great seven-foot centers, Kurland carved out one of the most impressive amateur careers ever. At Oklahoma State, he led his squad to NCAA titles in 1945 and '46, leading the nation in scoring the latter year. He later played six seasons of AAU ball and was an Olympian in 1948 and '52. (1961)

BOB LANIER

Center: A two-time All-American at St. Bonaventure, Lanier debuted with Detroit in 1970. A strong, no-nonsense center, Lanier played in eight All-Star Games and tallied 19,248 points and 9,698 rebounds in his career. In each of Lanier's five seasons in Milwaukee, the Bucks won the Central Division title. (1992)

JOE LAPCHICK

Center: The son of immigrants, Lapchick began playing professional basketball at age 17. The 6'5" center played in several leagues and centered the Original Celtics from 1923-27. Later, he became a great coach, leading St. John's to four NIT titles. He also coached the New York Knicks for nine seasons. (1966)

CLYDE LOVELLETTE

Center: Lovellette was a winner wherever he played. As a college star at Kansas, he was a three-time All-American (1950-52). In 1952, he led the nation in scoring and guided the Jayhawks to the NCAA title. He played for the 1952 gold-medal Olympic team before starting an 11-year NBA career. He played with the champion Minneapolis Lakers in 1954 and later won titles with the 1963 and '64 Boston Celtics. (1987)

JERRY LUCAS

Forward: A fine shooter, passer, and defensive ace, Lucas was a two-time college Player of the Year at Ohio State, where his team captured an NCAA title. He also helped the U.S. win the gold in the 1960 Olympics. In 1963-64 with Cincinnati, Lucas was the NBA's Rookie of the Year. He went on to play in seven All-Star Games and was part of the New York Knicks' 1973 championship team. He finished with 14,053 points and 12,942 rebounds. (1979)

HANK LUISETTI

Forward: Luisetti broke old standards by developing a one-handed shot. In three seasons at Stanford, Hank led his squad to successive Pacific Coast Conference titles. An All-American in 1937 and '38, Luisetti was the first college player ever to score 50 points in a game. He later starred on the AAU scene. (1959)

ED MACAULEY

Forward: "Easy Ed" Macauley was a four-time All-American at St. Louis (1946-49). In 1947, he led the nation with a .524 shooting percent-

age, and he was MVP of the NIT the following year. Macauley played ten NBA seasons, earning seven All-Star Game appearances. (1960)

PETE MARAVICH

Forward: Maravich, one of the greatest gunners in history, shattered many NCAA records, including highest career scoring average (44.2). Maravich starred at Louisiana State, earning college Player of the Year honors in 1970. "Pistol Pete" played NBA ball with Atlanta, the Jazz, and Boston. In 658 NBA games, he averaged 24.2 PPG. In 1976-77, he led the league in scoring with a 31.1 average. (1986)

SLATER MARTIN

Guard: At 5'10", "Dugie" Martin was the first "small superstar" of the NBA. After three outstanding years at Texas, Martin joined the NBA. He played for four league championship teams in Minneapolis before moving to St. Louis, where he helped the Hawks win the 1958 title. In 11 seasons, he tallied 3,160 assists and earned a reputation as a defensive genius. (1981)

BRANCH McCRACKEN

Forward: McCracken starred for three years at Indiana University, winning the conference MVP Award in 1928. During his career, he scored nearly one-third of all the points recorded by the Hoosiers. He later had great success as a coach, winning four Big Ten and two NCAA titles at Indiana. (1960)

JACK McCRACKEN

Center: A two-time All-American at N.W. Missouri State (1931-32), McCracken was known for his outstanding passing and domination of the backboards. As a star of the AAU circuit, he was an eight-time All-American between 1932 and 1945 and won two AAU championships. (1962)

BOBBY McDERMOTT

Forward: McDermott turned pro as a teenager and played for 17 years. He was a seven-time NBL All-Star, won five straight MVP Awards, and led the league twice in scoring. He was a champion with Brooklyn, Fort Wayne, Chicago, and the Original Celtics. (1987)

DICK McGUIRE

Guard: McGuire, an All-American at St. John's, helped the New York Knicks to three straight

NBA Finals (1951-53). Though he averaged just 8.0 PPG in 11 NBA seasons with New York and Detroit, McGuire made seven All-Star Games thanks to his point-guard skills. (1993)

ANN MEYERS

Guard: Meyers, of UCLA, was women's basketball's first four-time All-American. She also helped the 1976 Olympic team to a silver medal. In 1979, Meyers became the first and only woman to sign with an NBA club (Indiana), although she didn't make the team. (1993)

VERN MIKKELSEN

Forward: Out of tiny Hamline University, Mikkelsen went on to become one of the NBA's first power forwards. He helped Minneapolis to four NBA championships and was selected to six All-Star teams, averaging 14.4 PPG and 8.4 RPG over his career. (1995)

GEORGE MIKAN

Center: The game's first dominating big man, the 6'10" Mikan was a three-time NBA scoring leader. Previously, he was a three-time All-American at DePaul and twice was named college Player of the Year (1945 and '46), leading the nation in scoring in both of those years. Mikan played on five NBA title teams. (1959)

CHERYL MILLER

Forward: The owner of a 105-point game in high school, Miller was a four-time high school and four-time college All-American. At Southern Cal., she won two NCAA titles (1983-84) and three Naismith Awards. She averaged 23.6 PPG and 12.0 RPG in her career. (1995)

EARL MONROE

Guard: Earl "The Pearl" Monroe's slick ball-handling and dead-eye shooting made him a prolific scorer and crowd-pleaser. A two-time All-American at Winston-Salem State, he was drafted by Baltimore and was the NBA Rookie of the Year in 1968. He spent 13 years in the NBA and helped the New York Knicks win the 1973 league title. (1989)

CALVIN MURPHY

Guard: The 5'9" Murphy was a brilliant free throw shooter, canning 78 straight with Houston in 1980-81. The mighty mite averaged 33.1 PPG as a three-time All-American at Niagara. He scored 17.9 per game in his 13 NBA seasons, all with the Rockets. (1993)

STRETCH MURPHY

Center: Murphy was one of the most feared big men of his time, as he helped Purdue to a Big Ten title in 1928. A two-time All-American, Murphy set a Big Ten scoring mark in 1929. In his senior year, 1930, he captained Purdue to an undefeated record. (1960)

PAT PAGE

Forward: An outstanding defensive player and a star in three sports, Page led his University of Chicago squad to Western Conference titles in 1907, 1909 (when they were undefeated), and 1910. In 1910, Page was named college Player of the Year. (1962)

BOB PETTIT

Forward: A three-time All-American at Louisiana State (1952-54), Pettit played ten NBA seasons with the St. Louis Hawks. He was named NBA MVP in 1956 and '59. He led the Hawks to the league title in 1958. He finished as the greatest scorer in league history with 20,880 points. (1970)

ANDY PHILLIP

Guard: One of the stars of the University of Illinois' "Whiz Kids," Phillip set Big Ten scoring marks in 1942 and '43 and once scored 40 points in a game. He later played in the BAA and NBA for more than a decade. (1961)

JIM POLLARD

Forward: Pollard led Stanford to an NCAA championship in 1942 and later starred in the AAU circuit, winning MVP honors in 1947 and '48. He joined the Minneapolis Lakers in 1949 and helped them to five league titles. (1977)

FRANK RAMSEY

Guard: A two-time All-American while playing at Kentucky (1952 and '54), Ramsey joined the Boston Celtics and revolutionized the game by "inventing" the sixth-man position. Ramsey won seven titles in nine NBA seasons. He was called "the most versatile player in the NBA" by his longtime coach, Red Auerbach. (1981)

WILLIS REED

Center: One of the most intense competitors of his time, Reed began as a two-time All-American at Grambling. In ten pro seasons with the New York Knicks, he won two NBA titles (1970 and '73) and played in seven All-Star Games. He averaged 18.7 PPG in his career. (1981)

OSCAR ROBERTSON

Guard: One of the greatest all-around players ever, "The Big O." starred at the University of Cincinnati, where he was a two-time college Player of the Year and a three-time scoring leader. As a pro for Cincinnati, he was league MVP in 1964. Later, he led the Milwaukee Bucks to the 1971 NBA title. He finished his career with 26,710 points (25.7 PPG) and set an NBA record with 9,887 assists. (1979)

JOHN ROOSMA

Forward: Roosma made his mark as a member of the U.S. Army squad. In his Army career, he scored more than 1,000 points. Roosma, whose Army team went 70-3 during his tenure, served in the military for 30 years and retired as an Army colonel in 1956. (1961)

BILL RUSSELL

Center: Russell reigns as one of the great winners and rebounders of all time. As a collegian, he was Player of the Year in 1956 for San Francisco and also led his school to two NCAA titles. He then led the U.S. to gold in the 1956 Olympic Games. As a pro, he helped the Celtics to eight straight NBA crowns (1959-66) and 11 in 13 years. He collected 21,620 rebounds, averaged 15.1 PPG, and was league MVP five times. As player/coach, he led the Celts to titles in 1968 and '69. (1974)

HONEY RUSSELL

Guard: A great defensive player, John "Honey" Russell played in virtually every pro league during his 28-year career. He led the Cleveland Rosenblums to five straight titles (1925-29) and later coached his alma mater, Seton Hall, to 44 straight wins. In 1946-47, he became the first coach of the NBA Boston Celtics. (1964)

DOLPH SCHAYES

Forward: Schayes played his college ball at New York University, where he was an All-American in 1948. In 15 seasons with the Syracuse Nationals, he chalked up 19,249 points (18.2 per game). From February 1952 to December 1961, he played in a record 765 straight games. Later, he guided the Philadelphia 76ers to a division title. (1972)

ERNEST SCHMIDT

Forward: Schmidt was known as "One Grand Schmidt" after scoring 1,000 career points in his Kansas State Teachers College days. He was a four-time conference all-star in the early 1930s and was widely recognized as the greatest player ever to come out of the Missouri Valley. Later, he suited up for three seasons on the AAU circuit. (1973)

JOHN SCHOMMER

Center: A star in basketball, football, baseball, and track, Schommer led the Chicago Maroon basketball squad to three straight Big Ten titles (1907-09) and was the conference scoring leader all three years. He also enjoyed a 47-year career as athletic director, coach, and teacher at Illinois Institute of Technology. In 1949, the Helms Foundation named him a center on its All-Time All-America Team. (1959)

BARNEY SEDRAN

Guard: At 5'4", Sedran proved that size truly wasn't everything. Despite being banished from high school basketball, Sedran starred at City College of New York and was his team's leading scorer three years in a row. Upon his graduation in 1911, he embarked on a 15-year pro career that included ten championships. He later coached for another 20 years. (1962)

JULIANA SEMENOVA

Center: The Soviet seven-footer dominated her opponents, winning two Olympic golds (1976 and 1980) and three world championship golds. Semenova never lost a game in 18 years of international competition. (1993)

BILL SHARMAN

Guard: After two All-America years at Southern California, the sharp-shooting Sharman enjoyed an 11-year stint in the NBA, where he played on four championship Boston Celtics teams in the 1950s and early 1960s. Sharman's secret weapon was free throw shooting. After retiring with 12,665 points, he won titles as a coach in the ABA and NBA. (1975)

CHRISTIAN STEINMETZ

Guard: Steinmetz turned basketball into a recognized sport at the University of Wisconsin. As a senior in 1905, he set school scoring records (some of which would stand for the next 50 years), including most points in a game (50) and most points in a season (462). (1961)

JOHN THOMPSON

Guard: A star at Montana State, John "Cat" Thompson was selected to All-Rocky Mountain

Conference teams for four years in a row. In 1929, they were the Helms national champions and the Cat was named Player of the Year. Thompson eventually became a coach, where he remained for 14 years. (1962)

NATE THURMOND
Center: An All-American at Bowling Green, Thurmond was a defensive genius with strong shooting skills. In his 14-year NBA career, he averaged 15 points and 15 rebounds per game. In a 1974 game, he became the first to record a "quadruple-double." Playing for several NBA teams, Thurmond was named to seven All-Star Games. (1984)

JACK TWYMAN
Forward: An All-American at Cincinnati, Twyman joined the Rochester Royals in 1955-56. In 11 NBA seasons, he scored 15,840 points. A durable forward with precision shooting skills, Twyman played 823 games (including a stretch of 609 consecutively) and averaged 19.2 PPG. (1982)

WES UNSELD
Center: After an explosive career at Louisville, where he was an All-American in 1967 and '68, Unseld entered the NBA with an equally loud bang in 1968-69, when he was the NBA's MVP for the Baltimore Bullets. Unseld led the Bullets to an NBA title in 1978. In his career, he averaged 14 boards a game. He also served as coach of the Washington Bullets. (1987)

FUZZY VANDIVIER
Guard: Robert "Fuzzy" Vandivier became one of the greatest players in the history of Indiana basketball. He took his perennial-champion Franklin High School team directly to Franklin College in 1922 and helped establish a legendary squad. He is a member of the All-Time All-Star Five of Indiana. (1974)

ED WACHTER
Center: As a turn-of-the-century player, Wachter starred on nearly every team in the Eastern circuit. He was an annual scoring champion and a member of more title-winning clubs than anyone else of his time. Later, as a coach at Harvard, he founded the New England Basketball Association and struggled to gain national uniformity of rules and regulations. (1961)

BILL WALTON
Center: The big redhead carried UCLA to an 86-4 record and two NCAA titles (1972-73), earning college Player of the Year awards from 1972-74. Though he sat out four different NBA seasons because of injuries, he helped both Portland (1977) and Boston (1986) to NBA titles. Walton was named league MVP in 1977-78 with Portland. (1993)

BOBBY WANZER
Guard: An All-American at Seton Hall in 1946, Wanzer played for ten seasons with the Rochester Royals. He was the NBA's MVP in 1952-53, two years after helping the Royals win the 1951 NBA title. An outstanding shooter, Wanzer led the league in free throw accuracy (90 percent) in 1951-52. (1986)

JERRY WEST
Guard: One of the greatest high-pressure performers of all time, West earned his nickname "Mr. Clutch" during 14 seasons with the Los Angeles Lakers. A two-time All-American at West Virginia, West averaged 27.0 PPG in the NBA. He was also named to 14 All-Star Games and led L.A. to the 1972 NBA title. (1979)

NERA WHITE
Center: The 6'1" White was one of the most complete female players of all time. From 1955-69, she led a team sponsored by Nashville Business College to ten AAU national championships. She was named the AAU tournament's MVP ten times. In 1957-58, White led the U.S. to the world championship. (1992)

LENNY WILKENS
Guard: Wilkens enjoyed success at every level of the game. As an All-American at Providence College, he was the 1960 NIT MVP. Wilkens, a 6'1" guard, went on to play 15 seasons in the NBA, making nine All-Star appearances. He later coached Seattle, one of his former teams, to the 1979 NBA championship. As an NBA coach, he has won over 900 games. (1988)

JOHN WOODEN
Forward: Before becoming one of basketball's greatest coaches, Wooden was an outstanding player in his own right. A three-time All-American at Purdue (1930-32) and college Player of the Year (1932), he set a Big Ten scoring record in his senior year and led his team to the national title. (1960)

REMAINING MEMBERS OF THE BASKETBALL HALL OF FAME

COACHES
Phog Allen (1959)
Harold Anderson (1984)
Red Auerbach (1968)
Sam Barry (1978)
Ernest Blood (1960)
Howard Cann (1967)
H. Clifford Carlson (1959)
Lou Carnesecca (1992)
Ben Carnevale (1969)
Everett Case (1981)
Denny Crum (1994)
Chuck Daly (1994)
Everett Dean (1966)
Ed Diddle (1971)
Bruce Drake (1972)
Clarence Gaines (1981)
Jack Gardner (1983)
Slats Gill (1967)
Aleksandr Gomelsky (1995)
Marv Harshman (1984)
Eddie Hickey (1978)
Howard Hobson (1965)
Red Holzman (1985)
Hank Iba (1968)
Doggie Julian (1967)
Frank Keaney (1960)
George Keogan (1961)
Bob Knight (1991)
John Kundla (1995)
Ward Lambert (1960)
Harry Litwack (1975)
Kenneth Loeffler (1964)
Dutch Lonborg (1972)
Arad McCutchan (1980)
Al McGuire (1992)
Frank McGuire (1976)
John McLendon (1978)
Walter Meanwell (1959)
Ray Meyer (1978)
Ralph Miller (1987)
Pete Newell (1978)
Jack Ramsay (1992)
Cesare Rubini (1994)
Adolph Rupp (1968)
Leonard Sachs (1961)
Everett Shelton (1979)
Dean Smith (1982)
Fred Taylor (1985)
Margaret Wade (1984)
Stanley Watts (1985)
John Wooden (1972)
Phil Woolpert (1992)

CONTRIBUTORS
Senda Abbott (1984)
Clair Bee (1967)
Walter Brown (1965)
John Bunn (1964)
Bob Douglas (1971)
Al Duer (1981)
Clifford Fagan (1983)
Harry Fisher (1973)
Larry Fleisher (1991)
Eddie Gottlieb (1971)
Luther Gulick (1959)
Lester Harrison (1979)
Ferenc Hepp (1980)
Edward Hickox (1959)
Tony Hinkle (1965)
Ned Irish (1964)
R. William Jones (1964)
J. Walter Kennedy (1980)
Emil Liston (1974)
Bill Mokray (1965)
Ralph Morgan (1959)
Frank Morgenweck (1962)
James Naismith (1959)
John O'Brien (1961)
Larry O'Brien (1991)
Harold Olsen (1959)
Maurice Podoloff (1973)
Henry Porter (1960)
William Reid (1963)
Elmer Ripley (1972)
Lynn St. John (1962)
Abe Saperstein (1970)
Arthur Schabinger (1961)
Amos Alonzo Stagg (1959)
Boris Stankovic (1991)
Edward Steitz (1983)
Chuck Taylor (1968)
Bertha Teague (1984)
Oswald Tower (1959)
Arthur Trester (1961)
Clifford Wells (1971)
Lou Wilke (1982)

REFEREES
Jim Enright (1978)
George Hepbron (1960)
George Hoyt (1961)
Pat Kennedy (1959)
Lloyd Leith (1982)
Red Mihalik (1985)
John Nucatola (1977)
Ernest Quigley (1961)
J. Dallas Shirley (1979)
Earl Strom (1995)
David Tobey (1961)
David Walsh (1961)

TEAMS
Buffalo Germans (1961)
First Team (1959)
New York Rens (1963)
Original Celtics (1959)

Note: Year of election in parentheses.

100 Top College Stars & 64 Top College Teams

The following two sections evaluate the best players and teams in college basketball. Of the thousands of players in the college ranks, you'll read about the 100 that are expected to make the biggest impact in 1995-96. You'll also find season previews on the top 64 teams in the country.

Each player's scouting report begins with his vital stats, such as school, position, and height. Next comes a four-part evaluation of the player. "Background" reviews the player's career, starting with high school and continuing up through the 1994-95 season. "Strengths" examines his best assets, and "weaknesses" pinpoints his significant flaws. "Analysis" tries to put the player's whole game into perspective.

For a quick rundown on each player, you'll find a "player summary" box. You'll also get the player's career statistics. The stats include games (G), field goal percentage (FGP), free throw percentage (FTP), rebounds per game (RPG), assists per game (APG), and points per game (PPG).

Each of the 64 teams receives a one-page season preview. It begins with the basics, including 1994-95 overall record (this record includes NCAA or NIT games). It also lists the team's record in 1995 tournament play ("NCAAs: 2-1" means the team won two NCAA Tournament games and then lost the third). The coach's career Division I record is also listed.

Each season preview begins with an "opening line," which discusses the players it lost and the newcomers that are coming in. The preview then rates the team at each position—guard, forward, and center. "Analysis" evaluates the team's strengths and weaknesses and puts it all into perspective.

Finally, each preview contains the team's 1995-96 roster, which includes the team's top 12 players. The roster lists each player's 1994-95 statistics. The stats include field goal percentage (FGP), free throw percentage (FTP), 3-point field goals/attempts (3-PT), rebounds per game (RPG), assists per game (APG), and points per game (PPG).

SHAREEF ABDUR-RAHIM

School: California
Year: Freshman
Position: Forward
Height: 6'10" **Weight:** 230
Birthdate: December 11, 1976
Hometown: Marietta, GA

PLAYER SUMMARY	
Will	zip down the floor
Can't	be a classic post
Expect	immediate impact
Don't Expect	missed free throws

Background: Rated the top forward in the nation by most recruiting publications, Abdur-Rahim was a member of the 1994 U.S. junior national team. Wheeler High School's all-time leading scorer represented his school in both the 1995 McDonald's game and Magic's Roundball Classic.

Strengths: Abdur-Rahim was in great demand because he is the essence of the modern power-forward prospect. Agile and athletic, he moves quickly up and down the floor. Long arms make him appear taller than 6'10", and he uses a soft shooting touch to score over defenders. His unselfishness often results in easy scores for his mates.

Weaknesses: Being a new-age power forward means that the individual does not limit himself to the interior. That can have its downsides, as it does with Abdur-Rahim. Sometimes he becomes too enamored with his perimeter skill offensively when his size could be put to better use down low.

Strengths: The battle for Abdur-Rahim's services was spirited. He surprised many by declaring for California—Georgia Tech loomed as the favorite—and the NCAA was reportedly interested enough to take a look at how Abdur-Rahim was transported to visit a school 2,000 miles from home. He's a talent and will help California immensely.

DANYA ABRAMS

School: Boston College
Year: Junior
Position: Forward
Height: 6'7" **Weight:** 265
Birthdate: September 24, 1974
Hometown: Greenburgh, NY

PLAYER SUMMARY	
Will	create space inside
Can't	get sufficient help
Expect	lots of contact
Don't Expect	him to back down

Background: Lacking a major profile as a high school player, Abrams nonetheless made an immediate impact as a freshman at Boston College. He filled an essential need in the Eagles' 1993-94 run to the NCAA Tournament's Elite Eight. As a sophomore, he led the Big East in scoring.

Strengths: The Big East has earned a reputation as one of America's most physical leagues and Abrams is the embodiment of that. He loves to post up and use his considerable bulk to create working space in the lane. Quick feet and a soft release allow him to finish many plays with a score. He's also a very willing rebounder.

Weaknesses: Abrams's offensive game is limited to the lane. He faced many more double-teams last winter as he became the focal point of B.C.'s attack, and Abrams sometimes turned the ball over. Because of the physical nature of his game, foul trouble is a constant danger.

Analysis: Abrams was a marked man last year as the Eagles' lone scoring threat. However, he responded well to the greater scrutiny. He will continue to terrorize foes on the interior in the face of sagging defensive attention.

COLLEGE STATISTICS

		G	FGP	FTP	RPG	APG	PPG
93-94	BC	34	.464	.585	7.1	0.7	10.4
94-95	BC	28	.514	.720	9.1	1.6	22.1
Totals		62	.494	.667	8.0	1.1	15.7

RAY ALLEN
School: Connecticut
Year: Junior
Position: Forward/Guard
Height: 6'5" **Weight:** 202
Birthdate: July 20, 1975
Hometown: Dalzell, SC

PLAYER SUMMARY	
Will ....explode off dribble
Can't...............pound people inside
Expect ....a major NBA future
Don't Expect ....missed free throws

Background: Like the man whose U.S. Olympic Festival scoring record he broke in the summer of 1994, Shaquille O'Neal, Allen is the product of a military family. As a freshman at UConn, he was a unanimous pick for the Big East All-Rookie team.

Strengths: Polished as they come, Allen's athletic talent and skill level are awesome. A tremendous first step allows him to turn the corner on defenders, and strong hands make him an excellent finisher near the goal. Unlike many of today's athletic types, though, Allen is also comfortable on the perimeter. He has a sweet shooting stroke.

Weaknesses: Forced to play out of position at small forward most of last season, Allen faced some matchup problems defensively. Stronger, physical players were a nuisance. More time at off guard would allow his natural defensive skill to show.

Analysis: Some NBA types suggested Allen might have been the second perimeter player taken in the NBA draft had he declared. He offers the total package and is in a system that accents his strengths. This man could enjoy the kind of junior campaign that former teammate Donyell Marshall did.

COLLEGE STATISTICS

	G	FGP	FTP	RPG	APG	PPG
93-94 CONN	34	.510	.792	4.6	1.6	12.6
94-95 CONN	32	.489	.727	6.8	2.3	21.1
Totals	66	.497	.758	5.7	1.9	16.7

RAYSHARD ALLEN
School: Tulane
Year: Junior
Position: Center/Forward
Height: 6'7" **Weight:** 245
Birthdate: October 9, 1975
Hometown: Marrerro, LA

PLAYER SUMMARY	
Will ....fight for boards
Can't...............take area-code "J's"
Expect ....a high field goal pct.
Don't Expect....................much rest

Background: Tulane's recruiting class of 1993 was rated one of America's 20 best by *Basketball Times*, and Allen had a lot to do with that. The graduate of John Ehret High School became an immediate contributor in college, joining teammate Jerald Honeycutt on the All-Metro Freshman team.

Strengths: A wide frame gives Allen some advantages underneath, and he understands how to use them. In the post position, he has excellent quickness to go with muscle and creates scoring chances for himself. When the ball goes up, he knows how to position himself for caroms.

Weaknesses: Depth was not what it once was at Tulane last year and Allen was forced to log heavy minutes. That's not always good for a big man, especially on defense. Fatigue also led to shots that missed their mark.

Analysis: No one outside of New Orleans paid Tulane much heed, but the Green Wave advanced to the second round of the NCAA Tournament against Kentucky. Allen proved in that game that he's capable of thriving when the foe is among the nation's best. He'll get more chances this year.

COLLEGE STATISTICS

	G	FGP	FTP	RPG	APG	PPG
93-94 TUL	29	.547	.611	5.1	0.7	8.8
94-95 TUL	32	.610	.564	7.8	1.1	16.4
Totals	61	.588	.580	6.5	0.9	12.8

DEREK ANDERSON

School: Kentucky
Year: Junior
Position: Forward
Height: 6'6" **Weight:** 185
Birthdate: July 18, 1974
Hometown: Louisville, KY

PLAYER SUMMARY	
Will	thrive in transition
Can't	overpower people
Expect	lots of steals
Don't Expect	much rust

Background: This one-time star at Doss High School enrolled at Ohio State after that school pursued him with vigor. He started immediately and was one of the Big Ten's developing stars when he broke his leg in a game at Illinois in February 1994. In August 1994, Anderson transferred back home to Kentucky.

Strengths: An athletically gifted swingman, Anderson runs the floor exceptionally well. His explosive leaping ability and strong hands make him an effective finisher. He has the quickness to pick an opponent's pocket. He'll also find the open man.

Weaknesses: Anderson is a slasher more than he is a pure shooter. That makes him something of an oddity in Rick Pitino's system, where the long bomb is prized. There's also the issue of how the layoff will affect him and how quickly he'll adapt to his new surroundings.

Analysis: Perhaps the most devastating blow to Randy Ayers's future at Ohio State was this man's exit. This was the heir to Jimmy Jackson, and his switch to Kentucky was the final blow in the anguished summer of '94 in Columbus. He'll make fast friends in Lexington.

COLLEGE STATISTICS

		G	FGP	FTP	RPG	APG	PPG
92-93	OSU	22	.456	.809	3.3	2.7	10.2
93-94	OSU	22	.466	.814	4.9	4.9	15.0
Totals		44	.462	.812	4.1	3.8	12.6

SHANDON ANDERSON

School: Georgia
Year: Senior
Position: Guard/Forward
Height: 6'6" **Weight:** 205
Birthdate: December 31, 1973
Hometown: Atlanta, GA

PLAYER SUMMARY	
Will	play three spots
Can't	stay under control
Expect	open-court excitement
Don't Expect	safe passes

Background: From the outset of his career, Anderson has been cast in the lengthy shadow of brother Willie Anderson, a former Georgia star who plays for the NBA's Toronto Raptors. Shandon Anderson enjoyed a solid career at Crim High School and has been a three-year fixture for the Bulldogs.

Strengths: A good ball-handler for his size, Anderson sees the floor well. His game is predicated on using his size to take smaller foes inside or beat them down the court. Although not a pure point guard, Anderson can play that spot as well as second guard, small forward, or, in a pinch, big forward.

Weaknesses: Anderson has a collection of good skills but none stands out. There is no one gift that can lift him above the rest of the pack, and that hurts Georgia at crunch time. Additionally, there are moments when Anderson is operating at 100 miles per hour on the floor when the speed limit is 55.

Analysis: A career that has had its share of highs and lows could be prepared for a big finish. New coach Tubby Smith can bring some focus to Anderson's game, and that would allow his multiple skills to thrive.

COLLEGE STATISTICS

		G	FGP	FTP	RPG	APG	PPG
92-93	GEOR	29	.493	.610	3.6	1.5	9.3
93-94	GEOR	30	.485	.660	5.6	3.8	13.8
94-95	GEOR	28	.473	.589	5.2	3.0	13.3
Totals		87	.482	.625	4.8	2.8	12.1

CHUCKY ATKINS

School: South Florida
Year: Senior
Position: Guard
Height: 5'10" **Weight:** 160
Birthdate: August 14, 1974
Hometown: Orlando, FL

PLAYER SUMMARY	
Will	spearhead the attack
Can't	grab offensive boards
Expect	clutch shots
Don't Expect	stingy passing

Background: Dubbed "Chucky" in honor of his father, who goes by the same name, Atkins's first birthday present was a basketball. At Maynard Evans High School, he was a first-team all-state pick and the Most Valuable Player for the North in the 1992 Florida High School Coaches Association Game.

Strengths: Atkins loves the challenge of running an offense. He took charge of USF's offense as a freshman and never relinquished the reins. At high speeds, he handles the basketball well and loves to operate the break. He'll fly past defenders on the wings of a quick first step.

Weaknesses: Described as cocky by some, Atkins sometimes attempts to take too much on his shoulders. Personal duels can take precedence over team goals. As accomplished a scorer as Atkins is, he's not a pure shooter. His perimeter jumper is streaky.

Analysis: Though the rest of the world may be unfamiliar with Atkins, the powers that be are not—he was one of the 42 amateur players invited to try out for the U.S. national team this past summer. This gifted penetrator has a flair for the dramatic.

COLLEGE STATISTICS

		G	FGP	FTP	RPG	APG	PPG
92-93	SF	27	.425	.639	3.4	4.0	10.2
93-94	SF	26	.357	.745	2.4	4.0	11.5
94-95	SF	30	.414	.748	3.2	6.5	16.8
Totals		83	.399	.731	3.0	4.9	13.0

TOBY BAILEY

School: UCLA
Year: Sophomore
Position: Guard
Height: 6'5" **Weight:** 185
Birthdate: November 19, 1975
Hometown: Los Angeles, CA

PLAYER SUMMARY	
Will	dunk with flair
Can't	dominate defensively
Expect	explosive offense
Don't Expect	dull play

Background: As a teenager, Bailey often spent hours playing Cal's Jelani Gardner in one-on-one duels in Bailey's driveway. Bailey began last season on the bench and slowly worked his way into the starting lineup. He scored 26 points in the NCAA title game against Arkansas.

Strengths: Bailey is a terrific threat in the open floor. A competent ball-handler, he has the skill to slice to the goal and finish plays with authority. His dunks are momentum shifters in many instances. He also makes good use of his leaping ability on the boards, where he's an important contributor.

Weaknesses: Three-point shooting is an area Bailey needs to address. He makes the occasional 3 but there are too many others that don't go down. His motion is good, though, and a bit of toil should make him a more viable threat from deep. His free throw shooting also needs work.

Analysis: Throughout the season, Bailey attracted little notice in the shadows of Tyus Edney and the O'Bannon brothers. In the postseason that changed, as Bailey delivered several eye-opening performances. This youngster has superb skills and will be a major part of UCLA's defense of its national title.

COLLEGE STATISTICS

		G	FGP	FTP	RPG	APG	PPG
94-95	UCLA	33	.484	.564	4.8	1.9	10.5
Totals		33	.484	.564	4.8	1.9	10.5

DREW BARRY

School: Georgia Tech
Year: Senior
Position: Guard
Height: 6'5" **Weight:** 182
Birthdate: February 17, 1973
Hometown: Danville, CA

PLAYER SUMMARY	
Will	not lack for intensity
Can't	rely on raw tools
Expect	creative scoring
Don't Expect	Dad's jumper

Background: The fourth of Rick Barry's sons to play Division I basketball (the others being Scooter, Jon, and Brent) played his prep basketball at DeLaSalle High School. He redshirted in 1991-92 to develop strength and became a starter midway through his freshman season.

Strengths: Intangibles are not taken for granted here. Barry plays with reckless abandon and has terrific instincts. A superb passer, he knows when and how to deliver the basketball to his mates. Although he spurns his dad's underhand motion, Drew Barry is a fine free throw shooter.

Weaknesses: A classic shooter Barry is not. His form is erratic and he misses too many open 3's for an off guard. At the defensive end, his intensity and aggressiveness can lead to fouls. Because of his style, injuries are always a concern.

Analysis: Bobby Cremins's Yellow Jackets have endured two consecutive seasons without an NCAA Tournament bid. Tech would be well served if it took on some of Barry's traits and became a scrappier club than it has been. Barry needs to set the tone for Georgia Tech to return to prominence.

COLLEGE STATISTICS

		G	FGP	FTP	RPG	APG	PPG
92-93	GT	30	.468	.805	3.4	5.5	7.3
93-94	GT	24	.421	.776	3.4	5.9	8.1
94-95	GT	27	.513	.753	4.9	6.7	13.4
Totals		81	.474	.770	3.9	6.0	9.5

ISHUA BENJAMIN

School: North Carolina St.
Year: Sophomore
Position: Guard/Forward
Height: 6'5" **Weight:** 175
Birthdate: October 7, 1975
Hometown: Concord, NC

PLAYER SUMMARY	
Will	drive and dish
Can't	get much support
Expect	heady defense
Don't Expect	widespread notice

Background: The *Charlotte Observer* selected Benjamin as North Carolina's Mr. Basketball in his senior year at Concord High School. Benjamin was the cornerstone of a Charlotte AAU team that captured both the 17-and-under and 19-and-under national tournaments. He was named to the ACC All-Freshman team.

Strengths: Benjamin's game is exceptionally diversified. Coach Les Robinson can use him at any of three perimeter spots with confidence. Benjamin is a fine ball-handler who locates the open man well. Athletically gifted, Benjamin is a superb defender.

Weaknesses: If there is a void in Benjamin's game, it is at the offensive end. Benjamin is much more comfortable with drives down the lane and short jumpers than he is on the wing. His standstill jumper is shaky and needs to be more consistent if he is to continue to grow.

Analysis: In another dark year at N.C. State, Benjamin was a beacon. He is clearly the best player to enter the program in Robinson's reign, and the season's biggest scare came when rumors circulated that he was pondering a transfer. That story was denied and no one is more relieved than Robinson, for this is his main attraction.

COLLEGE STATISTICS

		G	FGP	FTP	RPG	APG	PPG
94-95	NCS	27	.389	.730	2.1	4.6	14.0
Totals		27	.389	.730	2.1	4.6	14.0

EDDIE BENTON

School: Vermont
Year: Senior
Position: Guard
Height: 5'11" **Weight:** 175
Birthdate: February 16, 1975
Hometown: Pittsburgh, PA

PLAYER SUMMARY	
Will	score in bunches
Can't	shoot enough
Expect	high-speed excitement
Don't Expect	forced shots

Background: From Perry Traditional High School, Benton was steered to Vermont by Massachusetts coach John Calipari. He was the New England Division I Rookie of the Year in 1992-93 and became only the third player in NCAA history to score 1,000 points before his 19th birthday.

Strengths: Breaking down foes off the dribble is one of Benton's specialties. He has excellent quickness and knows how to score or get to the free throw line once past the initial defender. From the perimeter, he can swish 3's in a hurry. He is a first-rate free throw shooter.

Weaknesses: Benton draws a great deal of attention from defenders, and in response often launches poor shots. Turnovers remain a problem and Benton seems to pay little heed to his responsibilities at the defensive end.

Analysis: Already Vermont's most decorated player, Benton craves a shot at an NCAA Tournament berth. The Catamounts have improved and Benton has reduced his scoring so that there is more balance. He'll gladly trade numbers for a shot at postseason glory.

COLLEGE STATISTICS

	G	FGP	FTP	RPG	APG	PPG
92-93 VERM	26	.414	.837	3.0	4.5	23.8
93-94 VERM	26	.385	.833	2.5	3.8	26.4
94-95 VERM	26	.360	.800	2.5	3.9	20.5
Totals	78	.385	.825	2.7	4.1	23.6

JOSEPH BLAIR

School: Arizona
Year: Senior
Position: Center
Height: 6'10" **Weight:** 265
Birthdate: June 12, 1974
Hometown: Houston, TX

PLAYER SUMMARY	
Will	display light touch
Can't	pass from post
Expect	high-percentage shots
Don't Expect	total health

Background: This communications major earned three letters in basketball at C.E. King High School, where he was named Texas Player of the Year as a senior. At Arizona, he was a *Basketball Weekly* Freshman All-American and became a regular starter as a sophomore.

Strengths: Today, there are many big men who fancy themselves as jump-shooters. The list does not include Blair. He understands his limits and sticks to interior post-up moves and short jumpers. A hungry rebounder, he gets off the floor quickly to seize control. Foes must account for him at the defensive end, lest he block their shot.

Weaknesses: Injuries have slowed Blair lately. They've cut into his effectiveness and durability. Shaky free throw shooting has also plagued Blair during his career. He is also a weak passer when teams double down on him.

Analysis: A key on Arizona's 1994 Final Four team, Blair has teased fans in Tucson with how good he can be. To date, he has not consistently produced due to some nagging injuries. This is his chance to show what he can really do.

COLLEGE STATISTICS

	G	FGP	FTP	RPG	APG	PPG
92-93 ARIZ	28	.652	.596	3.8	0.4	7.1
93-94 ARIZ	34	.607	.435	7.2	0.6	10.1
94-95 ARIZ	28	.559	.465	7.0	0.9	12.0
Totals	90	.597	.480	6.1	0.6	9.8

JARON BOONE

School: Nebraska
Year: Senior
Position: Guard
Height: 6'6" **Weight:** 200
Birthdate: May 23, 1974
Hometown: Salt Lake City, UT

PLAYER SUMMARY	
Will	swish lengthy "J's"
Can't	be careless with ball
Expect	free throws to fall
Don't Expect	rough edges

Background: Jaron's dad, Ron, played 13 seasons of professional basketball, most notably with the Utah Stars of the American Basketball Association. Boone was raised in Salt Lake City and went on to star at Skyline High School.

Strengths: Ron Boone was a tremendous shooter, and it's clear the gene pool has been kind to his offspring. Jaron has the kind of range that extends defenses. He knows how to get open coming off the screen and is a good enough ball-handler to create shots for himself.

Weaknesses: Although he sees action at both guard spots, he is better equipped to play off the basketball than he is to direct a team. Boone lacks the natural point-guard instincts others have. He tends to force the action when running the offense and turnovers often result. More consistency on his jumper would also be a plus.

Analysis: This decorated prepster has enjoyed a solid career for the Cornhuskers. The new season offers him a chance to take a step beyond that. He'll get the opportunity to be the kind of leader Eric Piatkowski became for Nebraska in his senior campaign.

COLLEGE STATISTICS

	G	FGP	FTP	RPG	APG	PPG
92-93 NEBR	31	.411	.821	2.3	2.8	6.9
93-94 NEBR	30	.476	.705	2.6	3.6	12.2
94-95 NEBR	32	.437	.679	3.3	3.6	17.5
Totals	93	.444	.716	2.8	3.4	12.3

MARCUS BROWN

School: Murray St.
Year: Senior
Position: Guard
Height: 6'3" **Weight:** 185
Birthdate: April 3, 1974
Hometown: West Memphis, AR

PLAYER SUMMARY	
Will	make free throws
Can't	intimidate defensively
Expect	OVC kudos
Don't Expect	bad shot choices

Background: This three-time all-state selection helped Arkansas win two AAU national championships. After pondering a track scholarship offer from Arkansas, Brown signed to play basketball at Murray State. Last year, he was cited as the Ohio Valley Conference Player of the Year.

Strengths: A great athlete, Brown is an exceptional leaper. He displays terrific quickness and knows how to use it to gain an edge. Unlike many prolific scorers, Brown doesn't need an inordinate amount of shots to produce. He's very effective in transition and has improved his 3-point accuracy.

Weaknesses: Brown likes to drive the lane, and that aggressiveness used to land him in frequent foul trouble. There are still occasions when he takes unnecessary gambles, especially defensively.

Analysis: Those Arkansas AAU teams—which also included Corliss Williamson—were some of the most successful in recent times, and now we know why. Brown is a standout, an explosive scorer who will pick an opponent's pocket. Each year he's added new twists to his game, and the only item missing now is acclaim.

COLLEGE STATISTICS

	G	FGP	FTP	RPG	APG	PPG
92-93 MSU	30	.488	.789	2.8	1.1	8.9
93-94 MSU	29	.503	.839	3.8	2.7	18.1
94-95 MSU	30	.510	.896	4.9	2.1	22.4
Totals	89	.503	.853	3.8	2.0	16.5

GREG BUCKNER

School: Clemson
Year: Sophomore
Position: Guard
Height: 6'4" **Weight:** 180
Birthdate: September 16, 1976
Hometown: Hopkinsville, KY

PLAYER SUMMARY	
Will	guard closely
Can't	win ACC title
Expect	more points
Don't Expect	wide notice

Background: Recruited by Rick Barnes when he was coaching at Providence, Buckner was granted a release from his letter of intent by new Friar coach Pete Gillen so that he could follow Barnes to Clemson. Buckner became an instant starter and the first Clemson Tiger in history to be named ACC Rookie of the Year.

Strengths: A powerful frame allows Buckner to work on the interior if he chooses. He can take the basketball into the lane and get his shot off. In addition, he has a jumper that is usually dependable. As his career progresses, he could become one of the nation's top defenders.

Weaknesses: There's some polish lacking in Buckner's game. He is devoid of consistency at times and is often too eager to make a play. He should improve with more experience.

Analysis: Buckner was little more than a curiosity entering college but became much more in his debut. Despite little experience, he made good decisions and emerged as the focal point of a Tiger attack that was strong enough to land an NIT bid. He was overshadowed by the likes of Jerry Stackhouse, Joe Smith, and Rasheed Wallace as a newcomer. Not so this time.

COLLEGE STATISTICS

	G	FGP	FTP	RPG	APG	PPG
94-95 CLEM	28	.526	.513	5.9	2.1	12.0
Totals	28	.526	.513	5.9	2.1	12.0

MARCUS CAMBY

School: Massachusetts
Year: Junior
Position: Center
Height: 6'11" **Weight:** 220
Birthdate: March 22, 1974
Hometown: Hartford, CT

PLAYER SUMMARY	
Will	alter game plans
Can't	back foes in
Expect	more muscle
Don't Expect	bad hands

Background: Some of the major schools in the region overlooked Camby when he sat out his junior season at Hartford Public High School. Former Massachusetts aide Bill Bayno kept close tabs on Camby and was rewarded when he signed with the Minutemen.

Strengths: Camby has natural shot-blocking talent. Along with fine leaping ability, he has long arms and a knack for knowing when to make his move. Offensively, he has the skills of a much smaller man. He's a good ball-handler and is most comfortable taking medium-distance jumpers.

Weaknesses: Although he's a superior shot-blocker, Camby's lack of strength puts him at a sizable disadvantage against powerful centers. Camby also lacks low-post moves and seems lost when playing with his back to the goal.

Analysis: After a strong freshman debut, Camby endured an uneven campaign. On occasion, he appeared to be an All-American. Other times he looked lost. No one questions his tools, and under the demanding watch of John Calipari, the guess is that he'll step forward as a major weapon this time out.

COLLEGE STATISTICS

	G	FGP	FTP	RPG	APG	PPG
93-94 MASS	29	.494	.596	6.4	1.2	10.2
94-95 MASS	30	.550	.643	6.2	1.2	13.9
Totals	59	.525	.622	6.3	1.2	12.1

JEFF CAPEL

School: Duke
Year: Junior
Position: Guard
Height: 6'5" **Weight:** 195
Birthdate: February 12, 1975
Hometown: Fayetteville, NC

PLAYER SUMMARY	
Will	see the floor
Can't	create consistently
Expect	explosive drives
Don't Expect	blocked shots

Background: The son of Jeff Capel Sr., presently the coach at Old Dominion, has been around basketball throughout his life. He was an All-American at South View High School. As a freshman, he was the starting point guard as the Blue Devils advanced to the NCAA finals.

Strengths: This quality athlete brings many skills to the table. He's a capable ball-handler who can turn the corner on defenders. Defensively, he has good size and moves his feet well. He's comfortable playing either guard position and rebounds well.

Weaknesses: Although a capable point guard, Capel is not a natural at that position. He doesn't have the instinctive feel for the other players on the court that his predecessor Bobby Hurley did. Pressure defense can force him to turn the ball over, and his jump shot tends to come and go.

Analysis: Capel appeared poised to take a significant step forward after a superb 1994 NCAA Tournament. The absence of coach Mike Krzyzewski seemed to affect him as much as anyone. He often appeared unsure of himself. Krzyzewski's return and the experience of 1994-95, though, should put him back on solid ground.

COLLEGE STATISTICS

	G	FGP	FTP	RPG	APG	PPG
93-94 DUKE	34	.458	.656	2.7	3.2	8.6
94-95 DUKE	31	.446	.643	2.7	4.1	12.5
Totals	65	.451	.650	2.7	3.6	10.4

VINCE CARTER

School: North Carolina
Year: Freshman
Position: Guard/Forward
Height: 6'6" **Weight:** 198
Hometown: Daytona Beach, FL

PLAYER SUMMARY	
Will	dribble penetrate
Can't	apply much bulk
Expect	versatility
Don't Expect	a long adjustment

Background: A well-rounded athlete, Carter has played football and volleyball and has been a high-jumper in track in addition to his signature sport. As a senior at Mainland High School, he averaged 22 PPG and 11 RPG while gaining recognition as a McDonald's All-American. He picked North Carolina over Florida and Florida State.

Strengths: This is a complete athlete. Carter possesses a thunderous first step that usually gets him past taller defenders. Once near the goal, he completes the play with authority. His dunking skills are at times breathtaking. From long distance, he is usually an accurate shooter.

Weaknesses: Carter figures to spend a good bit of time in the weight room in Chapel Hill. The natural maturation process and the iron pumping will help Carter become more effective inside at the collegiate level. He also has a bit of work to do to enhance his defensive game.

Analysis: When coaches made out their recruiting wish lists last year, this youngster was atop many polls. He and Ron Mercer of Kentucky are probably the top wing prospects in the class. Carter will fill the void at North Carolina created by Donald Williams's exit.

DION CROSS

School: Stanford
Year: Senior
Position: Guard
Height: 6'2" **Weight:** 175
Birthdate: August 5, 1974
Hometown: Woodson, AR

PLAYER SUMMARY	
Will	shoot often
Can't	help on boards
Expect	thunderous shot-making
Don't Expect	great ball-handling

Background: Cross was one of five starters at Parkview High School in Arkansas to sign with Division I schools. During his final state tournament, Corliss Williamson was so impressed by Cross that he gave his rival the MVP trophy that had been awarded to him.

Strengths: Opposing defenses know better than to leave Cross unattended on the perimeter. His quick-release jump shot is very accurate and he is not afraid to launch it. When the Cardinal needs a basket, it tends to look for Cross first. He also is a terrific free throw shooter.

Weaknesses: Dribble penetration would add another dimension to Cross's game. Sometimes he is too content to take long bombs. Although he can play the point, it's not his best spot due to spotty ball-handling. Cross also must become a better defender if he hopes to advance to the next level.

Analysis: While it doesn't get the recognition of some tandems, the backcourt combination of Cross and Brevin Knight is one of the nation's best. The two complement each other well and are the catalysts for a strong Stanford club that won its first NCAA Tournament game since 1942 last March.

COLLEGE STATISTICS

		G	FGP	FTP	RPG	APG	PPG
92-93	STAN	29	.473	.825	1.3	0.8	10.6
93-94	STAN	28	.444	.792	2.7	1.3	15.1
94-95	STAN	29	.437	.827	1.8	1.1	16.8
Totals		86	.449	.814	1.9	1.1	14.1

ACE CUSTIS

School: Virginia Tech
Year: Junior
Position: Forward
Height: 6'7" **Weight:** 206
Birthdate: May 24, 1974
Hometown: Eastville, VA

PLAYER SUMMARY	
Will	fly to the ball
Can't	make from downtown
Expect	hustling athleticism
Don't Expect	sharp passes

Background: During his career at Northampton High School, Custis played mostly center, with his back to the basket. Hence, major programs were a bit reluctant to recruit him. He landed at Virginia Tech where he injured a knee in fall practice, which required reconstructive surgery. He made the Metro Conference All-Freshman team in 1993-94.

Strengths: Custis calls the shadow of the basket home. He slices between opponents to carve out rebounding position. A relentless approach serves him well, and he gets many of his points off putbacks. He doesn't force bad shots and can get his soft shot off in congested areas of the paint.

Weaknesses: Custis has difficulty adding weight. That's a problem for a performer who likes to make the painted area his home. To offset that, he must develop more of a perimeter dimension so that he can step out and make 15-footers consistently.

Analysis: Virginia Tech enjoyed a fine run to the NIT crown, and Custis was the Hokies' ringleader. Basketball smarts, athletic skills, and desire are all a part of the Custis package. Look for his stature to grow as VTU begins its stint in the Atlantic 10.

COLLEGE STATISTICS

		G	FGP	FTP	RPG	APG	PPG
93-94	VT	28	.523	.693	9.1	2.1	10.9
94-95	VT	35	.533	.669	10.5	2.5	15.8
Totals		63	.529	.676	9.9	2.3	13.7

ERICK DAMPIER

School: Mississippi St.
Year: Junior
Position: Center
Height: 6'11" **Weight:** 255
Birthdate: July 14, 1974
Hometown: New Hebron, MS

PLAYER SUMMARY	
Will	protect the goal
Can't	drift outside
Expect	All-SEC first team
Don't Expect	showy moves

Background: Along with Mississippi State teammate Vandale Thomas, Dampier sparked Lawrence County High School to a three-year record of 103-12, which included two state titles. He was an All-Southeastern Conference second-team choice as a freshman and an All-South pick of *Basketball Times* last season.

Strengths: Long before he was considered an offensive threat, Dampier was acknowledged as a defensive presence. It remains the backbone of his game. Excellent foot movement and solid leaping ability make him an intimidating shot-blocker. He's a dutiful rebounder and has improved his offensive skills in his two years of college.

Weaknesses: Dampier is not a finished product. Offensively, he is limited to a few interior moves and putbacks. Double-teams can confuse him, and he doesn't always choose the proper outlet man. His free throw shooting also requires further attention.

Analysis: No one expected Dampier to make the kind of impact he has made at MSU. Hard work has helped him marry physical tools with quality play. His growth chart should continue to move upward, and an NBA future looms.

COLLEGE STATISTICS

		G	FGP	FTP	RPG	APG	PPG
93-94	MSU	29	.588	.491	8.7	0.8	11.9
94-95	MSU	30	.640	.596	9.7	0.9	13.1
Totals		59	.615	.541	9.2	0.9	12.5

DEVIN DAVIS

School: Miami (OH)
Year: Junior
Position: Forward
Height: 6'7" **Weight:** 215
Birthdate: December 27, 1974
Hometown: Miami, FL

PLAYER SUMMARY	
Will	chase rebounds
Can't	step back for 3's
Expect	greater notoriety
Don't Expect	shyness underneath

Background: In a fitting bit of irony, Miami of Ohio's top player is actually a native of the Florida city of the same name. He averaged 16 PPG and ten RPG in his final season at Miami Senior High School. In Ohio, he was named to the Mid-American Conference All-Freshman team and was an All-Mideast selection by *Basketball Times* last year.

Strengths: Aggressiveness and courage serve Davis well. He is not easily intimidated and loves to operate in the paint. Strong hands and quickness off the floor make him a superb rebounder. Many of his points come off putbacks. He has a nice touch from short range too.

Weaknesses: The same aggressiveness and enthusiasm that aid Davis also work against him in some instances. Foul trouble is always a concern.

Analysis: America discovered Davis, he of the dreadlock hair, in the NCAA Tournament when Miami upended Arizona and gave Virginia a mighty push. This athlete is more than a hairstyling curiosity. He's an enthusiastic performer who loves to rebound, play defense, and score when he can. With Gary Trent gone, he's the MAC's main man.

COLLEGE STATISTICS

		G	FGP	FTP	RPG	APG	PPG
93-94	MIAM	30	.489	.622	7.7	1.3	10.0
94-95	MIAM	30	.491	.692	7.5	1.5	16.9
Totals		60	.491	.666	7.6	1.4	13.4

HAROLD DEANE

School: Virginia
Year: Junior
Position: Guard
Height: 6'1" **Weight:** 177
Birthdate: September 11, 1974
Hometown: Petersburg, VA

PLAYER SUMMARY	
Will	harass other guards
Can't	shoot a lofty percentage
Expect	smart decisions
Don't Expect	lazy passes

Background: After beginning his high school career at Matoaca High in Virginia, Deane completed his prep work at Fork Union Military Academy. Deane stepped in for Cory Alexander in 1993-94 and became a third-team Freshman All-America pick of *Basketball Weekly*.

Strengths: While he didn't spend much time in high school as a point guard, Deane certainly looks the part now. His ball-handling is very reliable and he distributes the ball evenly among his Cavalier mates. Traps are handled with aplomb and his perimeter shooting must be respected. On defense, he's a nuisance.

Weaknesses: A lack of size makes Deane vulnerable to post-up moves by other point guards. At the offensive end, he is not a high-percentage shooter. That's the product of a jump shot that tends to run hot and cold.

Analysis: Deane has come a long way in two years at UVA. The plain truth was that the Cavaliers played better in 1994-95 with Deane running the show than they did when the more ballyhooed Alexander was in charge. That says much about Deane's unselfishness and consistent defensive effort.

COLLEGE STATISTICS

	G	FGP	FTP	RPG	APG	PPG
93-94 VIRG	31	.368	.706	3.5	2.8	12.3
94-95 VIRG	34	.392	.795	3.0	4.3	16.0
Totals	65	.381	.759	3.2	3.6	14.2

TONY DELK

School: Kentucky
Year: Senior
Position: Guard
Height: 6'1" **Weight:** 194
Birthdate: January 28, 1974
Hometown: Covington, KY

PLAYER SUMMARY	
Will	launch triples
Can't	play the point
Expect	creative offense
Don't Expect	laziness

Background: From his days at Haywood High School, Delk's calling card has been his explosive scoring touch. He led the state of Tennessee in scoring twice as a prepster, and he topped the Wildcats in his sophomore and junior seasons at Kentucky.

Strengths: The man known as "T.D." has developed into Rick Pitino's most reliable offensive weapon at Kentucky. A pure shooter, Delk has a quick release and accurate stroke from long range. He'll also draw defenders to him and use his quickness to go by.

Weaknesses: Pitino attempted to use Delk as a point guard during his freshman season and the experiment was a failure. Unfortunately, that is the position Delk must play if he is to have an NBA future. He needs to develop his ball-handling capacity and learn how to involve others.

Analysis: Delk is the Wildcats' designated go-to man. He likes the pressure and understands the demands of Pitino's system. Kentucky's deep bench probably means he won't get the minutes other All-America candidates will, but this man is a first-class college player.

COLLEGE STATISTICS

	G	FGP	FTP	RPG	APG	PPG
92-93 KENT	30	.452	.727	1.9	0.7	4.5
93-94 KENT	34	.455	.639	4.5	1.7	16.6
94-95 KENT	33	.478	.674	3.3	2.0	16.7
Totals	97	.465	.665	3.3	1.5	12.9

CAMERON DOLLAR

School: UCLA
Year: Junior
Position: Guard
Height: 6'1" **Weight:** 173
Birthdate: December 9, 1975
Hometown: Atlanta, GA

PLAYER SUMMARY	
Will	cope with pressure
Can't	snag rebounds
Expect	calm leadership
Don't Expect	porous defense

Background: After debuting at Douglass High School, Dollar switched to St. John's Prospect Hall in Frederick, Maryland. He led St. John's to the No. 8 national ranking as a senior and carried a 3.8 grade-point average too. As a freshman at UCLA, he emerged as the team's valued sixth man.

Strengths: This right-hander dribbles well and deals with double-teams effectively. Pressure doesn't fluster Dollar as he patiently seeks out the openings in the defense. Though not the scorer his predecessor Tyus Edney was, Dollar drives the lane well and can kiss the ball off the glass for a score.

Weaknesses: Essentially sound defensively, Dollar's lack of height does present some problems when checking foes. That is particularly evident when he plays the off-guard spot and is forced to deal with potent scorers.

Analysis: UCLA fans nearly panicked when it became apparent that Edney wouldn't be able to return to the NCAA final against Arkansas because of a wrist injury. Dollar saved the Bruins, though. He's steady and sure, commodities that will aid him as he attempts to permanently fill Edney's shoes.

COLLEGE STATISTICS

		G	FGP	FTP	RPG	APG	PPG
93-94	UCLA	28	.468	.589	1.5	2.7	3.9
94-95	UCLA	33	.354	.659	1.9	3.1	3.4
Totals		61	.410	.630	1.7	2.9	3.6

TIM DUNCAN

School: Wake Forest
Year: Junior
Position: Center/Forward
Height: 6'10" **Weight:** 238
Birthdate: April 25, 1976
Hometown: St. Croix, Virgin Islands

PLAYER SUMMARY	
Will	deflect shots
Can't	get into foul trouble
Expect	an All-American
Don't Expect	backcourt support

Background: Duncan's athletic career began in the swimming pool, where he was once listed among the top high school performers in the 400 freestyle. He only began playing basketball in the ninth grade. He was a first-team All-ACC pick in 1994-95.

Strengths: Around the goal, there are none better defensively. Duncan rarely goes for ball fakes yet manages to get into the air to block shots. He's able to be aggressive without committing a lot of fouls. On the backboards, he brings a tireless work ethic to the proceedings. He also has a soft shooting touch around the hoop.

Weaknesses: The occasions when Duncan is rested are few and far between. Although he possesses superb endurance, more breaks would allow him to remain fresh. The likelihood is, though, that his minutes will increase in the new campaign.

Analysis: Previously billed as one of the nation's hidden gems, that no longer is the case. In the minds of many scouts, Duncan is on level footing with Jerry Stackhouse, Joe Smith, and Rasheed Wallace, all of whom left for the NBA. Duncan's just 19 and likely a future top-five choice, perhaps even first overall, in the NBA draft.

COLLEGE STATISTICS

		G	FGP	FTP	RPG	APG	PPG
93-94	WF	33	.545	.745	9.6	0.9	9.8
94-95	WF	32	.591	.742	12.5	2.1	16.8
Totals		65	.573	.743	11.0	1.5	13.2

DAN EARL

School: Penn St.
Year: Junior
Position: Guard
Height: 6'3" **Weight:** 175
Birthdate: December 10, 1974
Hometown: Medford Lakes, NJ

PLAYER SUMMARY	
Will	penetrate and score
Can't	wear down foes
Expect	steady marksmanship
Don't Expect	turnovers

Background: The all-time leading scorer in Burlington County, New Jersey, Earl was the 1993 *USA Today* New Jersey Player of the Year. He sparked Shawnee High School to a 107-10 record during his career and won the state Tournament of Champions in 1992. At Penn State, Earl was an immediate starter.

Strengths: This fine ball-handler is an excellent quarterback for Penn State's patient offense. He locates the open man and feeds the post well. If defenders lay off, he can convert 3-point shots. Well schooled in the basics, Earl gets good defensive position and forces the occasional steal.

Weaknesses: The Big Ten is one of the land's most physical leagues, and even point guards are subjected to punishment. Earl's thin frame makes him vulnerable to powerful guards in one-on-one situations. He also can wear down at times from fatigue.

Analysis: The Nittany Lions are gradually learning to compete in the Big Ten. Earl is at the center of that revival. His sharp ball skills and calm demeanor make the Lions go. He'll likely score more this season as Penn State players look to compensate for the graduated John Amaechi.

COLLEGE STATISTICS

		G	FGP	FTP	RPG	APG	PPG
93-94	PSU	27	.386	.652	2.5	4.2	8.4
94-95	PSU	32	.424	.835	2.3	5.7	9.3
Totals		59	.406	.743	2.4	5.0	8.9

ERIC EBERZ

School: Villanova
Year: Senior
Position: Forward
Height: 6'7" **Weight:** 210
Birthdate: March 31, 1974
Hometown: Buffalo, NY

PLAYER SUMMARY	
Will	launch missiles
Can't	bang effectively
Expect	expert marksmanship
Don't Expect	flashy moves

Background: Eberz toiled in relative obscurity at St. Joseph's Collegiate Institute and was not viewed as a prize catch when he signed with the Wildcats. After making only one start as a freshman, Eberz came on strong in 1993-94 for Villanova's NIT championship team. Last year, he was a second-team All-Big East pick.

Strengths: Put simply, Eberz lives up to the nickname coach Steve Lappas attached to him—"The Assassin." Coolly efficient, Eberz has one of the sweetest strokes in the college game. He has a fast release and is deadly when left alone beyond the arc. He'll also react with a sharp pass if the shot is not available.

Weaknesses: Speed is somewhat lacking in Eberz's game. Athletic forwards can prove troublesome for him in one-on-one situations at the defensive end. Eberz will launch the occasional bad shot.

Analysis: Few appreciate Eberz beyond the Main Line. However, he is a fine shooter in an era when there aren't nearly the number of quality bombers there used to be. He keeps defenses honest and Jason Lawson free inside by spotting up from the perimeter.

COLLEGE STATISTICS

		G	FGP	FTP	RPG	APG	PPG
92-93	VILL	23	.327	.714	1.2	0.7	2.0
93-94	VILL	32	.450	.754	4.3	1.4	12.6
94-95	VILL	33	.476	.734	4.4	1.6	15.7
Totals		88	.455	.743	3.5	1.3	11.0

BRIAN EVANS

School: Indiana
Year: Senior
Position: Forward
Height: 6'8" **Weight:** 211
Birthdate: September 13, 1973
Hometown: Terre Haute, IN

PLAYER SUMMARY	
Will.........create matchup problems	
Can't..........use speed as a weapon	
Expect..................heady leadership	
Don't Expect ....lazy defense	

Background: In the town where one-time Indiana recruit Larry Bird came to prominence, Evans was a prep star. He sat out a redshirt year at Indiana after earning all-state honors at Terre Haute South High School. He's made a gradual progression from role-player to team leader and All-Big Ten threat over the course of his career.

Strengths: This left-hander possesses a smooth stroke from long range. When given time to set, he is deadly. Unselfish by nature, Evans will make the extra pass to find the open man. At the other end, Evans is fundamentally sound and a willing worker.

Weaknesses: Evans's eager style of play makes him susceptible to injuries. Even when those ailments don't sideline him, they do detract from his effectiveness. He can't rely on quickness to beat defenders and is not a shot-blocker.

Analysis: Last year won't be recalled as one of Indiana's greatest, and surely coach Bob Knight will challenge Evans and his fellow seniors to do better. Evans has a great wealth of experience and enough shot-making skill to make the Hoosiers a legitimate threat in the Big Ten title pursuit.

COLLEGE STATISTICS

		G	FGP	FTP	RPG	APG	PPG
92-93	IND	35	.425	.685	3.9	1.3	5.3
93-94	IND	27	.448	.793	6.8	2.2	11.9
94-95	IND	31	.462	.783	6.7	3.3	17.4
Totals		93	.451	.766	5.7	2.2	11.2

HESHIMU EVANS

School: Manhattan
Year: Sophomore
Position: Forward
Height: 6'6" **Weight:** 205
Birthdate: May 8, 1975
Hometown: Bronx, NY

PLAYER SUMMARY	
Will ....punctuate the break	
Can't....................................drain 3's	
Expect ....MAAC brilliance	
Don't Expect...expert ball-handling	

Background: The major schools ignored Evans long enough so that Manhattan coach Fran Fraschilla could score a major recruiting triumph. Evans's high school credentials were impeccable. He averaged 22.7 points and 12.7 rebounds at Trinity Pawling School after a four-year stint at Evander Childs High School.

Strengths: This is an exceptional athlete. Evans's lean frame permits him to beat most foes down the court. Agile, he owns a speedy first step that most defenders struggle to halt. Once in the lane, he understands how to complete the play. His medium-range jumper is reliable too.

Weaknesses: If there is anything lacking in Evans's game, it is polish. At times, he gets out of the offensive flow and minutes go by without him taking a shot. His ball-handling needs to improve if he is to operate on the perimeter, and he could use another five or six feet of range on his jumper.

Analysis: The Manhattan club that upset Oklahoma was an exceptionally balanced one. No one possessed great individual statistics, yet there were standouts and this was one of them. Evans has all the tools to be the scoring force at Manhattan.

COLLEGE STATISTICS

		G	FGP	FTP	RPG	APG	PPG
94-95	MANH	27	.519	.636	5.0	2.1	12.4
Totals		27	.519	.636	5.0	2.1	12.4

KWAME EVANS

School: George Washington
Year: Senior
Position: Guard
Height: 6'6" **Weight:** 190
Birthdate: December 29, 1973
Hometown: Baltimore, MD

PLAYER SUMMARY	
Will	shoot with grace
Can't	avoid cold streaks
Expect	versatile scoring
Don't Expect	breathtaking passes

Background: Evans, who aspires to one day own a restaurant, was recruited out of Baltimore Southern High School by Temple, Penn State, and Providence in addition to George Washington. He was the Colonials' leading scorer in the 1993 NCAA Tournament.

Strengths: When Evans is in a groove, he is most difficult to handcuff. He is a confident shooter from beyond the 3-point arc and can create a shot for himself as well. Defensively, he has made strides, and his lithe frame gives other wing players trouble.

Weaknesses: Shot selection can be a problem at times. Evans sometimes forces jumpers that aren't really there. He's also prone to carelessness with the basketball, as his ball-handling skills are only average.

Analysis: Along with teammate Vaughn Jones and the departed Yinka Dare, Evans is one-third of what may go down as George Washington's most significant recruiting class ever. G.W. has three NCAA Tournament wins in his career and appears positioned to add more in 1995-96. Evans is a sharp, experienced veteran whose range is vital to one of the Atlantic 10's best squads.

COLLEGE STATISTICS

		G	FGP	FTP	RPG	APG	PPG
92-93	GW	26	.403	.743	1.7	0.5	5.6
93-94	GW	30	.376	.725	4.7	1.7	13.2
94-95	GW	32	.416	.724	5.7	2.4	19.4
Totals		88	.400	.726	4.2	1.6	13.2

DAMON FLINT

School: Cincinnati
Year: Junior
Position: Forward/Guard
Height: 6'5" **Weight:** 191
Birthdate: October 21, 1973
Hometown: Cincinnati, OH

PLAYER SUMMARY	
Will	sky high
Can't	depend on jumper
Expect	sweet passes
Don't Expect	shaky defense

Background: One of Ohio's premier players at Woodward High School, Flint originally signed with Ohio State. However, recruiting violations on OSU's part reopened the process and Flint chose his hometown school. Flint made the starting lineup early in his freshman season and has been a fixture there ever since.

Strengths: This well-rounded athlete fills a variety of roles for coach Bob Huggins. He's probably at his best filling the lane on the break, where his athleticism and leaping ability stand out. Yet he can also direct the offense from the point-guard position thanks to competent ball-handling skills and excellent court vision.

Weaknesses: When the game drops to a slower pace offensively, Flint can struggle. His perimeter jumper is streaky and defenses will lay off him at times to protect against drives. Turnovers crop up too when he runs the offense.

Analysis: Cincinnati has continued to be a presence on the national scene in the past two seasons. Flint's had a lot to do with that. His athleticism and speed make him a nice fit for Huggins's system, and as he matures he'll emerge as one of the Midwest's best.

COLLEGE STATISTICS

		G	FGP	FTP	RPG	APG	PPG
93-94	CINC	32	.375	.588	3.8	2.8	12.6
94-95	CINC	31	.398	.623	2.2	2.5	7.0
Totals		63	.382	.601	3.0	2.6	9.8

DANNY FORTSON

School: Cincinnati
Year: Sophomore
Position: Forward
Height: 6'8" **Weight:** 245
Birthdate: March 27, 1976
Hometown: Pittsburgh, PA

PLAYER SUMMARY	
Will	expend energy
Can't	swing to backcourt
Expect	determined rebounding
Don't Expect	rainbow "J's"

Background: Fortson began his high school hoops career at Altoona High School before moving to Pittsburgh prior to his junior year. His transfer to Shaler High School became the subject of controversy, and he was forced to sit out a year by the state's athletic governing body. The year off didn't deter recruiters, as Michigan and Cincinnati were among the suitors.

Strengths: A powerful frame enables Fortson to operate effectively in the lane. He doesn't shy away from contact and understands the significance of rebounding. His shooting touch is sweet around the goal, and he uses a variety of low-post moves to free himself for opportunities.

Weaknesses: Although he's not a liability defensively, there's room for improvement. Fortson must learn to be aggressive without fouling. As he develops offensively, he'll likely add range to a jumper that is presently somewhat limited.

Analysis: If you were creating an ideal power forward, you could do worse than copy from Fortson's package of gifts. He's strong, tough, and willing to do the dirty work inside. Stamina and consistency are keys as he prepares for what should be a terrific year in the Queen City.

COLLEGE STATISTICS

		G	FGP	FTP	RPG	APG	PPG
94-95	CINC	34	.535	.684	7.6	1.1	15.1
Totals		34	.535	.684	7.6	1.1	15.1

TREMAINE FOWLKES

School: California
Year: Sophomore
Position: Guard/Forward
Height: 6'7" **Weight:** 215
Birthdate: April 11, 1976
Hometown: Los Angeles, CA

PLAYER SUMMARY	
Will	hustle for rebounds
Can't	depend on muscle
Expect	transition scores
Don't Expect	laziness

Background: Crenshaw High School has a rich athletic history that includes Marques Johnson and Darryl Strawberry, and Fowlkes created his own niche in that lineup. He was the second-leading scorer on the United States junior national team that competed in Argentina in the fall of 1994.

Strengths: The open floor is an inviting place for Fowlkes. He runs the court exceptionally well and can complete plays when he is on the receiving end of the pass. In the halfcourt game, he breaks defenders down off the dribble and has the potential to be a reliable jump-shooter. He is an excellent rebounder for a swingman.

Weaknesses: Inconsistency was an issue for Fowlkes as a freshman. His energy and effort sometimes got ahead of his skill level and that caused turnovers. An off-season goal should be plenty of long-range jumpers.

Analysis: California's coaching staff likened Fowlkes to first-round NBA draft pick Lamond Murray at the same stage, and nothing that happened in 1994-95 caused them to reevaluate their assessment. He's a hardworking performer with the athletic tools necessary to become a standout for a Golden Bear team that should rebound from a disappointing year.

COLLEGE STATISTICS

		G	FGP	FTP	RPG	APG	PPG
94-95	CAL	27	.455	.639	6.7	1.0	13.4
Totals		27	.455	.639	6.7	1.0	13.4

ADONAL FOYLE

School: Colgate
Year: Sophomore
Position: Center
Height: 6'10" **Weight:** 260
Birthdate: March 9, 1975
Hometown: Canouan, Grenadines

PLAYER SUMMARY	
Will	intimidate shooters
Can't	shoot from deep
Expect	tons of caroms
Don't Expect	offensive polish

Background: Foyle lived on the Grenadines Islands until he was 15, then moved to the United States. His legal guardians, Joan and Jay Mandle, are professors at Colgate. That's largely why Foyle spurned the likes of Duke and Syracuse to enroll in Hamilton. Foyle lived up to all the hype, earning Freshman All-America honors from *Basketball Times.*

Strengths: Great timing and athletic skills make Foyle a force in the paint. He's very quick off the floor and knows how to deflect shots. On the glass, he is utterly tenacious. Powerful hands allow him to snatch balls away from smaller foes.

Weaknesses: Offensively, Foyle has yet to develop fully. His range is limited and he needs to have a better feel of when and how to pass out of the inevitable double-teams he faces. Improvement at the free throw stripe would bolster his scoring production.

Analysis: He may have shocked the recruiting world with his decision to attend Colgate, but his success there caught no one off guard. The Red Raiders survived a brutal December schedule to win the Patriot League and Foyle was the major reason why. He'll one day begin a long pro career.

COLLEGE STATISTICS

	G	FGP	FTP	RPG	APG	PPG
94-95 COLG	30	.559	.500	12.4	1.2	17.0
Totals	30	.559	.500	12.4	1.2	17.0

JELANI GARDNER

School: California
Year: Sophomore
Position: Guard
Height: 6'6" **Weight:** 205
Birthdate: December 26, 1975
Hometown: Inglewood, CA

PLAYER SUMMARY	
Will	spot the open man
Can't	rely on quickness
Expect	more consistency
Don't Expect	any fear

Background: *FutureStars* rated Gardner as the No. 2 point guard entering college a year ago, and the graduate of St. John Bosco High School demonstrated flashes of excitement as a freshman. Gardner was among the Pac-10's assist leaders in his debut and a *Basketball Times* Freshman All-American.

Strengths: Gardner was coveted by most West Coast schools for the variety of his offensive game. He is a quality outside shooter who also possesses the acceleration to drive to the basket. When double-teamed, he can locate the open man and hit him. He dishes off well in the lane too.

Weaknesses: Most high school scoring stars aren't great defenders and that describes Gardner. He has trouble with quicker guards and can be beaten off the dribble. His deficiencies will be especially notable since he arrived as the heir to Jason Kidd, a first-rate ballhawk.

Analysis: It was an uneven year for California and Gardner. Both were unpredictable and prone to inconsistency. A year of maturity should work wonders. As he gains a better understanding of what it takes to succeed in college, Gardner will develop into one of the Pac-10's top talents.

COLLEGE STATISTICS

	G	FGP	FTP	RPG	APG	PPG
94-95 CAL	27	.409	.661	2.5	6.5	10.7
Totals	27	.409	.661	2.5	6.5	10.7

CHRIS GARNER

School: Memphis
Year: Junior
Position: Guard
Height: 5'10" **Weight:** 156
Birthdate: February 23, 1975
Hometown: Memphis, TN

PLAYER SUMMARY	
Will	handle the pressure
Can't	help much on glass
Expect	creative quickness
Don't Expect	foul woes

Background: Treadwell High School has provided Memphis its last three point guards—Elliot Perry, Anfernee Hardaway, and now Garner. As a senior, Garner was Treadwell's leading scorer at 22 PPG. He became a starter midway through his freshman season at Memphis and was named to the Great Midwest All-Newcomer team.

Strengths: Garner doesn't quake at the sight of pressure. He can use the dribble to turn the corner, and he splits defenses with style. On the fastbreak, he spots the open man and delivers the ball. Although not a pure shooter, he's a good enough scorer to keep defenses honest.

Weaknesses: Directing an offense at high speeds carries the risk of turnovers, and Garner has made his share. His decision-making has improved during his career but there are still times when he attempts to make plays that aren't available.

Analysis: He was one of the least publicized recruits in Memphis' class of 1997, yet he has become its most influential member. The Tigers didn't click in 1993-94 until Garner took the wheel, and they've thrived ever since. He'll get the ball to Lorenzen Wright and spark another superb season.

COLLEGE STATISTICS

	G	FGP	FTP	RPG	APG	PPG
93-94 MEMP	28	.391	.650	2.8	4.4	6.4
94-95 MEMP	34	.421	.485	3.4	6.4	6.6
Totals	62	.407	.532	3.1	5.5	6.5

KIWANE GARRIS

School: Illinois
Year: Junior
Position: Guard
Height: 6'2" **Weight:** 176
Birthdate: September 24, 1974
Hometown: Chicago, IL

PLAYER SUMMARY	
Will	dribble penetrate
Can't	develop consistency
Expect	free throw excellence
Don't Expect	much bench time

Background: This Chicago native was a standout at Westinghouse High School and a priority for the Illinois coaching staff. *FutureStars* listed him among its top 30 prospects in 1993, and Garris stepped into the starting point-guard position as a rookie at Illinois.

Strengths: Garris loves to handle the basketball and does it well. An explosive first step enables him to get into the lane. He's capable of making the spectacular shot in traffic or laying it off to an open teammate when the defense collapses on him. At the free throw line, he is deadly accurate.

Weaknesses: Sometimes Garris handles the basketball too much, leaving teammates standing around in the process. Defenses had some success double-teaming him last year, and he must do a better job of recognizing traps and surrendering the basketball sooner. His perimeter jumper needs work too.

Analysis: Garris is Illinois' clear leader and catalyst and a serious candidate for first-team All-Big Ten honors. A big year from Garris would go a long way toward giving a slumping league a star where it needs one—in the backcourt.

COLLEGE STATISTICS

	G	FGP	FTP	RPG	APG	PPG
93-94 ILL	28	.433	.803	3.5	3.8	15.9
94-95 ILL	31	.439	.831	2.8	3.8	15.9
Totals	59	.436	.817	3.2	3.8	15.9

ADRIAN GRIFFIN

School: Seton Hall
Position: Forward
Year: Senior
Height: 6'5" **Weight:** 217
Birthdate: July 4, 1974
Hometown: Wichita, KS

PLAYER SUMMARY	
Will	defend in style
Can't	rain down 3's
Expect	constant effort
Don't Expect	many headlines

Background: A two-time all-state selection at Wichita East High School, Griffin averaged 25.5 points and 11.6 rebounds as a prep senior. He debuted as a key reserve on a Pirate team that captured the Big East championship. Last year, he was a third-team All-Big East selection.

Strengths: The phrase "blue collar" applies to Griffin. It was his defense that first earned him minutes at the Hall, and he's one of the Big East's top stoppers today. At 6'5", he's capable of guarding a variety of men. Long arms and good timing help make him a menace. He's also an excellent rebounder for his position.

Weaknesses: Although he's a capable scorer, Griffin's offensive game has limitations. When he wanders out past the 3-point line, teams do not respect his long-range shot. As a wing player, he does not handle the basketball especially well.

Analysis: Seton Hall was a gritty team that made an NIT appearance largely on effort. Griffin sets the tone for the Pirates. His work ethic and desire have made him one of the Big East's top players. He is the defender no star wants to face on game night.

COLLEGE STATISTICS

		G	FGP	FTP	RPG	APG	PPG
92-93	SH	35	.506	.585	3.5	0.8	3.4
93-94	SH	30	.473	.603	7.8	2.2	9.7
94-95	SH	30	.554	.723	7.2	2.8	15.3
Totals		95	.519	.648	6.0	1.9	9.1

JEROD HAASE

School: Kansas
Year: Junior
Position: Guard
Height: 6'3" **Weight:** 185
Birthdate: April 1, 1974
Hometown: South Lake Tahoe, CA

PLAYER SUMMARY	
Will	collect floor burns
Can't	stay under control
Expect	3-point accuracy
Don't Expect	timid play

Background: After signing with California out of high school, Haase spent one year in Berkeley, where he started alongside Jason Kidd on a team that advanced to the Sweet 16 of the NCAA Tournament. He transferred to Kansas and, following a one-year layoff, was recognized as Big Eight Newcomer of the Year.

Strengths: Intensity is a given for Haase. His enthusiasm and willingness to sacrifice his body serve as the emotional catalyst for the Jayhawks. Loose balls are pursued with vigor and charges taken frequently. He's a talent too, with an excellent shooting touch from long range and the courage to drive the lane.

Weaknesses: K.U. coach Roy Williams wants Haase to understand that he doesn't have to punish his body at every turn. Reckless abandon can lead to injuries and Haase has had his share. When he gets moving too quickly, turnovers become an issue.

Analysis: Haase led the Jayhawks in scoring and sets the tone for their defensive attack. He's a threat from long range and can finish plays around the basket. When he stays under control, he is one of the Big Eight's elite performers.

COLLEGE STATISTICS

		G	FGP	FTP	RPG	APG	PPG
92-93	CAL	30	.389	.789	1.6	2.6	7.2
94-95	KANS	31	.436	.734	4.3	3.5	15.0
Totals		61	.420	.752	3.0	3.0	11.2

STEVE HAMER

School: Tennessee
Year: Senior
Position: Center
Height: 7'0" **Weight:** 240
Birthdate: November 13, 1973
Hometown: Grand Junction, TN

PLAYER SUMMARY	
Will	make smooth moves
Can't	pass from post
Expect	quality shots
Don't Expect	many victories

Background: Tennessee's Class A Mr. Basketball, Hamer made 19 starts as a freshman and became the Volunteers' regular center in 1993-94. Last year, he was an honorable-mention All-South selection of *Basketball Times*.

Strengths: Most seven-footers lack Hamer's touch around the basket. He's smooth and can make the face-up jumper to 12 feet. When the ball is delivered to him, he catches it well, a task that may sound small but is not for some centers. Opponents must also respect his shot-blocking gifts.

Weaknesses: Bad knees hamper Hamer's mobility. So too does a laid-back attitude that occasionally infuriates coach Kevin O'Neill. On the backboards, Hamer is not as aggressive as he should be, often allowing smaller players to sneak underneath.

Analysis: The Volunteers haven't won much in Hamer's career, and that obscures much of what he has accomplished. O'Neill's energy helped Hamer, increasing his intensity level and production. Further progress could result in an NBA future for this pivot. Size and skill of this type are hard to find.

COLLEGE STATISTICS

	G	FGP	FTP	RPG	APG	PPG
92-93 TENN	26	.544	.635	4.6	0.3	7.0
93-94 TENN	24	.578	.802	5.8	0.8	13.9
94-95 TENN	25	.529	.641	8.8	0.6	15.0
Totals	75	.549	.698	6.4	0.5	11.9

ZENDON HAMILTON

School: St. John's
Year: Sophomore
Position: Center/Forward
Height: 6'11" **Weight:** 215
Birthdate: April 27, 1975
Hometown: Floral Park, NY

PLAYER SUMMARY	
Will	glide gracefully
Can't	crunch inside
Expect	quick feet
Don't Expect	perimeter accuracy

Background: This product of Sewanhaka High School was a McDonald's All-American and the top center prospect in the nation as a senior. A fierce recruiting battle came down to St. John's and Syracuse with Hamilton signing with the Red Storm in the spring. He was named to the Big East All-Rookie team in 1994-95.

Strengths: Long and lean, Hamilton has impressive skills for a center. Few opposing big men can beat him down the floor, and he has the smooth moves needed to capitalize when he gets near the basket. He can score facing up with short jumpers or by beating his man off the dribble.

Weaknesses: Muscle is in short supply here. Hamilton gets pushed around too easily, and that's a major problem at the defensive end. He is not the kind of rebounder he should be, either, thanks in no small part to the lack of bulk.

Analysis: Make no mistake, Hamilton is a talent. However, he needs to become more comfortable with the physical nature of play in the Big East to reach his full potential. A year of experience and a summer in the weight room should help him take a step forward in 1995-96.

COLLEGE STATISTICS

	G	FGP	FTP	RPG	APG	PPG
94-95 STJ	28	.523	.617	5.0	0.6	11.4
Totals	28	.523	.617	5.0	0.6	11.4

MATT HARPRING

School: Georgia Tech
Year: Sophomore
Position: Forward
Height: 6'6" **Weight:** 202
Birthdate: May 31, 1976
Hometown: Dunwoody, GA

PLAYER SUMMARY	
Will	shoot smoothly
Can't	sky high
Expect	sound fundamentals
Don't Expect	flash and dash

Background: There is a long history of athletic success in the Harpring family, though most of it occurred on the gridiron. Harpring's father played football at Michigan, his grandfather at Navy, and his brothers at Northwestern and Akron. This youngster was also offered a football scholarship by Northwestern but chose to play hoops in Atlanta.

Strengths: All of the basics are covered by Harpring. He has an accurate jump shot and rarely forces it. A first-rate athlete, he defends well for a young player and does not shy away from the dirty work of rebounding. He loves to compete.

Weaknesses: Due to his youth, Harpring frequently deferred to his older mates last season. He needs to be more assertive offensively. At the other end, Harpring will become a better defender as he gains experience.

Analysis: One of the ACC's top newcomers, Harpring appears to be a rising star in one of America's top leagues. He's very sound and athletically gifted. More shot opportunities are sure to come his way, and that will translate into increased scoring productivity. This is a good one.

COLLEGE STATISTICS

	G	FGP	FTP	RPG	APG	PPG
94-95 GT	29	.484	.736	6.2	2.3	12.1
Totals	29	.484	.736	6.2	2.3	12.1

OTHELLA HARRINGTON

School: Georgetown
Year: Senior
Position: Center
Height: 6'9" **Weight:** 240
Hometown: Jackson, MS

PLAYER SUMMARY	
Will	fire strong outlet passes
Can't	chase quicker centers
Expect	renewed confidence
Don't Expect	another down year

Background: This was the most sought-after recruit in the prep class of 1992. A McDonald's All-American, Harrington was the Big East Rookie of the Year in 1992-93 and a second-team All-Big East choice as a sophomore.

Strengths: A classic center, Harrington plays effectively with his back to the basket. He doesn't shy away from contact and rebounds well. His best attribute at the offensive end is his soft touch around the goal. Defensively, he is a presence in the lane.

Weaknesses: Harrington's offensive game hasn't grown much since his days at Murrah High School. He lacks a signature offensive move. His game is not suited to transition basketball, which is why he suffered when coach John Thompson chose to go to a faster pace in 1994-95 to accommodate Allen Iverson's gifts.

Analysis: Put simply, Harrington's junior season was the worst of his three years. He didn't get the shots he had in the past, and when he did get the ball in the post he appeared tentative. A summer of work with Patrick Ewing and the other alums should reinforce that this is still a gifted pivot, one capable of a fine farewell campaign.

COLLEGE STATISTICS

	G	FGP	FTP	RPG	APG	PPG
92-93 GEOR	33	.573	.746	8.8	1.0	16.8
93-94 GEOR	31	.551	.733	8.0	1.2	14.7
94-95 GEOR	31	.559	.706	6.0	0.8	12.2
Totals	95	.562	.730	7.6	1.0	14.6

J.R. HENDERSON

School: UCLA
Year: Sophomore
Position: Forward
Height: 6'9" **Weight:** 215
Birthdate: October 30, 1976
Hometown: Bakersfield, CA

PLAYER SUMMARY	
Will	make smooth moves
Can't	take over a game
Expect	subtle grace
Don't Expect	fiery antics

Background: Long a target of college recruiters, Henderson's stock sank during an injury-plagued summer between his junior and senior years at East Bakersfield High School. He closed his prep career with a burst, though, averaging 27 PPG. In his second college game, Henderson hit two free throws with less than one second left to help UCLA defeat Kentucky on national T.V.

Strengths: Rarely flustered, Henderson has the skills to play any position on the floor. Against Oklahoma State in the Final Four, he filled in at center for foul-plagued George Zidek and held his own against Bryant Reeves. A first-rate defender, Henderson is often matched against the opponent's top scorer.

Weaknesses: The knock on Henderson as a prepster was that he did not always play hard. Part of that perception is no doubt based on Henderson's laconic nature—he's the essence of laid-back. He's not yet a 3-point threat.

Analysis: Henderson was a typical freshman in that he usually followed a great night with a mediocre one. Few dispute the notion that he'll one day be a star. His athletic versatility and ability to score in the paint make him one to watch.

COLLEGE STATISTICS

		G	FGP	FTP	RPG	APG	PPG
94-95	UCLA	33	.547	.675	4.2	1.3	9.2
Totals		33	.547	.675	4.2	1.3	9.2

RONNIE HENDERSON

School: LSU
Year: Junior
Position: Guard
Height: 6'4" **Weight:** 190
Birthdate: March 29, 1974
Hometown: Jackson, MS

PLAYER SUMMARY	
Will	tickle the twines
Can't	set himself up
Expect	a fast draw
Don't Expect	spectacular "D"

Background: Henderson missed most of his senior season of high school basketball with a separated shoulder. Nevertheless, the Murrah High School alum was rated the top off-guard prospect in the land by *FutureStars*. At LSU, he was an honorable-mention Freshman All-America pick.

Strengths: The item that first drew recruiters to Henderson was his shooting stroke. It features a textbook release and smooth finishing motion. Henderson can lift it effectively in traffic. He'll also make the occasional foray to the basket.

Weaknesses: No one has been more hampered by the inability of point guard Randy Livingston to stay healthy than Henderson. Henderson needs an assist expert like Livingston to get him the ball in areas where he's comfortable. At the other end, he is not a skilled man-to-man defender.

Analysis: Injuries have done much to keep Henderson from reaching his potential. First came his own shoulder injury and then came the knee problems that have robbed him of Livingston. This pair still has what it takes to become an elite tandem, and the expectation that Livingston will be ready to go in 1995-96 is good news for Henderson.

COLLEGE STATISTICS

		G	FGP	FTP	RPG	APG	PPG
93-94	LSU	26	.385	.711	3.7	1.2	16.5
94-95	LSU	27	.429	.734	5.3	2.2	23.3
Totals		53	.410	.726	4.5	1.7	20.0

MARK HENDRICKSON

School: Washington St.
Year: Senior
Position: Forward
Height: 6'9" **Weight:** 245
Birthdate: June 23, 1974
Hometown: Mount Vernon, WA

PLAYER SUMMARY	
Will	make smart moves
Can't	excite the masses
Expect	sound fundamentals
Don't Expect	huge scoring

Background: A fine all-around athlete, Hendrickson has been drafted by three different major-league baseball organizations as a pitcher. Hendrickson was a member of the Pac-10 All-Freshman team in 1992-93. The following year, he helped WSU to the NCAA Tournament.

Strengths: This left-hander is a solid shooter to 15 feet. He takes shots within the offense and doesn't look to freelance. On the glass, his effort is consistent. He possesses good timing and boxes out opponents well.

Weaknesses: Hendrickson falls into the category of a jack-of-all-trades, master of none. His lack of bulk has created problems for him on defense, but he reportedly muscled up over the summer. Quicker big men have also provided a defensive challenge for him.

Analysis: Although not a crowd-pleaser, Hendrickson accomplishes much with a versatile game that relies on smarts and skill. Washington State isn't a high-octane offense, so Hendrickson's numbers don't figure to be huge. But he's a gritty winner and one of the more underrated athletes in the nation.

COLLEGE STATISTICS

	G	FGP	FTP	RPG	APG	PPG
92-93 WSU	27	.556	.712	8.0	1.9	12.6
93-94 WSU	28	.485	.714	7.9	1.6	10.5
94-95 WSU	30	.667	.794	9.0	1.3	16.1
Totals	85	.565	.741	8.3	1.6	13.1

DAMETRI HILL

School: Florida
Year: Senior
Position: Forward/Center
Height: 6'7" **Weight:** 290
Birthdate: January 8, 1974
Hometown: St. Petersburg, FL

PLAYER SUMMARY	
Will	hit the hook
Can't	let weight creep up
Expect	a nose guard in shorts
Don't Expect	exceptional speed

Background: Although he looks more like a gridiron star, it's always been the basketball court that Hill has liked most. Viewed as the top frontcourt prospect in Florida, he helped take the Gators to the 1994 Final Four.

Strengths: One of the lost art forms in basketball today is the hook shot. It can be a very effective weapon for a center, and Hill figured that out at a young age. He calls his "Da Meat Hook" and it is a shot that allows him to score over taller centers. Hill's got a nice touch around the goal and will put a body on foes at the defensive end.

Weaknesses: It's a familiar plot line here—if Hill can control his weight, he'll be a major force. He has experienced only intermittent success in that regard and that has held him back. When he gets up above the 300-pound mark, he has trouble keeping pace at both ends.

Analysis: One of the most endearing characters during March 1994 slipped back into the shadows last winter. The Gators struggled to reach the NCAA Tournament and didn't last long once there. If Hill is to be more than a curiosity, he must keep his weight down.

COLLEGE STATISTICS

	G	FGP	FTP	RPG	APG	PPG
92-93 FLOR	16	.333	.636	0.6	0.2	1.1
93-94 FLOR	37	.513	.657	4.9	0.6	12.7
94-95 FLOR	29	.525	.686	5.9	1.1	13.7
Totals	82	.514	.668	4.4	0.7	10.8

EXREE HIPP

School: Maryland
Year: Senior
Position: Forward
Height: 6'8" **Weight:** 205
Birthdate: November 22, 1973
Hometown: Washington, DC

PLAYER SUMMARY	
Will	glide down the floor
Can't	push and shove
Expect	increased scoring
Don't Expect	humility

Background: This product of Washington, D.C., was named Mr. Basketball in his hometown in the wake of a terrific senior season at Harker Prep. At Maryland, he started from the outset and was on the Atlantic Coast Conference All-Freshman team. As a sophomore, he was an honorable-mention All-ACC pick.

Strengths: A hallmark of Hipp's game has been its consistency. Despite his height, Hipp is a finesse player who is most comfortable operating away from the basket. In the open court, he is comfortable handling the basketball and filling a lane on the break.

Weaknesses: Maryland's lack of size means Hipp usually has to match up with other forwards. He is thin and struggles with more physical foes. Although earnest on the backboards, he simply gets outmuscled underneath on many occasions.

Analysis: His brash manner has turned off some, but Hipp's career has been a strong one. He has been an integral ingredient in Maryland's climb back toward the top of the ACC. Look for a bit more scoring and an essential role on one of college basketball's better units.

COLLEGE STATISTICS

		G	FGP	FTP	RPG	APG	PPG
92-93	MARY	28	.481	.643	4.9	3.1	11.3
93-94	MARY	30	.472	.688	4.0	2.5	13.2
94-95	MARY	34	.514	.656	4.1	3.2	13.6
Totals		92	.490	.663	4.3	3.0	12.8

ODELL HODGE

School: Old Dominion
Year: Junior
Position: Center
Height: 6'9" **Weight:** 260
Birthdate: March 26, 1973
Hometown: Martinsville, VA

PLAYER SUMMARY	
Will	return to form
Can't	extend a defense
Expect	powerful moves
Don't Expect	running speed

Background: A two-time Virginia Player of the Year as a prepster, Hodge paid immediate dividends when he signed with Old Dominion. In 1992-93, he was the Colonial Athletic Association's Rookie of the Year, and a year later he was that loop's Player of the Year. A knee injury forced him to redshirt in 1994-95.

Strengths: Consistency helps make Hodge special. He never takes a night off, providing constant effort and production. In the lane, he is effective at using his size to rebound and post up. Excellent hands allow him to convert in traffic or at the line. He'll also redirect shots at the defensive end.

Weaknesses: A knee injury is always tough, especially on a large man like Hodge. It has the potential to reduce Hodge's mobility, which wasn't special in the first place. There's likely to be some rust on his shooting skills too.

Analysis: Perhaps the CAA's best player since David Robinson, Hodge watched his teammates go to the NCAA Tournament and upset Villanova. Clearly he's eager to go, and he should again wreak havoc in the lane for the Monarchs.

COLLEGE STATISTICS

		G	FGP	FTP	RPG	APG	PPG
92-93	OD	29	.560	.762	9.1	0.7	14.7
93-94	OD	31	.547	.682	9.0	1.4	19.4
94-95	OD	4	.568	.833	7.3	0.5	13.0
Totals		64	.553	.720	8.9	1.0	16.9

JERALD HONEYCUTT

School: Tulane
Year: Junior
Position: Forward
Height: 6'9" **Weight:** 245
Birthdate: October 20, 1974
Hometown: Grambling, LA

PLAYER SUMMARY	
Will	slam with thunder
Can't	commit silly fouls
Expect	multi-faceted scores
Don't Expect	defensive prowess

Background: Billed as the top recruit in Louisiana as a senior at Grambling High School, Honeycutt was expected to sign with Dale Brown at Louisiana State. Honeycutt chose Tulane instead. He was a second-team All-Metro Conference choice as a rookie and a first-team pick last winter.

Strengths: Throughout his career, Honeycutt has had defenders draped around him and has grown accustomed to making shots in traffic. His soft touch allows him to also step out to 3-point territory, where he must be guarded. He'll also slash to the basket and finish with flair. Increased upper-body strength improved his rebounding last year.

Weaknesses: A gifted scorer, Honeycutt sometimes suffers defensive lapses. He's occasionally too eager to make an exciting block. Against Kentucky in the NCAA Tournament, he took himself out of the game and virtually ended Tulane's hopes with early fouls.

Analysis: When he was a prep senior, the world was Honeycutt's oyster, and it's become apparent why that was so. Added strength and maturity make him a legitimate threat for national honors, and it will shock no one if he takes his game to the next level.

COLLEGE STATISTICS

		G	FGP	FTP	RPG	APG	PPG
93-94	TUL	29	.403	.680	6.7	1.9	15.3
94-95	TUL	33	.446	.659	7.5	3.4	17.3
Totals		62	.426	.668	7.1	2.7	16.4

DEREK HOOD

School: Arkansas
Year: Freshman
Position: Forward
Height: 6'7" **Weight:** 210
Hometown: Kansas City, MO

PLAYER SUMMARY	
Will	swipe the ball
Can't	drain free throws
Expect	sudden impact
Don't Expect	self-promotion

Background: Among the prep-class elite of 1995, Hood carried one of the lower profiles. His credits include berths on the McDonald's and *Parade* All-America teams. As a senior at Central High School, he averaged 14 points and 17 rebounds after signing with Arkansas in November of 1994.

Strengths: Arkansas in the Nolan Richardson era has been recognized as one of the nation's most athletic teams, and Hood fits perfectly here. He's gracefully quick and can pull up and connect on the kind of 3-point shots the Razorbacks love. If foes crowd him, he can also swoop by and finish the play with a slam.

Weaknesses: Richardson's system demands defensive heat the likes of which is foreign to most high school players. Hood has the requisite tools to be a serious defender but must learn to take fewer risks and improve his man-to-man skills.

Analysis: Labeled the best player in the state of Missouri by one publication, Hood is the featured attraction in one of America's best recruiting classes. Look for Hood to assume Scotty Thurman's mantle as the starting wing forward for the Razorbacks and have the kind of impressive debut Thurman enjoyed in 1992-93.

ALLEN IVERSON

School: Georgetown
Year: Sophomore
Position: Guard
Height: 6'1" **Weight:** 175
Hometown: Hampton, VA

PLAYER SUMMARY	
Will	fly in open floor
Can't	depend on jumper
Expect	Player of Year votes
Don't Expect	to be bored

Background: Perhaps the most coveted player in his class as a junior, Iverson took a serious detour when he was convicted for his role in a bowling alley brawl. After spending time in a correctional facility, Iverson was released and completed work on his high school degree. A call from his mother to John Thompson resulted in his enrollment at Georgetown.

Strengths: No one is faster with the basketball in the college game today than Iverson. Most guards cannot handle Iverson in one-on-one situations. He is at his best breaking down a defense and completing the play with a nifty move toward the goal.

Weaknesses: Iverson is adept at creating scoring opportunities for himself, but he hasn't mastered the art of doing the same for his teammates. He tends to become preoccupied with his own acrobatics. His shot selection could stand improvement too.

Analysis: Providence coach Pete Gillen likens Iverson to Isiah Thomas at the same stage. Both are entertaining lead guards and Iverson might be faster than Thomas was with the ball. If he develops the kind of court vision Thomas had, he too could become one for the ages.

COLLEGE STATISTICS

	G	FGP	FTP	RPG	APG	PPG
94-95 GEOR	30	.390	.688	3.3	4.5	20.4
Totals	30	.390	.688	3.3	4.5	20.4

DEON JACKSON

School: Bradley
Year: Senior
Position: Forward
Height: 6'6" **Weight:** 220
Birthdate: August 17, 1974
Hometown: Dayton, OH

PLAYER SUMMARY	
Will	convert short "J's"
Can't	maintain consistency
Expect	flashes of dominance
Don't Expect	defensive rebounds

Background: Jackson was something of a late bloomer at Patterson High School. Upon setting foot in Peoria, Jackson emerged as Bradley's leading scorer and the Missouri Valley Conference's Freshman of the Year.

Strengths: Multiple scoring skills define Jackson's game. He's comfortable in the open court, where he can slice to the basket and finish the play with power. He's a major nuisance to foes on the offensive glass. He finds crevices and uses his athletic skills to grab the basketball.

Weaknesses: Inconsistency has cropped into Jackson's game, often at the most inopportune moments. Jackson was ineffective in his first two cracks at the Missouri Valley Conference Tournament and received a good deal of heat for it. His defensive work is not exceptional in any way.

Analysis: Jim Molinari has restored some of the luster to the Bradley program that existed in the heyday of Hersey Hawkins in the late 1980s. Jackson's not in the class of a Hawkins, but he is a strong college player who has a chance to again lead the Braves into the postseason.

COLLEGE STATISTICS

	G	FGP	FTP	RPG	APG	PPG
92-93 BRAD	27	.523	.583	4.6	1.3	12.3
93-94 BRAD	31	.477	.672	5.1	1.3	14.3
94-95 BRAD	30	.480	.703	4.8	1.3	12.8
Totals	88	.491	.659	4.8	1.3	13.2

BRANDON JESSIE

School: Utah
Year: Senior
Position: Guard
Height: 6'5" **Weight:** 225
Birthdate: May 20, 1974
Hometown: Huntington Beach, CA

PLAYER SUMMARY	
Will	remain focused
Can't	resist a shot
Expect	rebounding
Don't Expect	mental weakness

Background: As a teen, Jessie split his time between the hardwood and the gridiron, which makes sense since his father is former NFL wide receiver Ron Jessie. In college, though, Jessie stuck to basketball. He played his first two seasons at Ventura Junior College before transferring to Utah for the 1994-95 campaign.

Strengths: A bright student of the game, Jessie adapted his game quickly to the major-college level. He's a competent shooter around the basket and is very muscular for a backcourt player. That strength allows him to post up smaller foes and rebound over them. He's also a willing passer.

Weaknesses: Plagued throughout 1994-95 by a persistent shoulder injury that required off-season surgery, Jessie had difficulty hitting long-range jumpers. In junior college, Jessie spent much of the time with his back to the basket. Now, though, he plays facing the goal, and that demands improved ball-handling and shooting.

Analysis: The WAC's Newcomer of the Year is poised for a big finish to his collegiate career. Soft-spoken by nature, Jessie makes a huge statement with his game on the floor. Along with Keith Van Horn, he figures to keep the Utes at the top of the WAC.

COLLEGE STATISTICS

	G	FGP	FTP	RPG	APG	PPG
94-95 UTAH	34	.481	.706	5.9	2.4	16.1
Totals	34	.481	.706	5.9	2.4	16.1

T.J. JOHNSON

School: Xavier
Year: Sophomore
Position: Forward
Height: 6'6" **Weight:** 245
Birthdate: April 27, 1976
Hometown: Charlotte, NC

PLAYER SUMMARY	
Will	fly to the ball
Can't	bank on finesse
Expect	foul line visits
Don't Expect	sluggishness

Background: After beginning his prep basketball career at East Mecklenberg High School in Charlotte, Johnson transferred to Oak Hill Academy. In 1992-93, he was the only non-senior starter on a club that included Jerry Stackhouse and Jeff McInnis. He chose Xavier over Marquette, East Carolina, and Rutgers.

Strengths: Brute force helps Johnson move bodies inside. A quick first step gets him off the floor in a hurry, which is a major rebounding advantage. In the lane, he features a strong post-up game. A muscular frame allows him to take plenty of pounding and get to the charity stripe.

Weaknesses: Johnson's affinity for contact can cause foul woes. That is an area that must be addressed this year because the Musketeers do not have the kind of interior depth to survive for long stretches in a game without him. As the double-teams begin coming his way, Johnson will have to learn how to adjust.

Strengths: Twenty-three wins put Xavier into the NCAA Tournament and Johnson was a vital ingredient. This time, his significance will be even larger. He's now a team linchpin as X.U. makes its debut in the Atlantic 10.

COLLEGE STATISTICS

	G	FGP	FTP	RPG	APG	PPG
94-95 XAV	28	.577	.675	5.3	0.7	11.9
Totals	28	.577	.675	5.3	0.7	11.9

KERRY KITTLES

School: Villanova
Year: Senior
Position: Guard
Height: 6'5" **Weight:** 179
Birthdate: June 12, 1974
Hometown: New Orleans, LA

PLAYER SUMMARY	
Will	make it look easy
Can't	act as offensive Q.B.
Expect	T.V. exposure
Don't Expect	3-point shyness

Background: After originally signing with Rollie Massimino, Kittles contemplated a transfer following Massimino's exit at Villanova. New coach Steve Lappas convinced him to stay, and he has emerged as one of the finest players in school history. The Big East Player of the Year was a second-team All-America pick of *Basketball Times*.

Strengths: Kittles's effortless style belies a quickness and scoring touch matched by few at the collegiate level. An accurate jump-shooter, he is at ease stepping out from behind a screen or pulling up for a shot off the dribble. He eludes defenders with an excellent first step and is one of the nation's more acrobatic dunkers.

Weaknesses: A quiet sort, Kittles sometimes allows the game to flow past him. With his repertoire, he must touch the basketball in every offensive sequence.

Analysis: If one were charting this man's collegiate growth chart, the line would move steadily upward. Each season, Kittles has made significant strides in his game. He'll be confronted with lofty expectations, yet he's got the firepower and know-how to take another step up the ladder.

COLLEGE STATISTICS

	G	FGP	FTP	RPG	APG	PPG
92-93	VILL	27	.482	.673	3.5	2.9	10.9
93-94	VILL	32	.452	.705	6.5	3.4	19.7
94-95	VILL	33	.524	.767	6.1	3.5	21.4
Totals		92	.486	.724	5.5	3.3	17.7

BREVIN KNIGHT

School: Stanford
Year: Junior
Position: Guard
Height: 5'10" **Weight:** 155
Birthdate: November 8, 1975
Hometown: East Orange, NJ

PLAYER SUMMARY	
Will	make wise choices
Can't	strike fear with "J"
Expect	excellent quickness
Don't Expect	errant passes

Background: Brevin's father, Melvin Knight, was an assistant to Bill Raftery at Seton Hall for six years in the 1970s. The younger Knight averaged 20 PPG at Seton Hall Prep as a senior and was a member of the Dean's List. He was an immediate starter at Stanford and led the Cardinal to the NCAA Tournament in 1994-95.

Strengths: Speed kills, and Knight has it in abundance. His quickness with the basketball allows him to frequently beat fullcourt traps on his own. Opposing guards must always be alert, for Knight is adept at swiping the basketball. He does a good job of getting Stanford into its pattern offense.

Weaknesses: A lithe frame makes Knight susceptible to being overpowered at the defensive end in one-on-one situations. Offensively, he does everything well but shoot consistently from the perimeter. Defenders tend to lay off him to protect against drives.

Analysis: Though overshadowed by the likes of Tyus Edney and Jason Kidd in his first two seasons, Knight is one of the West's top point guards. He sets the table for all that the Cardinal does offensively, and he effectively contains other guards. All this guy is lacking is some national exposure.

COLLEGE STATISTICS

	G	FGP	FTP	RPG	APG	PPG
93-94	STAN	28	.354	.756	3.9	5.4	11.1
94-95	STAN	28	.455	.750	3.9	6.6	16.6
Totals		56	.410	.753	3.9	6.0	13.9

CHUCK KORNEGAY

School: Villanova
Year: Junior
Position: Forward
Height: 6'9" **Weight:** 225
Birthdate: September 28, 1974
Hometown: Dudley, NC

PLAYER SUMMARY	
Will	power to glass
Can't	let if fly from deep
Expect	active rebounding
Don't Expect	superior passing

Background: At Southern Wayne High School, Kornegay was a four-year starter and a valued prospect. He signed with North Carolina State, starting in seven games before departing. After pondering a move to the pros, Kornegay transferred to Villanova. He debuted in 1994-95 and became a fixture in Steve Lappas's lineup.

Strengths: Shawn Kemp is Kornegay's favorite pro and he has some of Kemp's raw power. A ferocious finisher, Kornegay takes it up in traffic and gets to the free throw line. He's quick off the floor and boxes out well. Defensively, he is willing and able to deal with either centers or power forwards.

Weaknesses: A year's layoff generally leaves some rust, and Kornegay was not immune. He endured some peaks and valleys in acclimating himself to his new team. Because he frequently gets fouled inside, Kornegay needs to bolster his free throw shooting skills.

Analysis: Don't let Villanova's early exit from the NCAA Tournament discourage you—this is an excellent club and Kornegay is a major reason why. He won't be asked to score all that many points, but his strength inside is vital.

COLLEGE STATISTICS

	G	FGP	FTP	RPG	APG	PPG
92-93 NCS	7	.558	.700	4.9	1.4	8.9
94-95 VILL	26	.484	.586	6.3	2.5	8.4
Totals	**33**	**.498**	**.615**	**6.0**	**2.4**	**8.5**

RAEF LaFRENTZ

School: Kansas
Year: Sophomore
Position: Forward
Height: 6'11" **Weight:** 220
Birthdate: May 29, 1976
Hometown: Hampton, IA

PLAYER SUMMARY	
Will	expand his role
Can't	run with the deer
Expect	rebounding tenacity
Don't Expect	bad shots

Background: LaFrentz was billed as perhaps the greatest prep player in Iowa history. The announcement of his college choice was broadcast live on an area radio station. He started every game for the Jayhawks last year, averaging 24 minutes per game, and was tabbed Big Eight Freshman of the Year.

Strengths: LaFrentz has unusual skills for a man of his size. He will score in close or will step outside to 15 feet and fire accurately. His high-release jumper is difficult to block. Unlike some tall types who have skills, he's quite willing to bang inside and rebound. He also possesses superb instincts and a nose for the basketball.

Weaknesses: Quick, athletic power forwards can be a headache for LaFrentz at the defensive end. He demonstrated defensive improvement as 1994-95 unfolded but room for further development remains. A bout with mononucleosis seemed to impact LaFrentz's game down the stretch.

Analysis: This Iowan is a complete big man. Like most freshmen, he endured peaks and valleys. Yet he demonstrated that he could develop into an All-America caliber performer on the strength of his scoring tools and rebounding grit.

COLLEGE STATISTICS

	G	FGP	FTP	RPG	APG	PPG
94-95 KANS	31	.534	.637	7.5	0.5	11.4
Totals	**31**	**.534**	**.637**	**7.5**	**0.5**	**11.4**

TRAJAN LANGDON

School: Duke
Year: Sophomore
Position: Guard
Height: 6'4" **Weight:** 185
Birthdate: May 13, 1976
Hometown: Anchorage, AK

PLAYER SUMMARY	
Will	appear effortless
Can't	thrive inside
Expect	steady shooting
Don't Expect	stifling defense

Background: Alaska has produced few Division I stars and Langdon is clearly the best of the bunch. He was a McDonald's All-American at East Anchorage High School and an accomplished baseball player as well. He is technically a non-scholarship athlete at Duke because he's signed with the San Diego Padres.

Strengths: Langdon's trademark is his excellent shooting touch. He can spot up from deep and connect with a hand in his face. Opponents must respect him beyond the arc. Built solidly, Langdon is willing to enter the fray on the backboards.

Weaknesses: During its run to seven Final Fours, the Blue Devils created an identity as a defensive terror, particularly on the perimeter. That ball pressure was absent in 1994-95 and Langdon was one of the reasons why. Lacking great quickness, he had trouble blanketing foes in the manner Duke fans had grown accustomed to.

Analysis: One of the few bright spots in an otherwise tortured campaign in Durham, Langdon should be even better this year. No one questions his shooting touch or passing skill. The hope there is that Mike Krzyzewski can take this eager student and polish him into an All-America caliber player.

COLLEGE STATISTICS

	G	FGP	FTP	RPG	APG	PPG
94-95 DUKE	31	.453	.786	2.1	1.5	11.3
Totals	31	.453	.786	2.1	1.5	11.3

MIKKEL LARSEN

School: Iona
Year: Senior
Position: Center
Height: 6'10" **Weight:** 235
Birthdate: November 10, 1973
Hometown: Hellested, Denmark

PLAYER SUMMARY	
Will	post large numbers
Can't	thrive outside
Expect	inside intimidation
Don't Expect	glamorous hype

Background: As a youngster, Larsen was a swimmer and a soccer player in his native Denmark. After making minimal contributions as a freshman, Larsen was an All-East pick of *Eastern Basketball* last year.

Strengths: Larsen's arsenal consists of many of the classic post-up moves. He moves people out with a bulky frame and completes the play with a soft shooting touch. Although not blessed with tremendous speed, Larsen does a better job filling the lane in fastbreak situations than his size would suggest.

Weaknesses: At times, Larsen still forces shots. Iona has struggled in recent years and this man occasionally tries to shoulder too heavy a burden. It would be a big plus if he were to become a more accomplished passer out of traps.

Analysis: He arrived with no hoops pedigree and most basketball fans nationally still aren't familiar with him. However, Larsen is a force in the Metro Atlantic Athletic Conference. He will be the centerpiece as new head coach Tim Welsh attempts to reestablish the Iona that Jim Valvano and Pat Kennedy created in the 1970s and '80s.

COLLEGE STATISTICS

	G	FGP	FTP	RPG	APG	PPG
92-93 IONA	20	.382	.500	1.4	0.2	1.8
93-94 IONA	27	.487	.679	6.7	1.1	17.6
94-95 IONA	26	.526	.683	6.3	0.7	17.5
Totals	73	.500	.676	5.1	0.7	13.2

JASON LAWSON

School: Villanova
Year: Junior
Position: Center
Height: 6'11" **Weight:** 226
Birthdate: September 2, 1974
Hometown: Philadelphia, PA

PLAYER SUMMARY	
Will	pound in paint
Can't	avoid fouls
Expect	interior intimidation
Don't Expect	bad shots

Background: Lawson played in the shadow of Rasheed Wallace as a prepster. Once at Villanova, though, he stepped into the limelight. He's started every game of his college career and led the Wildcats in rebounding as both a freshman and sophomore.

Strengths: While some modern centers bank on finesse, Lawson likes contact. He never shies away from it and is most comfortable receiving the ball down low. Good hands help him catch the ball, and he's got a soft shooting touch around the basket. On defense, he is a classic shot-blocker with excellent timing.

Weaknesses: Lawson's willingness to play a physical game can lead to foul trouble. Through experience he's improved, but he can still be drawn into difficulty when teams come right at him. He must learn when to attempt to block the shot and when to sit back.

Analysis: This is the Big East's best center. Fundamentally sound, Lawson makes great use of his bulk and height to force teams to sag toward him. As good as Kerry Kittles is, this guy might be the most vital ingredient for a Villanova club with national championship aspirations.

COLLEGE STATISTICS

		G	FGP	FTP	RPG	APG	PPG
93-94	VILL	32	.523	.583	6.6	1.2	10.1
94-95	VILL	33	.595	.730	6.7	1.5	12.9
Totals		65	.562	.656	6.7	1.4	11.5

RANDY LIVINGSTON

School: LSU
Year: Sophomore
Position: Guard
Height: 6'4" **Weight:** 194
Birthdate: April 2, 1975
Hometown: New Orleans, LA

PLAYER SUMMARY	
Will	play through pain
Can't	avoid injury bug
Expect	savvy leadership
Don't Expect	speedy cuts

Background: A McDonald's All-American, Livingston was judged to be the top point-guard prospect in the class of 1993 by *Basketball Times* and *FutureStars*. He sat out 1993-94 with a knee injury suffered while working a summer basketball camp.

Strengths: When in top form, Livingston is the consummate floor general. He sees the floor and can think one or two moves ahead of everyone else out there. Passing is his special gift, and he knows how to create easy shots for his mates. He's a talented scorer who can drive the lane or make the 3-point goal.

Weaknesses: During the last two years, Livingston has battled major knee injuries. They have had a major impact on his speed and ability to make the cuts necessary in basketball. His quickness is not what it once was, and that's a liability that really hampers him defensively.

Analysis: This has been one of the sadder tales in major-college basketball over the past two seasons. After rehabilitating the first knee injury last summer, Livingston was again felled during 1994-95. He limped through the season and no one knows how close to his former self he'll be. If healed, he's a superstar.

COLLEGE STATISTICS

		G	FGP	FTP	RPG	APG	PPG
94-95	LSU	16	.438	.677	4.0	9.4	14.0
Totals		16	.438	.677	4.0	9.4	14.0

MICHAEL LLOYD

School: Syracuse
Year: Senior
Position: Guard
Height: 6'2" **Weight:** 190
Birthdate: November 2, 1972
Hometown: Baltimore, MD

PLAYER SUMMARY	
Will	zip down the floor
Can't	throttle down
Expect	plenty of turnovers
Don't Expect	cautious play

Background: One of the sparks of *USA Today's* national-championship team as a senior at Dunbar High School, Lloyd originally committed to attend Arkansas. He subsequently enrolled at San Jacinto Junior College, where he twice led the nation in junior college scoring.

Strengths: When the game is played in the open court, Lloyd can be a terror with the basketball. He can find and feed the open man or convert on a drive of his own. Exceptionally quick, he beats foes off the dribble frequently. He handled the point-guard position last year but has enough shooting skill to play off guard too.

Weaknesses: Too often Lloyd is out of control. His shot selection is spotty, and when running the offense he sometimes becomes more concerned with getting his own attempt rather than setting up his mates. He also committed far too many turnovers last year.

Analysis: Major things were expected from this one-time McDonald's All-American at Syracuse, but Lloyd's chart reads like a Wall Street report—up one day, down the next. He must learn how to channel some of his energy and talent to effectively lead the Orange now that Lawrence Moten has exited.

COLLEGE STATISTICS

		G	FGP	FTP	RPG	APG	PPG
94-95	SYR	30	.458	.634	3.2	5.2	12.5
Totals		30	.458	.634	3.2	5.2	12.5

FELIPE LOPEZ

School: St. John's
Year: Sophomore
Position: Guard/Forward
Height: 6'5" **Weight:** 178
Birthdate: December 19, 1974
Hometown: New York, NY

PLAYER SUMMARY	
Will	fire breathtaking passes
Can't	confidently stroke "J"
Expect	All-Big East acclaim
Don't Expect	too much

Background: This native of the Dominican Republic was rated as the top player in the class of 1994 while at New York's Rice High School. He led Rice to a city and state crown and then signed with St. John's. In his debut, he was voted a third-team All-Big East selection.

Strengths: It's called a "feel for the game," and Lopez has it. He sees the court well, is a very good ball-handler for his size, and has a knack for understanding when and where to deliver the basketball to his teammates. As a rookie, Lopez was a solid free throw shooter.

Weaknesses: Never a great shooter, Lopez was the subject of criticism in some quarters for that part of his game. He needs to develop more consistency in his release so that he can bury open jumpers. Turnovers are an issue too.

Analysis: A *Sports Illustrated* cover boy before he ever played a college game, Lopez faced incredibly unrealistic expectations in New York. For the most part, he held up well. This is a very talented chap who has plenty of time to fulfill the dreams of New York's Dominican community, to whom he is an idol.

COLLEGE STATISTICS

		G	FGP	FTP	RPG	APG	PPG
94-95	STJ	28	.411	.753	5.7	2.8	17.8
Totals		28	.411	.753	5.7	2.8	17.8

COREY LOUIS

School: Florida St.
Year: Sophomore
Position: Center
Height: 6'10" **Weight:** 220
Birthdate: February 12, 1977
Hometown: Miami, FL

PLAYER SUMMARY	
Will	patrol the paint
Can't	resist shot blocks
Expect	him to clean glass
Don't Expect	pretty passes

Background: Keeping this product of Northwestern High School at home was a major priority for Seminole coach Pat Kennedy. He succeeded in no small part because of Louis's eagerness to test himself in the Atlantic Coast Conference. In his initial campaign, Louis was an honorable-mention All-East choice of *Eastern Basketball.*

Strengths: Speed is uncommon for men this size, but Louis is an obvious exception to that rule. He runs the floor with grace and leaps high. He'll often beat his foe down the floor and finish a play with authority. Louis's springs make him a quality rebounder.

Weaknesses: While skilled, Louis remains something of an unpolished gem. More experienced pivots were able to lean on him and create problems. Time in the weight room would be a major plus. It would help alleviate the fatigue that seemed to wear on the lithe center as 1994-95 unfolded.

Analysis: There was some thought that Louis could have the kind of impact as a freshman that Joe Smith did at Maryland in 1993-94. It didn't happen, as FSU endured an uneven campaign. Louis showed plenty of ability, however, and the hope is that steadier backcourt play will allow him to generate more consistent offense.

COLLEGE STATISTICS

		G	FGP	FTP	RPG	APG	PPG
94-95	FSU	27	.449	.711	7.8	0.7	10.9
Totals		27	.449	.711	7.8	0.7	10.9

STEPHON MARBURY

School: Georgia Tech
Year: Freshman
Position: Guard
Height: 6'2" **Weight:** 175
Birthdate: February 20, 1977
Hometown: Brooklyn, NY

PLAYER SUMMARY	
Will	electrify Thrillerdome
Can't	stay within himself
Expect	another Tech star
Don't Expect	any flaws

Background: Long acknowledged as the top guard in the incoming freshman class, Marbury led Lincoln High School to both city and state championships as a senior. He was one of only three prep players selected to the national Junior Olympic team and received both the *Parade* and Gatorade national prep Player of the Year awards.

Strengths: Many lead guards today are fast off the dribble but have trouble if defenses sag to protect the drive. Not Marbury. In addition to excellent quickness and ball-handling skill, Marbury is a first-rate shooter. He can step back to nail a 20-foot jumper, meaning teams cannot ease off him on the perimeter. Fast hands make him a defensive troublemaker.

Weaknesses: A cool customer, Marbury sometimes is too nonchalant on the court. At times during his prep career, it almost seemed as though he was bored by it all. A few knocks in the ACC ought to cure him of that.

Analysis: Georgia Tech has produced three fine point guards in the Bobby Cremins era: Mark Price, Kenny Anderson, and Travis Best. Now it's Marbury's turn, and he appears ready to take his place in that kind of fast company. He'll make an enormous impact.

JEFF McINNIS

School: North Carolina
Year: Junior
Position: Guard
Height: 6'4" **Weight:** 182
Birthdate: October 22, 1974
Hometown: Charlotte, NC

PLAYER SUMMARY	
Will	distribute smartly
Can't	become impatient
Expect	increased scoring role
Don't Expect	shoddy defense

Background: McInnis began his prep career at West Charlotte High School before transferring to Oak Hill Academy. He teamed with Jerry Stackhouse for a 36-0 record and a national championship as a senior. In Chapel Hill, he spent a year caddying for Derrick Phelps before assuming the starting point-guard role in 1994-95.

Strengths: More offensive-minded than his predecessor Phelps, McInnis keeps defenders honest with a strong perimeter jumper. He has good range and is a viable threat from beyond the 3-point line. On the opposite end of the floor, McInnis is a fine ballhawk, moving his feet well.

Weaknesses: McInnis sometimes rushes things offensively. At times, he loses patience and forces passes that aren't open. His off-the-ball defense, though improved, still could use some shoring up.

Analysis: Obscured by more heralded classmates Stackhouse and Rasheed Wallace, McInnis nonetheless was an essential ingredient as North Carolina advanced to the Final Four. He is a multi-faceted operator whose skills will be more obvious as the Tar Heels take on a fresh look without Donald Williams.

COLLEGE STATISTICS

		G	FGP	FTP	RPG	APG	PPG
93-94	NC	35	.458	.638	1.7	2.4	5.6
94-95	NC	34	.491	.667	4.1	5.3	12.4
Totals		69	.480	.658	2.8	3.8	8.9

RON MERCER

School: Kentucky
Year: Freshman
Position: Forward
Height: 6'7" **Weight:** 200
Hometown: Madison, TN

PLAYER SUMMARY	
Will	execute fundamentals
Can't	gain enough strength
Expect	Freshman of Year votes
Don't Expect	verbose speeches

Background: Like most modern standouts, Mercer first made his mark in summer camp and AAU competition. Following his junior season at Good Pasture High School, he switched to Oak Hill Academy. At Oak Hill, he averaged 28 points, eight rebounds, and six assists for a 31-3 team.

Strengths: This is an extraordinarily well-rounded performer. Smooth and efficient, Mercer is capable of scoring from a variety of spots on the floor. If defenses press him tightly, he is agile enough to go by them and finish in traffic. Should they lay off, he makes foes pay with an accurate jumper good to the NBA 3-point line. He's also a helpful rebounder.

Weaknesses: Mercer's defense took a step up during the year at Oak Hill, but he is not yet where he needs to be to please coach Rick Pitino. A back injury plagued Mercer in the second half of 1994-95, and such woes can become nagging if not treated properly.

Analysis: He was somewhat overshadowed by the flashy Stephon Marbury and the mercurial Kevin Garnett, but Mercer might be the top talent in the class of 1999. It's a testament to his gifts that Pitino essentially showed Rodrick Rhodes the door to create a place for him.

RYAN MINOR

School: Oklahoma
Year: Senior
Position: Forward
Height: 6'7" **Weight:** 220
Birthdate: January 5, 1974
Hometown: Canton, OH

PLAYER SUMMARY	
Will ....connect from long range
Can't ....hit the curve
Expect ......All-America recognition
Don't Expect................silly passes

Background: This is a legitimate two-sport star. A product of Hammon High School, Minor was recruited to Oklahoma to play both basketball and baseball. On the diamond, he helped Oklahoma to the 1994 national championship. He was a 1994-95 third-team *Basketball Times* All-American.

Strengths: Few players in the nation are as well-rounded athletically as this man. Extremely versatile, Minor is as adept at posting up smaller foes for scores as he is at stepping out to the arc to drain a 3-pointer. He can swipe the ball from opponents.

Weaknesses: An aggressive sort, Minor can collect some fouls—although it's not quite the problem it was earlier in his career. A pedestrian surrounding cast sometimes leads him to try to do too much at the offensive end.

Analysis: In each of the past two seasons, Minor has made significant strides. He was a primary force in moving the Sooners from Big Eight also-ran status to a No. 4 seed in the Southeast Region of the NCAA Tournament. It was his court vision and all-around skill that lifted the Sooners on many nights. He's fully capable of doing it again.

COLLEGE STATISTICS

	G	FGP	FTP	RPG	APG	PPG
92-93 OKLA	31	.433	.667	2.7	1.0	4.7
93-94 OKLA	25	.498	.773	7.4	1.8	16.2
94-95 OKLA	32	.392	.823	8.4	2.2	23.6
Totals	88	.454	.787	6.1	1.7	14.9

STEVE NASH

School: Santa Clara
Year: Senior
Position: Guard
Height: 6'3" **Weight:** 185
Birthdate: February 7, 1974
Hometown: Victoria, BC

PLAYER SUMMARY	
Will ....deal assists
Can't ....operate among trees
Expect ....WCC Player of Year
Don't Expect ......intensity to waver

Background: Santa Clara's first recruit ever from Canada played his prep basketball at St. Michael's University High School. As a freshman at Santa Clara, he was the team's fourth-leading scorer. He also has extensive international experience with the Canadian national team.

Strengths: Although not a pure point guard, Nash comprehends how to direct an offense. He is very dangerous with the basketball, adept at driving the lane and feeding teammates or stepping into a 3-point effort. He loves to take risks in fastbreak situations and will not back down from a challenge.

Weaknesses: The fact that Nash loves to play at high speeds makes him susceptible to some bad passes. There are times when Nash is a bit too anxious to launch his patented jumper. Opponents will try to post him at the defensive end.

Analysis: He lacks a national identity and probably won't acquire one this winter. Yet Nash is a keeper, a workaholic who spends countless hours fine-tuning his game. He's the WCC's best and Santa Clara's key if it is to spring a postseason upset or two come March.

COLLEGE STATISTICS

	G	FGP	FTP	RPG	APG	PPG
92-93 SC	31	.424	.825	2.6	2.2	8.1
93-94 SC	26	.414	.831	2.5	3.7	14.6
94-95 SC	27	.445	.879	3.8	6.4	20.9
Totals	84	.429	.856	2.9	4.0	14.2

JEFF NORDGAARD

School: Wisconsin-Green Bay
Year: Senior
Position: Center/Forward
Height: 6'6" **Weight:** 226
Birthdate: February 23, 1973
Hometown: Dawson, MN

PLAYER SUMMARY	
Will	set smart screens
Can't	leap through roof
Expect	head fakes
Don't Expect	weak defense

Background: Minnesota has a spotty history of producing great basketball players, yet Nordgaard has been exceptional at Green Bay. The graduate of Dawson-Boyd High School is a three-year starter and was a first-team All-MCC pick last year.

Strengths: Fundamentally sharp play makes Nordgaard perfect for the Phoenix. Owning only marginal athletic skills, he is effective in no small part because of his feel for the game. He lures opposing big men out on the floor with an accurate jumper. From that vantage point, he is also an expert high-post passer.

Weaknesses: Because he is forced to play center, Nordgaard is at a height disadvantage virtually every night. He cannot be a presence in the lane due to his lack of leaping ability. The best he can hope for is to control his own man and get good rebounding position.

Analysis: Lacking size, quickness, and speed, Nordgaard is nonetheless an extraordinarily effective player. It is no coincidence that UWGB has had its greatest success, including two straight NCAA tourney trips, during Nordgaard's career.

COLLEGE STATISTICS

	G	FGP	FTP	RPG	APG	PPG
92-93 WBG	27	.507	.464	2.9	1.1	6.1
93-94 WGB	34	.590	.768	6.4	2.1	15.6
94-95 WGB	30	.547	.788	7.5	2.3	18.6
Totals	91	.557	.764	5.7	1.9	13.8

CHARLES O'BANNON

School: UCLA
Year: Junior
Position: Forward
Height: 6'7" **Weight:** 205
Birthdate: February 22, 1975
Hometown: Lakewood, CA

PLAYER SUMMARY	
Will	be a leader
Can't	fall into old habits
Expect	All-America attention
Don't Expect	physical play

Background: The brother of Final Four MVP Ed O'Bannon was a critical recruit for UCLA coach Jim Harrick. He got O'Bannon in 1993, and the Artesia High School grad was a key component of the national championship team as a sophomore.

Strengths: Athletic tools are O'Bannon's gift. He glides down the court with an effortless gait and accepts the ball well on the wing. His pull-up jumper is sound and he's got range to 15 feet. As he's developed more upper-body strength, he's also become an able rebounder.

Weaknesses: There's a bit of "cool" to O'Bannon's game, though not as much as there was in 1993-94. On occasion, he can drift to the fringe of action while others assert themselves. He's not yet a serious 3-point threat, a dimension that would give him more space to operate in the lane.

Analysis: In his first two collegiate seasons, O'Bannon deferred to his elders with exceptional results. Now it is his turn to take the lead. No one doubts O'Bannon's skills. A bit of refining and attention to detail could give the younger O'Bannon some All-America hardware of his own.

COLLEGE STATISTICS

	G	FGP	FTP	RPG	APG	PPG
93-94 UCLA	28	.514	.647	6.8	1.6	11.6
94-95 UCLA	33	.554	.739	6.1	3.3	13.6
Totals	61	.536	.705	6.4	2.6	12.7

ANDRAE PATTERSON

School: Indiana
Year: Sophomore
Position: Forward
Height: 6'8" **Weight:** 220
Birthdate: November 12, 1975
Hometown: Abilene, TX

PLAYER SUMMARY	
Will	rebound aggressively
Can't	roam defensively
Expect	more point production
Don't Expect	lackadaisical play

Background: This man was the main lure for coaches from coast to coast during his senior season at Cooper High School. Patterson was a McDonald's All-American and a contributor in his first season at Indiana.

Strengths: In terms of athletic tools, Patterson offers an attractive package. He's explosive off the floor, which makes him both a shot-blocking and rebounding factor. From one end to the other, he is faster than most forwards. Around the basket, he has a nice shooting touch.

Weaknesses: There are intricacies in Indiana's cut-and-pass system, and Patterson didn't always grasp them. He has to be more consistent in that department if he is to earn coach Bob Knight's implicit trust. Patterson still has strides to make in man-to-man defense too.

Analysis: The Hoosiers endured what was for them an unusual campaign—there was no Big Ten title and a first-round NCAA Tournament exit soon followed. Patterson mirrored the squad—he had his moments but was inconsistent. He has the capacity to achieve great things, though, and will be a key as Indiana attempts to replace Alan Henderson.

COLLEGE STATISTICS

	G	FGP	FTP	RPG	APG	PPG
94-95 IND	28	.494	.689	3.9	0.8	7.3
Totals	28	.494	.689	3.9	0.8	7.3

TOM PIPKINS

School: Duquesne
Year: Junior
Position: Guard
Height: 6'3" **Weight:** 185
Birthdate: June 24, 1975
Hometown: New Kensington, PA

PLAYER SUMMARY	
Will	play through pain
Can't	run the show
Expect	A-10 first-team votes
Don't Expect	scoring droughts

Background: At Valley High School, Pipkins was the all-time leading scorer in Western Pennsylvania. He was an immediate starter for the Dukes, earning a spot on the Atlantic 10 All-Freshman team. He was an honorable-mention All-East choice by *Eastern Basketball* in 1994-95.

Strengths: No need for a map to the goal for Pipkins—this scorer knows the route. A muscular frame allows Pipkins to post up smaller foes to score inside if he chooses. On other occasions, he will use a reliable jumper with range to 21 feet to put the ball into the basket. He's in good condition and can log heavy minutes.

Weaknesses: Great scorers are rarely breathtaking defenders and that description fits here. Under former head coach John Carroll, Duquesne played a good bit of zone, a luxury Pipkins may not have under new mentor Scott Edgar. He needs to improve his footwork.

Analysis: One of the elite players in the Atlantic 10, Pipkins hasn't gotten a great deal of attention because the Dukes haven't risen above mediocrity in his two years. Edgar hopes to change that and Pipkins will be his mainstay.

COLLEGE STATISTICS

	G	FGP	FTP	RPG	APG	PPG
93-94 DUQ	30	.403	.744	4.7	2.7	14.5
94-95 DUQ	28	.367	.736	4.4	2.1	17.4
Totals	58	.384	.740	4.5	2.4	16.0

VITALY POTAPENKO

School: Wright St.
Year: Junior
Position: Center
Height: 6'10" **Weight:** 270
Birthdate: March 21, 1975
Hometown: Kiev, Ukraine

PLAYER SUMMARY	
Will	bruise foes
Can't	ball-handle with flair
Expect	MCC dominance
Don't Expect	subtle moves

Background: A European friend of Wright State coach Ralph Underhill tipped the Raider coach off about Potapenko in the summer of 1993. Underhill then visited Potapenko in Kiev and later signed him. In his first year at WSU, Potapenko was named MCC Newcomer of the Year.

Strengths: In addition to his obvious size, Potapenko has an array of tools. He's very agile, runs the floor well, and possesses a soft shooting touch. Fundamentally sound, he rarely takes bad shots. Unlike some European players, he does not shun the kind of physical contact post players in America must endure.

Weaknesses: Aggressiveness is his largest hurdle. He averaged nearly four fouls a game last winter and that won't help Underhill, who needs him on the floor. At the defensive end, he must learn when to stay still and when a foul is worth surrendering.

Analysis: You've likely not heard much about this fellow, but then no one outside the Ukraine had prior to 1994-95. One rival coach suggests he's already better than Eric Montross and Bryant Reeves. WSU nearly sneaked into the NCAA Tournament last year, and this chap gives them a good chance to make it this time.

COLLEGE STATISTICS

	G	FGP	FTP	RPG	APG	PPG
94-95 WSU	30	.602	.733	6.4	1.4	19.2
Totals	30	.602	.733	6.4	1.4	19.2

JOHNNY RHODES

School: Maryland
Year: Senior
Position: Guard
Height: 6'5" **Weight:** 205
Birthdate: September 13, 1972
Hometown: Washington, DC

PLAYER SUMMARY	
Will	apply defensive pressure
Can't	shoot a lofty percentage
Expect	athletic drives
Don't Expect	a pretty stroke

Background: In his final season at Washington's Dunbar High School in 1991, Rhodes led that club to a city title. He spent a year at Maine Central Institute, where coach Max Good labeled him the best all-around player he had ever coached. Rhodes is a three-year starter and Maryland's all-time leader in steals.

Strengths: Nominated for the 1995 Henry Iba Corinthian Award as the national Defensive Player of the Year, Rhodes is a menace. His hands are very quick and that creates turnovers. With the ball in his hands, Rhodes is an excellent passer who can complete plays in transition.

Weaknesses: While Rhodes is a productive scorer, he is not a great shooter. Too often last year, defenses had the luxury of laying off him and sagging on Terrapin All-American Joe Smith. There are also too many stretches where Rhodes vanishes.

Analysis: With Smith in the NBA, Rhodes is now on center stage. If he can develop into a steady perimeter and medium-range jump-shooter, he'll be one of the ACC's best, for his defense and rebounding ability are already established.

COLLEGE STATISTICS

	G	FGP	FTP	RPG	APG	PPG
92-93 MARY	28	.420	.530	5.2	3.3	14.0
93-94 MARY	30	.419	.623	6.8	4.1	12.5
94-95 MARY	34	.525	.694	5.3	3.7	14.0
Totals	92	.455	.618	5.7	3.7	13.5

RON RILEY

School: Arizona St.
Year: Senior
Position: Guard/Forward
Height: 6'5" **Weight:** 200
Birthdate: December 27, 1973
Hometown: Las Vegas, NV

PLAYER SUMMARY	
Will	leap to the rafters
Can't	stroke the "J"
Expect	some turnovers
Don't Expect	slow play

Background: This 1992 graduate of Clark High School was voted Nevada's Player of the Year as a senior. At Arizona State, he was the Pac-10's leading scorer among freshmen in 1992-93 and was an honorable-mention All-West pick by *Basketball Times* the past two years.

Strengths: Arizona State under Bill Frieder loves to use all 94 feet of the court, and that suits Riley. He is very athletic and can beat defenders down the floor in transition. Because ASU has been undersized, Riley has been asked to chip in on the backboards and has done a competent job.

Weaknesses: When the pace slows, Riley's effectiveness is reduced. He's not nearly as comfortable in the halfcourt setting, for his jumper is not the most reliable portion of his game. A bad back limited Riley as a defender down the stretch in 1994-95.

Analysis: In an ASU saga filled with injuries, Riley has been one of the few constants. He gives Frieder a slashing wing player who finishes plays with authority. It figures to be another deep year for pro prospects in the Pac-10, and Riley is one of those who will attract some notice.

COLLEGE STATISTICS

		G	FGP	FTP	RPG	APG	PPG
92-93	ASU	28	.355	.660	3.5	1.8	13.0
93-94	ASU	28	.363	.670	5.0	2.5	14.2
94-95	ASU	33	.439	.744	5.3	1.5	16.0
Totals		89	.388	.696	4.6	1.9	14.5

CHRIS ROBINSON

School: Western Kentucky
Year: Senior
Position: Forward
Height: 6'5" **Weight:** 205
Birthdate: April 2, 1974
Hometown: Macon, GA

PLAYER SUMMARY	
Will	shine off Broadway
Can't	handle the rock
Expect	Sun Belt dominance
Don't Expect	any backsliding

Background: Robinson was not an elite recruiting prize entering college. He debuted with a strong ten-point performance against Jackson State and never looked back. Robinson was selected as one of the nation's most underrated players by *Basketball Times* in 1994-95.

Strengths: An explosive first step is Robinson's trademark. It gives him an edge against most foes and allows him to break down a defense from the wing. He finishes well around the hole. In addition, he rebounds well for a small forward.

Weaknesses: Robinson is more of a scorer than he is a long-range shooter. At times, he can be pressured into surrendering the basketball. His ball-handling skills are merely adequate.

Analysis: His isn't a household name and probably won't become one in 1995-96. However, Robinson is a gifted athlete who makes the Hilltoppers a valid threat to crack the Top 25. He's the cornerstone of a squad that captured the Sun Belt Conference and defeated Michigan in the opening round of the NCAA Tournament.

COLLEGE STATISTICS

		G	FGP	FTP	RPG	APG	PPG
92-93	WKU	32	.509	.641	3.4	1.2	7.3
93-94	WKU	31	.478	.721	5.7	2.0	14.7
94-95	WKU	31	.453	.711	6.7	2.2	17.0
Totals		94	.472	.696	5.3	1.8	13.0

MALIK ROSE

School: Drexel
Year: Senior
Position: Center
Height: 6'7" **Weight:** 250
Birthdate: November 23, 1974
Hometown: Philadelphia, PA

PLAYER SUMMARY	
Will	accumulate boards
Can't	extend to 15 feet
Expect	NAC Player of Year
Don't Expect	much finesse

Background: A first-team All-Public League pick at Philadelphia's Overbrook High School, Rose also made a mark as a musician—he was selected to play the tuba in the Pennsylvania State Band. At Drexel, he was the North Atlantic Conference Player of the Year in 1994-95.

Strengths: This powerfully built specimen has quick feet and strong athletic skills. He puts his frame to good use in the paint, sealing off defenders and setting crunching screens. At one time he was a poor free throw shooter, but today he's steady. In addition, he is a relentless rebounder.

Weaknesses: When Drexel steps up against larger schools, Rose can have trouble. Taller centers create problems because his limited range doesn't allow him to step outside, and he lacks the quickness to beat them on the box. Passing out of double-teams can be trouble at times too.

Analysis: Rose has been a star at Drexel throughout his career and will be again. He's a fine student and has a chance to be remembered as the top Dragon ever. If he can add more range to his game, he'll get a solid look from NBA scouts.

COLLEGE STATISTICS

		G	FGP	FTP	RPG	APG	PPG
92-93	DREX	29	.502	.563	11.4	0.3	13.6
93-94	DREX	30	.520	.545	12.4	0.7	13.9
94-95	DREX	30	.563	.714	13.5	1.2	19.5
Totals		89	.532	.610	12.4	0.7	15.7

JASON SASSER

School: Texas Tech
Year: Senior
Position: Forward
Height: 6'7" **Weight:** 210
Birthdate: January 1, 1974
Hometown: Dallas, TX

PLAYER SUMMARY	
Will	compete vigorously
Can't	be a shot-blocker
Expect	lots of double-teams
Don't Expect	national notoriety

Background: At Kimball High School, Sasser was the Class 5A Player of the Year in the state of Texas. At Texas Tech, he made 19 starts as a freshman and was a first-team All-Southwest Conference pick in each of the past two years.

Strengths: A determined sort, Sasser won't run from a big shot. In the open court, Sasser is very dangerous. He runs well and can pull up for the short jumper. That same jumper is also effective in the halfcourt game as Sasser comes off screens.

Weaknesses: Sasser takes gambles defensively in an effort to make steals, and that leaves the Red Raiders vulnerable at times. He is a scorer and doesn't always stay focused at the other end of the floor. If he aspires to an NBA career, Sasser must extend the range on his shot.

Analysis: A quiet force in the SWC, Sasser hopes to take his game to a higher level in 1995-96. He'll have to if the Red Raiders are to make any postseason plans—key contributors Mark Davis and Lance Hughes are gone. This will be Sasser's most challenging campaign yet, as defenses will undoubtedly swarm to him.

COLLEGE STATISTICS

		G	FGP	FTP	RPG	APG	PPG
92-93	TT	30	.434	.629	5.1	1.6	10.6
93-94	TT	28	.482	.710	9.4	2.9	20.6
94-95	TT	30	.510	.793	7.8	2.9	20.1
Totals		88	.481	.727	7.4	2.5	17.0

SHEA SEALS
School: Tulsa
Year: Junior
Position: Guard
Height: 6'5" Weight: 210
Birthdate: August 26, 1975
Hometown: Tulsa, OK

PLAYER SUMMARY	
Will	attract more attention
Can't	direct the offense
Expect	scoring fireworks
Don't Expect	lax rebounding

Background: The Oklahoma High School Player of the Year was a big recruiting plus for then-Tulsa coach Tubby Smith. He was a third-team Freshman All-America choice of *Basketball Times* and an All-Missouri Valley Conference pick last winter.

Strengths: Seals lists Scottie Pippen as his favorite pro player and his game has some parallels to the Chicago Bulls star. The McLain High School product can score from all spots on the floor. He'll slash to the goal or will pull up for a jump shot. When his path is blocked, he'll find the open man—plus he's a first-rate rebounder for his size.

Weaknesses: His grab bag of skills is such that Seals can try to do too much. At times he grows frustrated with all of the defensive attention he now receives and lets loose with a bad shot. His perimeter jumper can be prone to long cold spells.

Analysis: Since Seals arrived on campus, the Golden Hurricane has twice advanced to the Sweet 16 round of the NCAA Tournament. That's a major statement about this man's tools because Tulsa is not the kind of school that can seriously hope to pursue a national title. Seals will garner some preseason All-America votes.

COLLEGE STATISTICS

		G	FGP	FTP	RPG	APG	PPG
93-94	TULS	28	.426	.748	6.5	3.5	16.8
94-95	TULS	32	.389	.793	6.9	4.0	18.8
Totals		60	.405	.776	6.7	3.7	17.9

JESS SETTLES
School: Iowa
Year: Junior
Position: Forward
Height: 6'7" Weight: 220
Birthdate: July 7, 1974
Hometown: Winfield, IA

PLAYER SUMMARY	
Will	take quality shots
Can't	depend on his back
Expect	greater recognition
Don't Expect	public bravado

Background: Settles earned a Big Ten scholarship on the strength of a superb work ethic honed in backyard games with his father and brother. As a rookie at Iowa, Settles was a revelation. He was named the Big Ten's Freshman of the Year in 1993-94.

Strengths: Combining smarts and size, Settles might be the Big Ten's most well-rounded player. Extremely versatile, Settles is at his best in traffic, creating openings and knifing into the hole. This reliable free throw shooter is nearly as adept at stepping outside to launch the 3. He is also a skilled ball-handler.

Weaknesses: One of the reasons Settles was overlooked in high school is that he is not an overwhelming athletic presence. He does not possess great foot speed, and quick forwards can be a handful for him defensively—especially if his mobility is limited by a bad back.

Analysis: It is not a coincidence that Iowa's midseason slump occurred when Settles was sidelined with an aching back. When healthy, he is one of the nation's most complete players. He has a knack for finding the open man and making the kinds of plays that win games.

COLLEGE STATISTICS

		G	FGP	FTP	RPG	APG	PPG
93-94	IOWA	27	.574	.789	7.5	2.3	15.3
94-95	IOWA	26	.469	.802	6.2	2.0	15.6
Totals		53	.519	.796	6.9	2.2	15.5

DORON SHEFFER

School: Connecticut
Year: Junior
Position: Guard
Height: 6'5" **Weight:** 200
Birthdate: March 12, 1972
Hometown: Ramat Efal, Israel

PLAYER SUMMARY	
Will	find the open man
Can't	shoot without space
Expect	smooth drives
Don't Expect	quick feet

Background: A native of Israel, Sheffer came to Connecticut with extensive international experience. In 1992-93, he was voted Most Valuable Player of the Israeli club league, and he's a member of the Israeli national team. He was a second-team All-Big East selection in 1994-95.

Strengths: Excellent court vision allows Sheffer to see scoring opportunities develop before the defense can react. He is a confident ball-handler who understands how to attack a fullcourt trap. Shots are rarely forced as Sheffer likes to let the action flow to him. His understanding of the game helps him create steals.

Weaknesses: It takes Sheffer more time than most to launch his jumper. Even when he is open, Sheffer often passes the shot up. A prolonged slump in midseason shook his confidence, and the Huskies need him to make those open medium-range jumpers.

Analysis: After a sluggish start, Sheffer recovered to enjoy a solid finish to his second season. With the exit of point guard Kevin Ollie, Sheffer becomes critical to coach Jim Calhoun as the only experienced ball-handler on the scene. He's got the tools to keep UConn thriving in the fast lane.

COLLEGE STATISTICS

		G	FGP	FTP	RPG	APG	PPG
93-94	CONN	34	.505	.735	3.8	4.8	11.9
94-95	CONN	33	.401	.752	4.7	5.5	11.1
Totals		67	.451	.744	4.2	5.2	11.5

CHARLES SMITH

School: Rider
Year: Junior
Position: Forward
Height: 6'6" **Weight:** 200
Birthdate: October 23, 1975
Hometown: Boothwyn, PA

PLAYER SUMMARY	
Will	soar for swats
Can't	lean on big centers
Expect	rugged rebounding
Don't Expect	big muscles

Background: This late bloomer came on strong in his senior season at Chichester High School, earning Player of the Year honors in Delaware County. At Rider, he enjoyed a stellar debut. He was named both the Northeast Conference and Metropolitan New York-New Jersey Newcomer of the Year in 1993-94.

Strengths: Smith is a forward with guard-type skills. A sound shooting stroke makes him a threat from in tight and on medium-range jumpers. An authoritative first step makes him difficult for bulky big men to cope with. He finishes well around the goal and is a good free throw shooter.

Weaknesses: Although he's a shot-blocker, Smith is not an overly physical player. Upper-body strength would help him against strong interior types, who tend to move him around. As more double-teams come, Smith must do a better job of anticipating them.

Analysis: Lightly recruited, Smith has developed nicely in the "Broncs Zoo," Rider's tiny homecourt. He has been Rider's answer man since early in his freshman season and will be that again. As he matures and develops more perimeter skills, he could emerge as one of the NEC's finest ever.

COLLEGE STATISTICS

		G	FGP	FTP	RPG	APG	PPG
93-94	RIDE	30	.543	.757	7.2	1.5	16.9
94-95	RIDE	29	.484	.713	5.6	2.3	19.8
Totals		59	.511	.734	6.4	1.9	18.3

CURTIS STAPLES

School: Virginia
Year: Sophomore
Position: Guard
Height: 6'3" **Weight:** 175
Birthdate: July 14, 1976
Hometown: Roanoke, VA

PLAYER SUMMARY	
Will	hit area-code "J's"
Can't	operate inside
Expect	additional minutes
Don't Expect	rims to clang

Background: There was something of a gypsy flavor to Staples's prep career—he attended three schools in four years. He concluded at the famed Oak Hill Academy, where he was listed as the fifth-best big-guard prospect in the land by *FutureStars*. Staples moved into the Virginia starting lineup in February.

Strengths: A tireless worker, Staples spent many hours of his youth shooting baskets. The result is one of the purest jump shots in the college game. Staples has range to the NBA 3-point line and can connect under duress. He doesn't force many shots and contributes on the glass too.

Weaknesses: Virginia takes considerable pride in its defense, and that is an area Staples can bolster. Sometimes Staples gambles on a steal when it would be more prudent to hold his position. Cavalier guards don't have the luxury of taking such risks because there is no big man underneath to block shots.

Analysis: No one doubted Staples was a shooter. What attracted notice was the entirety of his game. He's quick and meshed well with Harold Deane in the backcourt. Look for his point total to rise dramatically on a wave of 3's.

COLLEGE STATISTICS

	G	FGP	FTP	RPG	APG	PPG
94-95 VIRG	34	.416	.755	3.0	0.8	11.9
Totals	34	.416	.755	3.0	0.8	11.9

LYNARD STEWART

School: Temple
Year: Sophomore
Position: Forward
Height: 6'7" **Weight:** 190
Birthdate: May 12, 1976
Hometown: Philadelphia, PA

PLAYER SUMMARY	
Will	convert in lane
Can't	swing to guard
Expect	a scoring upgrade
Don't Expect	good ball-handling

Background: Simon Gratz High School has a rich hoops history and lately has produced some excellent stars, Aaron McKie and Rasheed Wallace among them. Stewart averaged 15 PPG and 13 RPG as a senior at Gratz. Stewart's pedigree also includes two older brothers, Larry and Stephen, who starred at Coppin State.

Strengths: The matchup zone that Temple favors generally inhibits good rebounding, yet Stewart overcomes the natural tendency to let opponents sneak in for boards. He's a quick leaper with a sense for understanding where caroms will land. On offense, he's got a nice short-range jumper.

Weaknesses: Visits to the weight room will enhance Stewart's game. Another 15 to 20 pounds of muscle should help Stewart survive as a power forward rather than as a small forward. While he possesses a good feel around the basket, Stewart needs to improve his ball skills to become a threat on the wing.

Analysis: The Owls are consistently a factor in the Atlantic 10, and this team will go as far as Stewart and classmate Johnny Miller can take it. Stewart demonstrated that he has the gifts that will keep Temple strong. He's one of the Atlantic 10's young stars.

COLLEGE STATISTICS

	G	FGP	FTP	RPG	APG	PPG
94-95 TEMP	29	.437	.533	4.5	0.5	7.2
Totals	29	.437	.533	4.5	0.5	7.2

MAURICE TAYLOR

School: Michigan
Year: Sophomore
Position: Forward/Center
Height: 6'9" **Weight:** 230
Birthdate: October 30, 1976
Hometown: Detroit, MI

PLAYER SUMMARY	
Will	post up
Can't	drill 3's
Expect	electric dunks
Don't Expect	great stamina

Background: One of the lesser known members of the "Fresh Five," the heirs to Michigan's famed "Fab Five" recruiting class, Taylor had the best year of any Wolverine frosh. He was a first-team Freshman All-America pick of *Basketball Times*.

Strengths: Taylor runs the floor as well as any big man in the Big Ten. He is a presence at the defensive end in the lane with superb timing on shot blocks. On the backboards, he has a knack for coming up with the basketball. He gets off the ground quickly and is virtually unstoppable when he goes back up with the ball.

Weaknesses: As Taylor fills out, he'll become an even better rebounder. At times he became fatigued, and that led to some reaching fouls on defense. A bit more polish will also benefit his interior game, which is still somewhat raw.

Analysis: Despite the fact that he was a touted recruit—MVP of the West team in the 1994 Magic's Roundball Classic—Taylor did not arrive in Ann Arbor with the hype of classmates Willie Mitchell or Jerod Ward. Yet he outshone them both. He's capable of much more and reminds Michigan fans of current Los Angeles Clipper and ex-Wolverine Loy Vaught.

COLLEGE STATISTICS

	G	FGP	FTP	RPG	APG	PPG
94-95 MICH	31	.471	.602	5.1	1.2	12.4
Totals	31	.471	.602	5.1	1.2	12.4

KELLY THAMES

School: Missouri
Year: Sophomore
Position: Forward
Height: 6'7" **Weight:** 207
Birthdate: April 13, 1975
Hometown: St. Louis, MO

PLAYER SUMMARY	
Will	overcome pain
Can't	leap like before
Expect	a polished game
Don't Expect	tons of minutes

Background: Chosen Mr. Show-Me Basketball as a senior at Jennings High School, Thames made a fast adjustment to the college game. He was tabbed the Big Eight Freshman of the Year in 1993-94. Before practice began, he tore the posterior cruciate ligament in his knee and sat out all of last season.

Strengths: This well-rounded player offers a variety of skills. From the wing, he beats his man off the dribble or stops and connects on the jump shot. Thames uses his quickness and smart positioning to help Missouri on the glass.

Weaknesses: Much of Thames's offensive game prior to the knee injury was predicated on his explosive first step. It's difficult to gauge what effect the ligament tear will have. At the very least, it will probably create a measure of uncertainty.

Analysis: Tiger coach Norm Stewart received some attention in national Coach of the Year balloting because he managed to take Mizzou to the NCAA Tournament without this star. Thames was to be the main man for the Tigers. The injury raises questions, but this youngster's work ethic and skills should help him answer those.

COLLEGE STATISTICS

	G	FGP	FTP	RPG	APG	PPG
93-94 MISS	32	.514	.729	7.1	1.2	12.2
Totals	32	.514	.729	7.1	1.2	12.2

ROBERT TRAYLOR

School: Michigan
Year: Freshman
Position: Center/Forward
Height: 6'9" **Weight:** 275
Birthdate: February 1, 1977
Hometown: Detroit, MI

PLAYER SUMMARY	
Will	eat space
Can't	log tons of minutes
Expect	smooth moves inside
Don't Expect	expert conditioning

Background: Traylor made his first impression at a summer camp following his sophomore season at Murray-Wright High School. He later played for the United States team that won the men's junior world championship qualifying tournament in Argentina. He was tabbed Michigan's Mr. Basketball last March.

Strengths: They call him "Tractor" for his size, but it is Traylor's grace that captivates. He is very agile for someone so large and has inspired comparisons to Charles Barkley. He has a soft shooting touch, is a powerful leaper, and understands how to use his frame to carve space for himself in the post. Shot blocks are part of his repertoire too.

Weaknesses: At the close of his senior season in high school, Traylor was overweight. He was easily winded in several postseason all-star affairs. A loss of excess pounds would be an enormous help. It would make him quicker defensively and keep him in the game longer.

Analysis: Considered one of the top big men in the freshman class, Traylor is a rare combination of size and speed. He intimidates in the lane and is a tremendous passer. If he can shed the excess weight, he'll be an immediate force at Michigan.

KEITH VAN HORN

School: Utah
Year: Junior
Position: Forward
Height: 6'9" **Weight:** 227
Birthdate: October 25, 1975
Hometown: Diamond Bar, CA

PLAYER SUMMARY	
Will	rebound eagerly
Can't	add enough weight
Expect	straight shooting
Don't Expect	inconsistency

Background: The top prospect in Utah's outstanding recruiting class of 1993, Van Horn stepped in to make 24 starts as a freshman. He led the Utes in both scoring and rebounding, becoming the first freshman to lead Utah in points since Luther Burden did it in 1972-73. Last season, he was a first-team All-WAC selection.

Strengths: Van Horn's game is a well-rounded one. He's capable of scoring from the interior or perimeter, as he possesses a nifty jumper. On the inside, he's a bright student of the game who finds the gaps to position himself for rebounds. On the wing, he makes good use of his vision to get the ball to his mates.

Weaknesses: Although he's a player in the truest sense of the word, Van Horn does not have the ideal body for grappling inside. He's thin and can be moved around by opposing big men. Defensively, he struggles with footwork and is not much of a presence.

Analysis: Utah doesn't receive much national attention except for its coach, the entertaining and gifted Rick Majerus. But one of the reasons Majerus has won these past two seasons is that Van Horn has been a complete player, worthy of wider acclaim.

COLLEGE STATISTICS

	G	FGP	FTP	RPG	APG	PPG
93-94 UTAH	25	.516	.775	8.3	0.8	18.3
94-95 UTAH	33	.545	.856	8.5	1.4	21.0
Totals	58	.533	.821	8.4	1.1	19.8

JACQUE VAUGHN

School: Kansas
Year: Junior
Position: Guard
Height: 6'1" **Weight:** 195
Birthdate: February 11, 1975
Hometown: Los Angeles, CA

PLAYER SUMMARY	
Will	hit the books
Can't	consistently hit 3's
Expect	heady play
Don't Expect	turnovers

Background: As a prepster, Vaughn received nearly as much notoriety for his academic work as he did for his hoops skill. One B in tenth grade prevented him from graduating from John Muir High School with a perfect 4.0 grade-point average. This coveted prospect was the 1993-94 Big Eight Newcomer of the Year.

Strengths: This is a point guard in the purest sense of the term. Scoring is secondary to Vaughn. He prefers setting up his mates and is very good at it. Backcourt pressure doesn't disturb him and he has a knack for feeding the post effectively. He also understands his own offensive limitations.

Weaknesses: The knock on Vaughn is that he is not a consistent threat from the perimeter. A telling statistic is that when Vaughn shot better than 50 percent from the floor, Kansas was unbeaten. When Vaughn makes shots, it opens passing lanes.

Analysis: Vaughn and Allen Iverson enter the campaign as the premier point guards in the land. Vaughn is not a scorer but is under far greater control than Georgetown's star. Vaughn logged 33.5 minutes per game last winter, the most ever by a Jayhawk under Roy Williams.

COLLEGE STATISTICS

	G	FGP	FTP	RPG	APG	PPG
93-94 KANS	35	.467	.670	2.5	5.2	7.8
94-95 KANS	31	.452	.687	3.7	7.7	9.7
Totals	66	.459	.680	3.1	6.3	8.7

ANTOINE WALKER

School: Kentucky
Year: Sophomore
Position: Forward
Height: 6'8" **Weight:** 217
Birthdate: August 12, 1976
Hometown: Chicago, IL

PLAYER SUMMARY	
Will	feed the open man
Can't	afford to coast
Expect	steadier minutes
Don't Expect	a tiger on "D"

Background: This four-year starter at Mt. Carmel High School was named Mr. Basketball in the state of Illinois in 1994. *USA Today* selected him as a third-team prep All-American and Walker picked Kentucky over UNLV, Illinois, Michigan, and California. He was a second-team Freshman All-America choice of *Basketball Times*.

Strengths: Kentucky coach Rick Pitino says he's had no one of Walker's size who handles the basketball the way this youngster does. Given Pitino's NBA experience, that's a strong endorsement. Walker is extremely comfortable on the perimeter and can convert a medium-range wing jumper. He's also a solid rebounder.

Weaknesses: Inconsistency was a problem for Walker during his debut. Outstanding performances were followed by ones where you needed a program to know Walker was on the floor. Some feel Walker is too perimeter-oriented and a bit soft defensively.

Analysis: Since Jamal Mashburn exited for the NBA, Kentucky has lacked a great individual athlete who can take over a game. It was to be Rod Rhodes, but he never emerged. This is the best candidate on the present roster to assume the role. Walker has every tool needed.

COLLEGE STATISTICS

	G	FGP	FTP	RPG	APG	PPG
94-95 KENT	33	.419	.712	4.5	1.4	7.8
Totals	33	.419	.712	4.5	1.4	7.8

SAMAKI WALKER

School: Louisville
Year: Sophomore
Position: Forward
Height: 6'9" **Weight:** 220
Birthdate: February 25, 1976
Hometown: Columbus, OH

PLAYER SUMMARY	
Will	dunk over foes
Can't	shut down centers
Expect	superb interior passing
Don't Expect	poor rebounding

Background: Despite playing only nine contests as a senior at Whitehall High School, Walker was cited as a *Parade* All-American. He also scored 21 points in the Magic Johnson Roundball Classic at the close of his senior year. He then selected Louisville over Michigan, Kentucky, and North Carolina.

Strengths: Size and skill give Walker a major advantage inside. A first-rate drop step gets him to the hole, and a deft touch allows him to complete the score. He goes hard to the glass and uses his bulk and quickness off the floor to secure caroms. Excellent leaping ability makes him a defensive presence in the lane.

Weaknesses: Walker is not yet to the point where he is a strong one-on-one defender. He must improve his footwork and reach less to improve in that area. As it is, Louisville makes liberal use of a 2-3 zone in part to protect Walker from foul woes.

Analysis: A Freshman All-American, Walker has a future that looks limitless. He possesses scoring and rebounding tenacity, and only an injury interrupted an excellent rookie outing. Now healthy, Walker appears to be a prototype power forward in the tradition of Louisville greats like Rodney McCray.

COLLEGE STATISTICS

	G	FGP	FTP	RPG	APG	PPG
94-95 LOU	29	.548	.537	7.2	1.3	13.7
Totals	29	.548	.537	7.2	1.3	13.7

JOHN WALLACE

School: Syracuse
Position: Forward
Year: Senior
Height: 6'8" **Weight:** 225
Birthdate: February 9, 1974
Hometown: Rochester, NY

PLAYER SUMMARY	
Will	take wise shots
Can't	stop talking trash
Expect	quality rebounding
Don't Expect	long bombs

Background: New York's Mr. Basketball as a senior at Greece-Athena High School, Wallace was rated as the East's top forward prospect by *Eastern Basketball* in 1991-92. He was a consensus Freshman All-American in his debut at Syracuse and a first-team All-Big East choice in 1994-95.

Strengths: Wallace does his best work around the glass. He is not an overpowering rebounder; instead, he relies on smart positioning to gather caroms. He is very adept at getting offensive putbacks off rebounds. Scoring also comes when he uses a soft face-up jump shot.

Weaknesses: For all of his offensive skill, Wallace rarely takes over a game. He seems content to fade in and out, picking up points only off rebounds. If the Orange are to remain a threat to win the Big East, Wallace must shoulder a heavier burden.

Analysis: He came to the Carrier Dome billed as the second coming of Derrick Coleman and even took his idol's uniform number (44). Wallace, though, is not Coleman. What he is, however, is a strong interior player who needs consistency and drive to become a contender for All-America votes.

COLLEGE STATISTICS

	G	FGP	FTP	RPG	APG	PPG
92-93 SYR	29	.526	.718	7.6	1.3	11.1
93-94 SYR	30	.566	.761	9.0	1.7	15.0
94-95 SYR	30	.588	.679	8.2	2.6	16.8
Totals	89	.563	.720	8.3	1.9	14.3

DeJUAN WHEAT

School: Louisville
Year: Junior
Position: Guard
Height: 6'0" **Weight:** 160
Birthdate: October 14, 1973
Hometown: Louisville, KY

PLAYER SUMMARY	
Will	penetrate for points
Can't	post up
Expect	clutch performances
Don't Expect	shaky ball-handling

Background: A local product of Ballard High School, Wheat enrolled at Louisville as a part-time student and began his freshman year as a full-time student in 1993-94. He did not play basketball in 1992-93 but the layoff was not evident when he debuted as a Cardinal. He was *Basketball Times'* 1993-94 national Newcomer of the Year.

Strengths: This smooth guard is most comfortable with the basketball in his hands. He deals with traps well and knows how to get the ball to Louisville's big men. Defenders must respect his perimeter jumper too. It's soft and generally accurate. He's also a fine free throw shooter.

Weaknesses: Muscular guards are an obstacle for Wheat. He simply lacks the size to cope with powerful foes. Defensively, he is pesky but not much more.

Analysis: Louisville needed a late rally in the Metro Conference Tournament to reach the NCAA Tournament, so Wheat didn't receive the acclaim he deserved. This is a superior lead guard because he is both a gifted penetrator and long-range shooter. He can't be easily marked, and more observers will discover that as the Cardinals continue their return to national prominence.

COLLEGE STATISTICS

	G	FGP	FTP	RPG	APG	PPG
93-94 LOU	34	.450	.769	2.1	3.2	12.6
94-95 LOU	33	.487	.796	2.7	3.2	16.5
Totals	67	.471	.782	2.4	3.2	14.5

KENYA WILKINS

School: Oregon
Year: Junior
Position: Guard
Height: 5'10" **Weight:** 154
Birthdate: July 2, 1975
Hometown: Los Angeles, CA

PLAYER SUMMARY	
Will	fake with the dribble
Can't	attempt blocks
Expect	All-Pac-10 status
Don't Expect	fear

Background: A prep career at Dorsey High School was highlighted by a summer championship between his junior and senior seasons. Upon his arrival in Oregon, Wilkins set a freshman assist record. Last season, he quarterbacked the Ducks to their first NCAA Tournament appearance since 1961.

Strengths: Wilkins sets the tone for the Ducks and reminds some of former UCLA guard Tyus Edney. Defenders have a difficult time coping with his quickness with the basketball, as he often breaks defenses down with dribble penetration. Wilkins can spot the open man and get the ball to him. He's also a dangerous 3-point shooter.

Weaknesses: There are moments when Wilkins operates too quickly. In his rush to make something happen, he'll often attempt to feed men who are not open or get himself airborne with nowhere to land. Defense is an uphill fight because of his small stature.

Analysis: Oregon was one of the surprise teams in America, yet—because it didn't last long in the postseason—many fans weren't introduced to its stars. This is one of them. He's won at every level, and the expectation is that he'll keep the Ducks swimming upstream.

COLLEGE STATISTICS

	G	FGP	FTP	RPG	APG	PPG
93-94 OREG	27	.360	.709	3.3	5.3	11.5
94-95 OREG	28	.366	.735	3.2	6.1	12.1
Totals	55	.363	.722	3.2	5.7	11.8

JEROME WILLIAMS
School: Georgetown
Year: Senior
Position: Forward
Height: 6'9" **Weight:** 200
Hometown: Germantown, MD

PLAYER SUMMARY	
Will	generate energy
Can't	excel outside
Expect	rebounding supremacy
Don't Expect	dreary efforts

Background: There aren't many athletes in this age of intense recruiting analysis who slip through the cracks, but Williams did. After prepping at Magruder High School, Williams moved on to Montgomery College, where he was the junior college Most Valuable Player in Maryland. In 1994-95, he led the Big East in rebounding.

Strengths: An enthusiastic demeanor helps Williams inside. He loves to go after the basketball and usually grabs it. Defensively, he is quick enough to handle smaller forwards and eager enough to deal with the larger ones. He'll also challenge shots and block more than his share.

Weaknesses: For all of his energy, Williams is devoid of much offensive polish. He must rely upon offensive rebounds and putbacks to generate offense. He is not a great passer and—in his zest to get moving—sometimes rushes things, leading to turnovers.

Analysis: When Othella Harrington slumped, Williams picked up much of the inside slack for the Hoyas last year. His speed fits well with catalyst Allen Iverson, and on a team that shoots as poorly as the Hoyas, quality board work is essential. Williams could challenge for national rebounding honors.

COLLEGE STATISTICS

	G	FGP	FTP	RPG	APG	PPG
94-95 GEOR	31	.500	.629	10.0	1.5	10.9
Totals	31	.500	.629	10.0	1.5	10.9

LORENZEN WRIGHT
School: Memphis
Year: Sophomore
Position: Center
Height: 6'11" **Weight:** 225
Birthdate: November 4, 1975
Hometown: Memphis, TN

PLAYER SUMMARY	
Will	work tirelessly
Can't	bomb from the arc
Expect	forceful rebounding
Don't Expect	ill-advised shots

Background: This decorated prepster was a consensus All-American at Booker T. Washington High School and the Tennessee Player of the Year as selected by *USA Today*. At Memphis, he immediately assumed the starting-center spot and was named a first-team Freshman All-American by *Basketball Weekly*.

Strengths: A throwback, Wright loves the business of playing center. He is a presence in the lane defensively, blocking shots and deterring others. Few big men possess his quickness and leaping ability and that makes him a problem to defend. Wright finishes well around the goal and rarely forces a shot when it is not available.

Weaknesses: Like many young pivots, Wright still must learn how to react to double- and triple-teams. He doesn't always make the right choice and sometimes that creates turnovers. Free throw improvement could add two to four points to his average.

Analysis: Though much more attention was paid to classmates Allen Iverson and Felipe Lopez, this youngster enjoyed a debut outing that was nearly as good. He possesses tremendous skills and a work ethic that should insure a profitable NBA future. This is a potential top-five pick in the NBA draft.

COLLEGE STATISTICS

	G	FGP	FTP	RPG	APG	PPG
94-95 MEMP	34	.561	.626	10.2	1.5	14.8
Totals	34	.561	.626	10.2	1.5	14.8

ALABAMA

Conference: Southeastern
1994-95: 23-10, 3rd SEC West

1994-95 NCAAs: 1-1
Coach: David Hobbs (59-33)

Opening Line: With four seniors on his 1994-95 roster, including two key operatives, David Hobbs understood there would be a fair degree of rebuilding in 1995-96. When Antonio McDyess declared for the NBA draft in May, however, this became a major overhaul. Still, the Crimson Tide has an experienced backcourt and has recruited well enough to remain a contender for a postseason bid.

Guard: It is ironic that the area considered most vulnerable entering 1994-95 is now the Tide's greatest strength. Senior Marvin Orange is a steady hand at the point. His jumper is much improved over what it was earlier in his career. Eric Washington will begin the season as a starter. Yet a man to watch may be 6'3" Anton Reese, an excellent prep scorer from Georgia. Transfer Damon Bacote, late of Richmond, adds all-around skills too. Freshman Brian Williams brings a great first step and ball-handling skills.

Forward: In addition to McDyess, the Tide lost wing forward Jamal Faulkner and power man Jason Caffey. One man who will see plenty of action is Thalamus McGhee, a 6'9" graduate of Trinity Valley C.C. At 280 pounds, McGhee was a rebounding terror in junior college. Veteran Anthony Brown isn't the scorer Faulkner was, but his experience insures he'll have a role on the wing.

Center: At 6'9", 212 pounds, Roy Rogers is not well suited to the post. However, some of his best work came when McDyess was injured, and the hope now is that he'll elevate his play with the Tide star now in the NBA.

Analysis: Don't be fooled by the exit of McDyess and friends. Hobbs has proven to be an excellent recruiter since assuming the reins of command from former boss Wimp Sanderson in 1992, and he's assembled a superior corps of replacements. Holdovers Washington and Orange will be pushed hard by Reese and Williams, while McGhee will be an instant factor up front.

1995-96 ROSTER

	POS	HT	YR	FGP	FTP	3-PT	RPG	APG	PPG
Eric Washington	G/F	6'3"	Jr.	.46	.81	69/172	3.9	0.8	11.9
Marvin Orange	G	6'0"	Sr.	.32	.68	45/153	1.7	4.2	6.7
Roy Rogers	C	6'9"	Sr.	.51	.55	—	3.6	0.6	3.5
Anthony Brown	F	6'5"	Sr.	.48	.73	2/7	1.3	0.5	3.2
Marco Whitfield	G	5'11"	Sr.	.41	.50	5/18	0.9	1.4	2.1
Wade Kaiser	C	6'9"	Jr.	1.00	.50	—	0.7	0.1	0.6
Damon Bacote	G	6'3"	So.	—	—	—	—	—	—
M.C. Mazique	F	6'9"	Fr.	—	—	—	—	—	—
Thalamus McGhee	F/C	6'9"	Jr.	—	—	—	—	—	—
Anton Reese	G	6'3"	Fr.	—	—	—	—	—	—
Blake Thrasher	G	6'3"	Fr.	—	—	—	—	—	—
Brian Williams	G	6'2"	Fr.	—	—	—	—	—	—

ARIZONA

Conference: Pac-10   **1994-95 NCAAs:** 0-1
1994-95: 23-8, 2nd Pac-10   **Coach:** Lute Olson (481-187)

Opening Line: One year after reaching the NCAA Final Four in Charlotte, Arizona returned to familiar terrain—a first-round loss to an unheralded school, Miami of Ohio. The Wildcats' regular season wasn't a washout, though, as Damon Stoudamire established himself as one of the nation's premier players. Stoudamire led the Pac-10 in scoring and was the chief reason Arizona was rated 15th in the final Associated Press poll. Now he must be replaced.

Guard: Stoudamire's likely heir, prep scoring sensation Michael Bibby (son of the former UCLA great), won't enroll at his intended college until 1996-97. So Olson must improvise. The backcourt will be shared by seniors Reggie Geary and Corey Williams. A tenacious defender, Geary is limited offensively. Williams potentially has more firepower but isn't much of a playmaker. And both are major liabilities at the free throw line.

Forward: As a freshman, Miles Simon gave hints that he may be on the verge of a terrific career. This superb athlete runs the floor gracefully and can make a 3-pointer. Look for him to be a major scoring threat. The enigmatic Ben Davis, who became eligible in late December, never quite dominated at power forward the way some thought he might. He can be a force when he's focused.

Center: If the Wildcats are to flourish, they need a healthy, consistent season from Joseph Blair. At times, he's appeared ready to turn the corner, but he has never quite accomplished the feat. He must use his size to control the interior for Arizona. A.J. Bramlett, a freshman, will be groomed as Blair's backup.

Analysis: Just when it appeared the Wildcats had shaken their troubled NCAA Tournament past, they stumbled again. The truth is that by season's end this was a one-man unit. If Stoudamire didn't score a lot, the Cats were in trouble. This year's edition should be a more balanced cast, with the production geared to the frontcourt. Geary and Williams hold the key to a run at the top of the Pac-10.

1995-96 ROSTER

	POS	HT	YR	FGP	FTP	3-PT	RPG	APG	PPG
Joseph Blair	C	6'10"	Sr.	.56	.46	—	7.0	0.9	12.0
Ben Davis	F	6'9"	Sr.	.54	.63	—	5.9	0.4	9.9
Miles Simon	F/G	6'5"	So.	.48	.77	29/65	3.7	2.6	8.9
Corey Williams	G/F	6'7"	Sr.	.47	.48	31/84	4.1	1.3	6.8
Reggie Geary	G	6'2"	Sr.	.41	.43	36/94	3.1	3.6	6.2
Michael Dickerson	F	6'6"	So.	.54	.68	10/19	2.0	0.6	4.8
Joe McLean	G	6'7"	Sr.	.31	.79	11/54	2.5	1.5	3.9
Kelvin Eafon	G	6'1"	So.	.30	.75	2/7	0.4	0.5	0.7
A.J. Bramlett	F/C	6'10"	Fr.	—	—	—	—	—	—
Donnell Harris	F	6'11"	Fr.	—	—	—	—	—	—
Jason Terry	G	6'2"	Fr.	—	—	—	—	—	—

ARIZONA STATE

Conference: Pac-10
1994-95: 24-9, 3rd Pac-10

1994-95 NCAAs: 2-1
Coach: Bill Frieder (302-159)

Opening Line: Long criticized for his team's shortfall in the postseason, coach Bill Frieder gained a measure of redemption with ASU's strong showing in the 1995 NCAA Tournament. The Sun Devils dominated Ball State and rallied to defeat a good Manhattan squad before Kentucky ended matters. The early entry of Mario Bennett into the NBA creates a massive problem in the middle, however.

Guard: Though two starters were subtracted in the off-season, ASU is in good shape here. Sophomore Jeremy Veal and junior Quincy Brewer saw extensive action last year, as Frieder made liberal use of a three-guard rotation. Brewer is a lefty who makes smart decisions on the floor and is a hardnosed defender. Veal can be explosive and is a viable threat from 3-point country. New arrival Lenny Holly is a point guard with good size. Gee Gervin will sit out the year to concentrate on academics.

Forward: Ron Riley is the club's top returning scorer. This athletic wing player is best suited for the three spot, though he was forced to battle many power forwards last year. Opposite Riley could be any number of candidates. Senior Joe Zaletel saw spot duty last year and demonstrated a decent medium-range jumper. Junior college signee Lamar Richardson can help on the glass, while freshman Okeme Oziwo is a bit raw.

Center: No one on the roster really qualifies as a center. Steve Walston, 6'8", was redshirted last year. He doesn't figure to make an impact. Not only did Bennett leave, but J.R. Cunningham transferred.

Analysis: ASU relied on its quickness, 3-point shooting, and Bennett to win 24 contests last year. Two of those elements are intact. The backcourt is quick and the Sun Devils will disrupt opponents' rhythm. Veal and Riley are capable marksmen. The critical area is the interior, where Bennett was invaluable. Several unheralded big men must make strides if ASU is to return to the NCAA field of 64.

1995-96 ROSTER

	POS	HT	YR	FGP	FTP	3-PT	RPG	APG	PPG
Ron Riley	F	6'5"	Sr.	.44	.74	80/222	5.3	1.5	16.0
Jeremy Veal	G	6'3"	So.	.41	.83	44/118	1.3	1.6	7.4
Quincy Brewer	G	6'5"	Jr.	.49	.34	0/5	5.3	1.6	6.7
Joe Zaletel	F	6'7"	Sr.	.54	.56	0/3	1.0	0.2	1.8
Duane Davis	G	5'11"	Fr.	—	—	—	—	—	—
Roger Farrington	F	6'7"	Fr.	—	—	—	—	—	—
Lenny Holly	G	6'5"	Jr.	—	—	—	—	—	—
Okeme Oziwo	F	6'8"	Fr.	—	—	—	—	—	—
Lamar Richardson	F/C	6'8"	Jr.	—	—	—	—	—	—
Silester Rivers	F	6'6"	Fr.	—	—	—	—	—	—
Steve Walston	F/C	6'8"	Jr.	—	—	—	—	—	—

ARKANSAS

Conference: Southeastern   **1994-95 NCAAs:** 5-1
1994-95: 32-7, T-1st SEC West   **Coach:** Nolan Richardson (371-119)

Opening Line: The Razorbacks learned just what goes into defending an NCAA championship last year. The Hogs were drilled by Massachusetts early in the season and lost to the likes of Mississippi State and Auburn in SEC play. The pattern continued in the NCAA Tournament with three close calls. Now it's a new era, with a busload of prize recruits replacing the school's top six scorers.

Guard: For so long, the Hogs were defined by Corey Beck's toughness. That luxury is no longer afforded them as Beck as well as Alex Dillard and Clint McDaniel have moved on. Of the fresh faces, the top candidate at lead guard is Kareem Reid. This dynamic leader needs only to remain under control to prosper. Jesse Pate is the front-runner at off guard thanks to superior scoring tools. Freshman Marlon Towns should be a factor too.

Forward: The most notable arrival is McDonald's All-American Derek Hood. The 6'8" product of Kansas City is an efficient scorer with a quality jumper. He gets first crack at Scotty Thurman's old small-forward post. Holdover Landis Williams will be one of those attempting to fill the void created by Corliss Williamson's exit. He'll be pushed by Nick Davis and Sunday Adebayo.

Center: This is the one spot where Richardson can call on some familiar faces. Juniors Lee Wilson and Darnell Robinson shared the position last year. Neither delivered on his potential. Wilson was undone by injuries while Robinson spun his wheels. Robinson in particular could be a major force if he bolsters his defense and loses his propensity for taking jumpers beyond his range.

Analysis: Program sales will be at an all-time high in Bud Walton Arena. There are ten newcomers on the roster attempting to make Hog fans forget the core of a unit that went to two NCAA championship games. Theirs is a daunting task. Yet this is the top recruiting class in the country, and one gets the sense that Richardson will enjoy the underdog role he'll experience in 1995-96.

1995-96 ROSTER

	POS	HT	YR	FGP	FTP	3-PT	RPG	APG	PPG
Darnell Robinson	C	6'11"	Jr.	.41	.44	14/40	3.8	0.9	6.4
Lee Wilson	C	6'11"	Jr.	.67	.52	—	2.4	0.3	4.1
Landis Williams	F	6'7"	So.	.64	.70	0/2	1.1	0.3	2.9
Sunday Adebayo	F	6'6"	Jr.	—	—	—	—	—	—
Pat Bradley	G	6'2"	Fr.	—	—	—	—	—	—
Nicky Davis	F	6'9"	So.	—	—	—	—	—	—
Derek Hood	F	6'8"	Fr.	—	—	—	—	—	—
Jesse Pate	G	6'4"	Jr.	—	—	—	—	—	—
Kareem Reid	G	5'10"	Fr.	—	—	—	—	—	—
Marcus Saxon	G	6'2"	Jr.	—	—	—	—	—	—
Ali Thompson	F	6'5"	Fr.	—	—	—	—	—	—
Marlon Towns	G	6'4"	Fr.	—	—	—	—	—	—

BRIGHAM YOUNG

Conference: Western Athletic   **1994-95 NCAAs:** 0-1
1994-95: 22-10, T-2nd WAC   **Coach:** Roger Reid (136-58)

Opening Line: It has become a rite of spring: When the NCAA Tournament committee announces its field, the BYU Cougars are located in the middle part of a regional bracket. Last year, BYU was awarded an eighth seed in the Southeast Region, where it fell to Tulane in the first round. The school has posted six straight 20-win seasons and appears primed to add another in 1995-96.

Guard: Skeptics sniggered when coach Reid chose sons Randy and Robbie as his starters last year. Yet the younger Reids were sound, delivering competent ball-handling, skilled passing, and long-range accuracy. Robbie, off on a church mission, will miss this season. Randy, the older of the two blonde bombers, will go it alone at off guard. He'll be asked to score more. Freshman Todd Christensen will take Robbie's place.

Forward: The graduated Russell Larson brought size and shooting touch inside. Newcomers Bryon Ruffner and Nathan Cooper will see action in Larson's stead. Sophomores Grant Berges and Justin Weidauer are thin but will get a crack at the starting lineup. Ruffner, a junior college import, probably has a slight edge. Kenneth Roberts, a 6'6" senior, is most comfortable at center but will see more action at power forward if Reid's young centers develop.

Center: Roberts is the guts of this team. He relishes the challenge of defending taller men and scores often around the basket. He's not pretty, but he's vital to the Cougars. Cory Reader transferred, while Bret Jepsen left on a mission.

Analysis: The Cougars aren't going to overwhelm foes with their open-court skill. However, they play sharp basketball, beat the teams they are supposed to beat, and defend with vigor. There's no doubt that the added maturity some of their players gain while on church missions helps. This edition will continue the tradition and—if they overcome a thinned-out roster—will reach postseason play.

1995-96 ROSTER

	POS	HT	YR	FGP	FTP	3-PT	RPG	APG	PPG
Kenneth Roberts	C/F	6'6"	Sr.	.56	.84	2/3	6.6	1.5	15.4
Randy Reid	G	6'2"	Sr.	.37	.85	30/91	2.6	2.8	8.6
Jeff Campbell	F	6'9"	Jr.	.58	.64	—	1.7	0.4	3.0
Grant Berges	F	6'8"	So.	.43	.71	2/10	1.0	0.1	1.8
Bryan Hofheins	G	5'10"	Sr.	.50	—	0/1	0.1	0.1	0.3
Matt Lohner	G	6'1"	Jr.	—	—	0/1	0.2	0.2	—
Lance Archibald	G	6'3"	Fr.	—	—	—	—	—	—
Todd Christensen	G	6'1"	Fr.	—	—	—	—	—	—
Nathan Cooper	G	6'5"	Fr.	—	—	—	—	—	—
Bryon Ruffner	F	6'6"	Jr.	—	—	—	—	—	—
Jay Thompson	C	6'8"	Sr.	—	—	—	—	—	—
Justin Weidauer	F	6'7"	So.	—	—	—	—	—	—

CALIFORNIA

Conference: Pac-10
1994-95: 13-14, T-8th Pac-10

1994-95 NCAAs/NIT: DNP
Coach: Todd Bozeman (46-24)

Opening Line: After losing only ten times in Bozeman's first 43 games as head coach, the Golden Bears fell upon hard times in 1994-95. The loss of top NBA draft choices Jason Kidd and Lamond Murray doomed the Golden Bears to the depths of the Pac-10. However, there were hints of promise from underclassmen like Tremaine Fowlkes and Jelani Gardner, two of the top freshman in America.

Guard: Four guards made more than ten starts in the backcourt as Bozeman never could settle on a set pair. All are back with the exception of K.J. Roberts, who transferred. Randy Duck is a bundle of determination but didn't make his shots from the perimeter often enough last year. Moreover, Gardner and Anwar McQueen converted only 41 percent of their attempts from the floor. Fewer turnovers and improved marksmanship are musts here.

Forward: Monty Buckley, Cal's most viable outside threat, has exited, so the focus turns to athletic sophomore Fowlkes and top freshman prospect Shareef Abdur-Rahim. Both thrive in the transition game and can alter shots. Tony Gonzalez brings a willingness to rebound off the bench.

Center: This is a spot where Cal also suffered. Incumbent Michael Stewart got few chances to score and often found himself on the sidelines in the second half. He must be more cognizant of his role, focusing primarily on rebounding and interior defense. Injuries have hampered Alfred Grigsby, yet his experience and rebounding could be invaluable plusses.

Analysis: It was a strange year for the Bears, with victories at Arizona and Cincinnati and losses at home to Washington and Oregon State. That's the mark of a young team, though, and Bozeman is banking on this club's inherent athletic skill to raise it back into postseason contention. Gardner, Fowlkes, and Abdur-Rahim are a superb foundation to build around. The onus is on the role-players to step it up.

1995-96 ROSTER

	POS	HT	YR	FGP	FTP	3-PT	RPG	APG	PPG
Tremaine Fowlkes	F	6'7"	So.	.45	.64	17/56	6.7	1.0	13.4
Jelani Gardner	G	6'6"	So.	.41	.66	28/80	2.5	6.5	10.7
Randy Duck	G	6'2"	Jr.	.39	.68	38/106	2.0	2.1	9.6
Tony Gonzalez	F	6'6"	So.	.64	.62	—	3.9	0.6	7.1
Alfred Grigsby	F/C	6'9"	Sr.	.68	.59	—	3.4	0.4	6.0
Anwar McQueen	G	6'1"	Jr.	.41	.57	13/40	1.6	1.2	4.2
Michael Stewart	C	6'10"	Jr.	.51	.46	—	4.3	0.3	3.9
Sean Marks	C	6'10"	So.	.51	.54	—	0.7	0.3	3.0
Shareef Abdur-Rahim	F	6'10"	Fr.	—	—	—	—	—	—
Ed Gray	G	6'3"	Jr.	—	—	—	—	—	—
Kenyon Jones	C	6'10"	Fr.	—	—	—	—	—	—
Prentice McGruder	G	6'3"	Jr.	—	—	—	—	—	—

CINCINNATI

Conference: Conference USA   **1994-95 NCAAs:** 1-1
1994-95: 22-12, T-3rd Great Midwest   **Coach:** Bob Huggins (235-104)

Opening Line: The early exit of Dontonio Wingfield after 1993-94 apparently benefitted neither Wingfield (who was not on the Seattle SuperSonics' playoff roster) nor the Bearcats. U.C. needed a late rally in the Great Midwest Conference Tournament to ensure a ticket to the NCAA Tournament. Inconsistency from a young cast was a problem.

Guard: Keith LeGree arrived last year to assume control of the point-guard slot. He displayed many of the same qualities he showed in his first two seasons at Louisville—scoring punch, inconsistent perimeter shooting, and a few too many turnovers. The other guard spot belongs to Damon Flint, a versatile slasher. Flint is an excellent passer who finishes plays with a flourish. Freshman Melvin Levett, another athletic scorer, will see plenty of action in a reserve capacity, and junior college product Marcus Moss will spell LeGree.

Forward: The much anticipated arrival of Danny Fortson eased the pain of Wingfield's loss. A gifted scorer, Fortson was willing to mix it up inside and gifted enough to complete scores. Sophomore Bobby Brannen uses his active body to contribute off the glass. He possesses a solid mid-range jumper. Small forward Keith Gregor is willing to scrap for loose balls and defend tenaciously.

Center: Huggins likes a shot-blocker in the middle, and senior Arthur Long is that. He and Fortson were involved in an off-court incident that placed his future at Cincinnati in some doubt. He has value to the Cats and the guess was he would retain his eligibility.

Analysis: After a trip to the Final Four in 1992 and a visit to the Final Eight in 1993, Cincinnati has leveled off to some degree. The Bearcats are a successful program that has a tough time luring the kind of dominant center needed to annually challenge for the national title. However, life is much better than it was prior to Huggins's arrival, and it's going to stay that way.

1995-96 ROSTER

	POS	HT	YR	FGP	FTP	3-PT	RPG	APG	PPG
Danny Fortson	F	6'7"	So.	.54	.68	0/1	7.6	1.1	15.1
Art Long	C	6'8"	Sr.	.52	.55	1/5	8.3	1.3	12.2
Damon Flint	G	6'5"	Jr.	.40	.62	27/92	2.2	2.5	7.0
Keith LeGree	G	6'0"	Sr.	.42	.54	2/13	2.4	4.5	6.6
Bobby Brannen	F	6'7"	So.	.52	.68	—	1.8	0.5	2.6
Keith Gregor	F	6'5"	Sr.	.44	.58	1/11	1.7	1.5	2.3
Terrence Davis	G	6'2"	Jr.	—	—	—	—	—	—
Ryan Fletcher	F	6'8"	Fr.	—	—	—	—	—	—
Jackson Julson	F	6'9"	So.	—	—	—	—	—	—
Melvin Levett	G	6'4"	Fr.	—	—	—	—	—	—
Rodrick Monroe	F	6'6"	Jr.	—	—	—	—	—	—
Marcus Moss	G	5'10"	Jr.	—	—	—	—	—	—

CLEMSON

Conference: Atlantic Coast
1994-95: 15-13, T-6th ACC

1994-95 NIT: 0-1
Coach: Rick Barnes (143-99)

Opening Line: Last year, new coach Rick Barnes cleared a few psychological barriers for a program that's accustomed to struggling in the ACC. There was a victory at Duke in the ACC opener and an aggressive attitude that drew notice in some rival quarters, most notably North Carolina. Barnes and Dean Smith got into a heated exchange during the ACC Tournament as Smith complained about a hard foul committed by Iker Iturbe. A young cast should benefit from the lessons of 1994-95.

Guard: Clemson's best hope for tomorrow is a promising tandem of Merl Code and Greg Buckner. Code directs the offense. He's a competent scorer with good quickness and ball-handling skills. Buckner is a versatile athlete with a knack for scoring. He can be a terrific defender too. Bill Harder contributes off the bench.

Forward: The Tigers sorely lacked size and Barnes addressed that in his recruiting. Andrius Jurkunas has a strong perimeter game, while 6'8" Harold Jamison likes to mix it up inside. Both will log heavy minutes as rookies. Freshman Tony Christie is an athletic wing player who will also receive a shot at the small-forward post. Classmate Patrick Garner may contribute in a reserve capacity.

Center: With Devin Gray out last year, Iker Iturbe was thrown into the void at center, although he's a natural forward. Iturbe scored well around the basket but had trouble with imposing foes like Rasheed Wallace and Tim Duncan. He'll probably slide back to forward with Jamison or Garner logging the most minutes in the middle.

Analysis: To judge by the record, there wasn't much progress made in Barnes's debut. However, that's a bit misleading. The Tigers' coach instilled a defensive discipline that was missing under Cliff Ellis. In the off-season, he went about correcting Clemson's talent shortfall, landing one of the top ten classes in America. Time is needed for experience, but Clemson is on the right track.

1995-96 ROSTER

	POS	HT	YR	FGP	FTP	3-PT	RPG	APG	PPG
Greg Buckner	G/F	6'4"	So.	.53	.51	13/44	5.9	2.1	12.0
Merl Code	G	6'2"	Jr.	.41	.81	40/121	3.8	4.0	11.8
Bill Harder	G	6'0"	Jr.	.46	.80	23/57	2.1	3.1	8.0
Iker Iturbe	F/C	6'7"	So.	.47	.60	16/45	3.8	2.0	6.5
Danny Johnson	G	6'3"	So.	.23	.78	0/15	1.0	0.3	0.9
Tony Christie	F	6'7"	Fr.	—	—	—	—	—	—
Patrick Garner	F/C	6'9"	Fr.	—	—	—	—	—	—
Harold Jamison	F/C	6'8"	Fr.	—	—	—	—	—	—
Ledarion Jones	F	6'6"	Fr.	—	—	—	—	—	—
Andrius Jurkunas	F	6'9"	Fr.	—	—	—	—	—	—
Terrell McIntyre	G	5'8"	Fr.	—	—	—	—	—	—
Tom Wideman	C	6'10"	Fr.	—	—	—	—	—	—

CONNECTICUT

Conference: Big East
1994-95: 28-5, 1st Big East

1994-95 NCAAs: 3-1
Coach: Jim Calhoun (440-233)

Opening Line: Long a national-title dreamer, this program has developed the substance to go with the hype. UConn has dominated Big East regular-season play in each of the past two seasons, losing just four league games in that stretch. The Huskies also earned their first No. 1 ranking in February and fell to eventual champion UCLA in the West Regional final of the NCAA Tournament. Graduation losses will hurt but the recruiting class is one of America's finest.

Guard: Had Doron Sheffer opted to return to Israel, this area could have presented a serious problem for coach Jim Calhoun. Sheffer and Kevin Ollie gave the Huskies two capable quarterbacks and the loss of both would have been a major blow. As it is, Sheffer is back. His presence allows 6'2" freshman slasher Ricky Moore to develop at his own pace. Another key figure is Rashamel Jones, a 6'5" wing rookie who loves the transition game UConn plays.

Forward: An enormous talent, Ray Allen could be on the verge of a superb season. This tremendous athlete sets the tone for the Huskies with his shooting, ball-handling, and passing. He'll see time here and at off guard. Rudy Johnson is a bruising defender who understands his role and must now step forward as a leader. Veteran Kirk King is a quality rebounder. He has an early edge on Antric Klaiber and Sam Funches, two incoming freshmen with tools.

Center: For two seasons, Travis Knight was something of an enigma to Husky fans who had expected a dominant pivot when he arrived from Utah. Knight's not that, yet he has become a reliable starting center. A soft shooting touch around the goal makes him a factor. Eric Hayward provides a different look as a backup.

Analysis: Connecticut will be hard-pressed to continue its dominance of the Big East. The competition is better and UConn is young. However, the Huskies don't figure to fall far. Calhoun's system is sound and the new prospects don't have to be stars. That's Allen's task.

1995-96 ROSTER

	POS	HT	YR	FGP	FTP	3-PT	RPG	APG	PPG
Ray Allen	G/F	6'5"	Jr.	.49	.73	85/191	6.8	2.3	21.1
Doron Sheffer	G	6'5"	Sr.	.40	.75	38/104	4.7	5.5	11.1
Travis Knight	C	7'0"	Sr.	.56	.65	—	8.2	1.2	9.1
Kirk King	F	6'8"	Jr.	.51	.71	0/1	2.7	0.2	3.2
Eric Hayward	C/F	6'7"	Sr.	.65	.69	—	2.3	0.3	3.0
Rudy Johnson	F	6'6"	Sr.	.48	.58	4/12	1.4	0.5	2.6
Ruslan Inyatkin	F	6'7"	So.	.40	—	0/1	0.8	0.2	0.6
Dion Carson	G	6'3"	Jr.	—	—	—	—	—	—
Sam Funches	F	6'8"	Fr.	—	—	—	—	—	—
Rashamel Jones	G/F	6'5"	Fr.	—	—	—	—	—	—
Antric Klaiber	F	6'10"	Fr.	—	—	—	—	—	—
Ricky Moore	G	6'2"	Fr.	—	—	—	—	—	—

DUKE

Conference: Atlantic Coast
1994-95: 13-18, 9th ACC

1994-95 NCAAs/NIT: DNP
Coach: Mike Krzyzewski (435-201)

Opening Line: That crash you heard was the Duke empire falling upon hard times. One year after reaching the NCAA final (their seventh Final Four appearance in nine seasons), Duke sank to ninth in the ACC. The season was marred by a slow recovery from back surgery that forced Mike Krzyzewski off the sidelines in early January and a string of tight losses. Krzyzewski has his health back and is eager to prove that last winter was an aberration.

Guard: The Bobby Hurley era probably spoiled Duke fans. It became an assumption that any point guard who dons the uniform would make sharp decisions. Jeff Capel struggled in that role, forcing passes and applying little of the defensive pressure foes had come to expect from Duke. Steve Wojciechowski appears to be a step slow, and Chris Collins has never become a consistent performer. The most reliable threat here is Trajan Langdon, a stealth-like scorer.

Forward: Billed as the next Grant Hill, Ricky Price demonstrated that he has an imposing collection of athletic moves. He's not Hill, though, and it's unfair to expect him to be. The power-forward post is a dilemma for Krzyzewski. Joey Beard and Greg Newton were supposed to be ready now but presently offer little. Beard transferred to Boston University and Newton's status is unclear after a charge of academic dishonesty was lodged against him.

Center: For all of his critics, the fact is that Cherokee Parks was a first-round NBA draft choice and there's no apparent successor. Freshman whiz Taymon Domzalski gets first crack at the assignment. Great instincts and a splendid shooting touch give him a chance to be special.

Analysis: Fact is, Duke earned its spot in the ACC basement. This group is not nearly as athletic as its predecessors and it doesn't have a clear offensive leader. Krzyzewski's coaching acumen should get the Blue Devils back into the NCAA Tournament, but it's unrealistic to anticipate much more.

1995-96 ROSTER

	POS	HT	YR	FGP	FTP	3-PT	RPG	APG	PPG
Jeff Capel	G	6'5"	Jr.	.45	.64	63/137	2.7	4.1	12.5
Trajan Langdon	G	6'4"	So.	.45	.79	59/138	2.1	1.5	11.3
Ricky Price	F	6'6"	So.	.47	.68	13/41	3.3	1.0	8.1
Steve Wojciechowski	G	5'11"	So.	.34	.58	27/76	1.4	2.9	4.0
Greg Newton	F/C	6'11"	Jr.	.66	.47	—	3.4	0.2	4.0
Chris Collins	G	6'3"	Sr.	.30	.77	17/73	1.1	1.7	3.9
Tony Moore	F	6'8"	Sr.	.67	.74	—	2.1	0.5	2.7
Carmen Wallace	F	6'6"	Jr.	.50	.71	2/5	1.1	0.2	1.9
Stan Brunson	F	6'6"	Sr.	—	—	—	—	—	—
Matt Christensen	F	6'10"	Fr.	—	—	—	—	—	—
Taymon Domzalski	C	6'10"	Fr.	—	—	—	—	—	—
Todd Singleton	F	6'5"	So.	—	—	—	—	—	—

FLORIDA

Conference: Southeastern
1994-95: 17-13, 3rd SEC

1994-95 NCAAs: 1-1
Coach: Lon Kruger (225-169)

Opening Line: Seven short months after reaching its highest hoops point at the 1994 Final Four, Florida encountered the dark side of fame. Expectations rose and the Gators weren't prepared to deal with them. It took a late surge just to reach the NCAA Tournament. The good news is that those lofty expectations have diminished greatly as we prepare for 1995-96, and the talent level is not that different from what it was at the close of 1994.

Guard: Dan Cross did not enjoy an outstanding senior season, yet his production won't be quickly replaced—nor will that of athletic Jason Anderson. The spotlight now swings to Cross's former understudy, Greg Williams. His best attribute might be that he values the basketball. Help will come from Oak Hill Academy product Mike McFarland and holdover Dan Williams.

Forward: Two seniors, Brian Thompson and Dametri Hill, have the inside track on starting spots. Yet each is in for a challenge from new personnel. Louisianan Kendrick Spruel is a razor-thin wing player with the kind of superior perimeter skills that will push Thompson. Antrone Lee, 6'7", is another quick forward. Lee is a superb passer. There's also talented sophomore LeRon Williams.

Center: One of the more underrated elements in Gator country was departed center Andrew DeClercq. In his absence, Kruger will look to sophomore Damen Maddox, undersized but bruising, and Greg Cristell, a raw rookie. Another possibility is veteran John Griffiths, a shot-blocking specialist.

Analysis: The season past was a bit of a letdown for Gator fans, but coach Lon Kruger did take advantage of the visibility the Final Four appearance provided by landing a first-rate recruiting class. Lee and Spruel will bring instant offense and strong shooting, two items that were in short supply last year. Hill must emerge as a leader for a young Gator squad.

1995-96 ROSTER

	POS	HT	YR	FGP	FTP	3-PT	RPG	APG	PPG
Dametri Hill	C/F	6'7"	Sr.	.53	.69	7/23	5.9	1.1	13.7
Greg Williams	G	6'2"	Jr.	.42	.78	28/78	2.7	4.0	8.4
Brian Thompson	F	6'6"	Sr.	.42	.51	2/6	3.6	0.8	2.6
LeRon Williams	F	6'7"	So.	.53	.58	—	2.1	0.1	2.6
Dan Williams	G	6'3"	So.	.41	.53	10/25	0.7	0.7	2.2
John Griffiths	C	6'10"	Jr.	.78	.75	—	0.9	—	0.7
Damen Maddox	C	6'8"	So.	.67	.33	—	0.2	—	0.5
Greg Cristell	C	6'10"	Fr.	—	—	—	—	—	—
Antrone Lee	G/F	6'7"	Fr.	—	—	—	—	—	—
Mike McFarland	G	6'3"	Fr.	—	—	—	—	—	—
Eddie Shannon	G	5'11"	Fr.	—	—	—	—	—	—
Kendrick Spruel	F	6'8"	Fr.	—	—	—	—	—	—

FLORIDA STATE

Conference: Atlantic Coast
1994-95: 12-15, 7th ACC

1994-95 NCAAs/NIT: DNP
Coach: Pat Kennedy (293-165)

Opening Line: The Seminoles endured their second consecutive season on the outside looking in at the NCAA Tournament. Entering the season, the hope was that FSU could blend a bountiful crop of newcomers with Bob Sura and make a push for the postseason. However, inconsistency and a so-so year from its star doomed the Seminoles.

Guard: It is said that a point guard sets the tone for an entire offense, and one of the chief reasons for FSU's sporadic play was instability at the position. Coach Pat Kennedy rotated three players at the spot with uneven results. Sophomore LaMarr Greer offers good size and passing but has a difficult time defending quicker point guards. Avery Curry handles that task but is prone to playing out of control. Senior Scott Shepherd seems physically overmatched in the ACC. The uncertainty at the point does nothing to James Collins, the incumbent off guard. This athletic scorer is the primary scoring option with Sura off to pro basketball.

Forward: New faces will alter the Seminoles' frontcourt look. Gentry Sparks, 6'8", was one of the land's most coveted junior college recruits. Athletically gifted, Sparks fits nicely into the kind of freelance style favored by FSU. Corey Louis will hold down the other forward spot. He too is a splendid athlete, fully capable of running the floor and finishing with a slam. Junior Derrick Carroll is a proven scorer.

Center: Kirk Luchman was Andre Reid's backup for two seasons. However, the likelihood is that he will not assume the starting center berth. Plodding by nature, Luchman is no match for freshman signee Randell Jackson.

Analysis: Kennedy is nearing a crossroads at FSU. Consecutive sub-.500 seasons and the revival of strong programs at Maryland, Wake Forest, and possibly Clemson could spell trouble for the Seminoles. However, Kennedy has recruited well and the exit of Sura may be addition by subtraction.

1995-96 ROSTER

	POS	HT	YR	FGP	FTP	3-PT	RPG	APG	PPG
James Collins	G	6'4"	Jr.	.51	.70	72/164	4.3	1.8	18.0
Corey Louis	F	6'9"	So.	.45	.71	1/4	7.8	0.7	10.9
Derrick Carroll	F	6'6"	Jr.	.42	.81	42/112	2.7	0.8	7.8
LaMarr Greer	G	6'5"	So.	.40	.75	24/66	2.9	3.0	5.6
Avery Curry	G	6'2"	So.	.31	.55	14/49	2.8	1.1	3.6
Kirk Luchman	F/C	6'10"	Jr.	.43	.50	—	3.2	0.5	3.5
Scott Shepherd	G	5'11"	Sr.	.41	.80	7/24	1.4	1.3	3.4
Tim Wooden	F	6'11"	Sr.	.53	.60	0/4	1.8	0.4	2.4
Geoff Brower	G	6'4"	Fr.	.17	—	0/5	1.5	0.5	1.0
Randell Jackson	F/C	6'11"	Fr.	—	—	—	—	—	—
Kelvin McClendon	G	6'5"	Jr.	—	—	—	—	—	—
Gentry Sparks	F	6'8"	So.	—	—	—	—	—	—

GEORGETOWN

Conference: Big East
1994-95: 21-10, 4th Big East

1994-95 NCAAs: 2-1
Coach: John Thompson (524-200)

Opening Line: Years of patient, walk-it-up-the-floor basketball were discarded when Allen Iverson arrived on the scene last year. Thompson turned his youthful dynamo loose and mostly liked the results. Suddenly, Georgetown was a much more viable offensive machine than it had been previously in the 1990s. The Hoyas defeated Xavier and Weber State in the NCAA Tournament before falling to North Carolina 74-64 in the round of 16.

Guard: Blessed with superior quickness, Iverson breaks down defenses off the dribble and can make long shots too. As he learns to spot his open mates, he'll make the Hoyas more dangerous. Thompson used a variety of partners with Iverson. Two, Eric Myles and Jerry Nichols, will see significant minutes this year. Both must upgrade their defense.

Forward: If Iverson's burst was expected, Jerome Williams's was not. Williams gained Thompson's trust with stellar defense and excellent rebounding. Like Williams, Boubacar Aw is raw offensively but a superb athlete who can keep up with the faster pace. His defense stood him in good stead. Cheikh Dia fits the same mold and will be in the rotation. Former prep star Jahidi White is suited to the halfcourt game, yet he could earn some of departed Don Reid's minutes.

Center: Othella Harrington never adapted to the up-tempo style and his game suffered for it. At times, he appeared lost on the floor. When Iverson matures, he'll understand there are times when a post-up game like Harrington's has value. As for Harrington, he must expand his offensive repertoire and not allow his offense to affect his defense.

Analysis: The Hoyas don't have a lot of shot-makers, but the quickened pace allows them to score more by beating teams down the court. Iverson's an All-American. As he develops, he'll draw more attention and open lanes for others. It's a different Georgetown than we've seen, but the changes are for the better.

1995-96 ROSTER

	POS	HT	YR	FGP	FTP	3-PT	RPG	APG	PPG
Allen Iverson	G	6'0"	So.	.39	.69	35/151	3.3	4.5	20.4
Othella Harrington	C/F	6'9"	Sr.	.56	.71	0/1	6.0	0.8	12.2
Jerome Williams	F/G	6'9"	Sr.	.50	.63	2/11	10.0	1.5	10.9
Eric Myles	G	5'10"	So.	.37	.56	34/85	0.7	0.8	5.3
Boubacar Aw	F	6'7"	So.	.52	.58	—	2.5	0.9	4.0
Jahidi White	F/C	6'9"	So.	.43	.37	—	1.8	0.1	2.3
Cheikh Dia	F/C	6'10"	Jr.	.44	1.00	—	1.8	0.3	1.6
Jerry Nichols	G	6'4"	So.	.26	.57	0/10	0.5	0.5	1.2
Daymond Jackson	G/F	6'4"	Fr.	—	—	—	—	—	—
Godwin Owinje	F	6'8"	Jr.	—	—	—	—	—	—
Joseph Toumou	G	6'1"	Fr.	—	—	—	—	—	—
Jameel Watkins	C	6'10"	Fr.	—	—	—	—	—	—

GEORGE WASHINGTON

Conference: Atlantic 10   **1994-95 NIT:** 0-1
1994-95: 18-14, T-2nd A-10   **Coach:** Mike Jarvis (193-110)

Opening Line: With CBS cameras looking on last March, coach Mike Jarvis and his Colonial team got the bad news on Selection Sunday that the school would not receive its third consecutive NCAA Tournament bid. George Washington was on the cusp of an invitation, but some damaging losses to foes with low power ratings sabotaged the effort. On a more upbeat note, G.W. did weather the loss of star pivot Yinka Dare with style.

Guard: One guard spot is secure. It belongs to Kwame Evans, a 6'7" scorer with great range on his jump shot. He'll have every opportunity to assert himself as the chief scoring option. The question is, who will set him up? Shawnta Rogers, a 5'4" dynamo, is the point guard of tomorrow, and Jarvis is hopeful he will be the point guard of today. As of late summer, though, Rogers struggled to maintain eligibility. Another option is 6'0" Rasheed Hazzard, the son of former UCLA great Walt Hazzard.

Forward: Nimbo Hammons was an anchor here for the majority of his college career. With his departure, Jarvis's options shrink. If someone emerges in the backcourt, Evans could slide to Hammons's old spot. Senior Vaughn Jones will control the other forward post. He's not really a power player, either. Look for 6'10" Ferdinand Williams and 7'0" Andrei Sviridov to see action at the power forward slot.

Center: To the astonishment of most observers, Jarvis found a capable replacement for Dare instantly. Alexander Koul, a 7'1", 265-pounder, brings strength and power to the middle. In many ways, he was more consistent than Dare had been, though he is not the defensive presence his predecessor was. Koul will continue to flourish, thanks to a solid fundamental base and soft shooting touch.

Analysis: Though many suspected G.W.'s ascension was tied to Dare, 1994-95 illustrated that this program is much more than an individual. Despite the NCAA Tournament snub, G.W. is in good shape. It possesses balance and scoring skill within a quality system. Depth is an issue, but otherwise the Colonials seem set to prove that last winter was an interruption, nothing more.

1995-96 ROSTER

	POS	HT	YR	FGP	FTP	3-PT	RPG	APG	PPG
Kwame Evans	G	6'7"	Sr.	.42	.72	74/225	5.7	2.4	19.4
Alexander Koul	C	7'1"	So.	.63	.58	—	6.6	0.5	12.8
Vaughn Jones	F/G	6'5"	Sr.	.44	.72	22/56	5.2	3.4	12.8
Darin Green	F	6'5"	So.	.21	.67	1/3	0.6	0.3	1.0
Ferdinand Williams	F	6'10"	Jr.	.40	—	—	0.8	—	0.5
Rasheed Hazzard	G	6'0"	So.	.25	.67	1/3	0.1	0.2	0.4
Andrei Sviridov	F/C	7'0"	So.	—	—	—	0.3	—	—
J.J. Brade	F	6'4"	Fr.	—	—	—	—	—	—

GEORGIA

Conference: Southeastern
1994-95: 18-10, 2nd SEC East

1994-95 NIT: 0-1
Coach: Tubby Smith (79-43)

Opening Line: Last year was to be a trial of sorts for longtime Bulldog coach Hugh Durham. If he failed to reach the NCAA Tournament, Durham's 17-year career would have likely been over. The Bulldogs' near miss was not enough to save Durham. In steps coach Tubby Smith, the architect of Tulsa's consecutive appearances in the NCAA's Sweet 16. A veteran core gives him the opportunity to make an impact quickly.

Guard: An athletic group, the Bulldogs much prefer operating in transition and slashing to the goal to arching 3's. This applies to seniors Katu Davis and Shandon Anderson. Davis is a competent ball-handler who can beat defenders off the dribble. Versatility and multiple skills are Anderson's trademarks. Lefty Pertha Robinson offers exceptional playmaking skills. Freshman Michael Chadwick, 6'4", will log many minutes if he's consistent, for Smith likes to use his bench.

Forward: Steve Jones is much like the other Bulldogs—quick, athletic, and shaky when shooting from deep. His experience and suitability for Smith's system will make him a major factor. At the other forward position is senior Carlos Strong. One of Smith's primary goals is to convince Strong he can dominate. At a chiseled 6'8", 230 pounds, Strong has the goods to wreak havoc in the lane.

Center: Finally, the Charles Claxton watch is complete. The talented pivot never quite completed the climb that his potential suggested was possible. Filling Claxton's shoes is Terrell Bell, a 6'10" senior. Bell is a defensive menace. His shot-blocking gives the Bulldogs interior defensive strength.

Analysis: The ranks are thin, and the Bulldogs' perimeter shooting woes make them vulnerable to zone defenses. Yet Smith is a superb motivator and the energy supplied by the new coaching staff will be a major boost for this program, which had lapsed into mediocrity. An NCAA Tournament bid would be the school's first in five seasons.

1995-96 ROSTER

	POS	HT	YR	FGP	FTP	3-PT	RPG	APG	PPG
Carlos Strong	F	6'8"	Sr.	.47	.68	9/25	6.9	1.3	14.2
Shandon Anderson	F/G	6'6"	Sr.	.47	.59	17/53	5.2	3.0	13.3
Katu Davis	G	6'2"	Sr.	.42	.82	24/83	3.3	2.1	11.0
Pertha Robinson	G	6'1"	Sr.	.37	.71	20/66	4.0	6.3	6.1
Terrell Bell	C/F	6'10"	Sr.	.52	.58	1/2	3.2	0.3	3.7
Steve Jones	F/G	6'6"	Sr.	.53	.70	0/4	2.0	0.9	3.4
Brian Peterson	G	6'3"	Sr.	.44	1.00	4/5	0.5	0.3	2.0
Kris Nordholz	G	5'10"	Sr.	.50	.50	1/4	0.4	0.7	1.0
Michael Chadwick	G	6'4"	Fr.	—	—	—	—	—	—
Ray Harrison	G	6'3"	Fr.	—	—	—	—	—	—
Jon Nordin	F	6'8"	Fr.	—	—	—	—	—	—
Orlando Smith	G	5'11"	Fr.	—	—	—	—	—	—

GEORGIA TECH

Conference: Atlantic Coast   **1994-95 NCAAs/NIT:** DNP
1994-95: 18-12, 5th ACC   **Coach:** Bobby Cremins (374-230)

Opening Line: Based on its record, Tech should have made last year's NCAA Tournament. However, a late-season slump and an uninspired loss to Virginia in the opening round of the ACC Tournament soured the NCAA tourney selection committee on Georgia Tech. The Yellow Jackets were left off the NCAA's guest list and they subsequently declined an NIT bid. This year, they'll attempt to break the pattern of near misses with several key veterans and a coveted rookie.

Guard: As a youngster, Stephon Marbury worshipped fellow New Yorker Kenny Anderson. Now Marbury's assignment is to replace Anderson's replacement, Travis Best. Marbury brings a complete package of skills to the table, including excellent perimeter-shooting skills. He needs only to remain intense at all times to flourish. Off guard Drew Barry provides leadership and fine all-around skills.

Forward: Although not highly touted, Matt Harpring emerged as a starter and perhaps the most consistent newcomer in the ACC last year. Wise beyond his years, Harpring offers a wide range of skills. Michael Maddox served as James Forrest's backup and now gets first crack at the power-forward berth. Another possibility is freshman Juan Gaston, who can contribute off the glass. Rookie Gary Saunders is an athletic wing type who can also help at off guard.

Center: Coach Bobby Cremins likens Eddie Elisma to former Georgia Tech star John Salley. Elisma lacks great offensive tools but will alter shots and do the obligatory dirty work. Like Salley, Elisma is thin, and that's a problem when he's confronted with powerful pivots. Cremins likes Bucky Hodge's potential too.

Analysis: There was a bad taste in people's mouths in Atlanta after Georgia Tech slipped late in the season. The Yellow Jackets underachieved, again, and it kept them out of the NCAA Tournament. It's time for some new energy, and the guess is that the electric Marbury will provide it.

1995-96 ROSTER

	POS	HT	YR	FGP	FTP	3-PT	RPG	APG	PPG
Drew Barry	G	6'5"	Sr.	.51	.75	50/117	4.9	6.7	13.4
Matt Harpring	G/F	6'7"	So.	.48	.74	28/73	6.2	2.3	12.1
Michael Maddox	F	6'8"	So.	.45	.57	26/68	4.51	1.2	9.1
Eddie Elisma	F/C	6'9"	Jr.	.52	.51	—	5.0	0.5	5.8
C.J. Williams	G	6'2"	Jr.	.49	.81	8/27	1.3	0.8	3.7
Bryan Brennan	G	6'4"	So.	.39	1.00	3/12	0.5	0.32	2.1
Bucky Hodge	F/C	6'9"	So.	.32	.75	1/2	1.4	0.21	1.1
Ryan Murphy	G	6'3"	So.	.25	.50	1/2	0.3	0.1	0.4
Juan Gaston	F	6'7"	Fr.	—	—	—	—	—	—
Stephon Marbury	G	6'1"	Fr.	—	—	—	—	—	—
Gary Saunders	G/F	6'5"	Fr.	—	—	—	—	—	—
Ajani Williams	F	6'8"	Fr.	—	—	—	—	—	—

ILLINOIS

Conference: Big Ten
1994-95: 19-12, T-5th Big Ten

1994-95 NCAAs: 0-1
Coach: Lou Henson (645-318)

Opening Line: The Fighting Illini were a young team in 1994-95 and it showed. Bouts of inconsistency held a talented unit back in a year in which there was no dominant team in the Big Ten. This year's edition, built around All-Big Ten pick Kiwane Garris, seems ready to contend for the upper division of the conference.

Guard: There can be no argument that Garris is the Fighting Illini's main man. One has to look no further than the court, where Garris constantly draws double-teams. A sweet shooting season from Richard Keene would help alleviate the pressure on Garris. Keene has never delivered on the promise he showed in high school. Bryant Notree is an athletic option as the third guard.

Forward: After a freshman campaign of tantalizing hope, Jerry Hester leveled off in 1994-95. Excellent in transition, Hester was too often stymied when the game slowed to a half-court tempo. If his jumper from medium range is reliable, he can be dangerous. Sophomore Jerry Gee, once a valued recruit himself, offered glimpses of a fine power game. However, he'll get a strong push from Ryan Blackwell, a 6'8" star from Pittsford, New York. Blackwell runs the floor well and is very smooth at the offensive end.

Center: The departed Shelly Clark was a disappointment in the middle, yet there's no obvious replacement on hand. The duty probably will fall to Chris Gandy, a natural power forward whose strength is rebounding. Brett Robisch, 6'11", is a raw prospect who will get a chance too.

Analysis: Critics charged that the Fighting Illini underachieved in 1994-95, and to some extent they did. Illinois was never able to challenge the top teams in the conference, largely because it didn't find enough help for Garris. The onus is now on men like Hester and Keene to regain the momentum of the early stages of their respective careers so that foes can't hound Garris.

1995-96 ROSTER

	POS	HT	YR	FGP	FTP	3-PT	RPG	APG	PPG
Kiwane Garris	G	6'2"	Jr.	.44	.83	46/119	2.8	3.8	15.9
Richard Keene	G	6'6"	Sr.	.38	.66	63/173	3.8	3.6	10.9
Jerry Hester	F	6'6"	Jr.	.46	.53	38/94	4.8	1.9	10.8
Jerry Gee	F	6'8"	So.	.46	.64	—	3.4	0.2	6.0
Chris Gandy	F	6'9"	Jr.	.55	.75	2/6	2.2	—	3.1
Kevin Turner	G	6'2"	So.	.33	.41	14/38	0.7	0.6	2.7
Bryant Notree	G	6'4"	So.	.36	.30	2/12	2.1	0.5	2.6
Brian Johnson	F	6'6"	So.	.55	.71	1/5	1.0	0.4	2.1
Brett Robisch	C	6'11"	So.	.59	.25	1/5	0.7	—	1.3
Matt Heldman	G	6'0"	So.	.30	.86	0/2	0.6	0.2	0.9
Ryan Blackwell	F	6'8"	Fr.	—	—	—	—	—	—
Willie Coleman	G	6'1"	Fr.	—	—	—	—	—	—

INDIANA

Conference: Big Ten   **1994-95 NCAAs:** 0-1
1994-95: 19-12, T-3rd Big Ten   **Coach:** Bob Knight (659-235)

Opening Line: In truth, the Hoosiers' 1994-95 fortunes began to unravel in the 1994 NCAA Tournament. When Sherron Wilkerson crashed to the court at the USAir Arena with a broken leg, it left a gaping hole in the Indiana backcourt that was never adequately filled. Without solid guard play last year, the Hoosiers never managed to exploit their superior frontcourt.

Guard: Among last year's ballyhooed freshman class, 6'2" Neil Reed was the most productive. He proved capable of directing the offense while making enough jumpers to keep defenses honest. Wilkerson is expected back, though no one is quite sure how effective he'll be. Prior to the injury, he was beginning to assert himself offensively. Steve Hart will be a factor, especially if he improves his perimeter jumper, as will newcomer Chris Rowles.

Forward: As dependable as Alan Henderson was throughout his career, he never became the kind of dominant force Calbert Cheaney was in his final two seasons. Certainly Brian Evans does not possess the kind of ability needed to control a game. Yet he is a fifth-year senior with a sharp shooting eye who will be asked to lead. Sophomore Andrae Patterson steps in for Henderson. Consistency, particularly on the backboards, is a key for this gifted Texan. Junior college imports Louis Moore and Haris Mujezinovic could step forward in reserve roles, and athletic Charlie Miller still has tons of potential at small forward.

Center: Todd Lindeman is not destined for the All-America awards banquet. He's very mechanical and gets pushed around inside. However, he's got a soft shooting touch and knows his limitations. Frosh Larry Richardson will caddy for him.

Analysis: There is no larger hurdle to clear than shaky guard play, even for a coach as accomplished as Bob Knight. If Reed develops and Wilkerson returns to form, the Hoosiers will regain much of the luster that was lost in 1994-95.

1995-96 ROSTER

	POS	HT	YR	FGP	FTP	3-PT	RPG	APG	PPG
Brian Evans	F	6'8"	Sr.	.46	.78	58/139	6.7	3.3	17.4
Andrae Patterson	F	6'8"	So.	.49	.69	4/8	3.9	0.8	7.3
Neil Reed	G	6'2"	So.	.38	.67	22/71	1.7	2.5	5.9
Charlie Miller	F/G	6'7"	So.	.47	.62	8/15	2.8	0.8	5.6
Todd Lindeman	C	7'0"	Sr.	.49	.57	—	3.1	0.4	4.9
Steve Hart	G	6'3"	Jr.	.46	.69	3/13	2.3	1.4	4.7
Richard Mandeville	C	7'0"	So.	—	—	—	—	—	—
Lou Moore	F/G	6'7"	So.	—	—	—	—	—	—
Haris Mujezinovic	F	6'9"	Jr.	—	—	—	—	—	—
Larry Richardson	F/C	6'9"	Fr.	—	—	—	—	—	—
Chris Rowles	G	6'1"	So.	—	—	—	—	—	—
Sherron Wilkerson	G	6'4"	So.	—	—	—	—	—	—

IOWA

Conference: Big Ten
1994-95: 21-12, T-7th Big Ten

1994-95 NIT: 2-1
Coach: Tom Davis (458-250)

Opening Line: A drubbing at the hands of Indiana (110-79) on the final day of the regular season is likely all that separated the Hawkeyes from an NCAA Tournament appearance. There was considerable regret in Iowa City, because prior to the defeat at I.U. the Hawkeyes were playing some of the best basketball in the conference. A major setback came in January when the club lost several close contests as star Jess Settles grappled with back woes.

Guard: Coach Tom Davis rotates a gifted group of players who bring different skills to the proceedings. One-time Nebraska guard Andre Woolridge is a playmaker, capable of steering the offense. Junior Chris Kingsbury is the mad bomber, more comfortable shooting from downtown than he is up close. Mon'ter Glasper is a quality defender who scores in transition.

Forward: When healthy, Settles is one of the most versatile performers in the Midwest. The junior is an excellent shooter from medium range and can make 3's on occasion. Rebounding is another of his strengths. Kenyon Murray isn't the scoring force he was envisioned to be when he arrived here, but he's a first-rate defender and contributes a variety of intangible ingredients. Freshman Alvin Robinson may chip in off the glass.

Center: The Iowa staff feels like it found a sleeper in 6'11" Guy Rucker. Limited offensively, Rucker can provide a shot-blocking presence the Hawkeyes haven't enjoyed in awhile. Russ Millard will see plenty of action here and at power forward. Frosh J.R. Koch gives Davis another big body with promise on the interior.

Analysis: The Hawkeyes appear on the verge of something special. Settles's health is an issue and the guard corps isn't overwhelming. Yet Iowa pressures the ball well and has the kind of front-line skill it needs to make a run at the top of the Big Ten.

1995-96 ROSTER

	POS	HT	YR	FGP	FTP	3-PT	RPG	APG	PPG
Chris Kingsbury	G	6'5"	Jr.	.40	.80	117/297	2.7	1.7	16.8
Jess Settles	F	6'7"	Jr.	.47	.80	32/91	6.2	2.0	15.6
Andre Woolridge	G	6'1"	Jr.	.48	.77	24/62	2.5	5.8	14.0
Kenyon Murray	F	6'5"	Sr.	.46	.59	26/80	4.2	1.2	11.5
Russ Millard	F/C	6'8"	Sr.	.51	.59	4/13	3.3	0.9	5.2
Ryan Bowen	F	6'9"	So.	.53	.59	0/1	4.5	0.5	4.6
Mon'ter Glasper	G	6'2"	Sr.	.44	.51	8/34	1.7	2.4	3.9
Greg Helmers	C	6'10"	So.	.69	.81	—	2.0	0.5	2.1
Trey Bullet	G	6'5"	Fr.	—	—	—	—	—	—
J.R. Koch	F/C	6'10"	Fr.	—	—	—	—	—	—
Alvin Robinson	F	6'9"	Fr.	—	—	—	—	—	—
Guy Rucker	C	6'11"	Fr.	—	—	—	—	—	—

IOWA STATE

Conference: Big Eight   **1994-95 NCAAs:** 1-1
1994-95: 23-11, 5th Big Eight   **Coach:** Tim Floyd (185-94)

Opening Line: Inheriting a veteran unit from his predecessor Johnny Orr, coach Tim Floyd brought a commitment to defense last year that aided the previously freewheeling Cyclones. Led by the veteran trio of Fred Hoiberg, Julius Michalik, and Loren Meyer, Iowa State advanced to the Big Eight Tournament final, where it fell to Oklahoma State, 62-53. Those frontcourt holdovers are gone, and the emphasis is on a crop of newcomers rated tops in the Big Eight by one service.

Guard: Juniors Jason Kimbrough and Jacy Holloway split time at the point-guard spot. Neither scored much, as their job description involved setting up the big three. Kimbrough transferred, so the job is now Holloway's to lose. Two junior college transfers, Shelby Walton and Carlo Walton, will challenge for minutes, especially if they bring more offense to the table. At off guard, junior college product Kenny Pratt has the inside track on another juco graduate, Anthony Mull.

Forward: This is an area of great need. Michalik and Hoiberg were anchors, four-year starters who took the big shots. Shawn Bankhead, a 6'5" wing player, arrives from the College of Southern Idaho. He finishes plays well and can stick the medium-range jumper. Jason Justus, another junior college import, also figures to be a factor, as does Iowa schoolboy star Klay Edwards.

Center: Floyd brought in two seven-footers with the hope that one day they would develop into the kind of dependable pivot Meyer was. That day won't come soon. Tyler Peterson is a bit more advanced than Tony Rampton, yet he has much to learn about positioning.

Analysis: This was a pivotal year for Floyd in terms of replenishing talent. According to the prep sleuths, he did a good job of that. The only negative is that he lured mostly juco products, meaning there will be more holes to fill two years hence. A key will be how quickly the new faces adjust to Floyd's patient system.

1995-96 ROSTER

	POS	HT	YR	FGP	FTP	3-PT	RPG	APG	PPG
Klay Edwards	F	6'6"	Fr.	.67	—	—	4.0	1.0	4.0
Joe Modderman	G	6'9"	Jr.	.42	.68	6/18	0.8	0.2	2.3
Jacy Holloway	G	6'0"	Jr.	.38	.73	0/4	1.3	4.9	1.8
Shawn Bankhead	F	6'5"	Jr.	—	—	—	—	—	—
Kelvin Cato	C	6'11"	Jr.	—	—	—	—	—	—
Jason Justus	F	6'7"	Jr.	—	—	—	—	—	—
Anthony Mull	G	6'4"	Jr.	—	—	—	—	—	—
Tyler Peterson	C	7'0"	Fr.	—	—	—	—	—	—
Kenny Pratt	G/F	6'5"	Jr.	—	—	—	—	—	—
Tony Rampton	C	6'11"	Fr.	—	—	—	—	—	—
Carlo Walton	G	6'0"	Jr.	—	—	—	—	—	—
Shelby Walton	G	5'9"	Jr.	—	—	—	—	—	—

KANSAS

Conference: Big Eight
1994-95: 25-6, 1st Big Eight
1994-95 NCAAs: 2-1
Coach: Roy Williams (184-51)

Opening Line: For the first time in the 1990s, the Jayhawks last year failed to record at least 27 wins. The season could hardly be viewed as a washout, though, as K.U. captured its fifth Big Eight crown of the decade and was the top seed in the Midwest Region of the NCAA Tournament before being felled by Virginia. Only two seniors depart and coach Roy Williams has an All-America caliber point guard to direct his attack.

Guard: It all begins with junior Jacque Vaughn, an intelligent student of the game who sets up his mates with style. The only drawback last year was that an injury to Calvin Rayford robbed Vaughn of an experienced backup. Rayford's back and that's a huge plus. Off the ball, Williams has a variety of options. Jerod Haase is the starter and a hustling presence with a jumper. Billy Thomas flashed promise as a rookie.

Forward: When Sean Pearson's jumper abandoned him in the postseason, Kansas was in trouble. Pearson needs to be more consistent from long range. Perhaps the push of California prep phenom Paul Pierce will help. The 6'6" rookie is very explosive taking it to the hole and can make perimeter shots too. Raef LaFrentz is the starting power forward and needs only to develop endurance to become a star. B.J. Williams is a role-player who contributes rebounding and shot-blocking.

Center: With Greg Ostertag gone, the burden now falls to understudy Scot Pollard. The junior should be ready—he played frequently when Ostertag was in foul trouble and displayed a soft shooting touch.

Analysis: K.U. may have peaked too soon in 1994-95, fading in the NCAA Tournament as LaFrentz and Vaughn wore down. They'll have more aid this time around, and that enhances Kansas's prospects in March. This is the Big Eight favorite and also a threat to reach the Meadowlands.

1995-96 ROSTER

	POS	HT	YR	FGP	FTP	3-PT	RPG	APG	PPG
Jerod Haase	G	6'3"	Jr.	.44	.73	67/180	4.3	3.5	15.0
Raef LaFrentz	C/F	6'11"	So.	.53	.64	2/5	7.5	0.5	11.4
Scot Pollard	C/F	6'10"	Jr.	.56	.65	—	6.2	0.5	10.2
Jacque Vaughn	G	6'1"	Jr.	.45	.69	20/58	3.7	7.7	9.7
Sean Pearson	F	6'5"	Sr.	.42	.63	41/128	3.0	1.1	9.6
Billy Thomas	G/F	6'4"	So.	.44	.76	49/126	2.2	0.6	7.3
B.J. Williams	F	6'8"	Jr.	.44	.51	0/6	3.3	0.5	4.4
T.J. Whatley	G	6'4"	Sr.	.27	.50	0/5	0.5	0.1	0.6
Paul Pierce	F	6'6"	Fr.	—	—	—	—	—	—
T.J. Pugh	F	6'9"	Fr.	—	—	—	—	—	—
Calvin Rayford	G	5'7"	Sr.	—	—	—	—	—	—
Ryan Robertson	G	6'5"	Fr.	—	—	—	—	—	—

KANSAS STATE

Conference: Big Eight
1994-95: 12-15, 8th Big Eight

1994-95 NCAAs/NIT: DNP
Coach: Tom Asbury (137-74)

Opening Line: After arriving from scenic Malibu, California, home of Pepperdine University, coach Tom Asbury last year discovered a unit that was too often over-matched in the Big Eight. The Wildcats lacked quality perimeter shooting, and that shortfall made points hard to come by. The prospects for this season are better, however. Sophomore Mark Young is coming on, and the recruiting effort landed some interior scorers.

Guard: Elliot Hatcher led the Cats in scoring after transferring from Grayson County (Texas) C.C. This point guard is a defensive ball-hawk who can score off penetration. Improved play from the frontcourt should create more openings for Hatcher. Opposite Hatcher is Young, a 6'6" leaper. This first-class athlete needs to bolster his perimeter game. Hatcher is backed up by senior Brian Gavin, a shooter who isn't a true point guard.

Forward: When Asbury began working in Manhattan, KSU was very small. That's no longer the case. One forward is Tyrone Davis—a 6'8", 240-pounder—who can score on the box. Davis is prone to turnovers, however, and must be more help on the glass (5.7 RPG). Newcomer Manny Dies could figure into the rotation as a freshman. So could 6'10" junior Shawn Rhodes as well as one of the centers.

Center: Asbury added two junior college products to help here. John Williams, 6'9", is very quick to the ball and has some scoring moves on the interior. Gerald Eaker, 6'11", began his career at Ohio State and has made strides since.

Analysis: During his stint at Pepperdine, Asbury came to be recognized as a superior recruiter. Those skills will be put to the test in Manhattan. KSU lacks the tradition of some of its Big Eight rivals and is far from a hoops hotbed. So Asbury needs help from the junior college ranks. It appears he got it this year, and the increased size should offset some spotty perimeter shooting.

1995-96 ROSTER

	POS	HT	YR	FGP	FTP	3-PT	RPG	APG	PPG
Elliot Hatcher	G	6'0"	Sr.	.42	.77	41/102	3.5	3.0	13.4
Tyrone Davis	F	6'8"	Sr.	.50	.65	—	5.7	0.9	11.5
Mark Young	G/F	6'6"	So.	.36	.60	12/48	3.8	2.4	6.9
Brian Gavin	G	6'1"	Sr.	.25	.89	6/37	1.7	1.0	2.8
Aaron Swartzendruber	G	6'2"	So.	.25	.63	4/13	1.1	0.7	1.7
George Hill	C	6'8"	Sr.	.32	.40	—	2.5	0.2	1.2
Manny Dies	F	6'8"	Fr.	—	—	—	—	—	—
Gerald Eaker	C	6'11"	Jr.	—	—	—	—	—	—
Chris Griffin	G	6'2"	So.	—	—	—	—	—	—
Anton Hubert	G	6'0"	Jr.	—	—	—	—	—	—
Shawn Rhodes	F/C	6'10"	Fr.	—	—	—	—	—	—
John Williams	C	6'9"	Jr.	—	—	—	—	—	—

KENTUCKY

Conference: Southeastern
1994-95: 28-5, 1st SEC East

1994-95 NCAAs: 3-1
Coach: Rick Pitino (283-117)

Opening Line: The Wildcats' season was defined by two heavyweight matchups. In the first, the Wildcats downed Arkansas in a thrilling SEC Final to secure the No. 1 seed in the Southeast Region of the NCAA Tournament. In the second, however, the Cats were sabotaged by poor perimeter shooting in the regional final against North Carolina. The chance for redemption is at hand, though, as only three letter-winners exit and two top newcomers arrive.

Guard: Senior Tony Delk is Kentucky's leader. His range is virtually limitless and he'll beat foes off the dribble. Junior Jeff Sheppard started opposite Delk and his trademark is a sweet jumper. However, he's not a pure point guard. That's where freshman Wayne Turner, the No. 2 rated distributor in the class of 1995, comes in. Quick and elusive, Turner can operate at the fast pace Pitino craves.

Forward: Does the word "loaded" suffice? The Cats are so stacked that Pitino could happily show one-time prep sensation Rodrick Rhodes the door to the pros. Senior Walter McCarty developed into a smooth wing player last winter. Antoine Walker, a sophomore, is a rebounding terror with great ball skills. Transfer Derek Anderson was one of the Big Ten's best small forwards before leaving Ohio State. And Ron Mercer is the top small-forward prospect entering college, according to *FutureStars* magazine.

Center: Though he has not posted the kind of numbers he did at Washington, senior Mark Pope is the kind of dependable pivot Pitino needs. Jared Prickett has a nose for the basketball around the basket.

Analysis: On paper, this appears to be Pitino's best team since arriving in 1989. He's made one Final Four appearance in that stretch, losing to Michigan in 1993, but in Kentucky you are defined by national championships won. The faithful expect a title, and this group is gifted enough to produce it.

1995-96 ROSTER

	POS	HT	YR	FGP	FTP	3-PT	RPG	APG	PPG
Tony Delk	G	6'1"	Sr.	.48	.67	77/197	3.3	2.0	16.7
Walter McCarty	F	6'10"	Sr.	.51	.73	28/77	5.61	1.5	10.5
Jeff Sheppard	G	6'3"	Jr.	.44	.75	28/78	2.3	2.7	8.3
Mark Pope	F/C	6'10"	Jr.	.51	.73	21/44	6.3	0.9	8.2
Antoine Walker	F	6'8"	So.	.42	.71	17/55	4.5	1.4	7.8
Jared Prickett	F/C	6'9"	Sr.	.53	.60	2/8	4.8	1.7	6.7
Anthony Epps	G	6'2"	Jr.	.41	.85	32/80	2.1	4.2	6.7
Derek Anderson	G/F	6'5"	Jr.	—	—	—	—	—	—
Ron Mercer	F	6'7"	Fr.	—	—	—	—	—	—
Nazr Mohammed	C	6'10"	Fr.	—	—	—	—	—	—
Oliver Simmons	F	6'9"	Fr.	—	—	—	—	—	—
Wayne Turner	G	6'2"	Fr.	—	—	—	—	—	—

LONG BEACH STATE

Conference: Big West　　　　**1994-95 NCAAs:** 0-1
1994-95: 20-10, T-2nd Big West　　**Coach:** Seth Greenberg (88-59)

Opening Line: A season-opening win on national television against Detroit last year marked the start of a new era at Long Beach, as the school christened its new arena, the Pyramid. Behind the play of seniors Terrance O'Kelley and Joe McNaull, Long Beach lost only two games at the facility all year and snared an NCAA Tournament bid by winning the Big West Tournament.

Guard: Senior Rasul Salahuddin is a workhorse, driving the lane and applying excellent defensive pressure on the ball-handlers. His only drawback is that he is not a major threat from beyond the 3-point arc. Senior Jamie Davis averaged 6.5 PPG in less than 20 minutes of action per night, but he must reduce his turnovers. Senior Eric Brown provides a lift off the bench with his intensity.

Forward: Entering 1994-95, Greenberg felt James Cotton—1993-94's Big West Freshman of the Year—would be one of the league's top players. However, he saw only 29 minutes of action all season due to injury. So Greenberg improvised. He made extensive use of Juaquin Hawkins, who made enormous defensive contributions. He is the club's stopper. O'Kelley's exit creates a need at power forward. That's where 6'9" rebounding demon Marcus Johnson will operate this winter. Freshman D'Cean Bryant is also a candidate for minutes.

Center: Akeli Jackson, now a sophomore, served as McNaull's backup. A sweet touch around the goal will earn him many more than the 11 minutes per outing he received in 1994-95. Senior Brian Yankelevitz did not see much action. He's got size, though, and decent offensive skills.

Analysis: Very astutely, Greenberg has created a Big West power threat where there was none. Only New Mexico State can presently lay claim to a similar stockpile of talent. The Niners will crop up more often on television as the nation grows more familiar with this ascending regional presence.

1995-96 ROSTER

	POS	HT	YR	FGP	FTP	3-PT	RPG	APG	PPG
James Cotton	G/F	6'5"	So.	.30	.80	0/7	1.0	3.0	14.0
Rasul Salahuddin	G	6'3"	Sr.	.44	.67	28/95	2.4	5.3	9.3
Eric Brown	G	6'6"	Sr.	.45	.60	32/84	1.9	0.8	7.7
Jamie Davis	G/F	6'5"	Sr.	.38	.66	20/76	2.0	1.8	6.5
Juaquin Hawkins	F	6'7"	Sr.	.41	.50	3/27	3.2	2.2	5.8
Akeli Jackson	F/C	6'8"	So.	.55	.57	0/1	2.3	0.4	3.9
Brian Yankelevitz	C	6'8"	Jr.	.60	.63	—	2.2	0.3	1.9
D'Cean Bryant	F	6'7"	Fr.	—	—	—	—	—	—
Scott Catania	F	6'9"	Jr.	—	—	—	—	—	—
Marcus Johnson	F	6'9"	So.	—	—	—	—	—	—
Corey Saffold	G/F	6'7"	So.	—	—	—	—	—	—
Brandon Titus	G	6'4"	Jr.	—	—	—	—	—	—

LOUISIANA STATE

Conference: Southeastern   **1994-95 NCAAs/NIT:** DNP
1994-95: 12-15, 5th SEC West   **Coach:** Dale Brown (426-264)

Opening Line: If one listens closely, the sounds of grumbling can be heard in Baton Rouge. The Tigers have two consecutive sub-.500 seasons on the books and their record in recruiting is spotty. Coach Dale Brown believes a return to health of star guard Randy Livingston and some key additions will put LSU back on the winning track.

Guard: Any hope the Tigers had of earning a postseason invitation last year crumbled in late January. That's when Livingston, who had missed the previous season with a knee injury, went down with a broken kneecap. It is expected he will be back in form for the start of practice. That's a huge plus. His rapport with sweet-shooting junior Ronnie Henderson is exceptional. Former prep All-American Sylvester "Deuce" Ford is a nifty insurance policy for Livingston. Swingman Landers Nolley and freshman Maurice Carter offer great depth.

Forward: Stalwart Clarence Ceasar, the last playing link to the Shaquille O'Neal era, is gone. The logical heir is Duane Spencer, a 6'10" junior, who started as a freshman at Georgetown. Spencer is not much for the nasty stuff inside, but he is a graceful big man with a sweet medium-range jumper. It would be a shock if he does not benefit from many Livingston feeds. Garrick Scott is a bruiser who will assist on the boards. Roman Rubchenko is a viable 3-point threat.

Center: Senior Misha Mutavdzic is on center stage. This ex-star at Wagner College found the adjustment to high Division I daunting at times. However, he possesses a soft touch around the goal and is Brown's only legitimate pivot.

Analysis: The last two seasons have offered Tiger fans some harsh medicine. Injuries and a weak interior game have doomed LSU to second-division status in a rugged league. Brown is convinced the newcomers can provide sufficient firepower to mesh with Livingston and Henderson.

1995-96 ROSTER

	POS	HT	YR	FGP	FTP	3-PT	RPG	APG	PPG
Ronnie Henderson	G	6'4"	Jr.	.43	.73	68/212	5.3	2.2	23.3
Randy Livingston	G	6'4"	So.	.44	.68	20/65	4.0	9.4	14.0
Landers Nolley	G/F	6'7"	Sr.	.43	.75	37/88	4.7	2.1	10.7
Roman Rubchenko	F	6'8"	Sr.	.50	.63	16/44	5.9	1.1	9.8
Misha Mutavdzic	C	6'10"	Sr.	.53	.60	—	4.5	0.4	7.1
Garrick Scott	F	6'9"	Sr.	.40	.46	—	3.1	0.3	2.3
Maurice Carter	G	6'5"	Fr.	—	—	—	—	—	—
Deuce Ford	G	6'7"	Jr.	—	—	—	—	—	—
Bob Hall	C	6'10"	Jr.	—	—	—	—	—	—
Nick Sheppard	C	6'10"	Fr.	—	—	—	—	—	—
Duane Spencer	F	6'10"	Jr.	—	—	—	—	—	—
Rogers Washington	F	6'6"	Fr.	—	—	—	—	—	—

LOUISVILLE

Conference: Conference USA   **1994-95 NCAAs:** 0-1
1994-95: 19-14, T-2nd Metro   **Coach:** Denny Crum (565-212)

Opening Line: An early move by Clifford Rozier to the NBA draft last year left the Cardinals with an unusually youthful cast. There were no seniors on the roster, and that inexperience manifested itself in an up-and-down campaign. Louisville rallied in the final Metro Conference Tournament game behind DeJuan Wheat to gain an NCAA Tournament bid. However, Memphis quickly dispatched the Cards in opening-round play.

Guard: As he begins his junior year, Wheat is on the verge of national acclaim. A shrewd point guard, Wheat makes excellent passes, penetrates, and provides steady shooting from the perimeter. He is a legitimate 3-point threat. Occupying the other guard spot is Tick Rogers, an effective slasher and defender. Alvin Sims is a quality defender who lends a hand off the bench.

Forward: Jason Osborne is one of the best passing forwards in the country. He's also a potent offensive weapon, capable of scoring from medium range or in transition. Power forward might belong to Alex Sanders, who sat out last winter. At 245 pounds, he has the kind of rebounding muscle that can free up Samaki Walker. Brian Kiser is a long-range shooter who makes frequent contributions.

Center: He's listed as a forward, his natural position, but the reality is that Walker patrols the middle for the Cardinals. A Freshman All-America pick of *Basketball Times,* Walker is a superb post-up player and a major shot-blocking presence on the interior. He's aided by Beau Zach Smith.

Analysis: "Consistent" the Cardinals were not a year ago. In fact, prior to the Metro Conference Tournament, it appeared they would miss the NCAA Tournament. Louisville now has skill and improved depth. The knowledge gained last year will be a plus as well. In Wheat, Walker, and Osborne, they have a terrific trio around whom to build. What's more, the role-players are solid too.

1995-96 ROSTER

	POS	HT	YR	FGP	FTP	3-PT	RPG	APG	PPG
DeJuan Wheat	G	6'0"	Jr.	.49	.80	84/195	2.7	3.2	16.5
Samaki Walker	F/C	6'9"	So.	.55	.54	2/6	7.2	1.3	13.7
Jason Osborne	F	6'8"	Jr.	.43	.67	37/123	5.6	3.1	11.6
Tick Rogers	G	6'5"	Sr.	.46	.77	16/51	4.3	2.6	9.5
Brian Kiser	F	6'7"	Sr.	.44	.69	55/120	2.2	1.7	6.7
Alvin Sims	G/F	6'4"	Jr.	.49	.73	13/47	3.1	1.7	6.4
Eric Johnson	G/F	6'3"	So.	.49	.60	3/18	2.2	0.5	5.3
B.J. Flynn	G	6'2"	Jr.	.41	.72	6/25	1.5	1.0	3.9
Damion Dantzler	F	6'7"	So.	.40	.60	12/38	1.6	0.4	2.6
Beau Zach Smith	F/C	6'8"	Jr.	.40	.75	1/1	1.8	0.3	2.0
Craig Farmer	G/F	6'5"	So.	.50	.33	0/3	0.8	0.2	0.8
Alex Sanders	F/C	6'7"	So.	—	—	—	—	—	—

MANHATTAN

Conference: Metro Atlantic   **1994-95 NCAAs:** 1-1
1994-95: 26-5, 1st MAAC   **Coach:** Fran Fraschilla (68-23)

Opening Line: Widely derided when awarded an at-large bid last year, Manhattan proved the skeptics wrong by upsetting No. 4 seed Oklahoma in the opening round of the NCAA Tournament. The Jaspers also gave a quality performance in falling to Arizona State in the next round. Coach Fran Fraschilla welcomes back virtually everybody and is a heavy favorite to repeat as Metro Atlantic champion.

Guard: Fraschilla is blessed with a deep bench and uses it extensively. At the point, Fraschilla platoons senior Keaton Hyman and junior Tarik Thacker. Hyman is an excellent distributor who averaged seven assists per game during the MAAC Tournament. Leading scorer Ted Ellis is a dangerous 3-point shooter. He will also find the open man when defenses react to him on the perimeter.

Forward: Sophomore Heshimu Evans is a burgeoning star at one forward spot. His superior first step and leaping ability make him a candidate to become the kind of go-to man the Jaspers need. Junior Jason Hoover is a bit undersized at 6'5", yet he rarely forces bad shots and is a solid defender. He contributed more than six boards per game last year. Jeronimo Bucero came up big against Oklahoma. He's a legitimate 3-point threat, though he's not much of a rebounder.

Center: The only departure of note comes here, where Jamal Marshall patrolled the lane for the Jaspers. In his absence, Fraschilla will turn to his erstwhile backup, senior Justin Phoenix. Phoenix averaged 15 minutes a game last winter, so he's not unprepared for this assignment. Spelling Phoenix will be freshman Konata Springer, a 6'9" raw talent with limited offensive weapons.

Analysis: Fraschilla stamped himself as one of the sport's rising coaches with the Jaspers' NCAA effort. It might be hard to win as many games as Manhattan did a year ago, but the Jaspers will be one of the East's finest units. They are very sound defensively and have a potential star in Evans.

1995-96 ROSTER

	POS	HT	YR	FGP	FTP	3-PT	RPG	APG	PPG
Ted Ellis	G	6'2"	Sr.	.45	.76	66/168	3.5	2.3	14.0
Heshimu Evans	F	6'6"	So.	.52	.64	9/29	5.0	2.1	12.4
Jason Hoover	F	6'5"	Jr.	.54	.65	—	6.4	1.0	8.8
Keaton Hyman	G	5'11"	Sr.	.40	.58	8/32	4.3	4.9	6.2
Tarik Thacker	G	6'2"	Jr.	.41	.71	18/52	2.2	2.3	6.2
Justin Phoenix	C/F	6'8"	Sr.	.53	.69	2/5	3.2	0.4	5.9
Jeronimo Bucero	F	6'6"	Jr.	.42	.79	28/76	1.8	1.5	5.2
Travis Lyons	F	6'4"	So.	.55	.74	—	2.4	0.7	3.9
Steve McDowell	G	6'1"	So.	.43	.25	11/19	0.5	0.3	2.4
Kyle Dye	G	6'3"	Fr.	—	—	—	—	—	—
Brendan O'Brien	F	6'9"	So.	—	—	—	—	—	—
Konata Springer	C	6'9"	Fr.	—	—	—	—	—	—

MARYLAND

Conference: Atlantic Coast   **1994-95 NCAAs:** 2-1
1994-95: 26-8, T-1st ACC   **Coach:** Gary Williams (312-205)

Opening Line: It wasn't until his fifth season at Maryland that coach Gary Williams was finally able to overcome probation and the Len Bias tragedy to lift Maryland back into the Top 25. Last year, the Terrapins established that they were not a one-year sensation, capturing a share of the ACC title for the first time since 1980. Joe Smith was selected the national Player of they Year before announcing he would make himself available for the NBA draft.

Guard: Together, Duane Simpkins and Johnny Rhodes have logged an enormous amount of minutes throughout their careers here. Rhodes has been a starter since his freshman season and Simpkins moved into the lineup on a regular basis as a sophomore. Both have been brilliant at times. In the post-Smith era, they each need to offer Williams more consistency. If Terrell Stokes is eligible, he'll be groomed as Simpkins's heir. Sarunas Jasikevicius is a strong shooter whose role could grow.

Forward: The Terps' third key senior is Exree Hipp. The lithe wing player is much like his classmates in that he's prone to ups and downs. Another forward who must be more assertive is junior power man Keith Booth. Williams will demand a large effort from Booth, especially on the glass. Veteran Mario Lucas is a workmanlike athlete who can fill in at either spot.

Center: So who moves into Smith's spot? In truth, there are no pure centers on the roster. Sophomore Rodney Elliott is the odds-on pick to take Smith's spot in the starting lineup. Strong and eager, Elliott must avoid foul trouble and be cognizant of his limitations offensively. Newcomer Obinna Ekezie is raw but might be able to help.

Analysis: No one will deny Smith's enormous role in Maryland's success. Still, the Terps' experience, Williams's savvy, and some promising untested performers should be enough to keep this club in the NCAA Tournament picture.

1995-96 ROSTER

	POS	HT	YR	FGP	FTP	3-PT	RPG	APG	PPG
Johnny Rhodes	G	6'4"	Sr.	.52	.69	45/120	5.3	3.7	14.0
Exree Hipp	F	6'8"	Sr.	.51	.66	22/69	4.2	3.2	13.6
Keith Booth	F	6'5"	Jr.	.45	.70	3/23	7.3	2.2	10.9
Duane Simpkins	G	6'0"	Sr.	.45	.84	40/105	2.1	4.8	10.5
Mario Lucas	F	6'8"	Sr.	.42	.58	22/57	3.7	0.7	7.1
Sarunas Jasikevicius	G	6'4"	So.	.45	.81	14/37	0.7	0.8	3.1
Rodney Elliott	F	6'8"	So.	.50	.52	1/5	1.5	0.4	1.4
Matt Raydo	G	5'10"	Jr.	.44	.80	0/3	0.5	0.7	1.0
Matt Kovarik	G	6'5"	Jr.	.31	.65	1/5	0.9	0.9	0.7
Obinna Ekezie	F/C	6'10"	Fr.	—	—	—	—	—	—
LaRon Profit	F/G	6'6"	Fr.	—	—	—	—	—	—
Terrell Stokes	G	6'0"	Fr.	—	—	—	—	—	—

MASSACHUSETTS

Conference: Atlantic 10   **1994-95 NCAAs:** 3-1
1994-95: 29-5, 1st Atlantic 10   **Coach:** John Calipari (158-69)

Opening Line: It was a year replete with milestones for UMass, though not the one the folks of Western Massachusetts coveted. The Minutemen defeated No. 1 Arkansas to open last season and reached the top spot themselves for the first time in school history. In the NCAA Tournament, they advanced to the final eight before falling to Oklahoma State.

Guard: Departed starting guard Derek Kellogg was undervalued by all but coach John Calipari. In his absence, the playmaking duties will be spread out. Edgar Padilla is a strong shooter who can handle the basketball too. Carmelo Travieso is streakier with his shot but will contribute. Freshman Charlton Clarke is a terrific defender and slashing scorer. Andre Burks is a pure point who has had some off-court trouble.

Forward: Lou Roe's void is huge. His enormous heart and rebounding grit cannot be duplicated. As with the guards, Calipari looks for help by committee. Dana Dingle and Donta Bright are slashing scorers who must be more consistent with their perimeter jumpers. Neither is a great passer. For rebounding, Calipari will turn to Tyrone Weeks, a muscular 6'7" ball-hawk who improved as the season went on. And Inus Norville displayed flashes of excellence early in 1994-95.

Center: That sigh of relief was Calipari's when it was announced that Marcus Camby would not enter the NBA draft. Although Camby remains a raw talent, he is vital to UMass' success. He offers an interior scoring option, and his shot-blocking skills allow UMass to defend aggressively on the perimeter. Freshman Lari Ketner could be the starter when Camby exits, which is probably next year.

Analysis: Roe and Kellogg helped UMass go from a strong regional force to a national one. The Minutemen won't begin the year in the Top 10, but they aren't going to slip into oblivion. There's too much skill and Calipari is one of the country's top motivators. Another Atlantic 10 crown seems likely.

1995-96 ROSTER

	POS	HT	YR	FGP	FTP	3-PT	RPG	APG	PPG
Marcus Camby	C	6'11"	Jr.	.55	.64	1/1	6.2	1.2	13.9
Donta Bright	F	6'6"	Sr.	.48	.68	3/13	4.6	2.2	9.2
Edgar Padilla	G	6'1"	Jr.	.41	.77	35/109	1.8	3.0	7.1
Dana Dingle	F	6'6"	Sr.	.50	.55	4/15	5.5	1.5	7.0
Carmelo Travieso	G	6'2"	Jr.	.36	.48	38/113	2.3	1.0	5.3
Tyrone Weeks	F	6'7"	Jr.	.45	.64	—	4.9	0.5	4.3
Inus Norville	F	6'8"	So.	.54	.47	—	2.4	0.1	2.8
Rigoberto Nunez	F	6'7"	Sr.	.39	.75	2/10	0.9	0.4	1.3
Andre Burks	G	6'1"	So.	.20	—	1/4	0.5	0.8	1.2
Ted Cottrell	C/F	6'9"	Sr.	.31	.25	0/1	0.7	—	0.7
Charlton Clarke	G	6'3"	Fr.	—	—	—	—	—	—
Lari Ketner	F	6'10"	Fr.	—	—	—	—	—	—

MEMPHIS

Conference: Conference USA   **1994-95 NCAAs:** 2-1
1994-95: 24-10, 1st Great Midwest   **Coach:** Larry Finch (182-107)

Opening Line: Eager for redemption in the wake of an uncharacteristic 13-16 outing in 1993-94, Memphis earned it with a Great Midwest title in that league's farewell. The Tigers then drubbed Louisville in the opening round of the NCAA Tournament before eliminating Purdue. Only a questionable foul call kept the Tigers from sending Arkansas home in the Sweet 16 round.

Guard: When the Tigers struggled two seasons ago, one of the reasons was shaky guard play. Mingo Johnson and Chris Garner corrected that. Johnson, a Nashville native, supplies long-range shooting accuracy. He led the Tigers in 3-point shooting, connecting on 40.4 percent of his attempts. At the point, Garner is an effective dribbler who has learned to control his game. Memphis will have to replace the intensity provided by the departed Justin Wimmer.

Forward: There may be no more energetic twosome on the major-college scene than senior Michael Wilson and junior Cedric Henderson. The former may be the best leaper in the nation. Wilson led the Tigers in field goal shooting (57.3 percent) and lends a tremendous shot-blocking dimension. Henderson can also alter shots and score from on the box or beyond the 3-point arc. Newcomers Dorian Davis and James Newman will be asked to help swingman Rodney Newsom in a reserve capacity.

Center: In his debut, Lorenzen Wright came in and eclipsed David Vaughn, a man many believed would become an All-American. With Vaughn now gone, Wright's the one who looks like the standout.

Analysis: The critics have long derided Larry Finch in his native Memphis and were out in force after the 13-16 debacle that featured selfish play and bickering. Finch, though, proved resilient and steered the Tigers back into the national Top 25. With Wright in the middle, Memphis appears ready to take charge of its new conference in year one.

1995-96 ROSTER

	POS	HT	YR	FGP	FTP	3-PT	RPG	APG	PPG
Lorenzen Wright	C	6'10"	So.	.56	.63	0/1	10.2	1.5	14.8
Cedric Henderson	F	6'6"	Jr.	.44	.58	23/77	5.1	1.4	12.9
Mingo Johnson	G	6'2"	Sr.	.40	.64	72/178	2.1	3.7	10.7
Michael Wilson	F	6'7"	Sr.	.57	.74	1/5	3.2	0.5	7.9
Chris Garner	G	5'10"	Jr.	.42	.48	7/49	3.4	6.4	6.6
Rodney Newsom	G/F	6'6"	Sr.	.38	.82	34/88	3.0	0.8	5.9
Rob Forrest	G	5'11"	Sr.	.33	.60	1/2	0.2	0.3	1.7
Jason Smith	F	6'6"	Sr.	.64	.33	—	1.2	0.4	1.3
Chad Allen	C	6'10"	Jr.	—	—	—	—	—	—
Dorian Davis	G/F	6'7"	Fr.	—	—	—	—	—	—
Cody Hopson	G/F	6'5"	Jr.	—	—	—	—	—	—
James Newman	F	6'7"	Jr.	—	—	—	—	—	—

MIAMI OF FLORIDA

Conference: Big East
1994-95: 15-13, 5th Big East

1994-95 NIT: 0-1
Coach: Leonard Hamilton (105-156)

Opening Line: Entering 1994-95, coach Leonard Hamilton's job appeared to be very much on the line. After demonstrating promise in 1992-93, the Hurricanes failed to win a Big East Conference game in 1993-94. Miami responded to the challenge, reaching .500 in Big East play for the first time since joining the league. Hamilton was rewarded with a new contract in the off-season.

Guard: A large measure of credit for the turnaround goes to the shortest man on the roster. Kevin Norris, 5'9", gave the Hurricane attack the purpose and direction it had previously lacked. Senior Steve Edwards bounced back from a disappointing year to provide an exterior shooting presence. Mitchell Dunn is a solid all-around performer, while Steve Frazier must play more under control.

Forward: Perhaps the area of greatest improvement came at the defensive end, courtesy of forwards like Steve Rich and Alex Fraser. Hamilton likes to use a three-guard alignment, so Edwards will see plenty of time at the three spot. Two freshmen loom as impact forwards. Tim James was one of the most coveted players in talent-rich Florida. His explosive first step and athletic ability will earn him plenty of minutes. Junior college transfer Clifton Clark knows how to score, and his experience will serve him well.

Center: Constantin Popa was an underrated presence in the lane. At 7'2", he altered many shots and anchored Miami's defense. There really is no apparent heir. Rich is destined to slide over into the middle to duel 7'0" junior William Davis. Davis can be a factor defensively if he avoids foul trouble.

Analysis: Just when it appeared all of this program's promise was on the verge of disintegrating, Miami stepped back from the edge of the cliff with an encouraging outing. Hamilton's knack for finding talent means the Hurricanes will be able to contend for a second consecutive postseason bid. And, if James is a smash, they could go higher.

1995-96 ROSTER

	POS	HT	YR	FGP	FTP	3-PT	RPG	APG	PPG
Steven Edwards	G/F	6'6"	Sr.	.36	.77	64/195	4.5	2.2	12.8
Mitchell Dunn	G	6'0"	Sr.	.38	.59	26/72	3.1	2.4	8.1
Kevin Norris	G	5'9"	So.	.36	.73	26/87	3.3	3.6	7.8
Steve Rich	F	6'9"	Sr.	.46	.68	—	4.9	0.2	7.5
Alex Fraser	F	6'8"	Jr.	.43	.58	0/2	5.4	0.8	7.4
Steve Frazier	G	6'2"	Jr.	.28	.53	20/75	2.5	1.8	4.9
Lorenzo Pearson	F	6'8"	Sr.	.41	.43	—	3.0	0.2	3.5
Anthony Rosa	G	5'9"	Jr.	.38	.44	12/37	0.9	1.3	2.2
Clifton Clark	G/F	6'5"	Jr.	—	—	—	—	—	—
Kenny Davis	G	6'0"	Jr.	—	—	—	—	—	—
Will Davis	C	7'0"	Jr.	—	—	—	—	—	—
Tim James	F	6'8"	Fr.	—	—	—	—	—	—

MIAMI OF OHIO

Conference: Mid-American
1994-95: 23-7, 1st MAC

1994-95 NCAAs: 1-1
Coach: Herb Sendek (42-18)

Opening Line: Like the rest of the Mid-American Conference, the Redskins were rated as underdogs last year to prohibitive favorite Ohio University. Yet Miami found an answer for Gary Trent and cruised to the MAC regular-season title. Despite a loss in the MAC Tournament semifinal, the Redskins received an at-large bid to the NCAA Tournament, where they upset Arizona.

Guard: The Redskins will miss the quickness and leadership of Derrick Cross at the point. However, coach Herb Sendek can turn to several tested veterans in Cross's absence. One is 5'10" senior Chris McGuire, who played two seasons at Wright State before transferring to Miami in 1993. Sophomore Kenneth Bozeman brings quickness and ball-handling to the table. At off guard, Landon Hackim is one of the most dangerous 3-point shooters in the MAC. His stroke is pure and he can release the basketball quickly.

Forward: The story in the NCAA Tournament was Devin Davis, a rebounding terror who flourished in the glare of March. Jamie Mahaffey was a major plus at the other forward. His eligibility is complete, and now it's a wide-open affair for his minutes. A newcomer could make an impact. One is Ira Newble, a 6'6" product of Gulf Coast Junior College. He has a nose for the basketball in rebounding situations. Sendek loves his potential.

Center: Senior Kevin Beard isn't an offensive terror and could use additional bulk. However, he is a shot-blocker and a sound rebounder. Junior Chad Allen, 7'0", is rangy and raw. Newble could see action here.

Analysis: Sendek tore a page from mentor Rick Pitino's bible and made believers out of the people of Southern Ohio. His up-tempo attack relies heavily on the 3, and the defense offers a variety of looks to opponents. Led by the talented Davis, Miami has the inside track on another MAC crown.

1995-96 ROSTER

	POS	HT	YR	FGP	FTP	3-PT	RPG	APG	PPG
Devin Davis	F	6'7"	Jr.	.49	.69	0/1	7.5	1.5	16.9
Landon Hackim	G	5'10"	Sr.	.40	.78	65/186	2.0	1.4	14.0
Kevin Beard	C	6'7"	Sr.	.49	.70	3/5	5.5	1.0	7.2
Kenneth Bozeman	G/F	6'1"	So.	.46	.67	12/25	2.7	1.3	5.9
Chris McGuire	G	5'10"	Sr.	.46	.55	19/45	1.0	1.3	3.5
Jermaine Henderson	G	6'2"	Jr.	.26	.88	1/13	0.8	0.6	1.4
Chad Allen	C	7'0"	Jr.	.48	.27	0/1	1.2	—	1.0
Damon Frierson	G	6'4"	Fr.	—	—	—	—	—	—
Doug Johnson	F	6'5"	Fr.	—	—	—	—	—	—
Rob Mestas	G	5'10"	Fr.	—	—	—	—	—	—
Ira Newble	F	6'6"	Jr.	—	—	—	—	—	—
Wally Szczerbiak	F/G	6'6"	Fr.	—	—	—	—	—	—

MICHIGAN

Conference: Big Ten   **1994-95 NCAAs:** 0-1
1994-95: 17-14, T-3rd Big Ten   **Coach:** Steve Fisher (140-59)

Opening Line: The Fab Five era ended in the relative calm of Dayton, Ohio, last spring. The two holdovers from the original Fabs, Ray Jackson and Jimmy King, played their final college game as Michigan fell to Western Kentucky in the first round of the NCAA Tournament. Even reaching that plateau was a struggle, as the Wolverines battled offensive woes and poor chemistry throughout the year. Another top-three recruiting class arrives to add some more spice to matters.

Guard: It was on the perimeter where the Wolverines stalled. The starters, King and Dugan Fife, endured miserable shooting seasons. Fife is ostensibly the starter at point guard, but he'll get a big push from sophomore Travis Conlan and newcomer Louis Bullock. Bullock will be a welcome addition if he drains the jumper as he did in high school. King's job is ticketed for one of two talented sophomores, Jerod Ward or Willie Mitchell. Neither is a great ball-handler.

Forward: The loser of the Ward/Mitchell duel at off guard might well end up starting at small forward. The chief competition will be provided by freshman Albert White, a 6'6" athletic wing who thrives in transition. Power forward belongs to Maurice Taylor, a 6'9" sophomore who is terrific around the basket. He's complemented by classmate Maceo Baston. Baston's thin frame needs bulk, but he runs the floor exceptionally well.

Center: Makhtar Ndiaye left school unexpectedly, so freshman Robert Traylor looms as the man in the middle. Wide and graceful, Traylor explodes to the goal and can block shots. He needs only to shed some baby fat to become a star. Baston and Taylor can rotate to center.

Analysis: The recruiting analysts keep telling us about Michigan's triumphs on that front, and certainly the Wolverines have collected terrific athletes. However, there seems to be few role-players on hand. The Wolverines will win a lot of games on skill alone. If they are to go beyond the early rounds of the NCAA Tournament, though, the production of some manual laborers is essential.

1995-96 ROSTER

	POS	HT	YR	FGP	FTP	3-PT	RPG	APG	PPG
Maurice Taylor	F/C	6'9"	So.	.47	.60	3/7	5.1	1.2	12.4
Maceo Baston	F/C	6'9"	So.	.67	.55	—	5.5	0.2	7.7
Jerod Ward	F/G	6'9"	So.	.36	.68	10/31	3.7	0.6	6.0
Willie Mitchell	F/G	6'8"	So.	.36	.58	11/42	2.8	0.6	5.3
Dugan Fife	G	6'3"	Sr.	.32	.68	23/84	1.8	1.9	3.4
Travis Conlan	G	6'5"	So.	.35	.31	6/21	1.2	1.4	1.4
Neal Morton	G/F	6'5"	Sr.	—	1.00	—	0.3	—	0.3
Louis Bullock	G	6'2"	Fr.	—	—	—	—	—	—
Robert Traylor	C	6'9"	Fr.	—	—	—	—	—	—
Albert White	F/G	6'6"	Fr.	—	—	—	—	—	—

MICHIGAN STATE

Conference: Big Ten
1994-95: 22-6, 2nd Big Ten

1994-95 NCAAs: 0-1
Coach: Tom Izzo (0-0)

Opening Line: If not the greatest of his 19 seasons at Michigan State, 1994-95 was certainly coach Jud Heathcote's most profitable. In his final year as head coach, Heathcote received gifts at every stop on the Big Ten circuit. He nearly earned a Big Ten title to go with it, as the Spartans rode the explosive scoring of Shawn Respert and the defense of Eric Snow to 22 victories.

Guard: Respert and Snow were a dynamic combination that can't be quickly replaced. The best new coach Tom Izzo can hope for is competence. Junior Ray Weathers, who served as the third guard last year, steps in for Respert. A gutty scorer, he needs to refine his perimeter shot. Thomas Kelley, a speedy ball-handler, must remain under control and learn to set up his mates for scores.

Forward: Call this the Dow Jones Report. Three veterans held down two positions last year, and the coaching staff was never quite sure what to expect from any member of the trio. Daimon Beathea converted a corner jumper to beat Oklahoma State at the wire. Both he and 6'9" junior Jon Garavaglia must be more assertive offensively. Quinton Brooks was the steadiest of the bunch. Two freshmen, Morris Peterson and Jason Klein, will get an early look.

Center: Though undersized for the position, senior Jamie Feick developed into a reliable pivot for the Spartans. He willingly scraps on the glass for rebounds and gets good defensive position in the post. He also has a soft mid-range jumper. Antonio Smith, a 6'8" freshman, will be groomed to replace Feick in a year.

Analysis: Despite MSU's shocking first-round loss in the NCAA Tournament to Weber State, it is difficult to characterize 1994-95 as anything less than a success. Izzo's job is to see that the slippage isn't too great in his debut. Backcourt inexperience won't help. Still, the enthusiasm generated by a new coach and a faster pace should keep MSU in the hunt for another NCAA bid.

1995-96 ROSTER

	POS	HT	YR	FGP	FTP	3-PT	RPG	APG	PPG
Quinton Brooks	F	6'7"	Sr.	.53	.61	1/10	5.2	0.9	11.3
Jamie Feick	C	6'9"	Sr.	.62	.58	—	10.0	1.0	9.9
Jon Garavaglia	F	6'9"	Jr.	.48	.59	10/31	5.1	0.6	7.6
Daimon Beathea	F	6'7"	Sr.	.48	.34	1/5	3.5	1.0	5.0
Ray Weathers	G	6'3"	Jr.	.41	.63	7/19	2.0	0.7	3.5
Steve Polonowski	F	6'9"	Jr.	.48	.70	2/9	1.4	0.6	2.2
Thomas Kelley	G	6'2"	So.	.45	.50	0/1	0.5	0.5	1.4
Mike Respert	G	5'11"	Jr.	.43	.75	0/2	0.1	0.3	1.3
Steve Nicodemus	G	6'4"	Sr.	.40	1.00	3/8	0.5	0.2	1.2
Jason Klein	G/F	6'7"	Fr.	—	—	—	—	—	—
Morris Peterson	F	6'6"	Fr.	—	—	—	—	—	—
Antonio Smith	F	6'8"	Fr.	—	—	—	—	—	—

MINNESOTA

Conference: Big Ten   **1994-95 NCAAs:** 0-1
1994-95: 19-12, T-5th Big Ten   **Coach:** Clem Haskins (252-197)

Opening Line: What appeared to be a total rebuilding project last year took on a vastly different appearance when Voshon Lenard returned to school. Lenard, the club's leading scorer, made himself available for the NBA draft and wasn't chosen until the second round by the Milwaukee Bucks. So he came back and led the Gophers to an NCAA Tournament appearance. Lenard is gone for good now, however, and coach Clem Haskins must develop a new look.

Guard: In addition to Lenard, the Gophers lose Townsend Orr. Sam Jacobson is a leaper who's the team's leading returning scorer. Haskins brought in two newcomers, junior college transfer Bobby Jackson and freshman Charles Thomas, to compete with holdovers Micah Watkins and Eric Harris for minutes. Jackson brings quickness and experience, which might give him an edge at point guard.

Forward: The Golden Gophers need to replenish here too. Neither Jayson Walton nor Chad Kolander was as spectacular as Lenard, but both made valuable contributions. David Grim, a 6'7" senior, should hold down one spot. This wing forward fits into Haskins's up-tempo attack with his slashing game. Quincy Lewis, a 6'7" native of Arkansas, may have the inside track on a starting spot. Mark Jones, another junior college transfer, is a shot-maker, while Miles Tarver and Courtney James can bid for rebounds.

Center: Juniors John Thomas and Trevor Winter are prime options here. Neither is very advanced offensively. At 7'0", Winter must avoid foul woes to stay on the floor. Defense and rebounding are the essential elements for whomever starts.

Analysis: In a sense, Lenard's surprise return forestalled the rebuilding process for one year. Now it begins in earnest. The Golden Gophers are without much proven talent. However, the recruiting class offers promise. If the two junior college transfers contribute immediately, Minnesota might surprise people.

1995-96 ROSTER

	POS	HT	YR	FGP	FTP	3-PT	RPG	APG	PPG
Sam Jacobson	G/F	6'6"	So.	.46	.67	17/53	4.8	1.2	7.7
John Thomas	F/C	6'9"	Jr.	.47	.54	—	4.6	0.7	7.3
David Grim	F	6'7"	Sr.	.39	.71	19/61	3.3	1.2	5.2
Trevor Winter	C	7'0"	Jr.	.54	.70	—	3.1	0.6	3.5
Eric Harris	G	6'2"	So.	.36	.68	1/8	1.0	1.5	2.3
Micah Watkins	G	6'4"	So.	.67	.33	0/1	0.5	0.2	0.4
Bobby Jackson	G	6'1"	Jr.	—	—	—	—	—	—
Courtney James	F	6'8"	Fr.	—	—	—	—	—	—
Mark Jones	G/F	6'6"	Jr.	—	—	—	—	—	—
Quincy Lewis	G/F	6'7"	Fr.	—	—	—	—	—	—
Miles Tarver	F	6'8"	Fr.	—	—	—	—	—	—
Charles Thomas	G	6'4"	Fr.	—	—	—	—	—	—

MISSISSIPPI STATE

Conference: Southeastern   **1994-95 NCAAs:** 2-1
1994-95: 22-8, T-1st SEC West   **Coach:** Richard Williams (138-122)

Opening Line: MSU posted a 22-victory season last year, and it was a campaign that will long be recalled fondly in Starkville. The Bulldogs won at Kentucky for the first time in a generation, and then picked up two victories in the NCAA Tournament. Two of the key components to that club, center Erick Dampier and Darryl Wilson (both All-SEC choices), return to anchor the 1995-96 club.

Guard: If Richard Williams has a concern, it is point guard, where T.J. Honore was an able leader for this club. Though Wilson is a potent scorer, he is not really equipped to direct the attack. He is more comfortable operating without the basketball. Freshman Bart Hyche may not be ready to handle the chore, either, so it's probably up to Wilson to adapt. Sophomore Marcus Bullard provides 3-point shooting at off guard.

Forward: Another unheralded contributor, Marcus Grant, must be replaced here. Sophomore Whit Hughes can connect from long range and will recieve a look. Senior Jay Walton is a trusted veteran who doesn't shy from the dirty work inside. Newcomer Dontae Jones, a 6'7" power forward from Northeast Mississippi C.C., will make an impact. Jones is a power player who will fit nicely alongside Dampier in the middle.

Center: NBA scouts are paying close attention to Dampier. He's made consistent progress with a collection of low-post moves. As he matures, he will become more of a force. He's ably relieved by Bubba Wilson, a junior with a quality medium-range jumper. Wilson will also see action at forward. Freshman Tyrone Washington, 6'10", could be a good one when Dampier is done here.

Analysis: There have been few seasons in the long history of MSU basketball as glorious as the one just past. Williams appears to have laid a solid foundation for tommorrow as well. If he can find someone to steer the offense as efficiently as Honore did, the Bulldogs will push Arkansas in the SEC West.

1995-96 ROSTER

	POS	HT	YR	FGP	FTP	3-PT	RPG	APG	PPG
Darryl Wilson	G	6'1"	Sr.	.42	.83	94/227	4.7	2.5	17.8
Erick Dampier	C	6'11"	Jr.	.64	.60	—	9.7	0.9	13.1
Marcus Bullard	G	6'3"	So.	.42	.67	29/71	2.2	1.8	5.4
Russell Walters	F/C	6'10"	Sr.	.54	.53	—	3.9	0.6	4.8
Bubba Wilson	F/C	6'10"	Sr.	.44	.64	—	1.9	—	3.1
Jay Walton	F	6'7"	Sr.	.38	.75	0/5	2.1	0.4	1.4
Whit Hughes	F/G	6'5"	So.	.43	.73	2/11	1.6	0.8	1.4
Bart Hyche	G	5'11"	Fr.	—	—	—	—	—	—
Dontae Jones	F	6'7"	Jr.	—	—	—	—	—	—
David Rula	G	6'3"	Fr.	—	—	—	—	—	—
Early Smith	F	6'8"	Fr.	—	—	—	—	—	—
Tyrone Washington	C/F	6'10"	Fr.	—	—	—	—	—	—

MISSOURI

Conference: Big Eight
1994-95: 20-9, 4th Big Eight

1994-95 NCAAs: 1-1
Coach: Norm Stewart (660-319)

Opening Line: Coach Norm Stewart has made a career-long habit of defying the experts. He did so again in 1994-95. In September, forward Kelly Thames went down for the season with a knee injury, adding to a list of personnel losses that included 1993-94 Big Eight Player of the Year Melvin Booker. Missouri hardly missed a beat, though, earning an NCAA Tournament bid. Only a miracle drive by UCLA's Tyus Edney kept the Tigers from upending the eventual champions.

Guard: In his two seasons after transferring here, Paul O'Liney was a potent offensive weapon. He's gone now, however, so the burden falls to senior Julian Winfield and junior Jason Sutherland. Winfield is the club's defensive stopper and an efficient offensive player. Sutherland is an undersized guard with a dangerous jumper. Sophomore Kendrick Moore has the potential to grow into a key role, while junior Corey Tate has the explosiveness to mimic O'Liney.

Forward: Tate and Winfield will see some action here too. The most encouraging news for Stewart is that Thames is due back. It may take him some time to scrape off the rust accumulated from a year of rehabilitating his knee, but he's a major talent who makes the Tigers better. Scott Combs does many of the little things needed to win, while Derek Grimm rebounds and has good touch.

Center: Stewart conceded early in 1994-95 that he couldn't always tell the Haley twins apart. Sammie Haley is the left-hander who is a bit more advanced offensively. Simeon's a right-hander who is more comfortable at the defensive end of the floor. While unpolished offensively, both are shot-blockers.

Analysis: Try though they might, no one in the Big Eight can remove Missouri from title contention. The Tigers enter the new season with considerably brighter prospects than they did a year ago. This is a gutty, veteran team that trails only Kansas in the Big Eight talent pool.

1995-96 ROSTER

	POS	HT	YR	FGP	FTP	3-PT	RPG	APG	PPG
Julian Winfield	G/F	6'5"	Sr.	.54	.59	3/12	7.6	2.7	11.1
Derek Grimm	F	6'9"	Jr.	.52	.78	38/80	5.3	0.6	10.8
Jason Sutherland	G	6'1"	Jr.	.37	.84	44/113	2.0	1.6	8.7
Sammie Haley	F/C	7'1"	Sr.	.53	.51	—	5.3	0.7	8.0
Kendrick Moore	G	6'2"	So.	.44	.67	5/14	2.8	2.4	6.4
Corey Tate	G/F	6'4"	Jr.	.40	.65	3/20	4.7	1.6	5.8
Simeon Haley	F/C	7'0"	Sr.	.40	.60	—	3.5	0.3	4.5
Scott Combs	F	6'7"	So.	.53	.78	2/5	0.9	0.2	1.5
Monte Hardge	C	6'11"	Fr.	.40	.25	—	2.3	0.3	1.5
Desmond Ferguson	G/F	6'5"	Fr.	—	—	—	—	—	—
L. Dee Murdock	F	6'9"	Fr.	—	—	—	—	—	—
Kelly Thames	F	6'7"	So.	—	—	—	—	—	—

NEBRASKA

Conference: Big Eight
1994-95: 18-14, 7th Big Eight

1994-95 NIT: 1-1
Coach: Danny Nee (271-184)

Opening Line: With only one senior on the roster last year, Nebraska never could produce the kind of winning stretch it needed to move up in the Big Eight. Thus, it ended up with a ticket to the NIT. For the first time in his nine seasons at Nebraska, Danny Nee heard criticism for failing to steer his squad into the NCAA Tournament. Virtually everyone returns, so the expectations won't subside.

Guard: Jaron Boone directs the attack. His package of skills is exceptional, though he may not be ideally suited to the running the show. Senior Erick Strickland sees many minutes at the off-guard position. His calling card is defense. Long arms and superior anticipation make him a headache for opponents. For scoring punch, Nee calls on Tom Wald and Chester Surles.

Forward: The absence of former Husker star Eric Piatkowski was noticeable here last season. Nebraska missed the scoring and leadership traits he brought to the floor. Terrance Badgett is a competent forward, though not an offensive force. Nee hopes to plug in 6'7" junior college transfer Bernard Garner at power forward alongside Badgett. Rebounding is an area of need, and that's one of Garner's strong suits.

Center: This is a place where Nebraska has trouble against elite competition. Three holdovers will log minutes, though none figures to dominate. Senior Chris Sallee is the most physical. Mikki Moore needs more bulk to improve.

Analysis: Nee has established Nebraska as a solid Big Eight entry. Luring the kind of big men needed to step above that won't be easy, though. This edition should be more consistent than last year's and should get Nebraska back into the NCAA Tournament. Boone's got prime-time skills, and if he gets some assistance from the big men, Nebraska has a chance to end its string of four consecutive first-round defeats in NCAA tourney play.

1995-96 ROSTER

	POS	HT	YR	FGP	FTP	3-PT	RPG	APG	PPG
Jaron Boone	G	6'6"	Sr.	.44	.68	70/182	3.3	3.6	17.5
Erick Strickland	G	6'3"	Sr.	.44	.73	54/160	5.4	4.3	16.3
Tom Wald	G	6'0"	Sr.	.47	.83	12/50	2.3	4.0	8.4
Terrance Badgett	F	6'6"	Sr.	.50	.63	1/9	5.3	1.8	8.1
Mikki Moore	C	6'11"	Jr.	.50	.55	2/8	6.2	0.8	8.0
Chris Sallee	C	6'10"	Sr.	.56	.62	—	4.7	0.4	5.8
Jason Glock	G	6'5"	Sr.	.52	.88	13/35	1.9	1.4	5.1
Chester Surles	G	6'7"	So.	.40	.62	7/20	1.7	0.5	3.2
Larry Florence	G/F	6'6"	Fr.	—	—	—	—	—	—
Bernard Garner	F	6'7"	Jr.	—	—	—	—	—	—
Chad Ideus	F	6'7"	Fr.	—	—	—	—	—	—
Andy Markowski	F	6'8"	Fr.	—	—	—	—	—	—

NORTH CAROLINA

Conference: Atlantic Coast
1994-95: 28-6, T-1st ACC

1994-95 NCAAs: 4-1
Coach: Dean Smith (830-236)

Opening Line: Fresh from a disquieting second-round NCAA Tournament loss to Boston College in 1994, North Carolina rebounded to make its third Final Four appearance in five seasons. The Tar Heels built their attack around sophomores Jerry Stackhouse and Rasheed Wallace along with senior Donald Williams. All three are gone, and for the first time in years there are doomsayers who wonder if Carolina can win its customary 20 games.

Guard: The lone holdover from the Tar Heels' blue-chip recruiting class of 1993, Jeff McInnis, now moves to center stage. Previously, his task was to feed the scorers. He'll be asked to score more and he's capable of that. Opposite McInnis is the man who might be this school's next great one, 6'5" Vince Carter. The freshman is an awesome leaper who can stick the jumper as well. Relief work will be entrusted to Shammond Williams and Ryan Sullivan.

Forward: In the Tar Heels' national semifinal loss to Arkansas, Dante Calabria endured a horrific shooting effort. That's most unusual from a senior who is among the nation's premier 3-point artists. He won't get as many wide-open looks, though, as he did when surrounded by Stackhouse, Wallace, et al. Power forward is a problem for Smith. The best bets are holdover Ed Geth, once a Top 50 prospect, and freshman Antawn Jamison. Jamison played well in postseason all-star tilts and could add a rebounding presence Carolina desperately desires.

Center: When Wallace was forced out of action in the opening round of the NCAA Tournament, 7'2" Serge Zwikker stepped up with a strong performance. Yet Zwikker is not a quality ACC center. So slow is he that Smith felt he had to use a zone whenever Zwikker was on the floor.

Analysis: Depth was a major issue for the Tar Heels last year, one that Smith gracefully camouflaged. It won't be nearly as simple this time because UNC lacks a superstar of Stackhouse and Wallace's ilk. Carolina won't stumble too far, however, and should remain in the Top 25 picture.

1995-96 ROSTER

	POS	HT	YR	FGP	FTP	3-PT	RPG	APG	PPG
Jeff McInnis	G	6'4"	Jr.	.49	.67	44/112	4.1	5.3	12.4
Dante Calabria	G/F	6'4"	Sr.	.51	.72	66/133	4.8	2.7	10.5
Serge Zwikker	C	7'2"	Jr.	.49	.68	—	3.0	0.3	2.9
Ed Geth	F	6'8"	Jr.	.54	.27	—	1.4	0.1	1.9
Shammond Williams	G	6'3"	So.	.39	.86	6/20	0.4	0.7	1.7
Vince Carter	G/F	6'5"	Fr.	—	—	—	—	—	—
Antawn Jamison	F	6'7"	Fr.	—	—	—	—	—	—
Ademola Okulaja	F	6'7"	Fr.	—	—	—	—	—	—
Ryan Sullivan	G	6'2"	Fr.	—	—	—	—	—	—

NORTH CAROLINA-CHARLOTTE

Conference: Conference USA
1994-95: 19-9, 1st Metro

1994-95 NCAAs: 0-1
Coach: Jeff Mullins (168-127)

Opening Line: Sparked by senior captains Jarvis Lang and Jermaine Parker, the 49ers advanced to the NCAA Tournament last year for the third time in coach Jeff Mullins's successful ten-year run at the school. Among the highlights were wins at New Mexico and at Tulane. Lang's brilliant career ended in a 70-68 loss to Stanford in the opening round of the NCAA Tournament.

Guard: Last year, Mullins used a platoon system here, spreading the wealth among four guards. Fast off the dribble, Roderick Howard can beat foes in the lane. Shot selection is a problem for Howard, however. Junior Shanderic Downs averaged 7.7 PPG. If given the opportunity, he can score in bunches. Mullins also made liberal use of Bruce Patterson and Ponce James. Patterson is an excellent free throw shooter, while James must take better care of the basketball.

Forward: While not likely to be described as pretty, senior Bobby Kummer is effective. An excellent passer, he locates the open man and doesn't look for his own shot. The pick for the other forward spot might be 6'8" sophomore DeMarco Johnson. The only 49er to make better than 50 percent of his attempts from the floor, Johnson averaged 8.6 PPG and 4.6 RPG. He's the best bet to fill Lang's shoes. Swingmen Downs and Patterson provide depth.

Center: Though not glamorous, Parker was effective in this system. Mullins's sole recruit, junior college transfer Alexander Kuehl, 7'2", is penciled in as the new man in the middle. Kuehl will focus on defense and rebounding.

Analysis: Through patience and rebounding, UNC-Charlotte enjoyed an exemplary campaign. Lang was that edition's heart and soul, a player deemed the hardest working man in the Metro Conference by his peers. That tenacity must remain if the 49ers are to make a run at another postseason bid, because the perimeter shooting is poor. There is enough here to keep the momentum alive.

1995-96 ROSTER

	POS	HT	YR	FGP	FTP	3-PT	RPG	APG	PPG
Roderick Howard	G	5'10"	Jr.	.33	.86	46/134	1.8	3.1	9.9
DeMarco Johnson	F	6'8"	So.	.50	.72	0/2	4.6	0.7	8.6
Shanderic Downs	G/F	6'5"	Jr.	.37	.63	43/121	2.9	2.1	7.7
Bobby Kummer	G/F	6'6"	Sr.	.43	.62	25/63	3.4	2.7	6.3
Bruce Patterson	G/F	6'4"	Sr.	.42	.83	5/21	3.6	1.1	5.7
Ponce James	G	6'2"	Sr.	.39	.81	3/15	2.9	2.2	4.9
Roy Wells	F	6'6"	Sr.	.44	.47	9/24	1.3	0.9	3.4
Pino Pipes	F	6'7"	Jr.	.54	.50	—	0.9	0.1	1.2
Robert Price	G	5'11"	Sr.	.17	1.00	0/1	—	0.1	0.6
Andre Davis	G	6'1"	Jr.	—	—	—	—	—	—
Alexander Kuehl	C	7'2"	Jr.	—	—	—	—	—	—
T.J. Tison	F	6'8"	So.	—	—	—	—	—	—

NOTRE DAME

Conference: Big East
1994-95: 15-12

1994-95 NCAAs/NIT: DNP
Coach: John MacLeod (144-131)

Opening Line: The last of the great independents played its final conference-free campaign in virtual obscurity. Television appearances were infrequent and the schedule was weak by this school's standards. The energy within the program should be much higher this year, though, as the Fighting Irish make their bow in the Big East. The benefits of the move have already been felt in recruiting.

Guard: Ryan Hoover has virtually no national profile while playing at America's most famous athletic institution. That may change now. While not an impressive physical presence, Hoover is a gifted long-range shooter. Sidekick Admore White is a pesky defender and sound passer. Senior Keith Kurowski has been plagued by injuries. Freshman Antoni Wyche is the kind of gifted athletic force this program hasn't known in recent years. He'll see plenty of action. Point guard Doug Gottlieb will be White's apprentice.

Forward: The Irish are on the small size. Freshman Gary Bell will probably earn a starting nod at small forward. He brings scoring punch. At the power spot, coach John MacLeod looks to 6'9" junior Marcus Young. He tends to play in spurts. Another option is sophomore Pat Garrity. Garrity's game is well-rounded, and work in the weight room should be a major plus for him.

Center: This was a major problem for the Irish, and MacLeod hopes he's found the answer in Phil Hickey, a 6'11" freshman. Hickey is a bit raw, however. Junior Matt Gotsch is thin and will struggle against the wide-bodies in the Big East.

Analysis: Notre Dame basketball has paid dearly for its administration's reluctance to join a conference. The talent well dried up and this program became irrelevant nationally. The affiliation with the Big East is a godsend. Unfortunately, the talent on the roster won't allow the Irish to be a contender in their debut. The guards are steady but the frontcourt figures to be overmatched.

1995-96 ROSTER

	POS	HT	YR	FGP	FTP	3-PT	RPG	APG	PPG
Pat Garrity	F	6'8"	So.	.52	.77	7/18	5.1	1.3	13.4
Ryan Hoover	G	6'1"	Sr.	.36	.85	51/145	2.3	3.0	9.9
Keith Kurowski	G	6'2"	Sr.	.44	.78	11/35	1.2	1.7	9.7
Matt Gotsch	C	6'11"	Jr.	.54	.63	1/5	4.3	0.5	7.0
Derek Manner	F	6'7"	So.	.43	.65	2/6	2.1	1.0	4.6
Marcus Young	C/F	6'9"	Jr.	.64	.26	—	5.3	0.9	4.3
Pete Miller	G	6'4"	Jr.	.41	.65	12/34	0.9	0.7	3.2
Admore White	G	6'4"	Jr.	.45	.67	5/14	1.4	1.4	2.2
Gary Bell	F	6'5"	Fr.	—	—	—	—	—	—
Doug Gottlieb	G	6'1"	Fr.	—	—	—	—	—	—
Phil Hickey	C	6'11"	Fr.	—	—	—	—	—	—
Antoni Wyche	G	6'4"	Fr.	—	—	—	—	—	—

OKLAHOMA

Conference: Big Eight
1994-95: 23-9, 3rd Big Eight

1994-95 NCAAs: 0-1
Coach: Kelvin Sampson (126-112)

Opening Line: A season that was supposed to be one of transition turned into much more. Behind All-Big Eight player Ryan Minor, the Sooners charged through February to earn a No. 4 seed in the Southeast Region of the NCAA Tournament. Although they were upset by Manhattan in the first round, coach Kelvin Sampson emphasized that he felt his club had achieved its full potential.

Guard: John Ontjes performed an essential task for the Sooners in 1994-95, distributing the basketball and finding Minor. His exit means that this critical position is now up for grabs. Dion Barnes is a first-rate defender who can play either backcourt post. Newcomers Tyrone Foster, a 5'11" junior college transfer, and 6'5" Nate Erdmann offer terrific skills and should compose two-thirds of the three-guard rotation. Dandy point guard Prince Fowler transferred.

Forward: Minor is set in one of these places. His wide array of skills, including strong post-up and perimeter games, make him the focal point of this team's attack. Senior Ernie Abercrombie provides muscle and rebounding off the bench. Departed Calvin Curry held down the other starting berth last year. That looks like it will go to 6'7" freshman Eduardo Najera of San Antonio.

Center: The Sooners didn't get much production out of this position last year. That could change, though, with the arrival of Top 100 freshman Bobby Joe Evans. At 6'9", he has the kind of offensive skills his predecessor, James Mayden, lacked. He's got a nice drop-step move in the post and rebounds aggressively. Senior Jason Yanish will back him up.

Analysis: Despite the distasteful loss to Manhattan, it was a pleasant year in Norman. Sampson preached discipline and defense, and that aided a club that gave up too many easy scores in recent years. This recruiting class is filled with quality help and the kind of athleticism that was lacking last winter. Plus, Minor's a legitimate All-American.

1995-96 ROSTER

	POS	HT	YR	FGP	FTP	3-PT	RPG	APG	PPG
Ryan Minor	F	6'7"	Sr.	.49	.82	69/176	8.4	2.2	23.6
Dion Barnes	G	6'1"	Sr.	.47	.78	33/96	3.0	2.0	11.2
Ernie Abercrombie	F	6'4"	Sr.	.49	.67	4/10	6.2	1.0	10.5
Jason Yanish	C	6'11"	Sr.	.51	.66	—	2.8	0.4	4.0
Robert Allison	G	6'5"	Jr.	—	—	—	—	—	—
Michael Cotton	G	6'5"	Fr.	—	—	—	—	—	—
Nate Erdmann	G	6'5"	Jr.	—	—	—	—	—	—
Bobby Joe Evans	C	6'9"	Fr.	—	—	—	—	—	—
Tyrone Foster	G	5'11"	Jr.	—	—	—	—	—	—
Eduardo Najera	F	6'7"	Fr.	—	—	—	—	—	—
Evan Wiley	C	6'11"	So.	—	—	—	—	—	—

OKLAHOMA STATE

Conference: Big Eight
1994-95: 27-10, 2nd Big Eight

1994-95 NCAAs: 4-1
Coach: Eddie Sutton (553-209)

Opening Line: The Cowboys last year reached the NCAA Tournament for the fifth consecutive season, a first in school history. Once there, they enjoyed themselves totally. Led by senior All-American Bryant "Big Country" Reeves and classmate Randy Rutherford, the Cowboys defeated top seed Wake Forest and then UMass to reach the Final Four, where they lost to UCLA in the semis.

Guard: Despite some early struggles, Andre Owens emerged in last season's second half as a dependable point guard. What he lacks in flash he makes up for with lower-body strength and ball-handling. He's a decent perimeter jump-shooter too. Opposite Owens might be another junior college product, 6'4" Marlon Dorsey. Dorsey doesn't have Rutherford's long-range accuracy, but he's an explosive player who attacks the goal.

Forward: One of the Cowboys' wild cards in the run to the Final Four was junior swingman Chianti Roberts. He ranged from very effective to almost invisible. Consistency will be the key as Roberts takes on a heavier load. Sophomore Jason Skaer also will be asked to do more in the way of scoring. A most important addition is ex-Baylor star Jerome Lambert. In his one year of eligibility, he will be asked to dominate on the glass and score inside, goals that are easily within his reach. Martin Lewis will get a long look at wing forward.

Center: Here's the major void. Reeves played virtually all the minutes at center, leaving no time for his apprentice, 6'11" sophomore John Nelson. Nelson will get a trial by fire. Look for Lambert to also see action in the middle.

Analysis: It was a remarkable ride to the Final Four, particularly for Sutton. When he left Kentucky in 1989, it appeared his coaching career might be over. He was hired at his alma mater and it's proven to be a great marriage. The "Big Country" era was a marvelous one. The post-Country years won't be bad either.

1995-96 ROSTER

	POS	HT	YR	FGP	FTP	3-PT	RPG	APG	PPG
Andre Owens	G	5'11"	Sr.	.43	.69	22/60	3.4	6.9	7.6
Chianti Roberts	G/F	6'5"	Jr.	.59	.47	8/30	3.4	2.4	6.6
Jason Skaer	F	6'7"	So.	.46	.62	20/50	2.5	0.7	5.0
John Nelson	C	6'11"	So.	.56	.50	—	2.2	1.0	2.6
Kevin Miles	F	6'8"	Jr.	.55	.62	—	1.2	0.3	1.7
Chad Alexander	G	6'3"	So.	.33	.56	6/20	0.6	0.3	1.2
Marlon Dorsey	G	6'4"	Jr.	—	—	—	—	—	—
Jerome Lambert	F	6'8"	Sr.	—	—	—	—	—	—
Martin Lewis	G/F	6'5"	Jr.	—	—	—	—	—	—
Adrian Peterson	G	6'4"	Fr.	—	—	—	—	—	—
Maurice Robinson	F	6'7"	Jr.	—	—	—	—	—	—
Tommy Warner	G	6'0"	Fr.	—	—	—	—	—	—

OLD DOMINION

Conference: Colonial Athletic   **1994-95 NCAAs:** 1-1
1994-95: 21-12, 1st CAA   **Coach:** Jeff Capel (37-26)

Opening Line: The early days of coach Jeff Capel's first year at ODU did not offer much hint of hope. Star center Odell Hodge went down with a season-ending injury, which contributed to a 5-8 start. However, ODU rallied behind seniors Petey Sessoms and Mike Jones to capture the CAA crown and earn an automatic bid to the NCAA Tournament. There they defeated Villanova in a triple-overtime thriller that might have been the best game of the entire 1995 event.

Guard: While most of the fireworks were provided by the frontcourt, the Monarchs received sound guard play. Duffy Samuels can beat defenders off the dribble and make shots in traffic. E.J. Sherod's father, Edmund, played in the NBA, and the younger Sherod can score in transition. Sophomore Brion Dunlap is ready if those two falter.

Forward: Sessoms was the CAA Player of the Year and teamed with Jones to offer a winning edge. The leading candidate to fill his spot in the starting lineup is Radee Benson, a 6'5" freshman. Benson is a superior scorer and was pursued by a number of high-profile programs. Improved ball-handling, though, is a must. Opposite Benson is Mario Mullen, a gritty defender and hustling rebounder.

Center: This is where ODU gets better in a hurry. After redshirting, a healthy Hodge is back to patrol the middle for the Monarchs. Capel had to rely on over-achievers here last year, but that's no longer the case. Freshman Cal Bowdler, 6'10", is an intriguing backup.

Analysis: Capel weathered a stormy first six weeks to thrive. That he did so without Hodge says something about his coaching acumen. The star is back now and the timing could not be any better, as the recruiting class Capel has assembled is the best in the CAA. There may be some bumps in the road early, but this club should be a threat to big-name schools by March.

1995-96 ROSTER

	POS	HT	YR	FGP	FTP	3-PT	RPG	APG	PPG
Odell Hodge	C/F	6'9"	Jr.	.57	.83	—	7.3	0.5	13.0
Mario Mullen	F	6'6"	So.	.53	.74	19/47	5.7	2.0	12.9
E.J. Sherod	G	6'4"	Jr.	.40	.59	18/56	2.7	1.5	5.1
Duffy Samuels	G	5'9"	Jr.	.42	.68	6/22	1.2	1.9	4.1
Brion Dunlap	G	5'11"	So.	.31	.63	8/42	1.9	5.8	4.1
Reggie Bassette	C	6'9"	Fr.	—	—	—	—	—	—
Radee Benson	G/F	6'5"	Fr.	—	—	—	—	—	—
Cal Bowdler	F/C	6'10"	Fr.	—	—	—	—	—	—
Joe Bunn	F	6'6"	So.	—	—	—	—	—	—
Mike Byers	G	6'2"	Fr.	—	—	—	—	—	—
Mark Poag	F	6'6"	Fr.	—	—	—	—	—	—
Skipper Youngblood	F	6'8"	Fr.	—	—	—	—	—	—

PENN STATE

Conference: Big Ten
1994-95: 21-11, T-7th Big Ten

1994-95 NIT: 3-1
Coach: Bruce Parkhill (270-244)

Opening Line: Penn State's third season in the Big Ten was its most competitive. The Nittany Lions defeated the likes of Michigan at aging Rec Hall and garnered their first postseason bid as a member of the Big Ten. In fact, PSU was the last league member standing, as it advanced to the Final Four of the NIT. Center John Amaechi must be replaced, but coach Bruce Parkhill and friends believe they've turned a corner as they prepare for the opening of their new home arena, the 15,000-seat Bryce Jordan Center.

Guard: Perhaps the most encouraging development of the NIT jaunt was the work of Dan Earl. The junior emerged as a first-rate floor general. His sound jumper works well in conjunction with his smart decision-making skills. Sophomore Pete Lisicky announced his arrival at off guard. He's a threat from beyond the arc and will score on drives to the goal too.

Forward: After transferring from Syracuse, Glenn Sekunda became a reliable offensive weapon. He possesses a sweet shooting stroke and converts his free throw attempts. Rahsaan Carlton is on the thin side and isn't a pure shooter. This slasher knows how to finish plays in the paint, though, and understands Parkhill's defensive demands. Junior Phil Williams offers a rebounding presence.

Center: Help will have to come from within as 6'8" Aaron Jack is at least a year away from helping in a conference like the Big Ten. Amaechi's understudy, 6'11" Calvin Booth, offers size and decent athleticism. However, he has none of Amaechi's post-up skill. Look for Williams to see some action here too.

Analysis: Clearly, the Lions made progress in 1994-95. Parkhill has proven that Penn State can compete, if not excel, in the Big Ten. Taking the next step won't be easy without Amaechi. The lack of a strong interior presence is especially detrimental in a physical loop like the Big Ten.

1995-96 ROSTER

	POS	HT	YR	FGP	FTP	3-PT	RPG	APG	PPG
Glenn Sekunda	F	6'7"	Sr.	.46	.85	26/84	6.3	1.6	12.8
Pete Lisicky	G	6'4"	So.	.39	.83	58/173	2.0	1.6	9.7
Dan Earl	G	6'3"	Jr.	.42	.84	50/123	2.3	5.7	9.3
Rahsaan Carlton	F	6'6"	Sr.	.40	.65	29/95	3.1	0.9	8.6
Phil Williams	F	6'8"	Jr.	.50	.54	—	4.0	0.3	3.5
Damien McKnight	G	6'2"	So.	.38	.45	4/16	0.6	1.2	2.8
Calvin Booth	C	6'11"	Fr.	—	—	—	—	—	—
Aaron Jack	F/C	6'8"	Fr.	—	—	—	—	—	—
Carlton Langley	G	5'11"	So.	—	—	—	—	—	—
Jeremy Metzger	C/F	6'10"	Jr.	—	—	—	—	—	—
Joseph Pryor	G	6'4"	Fr.	—	—	—	—	—	—
Jarrett Stephens	F	6'7"	Fr.	—	—	—	—	—	—

PROVIDENCE

Conference: Big East   **1994-95 NIT:** 1-1
1994-95: 17-13, 6th Big East   **Coach:** Pete Gillen (219-88)

Opening Line: In his debut, coach Pete Gillen used a patchwork lineup that propelled the Friars to a strong start (10-2) that included a victory over Oklahoma State. Yet the lack of athleticism and a point guard derailed the Friars in Big East play, and they soon faded. A strong Big East Tournament and first-rate recruiting left the Friar faithful in an optimistic frame of mind.

Guard: No failing did more to undermine P.C. in 1994-95 than the lack of a true point guard. Gillen used Michael Brown and Borja Larragan at that spot and neither possessed the instincts or ball-handling skills necessary to effectively steer the offense. The remedy to that ailment came when Shammgod Wells announced he would attend P.C. Wells is exceptionally quick and was more under control last season than he was in the past. Jason Murdock is set at off guard, though he needs to be more consistent with his shot.

Forward: Eric Williams bore a heavy scoring load that will have to be split among several front-liners. After an early slump, 6'9" Austin Croshere showed the kind of soft shooting touch he had displayed as a freshman in the Big East Tournament. He's a finesse-oriented player who will be challenged by Gillen's recruits. Llewellyn Cole and Jamel Thomas come with the most impressive resumes, while junior college products Derrick Brown and Ruben Garces have the most experience.

Center: Croshere could spend some time here if Piotr Szybilski is not ready for the travails of Big East banging. He doesn't have the raw strength that last year's pivot, Troy Brown, possessed and that's a concern in a physical league.

Analysis: Gillen inherited a limited group and got about as much out of it as P.C. fans could have hoped. Now he's assembled a unit more to his liking. It can play the open-court style and apply fullcourt pressure. Experience is all that is lacking.

1995-96 ROSTER

	POS	HT	YR	FGP	FTP	3-PT	RPG	APG	PPG
Austin Croshere	F	6'9"	Jr.	.46	.78	29/85	4.9	1.1	10.2
Michael Brown	G	6'1"	Sr.	.40	.80	38/101	3.1	3.9	8.3
Jason Murdock	G	6'3"	Jr.	.37	.69	17/63	2.7	2.3	7.4
Borja Larragan	G	6'2"	So.	.39	.70	24/64	1.1	2.4	3.7
Piotr Szybilski	C	6'10"	So.	.50	.69	1/2	1.8	0.2	2.4
Jason Evans	C	7'0"	So.	.56	.33	—	0.9	—	1.3
Mark Adams	G	6'3"	So.	—	—	0/1	—	—	—
Derrick Brown	F	6'6"	Jr.	—	—	—	—	—	—
Llewellyn Cole	F	6'6"	Fr.	—	—	—	—	—	—
Ruben Garces	F/C	6'9"	Jr.	—	—	—	—	—	—
Jamel Thomas	F	6'6"	Fr.	—	—	—	—	—	—
Shammgod Wells	G	6'0"	Fr.	—	—	—	—	—	—

PURDUE

Conference: Big Ten   **1994-95 NCAAs:** 1-1
1994-95: 25-7, 1st Big Ten   **Coach:** Gene Keady (360-161)

Opening Line: The year following Glenn Robinson's departure was viewed by most as a rebuilding campaign in West Lafayette, but coach Gene Keady delivered another Big Ten championship. Keady received maximum effort from veterans such as Matt Waddell and Cuonzo Martin. Yet Purdue didn't have the tools to make much NCAA Tournament noise, barely escaping an upset to Wisconsin-Green Bay before falling to Memphis in Round 2.

Guard: Although Waddell's wisdom and shooting touch were important, Keady feels he's got plenty of backcourt firepower to replace him. Porter Roberts saw plenty of action alongside Waddell. The most athletic Boilermaker guard, Roberts is a fine defender and stays within the system. Todd Foster is a gritty worker with heart and hustle. Chad Austin and Alan Eldridge should be in the rotation and either might start with a strong preseason. Herb Dove is another tough defender.

Forward: There are two candidates to step in for Martin. One is holdover Justin Jennings, an excellent defender and rebounder. He lacks Martin's scoring touch, though. Freshman Luther Clay can put points up and rebound. Defense is more of a challenge for him. Former junior college Player of the Year Roy Hairston appears ready for a strong year at power forward now that he's adjusted to Division I play. Brandon Brantley is around to contribute at power forward and center.

Center: One of the more pleasant surprises last year was rookie Brad Miller. Fundamentally sound, he uses his size effectively and can make shots in the post area. He'll be a solid all-league caliber player by the time he's a senior.

Analysis: While the roster never overwhelms the reader with its individual parts, the sum always adds up to much more. Credit Keady, one of the sport's underrated gems. Purdue will guard teams closely, force turnovers, and produce just enough offense to be in the hunt for the top spot in the Big Ten.

1995-96 ROSTER

	POS	HT	YR	FGP	FTP	3-PT	RPG	APG	PPG
Brandon Brantley	F/C	6'8"	Sr.	.56	.82	0/1	6.1	0.4	10.0
Roy Hairston	F	6'8"	Sr.	.51	.49	13/48	4.5	1.3	9.6
Brad Miller	C	6'11"	So.	.58	.66	—	4.8	1.2	6.5
Justin Jennings	F	6'6"	Sr.	.60	.44	—	3.1	0.4	6.2
Chad Austin	G	6'2"	So.	.46	.66	22/54	2.0	2.0	5.7
Porter Roberts	G	6'3"	Sr.	.41	.63	8/37	4.0	3.8	4.9
Herb Dove	G/F	6'5"	Sr.	.57	.69	—	1.5	0.5	3.1
Todd Foster	G	6'1"	Sr.	.34	.69	14/46	0.8	1.1	2.0
David Lesmond	F	6'8"	So.	.27	.50	1/7	0.5	0.1	0.6
Brian Cardinal	F	6'8"	Fr.	—	—	—	—	—	—
Luther Clay	F	6'8"	Fr.	—	—	—	—	—	—
Alan Eldridge	G	6'1"	Fr.	—	—	—	—	—	—

ST. JOHN'S

Conference: Big East
1994-95: 14-14; T-6th Big East

1994-95 NIT: 0-1
Coach: Brian Mahoney (61-104)

Opening Line: A year that began with the Red Storm's new star, Felipe Lopez, on the cover of *Sports Illustrated's* college basketball preview issue closed quietly in the National Invitation Tournament. Despite an influx of badly needed talent, St. John's bore the mark of a youthful squad, struggling with consistency. The year's lessons should prove invaluable.

Guard: Although some were disappointed he couldn't lead them further, it's hard to argue that Lopez didn't deliver on his enormous prep promise. He averaged a shade under 18 points and was unafraid of taking the big shot. His passing skills made his teammates better too. Lopez isn't a great perimeter shooter, and that's an area he should address. Point guard was shared by Maurice Brown and Tarik Turner and each played sporadically. Both must be more careful with the ball.

Forward: James Scott has exited and the logical successor, Roshown McLeod, transferred. Lopez could see some action at small forward in concert with Rowan Barrett, a journeyman type who knows the system. Power forward is the domain of Charles Minlend, a sturdy senior whose game suffered some with Zendon Hamilton playing alongside him. Minlend needs to focus on the essential dirty work of interior play.

Center: Obscured by classmate Lopez, Hamilton nonetheless enjoyed a productive debut campaign too, making the Big East All-Rookie team. A first-rate shot-blocker, Hamilton held his own on the glass and emerged as a medium-range offensive weapon. However, he can be overpowered inside by bulkier big men.

Analysis: Expectations in New York far outstripped what realistically could be anticipated from a youthful bunch. If the Red Storm gets some consistency from Turner or Brown, it can get back to NCAA Tournament play. Lopez and Hamilton will keep things exciting.

1995-96 ROSTER

	POS	HT	YR	FGP	FTP	3-PT	RPG	APG	PPG
Felipe Lopez	G	6'5"	So.	.41	.75	35/114	5.7	2.8	17.8
Charles Minlend	F	6'6"	Sr.	.52	.74	1/7	8.5	1.1	12.7
Zendon Hamilton	C	6'11"	So.	.52	.62	0/1	5.0	0.6	11.4
Rowan Barrett	G/F	6'5"	Sr.	.42	.74	21/43	2.4	1.1	6.5
Maurice Brown	G	5'9"	Sr.	.45	.59	21/53	2.3	3.2	4.5
Tarik Turner	G	6'5"	So.	.46	.43	14/29	2.3	2.3	3.8
Tom Bayne	C	6'10"	Jr.	.61	—	—	0.9	—	1.6
Derek Brown	G	6'3"	Sr.	—	—	—	—	—	—
Ed Brown	F	6'8"	Fr.	—	—	—	—	—	—
Tyrone Grant	F	6'7"	Fr.	—	—	—	—	—	—
Fred Lyson	F/G	6'7"	Sr.	—	—	—	—	—	—
Mike Menniefield	F	6'8"	Jr.	—	—	—	—	—	—

SANTA CLARA

Conference: West Coast
1994-95: 21-7, 1st WCC

1994-95 NCAAs: 0-1
Coach: Dick Davey (53-33)

Opening Line: One year after eliminating Arizona in the opening round of the NCAA Tournament, the Broncs fell apart in 1993-94, falling below .500. So it was a mild surprise to see this unit revive so quickly. The Broncs dominated the WCC last year, falling only at Portland and Pepperdine in the regular season.

Guard: Santa Clara's tandem of Steve Nash and Marlon Garnett is clearly the class of the WCC. Nash is the speedy ball-handler who already owns the school record for 3-point field goals. Garnett is a quality long-range shooter too, connecting on 43 percent of his attempts from 3-point land last season. The only negative is that there isn't much depth behind those two.

Forward: The guards carry most of the scoring burden for the Broncs, so the roles of those in the frontcourt are to contribute rebounding and defensive support. Senior Kevin Dunne is steady, rarely forces bad shots, and rebounds well for a small forward (6.2 RPG). For the power-forward spot, coach Dick Davey calls on Drew Zurek, a 6'9" junior. Zurek's not very physical but has a soft scoring touch from medium range. Jason Sedlock is the first forward off the bench.

Center: No Bronc made greater strides last year than pivot Brendan Graves. He's not the quickest pivot around, but he gets good position and is a viable alternative if defenses hound the guards too closely. In reserve is 6'11" Phil Von Buchwaldt, a native of France.

Analysis: That the '95 Broncos were able to gain an at-large berth in the field of 64 NCAA teams is an indicator that this club has come far in recent years. The Broncs scored impressive wins over Oregon and Illinois State and played well in an 80-75 defeat at Kansas. Good guard play is essential and Santa Clara can count on that. This school has a history of following good years with bad ones, but that trend figures to cease here.

1995-96 ROSTER

	POS	HT	YR	FGP	FTP	3-PT	RPG	APG	PPG
Steve Nash	G	6'3"	Sr.	.44	.88	84/185	3.8	6.4	20.9
Marlon Garnett	G	6'2"	Jr.	.44	.85	63/146	3.9	1.7	13.6
Kevin Dunne	F	6'6"	Sr.	.54	.67	14/32	6.2	1.6	9.4
Brendan Graves	C	6'10"	Sr.	.45	.64	—	5.6	0.5	7.8
Drew Zurek	F	6'9"	Jr.	.52	.69	4/23	4.0	0.5	7.3
Jason Sedlock	F	6'7"	Jr.	.41	.82	11/47	3.6	1.3	6.6
Lloyd Pierce	G	6'3"	So.	.35	.52	1/3	2.7	0.5	4.0
Adam Anderson	G/F	6'5"	Sr.	.49	.42	4/18	2.0	0.4	3.0
Phil Von Buchwaldt	C	6'11"	Sr.	.32	.50	—	3.4	0.5	2.8
Nathan Fast	G	6'4"	Fr.	—	—	—	—	—	—
Craig Johnson	G	6'4"	Jr.	—	—	—	—	—	—
Todd Wuschnig	F	6'7"	Fr.	—	—	—	—	—	—

SETON HALL

Conference: Big East   **1994-95 NIT:** 0-1
1994-95: 16-14, T-6th Big East   **Coach:** George Blaney (410-330)

Opening Line: Written off by most pundits in last year's preseason, the Hall played surprisingly well through January. Matters deteriorated later, though, as the Pirates lost seven of their last eight, including their Big East Tournament opener. That prevented them from making an NCAA Tournament appearance. Still, there were enough bright spots in George Blaney's debut at the Hall to offer encouragement for 1995-96.

Guard: Tormented by expectations in his first two seasons at Seton Hall, Danny Hurley returned from a sabbatical to become a fine guard. He is not his brother Bobby and, fortunately, no longer attempts to be. This defensive ball-hawk committed fewer turnovers last year thanks to better decision-making. Hurley may spend more time at off guard as Levell Sanders expands his role. Junior Andre Brown is a physical defender who will see plenty of action.

Forward: Adrian Griffin is a cornerstone at one forward position. One of the Big East's best defensive forwards, he understands how to score too. Donnell Williams is the incumbent at the other forward berth. He made the Big East All-Rookie team thanks to a soft shooting touch and wise instincts in the lane. Roy Leath will see spot duty as a frosh along with hard-working Roger Ingraham.

Center: There's a void in the post that will be filled by junior college transfer Kelland Payton, 6'10", and sophomore Jacky Kaba. Both have powerful frames. Payton has a more imposing offensive game at this stage.

Analysis: The expansion of the Big East is not good news for the Hall, a small, private Catholic institution that formerly had New Jersey all to itself. Rutgers is now in the fold and Notre Dame has a strong recruiting base in the East. Blaney will have to toil diligently to keep the Hall in the league's upper division. This unit will defend well, but producing sufficient offense could be a problem.

1995-96 ROSTER

	POS	HT	YR	FGP	FTP	3-PT	RPG	APG	PPG
Adrian Griffin	F/G	6'5"	Sr.	.55	.72	6/20	7.2	2.8	15.3
Danny Hurley	G	6'2"	Sr.	.37	.70	40/132	2.7	5.3	13.8
Donnell Williams	F	6'7"	So.	.40	.68	52/135	6.0	1.6	13.1
Roger Ingraham	F	6'8"	Sr.	.58	.57	—	5.4	0.8	8.4
Levell Sanders	G	6'2"	So.	.42	.69	17/48	2.2	1.3	6.4
Jacky Kaba	F/C	6'10"	So.	.50	.35	—	4.6	0.3	5.4
Jearwaun Tuck	G	5'10"	Sr.	.33	.64	5/28	0.8	1.4	2.0
Andre Brown	G	6'3"	Jr.	—	—	—	—	—	—
Duane Jordan	F	6'6"	Fr.	—	—	—	—	—	—
Roy Leath	F	6'7"	Fr.	—	—	—	—	—	—
Kelland Payton	F/C	6'10"	Fr.	—	—	—	—	—	—
Bayonne Taty	F	6'10"	Jr.	—	—	—	—	—	—

STANFORD

Conference: Pac-10   **1994-95 NCAAs:** 1-1
1994-95: 20-9, T-5th Pac-10   **Coach:** Mike Montgomery (316-188)

Opening Line: In a very quiet manner, the Cardinal made its seventh postseason trip in eight seasons with a bid to last year's NCAA Tournament. A 10-0 start lifted Stanford to the No. 23 spot in the Associated Press poll and they were ranked as high as 15th at one point.

Guard: This is where Stanford has an edge on most clubs. The combination of Dion Cross and Brevin Knight lacks a national profile but is a handful for defenders. The two average 33 points a night between them. Cross does it with a superior perimeter scoring touch and excellent free throw shooting (82.7 percent). Knight is the floor general who distributes the basketball efficiently.

Forward: Lacking great athleticism, Stanford's forwards rely more on guile than gifts. Senior Andy Poppink is two years removed from a major back injury but looks none the worse for wear. He averaged 10.8 PPG last year and was the club's second-leading rebounder. Darren Allaway is the other returning starter, but foul trouble is his greatest enemy—he was disqualified six times last year. Senior swingman David Harbour, who comes off the bench, actually averages more minutes than Allaway.

Center: Tim Young was overshadowed by the league's more demonstrative freshmen (Jelani Gardner, Toby Bailey, Tremaine Fowlkes), yet he had a terrific debut campaign. Soft hands make him a viable low-post alternative to Cross and Knight, which gives the Cardinal excellent floor balance. Freshman Andy McClelland will spell Young when he encounters foul trouble.

Analysis: Stanford proved its worth when it defeated UNC-Charlotte in the opening round of the NCAA Tournament. Montgomery's program probably doesn't have the athletes to overtake UCLA or Arizona in the Pac-10. However, it's a very sound unit that will scale the 20-win plateau and return to the NCAA field.

1995-96 ROSTER

	POS	HT	YR	FGP	FTP	3-PT	RPG	APG	PPG
Dion Cross	G	6'2"	Sr.	.44	.83	82/171	1.8	1.1	16.8
Brevin Knight	G	5'10"	Jr.	.45	.75	19/51	3.9	6.6	16.6
Tim Young	C	7'1"	So.	.50	.69	—	8.6	0.4	12.3
Andy Poppink	F	6'7"	Sr.	.44	.73	10/38	5.9	2.6	10.8
David Harbour	G/F	6'3"	Sr.	.42	.73	25/63	3.2	1.4	9.6
Darren Allaway	F	6'8"	Sr.	.48	.71	—	4.4	0.3	6.0
Rich Jackson	F	6'6"	Jr.	.26	.38	4/17	1.0	0.2	1.3
Arthur Lee	G	6'0"	Fr.	—	—	—	—	—	—
Andy McClelland	C	6'10"	Fr.	—	—	—	—	—	—
Pete Sauer	F	6'8"	Fr.	—	—	—	—	—	—
Mark Seaton	F	6'9"	Fr.	—	—	—	—	—	—
Kris Weems	G	6'3"	Fr.	—	—	—	—	—	—

SYRACUSE

Conference: Big East
1994-95: 20-10, 3rd Big East

1994-95 NCAAs: 1-1
Coach: Jim Boeheim (454-150)

Opening Line: Were it not for an ill-timed timeout signalled for by Lawrence Moten, Syracuse would have eliminated Arkansas in the second round of the NCAA Tournament. Instead, the Orange fell 96-94 in overtime. Syracuse was also frustrated on the recruiting front. S.U. came in second on several top prepsters, including Ryan Blackwell (Illinois) and Stephon Marbury (Georgia Tech).

Guard: Filling Moten's void will be a chore. It was hoped that S.U. would attract a point guard to allow Michael Lloyd to slide to off guard. Yet Syracuse failed in bids to land Marbury, Wayne Turner, and Terrell Stokes, so Lloyd may be asked to shoulder distribution duties. He must learn to play more under control than he did last winter and force fewer shots. The door is open for Todd Burgan and Lazarus Sims to step up at off guard.

Forward: Underrated Lucious Jackson completed his eligibility, so now coach Jim Boeheim turns to several untested performers. Sophomore Bob Lazor, a thin forward, and transfer Jason Cipolla are in line to take over in the frontcourt. Cipolla was a highly rated prep recruit who spent time in junior college before coming to S.U. Opposite those two is John Wallace, a first-team All-Big East player who will take charge around the rim.

Center: J.B. Reafsnyder and Otis Hill split the position last year, and that's the blueprint Boeheim figures to follow again in 1995-96. Hill is the more powerful of the two, a good rebounder who is prone to foul trouble. Reafsnyder is steady and able to make soft shots around the basket.

Analysis: The near misses in recruiting were frustrating for Boeheim, but he did get a break when Wallace opted for the NBA draft and then came back to school. Wallace and Lloyd give the Orange two horses to ride. Syracuse will contend in the Big East before tangoing in the Big Dance.

1995-96 ROSTER

	POS	HT	YR	FGP	FTP	3-PT	RPG	APG	PPG
John Wallace	F	6'8"	Sr.	.59	.68	4/14	8.2	2.6	16.8
Michael Lloyd	G	6'2"	Sr.	.46	.63	23/71	3.2	5.2	12.5
Otis Hill	C	6'8"	Jr.	.52	.66	—	4.4	0.7	6.5
J.B. Reafsnyder	C	6'11"	Sr.	.48	.63	—	4.3	1.0	5.8
Todd Burgan	G/F	6'7"	So.	.48	.66	12/31	2.2	0.5	4.0
Lazarus Sims	G	6'2"	Sr.	.53	.47	10/29	1.4	2.6	3.0
Marius Janulis	G/F	6'5"	So.	.28	.83	5/15	1.1	0.7	2.8
Bobby Lazor	F	6'8"	So.	.51	.43	0/2	1.8	0.3	2.4
Jason Cipolla	G/F	6'7"	Jr.	—	—	—	—	—	—
LaSean Howard	F	6'5"	Fr.	—	—	—	—	—	—
Elvir Ovcina	C/F	6'11"	Fr.	—	—	—	—	—	—
David Patrick	G	5'11"	Fr.	—	—	—	—	—	—

TEMPLE

Conference: Atlantic 10
1994-95: 19-11, T-2nd A-10

1994-95 NCAAs: 0-1
Coach: Don Chaney (295-116)

Opening Line: Coach Don Chaney knew last year that replacing the departed Eddie Jones and Aaron McKie would be a major task, and his suspicions proved correct. The Owls struggled into the middle part of January, particularly at the offensive end. The development of freshmen Johnny Miller and Lynard Stewart, along with the play of veteran Rick Brunson, allowed the Owls to make a push to reach the NCAA Tournament.

Guard: Brunson rarely left the floor last year, so there's one major hole to fill. The two men who shared the spot opposite Brunson loom as the likely starters. One is Miller. This dynamic ball-handler and driver seemed perplexed by Chaney's patient attack early, then grew more comfortable. Levan Alston is not an exceptional scorer. He defends well, understands his role, and makes wise choices. The first guard off the bench could be recruit Rasheed Brokenborough, a quality shooter and finisher, although he was fighting to maintain eligibility.

Forward: The story here was Stewart. He emerged as a dependable rebounder and medium-range shooter. Chaney likes Jason Ivey's athleticism and smarts at the small-forward spot. He can make the open jumper, though his range is limited. He avoids critical mistakes and plays hurt. Derrick Battie is the incumbent power forward, but it's likely he'll spend a lot of time in the middle because Chaney's patience with William Cunningham has dwindled.

Center: Neither Cunningham nor Battie has developed to Chaney's liking. Battie has contributed more, though he remains limited offensively. Cunningham has poor hands and seems astonished when a pass comes his way.

Analysis: This wasn't a classic Temple unit in 1994-95. It lacked punch and was prone to silly errors. Yet Chaney adroitly steered the club to the NCAA Tournament. This edition appears to be better equipped to dethrone Massachusetts in the A-10. Stewart and Miller should blossom and Brokenborough, if he gains his eligibility, can bring some offense to a group that can use it.

1995-96 ROSTER

	POS	HT	YR	FGP	FTP	3-PT	RPG	APG	PPG
Johnny Miller	G	6'1"	So.	.34	.48	73/239	2.3	2.1	11.0
Levan Alston	G	6'3"	Sr.	.39	.73	52/142	3.9	3.4	10.1
Lynard Stewart	F	6'8"	So.	.44	.53	0/1	4.5	0.5	7.2
Jason Ivey	F	6'6"	Sr.	.45	.55	—	5.3	0.6	7.0
Derrick Battie	F/C	6'9"	Sr.	.42	.52	—	3.1	0.1	4.7
Huey Futch	F	6'7"	Jr.	.39	.60	8/29	3.1	0.3	3.2
William Cunningham	C	6'11"	Sr.	.48	.54	—	4.0	0.2	2.9
Lamond Adams	G	5'9"	So.	.15	.50	2/11	0.2	0.2	0.4
Marco Van Velsen	F	6'10"	Sr.	.25	—	—	—	—	0.3
Marc Jackson	F	6'10"	So.	—	—	—	—	—	—

TEXAS

Conference: Southwest   **1994-95 NCAAs:** 1-1
1994-95: 23-7, T-1st SWC   **Coach:** Tom Penders (371-262)

Opening Line: For the sixth time in coach Tom Penders's seven years in Austin, the Longhorns passed the 20-win mark last year. Fueled by the dynamic guard tandem of Roderick Anderson and Terrence Rencher, who combined for 41 PPG, Texas drilled Oregon 90-73 in the first round of the NCAA Tournament.

Guard: In the Penders era, the Longhorns have always featured superior guard play. Now he must find successors for Anderson and Rencher, which is no small task. Reggie Freeman lofted 300 3-pointers a day during the summer of 1994 and the benefits were evident in 1994-95. He became a starter at small forward, although he'll now likely shift to the off-guard slot. Sophomore Brandy Perryman drained a number of key shots off the bench for the Longhorns. He's an excellent free throw shooter but not a great passer. Freshmen DeJuan Vazquez and 5'10" lead guard Titus Warmsley will both log heavy minutes too, possibly as starters.

Forward: One of the top players in Texas schoolboy history, Kris Clack figures into the equation here. Listed as a guard, he could see time at small forward or on the backline. This McDonald's All-American is a superb rebounder for a wing player. Seniors Sonny Alvarado and Nathion Gilmore will likely split time at power forward. Swingman Carlton Dixon will also be called upon.

Center: Newcomer Dennis Jordan is the top choice here. A junior college All-American, Jordan scores well inside and adds a shot-blocking element to the Longhorns' interior defense. Sheldon Quarles is another shot-swatter.

Analysis: Texas suffered some major personnel losses but recruited exceptionally well. In fact, this might be Penders's finest recruiting class since coming to Texas. The new talent will be needed as the Horns look to life in the Big 12 beginning in 1996-97. This season affords the newcomers an opportunity to get acclimated to the faded SWC before stepping up into tougher terrain.

1995-96 ROSTER

	POS	HT	YR	FGP	FTP	3-PT	RPG	APG	PPG
Reggie Freeman	G	6'5"	Jr.	.44	.66	74/191	4.1	1.0	14.7
Brandy Perryman	G	6'2"	So.	.45	.89	44/99	0.6	0.6	5.5
Carlton Dixon	F/G	6'5"	So.	.49	.61	1/7	1.7	0.3	4.1
Sonny Alvarado	F	6'7"	Sr.	.52	.58	—	2.3	0.2	3.6
Cal Varner	G	6'3"	Sr.	.40	—	4/10	0.3	0.2	1.8
Nathion Gilmore	C	6'9"	Sr.	.43	.17	—	1.2	—	0.8
Kris Clack	G	6'5"	Fr.	—	—	—	—	—	—
Dennis Jordan	C	6'9"	Jr.	—	—	—	—	—	—
David Phillip	F	6'6"	Fr.	—	—	—	—	—	—
Sheldon Quarles	F/C	6'10"	Jr.	—	—	—	—	—	—
DeJuan Vazquez	G	6'4"	Fr.	—	—	—	—	—	—
Titus Warmsley	G	5'10"	Fr.	—	—	—	—	—	—

TULANE

Conference: Conference USA
1994-95: 23-10, T-2nd Metro

1994-95 NCAAs: 1-1
Coach: Perry Clark (104-76)

Opening Line: The ultimate compliment to coach Perry Clark is that just five years after reviving the moribund program, Tulane is now an expected guest at each NCAA Tournament. The Green Wave reached that plateau last winter largely on the strength of its 1-2 inside duo of Jerald Honeycutt and Rayshard Allen. Most of the squad that defeated BYU in the opening round of NCAA play returns.

Guard: Despite being overshadowed by Tulane's big men, the guard corps is productive and, at times, exciting. LeVeldro Simmons is an exceptional defender and can make the 3. His game is very well-rounded. Chris Cameron is not a pure jump-shooter, yet he's a handful for the opposition due to his slashing ability. He draws fouls and can pressure the basketball at the other end of the floor.

Forward: Honeycutt is one of the top forwards in the nation and will likely score 20 PPG. He's capable of working on the box or inside. Allen is a classic low-post banger who beats people in the post area and with tenacious rebounding. If it's instant offense Clark craves, he can call on Correy Childs. This Michigan native is explosive and has done some of his best work for the Green Wave off the bench. He is capable of creating his own shot and making it under duress.

Center: Razor thin, Lawrence Nelson nonetheless made a contribution as a freshman. On most nights, Allen is Tulane's center, but Nelson gives Clark the luxury of resting either Honeycutt or Allen for stretches. Nelson has soft hands and runs the floor well.

Analysis: Tulane has positioned itself as one of the nation's top 40 programs on an annual basis. Clark's a first-rate recruiter and Dale Brown can only fantasize about how good LSU would be with Honeycutt in its lineup instead of the Green Wave's. Tulane will pressure foes into turnovers, score in transition, and entertain its fans with another postseason trip.

1995-96 ROSTER

	POS	HT	YR	FGP	FTP	3-PT	RPG	APG	PPG
Jerald Honeycutt	F	6'9"	Jr.	.45	.66	43/138	7.5	3.4	17.3
Rayshard Allen	F/C	6'7"	Jr.	.61	.56	6/15	7.8	1.1	16.4
LeVeldro Simmons	G	6'4"	Sr.	.43	.73	34/92	3.4	4.0	13.8
Correy Childs	F	6'6"	Jr.	.51	.40	12/35	2.4	1.8	7.2
Chris Cameron	G	6'4"	Jr.	.44	.68	10/47	2.6	1.4	5.7
Lawrence Nelson	C	6'10"	So.	.34	.39	—	2.1	0.3	2.1
Dan Smith	G	6'0"	So.	1.00	—	—	—	—	2.0
Keith Harris	F	6'7"	Fr.	—	—	—	—	—	—
Patrick Lewis	G	6'2"	Jr.	—	—	—	—	—	—
Derrick Moore	G	6'1"	Fr.	—	—	—	—	—	—
Shun Sheffield	C	6'10"	Sr.	—	—	—	—	—	—

TULSA

Conference: Missouri Valley   **1994-95 NCAAs:** 2-1
1994-95: 24-8, 1st MVC   **Coach:** Steve Robinson (0-0)

Opening Line: The Golden Hurricane made it two consecutive appearances in the NCAA Tournament's regional semifinals by defeating Illinois and Old Dominion in the first two rounds last year. The mood grew a bit more somber at season's end when the man who steered the ship, Tubby Smith, left for Georgia. Former Kansas aide Steve Robinson assumes command.

Guard: One of the men most responsible for the spectacular work of the past two seasons, Alvin "Pooh" Williamson, is gone. So the Hurricanes are in the market for a new quarterback. One possibility is sophomore Jamie Gillin, a prodigious prep scorer who can also pass the basketball. Another is Jason Williams, a true floor general who looks to set up others first. Whoever gets the job will be required to set up 6'5″ star Shea Seals, the starter at off guard. Cordell Love (8.5 PPG) will play often when Seals slides to small forward.

Forward: Kwanza Johnson must be replaced, and Craig Hernadi could be the man. The 6'7″ senior must improve his 3-point shooting accuracy. Senior Ray Poindexter takes good shots and is a fine free throw shooter. He must commit fewer turnovers when pressed inside. Rafael Maldonado, 6'11″, is a rebounding presence who encountered much foul trouble last winter.

Center: Jeremy Rollo gets most of the work here, though Maldonado and Poindexter step in at times. Rollo's a diligent worker on the boards and can make shots around the glass.

Analysis: Though Smith has moved on, the prospects for continued excitement are good. Robinson is a bright, young coaching prospect with an impeccable pedigree, and a shift to the more prestigious Western Athletic Conference is only a year away. The cupboard is filled, and Tulsa could again prove to be an early-round NCAA Tournament scourge.

1995-96 ROSTER

	POS	HT	YR	FGP	FTP	3-PT	RPG	APG	PPG
Shea Seals	G/F	6'5″	Jr.	.39	.79	80/238	6.9	4.0	18.8
Cordell Love	G	6'3″	Sr.	.35	.88	54/165	2.0	1.1	8.5
J.R. Rollo	C	6'10″	Sr.	.48	.52	—	5.0	0.5	5.8
Ray Poindexter	F/C	6'11″	Sr.	.50	.78	—	4.9	1.3	5.5
Rafael Maldonado	F/C	6'11″	Jr.	.54	.64	2/2	4.2	0.6	5.4
Craig Hernadi	F	6'7″	Sr.	.39	.73	4/19	2.7	0.5	4.7
Dewayne Bonner	F/G	6'5″	Sr.	.39	.67	1/5	1.5	0.5	2.1
Jamie Gillin	G	6'4″	So.	.35	.36	8/27	0.5	0.3	2.0
Jason Williams	G	6'2″	Fr.	—	—	0/1	0.5	1.0	—
Zac Bennett	F	6'8″	Fr.	—	—	—	—	—	—
John Cornwell	F	6'9″	Fr.	—	—	—	—	—	—
Michael Ruffin	F/C	6'8″	Fr.	—	—	—	—	—	—

UCLA

Conference: Pac-10   **1994-95 NCAAs:** 6-0
1994-95: 31-2, 1st Pac-10   **Coach:** Jim Harrick (335-152)

Opening Line: Twenty years of frustration came to an end last year in Seattle when the Bruins beat Arkansas to grab their first NCAA title in two decades. Led by seniors Tyus Edney and Ed O'Bannon, UCLA survived a second-round scare against Missouri and then marched convincingly to the ultimate victory. Those two have exited, along with starting center George Zidek, but it is not time to stuff the Bruins back in the bottle for another 20 years.

Guard: Neither man loomed as a headliner as the fans filed into the Kingdome on that fateful Monday night. Yet both Cameron Dollar and Toby Bailey played huge roles as the Bruins held off the Razorbacks. Dollar effectively handled Arkansas' famous pressure. Bailey scored 26 points, many on feeds from Dollar. The two were unflappable on center stage. Sophomore Kris Johnson, lost in the numbers game last year, gets a shot as the first guard off the bench.

Forward: For two seasons, Charles O'Bannon mostly deferred to older brother Ed. That luxury is no longer an option. O'Bannon must now step forward as the kind of forceful captain his brother was. At the other forward spot will be J.R. Henderson. With more consistency, he too could be a standout. omm'A Givens, who arrived with impressive credentials, might break through if he matures.

Center: Ostensibly, Ike Nwankwo was Zidek's backup. Yet it was Henderson who was usually on the front line with the O'Bannon brothers when Zidek needed a rest. The best bet at center may actually be freshman Jelani McCoy. This San Diego product is very athletic for his size and is comfortable in the post.

Analysis: The national title was not an accident. Coach Jim Harrick has built a sound program and has the ingredients needed to retool quickly. There will be some ups and downs as the younger athletes adjust to leadership roles, but this program is in a smooth groove.

1995-96 ROSTER

	POS	HT	YR	FGP	FTP	3-PT	RPG	APG	PPG
Charles O'Bannon	F	6'7"	Jr.	.55	.74	6/29	6.1	3.3	13.6
Toby Bailey	G	6'5"	So.	.48	.56	20/73	4.8	1.9	10.5
J.R. Henderson	F	6'9"	So.	.55	.67	3/10	4.2	1.3	9.2
Cameron Dollar	G	6'1"	Jr.	.35	.66	2/16	1.9	3.1	3.4
Ike Nwankwo	C	6'11"	Jr.	.57	.54	—	1.6	0.1	2.7
Kris Johnson	G/F	6'4"	So.	.42	.71	0/3	1.7	0.3	2.6
Kevin Dempsey	F	6'6"	Sr.	.47	.50	3/9	0.8	0.4	1.7
omm'A Givens	C/F	6'10"	So.	.38	.56	—	1.3	0.1	1.6
Bob Myers	F	6'6"	Jr.	.17	1.00	0/2	0.5	0.1	0.3
Brandon Loyd	G	6'0"	Fr.	—	—	—	—	—	—
Jelani McCoy	C	6'10"	Fr.	—	—	—	—	—	—
Tommy Prince	F/G	6'5"	Fr.	—	—	—	—	—	—

UTAH

Conference: Western Athletic
1994-95: 28-6, 1st WAC

1994-95 NCAAs: 1-1
Coach: Rick Majerus (223-96)

Opening Line: After an uncharacteristically mediocre campaign in 1993-94, the Utes responded with a WAC title. Keyed by the tandem of Keith Van Horn and Brandon Jessie, the Utes earned the fourth seed in the West Region of the NCAA Tournament. Utah defeated Long Beach State before falling to Mississippi State in the second round. Coach Rick Majerus is grateful that Van Horn and Jessie are back in the fold.

Guard: At the wheel for the Utes is 6'1" senior Mark Rydalch. Though not especially quick after undergoing knee surgery as a freshman, Rydalch finds the open man and is a superior free throw shooter. His running mate, Jessie, was one of the West Coast's top newcomers last year. This explosive scorer is a tremendous athlete who needs only to develop a steady jumper to have an NBA future.

Forward: One forward spot belongs to Van Horn, the underrated scorer from Diamond Bar, California. Majerus counts on Van Horn to score in the neighborhood of 20 points a game. Senior Michael Doleac, a 6'11" forward/center, is productive and plays with a lot of heart. Freshman Will Carlton can contribute in a limited role.

Center: Ben Melmeth was force-fed as a freshman. At the offensive end, he's unpolished. However, his bulk is essential as the Utes look to duel the rugged Brigham Young Cougars in the WAC. If he adds a few post-up moves, Melmeth could be a solid center in the latter part of his career in Salt Lake City.

Analysis: In the early portion of 1994-95, Majerus assessed his young squad and determined that it was a year away from greatness. It then went on to win 28 games. This year's Utes might be even better. Van Horn and Jessie provide a level of athleticism the Utes have lacked historically and could take this unit deep into the NCAA Tournament.

1995-96 ROSTER

	POS	HT	YR	FGP	FTP	3-PT	RPG	APG	PPG
Keith Van Horn	F	6'9"	Jr.	.55	.86	59/153	8.5	1.4	21.0
Brandon Jessie	G	6'5"	Sr.	.48	.71	27/95	5.9	2.4	16.1
Michael Doleac	F/C	6'11"	Sr.	.45	.74	0/1	4.5	0.2	7.3
Mark Rydalch	G	6'1"	Sr.	.46	.84	36/79	1.6	3.1	7.2
Ben Melmeth	F/C	6'10"	So.	.47	.66	—	4.7	1.0	5.9
Terry Preston	G	5'11"	Jr.	.46	.75	28/67	1.7	2.4	4.8
Doug Chapman	F	6'7"	Sr.	.42	.56	—	1.6	0.2	1.3
Drew Hansen	F	6'5"	So.	.34	.68	7/25	1.1	0.9	1.3
Will Carlton	F	6'9"	Fr.	—	—	—	—	—	—
Ben Caton	G	6'4"	Jr.	—	—	—	—	—	—
Paul Jonas	G	6'3"	Fr.	—	—	—	—	—	—
Adam Sharp	G	6'3"	Fr.	—	—	—	—	—	—

VILLANOVA

Conference: Big East   **1994-95 NCAAs:** 0-1
1994-95: 25-8, 2nd Big East   **Coach:** Steve Lappas (109-101)

Opening Line: The Wildcats, winners of the 1994 NIT, built momentum last February and rolled to their first Big East Conference Tournament title in early March. Seeded third, 'Nova's campaign came to a crashing halt in the opening round of the NCAA Tournament when Old Dominion edged the Cats in a triple-overtime thriller. Yet this was essentially a young team, one that will build on that disappointment.

Guard: The only noticeable void to be filled is at point guard, where Jonathan Haynes held fort for the past three seasons. Alvin Williams, a 6'4" junior, spent the past two seasons prepping as the sixth man and now assumes command. Off guard is the domain of Kerry Kittles, the Big East Player of the Year and an All-American. Stepping into Williams's role off the bench is freshman John Celestand, who can handle the basketball and score.

Forward: They tend to be overshadowed by Kittles, but both starters perform admirably. Eric Eberz is a veteran marksman who relieves pressure on Kittles and center Jason Lawson with 3-point accuracy. Chuck Kornegay became eligible in December and was the final piece in this puzzle. He provides rebounding assistance for Lawson and scores well off putbacks. Zeffy Penn steps in to relieve Eberz and contributes intangible elements.

Center: It's all Lawson here. Indeed, when he fouled out against Old Dominion, the Cats were done. He's powerful, takes good shots, and gives Kittles the freedom to operate on the perimeter or swoop in for drives.

Analysis: Kittles mulled a move to the NBA. He stayed and that cemented Villanova's status as a national-title contender. Forget the first-round pratfall. This is a sound club with two major stars and a number of supporting players. Few teams are as well stocked.

1995-96 ROSTER

	POS	HT	YR	FGP	FTP	3-PT	RPG	APG	PPG
Kerry Kittles	G	6'5"	Sr.	.52	.77	86/209	6.1	3.5	21.4
Eric Eberz	F	6'7"	Sr.	.48	.73	94/214	4.4	1.6	15.7
Jason Lawson	C	6'11"	Jr.	.60	.73	—	6.7	1.5	12.9
Chuck Kornegay	F	6'9"	Jr.	.48	.59	—	6.3	2.5	8.4
Alvin Williams	G	6'4"	Jr.	.41	.74	15/57	3.5	4.8	7.1
Zeffy Penn	F	6'6"	Jr.	.50	.77	0/1	2.1	0.7	2.9
Adam Shafer	G	6'5"	So.	.15	.73	1/6	0.6	0.1	1.2
Kevin Cox	G	6'3"	Sr.	.27	1.00	1/4	0.3	0.3	1.0
Jaime Gregg	F	6'8"	Sr.	.25	.50	—	0.6	—	0.6
Rafal Bigus	C	7'1"	Fr.	—	—	—	—	—	—
Howard Brown	G	6'5"	Fr.	—	—	—	—	—	—
John Celestand	G	6'3"	Fr.	—	—	—	—	—	—

VIRGINIA

Conference: Atlantic Coast   **1994-95 NCAAs:** 3-1
1994-95: 25-9, T-1st ACC   **Coach:** Jeff Jones (105-57)

Opening Line: When Terry Holland retired in 1990, this program conducted a wide search for a successor. In the end, UVA turned to Holland's aide, Jeff Jones, to do the job. It's worked to perfection. The ex-Cavalier point guard has taken this squad to four NCAA Tournaments in five seasons, including last season's run to the Elite Eight. Now Holland is back as athletic director to watch the Cavs pursue an ACC title.

Guard: The wildcard in this deck, the gifted but enigmatic Cory Alexander, is gone to the NBA. Fact is, the Cavs were better off when Alexander was sidelined late in the year and Jones turned the offense over to Harold Deane. Deane understands UVA's offense and is very unselfish. Stepping in for Alexander in the backcourt was Curtis Staples, a fabulous outside shooter. He opens the lane up for Deane's drives. Courtney Alexander can produce points too.

Forward: For four seasons, Junior Burrough was a fixture in the lane. In his absence, Jones will use sophomore Norman Nolan. He can crash the glass but needs to adopt some of Burroughs's relentless intensity near the shadow of the goal. Jason Williford was an excellent defender, and that role now belongs to junior Jamal Robinson. Robinson's athleticism makes him a dangerous offensive weapon too. Depth could be a problem.

Center: If there was any position that weakened the Cavs, it was this one. Chris Alexander starts, but he is no threat offensively. Freshman Chase Metheney was redshirted so he could fill out his thin frame.

Analysis: Virginia doesn't garner much ink, yet the Cavs are 6-4 in NCAA Tournament play under Jones. This group won't beat itself and can use a potent backcourt combination to overwhelm foes. The Cavs should be an imposing roadblock come NCAA Tournament time.

1995-96 ROSTER

	POS	HT	YR	FGP	FTP	3-PT	RPG	APG	PPG
Harold Deane	G	6'1"	Jr.	.39	.79	69/196	3.0	4.3	16.0
Curtis Staples	G	6'3"	So.	.42	.76	103/244	3.0	0.8	11.9
Jamal Robinson	G/F	6'7"	Jr.	.36	.82	16/57	2.9	1.3	5.4
Norman Nolan	F	6'8"	So.	.48	.55	—	2.2	—	2.6
Chris Alexander	F/C	6'9"	Sr.	.57	.48	—	4.0	0.6	2.5
Maurice Watkins	F/G	6'5"	Jr.	.45	.17	—	0.4	0.2	1.1
Percy Ellsworth	G	6'3"	Jr.	.67	1.00	—	0.5	0.2	0.8
Martin Walton	F	6'9"	Jr.	.33	—	—	1.4	0.3	0.2
Courtney Alexander	G	6'5"	Fr.	—	—	—	—	—	—
Scott Johnson	F	6'9"	Fr.	—	—	—	—	—	—
Chase Metheney	C	7'4"	Fr.	—	—	—	—	—	—
Darryl Presley	F	6'6"	Fr.	—	—	—	—	—	—

VIRGINIA TECH

Conference: Atlantic 10
1994-95: 25-10, T-4th Metro

1994-95 NIT: 5-0
Coach: Bill Foster (494-303)

Opening Line: A first-round blowout loss to Southern Mississippi in the Metro Conference Tournament last year ended any Hokie hopes of reaching the NCAA Tournament. However, Tech made the most of its invitation to the NIT, defeating Clemson, Providence, and New Mexico State en route to the title in New York. Every significant player returns as VTU begins play in the Atlantic 10.

Guard: The combination of Shawn Good and Damon Watlington offers quality and balance. Good is the lead guard, a superb leaper who distributes the ball well. Watlington is a classy shooter who also locates the open man. David Jackson, who spent one year at UNC-Asheville before transferring, gives coach Bill Foster good minutes off the bench. And his twin brother Jim could provide more help than last year, when he was still dealing with the effects of back surgery.

Forward: Ace is the place. That's Ace Custis, VTU's go-to man. One underrated aspect of Custis's game is his first-rate defense. Shawn Smith plays opposite Custis. The 6'6" senior capped a fine campaign with a 24-point, 12-rebound outing in the 65-64 overtime victory over Marquette in the NIT final. He's a confident shooter who won't shy away from tense moments. Freshman Andre Ray will get a look as Custis's understudy.

Center: Travis Jackson's game has developed nicely. At 6'8", 220 pounds, Jackson is an able rebounder who can make shots around the goal. With Custis and Smith on hand, though, his opportunities to score are limited. Rookie Alvaro Tor has much learning to do before he becomes a factor.

Analysis: The Hokies hit their stride in the '95 postseason, and there's no reason to suspect they will stumble in their new league. VTU brings size, balance, and depth to the floor each night. A good crop of shooters and a potential star in Custis give this team the look of an NCAA Tournament threat.

1995-96 ROSTER

	POS	HT	YR	FGP	FTP	3-PT	RPG	APG	PPG
Shawn Smith	F	6'6"	Sr.	.48	.67	11/43	6.7	2.9	16.0
Ace Custis	F	6'7"	Jr.	.53	.67	5/16	10.5	2.5	15.8
Damon Watlington	G	6'2"	Sr.	.45	.76	60/158	3.8	3.1	13.8
Shawn Good	G	6'3"	Sr.	.54	.63	34/74	4.7	3.1	12.9
David Jackson	G/F	6'5"	Jr.	.39	.80	32/106	3.0	1.4	8.5
Travis Jackson	C	6'8"	Sr.	.42	.69	8/27	4.7	0.5	6.4
Myron Guillory	G	6'1"	So.	.38	.48	8/16	0.6	0.5	1.7
Shawn Browne	F	6'6"	Fr.	—	—	—	—	—	—
Jim Jackson	F	6'5"	Jr.	—	—	—	—	—	—
Keefe Matthews	C/F	6'8"	Jr.	—	—	—	—	—	—
Andre Ray	F	6'4"	Fr.	—	—	—	—	—	—
Alvaro Tor	C/F	6'9"	Fr.	—	—	—	—	—	—

WAKE FOREST

Conference: Atlantic Coast   **1994-95 NCAAs:** 2-1
1994-95: 26-6, T-1st ACC   **Coach:** Dave Odom (153-108)

Opening Line: For the first time since the NCAA Tournament began seeding teams in the late 1970s, Wake Forest earned a No. 1 seed last year. It won that distinction with a stellar performance in the ACC Tournament. Randolph Childress set a tournament scoring record and pushed the school to its first crown since 1962. The Demon Deacons received good news after the season when center sensation Tim Duncan declared he would return for the 1995-96 season.

Guard: There is a huge chasm to be filled. Childress's grit and heart defined the 1994-95 Deacons. Two holdovers are sophomore Jerry Braswell and Rusty LaRue. These two shared the off-guard post last season. Now Braswell will be asked to run the offense while LaRue will be called on to make 3's. Sophomore Tony Rutland displayed playmaking ability that will earn him a look as well.

Forward: Coach Dave Odom desperately needs Ricardo Peral to assert himself. He is a smooth shooter who can draw defenders away from the goal. Consistency is all that is lacking in his game. The Deacons will miss unheralded Travis Banks. He brought interior defense and toughness to the arena. The favorite to assume his post is William Stringfellow, an underrated 6'8" freshman. Classmate Rodney West is an explosive rebounder.

Center: Some pro sleuths believe Duncan may have been the top selection in the NBA draft had he made himself available. His shot-blocking and rebounding are vital for a team that doesn't have great size or depth up front.

Analysis: Duncan's decision to stay was an enormous triumph for Odom. It means there shouldn't be much slippage for one of America's great understated programs. Childress's intangible gifts may be more difficult to replace than people suspect, but there's good talent here. Peral can produce points and the freshmen should help immediately.

1995-96 ROSTER

	POS	HT	YR	FGP	FTP	3-PT	RPG	APG	PPG
Tim Duncan	C	6'10"	Jr.	.59	.74	3/7	12.5	2.1	16.8
Ricky Peral	F	6'10"	Jr.	.52	.60	12/35	3.6	0.9	6.7
Rusty LaRue	G	6'2"	Sr.	.42	.93	45/118	1.9	0.9	6.0
Tony Rutland	G	6'2"	So.	.32	.81	33/103	1.9	1.6	5.8
Jerry Braswell	G	6'1"	So.	.40	.83	21/60	1.1	0.6	3.9
Steven Goolsby	G	6'4"	So.	.44	.80	10/22	0.6	0.1	2.7
Antonio Jackson	F	6'8"	So.	.53	.67	—	1.1	0.1	1.5
Barry Canty	G	6'4"	Sr.	.30	.67	4/14	0.8	0.4	1.5
Joseph Amonett	G/F	6'5"	Fr.	—	—	—	—	—	—
William Stringfellow	F	6'8"	Fr.	—	—	—	—	—	—
Rodney West	F/C	6'10"	Fr.	—	—	—	—	—	—
Armond Wilson	G	6'2"	Fr.	—	—	—	—	—	—

WASHINGTON STATE

Conference: Pac-10
1994-95: 18-12, T-5th Pac-10

1994-95 NIT: 2-1
Coach: Kevin Eastman (142-87)

Opening Line: When WSU head coach Kelvin Sampson accepted the Oklahoma coaching position, many presumed Washington State would slide back into isolation. It did not happen, though, as Kevin Eastman artfully constructed a solid unit that was on the cusp of the NCAA Tournament. The Cougars then demonstrated their pluck with two wins in the NIT. The top six scorers are back.

Guard: Here lies WSU's strength. By necessity, Eastman makes use of three guards in the backcourt. Junior Isaac Fontaine led the club in scoring from a wing spot. He's a fine shooter, converting 45 percent of his attempts from 3-point range. Dominic Ellison does most of the ball-handling and keeps opponents honest from long range (41-percent accuracy on 3's). The third option is senior Shamon Antrum, the Pac-10's Newcomer of the Year, who exploded for 29 points in one meeting with UCLA.

Forward: Senior Mark Hendrickson sets the tone for WSU. Smart and dependable, Hendrickson rarely lifts a bad shot and is a superb rebounder. He's not much of a shot-blocker, though, which hurts the interior defense. Sophomore Carlos Daniel made eight starts and will likely be a regular starter this year. He needs to upgrade his free throw shooting.

Center: Eastman asked junior Tavares Mack to do battle with opposing big men and the results were uneven. Mack understands his offensive limitations and takes good shots. However, foul woes plagued him as did his relative lack of strength.

Analysis: This was one of the more productive teams in the nation in terms of potential reached. Each night, the Cougars play hard, take good shots, and execute offensively. What keeps them out of the elite is that they are without much size or bulk inside. There is no viable shot-blocker and larger units can take advantage of that. An NCAA bid looks like a realistic goal.

1995-96 ROSTER

	POS	HT	YR	FGP	FTP	3-PT	RPG	APG	PPG
Isaac Fontaine	G	6'4"	Jr.	.53	.77	36/80	4.5	2.9	18.5
Mark Hendrickson	F	6'9"	Sr.	.63	.79	14/34	9.0	1.3	16.1
Shamon Antrum	G	6'0"	Sr.	.43	.76	59/151	4.3	3.1	13.7
Dominic Ellison	G	5'10"	Jr.	.46	.75	46/113	2.0	6.9	11.3
Tavares Mack	F/C	6'9"	Jr.	.61	.59	—	4.8	0.7	8.6
Carlos Daniel	F	6'7"	So.	.55	.42	—	2.9	0.4	4.4
Ryan Topper	G	6'4"	Sr.	.27	—	3/8	—	0.6	1.0
Bill Coby	F/C	6'8"	Fr.	—	—	—	—	—	—
Kareem Jackson	G	6'3"	Jr.	—	—	—	—	—	—
Cameron Johnson	F	6'7"	Jr.	—	—	—	—	—	—
Chris Scott	G	6'3"	Jr.	—	—	—	—	—	—

WESTERN KENTUCKY

Conference: Sun Belt
1994-95: 27-4, 1st Sun Belt

1994-95 NCAAs: 1-1
Coach: Matt Kilcullen (89-102)

Opening Line: Despite losing head coach Ralph Willard to Pittsburgh, Western Kentucky responded last year with its 32nd 20-win season. Only Kentucky, North Carolina, Louisville, UCLA, and St. John's have had more. The highlight came in the first round of the NCAA Tournament when the Hilltoppers defeated Michigan in overtime. Now Matt Kilcullen must mold nine newcomers with the holdovers.

Guard: At 6'1", 165 pounds, lead guard Michael Fraliex doesn't intimidate through appearance. He's a sharp player, however, who distributes the ball effectively and is a reliable outside shooter. The other guard position is up for grabs. Freshmen Joe Harney and Melvin Adams are candidates. If Rob Williams, of famed Oak Hill Academy, can handle the point-guard slot, Fraliex might slide to second guard.

Forward: Sun Belt Player of the Year Chris Robinson is Kilcullen's cornerstone. The entire offense will be funneled through this electric wing player who keeps improving. He cannot allow himself to become frustrated with the amount of double-teaming he'll see this winter. Freshman Ravon Farris and Tony Lovan will duel for minutes at the other forward post with holdover Pop Thornton.

Center: Though just 6'6", Deon Jackson was mobile and understood the need to contribute on the glass. Now Kilcullen looks to 6'10" juco product Robert Marchant as his top candidate. Marchant won't score much, but if he defends and rebounds, Kilcullen will be happy. Farris and Thornton will see time here too.

Analysis: Kilcullen did a superb job winning with Willard's players. Now we'll see how he integrates his recruits with the holdovers. The system is sound, though, and in Robinson there's a go-to man to bail the Hilltoppers out when the offense stalls. There won't be 27 wins, but Western Kentucky still appears to be the class of the Sun Belt.

1995-96 ROSTER

	POS	HT	YR	FGP	FTP	3-PT	RPG	APG	PPG
Chris Robinson	F/G	6'5"	Sr.	.45	.71	35/110	6.7	2.2	17.0
Michael Fraliex	G	6'1"	Sr.	.42	.73	74/178	2.4	3.4	12.2
Pop Thornton	F	6'7"	Sr.	.48	.54	0/4	3.0	0.4	3.7
Carl Thomas	F	6'6"	So.	.32	.27	2/11	1.0	—	0.9
Melvin Adams	F	6'6"	Fr.	—	—	—	—	—	—
Kyle Chapman	G	6'5"	Fr.	—	—	—	—	—	—
Brad Divine	G	6'0"	Jr.	—	—	—	—	—	—
Ravon Farris	C	6'8"	Fr.	—	—	—	—	—	—
Joe Harney	G	6'4"	Fr.	—	—	—	—	—	—
Tony Lovan	F	6'6"	Jr.	—	—	—	—	—	—
Robert Marchant	C	6'10"	Jr.	—	—	—	—	—	—
Rob Williams	G	5'10"	Fr.	—	—	—	—	—	—

College Basketball Review

The final section in the book reviews the 1994-95 college basketball season and lists important historical information.

First, you'll find the final 1994-95 standings of 33 conferences in Division I. Their conference records include regular-season conference games only. Their overall records include all postseason tournament games, including conference tournaments, the NCAA, and the NIT. The standings indicate the teams that made the NCAA Tournament (*) and those that won their conference tournaments (#).

The recap of the 1994-95 season also includes the following:

- final A.P. poll and A.P. All-Americans
- Division I statistical leaders
- NCAA Tournament game-by-game results
- NCAA finals boxscore
- NIT results
- final A.P. women's poll
- women's NCAA tourney results

Finally, you'll find Division I historical information, including the following:

- national champions (1901-95)
- Final Four results (1939-95)
- Division I career leaders
- Division I season records
- Division I game records
- winningest Division I teams

The NCAA Tournament didn't begin until 1939. Prior to that, there were no official national champions. However, the Helms Foundation selected national champs retroactively for the years 1901-38. These are the teams that are listed in the national champions chart.

DIVISION I FINAL STANDINGS, 1994-95

American West

	Conference			Overall		
	W	L	Pct.	W	L	Pct.
#Southern Utah	6	0	1.00	17	11	.607
Cal. St.-Northr.	4	2	.667	8	20	.286
Cal. St.-Sacra.	2	4	.333	6	21	.222
Cal. Poly-SLO	0	6	.000	1	26	.037

Atlantic Coast

	Conference			Overall		
	W	L	Pct.	W	L	Pct.
*#Wake Forest	12	4	.750	26	6	.813
*North Carolina	12	4	.750	28	6	.824
*Maryland	12	4	.750	26	8	.765
*Virginia	12	4	.750	25	9	.735
Georgia Tech	8	8	.500	18	12	.600
Clemson	5	11	.313	15	13	.536
Florida St.	5	11	.313	12	15	.444
N. Carolina St.	4	12	.250	12	15	.444
Duke	2	14	.125	13	18	.419

Atlantic 10

	Conference			Overall		
	W	L	Pct.	W	L	Pct.
*#Massachusetts	13	3	.813	29	5	.853
George Wash.	10	6	.625	18	14	.563
*Temple	10	6	.625	19	11	.633
St. Bonaventure	9	7	.563	18	13	.581
St. Joseph's	9	7	.563	17	12	.586
West Virginia	7	9	.438	13	13	.500
Rutgers	7	9	.438	13	15	.464
Duquesne	5	11	.313	10	18	.357
Rhode Island	2	14	.125	7	20	.259

Big East

	Conference			Overall		
	W	L	Pct.	W	L	Pct.
*Connecticut	16	2	.889	28	5	.848
*#Villanova	14	4	.778	25	8	.758
*Syracuse	12	6	.667	20	10	.667
*Georgetown	11	7	.611	21	10	.677
Miami (FL)	9	9	.500	15	13	.536
Providence	7	11	.389	17	13	.567
Seton Hall	7	11	.389	16	14	.533
St. John's	7	11	.389	14	14	.500
Pittsburgh	5	13	.278	10	18	.357
Boston College	2	16	.111	9	19	.321

Big Eight

	Conference			Overall		
	W	L	Pct.	W	L	Pct.
*Kansas	11	3	.786	25	6	.806
*#Oklahoma St.	10	4	.714	27	10	.730
*Oklahoma	9	5	.643	23	9	.719
*Missouri	8	6	.571	20	9	.690
*Iowa St.	6	8	.429	23	11	.676
Colorado	5	9	.357	15	13	.536
Nebraska	4	10	.286	18	14	.563
Kansas St.	3	11	.214	12	15	.444

Big Sky

	Conference			Overall		
	W	L	Pct.	W	L	Pct.
*#Weber St.	11	3	.786	21	9	.700
Montana	11	3	.786	21	9	.700
Montana St.	8	6	.571	21	8	.724
Boise St.	7	7	.500	17	10	.630
Idaho St.	7	7	.500	18	10	.643
Idaho	6	8	.429	12	15	.444
Northern Arizona	4	10	.286	8	18	.308
E. Washington	2	12	.143	6	20	.231

Big South

	Conference			Overall		
	W	L	Pct.	W	L	Pct.
N.C.-Greensboro	14	2	.875	23	6	.793
#Charleston South.	12	4	.750	19	10	.655
Maryl.-Balt. Cnty.	10	6	.625	13	14	.481
Radford	9	7	.563	16	12	.571
Liberty	7	9	.438	12	16	.429
N.C.-Asheville	7	9	.438	11	16	.407
Towson St.	6	10	.375	12	15	.444
Winthrop	4	12	.250	7	20	.259
Coastal Carol.	3	13	.188	6	20	.231

Big Ten

	Conference			Overall		
	W	L	Pct.	W	L	Pct.
*Purdue	15	3	.833	25	7	.781
*Michigan St.	14	4	.778	22	6	.786
*Indiana	11	7	.611	19	12	.613
*Michigan	11	7	.611	17	14	.548
*Illinois	10	8	.556	19	12	.613
*Minnesota	10	8	.556	19	12	.613
Iowa	9	9	.500	21	12	.636
Penn St.	9	9	.500	21	11	.656
Wisconsin	7	11	.389	13	14	.481
Ohio St.	2	16	.111	6	22	.214
Northwestern	1	17	.056	5	22	.185

Big West

	Conference			Overall		
	W	L	Pct.	W	L	Pct.
Utah St.	14	4	.778	21	8	.724
New Mexico St.	13	5	.722	25	10	.714
*#Long Beach St.	13	5	.722	20	10	.667
Nevada	12	6	.667	18	11	.621
Pacific	9	9	.500	14	13	.519
Cal.-Santa Barb.	8	10	.444	13	14	.481
UNLV	7	11	.389	12	16	.429
Cal.-Irvine	6	12	.333	13	16	.448
Fullerton St.	5	13	.278	7	20	.259
San Jose St.	3	15	.167	4	23	.148

Colonial Athletic

	Conference			Overall		
	W	L	Pct.	W	L	Pct.
*#Old Dominion	12	2	.857	21	12	.636
N.C.-Wilmington	10	4	.714	16	11	.593
James Madison	9	5	.643	16	13	.552
East Carolina	7	7	.500	18	11	.621
American	7	7	.500	9	19	.321
William & Mary	6	8	.429	8	19	.296
Richmond	3	11	.214	8	20	.286
George Mason	2	12	.143	7	20	.259

Great Midwest

	Conference			Overall		
	W	L	Pct.	W	L	Pct.
*Memphis	9	3	.750	24	10	.706
*St. Louis	8	4	.667	23	8	.742
Marquette	7	5	.583	21	12	.636
*#Cincinnati	7	5	.583	22	12	.647
DePaul	6	6	.500	17	11	.607
Alabama-Birm.	5	7	.417	14	16	.467
Dayton	0	12	.000	7	20	.259

Ivy League

	Conference			Overall		
	W	L	Pct.	W	L	Pct.
*Pennsylvania	14	0	1.00	22	6	.786
Princeton	10	4	.714	16	10	.615
Dartmouth	10	4	.714	13	13	.500
Brown	8	6	.571	13	13	.500
Yale	5	9	.357	9	17	.346
Cornell	4	10	.286	9	17	.346
Harvard	4	10	.286	6	20	.231
Columbia	1	13	.071	4	22	.154

Metro

	Conference			Overall		
	W	L	Pct.	W	L	Pct.
*N.C.-Charlotte	8	4	.667	19	9	.679
*#Louisville	7	5	.583	19	14	.576
*Tulane	7	5	.583	23	10	.697
Virginia Tech	6	6	.500	25	10	.714
S. Mississippi	6	6	.500	17	13	.567
South Florida	5	7	.417	18	12	.600
Virginia Common.	3	9	.250	16	14	.533

Metro Atlantic Athletic

	Conference			Overall		
	W	L	Pct.	W	L	Pct.
*Manhattan	12	2	.857	26	5	.839
*#St. Peter's	10	4	.714	19	11	.633
Canisius	10	4	.714	21	14	.600
Fairfield	6	8	.429	13	15	.464
Iona	6	8	.429	10	17	.370
Loyola (MD)	5	9	.357	9	18	.333
Siena	5	9	.357	8	19	.296
Niagara	2	12	.143	5	25	.167

Mid-American

	Conference			Overall		
	W	L	Pct.	W	L	Pct.
*Miami (OH)	16	2	.889	23	7	.767
Ohio	13	5	.722	24	10	.706
Eastern Michigan	12	6	.667	20	10	.667
*#Ball St.	11	7	.611	19	11	.633
Bowling Green	10	8	.556	16	11	.593
Toledo	10	8	.556	16	11	.593
Western Michigan	9	9	.500	14	13	.519
Kent	5	13	.278	8	19	.296
Akron	4	14	.222	8	18	.308
Central Michigan	0	18	.000	3	23	.115

Mid-Continent

	Conference			Overall		
	W	L	Pct.	W	L	Pct.
#Valparaiso	14	4	.778	20	8	.714
Western Illinois	13	5	.722	20	8	.714
Buffalo	12	6	.667	18	10	.643
Youngstown St.	10	8	.556	18	10	.643
Troy St.	10	8	.556	11	16	.407
Eastern Illinois	10	8	.556	16	13	.552
Missouri-K.C.	7	11	.389	7	19	.269
Central Conn. St.	6	12	.333	8	18	.308
Chicago St.	6	12	.333	6	20	.231
N.E. Illinois	2	16	.111	4	22	.154

Mid-Eastern Athletic

	Conference			Overall		
	W	L	Pct.	W	L	Pct.
Coppin St.	15	1	.938	21	10	.677
S. Carolina St.	11	5	.688	15	13	.536
*#N. Carolina A&T	10	6	.625	15	15	.500
Bethune-Cookman	9	7	.563	12	16	.429
Maryl.-E. Shore	9	7	.563	13	14	.481
Howard	8	8	.500	9	18	.333
Morgan St.	5	11	.313	5	22	.185
Delaware St.	3	13	.188	7	21	.250
Florida A&M	2	14	.125	5	22	.185

Midwestern Collegiate

	Conference			Overall		
	W	L	Pct.	W	L	Pct.
*Xavier	14	0	1.00	23	5	.821
*#Wis.-Green Bay	11	4	.733	22	8	.733
Illinois-Chicago	11	4	.733	18	9	.667
Detroit	9	5	.643	13	15	.464
Butler	8	7	.533	15	12	.556
La Salle	7	7	.500	13	14	.481
Northern Illinois	7	8	.467	19	10	.655
Wright St.	6	8	.429	13	17	.433
Cleveland St.	3	11	.214	10	17	.370
Loyola (IL)	2	13	.133	5	22	.185
Wisc.-Milwaukee	2	13	.133	3	24	.111

Missouri Valley

	Conference			Overall		
	W	L	Pct.	W	L	Pct.
*Tulsa	15	3	.833	24	8	.750
*#South. Illinois	13	5	.722	23	9	.719
Illinois St.	13	5	.722	20	13	.606
Bradley	12	6	.667	20	10	.667
Evansville	11	7	.611	18	9	.667
S.W. Missou. St.	9	9	.500	16	11	.593
Drake	9	9	.500	12	15	.444
Wichita St.	6	12	.333	13	14	.481
Northern Iowa	4	14	.222	8	20	.286
Creighton	4	14	.222	7	19	.269
Indiana St.	3	15	.167	7	19	.269

North Atlantic

	Conference			Overall		
	W	L	Pct.	W	L	Pct.
*#Drexel	12	4	.750	22	8	.733
New Hampshire	11	5	.688	19	9	.679
Northeastern	10	6	.625	18	11	.621
Hartford	7	9	.438	11	16	.407
Boston U.	7	9	.438	15	16	.484
Vermont	7	9	.438	14	13	.519
Delaware	7	9	.438	12	15	.444
Maine	6	10	.375	11	16	.407
Hofstra	5	11	.313	10	18	.357

Northeast

	Conference			Overall		
	W	L	Pct.	W	L	Pct.
Rider	13	5	.722	18	11	.621
*#Mt. St. Mary's	12	6	.667	17	13	.567
Marist	12	6	.667	17	11	.607
Monmouth	11	7	.611	13	14	.481
Fairleigh Dickin.	11	7	.611	16	12	.571
Wagner	9	9	.500	10	17	.370
LIU-Brooklyn	8	10	.444	11	17	.393
St. Francis (PA)	7	11	.389	12	16	.429
St. Francis (NY)	5	13	.278	9	18	.333
Robert Morris	2	16	.111	4	23	.148

Ohio Valley
Conference

	Conference			Overall		
	W	L	Pct.	W	L	Pct.
*#Murray St.	11	5	.688	21	9	.700
Tennessee St.	11	5	.688	17	10	.630
Morehead St.	10	6	.625	15	12	.556
Tennessee Tech	9	7	.563	13	14	.481
Austin Peay	8	8	.500	13	16	.448
S.E. Missouri St.	7	9	.438	13	14	.481
Eastern Kentucky	6	10	.375	9	19	.321
Middle Tenn. St.	5	11	.313	12	15	.444
Tenn.-Martin	5	11	.313	7	20	.259

Pacific-10
Conference

	Conference			Overall		
	W	L	Pct.	W	L	Pct.
*UCLA	16	2	.889	31	2	.939
*Arizona	13	5	.722	23	8	.742
*Arizona St.	12	6	.667	24	9	.727
*Oregon	11	7	.611	19	9	.679
*Stanford	10	8	.556	20	9	.690
Washington St.	10	8	.556	18	12	.600
Oregon St.	6	12	.333	9	18	.333
California	5	13	.278	13	14	.481
Washington	5	13	.278	9	18	.333
Southern Cal.				7	21	.250

Patriot League
Conference

	Conference			Overall		
	W	L	Pct.	W	L	Pct.
*#Colgate	11	3	.786	17	13	.567
Bucknell	11	3	.786	13	14	.481
Navy	10	4	.714	20	9	.690
Holy Cross	9	5	.643	15	12	.556
Fordham	6	8	.429	11	17	.393
Lehigh	5	9	.357	11	16	.407
Army	4	10	.286	12	16	.429
Lafayette	0	14	.000	2	25	.074

Southeastern
Eastern Division
Conference

	Conference			Overall		
	W	L	Pct.	W	L	Pct.
*#Kentucky	14	2	.875	28	5	.848
Georgia	9	7	.563	18	10	.643
*Florida	8	8	.500	17	13	.567
Vanderbilt	6	10	.375	13	15	.464
South Carolina	5	11	.313	10	17	.370
Tennessee	4	12	.250	11	16	.407

Western Division
Conference

	Conference			Overall		
	W	L	Pct.	W	L	Pct.
*Arkansas	12	4	.750	32	7	.821
*Mississippi St.	12	4	.750	22	8	.733
*Alabama	10	6	.625	23	10	.697
Auburn	7	9	.438	16	13	.552
Louisiana St.	6	10	.375	12	15	.444
Mississippi	3	13	.188	8	19	.296

Southern
North Division
Conference

	Conference			Overall		
	W	L	Pct.	W	L	Pct.
Marshall	10	4	.714	18	9	.667
E. Tenn. St.	9	5	.643	14	14	.500
Davidson	7	7	.500	14	13	.519
Virginia Military	6	8	.429	10	17	.370
Appalachian St.	4	10	.286	9	20	.310

South Division
Conference

	Conference			Overall		
	W	L	Pct.	W	L	Pct.
*#Tenn.-Chatt.	11	3	.786	19	11	.633
Western Carolina	8	6	.571	14	14	.500
Citadel	6	8	.429	11	16	.407
Furman	6	8	.429	10	17	.370
Georgia Southern	3	11	.214	8	20	.286

Southland
Conference

	Conference			Overall		
	W	L	Pct.	W	L	Pct.
*#Nicholls St.	17	1	.944	24	6	.800
N.E. Louisiana	11	7	.611	14	18	.438
Texas-San Ant.	11	7	.611	15	13	.536
Stephen Austin	9	9	.500	14	14	.500
North Texas	9	9	.500	14	13	.519
Northwestern St.	8	10	.444	13	14	.481
Texas-Arlington	7	11	.389	10	17	.370
McNeese St.	7	11	.389	11	16	.407
S.W. Texas St.	7	11	.389	12	14	.462
Sam Houston St.	4	14	.222	7	19	.269

Southwest
Conference

	Conference			Overall		
	W	L	Pct.	W	L	Pct.
*#Texas	11	3	.786	23	7	.767
Texas Tech	11	3	.786	20	10	.667
Texas Christian	8	6	.571	16	11	.593
Rice	8	6	.571	15	13	.536
Texas A&M	7	7	.500	14	16	.467
Houston	5	9	.357	9	19	.321
Baylor	3	11	.214	9	19	.321
SMU	3	11	.214	7	20	.259

Southwestern Athletic
Conference

	Conference			Overall		
	W	L	Pct.	W	L	Pct.
*#Texas Southern	12	2	.857	22	7	.759
Missi. Valley St.	10	4	.714	17	11	.607
Alabama St.	8	6	.571	11	15	.423
Southern-B.R.	7	7	.500	13	13	.500
Jackson St.	7	7	.500	12	19	.387
Grambling	5	9	.357	11	17	.393
Alcorn St.	4	10	.286	7	19	.269
Prairie View	3	11	.214	6	21	.222

Sun Belt

	Conference			Overall		
	W	L	Pct.	W	L	Pct.
*#West. Kentucky	17	1	.944	27	4	.871
New Orleans	13	5	.722	20	11	.645
Jacksonville	12	6	.667	18	9	.667
Texas-Pan Am.	10	8	.556	14	14	.500
Louisiana Tech	9	9	.500	14	13	.519
Arkan.-Little Rock	9	9	.500	17	12	.586
South Alabama	7	11	.389	9	18	.333
Lamar	6	12	.333	11	16	.407
S.W. Louisiana	4	14	.222	7	22	.241
Arkansas St.	3	15	.167	8	20	.286

Trans America Athletic

	Conference			Overall		
	W	L	Pct.	W	L	Pct.
Charleston (SC)	15	1	.938	23	6	.793
Samford	11	5	.688	16	11	.593
Stetson	11	5	.688	15	12	.556
Mercer	8	8	.500	15	14	.517
S.E. Louisiana	7	9	.438	12	16	.429
Central Florida	7	9	.438	11	16	.407
Centenary	7	9	.438	10	17	.370
Georgia St.	6	10	.375	11	17	.393
*#Florida Intern.	4	12	.250	11	19	.367
Campbell	4	12	.250	8	18	.308
Florida Atlantic	0	0	.000	9	18	.333

West Coast

	Conference			Overall		
	W	L	Pct.	W	L	Pct.
*Santa Clara	12	2	.857	21	7	.750
Portland	10	4	.714	21	8	.724
St. Mary's	10	4	.714	18	10	.643
*#Gonzaga	7	7	.500	21	9	.700
San Diego	5	9	.357	11	16	.407
San Francisco	4	10	.286	10	19	.345
Pepperdine	4	10	.286	8	19	.296
Loyola Marymount	4	10	.286	13	15	.464

Western Athletic

	Conference			Overall		
	W	L	Pct.	W	L	Pct.
*#Utah	15	3	.833	28	6	.824
*Brigham Young	13	5	.722	22	10	.688
Texas-El Paso	13	5	.722	20	10	.667
Wyoming	9	9	.500	13	15	.464
New Mexico	9	9	.500	15	15	.500
Hawaii	8	10	.444	16	13	.552
Colorado St.	7	11	.389	17	14	.548
Fresno St.	7	11	.389	13	15	.464
San Diego St.	5	13	.278	11	17	.393
Air Force	4	14	.222	8	20	.286

Independents

	Overall		
	W	L	Pct.
Notre Dame	15	12	.556
Oral Roberts	10	17	.370

* Selected to the NCAA Tournament.
# Won postseason conference tournament. The Big Ten, Ivy League, and Pacific-10 did not hold tournaments.

Final A.P. Poll, 1994-95

	W–L	Points
1) UCLA (64)	25-2	1,624
2) Kentucky (1)	25-4	1,552
3) Wake Forest	24-5	1,473
4) North Carolina	24-5	1,347
5) Kansas	23-5	1,344
6) Arkansas	27-6	1,322
7) Massachusetts	26-4	1,256
8) Connecticut	25-4	1,123
9) Villanova	25-7	1,095
10) Maryland	24-7	986
11) Michigan St.	22-5	972
12) Purdue	24-6	929
13) Virginia	22-8	854
14) Oklahoma St.	23-9	736
15) Arizona	23-7	700
16) Arizona St.	22-8	638
17) Oklahoma	23-8	497
18) Mississippi St.	20-7	492
19) Utah	27-5	466
20) Alabama	22-9	306
21) Western Kentucky	26-3	248
22) Georgetown	19-9	220
23) Missouri	19-8	202
24) Iowa St.	22-10	194
25) Syracuse	19-9	103

A.P. ALL-AMERICA TEAMS

First Team
*Ed O'Bannon, UCLA
Jerry Stackhouse, North Carolina
#Joe Smith, Maryland
Damon Stoudamire, Arizona
Shawn Respert, Michigan St.

Second Team
Corliss Williamson, Arkansas
Lou Roe, Massachusetts
Rasheed Wallace, North Carolina
Randolph Childress, Wake Forest
Kerry Kittles, Villanova

*Winner of the Wooden Award as national Player of the Year.
#Winner of the Naismith Award and Rupp Trophy as national Player of the Year.

Poll taken prior to the NCAA Tournament and the NIT. Won-loss records reflect performances at the time the polls were taken. First-place votes are in parentheses.

DIVISION I LEADERS, 1994-95

SCORING

Kurt Thomas, Texas Christian	28.9
Frankie King, Western Carolina	26.5
Kenny Sykes, Grambling	26.3
Sherell Ford, Illinois-Chicago	26.2
Tim Roberts, Southern-Baton Rouge	26.2
Kareem Townes, La Salle	25.9
Joe Griffin, LIU-Brooklyn	25.8
Shawn Respert, Michigan St.	25.6
Rob Feaster, Holy Cross	24.9
Shannon Smith, Wisconsin-Milwaukee	24.5
Mark Lueking, Army	24.4
Otis Jones, Air Force	23.9
Ryan Minor, Oklahoma	23.6
Alan Henderson, Indiana	23.5
Ronnie Henderson, Louisiana St.	23.3
Scott Drapeau, New Hampshire	23.1
Tucker Neale, Colgate	23.1
Gary Trent, Ohio	22.9
Joe Wilbert, Texas A&M	22.9
Damon Stoudamire, Arizona	22.8
Marcus Brown, Murray St.	22.4
Matt Alosa, New Hampshire	22.3

REBOUNDS

Kurt Thomas, Texas Christian	14.6
Malik Rose, Drexel	13.5
Gary Trent, Ohio	12.8
Dan Callahan, Northeastern	12.6
Tim Duncan, Wake Forest	12.5
Adonal Foyle, Colgate	12.4
Tunji Awojobi, Boston U.	12.2
Kareem Carpenter, Eastern Michigan	11.8
Marcus Mann, Mississippi Valley St.	11.7
Chris Ensminger, Valparaiso	11.3

ASSISTS

Nelson Haggerty, Baylor	10.1
Curtis McCants, George Mason	9.3
Raimonds Miglinieks, California-Irvine	8.4
Eric Snow, Michigan St.	7.8
Jacque Vaughn, Kansas	7.7
Anthony Foster, South Alabama	7.5
Tony Miller, Marquette	7.5
Hassan Sanders, Southern-Baton Rouge	7.5
Ray Washington, Nicholls St.	7.3
Damon Stoudamire, Arizona	7.3

STEALS

Roderick Anderson, Texas	3.4
Greg Black, Texas-Pan American	3.4
Nate Langley, George Mason	3.3
Ray Washington, Nicholls St.	3.0
Clarence Ceasar, Louisiana St.	3.0
Allen Iverson, Georgetown	3.0
Shandue McNeill, St. Bonaventure	2.9
Dominick Young, Fresno St.	2.9
Erick Strickland, Nebraska	2.9
Gerald Walker, San Francisco	2.9

BLOCKED SHOTS

Keith Closs, Central Connecticut St.	5.3
Theo Ratliff, Wyoming	5.1
Adonal Foyle, Colgate	4.9
Pascal Fleury, Maryland-Baltimore County	4.6
Lorenzo Coleman, Tennessee Tech	4.5
Tim Duncan, Wake Forest	4.2
Brian Gilpin, Dartmouth	3.5
Mario Bennett, Arizona St.	3.5
Peter Aluma, Liberty	3.5
Marcus Camby, Massachusetts	3.4

FIELD GOAL PCT.

Shane Kline-Ruminski, Bowling Green	68.3
George Spain, Davidson	67.1
Rasheed Wallace, North Carolina	65.4
Erick Dampier, Mississippi St.	64.0
Alexander Koul, George Washington	63.2
Joe McNaull, Long Beach St.	62.9
Mark Hendrickson, Washington St.	62.7
Darnell McCulloch, Fresno St.	62.3
Lorenzo Coleman, Tennessee Tech.	62.2
Chuckie Robinson, East Carolina	61.8

FREE THROW PCT.

Greg Bibb, Tennessee Tech	90.6
Scott Hartzell, North Carolina-Greensboro	89.8
Marcus Brown, Murray St.	89.6
Keith Cornett, Texas-Arlington	88.6
Arlando Johnson, Eastern Kentucky	88.5
Danny Basile, Marist	88.1
Steve Nash, Santa Clara	87.9
John Rillie, Gonzaga	87.9
Lance Barker, Valparaiso	87.8
Michael Heary, Navy	87.5

3-PT. FIELD GOAL PCT.

Brian Jackson, Evansville	55.8
Scott Kegler, Pennsylvania	50.9
Chris Westlake, Wisconsin-Green Bay	50.0
Dante Calabria, North Carolina	49.6
Malik Hightower, Marshall	48.4
Jeremy Lake, Montana	48.4
Dion Cross, Stanford	48.0
Shawn Respert, Michigan St.	47.4
Daryl Christopher, Southern Utah	47.3
Rob Wooster, St. Francis (PA)	47.1

SCORING OFFENSE, TEAM

Texas Christian	93.7
Southern-Baton Rouge	93.3
Texas	92.9
George Mason	92.6
Troy St.	91.4
Nicholls St.	90.3
Texas Tech	88.8
Stephen F. Austin	87.9
Arkansas	87.6
UCLA	87.5

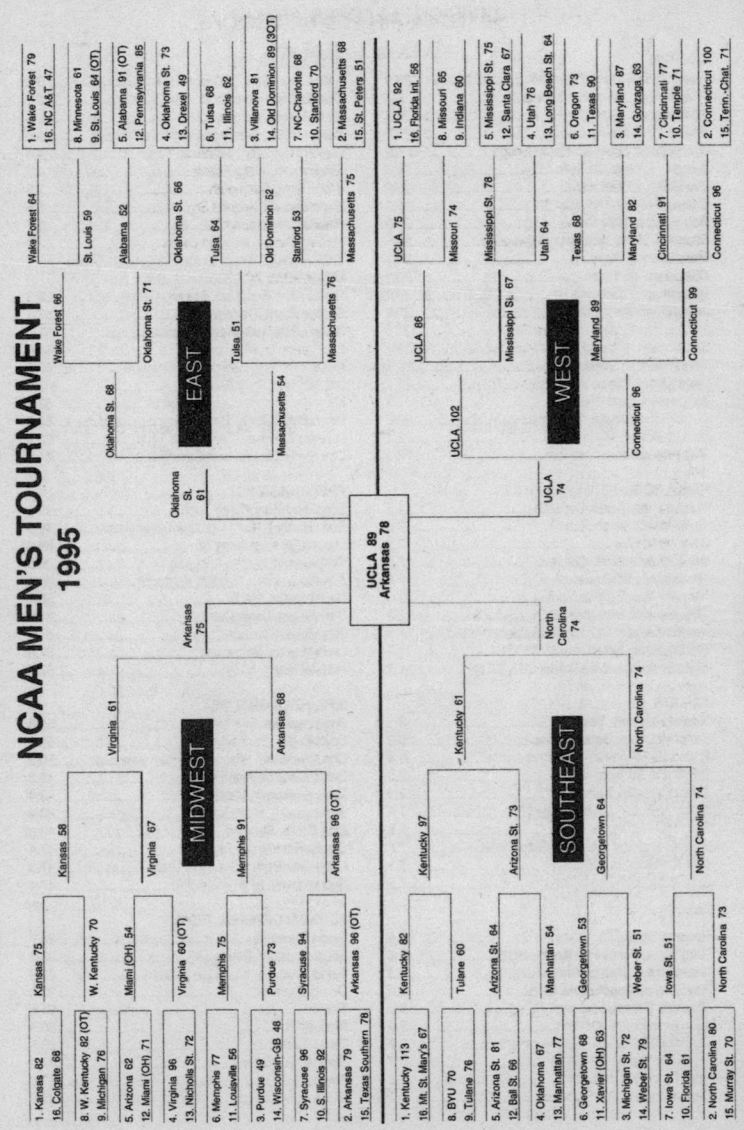

NCAA MEN'S TOURNAMENT 1995

1995 NCAA FINALS BOXSCORE

UCLA 89, Arkansas 78

Arkansas	MIN	FG-A	FT-A	REB	AST	PF	PTS
Thurman	32	2-9	0-0	3	1	2	5
Williamson	33	3-16	6-10	4	6	1	12
Martin	6	1-2	0-0	3	1	2	3
McDaniel	35	5-10	3-4	3	1	5	16
Beck	25	4-6	1-2	3	2	3	11
Stewart	22	5-10	1-2	5	0	4	12
Dillard	15	2-4	0-0	2	1	1	6
Robinson	10	2-3	0-0	2	0	3	4
Rimac	12	1-1	0-0	2	3	0	2
Wilson	7	3-4	1-2	0	0	1	7
Williams	1	0-0	0-0	0	0	0	0
Garrett	2	0-0	0-0	0	0	0	0
Totals	200	28-65	12-20	31	15	22	78

FGP—.431. FTP—.600. 3-PT FGP—10-28, .357
(Thurman 1-7, Martin 1-2, McDaniel 3-7, Beck 2-3,
Stewart 1-5, Dillard 2-3, Robinson 0-1).

UCLA	MIN	FG-A	FT-A	REB	AST	PF	PTS
E. O'Bannon	40	10-21	9-11	17	3	2	30
C. O'Bannon	36	4-10	3-4	9	6	1	11
Zidek	29	5-8	4-7	6	0	4	14
Bailey	39	12-20	1-2	9	3	3	26
Edney	3	0-0	0-0	0	0	0	0
Dollar	36	1-4	4-5	3	8	4	6
Henderson	17	1-5	0-0	2	1	1	2
Totals	200	33-68	21-29	46	21	15	89

FGP—.485. FTP—.724. 3-PT FGP—2-7, .286
(E. O'Bannon 1-4, Bailey 1-2, Dollar 0-1).

Halftime—UCLA 40, Arkansas 39.
Attendance—38,540 (Seattle Kingdome).

1995 NIT RESULTS

First Round
Marquette 68, Auburn 61
Coppin St. 75, St. Joseph's 68 (OT)
Penn St. 62, Miami (FL) 56
Canisius 83, Seton Hall 71
Iowa 96, DePaul 87
New Mexico St. 97, Colorado 83
Washington 94, Texas Tech 82
Ohio 83, George Washington 71
Providence 72, College of Charleston 67
St. Bonaventure 75, S. Mississippi 70
South Florida 74, St. John's 67
Bradley 86, Eastern Michigan 85 (2OT)
Nebraska 69, Georgia 61
Illinois St. 93, Utah St. 87 (OT)
Virginia Tech 62, Clemson 54
UTEP 90, Montana 60

Second Round
Virginia Tech 91, Providence 78
South Florida 75, Coppin St. 59
Washington St. 83, Illinois St. 80
Marquette 70, St. Bonaventure 61
Canisius 55, Bradley 53
New Mexico St. 92, UTEP 89 (OT)
Penn St. 65, Nebraska 59
Iowa 66, Ohio 62

Quarterfinals
Virginia Tech 64, New Mexico St. 61
Marquette 57, South Florida 50 (OT)
Canisius 89, Washington St. 80
Penn St. 67, Iowa 64

Semifinals
Virginia Tech 71, Canisius 59
Marquette 87, Penn St. 79

Finals
Virginia Tech 65, Marquette 64 (OT)

FINAL A.P. WOMEN'S POLL, 1994-95

1) Connecticut (32)	29-0	.800
2) Colorado	27-2	.746
3) Tennessee	29-2	.742
4) Stanford	26-2	.695
5) Texas Tech	30-3	.647
6) Vanderbilt	26-6	.644
7) Penn St.	25-4	.584
8) Louisiana Tech	26-4	.583
9) Western Kentucky	26-3	.557
10) Virginia	24-4	.522
11) North Carolina	28-4	.504
12) Georgia	24-4	.443
13) Alabama	20-8	.391
14) Washington	23-8	.364
15) Arkansas	22-6	.317
16) Purdue	21-7	.306
17) Florida	23-8	.281
18) George Washington	24-5	.276
19) Mississippi	21-7	.193
20) Duke	21-8	.186
21) Oregon St.	20-7	.158
22) San Diego St.	24-5	.116
23) Kansas	20-10	.95
24) N. Carolina St.	19-9	.58
25) Old Dominion	27-5	.27

Poll taken prior to the NCAA Tournament. Won-loss
records reflect performances at the time the poll was
taken. First-place votes in parentheses.

NCAA WOMEN'S TOURNAMENT

1995

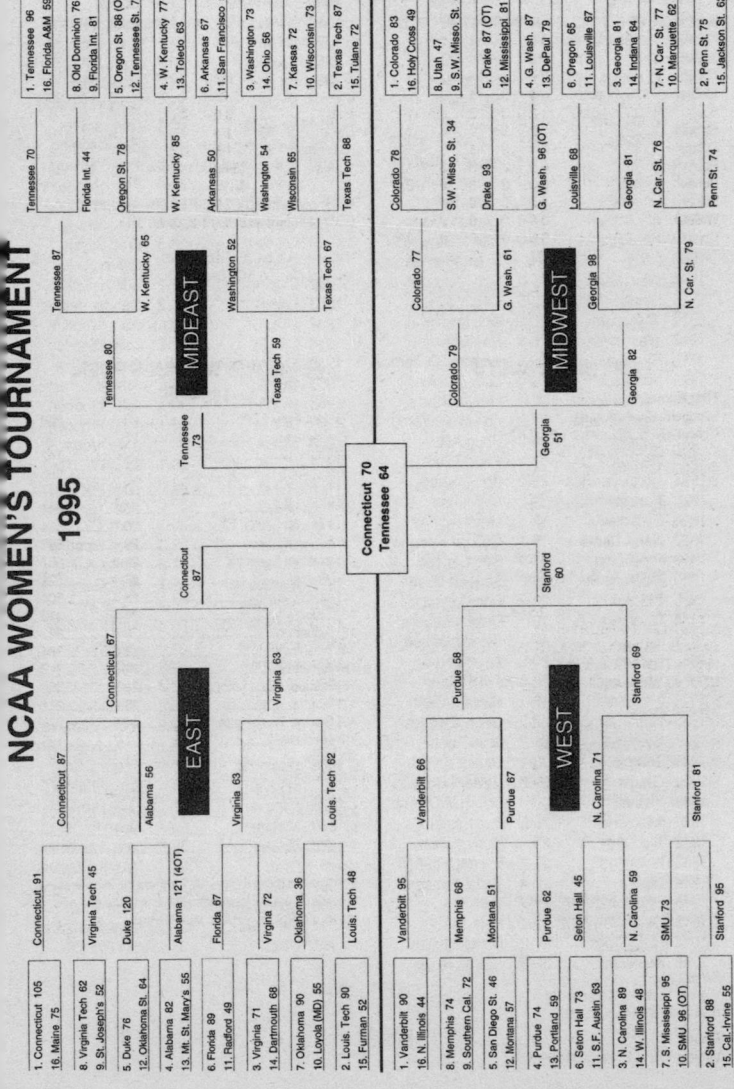

MIDEAST

1. Tennessee 96
16. Florida A&M 59
8. Old Dominion 76
9. Florida Int. 81
5. Oregon St. 88 (OT)
12. Tennessee St. 75
4. W. Kentucky 77
13. Toledo 63
6. Arkansas 67
11. San Francisco 58
3. Washington 73
14. Ohio 56
7. Kansas 72
10. Wisconsin 73
2. Texas Tech 87
15. Tulane 72

Tennessee 70
Florida Int. 44
Oregon St. 78
W. Kentucky 85
Arkansas 50
Washington 54
Wisconsin 65
Texas Tech 88

Tennessee 87
W. Kentucky 65
Washington 52
Texas Tech 67

Tennessee 80
Texas Tech 59

Tennessee 73

MIDWEST

1. Colorado 83
16. Holy Cross 49
8. Utah 47
9. S.W. Misso. St. 49
5. Drake 87 (OT)
12. Mississippi 81
4. G. Wash. 87
13. DePaul 79
6. Oregon 65
11. Louisville 67
3. Georgia 81
14. Indiana 64
7. N. Car. St. 77
10. Marquette 62
2. Penn St. 75
15. Jackson St. 62

Colorado 78
S.W. Misso. St. 34
Drake 93
G. Wash. 96 (OT)
Louisville 68
Georgia 81
N. Car. St. 76
Penn St. 74

Colorado 77
G. Wash. 61
Georgia 88
N. Car. St. 79

Colorado 79
Georgia 82

Georgia 51

Connecticut 70
Tennessee 64

Connecticut 87

Stanford 60

EAST

Connecticut 87
Virginia 63

Alabama 56

Virginia 63
Louis. Tech 62

Connecticut 67

Virginia 63

1. Connecticut 105
16. Maine 75
8. Virginia Tech 62
9. St. Joseph's 52
5. Duke 76
12. Oklahoma St. 64
4. Alabama 82
13. Mt. St. Mary's 55
6. Florida 89
11. Radford 49
3. Virginia 71
14. Dartmouth 68
7. Oklahoma 90
10. Loyola (MD) 55
2. Louis. Tech 90
15. Furman 52

Connecticut 91
Virginia Tech 45
Duke 120
Alabama 121 (4OT)
Florida 67
Virginia 72
Oklahoma 36
Louis. Tech 48

WEST

Vanderbilt 66

Purdue 67

Purdue 58

Stanford 69

N. Carolina 71

Stanford 81

1. Vanderbilt 90
16. N. Illinois 44
8. Memphis 74
9. Southern Cal. 72
5. San Diego St. 46
12. Montana 57
4. Purdue 74
13. Portland 59
6. Seton Hall 73
11. S.F. Austin 63
3. N. Carolina 89
14. W. Illinois 48
7. S. Mississippi 95
10. SMU 96 (OT)
2. Stanford 88
15. Cal-Irvine 55

Vanderbilt 95
Memphis 66
Montana 51
Purdue 62
Seton Hall 45
N. Carolina 59
SMU 73
Stanford 95

NATIONAL CHAMPIONS

YEAR	CHAMPION	RECORD	COACH	YEAR	CHAMPION	RECORD	COACH
1901	Yale	10-4	No coach	1949	Kentucky	32-2	Adolph Rupp
1902	Minnesota	11-0	Louis Cooke	1950	CCNY	24-5	Nat Holman
1903	Yale	15-1	W.H. Murphy	1951	Kentucky	32-2	Adolph Rupp
1904	Columbia	17-1	No coach	1952	Kansas	28-3	Phog Allen
1905	Columbia	19-1	No coach	1953	Indiana	23-3	Branch McCracken
1906	Dartmouth	16-2	No coach	1954	La Salle	26-4	Ken Loeffler
1907	Chicago	22-2	Joseph Raycroft	1955	San Francisco	28-1	Phil Woolpert
1908	Chicago	21-2	Joseph Raycroft	1956	San Francisco	29-0	Phil Woolpert
1909	Chicago	12-0	Joseph Raycroft	1957	North Carolina	32-0	Frank McGuire
1910	Columbia	11-1	Harry Fisher	1958	Kentucky	23-6	Adolph Rupp
1911	St. John's	14-0	Claude Allen	1959	California	25-4	Pete Newell
1912	Wisconsin	15-0	Doc Meanwell	1960	Ohio St.	25-3	Fred Taylor
1913	Navy	9-0	Louis Wenzell	1961	Cincinnati	27-3	Edwin Jucker
1914	Wisconsin	15-0	Doc Meanwell	1962	Cincinnati	29-2	Edwin Jucker
1915	Illinois	16-0	Ralph Jones	1963	Loyola (IL)	29-2	George Ireland
1916	Wisconsin	20-1	Doc Meanwell	1964	UCLA	30-0	John Wooden
1917	Washington St.	25-1	Doc Bohler	1965	UCLA	28-2	John Wooden
1918	Syracuse	16-1	Edmund Dollard	1966	Texas Western	28-1	Don Haskins
1919	Minnesota	13-0	Louis Cooke	1967	UCLA	30-0	John Wooden
1920	Pennsylvania	22-1	Lon Jourdet	1968	UCLA	29-1	John Wooden
1921	Pennsylvania	21-2	Edward McNichol	1969	UCLA	29-1	John Wooden
1922	Kansas	16-2	Phog Allen	1970	UCLA	28-2	John Wooden
1923	Kansas	17-1	Phog Allen	1971	UCLA	29-1	John Wooden
1924	North Carolina	25-0	Bo Shepard	1972	UCLA	30-0	John Wooden
1925	Princeton	21-2	Al Wittmer	1973	UCLA	30-0	John Wooden
1926	Syracuse	19-1	Lew Andreas	1974	N. Carol. St.	30-1	Norm Sloan
1927	Notre Dame	19-1	George Keogan	1975	UCLA	28-3	John Wooden
1928	Pittsburgh	21-0	Doc Carlson	1976	Indiana	32-0	Bobby Knight
1929	Montana St.	36-2	Shubert Dyche	1977	Marquette	25-7	Al McGuire
1930	Pittsburgh	23-2	Doc Carlson	1978	Kentucky	30-2	Joe B. Hall
1931	Northwestern	16-1	Dutch Lonborg	1979	Michigan St.	26-6	Jud Heathcote
1932	Purdue	17-1	Piggy Lambert	1980	Louisville	33-3	Denny Crum
1933	Kentucky	20-3	Adolph Rupp	1981	Indiana	26-9	Bobby Knight
1934	Wyoming	26-3	Dutch Witte	1982	North Carolina	32-2	Dean Smith
1935	New York	18-1	Howard Cann	1983	N. Carol. St.	28-8	Jim Valvano
1936	Notre Dame	22-2-1	George Keogan	1984	Georgetown	34-3	John Thompson
1937	Stanford	25-2	John Bunn	1985	Villanova	25-10	Rollie Massimino
1938	Temple	23-2	James Usilton	1986	Louisville	32-7	Denny Crum
1939	Oregon	29-5	Howard Hobson	1987	Indiana	30-4	Bobby Knight
1940	Indiana	20-3	Branch McCracken	1988	Kansas	27-11	Larry Brown
1941	Wisconsin	20-3	Bud Foster	1989	Michigan	30-7	Steve Fisher
1942	Stanford	28-4	Everett Dean	1990	UNLV	35-5	Jerry Tarkanian
1943	Wyoming	31-2	Everett Shelton	1991	Duke	32-7	Mike Krzyzewski
1944	Utah	22-4	Vadal Peterson	1992	Duke	34-2	Mike Krzyzewski
1945	Oklahoma A&M	27-4	Hank Iba	1993	North Carolina	34-4	Dean Smith
1946	Oklahoma A&M	31-2	Hank Iba	1994	Arkansas	31-3	Nolan Richardson
1947	Holy Cross	27-3	Doggie Julian	1995	UCLA	31-2	Jim Harrick
1948	Kentucky	36-3	Adolph Rupp				